JUSTICE SYSTEM

CORRECTIONS

SENTENCING & SANCTIONS | **PROBATION** | **PRISON** | **PAROLE**

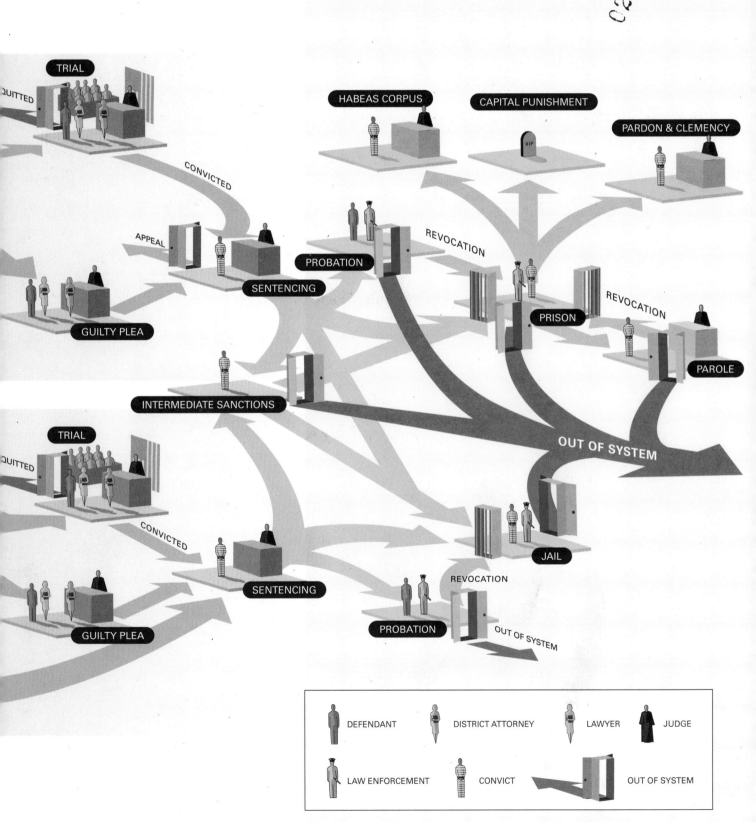

TRIAL

ACQUITTED

CONVICTED

HABEAS CORPUS

CAPITAL PUNISHMENT

PARDON & CLEMENCY

APPEAL

PROBATION

REVOCATION

REVOCATION

SENTENCING

GUILTY PLEA

PRISON

PAROLE

INTERMEDIATE SANCTIONS

OUT OF SYSTEM

TRIAL

ACQUITTED

CONVICTED

JAIL

REVOCATION

SENTENCING

PROBATION

OUT OF SYSTEM

GUILTY PLEA

Legend

DEFENDANT | DISTRICT ATTORNEY | LAWYER | JUDGE

LAW ENFORCEMENT | CONVICT | OUT OF SYSTEM

Welcome

TO THE 10th EDITION!

The following pages will introduce what's new in the

10th edition, as well as the hallmark features that have made

Criminal Justice Today the most widely used

introduction to criminal justice textbook in America today.

Lady Justice

As you read this text, note that the figure of Lady Justice is featured prominently throughout the design. She stands as the visual theme of the text because of her representation of the judicial ideal—fairness in the execution of the law.

Often she is depicted with a set of scales, a double-edged sword and a blindfold.

The scales measure the relative strength of the prosecutor's case versus the defense, and the sword signifies the power of justice and reason, which are objective and may support or condemn either party. The blindfold, especially common in European tradition, symbolizes that justice should be executed objectively.

Justice fountain, in Romerberg, a public square in Frankfurt, Germany.

Justice statue on top of Old Bailey, London, England

The depiction of Lady Justice with varying combinations of the scales, sword and blindfold was first seen in Greek and Roman iconography and reflects her mythological origins. She exhibits traits of the Greek goddess Themis, the scales-bearing Hellenic goddess of divine order and law who was advisor to Zeus, as well as Iustitia, the blindfolded Roman goddess of justice.

Although she has taken numerous forms throughout the ages and across cultures, as reflected in the variety of figures seen throughout the text, her symbolism has remained constant as the personification of the balanced moral spirit underpinning the legal system.

Justice statue in front of The Ministry of Justice Building, Brasilias, Brazil

Justice statue on the Albert V. Bryan Courthouse in Alexandria, Virginia

What's New

Juvenile Justice

Thoroughly revised juvenile justice chapter focusing on the latest issues facing juveniles and the juvenile justice system.

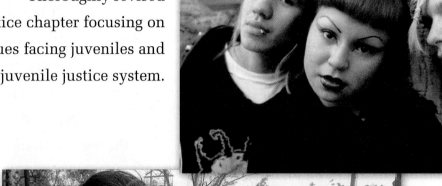

Intelligence-Led Policing

New thorough coverage of evidence-based and intelligence-led policing.

Uptick in Crime

Expanded coverage of the fear that violent crime is on the rise in big cities.

Theme

The always evolving theme of individual rights vs. public order has been a hallmark feature of Criminal Justice Today since the first edition and is more important now than ever before. The theme builds on the highest goals of the American criminal justice system, which are to achieve a just and orderly society in which people are free to pursue personal interests while remaining safe and secure.

Scales of Justice
Individual Rights vs. Public Order

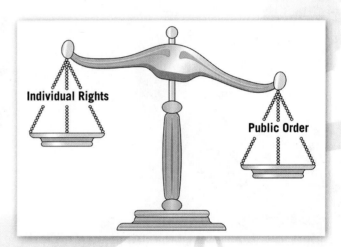

Freedom or Safety? Boxes
This critical thinking feature asks students to think about how the criminal justice system balances individual rights and public safety.

FREEDOM OR SAFETY?
You Decide

Giuliani Says: "Freedom Is about Authority"

As we move through the early years of the twenty-first century, the challenge for the criminal justice system, it seems, is to balance individual rights and personal freedoms with social control and respect for legitimate authority. Years ago, during the height of what was then a powerful movement to win back control of our nation's cities and to rein in skyrocketing crime rates, the *New York Post* sponsored a conference on crime and civil rights. The keynote speaker at that conference was New York City's Mayor Rudolph W. Giuliani. In his speech, Giuliani identified the tension between personal freedoms and individual responsibilities as the crux of the crime problem then facing his city and the nation. We mistakenly look to government and elected officials, Giuliani said, to assume responsi-

bility for solving the problem of crime when, instead, each individual citizen must become accountable for fixing what is wrong with our society. "We only see the oppressive side of authority. . . . What we don't see is that freedom is not a concept in which people can do anything they want, be anything they can be. Freedom is about authority. Freedom is about the willingness of every single human being to cede to lawful authority a great deal of discretion about what you do."

YOU DECIDE

What did Giuliani mean when he said, "What we don't see is that freedom is not a concept in which people can do anything they want, be anything they can be"? How can we, as a society, best balance individual rights and personal freedoms with social control and respect for legitimate authority?

Reference: Philip Taylor, "Civil Libertarians: Giuliani's Efforts Threaten First Amendment," Freedom Forum Online, http://www.freedomforum.org.

Timeliness

The Media, Celebrities, and Crime

Media and popular culture are having a greater influence on the criminal justice system.

Multiculturalism

American society is multicultural, composed of a wide variety of racial and ethic heritages, diverse religions, and distinct languages. How does the multicultural nature of our society impact the justice system?

The CSI Effect

Approximately 70% of the general public regularly watch CSI or similar shows. Some jury consultants think this is affecting deliberations in courts across the U.S.

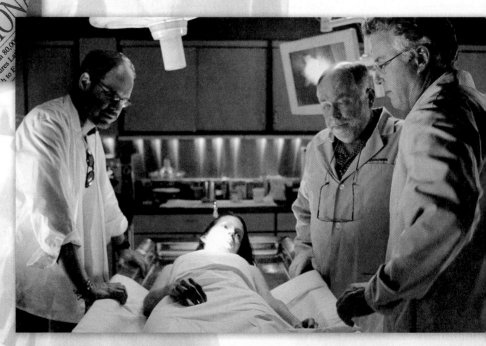

Technology

Cybercrime

Criminal buyers and sellers want your identity. Cybercrime is a growing area of concern in criminal justice today.

Instant Cell Phone Viruses

Computers can remotely send viruses to Bluetooth cell phones and corrupt the phone's operating system.

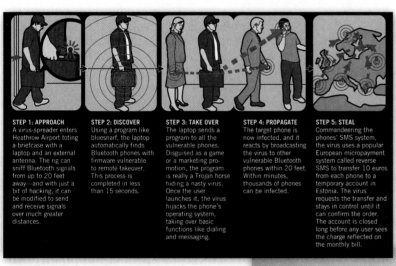

STEP 1: APPROACH
A virus-spreader enters Heathrow Airport toting a briefcase with a laptop and an external antenna. The rig can sniff Bluetooth signals from up to 20 feet away—and with just a bit of hacking, it can be modified to send and receive signals over much greater distances.

STEP 2: DISCOVER
Using a program like bluesnarf, the laptop automatically finds Bluetooth phones with firmware vulnerable to remote takeover. This process is completed in less than 15 seconds.

STEP 3: TAKE OVER
The laptop sends a program to all the vulnerable phones. Disguised as a game or a marketing promotion, the program is really a Trojan horse hiding a nasty virus. Once the user launches it, the virus hijacks the phone's operating system, taking over basic functions like dialing and messaging.

STEP 4: PROPAGATE
The target phone is now infected, and it reacts by broadcasting the virus to other vulnerable Bluetooth phones within 20 feet. Within minutes, thousands of phones can be infected.

STEP 5: STEAL
Commandeering the phones' SMS system, the virus uses a popular European micropayment system called reverse SMS to transfer 10 euros from each phone to a temporary account in Estonia. The virus requests the transfer and stays in control until it can confirm the order. The account is closed long before any user sees the charge reflected on the monthly bill.

Internet Use for al-Qaeda

Jihadists are using technology to spread their message and philosophy.

CRIMINAL JUSTICE TODAY

An Introductory Text for the 21st Century

TENTH EDITION

FRANK SCHMALLEGER, Ph.D.

Distinguished Professor Emeritus,
The University of North Carolina at Pembroke

PEARSON

Prentice
Hall

Upper Saddle River, New Jersey
Columbus, Ohio

Library of Congress Cataloging-in-Publication Data

Schmalleger, Frank
    Criminal justice today : an introductory text for the twenty-first century / Frank Schmalleger.—10th ed.
      p. cm.
    Includes bibliographical references and index.
    ISBN–13: 978–0–13–513030–8
    1. Criminal justice, Administration of—United States. I. Title.
    HV9950.S35 2009
    364.973—dc22

2007030427

Editor in Chief: Vernon R. Anthony
Senior Editor: Tim Peyton
Development Editor: Elisa Rogers
Editorial Assistant: Alicia Kelly
Project Managers: Barbara Marttine Cappuccio, Stephen C. Robb
Production Coordination: Janet Bolton
Art Director: Mary Siener
Interior Design: Ilze Lemesis
Cover Design: Ilze Lemesis
Cover Image: Corbis
Photographer: Dave Bartuff
Operations Supervisor: Patricia A. Tonneman
Director, Image Resource Center: Melinda Patelli
Manager, Rights and Permissions: Zina Arabia
Manager, Visual Research: Beth Brenzel
Manager, Cover Visual Research & Permissions: Karen Sanatar
Senior Image Permission Coordinator: Cynthia Vincenti
Photo Researcher: Jerry Marshall / Truitt and Marshall
Director of Marketing: David Gesell
Marketing Manager: Adam Kloza
Marketing Coordinator: Alicia Dysert
Copyeditor: Judith Mara Riotto
Proofreader: Maine Proofreading Services

Part and Chapter Opening Photo Credits:
Part 1: © Dave Bartruff/CORBIS. All rights reserved. Chapters: Comstock Images/Corbis—Comstock Images Royalty Free; Bob Daemmrich/Bob Daemmrich Photography, Inc.; © Jeff Tuttle/epa/CORBIS. All rights reserved. Part 2: © Skyscan/CORBIS. All rights reserved. Chapters: © Bettmann/CORBIS. All rights reserved; © Bernd Obermann/CORBIS. All rights reserved; © Mikael Karlson. All rights reserved; Librado Romero/New York Times Agency. Part 3: Arlene Jean Gee/Shutterstock. Chapters: Robert Llewellyn/Corbis Royalty Free; Tim Pannell/Corbis Royalty Free; Louis Lanzano/AP Wide World Photo. Part 4: ALBERT EINSTEIN and related rights™/© of The Hebrew University of Jerusalem, used under license. Represented exclusively by Corbis Corporation. Chapters: © Patti Sapone/*Star Ledger*/CORBIS. All rights reserved; Andrea Pistoles/Image Bank/Getty Images; Bill Curtsinger/Getty—National Geographic Society. Part 5: Sylvain Grandadam/Robert Harding World Imagery. Chapters: Daniel LeClair/Corbis/Reuters America LLC; HARTMUT SCHWAVZBACK/Peter Arnold, Inc.; Getty Images, Inc.; © Digital Art/CORBIS. All rights reserved.

This book was set in Bernhard Modern, Imago, and Melior by S4Carlisle Publishing Services. It was printed and bound by R.R. Donnelley & Sons, Company. The cover was printed by Phoenix Color Corp.

Pearson Education Ltd.
Pearson Education Singapore Pte. Ltd.
Pearson Education Canada, Ltd.
Pearson Education—Japan
Pearson Education Australia Pty. Limited
Pearson Education North Asia Ltd.
Pearson Educación de Mexico, S.A. de C.V.
Pearson Education Malaysia Pte. Ltd.

10 9 8 7 6 5 4 3 2 1
ISBN-13: 978-0-13-513757-4
ISBN-10:   0-13-513757-8

ISBN-13: 978-0-13-513030-8
ISBN-10:   0-13-513030-1

For Harmonie Star-Schmalleger,
my beautiful wife and other self

BRIEF CONTENTS

CONTENTS

PART 2   Policing   149

PART 3   Adjudication   307

PART 4   Corrections   427

PREFACE

The attacks of September 11, 2001, changed our nation's course and tested the moral fiber of Americans everywhere. Nowhere outside the armed forces has the terrorist threat been felt more keenly than in the criminal justice profession. The 2001 attacks led many to look to our system of justice, and to the people who serve it, for protection and reassurance—protection from threats both internal and external and reassurance that a justice system rooted in the ideals of democracy will continue to offer fairness and equality to all who come before the law.

In the years since September 11, strict new laws have been enacted, security efforts have been greatly enhanced, and practitioners of American criminal justice (especially those in law enforcement agencies) have recognized their important role as the first line of defense against threats to the American way of life. As a consequence, the study of criminal justice is more relevant today than ever before.

For many, personal involvement in the criminal justice field has become a way of serving our nation and helping to protect our communities. I understand that motivation and applaud it—partially because of the heroism and personal sacrifice it involves, but also because it adds to the important "moral sense" of what we, as Americans, are all about. The justice profession's service role has expanded to include college and university students who, in ever greater numbers, are declaring majors in criminal justice. Participation in the criminal justice system and in the study of criminal justice offers students a way of personally and meaningfully contributing to our society. It allows those who meet the challenging criteria for successful studies and employment to give something back to the nation and to the communities that nurtured them, and it reaffirms the American way of life by reinforcing the social values on which it is based.

Many students are also attracted to criminal justice because it provides a focus for the tension that exists within our society between individual rights and freedoms, on the one hand, and the need for public safety, security, and order, on the other. That tension—between individual rights and public order—is the theme around which all editions of this textbook have been built. That same theme is all the more relevant today because of the important question we have all been asking in recent years: "How much personal freedom are we willing to sacrifice to achieve a solid sense of security?"

While there are no easy answers to this question, this textbook guides criminal justice students in the struggle to find a satisfying balance between freedom and security. True to its origins, the tenth edition focuses on the crime picture in America and on the three traditional elements of the criminal justice system: police, courts, and corrections. This edition has been enhanced by additional "Freedom or Safety" boxes, which time and again question the viability of our freedoms in a world grown increasingly more dangerous. This edition also asks students to evaluate the strengths and weaknesses of the American justice system as it struggles to adapt to an increasingly multicultural society and to a society in which the rights of a few can threaten the safety of many.

It is my hope that this book will ground students in the important issues that continue to evolve from the tension between the struggle for justice and the need for safety. For it is on that bedrock that the American system of criminal justice stands, and it is on that foundation that the future of the justice system—and of this country—will be built.

Frank Schmalleger, Ph.D.
Distinguished Professor Emeritus,
The University of North Carolina at Pembroke

TO THE STUDENT

Exploring Criminal Justice Today

Anyone using this book is encouraged to visit the award-winning *Criminal Justice Today* site on the Web at cjtoday.com. This book's companion website provides a broad range of materials of relevance to the study of criminal justice and has links to many other criminal justice–related sites. Through the many "Web Extras" and "Library Extras" that are built into this text, and via the "Web Quests" found at the end of every chapter, the companion website provides substantially enhanced learning opportunities.

Hear the author discuss this chapter at cjtoday.com

Audio Extras let you hear the author introduce each chapter and provide a summary of important topics. Audio chapter introductions require Real Player™ or Windows Media Player™ software.

Keep up with the latest news and with pressing justice-related issues in the **CJ Today Blogspace**, with links to active blogs in criminal law, policing, the courts, drug control, sentencing, and corrections.

LIBRARY
Extra

Library Extras provide access to selected documents from the Bureau of Justice Statistics, the National Institute of Justice, the Bureau of Justice Assistance, the Federal Bureau of Investigation, and other important criminal justice agencies.

WEB
Extra

Web Extras provide virtual criminal justice tours of the Internet, with visits to significant police, courts, and corrections sites on the Web.

Join our **E-mail Discussion List** at http://groups.yahoo.com/group/CJToday, and stay abreast of what other students using this textbook are talking about.

ACKNOWLEDGMENTS

My thanks to all who assisted in so many different ways in the development of this textbook. The sacrifice of time made by my wife, Harmonie, as I worked endlessly in my office is very much appreciated. Thanks also to Karen Bretz, Barbara Cappuccio, Mary Carnis, Michelle Churma, Alicia Dysert, David Gesell, JoEllen Gohr, Sarah Holle, Alicia Kelly, Jerry Marshall, Stephen Robb, Elisa Rogers, Mary Siener, Pat Tonneman, and all the past and present Prentice Hall staff with whom I have worked. They are true professionals and have made the task of manuscript development enjoyable.

A very special thank-you goes to Robin Baliszewski, David Gesell, and Vern Anthony for their stewardship and support, and to my editor and friend, Tim Peyton, and marketing manager Adam Kloza for their invaluable insights, perseverance, and dedication to this project.

I am grateful to my supplements authors for their support of this new edition: Steve Chermak for the Student Study Guide; Sandy Boyd, Instructor's Resource Guide; David Graff, Companion Website; Kay Henriksen, TestGen and Test Item File; Carolyn D'Argenio, PowerPoints; Janet McNutt, PRS-enabled PowerPoints; and Naomi Sysak, Annotated Instructor's Edition. Thanks also to production coordinator Janet Bolton and personal assistant Laura Joyce for their very capable handling of numerous details. The keen eye of copy editor Judith Mara Riotto is beyond compare, and this book is much richer for her efforts. I am grateful, as well, to the manuscript reviewers involved in this and previous editions for holding me to the fire when I might have opted for a less rigorous coverage of some topics—especially Darl Champion of Methodist College, Jim Smith at West Valley College, Cassandra L. Renzi of Keiser University, and Bryan J. Vila at the National Institute of Justice, for their insightful suggestions as this book got under way.

Manuscript reviewers who have contributed to the development of *Criminal Justice Today* include

Howard Abadinsky
St. Johns University
Jamaica, NY

Reed Adams
Elizabeth City State
University
Elizabeth City, NC

Kevin Barrett
Palomar College
San Marcos, CA

Larry Bassi
State University of New
York (SUNY)–Brockport
Brockport, NY

Richard Becker
North Harris College
Houston, TX

Todd Beitzel
University of Findlay
Findlay, OH

Gad Bensinger
Loyola University–
Chicago
Chicago, IL

Michael Blankenship
Boise State University
Boise, ID

Mindy Bradley
University of Arkansas
Fayetteville, AR

Pauline Brennan
University of Nebraska
Omaha, NE

Theodore P. Byrne
California State
University–Dominguez
Hills
Carson, CA

W. Garret Capune
California State
University–Fullerton
Fullerton, CA

Mike Carlie
Southwest Missouri State
University
Springfield, MO

Geary Chlebus
James Sprunt Community
College
Kenansville, NC

Steven Christiansen
Joliet Junior College
Joliet, IL

Jon E. Clark
Temple University
Philadelphia, PA

Lora C. Clark
Pitt Community College
Greenville, NC

Warren Clark
California State
University–Bakersfield
Bakersfield, CA

Ellen G. Cohn
Florida International
University
Miami, FL

Gary Colboth
California State
University–Long Beach
Long Beach, CA

Kimberly Collica
Monroe College
Bronx, NY

Susan C. Craig
University of Central
Florida
Orlando, FL

Jannette O. Domingo
John Jay College of
Criminal Justice
New York, NY

Vicky Doworth
Montgomery College
Rockville, MD

Daniel P. Doyle
University of Montana
Missoula, MT

Steven Egger
University of
Houston–Clearlake
Houston, TX

Ron Fagan
Pepperdine University
Malibu, CA

Alan S. Frazier
Glendale Community
College
Glendale, CA

Harold A. Frossard
Moraine Valley
Community College
Palos Hills, IL

Barry J. Garigen
Genesee Community
College
Batavia, NY

Michael Gray
Wor-Wic Community
College
Salisbury, MD

Alex Greenberg
Niagara County
Community College
Sanborn, NY

Tim Griffin
St. Xavier University
Chicago, IL

Julia Hall
Drexel University
Philadelphia, PA

Ed Heischmidt
Rend Lake College
Ina, IL

Dennis Hoffman
University of Nebraska at
Omaha
Omaha, NE

Michael Hooper
California Department of
Justice
Sacramento, CA

William D. Hyatt
Western Carolina
University
Cullowhee, NC

Nicholas H. Irons
County College of Morris
Randolph, NJ

Galan M. Janeksela
University of Tennessee
at Chattanooga
Chattanooga, TN

Terry L. Johnson
Owens Community
College
Toledo, OH

Steve Johnson
Eastern Arizona College
Thatcher, AZ

David M. Jones
University of
Wisconsin–Oshkosh
Oshkosh, WI

Victor Kappeler
Eastern Kentucky State
University
Richmond, KY

P. Ray Kedia
Grambling State
University
Grambling, LA

Debra Kelly
Longwood University
Farmville, VA

Lloyd Klein
Louisiana State
University–Shreveport
Shreveport, LA

Sylvia Kuennen
Briar Cliff College
Sioux City, IA

Karel Kurst-Swanger
Oswego State University
of New York
Oswego, NY

Hamid R. Kusha
Texas A&M International
University
Laredo, TX

David S. Long
St. Francis College
Brooklyn, NY

Joan Luxenburg
University of Central
Oklahoma
Edmond, OK

Michael Lyman
Columbia College
Columbia, MO

Dena Martin
Ivy Tech Community
College of Indiana
Terre Haute, TN

Richard H. Martin
Elgin Community College
Elgin, IL

David C. May
Eastern Kentucky
University
Richmond, KY

G. Larry Mays
New Mexico State
University
Las Cruces, NM

Thomas P. McAninch
Scott Community College
Bettendorf, IA

William McGovern
Sussex County
Community College
Newton, NJ

Susan S. McGuire
San Jacinto College North
Houston, TX

Robert J. Meadows
California Lutheran
University
Thousand Oaks, CA

Jim Mezhir
Niagara County
Community College
Sanborn, NY

Rick Michelson
Grossmont College
El Cajon, CA

Jeffrey D. Monroe
Xavier University
Cincinnati, OH

Harvey Morley
California State
University–Long Beach
Long Beach, CA

Jacqueline Mullany
Indiana University
Northwest
Gary, IN

Roslyn Muraskin
C. W. Post Campus of
Long Island University
Brookville, NY

Charles Myles
California State
University–Los Angeles
Los Angeles, CA

Bonnie Neher
Harrisburg Area
Community College
Harrisburg, PA

David Neubauer
University of New
Orleans–Lakefront
New Orleans, LA

Ken O'Keefe
Prairie State College
Chicago Heights, IL

P. J. Ortmier
Grossmont College
El Cajon, CA

David F. Owens
Onondaga Community
College
Syracuse, NY

Michael J. Palmiotto
Wichita State University
Wichita, KS

Lance Parr
Grossmont College
El Cajon, CA

William H. Parsonage
Penn State University
University Park, PA

Allison Payne
Villanova University
Villanova, PA

Ken Peak
University of
Nevada–Reno
Reno, NV

Joseph M. Pellicciotti
Indiana University
Northwest
Gary, IN

Roger L. Pennel
Central Missouri State
University
Warrensburg, MO

Joseph L. Peterson
University of Illinois at
Chicago
Chicago, IL

Morgan Peterson
Palomar College
San Marcos, CA

Caryl Poteete
Illinois Central College
East Peoria, IL

Gary Prawel
Keuka College
Keuka Park, NY

Philip J. Reichel
University of Northern
Colorado
Greely, CO

Albert Roberts
Rutgers University
New Brunswick, NJ

Carl E. Russell
Scottsdale Community
College
Scottsdale, AZ

Paul Sarantakos
Parkland College
Champaign, IL

Wayne J. Scamuffa
ITT Technical Institute
Seattle, WA

Benson Schaffer
IVAMS Arbitration and
Mediation Services
Pomona, CA

Stephen J. Schoenthaler
California State
University–Stanislaus
Turlock, CA

Jeff Schrink
Indiana State University
Terre Haute, IN

Scott Senjo
Weber State University
Ogden, UT

Judith M. Sgarzi
Mount Ida College
Newton, MA

Louis F. Shepard
West Georgia Technical
College
LaGrange, GA

John Siler
Georgia Perimeter College
Clarkston, GA

Ira Silverman
University of South
Florida
Tampa, FL

Loretta J. Stalans
Loyola
University–Chicago
Chicago, IL

Domenick Stampone
Raritan Valley
Community College
Somerville, NJ

Z. G. Standing Bear
University of Colorado
Colorado Springs, CO

Mark A. Stetler
Montgomery College
Conroe, TX

B. Grant Stitt
University of
Nevada–Reno
Reno, NV

Norma Sullivan
College of DuPage
Glen Ellen, IL
and Troy University
Ft. Benning, GA

Robert W. Taylor
University of North Texas
Denton, TX

Lawrence F. Travis III
University of Cincinnati
Cincinnati, OH

Ron Vogel
California State
University–Long Beach
Long Beach, CA

John Vollmann, Jr.
Florida Metropolitan
University
Ft. Lauderdale, FL

David Whelan
Western Carolina
University
Cullowhee, NC

Dianne A. Williams
North Carolina A&T
State University
Greensboro, NC

Lois Wims
Salve Regina University
Newport, RI

L. Thomas Winfree, Jr.
New Mexico State
University
Las Cruces, NM

John M. Wyant
Illinois Central College
East Peoria, IL

Jeffrey Zack
Fayetteville Technical
Community College
Fayetteville, NC

My thanks to everyone! I would also like to extend a special thanks to the following individuals for their invaluable comments and suggestions along the way: Gordon Armstrong, Avon Burns, Kathy Cameron-Hahn, Alex Obi Ekwuaju, Gene Evans, Joe Graziano, Donald J. Melisi, Greg Osowski, Phil Purpura, John Robich, Barry Schreiber, Ted Skotnicki, Stewart Stanfield, Bill Tafoya, Tom Thackery, Joe Trevalino, Howard Tritt, Bill Tyrrell, Tim Veiders, and Bob Winslow.

Thanks are also due everyone who assisted in artistic arrangements, including Sergeant Michael Flores of the New York City Police Department's Photo Unit, Michael L. Hammond of the Everett (Washington) Police Department, Mikael Karlsson of Arresting Images, Assistant Chief James M. Lewis of the Bakersfield (California) Police Department, Tonya Matz of the University of Illinois at Chicago, and Monique Smith of the National Institute of Justice—all of whom were especially helpful in providing a wealth of photo resources. I am especially indebted to University of Illinois Professor Joseph L. Peterson for his assistance with sections on scientific evidence and to George W. Knox of the National Gang Crime Research Center for providing valuable information on gangs and gang activity.

I'd also like to acknowledge Chief J. Harper Wilson and Nancy Carnes of the FBI's Uniform Crime Reporting Program; Mark Reading of the Drug Enforcement Administration's Office of Intelligence; Kristina Rose at the National Institute of Justice; Marilyn Marbrook and Michael Rand at the Office of Justice Programs; Wilma M. Grant of the U.S. Supreme Court's Project Hermes; Ken Kerle at the American Jail Association; Lisa Bastian, survey statistician with the National Crime Victimization Survey Program; Steve Shackelton with the U.S. Parks Service; Ronald T. Allen, Steve Chaney, Bernie Homme, and Kenneth L. Whitman, all with the California Peace Officer Standards and Training Commission; Dianne Martin at the Drug Enforcement Administration; and George J. Davino of the New York City Police Department for their help in making this book both timely and accurate.

Last, but by no means least, Taylor Davis, H. R. Delaney, Jannette O. Domingo, Al Garcia, Rodney Hennigsen, Norman G. Kittel, Robert O. Lampert, and Joseph M. Pellicciotti should know that their writings, contributions, and valuable suggestions at the earliest stages of manuscript development continue to be very much appreciated. Thank you, everyone!

Frank Schmalleger, Ph.D.

ABOUT THE AUTHOR

Frank Schmalleger, Ph.D., is Distinguished Professor Emeritus at the University of North Carolina at Pembroke. He holds degrees from the University of Notre Dame and Ohio State University, having earned both a master's (1970) and a doctorate in sociology (1974) from Ohio State University with a special emphasis in criminology. From 1976 to 1994, he taught criminology and criminal justice courses at the University of North Carolina at Pembroke. For the last 16 of those years, he chaired the university's Department of Sociology, Social Work, and Criminal Justice. The university named him Distinguished Professor in 1991.

Schmalleger has taught in the online graduate program of the New School for Social Research, helping to build the world's first electronic classrooms in support of distance learning through computer telecommunications. As an adjunct professor with Webster University in St. Louis, Missouri, Schmalleger helped develop the university's graduate program in security administration and loss prevention. He taught courses in that curriculum for more than a decade. An avid Web user and website builder, Schmalleger is also the creator of a number of award-winning websites, including one that supports this textbook (http://www.cjtoday.com).

Frank Schmalleger is the author of numerous articles and more than 30 books, including the widely used *Criminal Justice: A Brief Introduction* (Prentice Hall, 2008), *Criminology Today* (Prentice Hall, 2009), and *Criminal Law Today* (Prentice Hall, 2006).

Schmalleger is also founding editor of the journal *Criminal Justice Studies*. He has served as editor for the Prentice Hall series *Criminal Justice in the Twenty-First Century* and as imprint adviser for Greenwood Publishing Group's criminal justice reference series.

Schmalleger's philosophy of both teaching and writing can be summed up in these words: "In order to communicate knowledge we must first catch, then hold, a person's interest—be it student, colleague, or policymaker. Our writing, our speaking, and our teaching must be relevant to the problems facing people today, and they must in some way help solve those problems." Visit the author's website at http://www.schmalleger.com.

Justice is truth in action!

—*Benjamin Disraeli (1804–1881)*

**Injustice anywhere is a threat
to justice everywhere.**

—*Martin Luther King, Jr. (1929–1968)*

PART 1
Crime in America

INDIVIDUAL RIGHTS VERSUS PUBLIC ORDER

The accused has these common law, constitutional, statutory, and humanitarian rights

- Justice for the individual
- Personal liberty
- Dignity as a human being
- The right to due process

Those individual rights must be effectively balanced against these community concerns

- Social justice
- Equality before the law
- The protection of society
- Freedom from fear

How does our system of justice work toward balance?

1

What Is Criminal Justice?

2

The Crime Picture

3

The Search for Causes

4

Criminal Law

The Will of the People Is the Best Law

The great American statesman and orator Daniel Webster (1782–1852) once wrote, "Justice is the great interest of man on earth. It is the ligament which holds civilized beings and civilized nations together." Although Webster lived in a relatively simple time with few problems and many shared rules, justice has never been easily won. Unlike Webster's era, society today is highly complex. It is populated by groups with a wide diversity of interests and faces threats and challenges unimaginable in Webster's day. It is within this challenging context that the daily practice of American criminal justice occurs.

The criminal justice system has three central components: police, courts, and corrections. The history, the activities, and the legal environment surrounding the police are discussed in Part 2 of this book. Part 3 describes the courts, and Part 4 deals with prisons, probation, and parole. Part 5 provides a guide to the future of the justice system and describes the impact of the threat of terrorism on enforcement agencies. We begin here in Part 1, however, with an overview of that grand ideal that we call *justice*, and we consider how the justice ideal relates to the everyday practice of criminal justice in the United States today. To that end, in the four chapters that make up this section, we will examine how and why laws are made. We will look at the wide array of interests that impinge

upon the justice system, and we will examine closely the dichotomy that distinguishes citizens who are primarily concerned with individual rights from those who emphasize the need for individual responsibility and social accountability—a dichotomy that has become especially significant in the wake of the September 11 terrorist attacks. In the pages that follow, we will see how justice can mean personal freedom and protection from the power of government to some people, and greater safety and security to others. In this section, we will also lay the groundwork for the rest of the text by painting a picture of crime in America today, suggesting possible causes for it, and showing how policies for dealing with crime have evolved.

As you read about the complex tapestry that is the practice of criminal justice in America today, you will learn of a system in flux, perhaps less sure of its purpose than at any time in its history. You may also catch the sense, however, that very soon a new and reborn institution of justice may emerge from the ferment that now exists. Whatever the final outcome, it can only be hoped that *justice*, as proffered by the American system of criminal justice, will be sufficient to hold our civilization together—and to allow it to prosper well into the twenty-first century and beyond.

CHAPTER 1

What Is Criminal Justice?

LEARNING OBJECTIVES

After reading this chapter, you should be able to

- Provide a brief history of crime in America.
- Identify the theme on which this textbook builds and highlight the differences between the individual-rights and public-order perspectives.
- Explain the relationship of criminal justice to social justice and to other wider notions of equity and fairness.
- Explain the structure of the American criminal justice system in terms of its major components and the functions they serve.
- Describe the process of American criminal justice, including the stages of criminal case processing.
- Explain the meaning of due process of law, and identify where due process guarantees can be found in the American legal system.
- Describe the role of research in contemporary criminal justice.
- Explain how multiculturalism and diversity present special challenges to, and opportunities for, the American system of criminal justice.

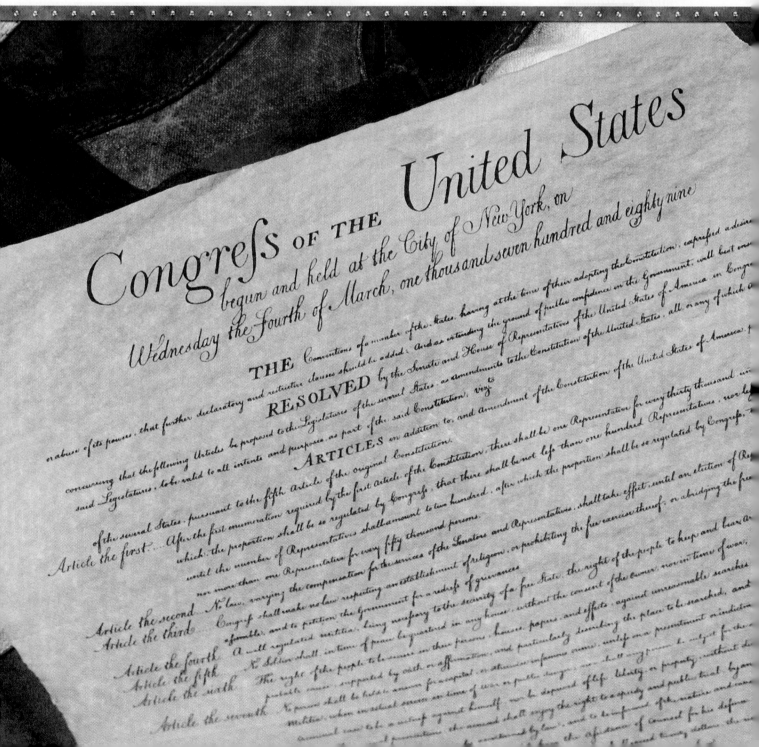

The rights guaranteed to criminal suspects, defendants, offenders, and prisoners were not included in the Bill of Rights for the benefit of criminals. They are fundamental political rights that protect all Americans from governmental abuse of power. These rights are found in the Fourth, Fifth, Sixth, Eighth, and Fourteenth Amendments. They include the guarantee against unreasonable search and seizure, the right to reasonable bail, the right to due process of law, and the right to be free from cruel and unusual treatment. This "bundle of rights" is indispensable to a free society.

—American Civil Liberties Union[1]

The Constitution is not a suicide pact.

—Former Secretary of State Warren Christopher, after terrorists destroyed the World Trade Center in New York City in 2001[2]

Hear the author discuss this chapter at cjtoday.com

Introduction

Five days after Hurricane Katrina made landfall near New Orleans in 2005, the *Washington Post* described the devastated metropolitan area as "a city of despair and lawlessness."[3] The *Wall Street Journal* ran headlines proclaiming that the city had "plunged into anarchy."[4] As the winds relented, looters ravaged stores, gunshots rang out, and armed gangs could be seen roaming the streets that hadn't been flooded. Some looters used forklifts and construction equipment to bust through storm shutters and steel doors protecting gun shops, liquor stores, and pharmacies.[5] The New Orleans Police Department, hamstrung by the absence of one-third of its 1,600 officers and the loss of critical communications channels and emergency equipment, struggled to keep control over its facilities. In one unflooded precinct, officers used an armored personnel carrier to survey the chaos.[6] Officers from another precinct were forced to barricade themselves into their three-story administrative center, renaming it Fort Apache after a film in which a police station is attacked. "You have to understand," said Juan Lopez, one of the officers who took refuge in the precinct house, "New Orleans was a violent place before the hurricane. After the hurricane, the city just let loose."[7]

The storm set into motion a number of events that are still sending shock waves throughout American society. The physical damage done by the hurricane, estimated at billions of dollars, was made worse by the massive social disorder that followed. Thousands of displaced people left their homes—with many never expected to return. Law enforcement and assistance agencies throughout the region suffered serious disruptions in their ability to provide services. Some officers walked off the job, and citizens were left to fend for themselves until thousands of National Guard troops armed with automatic weapons arrived to restore order in the wind- and flood-ravaged area.

The Katrina disaster, which created opportunities for those bent on criminal activity, illustrated the tenuous nature of social order. The social disorganization that followed Katrina continued long after the storm and involved a myriad of criminal offenses—including thousands of people arrested for defrauding the Federal Emergency Management Agency (FEMA), the government agency responsible for helping out after a disaster. FEMA fraud was so widespread that reports showed the number of households receiving FEMA emergency checks in four Louisiana parishes exceeded the number of households that existed there before the storm hit.[8] Almost 360,000 households applied for FEMA's Expedited Assistance payments in Orleans Parish alone—although the area had only 182,000 homes before Katrina. In one case that drew the attention of federal prosecutors, 33-year-old Kenneth McClain was charged with 14 counts of fraud in an elaborate conspiracy that allegedly scammed more than $10,000 in federal relief checks. McClain, who had 27 aliases and a number of open arrest warrants when caught, lived in Texas, far from the storm's wrath. He is accused of using stolen identities, some belonging to dead people, to file for assistance and then waiting in a Texas motel room for the aid checks to arrive.[9]

You're looking now not only at a rescue operation but a gigantic crime scene.

—Newscaster, ABC Nightly News, commenting on the World Trade Center site a few days after the September 11, 2001, attacks

New Orleans business owner Bob Rue standing in front of his rug store in the aftermath of Hurricane Katrina. His hastily created sign warns potential looters to stay away. Some say that the central purpose of the criminal justice system is the maintenance of social order. Others say that the justice system must respect the rights of those whom it processes. Are the two perspectives mutually exclusive?

Charlie Riedel/AP Wide World Photos

A very different kind of criminal event thrust itself on American society and our justice system with the September 11, 2001, terrorist attacks that targeted New York City's World Trade Center and the Pentagon. Those attacks, including one on an airliner that crashed in the Pennsylvania countryside, left nearly 3,000 people dead and caused billions of dollars in property damage. They have since been classified as the most destructive criminal activity ever to have been perpetrated on U.S. soil. The resulting "war on terrorism" changed the face of world politics and ushered in a new era in American society. Before the attacks, most Americans lived relatively secure lives, largely unfettered by fear of random personal attack. Following September 11, however, a heated debate has taken place between those wanting to enforce powerful crime-prevention and security measures and others seeking to preserve the individual rights and freedoms that have long been characteristic of American life. This issue, which has continued to feed TV talk shows and newspaper editorials nationwide, asks Americans to determine which rights, freedoms, and conveniences (if any) they are willing to sacrifice to increase personal and public safety. It also anticipates the theme on which this book is based—and which is discussed at length later in this chapter.

Regardless of your personal position in the ongoing debate between freedom and safety, it is important to recognize that terrorism is a potentially horrendous **crime**. Many states and the federal government have statutes outlawing terrorism, although terrorism itself can involve many other kinds of crimes. In the case of the World Trade Center and Pentagon attacks, for example, the crimes committed included murder, kidnapping, hijacking, grand theft, felonious assault, battery, conspiracy, and arson.

Crime does more than expose the weakness in social relationships; it undermines the social order itself, by destroying the assumptions on which it is based.

—James Q. Wilson, UCLA[ii]

crime

Conduct in violation of the criminal laws of a state, the federal government, or a local jurisdiction, for which there is no legally acceptable justification or excuse.[iii]

A Brief History of Crime in America

What we call *criminal activity* has undoubtedly been with us since the dawn of history, and crime control has long been a primary concern of politicians and government leaders worldwide. Still, the American experience with crime during the last half century has been especially influential in shaping the criminal justice system of today. In this country, crime waves have come and gone, including an 1850–1880 crime epidemic, which was apparently related to social upheaval caused by large-scale immigration and the Civil War.[10] A spurt of widespread organized criminal activity was associated with the Prohibition years of the early twentieth century. Following World War II, however, American crime rates remained relatively stable until the 1960s.

An artist's rendition of the New York City skyline as it will look once buildings envisioned by renowned architect Daniel Libeskind are constructed on the 16-acre World Trade Center site. The plan includes a soaring Freedom Tower that will stand 1,776 feet tall, several other towers, and a memorial to the nearly 3,000 people who were killed in the terrorist attacks that demolished the twin towers in 2001. How did those attacks change the American justice system?

Skidmore, Owings, & Merrill LLP/Getty Images

individual rights

The rights guaranteed to all members of American society by the U.S. Constitution (especially those found in the first ten amendments to the Constitution, known as the *Bill of Rights*). These rights are particularly important to criminal defendants facing formal processing by the criminal justice system.

The 1960s and 1970s saw a burgeoning concern for the rights of ethnic and racial minorities, women, people with physical and mental challenges, and many other groups. The civil rights movement of the period emphasized equality of opportunity and respect for individuals, regardless of race, color, creed, gender, or personal attributes. As new laws were passed and suits filed, court involvement in the movement grew. Soon a plethora of hard-won individual rights and prerogatives, based on the U.S. Constitution, the Bill of Rights, and new federal and state legislation, were recognized and guaranteed. By the 1980s, the civil rights movement had profoundly affected all areas of social life—from education and employment to the activities of the criminal justice system.

This emphasis on **individual rights** was accompanied by a dramatic increase in reported criminal activity. While some researchers doubted the accuracy of official accounts, reports by the Federal Bureau of Investigation of "traditional" crimes like murder, rape, and assault increased considerably during the 1970s and into the 1980s. Many theories were advanced to explain this leap in observed criminality. Some analysts of American culture, for example, suggested that the combination of newfound freedoms and long-pent-up hostilities of the socially and economically deprived worked to produce social disorganization, which in turn increased criminality.

By the mid-1980s, the dramatic increase in the sale and use of illicit drugs threatened the foundation of American society. Cocaine, and later laboratory-processed "crack," spread to every corner of America. The country's borders were inundated with smugglers intent on reaping quick fortunes. Large cities became havens for drug gangs, and many inner-city areas were all but abandoned to highly armed and well-financed drug racketeers. Cities experienced dramatic declines in property values, and residents wrestled with an eroding quality of life.

By the close of the 1980s, neighborhoods and towns were fighting for their communal lives. Huge rents had been torn in the national social fabric, and the American way of life, long taken for granted, was under the gun. Traditional values appeared in danger of going up in smoke along

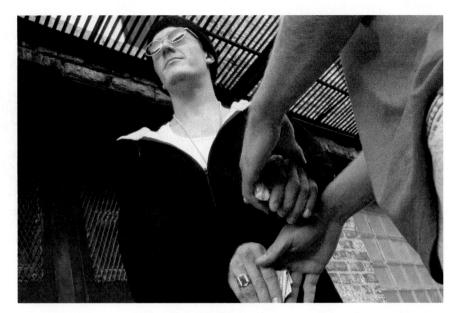

A street-corner drug deal. By the mid-1980s, the American criminal justice system had become embroiled in a war against illicit drugs, filling the nation's prisons and jails with drug dealers, traffickers, and users. Has the war been won?
Brand X Pictures/Robertstock.com

with the "crack" being consumed openly in some parks and resorts. Looking for a way to stem the tide of increased criminality, many took up the call for "law and order." In response, President Ronald Reagan created a cabinet-level "drug czar" position to coordinate the "war on drugs." Careful thought was given at the highest levels to using the military to patrol the sea-lanes and air corridors through which many of the illegal drugs entered the country. President George H. W. Bush, who followed Reagan into office, quickly embraced and expanded the government's antidrug efforts.

In 1992, the videotaped beating of Rodney King, an African American motorist, at the hands of Los Angeles–area police officers splashed across TV screens throughout the country and shifted the public's focus onto issues of police brutality and the effective management of law enforcement personnel. As the King incident seemed to show, when racial minorities came face to face with agents of the American criminal justice system, justice didn't always result. Although initially acquitted by a California jury—which contained no African American members—two of the officers who beat King were convicted in a 1993 federal courtroom of violating his civil rights.[11] The King incident and associated trials are described in more detail in Chapter 7.

Then, the very next year, law enforcement agencies were again criticized when agents of the Bureau of Alcohol, Tobacco, Firearms and Explosives (ATF) and the Federal Bureau of Investigation (FBI) faced off with David Koresh and members of his Branch Davidian cult in Waco, Texas. The conflict began when ATF agents assaulted Koresh's fortress-like compound, leaving four agents and six cult members dead. It ended 51 days later with the fiery deaths of Koresh and 71 of his followers, many of whom were children. The event led to a congressional investigation and charges that the ATF and the FBI had been ill prepared to deal successfully with large-scale domestic resistance and had reacted more out of alarm and frustration than wisdom. Attorney General Janet Reno refused to blame agents for misjudging Koresh's intentions, although 11 Davidians were later acquitted of charges that they had murdered the federal agents.

Soon afterward, a few spectacular crimes that received widespread coverage in the news media fostered a sense among the American public that crime in the United States was out of hand and that strict new measures were needed to combat it. One such crime was the 1995 bombing of the Alfred P. Murrah Federal Building in Oklahoma City by antigovernment extremists. Another was the 1999 Columbine High School massacre in Colorado that left 12 students and one teacher dead.[12]

The public's perception that crime rates were growing, coupled with a belief that offenders frequently went unpunished or received only a judicial slap on the wrist, led to a burgeoning emphasis on responsibility and punishment. By the late 1990s, a strong shift away from the claimed misdeeds of the criminal justice system was well under way, and a newfound emphasis on individual accountability began to blossom among an American public fed up with crime and fearful of its own victimization. Growing calls for enhanced responsibility quickly began to replace the previous emphasis on individual rights. As a juggernaut of conservative opinion made itself felt on the political scene, Senator Phil Gramm of Texas observed that the public wants to "grab violent criminals by the throat, put them in prison [and] stop building prisons like Holiday Inns."[13]

Then, in an event that changed the course of our society, public tragedy became forever joined with private victimization in our collective consciousness after a series of highly destructive and well-coordinated terrorist attacks on New York City and Washington, D.C., on September 11,

The current crisis in criminal and juvenile justice is fueled by the public's conviction that the system no longer represents an effective response to the problem of crime.

—Reinventing Probation Council

If you break the law, we're going to hold you accountable, and there will be tough consequences for your actions.

—North Carolina Governor Jim Hunt[iv]

People expect both safety and justice and do not want to sacrifice one for the other.

—Christopher Stone, President and Director, Vera Institute of Justice

2001. Those attacks resulted in the collapse and total destruction of the twin 110-story towers of the World Trade Center and a devastating explosion at the Pentagon. Thousands of people perished, and many were injured. Although law enforcement and security agencies were unable to prevent the September 11 attacks, many have since moved from a reactive to a proactive posture in the fight against terrorism—a change that is discussed in more detail in Chapter 6.

The September 11 attacks also made clear that adequate law enforcement involves a global effort at controlling crime and reducing the risk of injury and loss to law-abiding people both at home and abroad. The attacks showed that criminal incidents that take place on the other side of the globe can impact those of us living in the United States, and they illustrated how the acquisition of skills needed to understand diverse cultures can help in the fight against crime and terrorism.

An especially important new tool in the law enforcement arsenal is the federal **USA PATRIOT Act**,[14] enacted in 2001 as a legislative response to terrorism. The law, whose provisions were reauthorized by Congress with minor revisions in 2006, is officially known as the Uniting and Strengthening America by Providing Appropriate Tools Required to Intercept and Obstruct Terrorism Act of 2001 (from which the acronym *USA PATRIOT* is derived). The law dramatically increases the investigatory authority of federal, state, and local police agencies, although sometimes only temporarily. The expanded police powers created under the legislation are not limited to investigations of terrorist activity but apply to many different criminal offenses. Terrorism is discussed in more detail in Chapter 17. As that chapter points out, terrorism is a criminal act, and preventing terrorism and investigating terrorist incidents after they occur are highly important roles for local, state, and federal law enforcement agencies.

A different kind of offending, corporate and white-collar crime, took center stage in 2002 and 2003 as President George W. Bush called on Congress to stiffen penalties for unscrupulous business executives who knowingly falsify their company's financial reports.[15] The president's request came amidst declining stock market values, shaken investor confidence, and threats to the viability of employee pension plans in the wake of a corporate crime wave involving criminal activities that had been planned and undertaken by executives at a number of leading corporations. In an effort to restore order to American financial markets, President Bush signed the Sarbanes-Oxley Act on July 30, 2002.[16] The law, which has been called "the single most important piece of legislation affecting corporate governance, financial disclosure and the practice of public accounting since the US securities laws of the early 1930s,"[17] is intended to deter corporate fraud and to hold business executives accountable for their actions.

White-collar crime continues to be a focus of federal prosecutors, and in 2006 former Enron executives Kenneth Lay and Jeff Skilling were convicted of conspiracy to commit securities and wire fraud in what some called "the biggest business scandal in U.S. history"—the collapse of energy-trading giant Enron Corporation.[18] The company's troubles resulted in the loss of billions of dollars of investors' money. White-collar crime is discussed in more detail in Chapter 2.

For a detailed look at crimes that have shaped the past hundred years, see Web Extra 1–1 at cjtoday.com. Library Extra 1–1 at cjtoday.com also describes the changing nature of crime in America.

The Theme of This Book

This book examines the American system of criminal justice and the agencies and processes that constitute it. It builds on a theme that is especially valuable for studying criminal justice today: *individual rights versus public order.* This theme draws on historical developments that have shaped our legal system and our understandings of crime and justice. It is one of the primary determinants of the nature of contemporary criminal justice—including criminal law, police practice, sentencing, and corrections.

A strong emphasis on individual rights rose to the forefront of American social thought during the 1960s and 1970s, a period known as the *civil rights era.* The civil rights era led to the recognition of fundamental personal rights that had previously been denied illegally to many people on the basis of race, ethnicity, gender, sexual preference, or disability. The civil rights movement soon expanded to include the rights of many other groups, including criminal suspects, parolees and probationers, trial participants, prison and jail inmates, and victims. As the emphasis on civil rights grew, new laws and court decisions broadened the rights available to many.

The treatment of criminal suspects was afforded special attention by those who argued that the purpose of any civilized society should be to secure rights and freedoms for each of its citizens—including those suspected and convicted of crimes. Rights advocates feared unnecessarily restrictive government action and viewed it as an assault on basic human dignity and individual liberty. They believed that at times it was necessary to sacrifice some degree of public safety and

USA PATRIOT Act

A federal law (Public Law 107-56) enacted in response to terrorist attacks on the World Trade Center and the Pentagon on September 11, 2001. The law, officially titled the Uniting and Strengthening America by Providing Appropriate Tools Required to Intercept and Obstruct Terrorism Act, substantially broadened the investigative authority of law enforcement agencies throughout America and is applicable to many crimes other than terrorism. The law was slightly revised and reauthorized by Congress in 2006.

CJ BLOG

See our Rights versus Safety blogs.

WEB Extra   **LIBRARY** Extra

Prosecutors in the Enron Corporation case speaking to reporters in Houston in 2006 after a jury found two former chief executives guilty of fraud. Corporate and white-collar crime came under federal scrutiny after the "technology bubble" burst on Wall Street in 2000–2001. Should corporate criminals be treated differently from other offenders?

*Michael Stravato/*The New York Times

predictability to guarantee basic freedoms. Hence criminal rights activists demanded a justice system that limits police powers and that holds justice agencies accountable to the highest procedural standards.

During the 1960s and 1970s, the dominant philosophy in American criminal justice focused on guaranteeing the rights of criminal defendants while seeking to understand the root causes of crime and violence. The past 25 years, however, have witnessed increased interest in an ordered society, in public safety, and in the rights of crime victims. This change in attitudes was likely brought about by national frustration with the perceived inability of our society and its justice system to prevent crimes and to consistently hold offenders to heartfelt standards of right and wrong. Increased conservatism in the public-policy arena was given new life by the September 11, 2001,

I would rather be exposed to the inconveniences attending too much liberty than to those attending too small a degree of it.

—Thomas Jefferson

FREEDOM OR SAFETY?
You Decide

Giuliani Says: "Freedom Is about Authority"

As we move through the early years of the twenty-first century, the challenge for the criminal justice system, it seems, is to balance individual rights and personal freedoms with social control and respect for legitimate authority. Years ago, during the height of what was then a powerful movement to win back control of our nation's cities and to rein in skyrocketing crime rates, the *New York Post* sponsored a conference on crime and civil rights. The keynote speaker at that conference was New York City's Mayor Rudolph W. Giuliani. In his speech, Giuliani identified the tension between personal freedoms and individual responsibilities as the crux of the crime problem then facing his city and the nation. We mistakenly look to government and elected officials, Giuliani said, to assume re-

sponsibility for solving the problem of crime when, instead, each individual citizen must become accountable for fixing what is wrong with our society. "We only see the oppressive side of authority. . . .What we don't see is that freedom is not a concept in which people can do anything they want, be anything they can be. Freedom is about authority. Freedom is about the willingness of every single human being to cede to lawful authority a great deal of discretion about what you do."

YOU DECIDE

What did Giuliani mean when he said, "What we don't see is that freedom is not a concept in which people can do anything they want, be anything they can be"? How can we, as a society, best balance individual rights and personal freedoms with social control and respect for legitimate authority?

Reference: Philip Taylor, "Civil Libertarians: Giuliani's Efforts Threaten First Amendment," Freedom Forum Online, http://www.freedomforum.org.

terrorist attacks and by widely publicized instances of sexual offenses targeting children. It continues to be sustained by the many stories of violent victimization that seem to be the current mainstay of the American media.

Today, public perspectives have largely shifted away from seeing the criminal as an unfortunate victim of poor social and personal circumstances who is inherently protected by fundamental human and constitutional rights, to seeing him or her as a dangerous social predator who usurps the rights and privileges of law-abiding citizens. Reflecting the "get tough on crime" attitudes of today, many Americans demand to know how offenders can better be held accountable for violations of the criminal law. In 2006, for example, at least 14 governors signed laws designed to extend prison sentences for sex offenders, restrict where released sex offenders can live, and improve public notification of their whereabouts. More bills are pending as this book goes to press, including one in Louisiana that would require convicted offenders to carry bright orange driver's licenses stamped with the words "sex offender," and another in South Carolina that would make some molesters eligible for the death penalty.[19]

Even so, the tension between individual rights and social responsibility still forms the basis for most policy-making activity in the criminal justice arena. Those who fight for individual rights continue to carry the banner of civil and criminal rights for the accused and the convicted, while public-order activists loudly proclaim the rights of the victimized and call for an increased emphasis on social responsibility and criminal punishment for convicted criminals. In keeping with these realizations, the theme of this book can be stated as follows:

> There is widespread recognition in contemporary society of the need to balance (1) the freedoms and privileges of our nation's citizens and the respect accorded the rights of individuals faced with criminal prosecution against (2) the valid interests that society has in preventing future crimes, in public safety, and in reducing the harm caused by criminal activity. While the personal freedoms guaranteed to law-abiding citizens as well as to criminal suspects by the Constitution, as interpreted by the U.S. Supreme Court, must be closely guarded, the urgent social needs of communities for controlling unacceptable behavior and protecting law-abiding citizens from harm must be recognized. Still to be adequately addressed are the needs and interests of victims and the fear of crime and personal victimization that is often prevalent in the minds of many law-abiding citizens.

individual-rights advocate

One who seeks to protect personal freedoms within the process of criminal justice.

public-order advocate

One who believes that under certain circumstances involving a criminal threat to public safety, the interests of society should take precedence over individual rights.

Figure 1–1 represents our theme and shows that most people today who intelligently consider the criminal justice system assume one of two viewpoints. We will refer to those who seek to protect personal freedoms and civil rights within society, and especially within the criminal justice process, as **individual-rights advocates**. Those who suggest that under certain circumstances involving criminal threats to public safety, the interests of society (especially crime control and social order) should take precedence over individual rights will be called **public-order advocates**. Recently, retired U.S. Supreme Court Justice Sandra Day O'Connor summed up the differences between these two perspectives by asking, "At what point does the cost to civil liberties from legislation designed to prevent terrorism [and crime] outweigh the added security that that legislation provides?"[20] In this book, we seek to look at ways in which the individual-rights and

FIGURE 1–1

The theme of this book.

Balancing the concern for individual rights with the need for public order through the administration of criminal justice is the theme of this book.

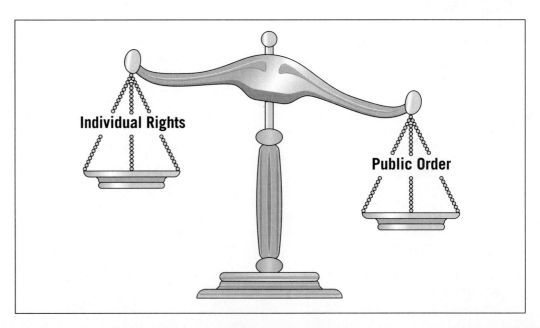

Individual Rights

Public Order

Demonstrators gathering on the steps of New York City's Federal Hall to protest provisions of the USA PATRIOT Act. Federal Hall served as the venue for President George Washington's inauguration in 1789 and was the meeting place of the First Congress, which wrote our nation's Bill of Rights. The PATRIOT Act was passed by Congress with little debate just 45 days after the terrorist attacks of September 11, 2001. Rights advocates claim that the act unfairly restricts individual liberties. What do you think?

Scout Tufankjian/AP Wide World Photos

public-order perspectives can be balanced to serve both sets of needs. Hence you will find our theme discussed throughout this text, within "Freedom or Safety" boxes, and highlighted in many of the Web Quest sections at the end of each chapter.

Social Justice

On September 20, 2001, in the immediate aftermath of the terrorist attacks on the World Trade Center and the Pentagon, President Bush delivered a televised address to the American people. In his rallying cry to a nation about to embark on a war against world terrorism, Bush said, "We will bring our enemies to justice; or we will bring justice to our enemies."[21] The word *justice* is powerful, and—at the time—the president's choice of words spoke to all Americans.

The reality, however, is that *justice* is an elusive term. As the "war on terrorism" began, for example, no one who heard the president's speech knew exactly what justice might mean and what

When you know both the accuser and the accused, as we so often do, the conflict between civil rights and victims' rights is seldom completely black or white. And it is the gray areas in between that make the debate so difficult.

—Columnist Vicki Williams, writing on crime in a small American town

A crowd reacting outside the San Mateo County (California) courthouse as guilty verdicts are returned in the 2005 California murder trial of Scott Peterson. Criminal justice and social justice are concepts that are closely tied in most people's minds. What does the word *justice* mean to you?

Justin Sullivan/AP Wide World Photos

CJ News

Who Watches the Watchers?

In some cities in Europe and the United States, a person can be videotaped by surveillance cameras hundreds of times a day, and it's safe to say that most of the time no one is actually watching.

But the advent of "intelligent video"—software that raises the alarm if something on camera appears amiss—means Big Brother will soon be able to keep a more constant watch, a prospect that is sure to heighten privacy concerns.

Combining motion detection technology with the learning capabilities of video game software, these new systems can detect people loitering, walking in circles or leaving a package.

New microphone technology can isolate the sound of a gunshot and direct the attached camera to swivel and zoom in on the source. Sensitivity may reach the point where microphones could pick out the word "explosives" spoken in a crowd.

"There's just not enough personnel to watch every single camera," said Chicago emergency operations chief Andrew Velasquez. "We are piloting analytic software right now . . . where you can set that particular camera to watch for erratic behavior, or someone leaving a suitcase on the sidewalk."

Since the attacks on the United States of September 11, 2001, sections of New York, Washington, Los Angeles, Chicago and even a few smaller U.S. towns have been blanketed with closed-circuit cameras. Privately owned cameras are also proliferating.

The encroachment on privacy in what civil libertarians call a "surveillance society" may be a price willingly paid by citizens who fear terrorism and crime.

A Chicago Police Department surveillance camera system and microphone unit positioned high above the street. This surveillance system includes a camera, high-bandwidth wireless communication, a strobe light, and a gunshot-recognition system, all in a bulletproof enclosure. The city is installing the surveillance system to spot crimes or terrorist activity. Do such units infringe on the personal freedoms of Chicago residents?

Safety Dynamics

But ever-alert software capable of maintaining a continuous "watch" on security cameras multiplies the risks of harassing innocent people, privacy experts say.

"I don't buy it. The number of false positives are going to be astronomical," said David Holtzman, author of "Privacy Lost." "It's extremely dangerous to abrogate legitimate law enforcement authority . . . to a camera."

In Chicago's darkened, windowless surveillance center, Velasquez looks forward to using new technology, which has had some success elsewhere.

The port of Jacksonville, Florida, has dispensed with human monitoring of cameras altogether by sending alerts and live video to the personal digital assistant of the nearest officer on patrol, according to a spokesman for ObjectVideo Inc.

ObjectVideo is one of two dozen companies seeking to perfect so-called intelligent video—an industry whose sales will grow from $60 million to $400 million within five years, according to global consulting group Frost & Sullivan.

Meanwhile, Texas is evaluating a pilot program in which it allowed Internet access to video of unmanned sections of its border with Mexico and urged viewers to send an e-mail if they spotted something.

"The cameras don't replace police officers. They are in essence a force multiplier. They serve as an extra set of eyes," Velasquez said.

The Chicago center is manned 24 hours a day by veteran police officers. A dozen screens depict a few street corners and a stadium, while others are tuned to cable news or Web sites.

They can retrieve video from thousands of cameras and their universe is expanded by private cameras owned by cooperating buildings and stores, but they can monitor only a few at a time.

Velasquez said his officers receive training on privacy and constitutional rights—for example it is illegal to look into private homes and offices—and digital recordings hold his officers accountable and prevent abuses that have occurred elsewhere.

In Britain, which has 4.2 million government security cameras, 2 million in London alone, a study showed that male surveillance workers sometimes ogled women on their screens, while others focused on minorities excessively.

But privacy experts also note another British study, from 2002, which said surveillance cameras did not lower overall crime rates and merely pushes crime elsewhere.

"Cameras are great tools for solving crime. They're not really that helpful in preventing crime," said Ed Yohnka of the American Civil Liberties Union.

Velasquez disputed the conclusion that cameras don't prevent crime, saying he constantly fields requests from residents asking for a camera to make their neighborhood safer.

He said cameras contributed to a drop in violent crime in the city of Chicago in recent years, a drop that is widely attributed to improved police work in countering gangs and street-corner drug dealing. At the same time, gang activity has surged in some Chicago suburbs.

The city's prosecutors said they rarely use video evidence in court from the cameras, which are encased in bulletproof boxes topped by blue flashing lights and are a common sight in crime-ridden neighborhoods.

CJ News (continued)

Downtown, the cameras are less obtrusive, though a pair mounted on a park fountain was removed after an outcry that they defiled the art.

Holtzman, the privacy expert, wondered where the line will be drawn if authorities opt to use the cameras to spy on suspects or to sniff out low-level crimes.

There are no legal barriers to video being subpoenaed by, for instance, a divorce lawyer seeking evidence of infidelity, he said.

"I think there's a certain amount of freedom you want to give people that live in the city to kind of screw up a little bit," he said.

For the latest in crime and justice news, visit the Talk Justice news feed at http://www.crimenews.info.

Source: Copyright 2007 Reuters. Reprinted with permission.

---

form it might eventually take. Even to those living within the same society, *justice* means different things. And just as *justice* can be an ambiguous term for politicians, even in times of war, it is not always clear how justice can be achieved in the criminal justice system. For example, is "justice for all" a reasonable expectation of today's—or tomorrow's—system of criminal justice? The answer is unclear because individual interests and social needs often diverge. From the perspective of a society or an entire nation, justice can look very different than it does from the perspective of an individual or a small group of people. Because of this dilemma, we now turn our attention to the nature of justice.

British philosopher and statesman Benjamin Disraeli (1804–1881) defined **justice** as "truth in action." A popular dictionary defines it as "the principle of moral rightness, or conformity to truth."[22] **Social justice** is a concept that embraces all aspects of civilized life. It is linked to notions of fairness and to cultural beliefs about right and wrong. Questions of social justice can arise about relationships between individuals, between parties (such as corporations and agencies of government), between the rich and the poor, between the sexes, between ethnic groups and minorities—between social connections of all sorts. In the abstract, the concept of social justice embodies the highest personal and cultural ideals.

Civil justice, one component of social justice, concerns itself with fairness in relationships between citizens, government agencies, and businesses in private matters, such as those involving contractual obligations, business dealings, hiring, and equality of treatment. **Criminal justice**, on the other hand, refers to the aspects of social justice that concern violations of the criminal law. As mentioned earlier, community interests in the criminal justice sphere demand the apprehension and punishment of law violators. At the same time, criminal justice ideals extend to the protection of the innocent, the fair treatment of offenders, and fair play by the agencies of law enforcement, including courts and correctional institutions.

Criminal justice, ideally speaking, is "truth in action" within the process that we call the **administration of justice**. It is therefore vital to remember that justice, in the truest and most satisfying sense of the word, is the ultimate goal of criminal justice—and of the day-to-day practices and challenges that characterize the American criminal justice system. Reality, unfortunately, typically falls short of the ideal and is severely complicated by the fact that justice seems to wear different guises when viewed from diverse vantage points. To some people, the criminal justice system and criminal justice agencies often seem biased in favor of the powerful. The laws they enforce seem to emanate more from well-financed, organized, and vocal interest groups than they do from any idealized sense of social justice. As a consequence, disenfranchised groups, those who do not feel as though they share in the political and economic power of society, are often wary of the agencies of justice, seeing them more as enemies than as benefactors.

On the other hand, justice practitioners, including police officers, prosecutors, judges, and corrections officials, frequently complain that their efforts to uphold the law garner unfair public criticism. The realities of law enforcement and of "doing justice," they say, are often overlooked by critics of the system who have little experience in dealing with offenders and victims. We must recognize, practitioners often tell us, that those accused of violating the criminal law face an elaborate process built around numerous legislative, administrative, and organizational concerns. Viewed realistically, although the criminal justice process can be fine-tuned to take into consideration the interests of ever-larger numbers of people, it rarely pleases everyone. The outcome of the criminal

justice

The principle of fairness; the ideal of moral equity.

social justice

An ideal that embraces all aspects of civilized life and that is linked to fundamental notions of fairness and to cultural beliefs about right and wrong.

civil justice

The civil law, the law of civil procedure, and the array of procedures and activities having to do with private rights and remedies sought by civil action. Civil justice cannot be separated from social justice because the justice enacted in our nation's civil courts reflects basic American understandings of right and wrong.

criminal justice

In the strictest sense, the criminal (penal) law, the law of criminal procedure, and the array of procedures and activities having to do with the enforcement of this body of law. Criminal justice cannot be separated from social justice because the justice enacted in our nation's criminal courts reflects basic American understandings of right and wrong.

administration of justice

The performance of any of the following activities: detection, apprehension, detention, pretrial release, post-trial release, prosecution, adjudication, correctional supervision, or rehabilitation of accused persons or criminal offenders.[vi]

justice process in any particular case is a social product, and like any product that is the result of group effort, it must inevitably be a patchwork quilt of human emotions, reasoning, and concerns.

Whichever side we choose in the ongoing debate over the nature and quality of criminal justice in America, it is vital that we recognize the plethora of pragmatic issues involved in the administration of justice while also keeping a clear focus on the justice ideal.[23] Was justice done, for example, in the 2005 criminal trial of pop music superstar Michael Jackson on charges of child molestation or in the 1995 murder trial of former football great O. J. Simpson? What about the trials of the Los Angeles police officers accused of beating Rodney King? Similarly, we might ask, was justice done in the arrest and lengthy detention of hundreds of Muslims after September 11, 2001—even though most were later released when no evidence could be found linking them to any crime?[24] While answers to such questions may reveal a great deal about the American criminal justice system, they also have much to say about the perspectives of those who provide them.

American Criminal Justice: System and Functions

The Consensus Model

criminal justice system

The aggregate of all operating and administrative or technical support agencies that perform criminal justice functions. The basic divisions of the operational aspects of criminal justice are law enforcement, courts, and corrections.

So far, we have described a **criminal justice system**[25] consisting of the component agencies of police, courts, and corrections. Each of these components can, in turn, be described in terms of its functions and purpose (Figure 1–2).

FIGURE 1–2

The core components of the American criminal justice system and their functions.

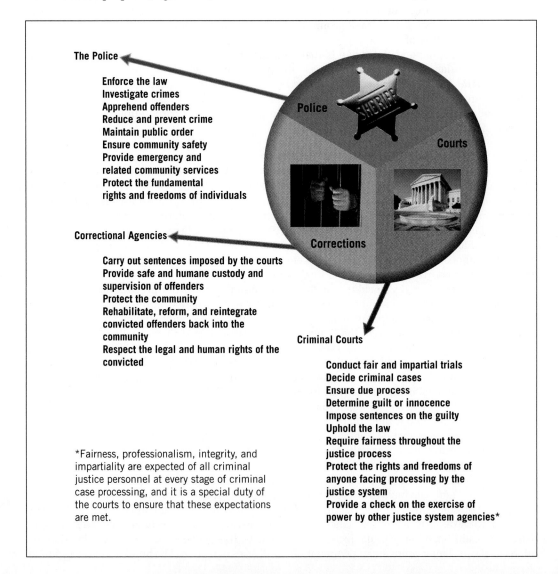

The Police

Enforce the law
Investigate crimes
Apprehend offenders
Reduce and prevent crime
Maintain public order
Ensure community safety
Provide emergency and
related community services
Protect the fundamental
rights and freedoms of individuals

Correctional Agencies

Carry out sentences imposed by the courts
Provide safe and humane custody and
supervision of offenders
Protect the community
Rehabilitate, reform, and reintegrate
convicted offenders back into the
community
Respect the legal and human rights of the
convicted

*Fairness, professionalism, integrity, and impartiality are expected of all criminal justice personnel at every stage of criminal case processing, and it is a special duty of the courts to ensure that these expectations are met.

Criminal Courts

Conduct fair and impartial trials
Decide criminal cases
Ensure due process
Determine guilt or innocence
Impose sentences on the guilty
Uphold the law
Require fairness throughout the
justice process
Protect the rights and freedoms of
anyone facing processing by the
justice system
Provide a check on the exercise of
power by other justice system agencies*

The systems perspective on criminal justice is characterized primarily by its assumption that the various parts of the justice system work together by design to achieve the wider purpose we have been calling *justice.* Hence the systems perspective on criminal justice generally encompasses a point of view called the **consensus model**. The consensus model assumes that each of the component parts of the criminal justice system strives toward a common goal and that the movement of cases and people through the system is smooth due to cooperation between the various components of the system.

The systems model of criminal justice is more an analytic tool than a reality, however. An analytic model, whether in the hard sciences or in the social sciences, is simply a convention chosen for its explanatory power. By explaining the actions of criminal justice officials—such as arrest, prosecution, and sentencing—as though they were systematically related, we are able to envision a fairly smooth and predictable process (which is described in more detail later in this chapter).

The systems model has been criticized for implying a greater level of organization and cooperation among the various agencies of justice than actually exists. The word *system* calls to mind a near-perfect form of social organization. The modern mind associates the idea of a system with machine-like precision in which the problems of wasted effort, redundancy, and conflicting actions are quickly corrected. In practice, the justice system has nowhere near this level of perfection, and the systems model is admittedly an oversimplification. Conflicts among and within agencies are rife; individual actors within the system often do not share immediate goals; and the system may move in different directions depending on political currents, informal arrangements, and personal discretion.

consensus model

A criminal justice perspective that assumes that the system's components work together harmoniously to achieve the social product we call *justice.*

The Conflict Model

The **conflict model** provides another approach to the study of American criminal justice. The conflict model says that the interests of criminal justice agencies tend to make actors within the system self-serving. According to this model, the goals of individual agencies often conflict, and pressures for success, promotion, pay increases, and general accountability fragment the efforts of the system as a whole, leading to a criminal justice *non*system.[26]

A classic study of clearance rates by criminologist Jerome H. Skolnick provides support for the idea of a criminal justice nonsystem.[27] Clearance rates are a measure of crimes solved by the police. The more crimes the police can show they have solved, the better they look to the public they serve. Skolnick discovered an instance in which a burglar was caught red-handed during the commission of a burglary. After his arrest, the police suggested that he confess to many unsolved burglaries that they knew he had not committed. In effect they said, "Help us out, and we will try to help you out!" The burglar did confess—to more than 400 other burglaries. Following the confession, the police were satisfied because they could say they had "solved" many burglaries, and the suspect was pleased as well because the police and the prosecutor agreed to speak on his behalf before the judge.

Both models have something to tell us. Agencies of justice with a diversity of functions (police, courts, and corrections) and at all levels (federal, state, and local) are linked closely enough for the term *system* to be meaningfully applied to them. On the other hand, the very size of the criminal justice undertaking makes effective cooperation between component agencies difficult. The police, for example, have an interest in seeing offenders put behind bars. Prison officials, on the other hand, are often working with extremely overcrowded facilities. They may favor early-release programs for certain categories of offenders, such as those judged to be nonviolent. Who wins out in the long run might just be a matter of internal politics and quasi-official wrangling. Everyone should be concerned, however, when the goal of justice is affected, and sometimes even sacrificed, because of conflicts within the system.

conflict model

A criminal justice perspective that assumes that the system's components function primarily to serve their own interests. According to this theoretical framework, justice is more a product of conflicts among agencies within the system than it is the result of cooperation among component agencies.

American Criminal Justice: The Process

Whether part of a system or a nonsystem, the agencies of criminal justice must process the cases that come before them. An analysis of criminal justice case processing provides both a useful guide to this book and a "road map" to the criminal justice system itself. The figure in the front of this book illustrates the processing of a criminal case through the federal justice system, beginning with the investigation of reported crimes. The process in most state systems is similar. See **Web Extra 1–2** at cjtoday.com for more information about the process shown in the figure.

WEB
Extra
■ ■ ■ ■

If we do not maintain Justice, Justice will not maintain us.

—*Francis Bacon*

warrant

In criminal proceedings, a writ issued by a judicial officer directing a law enforcement officer to perform a specified act and affording the officer protection from damages if he or she performs it.

Investigation and Arrest

The modern justice process begins with investigation. After a crime has been discovered, evidence is gathered at the scene when possible, and a follow-up investigation attempts to reconstruct the sequence of activities. Although a few offenders are arrested at the scene of the crime, most are apprehended later. In such cases, an arrest **warrant** issued by a judge provides the legal basis for an apprehension by police.

An arrest, in which a person is taken into custody, limits the arrestee's freedom. Arrest is a serious step in the process of justice and involves a discretionary decision made by the police seeking to bring criminal sanctions to bear. Most arrests are made peacefully, but if a suspect tries to resist, a police officer may need to use force. Only about half of all people arrested are eventually convicted, and of those, only about a quarter are sentenced to a year or more in prison.

During arrest and before questioning, defendants are usually advised of their constitutional rights, as enumerated in the famous U.S. Supreme Court decision of *Miranda* v. *Arizona*.[28] Defendants are told:

(1) "You have the right to remain silent." (2) "Anything you say can and will be used against you in court." (3) "You have the right to talk to a lawyer for advice before we ask you any questions, and to have him with you during questioning." (4) "If you cannot afford a lawyer, one will be appointed for you before any questioning if you wish." (5) "If you decide to answer questions now without a lawyer present, you will still have the right to stop answering at any time. You also have the right to stop answering at any time and may talk with a lawyer before deciding to speak again." (6) "Do you wish to talk or not?" and (7) "Do you want a lawyer?"[29]

Although popular television programs about the criminal justice system almost always show an offender being given a rights advisement at the time of arrest, the *Miranda* decision requires only that police advise a person of his or her rights prior to questioning. An arrest without questioning does not require a warning. When an officer interrupts a crime in progress, public-safety considerations may make it reasonable for the officer to ask a few questions prior to a rights advisement. Many officers, however, feel they are on sound legal ground only by advising suspects of their rights immediately after arrest. Investigation and arrest are discussed in detail in Chapter 7, "Policing: Legal Aspects."

Justice cannot be for one side alone, but must be for both.

—*Eleanor Roosevelt*

BOOKING

booking

A law enforcement or correctional administrative process officially recording an entry into detention after arrest and identifying the person, the place, the time, the reason for the arrest, and the arresting authority.

Following arrest, suspects are booked. During **booking**, which is an administrative procedure, pictures are taken, fingerprints are made, and personal information such as address, date of birth, weight, and height is gathered. Details of the charges are recorded, and an administrative record of the arrest is created. At this time suspects are often advised of their rights again and are asked to sign a form on which each right is written. The written form generally contains a statement acknowledging the advisement of rights and attesting to the fact that the suspect understands them.

Pretrial Activities

FIRST APPEARANCE

bail

The money or property pledged to the court or actually deposited with the court to effect the release of a person from legal custody.

Within hours of arrest, suspects must be brought before a magistrate (a judicial officer) for an initial appearance. The judge will tell them of the charges against them, will again advise them of their rights, and may sometimes provide the opportunity for **bail**.

Most defendants are released on recognizance into their own care or the care of another or are given the chance to post a bond during their first appearance. A bond may take the form of a cash deposit or a property bond in which a house or other property serves as collateral against flight. Those who flee may be ordered to forfeit the posted cash or property. Suspects who are not afforded the opportunity for bail because their crimes are very serious or who do not have the needed financial resources are taken to jail to await the next stage in the justice process.

If a defendant doesn't have a lawyer, one will be appointed at the first appearance. To retain a court-appointed lawyer, the defendant may have to demonstrate financial hardship. The names of assigned lawyers are usually drawn off the roster of practicing defense attorneys in the county. Some jurisdictions use public defenders to represent indigent defendants.

All aspects of the first appearance, including bail bonds and possible pretrial release, are discussed in detail in Chapter 10, "Pretrial Activities and the Criminal Trial."

PRELIMINARY HEARING

The primary purpose of a **preliminary hearing**, also sometimes called a *preliminary examination*, is to establish whether sufficient evidence exists against a person to continue the justice process. At the preliminary hearing, the hearing judge will seek to determine whether there is **probable cause** to believe that (1) a crime has been committed and (2) the defendant committed it. The decision is a judicial one, but the process provides the prosecutor with an opportunity to test the strength of the evidence at his or her disposal.

The preliminary hearing also allows defense counsel the chance to assess the strength of the prosecution's case. As the prosecution presents evidence, the defense is said to "discover" what it is. Hence the preliminary hearing serves a discovery function for the defense. If the defense attorney thinks the evidence is strong, he or she may suggest that a plea bargain be arranged. All defendants, including those who are indigent, have a right to be represented by counsel at the preliminary hearing.

INFORMATION OR INDICTMENT

In some states, the prosecutor may seek to continue the case against a defendant by filing an **information** with the court. An information, which is a formal written accusation, is filed on the basis of the outcome of the preliminary hearing.

Other states require that an **indictment** be returned by a **grand jury** before prosecution can proceed. The grand jury hears evidence from the prosecutor and decides whether the case should go to trial. In effect, the grand jury is the formal indicting authority. It determines whether probable cause exists to charge the defendant formally with the crime. Grand juries can return an indictment on less than a unanimous vote.

The grand jury system has been criticized because it is one-sided. The defense has no opportunity to present evidence; the grand jury is led only by the prosecutor, often through an appeal to emotions or in ways that would not be permitted in a trial. At the same time, the grand jury is less bound by specific rules than a trial jury. For example, a grand jury member once told the author that a rape case had been dismissed because the man had taken the woman to dinner first. Personal ignorance and subcultural biases are far more likely to play a role in grand jury hearings than in criminal trials. In defense of the grand jury system, however, defendants who are clearly innocent will likely not be indicted. A grand jury's refusal to indict can save the system considerable time and money by preventing cases lacking in evidence from further processing by the criminal justice system.

preliminary hearing

A proceeding before a judicial officer in which three matters must be decided: (1) whether a crime was committed, (2) whether the crime occurred within the territorial jurisdiction of the court, and (3) whether there are reasonable grounds to believe that the defendant committed the crime.

probable cause

A set of facts and circumstances that would induce a reasonably intelligent and prudent person to believe that a specified person has committed a specified crime. Also, reasonable grounds to make or believe an accusation. Probable cause refers to the necessary level of belief that would allow for police seizures (arrests) of individuals and full searches of dwellings, vehicles, and possessions.

information

A formal, written accusation submitted to a court by a prosecutor, alleging that a specified person has committed a specified offense.

indictment

A formal, written accusation submitted to the court by a grand jury, alleging that a specified person has committed a specified offense, usually a felony.

grand jury

A group of jurors who have been selected according to law and have been sworn to hear the evidence and to determine whether there is sufficient evidence to bring the accused person to trial, to investigate criminal activity generally, or to investigate the conduct of a public agency or official.

A criminal defendant at a preliminary hearing. Everyone facing criminal prosecution in the United States is guaranteed a constitutional right to due process, meaning that defendants must be afforded a fair opportunity to participate in every stage of criminal proceedings. Should due process rights extend to all offenders—even accused terrorists?
AP Wide World Photos

ARRAIGNMENT

The **arraignment** is "the first appearance of the defendant before the court that has the authority to conduct a trial."[30] At arraignment, the accused stands before a judge and hears the information, or indictment, against him as it is read. Defendants are again notified of their rights and are asked to enter a plea. Acceptable pleas generally include (1) not guilty, (2) guilty, and (3) no contest (*nolo contendere*), which may result in conviction but can't be used later as an admission of guilt in civil proceedings. Civil proceedings, or private lawsuits, while not covered in detail in this book, provide an additional avenue of relief for victims or their survivors. Convicted offenders increasingly face suits brought against them by victims seeking to collect monetary damages.

The Federal Rules of Criminal Procedure specify that "arraignment shall be conducted in open court and shall consist of reading the indictment or information to the defendant or stating to him the substance of the charge and calling on him to plead thereto. He shall be given a copy of the indictment or information before he is called upon to plead."[31]

Guilty pleas are not always accepted by the judge. If the judge believes a guilty plea is made under duress or is due to a lack of knowledge on the part of the defendant, the plea will be rejected and a plea of "not guilty" will be substituted for it. Sometimes defendants "stand mute," that is, they refuse to speak or to enter a plea of any kind. In that case, the judge will enter a plea of "not guilty" on their behalf.

The arraignment process is discussed in detail in Chapter 10, "Pretrial Activities and the Criminal Trial."

Everywhere across the nation, we are more concerned with ensuring that criminal activity does not repeat itself, rather than keeping criminal activity from occurring in the first place.

—Tony Fabelo, Executive Director, Texas Criminal Justice Policy Council

Adjudication

Under the Sixth Amendment to the U.S. Constitution, every criminal defendant has a right to a **trial** by jury. The U.S. Supreme Court, however, has held that petty offenses are not covered by the Sixth Amendment guarantee and that the seriousness of a case is determined by the way in which "society regards the offense." For the most part, "offenses for which the maximum period of incarceration is six months or less are presumptively petty."[32] In *Blanton* v. *City of North Las Vegas* (1989), the Court held that "a defendant can overcome this presumption and become entitled to a jury trial, only by showing that . . . additional penalties [such as fines and community service] viewed together with the maximum prison term, are so severe that the legislature clearly determined that the offense is a serious one."[33] The *Blanton* decision was further reinforced in the case of *U.S.* v. *Nachtigal* (1993).[34]

In most jurisdictions, many criminal cases never come to trial. The majority are "pleaded out," that is, they are dispensed of as the result of a bargained plea, or they are dismissed for one of a variety of reasons. Studies have found that as many as 82% of all sentences are imposed in criminal cases because of guilty pleas rather than trials.[35]

In cases that do come to trial, the procedures governing the submission of evidence are tightly controlled by procedural law and precedent. *Procedural law* specifies the type of evidence that may be submitted, the credentials of those allowed to represent the state or the defendant, and what a jury is allowed to hear.

While the federal government occasionally may make a great advance in the direction of civil liberties, they can also make a very disastrous reversal.

—Supreme Court Justice Robert H. Jackson[viii]

Precedent refers to understandings built up through common usage and also to decisions rendered by courts in previous cases. Precedent in the courtroom, for example, requires that lawyers request permission from the judge before approaching a witness. It also can mean that excessively gruesome items of evidence may not be used or must be altered in some way so that their factual value is not lost in the strong emotional reactions they may create.

Some states allow trials for less serious offenses to occur before a judge if defendants waive their right to a trial by jury. This is called a *bench trial*. Other states require a jury trial for all serious criminal offenses.

Trials are expensive and time-consuming. They pit defense attorneys against prosecutors. Regulated conflict is the rule, and jurors are required to decide the facts and apply the law as the judge explains it to them. In some cases, however, a jury may be unable to decide. Such a jury is said to be *deadlocked*, and the judge declares a mistrial. The defendant may be tried again when a new jury is impaneled.

The criminal trial and its participants are described fully in Chapter 9, "The Courts: Structure and Participants," and Chapter 10, "Pretrial Activities and the Criminal Trial."

Criminal justice cannot be achieved in the absence of social justice.

—American Friends' Service Committee[viii]

Sentencing

Once a person has been convicted, it becomes the responsibility of the judge to impose some form of punishment. The sentence may take the form of supervised probation in the community, a fine, a prison term, or some combination of these. Defendants will often be ordered to pay the costs of court or of their own defense if they are able.

Prior to sentencing, a sentencing hearing may be held in which lawyers on both sides present information concerning the defendant. The judge may also ask a probation or parole officer to compile a presentence report, which contains information on the defendant's family and business situation, emotional state, social background, and criminal history. This report helps the judge make an appropriate sentencing decision.

Judges traditionally have had considerable discretion in sentencing, although new state and federal laws now place limits on judicial discretion in some cases, requiring that a sentence "presumed" by law be imposed. Judges still retain enormous discretion, however, in specifying whether sentences on multiple charges are to run consecutively or concurrently. Offenders found guilty of more than one charge may be ordered to serve one sentence after another is completed, called a **consecutive sentence**, or may be told that their sentences will run at the same time, which is called a **concurrent sentence**.

Many convictions are appealed. The appeals process can be complex and can involve both state and federal judiciaries. An appeal is based on the defendant's claim that rules of procedure were not followed properly at some earlier stage in the justice process or that the defendant was denied the rights guaranteed by the U.S. Constitution.

Chapter 11, "Sentencing," outlines modern sentencing practices and describes the many modern alternatives to imprisonment.

Corrections

Once an offender has been sentenced, the corrections stage begins. Some offenders are sentenced to prison, where they "do time" for their crimes. Once in the correctional system, they are classified according to local procedures and are assigned to confinement facilities and treatment programs. Newer prisons today bear little resemblance to the massive bastions of the past, which isolated offenders from society behind huge stone walls. Many modern prisons, however, still suffer from a "lock psychosis" (a preoccupation with security) among top- and mid-level administrators as well as a lack of significant rehabilitation programs.

Chapter 13, "Prisons and Jails," discusses the philosophy behind prisons and sketches their historical development. Chapter 14, "Prison Life," portrays life on the inside and delineates the social structures that develop in response to the pains of imprisonment.

PROBATION AND PAROLE

Not everyone who is convicted of a crime and sentenced ends up in prison. Some offenders are ordered to prison only to have their sentences suspended and a probationary term imposed. They may also be ordered to perform community-service activities as a condition of their probation. During the term of probation, these offenders are required to submit to supervision by a probation officer and to meet other conditions set by the court. Failure to do so results in revocation of probation and imposition of the original prison sentence.

Offenders who have served a portion of their prison sentences may be freed on parole. They are supervised by a parole officer and assisted in their readjustment to society. As in the case of probation, failure to meet the conditions of parole may result in revocation of parole and a return to prison.

Chapter 11, "Sentencing," and Chapter 12, "Probation, Parole, and Community Corrections," deal with the practice of probation and parole and with the issues surrounding it. Learn more about the criminal justice process at Library Extra 1–2 at cjtoday.com. For a critical look at the justice system, visit Web Extra 1–3 at cjtoday.com.

Due Process and Individual Rights

The U.S. Constitution requires that criminal justice case processing be conducted with fairness and equity; this requirement is referred to as **due process**. Simply put, *due process* means procedural fairness.[36] It recognizes the individual rights of criminal defendants facing prosecution by a state or the federal government. Under the due process standard, rights violations may become the basis for the dismissal of evidence or of criminal charges, especially at the appellate level. Table 1–1 outlines the basic rights to which defendants in criminal proceedings are generally entitled.

Due process underlies the first ten amendments to the Constitution, which are collectively known as the *Bill of Rights*. It is specifically guaranteed by the Fifth, Sixth, and Fourteenth

The criminal justice system is composed of a sprawling bureaucracy with many separate agencies that are largely autonomous and independent.

—Gary LaFree, Ph.D., University of New Mexico

consecutive sentence

One of two or more sentences imposed at the same time, after conviction for more than one offense, and served in sequence with the other sentence. Also, a new sentence for a new conviction, imposed upon a person already under sentence for a previous offense, which is added to the previous sentence, thus increasing the maximum time the offender may be confined or under supervision.

concurrent sentence

One of two or more sentences imposed at the same time, after conviction for more than one offense, and served at the same time. Also, a new sentence for a new conviction, imposed upon a person already under sentence for a previous offense, served at the same time as the previous sentence.

LIBRARY **WEB**
Extra Extra

due process

A right guaranteed by the Fifth, Sixth, and Fourteenth Amendments of the U.S. Constitution and generally understood, in legal contexts, to mean the due course of legal proceedings according to the rules and forms established for the protection of individual rights. In criminal proceedings, due process of law is generally understood to include the following basic elements: a law creating and defining the offense, an impartial tribunal having jurisdictional authority over the case, accusation in proper form, notice and opportunity to defend, trial according to established procedure, and discharge from all restraints or obligations unless convicted.

TABLE 1–1   Individual Rights Guaranteed by the Bill of Rights[1]
A right to be assumed innocent until proven guilty
A right against unreasonable searches of person and place of residence
A right against arrest without probable cause
A right against unreasonable seizure of personal property
A right against self-incrimination
A right to fair questioning by the police
A right to protection from physical harm throughout the justice process
A right to an attorney
A right to trial by jury
A right to know the charges
A right to cross-examine prosecution witnesses
A right to speak and present witnesses
A right not to be tried twice for the same crime
A right against cruel or unusual punishment
A right to due process
A right to a speedy trial
A right against excessive bail
A right against excessive fines
A right to be treated the same as others, regardless of race, sex, religious preference, and other personal attributes

[1]As interpreted by the U.S. Supreme Court.

African-American men comprise less than 6% of the U.S. population and almost one-half of its criminal prisoners.

—Bureau of Justice Statistics

Amendments and is succinctly stated in the Fifth, which reads, "No person shall be . . . deprived of life, liberty, or property, without due process of law." The Fourteenth Amendment makes due process binding on the states, that is, it requires individual states to respect the due process rights of U.S. citizens who come under their jurisdiction.

The courts, and specifically the U.S. Supreme Court, have interpreted and clarified the guarantees of the Bill of Rights. The due process standard was set in the 1960s by the Warren Court (1953–1969), following a number of far-reaching Supreme Court decisions that affected criminal procedure. Led by Chief Justice Earl Warren, the Warren Court is remembered for its concern with protecting the innocent against the massive power of the state in criminal proceedings.[37] As a result of its tireless efforts to institutionalize the Bill of Rights, the daily practice of modern American criminal justice is now set squarely upon the due process standard.

The Role of the Courts in Defining Rights

Although the Constitution deals with many issues, what we have been calling *rights* are open to interpretation. Many modern rights, although written into the Constitution, would not exist in practice were it not for the fact that the U.S. Supreme Court decided, at some point in history, to recognize them in cases brought before it. In the well-known case of *Gideon* v. *Wainwright* (1963),[38] for example, the Supreme Court embraced the Sixth Amendment guarantee of a right to a lawyer for all criminal defendants and mandated that states provide lawyers for defendants who are unable to pay for them. Before *Gideon* (which is discussed in detail in Chapter 9), court-appointed attorneys for defendants unable to afford their own counsel were practically unknown, except in capital cases and in some federal courts. After the *Gideon* decision, court-appointed counsel became commonplace, and measures were instituted in jurisdictions across the nation to select attorneys fairly for indigent defendants. It is important to note, however, that while the Sixth Amendment specifically says, among other things, that "in all criminal prosecutions, the accused shall enjoy the right . . . to have the Assistance of Counsel for his defence," it does not say, in so many words, that the state is *required* to provide counsel. It is the U.S. Supreme Court, interpreting the Constitution, that has said that.

The U.S. Supreme Court is very powerful, and its decisions often have far-reaching consequences. The decisions rendered by the justices in cases like *Gideon* become, in effect, the law of the land. For all practical purposes, such decisions often carry as much weight as legislative ac-

CJ Careers

Why Study Criminal Justice?

As this chapter points out, criminal justice, as an academic area, is one of the fastest-growing disciplines in the United States. While the discipline has been expanding for more than a decade, much job growth is still to come, as the table in this box shows.

The events of September 11, 2001, have made the study of criminal justice more relevant than ever, and many of today's students use their criminal justice major as a path to a fulfilling job serving the nation and helping protect local communities. A criminal justice career offers students a way of contributing to society, and it permits them to give something back to the country and to the community that nurtured them. For many, a criminal justice ca-

reer reaffirms the American way of life by supporting the values on which it is based.

Other students are attracted to the study of criminal justice because it facilitates exploration of the tension that exists within American society between individual rights and freedoms, on the one hand, and the need for public safety and security, on the other. That tension—between individual rights and public order—forms the theme upon which this textbook is built, and it is discussed in detail elsewhere in this chapter.

For more information on rapidly expanding criminal justice careers, read *Where the Jobs Are: Mission Critical Opportunities for America*, available on the Web at http://www.justicestudies.com.jobs.htm.

Projected Occupation Growth, 2002–2012

Occupation	Federal Workforce (%)	Civilian Labor Force (%)
Criminal investigators	42.7	22.4
Management analysts	22.0	30.4
Biological scientists	20.8	19.0
Lawyers	10.7	17.0
Computer specialists	10.2	35.8
Production occupations	−4.2	3.2
Office clerks	−11.4	10.4
Secretaries	−17.2	4.5

Sources: Bureau of Labor Statistics, *Career Guide to Industries, 2004–2005*; and Bureau of Labor Statistics, *Occupational Projections and Training Data, 2004–2005*.

tion. For this reason, we speak of "judge-made law" (rather than legislated law) in describing judicial precedents that affect the process of justice.

Rights that have been recognized by court decisions are subject to continual refinement, and although the process of change is usually very slow, new interpretations may broaden or narrow the scope of applicability accorded to constitutional guarantees.

The Ultimate Goal: Crime Control through Due Process

Two primary goals were identified in our discussion of this book's theme: (1) the need to enforce the law and to maintain public order and (2) the need to protect individuals from injustice, especially at the hands of the criminal justice system. The first of these principles values the efficient arrest and conviction of criminal offenders. It is often referred to as the **crime-control model** of justice. The crime-control model was first brought to the attention of the academic community in Stanford University law professor Herbert Packer's cogent analysis of the state of criminal justice in the late 1960s.[39] For that reason, it is sometimes referred to as *Packer's crime-control model*.

The second principle is called the **due process model** because of its emphasis on individual rights. Due process is intended to ensure that innocent people are not convicted of crimes; it is a fundamental part of American criminal justice. It requires a careful and informed consideration of the facts of each individual case. Under the due process model, police are required to recognize the rights of suspects during arrest, questioning, and handling. Similarly, prosecutors and judges must recognize constitutional and other guarantees during trial and the presentation of evidence.

crime-control model

A criminal justice perspective that emphasizes the efficient arrest and conviction of criminal offenders.

due process model

A criminal justice perspective that emphasizes individual rights at all stages of justice system processing.

CJ Careers

U.S. Federal Government 2007 General Schedule Pay

Throughout this book, you will find a number of "CJ Careers" boxes showcasing job opportunities with various federal criminal justice agencies, such as the FBI, DEA, U.S. Secret Service, U.S. Marshals, and Bureau of Prisons. Those boxes describe agency-specific job requirements and list the federal pay levels at which successful appli-

cants might expect to be employed. Basic pay under the federal General Schedule (GS) pay plan is shown in the following table. Annual salaries for federal law enforcement officers, which are higher than for most other federal employees in the same grade, are also indicated.

For additional federal employment information, visit http://www.opm.gov, the official U.S. government website for job and employment information.

Salary Grade	Most Federal Employees	Federal Law Enforcement Personnel	Salary Grade	Most Federal Employees	Federal Law Enforcement Personnel	Salary Grade	Most Federal Employees*
GS-1	$16,630	NA	GS-6	$28,562	$33,322	GS-11	$46,974
GS-2	18,698	NA	GS-7	31,740	35,972	GS-12	56,301
GS-3	20,401	$24,481	GS-8	35,151	37,495	GS-13	66,951
GS-4	22,902	27,480	GS-9	38,824	40,412	GS-14	79,115
GS-5	25,623	31,601	GS-10	42,755	44,180	GS-15	93,063

*Includes law enforcement.

Note: GS pay is adjusted geographically, and most federal jobs pay a higher salary than that shown in the table. Locality payments in the continental United States range from 8.6% to 19%. Pay rates outside the continental United States are 10% to 25% higher. Also, certain hard-to-fill jobs, usually in the scientific, technical, and medical fields, may have higher starting salaries. Exact pay information can be found in federal position vacancy announcements. To view the most recent general federal pay scale and locality pay charts, go to http://www.opm.gov/oca.

Liberty is the perfection of civil society, but still authority must be acknowledged essential to its very existence.

—David Hume

social control

The use of sanctions and rewards within a group to influence and shape the behavior of individual members of that group. Social control is a primary concern of social groups and communities, and it is their interest in the exercise of social control that leads to the creation of both criminal and civil statutes.

The dual goals of crime control and due process are often assumed to be opposing goals. Indeed, some critics of American criminal justice argue that the practice of justice is too often concerned with crime control at the expense of due process. Other analysts of the American scene maintain that our type of justice coddles offenders and does too little to protect the innocent. While it is impossible to avoid ideological conflicts like these, it is also realistic to think of the American system of justice as representative of *crime control through due process*—that is, as a system of **social control** that is fair to those whom it processes. This model of *law enforcement infused with the recognition of individual rights* provides a workable conceptual framework for understanding the American system of criminal justice.

The Role of Research in Criminal Justice

The study of criminal justice as an academic discipline began in this country in the late 1920s, when August Vollmer (1876–1955), the former police chief of the Los Angeles Police Department (LAPD), persuaded the University of California to offer courses on the subject.[40] Vollmer was joined by his former student Orlando W. Wilson (1900–1972) and by William H. Parker (who later served as chief of the LAPD from 1950 to 1966) in calling for increased professionalism in police work through better training.[41] Largely as a result of Vollmer's influence, early criminal justice education was practice oriented; it was a kind of extension of on-the-job training for working practitioners. Hence, in the early days of the discipline, criminal justice students were primarily focused on the application of general management principles to the administration of police agencies. Criminal justice came to be seen as a practical field of study concerned largely with issues of organizational effectiveness.

criminology

The scientific study of the causes and prevention of crime and the rehabilitation and punishment of offenders.

By the 1960s, however, police training came to be augmented by criminal justice education[42] as students of criminal justice began to apply the techniques of social scientific research—many of them borrowed from sister disciplines like **criminology**, sociology, psychology, and political science—to the study of all aspects of the justice system. Scientific research into the operation of

CJ Futures

The National Law Enforcement and Corrections Technology Center

You will encounter a number of "CJ Futures" boxes in this book. These boxes illustrate a subtheme of your textbook: the future of crime and justice, including social issues and changing technology.

A major source of information about the impact of technology on the criminal justice system is the National Law Enforcement and Corrections Technology Center (NLECTC). This network of regional centers and specialty offices located across the country offers no-cost assistance to help law enforcement and corrections agencies implement current and emerging technologies. The system is composed of a national center located in Rockville, Maryland, and five regional centers in Rome, New York; Charleston, South Carolina; Denver, Colorado; El Segundo, California; and Anchorage, Alaska.

The NLECTC system also includes the Border Research and Technology Center in San Diego, California; the Office of Law Enforcement Standards in Gaithersburg, Maryland; the Office of Law Enforcement Technology Commercialization in Wheeling, West Virginia; and the Rural Law Enforcement Technology Center in Hazard, Kentucky.

NLECTC is supported by the National Institute of Justice (NIJ), an arm of the U.S. Department of Justice. It is overseen by the Office of Science and Technology within NIJ.

David G. Boyd, director of NIJ's Office of Science and Technology, is convinced of the important role that technology will continue to play in the fight against crime. According to Boyd, "The technological revolution that has swept society as a whole in recent years has also affected the criminal justice system. Some technologies that not long ago seemed advanced—vests that can stop bullets and electronic monitoring of probationers—today seem commonplace. But the revolution continues apace, with ever more spectacular advances now being made, or in the testing stages, or on the drawing board."

NLECTC provides a wealth of online information for anyone interested in technology assessment as applied to criminal justice. The agency's free newsletter, *TechBeat*, is published four times each year, both on paper and in electronic format. To request a subscription, e-mail asknlectc@nlectc.org. You can visit NLECTC on the Web via **Web Extra 1–4** at cjtoday. com. Once there, you will be able to search the site's Virtual Library, which offers hundreds of publications on topics ranging from Biological, Chemical and Radiological Defense to Transportation Infrastructure Security.

WEB Extra ▪▪▪▪

Reference: National Law Enforcement and Corrections Technology Center, June 2007.

the criminal justice system was encouraged by the 1967 President's Commission on Law Enforcement and Administration of Justice, which influenced passage of the Safe Streets and Crime Control Act of 1968. The Safe Streets Act led to the creation of the National Institute of Law Enforcement and Criminal Justice, which later became the National Institute of Justice (NIJ). As a central part of its mission, NIJ continues to support research in the criminal justice field through substantial funding for scientific explorations into all aspects of the discipline, and it funnels much of the $3 billion spent annually by the U.S. Department of Justice to local communities to help fight crime.

Scientific research has become a major element in the increasing professionalization of criminal justice, both as a career field and as a field of study. As you will learn in Chapter 5, there is a strong call today within criminal justice policy-making circles for the application of evidence-based practices in the justice field. As the word is used here, *evidence* does not refer to evidence of a crime but means, instead, *findings* that are supported by studies. Hence, *evidence-based practice* refers to crime-fighting strategies that have been scientifically tested and are based on social science research. As Chapter 5 points out, evidence-based practices can be expected to play an expanded role in policy making and in the administration of criminal justice for years to come.

Multiculturalism and Diversity in Criminal Justice

In late 2007, 58-year-old Tom Green, a Mormon sentenced in 2001 to a lengthy term in a Utah prison after being convicted of four counts of bigamy, was paroled.[43] Green, who had five wives, another five former wives, and 32 known children when he entered prison in 2001,[44] was also convicted of child rape arising from his marriage to a 13-year-old girl in 1986.

The Church of Jesus Christ of Latter-day Saints brought plural marriage to Utah in the early nineteenth century, but the state legislature banned the practice more than 100 years ago. Today,

CJ News

Police Recruits in Heavy Demand

Police departments, desperate to beef up their ranks, are using unprecedented recruiting tactics that include luring officer candidates from other cities and offering dramatically increased pay, housing allowances and other perks.

The aggressive recruiting efforts have become particularly common in cities such as Phoenix and Lexington, Ky., where local governments are emerging from budget slumps and hiring more officers to keep up with the public safety needs of rapidly growing areas.

To expand its pool of candidates for 500 jobs over the next two years, Phoenix's 2,969-officer department is recruiting on the Los

Los Angeles Police Department rookie officers applauding during their graduation ceremony at the police academy in the city's picturesque Elysian Park. Would you consider a job in policing?

J. Emilio Flores/LaOpinion/NewsCom

Angeles Police Department's turf in Southern California. The $300,000 campaign includes TV and newspaper ads that tout Phoenix's lower cost of living.

Los Angeles' 9,000-member department, which is seeking 720 officers, has responded by hiring its own recruiting strategist. "Southern California is a big market," Los Angeles Police Cmdr. Kenneth Garner says. "It's open season out here."

Honolulu's police department, which has struggled to find applicants on the Hawaiian Islands, is following a strategy similar to Phoenix's. The 1,800-officer department, trying to fill 200 openings, recently sent recruiters to San Diego and Portland, Ore., and got commitments from dozens of prospects.

Lexington raised starting salaries from $26,000 to $34,000 to help boost its 540-member force by 200 officers over four years. The city offers officers up to $7,400 for down payments on houses.

Other police agencies are dangling perks such as bonuses for recruits who speak foreign languages, says Elaine Deck, who tracks recruiting for the International Association of Chiefs of Police. Such perks have become more prevalent as departments have faced stiff competition for recruits in an economy that has created many higher-paying alternatives to police work.

"There are so many (departments) looking for officers," Deck says. The market is so competitive, she says, that departments for the first time are "recruiting whole families. . . . Everything is on the table: bilingual bonuses, housing allowances, you name it."

Some police departments have sent recruiters to other cities to sign up experienced officers from other agencies. Paul Schultz, police chief in Lafayette, Colo., says his 40-officer unit has been raided by larger agencies. "We've had officers go out on assignments where they have been recruited on the job."

For the latest in crime and justice news, visit the Talk Justice news feed at http://www.crimenews.info.

Source: Kevin Johnson, "Police Recruits in Heavy Demand," USA TODAY, November 11, 2005. Reprinted with permission.

E Pluribus Unum (Out of Many, One)

multiculturalism

The existence within one society of diverse groups that maintain unique cultural identities while frequently accepting and participating in the larger society's legal and political systems.[ix] *Multiculturalism* is often used in conjunction with the term *diversity* to identify many distinctions of social significance.

the church officially excommunicates polygamists, although the Fundamentalist Church of Jesus Christ of Latter Day Saints (FLDS), an offshoot of the mainstream church, practices polygamy as a central tenet.

Green was the first polygamist prosecuted in Utah in almost 50 years. The last major prosecution occurred in 1953, when the federal government raided the polygamous town of Short Creek, on the Utah-Arizona border. Images of children being torn away from their parents during that raid led to a public outcry. After that, the government largely ignored practitioners of plural marriage. Green's supporters claimed that it was because of the 2002 Winter Olympics held in Salt Lake City that polygamists, including Green, were targeted. In 2007, however, in a continuing crackdown on polygamists, Warren Steed Jeffs, a leader of the FLDS, was convicted of conspiring to rape a child and of being an accessory to child rape for performing a marriage involving a 14-year-old girl and her 19-year-old cousin. Jeffs, who was on the FBI's Ten Most Wanted list, is awaiting sentencing as this book goes to press. Some estimate the number of polygamists living in Utah and Arizona today at over 30,000,[45] and the existence of such alternative family lifestyles is just one indicator that the United States is a multicultural and diverse society.

Multiculturalism describes a society that is home to a multitude of different cultures, each with its own set of norms, values, and routine behaviors. While American society today is truly a multi-

A migrant worker in California holding a Spanish-English dictionary. American society is multicultural, composed of a wide variety of racial and ethnic heritages, diverse religions, incongruous values, disparate traditions, and distinct languages. What impact does the multicultural nature of our society have on the justice system?

Jae C. Hong/AP Wide World Photos

cultural society, composed of a wide variety of racial and ethnic heritages, diverse religions, incongruous values, disparate traditions, and distinct languages, multiculturalism in America is not new. For thousands of years before Europeans arrived in the Western Hemisphere, tribal nations of Native Americans each spoke their own language, were bound to customs that differed significantly from one another, and practiced a wide range of religions. European immigration, which began in earnest in the seventeenth century, led to greater diversity still. Successive waves of immigrants, along with the slave trade of the early and mid-nineteenth century,[46] brought a diversity of values, beliefs, and patterns of behavior to American shores that frequently conflicted with prevailing cultures. Differences in languages and traditions fed the American melting pot of the late nineteenth and early twentieth centuries and made effective communication between groups difficult.

The face of multiculturalism in America today is quite different than it was in the past, due largely to relatively high birthrates among some minority populations and the huge but relatively recent immigration of Spanish-speaking people from Mexico, Cuba, Central America, and South America. Part of that influx consists of substantial numbers of undocumented immigrants who have entered the country illegally and who, because of experiences in their home countries, may have a special fear of police authority and a general distrust for the law. Such fears make members of this group hesitant to report being victimized, and their undocumented status makes them easy prey for illegal scams like extortion, blackmail, and documentation crimes. Learn more about immigration and crime via Library Extra 1–3 at cjtoday.com.

LIBRARY
Extra
■ ■ ■ ■

Diversity characterizes both immigrant and U.S.-born individuals. Census Bureau statistics show that people identifying themselves as white account for 71% of the U.S. population—a percentage that has been dropping steadily for at least the past 40 years. People of Hispanic origin constitute approximately 12% of the population and are the fastest-growing group in the country. Individuals identifying themselves as African American make up another 12% of the population, and people of Asian and Pacific Island origin make up almost 4% of the total. Native Americans, including American Indians, Eskimos, and Aleuts, account for slightly less than 1% of all Americans.[47] Statistics like these, however, are only estimates, and their interpretation is complicated by the fact that surveyed individuals may be of mixed race. Nonetheless, it is clear that American society today is ethnically and racially quite diverse.

Race and *ethnicity* are only buzzwords that people use when they talk about multiculturalism. After all, neither race nor ethnicity determines a person's values, attitudes, or behavior. Just as there is no uniquely identifiable "white culture" in American society, it is a mistake to think that

America, known the world over as the land of the free, was founded on the principle of liberty and justice for all. . . . Yet, at the same time, some 2 million of our citizens are denied their freedom. . . . At some point we must ask ourselves: What is the moral price we pay as a nation for locking up our youth rather than lifting them up?

—Reverend Jesse L. Jackson, Sr.[x]

Without security, government cannot deliver, nor can the people enjoy, the prosperity and opportunities that flow from freedom and democracy.

—U.S. Attorney General Alberto Gonzales[xi]

all African Americans share the same values or that everyone of Hispanic descent honors the same traditions or even speaks Spanish.

Multiculturalism, as the term is used today, is but one form of *diversity.* Taken together, these two concepts—multiculturalism and diversity—encompass many distinctions of social significance. The broad brush of contemporary multiculturalism and social diversity draws attention to variety along racial, ethnic, subcultural, generational, faith, economic, and gender lines. Lifestyle diversity is also important. The fact that influential elements of the wider society are less accepting of some lifestyles than others doesn't mean that such lifestyles aren't recognized from the viewpoint of multiculturalism. It simply means that at least for now, some lifestyles are accorded less official acceptability than others. As a result, certain lifestyle choices, even within a multicultural society that generally respects and encourages diversity, may still be criminalized, as in the case of polygamy.

Multiculturalism and diversity will be discussed in various chapters throughout this textbook. For now, it is sufficient to recognize that the diverse values, perspectives, and behaviors characteristic of various groups within our society have a significant impact on the justice system. Whether it is the confusion that arises from a police officer's commands to a non-English-speaking suspect, the need for interpreters in the courtroom, a deep-seated distrust of the police in some minority communities, a lack of willingness among some immigrants to report crime, the underrepresentation of women in criminal justice agencies, or some people's irrational suspicions of Arab Americans following the September 11 terrorist attacks, diversity and multiculturalism present special challenges to the everyday practice of criminal justice in America. Finally, as we shall see, the demands and expectations placed on justice agencies in multicultural societies involve a dilemma that is closely associated with the theme of this text: how to protect the rights of individuals to self-expression while ensuring social control and the safety and security of the public.

SUMMARY

It is commonly assumed that these three components— law enforcement (police, sheriffs, marshals), the judicial process (judges, prosecutors, defense lawyers), and corrections (prison officials, probation, and parole officers)—add up to a "system" of criminal justice. A system implies some unity of purpose and organized interrelationship among component parts. In the typical American city and state, and under federal jurisdiction as well, no such relationship exists. There is, instead, a reasonably well-defined criminal process, a continuum through which each accused offender may pass: from the hands of the police, to the jurisdiction of the courts, behind the walls of a prison, then back onto the street.

—National Commission on the Causes and Prevention of Violence

- The American experience with crime during the last half century has been especially influential in shaping the criminal justice system of today. Although crime waves have come and gone, some events during the past century stand out as especially significant, including a spurt of widespread organized criminal activity associated with the Prohibition years of the early twentieth century; the substantial increase in "traditional" crimes during the 1960s and 1970s; the threat to the American way of life represented by illicit drugs around the same time; and the terrorist attacks of September 11, 2001.

- The theme of this book is one of individual rights versus public order. As this chapter points out, the personal freedoms guaranteed to law-abiding citizens as well as to criminal suspects by the Constitution must be closely guarded. At the same time, the urgent social needs of communities for controlling unacceptable behavior and protecting law-abiding citizens from harm must be recognized. This theme is represented by two opposing groups: individual-rights advocates and public-order advocates. The fundamental challenge facing the practice of American criminal justice is in achieving efficient enforce-

ment of the laws while simultaneously recognizing and supporting the legal rights of suspects and the legitimate personal differences and prerogatives of individuals.

- Although justice may be an elusive concept, it is important to recognize that criminal justice is tied closely to notions of social justice, including personal and cultural beliefs about equity and fairness. As a goal to be achieved, criminal justice refers to those aspects of social justice that concern violations of the criminal law. While community interests in the administration of criminal justice demand the apprehension and punishment of law violators, criminal justice ideals extend to the protection of the innocent, the fair treatment of offenders, and fair play by justice administration agencies.

- In this chapter, we described the process of American criminal justice as a system with three major components—police, courts, and corrections—all of which can be described as working together toward a common goal. We warned, however, that a systems viewpoint is useful primarily for the simplification that it provides. A more realistic approach to understanding criminal justice may be the nonsystem approach. As a nonsystem, the criminal justice process is depicted as a fragmented activity in which individuals and agencies within the process have interests and goals that at times coincide but often conflict.

- The stages of criminal case processing include investigation and arrest, booking, a first appearance in court, the defendant's preliminary hearing, the return of an indictment by the grand jury or the filing of an information by the prosecutor, arraignment of the defendant before the court, adjudication or trial, sentencing, and corrections. As a field of study, corrections includes jails, probation, imprisonment, and parole.

- The principle of due process, which underlies the first ten amendments to the U.S. Constitution, is central to American criminal justice. Due process (also called *due process of law*) means procedural fairness and requires that criminal case processing be conducted with fairness and equity. The ultimate goal of the criminal justice system in America is achieving crime control through due process.

- The study of criminal justice as an academic discipline began in this country in the late 1920s and is well established today. Scientific research has become a major element in the increasing professionalization of criminal justice, and there is an increasingly strong call for the application of evidence-based practices in the justice field. Evidence-based practices are crime-fighting strategies that have been scientifically tested and that are based on social science research.

- American society today is a multicultural society, composed of a wide variety of racial and ethnic heritages, diverse religions, incongruous values, disparate traditions, and distinct languages. Multiculturalism complicates the practice of American criminal justice since there is rarely universal agreement in our society about what is right or wrong or about what constitutes "justice." As such, multiculturalism represents both challenges and opportunities for today's justice practitioners.

KEY TERMS

administration of justice, 15

arraignment, 20

bail, 18

booking, 18

civil justice, 15

concurrent sentence, 21

conflict model, 17

consecutive sentence, 21

consensus model, 17

crime, 7

crime-control model, 23

criminal justice, 15

criminal justice system, 16

criminology, 24

due process, 21

due process model, 23

grand jury, 19

indictment, 19

individual rights, 8

individual-rights advocate, 12

information, 19

justice, 15

multiculturalism, 26

preliminary hearing, 19

probable cause, 19

public-order advocate, 12

social control, 24

social justice, 15

trial, 20

USA PATRIOT Act, 10

warrant, 18

QUESTIONS FOR REVIEW

1. Describe the American experience with crime during the last half century. What noteworthy criminal incidents or activities can you identify during that time, and what social and economic conditions might have produced them?

2. What is the theme of this book? According to that theme, what are the differences between the individual-rights perspective and the public-order perspective?

3. What is justice? What aspects of justice does this chapter discuss? How does criminal justice relate to social justice and to other wider notions of equity and fairness?

4. What are the main components of the criminal justice system? How do they interrelate? How might they conflict?

5. List the stages of case processing that characterize the American system of criminal justice, and describe each stage.

6. What is meant by *due process of law*? Where in the American legal system are guarantees of due process found?

7. What is the role of research in criminal justice? What is meant by the term *evidence-based practice*? How can research influence crime-control policy?

8. What is multiculturalism? What is social diversity? What impact do multiculturalism and diversity have on the practice of criminal justice in contemporary American society?

QUESTIONS FOR REFLECTION

1. Reiterate the theme of this textbook. How might this book's theme facilitate the study of criminal justice?

2. Why is public order necessary? Do we have enough public order or too little? How can we tell? What might a large, complex society like ours be like without laws and without a system of criminal justice? Would you want to live in such a society? Why or why not?

3. What must we, as individuals, sacrifice to facilitate public order? Do we ever give up too much in the interest of public order? If so, when?

4. This chapter describes two models of the criminal justice system. What are they, and how do they differ? Which model do you think is more useful? Which is more accurate? Why?

Discuss your answers to these questions and other issues on the CJ Today e-mail discussion list (join the list at ctoday.com).

WEB QUEST

Familiarize yourself with the *Criminal Justice Today* Companion Website and with its many features. To get there, point your browser to http://www.cjtoday.com. Once you've opened the site, you'll be able to read the latest crime and justice news, join the *Criminal Justice Today* e-mail discussion list, and research a wide variety of criminal justice topics. You can learn about your textbook's chapter objectives, practice with online review questions, preview chapter summaries, submit electronic homework to your instructor, and enjoy many Web-based criminal justice projects. (If your instructor decides to use the electronic homework feature of the site, it's always a good idea to keep a copy of any materials that you submit.) The site also allows you to listen to the author introduce each chapter.

Unique Web Extras and book-specific Library Extras substantially enhance the learning opportunities your text offers. Web Extras bring the justice system to life by providing a wealth of links to relevant and informative sites. Library Extras help you learn more about important topics in the justice field via the textbook's electronic library. Library Extras include the latest reports and bulletins from the Bureau of Justice Statistics, the National Institute of Justice, the Bureau of Justice Assistance, the FBI, the Department of Homeland Security, and other agencies. The author has selected each report to complement the textbook and to enhance your learning experience.

One Web resource of special importance is the Prentice Hall Criminal Justice Cybrary (*Cybrary* means "cyber-library"). Known to justice professionals as "the world's crime and justice directory," the Cybrary contains annotated links to more than 12,000 crime and justice sites throughout the nation and around the world. Because it is continually updated and fully searchable, the Cybrary can be an invaluable tool as you write term papers or do Web-based research on crime and justice. You can reach the Cybrary directly by going to http://www.cybrary.info.

To complete this Web Quest online, go to the Web Quest module in Chapter 1 of the *Criminal Justice Today* Companion Website at cjtoday.com.

CHAPTER 2

The Crime Picture

LEARNING OBJECTIVES

After reading this chapter, you should be able to

- Describe the history and nature of the FBI's UCR/NIBRS Program and explain what it can tell us about crime in the United States today.

- Describe the history and nature of the National Crime Victimization Survey Program and explain what it can tell us about crime in the United States today.

- Identify the special categories of crime discussed in this chapter and explain why they are of contemporary significance.

It may turn out that a free society cannot really prevent crime. Perhaps its causes are locked so deeply into the human personality, the intimate processes of family life, and the subtlest aspects of the popular culture that coping is the best that we can hope for.

—*James Q. Wilson, University of California, Los Angeles*[1]

No one way of describing crime describes it well enough.

—*President's Commission on Law Enforcement and Administration of Justice*

Hear the author discuss this chapter at cjtoday.com

Introduction

According to broadcast ratings guru *MediaWeek*, the most popular scripted show on television today is the CBS crime drama *CSI: Crime Scene Investigation*.[2] The series' top ranking would seem to be no small feat for a "cop show" that has to compete with the likes of widely watched offerings like *American Idol, Desperate Housewives, ER, Survivor*, and *Lost*. Until, that is, one realizes that the American public is fascinated with hard-hitting crime dramas. And that helps to explain the success of shows like the *CSI* spin-offs, *CSI: Miami* and *CSI: New York*, as well as to explain why the NBC-TV show *Law and Order* is the longest-running drama on television today and the second-longest running drama ever.[3] Like *CSI*, the *Law and Order* series has generated its own spin-offs, including *Law and Order: Criminal Intent* and *Law and Order: Special Victims' Unit*. Taken together, more than 600 original *Law and Order* segments have aired. Other crime and justice shows on TV today include *Blind Justice* (ABC), *Cold Case* (CBS), *Criminal Minds* (CBS), *The District* (CBS), *The Evidence* (ABC), *Hack* (CBS), *JAG* (CBS), *NCIS* (CBS), *Numb3rs* (CBS), *Prison Break* (Fox), *The Shield* (FX), *Wanted* (TNT), *The Wire* (HBO), and *Without a Trace* (CBS). Like this textbook, many of today's television shows deliver content across a variety of media. View the online CSI crime labs at Web Extra 2–1 at cjtoday.com, and see some real-life crime-prevention links sponsored by *Law and Order: SVU* at Web Extra 2–2. Visit a real cold case squad at Web Extra 2–3.

WEB
Extra
■ ■ ■ ■

The public's interest in crime has also given birth to reality TV crime shows, including *America's Most Wanted* (which premiered on Fox in 1988), *COPS, Crime and Punishment*, and *Wildest Police Videos*. Similarly, video magazine shows like *60 Minutes, 20/20*, and *Nightline* frequently focus on justice issues, and any number of recent movies—including films like *SWAT, Training Day, 2 Fast 2 Furious, The Green Mile, Runaway Jury*, and *Minority Report*—play off the public's fascination with crime and the personal drama it fosters.

This chapter has a dual purpose. First, it provides a statistical overview of crime in contemporary America by examining information on reported and discovered crimes. Second, it identifies special categories of crime that are of particular interest today, including crime against women, crime against the elderly, hate crime, corporate and white-collar crime, organized crime, gun crime, drug crime, cybercrime, and terrorism.

Although we will look at many crime statistics in this chapter, it is important to remember that statistical aggregates of reported crime, whatever their source, do not reveal the lost lives, human suffering, lessened productivity, and reduced quality of life that crime causes. Unlike the fictional characters on TV crime shows, real-life crime victims as well as real-life offenders lead intricate lives—they have families, hold jobs, and dream dreams. As we examine the crime statistics, we must not lose sight of the people behind the numbers.

Crime Data and Social Policy

We can have as much or as little crime as we please; depending on what we choose to count as criminal.

—*Herbert L. Packer*

Crime statistics provide an overview of criminal activity. If used properly, a statistical picture of crime can serve as a powerful tool for creating social policy. Decision makers at all levels, including legislators, other elected officials, and administrators throughout the criminal justice system, rely on crime data to analyze and evaluate existing programs, to fashion and design new crime-control initiatives, to develop funding requests, and to plan new laws and crime-control legislation. Many "get tough" policies, such as the three-strikes movement that swept the country during

The cast of the CBS-TV show *CSI.* The American public has long been enthralled with crime shows, and since the terrorist attacks of 2001, the public's concern with personal safety has surged. Why do so many people like to watch TV crime shows?

CBS/Landov LLC

the 1990s, have been based in large part on the measured ineffectiveness of existing programs to reduce the incidence of repeat offending.

However, some people question just how objective—and therefore how useful—crime statistics are. Social events, including crime, are complex and difficult to quantify. Even the decision of which crimes should be included and which excluded in statistical reports is itself a judgment reflecting the interests and biases of policymakers. Moreover, public opinion about crime is not always realistic. As well-known criminologist Norval Morris points out, the news media do more to influence public perceptions of crime than any official data do.[4] During the four-year period (in the mid-1990s) covered by Morris's study, for example, the frequency of crime stories reported in the national media increased fourfold. During the same time period, crime was at the top of the list in subject matter covered in news stories at both the local and national levels. The irony, says Morris, is that "the grossly increasing preoccupation with crime stories came at a time of steadily declining crime and violence." However, as Morris adds, "aided and abetted by this flood of misinformation, the politicians, federal and state and local, fostered the view that the public demands our present 'get tough' policies."

The Collection of Crime Data

Nationally, crime statistics come from two major sources: (1) the FBI's **Uniform Crime Reporting Program** (also known today as the UCR/NIBRS Program), which produces an annual overview of major crime entitled *Crime in the United States*; and (2) the **National Crime Victimization Survey (NCVS)** of the **Bureau of Justice Statistics (BJS)**. The most widely quoted numbers purporting to describe crime in America today probably come from the UCR/NIBRS Program, although the statistics it produces are based largely on *reports* to the police by victims of crime.

Recently, some professional organizations, most notably the Washington-based Police Executive Research Forum (PERF), have undertaken their own efforts to gather crime data. For example, PERF polled police departments across the country for data related to violent crime.[5] PERF surveys also ask police chiefs to provide subjective impressions of crime trends in their cities and towns.

The statistics gathered by PERF, similar to those in the UCR/NIBRS Program, are based on law enforcement agencies' reports of crimes. PERF notes, however, that because its "members

Uniform Crime Reporting (UCR) Program

A statistical reporting program run by the FBI's Criminal Justice Information Services (CJIS) division. The UCR Program publishes *Crime in the United States,* which provides an annual summation of the incidence and rate of reported crimes throughout the United States.

National Crime Victimization Survey (NCVS)

An annual survey of selected American households conducted by the Bureau of Justice Statistics to determine the extent of criminal victimization—especially unreported victimization—in the United States.

Bureau of Justice Statistics (BJS)

A U.S. Department of Justice agency responsible for the collection of criminal justice data, including the annual National Crime Victimization Survey.

are police chiefs, sheriffs, and other law enforcement executives, PERF is able to obtain official crime statistics from many of the nation's largest jurisdictions and to release those figures several months before the nationwide tallies are released by the FBI."[6]

A fourth source of crime data is offender self-reports based on surveys that ask respondents to reveal any illegal activity in which they have been involved. Offender self-reports are not discussed in detail in this chapter because surveys utilizing them are not national in scope and are not undertaken regularly. Moreover, offenders are often reluctant to accurately report ongoing or recent criminal involvement, making information derived from these surveys somewhat unreliable and less than current. However, the available information from offender self-reports reveals that serious criminal activity is considerably more widespread than most "official" surveys show (Figure 2–1).

Other regular publications also contribute to our knowledge of crime patterns throughout the nation. One such publication is the *Sourcebook of Criminal Justice Statistics*—an annual compilation of national information on crime and on the criminal justice system. The *Sourcebook* is produced by the BJS, and a Web-based version of the *Sourcebook* is continually updated as data become available. The National Institute of Justice (NIJ), which is the primary research arm of the U.S. Department of Justice, the Office of Juvenile Justice and Delinquency Prevention (OJJDP), the Federal Justice Statistics Resource Center, and the National Victim's Resource Center provide still more information on crime patterns. Visit Web Extra 2–4 at cjtoday.com for an overview of the many sources of crime data. The *Sourcebook* is available directly at Library Extra 2–1 at cjtoday.com.

WEB **LIBRARY**
Extra Extra
▪▪▪▪ ▪▪▪▪

FIGURE 2–1

The criminal justice funnel.

Source: Derived from Thomas H. Cohen and Brian Reaves, *Felony Defendants in Large Urban Countries, 2003* (Washington, DC: Bureau of Justice Statistics, 2006).

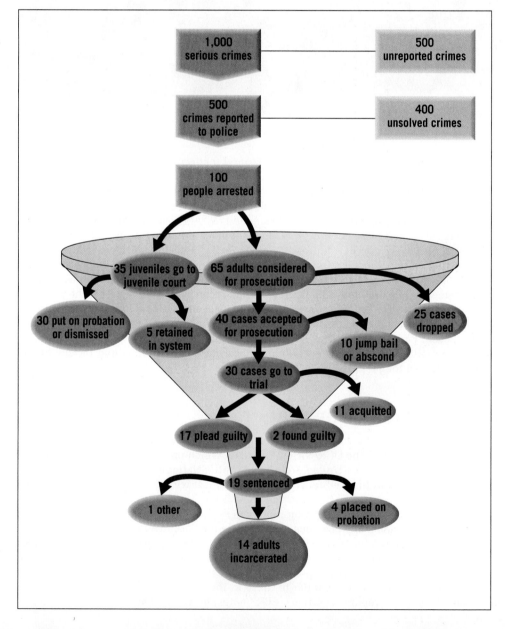

CJ News

Cities See Crime Surge as Threat to Their Revival

A minister who regularly conducts prayer vigils against violence and counsels crime victims is beaten by a gang of youths. Five people are shot and wounded at a community festival. A softball player is shot and wounded at a game, in front of 100 witnesses. One person is killed and four wounded in a shooting outside a funeral home as people gather for a wake.

These crimes happened in very public settings in Louisville, Kentucky, in 2006—two of them within 2 miles of the heart of this Ohio River city's downtown. Such incidents inevitably give communities the jitters, but cities are especially skittish now because the nation's violent crime rate is rising after more than a decade of decline, and the stakes are higher.

The drop in crime helped spark an urban revival that attracted thousands of residents and billions of dollars of investment to downtowns from Louisville to Miami, St. Louis and Denver. Now, city leaders across the nation are fearful that crime will kill the renaissance.

For a city such as Louisville, where downtown is flourishing, keeping crime in check is paramount. More than $1 billion has been invested in the commercial heart of the city this decade. By 2010, at least another $1 billion is expected to come in. Five hotels are set to open, and the 2000 housing units now downtown are expected to double by 2009.

Rising crime "has the potential of being damaging," says Jerry Abramson, mayor of Louisville from 1985 to 1998. He was elected again in 2002 after Louisville merged with surrounding Jefferson County; he was re-elected in 2006. "We all live day by day in terms

Los Angeles Sheriff's Department deputies and Compton Fire Department personnel working at the scene of a shooting in Compton, California, in 2006. Some experts fear that violent crime may be starting to rise in big cities after two decades of decline. What would be the consequences for American cities if crime were to increase?

Photo by Bob Riha, Jr./USA Today

of concern of some horrific thing happening in our central business district that would set us back."

Murders and robberies continued to rise nationwide during the first six months of 2006, according to the FBI, and violent crime overall appears headed for a second straight year of increases. Mayors and police chiefs regularly assure the public that violent crimes still are confined mostly to poorer drug- and gang-infested areas, but they are sounding alarms:

- One of the first sessions at the U.S. Conference of Mayors' winter meeting in January 2007 in Washington tackled initiatives to fight rising crime. Mayors are calling for a federal-local partnership to stem double-digit increases in murders, assaults and robberies in some cities.

- The National League of Cities has put the surge in violent crime on its legislative agenda, calling it one of the major challenges affecting quality of life.

- Mayors and police chiefs from about 55 cities . . . identified many factors pushing up crime rates: gangs, drugs, truancy, a growing culture of violence among youths, a profusion of illegal guns, unemployment and a wave of more than 600,000 ex-offenders finishing their prison terms and returning to the streets every year.

Abramson and some other mayors also blame the federal government for cutting funding for crime prevention and phasing out a Clinton administration program that added 100,000 police officers nationwide. They say Washington's focus has shifted to homeland security at the expense of hometown security.

"The consensus is that the federal government walked away from that partnership," Abramson says. "Crime all of a sudden begins to ratchet up but police on the street have ratcheted significantly down. We draw a correlation."

Justice Department spokesman Brian Roehrkasse disagrees. "The increase in violent crime in some areas does not appear to be related to federal spending for law enforcement," he says. "DOJ spending has never accounted for more than 4% of total spending on state and local law enforcement."

Trenton, N.J., Mayor Douglas Palmer, president of the Conference of Mayors, met with House Speaker Nancy Pelosi in January 2007. He hopes cities can gain more support now that Democrats control Congress.

"Over the '90s, cities have made great strides in coming back, revitalizing neighborhoods, but we've seen an escalation of violence," Palmer says.

"We have fewer police officers in our cities now than ever, with a greater proliferation of guns on the streets. . . . It is of the highest priority." Signs of the trend:

- The Police Executive Research Forum, a national police advocacy group, reported in October 2006 that murder, robbery and assaults had increased substantially in a cross-section of cities. The title of its report: *A Gathering Storm—Violent Crime in America.*

(continued)

CJ News (continued)

"There was a general sense that crime for most communities had dropped to such levels that it no longer was the issue that it was in the '90s and '80s," says Chuck Wexler, executive director of the police group. "We've seen a volatility in crime that we haven't seen in the previous eight years—and not just in the inner cities."

- FBI data . . . show that violent crime rose 2.2% nationwide in 2005, the largest annual increase in 14 years and the first since 2001. In the latest statistics available, violent crime rose 3.7% from January to June 2006 compared with the first six months of 2005. Murders went up 1.4%, felony assaults 1.2% and robberies 9.7%. Property crime dropped 2.6%.

- The FBI has directed more than 100 additional agents to help local authorities fight violent crime.

Justice Department teams visited 18 cities in November and December 2006 to determine why violent crime is spiking in some cities and not in others. They met with state and local law enforcement "to gain a better understanding of what is causing this increase and determine which efforts had been most effective in helping fight violent crime," Roehrkasse says.

- Orlando had 49 homicides in 2006, more than double the 22 in 2005. About 60% were linked to drugs. In Memphis, homicides rose from 118 in 2004 to 160 in 2006. Crime is down in Los Angeles and Chicago. In some cities, homicides are down, but robberies are up.

"We had a general rise in violent crime in not all but most cities in every region," says David Harris, professor of law and values at the University of Toledo College of Law.

Mayors find themselves in an awkward spot. On one hand, they want to publicize their crime problems to get more funding. On the other, they worry that too much crime talk will create a negative perception of cities and scare off people.

"It has a very detrimental effect on what mayors work on each and every day to try to entice businesses to come," Palmer says. "Perception is reality."

Adds Harris: "City officials are quite aware that whatever progress they've made in attracting new residents and bringing people back to live in the city would be at risk if people didn't feel safe."

Cities must deal with crime head-on, says urban historian Joel Kotkin, author of *The City*. "We all hoped that the days of relatively high crime rates had come and gone," he says. "We now know the problem is not going away."

MANY CITIES ARE TAKING ACTION

- In Trenton, homicides spiked to 31 in 2005 but dropped to 18 in 2006. More than 70% were gang-related, Palmer says. "We took down the leadership of nine gangs," he says. "They're in jail."

    The city is cracking down on truancy and providing job training while redeveloping deserted industrial areas, getting rid of 5,500 deserted properties and building 1,600 homes for working families.

"We're making our cities more livable, but it's all inextricably tied to the whole crime piece," Palmer says. "We need resources."

- In Milwaukee, 1993 saw 160 homicides, a record high. By 2004, it had a record low 88. They climbed the next year to 122, then inched down to 103 in 2006.

    "We did see probably a 20% increase in other categories of violent crime . . . an increase in armed robberies and shootings," says Mayor Tom Barrett, a former congressman.

    Barrett and other mayors are working to strengthen background checks of gun buyers. He launched a fatherhood initiative to address the problem of absentee dads. He cut firefighting staff to start 2007 with 1,970 sworn police officers, the highest number since 2000, but is struggling to fill almost 200 vacancies, he says.

    Downtown is thriving. About 14,000 people live there, 10 times more than a decade ago. Waterfront high-rises are going up. Work is starting on The Brewery, a multimillion-dollar conversion of the 26-acre old Pabst brewery complex into a residential and commercial center. The site borders downtown and inner-city neighborhoods.

    "Our downtown is very safe," Barrett says. "I'm concerned about violence that occurs in other parts of the city."

- In Miami, overall crime is down, but homicides are up.

    "The market is literally being flooded with assault weapons coming from Eastern Europe, the old Soviet bloc countries," Police Chief John Timoney says. Guns such as AK-47 rifles are selling for $150 to $200 compared with $700 or more not long ago, he says.

    "Every jerk who wants one can have one," Timoney says.

    Crime, he says, is not affecting Miami's downtown, where thousands of condominiums have been built or are planned. "But I was in New York when there was an all-time record high of homicides," he says. "Three kids were killed. Tourists from Utah were killed in the subway. When you start getting untraditional killings, that's when you get people's attention."

While violent crimes in Louisville have occurred away from downtown, the city has been proactive. Security cameras were installed in high-crime areas and neighborhood watch programs strengthened. Police on horses and bicycles patrol the Fourth Street Live area of clubs, stores and restaurants. The city has razed low-income housing and built mixed-income housing.

"Downtown is one of the, if not the, safest geographic areas in our community," Abramson says.

So far, 70 homicides in 2004 (the highest since 1997 when there were 85), 64 in 2005 and 51 in 2006 have not quelled downtown's resurgence. The Muhammad Ali Center opened in recent years, the convention center was expanded, and an arena is planned. The city soon will break ground on Museum Plaza, a $465 million, 61-story skyscraper that could transform Louisville's skyline.

Police Chief Robert White has reached out to the community since he arrived four years ago. "If we're going to have a long-term effect in fighting crime, we have to get people engaged," he says.

CJ News (continued)

Billboards across town advertise a 24-hour crime tip line, 574-LMPD. The first month in operation, 123 calls came in. Two years later, about 2,000 calls on average led to at least 30 arrests every month. Police credit the tip line with solving 18 homicides and shutting down three methamphetamine labs.

Donnie Morris, who lives in the high-crime West End, runs Prevention 2000 to teach children about gun safety, drugs and other threats. He and his wife, Jefferson County District Court Judge Joan Stringer, encourage churches to report anonymous crime tips they receive from their congregation.

"Areas that are most affected by crime are the ones that don't call the police, but they'll call their clergy," Morris says.

Phil and Kathy Scherer are the kind of empty nesters that many downtowns are attracting these days. The two had always been downtown boosters. After 33 years in the suburbs, they decided to "walk the walk," says Kathy, 58.

They bought a 3,000-square-foot penthouse in Preston Point, a striking modern building with a view of the river. She says she feels more comfortable being alone at night there than she did in her old suburban house.

Young people crowd the streets on their way to a skate park nearby. Joggers run by the waterfront. Mounted police trot past.

"We have always hoped that Louisville would have that 24-hour component," says Phil, 63, a city native and president of a commercial and industrial real estate firm. "I don't see crime as a deterrent."

Mayors hope it stays that way. The police executive association, however, expects the trend of rising crimes to continue this year.

"Robberies are occurring in parts of cities that didn't normally have robberies," Wexler says. "Cities are concerned."

For the latest in crime and justice news, visit the Talk Justice news feed at http://www.crimenews.info.

Source: Haya El Nasser, "Cities See Crime Surge as Threat to Their Revival," USA TODAY, January 25, 2007. Reprinted with permission.

The UCR/NIBRS Program

Development of the UCR Program

In 1930, Congress authorized the U.S. attorney general to survey crime in America, and the FBI was designated to implement the program. In short order, the bureau built on earlier efforts by the International Association of Chiefs of Police (IACP) to create a national system of uniform crime statistics. As a practical measure, IACP had recommended the use of readily available information, and so it was that citizens' crime reports to the police became the basis of the FBI's plan.[7]

During its first year of operation, the FBI's Uniform Crime Reporting Program received reports from 400 cities in 43 states. Twenty million people were covered by that first comprehensive survey. Today, approximately 16,000 law enforcement agencies provide crime information for the program, with data coming from city, county, and state departments. To ensure uniformity in reporting, the FBI has developed standardized definitions of offenses and terminologies used in the program. A number of publications, including the *Uniform Crime Reporting Handbook* and the *Manual of Law Enforcement Records*, are supplied to participating agencies, and training for effective reporting is available through FBI-sponsored seminars and instructional literature.

Following IACP recommendations, the original UCR Program was designed to permit comparisons over time through construction of a **Crime Index**. The index summed the occurrences of seven major offenses—murder, forcible rape, robbery, aggravated assault, burglary, larceny-theft, and motor vehicle theft—and expressed the result as a crime rate based on population. In 1979, by congressional mandate, an eighth offense—arson—was added to the index. The Crime Index, first published in *Crime in the United States* in 1960, was the title used for a simple aggregation of the seven main offense classifications (called Part I offenses). The Modified Crime Index refers to the original Crime Index offenses plus arson.

Over the years, however, concern grew that the Crime Index did not provide a clear picture of criminality because it was skewed by the offense with the highest number of reports—typically larceny-theft. The sheer volume of larceny-theft offenses overshadowed more serious but less frequently committed offenses, skewing perceptions of crime rates for jurisdictions with high numbers of larceny-thefts, but low numbers of serious crimes like murder and forcible rape. In June 2006, the FBI's Criminal Justice Information Services (CJIS) Advisory Policy Board officially discontinued the use of the Crime Index in the UCR/NIBRS Program and in its publications and

The typical mass murderer is extraordinarily ordinary.

—James Alan Fox, Northeastern University

Crime Index

A now defunct but once inclusive measure of the UCR Program's violent and property crime categories, or what are called *Part I offenses*. The Crime Index, long featured in the FBI's publication *Crime in the United States*, was discontinued in 2004. The index had been intended as a tool for geographic (state-to-state) and historical (year-to-year) comparisons via the use of crime rates (the number of crimes per unit of population). However, criticism that the index was misleading arose after researchers found that the largest of the index's crime categories, larceny-theft, carried undue weight and led to an underappreciation of changes in the rates of more violent and serious crimes.

New York Police Department crime-scene specialists collecting evidence in front of the British Consulate in May 2005 after two small makeshift bombs exploded outside the building. No one was injured in the blasts. What kinds of crimes are most likely to go unreported or undiscovered?

Mary Altaffer/AP Wide World Photos

directed the FBI to instead publish simple violent crime totals and property crime totals until a more viable index could be developed.[8]

Although work to develop such an index is still ongoing, UCR/NIBRS Program crime categories continue to provide useful comparisons of specific reported crimes over time and between jurisdictions. It is important to recognize, as you read through the next few pages, that today's UCR/NIBRS Program categories tend to parallel statutory definitions of criminal behavior, but they are not legal classifications—only conveniences created for statistical-reporting purposes. Because many of the definitions of crime used in this textbook are derived from official UCR/NIBRS Program terminology, you should remember that UCR/NIBRS terminology may differ from statutory definitions of crime.

The National Incident-Based Reporting System (NIBRS)

National Incident-Based Reporting System (NIBRS)

An incident-based reporting system that collects detailed data on every single crime occurrence. NIBRS data is replacing the kinds of summary data that have traditionally been provided by the FBI's Uniform Crime Reporting Program.

Beginning in 1988, the FBI's UCR Program initiated development of a new national crime-collection effort called the **National Incident-Based Reporting System (NIBRS)**. NIBRS represents a significant redesign of the original Uniform Crime Reporting Program. Whereas the original UCR system was "summary based," the newly enhanced National Incident-Based Reporting System is incident driven (Table 2–1). Under NIBRS, city, county, state, and federal law enforcement agencies throughout the country furnish detailed data on crime and arrest activities at the incident level either to the individual state incident-based reporting programs or directly to the federal NIBRS program.

NIBRS is not a separate report; rather it is the new methodology underlying the contemporary UCR system—hence our use of the term *UCR/NIBRS* in describing today's Uniform Crime Reporting Program. Whereas the old UCR system depended on statistical tabulations of crime data, which were often little more than frequency counts, the new UCR/NIBRS system gathers many details about each criminal incident. Included among them are information on place of occurrence, weapon used, type and value of property damaged or stolen, the personal characteristics of the offender and the victim, the nature of any relationship between the two, and the disposition of the complaint.

Under UCR/NIBRS, the traditional distinctions between Part I and Part II offenses are being replaced with 22 general offenses: arson, assault, bribery, burglary, counterfeiting, embezzlement, extortion, forcible sex offenses, fraud, gambling, homicide, kidnapping, larceny, motor vehicle theft, narcotics offenses, nonforcible sex offenses, pornography, prostitution, receiving stolen property, robbery, vandalism, and weapons violations. Other offenses on which UCR/NIBRS data are being gathered include bad checks, vagrancy, disorderly conduct, driving under the influence, drunkenness, nonviolent family offenses, liquor-law violations, "Peeping Tom" activity, runaways, trespass, and a general category of all "other" criminal law violations. UCR/NIBRS also

The public is properly obsessed with safety. Of industrialized countries, the U.S. has the highest rate of violent crime.

—Bob Moffitt, Heritage Foundation

TABLE 2–1 Differences between the Traditional UCR and Enhanced UCR/NIBRS Reporting

Traditional UCR	Enhanced UCR/NIBRS
Consists of monthly aggregate crime counts	Consists of individual incident records for the eight major crimes and 38 other offenses, with details on offense, victim, offender, and property involved
Records one offense per incident, as determined by the hierarchy rule, which suppresses counts of lesser offenses in multiple-offense incidents	Records each offense occurring in an incident
Does not distinguish between attempted and completed crimes	Distinguishes between attempted and completed crimes
Records rape of females only	Records rape of males and females
Collects assault information in five categories	Restructures definition of assault
Collects weapon information for murder, robbery, and aggravated assault	Collects weapon information for all violent offenses
Provides counts on arrests for the eight major crimes and 21 other offenses	Provides details on arrests for the eight major crimes and 49 other offenses

Source: Adapted from *Effects of NIBRS on Crime Statistics*, BJS Special Report (Washington, DC: Bureau of Justice Statistics, 2000), p. 1.

collects data on an expanded array of attributes involved in the commission of offenses, including whether the offender is suspected of using alcohol, drugs or narcotics, or a computer in the commission of the offense.

The FBI began accepting crime data in NIBRS format in January 1989. Although the bureau intended to have NIBRS fully in place by 1999, delays have been routine, and the NIBRS format has not yet been fully adopted. Because it is a flexible system, changes continue to be made in the data gathered under UCR/NIBRS. In 2003, for example, three new data elements were added to the survey to collect information on law enforcement officers killed and assaulted. Another new data element has been added to indicate the involvement of gang members in reported offenses.

The goals of the innovations introduced under NIBRS are to enhance the quantity, quality, and timeliness of crime-data collection by law enforcement agencies and to improve the methodology used for compiling, analyzing, auditing, and publishing the collected data. A major advantage of UCR/NIBRS, beyond the sheer increase in the volume of data collected, is the ability that NIBRS provides to break down and combine crime offense data into specific information.[9]

In keeping with the FBI's interest in technological improvements, and in order to make reports of crime data more widely available, in 2006 the FBI moved all UCR/NIBRS data reporting to the Internet and stopped paper production of its annual publication, *Crime in the United States*. Efforts to make the electronic versions more useful and searchable continue. The latest edition of *Crime in the United States* can be viewed at Library Extra 2–2 at cjtoday.com. To learn more about the effects of NIBRS innovations on crime statistics, including comparisons of traditional UCR summary data with the newer, more detailed UCR/NIBRS data, see Web Extra 2–5 at cjtoday.com. Finally, the Bureau of Justice Statistics provides an NIBRS information website, which can be accessed via Web Extra 2–6.

LIBRARY Extra

WEB Extra

Other changes in crime reporting were brought about by the 1990 Crime Awareness and Campus Security Act, which requires colleges to publish annual security reports.[10] Most campuses share crime data with the FBI, increasing the reported national incidence of a variety of offenses. The U.S. Department of Education reported that 48 murders and 3,680 forcible sex offenses occurred on and around college campuses in 2004. Also reported were 5,915 robberies, 7,076 aggravated assaults, 39,740 burglaries, and 13,874 motor vehicle thefts.[11] Although these numbers may seem high, it is important to realize that, except for the crimes of rape and sexual assault, college students experience violence at average annual rates that are lower than those for nonstudents in the same age group.[12] Rates of rape and sexual assault do not differ statistically between students and nonstudents. For the latest campus crime statistics, see Web Extra 2–7 at cjtoday.com. Library Extra 2–3 provides statistical information on the sexual victimization of college women.

WEB Extra   **LIBRARY** Extra

Historical Trends

Most UCR/NIBRS information is reported as a rate of crime. Rates are computed as the number of crimes *per* some unit of population. National reports generally make use of large units of population, such as 100,000 people. Hence, the rate of rape reported by the UCR/NIBRS Program for 2006 was 32.2 forcible rapes per every 100,000 inhabitants of the United States.[13] Rates allow for a meaningful comparison over areas and across time. The rate of reported rape for 1960, for example, was only about 10 per 100,000. We expect the number of crimes to increase as population grows, but rate increases are cause for concern because they indicate that reports of crime are increasing faster than the population is growing. Rates, however, require interpretation. Since the definition of rape that the FBI uses in reporting statistics on that crime includes only female victims, the rate of victimization might be more meaningfully expressed in terms of every 100,000 female inhabitants. Similarly, although there is a tendency to judge an individual's risk of victimization based on rates, such judgments tend to be inaccurate since they are based purely on averages and do not take into consideration individual life circumstances, such as place of residence, wealth, and educational level. While rates may tell us about aggregate conditions and trends, we must be very careful when applying them to individual cases.

Crime is like cutting grass. Just because you cut it down doesn't mean it's going to stay there.

—Senator Joseph R. Biden, Jr.[i]

Since the FBI's Uniform Crime Reporting Program began, there have been three major shifts in crime rates—and we now seem to be witnessing the beginning of a fourth. The first occurred during the early 1940s, when crime decreased sharply due to the large number of young men who entered military service during World War II. Young males make up the most "crime-prone" segment of the population, and their deployment overseas did much to lower crime rates at home. From 1933 to 1941, the Crime Index declined from 770 to 508 offenses per every 100,000 members of the American population.[14]

The second noteworthy shift in offense statistics was a dramatic increase in most forms of crime between 1960 and the early 1990s. Several factors contributed to the increase in reported crime during this period. One was also linked to World War II. With the end of the war and the return of millions of young men to civilian life, birthrates skyrocketed between 1945 and 1955, creating a postwar baby boom. By 1960, the first baby boomers were teenagers—and had entered a crime-prone age. This disproportionate number of young people produced a dramatic increase in most major crimes.

Other factors contributed to the increase in reported crime during the same period. Modified reporting requirements made it less stressful for victims to file police reports, and the publicity associated with the rise in crime sensitized victims to the importance of reporting. Crimes that might have gone undetected in the past began to figure more prominently in official statistics. Similarly, the growing professionalization of some police departments resulted in greater and more accurate data collection, making some of the most progressive departments appear to be associated with the largest crime increases.[15]

The 1960s were tumultuous years. The Vietnam War, a vibrant civil rights struggle, the heady growth of secularism, a dramatic increase in the divorce rate, diverse forms of "liberation," and the influx of psychedelic and other drugs all combined to fragment existing institutions. Social norms were blurred, and group control over individual behavior declined substantially. The "normless" quality of American society in the 1960s contributed greatly to the rise in crime.

From 1960 to 1980, crime rates rose from 1,887 to 5,950 offenses per every 100,000 U.S. residents. In the early 1980s, when postwar boomers began to age out of the crime-prone years and American society emerged from the cultural drift that had characterized the previous 20 years, crime rates leveled out briefly. Soon, however, an increase in drug-related criminal activity led crime rates—especially violent crime rates—to soar once again. Crime rates peaked during the early 1990s.

A third major shift came with a significant decline in the rates of most major crimes being reported between 1991 and 2006. During these years, the crime rate dropped from 5,897 to 3,835 offenses per every 100,000 residents—sending it down to levels not seen since 1975. The U.S. Department of Justice suggests various reasons for the decline, including[16]

- A coordinated, collaborative, and well-funded national effort to combat crime, beginning with the Safe Streets Act of 1968 and continuing through the USA PATRIOT Act of 2001
- Stronger, better-prepared criminal justice agencies, resulting from increased spending by federal and state governments on crime-control programs
- Growth in the popularity of innovative police programs, such as community policing (see Chapter 6)
- An aggressive approach to gun control, including the Brady Handgun Violence Prevention Act (discussed later in this chapter)

- A strong victims' movement and enactment of the 1984 federal Victims of Crime Act (see Chapter 11) and the 1994 Violence against Women Act (discussed later in this chapter), which established the Office for Victims of Crime in the U.S. Department of Justice

- Sentencing reform, including various "get tough on crime" initiatives (see Chapter 11)

- A substantial growth in the use of incarceration (see Chapter 13) due to changes in sentencing law practice (see Chapter 11)

- The "war on drugs," begun in the 1970s,[17] which resulted in stiff penalties for drug dealers and repeat drug offenders

- Increased use of the death penalty (see Chapter 11)

- Advances in forensic science and enforcement technology, including the increased use of real-time communications, the growth of the Internet, and the advent of DNA evidence (see Chapter 11)

The great 1990s crime drop ended with the 1990s. The new millennium brings a different picture.

—James Alan Fox, Northeastern University[ii]

More important than new strict laws, an expanded justice system and police funding, or changes in crime-fighting technologies, however, may have been influential economic and demographic factors that were largely beyond the control of policymakers but that combined to produce substantial decreases in rates of crime—including economic expansion and a significant shift in demographics caused by an aging of the population. During the 1990s, unemployment decreased by 36% in the United States, while the number of people ages 20 to 34 declined by 18%. Hence, it may have been the ready availability of jobs combined with demographic shifts in the population—not the official efforts of policymakers—that produced a noteworthy decrease in crime during the 1990s. Read noted criminologist Alfred Blumstein's analysis of crime's decline in Library Extra 2–4 at cjtoday.com to learn more about why crime rates fell during the 1990s.

A fourth shift in crime trends seems to be starting now. Some think that recent economic uncertainty, an increased jobless rate among unskilled workers, the growing number of ex-convicts who are back on the streets, the recent growth in the teenage population in this country, the increasing influence of gangs, copycat crimes, and the lingering social disorganization brought on by natural disasters like Hurricane Katrina in 2005 may lead to sustained increases in crime.[18] "We're probably done seeing declines in crime rates for some time to come," says Jack Riley, director of the Public Safety and Justice Program at RAND Corporation in Santa Monica, California. "The question," says Riley, "is how strong and how fast will those rates [rise], and what tools do we have at our disposal to get ahead of the curve."[19]

In 2006, in an effort to draw attention to spiking rates of violent crime in a number of major cities, the Police Executive Research Forum (PERF) released a report entitled *A Gathering Storm: Violence in America*. PERF was concerned that official FBI data would take too long to gather and might be released too late to effectively combat the growing trend in violence that it felt it had identified. The information used as the basis for the 2006 PERF report had been compiled from law enforcement executives at a "violent crime summit" held at the Mayflower Hotel in Washington, DC. PERF said that its data show that there are a number of cities across the country reporting large changes in the extent and nature of violent crime.

A second PERF report, this one entitled *Violent Crime in America: 24 Months of Alarming Trends*, was released in 2007 before full-year crime statistics were available from the FBI. It found even more reason for concern.[20] The report noted that urban violent crime increased significantly in 2006 and that "many cities experienced double-digit or even triple-digit percentage increases in homicides and other violence."

PERF authors said that the most recent crime statistics showed a worsening of a trend first identified by PERF in mid-2005, "when PERF began to hear rumblings from its members that 'violent crime is making a comeback.'" PERF statisticians found that, overall, homicides increased 2.9 percent over 2005 and robberies increased 6.5 percent. Although aggravated assaults declined 2.2 percent, aggravated assaults *committed with a firearm* increased 1.3 percent between 2005 and 2006. The statistics, said PERF, indicate a steady 24-month-long increase in violent crime rates in the nation's large cities.

Major cities across the United States that experienced an increase in murders in 2006 were New York (10% higher than a year earlier), Chicago (a 3.8% increase), Houston (an 11.9% increase), and Miami (a 42.6% increase). Jurisdictions that recorded their highest ever number of murders in 2006 include Newark, New Jersey; Orlando, Florida; and Prince William County, Virginia.

PERF notes that its findings "are not uniformly discouraging" and that some cities—like Dallas, Denver, and Washington, D.C.—had reduced homicide rates. "But overall," said the report's authors, "the 24-month trend, starting on January 1, 2005, is unmistakable." Some authorities, working independently from the FBI and PERF but using similar data, forecast a crime wave that

LIBRARY Extra ▪▪▪▪

FIGURE 2–2

Actual and projected rates of crime in the United States per 100,000 inhabitants, 1950–2010.

Source: Federal Bureau of Investigation, *Crime in the United States* (various years); and James Alan Fox, *Trends in Juvenile Violence: A Report to the United States Attorney General on Current and Future Rates of Offending* (Washington, DC: Bureau of Justice Statistics, 1996).

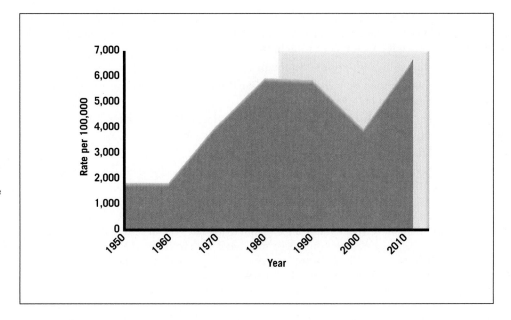

will peak around 2010.[21] Figure 2–2 shows historical rates of crime and projected rates through the end of this decade.

UCR/NIBRS in Transition

Reports of crime data available through the UCR/NIBRS program are now going through a transitional phase, as the FBI integrates more NIBRS-based data into its official summaries. The transition to NIBRS reporting is complicated by the fact that not only does NIBRS gather more kinds of data than the older summary UCR program did, but the definitions used for certain kinds of criminal activity under NIBRS are different from what they were under the traditional UCR program. The standard reference publication that the FBI designates for use by police departments in scoring and reporting crimes that occur within their jurisdiction is the *Uniform Crime Reporting Handbook*, and it is the most recent edition of that *Handbook* that guides and informs the discussion of crime statistics that you will find in the next few pages. You can access the entire 164-

FREEDOM OR SAFETY?
You Decide

A Dress Code for Bank Customers?

Dark glasses, a hooded sweatshirt, and a hat have been called the "uniform of choice" for bank robbers. In July 2002, in an effort to thwart a dramatic increase in robberies, some Massachusetts banks began posting requests for customers to remove hats, hoods, and sunglasses before entering financial establishments.

Not all banks, however, posted the signs. "I think what you have to weigh is convenience to customers versus the added benefits in terms of identifying suspects with a measure like this," said Melodie Jackson, spokeswoman for Citizens Bank of Massachusetts. "We're taking a very close look at things."

Banks in other parts of the country soon followed suit. By October 2002, 26 banks and credit unions with 141 locations in and around Springfield, Missouri, had posted signs asking visitors to remove sunglasses, hats, and anything that might hide their faces.

Today, such signs are commonplace at banks throughout the country, and it is likely that this request will soon become the *de facto* standard at banking and other financial venues.

YOU DECIDE

Are bank "dress codes" asking too much of customers? How would you feel about doing business with a bank that posts requests like those described here?

References: Michael S. Rosenwald and Emily Ramshaw, "Banks Post Dress Code to Deter Robbers," *Boston Globe*, July 13, 2002; and "Missouri Banks Attempt Unmasking Robbers," *Police Magazine* online, October 25, 2002, http://www.policemag.com/t_newspick.cfm?rank571952.

page *Uniform Crime Reporting Handbook* at Library Extra 2–5 at cjtoday.com. A thorough review of that document shows that much of the traditional UCR summary data-reporting terminology and structure remains in place. Learn more about the kinds of information recorded under NIBRS at Library Extra 2–6.

Figure 2–3 shows the FBI crime clock, which has long been calculated annually as a shorthand way of diagramming crime frequency in the United States. Note that crime clock data imply a regularity to crime that, in reality, does not exist.[22] Also, although the crime clock is a useful diagrammatic tool, it is not a rate-based measure of criminal activity and does not allow easy comparisons over time. Seven major crimes are included in the figure: murder, forcible rape, robbery, aggravated assault, burglary, larceny-theft, and motor vehicle theft.

The crime clock distinguishes between two categories of offenses: **violent crimes** and **property crimes**. The violent, or personal, crimes are murder, forcible rape, robbery, and aggravated assault. The property crimes, as Figure 2–3 shows, are burglary, larceny-theft, and motor vehicle theft. Other than the use of this simple dichotomy, UCR/NIBRS data do not provide a clear measure of the severity of the crimes they cover.

Like most UCR/NIBRS statistics, crime clock data are based on crimes reported to (or discovered by) the police. For a few offenses, the numbers reported are probably close to the numbers that actually occur. Murder, for example, is a crime that is difficult to conceal because of its seriousness. Even where the crime is not immediately discovered, the victim is often quickly missed by family members, friends, and associates, and someone files a "missing persons" report with the police. Auto theft is another crime that is reported in numbers similar to its actual rate of occurrence, probably because insurance companies require that the victim file a police report before they will pay the claim.

LIBRARY
Extra
■ ■ ■ ■

violent crime

A UCR/NIBRS summary offense category that includes murder, rape, robbery, and aggravated assault.

property crime

A UCR/NIBRS summary offense category that includes burglary, larceny-theft, motor vehicle theft, and arson.

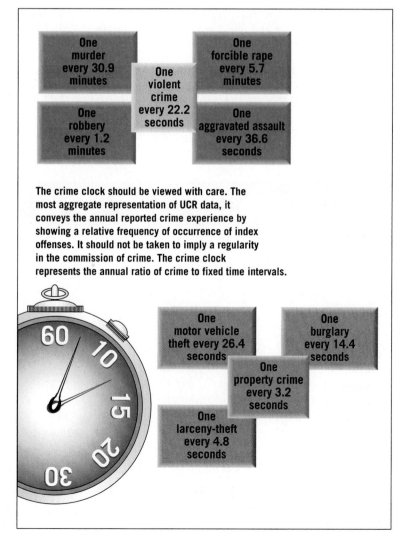

FIGURE 2–3

The FBI crime clock, which shows the frequency of commission of major crimes in 2006.

Source: Adapted from Federal Bureau of Investigation, *Crime in the United States, 2006*.

clearance rate

A traditional measure of investigative effectiveness that compares the number of crimes reported or discovered to the number of crimes solved through arrest or other means (such as the death of the suspect).

A commonly used term in today's UCR/NIBRS reports is **clearance rate**, which refers to the proportion of reported crimes that have been "solved." Clearances are judged primarily on the basis of arrests and do not involve judicial disposition. Once an arrest has been made, a crime is regarded as having been "cleared" for reporting purposes. Exceptional clearances (sometimes called *clearances by exceptional means*) can result when law enforcement authorities believe they know who committed a crime but cannot make an arrest. The perpetrator may, for example, have fled the country or died. Table 2–2 summarizes UCR/NIBRS program statistics for 2006.

Part I Offenses

MURDER

murder

The unlawful killing of a human being. *Murder* is a generic term that in common usage may include first- and second-degree murder, manslaughter, involuntary manslaughter, and other similar offenses.

Murder is the unlawful killing of one human being by another.[23] UCR/NIBRS statistics on murder describe the yearly incidence of all willful and unlawful homicides within the United States. Included in the count are all cases of nonnegligent manslaughter that have been reported to or discovered by the police. Not included in the count are suicides, justifiable homicides (that is, those committed in self-defense), deaths caused by negligence or accident, and murder attempts. In 2006, some 17,034 murders came to the attention of police departments across the United States. First-degree murder is a criminal homicide that is planned. Second-degree murder is an intentional and unlawful killing but one that is generally unplanned and that happens "in the heat of the moment."

Part I offenses

A UCR/NIBRS offense group used to report murder, rape, robbery, aggravated assault, burglary, larceny-theft, motor vehicle theft, and arson, as defined under the FBI's UCR/NIBRS Program.

Murder is the smallest numerical category in the **Part I offenses**. The 2006 murder rate was 5.7 homicides for every 100,000 residents of the United States. Generally, murder rates peak in the warmest months; in 2006, the greatest number of murders occurred in August. Geographically, murder is most common in the southern states. However, because those states are also the most populous, a meaningful comparison across regions of the country is difficult.

Age is no barrier to murder. Statistics for 2006 reveal that 203 infants (children under the age of one) were victims of homicide, as were 263 people age 75 and over.[24] Young adults between 20 and 24 were the most likely to be murdered. Murder perpetrators were also most common in this age group.

Firearms are the weapon used most often to commit murder. In 2006, guns were used in 58.3% of all killings. Handguns outnumbered shotguns almost 15 to 1 in the murder statistics, with rifles used almost as often as shotguns. Knives were used in approximately 12% of all murders. Other weapons included explosives, poison, narcotics overdose, blunt objects like clubs, and hands, feet, and fists.

TABLE 2–2	Major Crimes Known to the Police, 2006 (UCR/NIBRS Part I Offenses)		
Offense	**Number**	**Rate per 100,000**	**Clearance Rate**
Personal/Violent Crimes			
Murder	17,034	5.7	60.7%
Forcible rape	92,455	30.5	40.9
Robbery	447,403	149.4	25.2
Aggravated assault	860,853	287.5	54.0
Property Crimes			
Burglary	2,183,746	729.4	12.6
Larceny-theft	6,607,013	2,206.8	17.4
Motor vehicle theft	1,192,809	398.4	12.6
Arson[1]	69,055	26.8	18.0
U.S. Total	**11,470,368**	**3,834.5**	

[1]Arson can be classified as either a property crime or a violent crime, depending on whether personal injury or loss of life results from its commission. It is generally classified as a property crime, however. Arson statistics are incomplete for 2006.

Source: Adapted from Federal Bureau of Investigation, *Crime in the United States, 2006* (Washington, DC: U.S. Dept. of Justice, 2007).

Only 12.7% of all murders in 2006 were perpetrated by offenders classified as "strangers." In 45% of all killings, the relationship between the parties had not yet been determined. The largest category of killers was officially listed as "acquaintances," which probably includes a large number of former friends. Arguments cause most murders (40.6%), but murders also occur during the commission of other crimes, such as robbery, rape, and burglary. Homicides that follow from other crimes are more likely to be impulsive rather than planned.

Murders may occur in sprees, which "involve killings at two or more locations with almost no time break between murders."[25] One spree killer, John Allen Muhammad, 41, part of the "sniper team" that terrorized the Washington, D.C., area in 2002, was arrested along with 17-year-old Jamaican immigrant Lee Boyd Malvo in the random shootings of 13 people in Maryland, Virginia, and Washington over a three-week period. Ten of the victims died.[26] In 2003, Muhammad and Malvo were convicted of capital murder; Muhammad was sentenced to die. Malvo was given a second sentence of life without the possibility of parole in 2006 after he struck a deal with prosecutors in an effort to avoid the death penalty.[27]

In contrast to spree killing, mass murder entails "the killing of four or more victims at one location, within one event."[28] Recent mass murderers have included Seung-Hui Cho (who killed 33 people and wounded 20 on the campus of Virginia Polytechnic Institute and State University in Blacksburg, Virginia, in 2007); Timothy McVeigh (the antigovernment Oklahoma City bomber); Mohammed Atta and the terrorists whom he led in the September 11, 2001, attacks against American targets; and George Hennard (who killed 24 and wounded 20 at a Luby's Cafeteria in Killeen, Texas, in 1991).

Yet another kind of murder, serial murder, happens over time and officially "involves the killing of several victims in three or more separate events."[29] In cases of serial murder, days, months, or even years may elapse between killings.[30] Some of the more infamous serial killers of recent years are confessed Wichita BTK[31] murderer Dennis Rader; Jeffrey Dahmer, who received 936 years in prison for the murders of 15 young men (and who was himself later murdered in prison); Ted Bundy, who killed many college-aged women; Henry Lee Lucas, now in a Texas prison, who confessed to 600 murders but later recanted (yet was convicted of 11 murders and linked to at least 140 others); [32] Ottis Toole, Lucas's partner in crime; cult leader Charles Manson, still serving time for ordering followers to kill seven Californians, including famed actress Sharon Tate; Andrei Chikatilo, the Russian "Hannibal Lecter," who killed 52 people, mostly schoolchildren; [33] David Berkowitz, also known as the "Son of Sam," who killed six people on lovers' lanes around New York City; Theodore Kaczynski, the Unabomber, who perpetrated a series of bomb attacks on "establishment" figures; Seattle's Green River killer, Gary Leon Ridgway, a 54-year-old painter who in 2003 confessed to killing 48 women in the 1980s; and the infamous "railroad killer" Angel Maturino Resendiz. Although Resendiz was convicted of only one murder—that of Dr. Claudia Benton, which occurred in 1998—he is suspected of many more.[34]

Federal homicide laws changed in 2004, when President George Bush signed the Unborn Victims of Violence Act.[35] The act, which passed the Senate by only one vote, made it a separate federal crime to "kill or attempt to kill" a fetus "at any stage of development" during an assault on a pregnant woman. The fetal homicide statute, better known as Laci and Conner's Law, after homicide victims Laci Peterson and her unborn son (whom she had planned to name Conner),

If people here were not getting killed on the job in homicides, we would have quite a low rate of fatalities.

—Samuel Ehrenhalt, former Labor Department official, commenting on findings that show murder to be the top cause of on-the-job deaths in New York City

Self-confessed serial killer Gary L. Ridgway. The 54-year-old Ridgway, known as the Green River Strangler, is said to be the nation's worst captured serial killer. In 2003, Ridgway admitted to killing 48 women over a 20-year period in the Pacific Northwest. He is now serving life in prison without possibility of parole. What's the difference between serial killers and mass murderers?

Elaine Thompson/Reuters/Landov LLC

specifically prohibits the prosecution of "any person for conduct relating to an abortion for which the consent of the pregnant woman, or a person authorized by law to act on her behalf, has been obtained."

Because murder is such a serious crime, it consumes substantial police resources. Consequently, over the years the offense has shown the highest clearance rate of any index crime. Nearly 61% of all homicides were cleared in 2006. Figure 2–4 shows clearance rates for all Part I offenses except arson. Learn more about homicide trends in the United States at Library Extra 2–7 at cjtoday.com.

FORCIBLE RAPE

The term **rape** is often applied to a wide variety of sexual attacks, including same-sex rape and the rape of a male by a female. For statistical-reporting purposes, however, the term **forcible rape** has a specific and somewhat different meaning. The UCR/NIBRS Program defines *forcible rape* as "the carnal knowledge of a female forcibly and against her will."[36] By definition, rapes reported under the summary UCR Program are always of females. Although today our society acknowledges that males can be the victims of sexual assault, the *Uniform Crime Reporting Handbook*, which serves as a statistical-reporting guide for law enforcement agencies, says, "Sexual attacks on males are excluded from the rape category and should be classified as assaults or other sex offenses depending on the nature of the crime and the extent of the injury."[37] While it was not part of original UCR terminology, some jurisdictions refer to same-sex rape as **sexual battery**. Incidents of sexual battery are reportable under today's UCR/NIBRS Program as sexual offenses but do not enter the statistics on rape. Statutory rape, where no force is involved but the victim is younger than the age of consent, is not included in rape statistics, but attempts to commit the rape of a female by force or the threat of force are.

Forcible rape is the least reported of all violent crimes. Estimates are that only one out of every four forcible rapes is reported to the police. An even lower figure was reported by a 1992 government-sponsored study, which found that only 16% of rapes were reported.[38] The victim's fear of embarrassment was the most commonly cited reason for nonreports. In the past, reports of rapes were often handled in ways that made victims feel further victimized. Information was usually taken by desk sergeants or male detectives who were typically insensitive to victims' needs, and the physical examination victims had to endure was often a traumatizing experience in itself. Also, many states routinely permitted the woman's past sexual history to be revealed in detail in the courtroom if a trial ensued. But the past few decades have seen many changes designed to facilitate accurate reporting of rape and other sex offenses. Trained female detectives often interview the victims, physicians have become better educated in handling the psychological needs of victims, and sexual histories are no longer regarded as relevant in most trials.

UCR/NIBRS statistics show 92,455 reported forcible rapes for 2006, a slight decrease over the number of offenses reported for the previous year. Rape reports have generally increased, even in

LIBRARY
Extra
▪▪▪▪

rape

Unlawful sexual intercourse achieved through force and without consent. Broadly speaking, the term *rape* has been applied to a wide variety of sexual attacks and may include same-sex rape and the rape of a male by a female. Some jurisdictions refer to same-sex rape as *sexual battery*.

forcible rape (UCR/NIBRS)

The carnal knowledge of a female, forcibly and against her will. For statistical reporting purposes, the FBI defines *forcible rape* as "unlawful sexual intercourse with a female, by force and against her will, or without legal or factual consent." Statutory rape differs from forcible rape in that it generally involves nonforcible sexual intercourse with a minor.

sexual battery

Intentional and wrongful physical contact with a person, without his or her consent, that entails a sexual component or purpose.

FIGURE 2–4

Crimes cleared by arrest, 2006.

Source: Federal Bureau of Investigation, *Crime in the United States, 2006.*

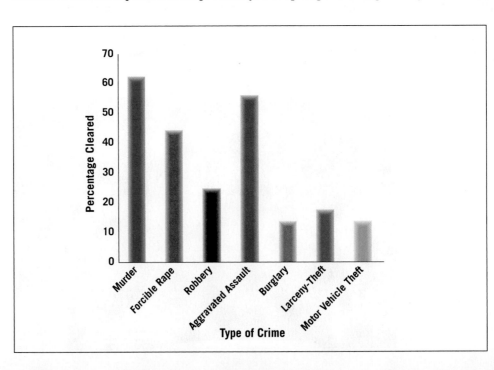

years when reports of other violent crimes have been on the decline. Figure 2–5 shows the rate of reported rape per 100,000 inhabitants. The offense of rape follows homicide in its seasonal variation. The greatest numbers of forcible rapes in 2006 were reported in the hot summer months, while the lowest numbers were recorded in January, February, November, and December.

Rape is frequently committed by a man known to the victim, as in the case of **date rape**. Victims may be held captive and subjected to repeated assaults.[39] In the crime of heterosexual rape, any female—regardless of age, appearance, or occupation—is a potential victim. Through personal violation, humiliation, and physical battering, rapists seek a sense of personal aggrandizement and dominance. Victims of rape often experience a lessened sense of personal worth; feelings of despair, helplessness, and vulnerability; a misplaced sense of guilt; and a lack of control over their personal lives.

Contemporary wisdom holds that forcible rape is often a planned violent crime that serves the offender's need for power rather than sexual gratification.[40] The "power thesis" has its origins in the writings of Susan Brownmiller, who argued in 1975 that the primary motivation leading to rape is the male desire to "keep women in their place" and to preserve gender inequality through violence.[41] Although many writers on the subject of forcible rape have generally accepted the power thesis, at least one study has caused some to rethink it. In a 1995 survey of imprisoned serial rapists, for example, Dennis Stevens found that "lust" was reported most often (41%) as "the primary motive for predatory rape."[42]

Statistically speaking, most rapes are committed by acquaintances of the victims and often betray a trust or friendship. Date rape, which falls into this category, appears to be far more common than previously believed. Recently, the growing number of rapes perpetrated with the use of the "date rape drug" Rohypnol have alarmed law enforcement personnel. Rohypnol, which is discussed in Chapter 16, is an illegal pharmaceutical substance that is virtually tasteless. Available on the black market, it dissolves easily in drinks and can leave anyone who consumes it unconscious for hours, making them vulnerable to sexual assault.

Rape within marriage, which has not always been recognized as a crime, is a growing area of concern in American criminal justice, and many laws have been enacted during the past few decades to deter it. Similarly, even though UCR/NIBRS Program statistics officially report only the rape or attempted rape of females, some state statutes criminalize the rape of a male by a female. When it occurs, this offense is typically statutory rape. In 2007, for example, sixth-grade Wilmington, Delaware, science teacher Rachel L. Holt, a 34-year-old divorcee, was sentenced to 10 years in prison after pleading guilty to second-degree rape. She had initially been charged with 28 counts of first-degree rape—which prosecutors said was based on the number of times she had

date rape

Unlawful forced sexual intercourse with a female against her will that occurs within the context of a dating relationship. Date rape, or acquaintance rape, is a subcategory of rape that is of special concern today.

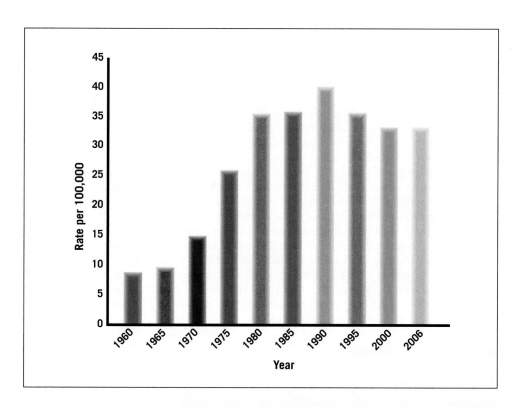

FIGURE 2–5

Rate of reported rape per 100,000 inhabitants, 1960–2006.

Source: Federal Bureau of Investigation, *Crime in the United States* (various years).

A crime in progress? Date rape is unlawful sexual intercourse with a female against her will that occurs within the context of a dating relationship. "Date rape drugs," like Rohypnol, are sometimes secretly placed in women's drinks, rendering them unable to resist. How can women guard against being victimized?

Peter Dokus/Getty Images Inc.– Stone Allstock

had sex with a 13-year-old male student whom she had plied with alcohol and let drive her car. The intense affair took place over a one-week period.

Learn more about the crime of rape and about what people can do to protect themselves at Web Extra 2–8 at cjtoday.com. Read about statistical measures relating to the sexual victimization of women at Library Extra 2–8 at cjtoday.com.

WEB
Extra
▪▪▪▪

LIBRARY
Extra
▪▪▪▪

ROBBERY

robbery (UCR/NIBRS)

The unlawful taking or attempted taking of property that is in the immediate possession of another by force or violence and/or by putting the victim in fear. Armed robbery differs from unarmed, or strong-arm, robbery in that it involves a weapon. Contrary to popular conceptions, highway robbery does not necessarily occur on a street—and rarely in a vehicle. The term *highway robbery* applies to any form of robbery that occurs outdoors in a public place.

Robbery is a personal crime involving a face-to-face confrontation between victim and perpetrator. It is often confused with burglary, which is primarily a property crime. (We'll examine burglary later.) Weapons may be used in robbery, or strong-arm robbery may occur through intimidation. Purse snatching and pocket picking are not classified as robbery by the UCR/NIBRS Program but are included under the category of larceny-theft.

In 2006, individuals were the most common target of robbers. Banks, gas stations, convenience stores, and other businesses were the second most common target, with residential robberies accounting for only 13.8% of the total. In 2006, 447,404 robberies were reported to the police. Of that number, 45% were highway robberies, meaning that the crime occurred outdoors, most commonly as the victim was walking. Strong-arm robberies, in which the victim was intimidated but no weapon was used, accounted for 33% of the total robberies reported. Guns were used in 35% of all robberies, and knives were used in 7%. Armed robbers are dangerous; guns are actually discharged in 20% of all robberies.[43]

When a robbery occurs, the UCR/NIBRS Program scores the event as one robbery, even when a number of victims were robbed during the event. With the move toward incident-driven reporting, however, the revised UCR/NIBRS Program will soon make data available on the number of individuals robbed in each incident. Because statistics on crime follow what's known as the *hierarchy rule*, they show only the most serious offense that occurred during a particular episode. Hence, robberies are often hidden when they occur in conjunction with more serious crimes. For example, 3% of robbery victims are also raped, and a large number of homicide victims are robbed.[44]

Robbery is primarily an urban offense, and most arrestees are young male minorities. The robbery rate in cities in 2006 was 207.5 per every 100,000 inhabitants, whereas it was only 15.9 in rural areas. Eighty-eight percent of those arrested for robbery in 2006 were male, 65% were under the age of 25, and 58% were minorities.[45]

AGGRAVATED ASSAULT

In April 2006, Arthur J. McClure, 22, of Fort Myers, Florida, was arrested when he allegedly took the head off of an Easter Bunny costume that he was wearing and punched Erin Johansson of Cape

Multiculturalism and Diversity

Race and the Criminal Justice System

Several years ago, Professor Lani Guinier of the University of Pennsylvania School of Law was interviewed on *Think Tank*, a public television show. Guinier was asked by Ben Wattenberg, the program's moderator, "When we talk about crime, crime, crime, are we really using a code for black, black, black?" Guinier responded this way: "To a great extent, yes, and I think that's a problem, not because we shouldn't deal with the disproportionate number of crimes that young black men may be committing, but because if we can't talk about race, then when we talk about crime, we're really talking about other things, and it means that we're not being honest in terms of acknowledging what the problem is and then trying to deal with it."[1]

Crimes, of course, are committed by individuals of all races. The link between crime—especially violent, street, and predatory crimes—and race, however, shows a striking pattern. In most crime categories, arrests of black offenders equal or exceed arrests of whites. In any given year, arrests of blacks account for more than 50% of all arrests for violent crimes. Blacks, however, comprise only 12% of the U.S. population. When *rates* (which are based upon the relative proportion of racial groups) are examined, the statistics are even more striking. The murder rate among blacks, for example, is ten times that of whites. Similar rate comparisons, when calculated for other violent crimes, show that far more blacks than whites are involved in other street crimes, such as assault, burglary, and robbery. Related studies show that 30% of all young black men in America are under correctional supervision on any given *day*—a far greater percentage than for members of any other race in the country.[2]

The real question for anyone interested in the justice system is how to explain such huge race-based disparities. Some authors maintain that racial differences in arrests and in rates of imprisonment are due to the differential treatment of African Americans at the hands of a discriminatory criminal justice system. Marvin D. Free, Jr., for example, says that the fact that African Americans are underrepresented as criminal justice professionals results in their being overrepresented in arrest and confinement statistics.[3] Some police officers, says Free, are more prone to arrest blacks than whites, frequently arrest blacks without sufficient evidence to support criminal charges, and overcharge in criminal cases involving black defendants—resulting in misleading statistical tabulations that depict blacks as being responsible for a greater proportion of crime than is, in fact, the case.

Other writers disagree. In *The Myth of a Racist Criminal Justice System*, for example, William Wilbanks claims that while the practice of American criminal justice may have been significantly racist in the past, and while some vestiges of racism may indeed remain, the system today is by and large objective in its processing of criminal defendants.[4] Using statistical data, Wilbanks shows that "at every point from arrest to parole there is little or no evidence of an overall racial effect, in that the percentage outcomes for blacks and whites are not very different."[5] Wilbanks claims to have reviewed "all the available studies that have examined the possible existence of racial discrimination from arrest to parole." In essence, he says, "this examination of the available evidence indicates that support for the 'discrimination thesis' is sparse, inconsistent, and frequently contradictory."

NAACP members protesting the police use of Tasers. Some claim that the justice system puts members of underrepresented groups at risk for unfair treatment. Others say the system is equitable. What do you think?

Rick Wood/Milwaukee Journal Sentinel/*NewsCom*

Wilbanks is careful to counter arguments advanced by those who continue to suggest that the system is racist. He writes, for example, "Perhaps the black/white gap at arrest is a product of racial bias by the police in that the police are more likely to select and arrest black than white offenders. The best evidence on this question comes from the National Crime Survey which interviews 130,000 Americans each year about crime victimization. . . . The percent of offenders described by victims as being black is generally consistent with the percent of offenders who are black according to arrest figures."

Contemporary research appears to discount claims that today's American justice system is racist. In 2006, for example, Pauline K. Brennan, a criminologist at the University of Nebraska at Omaha, examined the effects of race and ethnicity on the sentencing of female misdemeanants and found that "race/ethnicity did not directly affect sentencing."[6] Brennan discovered, however, that black and Hispanic females "were more likely to receive jail sentences than their White counterparts due to differences in" things like prior record and charge severity."

(continued)

Multiculturalism and Diversity (continued)

A fundamental critique of Wilbanks's thesis comes from Cora-mae Richey Mann, who says that his overreliance on quantitative or statistical data fails to capture the reality of racial discrimination within the justice system.[7] White victims, says Mann, tend to over-report being victimized by black offenders because they often mis-perceive Hispanic and other minority offenders as black. Similarly, she says, black victims are sometimes reluctant to report victimiza-tion—especially at the hands of whites.

Mann's arguments are discounted by those who point out that the statistics appear to be overwhelming. *If* they are accurate, then another question emerges: Why do blacks commit more crimes? Wilbanks says, "The assertion that the criminal justice system is not racist does not address the reasons why blacks appear to offend at higher rates than whites before coming into contact with the crimi-nal justice system. . . . It may be that racial discrimination in Ameri-can society has been responsible for conditions (for example, discrimination in employment, housing, and education) that lead to higher rates of offending by blacks."

Marvin Free, Jr., suggests that African Americans are still sys-tematically denied equal access to societal resources that would allow for full participation in American society—resulting in a higher rate of law violation. In a work that considers such issues in great detail, John Hagan and Ruth D. Peterson acknowledge the reality of higher crime rates among ethnic minorities and attribute them to (1) concentrated poverty, (2) joblessness, (3) family disruption, and (4) racial segregation.[8]

The question of *actual* fairness of the justice system can be quite different from one of *perceived* fairness. As University of Maryland Professor Katheryn K. Russell points out, "Study after study has shown that blacks and whites hold contrary views on the fairness of the criminal justice system's operation; blacks tend to be more cau-tious in their praise and frequently view the system as unfair and racially biased; by contrast whites have a favorable impression of the justice system. . . . The point is not that whites are completely satis-fied with the justice system, but rather that, relative to blacks, they have faith in the system."[9] One reason for such differences may be that blacks are more likely to be victims of police harassment and brutality or may know someone who has been.

Even if blacks do engage in more criminal activity than whites, says noted criminologist Thomas J. Bernard, higher rates of of-fending may be due, at least in part, to their perception that mem-bers of their group have historically been treated unfairly by agents of social control—resulting in anger and defiance, which express themselves in criminal activity.[10] Hence, says Bernard, crime—at least crime committed by minority group members—be-comes a kind of protest against a system that is perceived as fun-damentally unfair.

According to Russell, inequities in the existing system may pro-pel African Americans into crime and combine with stereotypical im-ages in the popular media to perpetuate what she calls the *criminalblackman* myth. The criminalblackman myth, says Russell, is a stereotypical portrayal of black men as *inherently* more sinister, evil, and dangerous than their white counterparts. The myth of the crim-inalblackman, adds Russell, is self-perpetuating, resulting in contin-ued frustration, more crime, and growing alienation among African Americans.

[1] Quoted in "For the Record," *Washington Post* wire service, March 3, 1994.

[2] Marvin D. Free, Jr., *African-Americans and the Criminal Justice System* (New York: Garland, 1996).

[3] Ibid.

[4] William Wilbanks, *The Myth of a Racist Criminal Justice System* (Monterey, CA: Brooks/Cole, 1987).

[5] William Wilbanks, "The Myth of a Racist Criminal Justice System," *Criminal Justice Research Bulletin*, Vol. 3, No. 5 (Huntsville, TX: Sam Houston State University, 1987), p. 2.

[6] Pauline K. Brennan, "Sentencing Female Misdemeanants: An Examination of the Direct and Indirect Effects of Race/Ethnicity," *Justice Quarterly*, Vol 23, No. 1 (March 2006), pp. 60–95.

[7] Coramae Richey Mann, "The Reality of a Racist Criminal Justice System," in Barry W. Hancock and Paul M. Sharp, eds., *Criminal Justice in America: Theory, Practice, and Policy* (Upper Saddle River, NJ: Prentice Hall, 1996), pp. 51–59.

[8] John Hagan and Ruth D. Peterson, *Crime and Inequality* (Stanford, CA: Stanford University Press, 1995).

[9] Katheryn K. Russell, "The Racial Hoax as Crime: The Law as Affirmation," *Indiana Law Journal*, Vol. 71 (1996), pp. 593–621.

[10] Thomas J. Bernard, "Angry Aggression among the 'Truly Disadvantaged,' " *Criminology*, Vol. 28, No. 1 (1990), pp. 73–96.

assault (UCR/NIBRS)

An unlawful attack by one person upon another. Historically, *assault* meant only the attempt to inflict injury on another person; a completed act constituted the separate offense of battery. Under modern statistical usage, however, attempted and completed acts are grouped together under the generic term *assault*.

Coral, Florida, after the young mother apparently became upset that a mall photo set was closing 10 minutes early.[46] The incident was witnessed by dozens of people, including many children who had gathered to have their pictures taken with the rabbit. McClure, who denied he struck Jo-hansson, was fired after the incident.

Assaults are of two types: simple (misdemeanor) and aggravated (felonious). For statistical-reporting purposes, simple assaults typically involve pushing and shoving. While simple assault may also at times include fistfights, the correct legal term to describe such incidents is *battery*. **Aggravated assaults** are distinguished from simple assaults in that either a weapon is used or the assault victim requires medical assistance. When a deadly weapon is employed, an aggravated assault may be charged as attempted murder even if no injury results.[47] In some cases, the UCR/NIBRS Program scores these attempted assaults as aggravated assault because of the poten-tial for serious consequences.

A man threatening a police officer with a beer bottle in Sydney, Australia, in December 2005, after ethnic tensions erupted into running battles between police and a mob of thousands of youths. An assault is an unlawful attack upon one person by another. What is the difference between assault and aggravated assault?

Rob Griffith/AP Wide World Photos

In 2006, 860,853 cases of aggravated assault were reported to law enforcement agencies in the United States. Assault reports were most frequent in summer months and least frequent in February, November, December, and January. Most aggravated assaults were committed with blunt objects or objects near at hand (34%), while hands, feet, and fists were also commonly used (25%). Less frequently used were knives (19%) and firearms (22%). Because those who commit assaults are often known to their victims, aggravated assaults are relatively easy to solve. About 54% of all aggravated assaults reported to the police in 2006 were cleared by arrest.

BURGLARY

Although it may involve personal and even violent confrontation, **burglary** is primarily a property crime. Burglars are interested in financial gain and usually fence (that is, illegally sell) stolen items, recovering a fraction of their cash value. About 2.2 million burglaries were reported to the police in 2006. Dollar losses to burglary victims totaled $4 billion, with an average loss per offense of $1,834.

The UCR/NIBRS Program employs three classifications of burglary: (1) forcible entry, (2) unlawful entry where no force is used, and (3) attempted forcible entry. In most jurisdictions, force need not be employed for a crime to be classified as burglary. Unlocked doors and open windows are invitations to burglars, and the legal essence of burglary consists not so much of a forcible entry as it does of the intent to trespass and steal. In 2006, 61.4% of all burglaries were forcible entries, 32.4% were unlawful entries, and 6.2% were attempted forcible entries.[48] The most dangerous burglaries were those in which a household member was home (about 10% of all burglaries).[49] Residents who were home during a burglary suffered a greater than 30% chance of becoming the victim of a violent crime.[50] However, while burglary may evoke images of dark-clothed strangers breaking into houses in which families lie sleeping, burglaries more often are of unoccupied homes and take place during daylight hours.

The clearance rate for burglary, as for other property crimes that we'll look at later, is generally low. In 2006, the clearance rate for burglary was only 12.6%. Burglars usually do not know their victims, and in cases where they do, burglars conceal their identity by committing their crime when the victim is not present.

LARCENY-THEFT

In 2002, 25-year-old Thad Roberts and 22-year-old Tiffany Fowler were arrested in Orlando, Florida, and charged with stealing moon rocks from the Johnson Space Center in Houston, Texas. Roberts had been working as a student intern at the center, and Fowler was a Space Center employee.[51] Officials realized that the lunar samples, along with a number of meteorites, were missing when they discovered that a 600-pound safe had disappeared from the Houston facility. They had been alerted to the loss by messages placed on a website run by a mineralogy club in Antwerp, Belgium, offering "priceless moon rocks collected by Apollo astronauts" for sale for up to $5,000 per gram. Roberts and Fowler were arrested by federal agents pretending to be potential purchasers.

aggravated assault

The unlawful, intentional inflicting, or attempted or threatened inflicting, of serious injury upon the person of another. While *aggravated assault* and *simple assault* are standard terms for reporting purposes, most state penal codes use labels like *first-degree* and *second-degree* to make such distinctions.

burglary (UCR/NIBRS)

The unlawful entry of a structure to commit a felony or a theft (excludes tents, trailers, and other mobile units used for recreational purposes). Under the UCR/NIBRS program, the crime of burglary can be reported if (1) an unlawful entry of an unlocked structure has occurred, (2) a breaking and entering (of a secured structure) has taken place, or (3) a burglary has been attempted.

Identity Theft: A New Kind of Larceny

In 2005, ChoicePoint, a personal-information clearinghouse with huge stores of private data on millions of Americans, announced that it had been the victim of a fraud perpetrated by thieves posing as legitimate business customers.[1] The firm quickly notified more than 145,000 people nationwide that critical personal information, including credit scores, Social Security numbers, street addresses, and more, had been stolen in what looked like a massive identity theft scheme. Later that year, more than 100,000 Bank of America and Wachovia customers were notified that their financial records might have been stolen.[2] MasterCard reported that 40 million credit card accounts had been compromised by a security breach at a payment-processing center.[3]

Identity theft, which involves obtaining credit, merchandise, or services by fraudulent personal representation, is a special kind of larceny. According to a recent Federal Trade Commission survey, identity theft has a direct impact on as many as 10 million victims annually, although most do not report the crime.[4] Identity theft became a federal crime in 1998 with the passage of the Identity Theft and Assumption Deterrence Act.[5] The law makes it a crime whenever anyone "knowingly transfers or uses, without lawful authority, a means of identifica-tion of another person with the intent to commit, or to aid or abet, any unlawful activity that constitutes a violation of federal law, or that constitutes a felony under any applicable state or local law."

The 2004 Identity Theft Penalty Enhancement Act[6] added two years to federal prison sentences for criminals convicted of using stolen credit card numbers and other personal data to commit crimes. It also prescribed prison sentences for those who use identity theft to commit other crimes, including terrorism, and it increased penalties for defendants who exceed or abuse the authority of their position in unlawfully obtaining or misusing means of personal identification.

Anyone can fall prey to identity theft—even celebrities. In 2000, for example, golfer Tiger Woods learned that his identity had been stolen and that credit cards taken out in his name had been used to steal $17,000 worth of merchandise, including a 70-inch TV, stereos, and a used luxury car. In 2001, the thief, 30-year-old Anthony Lemar Taylor, who looks nothing like Woods, was convicted of falsely obtaining a driver's license using the name of Eldrick T. Woods (Tiger's given name), Woods's Social Security number, and his birth date. Because Taylor already had 20 previous convictions of all kinds on his record, he was sentenced to 200 years in prison under California's three-strikes law.[7] Like Woods, most victims of identity theft do not even know that their identities have been stolen until they receive bills for merchandise they haven't purchased.

According to the National White Collar Crime Center, identity thieves use several common techniques. Some engage in "Dumpster diving," going through trash bags, cans, or Dumpsters to get copies of checks, credit card and bank statements, credit card applications, or other records that typically bear identifying information. Others use a technique called "shoulder surfing." It involves simply looking over the victim's shoulder as he or she enters personal information into a computer or on a written form. Eavesdropping is another simple, yet effective, technique that identity thieves often use. Eavesdropping can occur when the victim is using an ATM machine, giving credit card or other personal information over the phone, or dialing the number for their telephone calling card. Criminals can also obtain personal identifying information from potential victims through the Internet. Some Internet users, for example, reply to "spam" (unsolicited e-mail) that promises them all sorts of attractive benefits while requesting identifying data, such as checking account or credit card numbers and expiration dates, along with their name and address.[8] Identity theft perpetrated through the use of high technology depends on the fact that a person's legal and economic identity in contemporary society is largely "virtual" and supported by technology.

Learn more about identity thieves and how they operate via **Web Extra 2–9** and **Library Extra 2–9** at cjtoday.com.

World-renowned professional golfer Tiger Woods. In 2000, Woods became the victim of identity theft when 29-year-old Anthony Lemar Taylor of Sacramento, California, used Woods's identity to charge $17,000 on the golfer's charge cards. Why is identity theft so prevalent today? How can it be stopped?

AP Wide World Photos

WEB
Extra
▪▪▪▪

LIBRARY
Extra
▪▪▪▪

[1] John Waggoner, "ID Theft Scam Spreads across USA," *USA Today*, February 22, 2005, p. 1A.
[2] Paul Nowell, "Info on 100,000 Bank Users Possibly Stolen," *USA Today*, May 24, 2005, p. B6.
[3] Eric Dash and Tom Zeller, "MasterCard Says 40 Million Files Put at Risk," *New York Times*, June 18, 2005, p. A1.
[4] Christine Dugas, "Federal Survey: Identity Theft Hits 1 in 4 U.S. Households; Scope of Crime Much Worse Than Previously Thought," *USA Today*, September 4, 2003, p. B10.
[5] U.S. Code, Title 18, Section 1028.
[6] HR 1731 (2004).
[7] "Three Strikes, He's Out: Woods' Identity Thief Gets 200 Years-to-Life," Associated Press, April 28, 2001.
[8] Much of the information in this paragraph is adapted from National White Collar Crime Center, "WCC Issue: Identity Theft," http://www.nw3c.org/papers/Identity_Theft.pdf (accessed May 18, 2007).

Larceny is another name for theft, and the UCR/NIBRS Program uses the term **larceny-theft** to describe theft offenses. Some states distinguish between simple larceny and grand larceny, categorizing the crime based on the dollar value of what is stolen. Larceny-theft, as defined by the UCR/NIBRS Program, includes the theft of valuables of any dollar amount. The reports specifically list the following offenses as types of larceny (listed here in order of declining frequency):

- Thefts from motor vehicles
- Shoplifting
- Thefts from buildings
- Thefts of motor vehicle parts and accessories
- Bicycle thefts
- Thefts from coin-operated machines
- Purse snatching
- Pocket picking

Thefts of farm animals (known as *rustling*) and thefts of most types of farm machinery also fall into the larceny category. In fact, larceny is such a broad category that it serves as a kind of catchall in the UCR/NIBRS Program. In 1995, for example, Yale University officials filed larceny charges against 25-year-old student Lon Grammer, claiming that he had fraudulently obtained university funds.[52] The university maintained that Grammer had stolen his education by forging college and high school transcripts and concocting letters of recommendation prior to admission. Grammer's alleged misdeeds, which Yale University officials said misled them into thinking that Grammer, a poor student before attending Yale, had an exceptional scholastic record, permitted him to receive $61,475 in grants and loans during the time he attended the school. Grammer was expelled.

Reported thefts vary widely, in terms of both the objects stolen and their value. Stolen items range from pocket change to a $100 million aircraft. For reporting purposes, crimes entailing embezzlement, con games, forgery, and worthless checks are specifically excluded from the count of larceny. Because larceny has traditionally been considered a crime that requires physical possession of the item appropriated, some computer crimes, including thefts engineered through online access or thefts of software and information, have not been scored as larcenies unless computer equipment, electronic circuitry, or computer media were actually stolen. In 2004, however, the FBI confirmed that it was working with Cisco Systems, Inc., to investigate the possible theft of some of the company's intellectual property.[53] The theft involved approximately 800 megabytes of proprietary software code used to control the company's Internet routers. Since hardware manufactured by Cisco Systems accounts for more than 60% of all routers used on the Internet,[54] officials feared that the lost software could represent a major security threat for the entire Internet.

From a statistical standpoint, the most common form of larceny in recent years has been theft of motor vehicle parts, accessories, and contents. Tires, wheels, hubcaps, radar detectors, stereos, satellite radios, CD players, compact discs, and cellular phones account for many of the items reported stolen.

Reports to the police in 2006 showed 6,947,685 larcenies nationwide, with the total value of property stolen placed at $5.1 billion. Larceny-theft is the most frequently reported major crime, according to the UCR/NIBRS Program. It may also be the program's most underreported crime category because small thefts rarely come to the attention of the police. The average value of items reported stolen in 2006 was about $727.

MOTOR VEHICLE THEFT

For record-keeping purposes, the UCR/NIBRS Program defines *motor vehicles* as self-propelled vehicles that run on the ground and not on rails. Included in the definition are automobiles, motorcycles, motor scooters, trucks, buses, and snowmobiles. Excluded are trains, airplanes, bulldozers, most farm and construction machinery, ships, boats, and spacecraft; the theft of these would be scored as larceny-theft.[55] Vehicles that are temporarily taken by individuals who have lawful access to them are not thefts. Hence, spouses who jointly own all property may drive the family car, even though one spouse may think of the vehicle as his or her exclusive personal property.

As we said earlier, because most insurance companies require police reports before they will reimburse car owners for their losses, most occurrences of **motor vehicle theft** are reported to law enforcement agencies. Some reports of motor vehicle thefts, however, may be false. People who have damaged their own vehicles in solitary crashes or who have been unable to sell them may try to force insurance companies to "buy" them through reports of theft.

identity theft

A crime in which an imposter obtains key pieces of information, such as Social Security and driver's license numbers, to obtain credit, merchandise, and services in the name of the victim. The victim is often left with a ruined credit history and the time-consuming and complicated task of repairing the financial damage.[iii]

larceny-theft (UCR/NIBRS)

The unlawful taking or attempted taking, carrying, leading, or riding away of property, from the possession or constructive possession of another. Motor vehicles are excluded. Larceny is the most common of the eight major offenses, although probably only a small percentage of all larcenies are actually reported to the police because of the small dollar amounts involved.

motor vehicle theft (UCR/NIBRS)

The theft or attempted theft of a motor vehicle. *Motor vehicle* is defined as a self-propelled road vehicle that runs on land surface and not on rails. The stealing of trains, planes, boats, construction equipment, and most farm machinery is classified as larceny under the UCR/NIBRS Program, not as motor vehicle theft.

Motor vehicle theft or larceny? Even members of the FBI's Education and Training Services Unit in Washington, D.C., were unsure of how to classify the 1995 theft of this M-60 tank by Shawn Nelson, a former Army tank operator. Nelson drove the tank through the streets of San Diego before being shot and killed by police, who jumped on the tank and cut the hatch open with bolt cutters. In this photo, Nelson's body is being removed from the tank shortly after he was shot. How would you classify the crime for statistical reporting purposes? Would the classification differ if Nelson had lived?

David McNew/Corbis/Sygma

Those who insist that crime never pays have never met an identity thief. Identity theft not only pays, it pays extremely well.

—*Jonathan Turley*[iv]

In 2006, 1,192,809 motor vehicles were reported stolen. The average value per stolen vehicle was $6,649, making motor vehicle theft a $7.9 billion crime. The clearance rate for motor vehicle theft was only 12.6% in 2006. Large city agencies reported the lowest rates of clearance (9.4%), while rural counties had the highest rate (26%). Many stolen vehicles are quickly disassembled and the parts resold, since auto parts are much more difficult to identify and trace than are intact vehicles. In some parts of the country, chop shops—which take stolen vehicles apart and sell their components—operate like big businesses, and one shop may strip a dozen or more cars per day.

Motor vehicle theft can turn violent, as in cases of carjacking—a crime in which offenders usually force the car's occupants onto the street before stealing the vehicle. For example, in February 2000, Christy Robel watched helplessly as her six-year-old son Jake was dragged to his death after a man jumped behind the wheel of her car and sped off.[56] Robel had left the car running with the boy inside as she made a brief stop at a Kansas City sandwich shop. The carjacker, 35-year-old Kim L. Davis, tried to push Jake from the car as he made his escape, but the boy became entangled in his seat belt and was dragged for five miles at speeds of more than 80 mph. In October 2001, Davis was convicted of murder and was sentenced to spend the rest of his life in prison without possibility of parole.[57] The Bureau of Justice Statistics estimates that around 34,000 carjackings occur annually and account for slightly more than 1% of all motor vehicle thefts.[58]

Arrest reports for motor vehicle theft show that the typical offender is a young male. Fifty-seven percent of all arrestees in 2006 were under the age of 25, and 82.3% were male.

arson (UCR/NIBRS)

Any willful or malicious burning or attempt to burn, with or without intent to defraud, a dwelling house, public building, motor vehicle or aircraft, personal property of another, and so on. Some instances of arson result from malicious mischief, some involve attempts to claim insurance money, and some are committed in an effort to disguise other crimes, such as murder, burglary, or larceny.

ARSON

The UCR/NIBRS Program received crime reports from more than 16,000 law enforcement agencies in 2006.[59] Of these, only 13,943 submitted **arson** data. Even fewer agencies provided complete data as to the type of arson (the nature of the property burned), the estimated monetary value of the property, the ownership, and so on. Arson data include only the fires that are determined through investigation to have been willfully or maliciously set. Fires of unknown or suspicious origin are excluded from arson statistics.[60]

The intentional and unlawful burning of structures (houses, storage buildings, manufacturing facilities, and so on) was the type of arson reported most often in 2006 (25,919 instances). The arson of vehicles was the second most common category, with 17,259 such burnings reported. The average dollar loss per instance of arson in 2006 was $13,325, and total nationwide property damage was placed at close to $1 billion.[61] As with most property crimes, the clearance rate for arson was low—only 18% nationally. The crime of arson exists in a kind of statistical limbo. In 1979, Congress ordered that it be added as an eighth Part I offense. Today, however, many law enforcement agencies still have not begun making regular reports to the FBI on arson offenses in their jurisdictions.

Some of these difficulties have been resolved through the Special Arson Program, authorized by Congress in 1982. In conjunction with the National Fire Data Center, the FBI now operates a Special Arson Reporting System, which focuses on fire departments across the nation. The reporting system is designed to provide data to supplement yearly UCR arson tabulations.[62]

Part II Offenses

The Uniform Crime Reporting Program also includes information on what the FBI calls **Part II offenses**. Part II offenses, which are generally less serious than those that make up the Part I offense category, include a number of social-order, or so-called victimless, crimes. The statistics on Part II offenses are for recorded arrests, not for crimes reported to the police. The logic inherent in this form of scoring is that most Part II offenses would never come to the attention of the police were it not for arrests. Part II offenses are shown in Table 2–3, with the number of estimated arrests made in each category for 2006.

A Part II arrest is counted each time a person is taken into custody. As a result, the statistics in Table 2–3 do not report the number of suspects arrested but rather the number of arrests made. Some suspects were arrested more than once.

Part II offenses

A UCR/NIBRS offense group used to report arrests for less serious offenses. Agencies are limited to reporting only arrest information for Part II offenses, with the exception of simple assault.

The National Crime Victimization Survey

A second major source of statistical data about crime in the United States is the National Crime Victimization Survey, which is based on victim self-reports rather than on police reports. The NCVS is designed to estimate the occurrence of all crimes, whether reported or not.[63] The NCVS was first conducted in 1972. It built on efforts in the late 1960s by both the National Opinion Research Center and the President's Commission on Law Enforcement and the Administration of

TABLE 2–3 UCR/NIBRS Part II Offenses, 2006

Offense Category	Number of Arrests
Simple assault	1,305,757
Forgery and counterfeiting	108,823
Fraud	280,693
Embezzlement	20,012
Stolen property (e.g., receiving)	122,722
Vandalism	300,679
Weapons (e.g., carrying)	200,782
Prostitution and related offenses	79,673
Sex offenses (e.g., statutory rape)	87,252
Drug-law violations	1,889,810
Gambling	12,307
Offenses against the family (e.g., nonsupport)	131,491
Driving under the influence	1,460,498
Liquor-law violations	645,734
Public drunkenness	553,188
Disorderly conduct	703,504
Vagrancy	36,471
Curfew violation/loitering	159,907
Runaways	114,179

Source: Adapted from Federal Bureau of Investigation, *Crime in the United States, 2006* (Washington, DC: U.S. Dept. of Justice, 2007.

dark figure of crime

Crime that is not reported to the police and that remains unknown to officials.

Justice to uncover what some had been calling the **dark figure of crime**. This term refers to those crimes that are not reported to the police and that remain unknown to officials. Before the development of the NCVS, little was known about such unreported and undiscovered offenses.

Early data from the NCVS changed the way criminologists thought about crime in the United States. The use of victim self-reports led to the discovery that crimes of all types were more prevalent than UCR statistics indicated. Many cities were shown to have victimization rates that were more than twice the rate of reported offenses. Others, like Saint Louis, Missouri, and Newark, New Jersey, were found to have rates of victimization that very nearly approximated reported crime. New York, often thought of as a high-crime city, was discovered to have one of the lowest rates of self-reported victimization.

NCVS data are gathered by the Bureau of Justice Statistics through a cooperative arrangement with the U.S. Census Bureau.[64] Twice each year, Census Bureau personnel interview household members in a nationally representative sample of approximately 43,000 households (about 76,000 people). Approximately 150,000 interviews of individuals age 12 or older are conducted annually. Households stay in the sample for three years, and new households rotate into the sample regularly.

The NCVS collects information on crimes suffered by individuals and households, whether or not those crimes were reported to law enforcement. It estimates the proportion of each crime type reported to law enforcement, and it summarizes the reasons that victims give for reporting or not reporting. BJS statistics are published in annual reports entitled *Criminal Victimization* and *Crime and the Nation's Households.*

Using definitions similar to those employed by the UCR/NIBRS Program, the NCVS includes data on the national incidence of rape, sexual assault, robbery, assault, burglary, personal and household larceny, and motor vehicle theft. Not included are murder, kidnapping, and victimless crimes (crimes that, by their nature, tend to involve willing participants). Commercial robbery and the burglary of businesses were dropped from NCVS reports in 1977. The NCVS employs a hierarchical counting system similar to that of the pre-NIBRS system: It counts only the most "serious" incident in any series of criminal events perpetrated against the same individual. Both completed and attempted offenses are counted, although only people 12 years of age and older are included in household surveys.

NCVS statistics for recent years reveal the following:

- Approximately 15% of American households are touched by crime every year.
- About 16 million victimizations occur each year.
- City residents are almost twice as likely as rural residents to be victims of crime.
- About half of all violent crimes, and slightly more than one-third of all property crimes, are reported to police.[65]
- Victims of crime are more often men than women.
- Younger people are more likely than the elderly to be victims of crime.
- Blacks are more likely than whites or members of other racial groups to be victims of violent crimes.
- Violent victimization rates are highest among people in lower-income families.

A report by the Bureau of Justice Statistics found that in 2006, NCVS crime rates had reached their lowest level since the survey began.[66] Declines began in the mid-1990s, with violent crime rates dropping 57% between 1993 and 2006.[67] While these statistics indicate that in recent years crime rates have declined, UCR statistics, which go back almost another 40 years, show that today's crime rate is still many times what it was in the early and middle years of the twentieth century.[68] A comparison of UCR/NIBRS and NCVS data for 2006 can be found in Table 2–4. Explore the latest NCVS data at Web Extra 2–10 at cjtoday.com.

WEB
Extra
■ ■ ■ ■

LIBRARY
Extra
■ ■ ■ ■

Many researchers trust NCVS data more than UCR/NIBRS data because they believe that self-reports provide a more accurate gauge of criminal incidents than do police reports. Learn more about the use of self-report surveys in the measurement of crime and delinquency via Library Extras 2–10 and 2–11 at cjtoday.com.

As mentioned earlier in this chapter, crime statistics from the UCR/NIBRS and the NCVS reveal crime patterns that are often the bases for social policies created to deter or reduce crime. These policies also build on explanations for criminal behavior found in more elaborate interpretations of the statistical information. Unfortunately, however, researchers too often forget that statistics, which are merely descriptive, can be weak in explanatory power. For example, NCVS data show that "household crime rates" are highest for households (1) headed by blacks, (2) headed by younger people, (3) with six or more members, (4) headed by renters, and (5) located in cen-

TABLE 2–4   Comparison of UCR/NIBRS and NCVS Data, 2006

Offense	UCR/NIBRS	NCVS[1]
Personal/Violent Crimes		
Homicide	17,034	—
Forcible rape[2]	92,455	272,350
Robbery	447,403	711,570
Aggravated assault	860,853	1,354,750
Property Crimes		
Burglary[3]	2,183,746	3,539,760
Larceny	6,607,013	14,275,150
Motor vehicle theft	1,192,809	993,910
Arson[4]	69,055	—
Total of All Crimes Recorded	**11,470,368**	**21,147,490**

[1]NCVS data cover "households touched by crime," not absolute numbers of crime occurrences. More than one victimization may occur per household, but only the number of households in which victimizations occur enters the tabulations.

[2]NCVS statistics include both rape and sexual assault.

[3]NCVS statistics include only household burglary and attempts.

[4]Arson data are incomplete in the UCR/NIBRS and are not reported by the NCVS.

Source: Compiled from U.S. Department of Justice, *Criminal Victimization, 2006* (Washington, DC: Bureau of Justice Statistics, 2007); and Federal Bureau of Investigation, *Crime in the United States, 2006* (Washington, DC: U.S. Dept. of Justice, 2007).

tral cities.[69] Such findings, combined with statistics that show that most crime occurs among members of the same race, have led some researchers to conclude that values among certain black subcultural group members both propel them into crime and make them targets of criminal victimization. The truth may be, however, that crime is more a function of inner-city location than of culture. From simple descriptive statistics, it is difficult to know which is the case. Learn more about the UCR/NIBRS Program and the NCVS, and see how they compare, by viewing **Web Extra 2–11** at cjtoday.com.

WEB
Extra
■ ■ ■ ■

Problems with the UCR/NIBRS and the NCVS

Like most statistical data-gathering programs in the social sciences, the UCR/NIBRS and the NCVS programs are not without problems. Because UCR/NIBRS data are based primarily on citizens' crime reports to the police, there are several inherent difficulties. First, not all people report when they are victimized. Some victims are afraid to contact the police, while others may not believe that the police can do anything about the offense. Second, certain kinds of crimes are reported rarely, if at all. These include victimless crimes, also known as *social-order offenses*, such as drug use, prostitution, and gambling. Similarly, white-collar and high-technology offenses, such as embezzlement and computer crime—because they often go undiscovered—probably enter the official statistics only rarely. Third, victims' reports may not be entirely accurate. A victim's memory may be faulty, victims may feel the need to impress or please the police, or they may be under pressure from others to misrepresent the facts. Finally, all reports are filtered through a number of bureaucratic levels, which increases the likelihood that inaccuracies will enter the data. As noted methodologist Frank Hagan points out, "The government is very keen on amassing statistics. They collect them, add to them, raise them to the nth power, take the cube root, and prepare wonderful diagrams. But what you must never forget is that every one of these figures comes in the first instance from the *chowty dar* [village watchman], who puts down what he damn pleases."[70]

In contrast to the UCR/NIBRS dependence on crimes reported by victims who seek out the police, the National Crime Victimization Survey relies on door-to-door surveys and personal interviews for its data. Survey results, however, may be skewed for several reasons. First, no matter how objective survey questions may appear to be, survey respondents inevitably provide their personal interpretations and descriptions of what may or may not have been a criminal event. Second, by its very nature, the survey includes information from those people who are most willing to talk to surveyors; more reclusive people are less likely to respond regardless of the level of victimization they may have suffered. Also, some victims are afraid to report crimes even to nonpolice interviewers, while others may invent victimizations for the interviewer's sake. As the first page of the NCVS report admits, "Details about the crimes come directly from the victims, and no attempt is made to validate the information against police records or any other source."[71]

Finally, because both the UCR/NIBRS and the NCVS are human artifacts, they contain only data that their creators think appropriate. UCR/NIBRS statistics for 2001, for example, do not include a tally of those who perished in the September 11, 2001, terrorist attacks because FBI officials concluded that the events were too "unusual" to count. Although the FBI's 2001 *Crime in the United States* acknowledges "the 2,830 homicides reported as a result of the events of September 11, 2001," it goes on to say that "these figures have been removed" from the reported data.[72] Crimes that result from an anomalous event, but are excluded from reported data, highlight the arbitrary nature of the data-collection process itself.

Special Categories of Crime

crime typology

A classification of crimes along a particular dimension, such as legal categories, offender motivation, victim behavior, or the characteristics of individual offenders.

A **crime typology** is a classification scheme used in the study and description of criminal behavior. There are many typologies, all of which have an underlying logic. The system of classification that derives from any particular typology may be based on legal criteria, offender motivation, victim behavior, the characteristics of individual offenders, or the like. Criminologists Terance D. Miethe and Richard C. McCorkle note that crime typologies "are designed primarily to simplify social reality by identifying homogeneous groups of crime behaviors that are different from other clusters of crime behaviors."[73] Hence, one common but simple typology contains only two categories of crime: violent and property. In fact, many crime typologies contain overlapping or nonexclusive categories—just as violent crimes may involve property offenses, and property offenses may lead to violent crimes. Thus no one typology is likely to capture all of the nuances of criminal offending.

Social relevance is a central distinguishing feature of any meaningful typology, and it is with that in mind that the remaining sections of this chapter briefly highlight crimes of special importance today. They are crime against women, crime against the elderly, hate crime, corporate and white-collar crime, organized crime, gun crime, drug crime, cybercrime, and terrorism.

Crime against Women

The victimization of women is a special area of concern, and both the NCVS and the UCR/NIBRS contain data on gender as it relates to victimization. Statistics show that women are victimized less frequently than men in every major personal crime category other than rape.[74] The overall U.S. rate of violent victimization is about 25 per 1,000 males age 12 or older, and 18 per 1,000 females.[75] When women become victims of violent crime, however, they are more likely than men to be injured (29% versus 22%, respectively).[76] Moreover, a larger proportion of women than men make modifications in the way they live because of the threat of crime.[77] Women, especially those living in cities, have become increasingly careful about where they travel and the time of day they leave their homes—particularly if they are unaccompanied—and in many settings are often wary of unfamiliar males.

Date rape, familial incest, spousal abuse, **stalking**, and the exploitation of women through social-order offenses like prostitution and pornography are major issues facing American society today. Testimony before Congress tagged domestic violence as the largest cause of injury to American women.[78] Former Surgeon General C. Everett Koop once identified violence against women by their partners as the number one health problem facing women in America.[79] Findings from the National Violence against Women Survey (NVAWS) reveal the following:[80]

stalking

Repeated harassing and threatening behavior by one individual against another, aspects of which may be planned or carried out in secret. Stalking might involve following a person, appearing at a person's home or place of business, making harassing phone calls, leaving written messages or objects, or vandalizing a person's property. Most stalking laws require that the perpetrator make a credible threat of violence against the victim or members of the victim's immediate family.

- Physical assault is widespread among American women. Fifty-two percent of surveyed women said that they had been physically assaulted as a child or as an adult.

- Approximately 1.9 million women are physically assaulted in the United States each year.

- Eighteen percent of women experienced a completed or attempted rape at some time in their lives.

- Of those reporting rape, 22% were under 12 years old, and 32% were between 12 and 17 years old when they were first raped.

- Native American and Alaska Native women were most likely to report rape and physical assault, while Asian/Pacific Islander women were least likely to report such victimization. Hispanic women were less likely to report rape than non-Hispanic women.

- Women report significantly more partner violence than men. Twenty-five percent of surveyed women, and only 8% of surveyed men, said they had been raped or physically assaulted by a current or former spouse, cohabiting partner, or date.

- Violence against women is primarily partner violence. Seventy-six percent of the women who had been raped or physically assaulted since age 18 were assaulted by a current or former husband, cohabiting partner, or date, compared with 18% of the men.

- Women are significantly more likely than men to be injured during an assault. Thirty-two percent of the women and 16% of the men who had been raped since age 18 were injured during their most recent rape; 39% of the women and 25% of the men who were physically assaulted since age 18 were injured during their most recent physical assault.

- Eight percent of surveyed women and 2% of surveyed men said they had been stalked at some time in their lives. According to survey estimates, approximately 1 million women and 371,000 men are stalked annually in the United States.

A detailed BJS analysis found that women who are victims of violent crime are twice as likely to be victimized by strangers as by people whom they know.[81] However, they are far more likely than men to be victimized by a current or former intimate partner. When the perpetrators are known to them, women are most likely to be violently victimized by ex-husbands, boyfriends, and spouses (in descending order of incidence). The BJS study also found that separated or divorced women are six times more likely to be victims of violent crime than widows, four and a half times more likely than married women, and three times more likely than widowers and married men. Other findings indicate that (1) women living in central-city areas are considerably more likely to be victimized than women residing in the suburbs; (2) suburban women, in turn, are more likely to be victimized than women living in rural areas; (3) women from low-income families experience the highest amount of violent crime; (4) the victimization of women falls as family income rises; (5) unemployed women, female students, and those in the armed forces are the most likely of all women to experience violent victimization; (6) black women are victims of violent crime more frequently than are women of any other race; (7) Hispanic women are victimized more frequently than white women; and (8) women in the age range of 20 to 24 are most at risk for violent victimization, while those age 16 to 19 make up the second most likely group of victims. Learn more about violence against women via Library Extra 2–12 at cjtoday.com.

Survey findings like these show that more must be done to alleviate the social conditions that result in the victimization of women. Suggestions already under consideration call for expansion in the number of federal and state laws designed to control domestic violence, a broadening of the federal Family Violence Prevention and Services Act, federal help in setting up state advocacy offices for battered women, increased funding for battered women's shelters, and additional funds for prosecutors and courts to develop spousal abuse units. The federal Violent Crime Control and Law Enforcement Act of 1994 was designed to meet many of these needs through a subsection entitled the Violence against Women Act (VAWA). That act signified a major shift in our national response to domestic violence, stalking (which is often part of the domestic violence continuum), and sexual assault crimes. For the first time in our nation's history, violent crimes against women were addressed in relation to the more general problem of gender inequality.

The VAWA seeks to eradicate violence against women at all levels, and the act allocated $1.6 billion to fight violence against women. Included are funds to (1) educate police, prosecutors, and judges about the special needs of female victims; (2) encourage pro-arrest policies in cases of domestic abuse; (3) provide specialized services for female victims of crime; (4) fund battered women's shelters across the country; and (5) support rape education in a variety of settings nationwide. The law also extends "rape shield law" protections to civil cases and to all criminal cases in order to bar irrelevant inquiries into a victim's sexual history. VAWA was reauthorized by Congress in 2000. Read the text of the original VAWA legislation at Web Extra 2–12 at cjtoday.com.

Finally, the passage of antistalking legislation by all 50 states and the District of Columbia provides some measure of additional protection to women (since women comprise 80% of all stalking victims[82]). On the federal level, the seriousness of stalking was addressed when Congress passed the interstate stalking law in 1996.[83] The law[84] also addresses **cyberstalking**, or the use of the Internet by perpetrators seeking to exercise power and control over their victims by

Cyberspace has become a fertile field for illegal activity. With the use of new technology and equipment which cannot be policed by traditional methods, cyberstalking has replaced traditional methods of stalking and harassment. In addition, cyberstalking has led to offline incidents of violent crime. Police and prosecutors need to be aware of the escalating numbers of these events and devise strategies to resolve these problems through the criminal justice system.

—Linda Fairstein, Chief, Sex Crimes Prosecution Unit, Manhattan District Attorney's Office[v]

LIBRARY
Extra
■■■■

WEB
Extra
■■■■

cyberstalking

The use of the Internet, e-mail, and other electronic communication technologies to stalk another person.[vi]

Multiculturalism and Diversity

Gender Issues in Criminal Justice

The Violent Crime Control and Law Enforcement Act of 1994 included significant provisions intended to enhance gender equality throughout the criminal justice system. Title IV of the Violent Crime Control and Law Enforcement Act, known as the Violence against Women Act (VAWA) of 1994, contains the Safe Streets for Women Act. This act increased federal penalties for repeat sex offenders and requires mandatory restitution for sex crimes, including costs related to medical services (including physical, psychiatric, and psychological care); physical and occupational therapy or rehabilitation; necessary transportation, temporary housing, and child-care expenses; lost income; attorneys' fees, including any costs incurred in obtaining a civil protection order; and any other losses suffered by the victim as a result of the offense. The act also requires that compliance with a restitution order be made a condition of probation or supervised release (if such a sentence is imposed by the court) and provides that violation of the order will result in the offender's imprisonment.

Chapter 2 of VAWA provided funds for grants to combat violent crimes against women. The purpose of funding was to assist states and local governments to "develop and strengthen effective law enforcement and prosecution strategies to combat violent crimes against women, and to develop and strengthen victim services in cases involving violent crimes against women." The law also provided funds for the "training of law enforcement officers and prosecutors to more effectively identify and respond to violent crimes against women, including the crimes of sexual assault and domestic violence"; for "developing, installing, or expanding data collection and communication systems, including computerized systems, linking police, prosecutors, and courts or for the purpose of identifying and tracking arrests, protection orders, violations of protection orders, prosecutions, and convictions for violent crimes against women, including the crimes of sexual assault and domestic violence"; and for developing and strengthening "victim services programs, including sexual assault and domestic violence programs."

The act also created the crime of crossing state lines in violation of a protection order and the crime of crossing state lines to commit assault on a domestic partner. It established federal penalties for the latter offense of up to life in prison in cases where death results.

Chapter 3 of the act provided funds to increase the "safety for women in public transit and public parks." It authorized up to $10 million in grants through the Department of Transportation to enhance lighting, camera surveillance, and security telephones in public transportation systems used by women.

Chapter 5 of VAWA funded the creation of hot lines, educational seminars, informational materials, and training programs for professionals who provide assistance to victims of sexual assault. Another portion of the law, titled the Safe Homes for Women Act, increased grants for battered women's shelters, encouraged arrest in cases of

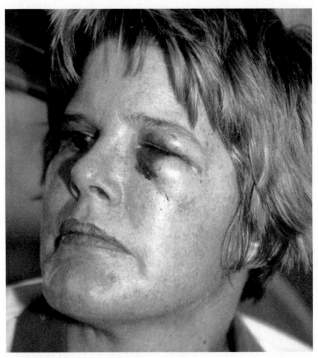

A battered woman posing for police photographers who are documenting her injuries. Intimate partner violence is a problem of special concern to the criminal justice system, and violence against women is an area that is receiving legislative attention, as evidenced by the federal Violence against Women Act. How might laws designed to protect women be improved?
Michael Newman/PhotoEdit Inc.

domestic violence, and provided for the creation of a national domestic violence hot line to provide counseling, information, and assistance to victims of domestic violence. The act also mandates that any protection order issued by a state court must be recognized by the other states and by the federal government and must be enforced "as if it were the order of the enforcing state."

VAWA was reauthorized by Congress in 2000 and again in 2005.[1] The 2000 reauthorization provided $3.3 billion in continuation funding and earmarked a portion of the money for programs that coordinate the work of victims' advocates, police, and prosecutors in the fight against domestic violence. The second reauthorization provided continuation monies for critical programs and funded the development of new services to respond to evolving community needs. In recognition of the fact that domestic violence sometimes leaves victims without homes, the 2006 legislation made funds available to expand services to the homeless, including the development of transitional housing options.

---

[1]VAWA 2005 was signed into law by President George W. Bush on January 5, 2006. It is officially known as the Violence against Women and Department of Justice Reauthorization Act of 2005 (Public Law 109–162).

threatening them directly or by posting misleading and harassing information about them. Cyberstalking can be especially insidious because it does not require that the perpetrator and the victim be in the same geographic area. Similarly, electronic communication technologies lower the barriers to harassment and threats; a cyberstalker does not need to confront the victim physically.[85] Learn more about stalking and cyberstalking at Library Extra 2–13 at cjtoday.com.

LIBRARY
Extra
■ ■ ■ ■

Crime against the Elderly

Relative to other age groups, older victims rarely appear in the crime statistics. Criminal victimization seems to decline with age, suggesting that older people are only infrequently targeted by violent and property criminals. Moreover, older people are more likely than younger individuals to live in secure areas and to have the financial means to provide for their own personal security.

Victimization data pertaining to older people come mostly from the NCVS, which, for such purposes, looks at people age 65 and older. The elderly generally experience the lowest rate of victimization of any age group in both violent and property crime categories.[86] Some aspects of crime against older people are worth noting. In general, elderly crime victims are more likely than younger victims to

- Be victims of property crime—nine out of ten crimes committed against the elderly are property crimes, compared to fewer than four in ten crimes against people between age 12 and 24
- Face offenders who are armed with guns
- Be victimized by strangers
- Be victimized in or near their homes during daylight hours
- Report their victimization to the police, especially when they fall victim to violent crime
- Be physically injured

In addition, elderly people are less likely to attempt to protect themselves when they are victims of violent crime. Only 49% of elderly victims attempt to protect themselves versus 70% of younger victims. Certain categories of elderly people are victimized disproportionately. Relative to their numbers, black men are more often victims, and separated or divorced people and urban residents have higher rates of victimization than do other elderly people. Even though their risk of victimization is considerably less, older people fear crime more than younger people; however, they are less likely to take crime-prevention measures than any other age group. Only 6% of households headed by people older than age 65 have an alarm, and only 16% of such households report engraving their valuables (versus a 25% national average).

The elderly face special kinds of victimizations that only rarely affect younger adults, such as physical abuse at the hands of caregivers. Criminal physical abuse of the elderly falls into two categories: domestic and institutional. Domestic abuse often occurs at the hands of caregivers who are related to their victims; institutional abuse occurs in residential settings like retirement centers, nursing homes, and hospitals. Both forms of elder abuse may also involve criminal sexual victimization. To learn more about domestic and institutional elder abuse, visit the National Center on Elder Abuse (NCEA) via Web Extra 2–13 at cjtoday.com.

WEB
Extra
■ ■ ■ ■

The elderly are also more often targeted by con artists. Confidence schemes center on commercial and financial fraud (including telemarketing fraud), charitable donation fraud, funeral and cemetery fraud, real estate fraud, caretaker fraud, automobile and home repair fraud, living trust fraud, health-care fraud (e.g., promises of "miracle cures"), and health-provider fraud (overbilling and unjustified repeat billing by otherwise legitimate health-care providers). "False friends" may intentionally isolate elderly targets from others in the hopes of misappropriating money through short-term secret loans or outright theft. Similarly, a younger person may feign romantic involvement with an elderly victim or pretend to be devoted to the senior in order to solicit money or receive an inappropriate gift or inheritance. The U.S. Senate's Special Committee on Aging provides additional information on such crimes at its Elder Justice Center website, which can be accessed via Web Extra 2–14 at cjtoday.com.

WEB
Extra
■ ■ ■ ■

Finally, crime against the elderly will likely undergo a significant increase as baby boomers enter their retirement years. Not only will the elderly comprise an increasingly larger segment of the population as boomers age, but it is anticipated that they will be wealthier than any preceding generation of retirees, making them attractive targets for scam artists and property criminals.[87]

Hate Crime

hate crime (UCR/NIBRS)

A criminal offense committed against a person, property, or society that is motivated, in whole or in part, by the offender's bias against a race, religion, disability, sexual orientation, or ethnicity/national origin.

A significant change in crime-reporting practices resulted from the Hate Crime Statistics Act,[88] signed into law by President George H. W. Bush in 1990. The act mandates a statistical tally of **hate crimes**; data collection under the law began in 1991. Congress defined *hate crime* as an offense "in which the defendant's conduct was motivated by hatred, bias, or prejudice, based on the actual or perceived race, color, religion, national origin, ethnicity, gender, or sexual orientation of another individual or group of individuals."[89] In 2006, police agencies reported a total of 7,722 hate-crime incidents, including 3 murders, across the country. As Figure 2–6 shows, approximately 19% of the incidents were motivated by religious bias, 51.8% were caused by racial hatred, and 12.7% were driven by prejudice against ethnicity or national origin. Another 15.5% of all hate crimes were based on sexual orientation, most committed against males believed by their victimizers to be homosexuals.[90] A relatively small number of hate crimes targeted people with physical or mental disabilities.

Following the terrorist attacks of September 11, 2001, authorities in some jurisdictions reported a dramatic shift in the nature of hate crime, with race-motivated crimes declining and crimes motivated by religion or ethnicity increasing sharply.[91] Islamic individuals, in particular, became the target of many such crimes.

Most hate crimes consist of intimidation, although vandalism, simple assault, and aggravated assault also account for a number of hate-crime offenses. A few robberies and rapes were also classified as hate crimes in 2006.

One particularly heinous and widely publicized hate crime culminated in death sentences for John William King, 24, and Lawrence Russell Brewer, 32, two white residents of Jasper County, Texas.[92] In separate trials in 1999, King and Brewer were found guilty of first-degree murder in the death of James Byrd, Jr., a 49-year-old black man. Using a chain, King and Brewer lashed Byrd to a pickup truck and dragged him over three miles of rural Texas asphalt to his death. If executed, King or Brewer will become only the second white person ever put to death in Texas for killing a black person. A third white supremacist, 24-year-old Shawn Allen Berry, was found guilty of participating in the crime and was sentenced to life in prison.

Although hate crimes are popularly conceived of as crimes motivated by racial enmity, the Violent Crime Control and Law Enforcement Act of 1994 created a new category of "crimes of violence motivated by gender." Congress defined this crime as "a crime of violence committed because of gender or on the basis of gender, and due, at least in part, to an animus based on the victim's gender." The 1994 act did not establish separate penalties for gender-motivated crimes, anticipating that they would be prosecuted as felonies under existing laws. The 1994 act also mandated that crimes motivated by biases against people with disabilities be considered hate crimes.

Hate crimes are sometimes called *bias crimes*. One form of bias crime that bears special mention is homophobic homicide. This term refers to the murder of homosexuals by those opposed to their lifestyles. Learn more about hate crime and what can be done to address it at Library Extras 2–14 and 2–15 at cjtoday.com.

LIBRARY
Extra

FIGURE 2–6

Motivation of hate-crime offenders, 2006.

Note: Total may be more than 100 percent due to rounding.

Source: Federal Bureau of Investigation, *Crime in the United States, 2006*.

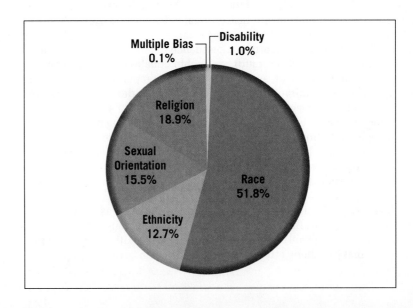

- Multiple Bias 0.1%
- Disability 1.0%
- Religion 18.9%
- Sexual Orientation 15.5%
- Race 51.8%
- Ethnicity 12.7%

Corporate and White-Collar Crime

Recently, a record number of corporations and their executives and former executives have faced high-profile criminal investigations and fraud charges. Between 2001 and 2003, accounting fraud and the ensuing bankruptcies of energy broker Enron Corporation and telecommunications giant WorldCom reduced the holdings of investment and retirement accounts across the country and around the world, wiping out hundreds of billions of dollars' worth of investor equity and taking a significant toll on the wealth of many Americans. Other publicly traded companies that have recently faced investigation include cable services provider Adelphia Communications Corporation (now part of Comcast Communications); French-based media conglomerate Vivendi Universal; national discount retailer Kmart; fiber optics giant Global Crossing; multinational conglomerate Tyco International; accounting firm Arthur Andersen (whose employees served as auditors and accountants for bankrupt Enron); Metabolife, a leading seller of products containing the herbal stimulant ephedrine, which faced a criminal investigation by the U.S. Justice Department into whether the company had lied about drug safety;[93] and London-based auction house Sotheby's. In 2004, Adelphia founder John Rigas and his son, former Adelphia chief financial officer Timothy Rigas, were found guilty of 18 counts of securities and bank fraud, of conspiring to loot the cable company of millions of dollars, and of misleading its investors.[94] Rigas, 80, was sentenced to 15 years in prison, while his son received a 20-year sentence.[95] In 2005, in a case that came to epitomize corporate greed, former Tyco CEO L. Dennis Kozlowski and former Tyco finance chief Mark H. Swartz were convicted of looting their former company of nearly $600 million.[96] About the same time, Bernard J. Ebbers, the 63-year-old former chief executive of WorldCom, was sentenced to serve 25 years behind bars for his role in the nation's largest account fraud. Finally, in 2006 former Enron executives Jeff Skilling and Kenneth Lay were convicted of conspiracy to commit securities and wire fraud in the collapse of energy-trading giant Enron Corporation.[97] The 52-year-old Skilling, Enron's former chief executive officer, received a 24-year sentence. Lay, 64, the company's founder, died from heart failure while awaiting sentencing.

Under the American system of criminal justice, corporations can be treated as separate legal entities and can be convicted of violations of the criminal law under a legal principle known as the *identification doctrine.* In 2002, for example, a federal jury convicted global accounting firm Arthur Andersen of obstruction of justice after its employees shredded documents related to Enron's bankruptcy in an effort to impede an investigation by securities regulators. The conviction, which was overturned by a unanimous U.S. Supreme Court in 2005,[98] capped the firm's demise, and it ended U.S. operations in August 2002.[99]

Although corporations may be convicted of a crime, the human perpetrators of **corporate crime** are business executives known as *white-collar criminals.* **White-collar crime** was first defined in 1939 by Edwin H. Sutherland in his presidential address to the American Sociological

With each arrest, indictment and prosecution, we sent this clear, unmistakable message: corrupt corporate executives are no better than common thieves.

—*U.S. Attorney General John Ashcroft, commenting on the arrests of former WorldCom executives[vii]*

corporate crime

A violation of a criminal statute by a corporate entity or by its executives, employees, or agents acting on behalf of and for the benefit of the corporation, partnership, or other form of business entity.[viii]

white-collar crime

Violations of the criminal law committed by a person of respectability and high social status in the course of his or her occupation. Also, nonviolent crime for financial gain utilizing deception and committed by anyone who has special technical or professional knowledge of business or government, irrespective of the person's occupation.

Society.[100] Sutherland proposed that "crime in the suites" (a reference to corporate offices) rivaled the importance of street crime in its potential impact on American society.

In July 2002, President George W. Bush unveiled plans to create a new Corporate Fraud Task Force within the federal government and proposed a new law providing criminal penalties for corporate fraud. He told corporate leaders on Wall Street, "At this moment, America's greatest economic need is higher ethical standards—standards enforced by strict laws and upheld by responsible business leaders."[101] A few months later, the president signed into law the Sarbanes-Oxley Act.[102] The new law created tough provisions designed to deter and punish corporate and accounting fraud and corruption and to protect the interests of workers and shareholders. Under the Sarbanes-Oxley Act, corporate officials (chief executive officers and chief financial officers) must personally vouch for the truth and accuracy of their companies' financial statements, and federal penalties for obstructing justice and, specifically, for shredding or destroying documents that might aid in a criminal investigation of business practices are substantially increased. Learn more about corporate and white-collar crime at the National White Collar Crime Center (NW3C) via **Web Extra 2–15** at cjtoday.com. Established in 1992, the NW3C provides a national support system for the prevention, investigation, and prosecution of multijurisdictional economic crimes. Learn more about how corporations can be held accountable from CorpWatch via **Web Extra 2–16**.

WEB
Extra

Organized Crime

organized crime

The unlawful activities of the members of a highly organized, disciplined association engaged in supplying illegal goods or services, including gambling, prostitution, loan-sharking, narcotics, and labor racketeering, and in other unlawful activities.[ix]

transnational organized crime

Unlawful activity undertaken and supported by organized criminal groups operating across national boundaries.

For many people, the term **organized crime** conjures up images of the Mafia (also called the *Cosa Nostra*) or the hit HBO TV series *The Sopranos*. Although organized criminal activity is decidedly a group phenomenon, the groups involved in such activity in the United States today display a great deal of variation. During the past few decades in the United States, the preeminence of traditional Sicilian American criminal organizations has fallen to such diverse criminal associations as the Black Mafia, the Cuban Mafia, the Haitian Mafia, the Colombian cartels, and Asian criminal groups like the Chinese Tongs and street gangs, Japanese yakuza, and Vietnamese gangs. Included here as well might be inner-city gangs, the best known of which are probably the Los Angeles Crips and Bloods and the Chicago Vice Lords, international drug rings, outlaw motorcycle gangs like the Hell's Angels and the Pagans, and other looser associations of small-time thugs, prison gangs, and drug dealers. Noteworthy among these groups—especially for their involvement in the lucrative drug trade—are the Latino organized bands, including the Dominican, Colombian, Mexican, and Cuban importers of cocaine, heroin, marijuana, and other controlled substances.

The unlawful activities of organized groups that operate across national boundaries are especially significant. Such activity is referred to as **transnational organized crime**. Transnational

Actor James Gandolfini (Tony Soprano) from HBO's hit series *The Sopranos*. The popular show explored the life of fictionalized organized crime figures in New Jersey. Why was the show such a hit with viewers?

HBO/Picture Desk, Inc./Kobal Collection

criminal associations worthy of special mention are the Hong Kong–based Triads, the South American cocaine cartels, the Italian Mafia, the Japanese yakuza, the Russian *Mafiya*, and the West African crime groups—each of which extends its reach well beyond its home country. In some parts of the world, close links between organized crime and terrorist groups involve money laundering, which provides cash to finance the activities of terrorist cells and to finance paramilitary efforts to overthrow established governments.

Former CIA Director R. James Woolsey points out that "while organized crime is not a new phenomenon today, some governments find their authority besieged at home and their foreign policy interests imperiled abroad. Drug trafficking, links between drug traffickers and terrorists, smuggling of illegal aliens, massive financial and bank fraud, arms smuggling, potential involvement in the theft and sale of nuclear material, political intimidation, and corruption all constitute a poisonous brew—a mixture potentially as deadly as what we faced during the cold war."[103] The challenge for today's criminal justice student is to recognize that crime does not respect national boundaries. Crime is global, and what happens in one part of the world could affect us all.[104]

Gun Crime

The 2007 shooting spree at the Virginia Polytechnic Institute and State University in Blacksburg, Virginia, in which 33 people died and 20 were wounded, led to one of the most intense debates over gun control in this country in decades. CJ Today Exhibit 2–2 provides additional information on the issue of gun control.

Constitutional guarantees of the right to bear arms have combined with historical circumstances to make ours a well-armed society. Guns are used in many types of crimes. Each year, approximately 1 million serious crimes—including homicide, rape, robbery, and assault—involve the use of a handgun. In a typical year, approximately 10,000 murders are committed in the United States with firearms. A recent report by the Bureau of Justice Statistics found that 18% of state prison inmates and 15% of federal inmates were armed at the time they committed the crime for which they were imprisoned.[105] Nine percent of those in state prisons said they fired a gun while committing the offense for which they were serving time.[106]

Both federal and state governments have responded to the public concern over the ready availability of handguns. In 1994, Congress passed the Brady Handgun Violence Prevention Act, which President Bill Clinton signed into law. The law was named for former Press Secretary James Brady, who was shot and severely wounded in an attempt on President Ronald Reagan's life on March 30, 1981. The law mandated a five-day waiting period before the purchase of a handgun, and it established a national instant criminal background check system that firearms dealers must use before selling a handgun. Under the system, licensed importers, manufacturers, and dealers are required to verify the identity of a firearm purchaser using a valid photo ID (such as a driver's license); must submit the purchaser's application to ensure that the applicant's receipt or possession of a handgun would not violate federal, state, or local law;[107] and must contact the system to receive a unique identification number authorizing the purchase before they transfer the handgun.

While the Brady law may limit retail purchases of handguns by felons, a BJS study found that most offenders obtain weapons from friends or family members or "on the street" rather than attempt to purchase them at retail establishments.[108] In 2001, undercover congressional investigators were able to show that applicants using fake forms of identification, such as counterfeit driver's licenses with fictitious names, could easily circumvent Brady law provisions.[109] Moreover, according to these studies, an ever-growing number of violent criminals are now carrying handguns.

In Congress, debate continues about whether to require gun manufacturers to create and retain "ballistic fingerprints" (the marks left on a bullet by the barrel of the gun from which it was fired) of each weapon they produce. Although a national ballistics fingerprinting requirement may still be years away, two states—Maryland and New York—already require that a record be kept of the "fingerprint" characteristics of each new handgun sold.[110] Learn more about promising strategies to reduce gun violence at Library Extra 2–16 at cjtoday.com. For the latest information on gun violence and gun laws, visit the Brady Center to Prevent Gun Violence via Web Extra 2–17 at cjtoday.com. The National Rifle Association site at Web Extra 2–18 provides support for responsible access to firearms.

LIBRARY Extra

WEB Extra

Drug Crime

Drug-law violations do not figure into Crime Index calculations. Unlike index crimes, however, drug-related crime continues to rise, lending support to the belief that the United States is experiencing more crime than traditional index tabulations show. The relentless increase in drug violations largely accounts for the continued growth in America's prison populations, even when

> *I'm signing a good bill.... It says loud and clear to corporate America, we expect you to be responsible, we expect you to be responsible with the people's money. We expect you to be responsible for the shareholders and your employees and if you're not, we're going to investigate you, arrest you and prosecute you.*
>
> —President George W. Bush, at the signing of the Sarbanes-Oxley Act of 2002[x]

CJ Today Exhibit 2–2

Gun Control

The Second Amendment to the U.S. Constitution reads, "A well regulated Militia, being necessary to the security of a free State, the right of the people to keep and bear Arms, shall not be infringed." For many years, the official position of the U.S. Justice Department had been that the Second Amendment merely gives states the collective right to organize and arm militias in order to protect the public interest and that it does not mean that individual citizens have a constitutional right to own firearms. On May 7, 2002, however, in two briefs filed with the U.S. Supreme Court by U.S. Solicitor General Theodore B. Olson, the Justice Department officially reversed course, declaring, "The current position of the United States . . . is that the Second Amendment more broadly protects the rights of individuals, including persons who are not members of any militia or engaged in active military service or training, to possess and bear their own firearms, subject to reasonable restrictions designed to prevent possession . . . of types of firearms that are particularly suited to criminal misuse."[1] Although the government's briefs did not ask the justices to take any action, they were seen by many as representing a significant victory for advocates of private gun ownership, such as the National Rifle Association (NRA). Nonetheless, few imagine that the apparent change in policy will lead to significant modifications in existing gun-control legislation, much of which was passed in the 1990s.

One of those laws, the Violent Crime Control and Law Enforcement Act of 1994,[2] regulated the sale of firearms within the United States and originally banned the manufacture of 19 military-style assault weapons, including those with specific combat features, such as high-capacity ammunition clips capable of holding more than ten rounds. The ban on assault weapons ended in 2004, however, when it was not renewed by Congress. The 1994 law also prohibited the sale or transfer of a gun to a juvenile, as well as the possession of a gun by a juvenile, and it prohibits gun sales to, and possession by, people subject to family violence restraining orders.

The 1996 Domestic Violence Offender Gun Ban[3] prohibits individuals convicted of misdemeanor domestic violence offenses from owning or using firearms. Soon after the law was passed, however, it became embroiled in controversy when hundreds of police officers across the country who had been convicted of domestic violence offenses were found to be in violation of the ban. A number of officers lost their jobs, while others were placed in positions that did not require them to carry firearms. While some legislators pushed to exempt police officers and military personnel from the ban's provisions, others argued that they should be included. Feminist Majority President Eleanor Smeal was angered. "Rather than trying to seek an exemption for police officers and military personnel who are abusers, we should be concerned with why we are recruiting so many abusers for these positions," she said.[4]

Following the 1999 Columbine High School shooting, a number of states moved to tighten controls over handguns and assault

Blacksburg (Virginia) police officers running toward a building on the Virginia Tech campus on April 16, 2007. That morning, Seung-Hui Cho, a student suffering from mental problems, shot and killed 33 people and wounded 20 in two separate shootings on the campus, leading some to brand Cho "the poster boy for gun control." Cho was armed with two semiautomatic handguns that he had recently purchased. He took his own life after firing more than 200 times at helpless students and professors, most of whom were in classrooms at the time of Cho's atttack. The shooting, which was quickly labeled the "worst mass shooting in American history," led to renewed calls for heightened gun-control measures throughout the United States. What is your position on the issue of gun control?
The Roanoke Times/*Matt Gentry/AP Wide World Photos*

weapons. The California legislature, for example, restricted gun purchases to one per month and tightened a ten-year-old ban on assault weapons. Similarly, Illinois passed a law requiring that gun owners lock their weapons away from anyone under age 14.

In 2004, at the urging of major police organizations, the U.S. Senate scuttled plans for a gun-industry protection bill. However, the bill was revived in 2005 and passed both houses of Congress before being signed into law by President George W. Bush on October 31. Known as the Protection of Lawful Commerce in Firearms Act, the law grants gunmakers and most gun dealers immunity from lawsuits brought by victims of gun crimes and their survivors. The law removes negligence as viable grounds for a civil suit against a gun dealer who carelessly sells a gun to someone who is at risk for using it in a crime; the law states that the dealer can be sued only if he or she knew of the gun buyer's criminal intent before the purchase. Gunmakers were made immune from suits alleging product liability for having manufactured potentially lethal items. Read the 2007 *Report to the President on Issues Raised by the Virginia Tech Tragedy* at **Library Extra 2-17** at cjtoday.com.

LIBRARY
Extra
■ ■ ■ ■

---

[1] "Justice Department Reverses Second-Amendment Interpretation," http://www.jointogether.org/gv/news/summaries/reader/0,2061,550836,00.html (accessed August 17, 2006).
[2] PL 103–322, 108 Stat. 1796 (codified as amended in scattered sections of 18, 21, 28, 42, etc., U.S.).
[3] PL 104–208, an amendment to U.S. Code, Title 18, Section 921(a). Also known as the Lautenberg Amendment.
[4] Jacob R. Clark, "Police Careers May Take a Beating from Fed Domestic-Violence Law," *Law Enforcement News,* Vol. 23, No. 461 (February 14, 1997), p. 1.

official crime rates (that is, index offenses) have been declining. Chapter 16 discusses illicit drugs and drug-law violations in detail. As that chapter shows, the rate of drug-related crime commission has more than doubled in the United States since 1975.

Alone, drug-law violations are themselves criminal, but more and more studies are linking drug abuse to other serious crimes. An early study by the RAND Corporation found that most of the "violent predators" among prisoners had extensive histories of heroin abuse, often in combination with alcohol and other drugs.[111] Some cities reported that a large percentage of their homicides were drug related.[112] More recent studies also link drug abuse to other serious crimes. Community leaders perceive, and data analyses confirm, that crack cocaine has a profound impact on violent crime, with homicide rates closely tracking cocaine use levels among adult male arrestees.[113] Prisoner survey data show that 19% of state inmates and 16% of federal prisoners reported committing their current offense to obtain money for drugs.[114] A 2000 study found that 13.3% of convicted jail inmates said that they had committed their offense to get money for drugs.[115]

Criminal justice system costs associated with the handling of drug offenders have increased substantially in recent years. Between 1984 and 2002, for example, the annual number of defendants charged with a drug offense in federal courts increased from 11,854 to more than 30,000.[116] Similarly, between 1984 and 2002, drug offenses accounted for an increased proportion of the federal criminal caseload, even when charges weren't brought. During 1984, 18% of referrals to U.S. attorneys were drug related, compared with 31% during 2002.[117] Some of the increase stems from changes in federal drug laws. Whatever the cause, the drug–crime link is costly to society and shows few signs of abating.

Cybercrime

Cybercrime, sometimes called *computer crime* or *information-technology crime*, uses computers and computer technology as tools in crime commission. Computer criminals manipulate the information stored in computer systems in ways that violate the law. (Thefts of computer equipment, although sometimes spectacular, are not computer crimes but are instead classified as larcenies.)

Many crimes committed via the Internet, such as prostitution, drug sales, theft, and fraud, are not new forms of offending. Rather, they are traditional offenses that use technology in their commission or that build on the possibilities for criminal activity that new technologies make possible. In 2004, for example, police and real estate agents in Australia and New Zealand issued warnings to people who had been using Web-based virtual tours to sell their houses.[118] Burglars "down under" had been using the tours, which provide 360-degree views of a home's interior, to target expensive houses, locate valuables, and identify and disarm security devices.

U.S. Customs and Border Protection Senior Special Agent Donald Daufenbach, an international expert in child pornography and the Internet, points out that "the Internet is like anything else: It can be bent or perverted for nefarious purposes. . . . The Internet has absolutely changed the way people communicate with each other, changed the way people conduct commerce, changed the way people do research, changed the way people entertain themselves and changed the way people break the law. . . . People are catching on pretty quick, but law enforcement is lagging behind miserably in this whole endeavor."[119]

cybercrime

Any crime perpetrated through the use of computer technology. Also, any violation of a federal or state cybercrime statute.

Microsoft technical analysts Bryan McDoweel (rear) and Liz Christopher (left) and FBI agents Dan Larkin and Tom Grasso training students at the National Cyber-Forensics and Training Alliance in Pittsburgh. How does this textbook define *cybercrime*? What kinds of crimes can be committed with the use of computers or through the Internet?

© 2004 Jason Cohn/Photo by www. jasoncohn.com

CJ News

Center Ties Hate Crimes to Border Debate

Tension over illegal immigration is contributing to a rise in hate groups and hate crimes across the nation, according to the Southern Poverty Law Center. It says that racist groups are using the immigration debate as a rallying cry.

The center—an Alabama-based non-profit organization that tracks racist, anti-immigrant and other extremist groups—says in a new report that there were 803 such hate groups in the USA in 2005, up from 762 in 2004 and a 33% jump since 2000.

The center's report says the national debate that has focused on Hispanic immigration has been "the single most important factor" in spurring activity among hate groups and has given them "an issue with real resonance."

The debate over immigration "has been critical to the growth of the hate movement," says Mark Potok, editor of the center's quarterly report on extremists. "More and more groups are turning to immigration to help recruitment."

Potok says the center has seen increasing signs that groups that have encouraged a particularly aggressive response to illegal immigration are working with neo-Nazi organizations to try to intimidate illegal immigrants.

He cites groups such as the Arizona-based Border Guardians, whose members burned a Mexican flag . . . in front of that nation's consulate in Tucson.

Border Guardians is a relatively new organization and was not included on the center's 2005 list of hate groups. Its director, Laine Lawless, disputes the center's report . . . that she has encouraged neo-Nazi groups to threaten and steal money from illegal immigrants. In an interview, Lawless said her group supports only "lawful actions."

Lawless said she gets "contacted by all sorts of groups" and "some of them are Nazis," but she said she does not recruit neo-Nazis. Lawless went on to describe the most vocal organizers of last month's immigrants' rights marches as militant "brown Nazis" whose activities threaten to ignite a "civil war" in America.

The building tension over illegal immigration's impact on America comes at a time when the FBI says that the number of hate-crime victims in 2004—the last year for which figures are available—was 9,528, up nearly 5% from 2003.

Members of the Minutemen anti-immigration group protesting the hiring of illegal day laborers outside a San Diego Home Depot in 2006, as Mexican day laborers looking for work counterprotest. How is illegal immigration tied to hate crimes?
UPI Photo/Earl S. Cryer/Landov LLC

The numbers don't approach the 12,020 hate-crime victims reported in 2001, when there was a rash of attacks against Muslims across the nation in the weeks after the Sept. 11 terrorist attacks.

There are about 12 million illegal immigrants in the USA.

Such immigrants—particularly Hispanics who cross from Mexico in search of work—also have become targets for private groups that have formed patrols along the southwestern border, usually against the wishes of law enforcement.

One of those groups is American Border Patrol. Its efforts have included rounding up illegal immigrants and turning them over to law enforcement. The Southern Poverty Law Center has accused ABP of abusing and illegally detaining immigrants, and the center lists ABP as a hate group.

ABP's director, Glenn Spencer, is a vocal critic of illegal immigration but says his group has done nothing wrong.

"Our borders are unprotected, and the (U.S.) Border Patrol is derelict in its duty," Spencer says. "We are trying to help by any means necessary."

For the latest in crime and justice news, visit the Talk Justice news feed at http://www.crimenews.info.

Source: Kevin Johnson, "Center Ties Hate Crimes to Border Debate," USA TODAY, May 17, 2006. Reprinted with permission.

WEB
Extra

Chapter 18 provides additional information about cybercrime, including computer malware, software piracy, and phishing, and the law enforcement technologies used to fight it. Learn more about cybercrime and efforts to combat it at **Web Extra 2–19** at **cjtoday.com**.

Terrorism

Following the September 11, 2001, attacks on the World Trade Center and the Pentagon, terrorism and its prevention became primary concerns of American justice system officials. Before Sep-

A commuter being helped away from the Edgware Road Underground Station following terrorist bombings in London's subway system in 2005. How might future acts of terrorism be prevented?

Jane Mingay/AP Wide World Photos

tember 11, however, terrorism was far from unknown. In 2001, for example, terrorist attacks totaled 864 worldwide—down from the 1,106 reported a year earlier.[120]

The great blackout of 2003, which affected as many as 50 million people in the United States and Canada, demonstrated the fragility of the nation's energy grid—another potential terrorist target. To assist in developing protection for the nation's critical infrastructure, the Homeland Security Act of 2002 created the Department of Homeland Security and made its director a Cabinet member. Similarly, in an effort to protect vital interests from future acts of terrorism, the U.S. government is building a whole new Internet of its own. Dubbed GOVNET, the service will provide secure voice and data communication by remaining physically and electronically separate from existing Internet routers and gateways.[121] Visit the Department of Homeland Security via Web Extra 2–20 at cjtoday.com. Terrorism and efforts to combat it are discussed in detail in Chapter 17.

WEB
Extra
■ ■ ■ ■

SUMMARY

- The FBI's Uniform Crime Reporting Program began in the 1930s when the Congress authorized the U.S. attorney general to survey crime in America. Today's UCR/NIBRS program provides annual data on the number of reported Part I offenses, or major crimes, as well as information about arrests that have been made for less serious Part II offenses. The Part I offenses are murder, forcible rape, robbery, aggravated assault, burglary, larceny-theft, motor vehicle theft, and arson. The Part II offense category covers many more crimes, including drug offenses, driving under the influence, and simple assault. Modifications to the UCR Program, which has traditionally provided only summary crime data, are occurring with the implementation of the new National Incident-Based Reporting System.

NIBRS, which represents a significant redesign of the original UCR Program, gathers many details about each criminal incident, such as place of occurrence, weapon used, type and value of property damaged or stolen, the personal characteristics of the offender and the victim, the nature of any relationship between the two, and the disposition of the complaint.

- The National Crime Victimization Survey is the second major source of statistical data about crime in the United States. The NCVS, which was first conducted in 1972, is based on victim self-reports rather than on police reports. The NCVS originally built on efforts by both the National Opinion Research Center and the 1967 President's Commission on Law Enforcement and the

Administration of Justice to uncover what some had been calling the *dark figure of crime*—that is, those crimes that are not reported to the police and that are relatively hidden from justice system officials. An analysis of victim self-report data led to the realization that crimes of all types were more prevalent than UCR statistics had previously indicated.

- This chapter discusses a number of special categories of crime, including crime against women, crime against the elderly, hate crime, corporate and white-collar crime, organized crime, gun crime, drug crime, cybercrime, and terrorism. Each of these categories is of special concern in contemporary society.

KEY TERMS

aggravated assault, 53

arson, 56

assault, 52

Bureau of Justice Statistics (BJS), 35

burglary, 53

clearance rate, 46

corporate crime, 65

Crime Index, 39

crime typology, 60

cybercrime, 69

cyberstalking, 61

dark figure of crime, 58

date rape, 49

forcible rape, 48

hate crime, 64

identity theft, 55

larceny-theft, 55

motor vehicle theft, 55

murder, 46

National Crime Victimization Survey (NCVS), 35

National Incident-Based Reporting System (NIBRS), 40

organized crime, 66

Part I offenses, 46

Part II offenses, 57

property crime, 45

rape, 48

robbery, 50

sexual battery, 48

stalking, 60

transnational organized crime, 66

Uniform Crime Reporting (UCR) Program, 35

violent crime, 45

white-collar crime, 65

QUESTIONS FOR REVIEW

1. Describe the historical development of the FBI's Uniform Crime Reporting Program, and list the crimes on which it reports. How is the ongoing implementation of the National Incident-Based Reporting System changing the UCR Program? How will data reported under the new UCR/NIBRS differ from the crime statistics reported under the traditional UCR Program?

2. Describe the history of the National Crime Victimization Survey. What do data from the NCVS tell us about crime in the United States today?

3. What are the special categories of crime discussed in this chapter? Why are they important?

QUESTIONS FOR REFLECTION

1. What can crime statistics tell us about the crime picture in America? How has that picture changed over time? What additional changes might be coming?

2. What are the potential sources of error in the nation's major crime reports? Can you think of some popular use of crime statistics today that might be especially misleading?

3. Why are many crime statistics expressed as rates? How does the use of crime rates instead of simple numerical tabulations improve the usefulness of crime data?

4. Do some property crimes have a violent aspect? Are there any personal crimes that could be nonviolent? If so, what might they be?

5. What is a clearance rate? What does it mean to say that a crime has been "cleared"? What are the different ways in which a crime can be cleared?

Discuss your answers to these questions and other issues on the CJ Today e-mail discussion list (join the list at cjtoday.com).

WEB QUEST

Visit the Prentice Hall Cybrary of Criminal Justice Links on the Web at http://www.cybrary.info, and familiarize yourself with the Cybrary's features. Note that a number of general categories are listed on the home page. (Click "Show All Categories" at the bottom of the page to see more.) The power of the Cybrary lies in its advanced search capabilities.

Practice using the Cybrary's search feature. Once you have become familiar with how the search feature works, use it to find links to the FBI's Uniform Crime Reporting Program (look for the FBI's home page), the *Sourcebook of Criminal Justice Statistics*, and data from the BJS National Crime Victimization Survey.

Visit all three sites to gather information on the crime of rape. Compare the availability of information on rape at these three sites. Compare the sites in other ways. Which do you find most useful? Why? Submit your answers to your instructor if asked to do so.

To complete this Web Quest online, go to the Web Quest module in Chapter 2 of the *Criminal Justice Today* Companion Website at cjtoday.com.

CHAPTER 3

The Search for Causes

LEARNING OBJECTIVES

After reading this chapter, you should be able to

- Explain the nature of criminological theory and discuss the role that social research plays in the development of such theory.

- Describe the Classical School of criminology, and show how it continues to influence criminological theorizing today.

- Describe the basic features of biological theories of crime causation, and know their shortcomings.

- Explain how the mapping of human DNA has enhanced contemporary psychobiological understandings of criminal behavior.

- Describe the fundamental assumptions of psychological explanations for crime, and know the shortcomings of such explanations.

- Describe the basic features of sociological theories of crime causation.

- Describe social process theories of criminology, and identify the kinds of crime-control policies that might be based on them.

- Describe conflict theories of criminality, and identify the kinds of crime-control policies that might be based on them.

- Identify three emergent theories of crime causation.

During the last several years, violent crime in America has been decreasing. And all Americans are grateful. . . . But, unfortunately, American society is still far too violent. The violent crime rate in the United States remains among the highest in the industrialized world.

—President George W. Bush[1]

I could kill everyone without blinking an eye!

—Charlie Manson[2]

Hear the author discuss this chapter at cjtoday.com

Introduction

In August 2006, well-known rapper Busta Rhymes was arrested by New York City police after he performed at the AmsterJam Music Festival. He was charged with assault for allegedly attacking a man who spit on his car.[3] A few months later, Rhymes—whose legal name is Trevor Smith—was accused of beating his former driver, Edward Hatchett, and of kicking him in the ribs during a dispute over back pay. The alleged attack, which was said to have taken place outside of Rhymes's Lower Manhattan office, left Hatchett with cuts, bruises, and substantial pain, according to a court complaint.[4]

Brushes with the law are nothing new to Rhymes. In February 2006, his bodyguard, 29-year-old Israel Ramirez, was shot to death outside a Brooklyn studio where Rhymes was recording a music video. About the same time, the performer and another of his bodyguards were sued by a fan who said the two men beat him after he asked for an autograph. Rhymes's arrest record extends back at least as far as 1998, when he and his manager were apprehended and charged with third-degree criminal possession of a concealed weapon. Police reportedly found an unregistered but loaded .45-caliber semiautomatic handgun in the singer's Mercedes after they stopped him for erratic driving.[5] Rhymes's most recent arrest came shortly before dawn on February 21, 2007, when he was stopped and taken into custody in Lower Manhattan for driving with a suspended license. According to police, Rhymes was pulled over for running a red light at 5:30 A.M.[6]

Rapper Busta Rhymes arriving at the 2006 BET Awards in Los Angeles. Rhymes has been arrested numerous times, leading some to claim that rap and some forms of hip-hop music lead to crime. What do you think?

Getty Images, Inc.

Rhymes is certainly not the only rapper to become acquainted with the criminal justice system. In April 2000, hip-hop artist Curtis "50 Cent" Jackson, a rising star in the world of hard-core rap music, was shot nine times in front of his grandmother's home in New York City.[7] One of the bullets hit him in the face. "50," as the singer is known to his fans, survived the shooting but spent months recovering. Two years later, 50 was back on the music scene, having recorded a top-selling album, *Get Rich or Die Tryin'*, propelled by his hit song "In Da Club." In 2002, he made headlines when he was arrested on New Year's Eve for illegal possession of a handgun.[8] 50 told fans that he'd had a bulletproof jacket made for his six-year-old son. In 2005, 50 released the album *The Massacre*, which quickly went Platinum, and his songs "Disco Inferno," "Candy Shop," and "P.I.M.P." topped the hip-hop charts.

As these stories illustrate, violent crime is no stranger to the world of hard-core rap music. Murdered rap stars include Tupac Shakur, Notorious B.I.G., Big L., and the Lost Boyz's hip-hop hype man Raymond "Freaky Tah" Rogers. Whether rap music merely reflects the social conditions under which its artists come of age or whether it is a direct cause of the violence that surrounds them is a question to which we will return shortly.

No discussion of crime and of the criminal justice system would be complete without considering the *causes* of crime and **deviance**. Criminologists search for answers to the fundamental questions about what causes crime: Why do people commit crime? What are the root causes of violence and aggression? Are people basically good, or are they motivated only by self-interest? More precisely, we might ask, "Why does a particular person commit a particular crime on a given occasion and under specific circumstances?"

In this chapter, we will look at the causes of crime. Before we begin, however, some brief definitions are in order. *Crime*, as noted in Chapter 1, is a violation of the criminal law without acceptable legal justification,[9] while *deviant behavior* is a violation of social norms that specify appropriate or proper behavior under a particular set of circumstances. Deviant behavior is a broad category that often includes crime.

Many theories have been advanced to explain all sorts of rule-violating behavior. Some observers of the contemporary scene, for example, blame much of today's crime on commonplace episodes of violence in the American media—especially on television, in music, and on film. Experts who study the media estimate that the average American child watches 8,000 murders and 100,000 acts of violence while growing up.[10] At an international conference, Suzanne Stutman, president of the Institute for Mental Health Initiatives, a nonprofit organization in Washington, D.C., reported that studies consistently show that the extent of exposure to television violence in childhood is a good predictor of future criminal behavior.[11] One particular study, released in 2002, found that watching just one hour of television a day can make a person more violent toward others.[12] The study, which was conducted over a 25-year period at New York's Columbia University, used police records to confirm that 45% of young men who had watched three or more hours of television a day went on to commit at least one aggressive act against another person, compared to 9% of young men who had watched for less than one hour per day.

Robert Brown, executive director of the Washington, D.C., Children's Trust Neighborhood Initiative, lays much of the blame for contemporary violence on rap music, especially "gangsta rap" and some forms of hip-hop. "So many of our young men," says Brown, "have accepted false icons of manhood for themselves . . . because the popular culture of videos and rap—Snoop Doggy Dogg and the rest—reinforces that this is the correct way to be. Guys . . . try to exude an aura that says, 'I am so bad that I am not afraid to take your life or to offer mine up in the process.' "[13]

An African American critic of gangsta rap puts it this way: "The key element is aggression—in rappers' body language, tone, and witty rhymes—that often leaves listeners hyped, on edge, angry about . . . something. Perhaps the most important element in gangsta rap is its messages, which center largely around these ideas: that women are no more than 'bitches and hos,' disposable playthings who exist merely for men's abusive delight; that it's cool to use any means necessary to get the material things you want; and most importantly, it's admirable to be cold-blooded and hard."[14] The Reverend Arthur L. Cribbs, Jr., an African American social critic, agrees. Cribbs calls gangsta rap "nothing but modern-day violence and vulgarity wrapped and packaged in blackface."[15]

Most people agree that media violence harms society. According to one survey, "57% of the public thinks violence in the media is a major factor in real-life violence" of all kinds.[16] But it is less than clear whether violence in the media and aggressive themes in popular music are indeed a cause of crime, as many believe, or merely a reflection of the social conditions that exist in many American communities today. Findings from studies on the effect of television viewing, for example, may be inadvertently spotlighting existing criminal tendencies among lower-class undereducated teenagers with enough time on their hands for extensive TV viewing. Hence, getting legislators to address the issue of violence in the media is difficult. For example,

deviance

A violation of social norms defining appropriate or proper behavior under a particular set of circumstances. Deviance often includes criminal acts.

The political right believes that the root cause of violent crime is bad genes or bad morals. Not so, says the left. The root cause of violent crime is bad housing or dead-end jobs. And I tell you that while doing something about the causes of violence surely requires a political ideology, the only way we can determine what those causes are in the first place is to check our ideologies at the door and to try to keep our minds open as wide, and for as long, as we can bear.

—John Monahan, speaking at the U.S. Sentencing Commission's Inaugural Symposium on Crime and Punishment

a proposed labeling system for video games and other forms of entertainment was advanced several years ago by Representatives Zach Wamp (R-Tenn.) and Bart Stupak (D-Mich.). They argued that the government requires warning labels on food, alcohol, and tobacco and should do likewise on sources of violence, but the proposal was voted down 266-161.[17]

Criminological Theory

It is easy to understand why the entertainment industry and the media are often targeted as the cause of crime and criminal violence. However, many other types of explanations for crime are also viable, such as genetic abnormalities, individual psychological differences, and variations in patterns of early socialization that may predispose some people to crime and violence. Likewise, it is prudent to examine social institutions such as the family, schools, and churches for their role in reducing or enhancing the likelihood of criminality among people.

One thing is certain: There is no single cause of crime; it is rooted in a diversity of causal factors and takes a variety of forms, depending on the situation in which it occurs. Nonetheless, some theories of human behavior help us understand why certain people engage in acts that society defines as criminal or deviant, while others do not. A **theory** is a kind of model. Theories posit relationships, often of a causal sort, between events and things under study. Formally, a complete theory consists of a series of interrelated propositions that attempt to describe, explain, predict, and ultimately control some class of events. A theory's explanatory power derives primarily from its inherent logical consistency, and theories are tested by how well they describe and predict reality. In other words, a good theory provides a relatively complete understanding of the phenomenon under study, and carefully made observations support predictions based on the theory. A good theory fits the facts, and it stands up to continued scrutiny. Figure 3–1 uses the association between poverty and crime as an example to diagram the important aspects of theory creation in the social sciences.

History is rife with theories purporting to explain rule-violating behavior. For example, an old Roman theory, based on ancient observations that more crime and deviance occur on nights with a full moon, proposed that the moon causes a kind of temporary insanity, or *lunacy*. According to this theory, deviant behavior isn't random; it waxes and wanes in cadence with the lunar cycle. Although modern statisticians have noted an association between phases of the moon and crime rates, the precise mechanism by which the moon influences behavior—if it does—has never been adequately explained.

As mentioned, a complete theory attempts to flesh out all of the causal links between phenomena that are associated or "correlated." For example, some comprehensive theories of lunacy suggest that light from the full moon stimulates the reticular-activating system (RAS) in the limbic portion of the human brain, which makes people more excitable and hyperactive—and thus more likely to behave in deviant ways and to commit crime. Others have suggested, quite simply, that people commit more crimes when the moon is full because it is easier to see.

Theories, once created, must be tested to determine whether they are valid, and modern criminology has become increasingly scientific.[18] Theory testing usually involves the development of **hypotheses** based on what the theory under scrutiny would predict. A theory of lunacy, for example, might be tested in a variety of ways, including (1) observing rates of crime and deviance on nights when the light of the full moon is obscured by clouds (we would expect no rise in crime rates if the RAS or visibility explanations are correct); and (2) examining city crime rates on full-moon nights—especially in well-lit city areas where the light of the moon hardly increases visibility. If the predictions made by a theory are validated by careful observation, the theory gains greater acceptability.

Generally accepted research designs—coupled with careful data-gathering strategies and statistical techniques for data analysis—have yielded considerable confidence in certain explanations for crime, while at the same time disproving others. Theories of crime causation that have met rigorous scientific tests for acceptability give policymakers the intellectual basis they need to create informed crime-control strategies. The ultimate goal of **research** and theory building in criminology is to provide models that permit a better understanding of criminal behavior and that enhance the development of strategies intended to address the problem of crime.

While we will use the word *theory* in describing various explanations for crime throughout this chapter, it should be recognized that the word is only loosely applicable to some of the perspectives we will discuss. As noted, many social scientists insist that to be considered "theories," explanations must consist of sets of clearly stated, logically interrelated, and measurable propositions. The fact that few of the "theories" that follow rise above the level of organized conjecture, and that many others are not readily amenable to objective scrutiny through scientific testing, is one of the greatest failures of social science today.

theory

A set of interrelated propositions that attempt to describe, explain, predict, and ultimately control some class of events. A theory is strengthened by its logical consistency and is "tested" by how well it describes and predicts reality.

hypothesis

An explanation that accounts for a set of facts and that can be tested by further investigation. Also, something that is taken to be true for the purpose of argument or investigation.[i]

research

The use of standardized, systematic procedures in the search for knowledge.

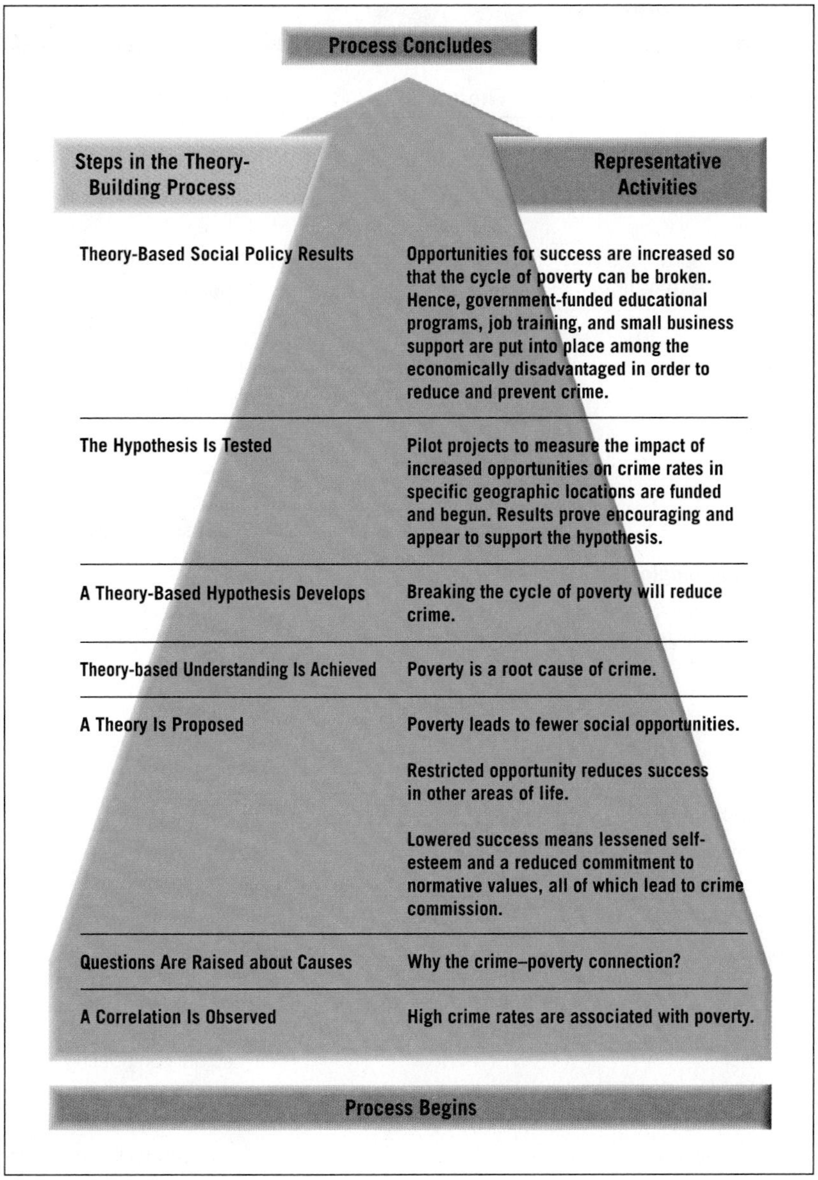

FIGURE 3-1

Steps in criminological
theory building and social
policy creation.

Process Concludes

Steps in the Theory-Building Process	Representative Activities
Theory-Based Social Policy Results	Opportunities for success are increased so that the cycle of poverty can be broken. Hence, government-funded educational programs, job training, and small business support are put into place among the economically disadvantaged in order to reduce and prevent crime.
The Hypothesis Is Tested	Pilot projects to measure the impact of increased opportunities on crime rates in specific geographic locations are funded and begun. Results prove encouraging and appear to support the hypothesis.
A Theory-Based Hypothesis Develops	Breaking the cycle of poverty will reduce crime.
Theory-based Understanding Is Achieved	Poverty is a root cause of crime.
A Theory Is Proposed	Poverty leads to fewer social opportunities. Restricted opportunity reduces success in other areas of life. Lowered success means lessened self-esteem and a reduced commitment to normative values, all of which lead to crime commission.
Questions Are Raised about Causes	Why the crime–poverty connection?
A Correlation Is Observed	High crime rates are associated with poverty.

Process Begins

Also, many contemporary theories of deviant and criminal behavior are far from complete, offering only limited ideas rather than complete explanations for the behavior in question. Moreover, when we consider the wide range of behaviors regarded as criminal—from murder to drug use to white-collar crime—it is difficult to imagine a theory that can explain them all.

For our purposes, explanations of criminal behavior fall into eight general categories:

- Classical
- Biological
- Psychobiological
- Psychological
- Sociological
- Social process
- Conflict
- Emergent

The differences among these approaches are summarized in Table 3–1. A ninth category could be **interdisciplinary theories**. These approaches integrate a variety of theoretical viewpoints in an attempt to explain crime and violence. Harvard University's Project on Human Development in

interdisciplinary theory

An approach that integrates a variety of theoretical viewpoints in an attempt to explain something, such as crime and violence.

TABLE 3–1 Types of Criminological Theory

Type	Theorists	Characteristics
Classical and Neoclassical		
Free will theories	Beccaria	Crime is caused by the individual exercise of free will.
Hedonistic calculus	Bentham	
Rational choice theory	Cohen & Felson	Prevention is possible through swift and certain punishment that offsets any gains to be had through criminal behavior.
Routine activities theory		
Biological		
Phrenology	Gall	"Criminal genes" cause deviant behavior. Criminals are identifiable through physical characteristics or genetic makeup. Treatment is generally ineffective, but aggression may be usefully redirected.
Atavism	Lombroso	
Criminal families	Dugdale; Goddard	
Somatotypes	Sheldon	
Psychobiological		
Chromosome theory	Jacobs	Human DNA, environmental contaminants, nutrition, hormones, physical trauma, and body chemistry play important and interwoven roles in producing human cognition, feeling, and behavior—including crime.
Biochemical approaches		
Heredity	Mednick; Wilson & Herrnstein	
Psychological		
Behavioral conditioning	Pavlov	Crime is the result of inappropriate behavioral conditioning or a diseased mind. Treatment necessitates extensive behavioral therapy.
Psychoanalysis	Freud	
Psychopathology	Cleckley	
Sociological		
Social disorganization	Park & Burgess; Shaw & McKay Durkheim; Merton	The structure of society and its relative degree of organization or disorganization are important actors contributing to the prevalence of criminal behavior.
Anomie		
Subcultures	Cohen	Group dynamics, group organization, and subgroup relationships form the causal nexus out of which crime develops. Effective social policy may require basic changes in patterns of socialization and an increase in accepted opportunities for success.
Focal concerns	Miller	
Subculture of violence	Wolfgang & Ferracuti	
Social Process		
Differential association	Sutherland	Crime results from the failure of self-direction, inadequate social roles, or association with defective others. Social policy places responsibility for change on the offender.
Social learning	Burgess & Akers	
Containment	Reckless	
Social control	Hirschi	
Neutralization	Sykes & Matza	
Labeling	Becker	The source of criminal behavior is unknown, but an understanding of crime requires recognition that the definition of crime is imposed on behavior by the wider society. Individuals defined as "criminal" may be excluded by society from "normal" opportunities. Therapy requires a total reorientation of the offender.

TABLE 3-1	Types of Criminological Theory	(continued)	
Type	**Theorists**	**Characteristics**	
Social development theory Life course perspective	Sampson & Laub	Human development occurs simultaneously on many levels, including psychological, biological, familial, interpersonal, cultural, societal, and ecological. The life course perspective notes that criminal behavior tends to follow an identifiable pattern throughout a person's life cycle.	
Conflict			
Radical criminology	Turk; Vold; Chambliss	Conflict is fundamental to social life. Crime is a natural consequence of social, political, and economic inequities.	
Peacemaking criminology	Pepinsky; Quinney	Fundamental changes to the structure of society are needed to eliminate crime.	
Emergent			
Feminist criminology	Adler; Simon; Daly & Chesney-Lind	Feminist criminology emphasizes the need for gender awareness in the criminological enterprise.	
Constitutive criminology	Henry & Milovanovic	Crime is a social phenomenon and, as such, is socially constructed.	
Postmodern criminology	Henry & Milovanovic	Deconstructionist approaches challenge existing theories in order to replace them with perspectives more relevant to the modern era.	

Chicago Neighborhoods is one example of an ongoing interdisciplinary study of the causes of crime. Described in more detail later in this chapter, the Harvard project is examining the roles of personality, school, and community as they contribute to juvenile delinquency and criminal behavior. See Web Extra 3–1 at cjtoday.com for more information on the project. Web Extra 3–2 leads to more information on the general categories of criminological theory mentioned here, and Library Extra 3–1 at cjtoday.com discusses recent theoretical developments in the field of criminological theory.

WEB Extra ▪▪▪▪ **LIBRARY** Extra ▪▪▪▪

The Classical School

Theories of the **Classical School** of crime causation dominated criminological thought for much of the late eighteenth and early nineteenth centuries. These theories represented a noteworthy advance over previous thinking about crime because they moved beyond superstition and mysticism as explanations for deviance. As noted criminologist Stephen Schafer puts it, "In the eighteenth-century individualistic orientation of criminal law, the act was judged and the man made responsible."[19] A product of the Enlightenment then sweeping through Europe, the Classical School demanded recognition of rationality and the ability to exercise informed choice in human social life.

Most classical theories of crime causation, both old and new, make certain basic assumptions. Among them are these:

- Crime is caused by the individual exercise of free will. Human beings are fundamentally rational, and most human behavior is the result of free will coupled with rational choice.

- Pain and pleasure are the two central determinants of human behavior.

- Crime erodes the bond that exists between individuals and society and is therefore an immoral form of behavior.

Classical School

An eighteenth-century approach to crime causation and criminal responsibility that grew out of the Enlightenment and that emphasized the role of free will and reasonable punishments. Classical thinkers believed that punishment, if it is to be an effective deterrent, has to outweigh the potential pleasure derived from criminal behavior.

- Punishment, a necessary evil, is sometimes required to deter law violators from repeating their crime and to serve as an example to others who would also violate the law.
- Crime prevention is possible through swift and certain punishment that offsets any gains to be had through criminal behavior.

Cesare Beccaria: Crime and Punishment

In 1764, Cesare Beccaria (1738–1794) published his *Essays on Crimes and Punishment.* The book was an immediate success and stirred a hornet's nest of controversy over the treatment of criminal offenders. Beccaria proposed basic changes in the criminal laws of his day to make them more "humanitarian." He called for the abolition of physical punishment and an end to the death penalty. Beccaria is best remembered for his suggestion that punishment should be just sufficient to deter criminal behavior but should never be excessive. Because Beccaria's writings stimulated many other thinkers throughout the eighteenth and early nineteenth centuries, he is referred to today as the founder of the Classical School of criminology.

Jeremy Bentham: Hedonistic Calculus

WEB
Extra

Among those influenced by Beccaria was the Englishman Jeremy Bentham (1748–1832). Bentham devised a "hedonistic calculus," which essentially said that the exercise of free will would cause an individual to avoid committing a crime as long as the punishment for committing that crime outweighed the benefits to be derived from committing it. Bentham termed this philosophy of social control *utilitarianism.* Both Bentham and Beccaria agreed that punishment had to be "swift and certain"—as well as just—to be effective. Learn more about Jeremy Bentham at Web Extra 3–3 at cjtoday.com.

The Neoclassical Perspective

neoclassical criminology

A contemporary version of classical criminology that emphasizes deterrence and retribution and that holds that human beings are essentially free to make choices in favor of crime and deviance or conformity to the law.

rational choice theory

A perspective on crime causation that holds that criminality is the result of conscious choice. Rational choice theory predicts that individuals will choose to commit crime when the benefits of doing so outweigh the costs of disobeying the law.

routine activities theory

A neoclassical perspective that suggests that lifestyles contribute significantly to both the amount and the type of crime found in any society.

A contemporary theory with roots in the Classical School, **neoclassical criminology** is a perspective that owes much to the early classical thinkers. Although classical criminology focuses primarily on pleasure and pain as motivators of human behavior, neoclassical criminology places greater emphasis on rationality and cognition. Central to such perspectives is **rational choice theory**, which holds that criminality is largely the result of conscious choices that people make. According to the theory, offenders choose to violate the law when they believe that the benefits of doing so outweigh the costs.

Rational choice theory is represented by a somewhat narrower perspective called **routine activities theory**. Routine activities theory was first proposed by Lawrence Cohen and Marcus Felson in 1979.[20] Cohen and Felson argued that lifestyles significantly affect both the amount and type of crime found in any society, and they noted that "the risk of criminal victimization varies dramatically among the circumstances and locations in which people place themselves and their property."[21] Lifestyles that contribute to criminal opportunities are likely to result in crime because they increase the risk of potential victimization.[22] For example, a person who routinely uses an ATM late at night in an isolated location is far more likely to be preyed on by robbers than is someone who stays home after dark. Rational choice theorists concentrate on "the decision-making process of offenders confronted with specific contexts" and have shifted "the focus of the effort to prevent crime . . . from broad social programs to target hardening, environmental design or any impediment that would [dissuade] a motivated offender from offending."[23]

Central to the routine activities approach is the claim that crime is likely to occur when a motivated offender and a suitable target come together in the absence of a *capable guardian.* Capable guardians are those who effectively discourage crime and prevent it from occurring. Members of neighborhood watch groups, for example, might be capable guardians. Capable guardians do not necessarily have to confront would-be offenders directly but might be people who have completed classes in crime prevention and who have taken steps to reduce their chances of victimization.

Social Policy and Classical Theories

[Television] poisons the minds of our young people . . . with destructive messages of casual violence and even more casual sex.

—Bob Dole, former Senator and Republican presidential candidate

Much of the practice of criminal justice in America today is built on concepts provided by Classical School theorists. Many contemporary programs designed to prevent crime, for example, have their philosophical roots in the classical axioms of deterrence and punishment. Modern heirs of the Classical School see punishment as central to criminal justice policy, use evidence of high crime rates to argue that punishment is a necessary crime preventive, and believe punishment is a natural and deserved consequence of criminal activity. Such thinkers call for greater prison capacity and new prison construction. In Chapter 1, we used the term *public-order advocate*, which can be applied to modern-day proponents of classical theory who frequently seek stiffer criminal laws and greater penalties for criminal activity. The emphasis on punishment as an appropriate response to crime, however, whether founded on principles of deterrence or revenge, and the resulting packed courtrooms and overcrowded prisons, has left many contemporary criminal justice policy initiatives foundering.

Biological explanations shaped criminology at its inception, and today they are reemerging with fresh vigor and increased potential.

—Nicole Rafter, Northeastern University[ii]

Biological Theories

Biological theories of crime causation, which had fallen into disrepute during the past few decades, are beginning to experience something of a contemporary resurgence. Most early theories of the **Biological School** of crime causation, which built on inherited or bodily characteristics and features, made certain fundamental assumptions. Among them are these:

- Basic determinants of human behavior, including criminal tendencies, are constitutionally or genetically based.
- The basic determinants of human behavior, including criminality, may be passed on from generation to generation. In other words, a penchant for crime may be inherited.
- At least some human behavior is the result of biological propensities inherited from more primitive developmental stages in the evolutionary process. Some human beings may be further along the evolutionary ladder than others, and their behavior may reflect it.

Biological School

A perspective on criminological thought that holds that criminal behavior has a physiological basis.

Franz Joseph Gall: Phrenology

The idea that the quality of a person can be judged by a study of the person's face is as old as antiquity. Even today, we often judge people on their looks, saying, "He has an honest face" or "She has tender eyes." Horror movies play on unspoken cultural themes to shape the way a "maniac" might look. Jack Nicholson's portrayal of a crazed killer in *The Shining* and Anthony Hopkins's role as a serial killer in *The Silence of the Lambs* turned that look into fortunes at the box office.

Franz Joseph Gall (1758–1828) was one of the first thinkers to theorize about the idea that bodily constitution might reflect personality. Gall was writing at a time when it was thought that organs throughout the body determined one's mental state and behavior. People were said to be "hard-hearted" or to have a "bad spleen" that filled them with bile. Gall focused on the head and the brain and called his approach *cranioscopy*. It can be summarized in four propositions:

- The brain is the organ of the mind.
- The brain consists of localized faculties or functions.
- The shape of the skull reveals the underlying development (or lack of development) of areas within the brain.
- The personality can be revealed by a study of the skull.

Gall never systematically tested his theory in a way that would meet contemporary scientific standards. Even so, his approach to predicting behavior, which came to be known as **phrenology**, quickly spread throughout Europe. Gall's student, Johann Gaspar Spurzheim (1776–1853), brought phrenology to America in a series of lectures and publications on the subject. By 1825, 29 phrenological journals were being produced in the United States and Britain.[24] Until the turn of the twentieth century, phrenology remained popular in some American circles, where it was used in diagnostic schemes to classify new prisoners.

phrenology

The study of the shape of the head to determine anatomical correlates of human behavior.

Cesare Lombroso: Atavism

Gall's theory was "deterministic" in the sense that it left little room for choice. What a person did depended more on the shape of the skull than on the exercise of free will. Other biological theories would soon build on that premise. One of the best known is that created by the Italian psychologist Cesare Lombroso (1835–1909).

Cesare Lombroso (left), who has been dubbed "the father of modern criminology," posing with friend Louis Lombard in a rare photograph from 1909. What concepts developed by Lombroso might still be applicable today?

Culver Pictures, Inc.

atavism

A condition characterized by the existence of features thought to be common in earlier stages of human evolution.

Lombroso began his criminal anthropology with a postmortem evaluation of famous criminals, including one by the name of Vilella. Before Vilella died, Lombroso had the opportunity to interview him on a number of occasions. After Vilella's death, Lombroso correlated earlier observations of personality traits with measurable physical abnormalities. As a result of this and other studies, Lombroso concluded that criminals were atavistic human beings—throwbacks to earlier stages of evolution who were not sufficiently mentally advanced for successful life in the modern world. **Atavism** was identifiable in suspicious individuals, Lombroso suggested, through measures designed to reveal "primitive" physical characteristics.

In the late nineteenth century, Charles Darwin's theory of evolution was rapidly being applied to a wide range of fields. It was not surprising, therefore, that Lombroso linked evolution and criminality. What separated Lombroso from his predecessors, however, was that he continually refined his theory through ongoing observation. Based on studies of known offenders, whom he compared to conformists, Lombroso identified a large number of atavistic traits, which, he claimed, characterized criminals. Among them were long arms, large lips, crooked noses, an abnormally large amount of body hair, prominent cheekbones, two eyes of different colors, and ears that lacked clearly defined lobes.

Atavism implies that certain people are born criminals. Throughout his life, Lombroso grappled with the task of determining what proportion of the total population of offenders were born criminals. His estimates ranged at different times between 70% and 90%. Career criminals and those who committed crimes of opportunity without atavistic features he termed *criminaloids*, and he recognized the potential causative roles of greed, passion, and circumstance in their behavior.

Positivist School

An approach to criminal justice theory that stresses the application of scientific techniques to the study of crime and criminals.

Today, Lombroso is known as the founder of the **Positivist School** of criminology because of the role observation played in the formulation of his theories. Stephen Schafer calls Lombroso "the father of modern criminology"[25] because most contemporary criminologists follow in the tradition that Lombroso began—scientific observation and a comparison of theory with fact.

THE EVIDENCE FOR AND AGAINST ATAVISM

After Lombroso died, two English physicians, Charles Goring and Karl Pearson, conducted a test of atavism, studying more than 3,000 prisoners and comparing them along physiological criteria to an army detachment known as the Royal Engineers. No significant differences were found between the two groups, and Lombroso's ideas rapidly began to fall into disrepute.

 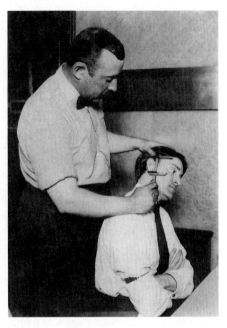

The Bertillion system of identification being applied to a subject in the years prior to the development of fingerprinting. The theory of atavism, based on the ideas of Charles Darwin, supported the use of physical anthropology in the identification of offenders. Why have sociological theories largely replaced simple biological approaches to explaining crime?

Courtesy of the Library of Congress

A further study of atavism was published in 1939 by Earnest A. Hooton, a distinguished Harvard University anthropologist. Hooton spent 12 years constructing anthropometric profiles—profiles based on human body measurements—of 13,873 male convicts in ten different American states. He measured each inmate in 107 different ways and compared them to 3,203 volunteers from National Guard units, firehouses, beaches, and hospitals. Surprisingly, Hooton did find some basis for Lombroso's beliefs, and he concluded that the inmate population in his study demonstrated a decided physical "inferiority."

However, Hooton never recognized that the prisoners he studied were only a subgroup of the population of all offenders throughout the country. They were, in fact, the least successful offenders—the ones who had been caught and imprisoned. Hooton may have unknowingly measured other criminals—the ones who had avoided capture—among his "conformist" population. Hence the "inferiority" Hooton observed may have been an artificial product of a process of selection (arrest) by the justice system.

Criminal Families

The concept of biological inheritance has been applied to "criminal families" as well as to individuals. The idea of mental degeneration as an inherited contributor to crime was first explored by Richard Dugdale.[26] Dugdale used the family tree method to study a family he called the Jukes, publishing his findings in 1877. The Juke lineage had its beginning in America with "Max" (whose last name is unknown), a descendant of Dutch immigrants to New Amsterdam in the early eighteenth century. Two of Max's sons married into the notorious "Juke family of girls," six sisters, all of whom were illegitimate. Male Jukes were reputed to have been "vicious," while Ada, one of the sisters, had an especially bad reputation and eventually came to be known as "the mother of criminals."

Dugdale found that, during the next 75 years, Ada's heirs included 1,200 people, most of whom were "social degenerates." Only a handful of socially productive progeny could be identified. In 1915, Dugdale's study of the Jukes was continued by Arthur A. Estabrook, who extended the line to include 2,094 descendants and found just as few conformists.

A similar study was published by Henry Goddard in 1912.[27] Goddard examined the Kallikak family, which contained two clear lines of descent. One emanated from an affair that Revolutionary War soldier Martin Kallikak had with a "feebleminded" barmaid. She bore a son, and the line eventually produced 480 identifiable descendants. After the war, Kallikak returned home and married a "virtuous" Quaker woman in Philadelphia. This legitimate line produced 496 offspring by 1912, of whom only three were abnormal; not one was criminal. The illegitimate group, however, contained over half "feebleminded" or deviant progeny.

The underlying suppositions of these studies are that degenerate and feebleminded people are produced and propagated through bad genetic material and that crime is an outlet for degenerate urges. However, these studies fail to recognize any effect that socialization and life circumstances have on the development of criminal behavior.

William Sheldon: Somatotypes

somatotyping

The classification of human beings into types according to body build and other physical characteristics.

"Constitutional" theories of crime causation refer to the *physical constitution*, or bodily characteristics, of offenders. The last of the famous constitutional theorists was William Sheldon (1893–1977), who developed the idea of **somatotyping**.

Sheldon studied 200 juvenile delinquents between the ages of 15 and 21 at the Hayden Goodwill Institute in Boston and decided that the young men possessed one of three somatotypes (or body types). The types of bodies described by Sheldon were (in his words):

- *Mesomorphs* with a relative predominance of muscle, bone, and connective tissue
- *Endomorphs* with a soft roundness throughout the various regions of the body; short tapering limbs; small bones; and soft, smooth, velvety skin
- *Ectomorphs* characterized by thinness, fragility, and delicacy of body

Sheldon developed a system of measurements by which an individual's physique could be expressed as a combination of three numbers, such as 4.0–4.0–3.5 (the representation of an average male). The numbers represented the degree of mesomorphy, endomorphy, and ectomorphy present in the individual on a scale of 0 to 7, where 0 indicates a complete lack of features of one category. American females were said to average 5.0–3.0–3.5 on the scale. Sheldon wrote that each somatotype was possessed of a characteristic personality, and he believed that predominantly mesomorphic individuals were most prone to aggression, violence, and delinquency.[28]

Social Policy and Biological Theories

Because traditional biological theories of crime causation attribute the cause of crime to fundamental physical characteristics that are not easily modified, they suggest the need for extreme social policies. During the 1920s and early 1930s, for example, biological theories of crime causation, especially those focusing on inherited mental degeneration, led to the eugenics movement, under which mentally handicapped women were sometimes sterilized to prevent them from bearing offspring. The eugenics movement was institutionalized by the 1927 U.S. Supreme Court case of *Buck* v. *Bell*, in which Justice Oliver Wendell Holmes, Jr., writing in support of a Virginia statute permitting sterilization, said, "It is better for all the world, if instead of waiting to execute degenerate offspring for crime, or to let them starve for their imbecility, society can prevent those persons who are manifestly unfit from continuing their kind."[29] Visit Web Extra 3–4 at cjtoday.com to learn more about biological theories of crime and violence.

WEB
Extra

Psychobiological Theories

During the past few decades, researchers have taken a sophisticated approach to biological theorizing about the causes of crime. Contemporary biochemical and physiological perspectives are sometimes termed *psychobiology*. The psychobiology of crime highlights the role of human DNA, environmental contaminants, nutrition, hormones, physical trauma (especially to the brain), and body chemistry in human cognition, feeling, and behavior.

Chromosome Theory

The detailed mapping of human DNA and other recent advances in the field of recombinant DNA have rekindled interest in genetic correlates of deviant behavior. More sophisticated than their historical counterparts, the biological theories of today often draw on the latest medical advances or build on popular health concerns.

The links between chromosome patterns and crime were first explored in the 1960s. A normal female has a chromosome structure often diagrammed as "XX" because of how the sex-determining gene pair looks in an electron microscope. A male has a Y chromosome in place of the second X, for a typical male XY pattern. Although it had been known for some time that a few people have abnormal patterns that include "extra" chromosomes (such as XXX females, XXY males with Kline-felter's syndrome, and XXYY "double males"), it wasn't until 1965 that the respected English journal *Nature* reported on the work of Patricia Jacobs, who identified **supermales**—men with an extra Y chromosome whose chromosome structure is diagrammed XYY. Jacobs found that supermales were more common in prisons than in the general population.[30]

Other early studies claimed that the XYY male was more aggressive than other males and that he possessed a number of specific physical and psychological traits, such as height (taller than 6 feet, 1 inch), thinness, acne, a tendency toward homosexuality, a somewhat low IQ, and "a marked tendency to commit a succession of apparently motiveless property crimes."[31] Later studies disputed many of these findings, and the significance of the XYY pattern for behavioral prediction is in doubt today.

Biochemical Factors and Imbalances

Research in the area of nutrition has produced some limited evidence that the old maxim "You are what you eat!" may contain more than a grain of truth. *Biocriminology* is a field of study that links violent or disruptive behavior to eating habits, vitamin deficiencies, genetics, and other conditions that affect body tissues.

One of the first studies to focus on chemical imbalances in the body as a cause of crime was reported in the British medical journal *Lancet* in 1943.[32] Authors of the study linked murder to hypoglycemia (low blood sugar), which is caused by too much insulin in the blood or by near starvation diets. Some researchers believe that hypoglycemia reduces the mind's capacity to reason effectively or to judge the long-term consequences of behavior.

Allergic reactions to common foods have been reported as the cause of violence and homicide in a number of studies.[33] Foods said to produce allergic reactions in sensitive individuals, leading to a swelling of the brain and brain stem, include milk, citrus fruit, chocolate, corn, wheat, and eggs. Involvement of the central nervous system in such allergies, it has been suggested, reduces the amount of learning that occurs during childhood and may contribute to delinquency as well as to adult criminal behavior. Some studies have implicated food additives, such as monosodium glutamate, dyes, and artificial flavorings, in producing criminal behavior.[34]

Other research has found that the amount of coffee and sugar consumed by inmates is considerably greater than in the outside population.[35] Theorists have suggested that high blood levels of caffeine and sugar produce antisocial behavior.[36] It is unclear whether inmates consume more coffee due to boredom or whether those with "excitable" personalities need the kind of stimulation coffee drinking produces. On the other hand, habitual coffee drinkers in nonprison populations have not been linked to crime, and other studies, such as that conducted by Mortimer Gross of the University of Illinois, show no link between the amount of sugar consumed and hyperactivity.[37] Similarly, studies "have not yielded evidence that a change in diet will result in [a] significant reduction in aggressive or antisocial behavior" among inmate populations.[38] Nonetheless, some prison programs have limited the intake of dietary stimulants through nutritional management and the substitution of artificial sweeteners for refined sugar.

Vitamins have also been examined for their impact on delinquency. Abram Hoffer found that disruptive children consumed far less than the optimum levels of vitamins B_3 and B_6 than did nonproblem youths.[39] He claimed that the addition of these vitamins to the diets of children who were deficient in them could control unruly behavior and improve school performance.

Overall, the role of food and diet in producing criminal behavior has not been well established. The American Dietetic Association and the National Council against Health Fraud have concluded that no convincing scientific relationship between crime and diet has yet been demonstrated.[40] Both groups are concerned that poor nutrition may result from programs that reduce or modify diets in an effort to affect behavior.

Hormones have also come under scrutiny as potential behavioral determinants. The male sex hormone, testosterone, has been linked to aggressiveness in males. Some studies of blood-serum levels of testosterone have shown a direct relationship[41] between the amount of hormone present and the degree of violence used by sex offenders,[42] and steroid abuse among bodybuilders has been linked to destructive urges and psychosis.[43] One 1998 study found that high levels of testosterone, especially when combined with low socioeconomic status, produced antisocial personalities, resulting in deviance and criminality.[44] In 2007, researchers at the University of Michigan at Ann Arbor found that the higher the blood levels of testosterone in young men, the more they enjoyed provoking anger in others.[45]

Some studies of brain chemistry have led researchers to conclude that low levels of certain neurotransmitters, especially serotonin, are directly related to a person's inability to control aggressive

supermale

A human male displaying the XYY chromosome structure.

impulses.[46] The presence of adequate serotonin levels in the human brain buffers irritating experiences that might otherwise result in anger and aggression. Low serotonin levels may result from the ingestion of toxic pollutants, such as the metals lead and manganese, according to one study.[47] Reduced serotonin levels, say other researchers, is sometimes found in men with an extra Y chromosome.[48]

Researchers have also implicated a malfunctioning endocrine system as a cause of physical abuse, antisocial behavior, and psychopathology. One Swedish study that focused on variations in blood-serum levels of two thyroid hormones, triiodothyronine (T_3) and thyroxine (FT_4), found that elevated T_3 levels were related to alcoholism and criminality.[49] Serum levels of FT_4 were found to be negatively correlated to such behavior.

Heredity and Other Physical Factors

Other physical factors have been shown to play a role in an individual's inclination toward criminality. Sarnoff Mednick, for example, found some basis for the claim that the autonomic nervous system (ANS) predisposes certain individuals toward criminality by limiting their ability to learn quickly.[50] He claims that those with a slow ANS are unable to inhibit antisocial behavior quickly enough to avoid punishment and stigmatization.[51] Physical trauma, especially brain injury, has also been shown to at times induce severe personality changes, including aggression and violent behavior in people with a previous behavioral history of neither.[52] Similarly, people born with certain abnormalities of the brain, especially frontal lobe dysfunction, may display a penchant for violence.[53] Frontal lobe dysfunction is sometimes caused by reduced cerebral blood flow.

Studies have shown that the behavior of biological children of criminals who are adopted at birth tends to reflect the criminality of biological parents, independent of the environment in which the children were raised.[54] Also, identical twins exhibit a greater similarity in behavior than do nonidentical (or "fraternal") twins, and a number of studies have shown that identical twins are more alike in patterns and degree of criminal involvement than are fraternal twins.[55]

Perhaps the best known of modern-day biological perspectives on crime was proposed by James Q. Wilson and Richard Herrnstein in their book *Crime and Human Nature*, published in 1985.[56] Wilson and Herrnstein argue that inherited traits, such as maleness, aggressiveness, mesomorphic body type, and low intelligence, combine with environmental influences, including poor schools and strained family life, to produce crime. Although the authors reject a firm determinism, asserting that it is the interaction between genetics and environment that determines behavior, they do claim that children who will eventually grow up to be criminals can sometimes be identified early in their lives. The most important factor in the diversion of potential offenders from lives of crime, according to Wilson and Herrnstein, is a healthy family life in which affection for others and conscience can develop.[57] Wilson and Herrnstein also use cross-cultural data from Japan, where crime rates are very low, to suggest that tendencies toward introversion among the Japanese result in fewer serious crimes than in the United States. The Wilson-Herrnstein thesis has been criticized for failing to explain crime that extends beyond "traditional lower-class street crime" and for failing to recognize the political nature of criminal definitions.[58]

Social Policy and Psychobiological Theories

Psychobiological theories often suggest modifying body chemistry to produce desirable behavioral changes. Hence, just as cancer researchers look for a "magic bullet" that might target defective chromosomes in the human immune system that allow for the growth of cancerous tissue, psychobiologists concerned with crime and its causes envision the day when similar techniques can be applied to the prevention and control of crime. If a gene for crime can be found, such researchers suggest, it might be turned off. In the meantime, psychobiologists have to be content with medicinal approaches to the treatment of crime and violence, such as employing tranquilizers, antipsychotic medications, mood-altering substances, and other drugs.

Studies show that drug treatments fashioned after psychobiological perspectives control aggressive and criminal behavior temporarily, but there is little evidence to suggest that they produce lasting results. In 1993, all biologically based theories of crime and violence were called into question by the National Academy of Sciences, whose review of hundreds of studies on the relationship among biology, violence, and crime concluded that "no patterns precise enough to be considered reliable biological markers for violent behavior have yet been identified."[59] The study did, however, find what it called "promising leads for future research."

Psychological Theories

Theories of the **Psychological School** of crime causation have an increasingly significant place in the criminological literature. Most psychological theories of crime make certain fundamental assumptions. Among them are these:

- The individual is the primary unit of analysis.
- Personality is the major motivational element within individuals, since it is the source of drives and motives.
- Crimes result from inappropriately conditioned behavior or from abnormal, dysfunctional, or inappropriate mental processes within the personality.
- Defective or abnormal mental processes may have a variety of causes, including a diseased mind and inappropriate learning or improper conditioning—often occurring in early childhood.

Psychological School

A perspective on criminological thought that views offensive and deviant behavior as the product of dysfunctional personality. Psychological thinkers identify the conscious, and especially the subconscious, contents of the human psyche as major determinants of behavior.

Behavioral Conditioning

Two threads were woven through early psychological theories. One emphasized **behavioral conditioning**, while the other focused mostly on personality disturbances and diseases of the mind. Taken together, these two foci constituted the early field of psychological criminology. Conditioning is a psychological principle that holds that the frequency of any behavior, including criminal or deviant behavior, can be increased or decreased through reward, punishment, and association with other stimuli. The concept of conditioned behavior was popularized through the work of the Russian physiologist Ivan Pavlov (1849–1936), whose work with dogs won him the Nobel Prize in physiology and medicine in 1904. Similarly, behavioral psychologists suggest that criminal behavior, which may be inherently rewarding under many circumstances, tends to be more common in those who are able to avoid punishment when involved in rule-breaking behavior.

behavioral conditioning

A psychological principle that holds that the frequency of any behavior can be increased or decreased through reward, punishment, and association with other stimuli.

Freudian Psychoanalysis

The name most widely associated with the field of psychology is that of Sigmund Freud (1856–1939). Freudian theory posits the existence of an id, an ego, and a superego within the personality.[60] The id is the source of drives, which are seen as primarily sexual. The ego is a rational mental entity, which outlines paths through which the desires of the id can be fulfilled. The ego is often called the *reality principle* because of the belief that it relates desires to practical behavioral alternatives. The superego is a guiding principle, often compared to conscience, that judges the quality of the alternatives presented by the ego according to the standards of right and wrong acquired by the personality of which it is a part. Freud wrote very little about crime, but his followers, who developed the school of Freudian **psychoanalysis**, believe that crime can result from at least three conditions.

The first possible source of criminal behavior is a weak superego, which cannot responsibly control the drives that emanate from the id. Sex crimes, crimes of passion, murder, and other violent crimes are thought to follow inadequate superego development. People who lack fully developed superegos are often called *psychopaths* or *sociopaths* to indicate that they cannot see beyond their own interests. Canadian criminologist Gwynn Nettler observes that "civilization is paid for through development of a sense of guilt."[61]

Freud also created the concept of sublimation to explain the process by which one thing is symbolically substituted for another. He believed that sublimation was necessary when the direct pursuit of one's desires was not possible. Freud suggested, for example, that many children learned to sublimate negative feelings about their mothers. In the society in which Freud developed his theories, mothers closely controlled the lives of their children, and Freud saw the developing child as continually frustrated in seeking freedom to act on his or her own. The strain produced by this conflict could not be directly expressed by the child because the mother also controlled rewards and punishments. Hence, dislike for one's mother (which Freud thought was especially strong in boys) might show itself symbolically later in life. Crimes against women could then be explained as being committed by men expressing a symbolic hatred.

A final Freudian explanation for criminality is based on the death instinct, or Thanatos, which Freud believed each of us carries. Thanatos is the often-unrecognized desire of animate matter to return to the inanimate. Potentially self-destructive activities, including smoking, speeding, skydiving,

psychoanalysis

A theory of human behavior, based on the writings of Sigmund Freud, that sees personality as a complex composite of interacting mental entities.

A battered woman turning away from her husband. When a woman is victimized, it is often at the hands of an "intimate other," such as a spouse or a boyfriend. Sigmund Freud suggested that a male batterer acts out a deep-seated resentment toward women that resulted from his childhood relationship with his mother. Why is this kind of theoretical perspective rarely given credence by criminologists today?

Francisco Cruz/SuperStock, Inc.

bad diets, "picking fights," and so on, can be explained by Thanatos. The self-destructive wish may also motivate offenders to commit crimes that are themselves dangerous or self-destructive—such as burglary, assault, murder, prostitution, and drug use—or it may result in unconscious efforts to be caught. Criminals who leave evidence behind may be responding to some basic need for apprehension and punishment.

Psychopathology and Crime

From a psychiatric point of view, crime might also occur because of a diseased mind or a disordered personality—conditions that may collectively be referred to as *psychopathy*. The study of psychopathic mental conditions is called **psychopathology**. The role of a disordered personality in crime causation was central to early psychiatric theorizing. In 1944, for example, the well-known psychiatrist David Abrahamsen wrote, "When we seek to explain the riddle of human conduct in general and of antisocial behavior in particular, the solution must be sought in the personality."[62] Later, some psychiatrists went so far as to claim that criminal behavior itself is only a symptom of a more fundamental psychiatric disorder.[63]

By the 1930s, psychiatrists had begun to develop the concept of a psychopathic personality. This personality type, which by its very definition is asocial, was fully developed by Hervey Cleckley in his 1941 book, *The Mask of Sanity*.[64] Cleckley described the **psychopath**, also called a *sociopath*, as a "moral idiot" whose central defining characteristic is the inability to accurately imagine how others think and feel. Hence, it becomes possible for a psychopath to inflict pain and engage in cruelty without appreciation for the victim's suffering. Charles Manson, for example, whom some have called a psychopath, once told a television reporter, "I could take this book and beat you to death with it, and I wouldn't feel a thing. It'd be just like walking to the drugstore." According to Cleckley, psychopathic indicators appear early in life, often in the teenage years. They include lying, fighting, stealing, and vandalism. Even earlier signs may be found, according to some authors, in bed-wetting, cruelty to animals, sleepwalking, and fire setting.[65]

While the terms *psychopath* and *criminal* are not synonymous, individuals manifesting characteristics of a psychopathic personality are likely, sooner or later, to run afoul of the law. As one writer says, "The impulsivity and aggression, the selfishness in achieving one's own immediate needs, and the disregard for society's rules and laws bring these people to the attention of the criminal justice system."[66]

Although much studied, the causes of psychopathy are unclear. Somatogenic causes, or those that are based on physiological aspects of the human organism, include (1) a malfunctioning central nervous system characterized by a low state of arousal, which drives the sufferer to seek excitement, and (2) brain abnormalities, which may be present in most psychopaths from birth.

psychopathology

The study of pathological mental conditions—that is, mental illness.

psychopath

A person with a personality disorder, especially one manifested in aggressively antisocial behavior, which is often said to be the result of a poorly developed superego.

I really truly tried to stop—but I couldn't.

—*Henry Louis Wallace, convicted killer of nine women, in a tape-recorded interview with police*

Charles Manson, one of the most photographed criminal offenders of all time, 20 years after he and his "family" shocked the world with their gruesome crimes. What do you think motivated Manson?

Grey Villet

Psychogenic causes, or those rooted in early interpersonal experiences, include the inability to form attachments to parents or other caregivers early in life, sudden separation from the mother during the first six months of life, and other forms of insecurity during the first few years of life. In short, a lack of love or the sensed inability to unconditionally depend on one central loving figure (typically the mother in most psychological literature) immediately following birth is often posited as a major psychogenic factor contributing to psychopathic development. Learn more about psychopathology and crime at Library Extra 3–2 at cjtoday.com. Read more about the Manson murders at Web Extra 3–5 at cjtoday.com.

LIBRARY Extra ▪ ▪ ▪ ▪

WEB Extra ▪ ▪ ▪ ▪

The Psychotic Offender

Another form of mental disorder is called **psychosis**. Psychotic people, according to psychiatric definitions, are out of touch with reality in some fundamental way. They may suffer from hallucinations, delusions, or other breaks with reality. For example, a psychotic may believe that he or she is a famous historical figure or may see spiders crawling on a bare wall. Psychoses may be either organic (that is, caused by physical damage to, or abnormalities in, the brain) or functional (that is, with no known physical cause). Psychotic people have also been classified as schizophrenic or paranoid schizophrenic. **Schizophrenics** are characterized by disordered or disjointed thinking, in which the types of logical associations they make are atypical of other people. Paranoid schizophrenics suffer from delusions and hallucinations.

Psychoses may lead to crime in a number of ways. Following the Vietnam War, for example, a number of former American soldiers suffering from a kind of battlefield psychosis killed friends and family members, thinking they were enemy soldiers. These men, who had been traumatized by battlefield experiences in Southeast Asia, relived their past on American streets.

Psychological Profiling

Psychological profiling is the attempt to derive a composite picture of an offender's social and psychological characteristics from the crime he or she committed and from the manner in which it was committed. Psychological profiling began during World War II as an effort by William Langer (1896–1977), a government psychiatrist hired by the Office of Strategic Services, to predict Adolf Hitler's actions.[67] Profiling in criminal investigations is based on the belief that criminality, because it is a form of behavior, can be viewed as symptomatic of the offender's

psychosis

A form of mental illness in which sufferers are said to be out of touch with reality.

schizophrenic

A mentally ill individual who suffers from disjointed thinking and possibly from delusions and hallucinations.

psychological profiling

The attempt to categorize, understand, and predict the behavior of certain types of offenders based on behavioral clues they provide.

personality. Psychological evaluations of crime scenes, including the analysis of evidence, are used to re-create the offender's frame of mind during the commission of the crime. A profile of the offender is then constructed to help in the investigation of suspects.

During the 1980s, the Federal Bureau of Investigation (FBI) led the movement toward psychological profiling[68] through its focus on violent sex offenses[69] and arson.[70] FBI profilers described "lust murderers" and serial arsonists. Often depicted as loners with an aversion to casual social contact, lust murderers were shown to rarely arouse suspicions in neighbors or employers. Other personality types became the focus of police efforts to arrest such offenders through a prediction of what they might do next.

New areas for psychological profiling include hostage negotiation[71] and international terrorism.[72] Right-wing terrorist groups in the United States have also been the subject of profiling efforts.

Social Policy and Psychological Theories

Crime-control policies based on psychological perspectives are primarily individualistic. They are oriented toward individualized treatment, characteristically exposing the individual offender to various forms of therapy intended to overcome the person's propensity for criminality.

Most crime-control strategies based on psychological theories emphasize assessing personal **dangerousness**, through psychological testing and other efforts to identify personality-based characteristics that predict interpersonal aggression. Although the ability to accurately predict future dangerousness is of great concern to today's policymakers, definitions of *dangerousness* are fraught with difficulty. As some authors have pointed out, "Dangerousness is not an objective quality like obesity or brown eyes; rather it is an ascribed quality like trustworthiness."[73] Hence, dangerousness is not necessarily a personality trait that is stable or easily identifiable. Even if it were, some studies of criminal careers show that involvement in crime decreases with age.[74] As one author puts it, if "criminality declines more or less uniformly with age, then many offenders will be 'over the hill' by the time they are old enough to be plausible candidates for preventive incarceration."[75]

Before crime-control policies can be based on present understandings of dangerousness, research must answer several questions: Can past behavior predict future behavior? Do former instances of criminality foretell additional ones? Are there other identifiable characteristics that violent offenders might manifest that could serve as warning signs to criminal justice decision makers faced with the dilemma of whether to release convicted felons?

dangerousness

The likelihood that a given individual will later harm society or others. Dangerousness is often measured in terms of recidivism, or the likelihood that an individual will commit an additional crime within five years following arrest or release from confinement.

Sociological Theories

Sociological theories are largely an American contribution to the study of crime causation. In the 1920s and 1930s, the famous **Chicago School** of sociology explained criminality as a product of society's impact on the individual. The structure of prevailing social arrangements, the interaction between individuals and groups, and the social environment were all seen as major determinants of criminal behavior.

Sociological perspectives on crime causation are quite diverse. Most, however, build on certain fundamental assumptions. Among them are these:

- Social groups, social institutions, the arrangements of society, and social roles all provide the proper focus for criminological study.

- Group dynamics, group organization, and subgroup relationships form the causal nexus out of which crime develops.

- The structure of society and the relative degree of social organization or **social disorganization** are important factors contributing to the prevalence of criminal behavior.

All sociological perspectives on crime share the foregoing characteristics, but particular theories may give greater or lesser weight to the following aspects of social life:

- The clash of norms and values among variously socialized groups

- Socialization and the process of association between individuals

- The existence of subcultures and varying types of opportunities

Chicago School

A sociological approach that emphasizes demographics (the characteristics of population groups) and geographics (the mapped location of such groups relative to one another) and that sees the social disorganization that characterizes delinquency areas as a major cause of criminality and victimization.

social disorganization

A condition said to exist when a group is faced with social change, uneven development of culture, maladaptiveness, disharmony, conflict, and lack of consensus.

CJ News

Was Eric Clark Insane or Just Troubled?

The phone roused Terry Clark from sleep. She eyed the clock: 5 A.M. Who could be calling at this hour?

"Flagstaff Police Department," a voice announced, abruptly. The next minutes and hours would pass like a slow-moving horror film where the evil emerges bit by bit.

At first, investigators told her only that a policeman had been shot.

She heard a name, Officer Jeff Moritz. He was called to the neighborhood after residents reported a pickup circling round and round, blaring loud music.

Her son Gentry's pickup sat abandoned—driver's-side door flung open, keys in the ignition, a Dr. Dre CD in the player—next to the sidewalk where the police officer had died.

Her son was the prime suspect. Not Gentry, though, who had been at home in bed, safe. Her other son. Eric. The one who had been a star football player and a good student with dreams.

The one who just two months earlier had called his mother and father aliens.

SLAYING SHOCKED TOWN

What happened in those early morning hours of June 21, 2000, left an entire town in shock. The victim was the only police officer ever killed in the line of duty in this mountain community north of Phoenix.

He was a caring cop who cut firewood for the handicapped and bought burgers for hungry transients he arrested. He was a husband and father with one young son and a second on the way.

The accused was a 17-year-old high school senior who had a history of marijuana use and had been arrested two months earlier for drunken driving and drug possession. Police had found two dozen hits of LSD in his car.

A portrait quickly emerged of a drug-crazed teen with no regard for life. But as the facts slowly surfaced so did a different picture of Eric Michael Clark—that of a decent boy from a stable family who had descended into schizophrenia.

With this revelation came a question: How do you measure justice when a killer is a mentally ill kid?

It took three years for Eric Clark to be found competent to stand trial. His lawyers pushed for a verdict of "guilty except insane," meaning incarceration in a psychiatric facility. Instead, a judge found him guilty of first-degree, intentional murder and sentenced him to life in prison, where treatment isn't assured.

On Wednesday, the U.S. Supreme Court is scheduled to take up the case of *Clark* v. *Arizona* and the issue of just how difficult states can make it for criminal defendants to prove insanity.

It's the first time the court has dealt with a direct constitutional challenge to the insanity defense since lawmakers around the country imposed new restrictions following John Hinckley's acquittal by reason of insanity in the 1981 shooting of President Reagan.

"When is it just to punish, or not?" says Richard Bonnie, director of the Institute of Law, Psychiatry and Public Policy at the University of Virginia. "There are some cases where a person was so mentally disturbed at the time of the offense that it would be inhumane and morally objectionable to convict and punish them."

Eric Clark leaving the Coconino County Courthouse in Arizona prior to sentencing. Clark was convicted of killing Flagstaff police officer Jeff Moritz but claimed that he saw the officer as an alien from outer space. At the time of the killing, Clark was just 17 years old. Should Clark be imprisoned, treated for his mental illness, or both?

*Courtesy Josh Biggs/*Arizona Daily Sun

SIGNPOSTS OF MENTAL ILLNESS

Looking back now, Terry Clark remembers things, little things, and wonders when it all started.

Eric was a gifted athlete who played soccer, baseball, basketball, football. As a running back at Flagstaff High, he was one of the young stars selected to play varsity and dreamed of becoming a professional athlete. Then he lost interest in sports.

He had been popular—a homecoming court nominee—but his friends quit calling. His grades, usually As and Bs, took a dive.

On June 21, 1999, Terry and her husband, Dave, had their son admitted to Aspen Hill, a local mental health facility. He'd abandoned his car on a road.

At Aspen Hill, Eric tested positive for marijuana, and Terry wondered whether drugs had triggered his behavior. But doctors alluded to something else—the possibility of schizophrenia. With no mental illness on either side of the family, Terry pushed that idea aside.

Eric seemed to improve and she had him discharged after only three days. "He's getting better," Terry convinced herself. He got worse.

That fall, Eric quit school. He became obsessed with Y2K, took his dad's debit card and charged $1,700 worth of survival gear. He wore layers upon layers of clothing and carried his possessions in a garbage bag.

When January 1, 2000, came and went, Eric's mood improved. He went back to high school. "He's getting better," Terry thought again—until Eric started mentioning "them."

That April, Eric suddenly referred to her as an alien. Eric called his father an alien, too. "If you'd go get some tools," he told them matter-of-factly, "I'd show you."

(continued)

CJ News (continued)

Terry now believed the doctors were right about schizophrenia. She was relieved when, that same month, Eric was arrested on drunken driving and drug charges; she thought that would lead to getting help. But authorities decided to postpone prosecution until Eric turned 18 later in the year.

She and Dave searched for counselors, but Eric refused to go. Terry left messages at treatment facilities that were never returned.

On June 19, 2000, Eric called his mother an alien again. "How would you like to be me," he said, "and never know who your real mother is?"

Terry contacted her lawyer and begged him to convince the county to pursue the drug charges. Prosecutors still wanted to wait until Eric was an adult, so he'd face longer prison time if convicted.

INTENT OR INSANITY?

Investigators surmise that sometime after 1:30 A.M. on June 21, 2000, Eric made his way home, sneaked into his brother Gentry's bedroom, took his keys and left in Gentry's truck.

What happened after that, and why, no one can know for certain; Eric never talked about the events of that morning.

At the 2003 trial, prosecutors and defense attorneys agreed that Eric suffered from paranoid schizophrenia and was mentally ill. But legal insanity is another matter; Arizona law spells out its limited use as a defense.

"A person may be found guilty except insane if, at the time of the commission of the criminal act, the person was afflicted with a mental disease or defect of such severity that the person did not know the criminal act was wrong," the law states.

The prosecutor, Assistant Attorney General David Powell, argued Eric did know. "Officer Moritz walked into . . . an ice-cold ambush," he said at trial.

Defense lawyers insisted Eric's psychosis was so severe he was incapable of hatching such a plan.

They noted that two months after the shooting, Eric called his parents from jail and told them Flagstaff was a "platinum city" inhabited by 50,000 aliens. Before hanging up, he added: "The only thing that will stop aliens are bullets."

In his appeal to the U.S. Supreme Court, lawyer David Goldberg asserts that Arizona law is so restrictive that it violates a mentally ill defendant's right to a fair trial.

For one, he says, Arizona law prohibited the trial court from considering Eric's mental illness in weighing whether he intentionally killed the police officer. Testimony about his mental illness was not permitted until the second phase of the two-part trial.

Goldberg also argues that Arizona's right-wrong test is too narrow in determining legal insanity. Eric might have known that killing was wrong in the abstract, Goldberg says, but if he believed Moritz was an alien, "he didn't understand the nature of what he was doing."

The Supreme Court's decision, expected later this year, could also mean a retrial for Eric Clark, something the Moritz family would see as unjust.

"An angry young man who sets out to kill a cop, or anybody else, ought to be locked up for the rest of his life," says the victim's father, Dan Moritz, a psychologist who questions whether Clark actually is a paranoid schizophrenic.

For the Clarks, a new trial would mean a chance for their son to receive psychiatric care.

"Lock him up for his crime," Terry Clark says, "but treat him for his mental illness, please. Eric didn't choose to be mentally ill. It chose him."

For the latest in crime and justice news, visit the Talk Justice news feed at http://www.crimenews.info.

Author's note: Eric Clark's conviction was upheld by the U.S. Supreme Court.
Source: "Was Eric Clark Insane or Just Troubled?" © April 15, 2006 by the Associated Press. Reprinted by permission.

Social Ecology Theory

In the 1920s, during the early days of sociological theorizing, the University of Chicago brought together such thinkers as Robert Park, Ernest Burgess,[76] Clifford Shaw, and Henry McKay.[77] Park and Burgess recognized that Chicago, like most cities, could be mapped according to its social characteristics. Their map resembled a target with a bull's-eye in the center. Shaw and McKay adapted these concentric zones to the study of crime when they realized that the zones nearest the center of the city had the highest crime rates. In particular, zone 2 (one removed from the center) consistently showed the highest crime rate over time, regardless of the groups or nationalities inhabiting it. This "zone of transition"—so called because new immigrant groups moved into it as earlier ones became integrated into American culture and moved out—demonstrated that crime was dependent to a considerable extent on aspects of the social structure of the city itself. Structural elements identified by Shaw and McKay included poverty, illiteracy, lack of schooling, unemployment, and illegitimacy. In combination, these elements were seen to lead to social disorganization, which in turn produced crime.

Anomie Theory

The French word **anomie** has been loosely translated as a condition of "normlessness." Anomie entered the literature as a sociological concept with the writings of Émile Durkheim (1858–1917) in the late nineteenth century.[78] Robert Merton (1910–2003) applied anomie to criminology in 1938 when he used the term to describe a disjunction between socially acceptable goals and means in American society.[79]

Merton believed that while the same goals and means are held out by society as desirable for everyone, they are not equally available to all. Socially approved goals in American society, for example, include wealth, status, and political power. The acceptable means to achieve these goals are education, wise investment, and hard work. Unfortunately, however, opportunities are not equally distributed throughout society, and some people turn to illegitimate means to achieve the goals they are pressured to reach. Still others reject both acceptable goals and legitimate means of reaching them.

Merton represented his theory with a chart, shown in Table 3–2. *Conformists* accept both the goals and means that society holds out as legitimate, while *innovators* accept the goals but reject the means, instead using illegal means to gain money, power, and success. It is the innovators whom Merton identified as criminal. The inherent logic of the model led Merton to posit other social types. *Ritualists* are those who reject success goals but still perform their daily tasks in conformity with social expectations. They might hold regular jobs but lack the desire to advance in life. *Retreatists* reject both the goals and the means and usually drop out of society by becoming derelicts, drug users, hermits, or the like. *Rebels* constitute a special category. Their desire to replace the existing system of socially approved goals and means with some other system more to their liking makes them the revolutionaries of the theory.

Merton believed that categories are not intentionally selected by the individuals who occupy them but rather are imposed on people by structural aspects of society. Where people live, how wealthy their family is, and what ethnic background they come from are all significant determinants of the "box" into which people are placed.

Modern writers on anomie recognize that normlessness is not likely to be expressed as criminality unless people who experience it also feel that they are capable of doing something to change their lives. As Catherine Ross and John Mirowsky put it, "A person who has high levels of normlessness and powerlessness is less likely to get in trouble with the law than a person who has a high level of normlessness and a high level of instrumentalism."[80]

Merton's anomie theory drew attention to the lack of equal opportunity that existed in society at the time he was writing. While considerable efforts have been made to eradicate it, much of that inequality continues today.

anomie

A socially pervasive condition of normlessness. Also, a disjunction between approved goals and means.

If we are ever to reduce the tragic toll of crime in society, we must compare the measured benefits of incarceration to less costly and more productive crime prevention strategies—especially those programs aimed at helping high-risk families and young people escape the hopelessness that surrounds their lives.

—Barry Krisberg, President, National Council on Crime and Delinquency

Subcultural Theory

Another sociological contribution to criminological theory is the idea of a subculture. A subculture is a group of people who participate in a shared system of values and norms that are at variance with those of the larger culture. Subcultural explanations of crime posit the existence of group values that support criminal behavior. Subcultures were first recognized in the enclaves formed by immigrants who came to America during the early part of the twentieth century. Statistics have shown that certain immigrant groups had low crime rates.[81] Among them were the

TABLE 3–2	Merton's Anomie Theory and Implied Types of Criminality		
Category	**Goals**	**Means**	**Examples**
Conformist	+	+	Law-abiding behavior
Innovator	+	−	Property offenses, white-collar crimes
Retreatist	−	−	Drug use/addiction, vagrancy, some "victimless" crimes
Ritualist	−	+	A repetitive and mundane lifestyle
Rebel	±	±	Political crime (for example, environmental activists who violate the law, violence-prone antiabortionists)

Source: Adapted with the permission of the Free Press, a division of Simon & Schuster Adult Publishing Group, from *Social Theory and Social Structure*, Revised and Enlarged Edition by Robert K. Merton. Copyright © 1967, 1968 by Robert K. Merton. All rights reserved.

The Physical Environment and Crime

Social ecology theory—an outgrowth of the Chicago School of sociological thought, which flourished during the 1920s and 1930s—posited a link between physical location and crime. A modern perspective, called *crime prevention through environmental design* (CPTED), bears a strong resemblance to earlier ecological theories. CPTED, which was first formulated in the 1960s and 1970s, focuses on the settings in which crimes occur and on techniques for reducing vulnerability within those settings. Because defensible space concepts are being increasingly applied to the design of physical facilities, including housing, parking garages, public buildings, and even entire neighborhoods, it is highly likely that applications of CPTED will accelerate throughout the twenty-first century.

Second-generation **defensible space theory**, upon which contemporary CPTED is built, developed around 1980 and considered more carefully how the impact of physical features on fear and victimization depends on other social and cultural features in the setting. Second-generation defensible space theory employed the **broken windows thesis**, which holds that physical deterioration and an increase in unrepaired buildings lead to increased concerns for personal safety among area residents. Heightened concerns, in turn, lead to further decreases in maintenance and repair and to increased delinquency, vandalism, and crime among local residents, which spawn even further deterioration both in a sense of safety and in the physical environment. Offenders from other neighborhoods are then increasingly attracted by the area's perceived vulnerability.

Research on CPTED has shown environmental design to be effective in lowering crime and crime-related public-order problems. Effective use of CPTED to alter features of the physical environment can affect potential offenders' perceptions about a possible crime site, their evaluations of the opportunities associated with that site, and the availability and visibility of one or more natural guardians at or near the site. CPTED is based on the belief that offenders decide whether to commit a crime in a particular location after they evaluate the area's features, including (1) the ease of entry to the area, (2) the visibility of the target to others—that is, the chance of being seen, (3) the attractiveness or vulnerability of the target, (4) the likelihood that criminal behavior will be challenged or thwarted if discovered, and (5) the ease of egress—that is, the ability to quickly and easily leave the area once the crime has been committed.

According to the National Institute of Justice, CPTED suggests four approaches to making a location more resistant to crime and to crime-related public-order problems:

- *Housing design or block layout*—making it more difficult to commit crimes by (1) reducing the availability of crime targets, (2) removing barriers that prevent easy detection of potential offenders or of an offense in progress, and (3) increasing physical obstacles to committing a crime.
- *Land use and circulation patterns*—creating safer use of neighborhood space by reducing routine exposure of potential of-

A run-down city street. To explain crime, criminologists sometimes use the "broken windows" approach, which says that neighborhood deterioration leads to rising crime rates. Similarly, poverty, unemployment, a relative lack of formal education, and low skill levels, which often characterize inner-city populations, seem to be linked to criminality. Why?
Peter Byron/PhotoEdit Inc.

fenders to crime targets. This can be accomplished through careful attention to walkways, paths, streets, traffic patterns, and locations and hours of operation of public spaces and facilities. Street closings or revised traffic patterns that decrease vehicular volume may, under some conditions, encourage residents to better maintain the sidewalks and streets in front of their houses.

- *Territorial features*—encouraging the use of territorial markers or fostering conditions that will lead to more extensive marking to indicate that the block or site is occupied by vigilant residents. Sponsoring cleanup and beautification contests and creating controllable, semiprivate outdoor locations may encourage such activities. This strategy focuses on small-scale, private, and semipublic sites, usually within predominantly residential locales. It is most relevant at the street-block level and below. It enhances the chances that residents themselves will generate semifixed features that demonstrate their involvement in and watchfulness over a particular delimited location.
- *Physical maintenance*—controlling physical deterioration to reduce offenders' perceptions that areas are vulnerable to crime and that residents are so fearful they would do nothing to stop a crime. Physical improvements may reduce the signals of vulnerability and increase commitment to joint protective activities. Physical deterioration, in all probability, not only influences the cognition and behavior of potential offenders but also shapes how residents behave and what they think about other residents.

For additional information on CPTED via the Crime Mapping Research Center, see Web Extra 3–6 at cjtoday.com.

WEB
Extra

References: Derek J. Paulsen and Matthew B. Robinson, *Spatial Aspects of Crime: Theory and Practice* (Boston: Allyn and Bacon, 2004); Oscar Newman, *Defensible Space* (New York: Macmillan, 1972); Oscar Newman, *Creating Defensible Space* (Washington, DC: HUD 1996); James Q. Wilson and George Kelling, "Broken Windows," *Atlantic Monthly,* March 1982; Dan Fleissner and Fred Heinzelmann, *Crime Prevention through Environmental Design and Community Policing* (Washington, DC: NIJ, 1996); Ralph B. Taylor and Adele V. Harrell, *Physical Environment and Crime* (Washington, DC: NIJ, 1996); Mary S. Smith, *Crime Prevention through Environmental Design in Parking Facilities* (Washington, DC: NIJ, 1996); and Corey L. Gordon and William Brill, *The Expanding Role of Crime Prevention through Environmental Design in Premises Liability* (Washington, DC: NIJ, 1996).

Scandinavians, Chinese, Dutch, Germans, and Japanese. Other immigrant groups, including Italians, Mexicans, Puerto Ricans, and Africans, demonstrated a significantly greater propensity for involvement in crime.[82]

Albert Cohen (b. 1918) coined the term **reaction formation** to encompass the rejection of middle-class values by status-seeking lower-class youths who find they are not permitted access to approved opportunities for success.[83] In Cohen's eyes, reaction formation leads to the development of gangs and perpetuates the existence of subcultures. Walter Miller described the focal concerns of subcultural participants in terms of "trouble," "toughness," "excitement," "smartness," "fate," and "autonomy."[84] It is a focus on such concerns, Miller suggested, that leads members of criminal subcultures into violations of the law. Richard Cloward and Lloyd Ohlin proposed the existence of an illegitimate opportunity structure that permits delinquent youths to achieve in ways that are outside of legitimate avenues to success.[85]

During the 1950s, Marvin Wolfgang and Franco Ferracuti examined homicide rates in Philadelphia and found that murder was a way of life among certain groups.[86] They discovered a "wholesale" and a "retail" price for murder—which depended on who was killed and who did the killing. Killings that occurred within violent subgroups were more likely to be partially excused than those that happened elsewhere. The term **subculture of violence** has come to be associated with their work and has since been applied to other locations across the country.

Critiques of subcultural theory have been numerous. A major difficulty for these theories lies in the fact that studies involving self-reports of crime commission have shown that much violence and crime occur outside of "criminal" subcultures. Many middle- and upper-class lawbreakers are able to avoid the justice system and therefore do not enter the "official" crime statistics. Hence, criminal subcultures may be those in which crime is more visible rather than more prevalent.

Social Policy and Sociological Theories

Theoretical approaches that fault the social environment as the root cause of crime point to social action as a panacea. A contemporary example of intervention efforts based on sociological theories can be found in Targeted Outreach,[87] a program operated by the Boys and Girls Clubs of America. The program's philosophy is based on studies undertaken at the University of Colorado that showed that at-risk youths could be effectively diverted from the juvenile justice system through the provision of positive alternatives. The program recruits at-risk youngsters—many as young as seven years old—and diverts them into activities that are intended to promote a sense of belonging, competence, usefulness, and power. Social programs like Targeted Outreach are intended to change the cultural conditions and societal arrangements that are thought to lead people into crime.

Social Process Theories

While psychological approaches to crime causation seek to uncover aspects of the personality hidden even from the mind in which they reside, and while sociological theories look to institutional arrangements in the social world to explain crime, social process approaches focus on the interaction between individuals and society. Most **social process theories** highlight the role of social learning. They build on the premise that behavior—both "good" and "bad"—is learned, and they suggest that "bad" behavior can be unlearned. Social process theories are often the most attractive to contemporary policymakers because they demand that responsibility be placed on the offender for actively participating in rehabilitation efforts and because they are consistent with popular cultural and religious values centered on teaching right from wrong.

Differential Association Theory

In 1939, Edwin Sutherland (1883–1950) published the third edition of his *Principles of Criminology*. It contained, for the first time, a formalized statement of his theory of differential association, a perspective that Sutherland based on the "laws of imitation" described by Gabriel Tarde (1843–1904), a French sociologist.

The theory of differential association explains crime as a natural consequence of the interaction with criminal lifestyles. Sutherland suggested that children raised in crime-prone environments were often isolated and unable to experience the values that would otherwise lead to conformity. Differential association provides the basis for much research in modern criminology.[88] Even popular stories of young drug pushers, for instance, often refer to the fact that inner-city

defensible space theory

The belief that an area's physical features may be modified and structured so as to reduce crime rates in that area and to lower the fear of victimization that residents experience.

broken windows thesis

A perspective on crime causation that holds that the physical deterioration of an area leads to higher crime rates and an increased concern for personal safety among residents.

reaction formation

The process whereby a person openly rejects that which he or she wants or aspires to but cannot obtain or achieve.

subculture of violence

A cultural setting in which violence is a traditional and often accepted method of dispute resolution.

social process theory

A perspective on criminological thought that highlights the process of interaction between individuals and society. Most social process theories highlight the role of social learning.

youths imitate what they see. Some residents of poverty-ridden ghettos learn quickly that fast money can be made in the illicit drug trade, and they tend to follow the examples of material "success" that they see around them.

Differential association views crime as the product of socialization and sees it as being acquired by criminals according to the same principles that guide the learning of law-abiding behavior in conformists. Differential association removes criminality from the framework of the abnormal and places it squarely within a general perspective applicable to all behavior. In the 1947 edition of his text, Sutherland wrote, "Criminal behavior is a part of human behavior, has much in common with non-criminal behavior, and must be explained within the same general framework as any other human behavior."[89] A study of the tenets of differential association (listed in Table 3–3) shows that Sutherland believed that even the sources of behavioral motivation are much the same for conformists and criminals, that is, both groups strive for money and success but choose different paths to the same goal.

However, differential association theory fails to explain why people have the associations they do and why some associations affect certain individuals more than others. Why, for example, are most prison guards unaffected by their constant association with offenders, while a few take advantage of their position to smuggle contraband? The theory has also been criticized for being so general and imprecise as to allow for little testing.[90] Complete testing of the theory would require that all of the associations a person has ever had be recorded and analyzed from the standpoint of the individual—a clearly impossible task.

Other theorists continue to build on Sutherland's early work. Robert Burgess and Ronald Akers, for example, have constructed a differential association–reinforcement theory that seeks to integrate Sutherland's original propositions with the work of American psychologist B. F. Skinner's work on conditioning.[91] Burgess and Akers suggest that although values and behavior patterns are learned in association with others, the primary mechanism through which such learning occurs is operant conditioning. Reinforcement is the key, they say, to understanding any social learning as it takes place. The name **social learning theory** has been widely applied to the work of Burgess and Akers. It is somewhat of a misnomer, however, since the term can easily encompass a wide range of approaches and should not be limited to one specific combination of the ideas found in differential association and reinforcement theory.

social learning theory

A psychological perspective that says that people learn how to behave by modeling themselves after others whom they have the opportunity to observe.

Restraint Theories

As we have seen throughout this chapter, most criminological theories posit a cause of crime.[92] Some theories, however, focus less on causes than on constraints—those forces that keep people from committing a crime. These theories are called *restraint theories*. However, since they focus primarily on why people do not break the law, restraint theories provide only half of the causal picture. They are especially weak in identifying the social-structural sources of motivations to commit crimes.[93] Also, the ways in which bonds with different institutions interact with one an-

TABLE 3–3 Sutherland's Principles of Differential Association
1. Criminal behavior is learned.
2. Criminal behavior is learned in interaction with others in a process of communication.
3. The principal part of the learning of criminal behavior occurs within intimate personal groups.
4. When criminal behavior is learned, the learning includes (a) techniques of committing the crime, which are sometimes very complicated, sometimes very simple, and (b) the specific direction of motives, drives, rationalizations, and attitudes.
5. The specific direction of motives and drives is learned from definitions of the legal codes as favorable or unfavorable.
6. A person becomes delinquent because of an excess of definitions favorable to violations of law over definitions unfavorable to violations of law.
7. Differential associations may vary in frequency, duration, priority, and intensity.
8. The process of learning criminal behavior by association with criminal and anticriminal patterns involves all the mechanisms that are involved in any other learning.
9. Although criminal behavior is an expression of general needs and values, it is not explained by those general needs and values since noncriminal behavior is an expression of the same needs and values.

Source: Edwin Sutherland, *Principles of Criminology*, 4th ed. (Chicago: J. B. Lippincott, 1947), pp. 6–7.

other and with personal attributes, as well as the variety of bonds that operate throughout the life cycle, have yet to be clarified.[94]

CONTAINMENT THEORY

Containment theory, a type of restraint theory offered by Walter Reckless (1899–1988), assumes that all of us are subject to inducements to crime.[95] Some of us resist these "pushes" toward criminal behavior, while others do not. The difference, according to Reckless, can be found in forces that contain, or control, behavior.

Reckless described two types of **containment:** outer and inner. Outer containment depends on social roles and the norms and expectations that apply to them. People who occupy significant roles in society find themselves insulated from deviant tendencies. A corporate executive, for example, is less apt to hold up a liquor store than is a drifter. The difference, according to Reckless, is not due solely to income, but also to the pressure the executive feels to conform.

Inner containment involves a number of factors, such as conscience, a positive self-image, a tolerance for frustration, and aspirations that are in line with reality. Reckless believed that inner containment is more powerful than outer containment; inner containment functions even in secret. For example, an inner-directed person who comes across a lost purse feels compelled to locate its rightful owner and return it. If theft or greed crosses the mind of an inner-directed person, he will say to himself, "I'm not that kind of person. That would be wrong."

Reckless studied small close-knit societies—including the Hutterites, Mennonites, and Amish—in developing his theory. He realized that the "containment of behavior . . . is . . . maximized under conditions of isolation and homogeneity of culture, class, and population."[96] Hence, its applicability to modern American society, with its considerable heterogeneity of values and perspectives, is questionable.

containment

The aspects of the social bond and of the personality that act to prevent individuals from committing crimes and engaging in deviance.

SOCIAL CONTROL THEORY

Travis Hirschi emphasized the bond between individuals and society as the primary operative mechanism in his *social control theory*.[97] Hirschi identified four components of that bond: (1) emotional attachments to significant others, (2) a commitment to appropriate lifestyles, (3) involvement or immersion in conventional values, and (4) a belief in the "correctness" of social obligations and the rules of the larger society. These components act as social controls on deviant and criminal behavior; as they weaken, social control suffers, and the likelihood of crime and deviance increases. Using self-reports of delinquency from high school students in California, Hirschi concluded that youngsters who were less attached to teachers and parents and who had few positive attitudes about their own accomplishments were more likely to engage in crime and deviance than were others.[98]

NEUTRALIZATION TECHNIQUES

Complementing restraint theory is the *neutralization approach* of Gresham Sykes and David Matza.[99] The neutralization approach centers on rationalizations that allow offenders to shed feelings of guilt and responsibility for their behavior. Sykes and Matza believed that most people drift into and out of criminal behavior but will not commit a crime unless they have available to them techniques of neutralization. Their study primarily concerned juveniles for whom, they suggested, neutralization techniques provided only a temporary respite from guilt. That respite, however, lasted long enough to avoid the twinges of conscience while a crime was being committed. Neutralization techniques include the following:

- Denial of responsibility ("I'm a product of my background.")
- Denial of injury ("No one was really hurt.")
- Denial of the victim ("They deserved it.")
- Condemnation of the condemners ("The cops are corrupt.")
- Appeal to higher loyalties ("I did it for my friends.")

Like containment theory, restraint theories tend to depend on a general agreement as to values, or they assume that offenders are simply conformists who suffer temporary lapses. Neutralization techniques, by definition, are only needed when the delinquent has been socialized into middle-class values or where conscience is well developed. Even so, neutralization techniques do not in themselves explain crime. Such techniques are available to us all, if we make only a slight effort to conjure them up. The real question is why some people readily allow proffered neutralizations to affect their behavior, while others effortlessly discount them.

Labeling Theory

labeling theory

A social process perspective that sees continued crime as a consequence of the limited opportunities for acceptable behavior that follow from the negative responses of society to those defined as offenders.

As we saw earlier in this chapter, the worth of any theory of behavior is proved by how well it reflects the reality of the social world. In practice, however, theoretical perspectives find acceptance in the academic environment via a number of considerations. **Labeling theory**, for example, became fashionable in the 1960s. Its popularity may have been due more to the cultural environment into which it was introduced rather than to any inherent quality of the theory itself.

Labeling theory was first introduced by Frank Tannenbaum (1893–1969) in 1938 under the rubric of *tagging*.[100] He wrote, "The young delinquent becomes bad because he is defined as bad and because he is not believed if he is good." He went on to say, "The process of making the criminal, therefore, is a process of tagging. . . . It becomes a way of stimulating . . . and evolving the very traits that are complained of. . . . The person becomes the thing he is described as being."[101] Tannenbaum focused on society's power to *define* an act or an individual as bad and drew attention to the group need for a scapegoat in explaining crime. The search for causes inherent in individuals was not yet exhausted, however, and Tannenbaum's theory fell mostly on deaf ears.

By the 1960s, the social and academic environments in America had changed, and the issue of responsibility was seen more in terms of the group than the individual. In his book *Outsiders*, published in 1963, Howard Becker pointed out that criminality is not a quality inherent in an act or in a person. Crime, said Becker, results from a social definition, through law, of unacceptable behavior. That definition arises through **moral enterprise**, by which groups on both sides of an issue debate and eventually legislate their notion of what is moral and what is not. Becker wrote, "The central fact about deviance [is that] it is created by society. . . . Social groups create deviance by making the rules whose infraction constitutes deviance."[102]

moral enterprise

The process undertaken by an advocacy group to have its values legitimated and embodied in law.

The criminal label, however, produces consequences for labeled individuals that may necessitate continued criminality. In describing the criminal career, Becker wrote, "To be labeled a criminal one need only commit a single criminal offense. . . . Yet the word carries a number of connotations specifying auxiliary traits characteristic of anyone bearing the label."[103] The first time a person commits a crime, the behavior is called *primary deviance* and may be a merely transitory form of behavior.

However, in the popular mind, a "known" criminal is not to be trusted, should not be hired because of the potential for crimes on the job, and would not be a good candidate for the military, marriage, or any position requiring responsibility. Society's tendency toward such thinking, Becker suggested, closes legitimate opportunities, ensuring that the only new behavioral alternatives available to the labeled criminal are deviant ones. Succeeding episodes of criminal behavior are seen as a form of secondary deviance that eventually becomes stabilized in the behavioral repertoire and self-concept of the labeled person.[104]

Labeling theory can be critiqued along a number of dimensions. First, it is not really a "theory" in that labeling does not uncover the genesis of criminal behavior. It is more useful in describing how such behavior continues than in explaining how it originates. Second, labeling theory does not recognize the possibility that the labeled individual may make successful attempts at reform and may shed the negative label. Finally, the theory does not provide an effective way of dealing with offenders. Should people who commit crimes not be arrested and tried so as to avoid the consequences of negative labels? It would be exceedingly naïve to suggest that all repeat criminal behavior would cease, as labeling theory might predict, if people who commit crimes are not officially "handled" by the system.

The Life Course Perspective

social development theory

An integrated view of human development that points to the process of interaction among and between individuals and society as the root cause of criminal behavior.

Some of the most recent perspectives on crime causation belong to a subcategory of social process thought called **social development theory**. According to the social development perspective, human development occurs simultaneously on many levels, including the psychological, biological, familial, interpersonal, cultural, societal, and ecological levels. Hence, social development theories tend to be integrated theories—that is, theories that combine various points of view on the process of development. Theories that fall into this category, however, highlight the process of interaction between individuals and society as the root cause of criminal behavior. In particular, they emphasize that a critical period of transition occurs in a person's life as he or she moves from childhood to adulthood.

life course perspective

An approach to explaining crime and deviance that investigates developments and turning points in the course of a person's life.

One social development perspective of special significance is the **life course perspective**. According to Robert Sampson and John Laub, who named the life course perspective in 1993, criminal behavior typically follows an identifiable pattern throughout a person's life cycle.[105] In the lives of those who eventually become criminal, crime-like or deviant behavior is relatively rare during early childhood, tends to begin as sporadic instances during early adolescence, becomes more common during the late-teen and early-adult years, and then gradually diminishes as the person gets older.

Sampson and Laub also use the idea of *transitions* in the life course, or turning points that identify significant events in a person's life and represent the opportunity for people to turn either away from or toward deviance and crime. An employer who gives an employee a second chance, for example, may provide a unique opportunity that helps determine the future course of that person's life. Similarly, the principle of *linked lives*, also common to life course theories, highlights the fact that no one lives in isolation. Events in the life course are constantly being influenced by family members, friends, acquaintances, employers, teachers, and so on. Not only might such influences determine the life course of any given individual, but they are active throughout the life course. Figure 3–2 diagrams some of the life course influences experienced by most adolescents. Also shown in the diagram are desired outcomes and positive and negative indicators of development.

In 1986, the federal Office of Juvenile Justice and Delinquency Prevention (OJJDP) began funding a study of life pathways as they lead to criminality. The Program of Research on the Causes and Correlates of Delinquency continues to produce results.[106] Researchers have been examining how delinquency, violence, and drug use develop within and are related to various social contexts, including the family, peer groups, schools, and the surrounding community. To date, the study has identified three distinct pathways to delinquency, which are shown in Figure 3–3. These pathways are not mutually exclusive and can sometimes converge:

- The *authority conflict pathway*, along which children begin to move during their early years (as early as three or four years old), involves stubborn behavior and resistance to parental authority. Defiance of authority begins around age 11, and authority avoidance (that is, truancy, running away) begins about the same time.

- The *covert pathway*, which starts around age ten with minor covert acts such as shoplifting and lying, quickly progresses to acts of vandalism involving property damage. Moderate to severe delinquency frequently begins a year or two later.

- The *overt pathway* is marked by minor aggression, such as bullying, that develops around age 11 or 12. The overt pathway leads to fighting and physical violence during the teenage years and tends to eventuate in serious violent criminality that may include rape, robbery, and assault.

A similar study is under way at the Project on Human Development in Chicago Neighborhoods (PHDCN), mentioned earlier in this chapter. PHDCN researchers are "tracing how criminal behavior develops from birth to age 32."[107] Participating researchers come from a variety of scientific backgrounds and include psychiatrists, developmental psychologists, sociologists, criminologists, physicians, educators, statisticians, and public health officials. The study focuses on the influence of communities, peers, families, and health-related, cognitive, and emotional factors to decipher the lines along which crime and delinquency are likely to develop. Learn more about the OJJDP's causes and correlates study at Web Extra 3–7 at cjtoday.com; find out more about the PHDCN project at Web Extra 3–8 and Library Extra 3–3; and read about the possible effects of childhood victimization on later criminality at Library Extra 3–4.

WEB Extra ▪▪▪▪ **LIBRARY** Extra ▪▪▪▪

Conflict Theories

Basic to the **conflict perspective** is the belief that conflict is a fundamental aspect of social life and can never be fully resolved. From the conflict point of view, formal agencies of social control at best merely coerce the unempowered or the disenfranchised to comply with the rules established by those in power. Laws become tools of the powerful, tools that are useful in keeping others from wresting control over important social institutions. Social order, rather than being the result of any consensus or process of dispute resolution, rests on the exercise of power through law. The conflict perspective can be described in terms of four key elements:[108]

- Society is composed of diverse social groups, and diversity is based on distinctions that people hold to be significant, such as gender, sexual orientation, and social class.

- Conflict among groups is unavoidable because of differing interests and differing values. Hence, conflict is inherent in social life.

- The fundamental nature of group conflict centers on the exercise of political power. Political power is the key to the accumulation of wealth and to other forms of power.

- Laws are the tools of power and further the interests of those powerful enough to make them. Laws allow those in control to gain what they define (through the law) as legitimate access to scarce resources and to deny (through the law) such access to the politically disenfranchised.

An honest and fully professional police community would acknowledge in its police education the root causes of crime—poverty, unemployment, underemployment, racism, poor health care, bad housing, weak schools, mental illness, alcoholism, addiction, single-parent families, teenage pregnancy, and a society of selfishness and greed.

—Patrick V. Murphy, former New York City Police Commissioner

conflict perspective

A theoretical approach that holds that crime is the natural consequence of economic and other social inequities. Conflict theorists highlight the stresses that arise among and within social groups as they compete with one another for resources and for survival. The social forces that result are viewed as major determinants of group and individual behavior, including crime.

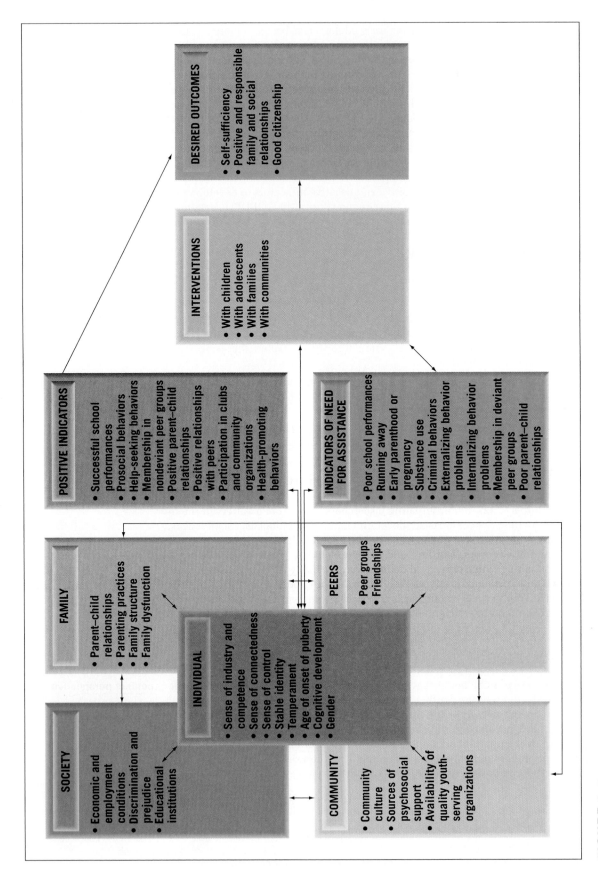

FIGURE 3–2

A conceptual model of adolescent development.

Source: Family and Youth Services Bureau, *Understanding Youth Development: Promoting Positive Pathways of Growth* (Washington, DC: U.S. Dept. of Health and Human Services, 2000).

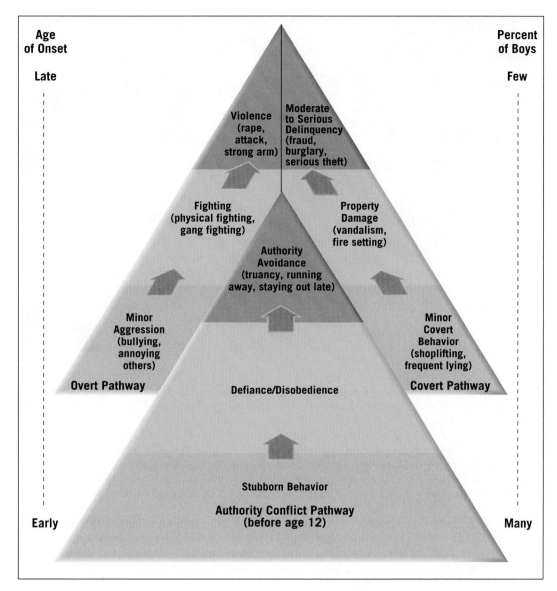

FIGURE 3–3

Three pathways to disruptive behavior and delinquency.

Source: Barbara Tatem Kelley et al., *Developmental Pathways in Boys' Disruptive and Delinquent Behavior* (Washington, DC: Office of Juvenile Justice and Delinquency Prevention, 1997).

Within the figure:

- Age of Onset (left axis): Late → Early
- Percent of Boys (right axis): Few → Many
- Violence (rape, attack, strong arm)
- Moderate to Serious Delinquency (fraud, burglary, serious theft)
- Fighting (physical fighting, gang fighting)
- Property Damage (vandalism, fire setting)
- Authority Avoidance (truancy, running away, staying out late)
- Minor Aggression (bullying, annoying others)
- Minor Covert Behavior (shoplifting, frequent lying)
- Overt Pathway
- Covert Pathway
- Defiance/Disobedience
- Stubborn Behavior
- Authority Conflict Pathway (before age 12)

Radical Criminology

Criminological theory took a new direction during the 1960s and 1970s, brought about in part by the turmoil that characterized American society during that period. **Radical criminology** placed the blame for criminality and deviant behavior squarely on officially sanctioned cultural and economic arrangements. The distribution of wealth and power in society was held to be the primary cause of criminal behavior, especially among those who were disenfranchised. Poverty and discrimination were seen to lead to frustration and pent-up hostilities that were expressed through murder, rape, theft, and other crimes.

Radical criminology had its roots in early conflict theories and in the thought of Dutch criminologist Willem Bonger. Some authors have distinguished between conflict theory and radical criminology by naming them "conservative conflict theory" and "radical conflict theory" respectively.[109] The difference between the two theories, however, is mostly in the rhetoric of the times. Conservative conflict theories held that conflict was a natural part of any society and that struggles for power and control would always occur. "Losers" of conflicts were defined as "criminal," and constraints on their behavior would be legislated. Characteristic of this perspective are the approaches of Austin Turk[110] (b. 1934) and George Vold (1896–1967). An even earlier conflict perspective can be found in the culture conflict notions of Thorsten Sellin, who was concerned with the clash of immigrant values and traditions with those of established American culture.[111]

Radical criminology went a step further. It recognized that the struggle to control resources is central to society, and it encompassed the notion that the law is a tool of the powerful. The focus

radical criminology

A conflict perspective that sees crime as engendered by the unequal distribution of wealth, power, and other resources, which adherents believe is especially characteristic of capitalist societies.

A homeless man walking by an expensive home. Radical criminologists claim that the inequitable distribution of wealth in society produces frustrations and pent-up hostilities that lead to criminality. In this view, the powerful use the criminal law as a tool to maintain their place in the social world. Do you agree? Why or why not?

Joel Stettenheim/Corbis/Bettmann

of radical criminology, however, was capitalism and the evils that capitalism was believed to entail. The ideas of Karl Marx (1818–1883) entered the field of criminology through the writings of William Chambliss[112] (b. 1933) and Richard Quinney[113] (b. 1934). According to Marx, the labor of the lower classes provides the basis for the accumulated wealth of the upper classes, and the lower classes are always exploited by the "owners" in society. The poor were trained to believe that capitalism was in their best interests and the working classes suffered under the consequences of a "false class consciousness" perpetrated by the powerful. Marx believed that only when the exploited workers realized their exploitation would they rebel and change society for the better.

American radical criminology built on the ideals of the 1960s and charged that the "establishment," controlled by the upper classes, perverted justice through the unequal application of judicial sanctions. As David Greenberg observes, "Many researchers attributed the overrepresentation of blacks and persons from impoverished family backgrounds in arrest and conviction statistics to the discriminatory practices of the enforcement agencies. It was not that the poor stole more, but rather that when they did, the police were more likely to arrest them."[114] Conflict theories of criminality face the difficulty of realistic implementation. Radical criminology, in particular, is flawed by its narrow emphasis on capitalist societies. It fails to recognize adequately the role of human nature in the creation of social classes and in the perpetuation of the struggle for control of resources. Radical criminology implies that a utopian social arrangement—perhaps communism—would eliminate most crime. Such a belief is contrary to historical experience: A close look at any contemporary communist society will reveal both social conflict and crime.

Peacemaking Criminology

peacemaking criminology

A perspective that holds that crime-control agencies and the citizens they serve should work together to alleviate social problems and human suffering and thus reduce crime.

Peacemaking criminology, which some theorists see as a mature expression of earlier conflict theories, holds that crime-control agencies and the citizens they serve should work together to alleviate social problems and human suffering and thus reduce crime.[115] Criminology as peacemaking has its roots in ancient Christian and Eastern philosophies, as well as in traditional conflict theory. Peacemaking criminology, which includes the notion of service and has also been called *compassionate criminology*, suggests that "compassion, wisdom, and love are essential for understanding the suffering of which we are all a part, and for practicing a criminology of nonviolence."[116] Peacemaking criminology also holds that official agents of social control need to work with both the victimized and the victimizers to achieve a new world order that is more just and fair to all who live in it. In a fundamental sense, peacemaking criminologists exhort their colleagues to transcend personal dichotomies to end the political and ideological divisiveness that separates people. "If we ourselves cannot know peace . . . how will our acts disarm hatred and violence?" they ask.[117]

Peacemaking criminology was popularized by the works of Harold Pepinsky[118] and Richard Quinney[119] beginning in 1986. Both Pepinsky and Quinney restate the problem of crime control from one of "how to stop crime" to one of "how to make peace" within society and among citizens and criminal justice agencies. Peacemaking criminology draws attention to many issues, among them the perpetuation of violence through the continuation of social policies based on dominant forms of criminological theory, the role of education in peacemaking, "commonsense theories of crime," crime control as human rights enforcement, and conflict resolution within community settings.[120]

Social Policy and Conflict Theories

Because radical and conflict criminologists view social inequality as the cause of crime, many suggest that the only way to achieve real change in the rate of crime is through revolution. Revolution—because it holds the promise of greater equality for underrepresented groups and because it mandates a redistribution of wealth and power—is thought necessary for any lasting reduction in crime.

Some contemporary writers on radical criminology, however, have attempted to address the issue of what can be done under our current system, because they recognize that a sudden and total reversal of existing political arrangements within the United States is highly unlikely. Hence, they have begun to focus on promoting "middle-range policy alternatives" to the present system, including "equal justice in the bail system, the abolition of mandatory sentences, prosecution of corporate crimes, increased employment opportunities, and promoting community alternatives to imprisonment."[121] Likewise, programs to reduce prison overcrowding, efforts to highlight injustices within the current system, the elimination of racism and other forms of inequality in the handling of both victims and offenders, growing equality in criminal justice system employment, and the like are all frequently mentioned as mid-range strategies for bringing about a justice system that is fairer and closer to the radical ideal.

Raymond Michalowski summarizes the policy directions envisioned by today's radical criminologists when he says, "We cannot be free from the crimes of the poor until there are no more poor; we cannot be free from domination of the powerful until we reduce the inequalities that make domination possible; and we cannot live in harmony with others until we begin to limit the competition for material advantage over others that alienates us from one another."[122]

Emergent Perspectives

A number of new and developing criminological perspectives deserve special mention. They include feminist criminology, constitutive criminology, and postmodern criminology. We will briefly discuss each in the sections that follow.

Feminist Criminology

As some writers in the developing field of **feminist criminology** have observed, "Women have been virtually invisible in criminological analysis until recently and much theorizing has proceeded as though criminality is restricted to men."[123] Another puts it this way: "[Traditional] criminological theory assumes a woman is like a man."[124] Feminist criminologists are now working to change long-cherished notions of crime and of criminal justice so that the role of women in both crime causation and crime control might be better appreciated.[125]

One of the first writers to attempt a definitive explanation of the criminality of women was Otto Pollak. Pollak's book, *The Criminality of Women*,[126] written in 1950, suggested that women commit the same number of offenses as men but that most of their criminality is hidden. Pollak claimed that women's roles at the time, primarily those of homemaker and mother, served to disguise their criminal undertakings. He also proposed that chivalrous treatment by a male-dominated justice system acted to bias every stage of criminal justice processing in favor of women. Hence, according to Pollak, although women are just as criminal as men, they are rarely arrested, tried, or imprisoned. In fact, although the criminality of women may approach or exceed that of men in selected offense categories, today it is safe to say that Pollak was incorrect in his assessment of the degree of female criminality; overall women commit far fewer crimes than men.

When internal cultures conflict, it can be as destructive as a collision between an iceberg and an ocean liner. Misunderstanding between two cultural groups can lead to conflict and, taken to the extreme, physical confrontations.

—Sherman Block, Los Angeles County Sheriff

feminist criminology

A developing intellectual approach that emphasizes gender issues in criminology.

Early works in the field of feminist criminology include Freda Adler's *Sisters in Crime*[127] and Rita Simon's *Women and Crime*.[128] Both books were published in 1975, and in them the authors claimed that the existing divergences in crime rates between men and women were due primarily to socialization rather than biology. Women, claimed these authors, were taught to believe in personal limitations, faced reduced socioeconomic opportunities, and, as a result, suffered from lowered aspirations. As gender equality increased, they said, it could be expected that male and female criminality would take on similar characteristics. More recent researchers, however, have not found this to be true; substantial differences between the criminality of men and women remain, even as gender equality grows.[129]

Contemporary feminist thinking in criminology is represented by the works of writers like Kathleen Daly and Meda Chesney-Lind.[130] Daly and Chesney-Lind emphasize the need for a "gender-aware" criminology and stress the usefulness of applying feminist thinking to criminological analysis. Gender, say these writers, is a central organizing principle of contemporary life. Feminist criminology suggests that theories of crime causation and prevention must include women and that more research on gender-related issues in the field is badly needed. Additionally, some authors say, "Criminologists should begin to appreciate that their discipline and its questions are a product of white, economically privileged men's experiences."[131] They suggest that rates of female criminality, which are lower than those of males, may show that criminal behavior is not as "normal" as once thought. Because modern-day criminological perspectives were mostly developed by white middle-class males, the propositions and theories they advance fail to take into consideration women's "ways of knowing."[132] Hence, the fundamental challenge posed by feminist criminology is this: Do existing theories of crime causation apply as well to women as they do to men? Or, as Daly and Chesney-Lind put it, given the current situation in theory development, "do theories of men's crime apply to women?"[133] Read some of Chesney-Lind's recent work via Library Extra 3–5 at cjtoday.com.

LIBRARY
Extra
■ ■ ■ ■

Recent perspectives on female criminality stress the fact "that a key to understanding and responding to women as offenders is understanding their status as crime victims."[134] Psychologist Cathy Spatz Widom, for example, examined the life cycle of female offenders, looking for links between childhood abuse and neglect and later criminality. Widom suggests that the successful socialization of girls can be "derailed" by early victimization through mechanisms such as "running away, deficits in cognitive ability and achievement, growing up without traditional social controls, engaging in relationships with deviant or delinquent individuals, and failing to learn the social and psychological skills necessary for successful adult development."[135]

Contemporary statistics tell us that although females make up 51% of the population of the United States, they are arrested for only 17.8% of all violent crimes and 31.6% of property crimes. The relatively limited involvement of women in the FBI's eight major crimes can be seen in Table 3–4. Data show that the number of female offenders is increasing faster than the number of male offenders, however. Between 1970 and 2000, the number of crimes committed by men grew by 46%, while crimes committed by women increased 144%. Violent crimes by men increased 82% during the period; by women, 260%. Property crimes perpetrated by men grew by 3%; by women, 85%.[136]

Relative increases in the FBI's Part II offenses tell a similar story. Arrests of women for embezzlement, for example, increased by more than 228% between 1970 and 2000, versus only 8.5% for men—reflecting women's increased entry into areas of financial responsibility. Arrests of women for drug abuse grew by 289%, and liquor-law violations by women increased 285% (versus 96% for men).[137] In two officially reported categories—prostitution and runaways—women outnumber men in the volume of offenses committed.[138] Other crimes in which significant numbers of women (relative to men) are involved include larceny-theft (where 38.5% of reported crimes are committed by women), forgery and counterfeiting (39.8%), fraud (44.9%), and embezzlement (50.4%).[139] Nonetheless, as Table 3–4 shows, female offenders still account for only a small proportion of all reported crimes. Statistics on female criminality are difficult to interpret since reports of increasing female criminality may reflect the greater equality of treatment accorded women in contemporary society more than they do actual increases in criminal activity. In the past, when women committed crimes, they were dealt with less formally than is likely to be the case today.

When women do commit serious crimes, they are more often followers than leaders. A study of women in correctional settings, for example, found that women are far more likely to assume "secondary follower roles during criminal events" than "dominant leadership roles."[140] Only 14% of women surveyed played primary roles, but those who did "felt that men had little influence in initiating or leading them into crime." African American women were found to be more likely to play "primary and equal crime roles" with men or with female accomplices than were white or Hispanic women. Statistics such as these dispel the myth that the female criminal in America has taken her place alongside the male offender—in terms of either leadership roles or the absolute number of crimes committed.

TABLE 3–4 Male and Female Involvement in Crime: Offense Patterns, 2006

UCR Index Crime	Percentage of All Arrests	
	Males	**Females**
Murder and nonnegligent manslaughter	89.1	10.9
Rape	98.7	1.3
Robbery	88.7	11.3
Aggravated assault	79.3	20.7
Burglary	85.5	14.5
Larceny-theft	62.3	37.7
Motor vehicle theft	82.3	17.7
Arson	83.0	17.0

Gender Differences

- Men are more likely than women to be arrested for serious crimes, such as murder, rape, robbery, and burglary.
- Arrest, jail, and prison data all suggest that more women than men who commit crimes are involved in property crimes, such as larceny, forgery, fraud, and embezzlement, and in drug offenses.

Source: Federal Bureau of Investigation, *Crime in the United States, 2006* (Washington, DC: U.S. Dept. of Justice, 2007).

Constitutive Criminology

In the early 1900s, George Herbert Mead[141] (1863–1931) set forth a theory called *symbolic interaction*, in which he demonstrated how people give meaning to the things around them and to their lives. About the same time, William Thomas[142] (1863–1947) explained that the significance of any human behavior is relative to the intentions behind it and to the situation in which it is interpreted. Hence, behavior that in one place or at one time is seen as acceptable, in another place or time may be perceived as deviant or even criminal. From this viewpoint, crime, like any other social phenomenon, is more a definition imposed by society on a particular type of activity than it is a quality inherent in the behavior itself. As a consequence, crime may mean different things to different people and is, no doubt, variously interpreted by the offender, by the victim, and by agents of social control. Seen this way, the significance of criminal behavior depends on one's interests in the crime and one's point of view and is ultimately knowable only to those who participate in it. Central to this way of thinking are the following principles:

- The significance of any behavior depends on a social consensus about what that behavior "means."
- Crime is the product of an active process of interpretation and social definition.
- Continued criminal activity may be more a consequence of the limited opportunities for acceptable behavior that are imposed on individuals defined as "criminal" than it is a product of choice.

Contemporary criminologists Stuart Henry and Dragan Milovanovic use the term **constitutive criminology** to refer to the process by which human beings create "an ideology of crime that sustains it as a concrete reality."[143] A central feature of constitutive criminology is its assertion that individuals shape their world while also being shaped by it. Constitutive criminology claims that crime and crime control are not "object-like entities" but constructions produced through a social process in which offender, victim, and society are all involved.[144] "We are concerned with the ways in which human agents actively coproduce that which they take to be crime," write Henry and Milovanovic. For these theorists, the idea of crime itself is a social construction, and researchers, they say, should recognize that criminals and victims are also "emergent realities." In short, constitutive criminology focuses on the social process by which crime and criminology become cultural realities.[145] Read some of Milovanovic's work via Library Extra 3–6 at cjtoday.com.

constitutive criminology

The study of the process by which human beings create an ideology of crime that sustains the notion of crime as a concrete reality.

LIBRARY
Extra
▪ ▪ ▪ ▪

postmodern criminology

A branch of criminology that developed after World War II and that builds on the tenets of postmodern social thought.

deconstructionist theory

One of the emerging approaches that challenges existing criminological perspectives to debunk them and that works toward replacing them with concepts more applicable to the postmodern era.

Postmodern Criminology

Before concluding this chapter, it is important to note that **postmodern criminology** is a term applied to a wide variety of novel perspectives that have developed in recent decades. It encompasses evolving paradigms with such intriguing names as *chaos theory*, *discourse analysis*, *topology theory*, *critical theory*, *realist criminology*, *constitutive theory*, and *anarchic criminology*.[146] Postmodern criminology builds on the belief that past criminological approaches have failed to realistically assess the true causes of crime and have therefore failed to offer workable solutions for crime control—or if they have, that such theories and solutions may have been appropriate at one time but no longer apply to the postmodern era. Because postmodern criminology challenges and debunks existing perspectives, it is referred to as *deconstructionist*, and such theories are sometimes called **deconstructionist theories**.

SUMMARY

- A theory is a proposed model of causal relationships between events and things under study. This chapter defines *theory* as a series of interrelated propositions that attempt to describe, explain, predict, and ultimately control some class of events. A good theory fits the facts and stands up to continued scrutiny. The goal of social research in criminology is to assist in the development of theoretical models that permit a better understanding of criminal behavior and that enhance the development of strategies intended to address the problem of crime.

- The Classical School of criminology, which was in vogue throughout the late eighteenth and early nineteenth centuries, held that crime is caused by the individual exercise of free will and that it can be deterred through the promise of swift and certain punishment. Classical criminology continues to be influential through today's neoclassical thought, represented by rational choice and routine activities theories.

- Biological theories posit a genetic or a physiological basis for deviant and criminal behavior. The notion of a "weak" gene that might predispose some people toward criminal activity has been expanded to include the impact of environmental contaminants, poor nutrition, and food additives on behavior. Studies of fraternal twins and chromosome structure have helped bring biological theories into the modern day. Such theories, however, have their shortcomings, including a lack of recognition of other perspectives that might help better explain criminality. Similarly, strict biological theories attribute the cause of crime to fundamental physical characteristics that are not easily modified.

- Psychobiological perspectives on crime causation note the role that human DNA, environmental contaminants, nutrition, hormones, physical trauma, and body chemistry play in behavior that violates the law. The detailed mapping of human DNA and other recent advances in the field of recombinant DNA have rekindled interest in genetic correlates of criminal behavior.

- Psychological explanations of crime are individualistic. Some psychoanalytic theories see offenders as psychotic, psychopathic, or sociopathic. Other psychological theories claim that criminal behavior is a type of conditioned response. The stimulus-response model sees criminal behavior as the consequence of a conditioning process that extends over the entire life span of an individual. As with most other theories, psychological perspectives remain plagued by shortcomings. Among them are questions about whether past behavior can accurately predict future behavior and whether there are identifiable characteristics that violent offenders might manifest that could serve as warning signs of impending criminal activity.

- Sociological theories hold that the individual is a product of his or her social environment. They emphasize the role that social structure, inequality, and socialization play in criminality. Although they are today's perspective of choice, the danger of most sociological approaches is that they tend to deny the significance of any influences beyond those that are mediated through social interaction.

- Social process theories of criminology claim that crime results from the failure of self-direction, from inadequate social roles, or from associating with others who are already criminal. Social policies based on such theories place responsibility for change largely on the offender.

- Conflict perspectives attempt to explain crime by noting that conflict is fundamental to social life and by claiming that crime is a natural consequence of social, political, and economic inequity. Conflict criminologists believe that fundamental changes in the structure of society are needed if crime is to be eliminated or curtailed.

- Included among emergent approaches to explaining crime are feminist criminology, constitutive criminology, and postmodern criminology. Feminist criminology challenges some long-held notions of crime and criminal justice that have been based solely on understandings of male criminality. Constitutive criminology highlights the fact that crime is a socially created phenomenon and that without some cultural agreements about right and wrong as reflected in the criminal laws of a society, crime, as we think of it, would not exist. Postmodern criminology, the last of the approaches discussed in this chapter, is often more an effort to debunk previous perspectives than it is a theoretical perspective in its own right.

KEY TERMS

anomie, 95

atavism, 84

behavioral conditioning, 89

Biological School, 83

broken windows thesis, 97

Chicago School, 92

Classical School, 81

conflict perspective, 101

constitutive criminology, 107

containment, 99

dangerousness, 92

deconstructionist theory, 108

defensible space theory, 97

deviance, 77

feminist criminology, 105

hypothesis, 78

interdisciplinary theory, 79

labeling theory, 100

life course perspective, 100

moral enterprise, 100

neoclassical criminology, 82

peacemaking criminology, 104

phrenology, 83

Positivist School, 84

postmodern criminology, 108

psychoanalysis, 89

psychological profiling, 91

Psychological School, 89

psychopath, 90

psychopathology, 90

psychosis, 91

radical criminology, 103

rational choice theory, 82

reaction formation, 97

research, 78

routine activities theory, 82

schizophrenic, 91

social development theory, 100

social disorganization, 92

social learning theory, 98

social process theory, 97

somatotyping, 86

subculture of violence, 97

supermale, 87

theory, 78

KEY NAMES

Freda Adler, 106

Cesare Beccaria, 82

Howard Becker, 100

Jeremy Bentham, 82

Ernest Burgess, 94

Meda Chesney-Lind, 106

Hervey Cleckley, 90

Albert Cohen, 97

Lawrence Cohen, 82

Kathleen Daly, 106

Marcus Felson, 82

Sigmund Freud, 89

QUESTIONS FOR REVIEW

1. What is a theory? Describe the steps in criminological theory building, and explain the role that social research plays in the development of theories about crime.

2. List the basic assumptions of classical theories of crime causation, and describe the neoclassical perspective.

3. Describe the basic features of biological theories of crime causation. What shortcomings of the biological perspective can you identify?

4. How has the mapping of human DNA enhanced contemporary psychobiological understandings of criminal behavior?

5. Describe the basic features of psychological explanations for crime. What are the shortcomings of this perspective?

6. Describe the basic features of sociological explanations for crime. What are the shortcomings of this perspective?

7. Describe social process theories of crime causation, including labeling theory and the life course perspective. What types of crime-control policies might be based on such theories?

8. Describe conflict theories of crime causation, including radical criminology and peacemaking criminology. What sorts of crime-control policies might be predicated on the basis of such theories?

9. What is meant by "emergent perspectives"? List and describe three emergent perspectives on crime causation.

QUESTIONS FOR REFLECTION

1. Chapter 1 referred briefly to evidence-based practices. What evidence-based practices might be developed as a result of the studies discussed in this chapter?

2. What is the relationship between punishment and classical and neoclassical thought? With what types of offenders might punishment be the most effective in reducing recidivism?

3. Do you think that biological theories successfully explain the causes of crime? Why or why not?

4. What role, if any, might psychobiological theories play in the development of crime-reduction strategies?

5. Do you think that psychological theories of crime causation are sound? Why or why not?

6. Do you think that sociological theories are sound? Why or why not?

Discuss your answers to these questions and other issues on the CJ Today e-mail discussion list (join the list at cjtoday.com).

WEB QUEST

One of the most informative criminal justice–related sites on the Web is the National Criminal Justice Reference Service (NCJRS). Visit the NCJRS at ncjrs.org, or use the Cybrary to locate the NCJRS. Once you have found NCJRS, explore each of the major informational categories it provides: Corrections, Courts, Crime, Crime Prevention, Drugs, Justice System, Juvenile Justice, Law Enforcement, and Victims.

Visit each category, and make a note of the features available. View at least one document from each category. Write a summary of each document (you should have a total of nine), and submit the summaries to your instructor if asked to do so.

Reenter each NCJRS category, and make a note of the websites referenced there. Visit at least three sites under each category, and write a brief description of each site (you should have a total of 27). Submit the descriptions to your instructor if asked to do so.

To complete this Web Quest online, go to the Web Quest module in Chapter 3 of the *Criminal Justice Today* Companion Website at cjtoday.com.

CHAPTER 4

Criminal Law

LEARNING OBJECTIVES

After reading this chapter, you should be able to

- Explain the nature and purpose of law.
- Discuss the nature of the rule of law, and describe its importance in Western democratic societies.
- Identify the various categories or types of law, and explain the purpose of each.
- List and describe the five categories of crime.
- List and describe the eight general features of crime.
- Explain what is meant by the *elements* of a specific criminal offense.
- Discuss the four broad categories of criminal defenses that our legal system recognizes.

Law is the art of the good and the fair.

—Ulpian, Roman judge (circa A.D. 200)

Every law is an infraction of liberty.

—Jeremy Bentham (1748–1832)

Law should be like death, which spares no one.

—Montesquieu (1689–1755)

Introduction

Hear the author discuss
this chapter at
cjtoday.com

*The greatest happiness of
the greatest number is the
foundation of morals and
legislation.*

—Jeremy Bentham

law

A rule of conduct, generally found
enacted in the form of a statute, that
proscribes or mandates certain
forms of behavior.

In 2003, after the American military had toppled the regime of Iraqi dictator Saddam Hussein but before the establishment of a new Iraqi government, soldiers of the U.S. Third Infantry Division had to release a man who had taken his beaten and bloodied wife to a Baghdad hospital for treatment and had continued to beat her while waiting for doctors to arrive.[1] When soldiers restrained the man, he exclaimed that he was exercising his marital rights under Islamic tradition and was beating his wife because she had interfered with his attempts to have intercourse with the couple's 14-year-old daughter. "The sad thing is there was nothing we could do," said Sergeant First Class Michael Shirley of Hinesville, Georgia, "apart from separate them and send her to her mother's house in a taxi, because there are no laws against domestic violence here. The women have to respect their husband's decisions. We can't get involved with religious or cultural beliefs."[2]

In contrast to prewar Iraq, modern postindustrial societies like the United States have developed highly formalized secular legal systems. Laws govern many aspects of our lives, and we are expected to know what the law *says* as it applies to our daily lives and to *follow* it. But do we really know what **law** is? The job of this chapter is to discuss the law both as a product of rule creation and as a guide for behavior. We will also examine criminal law in some detail, and we will discuss defenses commonly used by defendants charged with violations of the criminal law.

The Nature and Purpose of Law

Imagine a society without laws. Without civil law, people would not know what to expect from one another, nor would they be able to plan for the future with any degree of certainty. Without criminal law, people wouldn't feel safe because the more powerful could take what they wanted from the less powerful. Without constitutional law, people could not exercise the basic rights that are available to them as citizens of a free nation. A society needs laws to uphold fairness and to prevent the victimization of innocents.

statutory law

Written or codified law; the "law on
the books," as enacted by a
government body or agency having
the power to make laws.

LIBRARY
Extra
■ ■ ■ ■

penal code

The written, organized, and
compiled form of the criminal laws
of a jurisdiction.

case law

The body of judicial precedent,
historically built on legal reasoning and
past interpretations of statutory laws,
that serves as a guide to decision
making, especially in the courts.

Practically speaking, laws regulate relationships between people and also between parties, such as government agencies and individuals. They channel and simultaneously constrain human behavior, and they empower individuals while contributing to public order. Laws also serve other purposes. They ensure that the philosophical, moral, and economic perspectives of their creators are protected and made credible. They maintain values and uphold established patterns of social privilege. They sustain existing power relationships, and finally, they support a system for the punishment and rehabilitation of offenders. (See Table 4–1.) Modifications of the law, when gradually induced, promote orderly change in the rest of society.

Our laws are found in statutory provisions and constitutional enactments,[3] as well as in hundreds of years of rulings by courts at all levels. According to the authoritative *Black's Law Dictionary*, the word *law* "generally contemplates both statutory and case law."[4] **Statutory law** is "the law on the books." It results from legislative action and is often thought of as "the law of the land." Written laws exist in both criminal and civil areas and are called *codes*. Once laws have been written down in organized fashion, they are said to be *codified*. Federal statutes are compiled in the U.S. Code (U.S.C.), which is available online in its entirety at Library Extra 4–1 at cjtoday.com. State codes and municipal ordinances are also readily available in written, or statutory, form. The written form of the criminal law is called the **penal code. Case law**, which we will discuss in detail a bit later, is the law that results from judicial decisions.

But the laws of our country are not unambiguous. If all of "the law" could be found in written legal codes, it would be plain to nearly everyone, and we would need far fewer lawyers than are practicing today. But some laws—the precedents established by courts—do not exist "on the books," and even those that do are open to interpretation. This is where common law comes into

TABLE 4–1 What Do Laws Do?
• Laws maintain order in society.
• Laws regulate human interaction.
• Laws enforce moral beliefs.
• Laws define the economic environment.
• Laws enhance predictability.
• Laws support the powerful.
• Laws promote orderly social change.
• Laws sustain individual rights.
• Laws redress wrongs.
• Laws identify wrongdoers.
• Laws mandate punishment and retribution.

play. **Common law** is the traditional body of unwritten historical precedents created from everyday social customs, rules, and practices, many of which were supported by judicial decisions during early times. Common law principles are still used to interpret many legal issues in quite a few states. Hence, it is not uncommon to hear of jurisdictions within the United States referred to as "common law jurisdictions" or "common law states."

common law

Law originating from usage and custom rather than from written statutes. The term refers to an unwritten body of judicial opinion, originally developed by English courts, that is based on nonstatutory customs, traditions, and precedents that help guide judicial decision making.

The Rule of Law

The social, economic, and political stability of any society depends largely on the development and institutionalization of a predictable system of laws. Western democratic societies adhere to the **rule of law**, which is sometimes also referred to as the *supremacy of law*. The rule of law centers on the belief that an orderly society must be governed by established principles and known codes that are applied uniformly and fairly to all of its members. Under this tenet, no one is above the law, and those who make or enforce the law must also abide by it. The principle was well illustrated in 2002 when U.S. Representative James Traficant, a Democrat from Ohio, was expelled from Congress by fellow lawmakers after he was convicted in federal court of ten counts of bribery, tax evasion, and racketeering.[5] He was later sentenced to eight years in prison. Similarly, in 2007, former Ohio Republican Congressman Robert W. Ney was sentenced to 30 months in prison for corrupt dealings with convicted congressional lobbyist Jack Abramoff.[6] Other formerly powerful politicians who have recently served time in prison include former four-term South Dakota Governor Bill Janklow and former Connecticut Governor John G. Rowland.

The rule of law has been called the greatest political achievement of our culture. Without it, few other human achievements—especially those that require the coordinated efforts of a large number of people—would be possible. President John F. Kennedy eloquently explained the rule of law, saying, "Americans are free to disagree with the law, but not to disobey it; for [in] a government of laws and not of men, no man, however prominent and powerful, no mob, however unruly or boisterous, is entitled to defy a court of law."[7]

The rule of law has also been called "the foundation of liberties in the Western world,"[8] for it means that due process (which was discussed in Chapter 1) has to be followed in any criminal prosecution, and it is due process that serves as a check on arbitrary state power.

The American Bar Association notes that the rule of law includes these elements:[9]

- Freedom from private lawlessness provided by the legal system of a politically organized society

- A relatively high degree of objectivity in the formulation of legal norms and a like degree of evenhandedness in their application

- Legal ideas and juristic devices for the attainment of individual and group objectives within the bounds of ordered liberty

- Substantive and procedural limitations on governmental power in the interest of the individual for the enforcement of which there are appropriate legal institutions and machinery

Jurisprudence is the philosophy of law or the science and study of the law, including the rule of law. To learn more about the rule of law, including its historical development, visit Web Extra 4–1 at cjtoday.com.

rule of law

The maxim that an orderly society must be governed by established principles and known codes that are applied uniformly and fairly to all of its members.

The law isn't justice. It's a very imperfect mechanism. If you press exactly the right buttons and are also lucky, justice may show up in the answer. A mechanism is all the law was ever intended to be.

—Raymond Chandler[i]

jurisprudence

The philosophy of law. Also, the science and study of the law.

WEB
Extra

As the loss of political office suffered by former Connecticut Governor John G. Rowland and U.S. Representatives Bill Janklow (R-South Dakota), James Traficant (D-Ohio), and Robert W. Ney (R-Ohio) demonstrates, the *rule of law* means that no one is above the law—not even those who make it. Traficant (bottom left) was expelled from Congress in 2002 following his conviction on a number of federal crimes, including bribery, tax evasion, and racketeering. He is currently serving eight years in federal prison. Janklow (top right) was convicted of manslaughter in 2003 after he was involved in a traffic accident that killed a motorcyclist. A former four-term South Dakota governor, Janklow sped through a stop sign, causing the accident. He was forced to resign from Congress and was sentenced to serve 100 days in jail. Rowland (top left) entered federal prison in 2005 following a corruption conviction. Ney (bottom right), pleaded guilty in 2006 to influence peddling and corruption charges and entered federal prison in 2007. How would you explain the *rule of law* to someone who is unfamiliar with it?

Bob Child/AP Wide World Photos; Doug Dreyer/AP Wide World Photos; Summit County Jail/Getty Images, Inc.—Liaison; and Haraz N. Ghanbari/AP Wide World Photos

Types of Law

Criminal and civil law are the best-known types of modern law. However, scholars and philosophers have drawn numerous distinctions between categories of law which rest on the source, intent, and application of the law. Laws in modern societies can be usefully described in terms of the following groups:

- Criminal law
- Civil law
- Administrative law
- Case law
- Procedural law

This typology is helpful in understanding and thinking about the law. We will now discuss each type of law in some detail.

Criminal Law

Fundamental to the concept of **criminal law** is the assumption that criminal acts injure not just individuals, but society as a whole. Hence, we can define *criminal law* as the body of rules and regulations that define and specify the nature of, and punishments for, offenses of a public nature or for wrongs committed against the state or society. Criminal law is also called *penal law*.

Public order is compromised whenever a criminal act occurs. In old England, from which much of American legal tradition stems, offenders were said to have violated the "king's peace" when they committed a crime. They not only offended their victims but also disrupted the peaceful order established under the rule of the monarch. It is for this reason that in criminal cases the state, as the injured party, begins the official process of bringing the offender to justice. Even if the victim is dead and has no one to speak on his behalf, the agencies of justice will investigate the crime and file charges against the offender. Because crimes injure the fabric of society, the state—not the individual victim—is the plaintiff in criminal proceedings. Criminal court cases reflect this fact by being cited as follows: *State of New York* v. *Smith* (where state law has been violated) or *U.S.* v. *Smith* (where the federal government is the injured party).

Those found guilty of violating the criminal law are punished. Punishment is philosophically justified by the fact that the criminal *intended* the harm and is responsible for it. Punishment serves a variety of purposes, which we will discuss in a later chapter. When punishment is imposed in a criminal case, however, it is for one basic reason: to express society's fundamental displeasure with the offensive behavior and to hold the offender accountable for it. Punishment serves a variety of other purposes too, which we will discuss in Chapter 11. Criminal law, which is built on constitutional principles and which operates within an established set of procedures applicable to the criminal justice system, is composed of both statutory and case law.

Written law is of two types: substantive and procedural. **Substantive criminal law** describes what constitutes particular crimes, such as murder, rape, robbery, and assault, and specifies the appropriate punishment for each particular offense. Substantive criminal law deals directly with specifying the nature of, and appropriate punishment for, particular offenses. For example, every state in our country has laws against murder, rape, robbery, and assault. Differences in the law among these various jurisdictions can be studied in detail because each offense and the punishments associated with it are available in written form in the substantive criminal law. **Procedural laws**, on the other hand, specify acceptable methods for dealing with violations of substantive laws, especially within the context of a judicial setting. Learn more about the evolution of American criminal law at Library Extra 4–2 at cjtoday.com. Online criminal law journals may be accessed via Library Extras 4–3 and 4–4.

Civil Law

Civil law governs relationships between and among people, businesses and other organizations, and agencies of government. In contrast to the criminal law, whose violation is an offense against the state or against the nation, civil law governs relationships between parties. Civil law contains rules for contracts, divorce, child support and custody, the creation of wills, property transfers, negligence, libel, unfair practices in hiring, the manufacture and sale of consumer goods with hidden hazards for the user, and many other contractual and social obligations. When the civil law is violated, a civil suit may follow.

Typically, civil suits seek not punishment, but compensation, usually in the form of property or monetary damages. They may also be filed to achieve an injunction, or a kind of judicial cease-and-desist order. A violation of the civil law is not a crime. It may be a contract violation or a **tort**—a wrongful act, damage, or injury not involving a breach of contract. A tort involving, say, an automobile accident may give rise to civil liability under which the injured party may sue the person or entity that caused the injury and ask that the offending party be ordered to pay damages directly to the injured party. Because a tort is a personal wrong and not a crime, it is left to the aggrieved individual to set the machinery of the court in motion—that is, to bring a suit.

In 2005, for example, attorney Jack Thompson filed a $600 million lawsuit against video game maker Take-Two Interactive Software, claiming that the company's products, *Grand Theft Auto III* and *Grand Theft Auto: Vice City*, led to the shooting deaths of two Alabama police officers and

criminal law

The body of rules and regulations that define and specify the nature of and punishments for offenses of a public nature or for wrongs committed against the state or society. Also called *penal law*.

substantive criminal law

The part of the law that defines crimes and specifies punishments.

procedural law

The part of the law that specifies the methods to be used in enforcing substantive law.

LIBRARY
Extra
■ ■ ■ ■

civil law

The branch of modern law that governs relationships between parties.

tort

A wrongful act, damage, or injury not involving a breach of contract. Also, a private or civil wrong or injury.

FREEDOM OR SAFETY?
You Decide

Should Violent Speech Be Free Speech?

In 2005, a state jury in Alexandria, Virginia, convicted 42-year-old Muslim scholar Ali al-Timimi of a number of offenses, including the crime of incitement, conspiring to carry firearms and explosives, and soliciting others to make war against the United States. The U.S.-born Islamic spiritual adviser had spoken frequently at the Center for Islamic Information and Education—also known as the Dar al Arqam Islamic Center—in Falls Church, Virginia. Prosecutors told jurors that al-Timimi had verbally encouraged his followers to train with terrorist organizations and to engage in violent Jihad, or holy war, against America and its allies. Al-Timimi, who lived much of his life in the Washington, D.C., area, earned a doctorate in computational biology from George Mason University and is the author of at least twelve articles published in scientific journals, most dealing with how to use computers to analyze genes found in various kinds of cancer. As a teenager, Al-Timimi had spent two years in Saudi Arabia with his family, where he became interested in Islam.

Following conviction, al-Timimi was sentenced to life in prison without the possibility of parole, plus 70 years—a sentence meant to guarantee that he would never leave prison. He is currently appealing, and there is some chance that his case will be sent back for retrial based on claims that the National Security Agency illegally gathered information about his activities.

The al-Timimi case raises a number of interesting issues—among them the issue of when violent speech crosses the line from free expression into criminal advocacy.

The First Amendment to the U.S. Constitution guarantees the right to free speech. It is a fundamental guarantee of our democratic way of life. So, for example, the speech of those who advocate a new form of government in the United States is protected, even though their ideas may appear anti-American and ill considered.

In the 1957 case of *Roth* v. *United States*, the U.S. Supreme Court held that "the protection given speech and press was fashioned to assure unfettered interchange of ideas for the bringing about of political and social changes desired by the people."

It is important to remember, however, that constitutional rights are not without limit—that is, they have varying applicability under differing conditions. Some forms of speech are too dangerous to be allowed, even under our liberal rules.

Freedom of speech does not mean, for example, that you have a protected right to stand up in a crowded theater and yell "Fire!" That's because the panic that would follow such an exclamation would likely cause injuries and would put members of the public at risk of harm.

Hence, the courts have held that although freedom of speech is guaranteed by the Constitution, there are limits to it. (Shouting "Fire!" in a public park would likely not be considered an actionable offense.)

Similarly, saying, "The president deserves to die," horrific as it may sound, may be merely a matter of personal opinion. Anyone who says, "I'm going to kill the president," however, can wind up in jail because threatening the life of the president is a crime—as is the act of communicating threats of imminent violence in most jurisdictions.

Al-Timimi's mistake may have been the timing of his remarks, which were made to a public gathering in Virginia five days after the September 11, 2001, attacks. In his speech, al-Timimi called for a "holy war" and "violent Jihad" against the West. He was later quoted by converts with whom he met as referring to American forces in Afghanistan as "legitimate targets."

Critics of al-Timimi's conviction point to a seeming double standard under which people can be arrested for unpopular speech, but not for popular speech—regardless of the degree of violence it implies. They note, for example, that conservative columnist Ann Coulter has suggested in writing that "we should invade (Muslim) countries, kill their leaders and convert them to Christianity," but she was never arrested for what she said. More recently, Oklahoma Senator Tom Coburn's chief of staff, upset over decisions returned by the federal bench, proclaimed, "I don't want to impeach judges. I want to impale them!" Should he have been arrested for threatening the lives of judges?

The al-Timimi conviction may have a lot to say about the nature of a free society and only very little to say about al-Timimi himself, or what it was that he said.

YOU DECIDE

Should al-Timimi's advocacy of violence be unlawful? Why or why not? Might we have more to fear from the suppression of speech (even speech like al-Timimi's) than from its free expression? If so, how?

References: "Virginia Man Convicted of Urging War on U.S.," *USA Today*, April 27, 2005, p. 3A; Jonathan Turley, "When Is Violent Speech Still Free Speech?" *USA Today*, May 3, 2005, p. 13A; and Eric Lichtblau, "Administration Continues Eavesdropping Defense," *New York Times*, January 24, 2006.

---

a police dispatcher in 2003.[10] The lawsuit, which also named retailers Wal-Mart and Gamestop, which sold the games, alleges that 17-year-old Devin Thompson was mirroring violent acts that he had learned from the software when he grabbed an officer's gun, started firing, and then stole a patrol car. Thompson was an avid player of the games, which depict police killings and other violent acts. He had originally been taken into custody by officers on suspicion of driving a stolen automobile. According to press reports, Thompson, who was charged with murder, told the authorities who captured him, "Life is a video game. You gotta die sometime."

Civil law is more concerned with assessing liability than it is with intent. Civil suits arising from automobile crashes, for example, do not allege that the driver intended to inflict bodily harm. Nor do they claim that it was the driver's intent to damage either vehicle. However, when someone is injured or when property damage occurs, even in an accident, civil procedures make it possible to gauge responsibility and to assign liability to one party or the other. The parties to a civil suit are referred to as the *plaintiff*, who seeks relief, and the *defendant*, against whom relief is sought. Civil suits are also sometimes brought by crime victims against those whose criminal intent is clear. Once the perpetrator of a crime has been convicted, his victim may decide to seek monetary compensation from him through our system of civil laws.

Administrative Law

Administrative law is the body of regulations that governments create to control the activities of industry, business, and individuals. Tax laws, health codes, restrictions on pollution and waste disposal, vehicle registration laws, and building codes are examples of administrative laws. Other administrative laws cover practices in the areas of customs (imports and exports), immigration, agriculture, product safety, and most areas of manufacturing.

Administrative agencies will sometimes arrange settlements that fall short of court action but that are considered binding on individuals or groups that have not lived up to the intent of federal or state regulations. Education, environmental protection, and discriminatory hiring practices are all areas in which such settlements have been employed.

For the most part, a breach of administrative law is not a crime. However, criminal law and administrative regulations may overlap. For instance, organized criminal activity is on the rise in the area of toxic waste disposal—an area covered by many administrative regulations—which has led to criminal prosecutions in several states. The intentional and systematic denial of civil rights in areas generally thought to be administrative in nature, such as hiring, employment, and job compensation, may also lead to criminal sanctions through the federal system of laws.

Case Law

Case law comes from judicial decisions and is also referred to as the law of **precedent**. It represents the accumulated wisdom of trial and appellate courts (those that hear appeals) in criminal, civil, and administrative law cases over the years. Once a court decision is rendered, it is written down. At the appellate level, the reasoning behind the decision is recorded as well. Under the law of precedent, this reasoning should then be taken into consideration by other courts in settling similar future cases.

precedent

A legal principle that ensures that previous judicial decisions are authoritatively considered and incorporated into future cases.

Appellate courts have considerable influence on new court decisions at the trial level. The court with the greatest influence, of course, is the U.S. Supreme Court. The precedents it establishes are incorporated as guidelines into the process of legal reasoning by which lower courts reach conclusions.

The principle of recognizing previous decisions as precedents to guide future deliberations, called **stare decisis**, forms the basis for our modern law of precedent. Lief H. Carter, professor of political science at Colorado College, has pointed out that precedent operates along two dimensions, which he calls the *vertical* and the *horizontal*.[11] A vertical rule requires that decisions made by a higher court be taken into consideration by lower courts in their deliberations. Under this rule, state appellate courts, for example, are expected to follow the spirit of decisions rendered by the state supreme court. The horizontal dimension means that courts on the same level should be consistent in their interpretation of the law. The U.S. Supreme Court, operating under the horizontal rule, for example, should not be expected to change its ruling in cases similar to those it has already decided. *Stare decisis* makes for predictability in the law. Defendants walking into a modern courtroom are represented by lawyers who are trained in legal precedents as well as procedure. As a consequence, defendants have a good idea of what to expect about the manner in which their trial will proceed.

stare decisis

A legal principle that requires that, in subsequent cases on similar issues of law and fact, courts be bound by their own earlier decisions and by those of higher courts having jurisdiction over them. The term literally means "standing by decided matters."

Procedural Law

Procedural law is another kind of statutory law. It is a body of rules that determine the proceedings by which legal rights are enforced. The law of criminal procedure regulates the gathering of evidence and the processing of offenders by the criminal justice system. General rules of evidence, search and seizure, procedures to be followed in an arrest, trial procedures, and other

CJ News

$1B Judgment against Spammers

A federal judge has awarded an Internet service provider more than $1 billion in what is believed to be the largest judgment ever against spammers.

Robert Kramer, whose company provides e-mail service for about 5,000 subscribers in eastern Iowa, filed suit against 300 spammers after his inbound mail servers received up to 10 million spam e-mails a day in 2000, according to court documents.

Kramer said he was called away almost daily to repair downed e-mail servers that should run months without interruption.

U.S. District Judge Charles Wolle filed default judgments Friday against three of the defendants under the federal Racketeer Influenced and Corrupt Organizations Act (RICO) and the Iowa Ongoing Criminal Conduct Act.

AMP Dollar Savings of Mesa, Ariz., was ordered to pay $720 million, and Cash Link Systems of Miami was ordered to pay $360 million. The third company, Florida-based TEI Marketing Group, was ordered to pay $140,000.

"It's definitely a victory for all of us that open up our e-mail and find lewd and malicious and fraudulent e-mail in our boxes every day," Kramer told the *Quad-City Times* after the ruling. Kramer's attorney, Kelly Wallace, said he is unlikely to ever collect the judgment, which was made possible by an Iowa law that allows plaintiffs to claim damages of $10 per spam message. The judgments were then tripled under RICO.

"We hope to recover at least his costs," Wallace said.

Kramer's lawsuit was originally filed in October 2003 against 300 defendants then known only as John Does. There were no telephone listings for the three companies in Arizona and Florida. Nobody replied to an e-mail sent Saturday to Cash Link Systems.

According to court documents, no attorneys for the defendants were present during a bench trial in November.

The lawsuit continues against other named defendants.

Kramer's problems are linked to a CD-ROM sold to spammers that is called Bulk Mailing 4 Dummies, which includes a guide for sending spam and a large number of mainly fictitious e-mail addresses for some of the largest Internet providers in the nation, the judgment states.

While most of the addresses were for large providers such as America Online, Microsoft Network, Hotmail and EarthLink,

Laura Betterly, president of Data Resource Consulting, right, speaking at the Federal Trade Commission's Spam Forum in Washington, D.C., on May 1, 2003. Also pictured (from left to right) are Al DiGuido, CEO of Bigfoot Interactive, Lisa Pollock Mann, senior director of messaging at Yahoo! Inc., and Chris Lewis, security architect at Nortel Networks. The three-day forum explored possible government and business responses to spam. Should spamming be a criminal offense?

Charles Dharapak/AP Wide World Photos

Kramer's company—CIS Internet Services in Clinton—somehow had 2.8 million addresses entered on the CD-ROM, Wallace said.

Laura Atkins, president of SpamCon Foundation, an anti-spamming organization based in Palo Alto, Calif., said she believed it was the largest judgment ever in an anti-spam lawsuit. "This is just incredible," she said. "I'm not aware of anything that's been over $100 million."

For the latest in crime and justice news, visit the Talk Justice news feed at http://www.crimenews.info.

Source: "Internet Service Provider Wins $1B Judgment against Spammers," Associated Press, © December 20, 2004 by the Associated Press. Reprinted by permission.

specified processes by which the justice system operates are all contained in procedural law. Each state has its own set of criminal procedure laws, as does the federal government. Florida's laws of criminal procedure, for example, specify that a police officer making an arrest by a warrant "shall inform the person to be arrested of the cause of arrest and that a warrant has been issued, except when the person flees or forcibly resists before the officer has an opportunity to inform the person, or when giving the information will imperil the arrest." Florida law goes on to say that "the officer need not have the warrant in his or her possession at the time of arrest but on request of the person arrested shall show it to the person as soon as practicable."[12]

It is important to recognize that procedural laws are intended to protect the rights of criminal suspects while establishing a clear-cut series of formal proceedings through which the substantive criminal law can be enforced. In short, laws of criminal procedure balance a suspect's rights against the state's interests in the speedy and efficient processing of criminal defendants. Florida's laws of criminal procedure are available online at Library Extra 4–5 at cjtoday.com. View the Federal Rules of Criminal Procedure and the Federal Rules of Evidence at Library Extras 4–6 and 4–7.

LIBRARY
Extra
▪▪▪▪

General Categories of Crime

Violations of the *criminal* law can be of many different types and can vary in severity. Five categories of violations will be discussed in the pages that follow:

- Felonies
- Misdemeanors
- Offenses
- Treason and espionage
- Inchoate offenses

Felonies

Felonies are serious crimes; they include murder, rape, aggravated assault, robbery, burglary, and arson. Today, many felons receive prison sentences, although the range of potential penalties includes everything from probation and a fine to capital punishment in many jurisdictions. Under common law, felons could be sentenced to death, could have their property confiscated, or both. Following common law tradition, people who are convicted of felonies today usually lose certain privileges. Some states, for example, make a felony conviction and incarceration grounds for uncontested divorce. Others prohibit offenders from running for public office or owning a firearm and exclude them from some professions, such as medicine, law, and police work.

The federal government and many states have moved to a scheme of classifying the seriousness of felonies, using a number or letter designation. For purposes of criminal sentencing, for example, the federal system assigns a score of 43 to first-degree murder, while the crime of theft is only rated a "base offense level" of 4.[13] Attendant circumstances and the criminal history of the offender are also taken into consideration in sentencing decisions.

Because of differences among the states, a crime classified as a felony in one part of the country may be a misdemeanor in another, while in still other areas it may not be a crime at all! This is especially true of some drug-law violations and of certain other public-order offenses, such as homosexuality, prostitution, and gambling, which in a number of jurisdictions are perfectly legal, although such activity may still be subject to certain administrative regulations.

felony

A criminal offense punishable by death or by incarceration in a prison facility for at least one year.

Misdemeanors

Misdemeanors are relatively minor crimes, consisting of offenses such as petty theft, which is the theft of items of little worth; simple assault, in which the victim suffers no serious injury and in which none was intended; breaking and entering; the possession of burglary tools; disorderly conduct; disturbing the peace; filing a false crime report; and writing bad checks, although the amount for which the check is written may determine the classification of this offense.

In general, misdemeanors are any crime punishable by a year or less in prison. In fact, most misdemeanants receive suspended sentences involving a fine and supervised probation. If an "active sentence" is given for a misdemeanor violation of the law, it may involve time spent in a local jail, perhaps on weekends, rather than imprisonment in a long-term confinement facility. Alternatively, some misdemeanants are sentenced to perform community-service activities, such as washing school buses, painting local government buildings, and cleaning parks and other public areas.

Normally, a police officer cannot arrest a person for a misdemeanor unless the crime was committed in the officer's presence. If this requirement is not met, the officer must seek an arrest warrant from a magistrate or other judicial officer. Once a warrant has been issued, the officer may then proceed with the arrest.

misdemeanor

An offense punishable by incarceration, usually in a local confinement facility, for a period whose upper limit is prescribed by statute in a given jurisdiction, typically one year or less.

Offenses

offense

A violation of the criminal law. Also, in some jurisdictions, a minor crime, such as jaywalking, that is sometimes described as *ticketable.*

A third category of crime is the **offense**. Although, strictly speaking, all violations of the criminal law can be called *criminal offenses*, the term *offense* is sometimes used specifically to refer to minor violations of the law that are less serious than misdemeanors. When the term is used in that sense, it refers to such things as jaywalking, spitting on the sidewalk, littering, and committing certain traffic violations, including the failure to wear a seat belt. Another word used to describe such minor law violations is **infraction**. People committing infractions are typically ticketed and released, usually on a promise to appear later in court. Court appearances may often be waived through payment of a small fine that can be mailed.

infraction

A minor violation of state statute or local ordinance punishable by a fine or other penalty or by a specified, usually limited, term of incarceration.

Treason and Espionage

Felonies, misdemeanors, offenses, and the people who commit them constitute the daily work of the justice system. However, special categories of crime do exist and should be recognized. They include treason and espionage, two crimes that are often regarded as the most serious of felonies. **Treason** has been defined as "a U.S. citizen's actions to help a foreign government overthrow, make war against, or seriously injure the United States."[14] In addition to being a federal offense, treason is also a crime under the laws of most states. Hence, treason can be more generally defined as the attempt to overthrow the government of the society of which one is a member. The legislatures of some states, like California, have defined the crime of treason; in other states, the crime is defined in the state constitution. Florida's constitution, for example, which mirrors wording in the U.S. Constitution, says, "Treason against the state shall consist only in levying war against it, adhering to its enemies, or giving them aid and comfort, and no person shall be convicted of treason except on the testimony of two witnesses to the same overt act or on confession in open court."[15]

treason

A U.S. citizen's actions to help a foreign government overthrow, make war against, or seriously injure the United States.[ii] Also, the attempt to overthrow the government of the society of which one is a member.

Espionage, an offense akin to treason, but which can be committed by noncitizens, is the "gathering, transmitting, or losing" of information related to the national defense in such a manner that the information becomes available to enemies of the United States and may be used to their advantage.[16] In 1999, for example, one of the most significant espionage cases ever came to light. It involved the theft of highly classified American nuclear weapons secrets by spies working for the People's Republic of China. Over at least three decades, beginning in the 1960s, Chinese spies apparently stole enough weapons-related information to advance China's nuclear weapons program into the modern era. Were it not for the missile and bomb information gathered by the spies, congressional officials said, China's nuclear weapons technology might still be where America's was in the 1950s. See Web Extra 4–2 and Library Extra 4–8 at cjtoday.com for additional information on this very serious incident.

espionage

The "gathering, transmitting, or losing"[iii] of information related to the national defense in such a manner that the information becomes available to enemies of the United States and may be used to their advantage.

WEB
Extra
■ ■ ■ ■

LIBRARY
Extra
■ ■ ■ ■

Self-confessed FBI spy Robert Hanssen being arraigned before U.S. Magistrate Judge Theresa Buchanan in 2001. From left are Assistant U.S. Attorney Randy Bellows, defense attorney Plato Cacheris, Robert Hanssen, and defense attorney Preston Burton. What is the difference between treason and espionage?

AP Wide World Photos

Another example of espionage is the crime committed by former FBI agent Robert Hanssen. In July 2001, he pleaded guilty in U.S. District Court in Alexandria, Virginia, to 15 counts of espionage and conspiracy against the United States.[17] Hanssen admitted to having passed U.S. secrets to Moscow from about 1979 until 2001, when undercover investigators caught him leaving a package for his Russian handlers under a wooden footbridge in a Virginia park. The 25-year agency veteran had accepted more than $1.4 million in cash and diamonds from the Russians in return for disclosing secret and highly sensitive information, including U.S. nuclear warfare plans, advanced eavesdropping technology, and the identities of U.S. spies working overseas. Government officials feared that the information Hanssen provided had resulted in the deaths of a number of U.S. agents working in Russia. Prosecutors described the damage done to national security by Hanssen's spying as extremely grave. In return for his full cooperation in assessing the damage he had caused, Hanssen was spared the death penalty. Instead, he was sentenced to life in prison without possibility of parole. Learn more about Robert Hanssen and the crimes he committed at **Web Extra 4–3** at cjtoday.com.

Yet a third contemporary example of espionage was committed by a former Air Force intelligence analyst. In March 2003, Brian P. Regan was convicted of trying to sell classified documents to prewar Iraq and China.[18] Prior to sentencing, Regan made a deal with prosecutors to accept a sentence of life in prison in exchange for an agreement not to prosecute his wife, whom authorities claimed obstructed justice to help her husband. Prosecutors, who parlayed the impending war with Iraq into a background that emphasized the seriousness of the charges against Regan, had originally sought the death penalty.

> *One has not only a legal but a moral responsibility to obey just laws. Conversely, one has a moral responsibility to disobey unjust laws.*
>
> —*Martin Luther King, Jr.[iv]*

WEB
Extra
▪▪▪▪

Inchoate Offenses

Another special category of crime is called *inchoate.* The word *inchoate* means "incomplete or partial," and **inchoate offenses** are those that have not been fully carried out. Conspiracies are an example. When a person conspires to commit a crime, any action undertaken in furtherance of the conspiracy is generally regarded as a sufficient basis for arrest and prosecution. For instance, a woman who intends to kill her husband may make a phone call to find a hit man to carry out her plan. The call itself is evidence of her intent and can result in her imprisonment for conspiracy to commit murder.

Another type of inchoate offense is the attempt to commit a crime, which occurs when an offender is unable to complete a crime. For example, homeowners may arrive just as a burglar is beginning to enter their residence, causing the burglar to drop his tools and run. In most jurisdictions, this frustrated burglar can be arrested and charged with attempted burglary.

inchoate offense

An offense not yet completed. Also, an offense that consists of an action or conduct that is a step toward the intended commission of another offense.

General Features of Crime

From the perspective of Western jurisprudence, all crimes can be said to share certain features, and the notion of crime itself can be said to rest on such general principles. Taken together, these features, which are described in this section, make up the legal essence of the concept of crime. Conventional legal wisdom holds that the essence of crime consists of three conjoined elements: (1) the criminal act, which in legal parlance is termed the *actus reus*; (2) a culpable mental state, or *mens rea*; and (3) a concurrence of the two. Hence, as we shall see in the following pages, the essence of criminal conduct consists of a concurrence of a criminal act with a culpable mental state.

The Criminal Act (*Actus Reus*)

A necessary first feature of any crime is some act in violation of the law. Such an act is termed the **actus reus** of a crime. The term means "guilty act." Generally, a person must commit some voluntary act before he is subject to criminal sanctions. To *be something* is not a crime; to *do something* may be. For example, someone who is caught using drugs can be arrested, while someone who simply admits that he or she is a drug user (perhaps on a TV talk show) cannot be arrested on that basis. Police who hear the drug user's admission might begin gathering evidence to prove some specific law violation in that person's past, or perhaps they might watch that individual for future behavior in violation of the law. A subsequent arrest would then be based on a specific action in violation of the law pertaining to controlled substances.

Vagrancy laws, popular in the early part of the twentieth century, have generally been invalidated by the courts because they did not specify what act violated the law. In fact, the less

actus reus

An act in violation of the law. Also, a guilty act.

> *Justice is incidental to law and order.*
>
> —*J. Edgar Hoover[v]*

a person did, the more vagrant he or she was. An omission to act, however, may be criminal where the person in question is required by law to do something. Child-neglect laws, for example, focus on parents and child guardians who do not live up to their responsibility to care for their children.

Threatening to act can be a criminal offense. For example, threatening to kill someone can result in an arrest for the offense of communicating threats. Such threats against the president of the United States are taken seriously by the Secret Service, and individuals are arrested for boasting about planned violence directed at the president. Attempted criminal activity is also illegal. An attempt to murder or rape, for example, is a serious crime, even when the planned act is not accomplished.

Conspiracies, mentioned earlier in this chapter, are another criminal act. When a conspiracy unfolds, the ultimate act that it aims to bring about does not have to occur for the parties to the conspiracy to be arrested. When people plan to bomb a public building, for example, they can be legally stopped before the bombing. As soon as they take steps to "further" their plan, they have met the requirement for an act. Buying explosives, telephoning one another, and drawing plans of the building may all be actions in "furtherance of the conspiracy." But not all conspiracy statutes require actions in furtherance of the "target crime" before an arrest can be made. Technically speaking, crimes of conspiracy can be seen as entirely distinct from the target crimes that the conspirators are contemplating. For example, in 1994 the U.S. Supreme Court upheld the drug-related conviction of Reshat Shabani when it ruled that in the case of certain antidrug laws,[19] "it is presumed that Congress intended to adopt the common law definition of conspiracy, which does not make the doing of any act other than the act of conspiring a condition of liability."[20] Hence, according to the Court, "The criminal agreement itself," even in the absence of actions directed toward realizing the target crime, can be grounds for arrest and prosecution.

Similar to conspiracy statutes are many newly enacted antistalking laws, which are intended to prevent harassment and intimidation, even when no physical harm occurs. Antistalking statutes, however, still face the constitutional hurdle of attempting to prevent people not otherwise involved in criminal activity from walking and standing where they wish and from speaking freely. Ultimately, the U.S. Supreme Court will probably have to decide the legitimacy of such statutes.

A Guilty Mind (*Mens Rea*)

mens rea

The state of mind that accompanies a criminal act. Also, a guilty mind.

Mens rea is the second general component of crime. The term, which literally means "guilty mind," refers to the defendant's specific mental state at the time the behavior in question occurred. The importance of *mens rea* as a component of crime cannot be overemphasized. It can be seen in the fact that some courts have held that "[a]ll crime exists primarily in the mind."[21] The extent to which a person can be held criminally responsible for his or her actions generally depends on the nature of the mental state under which he or she was laboring at the time of the offense.

Four levels, or types, of *mens rea* can be distinguished: (1) purposeful (or intentional), (2) knowing, (3) reckless, and (4) negligent. Purposeful or intentional action is that which is undertaken to achieve some goal. Sometimes the harm that results from intentional action may be unintended; however, this does not reduce criminal liability. The doctrine of *transferred intent*, for example, which operates in all U.S. jurisdictions, holds a person guilty of murder if he took aim and shot at an intended victim but missed, killing another person instead. The philosophical notion behind the concept of transferred intent is that the killer's intent to kill, which existed at the time of the crime, transferred from the intended victim to the person who was struck by the bullet and died.

Knowing behavior is action undertaken with awareness. A person who acts purposefully always acts knowingly, but a person may act in a knowingly criminal way but for a purpose other than criminal intent. For example, an airline captain who allows a flight attendant to transport cocaine aboard an airplane may do so to gain sexual favors from the attendant, but without the purpose of drug smuggling. Knowing behavior involves near certainty. In this scenario, if the airline captain allows the flight attendant to carry cocaine aboard the plane, it *will* be transported, and the pilot knows it. In another example, if an HIV-infected individual knowingly has unprotected sexual intercourse with another person, the partner *will* be exposed to the virus.

reckless behavior

Activity that increases the risk of harm.

Reckless behavior is activity that increases the risk of harm. In contrast to knowing behavior, knowledge may be part of recklessness, but it exists more in the form of probability than certainty. As a practical example, reckless driving is a frequent charge in many jurisdictions; it is generally brought when a driver engages in risky activity that endangers others.

Nevertheless, *mens rea* is said to be present when a person should have known better, even if the person did not directly intend the consequences of his or her action. A person who acts negligently and thereby endangers others may be found guilty of **criminal negligence** when harm occurs, even though no negative consequences were intended. For example, a parent who leaves a 12-month-old child alone in the tub can be prosecuted for negligent homicide if the child drowns.[22] It should be emphasized, however, that negligence in and of itself is not a crime. Negligent conduct can be evidence of crime only when it falls below some acceptable standard of care. That standard is applied today in criminal courts through the fictional creation of a *reasonable person*. The question to be asked in a given case is whether a reasonable person, in the same situation, would have known better and acted differently from the defendant. The reasonable person criterion provides a yardstick for juries faced with thorny issues of guilt or innocence.

It is important to note that *mens rea*, even in the sense of intent, is not the same thing as motive. A **motive** refers to a person's reason for committing a crime. While evidence of motive may be admissible during a criminal trial to help prove a crime, motive itself is not an essential element of a crime. As a result, we cannot say that a bad or immoral motive makes an act a crime.

Mens rea is a tricky concept. Not only is it philosophically and legally complex, but a person's state of mind during the commission of an offense can rarely be known directly unless the person confesses. Hence, *mens rea* must generally be inferred from a person's actions and from all the circumstances surrounding those actions. Pure accident, however, which involves no recklessness or negligence, cannot serve as the basis for either criminal or civil liability. "Even a dog," the famous Supreme Court Justice Oliver Wendell Holmes once wrote, "distinguishes between being stumbled over and being kicked."[23]

STRICT LIABILITY AND *MENS REA*

A special category of crimes, called **strict liability** offenses, requires no culpable mental state and presents a significant exception to the principle that all crimes require a concurrence of *actus reus* and *mens rea*. Strict liability offenses, also called *absolute liability offenses*, make it a crime simply to *do* something, even if the offender has no intention of violating the law. Strict liability is philosophically based on the presumption that causing harm is in itself blameworthy, regardless of the actor's intent.

Routine traffic offenses are generally considered strict liability offenses. Driving 65 miles per hour in a 55-mph zone is a violation of the law, even though the driver may be listening to music, thinking, or simply going with the flow of traffic, entirely unaware that his or her vehicle is exceeding the posted speed limit. Statutory rape is another example of strict liability.[24] This crime generally occurs between two consenting individuals; it requires only that the offender have sexual intercourse with a person under the age of legal consent. Statutes describing the crime routinely avoid any mention of a culpable mental state. In many jurisdictions, it matters little whether the "perpetrator" knew the exact age of the "victim" or whether the "victim" lied about his or her age or had given consent, since statutory rape laws are "an attempt to prevent the sexual exploitation of persons deemed legally incapable of giving consent."[25]

Concurrence

The concurrence of an unlawful act and a culpable mental state provides the third basic component of crime. **Concurrence** requires that the act and the mental state occur together in order for a crime to take place. If one precedes the other, the requirements of the criminal law have not been met. A person may intend to kill a rival, for example. He drives to the intended victim's house, with his gun, fantasizing about how he will commit the murder. Just as he nears the victim's home, the victim crosses the street on the way to the grocery store. If the two accidentally collide and the intended victim dies, there has been no concurrence of act and intent.

Other Features of Crime

Some scholars contend that the three features of crime that we have just outlined—*actus reus*, *mens rea*, and concurrence—are sufficient to constitute the essence of the legal concept of crime. Other scholars, however, see modern Western law as more complex. They argue that recognition of five additional principles is necessary to fully appreciate contemporary understandings of crime. These five principles are (1) causation, (2) a resulting harm, (3) the principle of legality, (4) the principle of punishment, and (5) necessary attendant circumstances. We will now discuss each of these additional features in turn.

criminal negligence

Behavior in which a person fails to reasonably perceive substantial and unjustifiable risks of dangerous consequences.

motive

A person's reason for committing a crime.

strict liability

Liability without fault or intention. Strict liability offenses do not require *mens rea*.

concurrence

The coexistence of (1) an act in violation of the law and (2) a culpable mental state.

CAUSATION

Causation refers to the fact that the concurrence of a guilty mind and a criminal act may cause harm. While some statutes criminalize only conduct, others require that the offender *cause* a particular result before criminal liability can be incurred. Sometimes, however, a causal link is unclear. For example, let's consider a case of assault with a deadly weapon with intent to kill. A person shoots another, and the victim is seriously injured but is not immediately killed. The victim, who remains in the hospital, survives for more than a year. The victim's death occurs due to a blood clot that forms from lack of activity. In such a case, it is likely that defense attorneys will argue that the defendant did not cause the death; rather, the death occurred because of disease. If a jury agrees with the defense's claim, the shooter may go free or be found guilty of a lesser charge, such as assault.

legal cause

A legally recognizable cause. A legal cause must be demonstrated in court in order to hold an individual criminally liable for causing harm.

To clarify the issue of causation, the American Law Institute suggests use of the term **legal cause** to emphasize the notion of a legally recognizable cause and to preclude any assumption that such a cause must be close in time and space to the result it produces. Legal causes can be distinguished from those causes that may have produced the result in question but do not provide the basis for a criminal prosecution because they are too complex, too indistinguishable from other causes, not knowable, or not provable in a court of law.

HARM

A harm occurs in any crime, although not all harms are crimes. When a person is murdered or raped, harm can be clearly identified. Some crimes, however, can be said to be *victimless.* Perpetrators maintain that in committing such crimes they harm no one but themselves. Rather, they say, the crime is pleasurable. Prostitution, gambling, and drug use are commonly classified as "victimless." What these offenders fail to recognize, say legal theorists, is the social harm caused by their behavior. In areas afflicted with chronic prostitution, drug use, and illegal gambling, property values fall, family life disintegrates, and other, more traditional crimes increase as money is sought to support the "victimless" activities. Law-abiding citizens abandon the area.

In a criminal prosecution, however, it is rarely necessary to prove harm as a separate element of a crime since it is subsumed under the notion of a guilty act. In the crime of murder, for example, the "killing of a human being" brings about a harm but is, properly speaking, an act. When committed with the requisite *mens rea*, it becomes a crime. A similar type of reasoning applies to the criminalization of *attempts* that cause no harm. A scenario commonly raised to illustrate this dilemma is one in which attackers throw rocks at a blind person, but because of bad aim, the rocks hit no one, and the intended target remains unaware that anyone is trying to harm him. In such a case, should throwing rocks provide a basis for criminal liability? As one authority on the subject observes, "Criticism of the principle of harm has . . . been based on the view that the harm actually caused may be a matter of sheer accident and that the rational thing to do is to base the punishment on the *mens rea*, and the action, disregarding any actual harm or lack of harm or its degree."[26] This observation also shows why we have said that the essence of crime consists only of three things: (1) *actus reus*, (2) *mens rea*, and (3) the concurrence of an illegal act and a culpable mental state.

LEGALITY

The principle of legality is concerned with the fact that a behavior cannot be criminal if no law exists that defines it as such. For example, as long as you are of drinking age, it is all right to drink beer because there is no statute on the books prohibiting it. During Prohibition, of course, the situation was quite different. (In fact, some parts of the United States are still "dry," and the purchase or public consumption of alcohol can be a law violation regardless of age.) The principle of legality also includes the notion that **ex post facto** laws are not binding, which means that a law cannot be created tomorrow that will hold a person legally responsible for something she does today. Rather, laws are binding only from the date of their creation or from some future date at which they are specified as taking effect.[27]

ex post facto

Latin for "after the fact." The Constitution prohibits the enactment of *ex post facto* laws, which make acts committed before the laws in question were passed punishable as crimes.

PUNISHMENT

The principle of punishment holds that no crime can be said to occur where punishment has not been specified in the law. Larceny, for example, would not be a crime if the law simply said, "It is illegal to steal." Punishment for the crime must be specified so that if a person is found guilty of violating the law, sanctions can be lawfully imposed.

NECESSARY ATTENDANT CIRCUMSTANCES

Finally, statutes defining some crimes specify that additional elements, called **attendant circumstances**, must be present for a conviction to be obtained. Generally speaking, attendant circumstances are the "facts surrounding an event"[28] and include such things as time and place. Attendant circumstances that are specified by law as necessary elements of an offense are sometimes called *necessary attendant circumstances*, indicating that the existence of such circumstances is necessary, along with the other elements included in the relevant statute, for a crime to have been committed. Florida law, for example, makes it a crime to "[k]nowingly commit any lewd or lascivious act in the presence of any child under the age of 16 years."[29] In this case, the behavior in question might not be a crime if committed in the presence of someone who is older than 16.

Sometimes attendant circumstances increase the degree, or level of seriousness, of an offense. Under Texas law, for example, the crime of burglary has two degrees, defined by state law as follows: Burglary is a "(1) state jail felony if committed in a building other than a habitation; or (2) felony of the second degree [that is, a more serious crime] if committed in a habitation." Hence, the degree of the offense of burglary depends on the nature of the place burglarized.

Circumstances surrounding a crime can also be classified as aggravating or mitigating and may, by law, increase or lessen the penalty that can be imposed on a convicted offender. Aggravating and mitigating circumstances are not elements of an offense, however, since they are primarily relevant at the sentencing stage of a criminal prosecution. They are discussed in Chapter 11.

attendant circumstances

The facts surrounding an event.

Elements of a Specific Criminal Offense

Now that we have identified the principles that constitute the *general* notion of crime, we can examine individual statutes to see what particular statutory **elements** constitute a *specific* crime. Written laws specify exactly what conditions are necessary for a person to be charged in a given instance of criminal activity, and they do so for every offense. Hence, elements of a crime are specific legal aspects of a criminal offense that the prosecution must prove to obtain a conviction. In almost every jurisdiction in the United States, for example, the crime of first-degree murder involves four quite distinct elements:

element (of a crime)

In a specific crime, one of the essential features of that crime, as specified by law or statute.

1. An unlawful killing
2. Of a human being
3. Intentionally
4. With planning (or "malice aforethought")

The elements of any specific crime are the statutory minimum without which that crime cannot be said to have occurred. Since statutes differ between jurisdictions, the specific elements of a particular crime may vary. To convict a defendant of a particular crime, prosecutors must prove to a judge or jury that all of the required statutory elements are present[30] and that the accused was responsible for producing them. If even one element of an offense cannot be established beyond a reasonable doubt, criminal liability will not have been demonstrated, and the defendant will be found not guilty.

The Example of Murder

Every statutory element of a crime serves a purpose. As mentioned, the crime of first-degree murder includes an *unlawful killing* as one of its required elements. Not all killings are unlawful. In war, for instance, human beings are killed. These killings are committed with planning and sometimes with "malice." They are certainly intentional. Yet killing in war is not unlawful as long as the belligerents wage war according to international conventions.

The second element of first-degree murder specifies that the killing must be *of a human being*. People kill all the time. They kill animals for meat, they hunt, and they practice euthanasia on aged and injured pets. Even if the killing of an animal is planned and involves malice (perhaps a vendetta against a neighborhood dog that overturns trash cans), it does not constitute first-degree murder. Such a killing, however, may violate statutes pertaining to cruelty to animals.

The third element of first-degree murder, *intentionality*, is the basis for the defense of accident. An unintentional or nonpurposeful killing is not first-degree murder, although it may violate some other statute.

CJ Careers

U.S. Secret Service Uniformed Division

Name: Kevin S. Simpson

Position: Deputy Chief/White House Branch, U.S. Secret Service Uniformed Division

City: Washington, D.C.

College Attended: 1 year from completing associate's degree in criminal justice, with future plans to attend George Mason University.

Year Hired: 1988

"The U.S. Secret Service is recognized throughout the world as an elite law enforcement agency. As a member of this organization, I can assure you that the U.S. Secret Service offers a wide range of career opportunities that are both rewarding and fulfilling."

TYPICAL POSITION

Uniformed Division officer. Secret service agents provide personal protection for the president, vice president, president-elect, vice president-elect, and their immediate families; former presidents, their spouses, and minor children until the age of 16; visiting heads of foreign states and their spouses; major presidential and vice presidential candidates and their spouses; and others designated by law. They also work to suppress the counterfeiting of U.S. currency and to curtail financial crimes relating to banks, financial access devices (including credit and debit cards), computers, telecommunications, and telemarketing. In addition, Uniformed Division officers provide protection for the White House complex, the vice president's residence, the Main Treasury Building and Annex, and foreign diplomatic missions and embassies in the Washington, D.C., area. They travel in support of government missions of the president, vice president, and foreign heads of state, and they are responsible for the enforcement of mandated protective responsibilities, as described under U.S. Code, Title 3, Section 202.

EMPLOYMENT REQUIREMENTS

An applicant for the position of Uniformed Division officer must (1) be a U.S. citizen, (2) be between the ages of 21 and 37 at the time of appointment, and (3) hold a bachelor's degree from an accredited college or university; or have three years of work experience in the criminal investigative or law enforcement fields that required knowledge and application of laws relating to criminal violations; or demonstrate an equivalent combination of education and related experience. Applicants must also be in excellent health and physical condition and have uncorrected vision no worse than 20/60 binocular, correctable to 20/20 in each eye. (Lasik, ALK, RK, and PRK corrective eye surgeries are acceptable provided that applicants pass specific visual tests one year after surgery. Applicants who have undergone Lasik surgery may have visual tests three months after the surgery.) In addition, applicants must pass the Treasury Enforcement Agent (TEA) written examination and must successfully complete a background investigation that includes in-depth interviews, drug screening, medical examination, and polygraph examination.

Most positions are available only in Washington, D.C.; reasonable moving expenses are paid for out-of-area hires. The position of Uniformed Division officer is designated as a key position in accordance with Department of Defense Directive 1200.7. As such, employees occupying this position will have their military status changed to either Retired Reserve or Standby Reserve or may be discharged, as appropriate.

OTHER REQUIREMENTS

The position of Uniformed Division officer entails the following additional requirements: (1) long work hours in undesirable conditions on short notice, (2) frequent travel, and (3) the carrying of a firearm while on duty and the maintenance of firearms proficiency. Newly appointed Uniformed Division officers receive approximately eight weeks of intensive training at the Federal Law Enforcement Training Center (FLETC) in Glynco, Georgia, or Artesia, New Mexico. Upon successful completion of training at FLETC, they receive approximately 11 weeks of specialized instruction at the James J. Rowley Training Center in Laurel, Maryland.

SALARY

Uniformed Division officers are usually hired at the GS-5, GS-7, or GS-9 level, depending on qualifications and/or education. Special agents receive law enforcement availability pay (LEAP) that entitles them to receive an additional 25% of their annual base pay. A one-time recruitment bonus, 25% of basic annual pay, is paid to newly hired special agents who are identified as having a foreign language skill and can test at the required level.

BENEFITS

Benefits include (1) 13 days of accumulated sick leave annually, (2) two and a half to five weeks of paid vacation and ten paid federal holidays each year, (3) federal health and life insurance, (4) a comprehensive retirement program, (5) opportunity to participate in a Flexible Spending Account Program, (6) uniforms and equipment, (7) credit for prior federal civilian and military service, and (8) the opportunity for overtime work.

CJ Careers (continued)

DIRECT INQUIRIES TO:

U.S. Secret Service
Recruitment and Hiring Coordination Center (RHCC)
245 Murray Dr.
Building 410
Washington, DC 20223
202-406-5830

E-mail web form: http://www.secretservice.gov/contact_personnel.shtml

Website: http://www.secretservice.gov

To learn about the Secret Service's special agent, special officer, administrative, technical, and professional support positions, call 202-406-5830, visit http://www.secretservice.gov, or contact the nearest U.S. Secret Service field office.

For more information on the rapidly expanding criminal justice careers area, read *Where the Jobs Are: Mission Critical Opportunities for America,* available on the Web at http://www.justicestudies.com/jobs.htm.

Finally, murder has not been committed unless *malice* is involved. There are different kinds of malice. Second-degree murder involves malice in the sense of hatred or spite. A more extreme form of malice is necessary for a finding of first-degree murder. Sometimes the phrase used to describe this requirement is *malice aforethought.* This extreme kind of malice can be demonstrated by showing that planning was involved in the commission of the murder. Often, first-degree murder is described as "lying in wait," a practice that shows that thought and planning went into the illegal killing.

A charge of second-degree murder in most jurisdictions would necessitate proving that a voluntary (or intentional) killing of a human being had taken place—although without the degree of malice necessary for it to be classified as first-degree murder. A crime of passion is an example of second-degree murder. In a crime of passion, the malice felt by the perpetrator is hatred or spite, which is considered less severe than malice aforethought. Manslaughter, or third-degree murder, another type of homicide, can be defined simply as the unlawful killing of a human being. Not only is malice lacking in third-degree murder cases, but so is intention; in fact, the killer may not have intended that *any* harm come to the victim.

Manslaughter charges are often brought when a defendant acted in a negligent or reckless manner. The 2001 sentencing of 21-year-old Nathan Hall to 90 days in jail on charges of criminally negligent homicide following a fatal collision with another ski racer on Vail Mountain near Eagle, Colorado, provides such an example.[31] Hall had been tried on a more serious charge of reckless manslaughter, which carries a sentence of up to 16 years under Colorado law, but the jury convicted him of the lesser charge.

Manslaughter statutes, however, frequently necessitate some degree of negligence on the part of the killer. When a wanton disregard for human life is present—legally defined as "gross negligence"—some jurisdictions permit the offender to be charged with a more serious count of murder.

The *Corpus Delicti* of a Crime

The term **corpus delicti** literally means "the body of the crime." One way to understand the concept of *corpus delicti* is to realize that a person cannot be tried for a crime unless it can first be shown that the offense has, in fact, occurred. In other words, to establish the *corpus delicti* of a crime, the state has to demonstrate that a criminal law has been violated and that someone violated it. This term is often confused with the statutory elements of a crime, and sometimes the concept is mistakenly thought to refer to the body of a murder victim or some other physical result of criminal activity. It actually means something quite different.

There are two aspects to the *corpus delicti* of an offense: (1) that a certain result has been produced and (2) that a person is criminally responsible for its production. For example, the crime of larceny requires proof that the property of another has been stolen—that is, unlawfully taken by someone whose intent it was to permanently deprive the owner of its possession.[32] Hence, evidence offered to prove the *corpus delicti* in a trial for larceny is insufficient if it fails to prove that any property was stolen or if property found in a defendant's possession cannot be identified as having been stolen. Similarly, "[i]n an arson case, the *corpus delicti* consists of (1) a burned building or other

corpus delicti

The facts that show that a crime has occurred. The term literally means "the body of the crime."

BLOG

See our Criminal Law blogs.

defense (to a criminal charge)

Evidence and arguments offered by a defendant and his or her attorney to show why the defendant should not be held liable for a criminal charge.

alibi

A statement or contention by an individual charged with a crime that he or she was so distant when the crime was committed, or so engaged in other provable activities, that his or her participation in the commission of that crime was impossible.

justification

A legal defense in which the defendant admits to committing the act in question but claims it was necessary in order to avoid some greater evil.

excuse

A legal defense in which the defendant claims that some personal condition or circumstance at the time of the act was such that he or she should not be held accountable under the criminal law.

procedural defense

A defense that claims that the defendant was in some significant way discriminated against in the justice process or that some important aspect of official procedure was not properly followed in the investigation or prosecution of the crime charged.

property, and (2) some criminal agency which caused the burning. . . . In other words, the *corpus delicti* includes not only the fact of burning, but it must also appear that the burning was by the willful act of some person, and not as a result of a natural or accidental cause."[33]

We should note that the identity of the perpetrator is not an element of the *corpus delicti* of an offense. Hence, the fact that a crime has occurred can be established without having any idea who committed it or even why it was committed. This principle was clearly enunciated in a Montana case when that state's supreme court held that "the identity of the perpetrator is not an element of the corpus delicti." In *State* v. *Kindle* (1924),[34] the court said, "We stated that '[i]n a prosecution for murder, proof of the *corpus delicti* does not necessarily carry with it the identity of the slain nor of the slayer.' . . . The essential elements of the *corpus delicti* are . . . establishing the death and the fact that the death was caused by a criminal agency, nothing more." *Black's Law Dictionary* puts it another way: "The *corpus delicti* [of a crime] is the fact of its having been actually committed."[35]

Types of Defenses to a Criminal Charge

When a person is charged with a crime, he or she typically offers some defense. A **defense** consists of evidence and arguments offered by the defendant to show why he or she should not be held liable for a criminal charge. Our legal system generally recognizes four broad categories of defenses: (1) **alibi**, (2) **justifications**, (3) **excuses**, and (4) **procedural defenses**. An alibi, if shown to be valid, means that the defendant could not have committed the crime in question because he or she was somewhere else (and generally with someone else) at the time of the crime. When a defendant offers a justification as a defense, he or she admits committing the act in question but claims that it was necessary to avoid some greater evil. A defendant who offers an excuse as a defense, on the other hand, claims that some personal condition or circumstance at the time of the act was such that he or she should not be held accountable under the criminal law. Procedural defenses make the claim that the defendant was in some significant way discriminated against in the justice process or that some important aspect of official procedure was not properly followed in the investigation or prosecution of the crime charged. Table 4–2 lists the types of defenses that fall into these four categories. Each will be discussed in the pages that follow.

Alibi

A reference book for criminal trial lawyers says, "Alibi is different from all of the other defenses . . . because . . . it is based upon the premise that the defendant is truly innocent."[36] The defense of alibi

TABLE 4–2 **Types of Defenses**	
Alibi	
A claim of alibi	
Justifications	
Self-defense	Necessity
Defense of others	Consent
Defense of home and property	Resisting unlawful arrest
Excuses	
Duress	Provocation
Age	Insanity
Mistake	Diminished capacity
Involuntary intoxication	Mental incompetence
Unconsciousness	
Procedural Defenses	
Entrapment	Denial of a speedy trial
Double jeopardy	Prosecutorial misconduct
Collateral estoppel	Police fraud
Selective prosecution	

denies that the defendant committed the act in question. All of the other defenses we are about to discuss grant that the defendant committed the act, but they deny that he or she should be held criminally responsible. While justifications and excuses may produce findings of "not guilty," the defense of alibi claims outright innocence.

Alibi is best supported by witnesses and documentation. A person charged with a crime can use the defense of alibi to show that he or she was not present at the scene when the crime was alleged to have occurred. Hotel receipts, eyewitness identification, and participation in social events have all been used to prove alibis.

Justifications

As defenses, justifications claim a kind of moral high ground. Justifications may be offered by people who find themselves forced to choose between "two evils." Generally speaking, conduct that a person believes is necessary to avoid harm to himself or to another is justifiable if the harm he is trying to avoid is greater than the harm the law defining the offense seeks to avoid. For example, a firefighter might set a controlled fire to create a firebreak to head off a conflagration threatening a community. While intentionally setting a fire might constitute arson, destroying property to save a town by creating a firebreak may be justifiable behavior in the eyes of the community and in the eyes of the law. Included under the broad category of justifications are (1) self-defense, (2) defense of others, (3) defense of home and property, (4) necessity, (5) consent, and (6) resisting unlawful arrest.

SELF-DEFENSE

Self-defense is probably the best known of the justifications. This defense strategy makes the claim that it was necessary to inflict harm on another to ensure one's own safety in the face of near-certain injury or death. A person who harms an attacker can generally use this defense. However, the courts have held that where a "path of retreat" exists for a person being attacked, it should be taken. In other words, the safest use of self-defense is only when cornered, with no path of escape.

The amount of defensive force used must be proportional to the amount of force or the perceived degree of threat that one is seeking to defend against. Hence, **reasonable force** is the degree of force that is appropriate in a given situation and that is not excessive. Reasonable force can also be thought of as the minimum degree of force necessary to protect oneself, one's property, a third party, or the property of another in the face of a substantial threat. Deadly force, the highest degree of force, is considered reasonable only when used to counter an immediate threat of death or great bodily harm. Deadly force cannot be used against nondeadly force.

Force, as the term is used within the context of self-defense, means physical force and does not extend to emotional, psychological, economic, psychic, or other forms of coercion. A person who turns the tables on a robber and assaults him during a robbery attempt, for example, may be able to claim self-defense, but a businessperson who physically assaults a financial rival to prevent a hostile takeover of her company will have no such recourse.

Self-defense has been claimed in killings of abusive spouses. A jury is likely to accept as justified a killing that occurs while the physical abuse is in progress, especially where a history of such abuse can be shown. On the other hand, wives who suffer repeated abuse but coldly plan the killing of their husbands have not fared well in court.

DEFENSE OF OTHERS

The use of force to defend oneself has generally been extended to permit the use of reasonable force to defend others who are or who appear to be in imminent danger. The defense of others, sometimes called *defense of a third person*, is circumscribed in some jurisdictions by the **alter ego rule**. The alter ego rule holds that a person can only defend a third party under circumstances and only to the degree that the third party could act. In other words, a person who aids another whom he sees being attacked may become criminally liable if that person initiated the attack or if the assault is a lawful one—for example, an assault made by a law enforcement officer conducting a lawful arrest of a person who is resisting. A few jurisdictions, however, do not recognize the alter ego rule and allow a person to act in defense of another if the actor reasonably believes that his or her intervention is immediately necessary to protect the third person.

Defense of others cannot be claimed by an individual who joins an illegal fight merely to assist a friend or family member. Likewise, one who intentionally aids an offender in an assault, even though the tables have turned and the offender is losing the battle, cannot claim defense of others. Under the law, defense of a third person always requires that the defender be free from

self-defense

The protection of oneself or of one's property from unlawful injury or from the immediate risk of unlawful injury. Also, the justification that the person who committed an act that would otherwise constitute an offense reasonably believed that the act was necessary to protect self or property from immediate danger.

reasonable force

A degree of force that is appropriate in a given situation and is not excessive. Also, the minimum degree of force necessary to protect oneself, one's property, a third party, or the property of another in the face of a substantial threat.

alter ego rule

In some jurisdictions, a rule of law that holds that a person can only defend a third party under circumstances and only to the degree that the third party could legally act on his or her own behalf.

fault and that he act to aid an innocent person who is in the process of being victimized. The same restrictions that apply to self-defense also apply to the defense of a third party. Hence, a defender may act only in the face of an immediate threat to another person, cannot use deadly force against nondeadly force, and must act only to the extent and use only the degree of force needed to repel the attack.

DEFENSE OF HOME AND PROPERTY

In most jurisdictions, the owner of property can justifiably use reasonable, *nondeadly* force to prevent others from unlawfully taking or damaging it. As a general rule, the preservation of human life outweighs the protection of property, and the use of deadly force to protect property is not justified unless the perpetrator of the illegal act may intend to commit, or is in the act of committing, a violent act against another human being. A person who shoots and kills an unarmed trespasser, for example, could not claim "defense of property" to avoid criminal liability.[37] However, a person who shoots and kills an armed robber while being robbed can make such a claim.

The use of mechanical devices to protect property is a special area of law. Because deadly force is usually not permitted in defense of property, the setting of booby traps, such as spring-loaded shotguns, electrified gates, and explosive devices, is generally not permitted to protect property that is unattended and unoccupied. If an individual is injured as a result of a mechanical device intended to cause death or injury in the protection of property, criminal charges may be brought against the person who set the device.

On the other hand, acts that would otherwise be criminal may carry no criminal liability if undertaken to protect one's home. For purposes of the law, one's "home" is one's dwelling, whether owned, rented, or merely borrowed. Hotel rooms, rooms aboard vessels, and rented rooms in houses belonging to others are all considered, for purposes of the law, one's home. The retreat rule referred to earlier, which requires a person under attack to retreat when possible before resorting to deadly force, is subject to what some call the *castle exception*. The castle exception can be traced to the writings of the sixteenth-century English jurist Sir Edward Coke, who said, "A man's house is his castle—for where shall a man be safe if it be not in his house?"[38] The castle exception generally recognizes that a person has a fundamental right to be in his or her home and that the home is a final and inviolable place of retreat (that is, the home offers a place of retreat from which a person can be expected to retreat no further). Hence, it is not necessary for one to retreat from one's home in the face of an immediate threat, even where such retreat is possible, before resorting to deadly force in protection of the home. A number of court decisions have extended the castle exception to include one's place of business, such as a store or an office.

NECESSITY

Necessity, or the claim that some illegal action was needed to prevent an even greater harm, is a useful defense in cases that do not involve serious bodily harm. A famous but unsuccessful use of this defense occurred in *The Crown* v. *Dudly & Stephens* in the late nineteenth century.[39] This British case involved a shipwreck in which three sailors and a cabin boy were set adrift in a lifeboat. After a number of days at sea without food, two of the sailors decided to kill and eat the cabin boy. At their trial, they argued that it was necessary to do so, or none of them would have survived. The court, however, reasoned that the cabin boy was not a direct threat to the survival of the men and rejected this defense. Convicted of murder, they were sentenced to death, although they were spared the gallows by royal intervention. Although cannibalism is usually against the law, courts have sometimes recognized the necessity of consuming human flesh where survival was at issue. Those cases, however, involved only "victims" who had already died of natural causes.

CONSENT

The defense of consent claims that whatever harm was done occurred only after the injured person gave his or her permission for the behavior in question. In the late 1980s, for example, Robert Chambers pleaded guilty to first-degree manslaughter in the killing of 18-year-old Jennifer Levin. In what was dubbed the "Preppy Murder Case,"[40] Chambers had claimed that Levin died as a result of "rough sex," during which she had tied his hands behind his back and injured his testicles. Other cases involving sexual asphyxia (partial suffocation designed to heighten erotic pleasures) and bondage prompted a headline in *Time* heralding the era of the "rough-sex defense."[41] The magazine suggested that such a defense works best with a good-looking defendant who appears remorseful; a "hardened type of character," it said, could not effectively use the defense.[42]

In the "Condom Rapist Case," Joel Valdez was found guilty of rape in 1993 after a jury in Austin, Texas, rejected his claim that the act became consensual once he complied with his victim's request to use a condom. Valdez, who was drunk and armed with a knife at the time of the offense, claimed that his victim's request was a consent to sex. After that, he said, "we were making love."[43]

RESISTING UNLAWFUL ARREST

All jurisdictions make resisting arrest a crime. Resistance, however, may be justifiable, especially if the arresting officer uses excessive force. Some states have statutory provisions detailing the limits imposed on such resistance and the conditions under which it can be used. Such laws generally say that a person may use a reasonable amount of force, other than deadly force, to resist arrest or an unlawful search by a law enforcement officer if the officer uses or attempts to use greater force than necessary to make the arrest or search. Such laws are inapplicable in cases where the defendant is the first to resort to force. Deadly force to resist arrest is not justified unless the law enforcement officer resorts to deadly force when it is not called for.

> *No State shall make or enforce any law which shall abridge the privileges or immunities of citizens of the United States; nor shall any State deprive any person of life, liberty, or property, without due process of law; nor deny to any person within its jurisdiction the equal protection of the laws.*
>
> *—Fourteenth Amendment to the U.S. Constitution*

Excuses

In contrast to a justification, an excuse does not claim that the conduct in question is justified by the situation or that it is moral. An excuse claims, rather, that the actor who engaged in the unlawful behavior was, at the time, not legally responsible for his or her actions and should not be held accountable under the law. For example, a person who assaults a police officer, thinking that the officer is really a disguised space alien who has come to abduct him, may be found "not guilty" of the charge of assault and battery by reason of insanity. Actions for which excuses are offered do not morally outweigh the wrong committed, but criminal liability may still be negated on the basis of some personal disability of the actor or because of some special circumstances that characterize the situation. Excuses recognized by the law include (1) duress, (2) age, (3) mistake, (4) involuntary intoxication, (5) unconsciousness, (6) provocation, (7) insanity, (8) diminished capacity, and (9) mental incompetence.

DURESS

The defense of duress depends on an understanding of the situation. *Duress* has been defined as "any unlawful threat or coercion used by a person to induce another to act (or to refrain from acting) in a manner he or she otherwise would not (or would)."[44] A person may act under duress if, for example, he or she steals an employer's payroll to meet a ransom demand for kidnappers holding the person's children. Should the person later be arrested for larceny or embezzlement, the person can claim that he or she felt compelled to commit the crime to help ensure the safety of the children. Duress is generally not a useful defense when the crime committed involves serious physical harm, since the harm committed may outweigh the coercive influence in the minds of jurors and judges. Duress is sometimes also called *coercion*.

AGE

Age offers another kind of excuse to a criminal charge, and the defense of "infancy"—as it is sometimes known in legal jargon—has its roots in the ancient belief that children cannot reason logically until around the age of seven. Early doctrine in the Christian church sanctioned that belief by declaring that rationality develops around that age. As a consequence, only older children could be held responsible for their crimes.

The defense of infancy today has been expanded to include young people well beyond the age of seven. Many states set the sixteenth birthday as the age at which a person becomes an adult for purposes of criminal prosecution. Others use the age of 17, and still others 18. When a person younger than the age required for adult prosecution commits a "crime," it is termed a *juvenile offense*. He or she is not guilty of a criminal violation of the law by virtue of youth.

In most jurisdictions, children below the age of seven cannot be charged even with juvenile offenses, no matter how serious their actions may appear to others. However, in a rather amazing 1994 case, prosecutors in Cincinnati, Ohio, charged a 12-year-old girl with murder after she confessed to drowning her toddler cousin ten years earlier. The cousin, 13-month-old Lamar Howell, drowned in 1984 in a bucket of bleach mixed with water. Howell's drowning had been ruled an accidental death until his cousin came forward. In discussing the charges with the media, Hamilton (Ohio) County Prosecutor Joe Deters admitted that the girl could not be prosecuted successfully. "Frankly," he said, "anything under seven cannot be an age where you form criminal intent."[45] The prosecution's goal, claimed one of Deters's associates, was simply to "make sure she gets the counseling she needs."

CJ News

Courts Asked to Consider Culture

Santeria priest Ernesto Pichardo thought it was a good thing when fellow members of the Church of the Lukumi Babalu Aye began to leave the bodies of sacrificed chickens near the trees and bushes of Hialeah, Florida, the congregation's hometown, during the 1980s.

Others did not. The City Council in the city of 240,000 people, 11 miles northwest of Miami, rejected the church's contention that the ritual scatterings were a vital part of the Santeria religion and of the Afro-Cuban culture on which it is based. The city prosecuted the church under a law banning animal sacrifices that stood until 1993, when the U.S. Supreme Court struck it down as religious discrimination.

The sacrifices continue, although Pichardo says church members still are occasionally hassled by authorities.

"I learned one thing," says Pichardo, who as an orite, or special priest, is empowered to conduct the sacrifices. "When you bring something forward that is outside the Judeo-Christian tradition, the dominant culture is going to cause you problems."

Immigrants with roots in Africa, Asia and other non-Western cultures are winding up in America's courts after being charged with crimes for acts that would not be offenses in their home countries. In recent years, U.S. courts have been asked to decide the fates of defendants involved in animal sacrifices, ritual mutilations and other customs of foreign cultures.

Some legal analysts and academics say the phenomenon should lead U.S. courts to allow defendants from non-Western backgrounds to raise a **cultural defense** when they are charged with certain crimes. Legal traditionalists blanch at the idea, and courts here traditionally have been reluctant to allow such defenses.

"We say that as a society we welcome diversity, and in fact that we embrace it," says Alison Dundes Renteln, a political science professor at the University of Southern California and author of *The Cultural Defense,* a book that examines the influence of such cases on U.S. courts. "In practice, it's not that easy."

Recent cases bear that out:

- In Fresno in 1995, Thai Chia Moua, a Hmong shaman originally from Laos, ordered a German shepherd puppy beaten to death on his front porch while he chanted over its body. Moua later explained that he wanted the puppy's soul to hunt down an evil spirit that was tormenting his wife. He pleaded guilty to animal cruelty. He was sentenced to probation and community service.

- In San Mateo, Calif., in 2000, Taufui Piutau was arrested for driving under the influence of kava tea, a mild euphoric popular in his native Tonga. A hung jury led to a mistrial.

- Chewers of khat, a leaf grown in East Africa and Yemen that produces a caffeine-like stimulant buzz, have been prosecuted in Michigan, New York, Georgia, Connecticut and Minnesota since the mid-1990s. Khat is legal in Great Britain, but the U.S. government classifies it as a controlled substance in the same category as LSD and Ecstasy.

- In Sanford, N.C., in 2003, city officials banned the slaughter of goats and other farm animals. Mexican agricultural workers who

Santeria priest Ernesto Pichardo. The practice of animal sacrifice in Pichardo's Hialeah, Florida–based Church of the Lukumi Babalu Aye is protected under a U.S. Supreme Court decision, highlighting the possibility of raising cultural defenses against certain criminal charges. Cultural defenses have become especially important in recent years as immigrants with roots in Africa, Asia, and other non-Western cultures are being increasingly made to face criminal charges in the United States for acts that are legal in their home countries. Should cultural defenses offered by such immigrants be acceptable when American criminal laws have been violated?

Eliot J. Schechter/EJS Photo.Com, Inc.

had settled in the town had begun killing goats for backyard barbecues and nailing their heads to nearby trees.

- In Lawrenceville, Ga., in March, Ethiopian immigrant Khalid Adem was charged with child cruelty after his 4-year-old daughter was found to have undergone female circumcision. The practice, in which portions of the female genitals are removed, is condemned by the United Nations and is banned under a 1995 U.S. law, but it is common in some African cultures.

CIVIL LAWSUITS

Culture clashes also are producing civil lawsuits that run in the other direction: Recently arrived immigrants have filed claims against airlines and fast-food restaurants over conduct that was offensive in the immigrants' cultures.

CJ News (continued)

In 1988, the parents of Jasbir Singh, a Sikh, won $400,000 in court from Air Illinois after Singh, 26, was killed in a plane crash. An Illinois court ruled that the family was entitled to a larger-than-usual amount because Sikh custom would have required Singh to care for them in their old age.

Cultural claims have worked on occasion. In 1999, Mukesh Rai, a Carpenteria, Calif., pharmacist who is a vegetarian, accepted an undisclosed sum from Taco Bell after he mistakenly was served a beef burrito. Rai, a Hindu who had sued for $144,000, claimed that he was offended on cultural and religious grounds. He said the incident led him to consult a psychiatrist and to journey to India for a purifying bath in the Ganges River. Similar lawsuits by non-religious vegetarians usually fail, legal analysts say.

U.S. courts have dealt with similar pressures before.

In the early 20th century, Renteln says, Orthodox Jewish immigrants from Eastern Europe and Catholics from Italy brought religious and cultural practices that clashed with U.S. customs. Practices such as contracted or underage marriages, she says, were not protected under U.S. law and largely were eliminated.

Renteln wants courts to recognize what she calls America's "evolving definition of diversity." She says cultural defenses should be considered when determining guilt. But she does not say that those who commit culture-based crimes should always be found not guilty.

"Courts can judge on a case-by-case basis," Renteln says. "For instance, they could rule that it's OK for a Sikh man to wear a *kirpan* (a ceremonial dagger worn on or under the clothes) without endorsing female genital mutilation."

Legal traditionalists reject that notion. Michael Rushford, president of the Criminal Justice Legal Foundation, a conservative group, says that permitting cultural defenses would lead to a "legal relativism" in which "what's a crime for one person isn't for his neighbor. . . . The system we have is the best we can do to allow cultural differences without beating down basic human rights."

RELIGIOUS ASPECT IMPORTANT

Courts have long been reluctant to accept cultural defenses. Exceptions have come when groups have been able to argue that their religious as well as cultural rights have been violated.

In a case now before a U.S. appeals court, Albuquerque-based adherents of Uniao de Vegetal, a Brazilian religion, are claiming that restricting their access to the ayahuasca root violates a 1993 U.S. law that protects exotic religious practices. Tea brewed from the root produces a dreamlike state that is essential to their religion, the adherents say. The group won in federal trial court; the U.S. government has appealed.

Occasionally, lawyers have persuaded judges to go easy on defendants from other cultures.

In Brooklyn, N.Y., in 1989, Chinese-born Dong Lu Chen received probation for beating his wife to death with a claw hammer after she confessed to adultery. Chen's attorney, Stewart Orden, argued that the shame Chen felt was the result of his Chinese upbringing, and that it fed his frenzy.

"It was as much of a cultural explanation as cultural defense," says Orden, who says he has not used the strategy since the Chen case. "Culture may not excuse (a crime), but it can certainly shed light on things we may have difficulty understanding. Why shouldn't a court listen?"

For the latest in crime and justice news, visit the Talk Justice news feed at http://www.crimenews.info.

Source: Richard Willing, "Courts Asked to Consider Culture," USA TODAY, May 25, 2004. Reprinted with permission.

MISTAKE

Two types of mistake can serve as a defense. One is mistake of law, and the other is mistake of fact. Rarely is mistake of law held to be an acceptable defense. Most people realize that it is their responsibility to know the law as it applies to them. "Ignorance of the law is no excuse" is an old dictum still heard today. On occasion, however, cases do arise in which such a defense is accepted by authorities. For example, an elderly woman raised marijuana plants because they could be used to make a tea that relieved her arthritis pain. When her garden was discovered, she was not arrested but was advised as to how the law applied to her.

Mistake of fact is a much more useful form of the mistake defense. In 2000, for example, the statutory rape conviction of 39-year-old Charles Ballinger of Bradley County, Tennessee, was reversed by Tennessee's Court of Criminal Appeals at Knoxville on a mistake-of-fact claim.[46] Ballinger admitted that he had had sex with his 15-year-old neighbor, who was under the age of legal consent at the time of the act in 1998. In his defense, however, Ballinger claimed that he had had good reason to mistake the girl's age.

cultural defense

A defense to a criminal charge in which the defendant's culture is taken into account in judging his or her culpability.

INVOLUNTARY INTOXICATION

The claim of involuntary intoxication may form the basis for another excuse defense. Either drugs or alcohol may produce intoxication. Voluntary intoxication itself is rarely a defense to a criminal charge because it is a self-induced condition. It is widely recognized in our legal tradition that

Andrea Yates herself, in her interviews, said she knew it was wrong in the eyes of society. She knew it was wrong in the eyes of God, and knew it was illegal. And, you know, I don't know what wrong means if all those three things aren't factored in.

—A juror in Yates's first trial[vi]

an altered mental condition that is the product of voluntary activity cannot be used to exonerate guilty actions that follow from it. Some state statutes formalize this general principle of law and specifically state that voluntary intoxication cannot be offered as a defense against a charge of criminal behavior.[47]

Involuntary intoxication, however, is another matter. A person might be tricked into consuming an intoxicating substance. Secretly "spiked" punch, popular aphrodisiacs, or LSD-laced desserts might be ingested unknowingly. About ten years ago, for example, the Drug Enforcement Administration (DEA) began reporting that a powerful sedative manufactured by Hoffmann-LaRoche Pharmaceuticals and sold under the brand name Rohypnol was becoming popular with college students and with "young men [who] put doses of Rohypnol in women's drinks without their consent in order to lower their inhibitions."[48] Other behavioral effects of the drug are unknown, although its use has spread since the DEA first drew attention to it. On the street, Rohypnol is known as *roples*, *roche*, *ruffles*, *roofies*, and *rophies*.

Because the effects and taste of alcohol are so widely known in our society, the defense of involuntary intoxication due to alcohol consumption can be difficult to demonstrate.

UNCONSCIOUSNESS

A very rarely used excuse is that of unconsciousness. An individual cannot be held responsible for anything he or she does while unconscious. Because unconscious people rarely do anything at all, this defense is almost never seen in the courts. However, cases of sleepwalking, epileptic seizure, and neurological dysfunction may result in injurious, although unintentional, actions by people so afflicted. Under such circumstances, a defense of unconsciousness might be argued with success.

PROVOCATION

Provocation recognizes that a person can be emotionally enraged by another who intends to elicit just such a reaction. Should the person then strike out at the tormentor, some courts have held, he or she may not be guilty of criminality or may be guilty of a lesser degree of criminality than might otherwise be the case. The defense of provocation is commonly used in cases arising from barroom brawls in which a person's parentage was called into question, although most states don't look favorably on verbal provocation alone. This defense has also been used in some spectacular cases where wives have killed their husbands, or children their fathers, citing years of verbal and physical abuse. In these latter instances, perhaps because the degree of physical harm inflicted—the death of the husband or father—appears to be out of proportion to the abuse suffered by the wife or child, the courts have not readily accepted the defense of provocation. As a rule, the defense of provocation is generally more acceptable in minor offenses than in serious violations of the law.

INSANITY

From the point of view of the criminal law, *insanity* has a legal definition and not a medical one. This legal definition often has very little to do with psychological or psychiatric understandings of mental illness; rather, it is a concept developed to enable the judicial system to assign guilt or innocence to particular defendants. As a consequence, medical conceptions of mental illness do not always fit well into the legal categories of mental illness created by courts and legislatures. The differences between psychiatric and legal conceptualizations of insanity often lead to disagreements among expert witnesses who, in criminal court, may provide conflicting testimony as to the sanity of a defendant.

Consider, for example, the sad story of Andrea Pia Yates. The Texas mother was convicted in 2002 of the drowning murders of her five young children and ordered to serve life in prison. Evidence presented to the jury during Yates's trial established that she methodically killed the children one at a time and that she did so because she believed that it was the only way she could save them from the devil.

Prior to the killings, Yates, who has been described as devoutly Christian, had attempted suicide twice and had been hospitalized several times for mental illness. She had been diagnosed as schizophrenic and was known to be suffering from postpartum depression following the birth of her last child. At trial, both the prosecution and the defense agreed that she was severely mentally ill, and jurors were aware of the details of her mental illness. Nonetheless, given the differences between the psychiatric definition of mental illness and legal definition of insanity, Yates's attorneys could not convince the jury that their client was not guilty by reason of insanity. The jurors reasoned that Yates knew what she was doing because of the methodical nature of her actions, and they believed that she must have known her actions were wrong because she called the police immediately after she killed the children. Because the legal definition of insanity asks what a person knew or did not know at the time of the crime, they found her guilty.

Andrea Pia Yates, the Texas mother who admitted to drowning her five young children in a bathtub in 2001, conferring with attorney George Parnham at her retrial in 2006. Convicted of capital murder in 2002, she was found not guilty by reason of insanity in a retrial ordered by a three-judge panel of the First Texas Court of Appeals. In a civil action that followed her acquittal, Yates was ordered committed to the maximum-security North Texas State Hospital in Vernon, Texas. What does *insanity* mean for purposes of the criminal law?

Getty Images, Inc.

Critics of the original Yates decision, in which the insanity defense proved ineffective, have pointed out that while Andrea Yates may have known that society and the justice system would view her actions as "wrong," she may have believed that they were "right" and even necessary. In 2005, in what many saw as partial vindication of such a view, Yates's conviction was overturned by a Texas appeals court, and a new trial was ordered. The court found that false testimony by a prosecution psychiatrist had been instrumental in persuading the jury to reject Yates's claim of insanity. The testimony, by California psychiatrist Park Dietz, included a false assertion that he had consulted for an episode of the TV show *Law and Order* about a fictional case like that involving Yates.[49]

In 2006, Yates was retried, but this time she was found not guilty by reason of insanity. At the second trial, expert witness Dr. Phillip Resnick testified that Yates believed deeply that killing her children had been the right thing to do and that Yates thought that Satan had taken over her body and soul and was eyeing her children's souls next. In killing them, said Resnick, she believed that she was saving them from eternal damnation. Some speculated that jurors in Yates's new trial had been more sympathetic to her because a number of them had family members who suffered from mental illness. After trial, the jury foreman was asked if jurors had a message to send with their verdict. He replied, "Don't let this happen again. Do what you've got to do with the legislation, with insurance companies. Don't let this happen again."[50]

The **insanity defense** is given a lot of play in the entertainment industry; movies and television shows regularly employ it because it makes for good drama. In practice, however, the defense of insanity is rarely raised. According to an eight-state study funded by the National Institute of Mental Health, the insanity defense was used in less than 1% of the cases that came before county-level courts.[51] The study showed that only 26% of all insanity pleas were argued successfully and that 90% of those who employed the defense had been previously diagnosed with a mental illness. As the American Bar Association says, "The best evidence suggests that the mental nonresponsibility defense is raised in less than one percent of all felony cases in the United States and is successful in about a fourth of these."[52] Even so, there are several rules that guide the legal definition of insanity.

The M'Naghten Rule The insanity defense, as we know it today, was nonexistent prior to the nineteenth century. Until then, insane people who committed crimes were punished in the same way as other law violators. It was Daniel M'Naghten (sometimes spelled McNaughten or M'Naughten), a woodworker from Glasgow, Scotland, who, in 1844, became the first person to be found not guilty of a crime by reason of insanity. M'Naghten had tried to assassinate Sir Robert Peel, the British prime minister. He mistook Edward Drummond, Peel's secretary, for Peel himself and killed Drummond instead. At his trial, defense attorneys argued that M'Naghten suffered

What Yates knew is that others would deem her actions wrong. But as for herself, she was right. Her children were not "righteous." She was saving them from eternal damnation by sending them to heaven.

—Richard Cohen[vii]

insanity defense

A legal defense based on claims of mental illness or mental incapacity.

M'Naghten rule

A rule for determining insanity, which asks whether the defendant knew what he or she was doing or whether the defendant knew that what he or she was doing was wrong.

WEB
Extra

from vague delusions centered on the idea that the Tories, a British political party, were persecuting him. Medical testimony at the trial supported the defense's assertion that he didn't know what he was doing at the time of the shooting. The jury accepted M'Naghten's claim, and the insanity defense was born. Later, the House of Lords defined the criteria necessary for a finding of insanity. The **M'Naghten rule**, as it is called, holds that *a person is not guilty of a crime if, at the time of the crime, the person either didn't know what he or she was doing or didn't know that what he or she was doing was wrong.* The inability to distinguish right from wrong must be the result of some mental defect or disability.

Today, the M'Naghten rule is still followed in many U.S. jurisdictions (Figure 4–1). In those states, the burden of proving insanity falls on the defendant. Just as defendants are assumed to be innocent, they are also assumed to be sane at the outset of any criminal trial. Learn more about the M'Naghten rule at Web Extra 4–4 at cjtoday.com.

Irresistible Impulse   The M'Naghten rule worked well for a time. Eventually, however, some cases arose in which defendants clearly knew what they were doing, and they knew it was wrong. Even so, they argued in their defense that they couldn't stop doing what they knew was wrong. Such people are said to suffer from an *irresistible impulse*, and in a number of states today, they may be found not guilty by reason of that particular brand of insanity. Some states that do not use the irresistible-impulse test in determining insanity may still allow the successful demonstration of such an impulse to be considered in sentencing decisions.

In a spectacular 1994 Virginia trial, Lorena Bobbitt successfully employed the irresistible-impulse defense against charges of malicious wounding stemming from an incident in which she cut off her husband's penis with a kitchen knife as he slept. In the case, which made headlines around the world, Bobbitt's defense attorney told the jury, "What we have is Lorena Bobbitt's life juxtaposed against John Wayne Bobbitt's penis. The evidence will show that in her mind it was his penis from which she could not escape, that caused her the most pain, the most fear, the most humiliation."[53] The impulse to sever the organ, said the lawyer, became irresistible.

The irresistible-impulse test has been criticized on a number of grounds. Primary among them is the belief that all of us suffer from compulsions. Most of us, however, learn to control them. If we give in to a compulsion, the critique goes, then why not just say it was unavoidable so as to escape any legal consequences?

FIGURE 4–1

Standards for insanity determinations by jurisdiction.

Source: Adapted from David B. Rottman and Shauna M. Strickland, *State Court Organization 2004* (Washington, DC: Bureau of Justice Statistics, 2006), pp. 199–202.

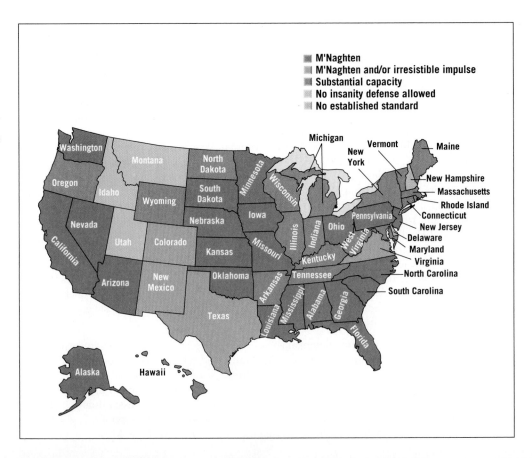

The Durham Rule Another rule for gauging insanity is called the *Durham rule.* Originally created in 1871 by a New Hampshire court, it was later adopted by Judge David Bazelon in 1954 as he decided the case of *Durham* v. *U.S.* for the court of appeals in the District of Columbia.[54] The Durham rule states that *a person is not criminally responsible for his or her behavior if the person's illegal actions were the result of some mental disease or defect.*

Courts that follow the Durham rule typically hear from an array of psychiatric specialists as to the mental state of the defendant. Their testimony is inevitably clouded by the need to address the question of cause. A successful defense under the Durham rule necessitates that jurors be able to see the criminal activity in question as the *product* of the defendant's mental deficiencies. And yet many people who suffer from mental diseases or defects never commit crimes. In fact, low IQ, mental retardation, and lack of general mental capacity are not allowable excuses for criminal behavior. Because the Durham rule is especially vague, it provides fertile ground for conflicting claims.

The Substantial-Capacity Test Nineteen states follow another guideline—the substantial-capacity test—as found in the Model Penal Code (MPC) of the American Law Institute (ALI).[55] Also called the *ALI rule* or the *MPC rule*, it suggests that insanity should be defined as the lack of a substantial capacity to control one's behavior. This test requires a judgment to the effect that the defendant either had or lacked "the mental capacity needed to understand the wrongfulness of his act or to conform his behavior to the requirements of the law."[56] The substantial-capacity test is a blending of the M'Naghten rule and the irresistible-impulse standard. "Substantial capacity" does not require total mental incompetence, nor does the rule require the behavior in question to live up to the criterion of total irresistibility. However, the problem of establishing just what constitutes "substantial mental capacity" has plagued this rule from its conception.

The Brawner Rule Judge Bazelon, apparently dissatisfied with the application of the Durham rule, created a new criterion for gauging insanity in the 1972 case of *U.S.* v. *Brawner.*[57] The Brawner rule, as it has come to be called, places responsibility for deciding insanity squarely with the jury. Bazelon suggested that the jury should be concerned with whether the defendant could justly be held responsible for the criminal act in the face of any claims of insanity. Under this proposal, juries are left with few rules to guide them other than their own sense of fairness.

The Insanity Defense and Social Reaction The insanity defense originated as a way to recognize the social reality of mental disease. However, the history of this defense has been rife with difficulty and contradiction. First, psychiatric testimony is expensive, and "expert" witnesses are often at odds with one another. Another difficulty with this defense is society's acceptance of it. When "not guilty due to insanity" findings have been made, the public has not always been satisfied that justice has been served. Dissatisfaction with the jumble of rules defining legal insanity peaked in 1982, when John Hinckley was acquitted of trying to assassinate then-President Ronald Reagan. At his trial, Hinckley's lawyers claimed that a series of delusions brought about by a history of schizophrenia left him unable to control his behavior. Government prosecutors were unable to counter defense contentions of insanity. The resulting acquittal shocked the nation and resulted in calls for a review of the insanity defense.

One response has been to ban the insanity defense from use at trial. A ruling by the U.S. Supreme Court in support of a Montana law allows states to prohibit defendants from claiming that they were insane at the time they committed their crimes. In 1994, without comment, the high court let stand a Montana Supreme Court ruling that held that eliminating the insanity defense does not violate the U.S. Constitution. Currently, only three states—Montana, Idaho, and Utah—bar use of the insanity defense.[58]

Guilty But Mentally Ill Another response to public frustration with the insanity and responsibility issue is the **guilty but mentally ill (GBMI)** verdict, now possible in at least 11 states. (In a few states, the finding is "guilty but insane.") A GBMI verdict means that a person can be held responsible for a specific criminal act even though a degree of mental incompetence may be present in his or her personality. In most GBMI jurisdictions, a jury must return a finding of "guilty but mentally ill" if (1) every element necessary for a conviction has been proved beyond a reasonable doubt, (2) the defendant is found to have been *mentally ill* at the time the crime was committed, and (3) the defendant was *not* found to have been *legally insane* at the time the crime was committed. The difference between mental illness and legal insanity is a crucial one, since a defendant can be mentally ill by standards of the medical profession but sane for purposes of the law.

Upon return of a GBMI verdict, a judge may impose any sentence possible under the law for the crime in question. Mandated psychiatric treatment, however, is often part of the commitment order. Once cured, the offender is usually placed in the general prison population to serve any remaining sentence.

Equal Justice Under Law

—Words inscribed above the entrance to the U.S. Supreme Court building

guilty but mentally ill (GBMI)

A verdict, equivalent to a finding of "guilty," that establishes that the defendant, although mentally ill, was in sufficient possession of his or her faculties to be morally blameworthy for his or her acts.

In 1997, Pennsylvania multimillionaire John E. du Pont was found guilty but mentally ill in the shooting death of former Olympic gold medalist David Schultz during a delusional episode. Although defense attorneys were able to show that du Pont sometimes saw Nazis in his trees, heard the walls talking, and had cut off pieces of his skin to remove bugs from outer space, he was held criminally liable for Schultz's death and was sentenced to 13 to 30 years in confinement.

As some authors have observed, the GBMI finding has three purposes: "first, to protect society; second, to hold some offenders who were mentally ill accountable for their criminal acts; [and] third, to make treatment available to convicted offenders suffering from some form of mental illness."[59] The U.S. Supreme Court case of *Ford* v. *Wainwright* recognized an issue of a different sort.[60] The 1986 decision specified that prisoners who become insane while incarcerated cannot be executed. Hence, although insanity may not always be a successful defense to criminal prosecution, it can later become a block to the ultimate punishment.

Temporary Insanity   Temporary insanity is another possible defense against a criminal charge. Widely used in the 1940s and 1950s, temporary insanity means that the offender claims to have been insane only at the time of the commission of the offense. If a jury agrees, the defendant goes free. The defendant is not guilty of the criminal action by virtue of having been insane at the time, yet he or she cannot be ordered to undergo psychiatric counseling or treatment because the insanity is no longer present. This type of plea has become less popular as legislatures have regulated the circumstances under which it can be made.

The Insanity Defense under Federal Law   Yet another response to the public's concern with the insanity defense and responsibility issues is the federal Insanity Defense Reform Act (IDRA). In 1984, Congress passed this act, which created major revisions in the federal insanity defense. Insanity under the law is now defined as a condition in which the defendant can be shown to have been suffering under a "severe mental disease or defect" and, as a result, "was unable to appreciate the nature and quality or the wrongfulness of his acts."[61] This definition of insanity comes close to that set forth in the old M'Naghten rule.

The act also places the burden of proving the insanity defense squarely on the defendant—a provision that has been challenged a number of times since the act was passed. The Supreme Court supported a similar requirement prior to the act's passage. In 1983, in the case of *Jones* v. *U.S.*,[62] the Court ruled that defendants can be required to prove their insanity when it becomes an issue in their defense. Shortly after the act became law, the Court held, in *Ake* v. *Oklahoma* (1985),[63] that the government must ensure access to a competent psychiatrist whenever a defendant indicates that insanity will be an issue at trial.

Consequences of an Insanity Ruling   The insanity defense today is not an "easy way out" of criminal prosecution, as some people assume. Once a verdict of "not guilty by reason of insanity" is returned, the judge may order the defendant to undergo psychiatric treatment until cured. Because psychiatrists are reluctant to declare any potential criminal "cured," such a sentence may result in more time spent in an institution than would have been spent in a prison. In *Foucha* v. *Louisiana* (1992),[64] however, the U.S. Supreme Court held that a defendant found not guilty by reason of insanity in a criminal trial could not thereafter be institutionalized indefinitely without a showing that he or she was either dangerous or mentally ill.

DIMINISHED CAPACITY

diminished capacity

A defense based on claims of a mental condition that may be insufficient to exonerate the defendant of guilt but that may be relevant to specific mental elements of certain crimes or degrees of crime.

Diminished capacity, or *diminished responsibility*, is a defense available in some jurisdictions. In 2003, the U.S. Sentencing Commission issued a policy statement saying that *diminished capacity* may mean that "the defendant, although convicted, *has a significantly impaired ability* to (A) understand the wrongfulness of the behavior comprising the offense or to exercise the power of reason; or (B) control behavior that the defendant knows is wrongful."[65] Still, "the terms 'diminished responsibility' and 'diminished capacity' do not have a clearly accepted meaning in [many] courts."[66] Some defendants who offer diminished-capacity defenses do so in recognition of the fact that such claims may be based on a mental condition that would not qualify as mental disease or mental defect nor be sufficient to support the defense of insanity but that might still lower criminal culpability. According to Peter Arenella, professor of law at UCLA, "the defense [of diminished capacity] was first recognized by Scottish common law courts to reduce the punishment of the 'partially insane' from murder to culpable homicide, a non-capital offense."[67]

The diminished-capacity defense is similar to the defense of insanity in that it depends on a showing that the defendant's mental state was impaired at the time of the crime. As a defense, diminished capacity is most useful when it can be shown that because of some defect of reason or mental shortcoming, the defendant's capacity to form the *mens rea* required by a specific crime was impaired. Unlike an insanity defense, however, which can result in a finding of "not guilty," a diminished-capacity defense is built on the recognition that "[m]ental condition, though insufficient to exonerate, may be relevant to specific mental elements of certain crimes or degrees of crime."[68] For example, a defendant might present evidence of mental abnormality in an effort to reduce first-degree murder to second-degree murder, or second-degree murder to manslaughter, when a killing occurs under extreme emotional disturbance. Similarly, in some jurisdictions, very low intelligence will, if proved, serve to reduce first-degree murder to manslaughter.[69]

As is the case with the insanity defense, some jurisdictions have entirely eliminated the diminished-capacity defense. The California Penal Code, for example, abolished the defense of diminished capacity,[70] stating that "[a]s a matter of public policy there shall be no defense of diminished capacity, diminished responsibility, or irresistible impulse in a criminal action or juvenile adjudication hearing."[71]

MENTAL INCOMPETENCE

In January 2007, King County (Washington) Superior Court Judge Helen Halpert dismissed murder charges against 39-year-old Marie Robinson, finding her mentally **incompetent to stand trial** in the deaths of her two baby sons.[72] The sons, 6-week-old Raiden and 16-month-old Justice, were found dead in Robinson's apartment by police who were called to check on the family. The boys were later determined to have died from starvation and dehydration, and Robinson was discovered passed out in a bedroom amid hundreds of empty beer cans. Her blood alcohol level at the time of discovery was five times Washington's legal limit for intoxication.

Although she was charged with two counts of second-degree murder, Halpert declared that "Ms. Robinson is clearly incompetent to stand trial. Every psychiatrist or psychologist who has examined her during the past two years has reached this conclusion." Interviews with Robinson showed that she believed her children were still alive and had been kidnapped by a secret police organization that wanted to prevent her from doing some kind of imagined scientific research.

Halpert found Robinson to be dangerously mentally ill and ordered her committed to a state mental hospital. Months later, however, doctors at Washington's Western State Hospital determined that she was not sick enough to be held for additional treatment, but they also reported that she had not made the necessary progress to face criminal proceedings. Although prosecutors have since refiled murder charges against her,[73] Washington law requires that Robinson's competence be restored before she can be tried—creating a dilemma that remains ongoing as this book goes to press.

In Washington, as in most states, a person deemed competent to stand trial must be capable of understanding the nature of the proceedings and must be able to assist in his or her own legal defense. Hence, while insanity refers to an assessment of the offender's mental condition at the time the crime was committed, mental incompetence refers to his or her condition immediately before prosecution.

Procedural Defenses

Procedural defenses make the claim that the defendant was in some manner discriminated against in the justice process or that some important aspect of official procedure was not properly followed. As a result, those offering this defense say, the defendant should be released from any criminal liability. The procedural defenses we will discuss here are (1) entrapment, (2) double jeopardy, (3) *collateral estoppel*, (4) selective prosecution, (5) denial of a speedy trial, (6) prosecutorial misconduct, and (7) police fraud.

ENTRAPMENT

Entrapment is an improper or illegal inducement to crime by enforcement agents. Entrapment defenses argue that enforcement agents effectively created a crime where there would otherwise have been none. For entrapment to occur, the idea for the criminal activity must originate with official agents of the criminal justice system. Entrapment can also result when overzealous undercover police officers convince a defendant that the contemplated law-violating behavior is not a crime. To avoid claims of entrapment, officers must not engage in activity that would cause a person to commit a crime that he or she would not otherwise commit. Merely providing an opportunity for a willing offender to commit a crime, however, is not entrapment.

One of the best-known entrapment cases of the twentieth century involved automaker John DeLorean. DeLorean was arrested in 1982 by federal agents near the Los Angeles airport.[74] A videotape, secretly made by the Federal Bureau of Investigation at the scene, showed him allegedly "dealing" with undercover agents and holding packets of cocaine, which he said were

No person shall be . . . twice put in jeopardy of life or limb.

—Fifth Amendment to the U.S. Constitution

incompetent to stand trial

In criminal proceedings, a finding by a court that, as a result of mental illness, defect, or disability, a defendant is incapable of understanding the nature of the charges and proceedings against him or her, of consulting with an attorney, and of aiding in his or her own defense.

entrapment

An improper or illegal inducement to crime by agents of law enforcement. Also, a defense that may be raised when such inducements have occurred.

Members of the New York City Police Department's Street Crimes Unit preparing for a day's work. Entrapment will likely not be an effective defense for muggers who attack these decoys. Why not?

Courtesy of the New York City Police Department

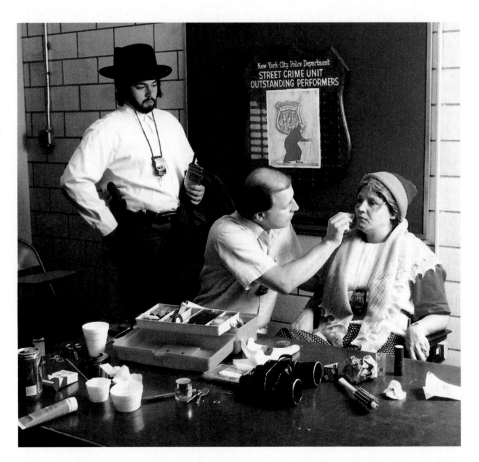

"better than gold." DeLorean was charged with narcotics-smuggling violations involving a large amount of drugs.

At his 1984 trial, DeLorean claimed that he had been set up by the police to commit a crime that he would not have been involved in were it not for their urging. DeLorean's auto company had fallen on hard times, and he was facing heavy debts. Federal agents, acting undercover, proposed to DeLorean a plan whereby he could make a great deal of money through drugs. Because the idea originated with the police, not with DeLorean, and because DeLorean was able to demonstrate successfully that he was repeatedly threatened by a police informant not to pull out of the deal, the jury returned a "not guilty" verdict.

The concept of entrapment is well summarized in a statement made by DeLorean's defense attorney to *Time* magazine before the trial: "This is a fictitious crime. Without the Government there would be no crime. This is one of the most insidious and misguided law-enforcement operations in history."[75]

DOUBLE JEOPARDY

The Fifth Amendment to the U.S. Constitution makes it clear that no person may be tried twice for the same offense. People who have been acquitted or found innocent may not again be "put in jeopardy of life or limb" for the same crime. The same is true of those who have been convicted: They cannot be tried again for the same offense. Cases that are dismissed for a lack of evidence also come under the double jeopardy rule and cannot result in a new trial. The U.S. Supreme Court has ruled that "the Double Jeopardy Clause protects against three distinct abuses: a second prosecution for the same offense after acquittal; a second prosecution for the same offense after conviction; and multiple punishments for the same offense."[76]

double jeopardy

A common law and constitutional prohibition against a second trial for the same offense.

Double jeopardy does not apply in cases of trial error. Hence, a defendant whose conviction was set aside because of some error in proceedings at a lower court level (for example, inappropriate instructions to the jury by the trial court judge) can be retried on the same charges. Similarly, when a defendant's motion for a mistrial is successful, or when members of the jury cannot agree on a verdict (resulting in a hung jury), a second trial may be held.

Defendants, however, may be tried in both federal and state courts without necessarily violating the principle of double jeopardy. For example, 33-year-old Rufina Canedo pleaded guilty to possession of 50 kilograms of cocaine in 1991 and received a six-year prison sentence from a California court.[77] Federal prosecutors, however, indicted her again—this time under a federal law—for the same offense. They offered her a deal: Testify against your husband, or face federal prosecution and the possibility of 20 years in a federal prison. Because state and federal statutes emanate from different jurisdictions, the Supreme Court has held this kind of dual prosecution to be constitutional. To prevent abuse, the U.S. Justice Department acted in 1960 to restrict federal prosecution in such cases to situations involving a "compelling federal interest," such as a civil rights violation. However, in the face of soaring drug-law violations in recent years, the restriction has been relaxed.

In 1992, in another drug case, the Supreme Court ruled that the Double Jeopardy Clause of the U.S. Constitution "only prevents duplicative prosecution for the same offense" but that "a substantive offense and a conspiracy to commit that offense are not the same offense for double jeopardy purposes." In that case, *U.S. v. Felix* (1992),[78] a Missouri man was convicted in that state of manufacturing methamphetamine and was then convicted again in Oklahoma of the "separate crime" of conspiracy to manufacture a controlled substance—in part based on his activities in Missouri.

Generally, because civil and criminal law differ as to purpose, it is possible to try someone in civil court to collect damages for a possible violation of civil law, even if they were found "not guilty" in criminal court, without violating the principle of double jeopardy. The well-known 1997 California civil trial of O. J. Simpson on grounds of wrongful death resulted in widespread publicity of just such a possibility.

Similarly, the 2005 civil trial of actor Robert Blake, following his acquittal at a criminal trial for murdering his wife, resulted in Blake's being ordered to pay $30 million to his wife's children.[79] In cases where civil penalties are "so punitive in form and effect as to render them criminal,"[80] however, a person sanctioned by a court in a civil case may not be tried in criminal court.

COLLATERAL ESTOPPEL

Collateral estoppel is similar to double jeopardy, but it applies to facts that have been determined by a "valid and final judgment."[81] Such facts cannot become the object of new litigation. For example, if a defendant has been acquitted of a murder charge by virtue of an alibi, it would not be permissible to try that person again for the murder of a second person killed along with the first.

SELECTIVE PROSECUTION

The procedural defense of selective prosecution is based on the Fourteenth Amendment's guarantee of "equal protection of the laws." This defense may be available where two or more individuals are suspected of criminal involvement, but not all are actively prosecuted. Selective prosecution based fairly on the strength of available evidence is not the object of this defense. But when prosecution proceeds unfairly on the basis of some arbitrary and discriminatory attribute, such as race, sex, friendship, age, or religious preference, this defense may offer protection. In 1996, however, in a case that reaffirmed reasonable limits on claims of selective prosecution, the U.S. Supreme Court ruled that for a defendant to successfully "claim that he was singled out for prosecution on the basis of his race, he must make a . . . showing that the Government declined to prosecute similarly situated suspects of other races."[82]

DENIAL OF A SPEEDY TRIAL

The Sixth Amendment to the Constitution guarantees a right to a speedy trial. The purpose of the guarantee is to prevent unconvicted and potentially innocent people from languishing in jail. The federal government[83] and most states have laws (generally referred to as *speedy trial acts*) that define the time limit necessary for a trial to be "speedy." They generally set a reasonable period, such as 90 or 120 days following arrest. Excluded from the total number of days are delays that result from requests by the defense to prepare the defendant's case. If the limit set by law is exceeded, the defendant must be set free, and no trial can occur.

Speedy trial claims became an issue in New Orleans after it was ravaged by Hurricane Katrina in August 2005 because hundreds of inmates in parish jails who had been arrested before the hurricane hit never came to trial. Nine months after the storm battered the city, Chief District Judge Calvin Johnson told reporters that his staff was continuing to find people who shouldn't be in jail and who were doing "Katrina time."[84] "We're still finding people—they bubble up weekly," Johnson said. Most pre-Katrina arrestees discovered by Johnson's staff had been taken into custody for misdemeanors before the storm hit, and the judge said that he releases them when they're found. "We can't have people in jail indeterminately," he said. Speedy trial laws are discussed in more detail in Chapter 10.

In all criminal prosecutions, the accused shall enjoy the right to a speedy and public trial, by an impartial jury.

—Sixth Amendment to the U.S. Constitution

PROSECUTORIAL MISCONDUCT

Another procedural defense is prosecutorial misconduct. Generally speaking, legal scholars use the term *prosecutorial misconduct* to describe actions undertaken by prosecutors that give the government an unfair advantage or that prejudice the rights of a defendant or a witness. Prosecutors are expected to uphold the highest ethical standards in the performance of their roles. When they knowingly permit false testimony, when they hide information that would clearly help the defense, or when they make unduly biased statements to the jury in closing arguments, the defense of prosecutorial misconduct may be available to the defendant.

The most famous instance of prosecutorial misconduct may have occurred during a convoluted 17-year-long federal case against former Cleveland autoworker John Demjanjuk. Demjanjuk, who was accused of committing war crimes as the notorious Nazi guard "Ivan the Terrible," was extradited in 1986 by the federal government to Israel to face charges there. In late 1993, however, the Sixth U.S. Circuit Court of Appeals in Cincinnati, Ohio, ruled that federal prosecutors, working under what the court called a "win-at-any-cost" attitude, had intentionally withheld evidence that might have exonerated Demjanjuk. Demjanjuk, who was stripped of his U.S. citizenship when extradited, later returned to the United States after the Supreme Court of Israel overturned his sentence there.[85]

POLICE FRAUD

During the 1995 double-murder trial of O. J. Simpson, defense attorneys suggested that evidence against Simpson had been concocted and planted by police officers with a personal dislike of the defendant. In particular, defense attorneys pointed a finger at Los Angeles Police Detective Mark Fuhrman, suggesting that he had planted a bloody glove at the Simpson estate and had tampered with bloodstain evidence taken from Simpson's white Ford Bronco. To support allegations that Fuhrman was motivated by racist leanings, defense attorneys subpoenaed tapes Fuhrman had made over a ten-year period with a North Carolina screenwriter who had been documenting life within the Los Angeles Police Department.

As one observer put it, however, the defense of police fraud builds on extreme paranoia about the government and police agencies. This type of defense, said Francis Fukuyama, carries "to extremes a distrust of government and the belief that public authorities are in a vast conspiracy to violate the rights of individuals."[86] It can also be extremely unfair to innocent people, for a strategy of this sort subjects otherwise well-meaning public servants to intense public scrutiny, effectively shifting attention away from criminal defendants and onto the police officers—sometimes with disastrous personal results. Anthony Pellicano, a private investigator hired by Fuhrman's lawyers, put it this way: "[Fuhrman's] life right now is in the toilet. He has no job, no future. People think he's a racist. He can't do anything to help himself. He's been ordered not to talk. His family and friends, he's told them not to get involved. . . . Mark Fuhrman's life is ruined. For what? Because he found a key piece of evidence."[87] The 43-year-old Fuhrman retired from police work before the Simpson trial concluded and has since written two books.

SUMMARY

- Laws are rules of conduct, usually found enacted in the form of statutes, that regulate relationships between people and also between parties. One of the primary functions of the law is to maintain public order. Laws also serve to regulate human interaction, enforce moral beliefs, define the economic environment of a society, enhance predictability, promote orderly social change, sustain individual rights, identify wrongdoers and redress wrongs, and mandate punishment and retribution. Because laws are made by those in power and are influenced by those with access to power brokers, they tend to reflect and support the interest of society's most powerful members.

- The rule of law, which is sometimes referred to as the *supremacy of law*, encompasses the principle that an orderly society must be governed by established principles and known codes that are applied uniformly and fairly to all of its members. It means that no one is above the law, and it mandates that those who make or enforce the law must also abide by it. The rule of law is regarded as a vital underpinning in Western democracies, for without it disorder and chaos might prevail.

- This chapter identified various types of law, including criminal law, civil law, administrative law, case law, and procedural law. We were concerned primarily with criminal law, which is that form of the law that defines, and specifies punishments for, offenses of a public nature or for wrongs committed against the state or against society.

- Violations of the criminal law can be of many different types and can vary in severity. Five categories of violations were discussed in this chapter: (1) felonies, (2) misdemeanors, (3) offenses, (4) treason and espionage, and (5) inchoate offenses.

- From the perspective of Western jurisprudence, all crimes can be said to share certain features. Taken together, these features make up the legal essence of the concept of crime. The essence of crime consists of three conjoined elements: (1) the criminal act, which in legal parlance is termed the *actus reus*, (2) a culpable mental state, or *mens rea*, and (3) a concurrence of the two. Hence, the essence of criminal conduct consists of a concurrence of a criminal act with a culpable mental state. Five additional principles, added to these three, allow us to fully appreciate contemporary understandings of crime. These five principles are (1) causation, (2) a resulting harm, (3) the principle of legality, (4) the principle of punishment, and (5) necessary attendant circumstances.

- Written laws specify exactly what conditions are required for a person to be charged in a given instance of criminal activity. Hence, the elements of a crime are specific legal aspects of the criminal offense that the prosecution must prove in order to obtain a conviction. Guilt can be demonstrated, and criminal offenders convicted, only if all of the statutory elements of the particular crime can be proved in court.

- Our legal system recognizes four broad categories of defenses to a criminal charge: (1) alibi, (2) justifications, (3) excuses, and (4) procedural defenses. An alibi, if shown to be valid, means that the defendant could not have committed the crime in question because he or she was not present at the time of the crime. When a defendant offers a justification as a defense, he or she admits committing the act in question but claims that it was necessary to avoid some greater evil. A defendant who offers an excuse as a defense claims that some personal condition or circumstance at the time of the act was such that he or she should not be held accountable under the criminal law. Procedural defenses make the claim that the defendant was in some significant way discriminated against in the justice process or that some important aspect of official procedure was not properly followed in the investigation or prosecution of the crime charged.

KEY TERMS

actus reus, 123

alibi, 130

alter ego rule, 131

attendant circumstances, 127

case law, 114

civil law, 117

common law, 115

concurrence, 125

corpus delicti, 129

criminal law, 117

criminal negligence, 125

cultural defense, 135

defense (to a criminal charge), 130

diminished capacity, 140

double jeopardy, 142

element (of a crime), 127

entrapment, 141

espionage, 122

excuse, 130

ex post facto, 126

felony, 121

guilty but mentally ill (GBMI), 139

inchoate offense, 123

incompetent to stand trial, 141

infraction, 122

insanity defense, 137

jurisprudence, 115

justification, 130

law, 114

legal cause, 126

mens rea, 124

misdemeanor, 121

M'Naghten rule, 138

motive, 125

offense, 122

penal code, 114

KEY CASES

QUESTIONS FOR REVIEW

1. What is the purpose of law? What would a society without laws be like?

2. What is the rule of law? What is its importance in Western democracies? What does it mean to say that "nobody is above the law"?

3. What types of law does this chapter discuss? What purpose does each serve?

4. What are the five categories of criminal law violations? Describe each, and rank the categories in terms of seriousness.

5. List and describe the eight general features of crime. What are the "three conjoined elements" that comprise the legal essence of the concept of crime?

6. What is meant by the *corpus delicti* of a crime? How does the *corpus delicti* of a crime differ from the statutory elements that must be proved to convict a particular defendant of committing that crime?

7. What four broad categories of criminal defenses does our legal system recognize? Under what circumstances might each be employed?

QUESTIONS FOR REFLECTION

1. What is common law? What impact does common law have on contemporary American criminal justice?

2. How does the legal concept of insanity differ from psychiatric explanations of mental illness?

3. Does the insanity defense serve a useful function today? If you could create your own rule for determining insanity in criminal trials, what would it be? How would it differ from existing rules?

4. Discuss your answers to these questions and other issues on the CJ Today e-mail discussion list (join the list at cjtoday.com).

WEB QUEST

Use the Cybrary (http://www.cybrary.info) to locate websites containing state criminal codes. Choose a state, and locate the statutes pertaining to the Federal Bureau of Investigation's (FBI's) eight major crimes. (Remember that the terminology may be different. Whereas the FBI uses the term *rape*, for example, the state you've selected may use *sexual assault*.) After studying the statutes, describe the *corpus delicti* of each major offense—that is, list the elements of each offense that a prosecutor must prove in court to obtain a conviction. Now choose a second state, preferably from a different geographic region of the country. Again, list the elements of each major offense. Compare the way in which those elements are described with the terminology used by the first state you chose. What differences, if any, exist? Submit your findings to your instructor if asked to do so.

To complete this Web Quest online, go to the Web Quest module in Chapter 4 of the *Criminal Justice Today* Companion Website at cjtoday.com.

PART 2
Policing

RIGHTS OF THE ACCUSED UNDER INVESTIGATION

The accused has these common law, constitutional, statutory, and humanitarian rights

- A right against unreasonable searches

- A right against unreasonable arrest

- A right against unreasonable seizures of property

- A right to fair questioning by authorities

- A right to protection from personal harm

These individual rights must be effectively balanced against these community concerns

- The efficient apprehension of offenders

- The prevention of crimes

How does our system of justice work toward balance?

5

Policing: History and Structure

6

Policing: Purpose and Organization

7

Policing: Legal Aspects

8

Policing: Issues and Challenges

To Protect and to Serve

Famed police administrator and former New York City Police Commissioner Patrick V. Murphy once said, "It is a privilege to be a police officer in a democratic society." While Murphy's words still ring true, many of today's law enforcement officers might hear in them only the echo of a long-dead ideal, unrealistic for today's times.

America's police officers form the front line in the unending battle against crime, drugs, and terrorism—a battle that seems to get more sinister and more demanding with each passing day. It is the police who are called when a crime is in progress or when one has been committed. They are the first responders to a terrorist event that strikes the homeland. The police are expected to objectively and impartially investigate law violations, gather evidence, solve crimes, and make arrests resulting in the successful prosecution of suspects—all the while adhering to the strict due process standards set forth in the U.S. Constitution and enforced by the courts. They are also expected to aid the injured, give succor to victims, and protect the innocent. The chapters in

this section of *Criminal Justice Today* provide an overview of the historical development of policing; describe law enforcement agencies at the federal, state, and local levels; explore issues related to police administration; and discuss the due process and legal environments surrounding police activity.

As you will see, although the police are ultimately charged with protecting the public, they often believe that members of the public do not accord them the respect they deserve, and they feel that the distance between the police and the public is not easily bridged. Within the last few decades, however, an image of policing has emerged that may do much to heal that divide. This model, known as *community policing*, goes well beyond traditional conceptions of the police as mere law enforcers and encompasses the idea that police agencies should take counsel from the communities they serve. Under this model, the police are expected to prevent crime, as well as solve it, and to help members of the community deal with other pressing social issues.

CHAPTER 5

Policing: History and Structure

LEARNING OBJECTIVES

After reading this chapter, you should be able to

- Summarize the historical development of policing in America, including the impact of the Prohibition era on American policing.

- Describe the three major levels of public law enforcement in the United States today.

- Identify significant federal law enforcement agencies and describe their responsibilities.

- Explain the role that state law enforcement agencies play in enforcing the law and identify the two major models of state law enforcement organization.

- Identify the various kinds of local law enforcement agencies and explain the role that local law enforcement agencies play in enforcing the law.

- Describe the nature and extent of private protective services in the United States today and describe the role these services might play in the future.

The police in the United States are not separate from the people. They draw their authority from the will and consent of the people, and they recruit their officers from them. The police are the instrument of the people to achieve and maintain order; their efforts are founded on principles of public service and ultimate responsibility to the public.

—*National Advisory Commission on Criminal Justice Standards and Goals*

Unlike the soldier fighting a war on foreign soil, police officers, who provide for our safety at home, have never been given the honor that was their due.

—*Hubert Williams, President, the Police Foundation*[1]

Hear the author discuss this chapter at cjtoday.com

Introduction

Many of the techniques used by today's police differ quite a bit from those employed in days gone by. Listen to how a policeman, writing in the mid-1800s, describes the way pickpockets were caught in London 200 years ago: "I walked forth the day after my arrival, rigged out as the very model of a gentleman farmer, and with eyes, mouth, and pockets wide open, and a stout gold-headed cane in my hand, strolled leisurely through the fashionable thoroughfares, the pump-rooms, and the assembly-rooms, like a fat goose waiting to be plucked. I wore a pair of yellow gloves well wadded, to save me from falling, through a moment's inadvertency, into my own snare, which consisted of about fifty fish-hooks, large black hackles, firmly sewn barb downward, into each of the pockets of my brand new leather breeches. The most blundering 'prig' alive might have easily got his hand to the bottom of my pockets, but to get it out again, without tearing every particle of flesh from the bones, was a sheer impossibility. . . . I took care never to see any of my old customers until the convulsive tug at one or other of the pockets announced the capture of a thief. I then coolly linked my arm in that of the prisoner, [and] told him in a confidential whisper who I was."[2]

British bobbies. Today's uniformed English police officers have a recognizable appearance rooted in the time of Sir Robert Peel. In what way were early American law enforcement efforts influenced by the British experience?

Comstock Images

Historical Development of the Police

Police tactics and strategy have changed substantially since historical times, and many different kinds of police agencies—some of them highly specialized—function within the modern criminal justice system. This chapter describes the development of organized policing in Western culture and discusses the function of contemporary American police forces at the federal, state, and local levels. Agency examples are given at each level. The promise held by private protective services, the recent rapid growth of private security organizations, and the quasi-private system of justice are also discussed.

If you want the present to be different from the past, study the past.

—Baruch Spinoza (1632–1677)

English Roots

The rise of the police as an organized force in the Western world coincided with the evolution of strong centralized governments. Although police forces have developed throughout the world, often in isolation from one another, the historical growth of the English police is of special significance to students of criminal justice in America, for it was on the British model that much of early American policing was based.

Law enforcement in early Britain, except for military intervention in the pursuit of bandits and habitual thieves, was not well organized until around the year A.D. 1200.[3] When a person committed an offense and could be identified, he or she was usually pursued by an organized posse. All able-bodied men who could hear a victim's cry for help were obligated to join the posse in a common effort to apprehend the offender. The posse was led by the shire reeve (the leader of the county) or by a mounted officer (the **comes stabuli**). Our modern words *sheriff* and *constable* are derived from these early terms. The *comites stabuli* (the plural form of the term) were not uniformed, nor were they numerous enough to perform all the tasks we associate today with law enforcement. This early system, employing a small number of mounted officers, depended for its effectiveness on the ability to organize and direct the efforts of citizens toward criminal apprehension.

The offender, cognizant of a near-certain end at the hands of the posse, often sought protection from trusted friends and family. As a consequence, feuds developed among organized groups of citizens, some seeking revenge and some siding with the offender. Suspects who lacked the shelter of a sympathetic group might flee into a church and invoke the time-honored custom of sanctuary. Sanctuary was rarely an ideal escape, however, as pursuers could surround the church and wait out the offender, preventing food and water from being carried inside. The offender, once caught, became the victim. Guilt was usually assumed, and trials were rare. Public executions, often involving torture, typified this early justice and served to provide a sense of communal solidarity as well as group retribution.

The development of law enforcement in English cities and towns grew out of an early reliance on bailiffs, or watchmen. Bailiffs were assigned the task of maintaining a **night watch**, primarily to detect fires and spot thieves. While too few in number to handle most emergencies, bailiffs were able to rouse the sleeping population, which could then deal with whatever crisis was at hand. Larger cities expanded the idea of bailiffs by creating both a night watch and a day ward.

British police practices became codified in the **Statute of Winchester**, written in 1285. The statute (1) specified the creation of the watch and the ward in cities and towns; (2) mandated the draft of eligible males to serve those forces; (3) institutionalized the use of the *hue and cry*, making citizens who disregarded a call for help subject to criminal penalties; and (4) required that citizens maintain weapons in their home for answering the call to arms.

Some authors have attributed the growth of modern police forces to the gin riots that plagued London and other European cities in the eighteenth and nineteenth centuries. The invention of gin around 1720 provided, for the first time, a potent and inexpensive alcoholic drink readily available to the massed populations gathered in the early industrial ghettos of eighteenth-century cities. Seeking to drown their troubles, huge numbers of people, far beyond the ability of the bailiffs to control, began binges of drinking and rioting. During the next hundred years, these gin riots created an immense social problem for British authorities. By this time, the bailiff system had broken down and was staffed by groups of woefully inadequate substitutes, hired by original draftees to perform duties in their stead. Incompetent and unable to depend on the citizenry for help in enforcing the laws, bailiffs became targets of mob violence and were often attacked and beaten for sport.

comes stabuli

A nonuniformed mounted law enforcement officer of medieval England. Early police forces were small and relatively unorganized but made effective use of local resources in the formation of posses, the pursuit of offenders, and the like.

night watch

An early form of police patrol in English cities and towns.

Statute of Winchester

A law, written in 1285, that created a watch and ward system in English cities and towns and that codified early police practices.

THE BOW STREET RUNNERS

The early eighteenth century saw the emergence in London of a large criminal organization led by Jonathan Wild. Wild ran a type of fencing operation built around a group of loosely organized robbers, thieves, and burglars who would turn their plunder over to him. Wild would then negotiate with the legitimate owners for a ransom of their possessions.

The police response to Wild was limited by disinterest and corruption. However, change began when Henry Fielding, a well-known writer, became the magistrate of the Bow Street region of London. Fielding attracted a force of dedicated officers, dubbed the **Bow Street Runners**, who soon stood out as the best and most disciplined enforcement agents that London had to offer. Fielding's personal inspiration and his ability to communicate what he saw as the social needs of the period may have accounted for his success.

Bow Street Runners

An early English police unit formed under the leadership of Henry Fielding, magistrate of the Bow Street region of London.

In February 1725, Wild was arrested and arraigned on the following charges: " (1) that for many years past he had been a confederate with great numbers of highwaymen, pick-pockets, house-breakers, shop-lifters, and other thieves, (2) that he had formed a kind of corporation of thieves, of which he was the head or director . . . , (3) that he had divided the town and country into so many districts, and appointed distinct gangs for each, who regularly accounted with him for their robberies . . . , (4) that the persons employed by him were for the most part felon convicts . . . , (5) that he had, under his care and direction, several warehouses for receiving and concealing stolen goods, and also a ship for carrying off jewels, watches, and other valuable goods, to Holland, where he had a superannuated thief for his benefactor, and (6) that he kept in his pay several artists to make alterations, and transform watches, seals, snuff-boxes, rings, and other valuable things, that they might not be known."[4] Convicted of these and other crimes, Wild attempted suicide by drinking a large amount of laudanum, an opium compound. The drug merely rendered him senseless, and he was hanged the following morning, having only partially recovered from its effects.

In 1754, Henry Fielding died. His brother John took over his work and occupied the position of Bow Street magistrate for another 25 years. The Bow Street Runners remain famous to this day for quality police work.

THE NEW POLICE

In 1829, Sir Robert Peel, who later became prime minister of England, formed what many have hailed as the world's first modern police force. The passage of the Metropolitan Police Act that year allocated the resources for Peel's force of 1,000 handpicked men. The London Metropolitan Police Force, also known as the **new police** or more simply the *Met*, soon became a model for police forces around the world.

new police

A police force formed in 1829 under the command of Sir Robert Peel. It became the model for modern-day police forces throughout the Western world.

Members of the Metropolitan Police were quickly dubbed **bobbies**, after their founder. London's bobbies were organized around two principles: the belief that it was possible to discourage crime, and the practice of preventive patrol. Peel's police patrolled the streets by walking beats. Their predecessors, the watchmen, had occupied fixed posts throughout the city, awaiting a public outcry. The new police were uniformed, resembling a military organization, and adopted a military administrative style.

bobbies

The popular British name given to members of Sir Robert (Bob) Peel's Metropolitan Police Force.

London's first two police commissioners were Colonel Charles Rowan, a career military officer, and Richard Mayne, a lawyer. Rowan believed that mutual respect between the police and the citizenry would be crucial to the success of the new force. As a consequence, early bobbies were chosen for their ability to reflect and inspire the highest personal ideals among young men in early-nineteenth-century Britain.

The new police were not immediately well received. Some elements of the population saw them as an occupying army, and open battles between the police and the citizenry ensued. The tide of sentiment turned, however, when an officer was viciously killed in the Cold Bath Fields riot of 1833. A jury, considering a murder charge against the killer, returned a verdict of "not guilty," inspiring a groundswell of public support for the much-maligned force.

The Early American Experience

Early American law enforcement efforts were based to some degree on the British experience. Towns and cities in colonial America depended on modified versions of the night watch and the day ward, but the unique experience of the American colonies quickly differentiated the needs of colonists from those of the masses remaining in Europe. Huge expanses of uncharted territory, vast wealth, a widely dispersed population engaged mostly in agriculture, and a sometimes ferocious frontier all combined to mold American law enforcement in a distinctive

An English policewoman directing subway riders in London following four explosions on the underground rail system and a bus in 2005. How has policing changed since the time of Sir Robert Peel?

Sang Tan/AP Wide World Photos

way. Recent writers on the history of the American police have observed that policing in America was originally "decentralized," "geographically dispersed," "idiosyncratic," and "highly personalized."[5]

THE FRONTIER

One of the major factors determining the development of American law enforcement was the frontier, which remained vast and wild until late in the nineteenth century. The backwoods areas provided a natural haven for outlaws and bandits. Henry Berry Lowery, a famous outlaw of the Carolinas, the James Gang, and many lesser-known desperadoes felt at home in the unclaimed swamps and forests.

Only the boldest of settlers tried to police the frontier. Among them was Charles Lynch, a Virginia farmer of the late eighteenth century. Lynch and his associates tracked and punished offenders, often according to the dictates of the still well-known lynch law, or vigilante justice, which they originated. Citizen posses and vigilante groups were often the only law available to settlers on the western frontier. Judge Roy Bean ("the Law West of the Pecos"), "Wild Bill" Hickok, Bat Masterson, Wyatt Earp, and Pat Garrett were other popular figures of the nineteenth century who took it upon themselves, sometimes in a semiofficial capacity, to enforce the law on the books as well as the standards of common decency.

Although today **vigilantism** has a negative connotation, most of the original vigilantes of the American West were honest men and women trying to forge an organized and predictable lifestyle out of the challenging situations that they encountered. Often faced with unscrupulous, money-hungry desperadoes, they did what they could to bring the standards of civilization, as they understood them, to bear in their communities.

vigilantism

The act of taking the law into one's own hands.

POLICING AMERICA'S EARLY CITIES

Small-scale organized law enforcement came into being quite early in America's larger cities. In 1658, paid watchmen were hired by the city of New York to replace drafted citizens.[6] By 1693, the first uniformed officer was employed by the city, and in 1731, the first neighborhood station, or precinct, was constructed. Boston, Cincinnati, and New Orleans were among the American communities to follow the New York model and hire a force of watchmen in the early nineteenth century.

In 1829, American leaders watched closely as Sir Robert Peel created London's new police. One year later, Stephen Girard, a wealthy manufacturer, donated a considerable amount of money to the city of Philadelphia to create a capable police force. The city hired 120 men to staff a night watch and 24 to perform similar duties during the day.

In 1844, New York's separate day and night forces were combined into the New York City Police Department. Boston followed suit in 1855. Further advances in American policing were precluded by the Civil War. Southern cities captured in the war came under martial law and were subject to policing by the military.

The coming of the twentieth century, coinciding as it did with numerous technological advances and significant social changes, brought a flood of reform. The International Association of Chiefs of Police (IACP) was formed in 1902; it immediately moved to create a nationwide clearinghouse for criminal identification. In 1915, the Fraternal Order of Police (FOP) initiated operations. It was patterned after labor unions but prohibited strikes; it accepted personnel of all ranks, from patrol officer to chief. In 1910, Alice Stebbins Wells became the first policewoman in the world, serving with the Los Angeles Police Department.[7] Prior to Wells's appointment, women had served as jail matrons, and widows had sometimes been carried on police department payrolls after their officer-husbands had died in the line of duty, but they had not been fully "sworn" with carrying out the duties of a police officer. Wells became an outspoken advocate for the hiring of more policewomen, and police departments across the country began to hire female officers, especially to provide police services to children and to women and to "protect male officers from delicate and troublesome situations"[8]—such as the need to physically restrain female offenders.

In 1915, the U.S. Census reported that 25 cities employed policewomen. In that year, coinciding with the creation of the FOP, the International Association of Policewomen (now the International Association of Women Police) was formed in the city of Baltimore. In 1918, Ellen O'Grady became the first woman to hold a high administrative post in a major police organization when she was promoted to the rank of deputy police commissioner for the city of New York. As Dorothy Moses Schulz, a contemporary commentator on women's entry into policing, has observed, "The Policewomen's movement was not an isolated phenomenon, but was part of women's movement into other newly created or newly professionalized fields."[9]

During the early twentieth century, telephones, automobiles, and radios all had their impact on the American police. Teddy Roosevelt, the twenty-sixth president of the United States, began his career by serving as a police commissioner in New York City from 1895 to 1897. While there, he promoted the use of a call-box system of telephones, which allowed citizens to report crimes rapidly and made it possible for officers to call quickly for assistance. As president, Roosevelt helped to organize the Bureau of Investigation, which later became the Federal Bureau of Investigation (FBI). Federal law enforcement already existed in the form of U.S. marshals, created by an act of Congress in 1789, and in the form of postal inspectors, authorized by the U.S. Postal Act of 1829. The FBI became a national investigative service designed to quickly identify and apprehend offenders charged with a growing list of federal offenses. Automobiles created an era of affordable, rapid transportation and gave police forces far-reaching powers and high mobility. Telephones and radios provided the ability to maintain regular communication with central au-

A New York City police officer "mugging" a prisoner in the early days of police photography. How have advances in technology shaped policing?

Courtesy of the Library of Congress

thorities. State police agencies arose to counter the threat of the mobile offender, with Massachusetts and Pennsylvania leading the way to statewide forces.

PROHIBITION AND POLICE CORRUPTION

A dark period for American law enforcement agencies began in 1920 with the passage of a constitutional prohibition against all forms of alcoholic beverages. Until Prohibition was repealed in 1933, most parts of the country were rife with criminal activity, much of it supporting the trade in bootlegged liquor. Bootleggers earned huge sums of money, and some of them became quite wealthy. Massive wealth in the hands of law violators greatly increased the potential for corruption among police officials, some of whom were "paid off" to support bootlegging operations.

In 1931, the **Wickersham Commission**, officially called the National Commission on Law Observance and Enforcement and led by former U.S. Attorney General George W. Wickersham, recognized that Prohibition was unenforceable and reported that it carried a great potential for police corruption.[10] The commission, which released a number of reports, also established guidelines for enforcement agencies that directed many aspects of American law enforcement until the 1970s. The most influential of the Wickersham Commission reports was entitled *Report on the Enforcement of the Prohibition Laws of the United States.* That report, the release of which became one of the most important events in the history of American policing, can be read in its entirety at Library Extra 5–1 at cjtoday.com.

Wickersham Commission

The National Commission on Law Observance and Enforcement. In 1931, the commission issued a report stating that Prohibition was unenforceable and carried a great potential for police corruption.

LIBRARY
Extra
■■■■

The Last Half of the Twentieth Century

The rapid cultural change that took place throughout America in the 1960s and 1970s forever altered the legal and social environment in which the police must work. During that period, in conjunction with a burgeoning civil rights movement, the U.S. Supreme Court frequently enumerated constitutionally based personal rights for those facing arrest, investigation, and criminal prosecution. Although a "chipping away" at those rights, which some say is continuing today, may have begun in the 1980s, the earlier emphasis placed on the rights of defendants undergoing criminal investigation and prosecution will have a substantial impact on law enforcement activities for many years to come.

The 1960s and 1970s were also a period of intense examination of police operations, from day-to-day enforcement decisions to administrative organization and police–community relations. In 1967, the President's Commission on Law Enforcement and Administration of Justice issued its report, *The Challenge of Crime in a Free Society,* which found that the police were often isolated from the communities they served.[11] In 1969, the **Law Enforcement Assistance Administration (LEAA)** was formed to assist police forces across the nation in acquiring the latest in technology

Law Enforcement Assistance Administration (LEAA)

A now-defunct federal agency established under Title I of the Omnibus Crime Control and Safe Streets Act of 1968 to funnel federal funding to state and local law enforcement agencies.

Detroit police officers inspecting equipment found in an illegal underground brewery during the Prohibition era. How did the constitutional prohibition against alcoholic beverages during the 1920s and early 1930s affect American policing?

© CORBIS

and in adopting new enforcement methods. In 1973, the National Advisory Commission on Criminal Justice Standards and Goals issued a comprehensive report detailing strategies for combating and preventing crime and for improving the quality of law enforcement efforts at all levels.[12] Included in the report was a call for greater participation in police work by women and ethnic minorities and the recommendation that a college degree be made a basic prerequisite for police employment by the 1980s. The creation of a third major commission, the National Commission on Crime Prevention and Control, was authorized by the federal Violent Crime Control and Law Enforcement Act of 1994, but the commission never saw the light of day.[13] Read about the crime commission that never was at Web Extra 5–1 at cjtoday.com.

WEB
Extra

Evidence-Based Policing

In 1969, with the passage of the Omnibus Crime Control and Safe Streets Act, the U.S. Congress created the Law Enforcement Assistance Administration (LEAA). LEAA was charged with combating crime through the expenditure of huge amounts of money in support of crime-prevention and crime-reduction programs. Some have compared the philosophy establishing LEAA to that which supported the American space program's goal of landing people on the moon: Put enough money into any problem, and it will be solved! Unfortunately, the crime problem was more difficult to address than the challenge of a moon landing; even after the expenditure of nearly $8 billion, LEAA had not come close to its goal. In 1982, LEAA expired when Congress refused it further funding.

The legacy of LEAA is an important one for police managers, however. The research-rich years of 1969 to 1982, supported largely through LEAA funding, have left a plethora of scientific findings relevant to police administration and, more importantly, have established a tradition of program evaluation within police management circles. This tradition, which is known as **scientific police management**, is a natural outgrowth of LEAA's insistence that every funded program contain a plan for its evaluation. *Scientific police management* refers to the application of social science techniques to the study of police administration for the purpose of increasing effectiveness, reducing the frequency of citizen complaints, and enhancing the efficient use of available resources. The heyday of scientific police management occurred in the 1970s, when federal monies were far more readily available to support such studies than they are today.

LEAA was not alone in funding police research during the 1970s. On July 1, 1970, the Ford Foundation announced the establishment of a Police Development Fund totaling $30 million, to be spent during the following five years to support major crime-fighting strategies of police departments. This funding led to the establishment of the Police Foundation, which continues to exist today with the mission of "foster[ing] improvement and innovation in American policing."[14] Police Foundation–sponsored studies during the past 20 years have added to the growing body of scientific knowledge about policing.

In 1973, LEAA established the **Exemplary Projects Program**, which was designed to recognize outstanding innovative efforts to combat crime and to provide assistance to crime victims so that such initiatives might serve as models for the nation. One project that won exemplary status early in the program was the Street Crimes Unit (SCU) of the New York City Police Department. The SCU disguised officers as potential mugging victims and put them in areas where they were most likely to be attacked. In its first year, the SCU made nearly 4,000 arrests and averaged a successful conviction rate of around 80%. Perhaps the most telling statistic was the "average officer days per arrest." The SCU invested only 8.2 days in each arrest, whereas the department average for all uniformed officers was 167 days per arrest.[15]

Today, federal support for criminal justice research and evaluation continues under the National Institute of Justice (NIJ) and the Bureau of Justice Statistics (BJS), both part of the Office of Justice Programs (OJP). OJP, created by Congress in 1984, provides federal leadership in developing the nation's capacity to prevent and control crime. The National Criminal Justice Reference Service (NCJRS), a part of NIJ, assists researchers nationwide in locating information applicable to their research projects. "Custom searches" of the NCJRS computer database can be done online and yield abundant information in most criminal justice subject areas. NIJ also publishes a series of informative periodic reports, such as the *NIJ Journal* and *NIJ Research in Review*, which serve to keep criminal justice practitioners and researchers informed about recent findings. View the NIJ online publication list at Web Extra 5–2 at cjtoday.com.

THE KANSAS CITY EXPERIMENT

By far the most famous application of social research principles to police management was the Kansas City preventive patrol experiment.[16] The results of the year-long **Kansas City experiment** were published in 1974. The study, sponsored by the Police Foundation, divided the southern

scientific police management

The application of social science techniques to the study of police administration for the purpose of increasing effectiveness, reducing the frequency of citizen complaints, and enhancing the efficient use of available resources.

Exemplary Projects Program

An initiative, sponsored by the Law Enforcement Assistance Administration, designed to recognize outstanding, innovative efforts to combat crime and to provide assistance to crime victims.

WEB
Extra

Kansas City experiment

The first large-scale scientific study of law enforcement practices. Sponsored by the Police Foundation, it focused on the practice of preventive patrol.

part of Kansas City into 15 areas. Five of these "beats" were patrolled in the usual fashion. In another group of five beats, patrol activities were doubled. The final third of the beats received a novel treatment indeed: No patrols were assigned to them, and no uniformed officers entered that part of the city unless they were called. The program was kept secret, and citizens were unaware of the difference between the patrolled and unpatrolled parts of the city.

The results of the Kansas City experiment were surprising. Records of "preventable crimes," those toward which the activities of patrol were oriented—such as burglary, robbery, auto theft, larceny, and vandalism—showed no significant differences in rate of occurrence among the three experimental beats. Similarly, citizens didn't seem to notice the change in patrol patterns in the two areas where patrol frequency was changed. Surveys conducted at the conclusion of the experiment showed no difference in citizens' fear of crime before and after the study. The 1974 study can be summed up in the words of the author of the final report: "The whole idea of riding around in cars to create a feeling of omnipresence just hasn't worked. . . . Good people with good intentions tried something that logically should have worked, but didn't."[17] This study has been credited with beginning the now-established tradition of scientific studies of policing.

A second Kansas City study focused on "response time."[18] It found that even consistently fast police response to citizen reports of crime had little effect on citizen satisfaction with the police or on the arrest of suspects. The study uncovered the fact that most reports made to the police came only after a considerable amount of time had passed. Hence, the police were initially handicapped by the timing of the report, and even the fastest police response was not especially effective.

EFFECTS OF THE KANSAS CITY STUDIES

The Kansas City studies greatly affected managerial assumptions about the role of preventive patrol and traditional strategies for responding to citizen calls for assistance. As Joseph Lewis, then director of evaluation at the Police Foundation, said, "I think that now almost everyone would agree that almost anything you do is better than random patrol."[19]

While the Kansas City studies called into question some basic assumptions about patrol, patrol remains the backbone of police work. New patrol strategies for the effective utilization of human resources have led to various kinds of **directed patrol** activities. One form of directed patrol varies the number of officers involved in patrolling according to the time of day or the frequency of reported crimes within an area, so as to put the most officers on the street where and when crime is most prevalent. Wilmington, Delaware, was one of the first cities to make use of split-force patrol, in which only a part of the patrol force performs routine patrol.[20] The remaining officers respond to calls for service, take reports, and conduct investigations.

In response to the Kansas City study on response time, some cities have prioritized calls for service,[21] ordering a quick police response only when crimes are in progress or when serious crimes have occurred. Less significant offenses, such as minor larcenies and certain citizen complaints, are handled using the mail or by having citizens come to the police station to make a report.

directed patrol

A police-management strategy designed to increase the productivity of patrol officers through the scientific analysis and evaluation of patrol techniques.

Members of the Kansas City (Missouri) Police Department being briefed on security measures for a planned visit by President George W. Bush. Scientific police management was supported by studies of preventive patrol undertaken in Kansas City in 1974. How does today's evidence-based policing build on that tradition?

Courtesy of the Media Office of the Kansas City Missouri Police Department

Early policing studies, such as the Kansas City patrol experiment, were designed to identify and probe some of the basic assumptions that guided police work. The initial response to many such studies was "Why should we study that? Everybody knows the answer already!" As in the case of the Kansas City experiment, however, it soon became obvious that conventional wisdom was not always correct. Scientific studies of special significance to law enforcement are summarized in Table 5–1.

EVIDENCE-BASED POLICING TODAY

At the close of the twentieth century, noted police researcher Lawrence W. Sherman addressed an audience of criminal justice policymakers, scholars, and practitioners at the Police Foundation in Washington, DC, and called for a new approach to American policing that would use research to guide and evaluate practice. "Police practices should be based on scientific evidence about what works best," Sherman told his audience. Sherman's lecture, entitled "Evidence-Based Policing: Policing Based on Science, Not Anecdote,"[22] popularized the term **evidence-based policing (EBP)**. EBP, says Sherman, "is the use of best available research on the outcomes of police work to implement guidelines and evaluate agencies, units, and officers."[23] In other words,

evidence-based policing (EBP)

The use of the best available research on the outcomes of police work to implement guidelines and evaluate agencies, units, and officers.[i]

TABLE 5–1	Selected Scientific Studies in Law Enforcement	
Year	**Study Name**	**Focus**
2005	Effectiveness of Designated Driver Programs	Designated driver campaigns to reduce highway accidents
2002	Reducing Gun Violence (Indianapolis)	Targeted police patrols to reduce gun crime and violence
2001	Boston's Operation Ceasefire Evaluation	Citywide effort to reduce gun violence, especially gang-related homicides
1999	National Evaluation of Weed-and-Seed Programs	Weed-and-seed programs in eight states
1998	Community Policing in Action (Indianapolis)	Police and citizen cooperation and neighborhood security
1994	Kansas City Gun Experiment	Supplemental police patrol to reduce gun crime
1992	New York City Police Department's Cadet Corps Study	Level of education among officers and hiring of minority officers
1992	Metro-Dade Spouse Abuse Experiment Replication (Florida)	Replication of a 1984 Minneapolis study
1991	Quality Policing in Madison, Wisconsin	Community policing and participatory police management
1990	Minneapolis "Hot Spot" Patrolling	Intensive patrol of problem areas
1987	Newport News Problem-Oriented Policing (Virginia)	Police solutions to community crime problems
1986	Crime Stoppers: A National Evaluation	Media crime-reduction programs
1986	Reducing Fear of Crime in Houston and Newark	Strategies for fear reduction among urban populations
1984	Minneapolis Domestic Violence Experiment	Effective police action in domestic violence situations
1981	Newark Foot Patrol Experiment	Costs versus benefits of foot patrol
1977	Cincinnati Team Policing Experiment	Team versus traditional policing
1977	Patrol Staffing in San Diego	One- versus two-officer units
1976	Police Response Time (Kansas City)	Citizen satisfaction with police response
1976	Police and Interpersonal Conflict	Police intervention in domestic and other disputes
1976	Managing Investigations	Detective/patrol officer teams
1976	Kansas City Peer Review Panel	Improvement in police behavior
1974	Kansas City Preventive Patrol Experiment	Effectiveness of police patrol

evidence-based policing uses research into everyday police procedures to evaluate current practices and to guide officers and police executives in future decision making. In any discussion of evidence-based policing, it is important to remember that the word *evidence* refers to scientific evidence, not criminal evidence.

"The basic premise of evidence-based practice," says Sherman, "is that we are all entitled to our own opinions, but not to our own facts."[24] Our own facts, or our beliefs about the way things should be done, says Sherman, often turn out to be wrong. During the civil rights movement of the 1960s and 1970s, for example, police executives in many areas took a heavy-handed approach in their attempts to control demonstrators. Images of tear-gas-filled streets, high-pressure fire hoses aimed at marchers, and police dogs biting fleeing demonstrators symbolize that era for many people. This heavy-handed approach had unintended consequences and served to inflame protesters. Situations that might have otherwise been contained with simple crowd-control tactics and the use of physical barriers became largely uncontrollable. Sherman reminds us that "the mythic power of subjective and unstructured wisdom holds back every field and keeps it from systematically discovering and implementing what works best in repeated tasks."

Today, the evidence-based policing model is gaining traction and has been called the single "most powerful force for change" in policing today.[25] Leading the movement toward evidence-based policing are organizations like the FBI's Futures Working Group and the Campbell Crime and Justice Group. FBI Supervisory Special Agent Carl J. Jensen III, a member of the Futures Working Group, notes that in the future "successful law enforcement executives will have to be consumers and appliers of research." They won't need to be researchers themselves, Jensen notes, "but they must use research in their everyday work."[26] The Campbell Crime and Justice Group, which emphasizes the use of experimental studies in crime and justice policymaking, can be accessed via Web Extra 5–3 at cjtoday.com.

> *Of all the ideas in policing, one stands out as the most powerful force for change: Police practices should be based on scientific evidence about what works best.*
>
> *—Lawrence W. Sherman*[ii]

WEB
Extra
▪▪▪▪

American Policing Today: From the Federal to the Local Level

The organization of American law enforcement has been called the most complex in the world. Three major legislative and judicial jurisdictions exist in the United States—federal, state, and local—and each has created a variety of police agencies to enforce its laws. Unfortunately, there has been little uniformity among jurisdictions as to the naming, function, or authority of enforcement agencies. The matter is complicated still more by the rapid growth of private security firms, which operate on a for-profit basis and provide services that have traditionally been regarded as law enforcement activities.

Federal Agencies

Dozens of **federal law enforcement agencies** are distributed among 14 U.S. government departments and 28 nondepartmental entities (Table 5–2). In addition to the enforcement agencies listed in the table, many other federal government offices are involved in enforcement through inspection, regulation, and control activities. At the beginning of 2007, the Government Accounting Office (GAO) reported that nonmilitary federal agencies employ a total of 139,929 law enforcement officers (LEOs), which it defined as individuals authorized to perform any of four specific functions: (1) conduct criminal investigations, (2) execute search warrants, (3) make arrests, or (4) carry firearms.[27]

Visit the home pages of many federal law enforcement agencies via Web Extra 5–4 at cjtoday.com. Learn more about staffing levels of federal criminal justice agencies at Library Extra 5–2.

federal law enforcement agency

A U.S. government agency or office whose primary functional responsibility is to enforce federal criminal laws.

 WEB
Extra
▪▪▪▪

 LIBRARY
Extra
▪▪▪▪

The Federal Bureau of Investigation

The Federal Bureau of Investigation may be the most famous law enforcement agency in the country and in the world. The FBI has traditionally been held in high regard by many Americans, who think of it as an example of what a law enforcement organization should be and who believe that FBI agents are exemplary police officers. William Webster, former director of the FBI, reflected this sentiment when he said, "Over the years the American people have come to expect the most professional law enforcement from the FBI. Although we use the most modern forms of management and technology in the fight against crime, our strength is in our people—in the character of the men and women of the FBI. For that reason we seek only those who have

TABLE 5-2   American Policing: Federal Law Enforcement Agencies

Department of Agriculture
U.S. Forest Service

Department of Commerce
Bureau of Export Enforcement
National Marine Fisheries Administration

Department of Defense
Air Force Office of Special Investigations
Army Criminal Investigation Division
Defense Criminal Investigative Service
Naval Investigative Service

Department of Energy
National Nuclear Safety Administration
Office of Mission Operations
Office of Secure Transportation

Department of Health and Human Services
Food and Drug Administration, Office of Criminal
    Investigations

Department of Homeland Security
Federal Law Enforcement Training Center
Federal Protective Service
Transportation Security Administration
U.S. Coast Guard
U.S. Customs and Border Protection (CBP)—
    includes U.S. Border Patrol
U.S. Immigration and Customs Enforcement (ICE)
U.S. Secret Service

Department of the Interior
Bureau of Indian Affairs
Bureau of Land Management
Fish and Wildlife Service
National Park Service
U.S. Park Police

Department of Justice
Bureau of Alcohol, Tobacco, Firearms, and
    Explosives
Bureau of Prisons
Drug Enforcement Administration
Federal Bureau of Investigation
U.S. Marshals Service

Department of Labor
Office of Labor Racketeering

Department of State
Diplomatic Security Service

Department of Transportation
Federal Air Marshals Program

Department of the Treasury
Internal Revenue Service–Criminal Investigation
    Division
Treasury Inspector General for Tax Enforcement

Department of Veterans Affairs
Office of Security and Law Enforcement

U.S. Postal Service
Postal Inspection Service

Other Offices with Enforcement Personnel
Administrative Office of the U.S. Courts
AMTRAK Police
Bureau of Engraving and Printing Police
Environmental Protection Agency–Criminal
    Investigations Division
Federal Reserve Board
Tennessee Valley Authority
U.S. Capitol Police
U.S. Mint
U.S. Supreme Court Police
Washington, D.C., Metropolitan Police
    Department

Note: Virtually every cabinet-level federal agency has its own Office of the Inspector General, which has enforcement authority.

Fidelity, bravery, and integrity.

—Motto of the Federal Bureau of Investigation

WEB
Extra

demonstrated that they can perform as professional people who can, and will, carry on our tradition of fidelity, bravery, and integrity."[28]

The history of the FBI spans about 100 years. It began as the Bureau of Investigation in 1908, when it was designed to serve as the investigative arm of the U.S. Department of Justice. The creation of the bureau was motivated, at least in part, by the inability of other agencies to stem the rising tide of American political and business corruption.[29] Learn about the history of the FBI at Web Extra 5–5.

The official purpose of today's FBI is succinctly stated in the agency's mission statement: "The Mission of the FBI is to protect and defend the United States against terrorist and foreign intelligence threats; to uphold and enforce the criminal laws of the United States; and to provide leadership and criminal justice services to federal, state, municipal, and international agencies and partners."[30] FBI special agents and administrators adhere to a set of core values officially stated as follows: (1) rigorous obedience to the Constitution of the United States, (2) respect for the dignity of all those we protect, (3) compassion, (4) fairness, (5) uncompromising personal integrity and institutional integrity, (6) accountability by accepting responsibility for our actions and decisions and the consequences of our actions and decisions, and (7) leadership, both personal and professional.[31]

CJ Careers

Federal Bureau of Investigation

Name: Kevin Kendrick

Position: Section Chief, Executive Development and Selection Program, Administrative Services Division

City: Washington, D.C.

College Attended: Wayne State University

Year Hired: 1981

"Seeing the good work that officers were doing when I was in school at Wayne State opened my eyes to the possibility of a career in law enforcement. I saw this as a wonderful opportunity to do something positive. Every day at the FBI is different. I can honestly say this is the greatest part of the job: the variety of assignments, the interaction with other agencies and the community. It's an incredible way to get things done. We do something that means something. We are having an impact on people's lives."

TYPICAL POSITIONS

Special agent, crime laboratory technician, ballistics technician, computer operator, fingerprint specialist, explosives examiner, document expert, and other nonagent technical positions. FBI activities include investigations into organized crime, white-collar crime, public corruption, financial crime, fraud against the government, bribery, copyright matters, civil rights violations, bank robbery, extortion, kidnapping, air piracy, terrorism, foreign counterintelligence, interstate criminal activity, fugitive and drug-trafficking matters, and other violations of federal statutes. The FBI also works with other federal, state, and local law enforcement agencies in investigating matters of joint interest and in training law enforcement officers from around the world.

EMPLOYMENT REQUIREMENTS

General employment requirements include (1) an age between 23 and 37; (2) excellent physical health; (3) uncorrected vision of not less than 20/200, correctable to 20/20 in one eye and at least 20/40 in the other eye; (4) good hearing; (5) U.S. citizenship; (6) a valid driver's license; (7) successful completion of a comprehensive background investigation; (8) a law degree or a bachelor's degree from an accredited college or university; (9) successful completion of an initial written examination; (10) an intensive formal interview; and (11) urinalysis. A polygraph examination may also be required.

OTHER REQUIREMENTS

Special-agent entry programs exist in the areas of law, accounting, languages, engineering/science, and a general "diversified" area. They require a minimum of three years of full-time work experience, preferably with a law enforcement agency. Candidates who otherwise meet entry requirements and who possess one or more of the following critical skills are currently deemed essential to address the agency's increasingly complex responsibilities and will be given priority in the hiring process: (1) computer science and other information technology specialties; (2) engineering; (3) physical sciences (physics, chemistry, biology, and so on); (4) foreign language proficiency (Arabic, Farsi, Pashtu, Urdu, Chinese [all dialects], Japanese, Korean, Russian, Spanish, and Vietnamese); (5) foreign counterintelligence; (6) counterterrorism; and (7) military intelligence experience. The FBI emphasizes education and especially values degrees in law, graduate studies, and business and accounting. Most nonagent technical career paths also require bachelor's or advanced degrees and U.S. citizenship.

SALARY

In mid-2007, Special Agent trainees at the FBI Academy were paid at GS-10, step 1 ($43,441) plus the Quantico, Virginia, locality adjustment (17.50%) during their time at the FBI Academy. This equated to $51,043 on an annualized basis. Newly assigned Special Agents are paid at GS-10, step 1 ($43,441) plus locality pay and availability pay. Locality pay (which ranges from 12.5% to 28.7% of base salary depending upon office assignment) is additional compensation to account for differences in the labor market between different areas. Availability pay is a 25% increase in adjusted salary (base salary plus locality pay) for all Special Agents due to their requirement to average a 50-hour workweek over the course of the year. Thus, with the locality and availability pay adjustments, new Special Agents in their first Field Offices earned between $61,100 and $69,900 in 2007. New Special Agents assigned to certain designated high-cost offices (New York, San Francisco, Los Angeles, San Diego, Washington, D.C., Boston, and Newark) may also be paid a one-time relocation bonus of approximately $22,000 to help offset higher real estate and living costs. Special agents can advance to GS-13 in field assignments and to GS-15 or higher in supervisory and management positions.

BENEFITS

Benefits include (1) 13 days of sick leave annually, (2) two and a half to five weeks of paid vacation and ten paid federal holidays each year, (3) federal health and life insurance, and (4) a comprehensive retirement program.

DIRECT INQUIRIES TO:

Federal Bureau of Investigation
J. Edgar Hoover Building
935 Pennsylvania Avenue, N.W.
Washington, DC 20535–0001

Phone: 202-324-3000, or check your local telephone book website: http://www.fbi.gov, or visit http://fbijobs.com

For more information on the rapidly expanding criminal justice careers area, read *Where the Jobs Are: Mission Critical Opportunities for America*, available on the Web at http://www.justicestudies.com/jobs.htm.

The most fundamental weakness in crime control is the failure of federal and state governments to create a framework for local policing. Much of what is wrong with the police is the result of the absurd, fragmented, unworkable nonsystem of more than 17,000 local departments.

—Patrick V. Murphy, former New York City Police Commissioner

FBI headquarters are located in the J. Edgar Hoover Building on Pennsylvania Avenue in Washington, D.C. Special agents and support personnel who work at the agency's headquarters organize and coordinate FBI activities throughout the country and around the world. Headquarters staffers determine investigative priorities, oversee major cases, and manage the organization's resources, technology, and personnel.

The daily work of the FBI is done by nearly 13,000 special agents assigned to 56 field offices and 400 satellite offices (known as *resident agencies*). A special agent in charge oversees each field office, except for the three largest field offices in Washington, D.C., Los Angeles, and New York City, each of which is headed by an assistant director.

The FBI also operates "legal attaché offices" (called *Legats*) in a number of major cities around the world, including London and Paris. Such offices permit the international coordination of enforcement activities and facilitate the flow of law enforcement–related information between the FBI and police agencies in host countries. In 1995, a few years after the end of the cold war, the FBI opened a legal attaché office in Moscow. The Moscow office assists Russian police agencies in the growing battle against organized crime in that country and helps American officials track suspected Russian criminals operating in the United States. Also in 1995, an Eastern European version of the FBI Academy, known as the International Law Enforcement Academy (ILEA), opened in Budapest, Hungary. Its purpose is to train police administrators from all of Eastern Europe in the latest crime-fighting techniques.[32]

A little over a decade ago, the FBI formed the National Computer Crime Squad (NCCS) to investigate violations of the federal Counterfeit Access Device and Computer Fraud and Abuse Act of 1984, the Computer Fraud and Abuse Act of 1986 (CFAA),[33] and other federal cybercrime laws. NCCS focuses on computer crimes like (1) intrusions of public switched networks (telephone company networks), (2) major computer network intrusions, (3) network integrity violations, (4) privacy violations, (5) industrial espionage, (6) pirated computer software, and (7) other crimes in which a computer is centrally involved. In recent years, the FBI has created individual cybercrime investigation teams in each of its field offices within the United States.

The FBI also operates the Combined DNA Index System (CODIS), a computerized forensic database of DNA "profiles" of offenders convicted of serious crimes (such as rape, other sexual assaults, murder, and certain crimes against children), as well as DNA profiles from unknown offenders.[34] CODIS, now a part of the National DNA Index System (NDIS), was formally authorized by the federal DNA Identification Act of 1994.[35] It is being enhanced daily through the work of federal, state, and local law enforcement agencies that take DNA samples from biological evidence gathered at crime scenes and from offenders themselves. The computerized CODIS system can rapidly identify a perpetrator when it finds a match between an evidence sample and a stored profile. By 1998, every state had enacted legislation establishing a CODIS database and requiring that DNA from offenders convicted of certain serious crimes be entered into the system. As of January 2006, the CODIS database contained more than 3 million DNA profiles.[36] Learn more about CODIS at Web Extra 5–6 at cjtoday.com.

WEB
Extra
■ ■ ■ ■

As the FBI has grown, some of its functions have become geographically dispersed. Headquartered in Clarksburg, West Virginia, the Criminal Justice Information Services (CJIS) Division serves as the central repository for criminal justice information services in the FBI. The FBI describes the division as "a customer-driven organization providing state-of-the-art identification and information services to local, state, federal, and international criminal justice communities." In support of these activities, CJIS has developed an advisory process that involves sharing management and policy-making decisions with local, state, and federal criminal justice agencies. The CJIS Division includes the Fingerprint Identification Program, the National Crime Information Center Program, the Uniform Crime Reporting Program, and the Integrated Automated Fingerprint Identification System (IAFIS)—a computer-based system that can store, process, analyze, and retrieve millions of fingerprints in a relatively short period of time.

The FBI Laboratory Division, located in Quantico, Virginia, operates one of the largest and most comprehensive crime laboratories in the world. It provides services related to the scientific solution and prosecution of crimes throughout the country. It is also the only full-service federal forensic laboratory in the United States. Laboratory activities include crime-scene searches, special surveillance photography, latent-fingerprint examination, forensic examination of evidence (including DNA testing), court testimony by laboratory personnel, and other scientific and technical services. The FBI offers laboratory services, free of charge, to all law enforcement agencies in the United States. Learn more about the FBI's administrative divisions, including the activities of each, via Web Extra 5–7 at cjtoday.com.

WEB
Extra
■ ■ ■ ■

The FBI also runs a National Academy Program, which is part of its Training Division. The program offered its first class in 1935 and had 23 students. It was then known as the FBI National Police Training School. In 1940, the school moved from Washington, D.C., to the U.S. Marine Am-

FBI agents taking part in an apartment arrest training exercise at the FBI Academy in Quantico, Virginia, as an instructor looks on. Student agents chosen for the course receive classroom and shooting-range instruction and act out crime and arrest scenarios at a mock-up town called Hogan's Alley. The academy, which began operations in 1935 in Washington, D.C., covers more than 300 acres and has produced more than 30,000 graduates. What are the core values of the FBI?

Vince Lupo/AP Wide World Photos

phibious Base at Quantico, Virginia. In 1972, the facility expanded to 334 acres, and the FBI Academy, as we know it today, officially opened.[37] According to the most recent statistics available, the academy program has produced 37,990 graduates since it began operations. This includes 2,475 international graduates from 151 foreign countries and 328 graduates from U.S. territories and possessions. More than 200 sessions have been offered since inception of the training program. Visit the FBI Academy on the Web via Web Extra 5–8 at cjtoday.com.

WEB
Extra
■ ■ ■ ■

THE FBI AND COUNTERTERRORISM

The FBI's counterterrorism efforts became especially important following the September 11, 2001, attacks on the World Trade Center in New York City and the Pentagon. Two months after the attacks, then-U.S. Attorney General John Ashcroft announced a major "reorganization and mobilization" of the FBI and other federal agencies, such as the Immigration and Naturalization Service (now U.S. Citizenship and Immigration Services—an office of the Department of Homeland Security). Speaking at a press conference in Washington, D.C., Ashcroft said, "Our strategic plan mandates fundamental change in several of the most critical components of American justice and law enforcement, starting with the organization that is at the center of our counterterrorism effort, the Federal Bureau of Investigation. In its history, the FBI has been many things: the protector of our institutions when they were under assault from organized crime; the keeper of our security when it was threatened by international espionage; and the defender of our civil rights when they were denied to some Americans on the basis of their race, color or creed. Today the American people call upon the Federal Bureau of Investigation to put prevention of terrorism at the center of its law-enforcement and national-security efforts."[38]

Since that time, the FBI has reshaped its priorities to focus on preventing future terrorist attacks. This effort is managed by the Counterterrorism Division at FBI headquarters and is emphasized at every field office, resident agency, and Legat. Headquarters administers a national threat warning system that allows the FBI to instantly distribute important terrorism-related bulletins to law enforcement agencies and public-safety departments throughout the country. "Flying Squads" provide specialized counterterrorism knowledge and experience, language capabilities, and analytic support as needed to FBI field offices and Legats.

To combat terrorism, the FBI's Counterterrorism Division collects, analyzes, and shares information and critical intelligence with various federal agencies and departments—including the Central Intelligence Agency (CIA), the National Security Agency (NSA), and the Department of Homeland Security (DHS)—and with law enforcement agencies throughout the country. An essential weapon in the FBI's battle against terrorism is the Joint Terrorism Task Force (JTTF). A National JTTF, located at the FBI's Washington headquarters, includes representatives from the Department of Defense, the Department of Energy, the Federal Emergency Management Agency, the Central Intelligence Agency, the Customs Service, the Secret Service, and U.S. Immigration and Customs Enforcement. In addition, through 66 local JTTFs, representatives from federal agen-

It remains the FBI's overriding priority to predict and prevent terrorist attacks. The threat posed by international terrorism, and in particular from Al Qaeda and related groups, continues to be the gravest we face.

—FBI Director Robert S. Mueller III[iii]

CJ News

New Breed of FBI Recruits Training to Take on Terror

Timothy Lauster hadn't fired a gun since he was 9. Tiffany Kelley never fired anything but a BB gun. Then they joined the FBI.

Lauster, 28, and Kelley, 31, represent a newer, more technically savvy breed of FBI agent. He's a computer specialist, and she's an electrical engineer.

They and others like them are changing the world's best-known law enforcement agency because they aren't the lawyers, accountants or ex-cops that the FBI traditionally has attracted and recruited.

"I felt that if I could help, I should," says Lauster, who has a computer science undergraduate degree and a master's in business administration. He says he took about a 50% cut in salary to leave a large financial strategies corporation to join the FBI.

Since the 9/11 terrorist attacks, the FBI has used radio and television ads, job fairs and its website to try to court computer-savvy men and women with multiple college degrees in sciences and languages as part of its emphasis on preventing terrorist attacks.

As of March 21, 2005, the FBI was about halfway toward meeting its annual goals for hiring agents with computer science, engineering and other science backgrounds. Karen Gardner, acting chief of the FBI's new agent training, says 30 engineers, 38 computer science experts and 28 science specialists had already been hired.

But the bureau continues to have difficulty recruiting people who are fluent in Arabic and other languages. By March 21, 2005, the FBI had hired only one Arabic speaker.

The FBI Academy, located on 547 acres of the U.S. Marine Corps base here in Quantico, Virginia, is key to the bureau's efforts to change its focus from crime solving to crime prevention.

The academy's curriculum has been under scrutiny by FBI Director Robert Mueller and other top bureau officials since the terrorist attacks because of the need to train a workforce well versed in counterterrorism, counterintelligence and information sharing. More than 3,400 new agents graduated from the FBI Academy from fiscal year 2002 to May 6, 2005. Up to 2,000 new agents will be trained in fiscal year 2007 alone.

The training is being done in the academy's 33-year-old decrepit buildings, which are crumbling and have cramped classrooms and stained carpets.

Congress has promised to pay for renovations, with $21 million allocated this year. But the academy cannot shut down even briefly because of the emphasis on training as many new agents as possible. The FBI is riding a post-9/11 boom in patriotism that's helped its recruitment efforts. Many of the new agents have left high-paying careers to join the fight against terrorism.

"This is a tremendous opportunity for the FBI to seize the moment . . . to show that they can do right," says Sen. Chuck Grassley, R-Iowa, a frequent FBI critic. "They just better not louse it up."

The pressure of preventing another catastrophic terrorist attack has changed the atmosphere at the FBI academy's bucolic campus, where Gardner says curriculum changes have taken on a new intensity.

"There's no margin for error," she says. "These kids have to hit the ground running."

An FBI firearms instructor taking aim at a target on the academy's range in Quantico, Virginia. What qualities is the FBI looking for in the agents it is hiring today?
Witt/SIPA Press

A key part of FBI training is teaching new agents the difference between intelligence and evidence, and ingraining in them the notion of sharing.

"We have the evidence mentality—that we can't release things because it would jeopardize the case," Gardner says. "But a lot of things ended up sitting in our files. We are shifting away from that need-to-know basis to a need-to-share basis."

New agents range in age from 23 to 37 with exceptions for law enforcement or other experience. The average age is 30.

FBI firearms instructors teach the art of shooting, starting with how to draw a gun while wearing a suit jacket—hand-me-downs that new agents wear while firing handguns or shotguns. Each new agent fires 3,000 to 4,000 rounds of ammunition before graduating.

When Gardner attended the academy in 1983, she says, "We were memorizing the five organized crime families in New York. We don't do that anymore." The FBI now wants "more independent, self-directed people" who are linear, logical thinkers, she says.

Since 9/11, Gardner says, there have been a few "lopsided" classes, with more than the usual numbers of computer scientists and engineers. "We're asking ourselves, 'Why are there so many geeks in this class?' It's because we're pushing to meet the (hiring) goals."

At Hogan's Alley, a small fake city on the academy's grounds, new agents learn from their mistakes.

On a recent day, a class of new agents in their eighth week at the academy struggled to operate a police car loudspeaker. They also experienced the consequences of failing to thoroughly search an armed "suspect," who pulled his blue plastic gun on a classmate.

And they learned about adrenaline rushes. Instructor Chris Robles, an 18-year veteran agent, covered his eyes as a car carrying several new agents came flying up one of Hogan's Alley's streets, jerking to a stop inches from the back bumper of a "suspect" vehicle.

"I was surprised at how real it felt," says Lauster, a member of the class. "They (instructors) assume you know nothing. In my case, that was a great assumption."

CJ News (continued)

New agents also learn how to enter a house and check rooms for armed perpetrators. "They do it wrong on TV," says David Linterman, 31, a mechanical engineer.

Chuck Taylor, the academy's resource management officer, says Hogan's Alley needs to be updated by adding, for example, an underground sewer so agents can learn how to deal with bioterrorism through fictitious releases of anthrax and other substances.

In defensive tactics instructor Jay Moeller's class, new agents work up a sweat. John Burns, 32, a mechanical engineer, says he thought he was in decent shape before he arrived at the academy.

"I'm not 18 anymore," he says. "It takes more time to recover."

For the latest in crime and justice news, visit the Talk Justice news feed at http://www.crimenews.info.

Source: Toni Locy, "New Breed of FBI Recruits Training to Take on Terror," USA TODAY. May 27, 2005. Reprinted with permission.

---

cies, state and local law enforcement personnel, and first responders coordinate efforts to track down terrorists and to prevent acts of terrorism in the United States.

In testimony before Congress in 2005, FBI Director Robert S. Mueller III identified three areas of special concern relative to the bureau's ongoing antiterrorism efforts. First, said Mueller, "is the threat from covert operatives who may be inside the U.S. who have the intention to facilitate or conduct an attack."[39] The very nature of trained covert operatives, said the director, is that they are difficult to detect. "I remain very concerned about what we are *not* seeing," said Mueller. Second, Mueller identified a concern "with the growing body of sensitive reporting that continues to show Al-Qaeda's clear intention to obtain and ultimately use some form of chemical, biological, radiological, nuclear or high-energy explosives (CBRNE) material in its attacks against America." Finally, said Mueller, "we remain concerned about the potential for Al-Qaeda to . . . exploit radical American converts and other indigenous extremists." Read more about Director Mueller's vision for the future of the FBI in the FBI's 132-page *Strategic Plan for 2004–2009* at Library Extra 5–3 at cjtoday.com.

BLOG

See our Policing blogs.

LIBRARY
Extra

State-Level Agencies

Most state police agencies were created in the late nineteenth or early twentieth century to meet specific needs. The Texas Rangers, created in 1835 before Texas attained statehood, functioned as a military organization responsible for patrolling the republic's borders. The apprehension of Mexican cattle rustlers was one of the main concerns.[40] Massachusetts, targeting vice control, was the second state to create a law enforcement agency. Today, a wide diversity of state policing agencies exists. Table 5–3 provides a list of typical state-sponsored law enforcement agencies.

FBI Director Robert S. Mueller III explaining his agency's shift in priorities following the 2001 terrorist attacks on the World Trade Center and the Pentagon. How has the FBI's mission changed since the events of September 11, 2001?

AP Wide World Photos

CJ Futures

The FBI's New Information Technology Tools

Since September 11, 2001, the FBI has recognized that the ability to assemble, analyze, and disseminate information both internally and with other intelligence and law enforcement agencies is essential to the nation's success in the "war on terrorism." Consequently, it has made modernization of its information technology (IT) systems a top priority.

According to FBI Director Robert S. Mueller III, the agency has recently taken a coordinated, strategic approach to IT, building a strategic IT plan and creating an internal system for managing IT projects at each stage of their life cycle. IT modernization is occurring under a multiphased program code-named Trilogy. As a result of Trilogy, the FBI has

1. Deployed a secure high-speed network that enables personnel in FBI offices around the country to share data, including audio, video, and image files.

2. Provided its agents and intelligence analysts with more than 30,000 new desktop computers running modern software applications, along with 3,700 printers, 1,600 scanners, 465 servers, and 1,400 routers.

3. Developed an IT infrastructure that provides for secure communication with FBI intelligence community partners.

The third phase of Trilogy included the virtual case file (VCF) system, which was intended to give the bureau's agents nearly instant access to all needed information in the agency's databases. VCF, however, encountered technical problems, some of which were related to requirements involving the sharing of information with other law enforcement and national security organizations. Consequently,

the VCF system was scrapped in 2005, and the FBI announced plans to use mostly off-the-shelf products that will allow agents to easily share information. The replacement system, called Sentinel, is based on a problem-solving framework known as the Federal Investigative Case Management Solution (FICMS). It is being developed by Lockheed Martin, a Maryland company engaged in the development and manufacture of advanced technology systems. Separate from the Trilogy/Sentinel program, the FBI has successfully deployed a number of new investigative and information-sharing capabilities, including the following:

- *Investigative Data Warehouse (IDW)*. IDW offers agents and analysts the technology needed to perform intelligent link analysis to uncover potential relationships that might exist between suspects, physical and information resources, and anticipated threats. IDW provides FBI users with a single access point to more than 47 sources of counterterrorism data, including information from FBI files, other government agency data, and open source news feeds, that were previously available only through separate proprietary information systems and laborious data-gathering efforts.

- *FBI Automated Messaging System (FAMS)*. FAMS began operations in December 2004 and now provides more than 300 FBI agents and intelligence analysts with the capability to send and receive critical organizational message traffic to any of the 40,000 or more addresses on the Defense Messaging System.

- *FBI Intelligence Information Reports Dissemination System (FIDS)*. FIDS is a Web-based software application that allows all FBI personnel with access to the FBI's internal intranet to create and disseminate standardized intelligence information reports quickly and efficiently to FBI agents and other law enforcement officers.

References: Testimony of Robert S. Mueller III, director of the Federal Bureau of Investigation, before the Committee on Intelligence of the U.S. Senate, February 16, 2005; Linda Rosencrance, "It's Official: FBI Scraps $170 Million Virtual Case File Project," *Computerworld,* March 9, 2005; "FBI Announces Award of Sentinel Contract," FBI press release, March 16, 2006; and "FBI Announces Deployment of Sentinel Phase I," FBI press release, June 19, 2007.

> *Every day [as a police officer] you get to be a different person. In that regard it is the best job in the world. You get to play many roles: rabbi, lawyer, social worker, psychiatrist.*
>
> —*New York police officer Salvatore Maniscalco*

Figure 5–1 shows that the number of full-time personnel employed by state law enforcement agencies is significantly less than the number employed by local police departments.

State law enforcement agencies are usually organized after one of two models. In the first, a centralized model, the tasks of major criminal investigations are combined with the patrol of state highways. Centralized state police agencies generally do the following:

- Assist local law enforcement departments in criminal investigations when asked to do so.
- Operate centralized identification bureaus.
- Maintain a centralized criminal records repository.

TABLE 5–3   American Policing: State Law Enforcement Agencies

Alcohol law enforcement agencies	Port authorities	State police
Fish and wildlife agencies	State bureaus of investigation	State university police
Highway patrol	State park services	Weigh station operations

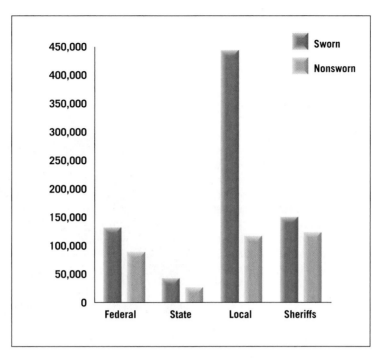

FIGURE 5–1

Federal, state, and local law enforcement employment in the United States, 2000.

Source: Brian A. Reaves and Matthew J. Hickman, *Law Enforcement Management and Administrative Statistics, 2000* (Washington, DC: Bureau of Justice Statistics, 2004); and Government Accounting Office, "Survey of Federal Civilian Law Enforcement Functions and Authorities" (GAO-07-121), December 2006.

- Patrol the state's highways.
- Provide select training for municipal and county officers.

The Pennsylvania Constabulary, known today as the Pennsylvania State Police, was the first modern force to combine these duties and has been called the "first modern state police agency."[41] Michigan, New Jersey, New York, Vermont, and Delaware are a few of the states that patterned their state-level enforcement activities after the Pennsylvania model.

The second state model, the decentralized model of police organization, characterizes operations in the southern United States but is found as well in the Midwest and in some western states. The model draws a clear distinction between traffic enforcement on state highways and other state-level law enforcement functions by creating at least two separate agencies. North Carolina, South Carolina, and Georgia are a few of the many states that employ both a highway patrol and a state bureau of investigation. The names of the respective agencies may vary, however, even though their functions are largely the same. In North Carolina, for example, the two major state-level law enforcement agencies are the North Carolina Highway Patrol and the State Bureau of Investigation. Georgia fields a highway patrol and the Georgia Bureau of Investigation, and South Carolina operates a highway patrol and the South Carolina Law Enforcement Division.

States that use the decentralized model usually have a number of other adjunct state-level law enforcement agencies. North Carolina, for example, has created a State Wildlife Commission with enforcement powers, a Board of Alcohol Beverage Control with additional agents, and a separate Enforcement and Theft Bureau for enforcing certain motor vehicle and theft laws. Learn more about state-level law enforcement agencies by visiting Web Extra 5–9 and Library Extra 5–4 at cjtoday.com.

WEB   **LIBRARY**
Extra   Extra

Local Agencies

Local police agencies, including city and county agencies, represent a third level of law enforcement activity in the United States. The term *local police* encompasses a wide variety of agencies. Municipal departments, rural sheriff's departments, and specialized groups like campus police and transit police can all be grouped under the "local" rubric. Large municipal departments are highly visible because of their vast size, huge budgets, and innovative programs. The nation's largest law enforcement agency, the New York Police Department (NYPD), for example, has about 45,000 full-time employees, including about 38,000 full-time **sworn officers**.[42]

Far greater in number, however, are small-town and county sheriff's departments. There are approximately 12,700 **municipal police departments** and 3,100 sheriff's departments in the United States.[43] Every incorporated municipality in the country has the authority to create its own police force. Some very small communities hire only one officer, who fills the roles of chief, investigator, and night watch—as well as everything in between. The majority of local agencies

sworn officer

A law enforcement officer who is trained and empowered to perform full police duties, such as making arrests, conducting investigations, and carrying firearms.[iv]

municipal police department

A city- or town-based law enforcement agency.

CJ News

Don't Even Ask about Extra Credit

They could be students in a classroom anywhere. The pupils sit in rows of chairs with fold-out desktops, taking and passing notes, eyeing wristwatches and cellphones. They laugh despite themselves when a classmate misreads the text aloud, substituting "pubic area" for "public area." They tap their feet impatiently and pass around packs of gum. Sometimes a tiny detail betrays them: a dull gleam of gunmetal at the hip, or a spoken reference to time on the 24-hour clock.

"If he were to say, 'I'm a Goodyear auto mechanic, and I'll fix your car in exchange for whatever sexual act,' I'd say yes," lectures Detective Jeffrey Etheridge, one of the instructors. As the giggling dies down, he adds, "This is more for academic discussion. This is never going to happen out on the street."

Call them the newest recruits for the oldest profession. The students—over a hundred of them, many female in their mid-20s—are all New York police officers who have volunteered to walk, or even strut, to the rhythm of an unusual beat. Hailing from precincts across the city, they've convened for a common purpose: to learn the tricks of the prostitute's trade and go undercover in a citywide sting called Operation Losing Proposition.

Their education is a single seven-hour session, traditionally offered twice or three times annually at the Police Academy on East 20th Street. The program began about a decade ago, and after a year's hiatus because of personnel and budget concerns, a pair of classes were taught late last year, preparing more than 200 new officers to walk the streets.

Some will tackle neighborhoods with the busiest corners in town, rough-and-tumble places like Hunts Point in the Bronx or Queens Plaza; the intersection of Weehawken and Christopher Streets in the West Village, popular among transvestites; or a notorious industrial strip in East New York, Brooklyn, between Flatlands Avenue and Linden Boulevard, that the police call the Pennsylvania Track.

But even in the busiest areas, busting a bona fide john is no easy task.

"You're going to get some very unusual requests: kissing, hugging, talking, medical procedures," Detective James Held of the Vice Division told his November class, adding that none of those requests was a crime. He offered an example: "What if someone comes up to you and says: 'Do you know what I want you to do? I want you to dress up like a girl and I want to go back to a hotel room, and I want you to paint my toenails. I'll pay you a thousand dollars for the hour.'"

"I'll bring the nail polish!" called out Tisjé Golden, an officer from the 25th Precinct in East Harlem. Laughter rippled outward from her seat and spread through the audience.

Still, Detective Held clarified, that's not a crime. Prostitution is not like a game of horseshoes. Close isn't good enough. To determine whether a suspect's behavior is illegal, officers must consult a rigorous recipe. The first ingredient is a sexual act, whether promised or performed. The latter, joked Detective Etheridge, who works in the Police Department's legal bureau, "is something you're not going to worry about, because you're not going to have sex, at least not on company time."

The second component is money, goods or services, including anything from a vial of crack to a ride across town. The final touch is

NYPD officers undergoing in-service tactical training in a Bronx classroom. What are these officers learning?

Photo by New York Police Department Photographic Unit

an agreement, verbal or otherwise (a simple nod of the head will do, the courts have concluded), to bind the service and fee together in a consensual exchange. To gather these elements, an experienced decoy will choreograph a suggestive verbal ballet, getting a john to articulate what he wants without being too pushy. Any aggressive or overly eager behavior, like offering repeated discounts or chasing down a customer, can be dismissed as entrapment.

Patronizing a prostitute is a Class B misdemeanor, punishable by up to three months in prison and a fine not to exceed $500. In certain cases, the police may even seize a john's car.

"Remember, as police, our role is to detect crime, not create crime," Detective Held gently reminded his charges. As the students listened, some thumbed through copies of a 46-page handbook that included a brief glossary of the prostitute's vernacular, a Kama Sutra of sexual slang. The lexicon included phrases like "john jams," or "lines of cars with tricks/johns to be serviced." It also named different types of prostitutes, from the "lot lizard," whose habitat is a truck stop, to the "bubble gum prostitute," who will sell herself for anything, accepting drugs, alcohol, or cigarettes in lieu of cash.

The curriculum also included tactics and equipment. Conversations with customers are recorded using a remote audio system called a Kel set. Before hitting the streets, students learned, a decoy hitches up to a transmitter, roughly the size of a pack of cigarettes, and snakes a microphone wire up the inside of his or her shirt. Sgt. Dan Farrell, an equipment expert, cautioned his students against leaning into the window of a john's vehicle while wearing a wire. It's a sloppy move that not only makes decoys vulnerable to getting grabbed by the hair, but also threatens to expose the wire.

Students learned how other officers play supporting roles, from the arrest team waiting nearby in unmarked cars, to the "ghost," an undercover officer who fades into the surroundings, ready to help a decoy in distress. Depending on the situation, a ghost may choose to pose as a pimp, a wino or a junkie.

Assuming a role in Operation Losing Proposition is strictly voluntary. That said, it is also equal-opportunity.

CJ News (continued)

"The decoy officer may be male or female," Detective Held announced, eliciting a chorus of groans and protests from the roughly 20 men in the class. "Sorry, guys. I used to say that, too," he quipped, "and then I was up on 43rd Street, shaking what mama gave me."

Officer Gamaliel Torres, 32, a broad-shouldered, soft-spoken officer from the Homeless Outreach Unit, said he was ribbed by colleagues when they heard he had signed up for the class. "I got a little hazing for it," he admitted.

Officer Taralee Gugliociello, 30, a former preschool teacher from a family of male police officers, said she was excited to try on the prostitute's role. "I'll be doing something my brothers can't do," she announced proudly, then reddened a bit. "I don't think they'd want to see," she confided. "My brothers would be like, 'Put some clothes on.'"

Not everyone shares the officers' ready spirit. "Is this really what our police department should be doing?" said Norman Siegel, a prominent civil rights lawyer and the former executive director of the New York Civil Liberties Union. "Look at the consensual nature of the crime, the fact that they're arresting the john—that's problematic in and of itself—and then seizing cars as a deterrent. It's disproportionate to the crime. History shows that it's very hard to deter this kind of activity."

Since the mid-1990s, precincts have conducted Operation Losing Proposition sporadically, usually in response to neighbors' complaints. Some complain more loudly than others. Detective Kevin Mannion, an instructor from the vice squad, told the class about an eccentric woman whose cruel habit—dumping a pot of scalding water from her window to disperse the prostitutes below—once misfired and splashed a cluster of undercover officers.

For the police, taking lumps is a part of getting into the act. "We're all actors or actresses in a way," mused Sgt. Joanne Riggs, who coordinates the training classes. "You've gotta be."

At the very least, undercover prostitution busts are more colorful than routine traffic stops.

"It breaks the monotony and it gives them great stories; cops love great stories," offered Eugene O'Donnell, an assistant professor of police studies at John Jay College of Criminal Justice. "What's a more bizarre way to make a living than standing out on a corner and talking to some guy in a limo?"

Toward the end of the class, Officer Golden offered her own take on getting into character. With a laugh and a slight shimmy, she suggested a sly motive. "Every woman," she said, "has a little prostitute in her."

For the latest in crime and justice news, visit the Talk Justice news feed at http://www.crimenews.info.

Source: Jessica Bruder, "Don't Even Ask about Extra Credit," *New York Times* online, February 13, 2005. Copyright © 2005 by the New York Times Co. Reprinted with permission.

---

employ fewer than ten full-time officers, and about three in eight agencies (more than 7,000 in all) employ fewer than five full-time officers. These smaller agencies include 2,245 (or 12%) with just one full-time officer and 1,164 (or 6%) with only part-time officers.[44] A few communities contract with private security firms for police services, and still others have no active police force at all, depending instead on local sheriff's departments to deal with law violators.

City police chiefs are typically appointed by the mayor or selected by the city council. Their departments' jurisdictions are limited by convention to the geographic boundaries of their communities. **Sheriffs**, on the other hand, are elected public officials whose agencies are responsible for law enforcement throughout the counties in which they function. Sheriff's deputies mostly patrol the "unincorporated" areas of the county, or those that lie between municipalities. They do, however, have jurisdiction throughout the county, and in some areas they routinely work alongside municipal police to enforce laws within towns and cities.

Sheriff's departments are generally responsible for serving court papers, including civil summonses, and for maintaining security within state courtrooms. Sheriffs also run county jails and are responsible for more detainees awaiting trial than any other type of law enforcement department in the country. For example, the Los Angeles County Jail System, operated by the Custody Operations Division of the L.A. County Sheriff's Department (LASD), is the largest in the world.[45] In 2003, with eight separate facilities, the custody division of the LASD had an average daily population of 18,423 inmates—considerably more than the number of inmates held in many state prison systems. More than 2,200 uniformed officers and 1,265 civilian employees work in the custody division of the LASD, and that division alone operates with a yearly budget in excess of $200 million.[46]

Sheriff's departments remain strong across most of the country, although in parts of New England, deputies mostly function as court agents with limited law enforcement duties. One report found that most sheriff's departments are small, with more than half of them employing fewer than 25 sworn officers.[47] Only 13 departments employ more than 1,000 officers. Even so, southern and western sheriffs are still considered the "chief law enforcement officers" in their counties. A list of conventional police agencies found at the local level is shown in Table 5–4. For information on

sheriff

The elected chief officer of a county law enforcement agency. The sheriff is usually responsible for law enforcement in unincorporated areas and for the operation of the county jail.

TABLE 5–4	American Policing: Local Law Enforcement Agencies	
Campus police	Housing authority agencies	Sheriff's departments
City/county agencies	Marine patrol agencies	Transit police
Constables	Municipal police departments	Tribal police
Coroners or medical examiners		

WEB Extra

LIBRARY Extra

selected local law enforcement agencies, view Web Extra 5–10 at cjtoday.com. Visit Library Extras 5–5 and 5–6 to learn more about staffing levels at local and state police agencies.

Private Protective Services

private protective service

An independent or proprietary commercial organization that provides protective services to employers on a contractual basis.

Private protective services constitute a fourth level of enforcement activity in the United States today. While public police are employed by the government and enforce public laws, private security personnel work for corporate employers and secure private interests.

Private security has been defined as "those self-employed individuals and privately funded business entities and organizations providing security-related services to specific clientele for a fee, for the individual or entity that retains or employs them, or for themselves, in order to protect their persons, private property, or interests from various hazards."[48] The growth in the size of private security in recent years has been phenomenal. In 2002, for example, $212.7 million was spent for security arrangements at the Olympic winter games in Salt Lake City, Utah—leading to the employment of more than 40,000 private security personnel in association with the event.[49] Only two years later, in 2004, however, official estimates put the total amount spent to secure the Olympic Games in Athens at $1.5 billion—or $283 per paid ticket.[50] Given Greece's geopolitical situation and its proximity to the Balkans and the Middle East, officials in Athens wanted to be sure they could prevent terrorist attacks.

ASIS International, with more than 33,000 members, is the preeminent international organization for private security professionals.[51] ASIS International members include corporate security managers and directors, as well as architects, attorneys, and federal, state, and local law enforcement personnel. Founded in 1955, ASIS International, formerly known as the American Society for Industrial Security, is dedicated to increasing the effectiveness and productivity of security professionals by developing educational and certification programs and training materials that address the needs of the security profession. ASIS also actively promotes the value of security management to business, the media, governmental entities, and the public. The organization publishes the industry magazine *Security Management*.

A group of Texas Rangers providing additional security during a scheduled execution at Huntsville, Texas, in 2000. The Texas Rangers have long been held in high regard among state police agencies. What are the two organizational models that characterize state law enforcement agencies today?

Bob Daemmrich/Stock Boston

A Daytona Beach, Florida, police officer ticketing a driver for a seat belt violation. Local police agencies, including city and county agencies, represent a third level of law enforcement activity in the United States. Why didn't the bumper sticker work?

*Nigel Cook/*Daytona Beach News–Journal/*AP Wide World Photos*

With 204 chapters worldwide, ASIS administers three certification programs: (1) the Certified Protection Professional (CPP) program, which provides for board certification in security management; (2) the Physical Security Professional (PSP) program, which provides a technical certification opportunity for specialists in physical plant security; and (3) the Professional Certified Investigator (PCI) program. Holders of PCI certification have satisfactorily demonstrated significant education and/or experience in the fields of case management, evidence collection, and case presentation. ASIS also promotes the importance of ethical standards in the private security sector. The ASIS International Code of Ethics can be found in the "Ethics and Professionalism" box in this chapter. ASIS can be reached online via **Web Extra 5–11** at cjtoday.com. The ASIS Security Toolkit, consisting of advisories, guidelines, case studies, information, news, and advice in the area of private security, can be seen at **Web Extra 5–12**.

WEB Extra

A report released by the National Institute of Justice in 2001, entitled *The New Structure of Policing,* found that "policing is being transformed and restructured in the modern world" in ways that were unanticipated only a few decades ago.[52] Much of the change is due to the development of private protective services as an important adjunct to public law enforcement activities in the United States and throughout much of the rest of the world. The NIJ report says that "the key to [understanding] the transformation is that policing, meaning the activity of making societies safe, is no longer carried out exclusively by governments" and that the distinction between private and public police has begun to blur. According to the NIJ, "gradually, almost imperceptibly, policing has been 'multilateralized,'" meaning that "a host of nongovernmental agencies have undertaken to provide security services." As a result, the NIJ report says, "policing has entered a new era, an era characterized by a transformation in the governance of security." The report concludes the following:

- In most countries, certainly in the democratic world, private police outnumber public police.

- In these same countries, people spend more time in their daily lives in places where visible crime prevention and control are provided by nongovernmental groups rather than by governmental police agencies.

- The reconstruction of policing is occurring worldwide despite differences in wealth and economic systems.

View the NIJ report in its entirety at **Library Extra 5–7** at cjtoday.com.

LIBRARY Extra

According to the National Center for Policy Analysis, private security personnel outnumber public law enforcement officers in the United States by nearly three to one.[53] The widely cited *Hallcrest Report II,*[54] another important document describing the private security industry, says that employment in the field of private security is anticipated to continue to expand by around 4% per year, whereas public police agencies are expected to grow by only 2.8% per year for the foreseeable future. Still faster growth is predicted in private security industry revenues, which are expected to increase about 7% per year, a growth rate almost three times greater than that projected for the gross national product. Table 5–5 lists the ten largest private security agencies in business today and some of the services they offer.

TABLE 5–5   American Policing: Private Security Agencies

The Largest Private Security Agencies in the United States

Advance Security, Inc.	Globe Security	Security Bureau, Inc.
Allied Security, Inc.	Guardsmark, Inc.	Wackenhut Corp.
American Protective Services	Pinkerton's, Inc.	Wells Fargo Guard Services
Burns International Security Services		

Private Security Services

Airport security	Computer/information security	Nuclear facility security
ATM services	Executive protection	Railroad detectives
Bank guards	Hospital security	School security
Company guards	Loss-prevention specialists	Store/mall security

Source: Adapted from William C. Cunningham, John J. Strauchs, and Clifford W. Van Meter, *The Hallcrest Report II: Private Security Trends, 1970–2000* (McLean, VA: Hallcrest Systems, 1990).

Major reasons for the quick growth of the American proprietary security sector include "(1) an increase in crimes in the workplace, (2) an increase in fear (real or perceived) of crime and terrorism, (3) the fiscal crises of the states, [which have] limited public protection, and (4) an increased public and business awareness and use of . . . more cost-effective private security products and services."[55]

FREEDOM OR SAFETY?
You Decide

The Conch Republic

The citizens of the tiny island town of Key West, Florida, have always prided themselves on being different. Hence, it should have come as no surprise when, on April 23, 1982, the island's mayor issued a proclamation seceding from the United States and declaring Key West a new nation named the Conch Republic. The decision to withdraw from the Union came in reaction to a 19-mile-long traffic jam created when authorities from the Task Force on South Florida Crime set up a checkpoint on U.S. 1—the only highway traversing the Florida Keys. Law enforcement officers used the checkpoint to examine the driver's licenses of travelers leaving the Keys and meticulously searched vehicles looking for contraband and illegal immigrants. At the time of the roadblock, at least one law enforcement official estimated that up to 80% of all marijuana and cocaine entering the nation was coming through south Florida, and Key West was said to be the "drug-smuggling capital of America."

In 1982, as today, the primary legal industry in Key West was tourism, and island officials feared that long delays at police roadblocks would keep visitors away. Protests about the roadblock were lodged with the White House, the Florida governor's office, and with U.S. congressional offices—all to no avail. Then-Vice President George H. W. Bush's press secretary issued a statement saying, "You have illegal immigrants and crime on the streets. . . . There's going to be some inconvenience. I think most people would want a little in-

convenience compared to having grocery stores held up and senior citizens mugged in the streets."

Island officials, however, didn't agree and hired an attorney to seek an injunction against the roadblock, arguing that it violated the Fourth Amendment's restriction against unreasonable search and seizure. "Unless they see the hand of a Haitian sticking out of the trunk or marijuana wafting out of the car, they don't have probable cause," said David Horan, the town's attorney. When the roadblock remained in place, island leaders issued a secession proclamation and promptly applied to the U.S. government for foreign aid.

For its part, the U.S. government ignored the secession movement, but the roadblock was quietly removed two months after it was put in place. Island residents, however, still celebrate April 23 as the day when, as one former Key West mayor put it, "the brave men and women of the Conch Republic gave up their lunch hour to secede from the United States."

YOU DECIDE

Although Key West's secession was never taken very seriously by the people involved in it 25 years ago, it illustrates an undeniable tension between freedom and security that continues to characterize American society today. How would you describe that tension in your own words? Are Americans today more or less willing to sacrifice some of their personal rights and freedoms in the interest of safety than they were 25 years ago?

Reference: Cynthia Crossen, "To Fight Car Searches, a Florida City Declared Itself a Foreign Nation," *Wall Street Journal* online, January 19, 2005, http://online.wsj.com/article_print/0,SB110609219909929528,00.html.

Private security guards aiming at targets during a training exercise in Israel. Why has the privatization of policing become a major issue facing governments and public justice agencies everywhere?
Ed Kashi/Corbis/Bettmann

Private agencies provide tailored policing funded by the guarded organization rather than through the expenditure of public monies. Experts estimate that the money spent on private security in this country exceeds the combined budgets of all law enforcement agencies—local, state, and federal.[56] Contributing to this vast expenditure is the federal government, which is itself a major employer of private security personnel, contracting for services that range from guards to highly specialized electronic snooping and computerized countermeasures at military installations and embassies throughout the world.

There are indications that private security activities are rapidly growing beyond traditional guard services to encompass dedicated efforts at security-related intelligence gathering. In August 2004, for example, the Department of Homeland Security warned that terrorists might be actively targeting Citigroup, Prudential, the New York Stock Exchange, and other large financial institutions on the East Coast of the United States. At the same time, however, Austin-based Stratfor, Inc., a low-profile private intelligence agency run by former CIA officers, was quietly assuring its clients that such an attack was very unlikely, saying that "Al Qaeda has never attacked into an alert."[57]

According to security investment firm Morgan Keegan, overall spending on corporate security, including intelligence, will amount to around $50 billion in 2005.[58] The total includes spending on physical security, Internet safeguards, staff screening and training, and terrorist and related intelligence analysis.

Integrating Public and Private Security

As the private security field grows, its relationship to public law enforcement continues to evolve. Some argue that "today, a distinction between public and private policing is increasingly meaningless."[59] As a result, the focus has largely shifted from an analysis of competition between the sectors to the recognition that each form of policing can help the other.

One government-sponsored report makes the following policy recommendations, which are designed to maximize the cooperative crime-fighting potential of existing private and public security resources:[60]

1. The resources of proprietary and contract security should be brought to bear in cooperative, community-based crime prevention and security awareness programs.

2. An assessment should be made of (1) the basic police services the public is willing to support financially, (2) the types of police services most acceptable to police administrators and the public for transfer to the private sector, and (3) which services might be performed for a lower unit cost by the private sector with the same level of community satisfaction.

3. With special police powers, security personnel could resolve many or most minor criminal incidents prior to police involvement. State statutes providing such powers could also provide for standardized training and certification requirements, thus assuring uniformity and precluding abuses. . . . Ideally, licensing and regulatory requirements would be the same for all states, with reciprocity for firms licensed elsewhere.

Law enforcement can ill afford to continue its traditional policy of isolating and even ignoring the activities of private security.

—*National Institute of Justice*[v]

Ethics and Professionalism

ASIS International Code of Ethics

PREAMBLE

Aware that the quality of professional security activity ultimately depends upon the willingness of practitioners to observe special standards of conduct and to manifest good faith in professional relationships, the American Society for Industrial Security adopts the following Code of Ethics and mandates its conscientious observance as a binding condition of membership in or affiliation with the Society:

CODE OF ETHICS

1. A member shall perform professional duties in accordance with the law and the highest moral principles.
2. A member shall observe the precepts of truthfulness, honesty, and integrity.
3. A member shall be faithful and diligent in discharging professional responsibilities.
4. A member shall be competent in discharging professional responsibilities.
5. A member shall safeguard confidential information and exercise due care to prevent its improper disclosure.
6. A member shall not maliciously injure the professional reputation or practice of colleagues, clients, or employers.

Article I

A member shall perform professional duties in accordance with the law and the highest moral principles.

Ethical Considerations

1. A member shall abide by the law of the land in which the services are rendered and perform all duties in an honorable manner.
2. A member shall not knowingly become associated in responsibility for work with colleagues who do not conform to the law and these ethical standards.
3. A member shall be just and respect the rights of others in performing professional responsibilities.

Article II

A member shall observe the precepts of truthfulness, honesty, and integrity.

Ethical Considerations

1. A member shall disclose all relevant information to those having the right to know.
2. A right to know is a legally enforceable claim or demand by a person for disclosure of information by a member. Such a right does not depend upon prior knowledge by the person of the existence of the information to be disclosed.
3. A member shall not knowingly release misleading information nor encourage or otherwise participate in the release of such information.

Article III

A member shall be faithful and diligent in discharging professional responsibilities.

Ethical Considerations

1. A member is faithful when fair and steadfast in adherence to promises and commitments.
2. A member is diligent when employing best efforts in an assignment.
3. A member shall not act in matters involving conflicts of interest without appropriate disclosure and approval.
4. A member shall represent services or products fairly and truthfully.

Article IV

A member shall be competent in discharging professional responsibilities.

Ethical Considerations

1. A member is competent who possesses and applies the skills and knowledge required for the task.
2. A member shall not accept a task beyond the member's competence nor shall competence be claimed when not possessed.

Article V

A member shall safeguard confidential information and exercise due care to prevent its improper disclosure.

Ethical Considerations

1. Confidential information is nonpublic information, the disclosure of which is restricted.
2. Due care requires that the professional must not knowingly reveal confidential information, or use a confidence to the disadvantage of the principal or to the advantage of the member or a third person, unless the principal consents after full disclosure of all the facts. This confidentiality continues after the business relationship between the member and his principal has terminated.
3. A member who receives information and has not agreed to be bound by confidentiality is not bound from disclosing it. A member is not bound by confidential disclosures made of acts or omissions which constitute a violation of the law.
4. Confidential disclosures made by a principal to a member are not recognized by law as privileged in a legal proceeding. The member may be required to testify in a legal proceeding to the information received in confidence from his principal over the objection of his principal's counsel.
5. A member shall not disclose confidential information for personal gain without appropriate authorization.

Article VI

A member shall not maliciously injure the professional reputation or practice of colleagues, clients, or employers.

Ethics and Professionalism (continued)

Ethical Considerations

1. A member shall not comment falsely and with malice concerning a colleague's competence, performance, or professional capabilities.
2. A member who knows, or has reasonable grounds to believe, that another member has failed to conform to the Society's Code of Ethics shall present such information to the Ethical Standards Committee in accordance with Article VIII of the Society's bylaws.

Source: ASIS International. Reprinted with permission.

THINKING ABOUT ETHICS

1. The ASIS code of ethics says, "A member shall observe the precepts of truthfulness, honesty, and integrity." Why are these qualities important in a security professional?
2. Why is it important for security personnel to "safeguard confidential information and exercise due care to prevent its improper disclosure"? What might happen if they didn't?

4. Law enforcement agencies should be included in the crisis-management planning of private organizations. . . . Similarly, private security should be consulted when law enforcement agencies are developing SWAT [special weapons and tactics] and hostage-negotiation teams. The federal government should provide channels of communication with private security with respect to terrorist activities and threats.

5. States should enact legislation permitting private security firms access to criminal history records in order to improve the selection process for security personnel and also to enable businesses to assess the integrity of key employees.

6. Research should . . . attempt to delineate the characteristics of the private justice system; identify the crimes most frequently resolved; assess the types and amount of unreported crime in organizations; quantify the redirection of [the] public criminal justice workload . . . and examine [the] . . . relationships between private security and . . . components of the criminal justice system.

7. A federal tax credit for security expenditures, similar to the energy tax credit, might be a cost-effective way to reduce police workloads.

One especially important policy area involves building private security/public policing partnerships to prevent terrorism and to respond to threats of terrorism. A 2004 national policy summit report, jointly authored by the International Association of Chiefs of Police and the 30,000-member ASIS International, says that despite similar interests in protecting people and

> *Without close scrutiny, it has become difficult to tell whether policing is being done by a government using sworn personnel, by a government using a private security company, by a private security company using civilian employees, by a private company using public police, or by a government employing civilians.*
>
> *—David H. Bayley and Clifford D. Shearing[vi]*

A private security officer conferring with a sworn public law enforcement officer. How can cooperation between private security agencies and public law enforcement offices help solve and prevent crimes?

Michael Newman/PhotoEdit Inc.

property in the United States, public police and private security agencies have rarely collaborated.[61] The report notes, however, that as much as 85% of the nation's critical infrastructure is protected by private security. It goes on to say that "the need for complex coordination, extra staffing, and special resources" in the light of possible terror attacks, "coupled with the significant demands of crime prevention and response, absolutely requires boosting the level of partnership between public policing and private security."[62] The full national policy summit report is available at Library Extra 5–8 at cjtoday.com.

LIBRARY
Extra
▪ ▪ ▪ ▪

SUMMARY

- American police departments owe a historical legacy to Sir Robert Peel and the London Metropolitan Police. Although law enforcement efforts in the United States were based to some degree on the British experience, the unique character of the American frontier led to the growth of a decentralized form of policing throughout the United States.

- Police agencies in the United States function to enforce the statutes created by lawmaking bodies, and differing types and levels of legislative authority are reflected in the diversity of police forces in our country today. Consequently, American policing presents a complex picture that is structured along federal, state, and local lines.

- Dozens of federal law enforcement agencies are distributed among 14 U.S. government departments and 28 nondepartmental entities, and each federal agency empowered by Congress to enforce specific statutes has its own enforcement arm. The FBI may be the most famous law enforcement agency in the country and in the world. The mission of the FBI is to protect and defend the United States against terrorist and foreign intelligence threats, to uphold and enforce the criminal laws of the United States, and to provide leadership and criminal justice services to federal, state, municipal, and international agencies and partners.

- State law enforcement agencies have numerous functions, including assisting local law enforcement departments in criminal investigations when asked to do so, operating centralized identification bureaus, maintaining a centralized criminal records repository, patrolling the state's highways, and providing select training for municipal and county officers. State law enforcement agencies are usually organized after one of two models. In the first, a centralized model, the tasks of major criminal investigations are combined with the patrol of state highways. The second state model, the decentralized model, draws a clear distinction between traffic enforcement on state highways and other state-level law enforcement functions by creating at least two separate agencies.

- Local police agencies represent a third level of law enforcement activity in the United States. They encompass a wide variety of agencies, including municipal police departments, rural sheriff's departments, and specialized groups like campus police and transit police.

- Private protective services constitute a fourth level of law enforcement. While public police are employed by the government and enforce public laws, private security personnel work for corporate or private employers and secure private interests. Private security personnel outnumber public law enforcement officers in the United States by nearly three to one, and private agencies provide tailored protective services funded by the guarded organization rather than by taxpayers.

KEY TERMS

bobbies, 154

Bow Street Runners, 154

comes stabuli, 153

directed patrol, 159

evidence-based policing (EBP), 160

Exemplary Projects Program, 158

federal law enforcement agency, 161

Kansas City experiment, 158

Law Enforcement Assistance
  Administration (LEAA), 157

municipal police department, 169

new police, 154

night watch, 153

private protective service, 172

scientific police management, 158

sheriff, 171

Statute of Winchester, 153
sworn officer, 169

vigilantism, 155
Wickersham Commission, 157

KEY NAMES

Henry Fielding, 154
Richard Mayne, 154

Robert Peel, 154
Charles Rowan, 154

QUESTIONS FOR REVIEW

1. Describe the historical development of policing in America. What impact did the Prohibition era have on the development of American policing?

2. What are the three levels of public law enforcement described in this chapter?

3. Identify a number of significant federal law enforcement agencies, and describe the responsibilities of each.

4. Explain the role that state law enforcement agencies play in enforcing the law, and describe the two major models of state law enforcement organization.

5. What different kinds of local law enforcement agencies exist in the United States today? What role does each agency have in enforcing the law?

6. Describe the nature and extent of private protective services in the United States today. What role do you think they will play in the future?

QUESTIONS FOR REFLECTION

1. Why are there so many different types of law enforcement agencies in the United States? What problems, if any, do you think are created by having such a diversity of agencies?

2. What is evidence-based policing? What assumptions about police work have scientific studies of law enforcement called into question? What other assumptions made about police work today might be similarly questioned or studied?

3. Contrast the current deployment of private security personnel with the number of public law enforcement personnel.

4. How can the quality of private security services be ensured?

5. What is the relationship between private security and public policing in America today? How might the nature of that relationship be expected to change over time? Why?

Discuss your answers to these questions and other issues on the CJ Today e-mail discussion list (join the list at ctoday.com).

WEB QUEST

Visit at least four of the federal law enforcement agencies listed under Web Extra 5–4 at cjtoday.com. Use the online information that each site provides to describe each agency in terms of its history, organization, and mission. Do the same with at least four of the state-level law enforcement agencies listed under Web Extra 5–9 and with at least four of the local law enforcement agencies listed under Web Extra 5–10. If you would like to use federal, state, or local agencies other than those listed at cjtoday.com, you can find many such sites in the Cybrary at http://www.cybrary.info.

CHAPTER 6

Policing: Purpose and Organization

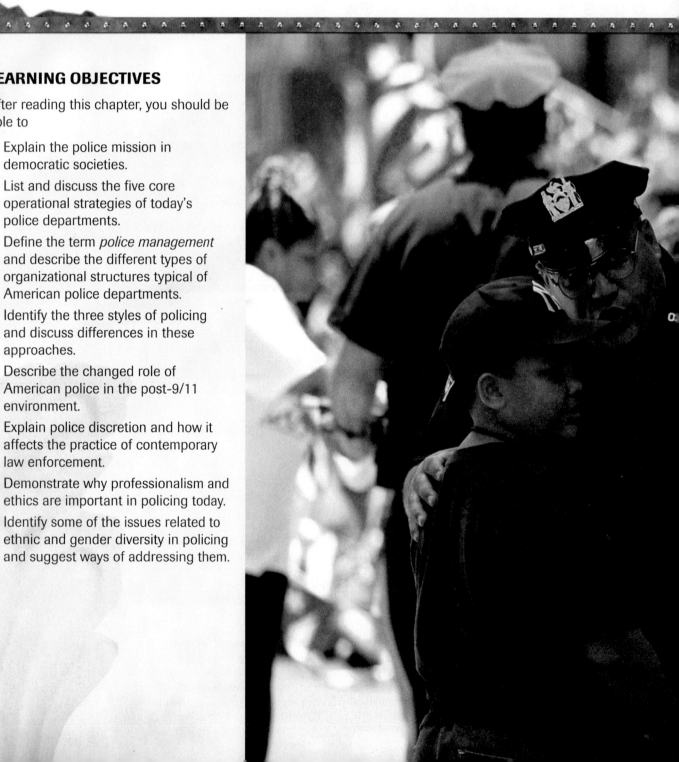

LEARNING OBJECTIVES

After reading this chapter, you should be able to

- Explain the police mission in democratic societies.
- List and discuss the five core operational strategies of today's police departments.
- Define the term *police management* and describe the different types of organizational structures typical of American police departments.
- Identify the three styles of policing and discuss differences in these approaches.
- Describe the changed role of American police in the post-9/11 environment.
- Explain police discretion and how it affects the practice of contemporary law enforcement.
- Demonstrate why professionalism and ethics are important in policing today.
- Identify some of the issues related to ethnic and gender diversity in policing and suggest ways of addressing them.

The purpose of the police service is to uphold the law fairly and firmly; to prevent crime; to pursue and bring to justice those who break the law; to keep the . . . peace; to protect, help and reassure the community; and to be seen to do this with integrity, common sense and sound judgment.

—United Kingdom Police Service,
Statement of Common Purpose

The tragedies of September 11, 2001, have forever changed the roles of traditional law enforcement in this country.

—Major Cities Chiefs Association[1]

Hear the author discuss
this chapter at
cjtoday.com

Introduction

In mid-November 2003, thousands of demonstrators protesting the proposed creation of the Free Trade Area of the Americas (FTAA) clashed with hundreds of Miami police officers equipped with riot gear. The protesters were targeting a meeting by foreign trade ministers to express concern that the creation of the 34-nation FTAA would send thousands of U.S. jobs overseas, exploit cheap labor, and waste natural resources.[2]

Although most demonstrators paraded peacefully and avoided confrontations, some pulled down crowd-control barriers with grappling hooks and scuffled with officers who were trying to maintain order. Before the melee ended, officers had to use batons, plastic shields, concussion grenades, pepper spray, and stun guns to regain control over the unruly protesters. Armored personnel carriers stood ready to move into hot spots. "We're basically trying to maintain the peace downtown," said police spokesperson Jorge Pino, as demonstrators advanced on police lines.[3] By the time the event ended, 74 people had been arrested and 42 protesters were injured, including 10 who had to be hospitalized. Three police officers were also hurt. As the Miami riots demonstrate, the maintenance of social order is an important part of police work today.

The Police Mission

The basic purposes of policing in democratic societies are to (1) enforce and support the laws of the society of which the police are a part, (2) investigate crimes and apprehend offenders, (3) prevent crime, (4) help ensure domestic peace and tranquility, and (5) provide the community with needed enforcement-related services. Simply put, as Sir Robert Peel, founder of the British system of policing, explained in 1822, "The basic mission for which the police exist is to reduce crime and disorder."[4]

In the paragraphs that follow, we turn our attention to these five basic elements of the police mission.

It shall be the mission of the Bradley County Sheriff's Office to consistently meet the public safety needs of all the people we serve, with integrity, respect, and fairness, within the resources allocated to us for this purpose. We shall strive to meet or exceed the expectations of those we serve, while enforcing the spirit of the law, and by always doing what is right.

—Mission statement, Bradley County (Tennessee) Sheriff's Office

Enforcing the Law

The police operate under an official public mandate that requires them to enforce the law. Collectively speaking, police agencies are the primary enforcers of federal, state, and local criminal laws. Not surprisingly, police officers see themselves as crime fighters, a view shared by the public and promoted by the popular media.

Although it is the job of the police to enforce the law, it is not their *only* job. Practically speaking, most officers spend the majority of their time answering nonemergency public-service calls,[5] controlling traffic, or writing tickets. Most are not involved in intensive, ongoing crime-fighting activities. Research shows that only about 10% to 20% of all calls to the police involve situations that actually require a law enforcement response—that is, situations that might lead to arrest and eventual prosecution.[6]

Miami riot police advancing through burning trash to control demonstrators protesting a meeting of foreign delegates who were attempting to negotiate an international free-trade agreement in 2003. Order maintenance is an important part of the police mission. What other aspects of the police mission can you identify?

David Adame/AP Wide World Photos

Even when the police are busy enforcing laws, they can't enforce them all. Police resources, including labor, vehicles, and investigative assets, are limited, causing officers to focus more on certain types of law violations than on others. Old laws prohibiting minor offenses like spitting on the sidewalk hold little social significance today and are typically relegated to the dustbin of statutory history. Even though they are still "on the books," few officers, if any, even think about enforcing such laws. Police tend to tailor their enforcement efforts to meet the contemporary concerns of the populace they serve.[7] For example, if a community is upset about a "massage parlor" operating in its neighborhood, the local police department may bring enforcement efforts to bear that lead to the relocation of the business. However, while community interests significantly influence the enforcement practices of police agencies, individual officers take their cue on enforcement priorities from their departments, their peers, and their supervisors. Learn more about how police supervisory styles influence patrol officer behavior at Library Extra 6–1 at cjtoday.com.

The police are expected not only to enforce the law but also to support it. The personal actions of law enforcement personnel should inspire others to respect and obey the law. Off-duty officers who speed down the highway or smoke marijuana at a party, for example, do a disservice to the police profession and engender disrespect for all agents of enforcement and for the law itself. Hence, in an important sense, we can say that respect for the law begins with the personal and public behavior of law enforcement officers.

LIBRARY
Extra
■ ■ ■ ■

Apprehending Offenders

Some offenders are apprehended during the commission of a crime or immediately afterward. Fleeing Oklahoma City bomber Timothy McVeigh, for example, was stopped by an Oklahoma Highway Patrol officer on routine patrol only 90 minutes after the destruction of the Alfred P. Murrah federal building[8] for driving a car with no license plate. When the officer questioned McVeigh about a bulge in his jacket, McVeigh admitted that it was a gun. The officer then took McVeigh into custody for carrying a concealed weapon. Typically, McVeigh would then have made an immediate appearance before a judge and have been released on bail. As fate would have it, however, the judge assigned to see McVeigh was involved in a protracted divorce case. The longer jail stay proved to be McVeigh's undoing. As the investigation into the bombing progressed, profiler Clinton R. Van Zandt of the Federal Bureau of Investigation's Behavioral Science Unit concluded that the bomber was likely a native-born white male in his twenties who had been in the military and was probably a member of a fringe militia group—all of which were true of McVeigh.[9] Working together, the FBI and the Oklahoma State Police realized that McVeigh was a likely suspect and questioned him. While McVeigh's capture was the result of a bit of good luck, many offenders are only caught as the result of extensive police work involving a painstaking investigation. (Investigation is described in more detail later in this chapter.)

Preventing Crime

crime prevention

The anticipation, recognition, and appraisal of a crime risk and the initiation of action to eliminate or reduce it.

Crime prevention is a proactive approach to the problem of crime; it is "the anticipation, recognition and appraisal of a crime risk and initiation of action to remove or reduce it."[10] In preventing crime, police agencies act before a crime happens, thus preventing victimization from occurring. Although the term *crime prevention* is relatively new, the idea is not. Securing valuables, limiting access to sensitive areas, and monitoring the activities of suspicious people are techniques used long before Western police forces were established in the 1800s.

Modern crime-prevention efforts aim not only to reduce crime and criminal opportunities and to lower the potential rewards of criminal activity, but also to lessen the public's fear of crime.[11] Crime-prevention efforts led by law enforcement include both techniques and programs. Techniques include access control, including barriers to entryways and exits; video and other types of surveillance; the use of theft-deterrence devices like locks, alarms, and tethers; lighting; and visibility landscaping. In contrast to techniques, crime-prevention programs are organized efforts that focus resources on reducing a specific form of criminal threat. The Philadelphia Police Department's Operation Identification, for example, is designed to discourage theft and to help recover stolen property.[12] The program educates citizens on the importance of identifying, marking, and listing their valuables to deter theft (because marked items are more difficult to sell) and to aid in their recovery. Through Operation Identification, the police department provides engraving pens, suggests ways of photographing valuables, and provides window decals and car bumper stickers that identify citizens as participants in the program. Other crime-prevention programs typically target school-based crime, gang activity, drug abuse, violence, domestic abuse, identity theft, vehicle theft, or neighborhood crimes, such as burglary.

Today's crime-prevention programs depend on community involvement and education and effective interaction between enforcement agencies and the communities they serve. For example, neighborhood watch programs build on active observation by homeowners and businesspeople on the lookout for anything unusual. Crime Stoppers International and Crime Stoppers USA are examples of privately sponsored programs that accept tips about criminal activity that they pass on to the appropriate law enforcement organization. Crime Stoppers International can be accessed via Web Extra 6–1 at cjtoday.com, and the National Crime Prevention Council can be found via Web Extra 6–2.

WEB Extra

PREDICTING CRIME

Law enforcement's ability to prevent crimes relies in part on the ability of police planners to predict when and where crimes will occur. Effective prediction means that limited police resources can be correctly assigned to the areas with the greatest need. One technique for predicting crim-

A warning sign telling looters to stay away from a flood-damaged home in Biloxi, Mississippi, following Hurricane Katrina in 2005. Effective law enforcement helps maintain social order and fills a critical need in the face of the widespread social disorganization that sometimes follows natural disasters or large-scale terrorist attacks. What other roles do the police fulfill?

Win McNamee/Getty Images, Inc.

inal activity is **CompStat**.[13] While CompStat may sound like a software program, it is actually a process of crime analysis and police management developed by the New York City Police Department in the mid-1990s[14] to help police managers better assess their performance and foresee the potential for crime. The CompStat process involves first collecting and analyzing the information received from 9-1-1 calls and officer reports.[15] Then, this detailed and timely information is mapped using special software developed for the purpose. The resulting map sequences, generated over time, reveal the time and place of crime patterns and identify "hot spots" of ongoing criminal activity. The maps also show the number of patrol officers active in an area, ongoing investigations, arrests made, and so on, thus helping commanders see which anticrime strategies are working.

CrimeStat, a Windows®-based spatial statistics-analysis software program for analyzing crime-incident locations, is a second technique for predicting criminal activity and produces results similar to CompStat's.[16] Developed by Ned Levine and Associates with grants from the National Institute of Justice (NIJ), CrimeStat provides statistical tools for crime mapping and analysis—including identification of crime hot spots, spatial distribution of incidents, and distance analysis—which help crime analysts target offenses that might be related to one another. CrimeStat software is available online via Web Extra 6–3 at cjtoday.com. Web Extra 6–4 provides a link to chicagocrime.org, which overlays crime statistics on maps of the city.

Preserving the Peace

Enforcing the law, apprehending offenders, and preventing crime are all daunting tasks for police departments because there are many laws and numerous offenders. Still, crimes are clearly defined by statute and are therefore limited in number. Peacekeeping, however, is a virtually limitless police activity involving not only activities that violate the law (and hence the community's peace) but many others as well. Law enforcement officers who supervise parades, public demonstrations, and picketing strikers, for example, attempt to ensure that the behavior of everyone involved remains "civil" so that it does not disrupt community life.

Robert Langworthy, who has written extensively about the police, says that keeping the peace is often left up to individual officers.[17] Basically, he says, departments depend on patrol officers "to define the peace and decide how to support it," and an officer is doing a good job when his or her "beat is quiet, meaning there are no complaints about loiterers or traffic flow, and commerce is supported."

Many police departments focus on quality-of-life offenses as a crime-reduction and peacekeeping strategy. **Quality-of-life offenses** are minor law violations, sometimes called *petty crimes*, that demoralize residents and businesspeople by creating disorder. Examples of petty crimes include excessive noise, graffiti, abandoned cars, and vandalism. Other quality-of-life offenses reflect social decay and include panhandling and aggressive begging, public urination, prostitution,

CompStat

A crime-analysis and police-management process, built on crime mapping, that was developed by the New York City Police Department in the mid-1990s.

WEB Extra

quality-of-life offense

A minor violation of the law (sometimes called a *petty crime*) that demoralizes community residents and businesspeople. Quality-of-life offenses involve acts that create physical disorder (for example, excessive noise or vandalism) or that reflect social decay (for example, panhandling and prostitution).

Chief Deputy Paula Townsend of the Watauga County, North Carolina, Sheriff's Department carrying 11-month-old Breanna Chambers to safety in 2005 after the capture of the child's parents. The parents, who were already wanted on charges related to methamphetamine manufacture, were charged with additional counts of child abduction, felonious restraint, and assault with a gun after they abducted Breanna and her two-year-old brother, James Paul Chambers, from a foster home. Today's police officers are expected to enforce the law while meeting the needs of the community. Do those goals conflict? If so, how?

Watauga Democrat/*Marie Freeman/AP Wide World Photos*

CJ News

Shaq Assists as Police Make Arrest

Shaquille O'Neal has been credited with an assist away from the basketball court, following a suspect who allegedly assaulted a gay couple and alerting police.

The 7-foot-1 Miami Heat center, who is in the process of becoming a Miami Beach reserve police officer, was driving on South Beach about 3 A.M. Sunday, September 11, 2005.

That's when he saw the man, riding as a passenger in a silver Honda, yell antigay slurs at the couple, said Bobby Hernandez, spokesman for the Miami Beach Police Department.

The man then got out of the car and threw a bottle, hitting one of the pedestrians, who was not seriously hurt. The suspect got back in the car and it sped off, but O'Neal followed.

"He flagged down the Miami Beach officer on duty there, and the officer was able to apprehend the subject," Hernandez said.

Michael Gonzalez, 18, was arrested on charges of aggravated assault and assault with a deadly weapon. A phone number for Gonzalez could not be located and it was not known if he has an attorney. The Honda's driver was not charged.

O'Neal, who hopes to be a police chief or county sheriff one day, was already being fitted for his Miami Beach police uniform before the incident.

"For this incident, I don't want to be credited as an individual who does police work," O'Neal said in a statement. "I want to be credited as a Miami Beach police officer."

For the latest in crime and justice news, visit the Talk Justice news feed at http://www.crimenews.info.

Basketball star and Los Angeles Port Police Officer Shaquille O'Neal receiving an award of appreciation at the Conference of the International Association of Airport and Seaport Police in Los Angeles in 2003. In 2005, O'Neal became a reserve officer in the Miami Beach Police Department and assisted in the arrest of a man accused of assaulting a gay couple. Might Shaq serve as a role model for others interested in police work?

Dan Steinberg/Getty Images

Source: "Shaq Assists as Police Arrest Man Accused of Assaulting Gay Couple," © September 14, 2005 by The Associated Press. Reprinted by permission.

---

roaming youth gangs, public consumption of alcohol, and street-level substance abuse.[18] Homelessness, while not necessarily a violation of the law unless it involves some form of trespass,[19] is also typically addressed under quality-of-life programs. Through police interviews, many of the homeless are relocated to shelters or hospitals or are arrested for some other offense. Some researchers claim that reducing the number of quality-of-life offenses in a community can restore a sense of order, reduce the fear of crime, and lessen the number of serious crimes that occur. However, quality-of-life programs have been criticized by those who say that the police should not be taking a law enforcement approach to social and economic problems.[20]

A similar approach to keeping the peace can be found in the broken windows model of policing.[21] This thesis (which is also discussed in the "CJ Futures" box in Chapter 3) is based on the notion that physical decay in a community, such as litter and abandoned buildings, can breed disorder and lead to crime by signaling that laws are not being enforced.[22] Such decay, the theory postulates, pushes law-abiding citizens to withdraw from the streets, which then sends a signal that lawbreakers can operate freely.[23] The broken windows thesis suggests that by encouraging the repair of rundown buildings and controlling disorderly behavior in public spaces, police agencies can create an environment in which serious crime cannot easily flourish.[24]

While desirable, public order has its own costs. Noted police author Charles R. Swanson says, "The degree to which any society achieves some amount of public order through police action depends in part upon the price that society is willing to pay to obtain it."[25] Swanson goes on to describe the price to be paid in terms of (1) police resources paid for by tax dollars and (2) "a reduction in the number, kinds, and extent of liberties" that are available to members of the public.

The sense of emergency in policing has crowded out our capacity to think about problems in the long term.

—Dan Reynolds[ii]

Providing Services

As writers for the National Institute of Justice observe, "any citizen from any city, suburb, or town across the United States can mobilize police resources by simply picking up the phone and placing a direct call to the police."[26] "Calling the cops" has been described as the cornerstone of policing in a democratic society. About 70% of the millions of daily calls to 9-1-1 systems across the country are directed to the police, although callers can also request emergency medical and fire services. Calls received by 9-1-1 operators are prioritized and then relayed to patrol officers, specialized field units, or other emergency personnel. For example, the Hastings (Minnesota) Police Department handled a total of 12,895 calls for service in 2001.[27] A breakdown of those calls shows that there were 1,837 calls related to serious crimes like arson, assault, auto theft, burglary, larceny, rape, and robbery. The remaining 11,058 calls were nonemergency calls about lost and found articles, minor motor vehicle accidents, barking dogs, suspicious persons, and parking and traffic law violation reports. Numbers like these have led some cities to adopt nonemergency "Citizen Service System" call numbers in addition to 9-1-1. More than a dozen metropolitan areas, including Baltimore, Dallas, Detroit, Las Vegas, New York, and San Jose, now staff 3-1-1 nonemergency systems around the clock. Plans are afoot in some places to adopt the 3-1-1 system statewide.

If you ever get lost, you can go find a policeman. The policeman will help you because he is your friend.

—A second-grade teacher

Operational Strategies

The police mission offers insight into general law enforcement goals, which help shape the various operational strategies that departments employ.[28] There are five core operational strategies—preventive patrol, routine incident response, emergency response, criminal investigation, and problem solving—and one ancillary operational strategy—support services.[29] The first four core strategies constitute the conventional way in which police have worked, at least since the 1930s; problem solving is relatively new. Each strategy has unique features, and each represents a particular way to approach situations that the police encounter. Operational strategies can be discussed along a number of dimensions. Table 6–1 describes each strategy in different ways, including the objectives, performance standards, and processes involved.

Preventive Patrol

Preventive patrol, the dominant operational policing strategy,[30] has been the backbone of police work since the time of Sir Robert Peel. Routine patrol activities, which place uniformed police officers on the street in the midst of the public, consume most of the resources of local and state-level police agencies.

Mounted Los Angeles Police Department officers patrolling a beach within the city limits. Patrol, a typical police function, can take a variety of forms. What kinds of patrol activities does the public expect from the police?

A. Ramey/PhotoEdit Inc.

TABLE 6–1   Operational Strategies of Police Work

Operational Strategy	Work Unit	Objectives	Record System	Reporting Requirements	Performance Standards	Specialized Training	Processes	Accountability
Preventive patrol	None—ongoing	Prevent and detect offenses, promote general feelings of security	Daily activity reports, patrol vehicle mileage	Daily activity reports	Absence of crime, low levels of citizen fear, high rate of police detection of certain types of offenses (e.g., commercial burglary)	Patrol methods (random, directed)	Limited—some officers use systematic area coverage patterns and plans	Limited—some expectation that officers will detect certain offenses on their beats, some command accountability for absence of citizen complaints about police presence
Routine incident response	Call	Record incident, resolve dispute, provide or take information	Dispatch records	Report or coded disposition	Complainant satisfaction, response time, fair treatment of parties, proper completion of report	Special training by type of incident	Procedures according to call type, reporting requirements	Code the call, file report, accountability rests with officer assigned and shift supervisor
Emergency response	Critical incident	Save life, interrupt crime, protect property, minimize injury	Dispatch records, after-action reports	Critical incident report	No deaths, minimal injuries, restoration of order	Vehicle operation, first aid, hostage rescue, SWAT, defensive tactics	First aid procedures, critical incident procedures, triage	Primary officer or scene commander, until incident ends (handed off, if necessary)
Criminal investigation	Case	Establish culpability, make prosecutable case, apprehend offender, clear case	Case files	Case report and file	Case filed by prosecutor, suspect apprehended	Death investigation, crime-scene analysis, forensics, interviewing	Criminal investigative procedures	Case file deadlines, case management (handed off, if necessary) rests with detective assigned, unit supervisor
Problem solving	Problem or project	Reduce harm, reduce incidence, eliminate problem, improve response	Project files	Sometimes none, project report	Significant reduction in harm, caused by intervention, for reasonable period of time	Problem-solving methods	SARA, CAPRA (see text)	Rests with police chief, district commander, supervisor, and officer
Support services	Program or procedure	Provide service, enhance police legitimacy	Program reports	Program or budget reports	Use/popularity of service	Specific procedures	Written procedure or curriculum	Fiscal

Source: Adapted from Michael S. Scott, *Problem-Oriented Policing: Reflections on the First 20 Years* (Washington, DC: U.S. Department of Justice, Office of Community Oriented Policing Services, 2000), p. 89.

The purpose of patrol is fourfold: to deter crimes, to interrupt crimes in progress, to position officers for quick response to emergency situations, and to increase the public's feelings of safety and security. Patrol is the operational mode uniformed officers are expected to work in when not otherwise involved in answering calls for service. Most departments use a computer-assisted dispatch (CAD) system to prioritize incoming service calls into different categories and to record dispatches issued, time spent on each call, the identities of responding personnel, and so on.

The majority of patrol activity is *interactive* because officers on patrol commonly interact with the public. Some forms of patrol, however, involve more interaction than others. The many types of patrol include foot, automobile, motorcycle, mounted, bicycle, boat, K-9, and aerial. Although some scientific studies of policing have questioned the effectiveness of preventive patrol in reducing crime (discussed in Chapter 5), most citizens expect police to patrol.

The spectacular and horrific nature of the September 11 terrorist attacks and the massive devastation and loss of life that they wrought have ushered in a new era of policing in the United States.

—International Association of Chiefs of Police[iii]

Routine Incident Response

Police officers on patrol frequently respond to routine incidents, such as minor traffic accidents. Routine incident responses comprise the second most common activity of patrol officers.[31] Officers responding to routine incidents must collect information and typically file a written report. As noted by the National Institute of Justice, "the specific police objective will . . . vary depending on the nature of the situation, but generally, the objective is to restore order, document information or otherwise provide some immediate service to the parties involved."[32]

One important measure of police success that is strongly linked to citizen satisfaction is **response time**—the time it takes for police officers to respond to calls for service. It is measured from the time a call for service is received by a dispatcher until an officer arrives on the scene.

During the first four months of the 2007 fiscal year, for example, police response times in New York City to crimes in progress averaged 7 minutes and 6 seconds—24 seconds better than the same period in the previous year. The average time required for a New York Police Department (NYPD) officer to arrive on the scene when responding to an incident rated by dispatchers as "critical" was 4.3 minutes. Response times to both critical incidents and crimes in progress in New York City in 2007 were the quickest times recorded in the city in more than a decade.[33]

response time

A measure of the time that it takes for police officers to respond to calls for service.

Emergency Response

In May 2003, Pomona, California, police officers on routine patrol responded to a dispatcher's instructions to assist in an emergency at a local coin-operated laundry.[34] On arrival, they found a two-year-old girl trapped inside an industrial-size washing machine. The officers used their batons to smash the locked glass-paned door. The girl, unconscious and nearly drowned when pulled from the machine, was taken to a local hospital where she was expected to recover. Her mother, 35-year-old Erma Osborne, was arrested at the scene and charged with child endangerment when the on-site video surveillance cameras showed her placing her daughter in the machine and shutting the door.

Although police respond to emergencies far less frequently than to routine incidents,[35] emergency response is a vital aspect of what police agencies do. Emergency responses, often referred to as *critical incidents*, are used for crimes in progress, traffic accidents with serious injuries, natural disasters, incidents of terrorism, officer requests for assistance, and other situations in which human life may be in jeopardy. Emergency responses take priority over all other police work, and until an emergency situation is secured and some order restored, the officers involved will not turn to other tasks. An important part of police training involves emergency response techniques, including first aid, hostage rescue, and the physical capture of suspects.

Criminal Investigation

The fourth operational strategy, criminal investigation, dominates media depictions of police work. Although central to the mission of the police, investigations actually constitute a relatively small proportion of police work. A **criminal investigation** is "the process of discovering, collecting, preparing, identifying, and presenting evidence to determine *what happened and who is responsible*"[36] when a crime occurs.

Criminal investigators are often referred to as *detectives*, and it is up to them to solve most crimes and to produce the evidence needed for the successful prosecution of suspects. But any

criminal investigation

"The process of discovering, collecting, preparing, identifying, and presenting evidence to determine *what happened and who is responsible*"[iv] when a crime has occurred.

police officer can be involved in the initial stages of the investigative process, especially those responding to critical incidents. First-on-the-scene officers, or first responders, can play a critical role in providing emergency assistance to the injured and in capturing suspects. First responders, however, also have an important responsibility to secure the crime scene, a duty that can later provide the basis for a successful criminal investigation. A **crime scene** is the physical area in which a crime is thought to have occurred and in which evidence of the crime is thought to reside (Figure 6–1). Securing the crime scene is particularly crucial, for when a crime takes place, especially a violent one, confusion often results. People at the scene and curious onlookers may unwittingly (and sometimes intentionally) destroy physical evidence, obliterating important clues like tire tracks, fingerprints, or footprints.

crime scene

The physical area in which a crime is thought to have occurred and in which evidence of the crime is thought to reside.

FIGURE 6–1

The crime-scene investigation process.

Note: This is not a real crime scene. This picture was fabricated by the Massachusetts State Police Crime Lab staff for demonstrative purposes.

Source: Courtesy of the Massachusetts State Police.

The Arson and Explosives Unit receives evidence recovered from crime scenes involving suspicious fires and explosions. The unit identifies ignitable liquid evidence recovered from a fire scene that may have been intentionally used to propagate a fire. The unit also identifies explosives or explosive residues recovered from a bombing scene and can reconstruct devices to assist investigators in identifying perpetrators and the source(s) of device components.

The Drug Unit analyzes all contraband seized by state police agencies and some local and federal agencies in Massachusetts. The most common substances analyzed at the laboratory are marijuana, cocaine, and heroin. To perform these analyses, the unit utilizes sensitive and selective instrumentation. This instrumentation allows the unit to identify and measure a wide range of illegal substances that have been seized.

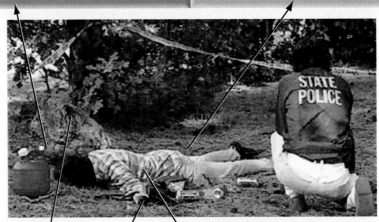

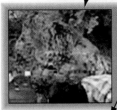

The Massachusetts State Police Crime Laboratory's DNA Unit processes forensic casework samples for STR (short tandem repeat) fragment analysis using a Perkin-Elmer 310 Genetic Analyzer. Thirteen specific locations on the molecule are tested for comparative DNA analysis of biological stains. DNA evidence is crucial to protect the unjustly accused and convict the guilty. Blood, such as that found on the rock in the mock crime scene, would be analyzed by the DNA Lab. Other biological materials—including saliva, semen, skin tissue, hair roots, and sweat— also contain nuclear DNA, which may lead to STR DNA profiles.

The Ballistics Section is responsible for conducting scientific examination, comparison, and identification of firearms and firearms-related evidence. Weapon operability must be demonstrated to support the successful prosecution of weapons-related offenses. Members respond to crime scenes to assist in determining what role, if any, a firearm has played in the commission of a crime. The section is also responsible for the destruction of firearms and ammunition as ordered by the court.

A victim's clothing would be logged in by the Evidence Control Unit. Clothing could also be of interest to the Criminalistics Unit and Trace Analysis Unit.

The preliminary investigation is an important part of the investigatory process. An effective preliminary investigation is the foundation on which the entire criminal investigation process is built.[37] The Florida Highway Patrol's policy manual provides a broad definition of a **preliminary investigation**, saying that it refers to all of the activities undertaken by a police officer who responds to the scene of a crime.[38] Those activities include the following:

1. Responding to immediate needs and rendering aid to the injured

2. Noting such facts as the position of victims or injured subjects, recording spontaneous statements, noting unusual actions or activities, and notifying headquarters with an assessment of the scene

3. Determining that a crime has been committed

4. Initiating enforcement action, such as arresting or pursuing the offender or dispatching apprehension information

5. Securing the crime scene and protecting evidence, including limiting access, identifying and isolating witnesses, and protecting all evidence, especially short-lived evidence (such as impressions in sand or mud)

6. Determining the need for investigative specialists and arranging for their notification

7. Compiling a thorough and accurate report of activities

A preliminary investigation begins when the call to respond has been received. Even before they arrive at the crime scene, officers may observe important events related to the offense, such as fleeing vehicles or the presence of suspicious people nearby. After they arrive, first responders begin collecting information through observation and possibly through conversations with others who are already at the scene. Typically, it is at this point that officers determine whether there are sufficient grounds to believe that a crime has actually occurred. Even in suspected homicides, for example, it is important to rule out accidental death, suicide, and death by natural causes before the investigation can proceed beyond the preliminary stage.

Next, specially trained crime-scene investigators arrive, and the detailed examination of a crime scene begins. **Crime-scene investigators** are expert in the use of specific forensics techniques, such as gathering DNA evidence, collecting fingerprints, photographing the scene, making sketches to show the position of items at the scene, and interviewing witnesses.

Crime-scene investigators are commonly promoted to their posts internally after at least a few years of patrol work. However, large local police departments and those at the state and federal levels may employ civilian crime-scene investigators. Follow-up investigations, based on evidence collected at the scene, are conducted by police detectives. Important to any investigation are solvability factors. A **solvability factor** is information about a crime that can provide a basis for determining the perpetrator's identity. If few solvability factors exist, a continuing investigation is unlikely to lead to an arrest. Learn more about crime-scene investigation at Library Extra 6–2 at cjtoday.com.

preliminary investigation

All of the activities undertaken by a police officer who responds to the scene of a crime, including determining whether a crime has occurred, securing the crime scene, and preserving evidence.

crime-scene investigator

An expert trained in the use of forensics techniques, such as gathering DNA evidence, collecting fingerprints, photographing the scene, sketching, and interviewing witnesses.

solvability factor

Information about a crime that forms the basis for determining the perpetrator's identity.

LIBRARY
Extra
■ ■ ■ ■

Problem Solving

The fifth operational strategy of police work is problem solving. Also called *problem-oriented policing*, problem solving seeks to reduce chronic offending in a community. NIJ authors note that "historically, it is the least well-developed by the police profession. While the police have always used the mental processes of problem-solving, problem-solving as a formal operational strategy of police work has gained some structure and systematic attention only in the past 20 years."[39]

The methodology of police problem solving is known by acronyms such as SARA (scanning, analysis, response, and assessment) or CAPRA (clients, acquired/analyzed, partnerships, respond, assess). CAPRA was developed by the Royal Canadian Mounted Police, who built on the earlier SARA process. This is the CAPRA process:[40]

- The police begin by communicating with the *clients* most affected by community problems.

- Information is *acquired* and *analyzed* to determine the problem's causes.

- Solutions are developed through community *partnerships*.

- The police *respond* with a workable plan.

- After plan implementation, the police periodically *assess* the situation to ensure progress.

Learn more about problem analysis in policing at Library Extra 6–3 at cjtoday.com.

The expectations of law enforcement as first responder for homeland security have put an almost unachievable burden on local law enforcement.

—Judith Lewis, Captain (retired), Los Angeles County Sheriff's Department

LIBRARY
Extra
■ ■ ■ ■

Support Services

Support services constitute the sixth operational strategy found in police organizations. They include such activities as dispatch, training, human resources management, property and evidence control, and record keeping. Support services keep police agencies running and help deliver the equipment, money, and resources necessary to support law enforcement officers in the field.

Managing Police Departments

police management

The administrative activities of controlling, directing, and coordinating police personnel, resources, and activities in the service of preventing crime, apprehending criminals, recovering stolen property, and performing regulatory and helping services.[v]

Police management entails administrative activities that control, direct, and coordinate police personnel, resources, and activities in an effort to prevent crime, apprehend criminals, recover stolen property, and perform a variety of regulatory and helping services.[41] Police managers include sworn law enforcement personnel with administrative authority, from the rank of sergeant to captain, chief, or sheriff, and civilians like police commissioners, attorneys general, state secretaries of crime control, and public-safety directors.

Police Organization and Structure

line operations

In police organizations, the field activities or supervisory activities directly related to day-to-day police work.

staff operations

In police organizations, activities (such as administration and training) that provide support for line operations.

Almost all American law enforcement organizations are formally structured among divisions and along lines of authority. Roles within police agencies generally fall into one of two categories: line and staff. **Line operations** are field or supervisory activities directly related to daily police work. **Staff operations** include support roles, such as administration. In organizations that have line operations only, authority flows from the top down in a clear, unbroken line;[42] no supporting elements (media relations, training, fiscal management divisions, and so on) exist. All line operations are directly involved in providing field services. Because almost all police agencies need support, only the smallest departments have just line operations.

Most police organizations include both line and staff operations. In such organizations, line managers are largely unencumbered with staff operations like budgeting, training, the scientific analysis of evidence, legal advice, shift assignments, and personnel management. Support personnel handle these activities, freeing line personnel to focus on the day-to-day requirements of providing field services.

In a line and staff agency, divisions are likely to exist within both line operations and staff operations. For example, field services, a line operation, may be broken down into enforcement and investigation. Administrative services, a staff operation, may be divided into human resources management, training and education, materials supply, finance management, and facilities management. The line and staff structure easily accommodates functional areas of responsibility within line and staff divisions. The organizational chart of the Elk Grove (California) Police Department shows this type of organization (Figure 6–2). A similar organizational chart showing the line and staff structure of the Los Angeles County Sheriff's Department (LASD)—the largest sheriff's department in the world[43]—is shown in Figure 6–3.

Chain of Command

chain of command

The unbroken line of authority that extends through all levels of an organization, from the highest to the lowest.

The organizational chart of any police agency shows a hierarchical **chain of command**, or the order of authority within the department. The chain of command clarifies who reports to whom. Usually, the chief of police or sheriff is at the top of the command chain—although his or her boss may be a police commissioner, city council, or mayor—followed by the subordinate leaders of each division. For example, in the Elk Grove Police Department's chain of command (see Figure 6–2), one assistant chief answers to the chief of police and oversees each of the department's divisions; a sergeant heads the administration division; and a lieutenant heads the other two divisions—field operations and investigations. Because field operations provides services 24 hours each day, a number of lieutenants are assigned to it, each in charge of an 8-hour shift. Within that division, the day watch is staffed by 26 enforcement personnel, while the night watch routinely has only 13 officers on duty (two sergeants and 11 patrol officers).

Because police departments employ a quasi-military chain-of-command structure, the titles assigned to personnel (captain, lieutenant, sergeant) are similar to those used by the military. It is important for individual personnel to know who is in charge; hence, unity of command is an important principle that must be firmly established within the department. When unity of command exists, every individual has only one supervisor to answer to and, under normal circum-

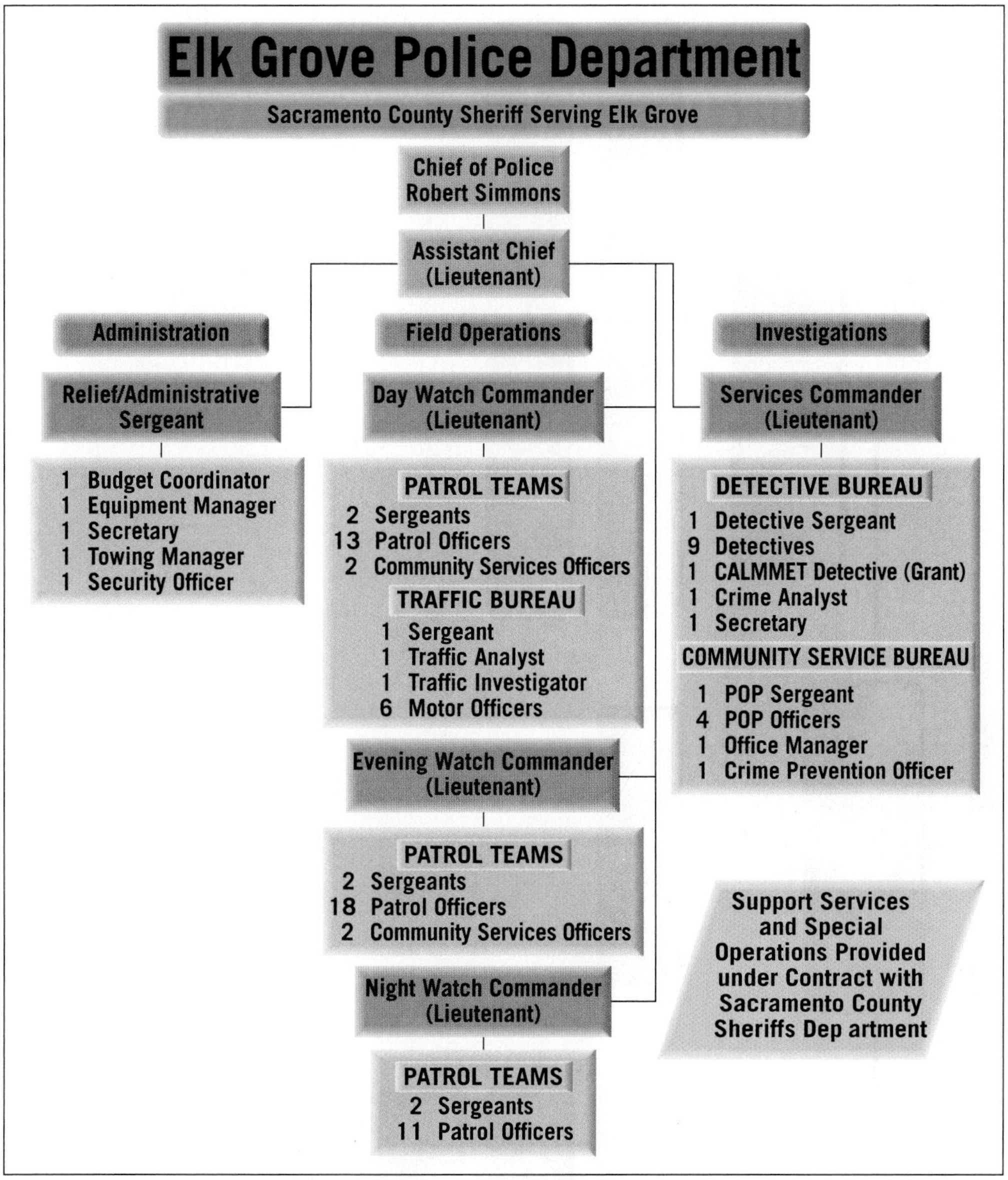

FIGURE 6–2

Organizational chart of the Elk Grove (California) Police Department.

Source: City of Elk Grove (California) Police Department. Reprinted with permission.

stances, to take orders from. **Span of control** refers to the number of police personnel or the number of units supervised by a particular commander. For example, one sergeant may be in charge of five or six officers; they represent the sergeant's span of control.

span of control

The number of police personnel or the number of units supervised by a particular commander.

Policing Styles

The history of American policing can be divided into four epochs,[44] each distinguishable by the relative dominance of a particular approach to police operations (Figure 6–4). The first period, the political era, was characterized by close ties between police and public officials. It began in the 1840s and ended around 1930. Throughout the period, American police agencies tended to serve the interests of powerful politicians and their cronies, providing public-order-maintenance services almost as an afterthought. The second period, the reform era, began in the 1930s and lasted until the 1970s. It was characterized by pride in professional crime fighting. Police departments during this period focused most of their resources on solving "traditional" crimes, such as murder, rape, and burglary, and on capturing offenders. The third period, which continues to characterize much of contemporary policing in America today, is the community policing era—an approach to policing that stresses the service role of police officers and envisions a partnership between police agencies and their communities.

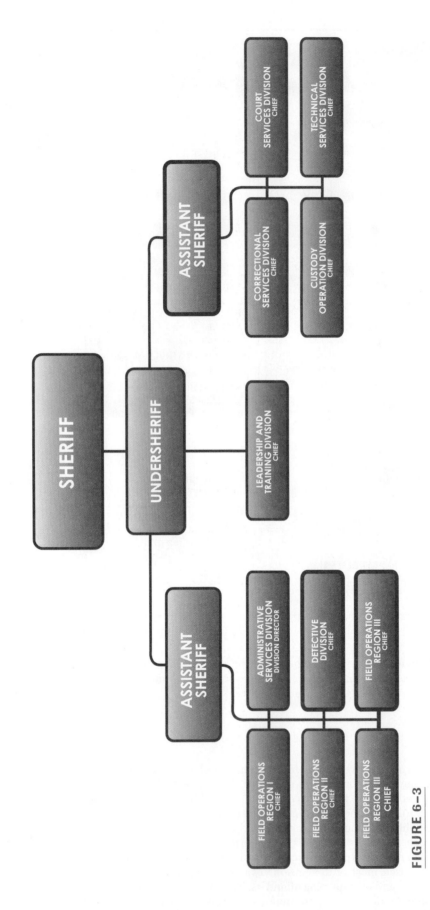

FIGURE 6–3

Organizational chart of the Los Angeles County Sheriff's Department.

Source: Los Angeles County Sheriff's Department. Reprinted with permission.

Era	Political Era	Reform Era	Community Era	Homeland Security Era
Time Period	1840s–1930	1930–1970s	1970s–Today	2001–Today
Characteristics	Close ties between the police and public officials. Uniformed officers in paramilitary-style organizations serving the interests of the politically powerful.	Pride in professional crime fighting. An emphasis on solving "traditional" crimes and capturing offenders.	Police departments work to identify and serve the needs of their communities. Envisions a partnership between local police agencies and their communities.	Policing to secure the homeland; emphasis on terrorism prevention. Builds on partnerships with the community to gather actionable intelligence to circumvent threats of terrorism.
Catalyst	The need for social order and security in a dynamic and rapidly changing society.	Citizen calls for reform and the development of police professionalism. The removal of politics from policing.	The realization that effective community partnerships can help prevent and solve crimes.	The terrorist attacks of September 11, 2001, and ongoing threats to the safety and security of all Americans.
Example	Police departments and officers were closely tied to their city's political system. Local "ward politicians" hired officers for their own purposes.	"G-men" and the crackdown on organized crime. Progressive policing, led by men like August Vollmer and O. W. Wilson.	A focus on quality-of-life offenses as a crime-reduction and peacekeeping strategy. The broken windows model of policing.	Creation of counterterrorism divisions and offices within departments. Collaboration between police agencies and the sharing of information needed to identify threats.

FIGURE 6–4

Historical eras in American policing.

The fourth period, policing to secure the homeland, is quite new and continues to evolve.[45] The homeland security era grew out of national concerns with terrorism prevention born of the terrorist attacks of September 11, 2001. As police scholar Gene Stephens explains it, "the twenty-first century has put policing into a whole new milieu—one in which the causes of crime and disorder often lie outside the immediate community, demanding new and innovative approaches."[46] A decline in street crime, says Stephens, has been replaced by concern with new and more insidious types of offending, including terrorism and Internet-assisted crimes. These new kinds of crimes, says Stephens, while they threaten the integrity of local communities, often involve offenders thousands of miles away. Nonetheless, as we shall see later in this chapter, the homeland security era builds substantially upon the community policing philosophy with which it coexists.

The influence of each of the first three historical phases survives today in what noted social commentator and Presidential Medal of Freedom recipient James Q. Wilson[47] calls "policing styles."[48] A style of policing describes how a particular agency sees its purpose and chooses the methods it uses to fulfill that purpose. Wilson's three policing styles—which he does not link to any particular historical era—are (1) the watchman style (characteristic of the political era), (2) the legalistic style (professional crime fighting of the reform era), and (3) the service style (which is becoming more common today). These three styles characterize nearly all municipal law enforcement agencies now operating in the United States, although some departments are a mixture of two or more styles.

The Watchman Style of Policing

watchman style

A style of policing marked by a concern for order maintenance. Watchman policing is characteristic of lower-class communities where police intervene informally into the lives of residents to keep the peace.

Police departments marked by the **watchman style** are chiefly concerned with achieving what Wilson calls "order maintenance" through control of illegal and disruptive behavior. Compared to the legalistic style, the watchman style uses discretion liberally. Watchman-style departments keep order through informal police "intervention," which may include persuasion, threats, or even "roughing up" disruptive people. Some authors condemn this style of policing, suggesting that it is typically found in lower- or lower-middle-class communities, especially where interpersonal relations include a fair amount of violence or physical abuse.

The watchman style was typified by the Los Angeles police officers who took part in the infamous beating of Rodney King in 1992. After the ensuing riots, the Christopher Commission, the independent commission on the Los Angeles Police Department (LAPD), found that the Los Angeles police "placed greater emphasis on crime control over crime prevention, a policy that distanced cops from the people they serve."[49]

The Legalistic Style of Policing

legalistic style

A style of policing marked by a strict concern with enforcing the precise letter of the law. Legalistic departments may take a hands-off approach to disruptive or problematic behavior that does not violate the criminal law.

Departments operating under the **legalistic style** enforce the letter of the law. For example, an officer who tickets a person going 71 miles per hour in a 70-mph speed zone is likely a member of a department that adheres to the legalistic style of policing. Conversely, legalistic departments routinely avoid community disputes arising from violations of social norms that do not break the law. Police expert Gary Sykes calls this enforcement style "laissez-faire policing" in recognition of its hands-off approach to behaviors that are simply bothersome or inconsiderate of community principles.[50]

The Service Style of Policing

service style

A style of policing marked by a concern with helping rather than strict enforcement. Service-oriented police agencies are more likely to use community resources, such as drug-treatment programs, to supplement traditional law enforcement activities than are other types of agencies.

In service-oriented departments, which strive to meet the needs of the community and serve its members, the police see themselves more as helpers than as soldiers in a war on crime. This type of department works with social services and other agencies to provide counseling for minor offenders and to assist community groups in preventing crimes and solving problems. Prosecutors may support the **service style** by agreeing not to prosecute law violators who seek psychiatric help or who voluntarily participate in programs like Alcoholics Anonymous, family counseling, or drug treatment. The service style is supported in part by citizens who seek to avoid the embarrassment that might result from a public airing of personal problems, thereby reducing the number of criminal complaints filed, especially in minor disputes. While the service style of policing may seem more appropriate to wealthy communities or small towns, it can also exist in cities whose police departments actively seek citizen involvement in identifying issues that the police can help address.

FREEDOM OR SAFETY?
You Decide

Watch Out: You're on Police TV

In 2007, officials in Los Angeles announced a plan to install video cameras in all 1,600 of the city's patrol cars within four years. "It's a good accounting of what happened at the scene," said Bob Baker, president of the Los Angeles Police Protective League. "I think it's great for the officers, great for the community and great for the city."

Patrol cars equipped with video cameras have been on the nation's highways since the late 1980s, and the footage they've produced has been a staple of real-life police TV shows for years. In 2002, following the nationally televised airing of what appeared to be the physical abuse of a teenage suspect by an Inglewood, California, arresting officer, Inglewood Mayor Roosevelt Dorn called for cameras to be installed in all of his city's patrol cars. The alleged abuse had been videotaped by a bystander.

Many people believe that camera-equipped cars will lead to a reduction in police abuses while serving to capture evidence of illegal behavior by suspects. Video footage can also be used for identification purposes and might be coupled with software that provides facial and license tag recognition, allowing officers to quickly identify stolen cars and wanted individuals.

Some, however, fear that the combination of video images and recognition software will lead to the creation of a suspect database that will inevitably include many otherwise innocent people, and which might be improperly shared with other agencies or the popular media.

Since 2000, the Justice Department's Office of Community-Oriented Policing Services has provided $15 million to state law enforcement agencies to equip 3,563 cruisers with cameras. A 2005 study by the International Association of Chiefs of Police surveyed 47 state law enforcement agencies that received federal grants to buy in-car cameras and concluded that such cameras substantially improved public trust in the police and protected officers against unfounded lawsuits.

YOU DECIDE

Do you think that equipping all of the nation's patrol cars with video cameras is a good idea? What negative impact, if any, might this initiative have on personal freedoms in our society? How might it impact policing?

References: International Association of Chiefs of Police, *The Impact of Video Evidence on Modern Policing* (Alexandria, VA: IACP, 2005); Patrick McMahon, "Increased Clamor for Cameras in Cop Cars," *USA Today*, July 18, 2002; and "LAPD to Put Cameras in Patrol Cars," *USA Today*, March 19, 2007, p. 3A.

Police–Community Relations

The 1960s were fraught with riots, unrest, and student activism as the war in Vietnam, civil rights concerns, and other social issues produced large demonstrations and marches. The police, generally inexperienced in crowd control, were all too often embroiled in tumultuous encounters—even pitched battles—with citizen groups that viewed the police as agents of "the establishment." To manage these new challenges, the legalistic style of policing, so common in America until then, began to yield to the newer service-oriented policing.

As social disorganization increased, police departments across the nation, seeking to understand and better cope with the problems they faced, created **police–community relations (PCR)** programs. PCR programs represented a movement away from an exclusive emphasis on the apprehension of law violators toward an effort to increase the level of positive police–citizen interaction. At the height of the PCR movement, city police departments across the country opened storefront centers where citizens could air complaints and interact easily with police representatives. As police scholar Egon Bittner recognized in 1976, PCR programs need to reach to "the grassroots of discontent," where citizen dissatisfaction with the police exists,[51] if they are to be truly effective.

In many contemporary PCR programs, public-relations officers are appointed to provide an array of services, such as neighborhood watch programs, drug-awareness workshops, Project ID—using police equipment and expertise to mark valuables for identification in the event of theft—and victims' assistance programs. Modern PCR programs, however, often fail to achieve their goal of increased community satisfaction with police services because they focus on servicing groups already well satisfied with the police. PCR initiatives that do reach disaffected community groups are difficult to manage and may even alienate participating officers from the communities they are assigned to serve. Thus, as Bittner noted, "while the first approach fails because it leaves out those groups to which the program is primarily directed, the second fails because it leaves out the police department."

police–community relations (PCR)

An area of police activity that recognizes the need for the community and the police to work together effectively. PCR is based on the notion that the police derive their legitimacy from the community they serve. Many police agencies began to explore PCR in the 1960s and 1970s.

Police officers serving food during an anticrime rally to encourage citizen involvement in crime fighting. Activities like this help foster the community policing ideal through which law enforcement officers and members of the public become partners in controlling crime and keeping communities safe. How does such a partnership help the police? The community?

Dale Stockton

TEAM POLICING

team policing

The reorganization of conventional patrol strategies into "an integrated and versatile police team assigned to a fixed district."[vi]

During the 1960s and 1970s, some communities experimented with **team policing**, which rapidly became an extension of the PCR movement. With team policing, a team of police officers was assigned semipermanently to particular neighborhoods, where it was expected they would become familiar with the inhabitants and with their problems and concerns. Patrol officers were given considerable authority in processing complaints, from receipt through resolution. Crimes were investigated and solved at the local level, with specialists called in only if the resources needed to continue an investigation were not available locally. Some authors called team policing a "technique to deliver total police services to a neighborhood."[52] Others, however, dismissed it as "little more than an attempt to return to the style of policing that was prevalent in the United States over a century ago."[53]

COMMUNITY POLICING

During the past 20 years, the role of the police in police–community relations has changed considerably. Originally, the PCR model was based on the fact that many police administrators saw police officers as enforcers of the law who were isolated from, and often in opposition to, the communities they policed. As a result, PCR programs were often a shallowly disguised effort to overcome public suspicion and community hostility.

Today, increasing numbers of law enforcement administrators embrace the role of service provider. Modern departments frequently help citizens solve a vast array of personal problems, many of which involve no law-breaking activity. For example, officers regularly aid sick or distraught people, organize community crime-prevention efforts, investigate domestic disputes, regulate traffic, and educate children and teens about drug abuse. Service calls far exceed calls directly related to law violations, and officers make more referrals to agencies like Alcoholics Anonymous, domestic violence centers, and drug-rehabilitation programs than they make arrests.

In contemporary America, some say, police departments function a lot like corporations. According to Harvard University's Executive Session on Policing, three generic kinds of "corporate strategies" guide American policing: (1) strategic policing, (2) problem-solving policing, and (3) community policing.[54]

strategic policing

A type of policing that retains the traditional police goal of professional crime fighting but enlarges the enforcement target to include nontraditional kinds of criminals, such as serial offenders, gangs and criminal associations, drug-distribution networks, and sophisticated white-collar and computer criminals. Strategic policing generally makes use of innovative enforcement techniques, including intelligence operations, undercover stings, electronic surveillance, and sophisticated forensic methods.

Strategic policing, something of a holdover from the reform era, "emphasizes an increased capacity to deal with crimes that are not well controlled by traditional methods."[55] Strategic policing retains the traditional police goal of professional crime fighting but enlarges the enforcement target to include nontraditional kinds of criminals, such as serial offenders, gangs and criminal associations, drug-distribution networks, and sophisticated white-collar and computer criminals. To meet its goals, strategic policing generally makes use of innovative enforcement techniques, including intelligence operations, undercover stings, electronic surveillance, and sophisticated forensic methods. The other two strategies give greater recognition to Wilson's service style. **Problem-solving policing** (sometimes called *problem-oriented policing*) takes the view that many crimes are caused by existing social conditions in the communities. To control crime, problem-oriented police managers attempt to uncover and effectively address these underlying social problems. Problem-solving policing makes thorough use of community resources, such as counseling centers, welfare programs, and job-training facilities. It also attempts to involve citizens in crime prevention through education, negotiation, and conflict management. For example, police may ask residents of poorly maintained housing areas to clean up litter, install better lighting, and provide security devices for their houses and apartments in the belief that clean, well-lighted, secure areas are a deterrent to criminal activity.

The third and newest strategy, **community policing** (sometimes called *community-oriented policing*), goes a step beyond the other two. It has been described as "a philosophy based on forging a partnership between the police and the community, so that they can work together on solving problems of crime, [and] fear of crime and disorder, thereby enhancing the overall quality of life in their neighborhoods."[56] This approach addresses the causes of crime to reduce the fear of crime and social disorder through problem-solving strategies and police–community partnerships.

The community policing concept evolved from the early works of police researchers George Kelling and Robert Trojanowicz. Their studies of foot-patrol programs in Newark, New Jersey,[57] and Flint, Michigan,[58] showed that "police could develop more positive attitudes toward community members and could promote positive attitudes toward police if they spent time on foot in their neighborhoods."[59] Trojanowicz's *Community Policing*, published in 1990,[60] may be the definitive work on this topic.

Community policing seeks to actively involve citizens in the task of crime control by creating an effective working partnership between citizens and the police.[61] Under the community policing ideal, the public and the police share responsibility for establishing and maintaining peaceful neighborhoods.[62] As a result, community members participate more fully than ever before in defining the police role. Police expert Jerome Skolnick says community policing is "grounded on the notion that, together, police and public are more effective and more humane coproducers of safety and public order than are the police alone."[63] According to Skolnick, community policing involves at least one of four elements: (1) community-based crime prevention, (2) the reorientation of patrol activities to emphasize the importance of nonemergency services, (3) increased police accountability to the public, and (4) a decentralization of command, including a greater use of civilians at all levels of police decision making.[64] As one writer explains it, "Community policing seeks to integrate what was traditionally seen as the different law enforcement, order maintenance and social service roles of the police. Central to the integration of these roles is a working partnership with the community in determining what neighborhood problems are to be addressed, and how."[65] Table 6–2 highlights the differences between traditional and community policing.

Community policing is a two-way street. It requires not only police awareness of community needs but also both involvement and crime-fighting action on the part of citizens themselves. As Detective Tracie Harrison of the Denver Police Department explains, "When the neighborhood takes stock in their community and they're serious [that] they don't want crime, then you start to see crime go down. . . . They're basically fed up and know the police can't do it alone."[66]

Police departments throughout the country continue to join the community policing bandwagon. A 2001 report by the Bureau of Justice Statistics (BJS) showed that state and local law enforcement agencies across the United States had nearly 113,000 full-time sworn personnel regularly engaged in community policing activities.[67] BJS noted that only about 21,000 officers would have been so categorized in 1997. At the time of the report, 64% of local police departments serving 86% of all residents had full-time officers engaged in some form of community policing activity, compared to 34% of departments serving 62% of all residents in 1997.

The Chicago Police Department launched its comprehensive community policing program, called Chicago's Alternative Policing Strategy (CAPS), in 1993. The development of a strategic plan for "reinventing the Chicago Police Department," from which CAPS evolved, included significant contributions by Mayor Richard M. Daley, who noted that community policing "means doing more than responding to calls for service and solving crimes. It means transforming the Department to support a new, proactive approach to preventing crimes before they occur. It means forging new partnerships among residents, business owners, community leaders, the police, and City services to solve long-range community problems."[68] Read the mayor's original report, written in conjunction with the Chicago Police Department, at Library Extra 6–4 at cjtoday.com.

problem-solving policing

A type of policing that assumes that crimes can be controlled by uncovering and effectively addressing the underlying social problems that cause crime. Problem-solving policing makes use of community resources, such as counseling centers, welfare programs, and job-training facilities. It also attempts to involve citizens in crime prevention through education, negotiation, and conflict management.

community policing

"A collaborative effort between the police and the community that identifies problems of crime and disorder and involves all elements of the community in the search for solutions to these problems."[vii]

LIBRARY
Extra
■ ■ ■ ■

TABLE 6–2   Traditional versus Community Policing

Question	Traditional Policing	Community Policing
Who are the police?	The police are a government agency principally responsible for law enforcement.	The police are the public, and the public are the police. Police officers are paid to give full-time attention to the duties of every citizen.
What is the relationship of the police force to other public-service departments?	Priorities often conflict.	The police are one department among many responsible for improving the quality of life.
What is the role of the police?	To solve crimes.	To solve problems.
How is police efficiency measured?	By detection and arrest rates.	By the absence of crime and disorder.
What are the highest priorities?	Crimes that are high value (for example, bank robberies) and those involving violence.	Whatever problems disturb the community most.
What do police deal with?	Incidents.	Citizens' problems and concerns.
What determines the effectiveness of police?	Response times.	Public cooperation.
What view do police take of service calls?	They deal with them only if there is no "real" police work to do.	They view them as a vital function and a great opportunity.
What is police professionalism?	Providing a swift, effective response to serious crime.	Keeping close to the community.
What kind of intelligence is most important?	Crime intelligence (study of particular crimes or series of crimes).	Criminal intelligence (information about the activities of individuals or groups).
What is the essential nature of police accountability?	Highly centralized; governed by rules, regulations, and policy directives; accountable to the law.	Local accountability to community needs.
What is the role of headquarters?	To provide the necessary rules and policy directives.	To preach organizational values.
What is the role of the press liaison department?	To keep the "heat" off operational officers so they can get on with the job.	To coordinate an essential channel of communication with the community.
How do the police regard prosecutions?	As an important goal.	As one tool among many.

Source: William R. Parks II, "Community Policing: A Foundation for Restorative Justice," http://www.realjustice.org/Pages /t2000papers/t2000_wparks.html (accessed March 25, 2006). Originally printed in Malcolm K. Sparrow, *Implementing Community Policing* (Washington, DC: National Institute of Justice, 1988), pp. 8–9.

WEB Extra   **LIBRARY** Extra

Today, CAPS functions on a department-wide basis throughout the city. Learn more about CAPS via Web Extra 6–5 at cjtoday.com. A review of Chicago's experience with community policing is available at Library Extra 6–5.

Although community policing efforts began in metropolitan areas, the community engagement and problem-solving spirit of these programs has spread to rural regions. Sheriff's departments operating community policing programs sometimes refer to them as "neighborhood-oriented policing" in recognition of the decentralized nature of rural communities. A Bureau of Justice Assistance (BJA) report on neighborhood-oriented policing notes that "the stereotypical view is that police officers in rural areas naturally work more closely with the public than do officers in metropolitan areas."[69] This view, warns the BJA, may not be entirely accurate, and rural departments would do well "to recognize that considerable diversity exists among rural communities and rural law enforcement agencies." Hence, as in metropolitan areas, effective community policing requires the involvement of all members of the community in identifying and solving problems.

The emphasis on community policing continues to grow. Title I of the Violent Crime Control and Law Enforcement Act of 1994, known as the Public Safety Partnership and Community Policing Act of 1994, highlighted community policing's role in combating crime and funded (among other things) "increas[ing] the number of law enforcement officers involved in activities that are focused on interaction with members of the community on proactive crime control and prevention by redeploying officers to such activities." The avowed purposes of the Community Policing Act were to (1) substantially increase the number of law enforcement officers interacting directly with the public (through a program known as Cops on the Beat); (2) provide additional and more effective training to law enforcement officers to enhance their problem-solving, service, and other skills needed in interacting with community members; (3) encourage development and implementation of innovative programs to permit community members to assist local law enforcement agencies in the prevention of crime; and (4) encourage development of new technologies to assist local law enforcement agencies in reorienting their emphasis from reacting to crime to preventing crime.

In response to the 1994 law, the U.S. Department of Justice created the Office of Community Oriented Policing Services (COPS). The COPS Office administered the funds necessary to add 100,000 community policing officers to our nation's streets—the number originally targeted by law. In 1999, the Department of Justice and COPS reached an important milestone by funding the 100,000th officer ahead of schedule and under budget. Although the Community Policing Act originally provided COPS funding only through 2000, Congress continued to fund the office after that, making another $500 million available for the hiring of an additional 50,000 officers.[70] Although COPS Office funding was cut substantially during the presidency of George W. Bush, it continues to function, and the office recently adopted the theme "Homeland Security through Community Policing." The theme emphasizes the crucial role of local police officers in gathering information on terrorist suspects—a topic that is discussed later in this chapter. The federal COPS Office can be found via Web Extra 6–6 at cjtoday.com.

WEB
Extra
▪ ▪ ▪ ▪

About the same time that the Violent Crime Control and Law Enforcement Act was passed, the Community Policing Consortium, based in Washington, D.C., began operations. Administered and funded by the Department of Justice's BJA, the consortium provides a forum for training and information exchange in the area of community policing. Members of the consortium include the International Association of Chiefs of Police, the National Sheriff's Association, the Police Executive Research Forum, the Police Foundation, and the National Organization of Black Law Enforcement Executives. Visit the Community Policing Consortium via Web Extra 6–7 at cjtoday.com.

WEB
Extra
▪ ▪ ▪ ▪

CRITIQUE OF COMMUNITY POLICING

As some authors have noted, "Community policing has become the dominant theme of contemporary police reform in America,"[71] yet problems have plagued the movement since its inception.[72] For one thing, the range, complexity, and evolving nature of community policing programs make their effectiveness difficult to measure.[73] Moreover, "citizen satisfaction" with police performance can be difficult to conceptualize and quantify. Most early studies examined citizens' attitudes developed through face-to-face interaction with individual police officers. They generally found a far higher level of dissatisfaction with the police among African Americans than among most other groups. Recent findings continue to show that the attitudes of African Americans toward the police remain poor. The wider reach of these studies, however, led evaluators to discover that this dissatisfaction may be rooted in overall quality of life and type of neighborhood.[74] Since, on average, African Americans continue to experience a lower quality of life than most other U.S. citizens, and because they often live in neighborhoods characterized by economic problems, drug trafficking, and street crime, recent studies conclude that it is these conditions of life, rather than race, that are most predictive of citizen dissatisfaction with the police.

Those who study community policing have often been stymied by ambiguity surrounding the concept of community.[75] Sociologists, who sometimes define a community as "any area in which members of a common culture share common interests,"[76] tend to deny that a community needs to be limited geographically. Police departments, on the other hand, tend to define communities "within jurisdictional, district or precinct lines, or within the confines of public or private housing developments."[77] Robert Trojanowicz and Mark Moore caution police planners that "the impact of

In the 21st Century the community policing philosophy is well positioned to take a central role in preventing and responding to terrorism and in efforts to reduce citizen fear.

—Matthew C. Scheider, Office of Community Oriented Policing Services[viii]

Los Angeles bike patrol officers conferring with a supervisor. The community policing concept requires that officers become an integral part of the communities they serve. How can community policing both help prevent and solve crimes?
Michael Newman/PhotoEdit Inc.

mass transit, mass communications and mass media have widened the rift between a sense of community based on geography and one [based] on interest."[78]

Researchers who follow the police definition of *community* recognize that there may be little consensus within and between members of a local community about community problems and appropriate solutions. Robert Bohm and colleagues at the University of Central Florida have found, for example, that while there may be some "consensus about social problems and their solutions . . . the consensus may not be community-wide." It may, in fact, exist only among "a relatively small group of 'active' stakeholders who differ significantly about the seriousness of most of the problems and the utility of some solutions."[79]

Finally, there is continuing evidence that not all police officers or managers are willing to accept nontraditional images of police work. One reason is that the goals of community policing often conflict with standard police performance criteria (such as arrests), leading to a perception among officers that community policing is inefficient at best and, at worst, a waste of time.[80] Similarly, many officers are loathe to take on new responsibilities as service providers whose role is more defined by community needs and less by strict interpretation of the law.

police subculture

A particular set of values, beliefs, and acceptable forms of behavior characteristic of American police. Socialization into the police subculture begins with recruit training and continues thereafter.

Some authors have warned that **police subculture** is so committed to a traditional view of police work, which is focused almost exclusively on crime fighting, that efforts to promote community policing can demoralize an entire department, rendering it ineffective at its basic tasks.[81] As the Christopher Commission found following the Rodney King riots, "Too many . . . patrol officers view citizens with resentment and hostility; too many treat the public with rudeness and disrespect."[82] Some analysts warn that only when the formal values espoused by today's innovative police administrators begin to match those of rank-and-file officers can any police agency begin to perform well in terms of the goals espoused by community policing reformers.[83]

Some public officials, too, are unwilling to accept community policing. Ten years ago, for example, New York City Mayor Rudolph W. Giuliani criticized the police department's Community Police Officer Program (CPOP), saying that it "has resulted in officers doing too much social work and making too few arrests."[84] Similarly, many citizens are not ready to accept a greater involvement of the police in their personal lives. Although the turbulent, protest-prone years of the 1960s and early 1970s are long gone, some groups remain suspicious of the police. No matter how inclusive community policing programs become, it is doubtful that the gap between the police and the public will ever be entirely bridged. The police role of restraining behavior that violates the law will always produce friction between police departments and some segments of the community. Learn more about measures of police effectiveness, including those related to community policing, at Library Extra 6–6 at cjtoday.com.

LIBRARY
Extra
■ ■ ■ ■

A Washington, D.C., Metro Transit police officer searching a train after subway bombings in London prompted increased security in 2005. How has the threat of terrorism altered the police role in America?
Reuters/Larry Downing/Landov LLC

Terrorism's Impact on Policing

In April 2005, three British nationals were charged with plotting to bomb five financial buildings in New York City, New Jersey, and Washington, D.C. The men, Dhiren Barot, 32, Nadeem Tarmohamed, 26, and Qaisar Shaffi, 25, allegedly served as al-Qaeda scouts and performed reconnaissance on the buildings.[85] The three had been arrested by British authorities in August 2004, and information gathered during the arrest led homeland security officials to convene a press conference at the Citigroup tower in Midtown Manhattan. The nation was told that known al-Qaeda operatives had conducted surveillance at several large New York financial centers, including the New York Stock Exchange.[86] Officials said that the terrorists may have been planning to use truck bombs targeting Wall Street in an effort to disrupt world financial markets. Outgoing Homeland Security Secretary Tom Ridge stressed the seriousness of the threat when he told reporters who had gathered for the briefing, "This is the most significant, detailed piece of information about any particular region that we have come across in a long, long time, perhaps ever."[87] In response to the announcement, the New York City Police Department set up barricades and vehicle checkpoints and mobilized heavily armed officers specially trained in antiterrorism tactics to patrol the financial district. Downtown city streets took on the embattled look of a city at war.

The incident made clear the changed role of American police agencies in the new era of international terrorism that began with the September 11, 2001, attacks on American targets. While the core mission of American police departments has not changed, law enforcement agencies at all levels now devote an increased amount of time and other resources to preparing for possible terrorist attacks and gathering the intelligence necessary to thwart them.

In today's post-9/11 world, local police departments play an especially important role in responding to the challenges of terrorism. They must help prevent attacks and respond when attacks occur, offering critical evacuation, emergency medical, and security functions to help stabilize communities following an incident. A recent survey of 250 police chiefs by the Police Executive Research Forum (PERF) found that the chiefs strongly believe that their departments can make valuable contributions to terrorism prevention by using community policing networks to exchange information with citizens and to gather intelligence.[88] Read the results of the PERF survey online at **Library Extra 6–7** at cjtoday.com.

To deal effectively with the threat of domestic terrorism, the police must be able to manage and coordinate different sources of data and intelligence, and then process them in such a way as to provide an enhanced understanding of actual or potential criminal activity.

—*COPS Office[ix]*

LIBRARY
Extra
▪▪▪▪

The Council on Foreign Relations, headquartered in New York City and Washington, D.C., agrees with PERF that American police departments can no longer assume that federal counterterrorism efforts alone will be sufficient to protect the communities they serve. Consequently, says the council, many police departments have responded by[89]

- Strengthening liaisons with federal, state, and local agencies, including fire departments and other police departments
- Refining their training and emergency response plans to address terrorist threats, including attacks with weapons of mass destruction
- Increasing patrols and shoring up barriers around landmarks, places of worship, ports of entry, transit systems, nuclear power plants, and so on
- More heavily guarding public speeches, parades, and other public events
- Creating new counterterrorism divisions and reassigning officers to counterterrorism from other divisions, such as drug enforcement
- Employing new technologies, including X-ray-like devices, to scan containers at ports of entry and using sophisticated sensors to detect a chemical, biological, or radiological attack

It is very important that our first line of defense against terrorism—the seven hundred thousand officers on the street—be given adequate training and background information on terrorism, the methods and techniques of the terrorists, and the likelihood of an imminent attack.

—Major Cities Chiefs Association[k]

The extent of local departments' engagement in such preventive activities depends substantially on budgetary considerations and is strongly influenced by the assessed likelihood of attack. The NYPD, for example, which has firsthand experience in responding to terrorist attacks (23 of its officers were killed when the World Trade Center towers collapsed), has created a special bureau headed by a deputy police commissioner responsible for counterterrorism training, prevention, and investigation.[90] One thousand officers have been reassigned to antiterrorism duties, and the department is training its entire 38,000-member force in how to respond to biological, radiological, and chemical attacks.[91] The NYPD has assigned detectives to work abroad with law enforcement agencies in Canada, Israel, Southeast Asia, and the Middle East to track terrorists who might target New York City,[92] and it now employs officers with a command of the Pashtun, Farsi, and Urdu languages of the Middle East to monitor foreign television, radio, and Internet communications. The department has also invested heavily in new hazardous materials protective suits, gas masks, and portable radiation detectors.

In November 2004, in an effort to provide the law enforcement community and policymakers with guidance on critical issues related to antiterrorism planning and critical incident response, the International Association of Chiefs of Police (IACP) announced its Taking Command Initiative. The IACP described the initiative as "an aggressive project to assess the current state of homeland security efforts in the United States and to develop and implement the actions necessary to protect our communities from the specter of both crime and terrorism."[93] Initial deliberations under the initiative led the IACP to conclude that "the current homeland security strategy is handicapped by a fundamental flaw: It was developed without sufficiently seeking or incorporating the advice, expertise, or consent of public safety organizations at the state, tribal or local level."[94] Building on that premise, the IACP identified five key principles that it says must form the basis of any effective national homeland security strategy:[95]

- Homeland security proposals must be developed in a local context, acknowledging that local, not federal, authorities have the primary responsibility for preventing, responding to, and recovering from terrorist attacks.
- Prevention, not just response and recovery, must be paramount in any national, state, or local security strategy. For too long, federal strategies have minimized the importance of prevention, focusing instead on response and recovery.
- Because of their daily efforts to combat crime and violence in their communities, state and local law enforcement officers are uniquely situated to identify, investigate, and apprehend suspected terrorists.
- Homeland security strategies must be coordinated nationally, not federally.
- A truly successful national strategy must recognize, embrace, and value the vast diversity among state and local law enforcement and public-safety agencies. A one-size-fits-all approach will fail to secure the nation.

Finally, in 2005, the IACP and its partners in the Post-9/11 Policing Project published *Assessing and Managing the Terrorism Threat*. The Post-9/11 Policing Project is a collaborative effort of the IACP, the National Sheriffs' Association (NSA), the National Organization of Black Law Enforcement Executives (NOBLE), the Major Cities Chiefs Association (MCCA), and the Police Foundation.[96] Learn more about the ongoing Taking Command initiative as its leaders work to "transform the concept of a locally designed, nationally coordinated homeland security strategy into a reality" via Web Extra 6–8 at cjtoday.com, and download the publication *Assessing and Managing the Terrorism Threat* at Library Extra 6–8 at cjtoday.com.

As the IACP recognizes, workable antiterrorism programs at the local level require effective sharing of critical information between agencies. FBI-sponsored Joint Terrorism Task Forces (JTTFs) facilitate this by bringing together federal and local law enforcement personnel to focus on specific threats. The FBI currently has established or authorized JTTFs in each of its 56 field offices. In addition to the JTTFs, the FBI has created Regional Terrorism Task Forces (RTTFs) to share information with local enforcement agencies. Through the RTTFs, FBI special agents assigned to terrorism prevention and investigation meet twice a year with their federal, state, and local counterparts for common training, discussion of investigations, and intelligence sharing. The FBI says that "the design of this non-traditional terrorism task force provides the necessary mechanism and structure to direct counterterrorism resources toward localized terrorism problems within the United States."[97] Six RTTFs are currently in operation: the Inland Northwest, South Central, Southeastern, Northeast Border, Deep South, and Southwest.

Another FBI counterterrorism component, Field Intelligence Groups (FIGs), were developed following recommendations of the 9/11 Commission. The commission said that the FBI should build a reciprocal relationship with state and local agencies, maximizing the sharing of information. FIGs, which now exist in all 56 FBI field offices, work closely with JTTFs to provide valuable services to law enforcement personnel at the state and local levels. According to the FBI, FIGs "generate intelligence products and disseminate them to the intelligence and law enforcement communities to help guide investigative, program, and policy decisions."[98]

Given the changes that have taken place in American law enforcement since the terrorist attacks of September 11, 2001, some say that traditional distinctions between crime, terrorism, and war are fading and that, at least in some instances, military action and civil law enforcement are becoming integrated. The critical question for law enforcement administrators in the near future may be one of discerning the role that law enforcement is to play in the emerging global context.

Intelligence-Led Policing and Antiterrorism

In 2005, the U.S. Department of Justice embraced the concept of **intelligence-led policing (ILP)** as an important technique to be employed by American law enforcement agencies in the battle against terrorism.[99] Intelligence is information that has been analyzed and integrated into a useful perspective. The information used in the development of effective intelligence is typically gathered from many sources, such as surveillance, covert operations, financial records, electronic eavesdropping, interviews, newspapers, the Internet, and interrogations. Law enforcement intelligence, or **criminal intelligence**, is the result of a "process that evaluates information collected from diverse sources, integrates the relevant information into a cohesive package, and produces a conclusion or estimate about a criminal phenomenon by using the scientific approach to problem solving."[100] While criminal investigation is typically part of the intelligence-gathering process, the intelligence function of a police department is more exploratory and more broadly focused than a single criminal investigation.[101]

ILP (also known as *intelligence-driven policing*) is the use of criminal intelligence to guide policing. A detailed description of ILP and its applicability to American law enforcement agencies is provided in the FBI publication *The Law Enforcement Intelligence Function* by David Carter of Michigan State University's School of Criminal Justice. The document is available at Library Extra 6–9 at cjtoday.com.

According to Carter, criminal intelligence "is a synergistic product intended to provide meaningful and trustworthy direction to law enforcement decision makers about complex criminality, criminal enterprises, criminal extremists, and terrorists." Carter goes on to point out that law enforcement intelligence consists of two types: tactical and strategic. Tactical intelligence "includes gaining or developing information related to threats of terrorism or crime and using this information to apprehend offenders, harden targets, and use strategies that will eliminate or mitigate the threat." Strategic intelligence, in contrast, provides information to decision makers about the changing nature of threats for the purpose of "developing response strategies and reallocating resources" to accomplish effective prevention.

Not every law enforcement agency has the staff or resources needed to create a dedicated intelligence unit. Even without an intelligence unit, however, a law enforcement organization

WEB Extra   **LIBRARY** Extra

intelligence-led policing (ILP)
The collection and analysis of information to produce an intelligence end product designed to inform police decision making at both the tactical and strategic levels.[xi]

criminal intelligence
Information compiled, analyzed, or disseminated in an effort to anticipate, prevent, or monitor criminal activity.[xii]

LIBRARY Extra

Cooperation of police at all levels along with coordination with other agencies will be necessary to cope with crime that is increasingly cross-jurisdictional.

—*Bud Levin, Blue Ridge Community College*

CJ News

Police Tactic against Terror: Let's Network

In January [2004], their mission was to speak before a mosquito sprayers' convention in Harrisburg, Pennsylvania. In April, the detectives attended a meeting of self-storage business owners in Atlanta. [In the summer of 2004], they were in Naples, Florida, mingling with propane gas vendors at their trade association's annual conference.

These are, admittedly, not the sort of assignments that investigators envision when they join the New York Police Department. But such missions, however mundane, have become as much a part of police counterterrorism efforts as the posting of detectives in places like Tel Aviv and Singapore, the planning for a bioterror attack or the identification of Arab speakers on the force.

Involving more grunt work than glamour, the city's counterterrorism effort has largely been built atop a nuts-and-bolts program of cultivating contacts with the businesses that might become unwitting parts of the next terror plot. Detectives visit scuba shops and hardware stores. They talk to parking garage attendants and plastic surgeons, hotel managers and tool rental companies, bulk fuel dealers and trade schools.

Police officials acknowledge that the program, which grew out of an effort two years ago to contact businesses that sold explosives, is something of a needle-in-a-haystack approach to stopping an attack or tracking down terrorist cells that may be plotting one. But in the post-9/11 world, in light of the failure of government agencies to act on a range of clues in the weeks and months before the attacks, they argue that no effort to develop this kind of early-warning system is wasted.

Called Operation Nexus, the program has focused on particular types of businesses based on intelligence that the department has culled from sources like an Al Qaeda manual for terrorist operatives and debriefings of some of the group's leaders and foot soldiers, said David Cohen, the deputy commissioner for intelligence.

Those debriefings and other evidence have suggested, among other things, that Al Qaeda has at least considered, if not plotted, using scuba divers to blow up bridges, riding in tourist helicopters for surveillance, turning trucks and limousines into rolling bombs and using special torches to cut the cables of the Brooklyn Bridge.

And Mr. Cohen noted that Al Qaeda members are trained to avoid the police.

"The next Mohamed Atta is far more likely to intersect with someone in the private sector than a law enforcement officer," he said, referring to the leader of the September 11 plot.

Mr. Cohen, a former deputy director of the Central Intelligence Agency, who oversees the program, said it is based on personal contact with people and repeated visits to various businesses. "If you take the time to talk to people, it leaves an imprint," he said.

The effort is focused largely in and around New York City, where six or so detectives have made close to 20,000 visits, returning to some businesses time and again to leave their business cards and the department's terrorism hot line number. The detectives are encouraged to spend time with the businesses, leaving an outline of what they describe as possibly suspicious activity tailored for each type of business: more than 60 altogether, said Lt. Christopher S.

Atlanta police officers, an FBI agent, and an ATF agent searching for evidence while investigating an Atlanta-area bombing. The fight against terrorism has enhanced the realization that law enforcement agencies at all levels need to work together. What forms might better cooperation take?

© Wally McNamee/Corbis

Higgins, whom police officials credit with developing the program from concept to reality.

At an agricultural or mosquito-spraying business, which the authorities fear could be used to spread a biological agent like anthrax, the detectives cite possible warning signs like the loss, theft or attempted theft of equipment or machine components. They tell business owners to call if they encounter evasive customers who inquire about equipment but seem to lack previous experience in the industry.

Businesses that offer used emergency vehicles for sale are told to watch for requests to buy fire or police vehicles with radios or other equipment intact. Army-Navy and uniform stores are warned to watch for people who say they are in the military or civil service but who make statements suggesting their stories are false.

"We're going to have eyeball-to-eyeball contact with that individual who may be approached by someone who wants to do harm to our city," Mr. Cohen said, noting that the business owners themselves can best spot an anomaly.

CJ News (continued)

Police Commissioner Raymond W. Kelly, who instituted the program, said it quickly expanded from its initial focus on explosives and marinas, at a time when there was heightened concern about terrorists using boats in attacks, to a wide range of other businesses. They include chemical and insecticide companies, livery car businesses, truck and van rentals, travel agencies and self-storage businesses, where the authorities fear terrorists could store explosives or radioactive materials for a dirty bomb.

"We're looking for anything that with a little thought could be used by a terrorist," Mr. Kelly said. Glenn Martin, a vice president of Helicopter Applications Inc., an agricultural spraying company in Pennsylvania, said that in a presentation to the Northeast Agricultural Aviation Association in Harrisburg this year, two Nexus detectives provided companies that do mosquito spraying and crop dusting with some insight into what they should look for. "It just drove the point home, basically," he said in a telephone interview. "We have to be more vigilant."

Other jurisdictions, including the Metropolitan Police in London, have studied New York's program and are trying to use it as a model in some fashion, Lieutenant Higgins said. The New York State Office of Public Security recently put in place a mirror image of the city's program across the state.

In at least one instance, though, the New York City detectives have raised the hackles of law enforcement authorities elsewhere. Last year, to test the program's effectiveness, detectives called scuba shops in New Jersey without identifying themselves and made several suspicious requests, seeking to pay cash for diving lessons and to avoid the required paperwork.

The store owners called the New Jersey authorities, who were unaware of the New York detectives' actions and were annoyed that they had not been notified, an official said.

Over all, the program has won high marks. Many current and former counterterrorism analysts say an aggressive approach, devised to provide an early warning that operatives or their supporters are already at work in this country, is critical to any antiterrorism effort.

"In today's day and age, where the ramifications of terrorism are so great, you've got to prevent," said Larry Mefford, who oversaw the FBI's counterterrorism and counterintelligence programs until he retired last year. "You can't wait for the attack, especially when you're talking about the future and the possible use of weapons of mass destruction.

"If you don't have a system like this, you're saying by default, 'They'll never get through our defenses,' and we obviously know from our past experience that that's not realistic."

As high as the stakes are, the work itself can be grindingly dull, visiting business after business and trying to remain energized. "This is the part of the business that is unrelenting and unglamorous," Mr. Cohen said.

Lieutenant Higgins said he usually fields three teams of two detectives each day, and they are expected to visit more than a dozen sites a day. Each visit is recorded in an extensive database that tracks the contacts, listing the detective assigned, the type of business, hours of operation, those who were spoken to, and whether they have any security equipment, like video cameras, that can capture images of people who come in.

Mr. Cohen said the program is a crucial part of the city's shield even if it is hard to quantify its effectiveness. For one thing, it is hard to know whether an attack has been prevented, officials noted.

For another, callers to the terrorism hot line do not generally identify whether their call was prompted by a Nexus visit.

"The risk is the farther we get from 9/11, complacency sets in, and we simply won't let that happen," Mr. Cohen said. "So we start out the day knowing that we are the bull's-eye. So how many have we stopped, we don't know. We do know a couple of things: We know we've been attacked; we know they have said very clearly they want to come back; we know we are high on the target list."

For the latest in crime and justice news, visit the Talk Justice news feed at http://www.crimenews.info.

Source: William K. Rashbaum, "Police Tactic against Terror: Let's Network," *New York Times*, August 14, 2004.

should have the ability to effectively utilize the information and intelligence products that are developed and disseminated by organizations at all levels of government. In other words, even though a police agency may not have the resources necessary to analyze all the information it acquires, it should still be able to mount an effective response to credible threat information that it receives. Learn more about the law enforcement intelligence function and intelligence-led policing at **Library Extra 6–10** at cjtoday.com.

LIBRARY
Extra
▪▪▪▪

Information Sharing and Antiterrorism

The need to effectively share criminal intelligence across jurisdictions and between law enforcement agencies nationwide became apparent with the tragic events of September 11, 2001. Consequently, governments at all levels are today working toward the creation of a fully integrated criminal justice information system. According to a recent task force report, a fully integrated criminal justice information system is "a network of public safety, justice and homeland security

NLETS

The International Justice and Public Safety Information Sharing Network.

computer systems which provides to each agency the information it needs, at the time it is needed, in the form that it is needed, regardless of the source and regardless of the physical location at which it is stored."[102] The information that is provided should be complete, accurate, and formatted in whatever way is most useful for the agency's tasks. In a fully integrated criminal justice information system, information would be made available at the practitioner's workstation, whether that workstation is a patrol car, desk, laptop, or judge's bench. Within such a system, each agency shares information not only with other agencies in its own jurisdiction but with multiple justice agencies on the federal, state, and local levels. In such an idealized justice information system, accurate information is also available to nonjustice agencies with statutory authority and a legal obligation to check criminal histories before licensing, employment, weapons purchase, and so on.

One widely used information sharing system is Law Enforcement Online (LEO). LEO, an Intranet intended exclusively for use by the law enforcement community, is a national interactive computer communications system and information service. This user-friendly system can be accessed by any approved employee of a duly constituted local, state, or federal law enforcement agency or by an approved member of an authorized law enforcement special-interest group. LEO provides a state-of-the-art communication mechanism to link all levels of law enforcement throughout the United States. Members use LEO to support investigative operations, send notifications and alerts, and remotely access a wide variety of law enforcement and intelligence systems and resources. LEO also allows federal agencies, including the FBI, to immediately disseminate sensitive but unclassified (SBU) information across agency boundaries.[103] The system includes password-accessed e-mail, Internet chat, an electronic library, an online calendar, special-interest topical focus areas, and self-paced distance learning modules.[104]

Another important information-sharing resource is available in **NLETS**, the International Justice and Public Safety Information Sharing Network. NLETS members include all 50 states, most federal agencies and territories, and the Royal Canadian Mounted Police. NLETS, which has been

The home page of the Multistate Anti-Terrorism Information Exchange (MATRIX), a pilot project in boundaryless policing and interagency information sharing. MATRIX ceased operation in 2005 after fielding almost 2 million queries from law enforcement investigators during its two years in existence. What is boundaryless policing?

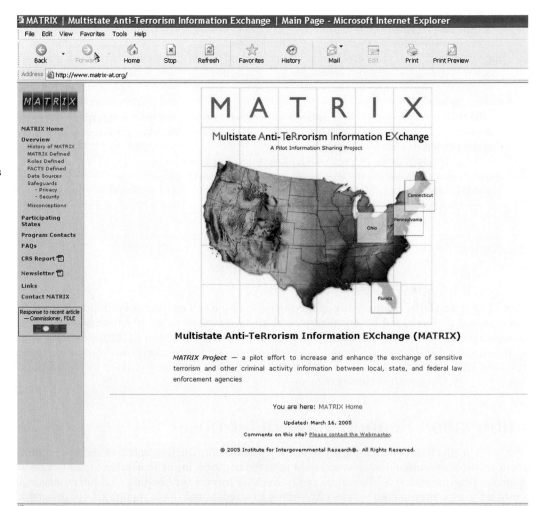

in operation for nearly 40 years, was formerly called the National Law Enforcement Telecommunications System. It has recently been enhanced to facilitate a variety of encrypted digital communications, and it now links 30,000 agencies and over half a million access devices in the United States and Canada. The system facilitates nearly 41 million transmissions each month. Information available through NLETS includes state criminal histories, homeland alert messages, immigration databases, driver records and vehicle registrations, aircraft registrations, Amber Alerts, weather advisories, and HAZMAT notifications and regulations. You can reach NLETS on the Web via Web Extra 6–9 at cjtoday.com.

Although both NLETS and LEO continue to evolve, most experts agree that a fully integrated nationwide criminal justice information system does not yet exist.[105] Efforts to create one, however, found their beginning in the 2003 National Criminal Intelligence Sharing Plan (NCISP). The NCISP was developed under the auspices of the U.S. Department of Justice's Global Justice Information Sharing Initiative and authored by its Global Intelligence Working Group (GIWG).[106] Federal, local, state, and tribal law enforcement representatives all had a voice in the development of the plan. The NCISP provides specific steps that can be taken by law enforcement agencies to participate in the sharing of critical law enforcement and terrorism prevention information.

Plan authors note that not every agency has the staff or resources needed to create a formal intelligence unit. However, the plan says that even without a dedicated intelligence unit, every law enforcement organization needs to have the ability to effectively consume the intelligence available from a wide range of organizations at all levels of government.[107] The NCISP is available in its entirety at Library Extra 6–11 at cjtoday.com.

WEB
Extra
■ ■ ■ ■

LIBRARY
Extra
■ ■ ■ ■

Discretion and the Individual Officer

Even as law enforcement agencies struggle to adapt to the threats posed by international terrorism, individual officers continue to retain considerable discretion in terms of their actions. **Police discretion** refers to the exercise of choice by law enforcement officers in the decision to investigate or apprehend, the disposition of suspects, the carrying out of official duties, and the application of sanctions. As one author has observed, "Police authority can be, at once, highly specific and exceedingly vague."[108] Decisions to stop and question someone, arrest a suspect, and perform many other police tasks are made solely by individual officers and must often be made quickly and in the absence of any close supervision. Kenneth Culp Davis, who pioneered the study of police discretion, says, "The police make policy about what law to enforce, how much to enforce it, against whom, and on what occasions."[109] To those who have contact with the police, the discretionary authority exercised by individual officers is of greater significance than all of the department manuals and official policy statements combined.

police discretion

The opportunity for police officers to exercise choice in their enforcement activities.

An officer writing a traffic ticket. Police officers wield a great amount of discretion, and an individual officer's decision to enforce a particular law or to effect an arrest is based not just on the law's applicability to a particular set of circumstances but also on the officer's subjective judgment about the nature of appropriate enforcement activity. What other factors influence discretion?

David Young-Wolff/PhotoEdit Inc.

Patrolling officers often decide against a strict enforcement of the law, preferring instead to handle situations informally. Minor law violations, crimes committed out of the officer's presence where the victim refuses to file a complaint, and certain violations of the criminal law where the officer suspects that sufficient evidence to obtain a conviction is lacking may all lead to discretionary action short of arrest. The widest exercise of discretion is in routine situations involving relatively less serious violations of the law, but serious criminal behavior may occasionally result in discretionary decisions not to make an arrest. Drunk driving, possession of controlled substances, and assault are examples of crimes in which on-the-scene officers may choose to issue a warning or offer a referral instead of making an arrest.

Studies of police discretion have found that a number of factors influence the discretionary decisions of individual officers. Here are some of those factors:

- *Background of the officer.* Law enforcement officers bring their life experience to the job. Values shaped through early socialization and attitudes acquired from ongoing socialization influence an officer's decisions. For example, if an officer learned prejudice against certain ethnic groups, that prejudice will likely manifest itself in enforcement decisions. An officer who values the nuclear family may handle spousal or child abuse and domestic disputes in predetermined ways.

- *Characteristics of the suspect.* Characteristics of a suspect that may influence police decisions include gender, demeanor, style of dress, and grooming.[110] Some officers treat men and women differently. Belligerent suspects are often seen as "asking for it" and as challenging police authority. Well-dressed suspects are likely to be treated with deference, but poorly groomed suspects can expect less respectful treatment. Suspects sporting personal styles with a message—biker's attire, unkempt beards, outlandish haircuts, gang-style clothes, and other nonconformist styles—are more likely to be arrested than are others.

- *Department policy.* Official policy rarely controls discretion, but it does influence it. For example, if department supervisors adhere to strict enforcement guidelines and closely monitor dispatches and other communications, individual officers will be less likely to release suspects at their own discretion.

- *Community interest.* Public attitudes toward certain crimes will increase the likelihood of arrest for suspected offenders. Contemporary attitudes toward crimes involving children—including child sex abuse, the sale of drugs to minors, domestic violence involving children, and child pornography—have all led to increased and strict enforcement of laws governing such offenses. Communities may identify specific problems affecting them and ask law enforcement to respond. Fayetteville, North Carolina, was plagued some years ago by a downtown area notorious for prostitution and massage parlors. Once the community voiced its concern over the problem and its economic impact on the city, the police responded with a series of highly effective arrests that eliminated massage parlors within the city limits. Departments that require officers to live in the areas they police recognize that community interests affect citizens and officers alike.

- *Pressure from victims.* Victims of certain crimes, such as spousal abuse and assaults on customers of prostitutes, commonly refuse to file a complaint. When victims refuse to cooperate, there is often little that police can do. However, some victims demand that their victimization be recognized and dealt with. Victims' assistance groups, such as People Assisting Victims and the Victim's Assistance Network, have sought to keep pressure on police departments and individual investigators to ensure the arrest and prosecution of suspects.

- *Disagreement with the law.* Some behaviors that are crimes in one area are not crimes in other areas. For example, gambling is now legal in many states, aboard cruise ships, and on some Native American reservations; many states have legalized homosexuality and most forms of consensual adult sexual behavior; prostitution is legal in portions of Nevada; and some drug offenses have been "decriminalized," with offenders being ticketed rather than arrested.

  Some laws lack a popular consensus, such as laws relating to many victimless offenses. Unpopular laws are not likely to get much attention from law enforcement officers. Sometimes such crimes are regarded as just "part of the landscape," or the law is thought to have not kept pace with a changing society. When an arrest does occur, it is often because individuals being investigated for more serious offenses were caught violating an unpopular statute. For example, drug offenders arrested in the middle of the night may be caught performing an illegal sexual act when the police break in. Charges may then include "crime against nature," as well as possession or sale of drugs.

  In some cases, discretionary police activity may take the form of "street justice" and may approach vigilantism. For example, certain lawful, even protected, behaviors may be annoying, offensive, or disruptive by the normative standards of a community or the personal standards of an officer. In these cases, the officer makes a personal decision about how to handle the disruption. Or an officer investigating a clear violation of the law may discover that he knows the guilty party. In some cases, officers have been known to render unusable the evidence needed for a conviction in court. In recognizing these possibilities, noted law enforcement scholar Gary Sykes says, "One of the major ambiguities of the police task is that officers are caught between two profoundly compelling moral systems: justice as due process . . . and conversely, justice as righting a wrong as part of defining and maintaining community norms."[111]

- *Available alternatives.* An officer's awareness of alternatives to arrest can influence discretion. Officers looking to avoid official action may turn to community treatment programs like outpatient drug or alcohol counseling and domestic dispute–resolution centers.

- *Personal practices of the officer.* Some officers view the violation of particular laws less seriously than other officers do. The police officer who smokes an occasional marijuana cigarette may deal less harshly with minor drug offenders than nonusing officers, and officers who routinely speed while driving the family car may be more lenient with speeders encountered while on duty.

Professionalism and Ethics

A profession is an organized undertaking characterized by a body of specialized knowledge acquired through extensive education[112] and by a well-considered set of internal standards and ethical guidelines that hold members of the profession accountable to one another and to society. Contemporary policing has many of the attributes of a profession.

Police professionalism requires that today's police officers have a great deal of specialized knowledge and that they adhere to the standards and ethics set out by the profession. Specialized knowledge in policing includes an understanding of criminal law, laws of procedure, constitutional guarantees, and relevant Supreme Court decisions; a working knowledge of weapons, hand-to-hand combat tactics, driving skills, vehicle maintenance, and radio communications; report-writing abilities; interviewing techniques; and media and human relations skills. Other specialized knowledge may include Breathalyzer operation, special weapons skills, polygraph operation, conflict resolution, and hostage negotiation. Supervisory personnel require an even wider range of skills, including administrative skills, management techniques, and strategies for optimum utilization of resources.

Police professionalism places important limits on the discretionary activities of individual enforcement personnel and helps officers and the departments they work for gain the respect and regard of the public they police. Police work is guided by an ethical code developed in 1956 by the Peace Officer's Research Association of California (PORAC) in conjunction with Dr. Douglas M. Kelley of Berkeley's School of Criminology.[113] The Law Enforcement Code of Ethics is reproduced in the "Ethics and Professionalism" box in this chapter.

Ethics training has been integrated into most basic law enforcement training programs, and calls for expanded training in **police ethics** are being heard from many corners. A comprehensive resource for enhancing awareness of law enforcement ethics, called the Ethics Toolkit, is available from the IACP and the federal Office of Community Oriented Policing Services via Web Extra 6–10 at cjtoday.com.

Many professional associations are associated with police work. One such organization, the Arlington, Virginia–based International Association of Chiefs of Police, has done much to raise professional standards in policing and continually strives for improvements in law enforcement nationwide. In like manner, the Fraternal Order of Police (FOP) is one of the best-known organizations of public-service workers in the United States. The FOP is the world's largest organization of sworn law enforcement officers, with more than 318,000 members in more than 2,100 lodges.

Accreditation is another avenue toward police professionalism. The Commission on Accreditation for Law Enforcement Agencies (CALEA) was formed in 1979. Police departments seeking accreditation through the commission must meet hundreds of standards in areas as diverse as day-to-day operations, administration, review of incidents involving the use of a weapon by officers, and evaluation and promotion of personnel. As of March 15, 2005, nearly 580 (3.3%) of the nation's 17,784 law enforcement agencies were accredited,[114] while a number of others were undergoing the accreditation process. Many accredited agencies are among the nation's largest; as a result, 25% of full-time law enforcement officers in the United States at the state and local levels are members of CALEA-accredited agencies.[115] Although accreditation makes possible the identification of high-quality police departments, it is often not valued by agency leaders because it offers few incentives. Accreditation does not guarantee a department any rewards beyond that of peer recognition. Visit CALEA online via Web Extra 6–11 at cjtoday.com.

police professionalism

The increasing formalization of police work and the accompanying rise in public acceptance of the police.

police ethics

The special responsibility to adhere to moral duty and obligation that is inherent in police work.

WEB Extra

WEB Extra

Ethics and Professionalism

The Law Enforcement Code of Ethics

As a Law Enforcement Officer, my fundamental duty is to serve mankind; to safeguard lives and property; to protect the innocent against deception, the weak against oppression or intimidation, and the peaceful against violence or disorder; and to respect the Constitutional rights of all men to liberty, equality, and justice.

I will keep my private life unsullied as an example to all; maintain courageous calm in the face of danger, scorn, or ridicule; develop self-restraint; and be constantly mindful of the welfare of others. Honest in thought and deed in both my personal and official life, I will be exemplary in obeying the laws of the land and the regulations of my department. Whatever I see or hear of a confidential nature or that is confided to me in my official capacity will be kept secret unless revelation is necessary in the performance of my duty.

I will never act officiously or permit personal feelings, prejudices, animosities, or friendships to influence my decisions. With no compromise for crime and with relentless prosecution of criminals, I will enforce the law courteously and appropriately without fear or favor, malice or ill will, never employing unnecessary force or violence and never accepting gratuities.

I recognize the badge of my office as a symbol of public faith, and I accept it as a public trust to be held so long as I am true to the ethics of the police service. I will constantly strive to achieve these objectives and ideals, dedicating myself before God to my chosen profession . . . law enforcement.

THINKING ABOUT ETHICS

1. Why does the Law Enforcement Code of Ethics ask law enforcement officers "to respect the Constitutional rights of all men to liberty, equality, and justice"? Does such respect further the goals of law enforcement? Why or why not?

2. Why is it important for law enforcement officers to "keep [their] private life unsullied as an example to all"? What are the potential consequences of *not* doing so?

Source: International Association of Chiefs of Police. Reprinted with permission.

Education and Training

WEB
Extra

peace officer standards and training (POST) program

The official program of a state or legislative jurisdiction that sets standards for the training of law enforcement officers. All states set such standards, although not all use the term *POST.*

Basic law enforcement training requirements were established in the 1950s by the state of New York and through a voluntary **peace officer standards and training (POST) program** in California. (Information on California's POST program can be accessed via Web Extra 6–12 at cjtoday.com.) Today, every jurisdiction mandates POST-like requirements, although these requirements vary considerably. Modern police education generally involves training in subjects as varied as human relations, firearms and weapons, communications, legal aspects of policing, patrol, criminal investigations, administration, report writing, and criminal justice systems. According to a 1999 Bureau of Justice Statistics report, the median number of hours of classroom training required of new officers is 823 in state police agencies, 760 in county departments, 640 in municipal departments, and 448 in sheriff's departments.[116] Standards continue to be modified. In 2002, for example, the California Commission on POST responded to statewide concerns over racial profiling by adding material to the police-training curriculum to ensure that all California law enforcement officers receive training "that reinforces the fact that racial profiling has a profound negative impact on communities and cannot be tolerated."[117]

Federal law enforcement agents receive schooling at the Federal Law Enforcement Training Center (FLETC) in Glynco, Georgia. The center provides training for about 60 federal law enforcement agencies, excluding the FBI and the Drug Enforcement Administration (DEA), which have their own training academies in Quantico, Virginia. FLETC also offers advanced training to state and local police organizations through the National Center for State and Local Law Enforcement Training, located on the FLETC campus. Specialized schools, like Northwestern University's Traffic Institute, are also credited with raising the level of police practice from purely operational concerns to a more professional level.

In 1987, in a move to further professionalize police training, the American Society for Law Enforcement Trainers was formed at the Ohio Peace Officer Training Academy. Now known as the American Society for Law Enforcement Training (ASLET), the Frederick, Maryland–based agency works to ensure quality in peace officer training and confers the title Certified Law Enforcement Trainer (CLET) on police-training professionals who meet its high standards. ASLET also works with the Police Training Network to provide an ongoing and comprehensive nationwide calendar of law enforcement training activities. Visit the network online via Web Extra 6–13 at cjtoday.com.

WEB
Extra

A recent innovation in law enforcement training is the Police Training Officer (PTO) program, whose development was funded by the COPS Office starting in 1999.[118] The PTO program was designed by the Reno (Nevada) Police Department, in conjunction with the Police Executive Research Forum, as an alternative model for police field training. In fact, it represents the first new postacademy field-training program for law enforcement agencies in more than 30 years. The PTO program uses contemporary methods of adult education and a version of problem-based learning that is specifically adapted to the police environment. It incorporates community policing and problem-solving principles and, according to the COPS Office, fosters "the foundation for life-long learning that prepares new officers for the complexities of policing today and in the future." Learn more about the PTO program at Library Extra 6–12 at cjtoday.com.

As the concern for quality policing builds, increasing emphasis is also being placed on the formal education of police officers. As early as 1931, the National Commission on Law Observance and Enforcement (the Wickersham Commission) highlighted the importance of a well-educated police force by calling for "educationally sound" officers.[119] In 1967, the President's Commission on Law Enforcement and Administration of Justice voiced the belief that "the ultimate aim of all police departments should be that all personnel with general enforcement powers have baccalaureate degrees."[120] At the time, the average educational level of police officers in the United States was 12.4 years—slightly beyond a high school degree. In 1973, the National Advisory Commission on Criminal Justice Standards and Goals made the following rather specific recommendation: "Every police agency should, no later than 1982, require as a condition of initial employment the completion of at least four years of education . . . at an accredited college or university."[121]

However, recommendations do not always translate into practice. A report found that 16% of state police agencies require a two-year college degree, and 4% require a four-year degree. County police are the next most likely to require either a two-year (13%) or four-year (3%) degree.[122] Among sheriff's departments, 6% require a degree, including 1% with a four-year degree requirement.[123] A 2002 report on police departments in large cities found that the percentage requiring new officers to have at least some college rose from 19% in 1990 to 37% in 2000, and the percentage requiring a two-year or four-year degree grew from 6% to 14% over the same period.[124] A Dallas Police Department policy requiring a minimum of 45 semester hours of successful college-level study for new recruits[125] was upheld in 1985 by the Fifth U.S. Circuit Court of Appeals in the case of *Davis* v. *Dallas*.[126]

An early survey of police departments by the Police Executive Research Forum found that police agencies that hire educated officers accrue these benefits:[127] (1) better written reports, (2) enhanced communications with the public, (3) more effective job performance, (4) fewer citizen complaints, (5) greater initiative, (6) wiser use of discretion, (7) heightened sensitivity to racial and ethnic issues, and (8) fewer disciplinary problems. However, there are drawbacks to having more educated police forces. Educated officers are more likely to leave police work, question orders, and request reassignment than noneducated officers.

Most federal agencies require college degrees for entry-level positions. Among them are the FBI, the DEA, the Bureau of Alcohol, Tobacco, Firearms, and Explosives (ATF), the Secret Service, the Bureau of Customs and Border Protection, and the Bureau of Immigration and Customs Enforcement (ICE).[128]

Recruitment and Selection

All professions need informed, dedicated, and competent personnel. In its 1973 report on the police, the National Advisory Commission on Criminal Justice Standards and Goals bemoaned the fact that "many college students are unaware of the varied, interesting, and challenging assignments and career opportunities that exist within the police service."[129] Today, police organizations consider education an important recruiting criterion, and they actively recruit new officers from two- and four-year colleges and universities, technical institutions, and professional organizations. The national commission report stressed the setting of high standards for police recruits and recommended a strong emphasis on minority recruitment, elimination of the requirement that new officers live in the area they were hired to serve, decentralized application and testing procedures, and various recruiting incentives.

A Bureau of Justice Statistics study published in 2006 found that local police departments use a variety of applicant-screening methods.[130] Nearly all use personal interviews, and a large majority use basic skills tests, physical agility measurements, medical exams, drug tests, psychological evaluations, and background investigations into the personal character of applicants (see Figure 6–5). Among departments serving 25,000 or more residents, about eight in ten use physical agility tests and written aptitude tests, more than half check credit records, and about half use

A good cop stays a rookie at heart, excited by every shift.

—A Nashville, Tennessee, police officer

LIBRARY
Extra
▪ ▪ ▪ ▪

La Toya Jackson showing off her wardrobe for the *Armed and Famous* TV show. The CBS series followed five stars through the Muncie, Indiana, police academy and onto patrol where they assisted in investigations and arrests. The show was cancelled in 2007, but not before it gained the attention of many "wannabe" officers. What are the attractions of police work?

CBS/Cliff Lipson/Landov LLC

personality inventories and polygraph exams. After training, successful applicants are typically placed on probation for one year. The probationary period in police work has been called the "first true job-related test . . . in the selection procedure,"[131] providing the opportunity for supervisors to gauge the new officer's response to real-life situations.

Effective policing, however, may depend more on innate personal qualities than on educational attainment or credit history. One of the first people to attempt to describe the personal attributes necessary for a successful police officer, famed 1930s police administrator August Vollmer, said that the public expects police officers to have "the wisdom of Solomon, the courage of David, the strength of Samson, the patience of Job, the leadership of Moses, the kindness of the Good Samaritan, the strategic training of Alexander, the faith of Daniel, the diplomacy of Lincoln, the tolerance of the Carpenter of Nazareth, and finally, an intimate knowledge of every branch of the natural, biological, and social sciences."[132] More practically, Orlando (O. W.) Wilson, the well-known police administrator of the 1940s and 1950s, once enumerated some "desirable personal qualities of patrol officers":[133] (1) initiative; (2) responsibility; (3) the ability to deal alone with emergencies; (4) the capacity to communicate effectively with people from di-

FIGURE 6–5

Percent of local police departments using various recruit-screening methods, 2003.

Source: Matthew J. Hickman and Brian A. Reaves, *Local Police Departments, 2003* (Washington, DC: Bureau of Justice Statistics, 2006), p. 8.

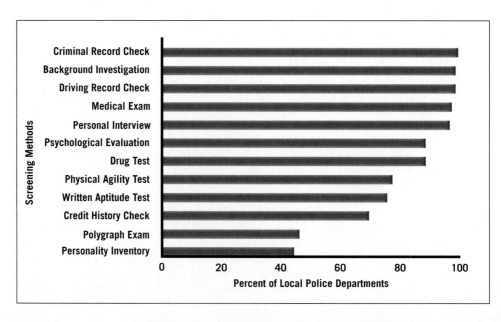

verse social, cultural, and ethnic backgrounds; (5) the ability to learn a variety of tasks quickly; (6) the attitude and ability necessary to adapt to technological changes; (7) the desire to help people in need; (8) an understanding of others; (9) emotional maturity; and (10) sufficient physical strength and endurance.

High-quality police recruits, an emphasis on training with an eye toward ethical aspects of police performance, and higher levels of education are beginning to raise police pay, which has traditionally been low. The acceptance of police work as a true profession should contribute to significantly higher rates of pay in coming years.

Ethnic and Gender Diversity in Policing

In 2003, Annetta W. Nunn took the reins of the Birmingham (Alabama) Police Department. For many, Nunn, a 44-year-old African American mother and Baptist choir singer, symbolizes the changes that have taken place in American policing during the past few decades. The new chief sits in a chair once occupied by Eugene "Bull" Connor, an arch segregationist and a national symbol of the South's fight against integration who jailed thousands of civil rights demonstrators during the 1960s. A 23-year veteran of the department, Nunn heads a force of 838 men and women.

A 1968 survey of police supervisors by the National Advisory Commission on Civil Disorders[134] (aka the Kerner Commission) found a marked disparity between the number of black and white officers in leadership positions. One of every 26 black police officers had been promoted to the rank of sergeant, while the ratio among whites was one in 12. Only one of every 114 black officers had become a lieutenant, while among whites the ratio was one in 26. At the level of captain, the disparity was even greater: One out of every 235 black officers had achieved the rank of captain, while one of every 53 whites had climbed to that rank.

Today, many departments, through dedicated recruitment efforts, have dramatically increased their complement of officers from underrepresented groups. The Metropolitan Detroit Police Department, for example, now has a force that is more than 30% black. Nationwide, racial and ethnic minorities comprised 22.7% of full-time sworn police personnel in 2000, up from 17.0% in 1990.[135] From 1990 to 2000, the number of African American local police officers increased by 13,300, or 35%, and the number of Hispanic officers increased by 17,600, or 93%. Moreover, a 2006 study of 123 African American police executives in the United States found that they were generally well accepted by their peers, well integrated into their leadership roles, and socially well adjusted.[136]

Although ethnic minorities are now employed in policing in numbers that approach their representation in the American population, women are still significantly underrepresented. The 2001 Status of Women in Policing Survey, conducted by the National Center for Women and

An advertisement for police professionals to work in Iraq. The acceptance of police work as a true profession will mean high pay and benefits—both at home and abroad—for those who embrace the professional ideals of training, education, and ethics. Is policing a true profession? Why or why not?

Courtesy of DynCorp International, LLC

Birmingham, Alabama, Chief of Police Annetta Nunn. Nunn's appointment in 2003 is indicative of expanded opportunities in policing for women and minorities. Nunn, who holds a bachelor's degree in criminal justice from the University of Alabama, was four years old in 1963 when thousands of civil rights demonstrators in Birmingham were beaten and arrested on orders of Police Chief Eugene "Bull" Connor. How do communities benefit from police agencies that are socially and culturally diverse?

Birmingham Police Department

Policing (NCWP), found that women fill only 12.7% of all sworn law enforcement positions nationwide.[137] On the other hand, the NCWP notes that women account for 46.5% of employed people over the age of 16 nationwide, meaning that they are "strikingly under-represented within the field of sworn law enforcement."[138] Key findings from the survey show the following:[139]

- Women currently fill about 12.7% of all sworn law enforcement positions among municipal, county, and state agencies in the United States with 100 or more sworn officers. Women of color hold 4.8% of these positions.

- Between 1990 and 2001, the representation of women in sworn law enforcement ranks increased from 9% to 12.7%—a gain of less than 4%, or less than 0.5% each year.

- If the slow growth rate of women in policing holds, women will not achieve equal representation within the police profession for another 70 years, and many experts caution that time alone may not be sufficient to substantially increase the number of female officers.

- Women hold 7.3% of sworn top command law enforcement positions, 9.6% of supervisory positions, and 13.5% of line operation positions. Women of color hold 1.6% of sworn top command positions, 3.1% of supervisory positions, and 5.3% of line operation positions.

- Fifty-six percent of the agencies surveyed reported no women in top command positions, and 88% of the agencies reported no women of color in their highest ranks.

- State agencies trail municipal and county agencies by a wide margin in hiring and promoting women. Specifically, 5.9% of the sworn law enforcement officers in state agencies are women, which is significantly lower than the percentage reported by municipal agencies (14.2%) and county agencies (13.9%).

- Consent decrees mandating the hiring and promotion of women and minorities significantly affected the gains women have made in law enforcement. Of the 25 agencies with the highest percentage of sworn women, ten are subject to such decrees. This contrasts sharply with just four of the 25 agencies with the lowest percentage of sworn women operating under consent decrees.

- On average, in agencies without a consent decree mandating the hiring and promotion of women and minorities, women comprise 9.7% of sworn personnel, whereas those agencies with a consent decree in force average 14.0% women in their ranks. The percentage of women of color is 6.3% in agencies without a consent decree and 11.7% in agencies operating under one.

It is unclear just how many women actually *want* to work in policing. Nonetheless, many departments aggressively recruit and retain women because they understand the benefits of having

African American and Hispanic police officers in Los Angeles. Ethnic minorities, while still underrepresented in the criminal justice field, have many opportunities for employment throughout the system. Can the same be said for women?

David R. Frazier Photolibrary/Photo Researchers, Inc.

more women as sworn officers. Because female officers tend to use less physical force than male officers, for example, they are less likely to be accused of using excessive force. Female officers are also better at defusing and de-escalating potentially violent confrontations, often possess better communications skills than their male counterparts, and are better able to facilitate the cooperation and trust required to implement a community policing model. Moreover, the NCWP says that "female officers often respond more effectively to incidents of violence against women—crimes that represent one of the largest categories of calls to police departments. Increasing the representation of women on the force is also likely to address another costly problem for police administrators—the pervasive problem of sex discrimination and sexual harassment—by changing the climate of modern law enforcement agencies."[140] Finally, "because women frequently have different life experiences than men, they approach policing with a different perspective, and the very presence of women in the field will often bring about changes in policies and procedures that benefit both male and female officers."[141] Additional information on how police departments can recruit and retain female officers can be found at Library Extra 6–13 at cjtoday.com.

LIBRARY
Extra
■ ■ ■ ■

Women as Effective Police Officers

One research report on female police officers in Massachusetts found that female officers (1) are "extremely devoted to their work," (2) "see themselves as women first, and then police officers," and (3) are more satisfied when working in nonuniformed capacities.[142] The researcher identified two groups of female officers: (1) those who felt themselves to be well integrated into their departments and were confident in their jobs and (2) those who experienced strain and on-the-job isolation. The officers' children were cited as a significant influence on their perceptions of self and their jobs. The demands of child rearing in contemporary society were found to be a major factor contributing to the resignation of female officers. The study also found that the longer female officers stayed on the job, the greater the stress and frustration they tended to experience, primarily because of the uncooperative attitudes of male officers. Some of the female officers identified networking as a potential solution to the stresses encountered by female officers but also said that when women get together to solve problems, they are seen as "crybabies" rather than professionals. Said one of the women in the study, "We've lost a lot of good women who never should have left the job. If we had helped each other, maybe they wouldn't have left."[143]

Some studies found that female officers are often underutilized and that many departments hesitate to assign women to patrol and other potentially dangerous field activities.[144] Consequently, some policewomen experience frustration and a lack of job satisfaction. An analysis of the genderization of the criminal justice workplace by Susan Ehrlich Martin and Nancy Jurik, for example, points out that gender inequality is part of a historical pattern of entrenched forms of gender interaction relating to the division of labor, power, and culture.[145] Martin and Jurik contend that women working in the justice system are viewed in terms of such historically developed filters, causing them to be judged and treated according to normative standards developed for men. As a result, formal and informal social controls continue to disenfranchise women who wish to work in the system and make it difficult to recognize the specific contributions that they make as women.

Increasing the Number of Minorities and Women in Police Work

To increase the representation of ethnic minorities and women in police work, the Police Foundation recommends (1) involving underrepresented groups in departmental affirmative action and long-term planning programs, (2) encouraging the development of an open promotion system whereby women can feel free to apply for promotion and in which qualified individuals of any race or gender will face equity in the promotion process, and (3) periodic audits to ensure that female officers are not being underutilized by ineffective tracking into clerical and support positions.[146]

Networking has taken root among the nation's female police officers, as attested to by the growth of organizations like the International Association of Women Police. Networks support female officers and help them deal with dilemmas on the job. Mentoring, another method for introducing women to police work,[147] creates semiformal relationships between experienced female officers and rookies through which problems can be addressed and experienced officers can guide junior partners through the maze of formal and informal expectations of policing.

Women today have entered the ranks of police administration. The 2,000-member International Association of Women Police estimates that there are more than 100 female chiefs of police throughout the country. The Women's Police Chief Association offers networking opportunities to women seeking and holding high rank in departments nationwide.[148] And the National Center for Women and Policing, a project of the Feminist Majority Foundation, provides a nationwide resource for law enforcement agencies, community leaders, and public officials seeking to increase the numbers of female police officers in their communities.

Barriers to diversity continue to fall. In 1979, for example, San Francisco became the first city in the world to actively recruit homosexuals for its police force. That action reduced the fear of reporting crimes among many homosexuals, who for years had been victims of organized assaults by bikers and street gangs. During the Clinton administration, Attorney General Janet Reno ordered all Justice Department agencies to end hiring discrimination based on sexual orientation.

SUMMARY

- The fundamental police mission in democratic societies includes five components: (1) enforcing the law (especially the criminal law), (2) investigating crimes and apprehending offenders, (3) preventing crime, (4) helping to ensure domestic peace and tranquility, and (5) providing the community with needed enforcement-related services.

- This chapter presents five core law enforcement strategies: (1) preventive patrol, (2) routine incident response, (3) emergency response, (4) criminal investigation, and (5) problem solving. Support, an ancillary operational strategy, is also discussed.

- Police management involves the administrative activities of controlling, directing, and coordinating police personnel, resources, and activities in the service of preventing crime, apprehending criminals, recovering stolen property, and performing regulatory and helping services. Virtually all American law enforcement organizations are formally structured among divisions and along lines of authority. Roles within police agencies usually fall into one of two categories: line and staff. Line operations are field or supervisory activities directly related to daily police work. Staff operations include support roles, such as administration.

- Three policing styles are identified in this chapter: (1) the watchman style, (2) the legalistic style, and (3) the service style. The style of policing that characterizes a community tends to flow from the lifestyles of those who live there. While the watchman style of policing, with its emphasis on order maintenance, was widespread during the mid-twentieth century, the service style, which is embodied in the community policing model, is commonplace today. Community policing is built on the principle that police departments and the communities they serve should work together as partners in the fight against crime.

- Policing in America was forever changed by the events of September 11, 2001. Local law enforcement agencies, many of which previously saw community protection and peacekeeping as their primary roles, are being called upon to protect against potential terrorist threats with international roots. The contemporary emphasis on terrorism prevention, alongside the need for a rapid response to threats of terrorism, has led to what some see as a new era of policing to secure the homeland. Homeland security policing builds upon the established framework of community policing for the purpose of gathering intelligence to prevent terrorism.

- Police discretion refers to the opportunity for police officers to exercise choice in their enforcement activities. Put another way, discretion refers to the exercise of choice by law enforcement officers in the decision to investigate or apprehend, the disposition of suspects, the carrying out of official duties, and the application of sanctions. The widest exercise of discretion can be found in routine situations involving relatively less serious violations of the law, but serious criminal behavior may also result in discretionary decisions not to make an arrest.

- Police professionalism requires that today's law enforcement officers adhere to ethical codes and standards established by the profession. Police professionalism places important limits on the discretionary activities of individual enforcement personnel and helps officers and the departments they work for gain the respect and regard of the public they police.

- This chapter points out that ethnic minorities are now employed in policing in numbers that approach their representation in the general population. Women, however, are still significantly underrepresented. Questions can be raised about the degree of minority participation in the command structure of law enforcement agencies, about the desire of significant numbers of women to work in policing, and the respect accorded to women and members of other underrepresented groups who work in law enforcement by their fellow officers.

KEY TERMS

chain of command, 192

community policing, 199

CompStat, 185

crime prevention, 184

crime scene, 190

crime-scene investigator, 191

criminal intelligence, 205

criminal investigation, 189

intelligence-led policing (ILP), 205

legalistic style, 196

line operations, 192

NLETS, 208

peace officer standards and training (POST) program, 212

police–community relations (PCR), 197

police discretion, 209

police ethics, 211

police management, 192

police professionalism, 211

police subculture, 202

preliminary investigation, 191

problem-solving policing, 199

quality-of-life offense, 185

response time, 189

service style, 196

solvability factor, 191

span of control, 193

staff operations, 192

strategic policing, 198

team policing, 198

watchman style, 196

QUESTIONS FOR REVIEW

1. What are the basic purposes of policing in democratic societies? How are they consistent with one another? In what ways might they be inconsistent?

2. What are the five core operational strategies that police departments use today? What is the ancillary operational strategy?

3. Define the term *police management*, and describe the different types of organizational structures typical of American police departments.

4. What are the three styles of policing described in this chapter? How do they differ? Which one characterizes the community in which you live?

5. What new responsibilities have American police agencies assumed since the September 11, 2001, terrorist attacks? What new challenges are they facing?

6. What is police discretion? How does the practice of discretion by today's officers reflect on their departments and on the policing profession as a whole?

7. What is police professionalism? How can you tell when police action is professional? Why are professionalism and ethics important in policing today?

8. What issues related to gender and ethnicity are important in American policing today? What problems still exist? How can those problems be addressed?

QUESTIONS FOR REFLECTION

1. Are there any aspects of the police mission that this chapter fails to recognize and that should be added to the basic purposes of policing identified here? If so, what are they?

2. How are police organizations managed? Might participatory or democratic management styles or the organizational styles of innovative high-technology firms be effective in policing? Why or why not?

3. What is community policing? How does it differ from what some might call traditional policing?

4. Does community policing offer an opportunity to improve policing services in the United States? Why or why not? Does it offer opportunities in the fight against terrorism? Why or why not?

5. Do you believe that policing is a true profession? How can the professionalism of today's law enforcement organizations be increased? Explain your answer.

Discuss your answers to these questions and other issues on the CJ Today e-mail discussion list (join the list at cjtoday.com).

WEB QUEST

Use the Web to find the home pages of three police departments (other than those described in this chapter) that have posted organizational charts showing their agency structure. The departments you find should include one big-city agency, a smaller town police department, and a sheriff's office. Compare the three organizational charts to see how they differ and how they are the same. Describe the differences and the similarities that you find, and submit your findings to your instructor if asked to do so.

To complete this Web Quest online, go to the Web Quest module in Chapter 6 of the *Criminal Justice Today* Companion Website at cjtoday.com.

CHAPTER 7

Policing: Legal Aspects

LEARNING OBJECTIVES

After reading this chapter, you should be able to

- Identify legal restraints on police action and be able to identify instances of the abuse of police power.

- Explain how the Bill of Rights and democratically inspired legal restraints help to protect personal freedoms in our society.

- Describe the circumstances under which police officers may properly conduct searches or seize property.

- Define *arrest* and describe how popular depictions of the arrest process may not be consistent with legal understandings of the term.

- Describe the intelligence function, including police interrogations, and explain the role of *Miranda* warnings.

OUTLINE

The touchstone of the Fourth Amendment is reasonableness. The Fourth Amendment does not proscribe all state-initiated searches and seizures. It merely proscribes those which are unreasonable.

—Florida *v.* Jimeno, *500 U.S. 248 (1991)*

"Yeah," the detective mumbled. "Fifteen guys. You might want to think about that. Only two of us . . ." He shook his head. "Sneaking a bunch of cops into a neighborhood like this is going to be like trying to sneak the sun past a rooster. . . ."

As he started up the stairs, Angelo reached not for his gun but for his wallet. He took out a Chase Manhattan calendar printed on a supple but firm slip of plastic. He flicked the card at Rand. "I'll open the door with this. You step in and freeze them."

"Jesus Christ, Angelo," the agent almost gasped. "We can't do that. We haven't got a warrant."

"Don't worry about it, kid," Angelo said, drawing up to the second door on the right on the second floor. "It ain't a perfect world."

—Larry Collins and Dominique Lapierre[1]

Hear the author discuss this chapter at cjtoday.com

Introduction

Early on a cold November morning in 2006, 23-year-old Sean Bell left a bachelor party at New York City's Kalua Cabaret strip club with two of his friends and climbed into his gray Nissan Altima. Although Bell, who was to be married later that day, didn't know it, undercover New York City Police Department (NYPD) officers had been staking out the club in an investigation into suspected drug and gun dealing there. What happened next remains unclear, but after a chaotic confrontation between Bell's group and the police, followed by a crash involving a van carrying some of the NYPD officers and Bell's car, officers opened fire on the vehicle, firing 50 rounds before the shooting ended. Bell died at the scene, and his friends were seriously injured. The officers later said that they thought Bell and his companions were armed and that they might have been drug dealers. It was not clear if Bell ever knew that the men, dressed in plain clothes, were police officers; he may have thought that he was being robbed or carjacked. On March 17, 2007, a Queens, New York, grand jury indicted three of the detectives involved in the case, charging two with first- and second-degree manslaughter, and a third with reckless endangerment.

Shortly after the indictments were handed down, demonstrators paraded through Queens demanding justice for Bell, who was African American, as were two of the three officers indicted in the shooting. New York City Mayor Michael R. Bloomberg urged residents to "respect the result of our justice system." He added, "It also needs to be said that being a police officer . . . is a very dangerous job. And although a trial will decide whether crimes were committed in this case, day in and day out the N.Y.P.D. does an incredible job under very difficult circumstances."[2]

The Bell shooting was reminiscent of the death of West African immigrant Amadou Diallo, who was killed in a hail of 41 bullets in 1999 as he stood in a New York City doorway and apparently reached for his identification after being told to raise his hands. Diallo reportedly had a poor command of the English language and may not have understood police commands to stay still. Officers had apparently mistaken him for a suspect they were pursuing. Although the officers who shot Diallo were charged with second-degree murder, they were later acquitted.[3] Law enforcement experts said that what happened in both the Bell and Diallo cases might be explained by "contagious shooting"—gunfire that spreads among officers "in the adrenaline-pumping, split-second heat of the moment"[4] who believe that they, or their colleagues, are facing a deadly threat.[5]

Not all questionable cases of police use of force involve shootings. Two months after Hurricane Katrina devastated New Orleans, for example, members of the city's overworked police department became embroiled in a public-relations nightmare when an Associated Press Television News (APTN) crew working in the French Quarter filmed two white officers beating an apparently dazed and unresisting 64-year-old African American retired elementary school teacher named Robert Davis. A third officer could be seen grabbing and shoving an APTN producer working with the news team. As the incident ended, Davis, whose family had property in the city, was arrested and charged with public intoxication, resisting arrest, battery on a police officer, and public intimidation. He later told reporters that he hadn't had an alcoholic drink in 25 years and that the trouble began when he asked a mounted officer for directions.[6] New Orleans Police Superintendent Warren Riley was quick to condemn the officers' behavior. "The actions that were observed on this video are certainly unacceptable [to] this department," Riley said as he announced the firings of officers Lance Schilling and Robert Evangelist and the suspension without pay of another officer, S. M. Smith. Soon afterward, the U.S. Department of Justice announced that it was opening a civil rights investigation into the incident. The case remains unresolved as this book goes to press.[7]

There is more law at the end of the policeman's nightstick than in all the decisions of the Supreme Court.

–Alexander "Clubber" Williams, late-nineteenth-century New York police officer

The Abuse of Police Power

National publicity surrounding the Davis beating was considerably less intense than that which centered on the 1991 videotaped beating of motorist Rodney King by Los Angeles Police Department (LAPD) officers. King, an unemployed 25-year-old African American man, was stopped by LAPD officers for an alleged violation of motor vehicle laws. Police said King had been speeding and had refused to stop for a pursuing patrol car. Officers claimed to have clocked King's 1988 Hyundai at 115 miles per hour on suburban Los Angeles's Foothill Freeway—even though the car's manufacturer later said the vehicle was not capable of speeds over 100 mph.

Eventually King did stop, but then officers of the LAPD appeared to attack him, shocking him twice with electronic stun guns and striking him with nightsticks and fists. Kicked in the stomach, face, and back, King was left with 11 skull fractures, missing teeth, a crushed cheekbone, and a broken ankle. A witness told reporters that she heard King begging officers to stop the beating but that they "were all laughing, like they just had a party."[8] King eventually underwent surgery

Protesters at a rally in Queens, New York, demanding answers for the fatal police shooting of Sean Bell as he left a bachelor's party on the night before his wedding in 2006. Bell, who was unarmed, was killed by NYPD officers who fired 50 rounds at him and two friends after they drove Bell's car into a minivan carrying plainclothes officers who were investigating the club where the party took place. Might "contagious shooting" explain what happened that night?

Reuters/Mike Segar/Landov LLC

[The police] are not perfect; we don't sign them up on some far-off planet and bring them into police service. They are products of society, and let me tell you, the human product today often is pretty weak.

—Former Los Angeles Police Chief
Daryl Gates

for brain injuries. Officers involved in the beating claimed that King, at 6 feet, 3 inches and 225 pounds, appeared strung out on PCP and that he and his two companions made the officers feel threatened.[9]

The entire incident was captured on videotape by an amateur photographer on a nearby balcony who was trying out his new night-sensitive video camera. The two-minute videotape was repeatedly broadcast over national television and was picked up by hundreds of local TV stations. The furor that erupted over the tape led to the ouster of LAPD Chief Daryl Gates and initiated a Justice Department review of law enforcement practices across the country.[10]

In 1992, a California jury found four police defendants not guilty—a verdict that resulted in days of rioting across Los Angeles. A year later, however, in the spring of 1993, two of the officers, Sergeant Stacey Koon and Officer Laurence Powell, were found guilty in federal court of denying King his constitutional right "not to be deprived of liberty without due process of law, including the right to be . . . free from the intentional use of unreasonable force."[11] Later that year, both were sentenced to two and a half years in prison, far less than might have been expected under federal sentencing guidelines. They were released from prison in December 1995, and a three-year court battle over whether federal sentencing guidelines were violated was resolved in the officers' favor the next year. Officers Theodore Briseno and Timothy Wind were exonerated at the federal level.

In 1994, King settled a civil suit against the city of Los Angeles for a reported $3.8 million. Observers later concluded that King himself was not a model citizen. At the time of the beating, he was on parole after having served time in prison for robbery. Since then he has been arrested on a variety of other charges, including battery, assault, drug use, and indecent exposure.[12] Regardless, King's 1991 beating continues to serve as a rallying point for individual-rights activists who want to ensure that citizens remain protected from the abuse of police power in an increasingly conservative society. Learn more about the Rodney King incident and its ramifications at **Web Extra 7–1** at cjtoday.com.

This chapter shows how no one is above the law—not even the police. It describes the legal environment surrounding police activities, from search and seizure through arrest and the interrogation of suspects. As we shall see throughout, democratically inspired legal restraints on the police help ensure individual freedoms in our society and prevent the development of a police state in America. Like anything else, however, the rules by which the police are expected to operate are in constant flux, and their continuing development forms the meat of this chapter. For a police perspective on these issues, visit **Web Extra 7–2** at cjtoday.com.

WEB
Extra
■■■■

WEB
Extra
■■■■

Police officers in the French Quarter of New Orleans repeatedly punching Robert Davis, 64, who was charged with public intoxication and resisting arrest. The beating, which took place following Hurricane Katrina in 2005, was videotaped by an Associated Press news crew that was in the area. The officers were later arrested and charged with battery. How can we establish effective limits on the police use of force to protect both officers and the public?

Mel Evans/AP Wide World Photos

A Changing Legal Climate

The Constitution of the United States is designed—especially in the **Bill of Rights**—to protect citizens against abuses of police power (Table 7–1). However, the legal environment surrounding the police in modern America is much more complex than it was just 45 years ago. Up until that time, the Bill of Rights was largely given only lip service in criminal justice proceedings around the country. In practice, law enforcement, especially on the state and local levels, revolved around tried-and-true methods of search, arrest, and interrogation that sometimes left little room for recognition of individual rights. Police operations during that period were often far more informal than they are today, and investigating officers frequently assumed that they could come and go as they pleased, even to the extent of invading someone's home without a search warrant. Interrogations could quickly turn violent, and the infamous "rubber hose," which was reputed to leave few marks on the body, was sometimes used during the questioning of suspects. Similarly, "doing things by the book" sometimes meant using thick telephone books to beat suspects, since the books spread out the force of blows and left few visible bruises. Although these abuses were not day-to-day practices in all police agencies and characterized just a small proportion of all officers, such conduct pointed to the need for greater control over police activities so that even the *potential* for abuse could be curtailed.

In the 1960s, the U.S. Supreme Court, under the direction of Chief Justice Earl Warren (1891–1974), accelerated the process of guaranteeing individual rights in the face of criminal prosecution. Warren Court rulings bound the police to strict procedural requirements in the areas of investigation, arrest, and interrogation. Later rulings scrutinized trial court procedure and enforced humanitarian standards in sentencing and punishment. The Warren Court also seized on the Fourteenth Amendment and made it the basis for judicial mandates requiring that both state and federal criminal justice agencies adhere to the Court's interpretation of the Constitution. The apex of the individual-rights emphasis in Supreme Court decisions was reached in the 1966 case of *Miranda* v. *Arizona*,[13] which established the famous requirement of a police "rights advisement" of suspects. In wielding its brand of idealism, the Warren Court (which held sway from 1953 until 1969) accepted that a few guilty people would go free in order to protect the rights of the majority of Americans.

In the decades since the Warren Court, a new conservative Court philosophy has resulted in Supreme Court decisions that have brought about what some call a "reversal" of Warren-era advances in the area of individual rights. By creating exceptions to some of the Warren Court's rules and restraints and by allowing for the emergency questioning of suspects before they are read their rights, a changed Supreme Court has recognized the realities attending day-to-day police work and the need to ensure public safety.

Bill of Rights

The popular name given to the first ten amendments to the U.S. Constitution, which are considered especially important in the processing of criminal defendants.

TABLE 7–1	Constitutional Amendments of Special Significance to the American System of Justice
This Right Is Guaranteed	**By This Amendment**
The right against unreasonable searches and seizures	Fourth
The right against arrest without probable cause	Fourth
The right against self-incrimination	Fifth
The right against "double jeopardy"	Fifth
The right to due process of law	Fifth, Sixth, Fourteenth
The right to a speedy trial	Sixth
The right to a jury trial	Sixth
The right to know the charges	Sixth
The right to cross-examine witnesses	Sixth
The right to a lawyer	Sixth
The right to compel witnesses on one's behalf	Sixth
The right to reasonable bail	Eighth
The right against excessive fines	Eighth
The right against cruel and unusual punishments	Eighth
The applicability of constitutional rights to all citizens, regardless of state law or procedure	Fourteenth

Individual Rights

The Constitution of the United States provides for a system of checks and balances among the legislative, judicial, and executive (presidential) branches of government. By this we mean that one branch of government is always held accountable to the other branches. The system is designed to ensure that no one individual or agency can become powerful enough to usurp the rights and freedoms guaranteed under the Constitution. Accountability rules out the possibility of a police state in which the power of law enforcement is absolute and is related more to political considerations and personal vendettas than to objective considerations of guilt or innocence.

Under our system of government, courts are the arena for dispute resolution, not just between individuals but between citizens and the agencies of government. People who feel they have not received the respect and dignity from the justice system that are due them under the law can appeal to the courts for redress. Such appeals are usually based on procedural issues and are independent of more narrow considerations of guilt or innocence in a particular case.

In this chapter, we focus on cases that are important for having clarified constitutional guarantees concerning individual liberties within the criminal justice arena. They involve issues that most of us have come to call *rights.* Rights are concerned with procedure, that is, with how police and other actors in the criminal justice system handle each part of the process of dealing with suspects. Rights violations have often become the basis for the dismissal of charges, the acquittal of defendants, or the release of convicted offenders after an appeal to a higher court.

Due Process Requirements

As you may recall from Chapter 1, the Fifth, Sixth, and Fourteenth Amendments to the U.S. Constitution require due process, which mandates that justice system officials respect the rights of accused individuals throughout the criminal justice process. Most due process requirements of relevance to the police pertain to three major areas: (1) evidence and investigation (often called *search and seizure*), (2) arrest, and (3) interrogation. Each of these areas has been addressed by a plethora of landmark U.S. Supreme Court decisions. **Landmark cases** produce substantial changes both in the understanding of the requirements of due process and in the practical day-to-day operations of the justice system. Landmark cases significantly clarify the "rules of the game"— the procedural guidelines by which the police and the rest of the justice system must abide.

The three areas we will discuss have been well defined by decades of court precedent. Keep in mind, however, that judicial interpretations of the constitutional requirement of due process are always evolving. As new decisions are rendered and as the composition of the Court itself changes, major changes and additional refinements may occur.

landmark case

A precedent-setting court decision that produces substantial changes in both the understanding of the requirements of due process and the practical day-to-day operations of the justice system.

An officer patting down a suspect. The legal environment in which the police work helps ensure proper official conduct. In a search like this, inappropriate behavior on the part of the officer can later become the basis for civil or criminal action against the officer and the police department. What might constitute "inappropriate behavior"?

John Boykin/PhotoEdit Inc.

Search and Seizure

The Fourth Amendment to the U.S. Constitution declares that people must be secure in their homes and in their persons against unreasonable searches and seizures. This amendment reads, "The right of the people to be secure in their persons, houses, papers, and effects, against unreasonable searches and seizures, shall not be violated, and no Warrants shall issue, but upon probable cause, supported by Oath or affirmation, and particularly describing the place to be searched, and the persons or things to be seized." The Fourth Amendment, a part of the Bill of Rights, was adopted by Congress and became effective on December 15, 1791.

The language of the Fourth Amendment is familiar to all of us. "Warrants," "probable cause," and other phrases from the amendment are frequently cited in editorials, TV news shows, and daily conversation about **illegally seized evidence**. It is the interpretation of these phrases over time by the U.S. Supreme Court, however, that has given them the impact they have on the justice system today.

illegally seized evidence

Evidence seized without regard to the principles of due process as described by the Bill of Rights. Most illegally seized evidence is the result of police searches conducted without a proper warrant or of improperly conducted interrogations.

The Exclusionary Rule

The first landmark case concerning search and seizure was *Weeks* v. *U.S.* (1914).[14] Freemont Weeks was suspected of using the U.S. mail to sell lottery tickets, a federal crime. Weeks was arrested, and federal agents went to his home to conduct a search. Since at the time investigators did not routinely use warrants, the agents had no search warrant. Still, they confiscated many incriminating items of evidence, as well as some of the suspect's personal possessions, including clothes, papers, books, and even candy.

Prior to trial, Weeks's attorney asked that the personal items be returned, claiming that they had been illegally seized under Fourth Amendment guarantees. A judge agreed and ordered the materials returned. On the basis of the evidence that was retained, however, Weeks was convicted in federal court and was sentenced to prison. He appealed his conviction through other courts, and his case eventually reached the U.S. Supreme Court, where his lawyer reasoned that if some of his client's belongings had been illegally seized, then all were taken improperly. The Court agreed and overturned Weeks's earlier conviction.

The *Weeks* case forms the basis of what is now called the **exclusionary rule**, which holds that evidence illegally seized by the police cannot be used in a trial. The rule acts as a control over police behavior and specifically focuses on the failure of officers to obtain warrants authorizing them either to conduct searches or to make arrests, especially where arrest may lead to the acquisition of incriminating statements or to the seizure of physical evidence.

It is important to note, incidentally, that Freemont Weeks could have been retried on the original charges following the Supreme Court decision in his case. He would not have faced double jeopardy because he was in fact not *finally* convicted on the earlier charges. His conviction was nullified on appeal, resulting in neither a conviction nor an acquittal. Double jeopardy becomes an issue only when a defendant faces retrial on the same charges following acquittal at his or her original trial or when the defendant is retried after having been convicted. The decision of the Supreme Court in the *Weeks* case was binding, at the time, only on federal officers because it was federal agents who were involved in the illegal seizure. Learn more about *Weeks* v. *U.S.* at Library Extra 7–1 at cjtoday.com.

exclusionary rule

The understanding, based on U.S. Supreme Court precedent, that incriminating information must be seized according to constitutional specifications of due process or it will not be allowed as evidence in a criminal trial.

LIBRARY
Extra
■ ■ ■ ■

PROBLEMS WITH PRECEDENT

The *Weeks* case demonstrates the Supreme Court's power to enforce the "rules of the game," as well as the much more significant role that it plays in rule creation. Until the *Weeks* case was decided, federal law enforcement officers had little reason to think they were violating due process because they were not required to obtain a warrant before conducting searches. The rule that resulted from *Weeks* was new, and it would forever alter the enforcement activities of federal officers.

The *Weeks* case reveals that the present appeals system, focusing as it does on the "rules of the game," presents a ready-made channel for the guilty to go free. There is little doubt that Freemont Weeks had violated federal law. A jury had convicted him. Yet he escaped punishment because of the illegal behavior of the police—behavior that, until the Court ruled, had been widely regarded as legitimate. Even if the police knowingly violate the principles of due process, which they sometimes do, our sense of justice is compromised when the guilty go free. Famed Supreme Court Justice Benjamin Cardozo (1870–1938) once complained, "The criminal is to go free because the constable has blundered."

Analysts of the criminal justice system have long considered three possible solutions to this problem. The first suggests that rules of due process, especially when newly articulated by the courts, should be applied only to future cases, not to the initial case in which they are stated. The justices in the *Weeks* case, for example, might have said, "We are creating the 'exclusionary rule' based on our realization in this case. Law enforcement officers are obligated to use it as a guide in all future searches. However, insofar as the guilt of Mr. Weeks was decided by a jury under rules of evidence existing at the time, we will let that decision stand."

A second solution would punish police officers or other actors in the criminal justice system who act illegally but would not allow the guilty defendant to escape punishment. This would allow the application of established precedent in cases where officers and officials had the benefit of clearly articulated rules and should have known better. Under this arrangement, any officer who intentionally violates due process guarantees might be suspended, be reduced in rank, lose pay, or be fired. Some authors have suggested that the decertification of police officers might serve as "an alternative to traditional remedies for police misconduct."[15] Because officers in every state except Hawaii[16] must meet the certification requirements of state boards to hold employment, some authors argue that decertification would have a much more personal (and therefore more effective) impact on individual officers than the exclusionary rule ever could.[17]

A third possibility would allow the Supreme Court to address theoretical questions involving issues of due process. Concerned supervisors and officials could ask how the Court would rule "if . . ." As things now work, the Court can only address real cases and does so on a **writ of *certiorari***, in which the Court orders the record of a lower court case to be prepared for review.

The difficulty with these solutions, however, is that they would substantially reduce the potential benefits available to defendants through the appeals process, effectively eliminating the process itself.

THE FRUIT OF THE POISONOUS TREE DOCTRINE

The Court continued to build on the rules concerning evidence with its ruling in *Silverthorne Lumber Co.* v. *U.S.* (1920).[18] In 1918, Frederick Silverthorne and his sons operated a lumber company and were accused of avoiding payment of federal taxes. When asked to turn over the company's books to federal investigators, the Silverthornes refused, citing their Fifth Amendment privilege against self-incrimination.

Shortly thereafter, federal agents descended on the lumber company and, without a search warrant, seized the company's books. The Silverthornes' lawyer appeared in court and asked that

writ of *certiorari*

A writ issued from an appellate court for the purpose of obtaining from a lower court the record of its proceedings in a particular case. In some states, this writ is the mechanism for discretionary review. A request for review is made by petitioning for a writ of *certiorari*, and the granting of review is indicated by the issuance of the writ.

FREEDOM OR SAFETY?

You Decide

Liberty Is a Double-Edged Sword

This chapter builds on the following theme: For police action to be "just," it must recognize the rights of individuals while holding them accountable to the social obligations defined by law. It is important to realize that many democratically inspired legal restraints on the police stem from the Bill of Rights, which comprises the first ten amendments to the U.S. Constitution. Such restraints help ensure individual freedoms in our society and prevent the development of a police state in America.

In police work and elsewhere, the principles of individual liberty and social justice are cornerstones on which the American way of life rests. Ideally, the work of police agencies, as well as the American system of criminal justice, is to ensure justice while guarding liberty. The liberty–justice issue is the dual thread that holds the tapestry of the justice system together—from the simplest daily ac-

tivities of police officers on the beat to the often complex and lengthy renderings of the U.S. Supreme Court.

For the criminal justice system as a whole, the question becomes, How can individual liberties be maintained in the face of the need for official action, including arrest, interrogation, incarceration, and the like? The answer is far from simple, but it begins with the recognition that liberty is a double-edged sword, entailing obligations as well as rights.

YOU DECIDE

What does it mean to say that "for police action to be 'just,' it must recognize the rights of individuals while holding them accountable to the social obligations defined by law"? How can police agencies accomplish this? What can individual officers do to help their agencies in this regard?

the materials be returned, citing the need for a search warrant, as had been established in the *Weeks* case. The prosecutor agreed, and the books were returned to the Silverthornes.

The Silverthornes went to trial thinking they would be acquitted because the evidence against them was no longer in the hands of prosecutors. In a surprise move, however, the prosecution introduced photographic copies of incriminating evidence, which they had made before returning the books. The Silverthornes were convicted in federal court. Their appeal eventually reached the U.S. Supreme Court. The Court ruled that just as illegally seized evidence cannot be used in a trial, neither can evidence be used that *derives* from an illegal seizure.[19] The conviction of the Silverthornes was overturned, and they were set free.

The *Silverthorne* case articulated a new principle of due process that today we call the **fruit of the poisonous tree doctrine**. This doctrine is potentially far-reaching. Complex cases developed after years of police investigative effort may be ruined if defense attorneys are able to demonstrate that the prosecution's case was originally based on a search or seizure that violated due process. In such cases, it is likely that all evidence will be declared "tainted" and will become useless.

fruit of the poisonous tree doctrine

A legal principle that excludes from introduction at trial any evidence later developed as a result of an illegal search or seizure.

The Warren Court (1953–1969)

Before the 1960s, the U.S. Supreme Court intruded only occasionally on the overall operation of the criminal justice system at the state and local levels. As one author observed, however, the 1960s were a time of idealism, and "without the distraction of a depression or world war, individual liberties were examined at all levels of society."[20] Hence, while the exclusionary rule became an overriding consideration in federal law enforcement from the time of its creation in 1914, it was not until 1961 that the Court, under Chief Justice Earl Warren, decided a case that changed the face of American law enforcement forever. Beginning with the now-famous *Mapp v. Ohio* (1961) case,[21] the Warren Court charted a course that would guarantee nationwide recognition of individual rights, as it understood them, by agencies at all levels of the criminal justice system.

APPLICATION OF THE EXCLUSIONARY RULE TO THE STATES

Mapp v. Ohio (1961) made the exclusionary rule applicable to criminal prosecutions at the state level. Dolree Mapp was suspected of harboring a fugitive who was wanted in a bombing. When Ohio police officers arrived at her house, she refused to admit them. Eventually, they forced their way in. During the search that ensued, pornographic materials were uncovered. Mapp was arrested and eventually convicted under a state law that made possession of such materials illegal.

Because of prior decisions by the U.S. Supreme Court, including *Wolf v. Colorado* (1949),[22] officers believed that the exclusionary rule did not apply to agents of state and local law enforcement. However, in a wide-reaching and precedent-setting decision, Mapp's conviction was overturned on appeal by a majority of Warren Court justices who decided that the U.S. Constitution, under the Fourteenth Amendment's due process guarantee, mandates that state and local

Police officers examining suspected controlled substances after a drug raid. The exclusionary rule means that illegally gathered evidence cannot be used later in court, requiring that police officers pay close attention to how they gather and handle evidence. How did the exclusionary rule come into being?

Chris O'Meara/AP Wide World Photos

law enforcement officers be held to the same standards of accountability as federal officers. The justices said that since the evidence against Mapp had been illegally obtained, it could not be used against her in any court of law in the United States. The precedent established in *Mapp* v. *Ohio* firmly applied the principles developed in *Weeks* and *Silverthorne* to trials in state courts, making police officers at all levels accountable to the rule of law, which, as embodied in the words of the Fourteenth Amendment, reads, "No State shall . . . deprive any person of life, liberty, or property, without due process of law; nor deny to any person within its jurisdiction the equal protection of the laws." Learn more about the case of *Mapp* v. *Ohio* at Library Extra 7–2 at cjtoday.com.

SEARCHES INCIDENT TO ARREST

Another important Warren-era case, *Chimel* v. *California* (1969),[23] involved both arrest and search activities by local law enforcement officers. Ted Chimel was convicted of the burglary of a coin shop based on evidence gathered at his home, where he was arrested. Officers, armed with an arrest warrant but not a search warrant, took Chimel into custody when they arrived at his residence and proceeded with a search of his entire three-bedroom house, including the attic, a small workshop, and the garage. Although officers realized that the search might be challenged in court, they justified it by claiming that it was conducted not so much to uncover evidence but as part of the arrest process. Searches that are conducted incident to arrest, they argued, are necessary for the officers' protection and should not require a search warrant. Coins taken from the burglarized coin shop were found in various places in Chimel's residence, including the garage, and were presented as evidence against him at trial.

Chimel's appeal eventually reached the U.S. Supreme Court, which ruled that the search of Chimel's residence, although incident to arrest, became invalid when it went beyond the person arrested and the area subject to that person's "immediate control." The thrust of the Court's decision was that searches during arrest can be made to protect arresting officers but that without a search warrant, their scope must be strongly circumscribed. The legal implications of *Chimel* v. *California* are summarized in Table 7–2.

The decision in the *Chimel* case built on the 1950 U.S. Supreme Court case of *U.S.* v. *Rabinowitz*.[24] Rabinowitz, a stamp collector, had been arrested and charged by federal agents with selling altered postage stamps to defraud other collectors. Employing a valid arrest warrant, officers arrested Rabinowitz at his place of employment and then proceeded to search his desk, file cabinets, and safe. They did not have a search warrant, but his office was small—only one room—and the officers conducted the search with a specific object in mind, the illegal stamps. Eventually, 573 altered postage stamps were seized in the search, and Rabinowitz was convicted in federal court of charges related to selling altered stamps.

Rabinowitz's appeal to the U.S. Supreme Court, based on the claim that the warrantless search of his business was illegal, was denied. The Court ruled that the Fourth Amendment provides protection against *unreasonable* searches but that the search in this case followed legally from the arrest of the suspect. In the language used by the Court, "It is not disputed that there may be reasonable searches, incident to arrest, without a search warrant. Upon acceptance of this established rule that some authority to search follows from lawfully taking the person into cus-

The public safety exception [to the exclusionary rule] was intended to protect the police, as well as the public, from danger.

—U.S. v. Brady, *819 F.2d 884 (1987)*

TABLE 7–2   Implications of *Chimel* v. *California* (1969)
What Arresting Officers May Search
The defendant
The physical area within easy reach of the defendant
Valid Reasons for Conducting a Search
To protect the arresting officers
To prevent evidence from being destroyed
To keep the defendant from escaping
When a Search Becomes Illegal
When it goes beyond the defendant and the area within the defendant's immediate control
When it is conducted for other than a valid reason

tody, it becomes apparent that such searches turn upon the reasonableness under all the circumstances and not upon the practicability of procuring a search warrant, for the warrant is not required."

Since the early days of the exclusionary rule, other court decisions have highlighted the fact that "the Fourth Amendment protects people, not places."[25] In other words, people can reasonably expect privacy in their *homes*—even if those homes are not houses. "Homes" of all sorts—including apartments, duplex dwellings, motel rooms, and even the cardboard boxes or makeshift tents of the homeless—are protected places under the Fourth Amendment. In *Minnesota* v. *Olson* (1990),[26] for example, the U.S. Supreme Court extended the protection against warrantless searches to overnight guests residing in the home of another. The capacity to claim the protection of the Fourth Amendment, said the Court, depends on whether the *person* who makes that claim has a legitimate expectation of privacy in the place searched.

In 1998, in the case of *Minnesota* v. *Carter*,[27] the Court held that for a defendant to be entitled to Fourth Amendment protection, "he must demonstrate that he personally has an expectation of privacy in the place searched, and that his expectation is reasonable." The Court noted that "the extent to which the Amendment protects people may depend upon where those people are. While an overnight guest may have a legitimate expectation of privacy in someone else's home . . . one who is merely present with the consent of the householder may not." Hence, an appliance repair person visiting a residence is unlikely to be accorded privacy protections while on the job.

In 2006, in the case of *Georgia* v. *Randolph*,[28] the Court ruled that police officers may not enter a home to conduct a warrantless search if one resident gives permission but the other refuses it. The *Randolph* case invalidated the use as evidence of a cocaine-coated straw that had been seized inside a home during a police search for which Scott Fitz Randolph's wife had given permission. At the time the search was conducted, Randolph and his wife were involved in a domestic dispute, and he was physically present as police searched the couple's residence. Randolph had already refused a police request for a search before his wife told officers that they could come inside and then led them to a bedroom and pointed out the straw. The *Randolph* ruling was a narrow one and centered on the stated refusal by a physically present co-occupant to permit warrantless entry in the absence of evidence of abuse or other circumstances that might otherwise justify an immediate police entry.[29]

The Burger Court (1969–1986) and the Rehnquist Court (1986–2005)

During the 1980s and 1990s, the United States experienced a swing toward conservatism, giving rise to a renewed concern with protecting the interests—financial and otherwise—of those who live within the law. The Reagan–Bush years, and the popularity of the two presidents who many thought embodied "old-fashioned" values, reflected the tenor of a nation seeking a return to "simpler," less volatile times.

Throughout the late 1980s, the U.S. Supreme Court mirrored the nation's conservative tenor by distancing itself from some earlier decisions of the Warren Court. While the Warren Court embodied the individual rights heyday in Court jurisprudence, Court decisions beginning in the 1970s were generally supportive of a "greater good" era—one in which the justices increasingly acknowledged the importance of social order and communal safety. Under Chief Justice Warren E. Burger, the new Court adhered to the principle that criminal defendants who claimed violations of their due process rights needed to bear most of the responsibility of showing that police went beyond the law in the performance of their duties. This tenet is still held by the Court today.

GOOD-FAITH EXCEPTIONS TO THE EXCLUSIONARY RULE

The Burger Court, which held sway from 1969 until 1986, "chipped away" at the strict application of the exclusionary rule originally set forth in the *Weeks* and *Silverthorne* cases. In the 1984 case of *U.S.* v. *Leon*,[30] the Court recognized what has come to be called the **good-faith exception** to the exclusionary rule. In this case, the Court modified the exclusionary rule to allow evidence that officers had seized in "reasonable good faith" to be used in court, even though the search was later ruled illegal. The suspect, Alberto Leon, was placed under surveillance for drug trafficking following a tip from a confidential informant. Burbank (California) Police Department investigators applied for a search warrant based on information gleaned from the surveillance, believing that they were in compliance with the Fourth Amendment requirement that "no Warrants shall issue, but upon probable cause." **Probable cause** is a tricky but important concept. Its legal criteria are based on facts and circumstances that would cause a reasonable person to believe that a

good-faith exception

An exception to the exclusionary rule. Law enforcement officers who conduct a search or who seize evidence on the basis of good faith (that is, when they believe they are operating according to the dictates of the law) and who later discover that a mistake was made (perhaps in the format of the application for a search warrant) may still provide evidence that can be used in court.

probable cause

A set of facts and circumstances that would induce a reasonably intelligent and prudent person to believe that a particular other person has committed a specific crime. Also, reasonable grounds to make or believe an accusation. Probable cause refers to the necessary level of belief that would allow for police seizures (arrests) of individuals and full searches of dwellings, vehicles, and possessions.

particular other person has committed a specific crime. Before a warrant can be issued, police officers must satisfactorily demonstrate probable cause in a written affidavit to a magistrate[31]—a low-level judge who ensures that the police establish the probable cause needed for warrants to be obtained. Upon a demonstration of probable cause, the magistrate will issue a warrant authorizing law enforcement officers to effect an arrest or conduct a search.

In *U.S.* v. *Leon*, a warrant was issued, and a search of Leon's three residences yielded a large amount of drugs and other evidence. Although Leon was convicted of drug trafficking, a later ruling in a federal district court resulted in the suppression of evidence against him on the basis that the original affidavit prepared by the police had not, in the opinion of the reviewing court, been sufficient to establish probable cause.

The federal government petitioned the U.S. Supreme Court to consider whether evidence gathered by officers acting in good faith as to the validity of a warrant should be fairly excluded at trial. The good-faith exception was presaged in the first sentences of the Court's written decision: "This case presents the question whether the Fourth Amendment exclusionary rule should be modified so as not to bar the use in the prosecution's case-in-chief of evidence obtained by officers acting in reasonable reliance on a search warrant issued by a detached and neutral magistrate but ultimately found to be unsupported by probable cause." The Court continued, "When law enforcement officers have acted in objective good faith or their transgressions have been minor, the magnitude of the benefit conferred on such guilty defendants offends basic concepts of the criminal justice system." Reflecting the renewed conservatism of the Burger Court, the justices found for the government and reinstated Leon's conviction.

In that same year, the Supreme Court case of *Massachusetts* v. *Sheppard* (1984)[32] further reinforced the concept of good faith. In the *Sheppard* case, officers executed a search warrant that failed to accurately describe the property to be seized. Although they were aware of the error, a magistrate had assured them that the warrant was valid. After the seizure was complete and a conviction had been obtained, the Massachusetts Supreme Judicial Court reversed the finding of the trial court. Upon appeal, the U.S. Supreme Court reiterated the good-faith exception and reinstated the original conviction.

The cases of *Leon* and *Sheppard* represented a clear reversal of the Warren Court's philosophy, and the trend continued with the 1987 case of *Illinois* v. *Krull*.[33] In *Krull*, the Court, now under the leadership of Chief Justice Rehnquist, held that the good-faith exception applied to a warrantless search permitted by an Illinois law related to automobile junkyards and vehicular parts sellers even though the state statute was later found to violate the Fourth Amendment. A 1987 Supreme Court case similar to *Sheppard*, *Maryland* v. *Garrison*,[34] supported the use of evidence obtained with a search warrant that was inaccurate in its specifics. In *Garrison*, officers had procured a warrant to search an apartment, believing it was the only dwelling on the building's third floor. After searching the entire floor, they discovered that it housed more than one apartment. Even so, evidence acquired in the search was held to be admissible based on the reasonable mistake of the officers.

The 1990 case of *Illinois* v. *Rodriguez*[35] further diminished the scope of the exclusionary rule. In *Rodriguez*, a badly beaten woman named Gail Fischer complained to police that she had been assaulted in a Chicago apartment. Fischer led police to the apartment—which she indicated she shared with the defendant—produced a key, and opened the door to the dwelling. Inside, investigators found the defendant, Edward Rodriguez, asleep on a bed, with drug paraphernalia and cocaine spread around him. Rodriguez was arrested and charged with assault and possession of a controlled substance.

Upon appeal, Rodriguez demonstrated that Fischer had not lived with him for at least a month and argued that she could no longer be said to have legal control over the apartment. Hence, the defense claimed, Fischer had no authority to provide investigators with access to the dwelling. According to arguments made by the defense, the evidence, which had been obtained without a warrant, had not been properly seized. The Supreme Court disagreed, ruling that "even if Fischer did not possess common authority over the premises, there was no Fourth Amendment violation if the police *reasonably believed* at the time of their entry that Fischer possessed the authority to consent."

In 1995, in the case of *Arizona* v. *Evans*, the U.S. Supreme Court created a "computer errors exception" to the exclusionary rule. In *Evans*, the Court held that a traffic stop that led to the seizure of marijuana was legal even though officers conducted the stop based on an arrest warrant that should have been deleted from their computer database. The arrest warrant reported to the officers by their computer had actually been quashed a few weeks earlier, but due to an oversight, a court employee had never removed it from the database.

In reaching its decision, the high court reasoned that police officers could not be held responsible for a clerical error made by a court worker and concluded that the arresting officers had acted in good faith. In addition, the majority opinion said that "the rule excluding evidence obtained without a warrant was intended to deter police misconduct, not mistakes by court employees."

Legal scholars have suggested that the exclusionary rule may undergo even further modification in the near future. Some analysts of the contemporary scene point to the fact that "the Court's majority is [now] clearly committed to the idea that the exclusionary rule is not directly part of the Fourth Amendment (and Fourteenth Amendment due process), but instead is an evidentiary device instituted by the Court to effectuate it."[36] In other words, if the Court should be persuaded that the rule is no longer effective or that some other strategy would better achieve the aim of protecting individual rights, the rule could be abandoned entirely. A general listing of established exceptions to the exclusionary rule, along with other investigative powers created by court precedent, is provided in Table 7–3.

During Rehnquist's tenure as chief justice, the Court invoked a characteristically conservative approach to many important criminal justice issues—from limiting the exclusionary rule[37] and generally broadening police powers, to sharply limiting the opportunities for state prisoners to bring appeals in federal courts.[38] Preventive detention, "no knock" police searches,[39] the death penalty,[40] and habitual offender statutes[41] (often known as *three-strikes laws*) all found decisive support under Chief Justice Rehnquist.[42] The particular cases in which the Court addressed these issues are discussed elsewhere in this text.

Following Rehnquist's death in 2005, President Bush nominated Judge John G. Roberts, Jr., to become the nation's seventeenth Chief Justice. Roberts, who had previously served as a judge on the U.S. Court of Appeals for the District of Columbia Circuit, was easily confirmed and assumed the bench in October 2005—in time for the Court's new term. Court watchers predict that Roberts is likely to continue the Rehnquist Court's conservative ways.

THE PLAIN-VIEW DOCTRINE

Police officers have the opportunity to begin investigations or to confiscate evidence, without a warrant, based on what they find in **plain view** and open to public inspection. The plain-view doctrine was succinctly stated in the U.S. Supreme Court case of *Harris* v. *U.S.* (1968),[43] in which a police officer inventorying an impounded vehicle discovered evidence of a robbery.[44] In the *Harris* case, the Court ruled that "objects falling in the plain view of an officer who has a right to be in the position to have that view are subject to seizure and may be introduced in evidence."[45]

The plain-view doctrine is applicable in common situations like crimes in progress, fires, accidents, and other emergencies. For example, police officers who enter a residence responding to a call for assistance and find drugs or other contraband in plain view are within their legitimate authority to confiscate the materials and to effect an arrest if the owner of the contraband can be identified. However, the plain-view doctrine applies only to sightings by the police under legal circumstances—that is, in places where the police have a legitimate right to be and, typically, only if the sighting was coincidental. Similarly, the incriminating nature of the evidence seized must have been "immediately apparent" to the officers making the seizure.[46] If officers conspired to avoid the necessity for a search warrant by helping to create a plain-view situation through surveillance, duplicity, or other means, the doctrine likely would not apply.

The plain-view doctrine was restricted by later federal court decisions. In the 1982 case of *U.S.* v. *Irizarry*,[47] the First Circuit Court of Appeals held that officers could not move objects to gain a view of evidence otherwise hidden from view. In the U.S. Supreme Court case of *Arizona* v. *Hicks* (1987),[48] the requirement that evidence be in plain view, without requiring officers to move or dislodge objects, was reiterated. In the *Hicks* case, officers responded to a shooting; a bullet fired in

plain view

A legal term describing the ready visibility of objects that might be seized as evidence during a search by police in the absence of a search warrant specifying the seizure of those objects. To lawfully seize evidence in plain view, officers must have a legal right to be in the viewing area and must have cause to believe that the evidence is somehow associated with criminal activity.

CJ Today Exhibit 7–1

Plain-View Requirements

Following the opinion of the U.S. Supreme Court in the case of *Horton* v. *California* (1990), items seized under the plain-view doctrine may be admissible as evidence in a court of law if both of the following conditions are met:

1. The officer who seized the evidence was in the viewing area lawfully.

2. The officer had probable cause to believe that the evidence was somehow associated with criminal activity.

TABLE 7–3 Selected Investigatory Activities Supported by Court Precedent

This Police Power	Is Supported By
Arrest based on computer error made by clerk	*Arizona* v. *Evans* (1995)
Authority to enter and/or search an "open field" without a warrant	*U.S.* v. *Dunn* (1987)
	Oliver v. *U.S.* (1984)
	Hester v. *U.S.* (1924)
Authority to search incident to arrest and/or to conduct a protective sweep in conjunction with an in-home arrest	*Maryland* v. *Buie* (1990)
	U.S. v. *Edwards* (1974)
	Chimel v. *California* (1969)
Gathering of incriminating evidence during interrogation in noncustodial circumstances	*Yarborough* v. *Alvarado* (2004)
	Thompson v. *Keohane* (1996)
	Stansbury v. *California* (1994)
	U.S. v. *Mendenhall* (1980)
	Beckwith v. *U.S.* (1976)
Gathering of incriminating evidence during *Miranda*-less custodial interrogation	*U.S.* v. *Patane* (2004)
Inevitable discovery of evidence	*Nix* v. *Williams* (1984)
"No-knock" searches or quick entry	*Brigham City* v. *Stuart* (2006)
	Hudson v. *Michigan* (2006)
	U.S. v. *Barnes* (2003)
	Richards v. *Wisconsin* (1997)
	Wilson v. *Arkansas* (1995)
Prompt action in the face of threat to public or personal safety or destruction of evidence	*U.S.* v. *Banks* (2003)
	Borchardt v. *U.S.* (1987)
	New York v. *Quarles* (1984)
	Warden v. *Hayden* (1967)
Seizure of evidence in good faith, even in the face of some exclusionary rule violations	*Illinois* v. *Krull* (1987)
	U.S. v. *Leon* (1984)
Seizure of evidence in plain view	*Horton* v. *California* (1990)
	Coolidge v. *New Hampshire* (1971)
	Harris v. *U.S.* (1968)
Stop and frisk/request personal identification	*Hiibel* v. *Sixth Judicial District Court of Nevada* (2004)
	Terry v. *Ohio* (1968)
Use of police informants in jail cells	*Arizona* v. *Fulminante* (1991)
	Illinois v. *Perkins* (1990)
	Kuhlmann v. *Wilson* (1986)
Warrantless naked-eye aerial observation of open areas and/or greenhouses	*Florida* v. *Riley* (1989)
	California v. *Ciraolo* (1986)
Warrantless search incident to a lawful arrest	*U.S.* v. *Rabinowitz* (1950)
Warrantless seizure of abandoned materials and refuse	*California* v. *Greenwood* (1988)
Warrantless vehicle search where probable cause exists to believe that the vehicle contains contraband and/or that the occupants have been lawfully arrested	*Thornton* v. *U.S.* (2004)
	Ornelas v. *U.S.* (1996)
	California v. *Acevedo* (1991)
	California v. *Carney* (1985)
	U.S. v. *Ross* (1982)
	New York v. *Belton* (1981)
	Carroll v. *U.S.* (1925)

a second-floor apartment had gone through the floor, injuring a man in the apartment below. When they entered, officers found the second-floor apartment in considerable disarray. While looking for the person who fired the weapon, they discovered and confiscated a number of guns and a stocking mask, like those used in robberies. Two expensive stereo sets lay in a corner of the apartment. Suspecting that the stereos were stolen, an officer looked over the equipment and was able to read the serial number of one of the components from where it rested. The other serial numbers, however, were not clearly visible, and the investigating officer moved some of the equipment in order to read them. When he called the numbers in to headquarters, he was told that the stereos indeed had been stolen. They were seized, and James Hicks, who lived in the apartment, was arrested. Hicks was eventually convicted on a charge of armed robbery, based on the evidence seized.

Upon appeal, the *Hicks* case reached the Supreme Court, which ruled that the officer's behavior had become illegal when he moved the stereo equipment to record the serial numbers. The Court held that people have a "reasonable expectation to privacy,"[49] which means that officers lacking a search warrant, even when invited into a residence, must act more like guests than inquisitors.

Most evidence seized under the plain-view doctrine is discovered "inadvertently"—that is, by accident.[50] However, in 1990, the U.S. Supreme Court ruled in the case of *Horton* v. *California*[51] that "even though inadvertence *is* a characteristic of most legitimate 'plain view' seizures, it is not a necessary condition."[52] In the *Horton* case, a warrant was issued authorizing the search of Terry Brice Horton's home for stolen jewelry. The affidavit, completed by the officer who requested the warrant, alluded to an Uzi submachine gun and a stun gun—weapons purportedly used in the jewelry robbery. It did not request that those weapons be listed on the search warrant. Officers searched the defendant's home but did not find the stolen jewelry. They did, however, seize a number of weapons, among them an Uzi, two stun guns, and a .38-caliber revolver. Horton was convicted of robbery in a trial in which the seized weapons were introduced into evidence. He appealed his conviction, claiming that officers had reason to believe that the weapons were in his home at the time of the search and were therefore not seized inadvertently. His appeal was rejected by the Court. As a result of the *Horton* case, inadvertence is no longer considered a condition necessary to ensure the legitimacy of a seizure that results when evidence other than that listed in a search warrant is discovered.

EMERGENCY SEARCHES OF PROPERTY AND EMERGENCY ENTRY

Certain emergencies may justify a police officer's decision to search or enter premises without a warrant. In 2006, for example, in the case of *Brigham City* v. *Stuart*,[53] the Court recognized the need for emergency warrantless entries under certain circumstances when it ruled that police

Latasha Smith (shown here sitting on a curb), who was arrested for failing to appear in court for a previous misdemeanor violation. Although the concept of plain view is difficult to define, Smith provides a personal example of the concept. After Dallas narcotics officers searched the house behind her for crack cocaine, they turned their attention to Smith and discovered the outstanding charges. How would you explain the concept of plain view?

AP Wide World Photos

officers "may enter a home without a warrant when they have an objectively reasonable basis for believing that an occupant is seriously injured or imminently threatened with such injury." The case involved police entry into a private home to break up a fight.

According to the Legal Counsel Division of the Federal Bureau of Investigation (FBI), there are three threats that "provide justification for emergency warrantless action."[54] They are clear dangers (1) to life, (2) of escape, and (3) of the removal or destruction of evidence. Any one of these situations may create an exception to the Fourth Amendment's requirement of a search warrant.

Emergency searches, or those conducted without a warrant when special needs arise, are legally termed *exigent circumstances searches*. When emergencies necessitate a quick search of premises, however, law enforcement officers are responsible for demonstrating that a dire situation existed that justified their actions. Failure to do so successfully in court will, of course, taint any seized evidence and make it unusable.

The U.S. Supreme Court first recognized the need for emergency searches in 1967 in the case of *Warden* v. *Hayden*.[55] In that case, the Court approved the warrantless search of a residence following reports that an armed robber had fled into the building. In *Mincey* v. *Arizona* (1978),[56] the Supreme Court held that "the Fourth Amendment does not require police officers to delay in the course of an investigation if to do so would gravely endanger their lives or the lives of others."[57]

A 1990 decision, rendered in the case of *Maryland* v. *Buie*,[58] extended the authority of police to search locations in a house where a potentially dangerous person could hide while an arrest warrant is being served. The *Buie* decision was meant primarily to protect investigators from potential danger and can apply even when officers lack a warrant, probable cause, or even reasonable suspicion.

In 1995, in the case of *Wilson* v. *Arkansas*,[59] the U.S. Supreme Court ruled that police officers generally must knock and announce their identity before entering a dwelling or other premises, even when armed with a search warrant. Under certain emergency circumstances, however, exceptions may be made, and officers may not need to knock or to identify themselves before entering.[60] In *Wilson*, the Court added that the Fourth Amendment requirement that searches be reasonable "should not be read to mandate a rigid rule of announcement that ignores countervailing law enforcement interests." Hence, officers need not announce themselves, the Court said, when suspects may be in the process of destroying evidence, officers are pursuing a recently escaped arrestee, or officers' lives may be endangered by such an announcement. Because the *Wilson* case involved an appeal from a drug dealer who was apprehended by police officers who entered her unlocked house while she was flushing marijuana down a toilet, some said that it establishes a "drug-law exception" to the knock-and-announce requirement.

In 1997, in *Richards* v. *Wisconsin*,[61] the Supreme Court clarified its position on "no knock" exceptions, saying that individual courts have the duty in each case to "determine whether the facts and circumstances of the particular entry justified dispensing with the requirement." The Court went on to say that "[a] 'no knock' entry is justified when the police have a reasonable suspicion that knocking and announcing their presence, under the particular circumstances, would be dangerous or futile, or that it would inhibit the effective investigation of the crime. This standard strikes the appropriate balance," said the Court, "between the legitimate law enforcement concerns at issue in the execution of search warrants and the individual privacy interests affected by no knock entries."

In 2001, in the case of *Illinois* v. *McArthur*,[62] the U.S. Supreme Court ruled that police officers with probable cause to believe that a home contains contraband or evidence of criminal activity may reasonably prevent a suspect found outside the home from reentering it while they apply for a search warrant; and in 2003, in a case involving drug possession, the Court held that a 15- to 20-second wait after officers knocked, announced themselves, and requested entry before breaking open a door was sufficient to satisfy Fourth Amendment requirements.[63]

In the 2006 case of *Hudson* v. *Michigan*,[64] the Court surprised many when it ruled that evidence found by police officers who enter a home to execute a warrant without first following the knock-and-announce requirement can be used at trial despite that constitutional violation. In the words of the Court, "The interests protected by the knock-and-announce rule include human life and limb (because an unannounced entry may provoke violence from a surprised resident), property (because citizens presumably would open the door upon an announcement, whereas a forcible entry may destroy it), and privacy and dignity of the sort that can be offended by a sudden entrance." But, said the Court, "the rule has never protected one's interest in preventing the government from seeing or taking evidence described in a warrant." The justices reasoned that the social costs of strictly adhering to the knock-and-announce rule are considerable and may include "the grave adverse consequence that excluding relevant incriminating evidence always entails—the risk of releasing dangerous criminals." In a ruling that some said signaled a new era of lessened restraints on the police, the Court's majority opinion said that since the interests vio-

---

emergency search

A search conducted by the police without a warrant, which is justified on the basis of some immediate and overriding need, such as public safety, the likely escape of a dangerous suspect, or the removal or destruction of evidence.

In this case, we hold that this common-law "knock and announce" principle forms a part of the reasonableness inquiry under the Fourth Amendment.

—Wilson v. Arkansas, *514 U.S. 927 (1995)*

lated by ignoring the knock-and-announce rule "have nothing to do with the seizure of the evidence, the exclusionary rule is inapplicable."

ANTICIPATORY WARRANTS

Anticipatory warrants are search warrants issued on the basis of probable cause to believe that evidence of a crime, while not presently at the place described, will likely be there when the warrant is executed. Such warrants anticipate the presence of contraband or other evidence of criminal culpability but do not claim that the evidence is present at the time that the warrant is requested or issued.

Anticipatory warrants are no different in principle from ordinary search warrants. They require an issuing magistrate to determine (1) that it is probable that (2) contraband, evidence of a crime, or a fugitive will be on the described premises (3) when the warrant is executed.

The constitutionality of anticipatory warrants was affirmed in 2006 in the U.S. Supreme Court case of *U.S.* v. *Grubbs*.[65] In *Grubbs*, an anticipatory search warrant had been issued for Grubbs's house based on a federal officer's affidavit stating that the warrant would not be executed until a parcel containing a videotape of child pornography—which Grubbs had ordered from an undercover postal inspector—was received at and physically taken into his residence. After the package was delivered, law enforcement officers executed the anticipatory search warrant, seized the videotape, and arrested Grubbs.

Arrest

Officers seize not only property but people as well—a process referred to as *arrest*. While many people think of arrest in terms of what they see on popular TV crime shows—the suspect is chased, subdued, and "cuffed" after committing a loathsome act in view of the camera—most arrests are far more mundane.

In technical terms, an **arrest** occurs whenever a law enforcement officer restricts a person's freedom to leave. There may be no yelling, "You're under arrest!" No *Miranda* warnings may be offered, and in fact, the suspect may not even consider himself or herself to be in custody. Some arrests evolve as a conversation between the officer and the suspect develops. Only when the suspect tries to leave and tests the limits of the police response may the suspect discover that he or she is really in custody. In the 1980 case of *U.S.* v. *Mendenhall*,[66] Justice Potter Stewart set forth the "free to leave" test for determining whether a person has been arrested. Stewart wrote, "A person has been 'seized' within the meaning of the Fourth Amendment only if in view of all the circumstances surrounding the incident, a reasonable person would have believed that he was not free to leave." The "free to leave" test "has been repeatedly adopted by the Court as the test for a seizure."[67] In 1994, in the case of *Stansbury* v. *California*,[68] the Court once again used such a test in determining the point at which an arrest had been made. In *Stansbury*, where the focus was on the interrogation of a suspected child molester and murderer, the Court ruled, "In determining whether an individual was in custody, a court must examine all of the circumstances surrounding the interrogation, but the ultimate inquiry is simply whether there [was] a formal arrest or restraint on freedom of movement of the degree associated with a formal arrest."

Youth and inexperience do not automatically undermine a reasonable person's ability to assess when they are free to leave. Hence, in the 2004 case of *Yarborough* v. *Alvarado*,[69] the U.S. Supreme Court found that a 17-year-old boy's two-hour interrogation in a police station without a *Miranda* advisement was not custodial, even though the boy confessed to his involvement in a murder and was later arrested. The boy, said the Court, had not actually been in police custody, even though he was in a building used by the police for questioning, because actions taken by the interviewing officer indicated that the juvenile had been free to leave. Whether a person is actually free to leave, said the Court, can only be determined by examining the totality of the circumstances surrounding the interrogation.[70]

Arrests that follow the questioning of a suspect are probably the most common type of arrest. When the decision to arrest is reached, the officer has come to the conclusion that a crime has been committed and that the suspect is probably the one who committed it. The presence of these elements constitutes the probable cause needed for an arrest. Probable cause is the basic minimum necessary for an arrest under any circumstances.

Arrests may also occur when the officer comes upon a crime in progress. Although such situations sometimes require apprehension of the offender to ensure the safety of the public, most arrests made during crimes in progress are for misdemeanors rather than felonies. In fact, many states do not allow arrest for a misdemeanor unless it is committed in the presence of an officer,

anticipatory warrants

Search warrants issued on the basis of probable cause to believe that evidence of a crime, while not presently at the place described, will likely be there when the warrant is executed.

arrest

The act of taking an adult or juvenile into physical custody by authority of law for the purpose of charging the person with a criminal offense, a delinquent act, or a status offense, terminating with the recording of a specific offense. Technically, an arrest occurs whenever a law enforcement officer curtails a person's freedom to leave.

since visible crimes in progress clearly provide the probable cause necessary for an arrest. In 2001, in a case that made headlines nationwide,[71] the U.S. Supreme Court upheld a warrantless arrest made by a Lago Vista, Texas, police officer for a seat belt violation. In what many saw as an unfair exercise of discretion, Patrolman Bart Turek stopped, then arrested, Gail Atwater, a young local woman whom he observed driving a pickup truck in which she and her two small children (ages three and five) were unbelted. Facts in the case showed that Turek verbally berated the woman after stopping her vehicle and that he handcuffed her, placed her in his squad car, and drove her to the local police station, where she was made to remove her shoes, jewelry, and eyeglasses and empty her pockets. Officers took her "mug shot" and placed her alone in a jail cell for about an hour, after which she was taken before a magistrate and released on $310 bond. Atwater was charged with a misdemeanor violation of Texas seat belt law. She later pleaded no contest and paid a $50 fine. Soon afterward, she and her husband filed a Section 1983 lawsuit against the officer, his department, and the police chief, alleging that the actions of the officer violated Atwater's Fourth Amendment right to be free from unreasonable seizures. The Court, however, concluded that "the Fourth Amendment does not forbid a warrantless arrest for a minor criminal offense, such as a misdemeanor seatbelt violation punishable only by a fine."

Most jurisdictions allow arrest for a felony without a warrant when a crime is not in progress, as long as probable cause can be established.[72] In jurisdictions that do require a warrant, arrest warrants are issued by magistrates when police officers can demonstrate probable cause. Magistrates will usually require that the officers seeking an arrest warrant submit a written affidavit outlining their reason for the arrest. In the case of *Payton* v. *New York* (1980),[73] the U.S. Supreme Court ruled that unless the suspect gives consent or an emergency exists, an arrest warrant is necessary if an arrest requires entry into a suspect's private residence.[74] In *Payton*, the justices held that "[a]bsent exigent circumstances," the "firm line at the entrance to the house . . . may not reasonably be crossed without a warrant." The Court reiterated its *Payton* holding in the 2002 case of *Kirk* v. *Louisiana*.[75] In *Kirk*, which involved an anonymous complaint about drug sales said to be taking place in the apartment of Kennedy Kirk, the justices reaffirmed their belief that "[t]he Fourth Amendment to the United States Constitution has drawn a firm line at the entrance to the home, and thus, the police need both probable cause to either arrest or search, and exigent circumstances to justify a nonconsensual warrantless intrusion into private premises."

Searches Incident to Arrest

The U.S. Supreme Court has established that police officers, to protect themselves from attack, have the right to conduct a search of a person being arrested, regardless of gender, and to search the area under the arrestee's immediate control. This rule regarding **search incident to an arrest**

search incident to an arrest

A warrantless search of an arrested individual conducted to ensure the safety of the arresting officer. Because individuals placed under arrest may be in possession of weapons, courts have recognized the need for arresting officers to protect themselves by conducting an immediate search of arrestees without obtaining a warrant.

An arresting officer patting down a drug suspect. The courts have generally held that to protect themselves and the public, officers have the authority to search suspects being arrested. What are the limits of such searches?

Craig Filipacchi/Getty Images, Inc.— Liaison

CJ News

Some Say Cop Videos Misleading

A series of recent videotaped arrests is providing an unfiltered look at often physical, sometimes brutal police work, due to the broadening technology of cellphone cameras and online video viewing.

Some law enforcement experts say the technology is shedding light on a long-standing if uncomfortable fact of life: Police frequently have to use force. And society and the law expect them to do so.

"The core function of police is, they're the ones who step up and use force when it is necessary," says Eugene O'Donnell, a former New York City police officer and prosecutor.

"The cops are doing our dirty work. And when someone puts it on camera and shoves it out there, we say, 'Isn't this terrible.'"

The tape of the beating of Rodney King by police in Los Angeles in 1991 had to be handed to television stations nationwide before the public saw it.

Nowadays, advances in computer technology and the advent of websites such as YouTube allow a person to post immediately a video online for millions of people to view.

In the latest videos:

- A man is seen being pepper-sprayed by officers in Venice Beach as he is put in a squad car. The incident happened [in 2005] but was posted online only recently.

- An officer is seen punching a suspect in the face while a fellow officer tries to handcuff him during a struggle on a Hollywood street in August of 2006.

- A UCLA student is seen being shocked with a Taser stun gun by a campus police officer during a library ID check.

Some defense lawyers say the videos are giving the American public a glimpse into brutality they never knew existed.

INCOMPLETE PICTURE?

"I can't see how anyone would think it would be OK to mete out punishment to someone who has been subdued and is not any threat," says John Raphling, lawyer for the man pepper-sprayed by officers.

The videos have been shocking to some Americans, a more raw real-life police drama than they may have expected after countless hours of television cop shows.

But the videos often provide an incomplete picture of events, police and law-enforcement advocates say—sometimes failing to show the actions that led to the confrontation and a suspect's behavior.

And after all, some experts say, a police officer's job is to control violent and potentially violent people. That generally requires using a level of force just above that used by the suspect.

"Somewhere in America, cops are beating up on somebody right now. It's legal and justifiable, even though it may be offensive to watch," says O'Donnell, professor of law and police studies at John Jay College of Criminal Justice.

Los Angeles Police Chief William Bratton says his officers were using justifiable force in subduing suspects in the Hollywood and Venice Beach incidents, even if the video strikes viewers as disturbing.

San Bernardino County Sheriff's Deputy Ivory Webb listens during his arraignment on charges of attempted voluntary manslaughter in March 2006, in a San Bernardino, California courtroom. Webb plead not guilty in the videotaped shooting of Senior Airman Elio Carrion on January 29, 2006. Why do some law enforcement experts say that video footage may sometimes provide an incomplete picture of what really happened?

Nick Ut/AP Wide World Photos

In the Venice Beach pepper-spraying, Bratton said county prosecutors examined the video and cleared officers of wrongdoing because the video showed the man was clearly combative.

"The officers showed remarkable restraint," Bratton said.

Likewise, the officers in the Hollywood incident were cleared after a court hearing.

Some experts say the number of videos is bound to increase, as will their impact on police work and the judicial system.

In January 2006, video captured a San Bernardino county sheriff's deputy shooting an unarmed Air Force airman after a chase in Chino, Calif. The footage appears to show the deputy firing three times as the suspect begins to comply with orders to get up from the ground. The officer was charged with attempted voluntary manslaughter.

A videotape of a Westminster, Colo., police takedown of a man after a seven-hour hostage drama drew attention when it was aired on TV and the Internet in 2005. The video appeared to show officers hitting the man after he was down.

In Inglewood, Calif., a jury . . . found in favor of two police officers who filed suit claiming they were unfairly disciplined after a videotaped beating of a teenager in a confrontation at a gas station in 2002.

"Because of the technology, everybody has a camera, and everybody's ready to use it," says Charles Whitebread, a professor of criminal procedure at the University of Southern California law school.

(continued)

CJ News (continued)

The impact could be especially significant in Los Angeles. The city has a long and troubled history with police, use of force, and arrest videos.

Rodney King's arrest and beating after a traffic stop, videotaped by a bystander, made nationwide news. Four officers were charged with using excessive force. Their acquittal in a 1992 trial sparked riots.

The Los Angeles Police Department is still feeling the effects of a 1999 scandal involving abuses by gang-control officers in the city's Rampart Division. The city agreed to comply with a federal court order that imposed numerous requirements for managing the force and reviewing instances of potential abuse. It is still in effect.

"EXCESSIVE FORCE" CULTURE?

Connie Rice, a civil rights lawyer who headed a review panel that investigated the scandal, credits the department with improvement in dealing with the public.

"I still think LAPD has an excessive force culture," she says. "LAPD needs to tell its officers you don't get to spray people just because they mouth off."

Whether the actions were justified or not, the videos have hurt the reputation of police, Whitebread says.

"It may well be that there are explanations. At first blush, it's pretty rough to look at," he says. "It can't do LAPD any good to have these videos disseminated."

Police are well aware of the power of such images. One response has been a move by some police forces around the country to install video cameras in police cars—allowing law enforcement to have its own more complete visual record of confrontations.

O'Donnell sees videos as possibly doing some good: They may help the public decide for itself what is reasonable force and what is not.

"People become used to the idea this is the police and what they do. . . . That may allow people to kind of clarify misconduct from things that are not misconduct.

"People see the police acting in a way that may not be pretty but may be justifiable," he said.

O'Donnell says the videos will also demonstrate that police are asked to bear a heavy burden in the criminal justice system, not just enforcing the law but acting as social workers with the mentally ill, the homeless and the addicted.

"It's a brutal system," says O'Donnell, "and cops bear the brunt of that brutality."

For the latest in crime and justice news, visit the Talk Justice news feed at http://www.crimenews.info.

Source: William M. Welch, "Some Say Cop Videos Misleading," USA TODAY, November 30, 2006. Reprinted with permission.

---

reasonable suspicion

The level of suspicion that would justify an officer in making further inquiry or in conducting further investigation. Reasonable suspicion may permit stopping a person for questioning or for a simple pat-down search. Also, a belief, based on a consideration of the facts at hand and on reasonable inferences drawn from those facts, that would induce an ordinarily prudent and cautious person under the same circumstances to conclude that criminal activity is taking place or that criminal activity has recently occurred. Reasonable suspicion is a *general* and reasonable belief that a crime is in progress or has occurred, whereas probable cause is a reasonable belief that a *particular* person has committed a *specific* crime.

was created in the *Rabinowitz* and *Chimel* cases discussed earlier. It became firmly established in other cases involving personal searches, such as the 1973 case of *U.S.* v. *Robinson*.[76] After Robinson had been stopped for a traffic violation, it was learned that his driver's license had expired. He was arrested for operating a vehicle without a valid license. Officers subsequently searched the defendant to be sure he wasn't carrying a weapon and discovered a substance that later proved to be heroin. He was convicted of drug possession but appealed. When Robinson's appeal reached the U.S. Supreme Court, the Court upheld an officer's right to conduct a search without a warrant for purposes of personal protection and to use the fruits of the search when it turns up contraband. In the words of the Court, "A custodial arrest of a suspect based upon probable cause is a reasonable intrusion under the Fourth Amendment; that intrusion being lawful, a search incident to the arrest requires no additional jurisdiction."[77]

The Court's decision in *Robinson* reinforced an earlier ruling in *Terry* v. *Ohio* (1968),[78] involving a seasoned officer who conducted a pat-down search of two men whom he suspected were casing a store, about to commit a robbery. The arresting officer was a 39-year veteran of police work who testified that the men "did not look right." When he approached them, he suspected they were armed. Fearing for his life, he quickly spun the men around, put them up against a wall, patted down their clothing, and found a gun on one of the men. The man, Terry, was later convicted in Ohio courts of carrying a concealed weapon.

Terry's appeal was based on the argument that the suspicious officer had no probable cause to arrest him and therefore no cause to search him. The search, he argued, was illegal, and the evidence obtained should not have been used against him. The Supreme Court disagreed, saying, "In view of these facts, we cannot blind ourselves to the need for law enforcement officers to protect themselves and other prospective victims of violence in situations where they may lack probable cause for an arrest."

The *Terry* case set the standard for a brief stop and frisk based on reasonable suspicion. Attorneys refer to such brief encounters as *Terry-type stops*. **Reasonable suspicion** can be defined as a belief, based on a consideration of the facts at hand and on reasonable inferences drawn from those facts, which would induce an ordinarily prudent and cautious person under the same circumstances to conclude that criminal activity is taking place or that criminal activity has recently occurred. It is the level of suspicion needed to justify an officer in making further inquiry or in conducting further investigation. Reasonable suspicion, which is a *general* and reasonable belief that a crime is in progress or has occurred, should be differentiated from probable cause. Probable cause, as noted earlier, is a reasonable belief that a *particular* person has committed a *specific* crime. It is important to note that the *Terry* case, for all the authority it conferred on officers, also made it clear that officers must have reasonable grounds for any stop and frisk that they conduct. Read more about the case of *Terry* v. *Ohio* at Library Extra 7–3 at cjtoday.com.

LIBRARY
Extra
▪ ▪ ▪ ▪

In 1989, in the case of *U.S.* v. *Sokolow*,[79] the Supreme Court clarified the basis on which law enforcement officers, lacking probable cause to believe that a crime has occurred, may stop and briefly detain a person for investigative purposes. In *Sokolow*, the Court ruled that the legitimacy of such a stop must be evaluated according to a "totality of circumstances" criterion—in which all aspects of the defendant's behavior, taken in concert, may provide the basis for a legitimate stop based on reasonable suspicion. In this case, the defendant, Andrew Sokolow, appeared suspicious to police because, while traveling under an alias from Honolulu, he had paid $2,100 in $20 bills (from a large roll of money) for two airplane tickets after spending a surprisingly small amount of time in Miami. In addition, the defendant was obviously nervous and checked no luggage. A warrantless airport investigation by Drug Enforcement Administration (DEA) agents uncovered more than 1,000 grams of cocaine in the defendant's belongings. In upholding Sokolow's conviction, the Court ruled that although no single behavior was proof of illegal activity, taken together his behaviors created circumstances under which suspicion of illegal activity was justified.

In 2002, the Court reinforced the *Sokolow* decision in *U.S.* v. *Arvizu* when it ruled that the "balance between the public interest and the individual's right to personal security"[80] "tilts in favor of a standard less than probable cause in brief investigatory stops of persons or vehicles . . . if the officer's action is supported by reasonable suspicion to believe that criminal activity may be afoot."[81] In the words of the Court, "This process allows officers to draw on their own experiences and specialized training to make inferences from and deductions about the cumulative information available."[82]

In 1993, in the case of *Minnesota* v. *Dickerson*,[83] the U.S. Supreme Court placed new limits on an officer's ability to seize evidence discovered during a pat-down search conducted for protective reasons when the search itself was based merely on suspicion and failed to immediately reveal the presence of a weapon. In this case, Timothy Dickerson, who was observed leaving a building known for cocaine trafficking, was stopped by Minneapolis police officers after they noticed him acting suspiciously. The officers investigated further and ordered Dickerson to submit to a pat-down search. The search revealed no weapons, but the officer conducting it testified that he felt a small lump in Dickerson's jacket pocket, believed it to be a lump of crack cocaine after examining it with his fingers, and then reached into Dickerson's pocket and retrieved a small bag of cocaine. Dickerson was arrested, tried, and convicted of possession of a controlled substance. His appeal, which claimed that the pat-down search had been illegal, eventually made its way to the U.S. Supreme Court. The high court ruled that "if an officer lawfully pats down a suspect's outer clothing and feels an object whose contour or mass makes its identity immediately apparent, there has been no invasion of the suspect's privacy beyond that already authorized by the officer's search for weapons." However, in *Dickerson*, the justices ruled, "the officer never thought that the lump was a weapon, but did not immediately recognize it as cocaine." The lump was determined to be cocaine only after the officer "squeezed, slid, and otherwise manipulated the pocket's contents." Hence, the Court held, the officer's actions in this case did not qualify under what might be called a "plain feel" exception. In any case, said the Court, the search in *Dickerson* went far beyond what is permissible under *Terry*, where officer safety was the crucial issue. The Court summed up its ruling in *Dickerson* this way: "While *Terry* entitled [the officer] to place his hands on respondent's jacket and to feel the lump in the pocket, his continued exploration of the pocket after he concluded that it contained no weapon was unrelated to the sole justification for the search under *Terry*" and was therefore illegal.

Just as arrest must be based on probable cause, officers may not stop and question an unwilling citizen whom they have no reason to suspect of a crime. In the case of *Brown* v. *Texas* (1979),[84] two Texas law enforcement officers stopped the defendant and asked for identification. Ed Brown, they later testified, had not been acting suspiciously, nor did they think he might have a weapon. The stop was made simply because officers wanted to know who he was. Brown was arrested under a Texas statute that required a person to identify himself properly and accurately when asked to do so by peace officers. Eventually, his appeal reached the U.S. Supreme Court, which ruled that under the circumstances of the *Brown* case, a person "may not be punished for refusing to identify himself."

In the 2004 case of *Hiibel* v. *Sixth Judicial District Court of Nevada*,[85] however, the Court upheld Nevada's "stop and identify" law that requires a person to identify himself to police if they encounter him under circumstances that reasonably indicate that he "has committed, is committing or is about to commit a crime." The *Hiibel* case was an extension of the reasonable suspicion doctrine set forth earlier in *Terry*.

In *Smith* v. *Ohio* (1990),[86] the Court held that an individual has the right to protect his or her belongings from unwarranted police inspection. In *Smith*, the defendant was approached by two officers in plain clothes who observed that he was carrying a brown paper bag. The officers asked him to "come here a minute" and, when he kept walking, identified themselves as police officers. The defendant threw the bag onto the hood of his car and attempted to protect it from the officers' intrusion. Marijuana was found inside the bag, and the defendant was arrested. Since there was little reason to stop the suspect in this case and because control over the bag was not thought necessary for the officers' protection, the Court found that the Fourth Amendment protects both "the traveler who carries a toothbrush and a few articles of clothing in a paper bag" and "the sophisticated executive with the locked attaché case."[87]

The following year, however, in what some Court observers saw as a turnabout, the Court ruled in *California* v. *Hodari D.* (1991)[88] that suspects who flee from the police and throw away items as they retreat may later be arrested based on the incriminating nature of the abandoned items. The significance of *Hodari* for future police action was highlighted by California prosecutors who pointed out that cases like *Hodari* occur "almost every day in this nation's urban areas."[89]

In 2000, the Court decided the case of William Wardlow.[90] Wardlow had fled upon seeing a caravan of police vehicles converge on an area of Chicago known for narcotics trafficking. Officers caught him and, searching for weapons, conducted a pat-down search of his clothing. After discovering a handgun, the officers arrested Wardlow on weapons charges, but his lawyer argued that police had acted illegally in stopping him since they did not have reasonable suspicion that he had committed an offense. The Illinois Supreme Court agreed with Wardlow's attorney, holding that "sudden flight in a high crime area does not create a reasonable suspicion justifying a *Terry* stop because flight may simply be an exercise of the right to 'go on one's way.' "[91] The case eventually reached the U.S. Supreme Court, which overturned the Illinois court, finding, instead, that the officers' actions did not violate the Fourth Amendment. In the words of the Court, "This case, involving a brief encounter between a citizen and a police officer on a public street, is governed by *Terry*, under which an officer who has a reasonable, articulable suspicion that criminal activity is afoot may conduct a brief, investigatory stop. While 'reasonable suspicion' is a less demanding standard than probable cause, there must be at least a minimal level of objective justification for the stop. An individual's presence in a 'high crime area,' standing alone, is not enough to support a reasonable, particularized suspicion of criminal activity, but a location's characteristics are relevant in determining whether the circumstances are sufficiently suspicious to warrant further investigation. . . . In this case, moreover, it was also Wardlow's unprovoked flight that aroused the officers' suspicions. Nervous, evasive behavior is another pertinent factor in determining reasonable suspicion . . . and headlong flight is the consummate act of evasion."[92]

Emergency Searches of Persons

> *Police work is the only profession that gives you the test first, then the lesson.*
>
> —*Anonymous*

Situations in which officers have to search people based on quick decisions do arise. An emergency search of a person may be warranted when, for example, he matches the description of an armed robber, he is found unconscious, or he has what appears to be blood on his clothes. Such searches can save lives by disarming fleeing felons or by uncovering a medical reason for an emergency situation. They may also prevent criminals from escaping or destroying evidence.

Emergency searches of persons, like those of premises, fall under the exigent circumstances exception to the warrant requirement of the Fourth Amendment. In the 1979 case of *Arkansas* v. *Sanders*,[93] the Supreme Court recognized the need for such searches "where the societal costs of obtaining a warrant, such as danger to law officers or the risk of loss or destruction of evidence, outweigh the reasons for prior recourse to a neutral magistrate."[94]

The 1987 case of *U.S.* v. *Borchardt*,[95] decided by the Fifth Circuit Court of Appeals, held that Ira Eugene Borchardt could be prosecuted for heroin uncovered during medical treatment, even though the defendant had objected to the treatment. Borchardt was a federal inmate when he was found unconscious in his cell. He was taken to a hospital, where tests revealed heroin in his blood. His heart stopped, and he was revived using cardiopulmonary resuscitation (CPR). Borchardt was given three doses of Narcan, a drug used to counteract the effects of heroin, and he improved, regaining consciousness. The patient refused requests to pump his stomach and began to become lethargic, indicating the need for additional Narcan. Eventually, he vomited nine plastic bags full of heroin, along with two bags that had burst. The heroin was turned over to federal officers, and Borchardt was eventually convicted of heroin possession. Attempts to exclude the heroin from evidence were unsuccessful, and the appeals court ruled that the necessity of the emergency situation overruled the defendant's objections to search his person.

The Legal Counsel Division of the FBI provides the following guidelines for conducting emergency warrantless searches of individuals, where the possible destruction of evidence is at issue.[96] (Keep in mind that there may be no probable cause to *arrest* the individual being searched.) All four conditions must apply:

1. At the time of the search there was probable cause to believe that evidence was concealed on the person searched.
2. At the time of the search there was probable cause to believe an emergency threat of destruction of evidence existed.
3. The officer had no prior opportunity to obtain a warrant authorizing the search.
4. The action was no greater than necessary to eliminate the threat of destruction of evidence.

Vehicle Searches

Vehicles present a special law enforcement problem. They are highly mobile, and when a driver or an occupant is arrested, the need to search the vehicle may be immediate.

The first significant Supreme Court case involving an automobile was *Carroll* v. *U.S.*[97] in 1925, in which a divided Court ruled that a warrantless search of an automobile or other vehicle is valid if it is based on a reasonable belief that contraband is present. In 1964, however, in the case of *Preston* v. *U.S.*,[98] the limits of warrantless vehicle searches were defined. Preston was arrested for vagrancy and taken to jail. His vehicle was impounded, towed to the police garage, and later searched. Two revolvers were uncovered in the glove compartment, and more incriminating evidence was found in the trunk. Preston, convicted on weapons possession and other charges, eventually appealed to the U.S. Supreme Court. The Court held that the warrantless search of Preston's vehicle had occurred while the automobile was in secure custody and had therefore been illegal. Time and circumstances would have permitted acquisition of a warrant to conduct the search, the Court reasoned.

When the search of a vehicle occurs after it has been impounded, however, that search may be legitimate if it is undertaken for routine and reasonable purposes. In the case of *South Dakota* v. *Opperman* (1976),[99] for example, the Court held that a warrantless search undertaken for purposes of inventorying and safekeeping the personal possessions of the car's owner was not illegal. The intent of the search, which turned up marijuana, had not been to discover contraband but to secure the owner's belongings from possible theft. Again, in *Colorado* v. *Bertine* (1987),[100] the Court supported the right of officers to open closed containers found in a vehicle while conducting a routine search for inventorying purposes. In the words of the Court, such searches are "now a well-defined exception in the warrant requirement." In 1990, however, in the precedent-setting case of *Florida* v. *Wells*,[101] the Supreme Court agreed with a lower court's suppression of marijuana evidence discovered in a locked suitcase in the trunk of a defendant's impounded vehicle. In *Wells*, the Court held that standardized criteria authorizing the search of a vehicle for inventorying purposes were necessary before such a discovery could be legitimate. Standardized criteria, said the Court, could take the form of department policies, written general orders, or established routines.

Generally speaking, where vehicles are concerned, an investigatory stop is permissible under the Fourth Amendment if supported by reasonable suspicion,[102] and a warrantless search of a stopped car is valid if it is based on probable cause.[103] Reasonable suspicion can expand into probable cause when the facts in a given situation so warrant. In the 1996 case of *Ornelas* v. *U.S.*,[104] for example, two experienced Milwaukee police officers stopped a car with California license plates that had been spotted in a motel parking lot known for drug trafficking after the Narcotics and Dangerous Drugs Information System (NADDIS) identified the car's owner as a known or suspected drug trafficker. One of the officers noticed a loose panel above an armrest in the vehicle's backseat and then searched the car. A package of cocaine was found beneath the panel, and the driver and a passenger were arrested. Following conviction, the defendants appealed to the U.S. Supreme Court, claiming that no probable cause to search the car existed at the time of the stop. The majority opinion, however, noted that in the view of the court that originally heard the case, "the model, age, and source-State origin of the car, and the fact that two men traveling together checked into a motel at 4 o'clock in the morning without reservations, formed a drug-courier profile and . . . this profile together with the [computer] reports gave rise to a reasonable suspicion of drug-trafficking activity. . . . [I]n the

CJ Careers

Bureau of Immigration and Customs Enforcement (ICE)

Name: Tamara N. Johnson

Position: Immigration Enforcement Agent

City: Dallas

College Attended: Northwestern State University

Year Hired: 2000

"I pursued a career in criminal justice because I believed that the criminal justice system lacked an effective form of rehabilitation. I wanted to make a difference and have an impact on repeat offenders in minority neighborhoods by establishing a form of rehabilitation that would not perpetuate criminal behavior. Recruiters [from the Immigration and Naturalization Service] came to my university and did a presentation. I applied and took the test."

"The greatest challenge of my job is being impartial, offering unbiased information and treating each detainee equally, regardless of their ethnicity, age, sex, or offense. It is also challenging working in a male-dominated career. Although I'm a female, I'm expected to respond to situations and provide backup for my male counterpart.

"The greatest reward of my job has been the opportunity to travel throughout the world. I've been exposed to many different cultures and customs. I've ridden a camel over the Sahara Desert and walked along the Nile River. I've learned survival skills and to always be prepared. The experiences and opportunities I have gained as an immigration enforcement officer have been priceless."

TYPICAL POSITIONS

Criminal investigator (special agent), immigration enforcement agent, detention enforcement agent, and deportation officer. The Bureau of Immigration and Customs Enforcement (ICE), a part of the Department of Homeland Security, focuses on the enforcement of immigration and customs laws within the United States, the protection of specified federal buildings, and air and marine enforcement.

EMPLOYMENT REQUIREMENTS

The applicant must be a U.S. citizen between 21 and 36 years of age, must be in good medical condition, and must possess a valid driver's license. General employment requirements include (1) a comprehensive written exam, (2) a structured employment interview, and (3) a background investigation. Appointment at the GS-5 level requires (1) a bachelor's degree from an accredited college or university; (2) three years of progressively responsible experience that demonstrates the ability to (a) analyze problems to identify significant factors, gather pertinent data, and recognize solutions, (b) plan and organize work, and (c) communicate effectively orally and in writing; or (3) an equivalent combination of education and experience.

OTHER REQUIREMENTS

Applicants are required to submit to urinalysis to screen for illegal drug use prior to appointment and will be subject to random testing after being hired. Selected candidates will attend basic training at the Immigration Officer Academy in Glynco, Georgia.

SALARY

Successful candidates are typically hired at the GS-5 or GS-7 level, depending on education and work experience.

BENEFITS

Benefits include (1) 13 days of sick leave annually, (2) two and a half to five weeks of paid vacation and ten paid federal holidays each year, (3) federal health and life insurance, and (4) a comprehensive retirement program.

DIRECT INQUIRIES TO:

Department of Homeland Security
Twin Cities Hiring Center, Recruitment Unit
One Federal Dr.
Fort Snelling, MN 55111-4055

Phone: 612-725-3496

Website: http://www.bice.gov

For more information on the rapidly expanding criminal justice careers area, read *Where the Jobs Are: Mission Critical Opportunities for America*, available on the Web at http://www.justicestudies.com/jobs.htm.

Source: Bureau of Immigration and Customs Enforcement.

court's view, reasonable suspicion became probable cause when [the deputy] found the loose panel."[105] Probable cause permits a warrantless search of a vehicle because it can quickly be driven out of a jurisdiction. This exception to the exclusionary rule is called the **fleeting-targets exception**.[106]

Warrantless vehicle searches can extend to any area of the vehicle if officers have probable cause to conduct a purposeful search or if officers have been given permission to search the vehicle. In the 1991 case of *Florida* v. *Jimeno*,[107] arresting officers stopped a motorist who gave them permission to search his car. A bag on the floor of the car was found to contain cocaine, and the defendant was later convicted on a drug charge. On appeal to the U.S. Supreme Court, however, he argued that the permission given to search his car did not extend to bags and other items within the car. In a decision that may have implications beyond vehicle searches, the Court held that "[a] criminal suspect's Fourth Amendment right to be free from unreasonable searches is not violated when, after he gives police permission to search his car, they open a closed container found within the car that might reasonably hold the object of the search. The amendment is satisfied when, under the circumstances, it is objectively reasonable for the police to believe that the scope of the suspect's consent permitted them to open the particular container."[108]

In *U.S.* v. *Ross* (1982),[109] the Court found that officers had not exceeded their authority in opening a bag in the defendant's trunk that was found to contain heroin. The search was held to be justifiable on the basis of information developed from a search of the passenger compartment. The Court said, "If probable cause justifies the search of a lawfully stopped vehicle, it justifies the search of every part of the vehicle and its contents that may conceal the object of the search."[110] Moreover, according to the 1996 U.S. Supreme Court decision in *Whren* v. *U.S.*,[111] officers may stop a vehicle being driven suspiciously and then search it once probable cause has developed, even if their primary assignment centers on duties other than traffic enforcement or "if a reasonable officer would not have stopped the motorist absent some additional law enforcement objective" (which in the *Whren* case was drug enforcement).

Motorists and their passengers may be ordered out of stopped vehicles in the interest of officer safety, and any evidence developed as a result of such a procedure may be used in court.[112] In 1997, for example, in the case of *Maryland* v. *Wilson*,[113] the U.S. Supreme Court overturned a decision by a Maryland court that held that crack cocaine found during a traffic stop was seized illegally when it fell from the lap of a passenger ordered out of a stopped vehicle by a Maryland state trooper. The Supreme Court cited concerns for officer safety and held that the activities of passengers are subject to police control. Similarly, in 2007, in the case of *People* v. *Brendlin,* the Court ruled that passengers in stopped vehicles are necessarily detained as a result of the stop, and that they should expect that, for safety reasons, officers will exercise "unquestioned police command" over them for the duration of the stop.

In 1998, however, the U.S. Supreme Court placed clear limits on warrantless vehicle searches. In the case of *Knowles* v. *Iowa*,[114] an Iowa policeman stopped Patrick Knowles for speeding, issued him a citation, but did not make a custodial arrest. The officer then conducted a full search of his car without Knowles's consent and without probable cause. Marijuana was found, and Knowles was arrested. At the time, Iowa state law gave officers authority to conduct full-blown automobile searches when issuing only a citation. The Supreme Court found, however, that while concern for officer safety during a routine traffic stop may justify the minimal intrusion of ordering a driver and passengers out of a car, it does not by itself justify what it called "the considerably greater intrusion attending a full field-type search." Hence, while a search incident to arrest may be justifiable in the eyes of the Court, a search incident to citation clearly is not.

In the 1999 case of *Wyoming* v. *Houghton*,[115] the Court ruled that police officers with probable cause to search a car may inspect any passengers' belongings found in the car that are capable of concealing the object of the search. *Thornton* v. *U.S.* (2004) established the authority of arresting officers to search a car without a warrant even if the driver had previously exited the vehicle.[116]

In 2005, in the case of *Illinois* v. *Caballes*,[117] the Court held that the use of a drug-sniffing dog during a routine and lawful traffic stop is permissible and may not even be a search within the meaning of the Fourth Amendment. In writing for the majority, Justice John Paul Stevens said that "the use of a well-trained narcotics-detection dog—one that does not expose noncontraband items that otherwise would remain hidden from public view—during a lawful traffic stop generally does not implicate legitimate privacy interests."

ROADBLOCKS AND MOTOR VEHICLE CHECKPOINTS

The Fourth and Fourteenth Amendments to the U.S. Constitution guarantee liberty and personal security to all people residing within the United States. Courts have generally held that, in the absence of probable cause to believe that a crime has been committed, police officers have no

fleeting-targets exception

An exception to the exclusionary rule that permits law enforcement officers to search a motor vehicle based on probable cause and without a warrant. The fleeting-targets exception is predicated on the fact that vehicles can quickly leave the jurisdiction of a law enforcement agency.

Every U.S. law enforcement officer takes an oath to defend and protect the Constitution. . . . We exist to protect the rights of the public. We are the first line of defense in protection of the Constitution and the Bill of Rights.

—Greenfield, California, Police Chief Joe Grebmeier[i]

A police officer searching a vehicle in San Diego, California. Warrantless vehicle searches, where the driver is suspected of a crime, have generally been justified by the fact that vehicles are highly mobile and can quickly leave police jurisdiction. Can passengers in the vehicle also be searched?

Mike Karlsson/Arresting Images

legitimate authority to detain or arrest people who are going about their business in a peaceful manner. In a number of instances, however, the U.S. Supreme Court has decided that community interests may necessitate a temporary suspension of personal liberty, even when probable cause is lacking. One such case is *Michigan Dept. of State Police* v. *Sitz* (1990),[118] which involved the legality of highway sobriety checkpoints, including those at which nonsuspicious drivers are subjected to scrutiny. In *Sitz*, the Court ruled that such stops are reasonable insofar as they are essential to the welfare of the community as a whole. That the Court reached its conclusion based on pragmatic social interests is clear from the words used by Chief Justice Rehnquist: "No one can seriously dispute the magnitude of the drunken driving problem or the States' interest in eradicating it. Media reports of alcohol-related death and mutilation on the Nation's roads are legion. Drunk drivers cause an annual death toll of over 25,000 and in the same time span cause nearly one million personal injuries and more than five billion dollars in property damage. . . . [T]he balance of the State's interest in preventing drunken driving, the extent to which this system can reasonably be said to advance that interest, and the degree of intrusion upon individual motorists who are briefly stopped, weighs in favor of the state program."[119]

In a second case, *U.S.* v. *Martinez-Fuerte* (1976),[120] the Court upheld brief suspicionless seizures at a fixed international checkpoint designed to intercept illegal aliens. The Court noted that "to require that such stops always be based on reasonable suspicion would be impractical because the flow of traffic tends to be too heavy to allow the particularized study of a given car necessary to identify it as a possible carrier of illegal aliens. Such a requirement also would largely eliminate any deterrent to the conduct of well-disguised smuggling operations, even though smugglers are known to use these highways regularly."[121]

In 2000, however, in what some people saw as a change in direction, the Court struck down a narcotics checkpoint program established by the Indianapolis Police Department in 1998. Under the program, stopped drivers were told that they were at a drug checkpoint, and officers examined each driver's license and registration while visually assessing the driver for signs of impairment. Drug-sniffing dogs were then walked around the vehicle's exterior. On average, motorists were stopped for three minutes. In ruling the program illegal, the justices held that the Fourth Amendment prohibits even a brief "seizure" of a motorist "under a program whose primary purpose is ultimately indistinguishable from the general interest in crime control." The Court's written opinion in this case, *Indianapolis* v. *Edmond*,[122] indicated that similar programs with the purpose of verifying driver's licenses and vehicle registrations would continue to be permissible because they were not intended to "detect evidence of ordinary criminal wrongdoing."

In fact, in 2004, in the case of *Illinois v. Lidster*,[123] the Court held that information-seeking highway roadblocks are permissible. In distinguishing this kind of stop from that in *Edmond*, the Court said that *Edmond*-type stops targeted motorists and were intended to determine whether a vehicle's occupants were committing a crime when stopped. The stop in *Lidster*, said the Court, was different because its intent was merely to solicit motorists' help in solving a crime. "The law," said the Court, "ordinarily permits police to seek the public's voluntary cooperation in a criminal investigation."

WATERCRAFT AND MOTOR HOMES

The 1983 case of *U.S. v. Villamonte-Marquez*[124] widened the *Carroll* decision (the first U.S. Supreme Court case involving a vehicle, which was discussed earlier) to include watercraft. The case involved an anchored sailboat occupied by Villamonte-Marquez, which was searched by a U.S. Customs officer after one of the crew members appeared unresponsive to being hailed. The officer thought he smelled burning marijuana after boarding the vessel and, through an open hatch, saw burlap bales that he suspected might be contraband. A search proved him correct, and the ship's occupants were arrested. Their conviction was overturned on appeal, but the U.S. Supreme Court reversed the appellate court. The Court reasoned that a vehicle on the water can easily leave the jurisdiction of enforcement officials, just as a car or truck can.

In *California v. Carney* (1985),[125] the Court extended police authority to conduct warrantless searches of vehicles to include motor homes. Earlier arguments had been advanced that a motor home, because it is more like a permanent residence than a vehicle, should not be considered a vehicle for purposes of search and seizure. In a 6–3 decision, the Court rejected those arguments, reasoning that a vehicle's appointments and size do not alter its basic function of providing transportation.

Houseboats were brought under the automobile exception to the Fourth Amendment warrant requirement in the 1988 Tenth Circuit Court case of *U.S. v. Hill*.[126] In this case, DEA agents believed that methamphetamine was being manufactured aboard a houseboat traversing Lake Texoma in Oklahoma. Because a storm warning had been issued for the area, agents decided to board and to search the boat prior to obtaining a warrant. During the search, an operating methamphetamine laboratory was discovered, and the boat was seized. In an appeal, the defendants argued that the houseboat search had been illegal because agents lacked a warrant to search their home. The appellate court, in rejecting the claims of the defendants, ruled that a houseboat, because it is readily mobile, may be searched without a warrant when probable cause exists to believe that a crime has been or is being committed.

Suspicionless Searches

In two 1989 decisions, the U.S. Supreme Court ruled for the first time that there may be instances when the need to ensure public safety provides a **compelling interest** that negates the rights of any individual to privacy, permitting **suspicionless searches**—those that occur when a person is not suspected of a crime. In the case of *National Treasury Employees Union v. Von Raab* (1989),[127] the Court, by a 5–4 vote, upheld a program of the U.S. Customs Service that required mandatory drug testing for all workers seeking promotions or job transfers involving drug interdiction and the carrying of firearms. The Court's majority opinion read, "We think the government's need to conduct the suspicionless searches required by the Customs program outweighs the privacy interest of employees engaged directly in drug interdiction, and of those who otherwise are required to carry firearms."

The second case, *Skinner v. Railway Labor Executives' Association* (1989),[128] was decided on the same day. In *Skinner*, the justices voted 7 to 2 to permit the mandatory testing of railway crews for the presence of drugs or alcohol following serious train accidents. The *Skinner* case involved evidence of drugs in a 1987 train wreck outside of Baltimore, Maryland, in which 16 people were killed and hundreds were injured.

The 1991 Supreme Court case of *Florida v. Bostick*,[129] which permitted warrantless "sweeps" of intercity buses, moved the Court deeply into conservative territory. The *Bostick* case came to the attention of the Court as a result of the Broward County (Florida) Sheriff's Department's routine practice of boarding buses at scheduled stops and asking passengers for permission to search their bags. Terrance Bostick, a passenger on one of the buses, gave police permission to search his luggage, which was found to contain cocaine. Bostick was arrested and eventually pleaded guilty to charges of drug trafficking. The Florida Supreme Court, however, found merit

compelling interest

A legal concept that provides a basis for suspicionless searches when public safety is at stake. (Urinalysis tests of train engineers are an example.) It is the concept on which the U.S. Supreme Court cases of *Skinner v. Railway Labor Executives' Association* (1989) and *National Treasury Employees Union v. Von Raab* (1989) turned. In those cases, the Court held that public safety may sometimes provide a sufficiently compelling interest to justify limiting an individual's right to privacy.

suspicionless search

A search conducted by law enforcement personnel without a warrant and without suspicion. Suspicionless searches are permissible only if based on an overriding concern for public safety.

in Bostick's appeal, which was based on a Fourth Amendment claim that the search of his luggage had been unreasonable. The Florida court held that "a reasonable passenger in [Bostick's] situation would not have felt free to leave the bus to avoid questioning by the police," and it overturned the conviction.

The state appealed to the U.S. Supreme Court, which held that the Florida Supreme Court had erred in interpreting Bostick's *feelings* that he was not free to leave the bus. In the words of the Court, "Bostick was a passenger on a bus that was scheduled to depart. He would not have felt free to leave the bus even if the police had not been present. Bostick's movements were 'confined' in a sense, but this was the natural result of his decision to take the bus." In other words, Bostick was constrained not so much by police action as by his own feelings that he might miss the bus were he to get off. Following this line of reasoning, the Court concluded that warrantless, suspicionless "sweeps" of buses, "trains, planes, and city streets" are permissible as long as officers (1) ask individual passengers for permission before searching their possessions, (2) do not coerce passengers to consent to a search, and (3) do not convey the message that citizen compliance with the search request is mandatory. Passenger compliance with police searches must be voluntary for the searches to be legal.

In contrast to the tone of Court decisions more than two decades earlier, the justices did not require officers to inform passengers that they were free to leave nor that they had the right to deny officers the opportunity to search (although Bostick himself was so advised by Florida officers). Any reasonable person, the Court ruled, should feel free to deny the police request. In the words of the Court, "The appropriate test is whether, taking into account all of the circumstances surrounding the encounter, a reasonable passenger would feel free to decline the officers' requests or otherwise terminate the encounter." The Court continued, "Rejected, however, is Bostick's argument that he must have been seized because no reasonable person would freely consent to a search of luggage containing drugs, since the 'reasonable person' test presumes an innocent person."

Critics of the decision saw it as creating new "gestapo-like" police powers in the face of which citizens on public transportation will feel compelled to comply with police requests for search authority. Dissenting Justices Harry Blackmun, John Paul Stevens, and Thurgood Marshall held that "the bus sweep at issue in this case violates the core values of the Fourth Amendment." The Court's majority, however, defended its ruling by writing, "[T]he Fourth Amendment proscribes unreasonable searches and seizures; it does not proscribe voluntary cooperation." In mid-2000, however, in the case of *Bond* v. *U.S.*,[130] the Court ruled that physical manipulation of a carry-on bag in the possession of a bus passenger without the owner's consent violates the Fourth Amendment's proscription against unreasonable searches.

In the case of *U.S.* v. *Drayton* (2002),[131] the U.S. Supreme Court reiterated its position that police officers are not required to advise bus passengers of their right to refuse to cooperate with officers conducting searches or of their right to refuse to be searched. In *Drayton*, the driver of a bus allowed three police officers to board the bus as part of a routine drug and weapons interdiction effort. One officer knelt on the driver's seat, facing the rear of the bus, while another officer stayed in the rear, facing forward. A third officer, named Lang, worked his way from back to front, speaking with individual passengers as he went. To avoid blocking the aisle, Lang stood next to or just behind each passenger with whom he spoke. He later testified that passengers who declined to cooperate or who chose to exit the bus at any time would have been allowed to do so without argument; that most people were willing to cooperate; that in his experience, passengers often leave buses for a cigarette or a snack while officers are on board; and that although he sometimes informed passengers of their right to refuse to cooperate, he did not do so on the day in question. As Lang approached Christopher Drayton and Clifton Brown, Jr., who were seated together, he held up his badge long enough for them to identify him as an officer. Speaking just loud enough for the two to hear, he declared that the police were looking for drugs and weapons and asked if respondents had any bags. When both of them pointed to a bag overhead, Lang asked if they minded if he checked it. Brown agreed, and a search of the bag revealed no contraband. Lang then asked Brown whether he minded if the officer checked his person. Brown agreed, and a pat-down search revealed hard objects similar to drug packages in both of Brown's thigh areas, resulting in his arrest. Lang then asked Drayton, "Mind if I check you?" When Drayton agreed, a pat-down revealed objects similar to those found on Brown, and Drayton was also arrested. A further search of the two men revealed that Drayton and Brown had taped cocaine between their legs. Both were charged with federal drug crimes. In court, their attorneys moved to suppress the cocaine as evidence, arguing that their consent to the pat-down searches was invalid. In denying the motions, the federal district court determined that the police conduct was not coercive and that the defendants' consent to the search had been voluntary. The Eleventh Circuit Court, however, reversed that finding based on the belief that bus passengers do not feel free to disregard officers' requests to search in the absence of some positive indication that consent may be refused.

CJ News

Legal Issues Being Raised in Subway Searches

Even more than security experts and intelligence analysts, one group of employees has become central to the new program of bag searches in the transit networks of the New York region: lawyers.

The decision in July 2005 to have police officers inspect the belongings of thousands of subway riders has opened a thicket of legal and constitutional issues, involving criminal procedure, transit security and concerns about potential misuse of the new tactic.

Donna Lieberman, the executive director of the New York Civil Liberties Union, said the organization had begun work on a federal lawsuit, which could be filed soon. Such a challenge will most likely claim that the policy violates the Fourth Amendment's prohibition against "unreasonable searches and seizures."

And at a news conference in Brooklyn, Capt. Eric Adams, the president of a group of black police officers, said its members were worried that riders of Middle Eastern, African or Asian descent would be disproportionately targeted in the searches, despite official assurances to the contrary.

New Jersey Transit and the Port Authority of New York and New Jersey started random searches on their trains and in their buses and stations, joining the city police and the Metropolitan Transportation Authority in conducting searches.

The four agencies have tried to sidestep a potential legal minefield by carefully specifying the limits and objectives of the policies, but the legality of the searches could well rest on subtle distinctions in the way they are carried out.

"It is by no means a foregone conclusion that these searches will be found reasonable under the Fourth Amendment," said Tracey Maclin, a law professor at Boston University. "The number of people involved, the nature and severity of the intrusions and the uncertain duration of the searches all make this fundamentally very different from anything we have seen before."

At least three United States Supreme Court cases will probably influence any judge assessing the searches.

In 1979, in *Delaware* v. *Prouse*, the court held that random traffic stops, left to the discretion of police officers, were unconstitutional. In 1990, in *Michigan* v. *Sitz*, the court upheld the legality of sobriety checkpoints in which a consistent proportion of drivers was stopped. The court ruled that such roadblocks were permitted as a way to prevent drunken driving.

The court has set limits on those roadblocks, however. In 2000, in *Indianapolis* v. *Edmond*, it struck down the use of traffic checkpoints to stop drivers so that trained dogs could sniff the vehicles for narcotics. Unlike checkpoints to make sure that drivers were sober or had valid licenses and registrations, the court said, roadblocks for general law enforcement were unconstitutional.

David D. Cole, a law professor at Georgetown University, said the government was likely to succeed in demonstrating a special need for the current searches in New York.

A judge evaluating a legal challenge, he said, would probably look at three factors: whether the searches are truly random or use standardized criteria; whether riders were given advance notice or

A police officer checking the bag of a subway rider at New York City's Forty-second Street/Bryant Park station. Should random bag checks be permitted, or do they unfairly impinge upon the rights of people wanting to ride the subway?

John Marshall Mantel/AP Wide World Photos

provided their consent to the searches; and the degree of intrusiveness. "It's very hard to predict how these cases will turn out, because it's such an open-ended balancing test," he said.

According to a two-page directive sent to all police commanders following the July 2005 subway bombings in London, the searches were begun "to increase deterrence and detection of potential terrorist activity and to give greater protection to the mass transit-riding public." The directive authorized the police to inspect "backpacks, containers and other carry-on items which are capable of containing explosive devices."

The policy includes several provisions that could help in defending the new searches from court challenges.

First, although Mayor Michael R. Bloomberg and Police Commissioner Raymond W. Kelly have described the searches as "random," they should rely on a precise frequency that is not subject to officers' discretion, according to the directive.

A supervisor at each checkpoint is supposed to determine the frequency of searches—1 in every 5, 12 or 20 passengers, for example—based on the volume of passengers, the number of officers available and the "flow of commuter traffic."

Second, extensive steps were taken to notify the public about the searches. At subway stations and train terminals, megaphone and public-address systems were used. Notices were handwritten on dry-erase boards in the booths in most subway stations. At many checkpoints, the police have set up signs on easels near the turnstiles.

The directive states that individuals who refuse to be searched can leave the subway system, and that such a refusal "shall not constitute probable cause for an arrest or reasonable suspicion for a forcible stop."

(continued)

CJ News (continued)

The degree of intrusiveness could become a thorny issue. The directive provides that officers may open a package and "physically inspect and manipulate the contents to ensure it does not contain an explosive device." Leaving aside the issue of illegal drugs or weapons, some riders have already voiced misgivings about having the police examine sensitive possessions, like medications and personal hygiene products.

Lawyers have been used extensively in writing the search policies. The deputy police commissioner for legal matters, S. Andrew Schaffer, formerly the general counsel for New York University, joined Mr. Kelly and top police commanders in completing their plans for the searches.

Similarly, Catherine A. Rinaldi, the general counsel for the Metropolitan Transportation Authority, was "intimately involved" in plans for searches on the Long Island Rail Road and Metro-North Commuter Railroad, according to Tom Kelly, a spokesman for the authority.

Ronald Susswein, an assistant attorney general in New Jersey, said that the New Jersey Transit searches would not be conducted arbitrarily. "This is not a criminal enforcement procedure," he said. "We're not trying to catch anyone. We're trying to deter terrorism."

While the majority of riders interviewed since the searches began said they supported the searches, a few have expressed concerns.

"For a split second, I thought that because of my skin complexion, they picked me," said James Hamilton, 38, whose attaché case was searched at Herald Square. "I'm not sure if I had brown hair and blue eyes, that that would have happened." He has black hair, dark brown eyes and a dark complexion.

Charles Wilson, 35, a schoolteacher whose bag was searched at Fulton Street in Lower Manhattan, said, "This is not going to make things better between the police and people of color." Mr. Wilson is black.

Captain Adams, whose organization, 100 Blacks in Law Enforcement Who Care, held a news conference immediately after the searches began, said he believed that discrimination was likely in practice, if not intent. "You can say 'no profiling,' but when you have a police department that has a history of profiling, it is going to practice what it knows," he said.

A police spokesman, Paul J. Browne, said he strongly disagreed. "These inspections are being conducted in a constitutional manner and have been met with enthusiastic cooperation by the overwhelming majority of riders we've come into contact with," he said.

For the latest in crime and justice news, visit the Talk Justice news feed at http://www.crimenews.info.

In 2004, the Court made it clear that suspicionless searches of vehicles at our nation's borders are permitted, even when the searches are extensive. In the case of *U.S.* v. *Flores-Montano*,[132] customs officials disassembled the gas tank of a car belonging to a man entering the country from Mexico and found that it contained 37 kilograms of marijuana. Although the officers admitted that their actions were not motivated by any particular belief that the search would reveal contraband, the Court held that Congress has always granted "plenary authority to conduct routine searches and seizures at the border without probable cause or a warrant." In the words of the Court, "the Government's authority to conduct suspicionless inspections at the border includes the authority to remove, disassemble and reassemble a vehicle's fuel tank."

High-Technology Searches

The burgeoning use of high technology to investigate crime and to uncover violations of the criminal law is forcing courts throughout the nation to evaluate the applicability of constitutional guarantees in light of high-tech searches and seizures. In 1996, the California appellate court decision in *People* v. *Deutsch*[133] presaged the kinds of issues that are likely to be encountered as American law enforcement expands its use of cutting-edge technology. In *Deutsch*, judges faced the question of whether a warrantless scan of a private dwelling with a thermal-imaging device constitutes an unreasonable search within the meaning of the Fourth Amendment. Such devices (also called *forward-looking infrared [FLIR] systems*) measure radiant energy in the radiant heat portion of the electromagnetic spectrum[134] and display their readings as thermographs. The "heat picture" that a thermal imager produces can be used, as it was in the case of Dorian Deutsch, to reveal unusually warm areas or rooms that might be associated with the cultivation of drug-bearing plants, such as marijuana. Two hundred cannabis plants, which were being grown hydroponically under high-wattage lights in two walled-off portions of Deutsch's home, were seized following an exterior

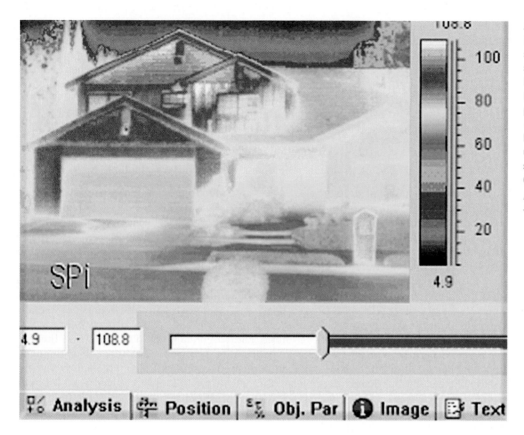

A photo created by a thermal-imaging device. The photo shows "hot spots" in a suspected marijuana grower's home that might be produced by lights used to grow the plants indoors. In *Kyllo* v. *U.S.* (2001), the U.S. Supreme Court held that the police may not use such devices without a search warrant. What was the Court's rationale?

Image compliments of Spi-www.x20.org

thermal scan of her home by a police officer who drove by at 1:30 in the morning. Because no entry of the house was anticipated during the search, the officer had acted without a search warrant. The California court ruled that the scan was an illegal search because "society accepts a reasonable expectation of privacy" surrounding "nondisclosed activities within the home."[135]

In a similar case, *Kyllo* v. *U.S* (2001),[136] the U.S. Supreme Court reached much the same conclusion. Based on the results of a warrantless search conducted by officers using a thermal-imaging device, investigators applied for a search warrant of Kyllo's home. The subsequent search uncovered more than 100 marijuana plants that were being grown under bright lights. In overturning Kyllo's conviction on drug-manufacturing charges, the Court held, "Where, as here, the Government uses a device that is not in general public use, to explore details of a private home that would previously have been unknowable without physical intrusion, the surveillance is a Fourth Amendment 'search,' and is presumptively unreasonable without a warrant."[137]

Learn more about the issues surrounding search and seizure at Web Extra 7–3 at cjtoday.com.

WEB Extra

The Intelligence Function

In law enforcement parlance, useful information is known as *intelligence*, and the need for intelligence leads police investigators to question both suspects and informants—and even more often, potentially knowledgeable citizens who may have been witnesses or victims. Data gathering is a crucial form of intelligence; without it, enforcement agencies would be virtually powerless to plan and effect arrests.

The importance of gathering intelligence in police work cannot be overstressed. Studies have found that the one factor most likely to lead to arrest in serious crimes is the presence of a witness who can provide information to the police. Undercover operations, neighborhood watch programs, "crime stopper" groups, and organized detective work all contribute this vital information.

Informants

Information gathering is a complex process, and many ethical questions have been raised about the techniques police use to gather information. The use of paid informants, for example, is an area of concern to ethicists who believe that informants are often paid while getting away with

The right of the people to be secure in their persons, houses, papers, and effects, against unreasonable searches and seizures, shall not be violated, and no Warrants shall issue, but upon probable cause, supported by Oath or affirmation, and particularly describing the place to be searched, and the persons or things to be seized.

—Fourth Amendment to the U.S. Constitution

minor crimes that investigators are willing to overlook. Another concern is the police practice (endorsed by some prosecutors) of agreeing not to charge one offender out of a group if he or she will "talk" and testify against the others.

As we have seen, probable cause is an important aspect of both police searches and legal arrests. The successful use of informants in supporting requests for a warrant depends on the demonstrable reliability of their information. The case of *Aguilar* v. *Texas* (1964)[138] clarified the use of informants and established a two-pronged test. The U.S. Supreme Court ruled that informant information can establish probable cause if both of the following criteria are met:

1. The source of the informant's information is made clear.
2. The police officer has a reasonable belief that the informant is reliable.

The two-pronged test of *Aguilar* v. *Texas* was intended to prevent the issuance of warrants on the basis of false or fabricated information. The case of *U.S.* v. *Harris* (1971)[139] provided an exception to the two-pronged *Aguilar* test. The *Harris* court recognized the fact that when an informant provides information that is damaging to him or her, it is probably true. In *Harris*, an informant told police that he had purchased non-tax-paid whiskey from another person. Since the information also implicated the informant in a crime, it was held to be accurate, even though it could not meet the second prong of the *Aguilar* test. "Admissions of crime," said the Court, "carry their own indicia of credibility—sufficient at least to support a finding of probable cause to search."[140]

In 1983, in the case of *Illinois* v. *Gates*,[141] the Court adopted a totality-of-circumstances approach, which held that sufficient probable cause for issuing a warrant exists where an informant can be reasonably believed on the basis of everything that the police know. The *Gates* case involved an anonymous informant who provided incriminating information about another person through a letter to the police. Although the source of the information was not stated and the police were unable to say whether the informant was reliable, the overall sense of things, given what was already known to police, was that the information supplied was probably valid. In *Gates*, the Court held that probable cause exists when "there is a fair probability that contraband or evidence of a crime will be found in a particular place."

In the 1990 case of *Alabama* v. *White*,[142] the Supreme Court ruled that an anonymous tip, even in the absence of other corroborating information about a suspect, could form the basis for an investigatory stop if the informant accurately predicted the *future* behavior of the suspect. The Court reasoned that the ability to predict a suspect's behavior demonstrates a significant degree of familiarity with the suspect's affairs. In the words of the Court, "Because only a small number of people are generally privy to an individual's itinerary, it is reasonable for the police to believe that a person with access to such information is likely to also have access to reliable information about that individual's illegal activities."[143]

In 2000, in the case of *Florida* v. *J. L.*,[144] the Court held that an anonymous tip that a person is carrying a gun does not, without more, justify a police officer's stop and frisk of that person. Ruling that such a search is invalid under the Fourth Amendment, the Court rejected the suggestion of a firearm exception to the general stop-and-frisk rule.[145] The identity of informants may be kept secret only if sources have been explicitly assured of confidentiality by investigating officers or if a reasonably implied assurance of confidentiality has been made. In *U.S. Dept. of Justice* v. *Landano* (1993),[146] the U.S. Supreme Court required that an informant's identity be revealed through a request made under the federal Freedom of Information Act. In that case, the FBI had not specifically assured the informant of confidentiality, and the Court ruled that "the government is not entitled to a presumption that all sources supplying information to the FBI in the course of a criminal investigation are confidential sources."

Police Interrogation

In 2003, Illinois became the first state in the nation to require the electronic recording of police interrogations and confessions in homicide cases.[147] State lawmakers hoped that the use of recordings would reduce the incidence of false confessions as well as the likelihood of convictions based on such confessions. Under the law, police interrogators must create videotape or audiotape recordings of any questioning of suspects. The law prohibits the courtroom introduction of statements and confessions that have not been taped. Proponents of the law say that it will prevent the police intimidation of murder suspects and will put an end to coerced confessions.

The U.S. Supreme Court has defined **interrogation** as any behaviors by the police "that the police should know are reasonably likely to elicit an incriminating response from the suspect."[148] Hence, interrogation may involve activities that go well beyond mere verbal questioning, and the Court has held that interrogation may include "staged lineups, reverse lineups, positing guilt,

interrogation

The information-gathering activity of police officers that involves the direct questioning of suspects.

minimizing the moral seriousness of crime, and casting blame on the victim or society." The Court has also held that "police words or actions normally attendant to arrest and custody do not constitute interrogation" unless they involve pointed or directed questions. Hence, an arresting officer may instruct a suspect on what to do and may chitchat with him or her without engaging in interrogation within the meaning of the law. Once police officers make inquiries intended to elicit information about the crime in question, however, interrogation has begun. The interrogation of suspects, like other areas of police activity, is subject to constitutional limits as interpreted by the courts, and a series of landmark decisions by the U.S. Supreme Court has focused on police interrogation.

PHYSICAL ABUSE

The first in a series of significant cases regarding police interrogation was *Brown* v. *Mississippi*,[149] decided in 1936. The *Brown* case began with the robbery of a white store owner in Mississippi in 1934 during which the store owner was killed. A posse formed and went to the home of a local African American man rumored to have been one of the perpetrators. They dragged the suspect from his home, put a rope around his neck, and hoisted and lowered him from a tree a number of times, hoping to get a confession from the man, but failing. The posse was headed by a deputy sheriff who then arrested other suspects in the case and laid them over chairs in the local jail and whipped them with belts and buckles until they "confessed." These confessions were used in the trial that followed, and all three defendants were convicted of murder. Their convictions were upheld by the Mississippi Supreme Court. In 1936, however, the case was reviewed by the U.S. Supreme Court, which overturned all of the convictions, saying that it was difficult to imagine techniques of interrogation more "revolting" to the sense of justice than those used in this case.

INHERENT COERCION

Interrogation need not involve physical abuse for it to be contrary to constitutional principles. In the case of *Ashcraft* v. *Tennessee* (1944),[150] the U.S. Supreme Court found that interrogation involving **inherent coercion** was not acceptable. Ashcraft had been charged with the murder of his wife, Zelma. He was arrested on a Saturday night and interrogated by relays of skilled interrogators until Monday morning, when he purportedly made a statement implicating himself in the murder. During questioning, he had faced a blinding light but was not physically mistreated. Investigators later testified that when the suspect requested cigarettes, food, or water, they "kindly" provided them. The Court's ruling, which reversed Ashcraft's conviction, made it plain that the Fifth Amendment guarantee against self-incrimination excludes any form of official coercion or pressure during interrogation.

A similar case, *Chambers* v. *Florida*, was decided in 1940.[151] In that case, four black men were arrested without warrants as suspects in the robbery and murder of an aged white man. After several days of questioning in a hostile atmosphere, the men confessed to the murder. The confessions were used as the primary evidence against them at their trial, and all four were sentenced to die. On appeal, the U.S. Supreme Court held that "the very circumstances surrounding their confinement and their questioning without any formal charges having been brought, were such as to fill petitioners with terror and frightful misgivings."[152] Learn more about the case of *Chambers* v. *Florida* at Library Extra 7–4 at cjtoday.com.

PSYCHOLOGICAL MANIPULATION

Not only must interrogation be free of coercion and hostility, but it also cannot involve sophisticated trickery designed to ferret out a confession. Interrogators do not necessarily have to be scrupulously honest in confronting suspects, and the expert opinions of medical and psychiatric practitioners may be sought in investigations. However, the use of professionals skilled in **psychological manipulation** to gain confessions was banned by the Court in the case of *Leyra* v. *Denno*[153] in 1954, during the heyday of psychiatric perspectives on criminal behavior.

In the *Leyra* case, detectives employed a psychiatrist to question Camilo Leyra, who had been charged with the hammer slayings of his parents. Leyra had been led to believe that the medical doctor to whom he was introduced in an interrogation room had actually been sent to help him with a sinus problem. Following a period of questioning, including subtle suggestions by the psychiatrist that he would feel better if he confessed to the murders, Leyra did indeed confess.

The Supreme Court, on appeal, ruled that the defendant had been effectively and improperly duped by the police. In the words of the Court, "Instead of giving petitioner the medical advice and treatment he expected, the psychiatrist by subtle and suggestive questions simply continued the police effort of the past days and nights to induce petitioner to admit his guilt. For an hour

inherent coercion

The tactics used by police interviewers that fall short of physical abuse but that nonetheless pressure suspects to divulge information.

LIBRARY
Extra
▪ ▪ ▪ ▪

psychological manipulation

Manipulative actions by police interviewers that are designed to pressure suspects to divulge information and that are based on subtle forms of intimidation and control.

and a half or more the techniques of a highly trained psychiatrist were used to break petitioner's will in order to get him to say he had murdered his parents."[154]

In 1991, in the case of *Arizona* v. *Fulminante*,[155] the U.S. Supreme Court further curtailed the use of sophisticated techniques to gain a confession. Oreste Fulminante was an inmate in a federal prison when he was approached by a fellow inmate who was an FBI informant. The informant told Fulminante that other inmates were plotting to kill him because of a rumor that he had killed a child. The informant offered to protect Fulminante if he divulged the details of his crime. Fulminante then described his role in the murder of his 11-year-old stepdaughter. He was charged with that murder, tried, and convicted.

On appeal to the U.S. Supreme Court, Fulminante's lawyers argued that their client's confession had been coerced because of the threat of violence communicated by the informant. The Court agreed that the confession had been coerced and ordered a new trial at which the confession could not be admitted into evidence. Simultaneously, however, the Court found that the admission of a coerced confession should be considered a harmless "trial error" that need not necessarily result in reversal of a conviction if other evidence still proves guilt. The decision was especially significant because it partially reversed the Court's earlier ruling, in *Chapman* v. *California* (1967),[156] where it was held that forced confessions were such a basic form of constitutional error that they automatically invalidated any conviction to which they related. Fulminante was convicted again at his second trial, where his confession was not entered into evidence, and he was sentenced to die. The Arizona Supreme Court, however, overturned his conviction, ruling that testimony describing statements the victim had made about fearing for her life prior to her murder, and which had been entered into evidence, were hearsay and had prejudiced the jury.[157]

The Right to a Lawyer at Interrogation

> *While every person is entitled to stand silent, it is more virtuous for the wrongdoer to admit his offense and accept the punishment he deserves. . . . It is wrong, and subtly corrosive of our criminal justice system, to regard an honest confession as a mistake.*
>
> —Justice Antonin Scalia, dissenting in Minnick v. Mississippi, 498 U.S. 146 (1990)

In 1964, in the case of *Escobedo* v. *Illinois*,[158] the Supreme Court recognized the right to have legal counsel present during police interrogation. Danny Escobedo was arrested for the murder of his brother-in-law. During the interrogation that followed, officers told him that they "had him cold" and that he should confess. Escobedo asked to see his lawyer but was told that an interrogation was in progress and that he couldn't see his lawyer. Soon the lawyer arrived and asked to see Escobedo. Police told him that his client was being questioned and could be seen after questioning concluded. Escobedo later claimed that while he repeatedly asked for his lawyer, he was told, "Your lawyer doesn't want to see you." Eventually, Escobedo confessed and was convicted at trial on the basis of his confession. Upon appeal, the U.S. Supreme Court overturned Escobedo's conviction, ruling that counsel is necessary at police interrogations to protect the rights of the defendant and should be provided when the defendant desires.

In 1981, the case of *Edwards* v. *Arizona*[159] established a "bright-line rule" (that is, specified a criterion that cannot be violated) for investigators to use in interpreting a suspect's right to counsel. In *Edwards*, the Supreme Court reiterated its *Miranda* concern that once a suspect who is in custody and is being questioned requests the assistance of counsel, all questioning must cease until an attorney is present. In 1990, the Court refined the rule in *Minnick* v. *Mississippi*,[160] when it held that after the suspect has had an opportunity to consult his or her lawyer, interrogation may not resume unless the lawyer is present. Similarly, according to *Arizona* v. *Roberson* (1988),[161] the police may not avoid the suspect's request for a lawyer by beginning a new line of questioning, even if it is about an unrelated offense.

In 1994, however, in the case of *Davis* v. *U.S.*,[162] the Court "put the burden on custodial suspects to make unequivocal invocations of the right to counsel." In the *Davis* case, a man being interrogated in the death of a sailor waived his *Miranda* rights but later said, "Maybe I should talk to a lawyer." Investigators asked the suspect clarifying questions, and he responded, "No, I don't want a lawyer." He appealed his conviction, claiming that interrogation should have ceased when he mentioned a lawyer. The Court, in affirming the conviction, stated that "it will often be good police practice for the interviewing officers to clarify whether or not [the suspect] actually wants an attorney."

Miranda warnings

The advisement of rights due criminal suspects by the police before questioning begins. *Miranda* warnings were first set forth by the U.S. Supreme Court in the 1966 case of *Miranda* v. *Arizona*.

Suspect Rights: The *Miranda* Decision

In the area of suspect rights, no case is as famous as *Miranda* v. *Arizona* (1966),[163] which established the well-known ***Miranda* warnings**. Many people regard *Miranda* as the centerpiece of the Warren Court due process rulings.

The case involved Ernesto Miranda, who was arrested in Phoenix, Arizona, and was accused of having kidnapped and raped a young woman. At police headquarters, he was identified by the victim. After being interrogated for two hours, Miranda signed a confession that formed the basis of his later conviction on the charges.

On appeal, the U.S. Supreme Court rendered what some regard as the most far-reaching opinion to have affected criminal justice in the last half century. The Court ruled that Miranda's conviction was unconstitutional because "[t]he entire aura and atmosphere of police interrogation without notification of rights and an offer of assistance of counsel tends to subjugate the individual to the will of his examiner."

The Court continued, saying that the suspect "must be warned prior to any questioning that he has the right to remain silent, that anything he says can be used against him in a court of law, that he has the right to the presence of an attorney, and that if he cannot afford an attorney one will be appointed for him prior to any questioning if he so desires. Opportunity to exercise these rights must be afforded to him throughout the interrogation. After such warnings have been given, and such opportunity afforded him, the individual may knowingly and intelligently waive these rights and agree to answer the questions or make a statement. But unless and until such warnings and waiver are demonstrated by the prosecution at the trial, no evidence obtained as a result of interrogation can be used against him."

To ensure that proper advice is given to suspects at the time of their arrest, the now-famous *Miranda* rights are read before any questioning begins. These rights, as found on a *Miranda* warning card commonly used by police agencies, appear in CJ Today Exhibit 7–2.

Once suspects have been advised of their *Miranda* rights, they are commonly asked to sign a paper that lists each right, in order to confirm that they were advised of their rights and that they understand each right. Questioning may then begin, but only if suspects waive their rights not to talk and to have a lawyer present during interrogation.

In 1992, *Miranda* rights were effectively extended to illegal immigrants living in the United States. In a settlement reached in Los Angeles of a class-action lawsuit with the Immigration and Naturalization Service, U.S. District Court Judge William Byrne, Jr., approved the printing of millions of notices in several languages to be given to arrestees. The approximately 1.5 million illegal aliens arrested each year must be told they may (1) talk with a lawyer, (2) make a phone call, (3) request a list of available legal services, (4) seek a hearing before an immigration judge, (5) possibly obtain release on bond, and (6) contact a diplomatic officer representing their country.[164] This was "long overdue," said Roberto Martinez of the American Friends Service Committee's

CJ Today Exhibit 7–2

The *Miranda* Warnings

ADULT RIGHTS WARNING

Suspects 18 years old or older who are in custody must be advised of the following rights before any questioning begins:

1. You have the right to remain silent.

2. Anything you say can be used against you in a court of law.

3. You have the right to talk to a lawyer and to have a lawyer present while you are being questioned.

4. If you want a lawyer before or during questioning but cannot afford to hire a lawyer, one will be appointed to represent you at no cost before any questioning.

5. If you answer questions now without a lawyer here, you still have the right to stop answering questions at any time.

WAIVER OF RIGHTS

After reading and explaining the rights of a person in custody, an officer must also ask for a waiver of those rights before any questioning. The following waiver questions must be answered affirmatively, either by express answer or by clear implication. Silence alone is not a waiver.

1. Do you understand each of these rights I have explained to you? (Answer must be YES.)

2. Having these rights in mind, do you now wish to answer questions? (Answer must be YES.)

3. Do you now wish to answer questions without a lawyer present? (Answer must be YES.)

   The following question must be asked of juveniles ages 14, 15, 16, and 17:

4. Do you now wish to answer questions without your parents, guardians, or custodians present? (Answer must be YES.)

Source: North Carolina Justice Academy. Reprinted with permission.

Ernesto Miranda, shown here after a jury convicted him for a second time. Miranda's conviction on rape and kidnapping charges after arresting officers failed to advise him of his rights led to the now-famous *Miranda* warnings. What do the *Miranda* warnings say?

AP Wide World Photos

Mexico-U.S. border program. "Up to now, we've had total mistreatment of civil rights of undocumented people."

When the *Miranda* decision was originally handed down, some hailed it as ensuring the protection of individual rights guaranteed under the Constitution. To guarantee those rights, they suggested, no better agency is available than the police themselves, since the police are present at the initial stages of the criminal justice process. Critics of *Miranda*, however, argued that the decision put police agencies in the uncomfortable and contradictory position not only of enforcing the law but also of having to offer defendants advice on how they might circumvent conviction and punishment. Under *Miranda*, the police partially assume the role of legal adviser to the accused.

In 1999, however, in the case of *U.S.* v. *Dickerson*,[165] the Fourth Circuit U.S. Court of Appeals upheld an almost-forgotten law that Congress had passed in 1968 with the intention of overturning *Miranda*. That law, Section 3501 of Chapter 223, Part II of Title 18 of the U.S. Code, says that "a confession . . . shall be admissible in evidence if it is voluntarily given." On appeal in 2000, the U.S. Supreme Court upheld its original *Miranda* ruling by a 7–2 vote and found that *Miranda* is a constitutional rule (that is, a fundamental right inherent in the U.S. Constitution) that cannot be dismissed by an act of Congress. "*Miranda* and its progeny," the majority wrote in *Dickerson* v. *U.S.* (2000), will continue to "govern the admissibility of statements made during custodial interrogation in both state and federal courts."[166]

Read the full text of the original *Miranda* decision, the text of Section 3501 of the U.S. Code, the Fourth Circuit Court's 1999 opinion in *Dickerson*, and the final U.S. Supreme Court majority and dissenting opinions at the *Miranda* Revisited website via Web Extra 7–4 at cjtoday.com.

WEB
Extra

WAIVER OF *MIRANDA* RIGHTS BY SUSPECTS

Suspects in police custody may legally waive their *Miranda* rights through a *voluntary* "knowing and intelligent" waiver. A *knowing waiver* can only be made if a suspect is advised of his or her rights and is in a condition to understand the advisement. A rights advisement made in English to a Spanish-speaking suspect, for example, cannot produce a knowing waiver. Likewise, an

A suspect being read his *Miranda* rights immediately after arrest. Officers often read *Miranda* rights from a card to preclude the possibility of mistake. What might be the consequences of a mistake?
Michael Newman/PhotoEdit Inc.

intelligent waiver of rights requires that the defendant be able to understand the consequences of not invoking the *Miranda* rights. In the case of *Moran* v. *Burbine* (1986),[167] the U.S. Supreme Court defined an intelligent and knowing waiver as one "made with a full awareness both of the nature of the right being abandoned and the consequences of the decision to abandon it." Similarly, in *Colorado* v. *Spring* (1987),[168] the Court held that an intelligent and knowing waiver can be made even though a suspect has not been informed of all the alleged offenses about which he or she is about to be questioned.

INEVITABLE-DISCOVERY EXCEPTION TO *MIRANDA*

The case of Robert Anthony Williams provides a good example of the change in the U.S. Supreme Court philosophy, alluded to earlier in this chapter, from an individual-rights perspective toward a public-order perspective. The case epitomizes what many consider a slow erosion of the advances in defendant rights, which reached their apex in *Miranda*. This case began in 1969, at the close of the Warren Court era. Williams was apprehended as a suspect in the murder of ten-year-old Pamela Powers around Christmas time and was advised of his rights. Later, as Williams rode in a car with detectives who were searching for the girl's body, one of the detectives made what has since become known as the "Christian burial speech." The detective told Williams that since Christmas was almost upon them, it would be "the Christian thing to do" to see to it that Pamela had a decent burial rather than having to lie in a field somewhere. Williams confessed and led detectives to the body. However, because Williams had not been reminded of his right to have a lawyer present during his conversation with the detective, the Supreme Court in *Brewer* v. *Williams* (1977)[169] overturned Williams's conviction, saying that the detective's remarks were "a deliberate eliciting of incriminating evidence from an accused in the absence of his lawyer."

In 1977, Williams was retried for the murder, but his remarks in leading detectives to the body were not entered into evidence. The discovery of the body was used, however, and Williams was convicted, prompting another appeal to the Supreme Court based on the argument that the body should not have been used as evidence since it was discovered due to the illegally gathered statements. This time, in the 1984 case of *Nix* v. *Williams*,[170] the Supreme Court affirmed Williams's second conviction, holding that the body would have been found anyway, since detectives were searching in the direction where it lay when Williams revealed its location. This ruling came during the heyday of the Burger Court and clearly demonstrates a tilt by the Court away from suspects' rights and an acknowledgment of the imperfect world of police procedure. The *Williams* case, as it was finally resolved, is said to have created the inevitable-discovery exception to the

Miranda requirements. The inevitable-discovery exception means that evidence, even if it was otherwise gathered inappropriately, can be used in a court of law if it would have invariably turned up in the normal course of events.

PUBLIC-SAFETY EXCEPTION TO *MIRANDA*

Also in 1984, the U.S. Supreme Court established what has come to be known as the *public-safety exception* to the *Miranda* rule. The case of *New York* v. *Quarles*[171] centered on a rape in which the victim told police her assailant had a gun and had fled into a nearby supermarket. Two police officers entered the store and apprehended the suspect. One officer immediately noticed that the man was wearing an empty shoulder holster and, fearing that a child might find the discarded weapon, quickly asked, "Where's the gun?" Quarles was convicted of rape but appealed his conviction, requesting that the weapon be suppressed as evidence because officers had not advised him of his *Miranda* rights before asking him about it. The Supreme Court disagreed, stating that considerations of public safety were overriding and negated the need for rights advisement prior to limited questioning that focused on the need to prevent further harm.

The U.S. Supreme Court has also held that in cases when the police issue *Miranda* warnings, a later demonstration that a person may have been suffering from mental problems does not necessarily negate a confession. *Colorado* v. *Connelly* (1986)[172] involved a man who approached a Denver police officer and said he wanted to confess to the murder of a young girl. The officer immediately informed him of his *Miranda* rights, but the man waived them and continued to talk. When a detective arrived, the man was again advised of his rights and again waived them. After being taken to the local jail, the man began to hear "voices" and later claimed that it was these voices that had made him confess. At the trial, the defense moved to have the earlier confession negated on the basis that it was not voluntarily or freely given because of the defendant's mental condition. On appeal, the U.S. Supreme Court disagreed, saying that "no coercive government conduct occurred in this case." Hence, "self-coercion," due to either a guilty conscience or faulty thought processes, does not bar prosecution based on information revealed willingly by a suspect.

The 1986 case of *Kuhlmann* v. *Wilson*[173] represents another refinement of *Miranda*. In this case, the Court upheld a police informant's lawful ability to gather information for use at a trial from a defendant while the two were placed together in a jail cell. The passive gathering of information was judged to be acceptable, provided that the informant did not make attempts to elicit information.

In the case of *Illinois* v. *Perkins* (1990),[174] the Court expanded its position to say that under appropriate circumstances, even the active questioning of a suspect by an undercover officer posing as a fellow inmate does not require *Miranda* warnings. In *Perkins*, the Court found that, lacking other forms of coercion, the fact that the suspect was not aware of the questioner's identity as a law enforcement officer ensured that his statements were freely given. In the words of the Court, "The essential ingredients of a 'police-dominated atmosphere' and compulsion are not present when an incarcerated person speaks freely to someone that he believes to be a fellow inmate."

MIRANDA AND THE MEANING OF INTERROGATION

Modern interpretations of the applicability of *Miranda* warnings turn on an understanding of interrogation. The *Miranda* decision, as originally rendered, specifically recognized the need for police investigators to make inquiries at crime scenes to determine facts or to establish identities. As long as the individual questioned is not yet in custody and as long as probable cause is lacking in the investigator's mind, such questioning can proceed without *Miranda* warnings. In such cases, interrogation, within the meaning of *Miranda*, has not yet begun.

The case of *Rock* v. *Zimmerman* (1982)[175] provides a different sort of example—one in which a suspect willingly made statements to the police before interrogation began. The suspect had set fire to his own house and shot and killed a neighbor. When the fire department arrived, he began shooting again and killed the fire chief. Cornered later in a field, the defendant, gun in hand, spontaneously shouted at police, "How many people did I kill? How many people are dead?"[176] This spontaneous statement was held to be admissible evidence at the suspect's trial.

It is also important to recognize that in the *Miranda* decision, the Supreme Court required that officers provide warnings only in those situations involving *both* arrest and custodial interrogation—what some call the **Miranda triggers**. In other words, it is generally permissible for officers to take a suspect into custody and listen, without asking questions, while he or she talks. Similarly, they may ask questions without providing a *Miranda* warning, even within the confines of a police station house, as long as the person questioned is not a suspect and is not under arrest.[177] Warnings are required only when officers begin to actively and deliberately elicit responses from a suspect whom they know has been indicted or who is in custody.

Miranda triggers

The dual principles of custody and interrogation, both of which are necessary before an advisement of rights is required.

Officers were found to have acted properly in the case of *South Dakota* v. *Neville* (1983)[178] when they informed a man suspected of driving while intoxicated (DWI), without reading him his rights, that he would stand to lose his driver's license if he did not submit to a Breathalyzer test. When the driver responded, "I'm too drunk. I won't pass the test," his answer became evidence of his condition and was permitted at trial.

A third-party conversation recorded by the police after a suspect has invoked the *Miranda* right to remain silent may be used as evidence, according to a 1987 ruling in *Arizona* v. *Mauro*.[179] In *Mauro*, a man who willingly conversed with his wife in the presence of a police tape recorder, even after invoking his right to keep silent, was held to have effectively abandoned that right.

When a waiver is not made, however, in-court references to a defendant's silence following the issuing of *Miranda* warnings are unconstitutional. In the 1976 case of *Doyle* v. *Ohio*,[180] the U.S. Supreme Court definitively ruled that "a suspect's [post-*Miranda*] silence will not be used against him." Even so, according to the Court in *Brecht* v. *Abrahamson* (1993),[181] prosecution efforts to use such silence against a defendant may not invalidate a finding of guilt by a jury unless the "error had substantial and injurious effect or influence in determining the jury's verdict."[182]

Of course, when a person is *not* a suspect and is *not* charged with a crime, *Miranda* warnings need not be given. Such logic led to what some have called a "fractured opinion"[183] in the 2003 case of *Chavez* v. *Martinez*.[184] The case involved Oliverio Martinez, who was blinded and paralyzed in a police shooting after he grabbed an officer's weapon during an altercation. An Oxnard, California, police officer named Chavez persisted in questioning Martinez while he was awaiting treatment despite his pleas to stop and the fact that he was obviously in great pain. The Court held that "police questioning in [the] absence of *Miranda* warnings, even questioning that is overbearing to [the] point of coercion, does not violate constitutional protections against self-incrimination, as long as no incriminating statements are introduced at trial."[185] Nonetheless, the Court found that Martinez could bring a civil suit against Chavez and the Oxnard Police Department for violation of his constitutional right to due process.

Gathering Special Kinds of Nontestimonial Evidence

The role of law enforcement is complicated by the fact that suspects are often privy to special evidence of a nontestimonial sort. Nontestimonial evidence is generally physical evidence, and most physical evidence is subject to normal procedures of search and seizure. A special category of nontestimonial evidence, however, includes very personal items that may be within or part of a person's body, such as ingested drugs, blood cells, foreign objects, medical implants, and human DNA. Also included in this category are fingerprints and other kinds of biological residue. The gathering of such special kinds of nontestimonial evidence is a complex area rich in precedent. The Fourth Amendment guarantee that people be secure in their homes and in their persons has generally been interpreted by the courts to mean that the improper seizure of physical evidence of any kind is illegal and will result in exclusion of that evidence at trial. When very personal kinds of nontestimonial evidence are considered, however, the issue becomes more complicated.

THE RIGHT TO PRIVACY

Two 1985 cases, *Hayes* v. *Florida*[186] and *Winston* v. *Lee*,[187] provide examples of limits the courts have placed on the seizure of very personal forms of nontestimonial evidence. The *Hayes* case established the right of suspects to refuse to be fingerprinted when probable cause necessary to effect an arrest does not exist. *Winston* demonstrated the inviolability of the body against surgical and other substantially invasive techniques that might be ordered by authorities against a suspect's will.

In the *Winston* case, Rudolph Lee, Jr., was found a few blocks from the scene of a robbery with a gunshot wound in his chest. The robbery had involved an exchange of gunshots by the store owner and the robber, with the owner noting that the robber had apparently been hit by a bullet. At the hospital, the store owner identified Lee as the robber. The prosecution sought to have Lee submit to surgery to remove the bullet in his chest, arguing that the bullet would provide physical evidence linking him to the crime. Lee refused the surgery, and in *Winston* v. *Lee*, the U.S. Supreme Court ruled that Lee could not be ordered to undergo surgery because intrusion into his body of that magnitude was unacceptable under the right to privacy guaranteed by the Fourth Amendment. The *Winston* case was based on precedent established in *Schmerber* v. *California* (1966).[188] The *Schmerber* case turned on the extraction against the defendant's will of a blood sample to be measured for alcohol content. In *Schmerber*, the Court ruled that warrants must be obtained for bodily intrusions unless fast action is necessary to prevent the destruction of evidence by natural physiological processes.

CJ Today Exhibit 7–3

Miranda Update

On June 28, 2004, the U.S. Supreme Court handed down two important decisions—*U.S.* v. *Patane*[1] and *Missouri* v. *Seibert*[2]—in a continuing refinement of its original 1966 ruling in *Miranda* v. *Arizona*.[3]

As described in this chapter, *Miranda* created a presumption of coercion in all custodial interrogations. Generally speaking, only a demonstration that *Miranda* warnings have been provided to a suspect has been sufficient to counter that presumption and to allow legal proceedings based on the fruits of an interrogation to move forward. Consequently, some scholars were surprised by *Patane*, in which the Court found that "a mere failure to give *Miranda* warnings does not, by itself, violate a suspect's constitutional rights or even the *Miranda* rule."

The *Patane* case began with the arrest of a convicted felon after a federal agent told officers that the man owned a handgun illegally. At the time of arrest, the officers tried to advise the defendant of his rights, but he interrupted them, saying that he already knew his rights. The officers then asked him about the pistol, and he told them where it was. After the weapon was recovered, the defendant was charged with illegal possession of a firearm by a convicted felon.

At first glance, *Patane* appears to contradict the fruit of the poisoned tree doctrine that the Court established in the 1920 case of *Silverthorne Lumber Co.* v. *U.S.*[4] and that *Wong Sun* v. *U.S.* (1963)[5] made applicable to verbal evidence derived immediately from an illegal search and seizure. An understanding of *Patane*, however, requires recognition of the fact that the *Miranda* rule is based on the self-incrimination clause of the Fifth Amendment to the U.S. Constitution. According to the Court in *Patane*, "that Clause's core protection is a prohibition on compelling a criminal defendant to testify against himself at trial." It cannot be violated, the Court said, "by the introduction of nontestimonial evidence obtained as a result of voluntary statements." In other words, according to the Court, only (1) coerced statements and (2) those voluntary statements made by

a defendant that might directly incriminate him or her at a later trial are precluded by a failure to read a suspect his or her *Miranda* rights. Such voluntary statements would, of course, include such things as an outright confession.

Significantly, however, oral statements must be distinguished, the Court said, from the "physical fruits of the suspect's unwarned but voluntary statements." In other words, if an unwarned suspect is questioned by police officers and tells the officers where they can find an illegal weapon or a weapon that has been used in a crime, the weapon can be recovered and later introduced as evidence at the suspect's trial. If the same unwarned suspect, however, tells police that he committed a murder, then his confession will not be allowed into evidence at trial. The line drawn by the court is against the admissibility of *oral statements* made by an unwarned defendant, not the *nontestimonial physical evidence* resulting from continued police investigation of such statements. Under *Patane*, the oral statements themselves cannot be admitted, but the physical evidence derived from them can be. "Thus," wrote the justices in *Patane*, "admission of nontestimonial physical fruits (the pistol here) does not run the risk of admitting into trial an accused's coerced incriminating statements against himself."

The *Seibert* case addressed a far different issue: that of the legality of a two-step police interrogation technique in which suspects were questioned and—if they made incriminating statements—were then advised of their *Miranda* rights and questioned again. The justices found that such a technique could not meet constitutional muster, writing, "When the [*Miranda*] warnings are inserted in the midst of coordinated and continuing interrogation, they are likely to mislead and deprive a defendant of knowledge essential to his ability to understand the nature of his rights and the consequences of abandoning them. . . . And it would be unrealistic to treat two spates of integrated and proximately conducted questioning as independent interrogations . . . simply because *Miranda* warnings formally punctuate them in the middle."

[1] *U.S.* v. *Patane*, 542 U.S. 630 (2004).
[2] *Missouri* v. *Seibert*, 542 U.S. 600 (2004).
[3] *Miranda* v. *Arizona*, 384 U.S. 436 (1966).
[4] *Silverthorne Lumber Co.* v. *U.S.*, 251 U.S. 385 (1920).
[5] *Wong Sun* v. *U.S.*, 371 US 471 (1963).

BODY-CAVITY SEARCHES

In early 2005, officers of the Suffolk County (New York) Police Department arrested 36-year-old Terrance Haynes and charged him with marijuana possession.[189] After placing him in the back of a patrol car, Haynes appeared to choke and had difficulty breathing. Soon his breathing stopped, prompting officers to use the Heimlich maneuver, which dislodged a plastic bag from Haynes's windpipe. The bag contained eleven packets of cocaine. Although Haynes survived the ordeal, he now faces up to 25 years in prison.

While some suspects might literally "cough up" evidence, some are more successful at hiding it *in* their bodies. Body-cavity searches are among the most problematic types of searches for police today. "Strip" searches of convicts in prison, including the search of body cavities, have generally been held to be permissible.

CJ News

Police DNA Collection Sparks Questions

When a 60-year-old man spat on the sidewalk, his DNA became as public as if he had been advertising it across his chest.

Police officers secretly following Leon Chatt [in August 2006] collected the saliva—loaded with Chatt's unique genetic makeup—to compare with DNA evidence from the scene of an old murder they believed he'd committed.

On Feb. 1, [2007,] Chatt was charged in one of Buffalo's oldest unsolved cases, the 1974 rape and stabbing of his wife's stepsister, Barbara Lloyd.

While secretly collecting a suspect's DNA may be an unorthodox approach to solving crimes, prosecutors say it crosses no legal boundaries—that when someone leaves their DNA in a public place via flakes of skin, strands of hair or saliva, for example, they give up any expectation of privacy.

But the practice has raised questions from Washington state to Florida, where similar collections are under scrutiny.

"If we felt it wasn't proper and we didn't have a strong legal foundation, we wouldn't have done it," Erie County [New York] District Attorney Frank Clark said, discussing another recent case involving secretly obtained DNA.

In that case, the smoking gun was tableware the suspect used during a night out with his wife. Undercover investigators had waited out Altemio Sanchez at the bar of a Buffalo restaurant one evening and moved in on his water glass and utensils after he'd gone.

Two days later, the 49-year-old factory worker and father of two was charged with being the elusive "Bike Path Rapist" believed responsible for the deaths of three women and rape of numerous others from the early 1980s through 2006.

Lawyers for Sanchez and Chatt say both men continue to profess their innocence. Both have pleaded not guilty to charges of second-degree murder and their cases are pending in the courts.

DNA, which is unique to every person, has become a cold case squad's best friend. Investigators can re-examine things like hair, blood, semen and carpet fibers from decades-old crime scenes and cross-reference the DNA with ever expanding databases kept by law enforcement.

"It's one of the greatest tools that law enforcement has today," said Dennis Richards, the Buffalo Police Department's chief of detectives.

New York state last year underscored the value of DNA by tripling, to about 46%, the number of people convicted of crimes who must submit a sample to the state's database.

To catch up on a backlog, Erie County in January conducted an unusual two-day DNA "blitz." Hundreds of convicts who "owed" a sample were summoned to a downtown courthouse, where an assembly line of sorts was set up to swab their mouths.

But it is the so-called "abandoned" DNA like that collected from Sanchez and Chatt—and suspects elsewhere arrested based on discarded cigarettes or chewing gum—that concerns people like Elizabeth Joh. The University of California law professor believes it is time legislators consider regulating such collections out of concerns for privacy.

Right now, police rely on abandoned DNA when they lack enough evidence to obtain a court-ordered sample.

Karin Strom, who authorities allege was strangled in her home almost 30 years ago by Utah resident Edward Owens, 56. Owens, who was in his twenties at the time of the murder, surrendered to police in 2007 after tests determined that it was his DNA that had been scraped from under the fingernails of Strom years ago. The sophisticated tests, which were not available at the time of the murder, used DNA from material that had been saved in an evidence locker. Owens was charged with first-degree felony murder in the death of Strom. His arrest, like others discussed in this box, has raised questions about how DNA samples can be collected from criminal suspects. Should "public" DNA be readily available to police officers, just like discarded trash?
Woods Cross Police Department

"If we look at this kind of evidence as abandoned, then it really permits the police to collect DNA from anyone—not just cold case issues—from anyone at any time and really for no good reason or any reason at all," Joh said.

"That's something that maybe sounds like a science fiction scenario—police running after people trying to get their DNA," she said, "but we really don't know where this could lead."

Asked whether there should be boundaries on such collections, Richards said, "That's one for the lawyers to argue in a court of law."

Chatt's attorney, John Jordan, said he would "absolutely" challenge the DNA evidence in his client's case in court but declined to elaborate.

(continued)

CJ News (continued)

Prosecutors tend to view abandoned DNA as akin to trash, which courts have upheld as fair game for investigators, Joh said.

She pointed to the case of *California* v. *Greenwood*, in which the U.S. Supreme Court ruled in 1988 that police did not need a warrant to search a suspected drug dealer's trash because he should have had no expectation of privacy when he placed it on the curb. Trash, the judges wrote, is "readily accessible to animals, children, scavengers, snoops, and other members of the public."

But Joh argued comparing DNA and trash is a poor analogy.

"Obviously, we might want to discard that cigarette, but do we really mean to give up all kinds of privacy claims in the genetic material that might lie therein?" she asked.

As advances in technology make DNA analysis faster and cheaper, "I think of it really as a kind of frontier issue," she said.

Richards, meanwhile, pointed out that while abandoned DNA can confirm a suspect's identity, it also works to the benefit of someone who is innocent.

"DNA rules people in, but it also rules people out," he said.

That point was not lost on the husband of murder victim Barbara Lloyd, who was questioned for hours after he reported his wife's death from 16 stab wounds in their bedroom that March 1974 morning. Police ruled Galan Lloyd out as a suspect after a few days.

Chatt's arrest, he said, proved that was the right decision.

"If there were people out there who still thought I did it, this should do it," Lloyd, now 59, told *The Buffalo News*.

Barbara Lloyd was killed as her then-3-year-old son, Joseph, and 14-month-old daughter, Kimberly, slept. The now-grown children recently persuaded police to take another look at the killing, leading police to close in on Chatt.

"We were very fortunate that at that time there was a detective in the evidence collection unit who was able to secure evidence from the scene which was later used for comparison," Richards said. "Here we are 30 years later, able to open up a box and submit some of the items that we found and to have a DNA analysis done."

Joh suggests proceeding with caution.

"My hope is there will be much greater awareness of what this means, not just for these particular cases, but for everyone," she said. "Is DNA sampling going to be ordinary and uncontroversial for the general population, in which case abandoned DNA may not be so alarming, or does it raise a whole host of privacy questions?"

For the latest in crime and justice news, visit the Talk Justice news feed at http://www.crimenews.info.

Source: Carolyn Thompson, "Police DNA Collection Sparks Questions," © March 17, 2007 by The Associated Press. Reprinted by permission.

Prosecutors and police perform the balancing test every day between individual rights and the right of citizens to be free of crime in their homes and neighborhoods, and they are watched over closely by our courts. For all in law enforcement, this balancing of rights is not an academic exercise, but a real test, where the consequence of being wrong is that a killer may go free, or even worse, an innocent man may be convicted.

—Cape Cod, Massachusetts, prosecutor Michael O'Keefe[ii]

The 1985 Supreme Court case of *U.S.* v. *Montoya de Hernandez*[190] focused on the issue of "alimentary canal smuggling," in which the offender typically swallows condoms filled with cocaine or heroin and waits for nature to take its course to recover the substance. In the *Montoya* case, a woman known to be a "balloon swallower" arrived in the United States on a flight from Colombia. She was detained by customs officials and given a pat-down search by a female agent. The agent reported that the woman's abdomen was firm and suggested that X-rays be taken. The suspect refused and was given the choice of submitting to further tests or taking the next flight back to Colombia. No flight was immediately available, however, and the suspect was placed in a room for 16 hours, where she refused all food and drink. Finally, a court order for an X-ray was obtained. The procedure revealed "balloons," and the woman was detained another four days, during which time she passed numerous cocaine-filled plastic condoms. The Court ruled that the woman's confinement was not unreasonable, based as it was on the supportable suspicion that she was "body-packing" cocaine. Any discomfort she experienced, the Court ruled, "resulted solely from the method that she chose to smuggle illicit drugs."[191]

Electronic Eavesdropping

Modern technology makes possible increasingly complex forms of communication. One of the first Supreme Court decisions involving electronic communications was the 1928 case of *Olmstead* v. *U.S.*[192] In *Olmstead*, bootleggers used their home telephones to discuss and transact business. Agents tapped the lines and based their investigation and ensuing arrests on conversations they overheard. The defendants were convicted and eventually appealed to the high court, arguing that the agents had in effect seized information illegally without a search warrant in violation of the defendants' Fourth Amendment right to be secure in their homes. The Court ruled, however, that telephone lines were not an extension of the defendants' homes and therefore were not protected by the constitutional guarantee of security. However, subsequent federal statutes have substantially modified the significance of *Olmstead*.

Recording devices carried on the body of an undercover agent or an informant were ruled to produce admissible evidence in *On Lee* v. *U.S.* (1952)[193] and *Lopez* v. *U.S.* (1963).[194] The 1967 case of *Berger* v. *New York*[195] permitted wiretaps and "bugs" in instances where state law provided for the use of such devices and where officers obtained a warrant based on probable cause.

The Court appeared to undertake a significant change of direction in the area of electronic eavesdropping when it decided the case of *Katz* v. *U.S.* in 1967.[196] Federal agents had monitored a number of Katz's telephone calls from a public phone using a device separate from the phone lines and attached to the glass of the phone booth. The Court, in this case, stated that a warrant is required to unveil what a person makes an effort to keep private, even in a public place. In the words of the Court, "The government's activities in electronically listening to and recording the petitioner's words violated the privacy upon which he justifiably relied while using the telephone booth and thus constituted a 'search and seizure' within the meaning of the Fourth Amendment."

In 1968, with the case of *Lee* v. *Florida*,[197] the Court applied the Federal Communications Act[198] to telephone conversations that might be the object of police investigation and held that evidence obtained without a warrant could not be used in state proceedings if it resulted from a wiretap. The only person who has the authority to permit eavesdropping, according to that act, is the sender of the message.

The Federal Communications Act, originally passed in 1934, does not specifically mention the potential interest of law enforcement agencies in monitoring communications. Title III of the Omnibus Crime Control and Safe Streets Act of 1968, however, mostly prohibits wiretaps but does allow officers to listen to electronic communications when (1) an officer is one of the parties involved in the communication, (2) one of the parties is not the officer but willingly decides to share the communication with the officer, or (3) officers obtain a warrant based on probable cause. In the 1971 case of *U.S.* v. *White*,[199] the Court held that law enforcement officers may intercept electronic information when one of the parties involved in the communication gives consent, even without a warrant.

In 1984, the Supreme Court decided the case of *U.S.* v. *Karo*,[200] in which DEA agents had arrested James Karo for cocaine importation. Officers placed a radio transmitter inside a 50-gallon drum of ether purchased by Karo for use in processing the cocaine. The device was placed inside the drum with the consent of the seller of the ether but without a search warrant. The shipment of ether was followed to the Karo house, and Karo was arrested and convicted of cocaine-trafficking charges. Karo appealed to the U.S. Supreme Court, claiming that the radio beeper had violated his reasonable expectation of privacy inside his premises and that, without a warrant, the evidence it produced was tainted. The Court agreed and overturned his conviction.

MINIMIZATION REQUIREMENT FOR ELECTRONIC SURVEILLANCE

The Supreme Court established a minimization requirement pertinent to electronic surveillance in the 1978 case of *U.S.* v. *Scott*.[201] *Minimization* means that officers must make every reasonable effort to monitor only those conversations, through the use of phone taps, body bugs, and the like, that are specifically related to the criminal activity under investigation. As soon as it becomes obvious that a conversation is innocent, then the monitoring personnel are required to cease their invasion of privacy. Problems arise if the conversation occurs in a foreign language, if it is "coded," or if it is ambiguous. It has been suggested that investigators involved in electronic surveillance maintain logbooks of their activities that specifically show monitored conversations, as well as efforts made at minimization.[202]

THE ELECTRONIC COMMUNICATIONS PRIVACY ACT OF 1986

Passed by Congress in 1986, the **Electronic Communications Privacy Act (ECPA)**[203] brought major changes in the requirements law enforcement officers must meet to intercept wire communications (those involving the human voice). The ECPA deals specifically with three areas of communication: (1) wiretaps and bugs, (2) pen registers, which record the numbers dialed from a telephone, and (3) tracing devices, which determine the number from which a call emanates. The act also addresses the procedures to be followed by officers in obtaining records relating to communications services, and it establishes requirements for gaining access to stored electronic communications and records of those communications. The ECPA basically requires that investigating officers must obtain wiretap-type court orders to eavesdrop on *ongoing communications*. The use of pen registers and recording devices, however, is specifically excluded by the law from court order requirements.[204]

How much of our freedom must we surrender in the name of preserving it?

—Letter to the editor, New York Times, July 28, 2005

Electronic Communications Privacy Act (ECPA)

A law passed by Congress in 1986 establishing the due process requirements that law enforcement officers must meet in order to legally intercept wire communications.

A related measure, the Communications Assistance for Law Enforcement Act (CALEA) of 1994,[205] appropriated $500 million to modify the U.S. phone system to allow for continued wiretapping by law enforcement agencies. The law also specifies a standard-setting process for the redesign of existing equipment that would permit effective wiretapping in the face of coming technological advances. In the words of the FBI's Telecommunications Industry Liaison Unit, "This law requires telecommunications carriers, as defined in the Act, to ensure law enforcement's ability, pursuant to court order or other lawful authorization, to intercept communications notwithstanding advanced telecommunications technologies."[206] In 2004, 1,710 wiretap requests were approved by federal and state judges, and approximately 5.2 million conversations were intercepted by law enforcement agencies throughout the country.[207]

THE TELECOMMUNICATIONS ACT OF 1996

Title V of the Telecommunications Act of 1996[208] made it a federal offense for anyone engaged in interstate or international communications to knowingly use a telecommunications device "to create, solicit, or initiate the transmission of any comment, request, suggestion, proposal, image, or other communication which is obscene, lewd, lascivious, filthy, or indecent, with intent to annoy, abuse, threaten, or harass another person." The law also provided special penalties for anyone who "makes a telephone call . . . without disclosing his identity and with intent to annoy, abuse, threaten, or harass any person at the called number or who receives the communication" or who "makes or causes the telephone of another repeatedly or continuously to ring, with intent to harass any person at the called number; or makes repeated telephone calls" for the purpose of harassing a person at the called number.

A section of the law, known as the Communications Decency Act (CDA),[209] criminalized the transmission to minors of "patently offensive" obscene materials over the Internet or other computer telecommunications service. Portions of the CDA were invalidated by the U.S. Supreme Court in the case of *Reno* v. *ACLU* (1997).[210]

THE USA PATRIOT ACT OF 2001

The USA PATRIOT Act of 2001, which is also discussed in CJ Today Exhibit 7–4, made it easier for police investigators to intercept many forms of electronic communications. Under previous federal law, for example, investigators could not obtain a wiretap order to intercept *wire* communications for violations of the Computer Fraud and Abuse Act.[211] In several well-publicized cases, hackers had stolen teleconferencing services from telephone companies and then used those services to plan and execute hacking attacks.

The act[212] added felony violations of the Computer Fraud and Abuse Act to Section 2516(1) of Title 18 of the U.S. Code—the portion of federal law that lists specific types of crimes for which investigators may obtain a wiretap order for wire communications.

President George W. Bush signing legislation renewing the USA PATRIOT Act on March 9, 2006. The president was joined by House and Senate representatives as he signed the new law in the East Room of the White House. How does the 2006 legislation differ from the original act, which was passed shortly after the terrorist attacks of 2001?

Mark Wilson/Getty Images

CJ Today Exhibit 7-4

The USA PATRIOT Act of 2001

On October 26, 2001, President George W. Bush signed into law the USA PATRIOT Act, also known as the Uniting and Strengthening America by Providing Appropriate Tools Required to Intercept and Obstruct Terrorism Act. The law, which was drafted in response to the September 11, 2001, terrorist attacks on the World Trade Center and the Pentagon, substantially increased the investigatory authority of federal, state, and local police agencies. The act permits longer jail terms for certain suspects arrested without a warrant, broadens **sneak and peek search** authority (searches conducted without prior notice and in the absence of the suspect), and enhances the power of prosecutors. The law also increases the ability of federal authorities to tap phones (including wireless devices), share intelligence information, track Internet usage, crack down on money laundering, and protect U.S. borders. Many of the crime-fighting powers created under the legislation are not limited to acts of terrorism but apply to many different kinds of criminal offenses. The 2001 law led individual-rights advocates to question whether the government unfairly expanded police powers at the expense of civil liberties. Major provisions of the law relevant to law enforcement investigations in general are shown in this box.

One Hundred Seventh Congress of the United States of America
AT THE FIRST SESSION
Begun and held at the City of Washington on Wednesday, the third day of January, two thousand and one
An Act
To deter and punish terrorist acts in the United States and around the world, to enhance law enforcement investigatory tools, and for other purposes.
Be it enacted by the Senate and House of Representatives of the United States of America in Congress assembled,

SECTION 1. SHORT TITLE AND TABLE OF CONTENTS.

(a) SHORT TITLE—This Act may be cited as the "Uniting and Strengthening America by Providing Appropriate Tools Required to Intercept and Obstruct Terrorism (USA PATRIOT Act) Act of 2001."

TITLE II—ENHANCED SURVEILLANCE PROCEDURES

SEC. 203. AUTHORITY TO SHARE CRIMINAL INVESTIGATIVE INFORMATION.

(b) AUTHORITY TO SHARE ELECTRONIC, WIRE, AND ORAL INTERCEPTION INFORMATION.—
(1) LAW ENFORCEMENT.—Section 2517 of title 18, United States Code, is amended by inserting at the end the following:
"(6) Any investigative or law enforcement officer, or attorney for the Government, who by any means authorized by this chapter, has obtained knowledge of the contents of any wire, oral, or electronic communication, or evidence derived therefrom, may disclose such contents to any other Federal law enforcement, intelligence, protective, immigration, national defense, or national security official to the

extent that such contents include foreign intelligence or counterintelligence (as defined in section 3 of the National Security Act of 1947 (50 U.S.C. 401a)), or foreign intelligence information (as defined in subsection 19 of section 2510 of this title), to assist the official who is to receive that information in the performance of his official duties. Any Federal official who receives information pursuant to this provision may use that information only as necessary in the conduct of that person's official duties subject to any limitations on the unauthorized disclosure of such information."

SEC. 213. AUTHORITY FOR DELAYING NOTICE OF THE EXECUTION OF A WARRANT.

Section 3103a of title 18, United States Code, is amended—
(1) by inserting "(a) IN GENERAL.—" before "In addition"; and
(2) by adding at the end the following:
"(b) DELAY.—With respect to the issuance of any warrant or court order under this section, or any other rule of law, to search for and seize any property or material that constitutes evidence of a criminal offense in violation of the laws of the United States, any notice required, or that may be required, to be given may be delayed if—
"(1) the court finds reasonable cause to believe that providing immediate notification of the execution of the warrant may have an adverse result (as defined in section 2705);
"(2) the warrant prohibits the seizure of any tangible property, any wire or electronic communication (as defined in section 2510), or, except as expressly provided in chapter 121, any stored wire or electronic information, except where the court finds reasonable necessity for the seizure; and
"(3) the warrant provides for the giving of such notice within a reasonable period of its execution, which period may thereafter be extended by the court for good cause shown."

What This Means

The USA PATRIOT Act amends Title 18, Section 3103, of the U.S. Code to create a uniform standard authorizing courts to delay notification of lawful searches if the court finds "reasonable cause" to believe that providing immediate notification of the execution of the warrant may have an "adverse result" (such as endangering the life or physical safety of an individual, flight from prosecution, evidence tampering, or witness intimidation) or might otherwise seriously jeopardize an investigation or unduly delay a trial. This section of the USA PATRIOT Act is primarily designed to authorize delayed notice of *searches* rather than delayed notice of *seizures*. The USA PATRIOT Improvement and Reauthorization Act of 2005, which became law in 2006, clarified *delayed notification* to mean 30 days after the search has been conducted, with the possibility of a delay of up to 90 days under special circumstances.

SEC. 216. MODIFICATION OF AUTHORITIES RELATING TO USE OF PEN REGISTERS AND TRAP AND TRACE DEVICES.

(b) ISSUANCE OF ORDERS.—
(1) IN GENERAL.—Section 3123(a) of title 18, United States Code, is amended to read as follows:
"(a) IN GENERAL.—

(continued)

CJ Today Exhibit 7–4 (continued)

"(1) ATTORNEY FOR THE GOVERNMENT.—Upon an application made under section 3122(a)(1), the court shall enter an *ex parte* order authorizing the installation and use of a pen register or trap and trace device anywhere within the United States, if the court finds that the attorney for the Government has certified to the court that the information likely to be obtained by such installation and use is relevant to an ongoing criminal investigation."

What This Means

Although Congress enacted a pen/trap statute in 1986 (which made possible the collection of noncontent traffic information associated with communications, such as the phone number dialed from a particular telephone), it could not anticipate the dramatic expansion in electronic communications that would occur in the next 15 years, including communications over computer networks.

Section 216 of the USA PATRIOT Act updates the pen/trap statute in three important ways: (1) The amendments clarify that law enforcement may use pen/trap orders to trace communications on the Internet and other computer networks; (2) pen/trap orders issued by federal courts now have nationwide effect; and (3) law enforcement authorities must file a special report with the court whenever they use a pen/trap order to install their own monitoring device on computers belonging to a public provider.

SEC. 219. SINGLE-JURISDICTION SEARCH WARRANTS FOR TERRORISM.

Rule 41(a) of the Federal Rules of Criminal Procedure is amended by inserting after "executed" the following: "and (3) in an investigation of domestic terrorism or international terrorism (as defined in section 2331 of title 18, United States Code), by a Federal magistrate judge in any district in which activities related to the terrorism may have occurred, for a search of property or for a person within or outside the district."

What This Means

Under prior law, Rule 41(a) of the Federal Rules of Criminal Procedure required that a search warrant be obtained within a dis-

trict for searches within that district. The only exception was for cases in which property or a person within the district might leave the district before the warrant could be executed. The rule created what some saw as unnecessary delays and burdens in the investigation of terrorist activities and networks that spanned a number of districts, because warrants had to be obtained separately in each district. Section 219 purports to solve that problem by providing that, in domestic or international terrorism cases, a search warrant may be issued by a magistrate judge in any district in which activities related to the terrorism have occurred for a search of property or persons located within or outside of the district.

CIVIL RIGHTS IMPLICATIONS

While many aspects of the USA PATRIOT Act have been criticized as potentially unconstitutional, Section 213, which authorizes delayed notice of the execution of a warrant, may be most vulnerable to challenge. The American Civil Liberties Union (ACLU) maintains that under this section, law enforcement agents could enter a house, apartment, or office with a search warrant while the occupant is away, search through his or her property, and take photographs without having to tell the suspect about the search until later.[1] The ACLU also believes that this provision is illegal because the Fourth Amendment to the Constitution protects against unreasonable searches and seizures and requires the government to obtain a warrant and to give notice to the person whose property will be searched before conducting the search. The notice requirement enables suspects to assert their Fourth Amendment rights.

Read the entire USA PATRIOT Act of 2001 at Library Extra 7–5 at cjtoday.com. Title 18 of the U.S. Code is available at Library Extra 7–6. The USA PATRIOT Improvement and Reauthorization Act of 2005 is available at Library Extra 7–7.

LIBRARY
Extra
■ ■ ■ ■

---

[1]Much of the information in this paragraph is taken from American Civil Liberties Union, *How the Anti-Terrorism Bill Expands Law Enforcement "Sneak and Peek" Warrants,* http://www.aclu.org/congress/1102301b.html (accessed February 12, 2005).

References: USA PATRIOT Improvement and Reauthorization Act of 2005 (Public Law 109-177); U.S. Department of Justice, *Field Guidance on Authorities (Redacted) Enacted in the 2001 Anti-Terrorism Legislation* (Washington, DC: Dept. of Justice, no date), http://www.epic.org/terrorism/DOJguidance.pdf (accessed August 28, 2007); USA PATRIOT Act, 2001 (Public Law 107-56); American Civil Liberties Union, *How the Anti-Terrorism Bill Expands Law Enforcement "Sneak and Peek" Warrants,* http://www.aclu.org/congress/1102301b.html (accessed August 28, 2007); and American Civil Liberties Union, *How the Anti-Terrorism Bill Limits Judicial Oversight of Telephone and Internet Surveillance,* http://www.aclu.org/congress/1102301g.html (accessed August 28, 2007).

---

sneak and peek search

A search that occurs in the suspect's absence and without his or her prior knowledge.

The USA PATRIOT Act also modified that portion of the ECPA that governs law enforcement access to stored electronic communications, such as e-mail, to include stored wire communications, such as voice mail. Before the modification, law enforcement officers needed to obtain a wiretap order rather than a search warrant to obtain unopened voice communications. Because today's e-mail messages may contain digitized voice "attachments," investigators were sometimes required to obtain both a search warrant and a wiretap order to learn the contents of a specific message. Under the act, the same rules now apply to both stored wire communications and stored electronic communications. Wiretap orders, which are often much more difficult to obtain than search warrants, are now only required to intercept real-time telephone conversations.

Before passage of the USA PATRIOT Act, federal law allowed investigators to use an administrative subpoena (that is, a subpoena authorized by a federal or state statute or by a federal or state grand jury or trial court) to compel Internet service providers to provide a limited class of information, such as a customer's name, address, length of service, and means of payment. Also under previous law, investigators could not subpoena certain records, including credit card numbers or details about other forms of payment for Internet service. Such information can be very useful in determining a suspect's true identity because, in some cases, users give false names to Internet service providers.

Previous federal law[213] was also technology specific, relating primarily to telephone communications. Local and long-distance telephone billing records, for example, could be subpoenaed, but not billing information for Internet communications or records of Internet session times and durations. Similarly, previous law allowed the government to use a subpoena to obtain the customer's "telephone number or other subscriber number or identity" but did not define what that phrase meant in the context of Internet communications.

The USA PATRIOT Act amended portions of this federal law[214] to update and expand the types of records that law enforcement authorities may obtain with a subpoena. "Records of session times and durations," as well as "any temporarily assigned network address" may now be gathered. Such changes should make the process of identifying computer criminals and tracing their Internet communications faster and easier.

Finally, the USA PATRIOT Act facilitates the use of roving, or multipoint, wiretaps. Roving wiretaps, issued with court approval, target a specific individual and not a particular telephone number or communications device. Hence, law enforcement agents armed with an order for a multipoint wiretap can follow the flow of communications engaged in by a person as he switches from one cellular phone to another or to a wired telephone.

In 2006, President George W. Bush signed the USA PATRIOT Improvement and Reauthorization Act of 2005[215] into law. Also referred to as PATRIOT II, the act made permanent 14 provisions of the original 2001 legislation that had been slated to expire and extended others for another four years (including the roving wiretap provision and a provision that allows authorities to seize business records). It also addressed some of the concerns of civil libertarians who had criticized the earlier law as too restrictive. Finally, the new law provided additional protections for mass transportation systems and seaports, closed some legal loopholes in laws aimed at preventing terrorist financing, and includes a subsection called the Combat Methamphetamine Act (CMA). The CMA contains significant provisions intended to strengthen federal, state, and local efforts designed at curtailing the spread of methamphetamine use.

Learn more about electronic surveillance and wiretapping in criminal cases via Web Extra 7–5 at cjtoday.com, and read the complete USA PATRIOT Act reauthorization legislation at Library Extra 7–7 at cjtoday.com.

WEB **LIBRARY**
Extra Extra

GATHERING ELECTRONIC EVIDENCE

The Internet, computer networks, and automated data systems present many new opportunities for committing criminal activity.[216] Computers and other electronic devices are increasingly being used to commit, enable, or support crimes perpetrated against people, organizations, and property. Whether the crime involves attacks against computer systems or the information they contain or more traditional offenses like murder, money laundering, trafficking, or fraud, **electronic evidence** is increasingly important.

Electronic evidence is "information and data of investigative value that is stored in or transmitted by an electronic device."[217] Such evidence is often acquired when physical items like computers, removable disks, CDs, DVDs, magnetic tape, flash memory chips, cellular telephones, personal digital assistants, and other electronic devices are collected from a crime scene or are obtained from a suspect.

Electronic evidence has special characteristics: (1) It is latent; (2) it can transcend national and state borders quickly and easily; (3) it is fragile and can easily be altered, damaged, compromised, or destroyed by improper handling or improper examination; and (4) it may be time sensitive. Like DNA or fingerprints, electronic evidence is **latent evidence** because it is not readily visible to the human eye under normal conditions. Special equipment and software are

electronic evidence

Information and data of investigative value that are stored in or transmitted by an electronic device.[iii]

latent evidence

Evidence of relevance to a criminal investigation that is not readily seen by the unaided eye.

required to "see" and evaluate electronic evidence. In the courtroom, expert testimony may be needed to explain the acquisition of electronic evidence and the examination process used to interpret it.

In 2002, in recognition of the special challenges posed by electronic evidence, the Computer Crime and Intellectual Property Section (CCIPS) of the Criminal Division of the U.S. Department of Justice released a how-to manual for law enforcement officers called *Searching and Seizing Computers and Obtaining Electronic Evidence in Criminal Investigations*.[218] The manual, which explains procedures for **digital criminal forensics**, can be accessed at Library Extra 7–9 at cjtoday.com.

About the same time, the Technical Working Group for Electronic Crime Scene Investigation (TWGECSI) released a detailed guide for law enforcement officers to use in gathering electronic evidence. The manual, *Electronic Crime Scene Investigation: A Guide for First Responders*,[219] grew out of a partnership formed in 1998 between the National Cybercrime Training Partnership, the Office of Law Enforcement Standards, and the National Institute of Justice. The working group was asked to identify, define, and establish basic criteria to assist federal and state agencies in handling electronic investigations and related prosecutions.

TWGECSI guidelines say that law enforcement must take special precautions when documenting, collecting, and preserving electronic evidence to maintain its integrity. The guidelines also note that the first law enforcement officer on the scene should take steps to ensure the safety of everyone at the scene and to protect the integrity of all evidence, both traditional and electronic. The entire TWGECSI guide, which includes many practical instructions for investigators working with electronic evidence, is available at Library Extra 7–10 at cjtoday.com.

Once digital evidence has been gathered, it must be analyzed. Consequently, in 2004, the government-sponsored Technical Working Group for the Examination of Digital Evidence (TWGEDE) published *Forensic Examination of Digital Evidence: A Guide for Law Enforcement*. Among the guide's recommendations are that digital evidence should be acquired in a manner that protects and preserves the integrity of the original evidence and that examination should be conducted only on a *copy* of the original evidence. The entire guide, which is nearly 100 pages long, can be accessed at Library Extra 7–11 at cjtoday.com. An even more detailed guide, entitled *Investigations Involving the Internet and Computer Networks*, was published by the National Institute of Justice in 2007 and is available at Library Extra 7–12.

Warrantless searches bear special mention in any discussion of electronic evidence. In the 1999 case of *U.S.* v. *Carey*,[220] a federal appellate court held that the consent a defendant had given to police for his apartment to be searched did not extend to the search of his computer once it was taken to a police station. Similarly, in *U.S.* v. *Turner*,[221] the First Circuit Court of Appeals held that the warrantless police search of a defendant's personal computer while in his apartment exceeded the scope of the defendant's consent.

LIBRARY
Extra
▪ ▪ ▪ ▪

digital criminal forensics

The lawful seizure, acquisition, analysis, reporting, and safeguarding of data from digital devices that may contain information of evidentiary value to the trier of fact in criminal events.[iv]

LIBRARY
Extra
▪ ▪ ▪ ▪

LIBRARY
Extra
▪ ▪ ▪ ▪

SUMMARY

- Legal restraints on police action stem primarily from the U.S. Constitution's Bill of Rights, especially the Fourth, Fifth and Sixth Amendments, which, along with the Fourteenth Amendment, require due process of law. Most due process requirements of relevance to police work concern three major areas: (1) evidence and investigation (often called *search* and *seizure*), (2) arrest, and (3) interrogation. Each of these areas has been addressed by a number of important U.S. Supreme Court decisions, and it is the discussion of those decisions and their significance for police work that makes up the bulk of this chapter's content.

- The Bill of Rights was designed to protect citizens against abuses of police power. It does so by guaranteeing due process of law for everyone suspected of having committed a crime and by ensuring the availability of constitutional rights to all citizens, regardless of state or local law or procedure. Within the context of criminal case processing, due process requirements mandate that all justice system officials, not only the police, respect the rights of accused individuals throughout the criminal justice process.

- The Fourth Amendment to the Constitution declares that people must be secure in their homes and in their persons against unreasonable searches and seizures. Consequently, law enforcement officers are generally required to demonstrate probable cause in order to obtain a search warrant if they are to legally conduct searches and seize the property of criminal suspects. The Supreme Court has established that police officers, in order to protect themselves from attack, have the right to search a person being arrested and to search the area under the arrestee's immediate control.

- An arrest takes place whenever a law enforcement officer restricts a person's freedom to leave. Arrests may occur when an officer comes upon a crime in progress, but most jurisdictions also allow warrantless arrests for felonies when a crime is not in progress, as long as probable cause can later be demonstrated.

- Information that is useful for law enforcement purposes is called *intelligence*, and as this chapter has shown, intelligence gathering is vital to police work. The need for useful information often leads police investigators to question suspects, informants, and potentially knowledgeable citizens. When suspects who are in custody become subject to interrogation, they must be advised of their *Miranda* rights before questioning begins. The *Miranda* warnings, which were mandated by the Supreme Court in the 1966 case of *Miranda* v. *Arizona*, are listed in this chapter. They ensure that suspects know their rights—including the right to remain silent—in the face of police interrogation.

KEY TERMS

anticipatory warrants, 239

arrest, 239

Bill of Rights, 227

compelling interest, 249

digital criminal forensics, 270

Electronic Communications Privacy Act (ECPA), 265

electronic evidence, 269

emergency search, 238

exclusionary rule, 229

fleeting-targets exception, 247

fruit of the poisonous tree doctrine, 231

good-faith exception, 233

illegally seized evidence, 229

inherent coercion, 255

interrogation, 254

landmark case, 228

latent evidence, 269

Miranda triggers, 260

Miranda warnings, 256

plain view, 235

probable cause, 233

psychological manipulation, 255

reasonable suspicion, 242

search incident to an arrest, 240

sneak and peek search, 268

suspicionless search, 249

writ of *certiorari*, 230

KEY CASES

Alabama v. *White*, 254

Arizona v. *Fulminante*, 256

Brecht v. *Abrahamson*, 261

Brown v. *Mississippi*, 255

California v. *Hodari D.*, 244

Carroll v. *U.S.*, 245

Chimel v. *California*, 232

Dickerson v. *U.S.*, 258

Escobedo v. *Illinois*, 256

Florida v. *Bostick*, 249

Horton v. *California*, 237

Illinois v. *Perkins*, 260

Indianapolis v. *Edmond*, 248

Kyllo v. *U.S.*, 253

Mapp v. *Ohio*, 231

Minnick v. *Mississippi*, 256

QUESTIONS FOR REVIEW

1. Name some of the legal restraints on police action, and list some types of behavior that might be considered abuse of police authority.

2. How do the Bill of Rights and democratically inspired legal restraints on the police help ensure personal freedoms in our society?

3. Describe the legal standards for assessing searches and seizures conducted by law enforcement agents.

4. What is arrest, and when does it occur? How do legal understandings of the term differ from popular depictions of the arrest process?

5. What is the role of interrogation in intelligence gathering? List each of the *Miranda* warnings. Which recent U.S. Supreme Court cases have affected *Miranda* warning requirements?

QUESTIONS FOR REFLECTION

1. What is the Bill of Rights, and how does it affect our understandings of due process?

2. On what constitutional amendments are due process guarantees based? Can we ensure due process in our legal system without substantially increasing the risk of criminal activity?

3. What is the exclusionary rule? What is the fruit of the poisonous tree doctrine? What is their importance in American criminal justice?

4. Under what circumstances may police officers search vehicles? What limits, if any, are there on such searches? What determines such limits?

5. What are suspicionless searches? How does the need to ensure public safety justify certain suspicionless searches?

6. What is electronic evidence? How should first-on-the-scene law enforcement personnel handle it?

Discuss your answers to these questions and other issues on the CJ Today e-mail discussion list (join the list at cjtoday.com).

WEB QUEST

Create a list of every U.S. Supreme Court decision discussed in this chapter. Group the cases by subject (that is, vehicle searches, searches following arrest, interrogation, and so on), and list them in order by year of decision. Use the Web to collect full-text opinions from the Court for as many of these cases as you can find. Visit the Legal Information Institute at Cornell University (http://www.law.cornell.edu) for some of the best Supreme Court information available anywhere. Submit the materials you find to your instructor if asked to do so.

Note: This is a large project, and your instructor may ask you to work with just one area (such as vehicle searches) or may assign the entire project to your class, asking individual students or groups of students to be responsible for separate subjects.

To complete this Web Quest online, go to the Web Quest module in Chapter 7 of the *Criminal Justice Today* Companion Website at cjtoday.com.

CHAPTER 8

Policing: Issues and Challenges

LEARNING OBJECTIVES

After reading this chapter, you should be able to

- Describe the police working personality and relate it to police culture.

- List and describe different types of police corruption and discuss possible methods for building police integrity.

- Explain the dangers of police work and discuss what can be done to reduce those dangers.

- Describe the situations in which police officers are most likely to use force and provide some guidelines for determining when too much force has been used.

- Describe racial profiling and biased policing and explain why they have become significant issues in policing today.

- Describe the civil liability issues associated with policing and identify common sources of civil suits against the police.

Respect and appreciation for diversity relating to gender, race, victims, and people with special needs are central to recognizing human rights. Police agencies that understand and value diverse communities create structures and systems that reach outward, enjoining and empowering police officers and citizens to collaborate in problem-solving on issues of crime and disorder.

—*Police Executive Research Forum*[1]

The police at all times should maintain a relationship with the public that gives reality to the historic tradition that the police are the public and that the public are the police.

—*Sir Robert Peel, 1829*[2]

Hear the author discuss this chapter at cjtoday.com

Introduction

Today's police officers and administrators face many complex issues. Some concerns, such as corruption, on-the-job dangers, and the use of deadly force, derive from the very nature of police work. Others, like racial profiling and exposure to civil liability, have arisen due to common practices, characteristic police values, public expectations, legislative action, and ongoing societal change. Certainly, one of the most significant challenges facing American law enforcement today is policing a multicultural society. All of these issues are discussed in the pages that follow. We begin, however, with the police recruit socialization process. It is vital to understand this process because the values and expectations learned through it not only contribute to the nature of many important police issues but also determine how the police view and respond to those issues.

Police Personality and Culture

New police officers learn what is considered appropriate police behavior by working with seasoned veterans. Through conversations with other officers in the locker room, in a squad car, or over a cup of coffee, a new recruit is introduced to the value-laden subculture of police work. A definition of *police subculture* was given in Chapter 6. It can also be understood as "the set of informal values which characterize the police force as a distinct community with a common identity."[3] This process of informal socialization plays a much bigger role than formal police academy training in determining how rookies come to see police work. Through it, new officers gain a shared view of the world that can best be described as "streetwise." Streetwise cops know what official department policy is, but they also know the most efficient way to get a job done. By the time rookie officers become streetwise, they know which of the various informal means of accomplishing the job are acceptable to other officers. The police subculture creates few real mavericks, but it also produces few officers who view their jobs exclusively in terms of public mandates and official dictums.

In the 1960s, renowned criminologist Jerome Skolnick described what he called the **police working personality**.[4] Skolnick's description of the police personality was consistent with William Westley's classic study of the Gary (Indiana) Police Department, in which he found a police culture with its own "customs, laws, and morality,"[5] and with Arthur Niederhoffer's observation that cynicism was pervasive among officers in New York City.[6] More recent authors have claimed that the "big curtain of secrecy" surrounding much of police work shields knowledge of the nature of the police personality from outsiders.[7] Taken in concert, these writers offer a picture of the police working personality shown in Table 8–1.

Some characteristics of the police working personality are essential for survival and effectiveness. For example, because officers are often exposed to highly emotional and potentially threatening confrontations with belligerent people, they must develop *efficient, authoritarian* strategies for gaining control over others. Similarly, a suspicious nature makes for a good police officer, especially during interrogations and investigations.

police working personality
All aspects of the traditional values and patterns of behavior evidenced by police officers who have been effectively socialized into the police subculture. Characteristics of the police personality often extend to the personal lives of law enforcement personnel.

TABLE 8-1	The Police Personality	
Authoritarian	Honorable	Loyal
Conservative	Hostile	Prejudiced
Cynical	Individualistic	Secret
Dogmatic	Insecure	Suspicious
Efficient		

However, other characteristics of the police working personality are not so advantageous. For example, many officers are cynical and some can be hostile toward members of the public who do not share their conservative values. These traits result from regular interaction with suspects, most of whom, even when they are clearly guilty in the eyes of the police, deny any wrongdoing. Eventually, personal traits that result from typical police work become firmly ingrained, setting the cornerstone of the police working personality.

There are at least two sources of the police personality. On the one hand, it may be that components of the police personality already exist in some individuals and draw them toward police work.[8] Supporting this view are studies that indicate that police officers who come from conservative backgrounds view themselves as defenders of middle-class morality.[9] On the other hand, some aspects of the police personality can be attributed to the socialization into the police subculture that rookie officers experience when they are inducted into police ranks.

Researchers have reported similar elements in police subculture throughout the United States. They have concluded that like all cultures, police subculture is a relatively stable collection of beliefs and values that is unlikely to change from within. Police subculture may, however, be changed through external pressures, such as new hiring practices, investigations into police corruption or misuse of authority, and commission reports that create pressures for police reform. Learn more about police subculture and police behavior at Web Extra 8–1 at cjtoday.com.

WEB
Extra
■■■■

Corruption and Integrity

Although most law enforcement officers perform their duties responsibly and with honor, some do not. In 2006, for example, Border Patrol Agent Oscar Antonio Ortiz pleaded guilty to charges of conspiracy to smuggle aliens into the United States, making a false claim to U.S. citizenship, making a false statement in the acquisition of a firearm, and being an illegal alien in possession of a firearm.[10] Ortiz, a Mexican citizen who was born in Tijuana, secured a job with the Border

New York City police officers celebrating after the completion of a training ceremony. The police working personality has been characterized as authoritarian, suspicious, and conservative. How does the police working personality develop?

AP Wide World Photos

Multiculturalism and Diversity

Policing a Multicultural Society

Members of some social groups have backgrounds, values, and perspectives that, although they do not directly support law breaking, contrast sharply with those of many police officials. Robert M. Shusta, a well-known writer on multicultural law enforcement, says that police officers "need to recognize the fact of poor police-minority relations historically, including *unequal* treatment under the law."[1] Moreover, says Shusta, "many officers and citizens are defensive with each other because their contact is tinged with negative historical 'baggage.'"

In other words, even though discrimination in the enforcement of the criminal law may not be commonplace today, it *was* in the past—and perceptions built on past experience are often difficult to change. Moreover, if the function of law enforcement is to "protect and serve" law-abiding citizens from all backgrounds, then it becomes vital for officers to understand and respect differences in habits, customs, beliefs, patterns of thought, and traditions.[2] Hence, as Shusta says, "the acts of approaching, communicating, questioning, assisting, and establishing trust with members of different groups require special knowledge and skills that have nothing to do with the fact that 'the law is the law' and must be enforced equally. Acquiring sensitivity, knowledge, and skills leads to [an increased appreciation for the position of others] that will contribute to improved communications with members of all groups."[3]

How can police officers acquire greater sensitivity to the issues involved in policing a diverse multicultural society? Some researchers suggest that law enforcement officers of *all* backgrounds begin by exploring their own prejudices. Prejudices, which are judgments or opinions formed before facts are known and which usually involve negative or unfavorable thoughts about groups of people, can lead to discrimination. Most people, including police officers, are able to reduce their tendency to discriminate against those who are different by exploring and uprooting their own personal prejudices.

One technique for identifying prejudices is cultural awareness training. As practiced in some police departments today, cultural awareness training explores the impact of culture on human behavior—and especially on law-breaking behavior. Cultural awareness training generally involves four stages:[4]

- *Clarifying the relationship between cultural awareness and police professionalism.* As Shusta explains it, "The more professional a police officer is, the more sophisticated he or she is in responding to people of all backgrounds and the more successful he or she is in cross-cultural contact."[5]

- *Recognizing personal prejudices.* In the second stage of cultural awareness training, participating officers are asked to recognize and identify their own personal prejudices and biases. Once prejudices have been identified, trainers strive to show how they can affect daily behavior.

- *Acquiring sensitivity to police–community relations.* In this stage of training, participating officers learn about historical and existing community perceptions of the police. Training can often be enhanced through the use of carefully chosen and well-qualified guest speakers or participants from minority communities.

- *Developing interpersonal relations skills.* The goal of this last stage of training is to help officers develop the positive verbal and nonverbal communications skills necessary for successful interaction with community members. Many trainers believe that basic skills training will result in the continuing development of such skills because officers will quickly begin to see the benefits (in terms of lessened interpersonal conflict) of effective interpersonal skills.

[1]Robert M. Shusta et al., *Multicultural Law Enforcement: Strategies for Peacekeeping in a Diverse Society,* 2nd ed. (Upper Saddle River, NJ: Prentice Hall, 2002), p. 4.
[2]Ibid., p. 16.
[3]Ibid., p. 4.
[4]Ibid., pp. 104–106.
[5]Ibid., p. 4.

Patrol in 2001 by using a fake birth certificate that listed Chicago as his place of birth. Court documents show that he conspired with at least one other border patrol agent to smuggle more than 100 Mexican nationals into the United States. Officials revealed that intercepted phone calls between Ortiz and another agent spoke of payments of up to $2,000 per person smuggled into the United States. The recorded calls also discussed rates that human traffickers working with the agents should be charged to secure the agents' cooperation.[11] On July 28, 2006, a federal district court judge sentenced Ortiz to serve 60 months in prison. He will likely be deported after his sentence is complete.

The kind of corruption seen in Ortiz's case pales alongside that of two retired New York City police detectives who were convicted in 2006 of giving confidential information to mob leaders and of misusing their authority as law enforcement officers to kidnap and kill rival gangsters.[12] Federal prosecutors successfully portrayed retired police investigator Louis Eppolito, 56, and his former partner, Stephen Caracappa, 63, as assassins working for the Luchese crime family. The two are suspected of killing at least eight men in one of the city's most notorious police corruption scandals ever. Their convictions, on 70 counts of racketeering, came 20 years after their first victim was gunned down in a New York City parking garage. Caracappa, who may have been the triggerman in most of the killings, was known for helping to create the New York Police Department's Organized Crime Homicide Unit and was described as "a gatekeeper of information about Mafia killings investigated by police." Although the jurors remained anonymous throughout the trial for protection from possible retaliation, one of them, a building safety official from Long Island, told reporters after the trial that he was shocked at the detectives for having broken their oath to uphold the law. "When you're given an oath, and an oath as precious as being a police officer, and a duty to protect and serve people, that is the highest oath ever," said the juror. "It's like, 'How dare you violate that oath?' . . . When you violate [that] oath, you lose the respect of the people you're sworn to protect."[13]

Police corruption has been a problem in American society since the early days of policing. The combination of power, authority, and discretion in police work produces great potential for abuse. In today's society, the personal and financial benefits of having the police "on your side" are greater than ever. Police officers face temptations that range from a small restaurant owner's offer of a free cup of coffee in exchange for the officer's future goodwill, perhaps for something as simple as a traffic ticket, to a drug dealer's huge monetary bribe to guarantee that the officer will look the other way when a shipment of cocaine arrives. As noted criminologist Carl Klockars says, policing, by its very nature, "is an occupation that is rife with opportunities for misconduct. Policing is a highly discretionary, coercive activity that routinely takes place in private settings, out of the sight of supervisors, and in the presence of witnesses who are often regarded as unreliable."[14]

The effects of police corruption are far-reaching. As Michael Palmiotto of Wichita State University notes, "Not only does misconduct committed by an officer personally affect that officer, it also affects the community, the police department that employs the officer and every police department and police officer in America. Frequently, negative police actions caused by inappropriate police behavior reach every corner of the nation, and at times, the world."[15]

Exactly what constitutes corruption is not always clear. Ethicists say that police corruption ranges from minor offenses to serious violations of the law. In recognition of what some have called corruption's "slippery slope,"[16] most police departments now explicitly prohibit officers from accepting even minor gratuities. The slippery slope perspective holds that even small thank-yous accepted from members of the public can lead to a more ready acceptance of larger bribes. An officer who begins to accept, and then expect, gratuities may soon find that his or her practice of policing becomes influenced by such gifts and that larger ones soon follow. At that point, the officer may easily slide to the bottom of the moral slope, which was made slippery by previous small concessions.

Thomas Barker and David Carter, who have studied police corruption in depth, make the distinction between "occupational deviance," which is motivated by the desire for personal benefit, and "abuse of authority, which occurs most often to further the organizational goals of law enforcement, including arrest, ticketing, and the successful conviction of suspects."[17]

police corruption

The abuse of police authority for personal or organizational gain.[i]

The Los Angeles Police Department's Rampart Station office, where a corruption scandal occurred in 2000 and 2001. A number of officers assigned to the Rampart Division were investigated on charges ranging from falsifying evidence to the theft and sale of illegal drugs. In what some have called "the biggest police scandal case in Los Angeles history," many criminal cases had to be dismissed. What other forms can police corruption take?

David McNew/Liaison/Getty Images, Inc.

FBI Special Agent Frank Perry, former chief of the bureau's ethics unit, distinguishes between police deviance and police corruption. Police deviance, according to Perry, consists of "unprofessional on- and off-duty misconduct, isolated instances of misuse of position, improper relationships with informants or criminals, sexual harassment, disparaging racial or sexual comments, embellished/falsified reporting, time and attendance abuse, insubordination, nepotism, cronyism, and noncriminal unauthorized disclosure of information."[18] Deviance, says Perry, is a precursor to individual and organizational corruption. It may eventually lead to outright corruption unless police supervisors and internal affairs units are alert to the warning signs and actively intervene to prevent corruption from developing.

Figure 8–1 sorts examples of police corruption in terms of seriousness, though not everyone would agree with this ranking. In fact, a survey of 6,982 New York City police officers found that 65% did not classify excessive force, which we define later in this chapter, as a corrupt behavior.[19] Likewise, 71% of responding officers said that accepting a free meal is not a corrupt practice. Another 15% said that personal use of illegal drugs by law enforcement officers should not be considered corruption.

Knapp Commission

A committee that investigated police corruption in New York City in the early 1970s.

In the early 1970s, Frank Serpico made headlines when he testified before the **Knapp Commission** on police corruption in New York City.[20] Serpico, an undercover operative within the police department, revealed a complex web of corruption in which money and services routinely changed hands in "protection rackets" created by unethical officers. The authors of the Knapp Commission report distinguished between two types of corrupt officers, which they termed "grass eaters" and "meat eaters."[21] "Grass eating," the more common form of police corruption, was described as illegitimate activity that occurs from time to time in the normal course of police work. It involves mostly small bribes or relatively minor services offered by citizens seeking to avoid arrest and prosecution. "Meat eating" is a much more serious form of corruption, involving an officer's actively seeking illicit moneymaking opportunities. Meat eaters solicit bribes

FIGURE 8–1

Types and examples of police corruption.

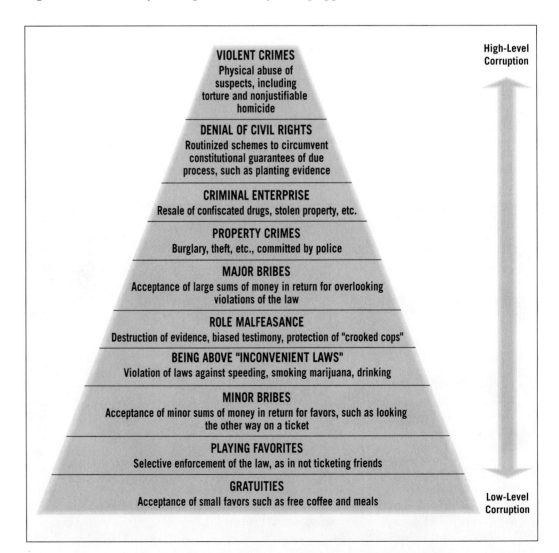

through threat or intimidation, whereas grass eaters commit the less serious offense of failing to refuse bribes that are offered.

In 1993, during 11 days of corruption hearings reminiscent of the Knapp Commission era, a parade of crooked New York police officers testified before a commission headed by former judge and Deputy Mayor Milton Mollen. Among the many revelations, officers spoke of dealing drugs, stealing confiscated drug funds, stifling investigations, and beating innocent people. Officer Michael Dowd, for example, told the commission that he had run a cocaine ring out of his station house in Brooklyn and had bought three homes on Long Island and a Corvette with the money he made. Most shocking of all, however, were allegations that high-level police officials attempted to cover up embarrassing incidents and that many officials may have condoned unprofessional and even criminal practices by the officers under their command. Honest officers, including internal affairs investigators, described how higher authorities had resisted their efforts to end corruption among their colleagues.

Repercussions from the Mollen Commission hearings continue to be felt. In 2004, for example, a New York State judge ruled that the city of New York must pay special disability benefits to former police officer Jeffrey W. Baird, who served as an informant for the commission. Baird helped uncover corruption while working as an internal affairs officer but suffered from posttraumatic stress disorder after fellow officers threatened him, vandalized his work area, and sent obscene materials to his home.[22]

See our Policing blogs.

Corruption in the Los Angeles Police Department's (LAPD) Rampart Division was slated to be fictionalized in a planned Franchise Pictures 2008 movie, *Notorious*.[23] The movie, in which Sylvester Stallone is expected to star as an LAPD detective, suggests that rappers Biggie Smalls (aka Notorious B.I.G.) and Tupac Shakur were killed as part of a conspiracy involving the police, gang members, and officials from the music industry. The true Rampart scandal, although it involved widespread and significant police corruption, was a somewhat more mundane affair.

The scandal began in mid-2000, when the LAPD became embroiled in accusations of corruption that centered on the Rampart Division's antigang unit, known as CRASH (Community Resources against Street Hoodlums).[24] Many of the unit's officers were accused of operating like a criminal organization to frame hundreds of people through threats and beatings, by planting evidence, and by committing perjury. They and other officers were alleged to be running a drug ring, eliminating competition from civilian dealers by framing them and seeing them sent to prison.[25] Seven shootings and at least two killings were among the illegal activities allegedly committed by officers. The scandal came to light after LAPD Officer Rafael Perez was caught stealing $1 million worth of cocaine from an evidence room. In exchange for an offer of leniency, Perez turned informant and cooperated with prosecutors. Perez, who was also accused of murder by a former girlfriend, provided investigators with details about ongoing corruption in the Rampart Division.[26] As events unfolded, prosecutors accused LAPD Chief Bernard Parks of withholding critical information needed to build a case against the accused officers. According to prosecutors, the LAPD, under the direction of Chief Parks, "failed to provide arrest reports, witness statements and background information." The prosecutors claimed that "on several occasions, the LAPD . . . actually hindered the progress of the investigation."[27] Parks was replaced as chief by William J. Bratton in 2002.

By 2005, more than 100 falsely obtained convictions had been thrown out, and 20 LAPD officers had left active duty.[28] Another seven officers were convicted of conspiring to frame innocent people, but a judge overturned three of the convictions on procedural grounds. The remaining four officers received sentences of up to five years in prison.[29] The Los Angeles city attorney agreed to pay a total of $70.2 million to settle approximately 214 lawsuits stemming from the corruption scandal. At the time of the settlement, the *Los Angeles Times* complained that much of the money, averaging $400,000 per settlement, went to "drug dealers, gang members and other criminals who said they had been framed, shot, beaten or otherwise mistreated by police."[30] The largest settlement, $15 million, went to former gang member Javier Francisco Ovando, who had been paralyzed by a police shooting. In responding to critics, Cindy Miscikowski, chairwoman of the Los Angeles city council's Public Safety Committee, pointed out that "regardless of who the plaintiffs were, there was evidence of wrongdoing. That's what we had to recognize. . . . Civil rights are civil rights," Miscikowski said, "and they apply to everyone across the board."[31]

The LAPD is now operating under a consent decree, a legally binding agreement with the U.S. Department of Justice that calls for major reforms. The decree requires the department to install a computer system to track complaints and disciplinary actions against LAPD officers; to collect data on the racial makeup of citizens stopped for traffic violations; and to create a special unit within the department to investigate shootings and beatings by police officers to determine whether excessive force was used.[32] Rafael Perez, sentenced to five years in prison, warned young officers as he was sentenced that "whoever chases monsters must see that he not become a monster himself."[33] Learn more about the Rampart scandal at Web Extra 8–2 at cjtoday.com.

WEB
Extra

Money—The Root of Police Evil?

Years ago, Edwin Sutherland applied the concept of *differential association* (discussed in Chapter 3) to the study of deviant behavior.[34] Sutherland suggested that frequent, continued association of one person with another makes the associates similar. Of course, Sutherland was talking about criminals, not police officers. Consider, however, the dilemma of average officers: Their job entails issuing traffic citations to citizens who try to talk their way out of a ticket, dealing with prostitutes who feel hassled by police, and arresting drug users who think it should be their right to do what they want as long as "it doesn't hurt anyone." Officers regularly encounter personal hostility and experience consistent and often quite vocal rejection of society's formalized norms. They receive relatively low pay, which indicates to them that their work is not really valued. By looking at the combination of these factors, it is easy to understand how officers often develop a jaded attitude toward the society they are sworn to protect.

Police officers' low pay may be a critical ingredient of the corruption mix. Salaries paid to police officers in this country have been notoriously low compared to those of other professions that require personal dedication, extensive training, high stress, and the risk of bodily harm. As police work becomes more professional, many police administrators hope that salaries will rise. However, no matter how much police pay increases, it will never be able to compete with the staggering amounts of money to be made through dealing in contraband. Working hand in hand with monetary pressures toward corruption are the moral dilemmas produced by unenforceable laws that provide the basis for criminal profit. During Prohibition, the Wickersham Commission warned of the potential for official corruption inherent in the legislative taboos on alcohol. The immense demand for drink called into question the wisdom of the law while simultaneously providing vast resources designed to circumvent it. Today's drug scene bears similarities to the Prohibition era. As long as there is a market for illegal drugs, the financial as well as societal pressures on the police to profit from the drug trade will remain substantial.

Building Police Integrity

The difficulties of controlling corruption can be traced to several factors, including the reluctance of police officers to report corrupt activities by their fellow officers, the reluctance of police administrators to acknowledge the existence of corruption in their agencies, the benefits of corrupt transactions to the parties involved, and the lack of immediate victims willing to report corruption. However, high moral standards embedded in the principles of the police profession and effectively communicated to individual officers through formal training and peer-group socialization can raise the level of integrity in any department. Some law enforcement training programs are increasingly determined to reinforce the high ideals many recruits bring to police

Iowa Governor Tom Vilsack presenting Governor's Awards of Valor to Mills County Deputy Eugene Goos (left) and Glenwood Police Officer Gary Chambers (center) at the statehouse in Des Moines in 2002. The officers were given the award for their arrest of an armed gunman in a Glenwood shooting. The appropriate and timely recognition of outstanding and professional police activity can go a long way toward building police integrity and offsetting possible temptations for individual officers to engage in inappropriate behavior. What kinds of activities should be rewarded?

AP Wide World Photos

work and to encourage veteran officers to retain their commitment to the highest professional standards. As one Federal Bureau of Investigation (FBI) publication explains it, "Ethics training must become an integral part of academy and in-service training for new and experienced officers alike."[35]

Ethics training, which was discussed in Chapter 6, is part of a "reframing" strategy that emphasizes integrity to target police corruption. In 1997, for example, the National Institute of Justice (NIJ) released a report entitled *Police Integrity: Public Service with Honor*.[36] The report, based on recommendations made by participants in a national symposium on police integrity, suggested (1) integrating ethics training into the programs offered by newly funded Regional Community Policing Institutes throughout the country, (2) broadening research activities in the area of ethics through NIJ-awarded grants for research on police integrity, and (3) conducting case studies of departments that have an excellent track record in the area of police integrity.

The NIJ report was followed in 2001 by a U.S. Department of Justice document entitled *Principles for Promoting Police Integrity*.[37] The foreword to that document states, "For . . . policing to be successful, and crime reduction efforts to be effective, citizens must have trust in the police. All of us must work together to address the problems of excessive use of force and racial profiling, and—equally important—the perceptions of many minority residents that law enforcement treats them unfairly, if we are to build the confidence in law enforcement necessary for continued progress. Our goal must be professional law enforcement that gives all citizens of our country the feeling that they are being treated fairly, equally and with respect." The report covered such topics as the use of force; complaints and misconduct investigations; accountability and effective management; training; nondiscriminatory policing; and recruitment, hiring, and retention. Read the full report, which provides examples of promising police practices and policies that promote integrity, at Library Extra 8–1 at cjtoday.com.

In 2000, the International Association of Chiefs of Police (IACP), in an effort to reinforce the importance of ethical standards in policing, adopted the Law Enforcement Oath of Honor, shown in the "Ethics and Professionalism" box in this chapter. The IACP suggests that the Law Enforcement Oath of Honor should be seen by individual officers as a statement of commitment to ethical behavior. It is meant to reinforce the principles embodied in the Law Enforcement Code of Ethics, which is printed in the "Ethics and Professionalism" box in Chapter 6.

In December 2005, the U.S. Department of Justice weighed in on the issue of police integrity with a Research for Practice report entitled *Enhancing Police Integrity*.[38] The report said that "an agency's culture of integrity, as defined by clearly understood and implemented policies and

Nothing's so sacred as honor.

—Inscription on Wyatt Earp's headstone

LIBRARY
Extra
■■■■

The ability of the police to fulfill their sacred trust will improve as a lucid sense of ethical standards is developed.

—Former New York City Police Commissioner Patrick V. Murphy

Ethics and Professionalism

The Law Enforcement Oath of Honor

On my honor, I will never
Betray my badge, my integrity,
My character or the public trust.
I will always have the courage to hold
Myself and others accountable for our actions.
I will always uphold the Constitution,
My community, and the agency I serve.

Honor means that one's word is given as a guarantee.

Betray is defined as breaking faith with the public trust.

Badge is the symbol of your office.

Integrity is being the same person in both private and public life.

Character means the qualities that distinguish an individual.

Public trust is a charge of duty imposed in faith toward those you serve.

Courage is having the strength to withstand unethical pressure, fear or danger.

Accountability means that you are answerable and responsible to your oath of office.

Community is the jurisdiction and citizens served.

THINKING ABOUT ETHICS

1. How is the Law Enforcement Oath of Honor similar to the Law Enforcement Code of Ethics found in Chapter 6? How does it differ?
2. How do the two support each other?

Source: "The Law Enforcement Oath of Honor," adopted at the 107th International Association of Chiefs of Police Annual Conference, November 15, 2000. Reprinted with permission.

internal affairs

The branch of a police organization tasked with investigating charges of wrongdoing involving members of the department.

rules, may be more important in shaping the ethics of police officers than hiring the 'right' people."[39] Report authors also noted that officers tend to evaluate the seriousness of various types of misconduct by observing and assessing their department's response in detecting and disciplining it. If unwritten policies conflict with written policies, the authors observed, then the resulting confusion undermines an agency's overall integrity-enhancing efforts. *Enhancing Police Integrity* is available online at Library Extra 8–2 at cjtoday.com.

Most large city law enforcement agencies have their own **internal affairs** divisions, which are empowered to investigate charges of wrongdoing made against officers. Where necessary, state police agencies may be called on to examine reported incidents. Federal agencies, including the FBI and the Drug Enforcement Administration (DEA), get involved when corruption violates federal statutes. The U.S. Department of Justice (DOJ), through various investigative offices, has the authority to examine possible violations of civil rights resulting from the misuse of police authority. The DOJ is often supported in these endeavors by the American Civil Liberties Union (ACLU), the National Association for the Advancement of Colored People (NAACP), and other watchdog groups.

Drug Testing of Police Employees

There is more to being a professional than just looking like one.

—Rob Edwards

On November 17, 2000, the U.S. Court of Appeals for the Fourth Circuit found that the chief of police in Westminster, Maryland, had acted properly in asking a doctor to test an officer's urine for the presence of heroin without the officer's knowledge.[40] Westminster Police Officer Eric Carroll had gone to the local hospital complaining of tightness in his chest and fatigue. The doctor who examined Carroll diagnosed him as suffering from high blood pressure. Carroll was placed on disability leave for three days. While Carroll was gone, the police chief received a call from someone who said that the officer was using heroin. The chief verified the caller's identity and then called the department doctor and asked him to test Carroll for drugs—but without informing the officer of the test. When Carroll returned to the physician for a follow-up visit, the doctor took a urine sample, saying that it was to test for the presence of blood. Although no blood was found in Carroll's urine, it did test positive for heroin. As a consequence, Officer Carroll's employment with the department was terminated. He then sued in federal court, alleging conspiracy, defamation, and violations of his constitutional rights. The Fourth Circuit Court of Appeals, however, determined that the chief's actions were reasonable because, among other things, Carroll had signed a preemployment waiver that permitted the department to conduct drug tests at any time, with or without cause.[41]

The widespread potential for police corruption created by illicit drugs has led to focused efforts to combat drug use by officers. Drug-testing programs in local police departments are an example of such efforts. The IACP has developed a model drug-testing policy for police managers. The policy, designed to meet the needs of local departments, suggests the following:[42]

- Testing all applicants and recruits for drug or narcotics use
- Testing current employees when performance difficulties or documentation indicates a potential drug problem
- Testing current employees when they are involved in the use of excessive force or when they suffer or cause an on-duty injury
- Routine testing of all employees assigned to special "high-risk" areas, such as narcotics and vice

The courts have supported drug testing based on a reasonable suspicion that drug abuse has been or is occurring,[43] although random testing of officers was banned by the New York State Supreme Court in the case of *Philip Caruso, President of P.B.A.* v. *Benjamin Ward, Police Commissioner* (1986).[44] Citing overriding public interests, a 1989 decision by the U.S. Supreme Court upheld the testing of U.S. Customs personnel applying for transfer into drug-law enforcement positions or into positions requiring a firearm.[45] Many legal issues surrounding employee drug testing remain to be resolved in court, however.

Complicating this issue is the fact that drug and alcohol addictions are "handicaps" protected by the Federal Rehabilitation Act of 1973. As such, federal law enforcement employees, as well as those working for agencies with federal contracts, are entitled to counseling and treatment before action can be taken toward termination.

Employee drug testing in police departments, as in many other agencies, is a sensitive subject. Some claim that existing tests for drug use are inaccurate, yielding a significant number of "false positives." Repeated testing and high threshold levels for narcotic substances in the blood may eliminate many of these concerns. Less easy to address, however, is the belief that drug testing intrudes on the personal rights and professional dignity of individual employees. Learn more about employee drug-testing policies in police departments at Web Extra 8–3 at cjtoday.com, and discover more about corruption and the continuing drive toward police integrity at Library Extras 8–3 and 8–4 at cjtoday.com.

WEB Extra

LIBRARY Extra

The Dangers of Police Work

On October 15, 1991, the National Law Enforcement Officers' Memorial was unveiled in Washington, D.C. The memorial contained the names of 12,561 law enforcement officers killed in the line of duty, including U.S. Marshals Service Officer Robert Forsyth, who in 1794 was the nation's first law enforcement officer to be killed on the job. Nearly 6,000 names have been added since opening day.[46] At the memorial, an interactive video system provides visitors with brief biographies and photographs of officers who have died. Tour the memorial by visiting Web Extra 8–4 at cjtoday.com.

WEB Extra

As the memorial proves, police work is, by its very nature, dangerous. Although many officers never once fire their weapons in the line of duty, some do die while performing their jobs. On-the-job police deaths occur from stress, training accidents, and auto crashes. However, it is violent death at the hands of criminal offenders that police officers and their families fear most.

Violence in the Line of Duty

At one o'clock on the morning of April 17, 2005, 50-year-old Providence (Rhode Island) Police Department Detective Sergeant James L. Allen was shot and killed with his own service weapon inside the Providence Public Safety Complex. Allen was in the process of questioning 26-year-old Esteban Carpio about the stabbing and robbery of an 86-year-old woman that had taken place the day before.[47] Carpio, who was not under arrest and whose handcuffs had been removed, apparently grabbed Allen's weapon during a brief struggle and shot the officer. After the killing, Carpio shot out a third-story window, jumped to the ground, and attempted to escape. Injured in the fall, he was apprehended a few blocks away. Detective Allen, whose father is a retired police captain, had served with the Providence Police Department for 27 years. He is survived by a wife and two daughters.[48]

Most officers who are shot are killed by lone suspects armed with a single weapon. In 2006, 146 American law enforcement officers were killed in the line of duty.[49] Figure 8–2 shows the

The flag-draped casket of slain Providence, Rhode Island, Police Detective James L. Allen being carried out of Providence's Saint Thomas Church following funeral services in 2005. Allen, 50, was questioning a suspect about the stabbing of an elderly woman when the man allegedly grabbed Allen's weapon and shot him. How might the dangers associated with police work be reduced?

Chitose Suzuki/AP Wide World Photos

FIGURE 8–2

U.S. law enforcement officers killed in the line of duty, 2006.

Source: Based on data from the Officer Down Memorial Page website, http://www.odmp.org.

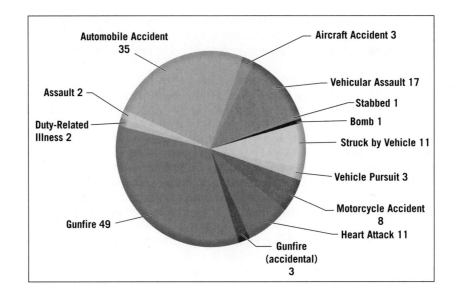

number of officers killed in different types of incidents. In 2001, the attacks on the World Trade Center resulted in the greatest ever annual loss of life of on-duty law enforcement officers when 72 police officers perished.[50]

A study by the FBI found that, generally, slain officers were good natured and conservative in the use of physical force, "as compared to other law enforcement officers in similar situations. They were also perceived as being well-liked by the community and the department, friendly to everyone, laid back, and easy going."[51] Finally, the study, which was published before the September 11, 2001, terrorist attacks, also found that most officers who were killed failed to wear protective vests.

For statistics on police killings to have meaning beyond the personal tragedy they entail, it is necessary to place them within a larger framework. There are approximately 730,000 state and local (full- and part-time) sworn police employees in this country,[52] along with another 88,000 federal agents.[53] Such numbers demonstrate that the rate of violent death among law enforcement officers in the line of duty is small indeed.

Risk of Disease and Infected Evidence

biological weapon

A biological agent used to threaten human life (for example, anthrax, smallpox, or any infectious disease).[iii]

Dangers other than violence also threaten law enforcement officers. The increase in serious diseases that can be transmitted by blood and other body fluids, the possible planned release of active **biological weapons** like anthrax or smallpox, and the fact that crime and accident scenes are inherently dangerous combine to make *caution* a necessary watchword among investigators and first responders. Routine criminal and accident investigations hold the potential for infection through minor cuts and abrasions resulting from contact with the broken glass and torn metal of a wrecked vehicle, the sharp edges of knives found at the scene of an assault or murder, and drug implements like razor blades and hypodermic needles secreted in vehicles, homes, and pockets. Such minor injuries, previously shrugged off by many police personnel, have become a focal point for warnings about the dangers of AIDS, hepatitis B, tuberculosis, and other diseases spread through contact with infected blood.

In 1988, in Sonoma County, California, Sheriff Dick Michaelson announced the first case of AIDS infection in an officer that was clearly caused by interaction with a suspect. A deputy in Michaelson's department had contracted AIDS a few years earlier when he was pricked by a hypodermic needle during a pat-down search.[54]

Infection can also occur from the use of breath alcohol instruments on infected persons, the handling of evidence of all types, seemingly innocuous implements like staples, the emergency delivery of babies in squad cars, and the attack (especially bites) by infected individuals who are being questioned or who are in custody. Understandably, officers are concerned about how to handle the threat of AIDS and other bloodborne diseases. However, as a publication of the New York City Police Department reminds its officers, "Police officers have a professional responsibility to render assistance to those who are in need of our services. We cannot refuse to help. Persons with infectious diseases must be treated with the care and dignity we show all citizens."[55]

Of equal concern is the threat of biological agents. Although crime scenes and sites known to harbor (or that are suspected of harboring) dangerous active biological agents require a response

The aftermath of a fiery truck crash on Interstate 95 in Connecticut in 2004. The intense heat caused part of the road to collapse. Law enforcement officers have a basic duty to render assistance to individuals in need of it and are often the first responders in emergencies. What kinds of unique challenges do police officers face as first responders?

Connecticut Post/*Christian Abraham/AP Wide World Photos*

by teams equipped with special protective equipment, all law enforcement officers should take reasonable precautions against exposure to the wide variety of infectious agents known to exist at even routine crime scenes. Emergency management agencies generally recommend a number of precautions, shown in Table 8–2, to defend against exposure to infectious substances.

To better combat the threat of infectious diseases among public-safety employees and health-care professionals, the federal Bloodborne Pathogens Act of 1991[56] requires that police officers receive proper training in how to prevent contamination by bloodborne infectious agents. The act also requires that police officers undergo an annual refresher course on the topic.

Police departments will face an increasing number of legal challenges in the years to come in cases of infectious diseases like AIDS and in cases involving the release of biological agents. Predictable areas of concern include (1) the need to educate officers and other police employees about AIDS, anthrax, and other serious infectious diseases; (2) the responsibility of police departments to prevent the spread of AIDS and other infectious diseases in police lockups; and (3) the necessity of effective and nondiscriminatory enforcement activities and lifesaving measures by police officers in environments contaminated with active biological agents. With regard to nondiscriminatory activities, the National Institute of Justice has suggested that legal claims in support of an officer's refusal to render assistance to people with AIDS would probably not be effective in court.[57] The reason is twofold: The officer has a basic duty to render assistance to individuals in need of it, and the possibility of AIDS transmission by casual contact has been scientifically established as extremely remote. A final issue of growing concern involves activities by police officers infected with the AIDS virus. Few statistics are currently available on the number of officers with AIDS, but public reaction to those officers may be a developing problem that police managers will soon need to address.

To introduce and implement new police ideas is not easy, but it is possible. More than that, it is essential if we are to achieve elementary public safety in American cities and confidence in the police by those who are being policed.

—Jerome H. Skolnick and David H. Bayley[iv]

Stress and Fatigue among Police Officers

In the week after Hurricane Katrina in 2005, two New Orleans police officers used their service weapons to take their own lives. One was Sergeant Paul Accardo, the department's spokesperson. The other was patrolman Lawrence Celestine, an officer described by Deputy Police Chief W. J. Riley as "an outstanding cop."[58] Feelings of powerlessness, personal loss, and an inability to help those in need all seriously heightened the level of stress felt by officers in New Orleans following the hurricane. "The most stressing part is seeing the citizens we serve every day being treated like refugees," said Riley. "There were cops walking through the crowd at the convention center and people were coming up to beg for food. Not being able to help is a difficult thing. People were calling our names because we knew them and to not be able to help, man, that's stressful."[59]

Traumatic events, like hurricanes, terrorist attacks, and violent confrontations, are instantly stressful. But long-term stress, whose debilitating effects accumulate over years, may be the most

Good cops always seem to be able to identify causes of problems and to come up with the least troublesome ways of solving them.

—Jerome Skolnick

TABLE 8–2 Biological Incident Law Enforcement Concerns

Suspicious material	Responding officers should not handle or come into close physical contact with suspicious material. If it is necessary to handle the material to evaluate it, officers should wear surgical gloves and masks and wash their hands thoroughly with soap and water after handling.
Human bites	The biter usually receives the victim's blood. Viral transmission through saliva is highly unlikely. If bitten by anyone, milk the wound to make it bleed, wash the area thoroughly, and seek medical attention.
Spitting	Viral transmission through saliva is highly unlikely.
Urine/feces	The virus has been isolated in only very low concentrations in urine and not at all in feces. No cases of AIDS or AIDS virus infection have been associated with either urine or feces.
Cuts/puncture wounds	Use caution in handling sharp objects and searching areas hidden from view. Needle-stick studies show risk of infection is very low.
CPR/first aid	To eliminate the already minimal risk associated with CPR, use masks/airways. Avoid blood-to-blood contact by keeping open wounds covered and wearing gloves when in contact with bleeding wounds.
Body removal	Observe crime-scene rules; do not touch anything. Those who must come in contact with blood or other body fluids should wear gloves.
Casual contact	No cases of AIDS or AIDS virus infection have been attributed to casual contact.
Any contact with blood or body fluids	Wear gloves if contact with blood or body fluids is considered likely. If contact occurs, wash thoroughly with soap and water; clean up spills with one part water to nine parts household bleach.
Contact with dried blood	No cases of infection have been traced to exposure to dried blood. The drying process itself appears to inactivate the virus. Despite low risk, however, caution dictates wearing gloves, a mask, and protective shoe coverings if exposure to dried blood particles is likely (for example, during a crime-scene investigation).

References: Michigan Department of Community Health, *Anthrax (Bacillus anthracis) Information for Health Care Providers,* http://www.michigan.gov/documents/Healthcare_provider_FAQ-anthrax_08-2004_104327_7.pdf (accessed June 11, 2007); Massachusetts Administrative Office of the Trial Court, *Personnel Policies and Procedures Manual,* Section 24.000 ("Statement of Policy and Procedures on AIDS"), http://www.state.ma.us/courts/admin/hr/section24.html (accessed January 5, 2004); and "Collecting and Handling Evidence Infected with Human Disease-Causing Organisms," *FBI Law Enforcement Bulletin,* July 1987.

insidious and least visible of all threats facing law enforcement personnel today. While some degree of stress can be a positive motivator, serious stress, over long periods of time, is generally regarded as destructive, even life threatening.

Stress is a natural component of police work.[60] The American Institute of Stress, based in Yonkers, New York, ranks policing among the top ten stress-producing jobs in the country.[61] The Bureau of Justice Statistics points out that "exposure to violence, suffering, and death is inherent to the profession of the law enforcement officer. There are other sources of stress as well. Officers who deal with offenders on a daily basis may perceive the public's opinion of police performance to be unfavorable; they often are required to work mandatory, rotating shifts; and they may not have enough time to spend with their families. Police officers also face unusual, often highly disturbing, situations, such as dealing with a child homicide victim or the survivors of vehicle crashes."[62]

Some stressors in police work are particularly destructive. One is frustration brought on by the inability to be effective, regardless of the amount of personal effort expended. Arrests may not lead to convictions. Evidence available to the officer may not be allowed in court. Imposed sentences may seem inadequate to the arresting officer. The feelings of powerlessness that come from seeing repeat offenders back on the streets and from witnessing numerous injustices to innocent victims may greatly stress police officers and cause them to question the purpose of their professional lives. These feelings of frustration and powerlessness may also lead to desperate attempts to find relief. As one researcher observes, "The suicide rate of police officers is more than twice that of the general population."[63]

Another source of stress—that of living with constant danger—is incomprehensible to most of us, even to the family members of many officers. As one officer says, "I kick in a door and I've gotta talk some guy into putting a gun down. . . . And I go home, and my wife's upset because the lawn isn't cut and the kids have been bad. Now, to her that's a real problem."[64] Yet the support of family and friends is crucial for handling stress.

Stress is not unique to the police profession, but because of the "macho" attitude that is traditionally associated with police work, police officers deny their stress more often than those in other occupations do. Some individuals are more susceptible to the negative effects of stress than others. The Type A personality, popularized 30 years ago, is most likely to perceive life in terms of pressure and performance. Type B people are more laid back and less likely to suffer from the negative effects of stress. Police ranks, drawn as they are from the general population, are filled with both stress-sensitive and stress-resistant personalities.

STRESS REDUCTION

It is natural to want to reduce stress.[65] Humor helps, even if it's somewhat cynical. Health-care professionals, for example, are noted for their ability to joke while caring for patients who are seriously ill or even dying. At times, police officers use humor similarly to defuse their reactions to dark or threatening situations. Keeping an emotional distance from stressful events is another way of coping with them, although such distance is not always easy to maintain. Police officers who have had to deal with serious cases of child abuse often report that they experience emotional turmoil as a consequence.

Exercise, meditation, abdominal breathing, biofeedback, self-hypnosis, guided imaging, induced relaxation, subliminal conditioning, music, prayer, and diet have all been cited as useful techniques for stress reduction. Devices to measure stress levels are available in the form of hand-held heart rate monitors, blood pressure devices, "biodots" (which change color according to the amount of blood flow in the extremities), and psychological inventories.

A new approach to managing stress among police officers holds that the amount of stress that officers experience is directly related to their reactions to potentially stressful situations.[66] Officers who can filter out extraneous stimuli and who can distinguish between truly threatening situations and those that are benign are much less likely to report job-related stressors than those lacking these

A New York Police Department officer showing obvious signs of fatigue while working at a traffic barrier. Stress and fatigue are common problems in police work and can result from long work hours, grueling investigations, traumatic experiences, and even boredom. How can boredom be combated?

Robert Brenner/PhotoEdit Inc.

abilities. Because stress-filtering abilities are often closely linked to innate personality characteristics, some researchers suggest careful psychological screening of police applicants to better identify those who have a natural ability to cope with situations that others might perceive as stressful.[67]

Police officers' family members often report feelings of stress that are directly related to the officers' work. As a result, some departments have developed innovative programs to allay family stress. The Collier County (Florida) Spousal Academy, for example, is a family support program that offers training to spouses and other domestic partners of deputies and recruits who are enrolled in the department's training academy. The ten-hour program deals directly with issues that are likely to produce stress and informs participants of department and community resources that are available to help them. Peer-support programs for spouses and life partners and for the adolescent children of officers are also beginning to operate nationwide. Library Extra 8–5 at cjtoday.com provides a comprehensive overview of issues related to police officer stress.

LIBRARY
Extra
■■■■

OFFICER FATIGUE

Like stress, fatigue can affect a police officer's performance. As criminologist Bryan Vila points out, "Tired, urban street cops are a national icon. Weary from overtime assignments, shift work, night school, endless hours spent waiting to testify, and the emotional and physical demands of the job, not to mention trying to patch together a family and social life during irregular islands of off-duty time, they fend off fatigue with coffee and hard-bitten humor."[68] Vila found levels of police officer fatigue to be six times as high as those of shift workers in industrial and mining jobs.[69] As Vila notes, few departments set work-hour standards, and fatigue associated with the pattern and length of work hours may be expected to contribute to police accidents, injuries, and misconduct.

To address the problem, Vila recommends that police departments "review the policies, procedures, and practices that affect shift scheduling and rotation, overtime moonlighting, the number of consecutive work hours allowed, and the way in which the department deals with overly tired employees."[70] Vila also suggests controlling the working hours of police officers, "just as we control the working hours of many other occupational groups."[71]

FREEDOM OR SAFETY?
You Decide

Protecting Public Places

In October 2004, a three-judge panel of the 11th U.S. Circuit Court of Appeals held that protesters could not be required to pass through metal detectors at a planned rally against a school for Latin American soldiers at Fort Benning in Columbus, Georgia. "In the absence of some reason to believe that international terrorists would target or infiltrate this protest, there is no basis for using September 11 as an excuse for searching the protesters," the court said. Protesters believe that the school, the Western Hemisphere Institute for Security Cooperation, teaches Latin American soldiers to violate the human rights of poor people in their home countries.

Fifteen thousand protesters routinely attend the annual vigil against the institute, which had previously been called the School of the Americas—and metal detectors had been used on the crowd in the past. Organizers claimed, however, that some security measures had been put in place merely to harass demonstrators and to keep people from participating in the protests.

The court seemed to agree. "We cannot simply suspend or restrict civil liberties until the War on Terror is over, because the War on Terror is unlikely ever to be truly over," said Judge Gerald Tjoflat, author of the 11th Circuit panel's opinion. "September 11, 2001, already a day of immeasurable tragedy, cannot be the day liberty perished in this country."

Columbus Mayor Bob Poydasheff noted that his city would abide by the court's order but called it "unreasonable." "I can't go into the 11th Circuit Court of Appeals without being scanned and having my briefcase searched," the mayor said. "They have every right to do that, to make sure they're protected. And I have every right to make sure my police are protected, and the citizens and other protesters are protected."

YOU DECIDE

Why did the court prohibit the use of metal detectors? Under what circumstances might the court allow their use? Do you agree with Mayor Poydasheff's argument that city officials should have the same right to protect public areas under their jurisdiction that the court has to protect its courtrooms?

Reference: "Terrorism Fears Not Sufficient Reason to Search Protesters, Appellate Court Rules," Associated Press, October 17, 2004.

Police Use of Force

Police use of force is defined as the use of physical restraint by a police officer when dealing with a member of the public.[72] Law enforcement officers are authorized to use the amount of force that is reasonable and necessary given the circumstances. Most officers are trained in the use of force and typically encounter numerous situations during their careers when the use of force is appropriate—for example, when making some arrests, restraining unruly combatants, or controlling a disruptive demonstration. Force may involve hitting; holding or restraining; pushing; choking; threatening with a flashlight, baton, or chemical or pepper spray; restraining with a police dog; or threatening with a gun. Some definitions of police use of force include handcuffing.

The National Institute of Justice estimates that over 43.5 million people nationwide have face-to-face contact with the police over a typical 12-month period (nearly 18 million as a result of traffic stops) and that approximately 1.6%, or about 700,000, of these people become subject to the use of force or the threat of force.[73] When handcuffing is included in the definition of force, the number of people subjected to force increases to 1.2 million, or slightly more than 2.5% of those having contact with the police. Other studies show that police use weaponless tactics in approximately 80% of use-of-force incidents and that about 88% of all use-of-force incidents involve merely grabbing or holding the suspect.[74]

Studies show that police use force in fewer than 20% of adult custodial arrests. Even in instances where force is used, the police primarily use weaponless tactics (Figure 8–3), and female officers are less likely to use physical force and firearms, and more likely to use chemical weapons (mostly pepper spray), than their male counterparts.[75] Figure 8–4 shows the types of encounters in which the use of force is most likely to be employed.

A more complex issue is the use of excessive force. The International Association of Chiefs of Police defines **excessive force** as "the application of an amount and/or frequency of force greater than that required to compel compliance from a willing or unwilling subject."[76] When excessive force is employed, the activities of the police often come under public scrutiny and receive attention from the media and from legislators. Police officers' use of excessive force can also result in lawsuits by members of the public who feel that they have been treated unfairly. Whether the use of excessive force is aberrant behavior on the part of an individual officer or is a practice of an entire law enforcement agency, both the law and public opinion generally condemn it.

Kenneth Adams, an associate dean at the University of Central Florida and an expert in the use of force by police, notes that there is an important difference between the terms *excessive force*, such as shoving or pushing when simply grabbing a suspect would be adequate, and the *excessive use of force*, which refers to the phenomenon of force being used unacceptably, often on a department-wide basis. The term, says Adams, "deals with relative comparisons among police agencies, and there are no established criteria for judgment." *Use of excessive force* and the *excessive use of force* may be distinguished from the *illegal use of force*, which refers to situations in which the use of force by police violates a law or statute.[77]

police use of force

The use of physical restraint by a police officer when dealing with a member of the public.[v]

excessive force

The application of an amount and/or frequency of force greater than that required to compel compliance from a willing or unwilling subject.[vi]

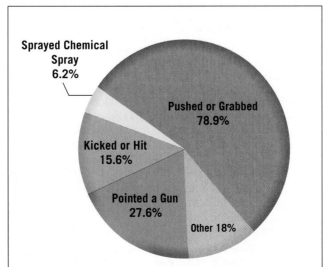

Sprayed Chemical Spray 6.2%
Pushed or Grabbed 78.9%
Kicked or Hit 15.6%
Pointed a Gun 27.6%
Other 18%

FIGURE 8–3

Citizen reports of types of force used by police officers during adult custodial arrests involving force.

Note: Percentages total more than 100 because some respondents reported more than one type of force.

Source: Matthew R. Durose et al., *Contacts between Police and Public 2005* (Washington, DC: Bureau of Justice Statistics, February 2007), p. 10.

FIGURE 8–4

Police use of force by type of encounter.

Source: International Association of Chiefs of Police, *Police Use of Force in America, 2001* (Alexandria, VA: IACP, 2001), p. iii. Printed by permission of the International Association of Chiefs of Police.

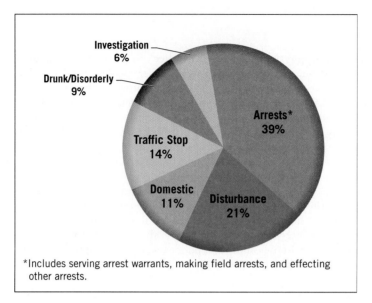

*Includes serving arrest warrants, making field arrests, and effecting other arrests.

In a study reported in 2001, Geoffrey Alpert and Roger Dunham found that the "force factor"—the level of force used by the police relative to the suspect's level of resistance—is a key element to consider in attempting to reduce injuries to both the police and suspects.[78] The force factor is calculated by measuring both the suspect's level of resistance and the officer's level of force on an equivalent scale and by then subtracting the level of resistance from the level of police force used. Results from the study indicate that, on average, the level of force that officers use is closely related to the type of training that their departments emphasize.

Excessive force can also be symptomatic of **problem police officers**. Problem police officers are those who exhibit problem behavior, as indicated by high rates of citizen complaints, frequent involvement in use-of-force incidents, and by other evidence.[79] The Christopher Commission, which studied the structure and operation of the Los Angeles Police Department in the wake of the Rodney King beating, found a number of "repeat offenders" on the LAPD force.[80] According to the commission, approximately 1,800 LAPD officers were alleged to have used excessive force or improper tactics between 1986 and 1990. Of these officers, more than 1,400 had only one or two allegations against them. Another 183 officers had four or more allegations, 44 had six or more, 16 had eight or more, and one had 16 such allegations. The commission also found that, generally speaking, the 44 officers with six complaints or more had received positive performance evaluations that failed to record "sustained" complaints or to discuss their significance.

Recent studies have found that problem police officers do not differ significantly in race or ethnicity from nonproblem officers, although they tend to be male and have disciplinary records that are more serious than those of other officers. Some departments are developing early-warning systems to allow police managers to identify potentially problematic officers and to reduce problem behavior. Learn more about police use of force, as well as force used against the police, from Library Extras 8–6 and 8–7 at cjtoday.com.

problem police officer

A law enforcement officer who exhibits problem behavior, as indicated by high rates of citizen complaints and use-of-force incidents and by other evidence.[vii]

LIBRARY
Extra
■ ■ ■ ■

Deadly Force

deadly force

Force likely to cause death or great bodily harm. Also, "the intentional use of a firearm or other instrument resulting in a high probability of death."[viii]

Generally speaking, **deadly force** is likely to cause death or significant bodily harm. The FBI defines *deadly force* as "the intentional use of a firearm or other instrument resulting in a high probability of death."[81] According to a report released by the Bureau of Justice Statistics in 2001, the number of justifiable homicides by police averages "nearly 400 felons each year."[82]

The use of deadly force by law enforcement officers, especially when it is *not* considered justifiable, is one area of potential civil liability that has received considerable attention in recent years. Historically, the fleeing-felon rule applied to most U.S. jurisdictions. It held that officers could use deadly force to prevent the escape of a suspected felon, even when that person represented no immediate threat to the officer or to the public.

The 1985 U.S. Supreme Court case of *Tennessee* v. *Garner*[83] specified the conditions under which deadly force could be used in the apprehension of suspected felons. Edward Garner, a 15-year-old suspected burglar, was shot to death by Memphis police after he refused their order to halt and attempted to climb over a chain-link fence. In an action initiated by Garner's father, who claimed that his son's constitutional rights had been violated, the Court held that the use of deadly force by the police to prevent the escape of a fleeing felon could be justified only where the suspect could reasonably be thought to represent a significant threat of serious injury or death to the public or to the officer and where deadly force is necessary to effect the arrest. In reaching its decision, the Court declared that "[t]he use of deadly force to prevent the escape of *all* felony suspects, whatever the circumstances, is constitutionally unreasonable."

In the 1989 case of *Graham* v. *Connor*,[84] the Supreme Court established the standard of "objective reasonableness." The Court said that whether deadly force has been used appropriately should be judged from the perspective of a reasonable officer on the scene and not with the benefit of "20/20 hindsight." The justices wrote, "The calculus of reasonableness must embody allowance for the fact that police officers are often forced to make split-second judgments—in circumstances that are tense, uncertain, and rapidly evolving—about the amount of force that is necessary in a particular situation."

In 1995, following investigations into the actions of federal agents at the deadly siege of the Branch Davidian compound at Waco, Texas, and the tragic deaths associated with a 1992 FBI assault on antigovernment separatists in Ruby Ridge, Idaho (a case that is discussed later in the chapter), the federal government announced that it was adopting an "imminent danger" standard for the use of deadly force by federal agents. The imminent danger standard restricts the use of deadly force to those situations in which the lives of agents or others are in danger. When the new standard was announced, federal agencies were criticized for taking so long to adopt them. The federal deadly force policy, as adopted by the FBI, contains the following elements:[85]

- *Defense of life.* Agents may use deadly force only when necessary—that is, only when they have probable cause to believe that the subject poses an imminent danger of death or serious physical injury to the agent or to others.

- *Fleeing subject.* Deadly force may be used to prevent the escape of a fleeing subject if there is probable cause to believe that the subject has committed a felony involving the infliction or threatened infliction of serious physical injury or death and that the subject's escape would pose an imminent danger of death or serious physical injury to the agent or to others.

- *Verbal warnings.* If feasible, and if doing so would not increase the danger to the agent or to others, a verbal warning to submit to the authority of the agent should be given prior to the use of deadly force.

- *Warning shots.* Agents may not fire warning shots.

- *Vehicles.* Agents may not fire weapons solely to disable moving vehicles. Weapons may be fired at the driver or other occupant of a moving motor vehicle only when the agent has probable cause to believe that the subject poses an imminent danger of death or serious physical injury to the agent or to others and when the use of deadly force does not create a danger to the public that outweighs the likely benefits of its use.

Studies of killings by the police have often focused on claims of discrimination—that is, that minority suspects are more likely to be shot than whites. But research has not provided solid support for such claims. While individuals shot by police are more likely to be minorities, an early study by James Fyfe found that police officers will generally respond with deadly force when mortally threatened and that minorities are considerably more likely to use weapons in assaults on officers than are whites.[86] Complicating the picture further, Fyfe's study showed that minority officers are involved in the shootings of suspects more often than other officers, a finding that may be due to the assignment of minority officers to inner-city and ghetto areas. However, a later study by Fyfe, which analyzed police shootings in Memphis, Tennessee, found that black property offenders were twice as likely as whites to be shot by police.[87]

Although relatively few police officers ever fire their weapons at suspects during the course of their careers, those who do may become embroiled in social, legal, and personal complications. It is estimated that in an average year, 600 suspects are killed by public police in America, while another 1,200 are shot and wounded, and 1,800 are shot at and missed.[88] The personal side of police shootings is well summarized in the title of an article that appeared in *Police Magazine*. The article, "I've Killed That Man Ten Thousand Times," demonstrates how police officers who have to use their weapons may be haunted by years of depression and despair.[89] Not long ago, according to author Anne Cohen, all departments did to help an officer who had shot someone was to "give him enough bullets to reload his gun." The stress and trauma that police officers suffer from having shot someone are only now being realized, and many departments have yet to develop mechanisms for adequately dealing with them.[90]

Police officers have particular difficulty dealing with instances of "suicide by cop," in which individuals bent on dying engage in behavior that causes responding officers to resort to deadly

The calculus of reasonableness must embody allowance for the fact that police officers are often forced to make split-second judgments—in circumstances that are tense, uncertain, and rapidly evolving—about the amount of force that is necessary in a particular situation.

—Graham *v.* Connor, *490 U.S. 386, 396–397 (1989)*

force. On March 10, 2005, for example, John T. Garczynski, Jr., a father of two preteen boys, died in a hail of 26 police bullets fired by officers who had surrounded his vehicle in a Boca Raton, Florida, condominium parking lot.[91] Garczynski, a Florida Power and Light Company employee, had been separated from his wife months earlier and appeared to have been despondent over financial problems and the breakup of his marriage. The night before his death, Garczynski met his wife at a bowling alley and handed her a packet containing a suicide note, a typed obituary, and a eulogy to be read at his funeral. After he left, Garczynski's wife called police, and officers used the help of a cell phone company to locate Garczynski. As deputies surrounded his 2003 Ford Explorer, he attempted to start the vehicle. One of the officers yelled "Freeze" and then "Let me see your hands." It was at that point, deputies said, that Garczynski pointed a gun at them and they fired.

Rebecca Stincelli, author of the book *Suicide by Cop: Victims from Both Sides of the Badge*,[92] says an incident like that involving Garczynski can be devastating for police officers. "In the past, people have used rope, a gun, gas, jumped off a building. A police officer is just another method," said Stincelli. "They say it's nothing personal. [But] they are wrong. It's very personal" for the officers involved.[93] The FBI says that "suicide-by-cop incidents are painful and damaging experiences for the surviving families, the communities, and all law enforcement professionals."[94]

A study of fatal shootings by Los Angeles police officers found that an astonishingly large number—more than 10%—could be classified as "suicide by cop."[95] Recently, researchers have identified three main "suicide by cop" categories: direct confrontations, in which suicidal subjects instigate attacks on police officers for the purpose of dying; disturbed interventions, in which potentially suicidal subjects take advantage of police intervention in their suicide attempt in order to die; and criminal interventions, in which criminal suspects prefer death to capture and arrest.[96]

> *Everyone is a prisoner of his own experiences. No one can eliminate prejudices—just recognize them.*
>
> *—Edward R. Murrow*

Less-Lethal Weapons

less-lethal weapon

A weapon that is designed to disable, capture, or immobilize—but not kill—a suspect. Occasional deaths do result from the use of such weapons, however.

Less-lethal weapons offer what may be a problem-specific solution to potential incidents of "suicide by cop," as well as a generic solution to at least some charges of use of excessive force. Less-lethal weapons are designed to disable, capture, or immobilize a suspect rather than kill him or her. Efforts to provide law enforcement officers with less-lethal weapons like stun guns, Tasers, rubber bullets, beanbag projectiles, and pepper spray began in 1987.[97] More exotic types of less-lethal weapons, however, are on the horizon. They include snare nets fired from shotguns, disabling sticky foam that can be sprayed from a distance, microwave beams that heat the tissue of people exposed to them until they desist in their illegal or threatening behavior or lose consciousness, and high-tech guns that fire bolts of electromagnetic energy at a target, causing painful sensory overload and violent muscle spasms. The National Institute of Justice says, "The goal is to give line officers effective and safe alternatives to lethal force."[98]

As their name implies, however, less-lethal weapons are not always safe. On October 21, 2004, for example, 21-year-old Emerson College student Victoria Snelgrove died hours after being hit in the eye with a plastic pepper-spray-filled projectile that police officers fired at a rowdy crowd celebrating the Red Sox victory over the New York Yankees in the final game of the American League Championship Series in 2004. Witnesses said that officers fired the projectile into the crowd after a reveler near Fenway Park threw a bottle at a mounted Boston police officer.[99]

Racial Profiling and Biased Policing

racial profiling

"Any police-initiated action that relies on the race, ethnicity, or national origin, rather than [1] the behavior of an individual, or [2] . . . information that leads the police to a particular individual who has been identified as being, or having been, engaged in criminal activity."[ix]

Racial profiling first received national attention in the late 1990s. Racial profiling can be defined as any police action initiated on the basis of the race, ethnicity, or national origin of a suspect, rather than on the behavior of that individual or on information that leads the police to a particular individual who has been identified as being, or having been, engaged in criminal activity.[100]

The alleged use by police of racial profiling may take a number of forms. Minority accounts of disparate treatment at the hands of police officers include being stopped for being "in the wrong car" (for example, a police stop of an African American youth driving an expensive late-model BMW); being stopped and questioned for being in the wrong neighborhood (that is, police stops of members of minority groups driving through traditionally white residential neighborhoods); and perceived harassment at the hands of police officers for petty traffic violations like underinflated tires, failure to signal properly before switching lanes, vehicle equipment failures, driving less than 10 miles per hour above the speed limit, or having an illegible license plate.[101]

Profiling was originally intended to help catch drug couriers attempting to enter the country. The U.S. Customs Service and the Drug Enforcement Administration developed a number of

CJ Careers

Bureau of Alcohol, Tobacco, Firearms, and Explosives (ATF)

Name: Robert M. Young, Jr.

Position: Special Agent/Criminal Investigator

City: Lexington, Kentucky

College Attended: Rider University

Year Hired: 1998

"I pursued a career in criminal justice because I am not the type of person who enjoys working a nine-to-five office job. I like having a career where each day presents its own unique challenges. For instance, there are days when I may be in court testifying, days investigating an arson or explosive incident, or days in the field participating in an undercover operation. I believe it is this ever-changing work environment that attracts such a diverse and unique group of individuals to careers in law enforcement. . . .
I believe the greatest challenge I have encountered in my job is the difficulty in trying to adequately balance the demands of the job with the demands of my personal life. . . .
There is no greater reward for a law enforcement officer than that of seeing the look of appreciation on the face of a crime victim after the defendant has been convicted and sentenced for the crime that was investigated."

TYPICAL POSITIONS

Special agent, explosives expert, criminal investigator, firearms specialist, bomb scene investigator, liquor law violations investigator, fingerprint identification specialist, intelligence research specialist, and forensic chemist. The Bureau of Alcohol, Tobacco, Firearms, and Explosives (ATF) has primary investigative jurisdiction among federal agencies for the investigation of international arms trafficking, illegal arms movement, and the illegal use of explosives.

EMPLOYMENT REQUIREMENTS

GS-5 ATF special agent applicants must meet the same employment requirements as most other federal agents, including (1) successful completion of the Treasury Enforcement Agent Examination, (2) a field interview, (3) a full field background investigation leading to successful certification for a top-secret clearance, and (4) a bachelor's degree from an accredited college or university or three years of general experience, one of which must be equivalent to at least the GS-4 level.

OTHER REQUIREMENTS

Other general requirements for employment as a federal officer apply. An applicant must (1) be a U.S. citizen, (2) be between 21 and 37 years old, (3) be in good physical health, (4) hold a current, valid U.S. driver's license, (5) pass a polygraph examination, and (6) have eyesight of no less than 20/100 uncorrected, and corrected vision of at least 20/30 in one eye and 20/20 in the other. New agents undergo eight weeks of specialized training at the Federal Law Enforcement Training Center in Glynco, Georgia.

SALARY

A bachelor's degree qualifies applicants for appointment at the GS-5 level, although appointments may be made at the GS-7 level for college graduates who are able to demonstrate superior academic achievement (that is, class standing in the upper third of their graduating class; a cumulative undergraduate grade point average of 2.95 or better; or membership in a national honor society recognized by the Association of College Honor Societies). GS-9 appointments require a master's degree, two full academic years of progressively higher-level graduate education, or one year of specialized experience equivalent to the next lower grade in the federal service. Depending on geographic area of assignment, this salary can be raised from 16% to 30% above the established base level.

BENEFITS

Benefits include (1) 13 days of sick leave annually, (2) two and a half to five weeks of paid vacation and ten paid federal holidays each year, (3) federal health and life insurance, and (4) a comprehensive retirement program.

DIRECT INQUIRIES TO:

Bureau of Alcohol, Tobacco, Firearms, and Explosives
Personnel Division
Room 4100
650 Massachusetts Ave., N.W.
Washington, DC 20226

Phone: 202-927-5690

Website: http://atf.treas.gov

For more information on the rapidly expanding criminal justice careers area, read *Where the Jobs Are: Mission Critical Opportunities for America,* available on the Web at http://www.justicestudies.com/jobs.htm.

Source: Bureau of Alcohol, Tobacco, Firearms, and Explosives.

"personal indicators" that seemed, from the agency's day-to-day enforcement experiences, to be associated with increased likelihood of law violation. Among the indicators were these: speaking Spanish; entering the United States on flights originating in particular Central and South American countries; being an 18- to 32-year-old male; having purchased tickets with cash; and having a short planned stay (often of only a day or two) in the United States. Federal agents frequently used these criteria in deciding which airline passengers to search and which bags to inspect.

Racial profiling has been derisively referred to as "driving while black" or "driving while brown," although it may also apply to situations other than those involving traffic violations. Racial profiling came to the attention of the public when police in New Jersey and Maryland were accused of unfair treatment of black motorists and admitted that race was a factor in traffic stops.

A 1999 report by the attorney general of New Jersey concluded that New Jersey state troopers *had* engaged in racial profiling along the New Jersey Turnpike.[102] The report, which tracked traffic stops between 1997 and 1998, found that people of color constituted 40.6% of the stops made on the turnpike. Although few stops resulted in a search, 77.2% of individuals searched were people of color. An analysis of these searches indicated that 10.5% of the searches that involved white motorists and 13.5% of the searches involving black motorists resulted in arrest or seizure.[103] An earlier racial profiling report, which had been compiled in support of a lawsuit against the state of New Jersey, showed that African Americans comprised 13.5% of New Jersey Turnpike users and 15% of drivers who were speeding.[104] At the same time, blacks represented 35% of those stopped and 73.2% of those arrested. The lawsuit resulted in the suppression of evidence in many criminal cases involving black motorists who had been arrested on the turnpike.

In 2003, in response to widespread public outcry over the use of racial profiling, the U.S. Department of Justice banned its practice in all federal law enforcement agencies, except in cases that involve the possible identification of terrorist suspects.[105] According to the DOJ, "the guidance provides that in making routine law enforcement decisions—such as deciding which motorists to stop for traffic infractions—consideration of the driver's race or ethnicity is absolutely forbidden."[106]

> *It is practically an article of faith among young, black males that they are more likely than whites to be stopped, frisked, spread-eagled, and arrested by the police, often on the flimsiest of charges.*
>
> —Hutchinson Report, July 2001

Those who defend the use of racial profiling by the police argue that it is not a bigoted practice when based on facts (such as when a police department decides to increase patrols in a housing area occupied primarily by minorities because of exceptionally high crime rates there) or when significant criminal potential exists among even a few members of a group. An example of the latter is the widespread public suspicions that focused on Arabs and Arab Americans following the terrorist attacks of September 11, 2001. As soon as it was publicly announced that the hijackers had been of Middle Eastern origin, some flight crews demanded that Arab-looking passengers be removed from their airplanes before takeoff, and passengers refused to fly with people who looked like Arabs.[107]

None of this is to say, of course, that race or ethnicity somehow inherently causes crime (or that it somehow causes poverty or increases the risk of victimization). If anything, race and ethnicity may simply display a significant correlation with certain types of crime, as they do with certain kinds of victimization. Hence, although the *real* causes of criminality may be socialization into criminal subcultures, economically deprived neighborhoods, a lack of salable job skills, and intergenerational poverty, and not race per se, to some law enforcement officers race provides one more indicator of the likelihood of criminality. David Cole, a professor at Georgetown University's Law Center, for example, notes that in the minds of many police officials, "racial and ethnic disparities reflect not discrimination [or bigotry] but higher rates of offenses among minorities."[108] "Nationwide," says Cole, "blacks are 13 times more likely to be sent to state prisons for drug convictions than are whites, so it would seem rational for police to assume that all other things being equal, a black driver is more likely than a white driver to be carrying drugs." Statistics like this, of course, may further enhance police focus on minorities and may result in even more arrests, thereby reinforcing the beliefs on which racial profiling by enforcement agents is based. Such observations led esteemed sociologist Amitai Etzioni to declare in 2001 that racial profiling is not necessarily racist.[109] Moreover, warned Etzioni, an end to racial profiling "would penalize those African-American communities with high incidences of violent crime" because they would lose the levels of policing that they need to remain relatively secure.

Regardless of arguments offered in support of racial profiling as an enforcement tool, the practice has been widely condemned as being contrary to basic ethical principles. National public opinion polls conducted by the Gallup Organization in 1999, for example, showed that 81% of respondents were morally opposed to the practice of racial profiling by the police.[110] Those participating in the survey generally felt that profiling is wrong because it is a form of race-based discrimination. Findings from the poll might be interpreted to mean that most people believe that racial discrimination of any kind is inherently unethical and not permissible in a free society. Moreover, as Christopher Stone, known for his writings on racial justice, explains, "Most people of all races and ethnic groups are never convicted of a crime, but stereotypes can work to brand all members of some groups with suspicion . . . putting an undue burden on innocent members of these groups."[111]

CJ News

As Shocks Replace Bullets, Questions Arise

The police in Seattle have had their share of high-profile violent or deadly run-ins with protesters, mentally ill suspects and other law-breakers. But in 2003, for the first time in 15 years, no one here was shot and killed by the police.

Miami, a city with a long history of police shootings and ensuing civil unrest, had no police shootings [in 2003], fatal or otherwise, for the first time in 14 years. In Phoenix, where such shootings reached a level over the last several years that far outpaced the rate of much larger cities, deadly police shootings fell sharply in 2003, to their lowest rate in 14 years.

In these cities and in a fast-growing number of the nation's police departments, officers are carrying a slick new weapon, the Taser gun, which looks a lot like a pistol but does not shoot to kill.

Though officials say the Taser gun, which fires a stunning jolt of electricity, is not solely responsible for a decline in police killings, many departments say it has made a huge difference. Its supporters say the Taser is saving lives, protecting officers and suspects in standoffs that might otherwise have left someone dead or seriously injured.

"This is 100 percent more humane," said Officer Tom Burns, who has carried a Taser gun for the past two and a half years on bicycle patrol in Seattle.

But as the Taser spreads rapidly, it is raising questions about whether the weapon, which can also be applied directly to the skin as a stun gun, could be abused by the police. The Taser zaps suspects with 50,000 volts of electricity, disabling them for five seconds at a time. Critics say the weapon is ripe for abuse because the shock leaves no obvious mark, other than what looks like a small bee sting. Human rights groups in the United States and abroad have called Tasers potential instruments of torture.

They are now being used by more than 4,000 police departments. Roughly 170 new departments are buying the high-tech electro-shock guns every month, and the Army has begun using them in Iraq, according to Taser International, the Arizona company that makes them. More than one-third of Seattle's 600 patrol officers carry Tasers. In Miami, Phoenix and a growing number of cities, every officer has one.

Tasers have often been introduced in the wake of public outcry over deadly police shootings. That was the case in Seattle, Denver, Austin, Tex., and Portland, Ore., as part of an effort to reduce killings through the use of training programs and "less lethal" weapons.

"You have to think about the alternatives," said Officer Burns, who also carries pepper spray and a .40-caliber Glock pistol. He said he had used the Taser five times on suspects who seemed eager to attack or were difficult to control. "And without this technology you might have to break it down to very brutal methods."

Officer Burns was on the scene in 1999 when Seattle police shot and killed a mentally ill man, a widely publicized incident that led to soul-searching in the department and a plan that among other things involved the purchase of Tasers.

The newest Tasers are an advanced version of technology that was developed in the 1970's but was not considered by the police to be effective until recently. The electrical pulses travel from the gun through

Shocking force

Taser International Inc., the maker of stun weapons, has watched its stock soar amidst growing concerns about whether the weapons are as non-lethal as advertised. In a recent report, Amnesty International says stun guns are being abused by police.

A Taser's electrical current overrides the central nervous system for five seconds, temporarily paralyzing targets

Use of force incidents

At the Orange County, Florida, Sheriff's Office Tasers were the most prevalent force option, constituting 68 percent of all use-of-force incidents in 2002.

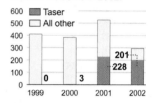

Dataport stores date and time of Taser firing

Insulated wires transmit 50,000 volts of electricity through up to two inches of clothing

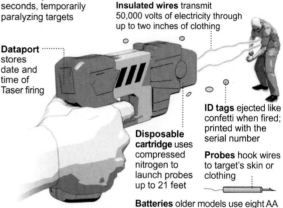

Disposable cartridge uses compressed nitrogen to launch probes up to 21 feet

ID tags ejected like confetti when fired; printed with the serial number

Probes hook wires to target's skin or clothing

Batteries older models use eight AA batteries, newer models are rechargeable

SOURCES: Amnesty International; Taser International

Source: Amnesty International; Taser International.

two 21-foot-long wires that look like a stretched-out Slinky tipped with barbed probes. If the probes pierce skin or a layer of clothing two inches thick or less, the jolt contracts the muscles and throws the suspect off balance. It makes the suspect unable to move and gives the police a full five seconds with every "tasing" to handcuff the suspect. The police say that 50,000 volts is a safe amount of electricity to absorb and that suspects shot with a Taser recover immediately.

But critics and watchdog groups say the Taser could be used to torture suspects and prison inmates to extract confessions or taunt them, and Amnesty International has called for a ban on their use pending studies on their long-term effects. Human rights and civil liberties groups are also questioning whether the electro-shocks that Tasers deliver are potentially deadly.

"Surely it's better than being killed," said Dan Handelman, a founder of Portland Copwatch, a group that has been critical of that city's growing use of Tasers over the last year. "But it's not necessarily an acceptable replacement because it's not being used—at least in Portland—in place of lethal force; it's being used for compliance."

Across the country in recent months, several suspects who were shot with Tasers, sometimes repeatedly, have died. But officials said other health problems, like heart conditions and drug overdoses, were the cause.

(continued)

A promotional photo showing the effects of Taser International's Advanced Taser®. This less-lethal weapon, intended for use in law enforcement and private security, incapacitates potential attackers by delivering an electrical shock to the person's nervous system. The technology is meant to reduce injury rates to both suspects and officers. When might the use of a Taser be appropriate?

TASER International (NASDAQ: TASR)

The American Civil Liberties Union of Colorado urged the Denver Police Department two weeks ago to limit its use of Tasers. The group cited a rising number of deaths nationally, saying 16 suspects in custody had died after being subdued with Tasers or stun guns in 2003, up from 10 in 2002 and 3 in 2001. But none of the deaths were officially attributed to the effect of the weapons.

In Las Vegas, William Lomax, 26, died last month after being arrested and, according to witnesses and the police, shot with a Taser four or five times, which critics of the Police Department said was an excessive use of force. Investigators said that Mr. Lomax had been under the influence of drugs, but that the cause of death was still under investigation.

Marsha Bell, 22, said she saw Mr. Lomax, her cousin, arrested on February 21 at her apartment complex, where he often visited his family. After he had a run-in with security guards, the police were called.

"He was on the ground," Ms. Bell said in a telephone interview. "He had two pairs of handcuffs on him, and I didn't know the Taser was being used until I heard him screaming. He kept screaming and screaming, saying, 'Oh God, Jesus, please no.' He was screaming in pain; he was hurt and he didn't resist."

Lt. Tom Monahan of the Las Vegas Metropolitan Police Department, which bought several hundred Tasers last year, said that Mr. Lomax had struggled with officers, security guards and paramedics, and that the Taser was used while officers were trying to handcuff him.

Officer Thomas Miller, who conducts Taser training for the Las Vegas department, said that there were clear guidelines on when Tasers should be used.

"In the past, an officer would have to fight," Officer Miller said. "Now we have an option to stop that before it gets to that point, greatly reducing the risk to the officer and the suspect."

The police do say that a Taser would never replace lethal weapons if an officer felt his life was in imminent danger, like when a suspect is wielding a knife or a gun at close proximity, or when no other officer is available to provide "lethal cover" for an officer using

the Taser. Most departments allow officers on the scene to make that judgment call.

In the New York City Police Department, supervisors and members of the large Emergency Service Unit, which helps patrol officers in violent situations, carry Tasers, but patrol officers do not, the police said.

The newest models cost $799 each, according to Taser International, the leading producer of the weapons. But company officials, who have seen their stock skyrocket over the last year, say the savings to police departments that might otherwise be sued over violent confrontations or shootings are potentially huge.

The police and other supporters of the new technology also say there are built-in safeguards to prevent abuse of the guns. Each Taser, which is powered by batteries, has a data port that records each shock and is used by police departments when they prepare incident reports, allowing supervisors to count how many times a Taser was fired.

Steve Tuttle, a spokesman for Taser International, which is based in Scottsdale, Ariz., said the company continually reviewed data and had found few instances among about 70,000 episodes so far of abuse or inappropriate use.

"If there's a bad apple out there, the technology we made will catch that bad apple," Mr. Tuttle said. "We've won the lottery in terms of great success, stock market-wise, but with that comes much more scrutiny."

Officer Burns of the Seattle department said the police could not deny that a misguided officer could abuse any weapon. But he said that there had been numerous instances in Seattle where officers had used the Taser instead of fists, nightsticks, guns or pepper spray, which can have much longer effects than Taser shocks, and that suspects had recovered immediately.

"Shooting someone is not a badge of honor," Officer Burns said. "It's something no one wants to do. No police officer in the world is paid to die; no police officer in the world is paid to get hurt."

For the latest in crime and justice news, visit the Talk Justice news feed at http://www.crimenews.info.

Author's Update: Amid continuing controversy over the safety of stun weapons, the two largest law enforcement divisions of the Department of Homeland Security—the Bureau of Immigration and Customs Enforcement (ICE) and the Bureau of Customs and Border Protection (CBP)—recently rejected the use of stun guns for about 20,000 agents and officers.

From a more pragmatic viewpoint, however, racial profiling is unacceptable because it weakens the public's confidence in the police, thereby decreasing police–citizen trust and cooperation. As some authors explain, "Truly effective policing will only be achieved when police both protect their neighborhoods from crime and respect the civil liberties of all residents. When law enforcement practices are perceived to be biased, unfair, or disrespectful, communities of color are less willing to trust and confide in police officers, report crimes, participate in problem-solving activities, be witnesses at trials, or serve on juries."[112] These authors summarize the current situation with regard to racial profiling this way: "The challenge that confronts American police organizations is how to sustain the historic decline in rates of criminal activity while enhancing police legitimacy in the eyes of the communities they serve. Appropriately addressing allegations of racial profiling is central to this new mission."[113] Learn more about racial profiling and police management via Library Extra 8–8 at cjtoday.com.

We must strive to eliminate any racial, ethnic, or cultural bias that may exist among our ranks.

—Los Angeles County Sheriff Sherman Block

LIBRARY
Extra
▪▪▪▪

Racially Biased Policing

In 2001, the Police Executive Research Forum (PERF) released a detailed report entitled *Racially Biased Policing: A Principled Response*.[114] PERF researchers surveyed more than 1,000 police executives, analyzed material from more than 250 law enforcement agencies, and sought input from law enforcement agency personnel, community activists, and civil rights leaders about racial bias in policing. Researchers concluded that "the vast majority of law enforcement officers—of all ranks, nationwide—are dedicated men and women committed to serving all citizens with fairness and dignity."[115] Most police officers, said the report, share an intolerance for racially biased policing. The report's authors noted that some police behaviors may be misinterpreted as biased when, in fact, the officer is just doing his or her job. "The good officer continually scans the environment for anomalies to normalcy—for conditions, people and behavior that are unusual for that environment," they said. "In learning and practicing their craft, officers quickly develop a sense for what is normal and expected, and conversely, for what is not."[116] Hence, for officers of any race to take special notice of unknown young white males who unexpectedly appear in a traditionally African American neighborhood, for example, might be nothing other than routine police procedure. Such an observation, however, is not in itself sufficient for an investigatory stop but might be used in conjunction with other trustworthy and relevant information already in the officer's possession—such as the officer's prior knowledge that young white men have been visiting a particular apartment complex in the neighborhood to purchase drugs—to justify such a stop.

The PERF report makes many specific recommendations to help police departments be free of bias. One recommendation, for example, says that "supervisors should monitor activity reports for evidence of improper practices and patterns. They should conduct spot-checks and regular sampling of in-car videotapes, radio transmissions, and in-car computer and central communications records to determine if both formal and informal communications are professional and free from racial bias and other disrespect."[117] Read the entire PERF report at Library Extra 8–9 at cjtoday.com.

LIBRARY
Extra
▪▪▪▪

Police Civil Liability

In 1996, 51-year-old Richard Kelley filed suit in federal court against the Massachusetts State Police and the Weymouth (Massachusetts) Police Department.[118] The suit resulted from an incident during which, Kelley alleged, state troopers and Weymouth police officers treated him as a drunk rather than recognizing that he had just suffered a stroke while driving. According to Kelley, following a minor traffic accident caused by the stroke, officers pulled him from his car, handcuffed him, dragged him along the ground, and ignored his pleas for help—forcing him to stay at a state police barracks for seven hours before taking him for medical treatment. Drunk-driving charges against Kelley were dropped after medical tests failed to reveal the presence of any intoxicating substances in his body.

Civil liability suits brought against law enforcement personnel are of two types: state and federal. Suits brought in state courts have generally been the more common form of civil litigation involving police officers. In recent years, however, an increasing number of suits have been brought in federal courts on the claim that the civil rights of the plaintiff, as guaranteed by federal law, were denied.

civil liability

Potential responsibility for payment of damages or other court-ordered enforcement as a result of a ruling in a lawsuit. Civil liability is not the same as criminal liability, which means "open to punishment for a crime."[x]

Common Sources of Civil Suits

Police officers may become involved in a variety of situations that could result in civil suits against the officers, their superiors, and their departments. Major sources of police civil liability are listed in Table 8–3. Charles Swanson, an expert in police procedure, says that the most

TABLE 8–3 Major Sources of Police Civil Liability

Failure to protect property in police custody	Negligence in the care of suspects in police custody
Failure to render proper emergency medical assistance	Failure to prevent a foreseeable crime
Lack of due regard for the safety of others	False imprisonment
Failure to aid private citizens	Unnecessary assault or battery
False arrest	Violations of constitutional rights
Inappropriate use of deadly force	Racial profiling
Malicious prosecution	Patterns of unfair and inequitable treatment

common sources of lawsuits against the police are "assault, battery, false imprisonment, and malicious prosecution."[119]

Of all complaints brought against the police, assault charges are the best known, being, as they are, subject to high media visibility. Less visible, but not uncommon, are civil suits charging the police with false arrest or false imprisonment. In the 1986 case of *Malley* v. *Briggs*,[120] the U.S. Supreme Court held that a police officer who effects an arrest or conducts a search on the basis of an improperly issued warrant may be liable for monetary damages when a reasonably well-

Multiculturalism and Diversity

Investigating Crime in a Multicultural Setting

In the mid-1990s, the Washington, D.C.–based National Crime Prevention Council (NCPC) published an important guide for American law enforcement officers who work with multicultural groups. The principles it contains can be applied equally to most foreign-born individuals living in the United States and are especially important to patrol officers and criminal investigators.

The NCPC guide points out that it is important for well-intentioned newcomers to this country to learn that the law enforcement system in the United States is not a national police force but a series of local, state, and federal agencies that take seriously their obligation to "serve and protect" law-abiding residents. Newcomers need to know that police officers can teach them how to protect themselves and their families from crime. Many immigrants, especially political refugees, come from countries in which the criminal justice system is based on tyranny, repression, and fear.

The NCPC suggests that law enforcement officers and other members of the criminal justice system can help ease this transition by working not only to communicate with immigrants but also to understand them and the complexities of their native cultures. The mere absence of conflict in a neighborhood does not mean that residents of different cultures have found harmony and a cooperative working relationship, says the NCPC. True multicultural integration occurs when various cultures reach a comfortable day-to-day interaction marked by respect, interest, and caring.

Communities in which immigrants and law enforcement have established close positive ties benefit considerably, according to the NCPC. Immigrants gain greater access to police and other services, such as youth programs, victim assistance, parenting classes, medical assistance programs, business networking, and neighborhood groups. Crime decreases in communities where law enforcement officers help immigrants learn to protect themselves against crime.

For police officers working in communities in which "language is a serious barrier between cultures," the NCPC suggests the following pointers for communicating more effectively:

- Be patient when speaking with someone who does not clearly understand your language. Speak slowly and distinctly. Be willing to repeat words or phrases if necessary. Remember that shouting never helps a nonnative speaker understand better.

- Be careful with your choice of words, selecting those that are clear, straightforward, and simple to understand. Avoid colloquialisms and slang.

- Allow extra time for investigation when the people involved have not mastered English.

- Be sure that anyone who serves as an interpreter is fully qualified and has had experience. Interpreting under pressure is a difficult task; lack of training can lead to mistakes.

- Be candid about your ability to speak or understand a language. Trying to "fake it" just leads to confusion, misunderstanding, and misspent time.

- Never assume that someone is less intelligent just because he or she doesn't speak English well.

Visit the National Crime Prevention Council via **Web Extra 8–5** at cjtoday.com.

Reference: Adapted from National Crime Prevention Council, *Building and Crossing Bridges: Refugees and Law Enforcement Working Together* (Washington, DC: NCPC, 1994).

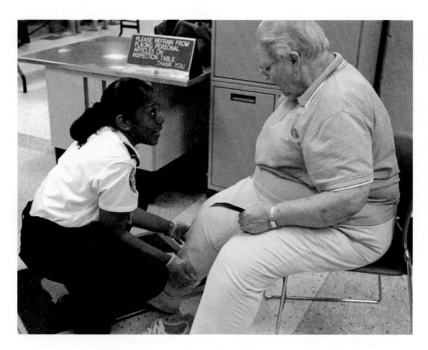

A passenger being subjected to a heightened security screening at Dallas-Forth Worth International Airport. Some people fear that the use of profiling techniques could unfairly discriminate against members of certain racial and ethnic groups. Others suggest that the careful use of profiling can provide an important advantage in an age of scarce resources. With which perspective do you agree?

Mark Williams

trained officer, under the same circumstances, "would have known that his affidavit failed to establish probable cause and that he should not have applied for the warrant." Significantly, the Court ruled that an officer "cannot excuse his own default by pointing to the greater incompetence of the magistrate."[121] That is, the officer, rather than the judge who issued the warrant, is ultimately responsible for establishing the basis for pursuing the arrest or search.

When an officer makes an arrest without just cause or simply impedes an individual's right to leave the scene without good reason, he or she may also be liable for the charge of false arrest. Officers who "throw their weight around" are especially subject to this type of suit, grounded as it is on the abuse of police authority. Because generally employers may be sued for the negligent or malicious actions of their employees, many police departments are being named as codefendants in lawsuits today.

Civil suits are also brought against officers whose actions are deemed negligent. High-speed vehicle pursuits are especially dangerous because of the potential for injury to innocent bystanders. In the case of *Biscoe* v. *Arlington County* (1984),[122] for example, Alvin Biscoe was awarded $5 million after he lost both legs as a consequence of a high-speed chase while he was waiting to cross the street. Biscoe, an innocent bystander, was struck by a police car that went out of control. The officer driving the car had violated department policies prohibiting high-speed chases, and the court found that he had not been properly trained.

Departments may protect themselves to some degree through training combined with regulations limiting the authority of their personnel. One year after the *Biscoe* case was decided, for example, a Louisiana police officer, who had an accident while driving 75 mph in a 40-mph zone, was found to be negligent and was held liable for damages.[123] However, the department was not held liable because it had a policy limiting emergency driving to no more than 20 mph over the posted speed limit and because officers were trained in that policy. In 2007, in the case of *Scott* v. *Harris,* the Supreme Court created a new rule shielding police officers involved in vehicle chases from liability if the motorist's actions during the chase threatened bystanders.

According to the FBI, "a traffic accident constitutes the most common terminating event in an urban pursuit."[124] Hence, some cities are actively replacing high-speed vehicle pursuits with surveillance technologies employing unmanned aerial vehicles (UAVs). Although helicopters have long been used in this capacity, the advent of UAV technology promises to make the tracking of fleeing suspects much quicker and far safer for all involved.

Law enforcement supervisors may be the object of lawsuits by virtue of the fact that they are responsible for the actions of their officers. If it can be shown that supervisors were negligent in hiring (as when someone with a history of alcoholism, mental problems, sexual deviance, or drug abuse is employed) or if supervisors failed in their responsibility to properly train officers before arming and deploying them, they may be found liable for damages.

In the 1989 case of the *City of Canton, Ohio* v. *Harris,*[125] the U.S. Supreme Court ruled that a "failure to train" can become the basis for legal liability on the part of a municipality where the "failure to train amounts to deliberate indifference to the rights of persons with whom the police

We depend on law enforcement officers to protect us. They have to make split-second decisions in the field. Would we want to put police officers in the position where they wouldn't (react) out of fear that three weeks later they'd be called a criminal?

—Florida defense attorney Michael Salnick, representing a police officer accused of manslaughter in the death of a fleeing suspect.[xi]

A police car destroyed during a high-speed chase. Research shows that most of the suspects chased by police are not violent criminals, and high-speed chases are especially dangerous because of their potential to injure innocent bystanders. When injuries do occur, a chase might provide a lawful basis for a civil suit against officers and their departments. How might a department protect itself from these kinds of suits?

© Luis Santana/911 Pictures

The twenty-first century police candidate must be carefully chosen and then trained and mentored to fill the role of modern policing. Only then will policing become a true profession; and only then will police be able to deliver on their mission to protect and serve the citizenry.

—Gene Stephens[xii]

come in contact."[126] In that case, Geraldine Harris was arrested and taken to the Canton, Ohio, police station. While at the station, she slumped to the floor several times. Officers left her on the floor and did not call for medical assistance. Upon release, Harris's family took her to a local hospital, where she was found to be suffering from several emotional ailments. Harris was hospitalized for a week and received follow-up outpatient treatment for the next year.

In the 1997 case of *Board of the County Commissioners of Bryan County, Oklahoma* v. *Brown*, however, the Supreme Court ruled that to establish liability, plaintiffs must show that "the municipal action in question was not simply negligent, but was taken with 'deliberate indifference' as to its known or obvious consequences."[127] In *Brown*, a deputy named Burns was hired by the sheriff of Bryan County, Oklahoma. Burns later used excessive force in arresting a woman, and the woman sued the county for damages, claiming that Deputy Burns had been hired despite his criminal record. In fact, some years earlier, Burns had pleaded guilty to various driving infractions and other misdemeanors, including assault and battery—a charge resulting from a college fight. At trial, a spokesperson for the sheriff's department admitted to receiving Burns's driving and criminal records but said he had not reviewed either in detail before the department decided to hire Burns. Nonetheless, the Supreme Court held that deliberate indifference on the part of the county had not been established because the plaintiff had not demonstrated that "Burns's background made his use of excessive force in making an arrest a plainly obvious consequence of the hiring decision." According to this decision, a municipality (in this case, a county) may not be held liable solely because it employs a person with an arrest record.

Federal Lawsuits

1983 lawsuit

A civil suit brought under Title 42, Section 1983, of the U.S. Code against anyone who denies others their constitutional right to life, liberty, or property without due process of law.

Civil suits alleging police misconduct that are filed in federal courts are often called **1983 lawsuits** because they are based on Section 1983 of Title 42 of the U.S. Code—an act passed by Congress in 1871 to ensure the civil rights of men and women of all races. That act requires due process of law before any person can be deprived of life, liberty, or property and specifically provides redress for the denial of these constitutional rights by officials acting under color of state law. It reads as follows:

> Every person who, under color of any statute, ordinance, regulation, custom, or usage, of any State or Territory, subjects, or causes to be subjected, any citizen of the United States or other person within the jurisdiction thereof to the deprivation of any rights, privileges, or immunities secured by the Constitution and laws, shall be liable to the party injured in an action at law, suit in equity, or other proper proceeding for redress.[128]

A 1983 suit may be brought, for example, against officers who shoot suspects under questionable circumstances, thereby denying them their right to life without due process. Similarly, an officer who makes an arrest based on accusations that he or she knows to be untrue may be subject to a 1983 lawsuit.

Bivens action

A civil suit, based on the case of *Bivens* v. *Six Unknown Federal Agents,* brought against federal government officials for denying the constitutional rights of others.

Another type of liability action, this one directed specifically at federal officials or enforcement agents, is called a **Bivens action**. The case of *Bivens* v. *Six Unknown Federal Agents* (1971)[129] established a path for legal action against agents enforcing federal laws, which is similar to that found in a 1983 suit. *Bivens* actions may be addressed against individuals but not against the United States or its agencies.[130] Federal officers have generally been granted a court-created qualified immunity and have been protected from suits where they were found to have acted in the belief that their action was consistent with federal law.[131]

In the past, the doctrine of sovereign immunity barred legal actions against state and local governments. Sovereign immunity was a legal theory that held that a governing body could not be sued because it made the law and therefore could not be bound by it. Immunity is a much more complex issue today. Some states have officially abandoned any pretext of immunity through legislative action. New York State, for example, has declared that public agencies are equally as liable as private agencies for violations of constitutional rights. Other states, like California, have enacted statutory provisions that define and limit governmental liability.[132] A number of state immunity statutes have been struck down by court decision. In general, states are moving in the direction of setting dollar limits on liability and adopting federal immunity principles to protect individual officers, including "good faith" and "reasonable belief" rules.

At the federal level, the concept of sovereign immunity is embodied in the Federal Tort Claims Act (FTCA),[133] which grants broad immunity to federal government agencies engaged in discretionary activities. When a federal employee is sued for a wrongful or negligent act, the Federal Employees Liability Reform and Tort Compensation Act of 1988, commonly known as the Westfall Act, empowers the attorney general to certify that the employee was acting within the scope of his or her office or employment at the time of the incident. Upon certification, the employee is dismissed from the action, and the United States is substituted as defendant. The case then falls under the governance of the FTCA.

The U.S. Supreme Court has supported a type of qualified immunity for individual officers (as opposed to the agencies for which they work). This immunity "shields law enforcement officers from constitutional lawsuits if reasonable officers believe their actions to be lawful in light of clearly established law and the information the officers possess." The Supreme Court has also described qualified immunity as a defense "which shields public officials from actions for damages unless their conduct was unreasonable in light of clearly established law."[134] According to the Court, "[T]he qualified immunity doctrine's central objective is to protect public officials from undue interference with their duties and from potentially disabling threats of liability."[135] In the context of a warrantless arrest, the Court said in *Hunter* v. *Bryant* (1991),[136] "even law enforcement officials who reasonably but mistakenly conclude that probable cause is present are entitled to immunity."[137]

The doctrine of qualified immunity, as it exists today, rests largely on the 2001 U.S. Supreme Court decision of *Saucier* v. *Katz*,[138] in which the Court established a two-pronged test for assessing constitutional violations by government agents.[139] First, the court hearing the case must decide whether the facts, taken in the light most favorable to the party asserting the injury, show that the defendant's conduct violated a constitutional right. Second, the court must then decide whether that right was clearly established. For a right to be clearly established, the Court ruled, "it would be clear to a reasonable [defendant] that his conduct was unlawful in the situation he confronted." In summary, qualified immunity protects law enforcement agents from being sued for damages unless they violate clearly established law which a reasonable official in the agent's position would have known.

Criminal charges can also be brought against officers who appear to overstep legal boundaries or who act in violation of set standards. In 2001, for example, in the case of *Idaho* v. *Horiuchi*,[140] the Ninth U.S. Circuit Court of Appeals ruled that federal law enforcement officers are not immune from state prosecution where their actions violate state law "either through malice or excessive zeal." The case involved FBI sharpshooter Lon Horiuchi, who was charged with negligent manslaughter by prosecutors in Boundary County, Idaho, following the 1992 incident at Ruby Ridge. Learn more about the Ruby Ridge incident at Library Extra 8–10 at cjtoday.com.

LIBRARY
Extra
■ ■ ■ ■

Today, most police departments at both state and federal levels carry liability insurance to protect themselves against the severe financial damage that can result from the loss of a large civil suit. Some officers also acquire private policies that provide coverage in the event they are named as individuals in a civil suit. Both types of insurance policies generally cover legal fees up to a certain amount, regardless of the outcome of the case. Police departments that face civil prosecution because of the actions of an officer may find that legal and financial liability extends to supervisors, city managers, and the community itself. Where insurance coverage does not exist or is inadequate, city coffers may be nearly drained to meet the damages awarded.[141]

A 2001 study of a large sample of police chiefs throughout Texas found that most believed that lawsuits or the threat of civil litigation against the police makes it harder for individual officers to do their jobs. Most of the chiefs espoused the idea that adequate training, better screening of applicants, close supervision of officers, and "treating people fairly" all reduced the likelihood of lawsuits.[142]

SUMMARY

- The police personality is created through informal pressures on officers by a powerful police subculture that communicates values that support law enforcement interests. This chapter described the police personality as, among other things, authoritarian, conservative, honorable, loyal, cynical, dogmatic, hostile, prejudiced, secret, and suspicious.

- Various types of police corruption were described in this chapter, including "grass eating," and "meat eating," which includes much more serious forms of corruption such as an officer's actively seeking illegal moneymaking opportunities through the exercise of his or her law enforcement duties. Ethics training was mentioned as part of a "reframing" strategy that emphasizes integrity in an effort to target police corruption. Also discussed was a recent U.S. Department of Justice report that focused on enhancing policing integrity and that cited a police department's culture of integrity as more important in shaping the ethics of police officers than hiring the "right" people.

- The dangers of police work are many and varied. They consist of violent victimization, disease, exposure to biological or chemical toxins, stressful encounters with suspects and victims, and on-the-job fatigue. Stress-management programs, combined with department policies designed to reduce exposure to dangerous situations and agency practices that support officers' needs, can all help combat the dangers and difficulties that police officers face in their day-to-day work.

- Law enforcement officers are authorized to use the amount of force that is reasonable and necessary in a particular situation. Many officers have encounters where the use of force is appropriate. Nonetheless, studies show that the police use force in fewer than 20% of adult custodial arrests. Even in instances where force is used, police officers primarily use weaponless tactics. Excessive force is the application of an amount and/or frequency of force greater than that required to compel compliance from a willing or unwilling subject.

- Racial profiling, or racially biased policing, is any police action initiated on the basis of the race, ethnicity, or national origin of a suspect rather than on the behavior of that individual or on information that leads the police to a particular individual who has been identified as being, or having been, engaged in criminal activity. Racial profiling is a bigoted practice unworthy of the law enforcement professional. It has been widely condemned as contrary to basic ethical principles. Further, it weakens the public's confidence in the police, thereby decreasing police–citizen trust and cooperation. This chapter pointed out, however, that racial or ethnic indicators associated with particular suspects or suspect groups may have a place in legitimate law enforcement strategies if they accurately relate to suspects who are being sought for criminal law violations.

- Civil liability issues are very important in policing. They arise because officers and their agencies sometimes inappropriately use power to curtail the civil and due process rights of criminal suspects. Both police departments and individual police officers can be targeted by civil lawsuits. Federal suits based on claims that officers acted with disregard for an individual's right to due process are called *1983 lawsuits* because they are based on Section 1983 of Title 42 of the U.S. Code. Another type of civil suit that can be brought specifically against federal agents is a *Bivens* action. Although the doctrine of sovereign immunity barred legal action against state and local governments in the past, recent court cases and legislative activity have restricted the opportunity for law enforcement agencies and their officers to exercise claims of immunity.

KEY TERMS

1983 lawsuit, 302

biological weapon, 286

Bivens action, 302

civil liability, 299

deadly force, 292

excessive force, 291

internal affairs, 284

Knapp Commission, 280

less-lethal weapon, 294

police corruption, 279

police use of force, 291

police working personality, 276

problem police officer, 292

racial profiling, 294

KEY CASES

Biscoe v. *Arlington County,* 301

Bivens v. *Six Unknown Federal Agents,* 302

City of Canton, Ohio v. *Harris,* 301

Graham v. *Connor,* 293

Hunter v. *Bryant,* 303

Idaho v. *Horiuchi,* 303

Malley v. *Briggs,* 300

Tennessee v. *Garner,* 292

QUESTIONS FOR REVIEW

1. What is the police working personality? What are its central features? How does it develop? How does it relate to police subculture?

2. What are the different types of police corruption? What themes run through the findings of the Knapp Commission and the Wickersham Commission? What innovative steps might police departments take to reduce or eliminate corruption among their officers?

3. What are the dangers of police work? What can be done to reduce those dangers?

4. In what kinds of situations are police officers most likely to use force? When has too much force been used?

5. What is racial profiling? Why has it become a significant issue in policing today?

6. What are some of the civil liability issues associated with policing? What are some of the common sources of civil suits against the police? How can civil liability be reduced?

QUESTIONS FOR REFLECTION

1. Do you think that this chapter has accurately described the police personality? Why or why not? Can you identify any additional characteristics of the police personality? Are there any listed here that you do not think are appropriate?

2. What strategies can you think of for helping build police integrity? How might those strategies differ from one agency to another or from the local to the state or federal level?

3. What is it about racial profiling that most people find unacceptable? Are there any situations in which law enforcement's use of racial features or ethnic characteristics may be appropriate in targeting suspected criminals? If so, what would those situations be?

Discuss your answers to these questions and other issues on the CJ Today e-mail discussion list (join the list at cjtoday.com).

WEB QUEST

Visit the National Criminal Justice Reference Service (NCJRS) at http://www.ncjrs.org. Click on "Advanced Search" and then on "Hints on Searching the NCJRS website" to view tips on performing effective searches, modifying search queries, and interpreting search results. Write a description of the search techniques available in the NCJRS database, including wild-card, proximity, concept, Boolean, and pattern searching. What does the help text suggest you do if you find too much in your search? If you find too little?

Revisit the NCJRS advanced search page, and click on the "Library/Abstracts" tab. What is the NCJRS Abstracts Database? How does it differ from the NCJRS full-text collection?

After you have become familiar with searching techniques, put your skills to use by conducting a search of the NCJRS site to identify documents on homeland security and policing. (You may have to develop your own search strategy using other keywords in combination with "security" or "police" to narrow down the results of your search.) What kinds of documents did you find? What conclusions, if any, did you come to about the police role in homeland security after reading these documents?

To complete this Web Quest online, go to the Web Quest module in Chapter 8 of the *Criminal Justice Today* Companion Website at cjtoday.com.

PART 3
Adjudication

RIGHTS OF THE ACCUSED BEFORE THE COURT

The accused has these common law, constitutional, statutory, and humanitarian rights

- The right to a speedy trial

- The right to legal counsel

- The right against self-incrimination

- The right not to be tried twice for the same offense

- The right to know the charges

- The right to cross-examine witnesses

- The right against excessive bail

These individual rights must be effectively balanced against these community concerns

- Conviction of the guilty

- Exoneration of the innocent

- The imposition of appropriate punishment

- The protection of society

- Efficient and cost-effective procedures

- Seeing justice done

How does our system of justice work toward balance?

9

The Courts: Structure and Participants

10

Pretrial Activities and the Criminal Trial

11

Sentencing

Equal Justice under the Law

The well-known British philosopher and statesman Benjamin Disraeli (1804–1881) once defined justice as "truth in action." The study of criminal case processing by courts at all levels provides perhaps the best opportunity available to us from within the criminal justice system to observe what should ideally be "truth in action." The courtroom search for truth, which is characteristic of criminal trials, pits the resources of the accused against those of the state. The ultimate outcome of such procedures, say advocates of our adversarial-based system of trial practice, should be both truth and justice.

Others are not so sure. British novelist William McIlvanney (1936–) once wrote, "Who thinks the law has anything to do with justice? It's what we have because we can't

have justice." Indeed, many critics of the present system claim that courts at all levels have become so concerned with procedure and with sets of formalized rules that they have lost sight of the truth. The chapters that make up this section of *Criminal Justice Today* provide an overview of American courts, including their history and present structure, and examine the multifaceted roles played by both professional and lay courtroom participants. Sentencing—the practice whereby juries recommend and judges impose sanctions on convicted offenders—is covered in the concluding chapter of this section. Whether American courts routinely uncover truth and therefore dispense justice, or whether they are merely locked into a pattern of hollow procedure that does little other than mock the justice ideal, will be for you to decide.

CHAPTER 9

The Courts: Structure and Participants

LEARNING OBJECTIVES

After reading this chapter, you should be able to

- Describe the development of American courts and explain the concept of the dual-court system.

- Describe a typical state court system and identify some of the differences between the state and federal court systems.

- Explain the structure of the federal court system and name and describe the various types of federal courts.

- Describe the courtroom work group and identify its members.

- Identify and explain the roles of professional members of the courtroom work group.

- Identify and explain the roles of nonjudicial or nonprofessional courtroom participants.

The criminal court is the central, crucial institution in the criminal justice system. It is the part of the system that is the most venerable, the most formally organized, and the most elaborately circumscribed by law and tradition. It is the institution around which the rest of the system has developed.

—President's Commission on Law Enforcement and Administration of Justice

Courts are one of the few institutions of American government that have outperformed our expectations. We've come to look at them as the ultimate safeguard of our rights.

—New York University law professor Burt Neuborne[1]

Hear the author discuss this chapter at cjtoday.com

Introduction

On March 11, 2005, rape suspect Brian Nichols grabbed a deputy's gun and shot her in the face as he was being prepared for transfer from a jail holding cell to an Atlanta courtroom.[2] Nichols, 33, then took the gun and crossed a pedestrian bridge into the courthouse area, where he entered the eighth-floor courtroom in which his trial was scheduled to be held. Once inside, he shot and killed Superior Court Judge Rowland Barnes and court reporter Julie Ann Brandau. Both were in the midst of a civil hearing, with no police officers present. Nichols then fled down a stairwell, shooting and killing Fulton County Deputy Sheriff Hoyt Teasley, whom he encountered along the way. Following several carjackings, Nichols came upon U.S. Customs Agent David Wilhelm as the agent worked on his house in Atlanta's Buckhead section. Nichols killed Wilhelm and took his truck, fleeing to the Atlanta suburb of Duluth. He became the focus of the largest manhunt in Georgia history before his capture a day later at a Gwinnett County condominium, where he had been holding 26-year-old Ashley Smith captive.

Nichols' courthouse rampage came only a week after the husband and elderly mother of federal Judge Joan Humphrey Lefkow were found shot to death in the basement of the family's Chicago home.[3] A few days later, the case seemed solved when 57-year-old Bart Ross shot himself to death during a Wisconsin traffic stop. Ross, stopped for having a burned-out taillight, left a suicide note saying that he had killed the judge's family. DNA from a cigarette butt found in the Lefkow house after the killings confirmed Ross's presence at the murder scene.[4] A medical malpractice case in which Ross had been the plaintiff, and that Judge Lefkow had earlier dismissed, apparently served as a motive in the killings.

Incidents like those in Atlanta and Chicago highlight the critical role that our nation's courts and the personnel who staff them play in the American system of justice. Breaches of courtroom security endanger courtroom participants and threaten the effective administration of justice. Without courts to decide guilt or innocence and to impose sentence on those convicted of crimes, the activities of law enforcement officials would become meaningless.

There are many different levels of courts in the United States, but they all dispense justice and help ensure that officials in the justice system work within the law when carrying out their duties. At many points in this textbook and in three specific chapters (Chapter 7, "Policing: Legal Aspects"; Chapter 12, "Probation, Parole, and Community Corrections"; and Chapter 13, "Prisons and Jails"), we take a close look at court precedents that have defined the legality of enforcement efforts and correctional action. In Chapter 4, "Criminal Law," we explored the law-making function of courts. This chapter provides a picture of how courts work by describing the American court system at both the state and federal levels. We will look at the roles of courtroom actors—from attorneys to victims and from jurors to judges. Then in Chapter 10, we will discuss pretrial activities and examine each of the steps in a criminal trial.

A deputy being wheeled into a waiting ambulance (top right) in the aftermath of shootings at the Fulton County Courthouse in Atlanta, Georgia, in 2005. The deputy later died. Also killed in the shootings were Superior Court Judge Rowland Barnes (bottom left) and court reporter Julie Ann Brandau (bottom right). The shooter, rape suspect Brian Nichols (top left), grabbed a deputy's gun as he was being transferred from a holding cell. He escaped after the shootings, only to be captured the next day at a nearby condominium. What can be done to improve the safety of our nation's courthouses?

John Bazemore/AP Wide World Photos, Photo by Ben Gray/The Atlanta Journal-Constitution, *and Photo by Brent Sanderlin/The* Atlanta Journal-Constitution.

History and Structure of the American Court System

Two types of courts function within the American criminal justice system: (1) state courts and (2) federal courts. Figure 9–1 outlines the structure of today's **federal court system**, and Figure 9–2 diagrams a typical **state court system**. This dual-court system is the result of general agreement among the nation's founders about the need for individual states to retain significant legislative authority and judicial autonomy separate from federal control. Under this concept, the United States developed as a relatively loose federation of semi-independent provinces. New states joining the union were assured of limited federal intervention into local affairs. State legislatures were free to create laws, and state court systems were needed to hear cases in which violations of those laws occurred.

In the last 200 years, states' rights have gradually waned relative to the power of the federal government, but the dual-court system still exists. Even today, state courts do not hear cases involving alleged violations of federal law, nor do federal courts get involved in deciding issues of state law unless there is a conflict between local or state statutes and federal constitutional guarantees. When such conflicts arise, claimed violations of federal due process guarantees—especially those found in the Bill of Rights—can provide the basis for appeals made to federal courts by offenders convicted in state court systems. Learn more about the dual-court system in America at Library Extra 9–1 at cjtoday.com.

This chapter describes both federal and state court systems in terms of their historical development, **jurisdiction**, and current structure. Because it is within state courts that the large majority of criminal cases originate, we turn our attention first to them.

federal court system

The three-tiered structure of federal courts, comprising U.S. district courts, U.S. courts of appeal, and the U.S. Supreme Court.

state court system

A state judicial structure. Most states have at least three court levels: trial courts, appellate courts, and a state supreme court.

LIBRARY Extra
■■■■

jurisdiction

The territory, subject matter, or people over which a court or other justice agency may exercise lawful authority, as determined by statute or constitution.

FIGURE 9–1

The structure of the federal courts.

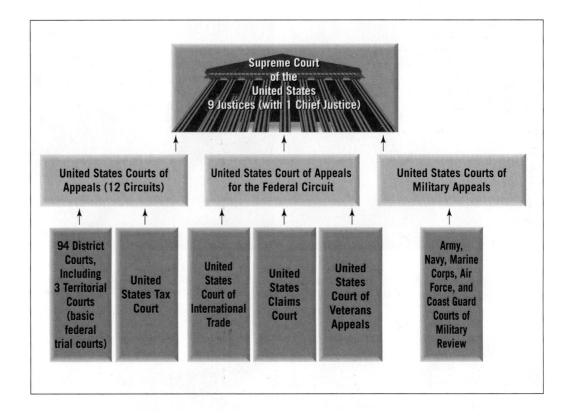

FIGURE 9–2

A typical state court system.

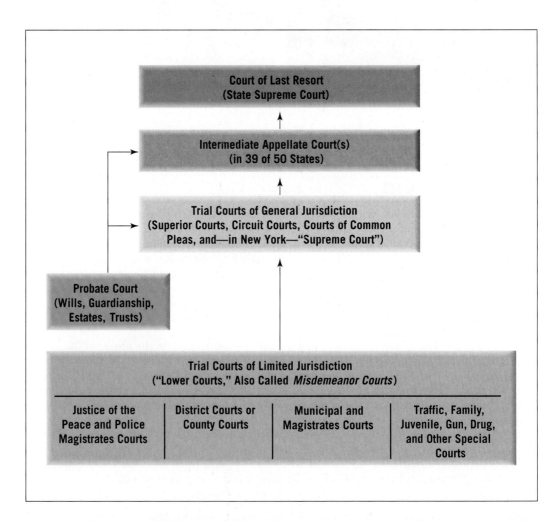

Junior high school children posing in the pillory in Williamsburg, Virginia. Just as criminal punishments have changed throughout the centuries, so too have criminal courts, which today provide civilized forums for exploring conflicting claims about guilt and innocence. How might our courts continue to evolve?
Jeff Greenberg/PhotoEdit Inc.

The State Court System

The Development of State Courts

Each of the original American colonies had its own court system for resolving disputes, both civil and criminal. As early as 1629, the Massachusetts Bay Colony created a General Court, composed of the governor, his deputy, 18 assistants, and 118 elected officials. The General Court was a combined legislature and court that made laws, held trials, and imposed sentences.[5] By 1639, as the colony grew, county courts were created, and the General Court took on the hearing of appeals as its primary job, retaining original jurisdiction only in cases involving "tryalls of life, limm, or banishment" and divorce.[6]

Pennsylvania began its colonial existence with the belief that "every man could serve as his own lawyer."[7] The Pennsylvania system utilized "common peacemakers" who served as referees in disputes. Parties to a dispute, including criminal suspects, could plead their case before a common peacemaker they had agreed on. The decision of the peacemaker was binding on the parties. Although the Pennsylvania referee system ended in 1766, lower-level judges are still referred to as *justices of the peace* in Pennsylvania and a few other states, though they are called *magistrates* in many other jurisdictions.

By 1776, all of the American colonies had established fully functioning court systems. The practice of law, however, was substantially inhibited by a lack of trained lawyers. A number of the early colonies even displayed a strong reluctance to recognize the practice of law as a profession. A Virginia statute enacted in 1645, for example, provided for the removal of "mercenary attorneys" from office and prohibited the practice of law for a fee. Most other colonies retained strict control over the number of authorized *barristers*—another name for lawyers—by requiring formal training in English law schools and appointment by the governor. New York, which provided for the appointment of "counselors at law," permitted a total of only 41 lawyers to practice law between 1695 and 1769[8]—in large part due to a widespread distrust of formally trained attorneys.

The tenuous status of lawyers in the colonies was highlighted by the 1735 trial of John Zenger in New York. Zenger was the editor of the newspaper *New York Journal* and was accused of slandering Governor William Cosby. When Cosby threatened to disbar any lawyer who defended Zenger, the editor hired Pennsylvania lawyer Andrew Hamilton, who was immune to the governor's threats because he was from out of state.[9]

Following the American Revolution, colonial courts provided the organizational basis for the growth of fledgling state court systems. Since there had been considerable diversity in the structure of colonial courts, state courts were anything but uniform. Initially, most states made no distinction between **original jurisdiction**, the lawful authority of a court to hear cases that arise within a specified geographic area or that involve particular kinds of law violations, and

original jurisdiction

The lawful authority of a court to hear or to act on a case from its beginning and to pass judgment on the law and the facts. The authority may be over a specific geographic area or over particular types of cases.

A criminal trial in progress. Why are courts sometimes called "the fulcrum of the criminal justice system"?

Ron Chapple/Taxi/Getty Images, Inc.—Taxi

appellate jurisdiction

The lawful authority of a court to review a decision made by a lower court.

appellate jurisdiction, the lawful authority of a court to review a decision made by a lower court. Many, in fact, had no provisions for appeal. Delaware, for example, did not allow appeals in criminal cases until 1897. States that did permit appeals often lacked any established appellate courts and sometimes used state legislatures for that purpose.

By the late nineteenth century, a dramatic increase in population, growing urbanization, the settlement of the West, and other far-reaching changes in the American way of life led to a tremendous increase in civil litigation and criminal arrests. Legislatures tried to keep pace with the rising tide of cases. States created a number of courts at the trial, appellate, and supreme court levels, calling them by a variety of names and assigning them functions that sometimes were completely different from those of similarly named courts in neighboring states. City courts, which were limited in their jurisdiction by community boundaries, arose to handle the special problems of urban life, such as disorderly conduct, property disputes, and the enforcement of restrictive and regulatory ordinances. Other tribunals, such as juvenile courts, developed to handle special kinds of problems or special clients. Some, like magistrate's courts or small-claims courts, handled only minor law violations and petty disputes. Still others, like traffic courts, were very narrow in focus. The result was a patchwork quilt of hearing bodies, some only vaguely resembling modern notions of a trial court.

State court systems developed by following several models. One was the New York State Field Code of 1848, which clarified jurisdictional claims and specified matters of court procedure. While many states copied the plan of the Field Code, it was later amended so extensively that its usefulness as a model dissolved. The federal Judiciary Act of 1789 and later the federal Reorganization Act of 1801 provided other models for state court systems. States that followed the federal model developed a three-tiered structure of (1) trial courts of limited jurisdiction, (2) trial courts of general jurisdiction, and (3) appellate courts.

State Court Systems Today

The three-tiered federal model was far from perfect, however. Within the structure it provided, many local and specialized courts proliferated. Traffic courts, magistrate's courts, municipal courts, recorder's courts, probate courts, and courts held by justices of the peace were but a few that functioned at the lower levels. In the early twentieth century, the American Bar Association (ABA) and the American Judicature Society led the movement toward simplification of state court structures. Proponents of state court reform sought to unify redundant courts that held overlapping jurisdictions. Most reformers suggested a uniform model for all states that would build on (1) a centralized court structure composed of a clear hierarchy of trial and appellate courts, (2) the consolidation of numerous lower-level courts with overlapping jurisdictions, and (3) a centralized state court authority that would be responsible for budgeting, financing, and managing all courts within a state.

The court reform movement continues today. Although reformers have made substantial progress in many states, there are still many differences between and among state court systems. Reform states, which early on embraced the reform movement, are now characterized by streamlined judicial systems consisting of precisely conceived trial courts of limited and general jurisdiction, supplemented by one or two appellate court levels. Nonreform, or traditional, states retain judicial systems that are a conglomeration of multilevel and sometimes redundant courts with poorly defined jurisdictions. Even in nonreform states, however, most criminal courts can be classified within the three-tiered structure of two trial court echelons and an appellate tier.

STATE TRIAL COURTS

Trial courts are where criminal cases begin. The trial court conducts arraignments, sets bail, takes pleas, and conducts trials. (We will discuss each of these functions in more depth in the next chapter.) If the defendant pleads guilty or is found guilty, the trial court imposes sentence. Trial courts of limited, or special, jurisdiction are also called *lower courts*. Lower courts are authorized to hear only less serious criminal cases, usually involving misdemeanors, or to hear special types of cases, such as traffic violations, family disputes, and small claims. Courts of limited jurisdiction, which are depicted in TV shows like *Judge Judy* and *Joe Brown*, rarely hold jury trials, depending instead on the hearing judge to make determinations of both fact and law. At the lower-court level, a detailed record of the proceedings is not maintained. Case files will only include information on the charge, the plea, the finding of the court, and the sentence. All but six of the states make use of trial courts of limited jurisdiction.[10]

These lower courts are much less formal than courts of general jurisdiction. In an intriguing analysis of court characteristics, Thomas Henderson, director of the National Center for State Courts, found that misdemeanor courts process cases according to a "decisional model."[11] The decisional model, said Henderson, is informal, personal, and decisive. It depends on the quick resolution of relatively uncomplicated issues of law and fact.

Trial courts of general jurisdiction—variously called *high courts*, *circuit courts*, or *superior courts*—are authorized to hear any criminal case. In many states, they also provide the first appellate level for courts of limited jurisdiction. In most cases, superior courts offer defendants whose cases originated in lower courts the chance for a new trial instead of a review of the record of the earlier hearing. When a new trial is held, it is referred to as **trial *de novo.***

Henderson describes courts of general jurisdiction according to a "procedural model."[12] Such courts, he says, make full use of juries, prosecutors, defense attorneys, witnesses, and all the other actors we usually associate with American courtrooms. The procedural model, which is far more formal than the decisional model, includes numerous court appearances to ensure that all of a defendant's due process rights are protected. The procedural model makes for a long, expensive, relatively impersonal, and highly formal series of legal maneuvers involving many professional participants—a fact clearly seen in the widely televised 1995 double-murder trial of famed athlete and media personality O. J. Simpson.

Trial courts of general jurisdiction operate within a fact-finding framework called the adversarial process. That process pits the interests of the state, represented by prosecutors, against the professional skills and abilities of defense attorneys. The adversarial process is not a free-for-all; rather, it is constrained by procedural rules specified in law and sustained through tradition. Take a virtual tour of California trial courts via **Web Extra 9–1** at cjtoday.com.

STATE APPELLATE COURTS

Most states today have an appellate division where people can appeal a decision against them, consisting of an intermediate appellate court (often called the *court of appeals*) and a high-level appellate court (generally termed the *state supreme court*). High-level appellate courts are referred to as **courts of last resort**, indicating that a defendant can go no further with an appeal within the state court system once the high court rules on a case. All states have supreme courts, although only 39 have intermediate appellate courts.[13]

An **appeal** by a convicted defendant asks that a higher court review the actions of a lower court. Once they agree to review a decision, or accept an appeal, courts within the appellate division do not conduct a new trial. Instead, they review the case on the record, examining the written transcript of lower-court hearings to ensure that those proceedings were carried out fairly and in accordance with proper procedure and state law. These courts may also allow attorneys for both sides to make brief oral arguments and will generally consider other briefs or information filed by the appellant (the party initiating the appeal) or the appellee (the side opposed to the

trial *de novo*

Literally, "new trial." The term is applied to cases that are retried on appeal, as opposed to those that are simply reviewed on the record.

WEB
Extra
∎ ∎ ∎ ∎

court of last resort

The court authorized by law to hear the final appeal on a matter.

appeal

Generally, the request that a court with appellate jurisdiction review the judgment, decision, or order of a lower court and set it aside (reverse it) or modify it.

appeal).State statutes generally require that sentences of death or life imprisonment be automatically reviewed by the state supreme court.

Most convictions are affirmed on appeal. Occasionally, however, an appellate court will determine that the trial court erred in allowing certain kinds of evidence to be heard, that it failed to properly interpret the significance of a relevant statute, or that some other impropriety occurred. When that happens, the verdict of the trial court will be reversed, and the case may be sent back for a new trial, or *remanded.* When a conviction is overturned by an appellate court because of constitutional issues or when a statute is determined to be invalid, the state usually has recourse to the state supreme court, or when an issue of federal law is involved, as when a state court has ruled a federal law unconstitutional, to the U.S. Supreme Court.

Defendants who are not satisfied with the resolution of their case within the state court system may attempt an appeal to the U.S. Supreme Court. For such an appeal to have any chance of being heard, it must be based on claimed violations of the defendant's rights, as guaranteed under federal law or the U.S. Constitution. Under certain circumstances, federal district courts, which we will look at later in the chapter, may also provide a path of relief for state defendants who can show that their federal constitutional rights were violated. However, in the 1992 case of *Keeney* v. *Tamayo-Reyes*, the U.S. Supreme Court ruled that a "respondent is entitled to a federal evidentiary hearing [only] if he can show cause for his failure to develop the facts in the state-court proceedings and actual prejudice resulting from that failure, or if he can show that a fundamental miscarriage of justice would result from failure to hold such a hearing."[14] Justice Byron White, writing for the Court, said, "It is hardly a good use of scarce judicial resources to duplicate fact-finding in federal court merely because a petitioner has negligently failed to take advantage of opportunities in state-court proceedings."

Likewise, in *Herrera* v. *Collins* (1993),[15] the Court ruled that new evidence of innocence is no reason for a federal court to order a new state trial if constitutional grounds are lacking. In *Herrera*, where the defendant was under a Texas death sentence for the murder of two police officers, the Court said, "Where a defendant has been afforded a fair trial and convicted of the offense for which he was charged, the constitutional presumption of innocence disappears. . . . Thus, claims of actual innocence based on newly discovered evidence have never been held [to be] grounds for relief, absent an independent constitutional violation occurring in the course of the underlying state criminal proceedings. To allow a federal court to grant relief . . . would in effect require a new trial 10 years after the first trial, not because of any constitutional violation at the first trial, but simply because of a belief that in light of his new found evidence a jury might find him not guilty at a second trial." The *Keeney* and *Herrera* decisions have severely limited access by state defendants to federal courts. See Library Extra 9–2 at cjtoday.com for additional information on challenging state court criminal convictions within the federal court system.

LIBRARY
Extra
■ ■ ■ ■

STATE COURT ADMINISTRATION

To function efficiently, courts require uninterrupted funding, adequate staffing, trained support personnel, a well-managed case flow, and coordination between levels and among jurisdictions. To oversee these and other aspects of judicial management, every state has its own mechanism for court administration. Most have **state court administrators** who manage these operational functions.

The following tasks are typical of state court administrators:[16]

state court administrator

A coordinator who assists with case-flow management, operating funds budgeting, and court docket administration.

- The preparation, presentation, and monitoring of a budget for the state court system
- The analysis of case flows and backlogs to determine where additional personnel, such as judges, prosecutors, and others, are needed
- The collection and publication of statistics describing the operation of state courts
- Efforts to streamline the flow of cases through individual courts and the system as a whole
- Service as a liaison between state legislatures and the court system
- The development or coordination of requests for federal and other outside funding
- The management of state court personnel, including promotions for support staff and the handling of retirement and other benefits packages for court employees
- The creation and coordination of plans for the training of judges and other court personnel (in conjunction with local chief judges and supreme court justices)
- The assignment of judges to judicial districts (especially in states that use rotating judgeships)
- The administrative review of payments to legal counsel for indigent defendants

State court administrators can receive assistance from the National Center for State Courts (NCSC) in Williamsburg, Virginia. The NCSC is an independent nonprofit organization dedicated to the improvement of the American court system. It was founded in 1971 at the behest of Chief Justice Warren E. Burger. The NCSC provides services to state courts, which include helping to

- Develop policies to enhance state courts
- Advance state courts' interests within the federal government
- Secure sufficient resources for state courts
- Strengthen state court leadership
- Facilitate state court collaboration
- Provide a model for organizational administration

You can visit the National Center for State Courts via Web Extra 9–2 at cjtoday.com.

At the federal level, the court system is administered by the Administrative Office of the United States Courts (AOUSC), in Washington, D.C. The AOUSC, created by Congress in 1939, prepares the budget and legislative agenda for federal courts. It also performs audits of court accounts, manages funds for the operation of federal courts, compiles and publishes statistics on the volume and type of business conducted by the courts, and recommends plans and strategies to efficiently manage court business. You can visit the Administrative Office of the United States Courts via Web Extra 9–3 at cjtoday.com.

WEB
Extra
▪▪ ▪▪

WEB
Extra
▪▪ ▪▪

DISPUTE-RESOLUTION CENTERS AND COMMUNITY COURTS

It is often possible to resolve minor disputes (in which minor criminal offenses might otherwise be charged) without a formal court hearing. Some communities have **dispute-resolution centers**, which hear victims' claims of minor wrongs such as passing bad checks, trespassing, shoplifting, and petty theft. Today, more than 200 centers throughout the country,[17] frequently staffed by volunteer mediators, work to resolve disagreements without assigning blame. Dispute-resolution programs began in the early 1970s, with the earliest being the Community Assistance Project in Chester, Pennsylvania; the Night Prosecutor Program in Columbus, Ohio; and the Arbitration as an Alternative Program in Rochester, New York. Following the lead of these programs, the U.S. Department of Justice helped promote the development of three experimental Neighborhood Justice Centers in Los Angeles, Kansas City (MO), and Atlanta. Each center accepted both minor civil and criminal cases.

Mediation centers are often closely integrated with the formal criminal justice process and may substantially reduce the caseload of lower-level courts. Some centers are, in fact, run by the courts and work only with court-ordered referrals. Others are semiautonomous but may be dependent on

dispute-resolution center

An informal hearing place designed to mediate interpersonal disputes without resorting to the more formal arrangements of a criminal trial court.

Graduates of a community dispute-resolution training program in Oakland County, Michigan, posing for a photo. Staffed largely by volunteers, dispute-resolution centers facilitate cooperative solutions to relatively low-level disputes in which minor criminal offenses might otherwise be charged. How do dispute-resolution centers help relieve some of the pressures facing our criminal courts?

Photo courtesy of Oakland Mediation Center, Bloomfield Hills, Michigan

courts for endorsement of their decisions; others function with complete autonomy. Rarely, however, do dispute-resolution programs entirely supplant the formal criminal justice mechanism, and defendants who appear before a community mediator may later be charged with a crime. Community mediation programs have become a central feature of today's restorative justice movement (discussed in more detail in Chapter 11).

Recently, the community justice movement has led to the creation of innovative low-level courts in some parts of the country. Unlike dispute-resolution centers, **community courts** are always *official* components of the formal justice system and can hand down sentences, including fines and jail time, without further judicial review. Community courts typically begin as grassroots movements undertaken by community residents and local organizations seeking to build confidence in the way offenders are handled for less serious offenses. Community courts generally sentence convicted offenders to work within the community, "where neighbors can see what they are doing."[18] Like dispute-resolution centers, community courts focus on quality-of-life crimes that erode a neighborhood's morale, emphasize problem solving rather than punishment, and build on restorative principles such as community service and restitution. A 2006 Center for Court Innovation study of the Red Hook Community Justice Center in Red Hook, New York, found that defendants considered the community court to be more fair than traditional courts.[19] According to the study, perceptions of fairness were primarily related to the more personal role played by community court judges, who dispense with much of the formality of traditional courts and who often offer support and praise to defendants who work within the parameters set by the court.

Both mediation centers and community courts have been criticized, however, because they typically work only with minor offenders and deny the opportunity for mediation to victims and offenders in more serious cases. They have also come under criticism because defendants may see them as just another form of criminal sanction rather than as a true alternative to processing by the criminal justice system.[20] Dispute-resolution centers, in particular, have been criticized for doing little more than providing a forum for shouting matches between the parties involved. Learn more about dispute-resolution centers and community courts at Library Extra 9–3 and Web Extra 9–4 at cjtoday.com.

community court

A low-level court that focuses on quality-of-life crimes that erode a neighborhood's morale. Community courts emphasize problem solving rather than punishment and build on restorative principles like community service and restitution.

LIBRARY Extra
WEB Extra

The Federal Court System

Whereas state courts evolved from early colonial arrangements, federal courts were created by the U.S. Constitution. Article III, Section 1, of the Constitution provides for the establishment of "one supreme Court, and . . . such inferior Courts as the Congress may from time to time ordain and establish." Article III, Section 2, specifies that such courts are to have jurisdiction over cases arising under the Constitution, federal laws, and treaties. Federal courts are also to settle disputes between states and to have jurisdiction in cases where one of the parties is a state.

Today's federal court system represents the culmination of a series of congressional mandates that have expanded the federal judicial infrastructure so that it can continue to carry out the duties envisioned by the Constitution. Notable federal statutes that have contributed to the present structure of the federal court system include the Judiciary Act of 1789, the Judiciary Act of 1925, and the Magistrate's Act of 1968.

As a result of constitutional mandates, congressional actions, and other historical developments, today's federal judiciary consists of three levels: (1) U.S. district courts, (2) U.S. courts of appeal, and (3) the U.S. Supreme Court. Each is described in turn in the following sections.

U.S. District Courts

The U.S. district courts are the trial courts of the federal court system.[21] Within limits set by Congress and the Constitution, the district courts have jurisdiction to hear nearly all categories of federal cases, including both civil and criminal matters. There are 94 federal judicial districts, including at least one district in each state (some states, like New York and California, have as many as four), the District of Columbia, and Puerto Rico. Each district includes a U.S. bankruptcy court as a unit of the district court. Three territories of the United States—the Virgin Islands, Guam, and the Northern Mariana Islands—have district courts that hear federal cases, including bankruptcy cases. There are two special trial courts that have nationwide jurisdiction over certain types of cases. The Court of International Trade addresses cases involving international trade and customs issues. The U.S. Court of Federal Claims has jurisdiction over most claims for monetary damages against the United States, disputes over federal contracts, unlawful "takings" of private property by the federal government, and a variety of other claims against the United States.

Federal district courts have original jurisdiction over all cases involving alleged violations of federal statutes. A district may be divided into divisions and may have several places where the court hears cases. District courts were first authorized by Congress through the Judiciary Act of 1789, which allocated one federal court to each state. Because of population increases over the years, new courts have been added in many states.

Nearly 650 district court judges staff federal district courts. Because some courts are much busier than others, the number of district court judges varies from a low of two in some jurisdictions to a high of 27 in others. District court judges are appointed by the president and confirmed by the Senate, and they serve for life. An additional 369 full-time and 110 part-time magistrate judges (referred to as *U.S. magistrates* before 1990) serve the district court system and assist the federal judges. Magistrate judges have the power to conduct arraignments and may set bail, issue warrants, and try minor offenders.

U.S. district courts handle tens of thousands of cases per year. For the 12 months ending September 30, 2006, for example, 56,532 criminal cases[22] and 259,541 civil cases[23] were filed in U.S. district courts. Drug prosecution, especially in courts located close to the U.S.–Mexican border, has led to considerable growth in the number of cases filed. Federal drug prosecutions in the border states of California, Arizona, New Mexico, and Texas more than doubled between 1994 and 2000, from 2,864 to 6,116, and immigration prosecutions increased more than sevenfold, from 1,056 to 7,613.[24] During the past 20 years, the number of cases handled by the entire federal district court system has grown exponentially. The hiring of new judges and the creation of new courtroom facilities have not kept pace with the increase in caseload, and questions persist as to the quality of justice that overworked judges can deliver.

One of the most pressing issues facing district court judges is the fact that their pay, which at around $152,000 in mid-2006[25] placed them in the top 1% of income-earning Americans, is low compared to what most could earn in private practice. Since 1992, the salaries of federal judges have remained relatively stagnant, leading many judges to leave the bench,[26] and in 2006, Chief Justice John Roberts called Congress's failure to raise judges' pay "a direct threat to judicial independence."[27] Because of low pay, said Roberts, "judges effectively serve for a term dictated by their financial position rather than for life." Learn more about the federal courts at Library Extra 9–4 at cjtoday.com.

LIBRARY
Extra
■ ■ ■ ■

U.S. Courts of Appeal

The 94 judicial districts are organized into 12 regional circuits, each of which has a U.S. court of appeals.[28] A court of appeals hears appeals from the district courts located within its circuit, as well as appeals from decisions of federal administrative agencies. The Court of Appeals for the Federal Circuit has nationwide jurisdiction to hear appeals in special cases, such as those involving patent laws and cases decided by the Court of International Trade and the U.S. Court of Federal Claims.

The U.S. Court of Appeals for the Federal Circuit and the 12 regional courts of appeal are often referred to as *circuit courts*. Early in the nation's history, the judges of the first courts of appeal visited each of the courts in one region in a particular sequence, traveling by horseback and riding the "circuit." Today, the regional courts of appeal review matters from the district courts of their geographic regions, from the U.S. Tax Court, and from certain federal administrative agencies. A disappointed party in a district court usually has the right to have the case reviewed in the court of appeals for the circuit. The First through Eleventh Circuits all include three or more states, as illustrated in Figure 9–3.

Each court of appeals consists of six or more judges, depending on the caseload of the court. Circuit court judges are appointed for life by the president with the advice and consent of the Senate. The judge who has served on the court the longest and who is under 65 years of age is designated as the chief judge and performs administrative duties in addition to hearing cases. The chief judge serves for a maximum term of seven years. There are 167 judges on the 12 regional courts of appeals.

The U.S. Court of Appeals for the District of Columbia, which is often called the Twelfth Circuit, hears cases arising in the District of Columbia and has appellate jurisdiction assigned by Congress in legislation concerning many departments of the federal government. The U.S. Court of Appeals for the Federal Circuit (in effect, the Thirteenth Circuit) was created in 1982 by the merging of the U.S. Court of Claims and the U.S. Court of Customs and Patent Appeals. The court hears appeals in cases from the U.S. Court of Federal Claims, the U.S. Court of International Trade, the U.S. Court of Veterans Appeals, the International Trade Commission, the Board of Contract Appeals, the Patent and Trademark Office, and the Merit Systems Protection Board. The Federal Circuit Court also hears appeals from certain decisions of the secretaries of the Department

Oyez, oyez, oyez! All persons having business before the honorable, the Supreme Court of the United States, are admonished to draw near and give their attention, for the court is now sitting. God save the United States and this honorable Court.

—Marshal's cry at the opening of public sessions of the U.S. Supreme Court

FIGURE 9–3

Geographic boundaries of the U.S. courts of appeal and U.S. district courts.

of Agriculture and the Department of Commerce and cases from district courts involving patents and minor claims against the federal government.

Almost all appeals from federal district courts go to the court of appeals serving the circuit in which the case was first heard. Federal appellate courts have mandatory jurisdiction over the decisions of district courts within their circuits. Mandatory jurisdiction means that U.S. courts of appeals are required to hear the cases brought to them. Criminal appeals from federal district courts are usually heard by panels of three judges sitting on a court of appeals rather than by all the judges of each circuit. A defendant's right to appeal, however, has been interpreted to mean the right to one appeal. Hence, the U.S. Supreme Court need not necessarily hear the appeals of defendants who are dissatisfied with the decision of a federal appeals court.

Federal appellate courts operate under the Federal Rules of Appellate Procedure, although each has also created its own separate Local Rules. Local Rules may mean that one circuit, such as the Second, will depend heavily on oral arguments, while others may substitute written summary depositions in their place. Appeals generally fall into one of three categories: (1) frivolous appeals, which have little substance, raise no significant new issues, and are generally disposed of quickly; (2) ritualistic appeals, which are brought primarily because of the demands of litigants, even though the probability of reversal is negligible; and (3) nonconsensual appeals, which entail major questions of law and policy and on which there is considerable professional disagreement among the courts and within the legal profession.[29] The probability of reversal is highest in the case of nonconsensual appeals.

Because of the constitutional guarantee of the right to an appeal, federal circuit courts face an ever-increasing workload. Between 2004 and 2005, the number of federal criminal appeals rose 28 percent, reaching record highs and marking a tenth consecutive record-breaking year.[30] Much of the growth in criminal appeals can be attributed to the U.S. Supreme Court decisions of *Blakely* v. *Washington* (2004)[31] and *U.S.* v. *Booker* (2005),[32] which brought into question the validity of many previously imposed federal criminal sentences.[33] (The *Blakely* and *Booker* cases are discussed in detail in Chapter 11.)

While the number of cases filed in both appellate courts and district courts continues to swell, the number of federal judges available to hear them has remained virtually unchanged, leading to huge increases in judicial workloads. Consequently, in 2005, the Judicial Conference of the United States, the primary policy-making arm of the federal courts, urged Congress to create 68 new federal judgeships in appellate and district courts.[34] The conference cited a need for 9 permanent and 3 temporary court of appeals judgeships, and 44 permanent and 12 temporary district judgeships. Congress has yet to act on the recommendation. Learn more about criminal appeals in federal courts via Library Extra 9–5 at cjtoday.com.

LIBRARY
Extra
■ ■ ■ ■

The U.S. Supreme Court

At the apex of the federal court system stands the U.S. Supreme Court. The Supreme Court is located in Washington, D.C., across the street from the U.S. Capitol. The Court consists of nine justices, eight of whom are associate justices. The ninth presides over the Court as the chief justice of the United States. Supreme Court justices are nominated by the president, are confirmed by the Senate, and serve for life. Lengthy terms of service are a tradition among justices. One of the earliest chief justices, John Marshall, served the Court for 34 years, from 1801 to 1835. The same was true of Justice Stephen J. Field, who sat on the bench between 1863 and 1897. Justice Hugo Black passed the 34-year milestone, serving an additional month, before he retired in 1971. Justice William O. Douglas set a record for longevity on the bench, retiring in 1975 after 36 years and six months of service. You can view the biographies of today's Supreme Court justices via Web Extra 9–5 at cjtoday.com.

The Supreme Court of the United States wields immense power. The Court's greatest authority lies in its capacity for **judicial review** of lower-court decisions and state and federal statutes. By exercising its power of judicial review, the Court decides what laws and lower-court decisions keep with the intent of the U.S. Constitution. The power of judicial review is not explicit in the Constitution but was anticipated by its framers. In the *Federalist Papers*, which urged adoption of the Constitution, Alexander Hamilton wrote that through the practice of judicial review, the Court would ensure that "the will of the whole people," as grounded in the Constitution, would be supreme over the "will of the legislature," which might be subject to temporary whims.[35] It was not until 1803, however, that the Court forcefully asserted its power of judicial review. In an opinion written for the case of *Marbury* v. *Madison* (1803),[36] Chief Justice John Marshall established the Court's authority as final interpreter of the U.S. Constitution, declaring, "It is emphatically the province of the judicial department to say what the law is."

INCREASING COMPLEXITY AND THE SUPREME COURT

The evolution of the U.S. Supreme Court provides one of the most dramatic examples of institutional development in American history. Sparsely described in the Constitution, the Court has grown from a handful of circuit-riding justices into a modern organization that wields tremendous legal power over all aspects of American life. Much of the Court's growth has been because it is increasingly willing to mediate fundamental issues of law and to act as a resort from arbitrary and capricious processing by the justice systems of the states and the national government.

The *Marbury* decision established the Court as a mighty force in the federal government by virtue of the power of judicial review. As we discussed in Chapter 7, the Court began to apply that power during the 1960s to issues of crime and justice at the state and local levels. You may recall that the Court signaled its change in orientation in 1961 with the case of *Mapp* v. *Ohio*,[37] which extended the exclusionary rule—which holds that evidence illegally seized by the police cannot

WEB
Extra
■ ■ ■ ■

judicial review

The power of a court to review actions and decisions made by other agencies of government.

Protesters in front of the U.S. Supreme Court in 2004. Highlighting its importance as our nation's premier legal institution, the Court became the backdrop for a rally against the USA PATRIOT Act. Protesters claimed that the act unfairly denies foreign terror suspects the right to a quick and impartial hearing. How does the Court serve to balance individual rights and freedoms with the need for public safety and social order?

© *William Philpott/Reuters/Corbis*

be used in a trial—to the states. Such extension, combined with the near-simultaneous end of the hands-off doctrine that had previously exempted state prison systems from Court scrutiny (and which is discussed in Chapter 14), placed the authority of the Court squarely over the activities of state criminal justice systems. From that time forward, the Court's workload became increasingly heavy, and today it shows few signs of abatement.

THE SUPREME COURT TODAY

The Supreme Court reviews the decisions of lower courts and may accept cases both from U.S. courts of appeal and from state supreme courts. It has limited original jurisdiction and does not conduct trials except in disputes between states and in some cases of attorney disbarment. For a case to be heard, at least four justices must vote in favor of a hearing. When the Court agrees to hear a case, it will issue a writ of *certiorari* to a lower court, ordering it to send the records of the case forward for review. Once having granted *certiorari*, the justices can revoke the decision. In such cases, a writ is dismissed by ruling that it was improvidently granted.

The U.S. Supreme Court may review any decision appealed to it that it decides is worthy of review. In fact, however, the Court elects to review only cases that involve a substantial federal question. Of approximately 5,000 requests for review received by the Court yearly, only about 200 are heard.

A term of the Supreme Court begins, by statute, on the first Monday in October and lasts until early July. The term is divided among sittings, when cases will be heard, and time for the writing and delivering of opinions. Between 22 and 24 cases are heard at each sitting (which may last days), with each side allotted 30 minutes for arguments before the justices. Intervening recesses allow justices time to study arguments and supporting documentation and to work on their opinions.

Decisions rendered by the Supreme Court are rarely unanimous. Instead, the opinion that a majority of the Court's justices agree on becomes the judgment of the Court. Justices who agree with the Court's judgment write concurring opinions if they agree for a different reason or if they feel that they have some new light to shed on a legal issue in the case. Justices who do not agree with the decision of the Court write dissenting opinions, which may offer new possibilities for successful appeals of future cases. Visit the U.S. Supreme Court via Web Extra 9–6 at cjtoday.com, and learn more about the federal judiciary via Library Extra 9–6 at cjtoday.com.

WEB
Extra
▪▪▪▪

LIBRARY
Extra
▪▪▪▪

U.S. Supreme Court Chief Justice John G. Roberts, Jr., walking past an official portrait of his predecessor, former Chief Justice William H. Rehnquist, who died in office in 2005. Roberts, who served on the U.S. Court of Appeals for the District of Columbia Circuit before joining the nation's highest court, was nominated in 2005 by President George W. Bush to succeed Rehnquist. Do you think that a justice's personal values and beliefs might influence his or her decisions on important matters that come before the court—or are such decisions always a matter of impersonal application of relevant law?

Charles Dharapak/Getty Images, Inc.

Thurgood Marshall (1908–1993), the nation's first African American U.S. Supreme Court justice. Why do some people argue that the nation's highest court needs to have more minority justices?

AP Wide World Photos

The Courtroom Work Group

In March 2005, Scott Peterson became the 641st person on California's death row in San Quentin State Prison. Peterson, 32, had been sentenced to die by San Mateo (California) Superior Court Judge Alfred Delucchi following his conviction for the 2002 murders of his pregnant 27-year-old wife, Laci, and the couple's unborn son, Conner. Laci Peterson disappeared on December 24, 2002. Her badly decomposed body and that of her fetus washed ashore in San Francisco Bay four months later near the marina where Peterson said he had taken his boat on a fishing trip the day his wife disappeared. Peterson, a former fertilizer salesman, was found guilty by a jury of six men and six women that heard testimony from 184 witnesses, including massage therapist Amber Frey with whom Peterson had been having an affair. The trial lasted 23 weeks, during which two jurors had to be replaced with alternates. Peterson's attorney, Mark Geragos, indicated that he would make those dismissals the basis for an appeal to California's Supreme Court. The Peterson case captivated the country and made headlines worldwide. See a copy of the criminal indictment against Scott Peterson at Library Extra 9–7 at cjtoday.com, and hear the verdicts against him being read at Web Extra 9–7 at cjtoday.com.

Like plays on a stage, criminal trials often entail quite a bit of drama and may involve many participants, each of whom has a different role to fill. Participants can be divided into two categories: professionals and outsiders. The professionals are the official courtroom actors and include judges, prosecuting attorneys, defense attorneys, public defenders, and others who earn a living serving the court. These professionals are called the **courtroom work group**. The courtroom work group is guided by statutory requirements and ethical considerations; members of the group also recognize informal rules of civility, the need for cooperation, and shared goals.[38] Hence, even within the adversarial framework of a criminal trial, the courtroom work group is dedicated to bringing the procedure to a successful close.[39]

In contrast, outsiders—those trial participants who are only temporarily involved with the court—are generally unfamiliar with courtroom organization and trial procedure. Outsiders, or nonjudicial personnel, include jurors and witnesses as well as defendants and victims. Although in this chapter we refer to these people as nonprofessional courtroom actors, they may have a greater personal investment in the outcome of the trial than anyone else. Learn more about professional and nonprofessional courtroom participants at Web Extra 9–8 at cjtoday.com.

When we have examined in detail the organization of the Supreme Court, and the entire prerogatives which it exercises, we shall readily admit that a more imposing judicial power was never constituted by any people.

—*Alexis de Tocqueville,* Democracy in America *(1835)*

courtroom work group

The professional courtroom actors, including judges, prosecuting attorneys, defense attorneys, public defenders, and others who earn a living serving the court.

Professional Courtroom Participants

The Judge

judge

An elected or appointed public official who presides over a court of law and who is authorized to hear and sometimes to decide cases and to conduct trials.

The trial **judge** has the primary duty of ensuring justice. The American Bar Association's *Standards for Criminal Justice* describes the duties of the trial judge as follows: "The trial judge has the responsibility for safeguarding both the rights of the accused and the interests of the public in the administration of criminal justice. . . . The purpose of a criminal trial is to determine whether the prosecution has established the guilt of the accused as required by law, and the trial judge should not allow the proceedings to be used for any other purpose."[40]

In the courtroom, the judge holds ultimate authority, ruling on matters of law, weighing objections from both sides, deciding on the admissibility of evidence, and disciplining anyone who challenges the order of the court. In most jurisdictions, judges also sentence offenders after a verdict has been returned; in some states, judges serve to decide guilt or innocence for defendants who waive a jury trial.

Most state jurisdictions have a chief judge who, besides serving as a trial judge, must also manage the court system. Management includes hiring staff, scheduling sessions of court, ensuring the adequate training of subordinate judges, and coordinating activities with other courtroom actors. Chief judges usually assume their position by virtue of seniority and rarely have any formal training in management. Hence, the managerial effectiveness of a chief judge is often a matter of personality and dedication more than anything else.

Scott Peterson (left) with defense attorney Mark Geragos; Scott's wife, Laci; and Judge Alfred A. Delucchi, who presided over Peterson's 2004 California murder trial. Peterson, 30, was convicted of killing his 27-year-old wife and their unborn son. Their bodies, which were dumped into San Francisco Bay on Christmas Eve 2002, washed ashore four months later near the spot where Peterson said he had been fishing when Laci disappeared. What was the evidence against Peterson?

Modesto Bee, Bart Ah You/AP Wide World Photos, Modesto Police Department Handout/AP Wide World Photos, and Tribune News/Nick Lammers/AP Wide World Photos

JUDICIAL SELECTION

As mentioned earlier, judges at the federal level are nominated by the president of the United States and take their place on the bench only after confirmation by the Senate. At the state level, things work somewhat differently. Depending on the jurisdiction, state judgeships are won either through popular election or by political (usually gubernatorial) appointment. The process of judicial selection at the state level is set by law.

Both judicial election and appointment have been criticized for allowing politics to enter the judicial arena, although in somewhat different ways. Under the election system, judicial candidates must receive the endorsement of their parties, generate contributions, and manage an effective campaign. Under the appointment system, judicial hopefuls must be in favor with incumbent politicians to receive appointments. Because partisan politics plays a role in both systems, critics have claimed that sitting judges can rarely be as neutral as they should be. They carry to the bench with them campaign promises, personal indebtedness, and possible political agendas.

To counter some of these problems, a number of states have adopted the Missouri Plan (or the Missouri Bar Plan) for judicial selection,[41] which combines elements of both election and appointment. It requires candidates for judicial vacancies to undergo screening by a nonpartisan state judicial nominating committee. Candidates selected by the committee are reviewed by an arm of the governor's office, which selects a final list of names for appointment. Incumbent judges must face the electorate after a specified term in office. They then run unopposed in nonpartisan elections in which only their records may be considered. Voters have the choice of allowing a judge to continue in office or asking that another be appointed to take his or her place. Because the Missouri Plan provides for periodic public review of judicial performance, it is also called the *merit plan of judicial selection.*

JUDICIAL QUALIFICATIONS

A few decades ago, many states did not require any special training, education, or other qualifications for judges. Anyone (even someone without a law degree) who won election or was appointed could assume a judgeship. Today, however, almost all states require that judges in general jurisdiction and appellate courts hold a law degree, be a licensed attorney, and be a member of their state bar association. Many states also require newly elected judges to attend state-sponsored training sessions on subjects like courtroom procedure, evidence, dispute resolution, judicial writing, administrative record keeping, and ethics.

While most states provide instruction to meet the needs of trial judges, some organizations also provide specialized training. The National Judicial College, located on the campus of the University of Nevada at Reno, is one such institution. It was established in 1963 by the Joint Committee for the Effective Administration of Justice, chaired by Justice Tom C. Clark of the U.S. Supreme Court.[42] More than 32,000 judges have enrolled in courses since the college began operation.[43] Visit the National Judicial College via Web Extra 9–9 at cjtoday.com.

In some parts of the United States, lower-court judges, such as justices of the peace, local magistrates, and "district" court judges, may still be elected without educational and other professional requirements. Today, in 43 states, some 1,300 nonlawyer judges are serving in mostly rural courts of limited jurisdiction.[44] In New York, for example, of the 3,300 judges in the state's unified court system, approximately 65% are part-time town or village justices, and about 80% of town and village justices are not lawyers.[45] The majority of cases that come before New York lay judges involve alleged traffic violations, although they may also include misdemeanors, small-claims actions, and civil cases of up to $3,000.

Even though some have defended lay judges as being closer to the citizenry in their understanding of justice,[46] in most jurisdictions, the number of lay judges is declining. States that continue to use lay judges in lower courts do require that candidates for judgeships not have criminal records, and most states require that they attend special training sessions if elected.

JUDICIAL MISCONDUCT

In June 1997, a bond hearing in West Virginia took a turn for the worse when Pleasant County Circuit Judge Joseph Troisi took off his robe, stepped to the front of the judge's bench, and bit defendant Bill Whittens on the nose. Whittens said the judge bit him after he directed a derogatory remark at him. Whittens required medical treatment at a local hospital. The Federal Bureau of Investigation (FBI) was called in to investigate, and Judge Troisi later resigned.[47]

Most judges are highly professional in and out of the courtroom. However, occasionally a judge oversteps the limits of his authority; some unprofessional judicial behavior may even

I left [the Supreme Court] . . . perfectly convinced that . . . a system so defective . . . would not obtain the energy, weight, and dignity which are essential to its affording due support to the national government, nor acquire the public confidence and respect which, as the last resort of the justice of the nation, it should possess.

—John Jay, first Chief Justice of the United States, in a letter to John Adams, 1801

We are under a Constitution, but the Constitution is what the judges say it is, and the judiciary is the safeguard of our liberty and of our property under the Constitution.

—Charles Evans Hughes, eleventh Chief Justice of the United States, in a speech before the Elmira, New York, Chamber of Commerce, 1907

WEB
Extra

violate the law. In 2002, for example, two men who were sentenced to death in Arizona in the 1980s asked an appellate court to reverse their sentences, claiming that the judge who sentenced them suffered from impaired judgment because he had used marijuana.[48] The judge, former Phoenix Superior Court Judge Philip Marquardt, had bought marijuana by mail using office stationery—with the court's return address printed on it—to make the purchases. He was removed from the bench in 1991 and lost his license to practice law following a second drug conviction. The judge, now a 69-year-old retired ski instructor, recently conceded in an interview that he had used marijuana regularly during the years in which he sentenced Richard Michael Rossi and Warren Summerlin to death. Rossi, interviewed from prison, said, "There is a lot of irony here. We both had addiction problems. I acknowledged mine. He didn't acknowledge his."

At the federal level, the Judicial Councils Reform and Judicial Conduct and Disability Act, passed by Congress in 1980, specifies the procedures necessary to register complaints against federal judges and, in serious cases, to begin the process of impeachment, or forced removal from the bench.

The Prosecuting Attorney

The **prosecutor**—called variously the *district attorney, state's attorney, county attorney, commonwealth attorney,* or *solicitor*—is responsible for presenting the state's case against the defendant. The prosecuting attorney is the primary representative of the people by virtue of the belief that violations of the criminal law are an affront to the public. Except for federal prosecutors (called *U.S. attorneys*) and solicitors in five states, prosecutors are elected and generally serve four-year terms with the possibility of continuing reelection.[49] Widespread criminal conspiracies, whether they involve government officials or private citizens, may require the services of a special prosecutor whose office can spend the time and resources needed for efficient prosecution.[50]

In many jurisdictions, because the job of prosecutor entails too many duties for one person to handle, prosecutors supervise a staff of assistant district attorneys who do most in-court work. Assistants are trained attorneys, usually hired directly by the chief prosecutor and licensed to practice law in the state in which they work. Approximately 2,300 chief prosecutors, assisted by 24,000 deputy attorneys, serve the nation's counties and independent cities.[51]

Another prosecutorial role has traditionally been that of quasi-legal adviser to local police departments. Because prosecutors are sensitive to the kinds of information needed for conviction, they may help guide police investigations and will exhort detectives to identify credible witnesses, uncover additional evidence, and the like. This role is limited, however. Police departments are independent of the administrative authority of the prosecutor, and cooperation between them, although based on the common goal of conviction, is purely voluntary. Moreover, close cooperation between prosecutors and police may not always be legal. A 1998 federal law known as the McDade-Murtha Law,[52] for example, requires that federal prosecutors abide by all state bar ethics rules. In late 2000, in a reflection of the federal sentiment, the Oregon Supreme Court temporarily ended police–prosecutor collaboration in that state in instances involving potential deception by law enforcement officers.[53] The court, ruling in the Oregon State Bar disciplinary case of *In re Gatti,*[54] held that all lawyers within the state, including government prosecutors overseeing organized crime, child pornography, and narcotics cases, must abide by the Oregon State Bar's strictures against dishonesty, fraud, deceit, and misrepresentation.[55] Under the court's ruling, a prosecutor in Oregon who encourages an undercover officer or an informant to misrepresent himself or herself could be disbarred and prohibited from practicing law. As a result of the highly controversial ruling, the FBI and the Drug Enforcement Administration ended all big undercover operations in Oregon, and local police departments cancelled many ongoing investigations. In 2002, the Oregon Supreme Court accepted an amendment to the state bar association's disciplinary rules to allow a lawyer to advise and to supervise otherwise lawful undercover investigations of violations of civil law, criminal law, or constitutional rights as long as the lawyer "in good faith believes there is a reasonable possibility that unlawful activity has taken place, is taking place or will take place in the foreseeable future."[56]

Once a trial begins, the job of the prosecutor is to vigorously present the state's case against the defendant. Prosecutors introduce evidence against the accused, steer the testimony of witnesses "for the people," and argue in favor of conviction. Because defendants are presumed innocent until proven guilty, the burden of demonstrating guilt beyond a reasonable doubt rests with the prosecutor.

Reporters shouting questions at Durham County (North Carolina) District Attorney Mike Nifong, right, after a community forum to discuss rape allegations that had been made against three members of the Duke University lacrosse team in 2006. Nifong, who would not abandon his quest to prosecute the men, even when the accuser was discredited and DNA evidence seemed to definitively show that the men were innocent, was disbarred following a 2007 ethics hearing by the North Carolina State Bar Association. How did Nifong's actions (rightly or wrongly) demonstrate the power wielded by local prosecutors throughout the United States?

Gerry Broome/AP Wide World Photos

PROSECUTORIAL DISCRETION

In May 2007, North Carolina Attorney General Roy A. Cooper dismissed rape charges that had been brought against three former members of the Duke University lacrosse team, saying that the players were innocent of all charges. Those charges had been brought by Durham County prosecutor Michael B. Nifong, after an exotic dancer who had performed at a house party in 2006 told police that she had been raped, sodomized, strangled, and beaten by the partygoers. Contradictions in the accuser's statements, however, along with a lack of DNA and other evidence, convinced Cooper that the attack had never occurred. Cooper told CBS's *60 Minutes* that Nifong should have seen the contradictions himself. Calling Nifong "a rogue prosecutor," Cooper said that "when you have a prosecutor who takes advantage of his enormous power and overreaches like this, then yes, it's offensive."[57] Cooper added that other prosecutors "were offended by a prosecutor who didn't take the time to make sure that he had all of the facts straight before leveling charges." A day later, Nifong apologized to the students, saying "to the extent that I made judgments that ultimately proved to be incorrect, I apologize to the three students that were wrongly accused." He added, "I also understand that when someone has been wrongly accused, the harm caused by the accusations might not be immediately undone merely by dismissing them. It is my sincere desire that the actions of Attorney General Cooper will serve to remedy any remaining injury that has resulted from these cases."[58] Calls for further action against Nifong led to his being disbarred in 2007 following an ethics hearing by the North Carolina Bar Association. He was later found guilty of criminal contempt of court, and spent one day in jail.

The "Duke rape case," as it came to be known in the media, highlights the fact that American prosecutors occupy a unique position in the nation's criminal justice system by virtue of the considerable **prosecutorial discretion** they exercise. As U.S. Supreme Court Justice Robert H. Jackson noted in 1940, "The prosecutor has more control over life, liberty, and reputation than any other person in America."[59] Before a case comes to trial, the prosecutor may decide to accept a plea bargain, divert the suspect to a public or private social service agency, ask the suspect to seek counseling, or dismiss the case entirely for lack of evidence or for a variety of other reasons. Studies have found that the prosecution dismisses from one-third to one-half of all felony cases before trial or before a plea bargain is made.[60] Prosecutors also play a significant role before grand juries. States that use the grand jury system depend on prosecutors to bring evidence before the grand jury and to be effective in seeing indictments returned against suspects.

In preparation for trial, the prosecutor decides what charges are to be brought against the defendant, examines the strength of the incriminating evidence, and decides which witnesses to call. Two important U.S. Supreme Court decisions have held that it is the duty of prosecutors to make available any evidence in their possession to, in effect, help the defense build its case. In

prosecutorial discretion

The decision-making power of prosecutors, based on the wide range of choices available to them, in the handling of criminal defendants, the scheduling of cases for trial, the acceptance of negotiated pleas, and so on. The most important form of prosecutorial discretion lies in the power to charge, or not to charge, a person with an offense.

the first case, *Brady* v. *Maryland* (1963),[61] the Court held that the prosecution is required to disclose to the defense evidence that directly relates to claims of either guilt or innocence. The second and more recent case is that of *U.S.* v. *Bagley*,[62] decided in 1985. In *Bagley*, the Court ruled that the prosecution must disclose any evidence that the defense requests. The Court reasoned that to withhold evidence, even when it does not relate directly to issues of guilt or innocence, may mislead the defense into thinking that such evidence does not exist.

In 2004, in a decision predicated upon *Brady*, the U.S. Supreme Court intervened to stop the execution of 45-year-old Texan Delma Banks ten minutes before it was scheduled to begin. In finding that prosecutors had withheld vital exculpatory information during Banks's trial for the 1980 shooting death of a 16-year-old boy, the Court said "a rule declaring 'prosecutor may hide, defendant must seek,' is not tenable in a system constitutionally bound to accord defendants due process."[63] Banks had spent 24 years on death row.

One special decision that the prosecutor makes concerns the filing of separate or multiple charges. The decision to try a defendant simultaneously on multiple charges allows for the presentation of a considerable amount of evidence and permits an in-court demonstration of a complete sequence of criminal events. This strategy has additional practical advantages: It saves time and money by substituting one trial for what might otherwise be a number of trials if each charge were to be brought separately before the court. From the prosecutor's point of view, however, trying the charges one at a time carries the advantage of allowing for another trial on a new charge if a "not guilty" verdict is returned.

The activities of the prosecutor do not end with a finding of guilt or innocence. Following conviction, prosecutors are usually allowed to make sentencing recommendations to the judge. For example, they can argue that aggravating factors (discussed in Chapter 11), prior criminal record, or the especially heinous nature of the offense calls for strict punishment. When a convicted defendant appeals, prosecutors may need to defend their own actions and, in briefs filed with appellate courts, to argue that the conviction was properly obtained. Most jurisdictions also allow prosecutors to make recommendations when defendants they have convicted are being considered for parole or for early release from prison.

Until relatively recently, prosecutors generally enjoyed much the same kind of immunity against liability in the exercise of their official duties that judges do. The 1976 Supreme Court case *Imbler* v. *Pachtman*[64] provided the basis for immunity with its ruling that "state prosecutors are absolutely immune from liability . . . for their conduct in initiating a prosecution and in presenting the State's case." However, in the 1991 case of *Burns* v. *Reed*,[65] the Court held that "[a] state prosecuting attorney is absolutely immune from liability for damages . . . for participating in a probable cause hearing, but not for giving legal advice to the police." The *Burns* case involved Cathy Burns of Muncie, Indiana, who shot her sleeping sons while laboring under a multiple personality disorder. To explore the possibility of multiple personality further, the police asked the prosecuting attorney if it would be appropriate for them to hypnotize the defendant. The prosecutor agreed that hypnosis would be a permissible avenue for investigation, and the suspect confessed to the murders while hypnotized. She later alleged in her complaint to the Supreme Court "that [the prosecuting attorney] knew or should have known that hypnotically induced testimony was inadmissible" at trial.[66]

THE ABUSE OF DISCRETION

Because prosecutors have so much discretion in their decision making, there is considerable potential for abuse. Many types of discretionary decisions are always inappropriate. Examples include accepting guilty pleas to drastically reduced charges for personal considerations, deciding not to prosecute friends or political cronies, and being overzealous in prosecuting to support political ambitions.

Administrative decisions such as case scheduling, which can wreak havoc with the personal lives of defendants and the professional lives of defense attorneys, can also be used by prosecutors to harass defendants into pleading guilty. Some forms of abuse may be unconscious. At least one study suggests that some prosecutors tend toward leniency where female defendants are concerned and tend to discriminate against minorities when deciding whether to prosecute.[67]

Although the electorate is the final authority to which prosecutors must answer, gross misconduct by prosecutors may be addressed by the state supreme court or by the state attorney general's office. Short of addressing *criminal* misconduct, however, the options available to the court and to the attorney general are limited.

THE PROSECUTOR'S PROFESSIONAL RESPONSIBILITY

As members of the legal profession, prosecutors are expected to abide by various standards of professional responsibility, such as those found in the American Bar Association (ABA) Model Rules of Professional Conduct. Most state bar associations have adopted their own versions of the ABA rules and expect their members to respect those standards. Consequently, serious violations of the rules may result in a prosecutor's being disbarred from the practice of law. Official ABA commentary on Rule 3.8, *Special Responsibilities of the Prosecutor*, says that "a prosecutor has the responsibility of a minister of justice and not simply that of an advocate; the prosecutor's duty is to seek justice, not merely to convict. This responsibility carries with it specific obligations to see that the defendant is accorded procedural justice and that guilt is decided upon the basis of sufficient evidence."[68] Hence, prosecutors are barred by the standards of the legal profession from advocating any fact or position that they know is untrue. Prosecutors have a voice in influencing public policy affecting the safety of America's communities through the National District Attorneys Association (NDAA). Visit the NDAA via **Web Extra 9–10** at cjtoday.com.

WEB
Extra

The Defense Counsel

The **defense counsel** is a trained lawyer who may specialize in the practice of criminal law. The task of the defense counsel is to represent the accused as soon as possible after arrest and to ensure that the defendant's civil rights are not violated during processing by the criminal justice system. Other duties of the defense counsel include testing the strength of the prosecution's case, taking part in plea negotiations, and preparing an adequate defense to be used at trial. In the preparation of a defense, criminal lawyers may enlist private detectives, experts, witnesses to the crime, and character witnesses. Some lawyers perform aspects of the role of private detective or investigator themselves. Defense attorneys also review relevant court precedents to identify the best defense strategy.

Defense preparation often entails conversations between lawyer and defendant. Such discussions are recognized as privileged communications protected under the umbrella of attorney–client confidentiality. In other words, lawyers cannot be compelled to reveal information that their clients have confided to them.[69]

If the defendant is found guilty, the defense attorney will be involved in arguments at sentencing, may be asked to file an appeal, and may counsel the defendant and the defendant's family about any civil matters (payment of debts, release from contractual obligations, and so on) that must be arranged after sentence is imposed. Hence, the work of the defense attorney encompasses many roles, including attorney, negotiator, investigator, confidant, family and personal counselor, social worker, and, as we shall see, bill collector.

defense counsel

A licensed trial lawyer hired or appointed to conduct the legal defense of a person accused of a crime and to represent him or her before a court of law.

From the moment you walk into the courtroom, you are the defendant's only friend.

—*Austin defense attorney Michael E. Tigar*

THE CRIMINAL LAWYER

Three major categories of defense attorneys assist criminal defendants in the United States: (1) private attorneys, usually referred to as *retained counsel*; (2) *court-appointed counsel*; and (3) *public defenders*.

Private attorneys either have their own legal practices or work for law firms in which they are partners or employees. Private attorneys' fees can be high; most privately retained criminal lawyers charge from $100 to $250 per hour. Included in their bill is the time it takes to prepare for a case, as well as time spent in the courtroom. High-powered criminal defense attorneys who have a reputation for successfully defending their clients can be far more expensive. Fees charged by famous criminal defense attorneys can run into the hundreds of thousands of dollars—and sometimes exceed $1 million—for handling just one case!

Few law students choose to specialize in criminal law, even though the job of a criminal lawyer may appear glamorous. One reason may be that the collection of fees can be a significant source of difficulty for many defense attorneys. Most defendants are poor. Those who aren't are often reluctant to pay what they believe is an exorbitant fee, and woe be it to the defense attorney whose client is convicted before the fee has been paid! Visit the National Association of Criminal Defense Lawyers (NACDL) via **Web Extra 9–11** and the Association of Federal Defense Attorneys (AFDA) via **Web Extra 9–12** at cjtoday.com to learn more about the practice of criminal law.

WEB
Extra

CRIMINAL DEFENSE OF THE POOR

The Sixth Amendment to the U.S. Constitution guarantees criminal defendants the effective assistance of counsel. A series of U.S. Supreme Court decisions has established that defendants who are unable to pay for private criminal defense attorneys will receive adequate representation at all stages of criminal justice processing. In *Powell* v. *Alabama* (1932),[70] the Court held that the Fourteenth Amendment requires state courts to appoint counsel for defendants in capital cases who are unable to afford their own. In 1938, in *Johnson* v. *Zerbst*,[71] the Court overturned the conviction of

O Lord, look down upon these the multitudes, and spread strife and dissension, so that this, Thy servant, might prosper.

—*Anonymous, "The Lawyer's Prayer"*

an indigent federal inmate, holding that his Sixth Amendment due process right to counsel had been violated. The Court declared, "If the accused . . . is not represented by counsel and has not competently and intelligently waived his constitutional right, the Sixth Amendment stands as a jurisdictional bar to a valid conviction and sentence depriving him of his life or his liberty." The decision established the right of indigent defendants to receive the assistance of appointed counsel in all criminal proceedings in federal courts. The 1963 case of *Gideon* v. *Wainwright*[72] extended the right to appointed counsel to all indigent defendants charged with a felony in state courts. In *Argersinger* v. *Hamlin* (1972),[73] the Court required adequate legal representation for anyone facing a potential sentence of imprisonment. Juveniles charged with delinquent acts were granted the right to appointed counsel in the case of *In re Gault* (1967).[74]

In 2002, a closely divided U.S. Supreme Court expanded the Sixth Amendment right to counsel, ruling that defendants in state courts who are facing relatively minor charges must be provided with an attorney at government expense even when they face only the slightest chance of incarceration. The case, *Alabama* v. *Shelton*,[75] involved defendant LeReed Shelton, who was convicted of third-degree assault after taking part in a fistfight with another motorist following a minor traffic accident. Shelton had been advised of his right to have an attorney represent him at trial, and the judge who heard his case repeatedly suggested that he should hire an attorney and warned him of the dangers of serving as his own attorney, but at no time did the judge offer Shelton assistance of counsel. Unable to afford an attorney, Shelton proceeded to represent himself and was convicted and sentenced to 30 days in the county jail. The sentence was suspended, and he was placed on two years of unsupervised probation, fined $500, and ordered to make restitution and to pay the costs of court. Shelton soon appealed on Sixth Amendment grounds, however, and the Alabama Supreme Court ruled in his favor, reasoning that a suspended sentence constitutes a "term of imprisonment" no matter how unlikely it is that the term will ever be served. On appeal by the state of Alabama, the case made its way to the U.S. Supreme Court, which agreed that "[a] suspended sentence is a prison term" and requires appointed counsel when an indigent defendant desires legal representation.

States have responded to the federal mandate for indigent defense in a number of ways. Most now use one of three systems to deliver legal services to criminal defendants who are unable to afford their own: (1) court-appointed counsel, (2) public defenders, and (3) contractual arrangements. Most systems are administered at the county level, although funding arrangements may involve state, county, and municipal monies—as well as federal grants and court fees.

Court-appointed defense attorneys, also called *assigned counsel*, are usually drawn from a roster of all practicing criminal attorneys within the jurisdiction of the trial court. Their fees are paid at a rate set by the state or local government. These fees are typically low, however, and may affect the amount of effort an assigned attorney puts into a case. In 2001, for example, New York's court-appointed attorneys were paid only $25 per hour for out-of-court preparation time and $40 an hour for time spent in the courtroom—a rate of pay that is 10 to 20 times less than what they normally earn for a private case.[76] So, although most attorneys assigned by the court to indigent defense take their jobs seriously, some feel only a loose commitment to their clients. Paying clients, in their eyes, deserve better representation.

public defender

An attorney employed by a government agency or subagency, or by a private organization under contract to a government body, for the purpose of providing defense services to indigents, or an attorney who has volunteered such service.

The second type of indigent defense, the **public defender** program, relies on full-time salaried staff. Staff members include defense attorneys, defense investigators, and office personnel. Defense investigators gather information in support of the defense effort. They may interview friends, family members, and employers of the accused, with an eye toward effective defense. Public defender programs have become popular in recent years, with approximately 64% of counties nationwide now funding them.[77] A 1996 Bureau of Justice Statistics (BJS) report found that a public defender system is the primary method used to provide indigent counsel for criminal defendants and that 28% of state jurisdictions nationwide use public defender programs exclusively to provide indigent defense.[78] Critics charge that public defenders, because they are government employees, are not sufficiently independent from prosecutors and judges. For the same reason, clients may be suspicious of public defenders, viewing them as state functionaries. Finally, because of the huge caseloads typical of public defenders' offices, there is pressure to use plea bargaining excessively.

Through a third type of indigent defense, contract attorney programs, county and state officials arrange with local criminal lawyers to provide for indigent defense on a contractual basis. Individual attorneys, local bar associations, and multipartner law firms may all be tapped to provide services. Contract defense programs are the least widely used form of indigent defense at present, although their popularity is growing.

Critics of the current system of indigent defense point out that the system is woefully underfunded. Findings from the most recent National Survey of Indigent Defense Systems were published in 2001.[79] The survey found that reporting states spent a total of $662,590,139 on indigent criminal defense in 1999. Most of the money ($337 million) went to fund public defender programs, while assigned counsel programs cost $191 million, and contract attorney fees totaled $53 million. New Jersey, the most populous of the states covered by the survey, spent the most money ($73 million) on indigent criminal defense. Although these figures may seem quite large, they total only about one-third the amount that reporting states spend every year to prosecute criminal defendants. As a result, the report of the National Symposium on Indigent Defense proclaimed in 2000, "Indigent defense today, in terms of funding, caseloads, and quality, is in a chronic state of crisis."[80] Some question the quality of services available through public defender systems due to the fact that entry-level public defenders are paid poorly in comparison to what new attorneys entering private law firms might earn. In 2004, for example, Avoyelles Parish in Louisiana hired a part-time attorney with no previous criminal defense experience to handle all court-assigned juvenile and misdemeanor cases and to handle all felony arraignments. The attorney, whose work load included 1,088 misdemeanor and 256 juvenile cases, was paid $19,200.[81] In 2004, entry-level assistant public defenders in Massachusetts earned $35,000,[82] those in Georgia made $44,000, and those in Kentucky were paid $33,425; attorneys entering private practice can make much more. Moreover, the cost to the states for representing an indigent defendant averages around $490, while private attorney fees are generally much higher.[83]

As a consequence of such limited funding, many public defender's offices employ what critics call a "plead 'em and speed 'em through" strategy, which can often mean that attorneys meet their clients for the first time in courtrooms as trials are about to begin and use plea bargaining to move cases along. Mary Broderick of the National Legal Aid and Defender Association says, "We aren't being given the same weapons. . . . It's like trying to deal with smart bombs when all you've got is a couple of cap pistols."[84] Proposed enhancements to indigent defense systems are offered by the National Legal Aid and Defender Association (NLADA). You can visit the NLADA via Web Extra 9–13 at cjtoday.com.

The entire 200-page report of the National Symposium on Indigent Defense is available at Library Extra 9–8 at cjtoday.com, and the Bureau of Justice Statistics 2001 overview of the National Survey of Indigent Defense Systems can be found at Library Extra 9–9. Library Extra 9–10 provides an overview of state-funded indigent defense services.

Although state indigent defense services are sometimes significantly underfunded, the same is not true of the federal system. The defense of indigent Oklahoma City bomber Timothy McVeigh, for example, cost taxpayers an estimated $13.8 million—which doesn't include the cost of his appeal or execution. McVeigh's expenses included $6.7 million for attorneys, $2 million for investigators, $3 million for expert witnesses, and approximately $1.4 million for office rent and secretarial assistance.[85]

In 2000, the Bureau of Justice Statistics (BJS) reported data on publicly financed counsel nationwide in two research reports that appear to conflict with the conclusions reached by the National Survey of Indigent Defense Systems.[86] BJS statisticians found that court-appointed defense attorneys represent 66% of federal felony defendants, as well as 82% of felony defendants in the nation's 75 most populous counties. The study also found that conviction rates for indigent defendants and for those with their own lawyers were about the same in both federal and state courts. About 90% of the federal defendants and 75% of defendants in the most populous counties were found guilty regardless of the type of attorney they had. However, the study showed that those found guilty and represented by publicly financed attorneys were incarcerated at a higher rate than those defendants who paid for their own legal representation—88% compared to 77% in federal courts and 71% compared to 54% in the most populous counties. On average, however, prison sentences for defendants with publicly financed attorneys were shorter than were those with hired counsel. In federal district court, convicted defendants who had publicly financed attorneys were sentenced to less than five years on average, and those with private attorneys to just over five years. In large counties, those with publicly financed attorneys were sentenced to an average of two and a half years, and those with private attorneys to three years.

Of course, defendants need not be represented by any counsel at all. Defendants may waive their right to an attorney and undertake their own defense—a right held by the U.S. Supreme Court to be inherent in the Sixth Amendment in the 1975 case of *Faretta* v. *California*.[87] Self-representation is uncommon, however, and only 1% of federal inmates and 3% of state inmates report having represented themselves.[88] Some famous instances of self-representation include the 1995 trial of Long Island Rail Road commuter train shooter Colin Ferguson, the 1999 assisted suicide trial of Dr. Jack Kevorkian, and the 2002 federal competency hearings of Zacarias Moussaoui.

Defendants who are not pleased with the lawyer appointed to defend them are in a somewhat different situation. They may request, through the court, that a new lawyer be assigned to represent them, as Timothy McVeigh did following his conviction and death sentence in the Oklahoma City bombing case. However, unless there is clear reason for reassignment, such as an obvious personality conflict

Even the intelligent and educated layman . . . requires the guiding hand of counsel at every step in the proceedings against him.

—Gideon v. Wainwright, 372 U.S. 335, 344 (1963)

WEB Extra

LIBRARY Extra

I truly believe he's innocent. And if I didn't convince 12 people of that, then I didn't do enough.

– Mark Geragos, attorney for Scott Peterson

CJ Today Exhibit 9–1

Gideon v. *Wainwright* and Indigent Defense

Today, about three-fourths of state-level criminal defendants and one-half of federal defendants are represented in court by publicly funded counsel.[1] As recently as 40 years ago, however, the practice of publicly funded indigent defense was uncommon. That changed in 1963 when, in the case of *Gideon* v. *Wainwright*,[2] the U.S. Supreme Court extended the right to legal counsel to indigent defendants charged with a criminal offense. The reasoning of the Court is well summarized in this excerpt from the majority opinion written by Justice Hugo Black:

> Governments, both state and federal, quite properly spend vast sums of money to establish machinery to try defendants accused of crime. Lawyers to prosecute are everywhere deemed essential to protect the public's interest in an orderly society. Similarly,

there are few defendants charged with crime, few indeed, who fail to hire the best lawyers they can get to prepare and present their defenses. That government hires lawyers to prosecute and defendants who have the money hire lawyers to defend are the strongest indications of the widespread belief that lawyers in criminal courts are necessities, not luxuries. The right of one charged with crime to counsel may not be deemed fundamental and essential to fair trials in some countries, but it is in ours. From the very beginning, our state and national constitutions and laws have laid great emphasis on procedural and substantive safeguards designed to assure fair trials before impartial tribunals in which every defendant stands equal before the law. This noble ideal cannot be realized if the poor man charged with crime has to face his accusers without a lawyer to assist him.

[1]Steven K. Smith and Carol J. DeFrances, *Indigent Defense* (Washington, DC: Bureau of Justice Statistics, 1996).
[2]*Gideon* v. *Wainwright*, 372 U.S. 335 (1963).

between defendant and attorney, few judges are likely to honor a request of this sort. Short of obvious difficulties, most judges will trust in the professionalism of appointed counselors.

State-supported indigent defense systems may also be called on to provide representation for clients upon appeal. An attorney who is appointed to represent an indigent defendant on appeal, however, may conclude that an appeal would be frivolous. If so, he or she may request that the appellate court allow him or her to withdraw from the case or that the court dispose of the case without requiring the attorney to file a brief arguing the merits of the appeal. In 1967, in the case of *Anders* v. *California*,[89] the U.S. Supreme Court found that to protect a defendant's constitutional right to appellate counsel, appellate courts must safeguard against the risk of accepting an attorney's negative assessment of a case where an appeal is not actually frivolous. The Court also found California's existing procedure for evaluating such requests to be inadequate, and the justices set forth an acceptable procedure. In 1979, in the case of *People* v. *Wende*,[90] the state of California adopted a new standardized procedure that, although not the same as the one put forth in *Anders*, was designed to protect the right of a criminal defendant to appeal.

The *Wende* standard was put to the test in the 2000 case of *Smith* v. *Robbins*.[91] The case began when convicted California murderer Lee Robbins told his court-appointed counsel that he wanted to file an appeal. His attorney concluded that the appeal would be frivolous and filed a brief with the state court of appeals to that effect. The court agreed with the attorney's assessment, and the appeal was not heard. The California Supreme Court denied further review of the case. After exhausting his state postconviction remedies, Robbins appealed to the federal courts, arguing that he had been denied effective assistance of appellate counsel because his counsel's brief did not comply with one of the requirements in *Anders*—specifically, the requirement that the brief must mention "anything in the record that might arguably support the appeal." A federal district court agreed, concluding that there were at least two issues that might have supported Robbins's appeal. The court found that the failure to include them in the brief deviated from the *Anders* procedure and thus amounted to deficient performance by counsel. The Ninth Circuit Court agreed, concluding that *Anders* established a mandatory procedure as a standard against which the performance of appointed counsel could be assessed. When the case finally reached the U.S. Supreme Court, the justices held that the *Anders* procedure is only one method of satisfying the Constitution's requirements for indigent criminal appeals and that the states are free to adopt different procedures as long as those procedures adequately safeguard a defendant's right to appellate counsel.

Finally, in 2001, in the case of *Texas* v. *Cobb*,[92] the Supreme Court ruled that the Sixth Amendment right to counsel is "offense specific" and applies only to the offense with which a defendant is charged—and not to other offenses, even if they are factually related to the charged offense. The case originated with the arrest of Raymond Cobb on charges of burglary. A woman and her 16-month-old daughter had disappeared from a house that had been burglarized, although it was unclear to investigators whether the burglary and the disappearances were related. Counsel was appointed to represent Cobb, who then confessed to the burglary but denied knowledge of the disappearance of the woman and child. While free on bond on the burglary charge, Cobb confessed to his father that he had killed the woman and child. His father then contacted the police, and Cobb was arrested. While in custody, Cobb waived his *Miranda* rights and confessed to the murders. He was later convicted of capital murder and was sentenced to death. On appeal to the Texas Court of Criminal Appeals, he argued that his confession should not have been admitted into evidence at his trial because it was obtained in violation of his Sixth Amendment right to counsel. That right, he claimed, stemmed from the fact that counsel had been appointed for him in the burglary case. The Texas court agreed with Cobb and reversed his conviction, finding that once the right to counsel attaches to the offense charged, it also attaches to any other offense that is very closely related factually to the offense charged. When the case reached the U.S. Supreme Court, however, the justices overturned the Texas court's ruling and held that the Sixth Amendment right to counsel is "offense specific" and does not necessarily extend to offenses that are "factually related" to those that have actually been charged.

THE ETHICS OF DEFENSE

The job of defense counsel, as we have already mentioned, is to prepare and offer a vigorous defense on behalf of the accused at trial and to appeal cases that have merit. A proper defense at trial often involves the presentation of evidence and the examination of witnesses, both of which require careful thought and planning. Good attorneys may become emotionally committed to the outcomes of trials in which they are involved. Some lawyers, however, cross the line when they lose their professional objectivity and embrace the wider cause of their clients. That's what happened to Lynne Stewart, 65, who was convicted in 2005 of smuggling messages from her jailed client, the radical Egyptian sheik Omar Abdel-Rahman (also known as the "blind sheik"), to his terrorist followers outside of prison.[93] Abdel-Rahman is serving life behind bars for his role in an unsuccessful 1993 plot to bomb New York City landmarks. Stewart, a 1960s-era radical, has often chosen to represent the most contemptible clients, believing that justice requires that everyone receive a vigorous defense. She was arrested after she issued a public statement on behalf of the sheik expressing her client's withdrawal of support for a cease-fire involving his supporters in Egypt. Stewart had known in advance that making the statement violated an order to restrict the sheik's communications, but she later testified that she believed that violence is sometimes necessary to achieve justice. Other evidence showed that she had facilitated forbidden communications

Defense attorney Lynne Stewart, 67, who was sentenced to prison in 2006 for smuggling messages from her jailed client, the radical Egyptian sheik Omar Abdel-Rahman (aka the "blind sheik"), to his terrorist followers outside of prison. Our adversarial system requires that attorneys sometimes defend unpopular clients, but the defense role is carefully prescribed by ethical and procedural standards. How did Stewart's actions violate those standards?

Stephen Chernin/AP Wide World Photos

Ethics and Professionalism

American Bar Association's Model Rules of Professional Conduct

To help attorneys understand what is expected of them, the American Bar Association (ABA) has provided significant guidance in the areas of legal ethics and professional responsibility. Specifically, the ABA has developed professional standards intended to serve as models for state bar associations and to guide legislative bodies focused on ensuring ethical behavior among attorneys.

The ABA's first major foray into the area of ethical guidelines resulted in the adoption of its original Canons of Professional Ethics on August 27, 1908. In 1913, in an effort to keep the association informed about state and local bar activities concerning professional ethics, the ABA established its Standing Committee on Professional Ethics. The name of the group was changed to the Committee on Ethics and Professional Responsibility in 1971, and the committee continues to function under that name today.

In 1969, the committee's Model Code of Professional Responsibility was formally adopted by the ABA. Eventually, the majority of state and federal jurisdictions adopted their own versions of the Model Code.

In 1977, the ABA Commission on Evaluation of Professional Standards was created and charged with rethinking the ethical problems of the legal profession. Over the next six years, the Commission drafted the Model Rules of Professional Conduct, which the ABA adopted on August 2, 1983. The Model Rules effectively supplanted the Model Code of Professional Responsibility, and today most state and federal jurisdictions have adapted the Model Rules to their own particular circumstances.

The Model Rules have been periodically amended—most significantly in 2002—but continue to provide the touchstone ethical standards of the American legal profession today. Visit the American Bar Association on the Internet at **Web Extra 9–14** at cjtoday.com, and learn about its Center for Professional Responsibility at **Web Extra 9–15**.

WEB Extra ▪▪▪▪

THINKING ABOUT ETHICS

1. Should a defense attorney represent a client whom he or she knows to be guilty? Explain.
2. Would it be unethical for an attorney to refuse to represent such a client? Why or why not?

Reference: American Bar Association, *Model Rules of Professional Conduct–Preface*, http://www.abanet.org/cpr/mrpc/preface.html (accessed May 17, 2007).

between Abdel-Rahman and a translator by using prearranged cues such as tapping on a table, shaking a water bottle, and uttering key terms like "chocolate" and "heart attack" during prison visits.

The nature of the adversarial process, fed by the emotions of the participants combined with the often privileged and extensive knowledge that defense attorneys have about their cases, is enough to tempt the professional ethics of some counselors. Because the defense counsel may often know more about the guilt or innocence of the defendant than anyone else prior to trial, the defense role is carefully prescribed by ethical and procedural considerations. Attorneys violate both law and the standards of their profession if they knowingly misrepresent themselves or their clients. As Michael Ratner, president of the Center for Constitutional Rights, put it when commenting on the Stewart case, "lawyers need to be advocates, but they don't need to be accomplices."[94]

To help attorneys understand what is expected of them, and what the appropriate limits of a vigorous defense might be, the American Bar Association provides significant guidance in the areas of legal ethics and professional responsibility. (See the "Ethics and Professionalism" box in this chapter.) Even so, some attorney–client interactions remain especially tricky. Defense attorneys, for example, are under no obligation to reveal information obtained from a client without the client's permission. However, all states permit defense lawyers to violate a client's confidentiality without fear of reprisal if they reasonably believe that doing so could prevent serious injury or death to another person. In 2004, with passage of a new evidence law broadening the state's evidence code, California joined the other 49 states in freeing attorneys to violate client confidentiality in such cases. California law makes disclosure discretionary, not mandatory. Kevin Mohr, a professor at Western State University College of Law in Fullerton, California, noted that the new law provides the first exception to the attorney–client privilege in California in more than 130 years. "A lawyer can now take action and intervene and prevent [a] criminal act from occurring," said Mohr.[95]

The California changes had been presaged by an action of the American Bar Association, which eased its secrecy rules surrounding attorney–client relationships in 2001.[96] Prior to that time, ABA rules permitted criminal defense attorneys to disclose incriminating information about a client only to prevent imminent death or substantial bodily harm. The 2001 rule change dispensed with the word *imminent*, allowing attorneys to reveal clients' secrets in order to stop future deaths or to prevent substantial bodily harm.

Somewhat earlier, the 1986 U.S. Supreme Court case of *Nix* v. *Whiteside*[97] clarified the duty of lawyers to reveal known instances of client perjury. The *Nix* case came to the Court upon the complaint of the defendant, Whiteside, who claimed that he was deprived of the assistance of effective counsel during his murder trial because his lawyer would not allow him to testify untruthfully. Whiteside wanted to testify that he had seen a gun or something metallic in his victim's hand before killing him. Before trial, however, Whiteside admitted to his lawyer that he had actually seen no weapon, but he believed that to testify to the truth would result in his conviction. The lawyer told Whiteside that, as a professional counselor, he would be forced to challenge Whiteside's false testimony if it occurred and to explain to the court the facts as he knew them. On the stand, Whiteside said only that he thought the victim was reaching for a gun but did not claim to have seen one. He was found guilty of second-degree murder and appealed to the Supreme Court on the claim of inadequate representation. The Court, recounting the development of ethical codes in the legal profession, held that a lawyer's duty to a client "is limited to legitimate, lawful conduct compatible with the very nature of a trial as a search for truth. . . . Counsel is precluded from taking steps or in any way assisting the client in presenting false evidence or otherwise violating the law."[98]

The Bailiff

The **bailiff**, another member of the professional courtroom work group, is usually an armed law enforcement officer. The job of the bailiff, also called a *court officer,* is to ensure order in the courtroom, to announce the judge's entry into the courtroom, to call witnesses, and to prevent the escape of the accused (if the accused has not been released on bond). The bailiff also supervises the jury when it is sequestered and controls public and media access to jury members. Bailiffs in federal courtrooms are deputy U.S. marshals.

Courtrooms can be dangerous places—as the story that opened this chapter showed—and bailiffs play a critical role in courtroom security. In an event that led to tightened courtroom security nationwide, George Lott opened fire in a courtroom in Tarrant County, Texas, in 1992, killing two lawyers and injuring three other people.[99] Lott, an attorney, was frustrated by the court's handling of his divorce and by child molestation charges that had been filed against him by his ex-wife. Lott was sentenced to die in 1993. Following the Lott incident and others like it, most courts began using metal detectors, and many now require visitors to leave packages, cellular phones, and objects that might conceal weapons in lockers or to check them with personnel before entering the courtroom.

A comprehensive courthouse security plan must, of course, extend beyond individual courtrooms. In 2005, around the time of the courthouse shootings in Atlanta, the National Center for State Courts (NCSC) released a comprehensive plan for improving security in state courthouses.[100] The plan contained a list of ten essential elements for court safety that include the need to (1) assess existing and potential threats, (2) identify physical strengths and weaknesses of existing courts, (3) develop a comprehensive emergency response plan, (4) be aware of the latest technologies in court security, and (5) build strong and effective partnerships among state courts, law enforcement agencies, and county commissioners. The complete list of NCSC recommendations is available at Library Extra 9–11 at cjtoday.com.

bailiff

The court officer whose duties are to keep order in the courtroom and to maintain physical custody of the jury.

LIBRARY
Extra
▪ ▪ ▪ ▪

The Local Court Administrator

Many states now employ local court administrators whose job is to facilitate the smooth functioning of courts in a judicial district or area. A major impetus for the hiring of local court administrators came from the 1967 President's Commission on Law Enforcement and Administration of Justice. Examining state courts, the commission found "a system that treats defendants who are charged with minor offenses with less dignity and consideration than it treats those who are charged with serious crimes."[101] A few years later, the National Advisory Commission on Criminal Justice Standards and Goals recommended that all courts with five or more judges create the position of trial court administrator.[102]

Court administrators provide uniform court management, assuming many of the duties previously performed by chief judges, prosecutors, and court clerks. Where court administrators operate, the ultimate authority for running the court still rests with the chief judge. Administrators,

Free and open access to justice requires a safe and secure environment in which all those who come to the courthouse are free from fear and intimidation. Judges, employees, and the public need to feel safe if they are to conduct themselves in a fair and impartial manner and in accordance with a sense of judicial decorum.

—*National Center for State Courts*[ii]

however, are able to relieve the judge of many routine and repetitive tasks, such as record keeping, scheduling, case-flow analysis, personnel administration, space utilization, facilities planning, and budget management. They may also take the minutes at meetings of judges and their committees.

Juror management is another area in which trial court administrators are becoming increasingly involved. Juror utilization studies can identify problems such as the overselection of citizens for the jury pool and the reasons for excessive requests to be excused from jury service. They can also suggest ways to reduce the time jurors waste waiting to be called or impaneled.

Effective court administrators are able to track lengthy cases and identify bottlenecks in court processing. They then suggest strategies to make the administration of justice more efficient for courtroom professionals and more humane for lay participants.

The Court Reporter

The role of the court reporter (also called the *court stenographer* or *court recorder*) is to create a record of all that occurs during a trial. Accurate records are very important in criminal trial courts because appeals may be based entirely on what went on in the courtroom. Especially significant are all verbal comments made in the courtroom, including testimony, objections, the judge's rulings, the judge's instructions to the jury, arguments made by lawyers, and the results of conferences between the lawyers and the judge. The official trial record, often taken on a stenotype machine or an audio recorder, may later be transcribed in manuscript form and will become the basis for any appellate review of the trial.

Today's court stenographers often employ computer-aided transcription (CAT) software, which translates typed stenographic shorthand into complete and readable transcripts. Court reporters may be members of the National Court Reporters Association, the United States Court Reporters Association, or the Association of Legal Administrators—all of which support the activities of these professionals. You can visit the National Court Reporters Association via **Web Extra 9–16** at cjtoday.com.

WEB
Extra
▪▪▪▪

The Clerk of Court

The jury is . . . a cornerstone of justice and the democratic process, [but] the jury process needs to be brought into the 21st Century.

—*Robert Grey, President of the American Bar Association*[iii]

The duties of the clerk of court (also known as the *county clerk*) extend beyond the courtroom. The clerk maintains all records of criminal cases, including all pleas and motions made both before and after the actual trial. The clerk also prepares a jury pool, issues jury summonses, and subpoenas witnesses for both the prosecution and the defense. During the trial, the clerk (or an assistant) marks physical evidence for identification as instructed by the judge and maintains custody of that evidence. The clerk also swears in witnesses and performs other functions as the judge directs. Some states allow the clerk limited judicial duties, such as the power to issue warrants, to handle certain matters relating to individuals declared mentally incompetent,[103] and to serve as judge of probate—overseeing wills and the administration of estates.

Expert Witnesses

expert witness

A person who has special knowledge and skills recognized by the court as relevant to the determination of guilt or innocence. Unlike lay witnesses, expert witnesses may express opinions or draw conclusions in their testimony.

Most of the "insiders" we've talked about so far either are employees of the state or have ongoing professional relationships with the court (as in the case of defense counsel). **Expert witnesses**, however, may not have that kind of status, although some do. Expert witnesses are recognized as having specialized skills and knowledge in an established profession or technical area. They must demonstrate their expertise through education, work experience, publications, and awards. Their testimony at trial provides an effective way of introducing scientific evidence in such areas as medicine, psychology, ballistics, crime-scene analysis, photography, and many other disciplines. Expert witnesses, like the other courtroom actors described in this chapter, are generally paid professionals. And like all other witnesses, they are subject to cross-examination. Unlike lay witnesses, they are allowed to express opinions and to draw conclusions, but only within their particular area of expertise.

One difficulty with expert testimony is that it can be confusing to the jury. Sometimes the trouble is due to the nature of the subject matter and sometimes to disagreements between the experts themselves. Often, however, it arises from the strict interpretation given to expert testimony by procedural requirements. The difference between medical and legal definitions of insanity, for example, points to a divergence in both history and purpose between the law and science. Courts that attempt to apply criteria like the M'Naghten rule (discussed in Chapter 4) in deciding claims of "insanity" are often faced with the testimony of psychiatric experts who refuse to even recog-

CJ Careers

U.S. Marshals Service

Name: Larry Harper

Position: Deputy U.S. Marshal, Operations Division

City: Albuquerque, New Mexico

College Attended: University of New Mexico

Year Hired: 2003

"I went into law enforcement because I wanted to do my part in making my community safe. Even when I was a child, I knew I wanted to go into law enforcement. When I saw the Marshals Service while doing an internship in college, I knew this was where I wanted to be. I enjoy the flexibility of the job. . . . It's not the same every day."

TYPICAL POSITIONS

Deputy U.S. marshal. The mission of the U.S. Marshals Service is to protect the federal courts and to ensure the effective operation of the judicial system. Deputy U.S. marshals are involved in court security, fugitive investigations, witness security, transportation and custody of federal prisoners, management of seized assets, and special operations.

EMPLOYMENT REQUIREMENTS

The applicant must be a U.S. citizen between 21 and 36 years of age, must be in excellent physical condition, and must possess a valid driver's license and a good driving record. General employment requirements include (1) a comprehensive written exam, (2) a structured employment interview, and (3) a background investigation. Appointment at the GS-5 level requires (1) a bachelor's degree from an accredited college or university or (2) three years of "responsible volunteer or paid experience" or (3) an equivalent combination of education and experience.

OTHER REQUIREMENTS

Successful applicants must complete ten weeks of rigorous training at the U.S. Marshals Service Training Academy in Glynco, Georgia.

Source: U.S. Department of Justice.

SALARY

Deputy U.S. marshals are typically hired at GS-5 or GS-7, depending on education and work experience.

BENEFITS

Benefits include (1) 13 days of sick leave annually, (2) two and a half to five weeks of paid vacation and ten paid federal holidays each year, (3) federal health and life insurance, and (4) a comprehensive retirement program.

DIRECT INQUIRIES TO:

U.S. Marshals Service

Human Resources Division–Law Enforcement Recruiting

Washington, DC 20530-1000

Phone: 202-307-9400

Website: http://www.usdoj.gov/marshals

For more information on the rapidly expanding criminal justice careers area, read *Where the Jobs Are: Mission Critical Opportunities for America*, available on the Web at http://www.justicestudies.com/jobs.htm.

---

nize the word. Such experts may prefer, instead, to speak in terms of *psychosis* and *neurosis*—words that have no place in legal jargon. Because of the uncertainties they create, legal requirements may pit experts against one another and may confound the jury.

Even so, most authorities agree that expert testimony is usually viewed by jurors as more trustworthy than other forms of evidence. In a study of scientific evidence, one prosecutor commented that if he had to choose between presenting a fingerprint or an eyewitness at trial, he would always go with the fingerprint.[104] As a consequence of the effectiveness of scientific evidence, the National Institute of Justice recommends that "prosecutors consider the potential utility of such information in all cases where such evidence is available."[105]

Some expert witnesses traverse the country and earn very high fees by testifying at trials. DNA specialist John Gerdes, for example, was paid $100 per hour for his work in support of the defense in the 1995 O. J. Simpson criminal trial, and New York forensic pathologist Michael Baden

A ballistics expert testifying on the witness stand in a criminal trial as jurors view evidence on nearby computer displays. Expert witnesses may express opinions and draw conclusions in their area of expertise; they need not limit their testimony to facts alone. Why are expert witnesses permitted such leeway?

© Royalty-Free/CORBIS

charged $1,500 per day for time spent working for Simpson in Los Angeles. Baden billed Simpson more than $100,000, and the laboratory for which Gerdes worked received more than $30,000 from Simpson's defense attorneys.[106]

Nonprofessional Courtroom Participants

Defendants, victims, jurors, and most witnesses are usually unwilling or inadvertent participants in criminal trials. Although they are outsiders who lack the status of paid professional participants, these are precisely the people who provide the grist for the judicial mill. The press, a willing player in many criminal trials, makes up another group of outsiders. Let's look now at each of these courtroom actors.

Lay Witnesses

lay witness

An eyewitness, character witness, or other person called on to testify who is not considered an expert. Lay witnesses must testify to facts only and may not draw conclusions or express opinions.

subpoena

A written order issued by a judicial officer or grand jury requiring an individual to appear in court and to give testimony or to bring material to be used as evidence. Some subpoenas mandate that books, papers, and other items be surrendered to the court.

Nonexpert witnesses, also known as **lay witnesses**, may be called to testify by either the prosecution or the defense. Lay witnesses may be eyewitnesses who saw the crime being committed or who came upon the crime scene shortly after the crime had occurred. Another type of lay witness is the character witness, who frequently provides information about the personality, family life, business acumen, and so on of the defendant in an effort to show that this is not the kind of person who would commit the crime with which he or she is charged. Of course, the victim may also be a witness, providing detailed and sometimes lengthy testimony about the defendant and the crime.

A written document called a **subpoena** officially notifies witnesses that they are to appear in court to testify. Subpoenas are generally served by an officer of the court or by a police officer, though they are sometimes mailed. Both sides in a criminal case may subpoena witnesses and might ask that individuals called to testify bring with them books, papers, photographs, videotapes, or other forms of physical evidence. Witnesses who fail to appear when summoned may face contempt-of-court charges.

A lay witness being sworn in before testifying in a criminal trial. Nonexpert witnesses must generally limit their testimony to facts about which they have direct knowledge. Why are such limits imposed?

© Royalty-Free/CORBIS

The job of a witness is to provide accurate testimony concerning only those things of which he or she has direct knowledge. Normally, witnesses are not allowed to repeat things that others have told them unless they must do so to account for certain actions of their own. Since few witnesses are familiar with courtroom procedure, the task of testifying is fraught with uncertainty and can be traumatizing.

Everyone who testifies in a criminal trial must do so under oath, in which some reference to God is made, or after affirmation,[107] which is a pledge to tell the truth used by those who find either swearing or a reference to God objectionable.

All witnesses are subject to cross-examination, a process that will be discussed in the next chapter. Lay witnesses may be surprised to find that cross-examination can force them to defend their personal and moral integrity. A cross-examiner may question a witness about past vicious, criminal, or immoral acts, even when such matters have never been the subject of a criminal proceeding.[108] As long as the intent of such questions is to demonstrate to the jury that the witness is not credible, the judge will normally permit them.

Witnesses have traditionally been shortchanged by the judicial process. Subpoenaed to attend court, they have often suffered from frequent and unannounced changes in trial dates. A witness who promptly responds to a summons to appear may find that legal maneuvering has resulted in unanticipated delays. Strategic changes by either side may make the testimony of some witnesses entirely unnecessary, and people who have prepared themselves for the psychological rigors of testifying often experience an emotional letdown.

To compensate witnesses for their time and to make up for lost income, many states pay witnesses for each day that they spend in court. Payments range from $5 to $30 per day,[109] although some states pay nothing at all. In a 2004 Chicago murder case in which Oprah Winfrey served as a juror, for example, all jurors, including Winfrey—a billionaire—were paid $17.20 a day for their services.[110] The 1991 U.S. Supreme Court case of *Demarest* v. *Manspeaker et al.*[111] held that federal prisoners subpoenaed to testify are entitled to witness fees just as nonincarcerated witnesses would be.

In an effort to make the job of witnesses less onerous, 39 states and the federal government have laws or guidelines requiring that witnesses be notified of scheduling changes and cancellations in criminal proceedings.[112] In 1982, Congress passed the Victim and Witness Protection Act, which required the U.S. attorney general to develop guidelines to assist victims and witnesses in meeting the demands placed on them by the justice system. A number of **victims-assistance programs**

> *From what I see in my courtroom every day, many American juries might as well be using Ouija boards.*
>
> —Judge Harold J. Rothwax

victim-assistance program

An organized program that offers services to victims of crime in the areas of crisis intervention and follow-up counseling and that helps victims secure their rights under the law.

(also called *victim/witness-assistance programs*) have also taken up a call for the rights of witnesses and are working to make the courtroom experience more manageable.

Jurors

*The highest act of
citizenship is jury service.*

—*President Abraham Lincoln*

juror

A member of a trial or grand jury who has been selected for jury duty and is required to serve as an arbiter of the facts in a court of law. Jurors are expected to render verdicts of "guilty" or "not guilty" as to the charges brought against the accused, although they sometimes fail to do so (as in the case of a hung jury).

The Cook County, Illinois, jury on which television host Oprah Winfrey served convicted a man of first-degree murder in 2004. "It was an eye-opener for all of us," Winfrey said after the three-day trial ended. "It was not an easy decision to make."[113]

Article III of the U.S. Constitution requires that "[t]he trial of all crimes . . . shall be by jury." States have the authority to determine the size of criminal trial juries. Most states use juries composed of 12 people and one or two alternates designated to fill in for **jurors** who are unable to continue due to accident, illness, or personal emergency. Some states allow for juries of fewer than 12, and juries with as few as six members have survived Supreme Court scrutiny.[114]

Jury duty is regarded as a responsibility of citizenship. Other than juveniles and people in certain occupations, such as police personnel, physicians, members of the armed services on active duty, and emergency services workers, those who are called for jury duty must serve unless they can convince a judge that they should be excused for overriding reasons. Aliens, convicted felons, and citizens who have served on a jury within the past two years are excluded from jury service in most jurisdictions.

The names of prospective jurors are often gathered from the tax register, motor vehicle records, or voter registration rolls of a county or municipality. Minimum qualifications for jury service include adulthood, a basic command of spoken English, citizenship, "ordinary intelligence," and local residency. Jurors are also expected to possess their "natural faculties," meaning that they should be able to hear, speak, see, move, and so forth. Some jurisdictions have recently allowed people with physical disabilities to serve as jurors, although the nature of the evidence to be presented in a case may preclude people with certain kinds of disabilities from serving.

Ideally, the jury should be a microcosm of society, reflecting the values, rationality, and common sense of the average person. The U.S. Supreme Court has held that criminal defendants have a right to have their cases heard before a jury of their peers.[115] Peer juries are those composed of a representative cross section of the community in which the alleged crime occurred and where the trial is to be held. The idea of a peer jury stems from the Magna Carta's original guarantee of jury trials for "freemen." Freemen in England during the thirteenth century, however, were more likely to be of similar mind than is a cross section of Americans today. Hence, although the duty of the jury is to deliberate on the evidence and, ultimately, to determine guilt or innocence, social dynamics may play just as great a role in jury verdicts as do the facts of a case.

In a 1945 case, *Thiel* v. *Southern Pacific Co.*,[116] the Supreme Court clarified the concept of a "jury of one's peers" by noting that while it is not necessary for every jury to contain representatives of every conceivable racial, ethnic, religious, gender, and economic group in the community, court officials may not systematically and intentionally exclude any juror solely because of his or her social characteristics.

In 2005, the American Bar Association released a set of 19 principles intended to guide jury reform.[117] ABA President Robert J. Grey, Jr., said that the principles were aimed at improving the courts' treatment of jurors and to "move jury service into the 21st Century." Some of the principles sounded like a juror's bill of rights and included provisions to protect jurors' privacy and personal information, to inform jurors of trial schedules, and to "vigorously promote juror understanding of the facts and the law." Courts should instruct jurors "in plain and understandable language," the ABA report said. When trials conclude, the report continued, jurors should be advised by judges that they have the right to talk to anyone, including members of the press, and that they also have the right to refuse to talk to anyone about their jury service. Practical recommendations included allowing jurors to take notes, educating jurors regarding the essential aspects of a jury trial, and providing them with identical notebooks containing the court's preliminary instructions and selected exhibits that have been ruled admissible. Read the ABA's entire report, *Principles for Juries and Jury Trials*, at Library Extra 9–12 at cjtoday.com, and learn more about what it's like to serve on a jury in a criminal trial at Web Extra 9–17 at cjtoday.com.

LIBRARY
Extra

WEB
Extra

The Victim

Not all crimes have clearly identifiable victims, and in a murder case, the victim does not survive. Where there is an identifiable surviving victim, however, he or she is often one of the most forgotten people in the courtroom. Although the victim may have been profoundly affected by

CJ News

"*CSI* Effect" Has Juries Wanting More Evidence

Like viewers across the nation, folks in Galveston, Texas, watch a lot of TV shows about crime-scene investigators. Jury consultant Robert Hirschhorn couldn't be happier about that.

Hirschhorn was hired [in 2003] to help defense attorneys pick jurors for the trial of Robert Durst, a millionaire real estate heir who was accused of murdering and dismembering a neighbor, Morris Black. It was a case in which investigators never found Black's head. The defense claimed that wounds to the head might have supported Durst's story that he had killed Black in self-defense.

Hirschhorn wanted jurors who were familiar with shows such as *CSI: Crime Scene Investigation* to spot the importance of such a gap in the evidence. That wasn't difficult: In a survey of the 500 people in the jury pool, the defense found that about 70% were viewers of CBS's *CSI* or similar shows such as Court TV's *Forensic Files* or NBC's *Law & Order.*

Durst was acquitted in November [2003]. To legal analysts, his case seemed an example of how shows such as *CSI* are affecting action in courthouses across the USA by, among other things, raising jurors' expectations of what prosecutors should produce at trial.

Prosecutors, defense lawyers and judges call it "the *CSI* effect," after the crime-scene shows that are among the hottest attractions on television. The shows—*CSI* and *CSI: Miami,* in particular—feature high-tech labs and glib and gorgeous techies. By shining a glamorous light on a gory profession, the programs also have helped to draw more students into forensic studies.

But the programs also foster what analysts say is the mistaken notion that criminal science is fast and infallible and always gets its man. That's affecting the way lawyers prepare their cases, as well as the expectations that police and the public place on real crime labs. Real crime-scene investigators say that because of the programs, people often have unrealistic ideas of what criminal science can deliver.

Like Hirschhorn, many lawyers, judges and legal consultants say they appreciate how *CSI*-type shows have increased interest in forensic evidence.

"Talking about science in the courtroom used to be like talking about geometry—a real jury turnoff," says Hirschhorn, of Lewisville, Texas. "Now that there's this almost obsession with the (TV) shows, you can talk to jurors about (scientific evidence) and just see from the looks on their faces that they find it fascinating."

But some defense lawyers say *CSI* and similar shows make jurors rely too heavily on scientific findings and unwilling to accept that those findings can be compromised by human or technical errors.

Prosecutors also have complaints: They say the shows can make it more difficult for them to win convictions in the large majority of cases in which scientific evidence is irrelevant or absent.

"The lesson that both sides can agree on is, what's on TV does seep into the minds of jurors," says Paul Walsh, chief prosecutor in New Bedford, Mass., and president of the National District Attorneys Association. "Jurors are going to have information, or what they think is information, in mind. That's the new state of affairs."

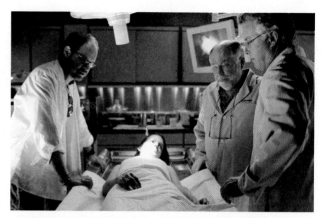

Actors David Berman (as assistant coroner David Phillips), Robert David Hall (as coroner Al Robbins), and William Petersen (as Gil Grissom) examining a corpse in a scene from *CSI: Crime Scene Investigation.* Why do experts fear that popular TV crime dramas like *CSI* have led to unrealistic expectations among today's criminal jurors?
© Neal Preston/Corbis

Lawyers and judges say the *CSI* effect has become a phenomenon in courthouses across the nation:

- In Phoenix [in 2004], jurors in a murder trial noticed that a bloody coat introduced as evidence had not been tested for DNA. They alerted the judge. The tests hadn't been needed because the defendant had acknowledged being at the murder scene. The judge decided that TV had taught jurors about DNA tests, but not enough about when to use them.

- [In 2001] in Richmond, Va., jurors in a murder trial asked the judge whether a cigarette butt found during the investigation could be tested for links to the defendant. Defense attorneys had ordered DNA tests but had not yet introduced them into evidence. The jury's hunch was correct—the tests exonerated the defendant, and the jury acquitted him.

- In Arizona, Illinois and California, prosecutors now use "negative evidence witnesses" to try to assure jurors that it is not unusual for real crime-scene investigators to fail to find DNA, fingerprints and other evidence at crime scenes.

- In Massachusetts, prosecutors have begun to ask judges for permission to question prospective jurors about their TV-watching habits. Several states already allow that.

- [In 2003] in Wilmington, Del., federal researchers studying how juries evaluate scientific evidence staged dozens of simulated trials. At one point, a juror struggling with especially complicated DNA evidence lamented that such problems never come up "on *CSI.*"

The *CSI* effect also is being felt beyond the courtroom. At West Virginia University, forensic science is the most popular undergraduate major for the second year in a row, attracting 13% of incoming freshmen this fall. In June, supporters of an Ohio library drew an

(continued)

CJ News (continued)

overflow crowd of 200-plus to a luncheon speech on DNA by titling it "CSI: Dayton."

The Los Angeles County Sheriff's Department crime lab has seen another version of the *CSI* effect. Four technicians have left the lab for lucrative jobs as technical advisers to crime-scene programs. "They found a way to make science pay," lab director Barry Fisher says.

SHOWS' POPULARITY SOARS

CSI ... was America's second-most-popular TV program during the 2004 season, after the Tuesday edition of *American Idol.*

CSI and a spinoff, *CSI: Miami* ... , have drawn an average of more than 40 million viewers a week. . . . *Law & Order*, whose plots sometimes focus on forensic evidence, has been the 13th-most-watched show during the 2003–04 season, averaging about 15 million viewers. On cable, the Discovery Channel, A&E and Court TV have programs that highlight DNA testing or the analysis of fingerprints, hair and blood-spatter patterns.

CSI: NY, set in New York City, [premiered] in September 2005. The *CSI* shows combine whiz-bang science with in-your-face interrogations to solve complex crimes. Some sample dialogue from actor David Caruso, the humorless monotone who plays investigator Horatio Caine on *CSI: Miami:* "He (the bad guy) doesn't know how evidence works, but you know what? He will."

The shows' popularity, TV historians say, is partly a result of their constant presence. Counting network and cable, at least one hour of crime-forensics programming airs in prime time six nights a week.

The stars of the shows often are the equipment—DNA sequencers, mass spectrometers, photometric fingerprint illuminators, scanning electron microscopes. But the technicians run a close second.

"It's 'geek chic,' the idea that kids who excel in science and math can grow up to be cool," says Robert Thompson, who teaches the history of TV programming at Syracuse University. "This is long overdue. . . . Cops and cowboys and doctors and lawyers have been done to death."

DEPARTING FROM REALITY

Some of the science on *CSI* is state-of-the-art. Real lab technicians can, for example, lift DNA profiles from cigarette butts, candy wrappers and gobs of spit, just as their Hollywood counterparts do.

But some of what's on TV is far-fetched. Real technicians don't pour caulk into knife wounds to make a cast of the weapon. That wouldn't work in soft tissue. Machines that can identify cologne from scents on clothing are still in the experimental phase. A criminal charge based on "neuro-linguistic programming"—detecting lies by the way a person's eyes shift—likely would be dismissed by a judge.

But real scientists say *CSI*'s main fault is this: The science is always above reproach.

"You never see a case where the sample is degraded or the lab work is faulty or the test results don't solve the crime," says Dan Krane, president and DNA specialist at Forensic Bioinformatics in Fairborn, Ohio. "These things happen all the time in the real world."

Defense lawyers say the misconception that crime-scene evidence and testing are always accurate helps prosecutors. "Jurors expect the criminal justice system to work better than it does," says Betty Layne DesPortes, a criminal defense lawyer in Richmond, Va., who has a master's degree in forensic science.

She notes that during the past 15 years, human errors and corruption have skewed test results in crime labs in West Virginia, Pennsylvania, California, Texas and Washington state.

But prosecutors say the shows help defense lawyers. Jurors who are regular viewers, they say, expect testable evidence to be present at all crime scenes.

In fact, they say, evidence such as DNA and fingerprints—the staple of *CSI* plots—is available in only a small minority of cases and can yield inconclusive results.

"Defense attorneys will get up there and bang the rail and say 'Where were the DNA tests?' to take advantage of the idea that's in the juror's mind," says Joshua Marquis, a prosecutor in Astoria, Ore. "You've got to do a lot of jury preparation to defeat that."

Some prosecutors have gone to great lengths to lower jurors' expectations about such evidence.

In Belleville, Ill., last spring, prosecutor Gary Duncan called on seven nationally recognized experts to testify about scientific evidence against a man accused of raping and murdering a 10-year-old girl. The witnesses included specialists in human and animal DNA, shoe-print evidence, population statistics and human mitochondrial DNA, genetic material that is inherited only from one's mother and that seldom is used in criminal cases. Duncan won a conviction.

"I wanted to be certain the jury was clear on the evidence and its meaning," he says. "These days, juries demand that."

CSI producers acknowledge that they take some liberties with facts and the capabilities of science, but they say it's necessary to keep their story lines moving.

Elizabeth Devine, a former crime-lab technician who writes and produces episodes of *CSI: Miami*, spoke at a training seminar for prosecutors last year in Columbia, S.C. She said that if the shows did not cut the time needed to perform DNA tests from weeks to minutes, a villain might not be caught before "episode five."

For all of *CSI*'s faults, some lab technicians say they have a soft spot for the TV version of their world. "It's great for getting people interested (in) careers" in forensic science, says Barbara Llewellyn, director of DNA analysis for the Illinois State Police.

Terry Melton, president of Mitotyping Technologies in State College, Pa., says the programs have made "jury duty something people now look forward to."

And Fisher says the shows have given "science types" like himself some unexpected cachet.

"When I tell someone what I do, I never have to explain it now," he says. "They know what a crime-scene (technician) does. At least, they think they do."

For the latest in crime and justice news, visit the Talk Justice news feed at http://www.crimenews.info.

Source: Richard Willing, " '*CSI* Effect' Has Juries Wanting More Evidence: People Expect Real Crime-Solving to Be Like the Hit TV Show," USA TODAY, May 5, 2004. Reprinted with permission.

the crime itself and is often emotionally committed to the proceedings and trial outcome, he or she may not even be permitted to participate directly in the trial process. Although a powerful movement to recognize the interests of victims is in full swing in this country, it is still not unusual for crime victims to be totally unaware of the final outcome of a case that intimately concerns them.[118]

Hundreds of years ago, the situation surrounding victims was far different. During the early Middle Ages in much of Europe, victims or their survivors routinely played a central role in trial proceedings and in sentencing decisions. They testified, examined witnesses, challenged defense contentions, and pleaded with the judge or jury for justice, honor, and often revenge. Sometimes they were even expected to carry out the sentence of the court by flogging the offender or by releasing the trapdoor used for hangings. This "golden age" of the victim ended with the consolidation of power into the hands of monarchs, who declared that vengeance was theirs alone.

Today, victims, like witnesses, experience many hardships as they participate in the criminal court process. These are a few of the rigors they endure:

- Uncertainty as to their role in the criminal justice process
- A general lack of knowledge about the criminal justice system, courtroom procedure, and legal issues
- Trial delays that result in frequent travel, missed work, and wasted time
- Fear of the defendant or of retaliation from the defendant's associates
- The trauma of testifying and of cross-examination

The trial process itself can make for a bitter experience. If victims take the stand, defense attorneys may test their memory, challenge their veracity, or even suggest that they were somehow responsible for their own victimization. After enduring cross-examination, some victims report feeling as though they, and not the offender, were portrayed as the criminal to the jury. The difficulties encountered by victims have been compared to a second victimization at the hands of the criminal justice system.

The Defendant

Generally, defendants must be present at their trials. The Federal Rules of Criminal Procedure, like state rules, require that a defendant must be present at every stage of a trial, except that a defendant who is initially present may be voluntarily absent after the trial has commenced.[119] In *Crosby* v. *U.S.* (1993),[120] the U.S. Supreme Court held that a defendant may not be tried in absentia, even if he or she was present at the beginning of a trial, if his or her absence is due to escape or failure to appear. In *Zafiro* v. *U.S.* (1993),[121] the justices held that, at least in federal courts, defendants charged with similar or related offenses may be tried together, even when their defenses differ substantially.

The majority of criminal defendants are poor, uneducated, and often alienated from the philosophy that undergirds the American justice system. Many are relatively powerless and are at the mercy of judicial mechanisms. However, experienced defendants, notably those who are career offenders, may be well versed in courtroom demeanor. As we discussed earlier, defendants in criminal trials may even choose to represent themselves, though such a choice may not be in their best interests.

Even without self-representation, every defendant who chooses to do so can substantially influence events in the courtroom. Defendants exercise choice in (1) selecting and retaining counsel, (2) planning a defense strategy in coordination with their attorney, (3) deciding what information to provide to (or withhold from) the defense team, (4) deciding what plea to enter, (5) deciding whether to testify personally, and (6) determining whether to file an appeal if convicted.

Nevertheless, even the most active defendants suffer from a number of disadvantages. One is the tendency of others to assume that anyone on trial must be guilty. Although a criminal defendant is "innocent until proven guilty," the very fact that the defendant is accused of an offense casts a shadow of suspicion that may foster biases in the minds of jurors and other courtroom actors. Another disadvantage lies in the often-substantial social and cultural differences that separate the offender from the professional courtroom staff. While lawyers and judges tend to identify with upper-middle-class values and lifestyles, few offenders do. The consequences of such a gap between defendant and courtroom staff may be insidious and far-reaching.

The beauty of the jury is their morality. Tap into it.

—San Francisco defense attorney
Tony Serra

My experience was like being in prison.

—Tracy Hampton, who was excused
from the Simpson criminal jury after
four months of sequestration

No citizen possessing all other qualifications which are or may be prescribed by law shall be disqualified for service as grand or petit juror in any court of the United States, or of any State on account of race, color, or previous condition of servitude.

—U.S. Code, Title 18, Section 243

Spectators and the Press

Spectators and the press are often overlooked because they do not have an official role in courtroom proceedings. Both spectators and media representatives may be present in large numbers at any trial. Spectators include members of the families of both victim and defendant, friends of either side, and curious onlookers—some of whom are avocational court watchers. Journalists, TV reporters, and other members of the press are apt to be present at "spectacular" trials (those involving an especially gruesome crime or a famous personality) and at those in which there is a great deal of community interest. The right of reporters and spectators to be present at a criminal trial is supported by the Sixth Amendment's requirement of a public trial.

Press reports at all stages of a criminal investigation and trial often create problems for the justice system. Significant pretrial publicity about a case may make it difficult to find jurors who have not already formed an opinion as to the guilt or innocence of the defendant. News reports from the courtroom may influence or confuse nonsequestered jurors who hear them, especially when they contain information brought to the bench but not heard by the jury.

In the 1976 case of *Nebraska Press Association* v. *Stuart*,[122] the U.S. Supreme Court ruled that trial court judges could not legitimately issue gag orders preventing the pretrial publication of information about a criminal case, as long as the defendant's right to a fair trial and an impartial jury could be ensured by traditional means.[123] These means include (1) a **change of venue**, whereby the trial is moved to another jurisdiction less likely to have been exposed to the publicity; (2) trial postponement, which would allow for memories to fade and emotions to cool; and (3) jury selection and screening to eliminate biased people from the jury pool. In 1986, the Court extended press access to preliminary hearings, which it said are "sufficiently like a trial to require public access."[124] In 1993, in the case of *Caribbean International News Corporation* v. *Puerto Rico*,[125] the Court effectively applied that requirement to territories under U.S. control.

Today, members of the press and their video, television, and still cameras are allowed into most state courtrooms. New York is one significant exception, and in 2004, a state court upheld the constitutionality of a 51-year-old law[126] prohibiting the use of cameras in that state's courts.[127] Forty-two states specifically allow cameras at most criminal trials,[128] although the majority require that permission be obtained from the judge before filming begins. Most states also impose restrictions on certain kinds of recording—of jurors or of juveniles, for example, or of conferences between an attorney and the defendant or between an attorney and the judge—although most states allow the filming of such proceedings without audio pickup. Only a few states ban television or video cameras outright. Indiana, Maryland, Mississippi, Nebraska, and Utah all prohibit audiovisual coverage of criminal trials. The District of Columbia prohibits cameras at trials and at appellate hearings.[129]

The U.S. Supreme Court has been far less favorably disposed to television coverage than have most state courts. In 1981, a Florida defendant appealed his burglary conviction to the Supreme Court,[130] arguing that the presence of television cameras at his trial had turned the court into a circus for attorneys and made the proceedings more a sideshow than a trial. The Supreme Court, recognizing that television cameras have an untoward effect on many people, found in favor of the defendant. In the words of the Court, "Trial courts must be especially vigilant to guard against any impairment of the defendant's right to a verdict based solely upon the evidence and the relevant law."

Cameras of all kinds have been prohibited in all federal district criminal proceedings since 1946 by Rule 53 of the Federal Rules of Criminal Procedure.[131] In 1972, the Judicial Conference of the United States adopted a policy opposing broadcast of civil proceedings in district courts, and that policy was incorporated into the Code of Conduct for United States Judges. Nonetheless, some district courts have local rules that allow photographs and filming during selected proceedings.

A three-year pilot project that allowed television cameras into six U.S. district courts and two appeals courts closed on December 31, 1994, when the Judicial Conference voted to end the project. Conference members expressed concerns that cameras were a distracting influence and were having a "negative impact on jurors [and] witnesses"[132] by exposing them to possible harm by revealing their identities. Still, some federal appellate courts have created their own policy on the use of cameras and broadcast equipment in the courtroom. The official policy of the U.S. Court of Appeals for the Ninth Circuit, for example, permits cameras and media broadcasts that meet certain rules. The policy stipulates, "Three business days advance notice is required from the media of a request to be present to broadcast, televise, record electronically, or take photographs at

---

change of venue

The movement of a trial or lawsuit from one jurisdiction to another or from one location to another within the same jurisdiction. A change of venue may be made in a criminal case to ensure that the defendant receives a fair trial.

We have a criminal jury system which is superior to any in the world; and its efficiency is only marred by the difficulty of finding twelve men every day who don't know anything.

—Mark Twain

a particular session. Such requests must be submitted to the Clerk of Court." The policy adds, "The presiding judge of the panel may limit or terminate media coverage, or direct the removal of camera coverage personnel when necessary to protect the rights of the parties or to assure the orderly conduct of the proceedings."[133]

Today's new personal technologies, however, which include cellular telephones with digital camera capabilities, streaming Web-based video, and miniaturized recording devices, all threaten courtroom privacy. For more information on technology trends that might affect the use of cameras in courtrooms, see Library Extra 9–13 at cjtoday.com.

LIBRARY
Extra
■ ■ ■ ■

SUMMARY

- In the United States, there are two judicial systems. One is a state system made up of state and local courts established under the authority of state governments. The other is the federal court system, created by Congress under the authority of the U.S. Constitution. This dual-court system is the result of general agreement among the nation's founders about the need for individual states to retain significant legislative authority and judicial autonomy separate from federal control.

- A typical state court system consists of trial courts of limited jurisdiction, trial courts of general jurisdiction, and appellate courts—usually including a state supreme court. State courts have virtually unlimited power to decide nearly every type of case, subject only to the limitations of the U.S. Constitution, their own state constitutions, and state law; and it is within state courts that the large majority of criminal cases originate.

- The federal court system consists of three levels: U.S. district courts, U.S. courts of appeal, and the U.S. Supreme Court. U.S. district courts are the trial courts of the federal system and are located principally in larger cities. They decide only those cases over which the Constitution gives them authority. The highest federal court,

the U.S. Supreme Court, is located in Washington, D.C., and hears cases only on appeal from lower courts.

- The courtroom work group is comprised of professional courtroom personnel, including the judge, the prosecuting attorney, the defense counsel, the bailiff, the local court administrator, the court reporter, the clerk of court, and expert witnesses. Also present in the courtroom for a trial are "outsiders"—nonprofessional courtroom participants like witnesses and jurors.

- The courtroom work group is guided by statutory requirements and ethical considerations, and its members are generally dedicated to bringing the criminal trial and other courtroom procedures to a successful close. This chapter describes the role that each professional participant plays in the courtroom. The judge, for example, has the primary duty of ensuring a fair trial—in short, seeing that justice prevails.

- Nonprofessional courtroom participants include lay witnesses, jurors, the victim, the defendant, and spectators and members of the press. Nonjudicial or nonprofessional courtroom personnel may be unwilling or inadvertent participants in a criminal trial.

KEY TERMS

appeal, 315

appellate jurisdiction, 314

bailiff, 335

change of venue, 344

community court, 318

court of last resort, 315

courtroom work group, 323

defense counsel, 329

dispute-resolution center, 317

expert witness, 336

federal court system, 311

judge, 324

judicial review, 321

jurisdiction, 311

juror, 340

lay witness, 338

original jurisdiction, 313

prosecutor, 326

prosecutorial discretion, 327

public defender, 330

state court administrator, 316

state court system, 311

subpoena, 338

trial *de novo*, 315

victim-assistance program, 339

KEY CASES

Argersinger v. *Hamlin,* 330

Burns v. *Reed,* 328

Crosby v. *U.S.,* 343

Demarest v. *Manspeaker et al.,* 339

Gideon v. *Wainwright,* 330

Herrera v. *Collins,* 316

Imbler v. *Pachtman,* 328

Keeney v. *Tamayo-Reyes,* 316

Marbury v. *Madison,* 321

Zafiro v. *U.S.,* 343

QUESTIONS FOR REVIEW

1. How did the American court system develop? What is the dual-court system? Why do we have a dual-court system in America?

2. What is a typical state court system like? What are some of the differences between the state and federal court systems?

3. How is the federal court system structured? What are the various types of federal courts?

4. What is meant by the *courtroom work group*? What two major subcategories comprise the courtroom work group?

5. Who are the professional members of the courtroom work group, and what are their roles?

6. Who are the nonprofessional courtroom participants, and what are their roles?

QUESTIONS FOR REFLECTION

1. What are the three forms of indigent defense used in the United States? Why might defendants prefer private attorneys over public counsel?

2. What is an expert witness? What is a lay witness? How might their testimony differ? What are some of the issues involved in deciding whether a person is an expert for purposes of testimony?

3. How do the professional and nonprofessional courtroom participants work together to bring most criminal trials to a successful close? What do you think a "successful close" might mean to the judge? To the defense attorney? To the prosecutor? To the jury? To the defendant? To the victim?

Discuss your answers to these questions and other issues on the CJ Today e-mail discussion list (join the list at cjtoday.com).

WEB QUEST

Take a virtual tour of the U.S. Supreme Court Building via the multimedia Oyez Project, available on the Web at http://www.oyez.org/tour/. Once there, use the tour contents menu to help you navigate the site. Take a closer look at almost any area of the building, and get a 360-degree view of almost every room by clicking on the picture (hold the mouse button down and drag it). For this assignment, make use of all of the navigational features available at the Oyez Project site to move through the Supreme Court Building. As you tour the building, write down what you see, and print out images of each room you visit. Submit these descriptions and images to your instructor if asked to do so. (You must have Apple's QuickTime installed on your computer to view the images described here.)

To complete this Web Quest online, go to the Web Quest module in Chapter 9 of the *Criminal Justice Today* Companion Website at cjtoday.com.

CHAPTER 10

Pretrial Activities and the Criminal Trial

LEARNING OBJECTIVES

After reading this chapter, you should be able to

- List and explain the steps typically taken during pretrial activities.
- Describe the nature and purpose of the criminal trial.
- Identify the various stages of a criminal trial.
- Describe methods that have been suggested for improving the adjudication process.

OUTLINE

- Introduction
- Pretrial Activities
- The Criminal Trial

- Stages of a Criminal Trial
- Improving the Adjudication Process

Lives are lost and won in the courts, lost and won in the law—every day, everywhere. Most of us seldom really think about this. But in the jury room, the thought cannot be avoided, since there you learn that justice doesn't merely happen (neatly, reliably, like a crystal taking shape in a distant vacuum); justice is, rather, done, made, manufactured. Made by imperfect, wrangling, venal and virtuous human beings, using whatever means are at their disposal. In the jury room, you discover that the whole edifice of social order stands, finally, on handicraft—there is no magic, no mathematics, no science, no angelic fixer who checks our juridical homework. This is a frightening thing, not least because any one of us could be accused of a crime.

—D. Graham Burnett, jury foreman[1]

Society asks much of the criminal court. The court is expected to meet society's demand that serious offenders be convicted and punished, and at the same time it is expected to insure that the innocent and unfortunate are not oppressed.

—The President's Commission on Law Enforcement and Administration of Justice

---

Hear the author discuss this chapter at cjtoday.com

Introduction

In March 2007, following a trial that lasted 17 days and brought some jurors to tears, a South Florida jury found 48-year-old John Evander Couey guilty of the 2005 kidnapping, sexual assault, and murder of his young neighbor, 9-year-old Jessica Lunsford. During the trial, police detectives testified that Couey tied the girl up with speaker wire and wrapped her in garbage bags before burying her near her home—still alive and clutching a stuffed dolphin. It took only four hours for jurors to return the guilty verdicts against Couey, a previously convicted sex offender who had admitted before the start of the trial that he had killed Lunsford. His confession was thrown out, however, when the judge ruled that the police had not honored Couey's request to have a lawyer present during the confession. Although a psychologist testified that Couey shows signs of mental illness and retardation, the jury that convicted him convened again in the trial's sentencing phase and recommended that he be put to death—a recommendation followed by Judge Richard Howard. For his part, Couey seemed distracted throughout much of the trial and spent his time drawing with colored pencils. Read an archived courtroom blog written as the trial progressed at Web Extra 10–1 at cjtoday.com.

Although the Couey trial was exceptional for the attention it received, it is typical in many other ways of the hundreds of criminal trials that take place every day throughout the United States.

WEB
Extra
▪ ▪ ▪ ▪

Pretrial Activities

The American criminal justice system is theater to the world.

—Harvard University law professor Alan Dershowitz

In this chapter, we will describe the criminal trial process, highlighting each important stage in the procedure. First, however, we look at the court-related activities that routinely take place *before* trial can begin. These activities (as well as the names given to them) vary among jurisdictions. They are described generally in the pages that follow.

John Evander Couey (left) using headphones to listen to motions made during jury selection at the start of his 2007 trial in Tavares, Florida, for the 2005 kidnapping, rape, and murder of 9-year-old Jessica Lunsford. Couey, who pleaded not guilty, was convicted and sentenced to die. Young Jessica is shown in the photo on the right, while the bottom photo shows candles, cards, and toys that well-wishers left near the Lunsford home as authorities searched for her after she was kidnapped. What steps in the criminal justice process did Couey likely experience prior to conviction?

Scott Iskowitz/AP Wide World Photos, UPI Photo/HO/Landov LLC, and Peter Cosgrove/AP Wide World Photos

The First Appearance

Following arrest, most defendants do not come into contact with an officer of the court until their **first appearance** before a magistrate or a lower-court judge.[2] A first appearance, sometimes called an *initial appearance* or *magistrate's review*, occurs when defendants are brought before a judge (1) to be given formal notice of the charges against them, (2) to be advised of their rights, (3) to be given the opportunity to retain a lawyer or to have one appointed to represent them, and (4) perhaps to be afforded the opportunity for bail.

According to the procedural rules of all jurisdictions, defendants who have been taken into custody must be offered an in-court appearance before a magistrate "without unnecessary delay." The 1943 U.S. Supreme Court case of *McNabb* v. *U.S.*[3] established that any unreasonable delay in an initial court appearance would make confessions inadmissible if interrogating officers obtained them during the delay. Based on the *McNabb* decision, 48 hours following arrest became the standard maximum time by which a first appearance should be held.

The first appearance may also involve a probable cause hearing, although such hearings may be held separately since they do not require the defendant's presence. (In some jurisdictions, a probable cause hearing may be combined with the preliminary hearing, which we will look at later in this chapter.) Probable cause hearings are necessary when arrests are made without a warrant.[4] During a probable cause hearing, also called a *probable cause determination*, a judicial officer will review police documents and reports to ensure that probable cause supported the arrest. The review of the arrest proceeds in a relatively informal fashion, with the judge seeking to decide whether, at the time of apprehension, the arresting officer had reason to believe both (1) that a crime had been or was being committed and (2) that the defendant was the person who committed it. Most of the evidence presented to the judge comes either from the arresting officer or from the victim. If probable cause is not found, the suspect is released. As with a first appearance, a probable cause hearing should take place within 48 hours.

In 1991, in a class-action suit entitled *County of Riverside* v. *McLaughlin*,[5] the U.S. Supreme Court imposed a promptness requirement on probable cause determinations for in-custody arrestees. The Court held that "a jurisdiction that provides judicial determinations of probable

first appearance

An appearance before a magistrate during which the legality of the defendant's arrest is initially assessed and the defendant is informed of the charges on which he or she is being held. At this stage in the criminal justice process, bail may be set or pretrial release arranged.

A bail hearing in progress. Standing before the judge are Julie Barnes and Thomas Levesque, a homeless pair accused of accidentally starting a warehouse blaze that led to the deaths of six Worcester, Massachusetts, firefighters. Levesque's bail was set at $250,000 cash, or $2.5 million with surety; Barnes's bail was set at $75,000 cash, or $750,000 with surety. In 2002, the two agreed to a plea agreement, and each was sentenced to five years of probation for involuntary manslaughter. What purpose does bail serve?

AP Wide World Photos

cause within 48 hours of arrest will, as a general matter, comply with the promptness requirement." The Court specified, however, that weekends and holidays could not be excluded from the 48-hour requirement (as they had been in Riverside County, California) and that, depending on the specifics of the case, delays of fewer than two days may still be unreasonable.

During a first appearance, the suspect is not given an opportunity to present evidence, although the U.S. Supreme Court has held that defendants are entitled to representation by counsel at their first appearance.[6] Following a reading of the charges and an advisement of rights, counsel may be appointed to represent indigent defendants, and proceedings may be adjourned until counsel can be obtained. In cases where a suspect is unruly, intoxicated, or uncooperative, a judicial review may take place without the suspect's presence.

Some states waive a first appearance and proceed directly to arraignment (discussed later), especially when the defendant has been arrested on a warrant. In states that move directly to arraignment, the procedures undertaken to obtain a warrant are regarded as sufficient to demonstrate a basis for detention before arraignment.

PRETRIAL RELEASE

pretrial release

The release of an accused person from custody, for all or part of the time before or during prosecution, on his or her promise to appear in court when required.

A significant aspect of the first appearance hearing is the consideration of **pretrial release**. Defendants charged with very serious crimes, or those who are thought likely to escape or to injure others, are usually held in jail until trial. Such a practice is called *pretrial detention*. The majority of defendants, however, are afforded the opportunity for release. Many jurisdictions make use of pretrial service programs, which may also be called *early-intervention programs*.[7] Such programs, which are typically funded by the states or by individual counties, perform two critical functions: (1) They gather and present information about newly arrested defendants and about available release options for use by judicial officers in deciding what (if any) conditions are to be set for the defendants' release prior to trial, and (2) they supervise defendants released from custody during the pretrial period by monitoring their compliance with release conditions and by helping to ensure that they appear for scheduled court events. Learn more about pretrial services at Library Extra 10–1 at cjtoday.com.

LIBRARY
Extra

The initial pretrial release/detention decision is usually made by a judicial officer or by a specially appointed hearing officer who considers background information provided by the pretrial service program, along with the representations made by the prosecutor and the defense attorney. In making this decision, judicial officers are concerned about two types of risk: (1) the risk of flight or nonappearance for scheduled court appearances and (2) the risk to public safety. In assessing these risks, judicial officers tend to focus on four key factors:

- The seriousness of the current charge, as set forth in the complaint and the representations of the prosecutor

- The defendant's prior criminal record, which is widely viewed as relevant to assessing the risk to public safety that would be posed by a decision to release or to set a relatively low money bond amount

- Information about the defendant, including community and family ties; employment status; housing; existence and nature of any substance abuse problems; and (if the defendant had been arrested before) record of compliance with conditions of release set on previous occasions, including any failures to appear
- Information about available supervisory options if the defendant is released

BAIL

Bail is the most common release/detention decision-making mechanism in American courts. Bail serves two purposes: (1) It helps ensure reappearance of the accused, and (2) it prevents unconvicted individuals from suffering imprisonment unnecessarily.

Bail involves the posting of a bond as a pledge that the accused will return for further hearings. **Bail bonds** usually involve cash deposits but may be based on property or other valuables. A fully secured bond requires the defendant to post the full amount of bail set by the court. The usual practice, however, is for a defendant to seek privately secured bail through the services of a professional bail bondsman. The bondsman will assess a percentage (usually 10% to 15%) of the required bond as a fee, which the defendant will have to pay up front. Those who "skip bail" by hiding or fleeing will sometimes be ordered by the court to forfeit their bail. Forfeiture hearings must be held before a bond can be taken, and most courts will not order bail forfeited unless it appears that the defendant intends to avoid prosecution permanently. Bail forfeiture will often be reversed if the defendant later appears willingly to stand trial.

In many states, bondsmen are empowered to hunt down and bring back defendants who have fled. In some jurisdictions, bondsmen hold virtually unlimited powers and have been permitted by courts to pursue, arrest, and forcibly extradite their charges from foreign jurisdictions without concern for the due process considerations or statutory limitations that apply to law enforcement officers.[8] Recently, however, a number of states have enacted laws that eliminate for-profit bail bond businesses, replacing them instead with state-operated pretrial service agencies. Visit the Professional Bail Agents of the United States via Web Extra 10–2 at cjtoday.com to learn more about the job of bail bondsmen and to view the group's code of ethics.

ALTERNATIVES TO BAIL

The Eighth Amendment to the U.S. Constitution does not guarantee the opportunity for bail but does state that "[e]xcessive bail shall not be required." Some studies, however, have found that many defendants who are offered the opportunity for bail are unable to raise the money. Thirty years ago, a report by the National Advisory Commission on Criminal Justice Standards and Goals found that as many as 93% of felony defendants in some jurisdictions were unable to make bail.[9]

To extend the opportunity for pretrial release to a greater number of nondangerous arrestees, many states and the federal government now offer various alternatives to the cash bond system,

bail bond

A document guaranteeing the appearance of a defendant in court as required and recording the pledge of money or property to be paid to the court if he or she does not appear, which is signed by the person to be released and anyone else acting on his or her behalf.

WEB
Extra

A typical bail bond office. Bail bond offices like this one are usually found near courthouses where criminal trials are held. Should all criminal suspects be afforded bail? Why or why not?
Mark Richards

such as (1) release on recognizance, (2) property bond, (3) deposit bail, (4) conditional release, (5) third-party custody, (6) unsecured bond, and (7) signature bond.

Release on Recognizance (ROR) **Release on recognizance (ROR)** involves no cash bond, requiring as a guarantee only that the defendant agree in writing to return for further hearings as specified by the court. Release on recognizance was tested during the 1960s in a social experiment called the Manhattan Bail Project.[10] In the experiment, those arrested for serious crimes, including murder, rape, and robbery, and those with extensive prior criminal records were excluded from participating in the project. The rest of the defendants were scored and categorized according to a number of "ideal" criteria used as indicators of both dangerousness and the likelihood of pretrial flight. Criteria included (1) no previous convictions, (2) residential stability, and (3) a good employment record. Those likely to flee were not released.

Studies of the bail project revealed that it released four times as many defendants before trial as had been freed under the traditional cash bond system,[11] and that only 1% of those released fled from prosecution—the same percentage as for those set free on cash bond.[12] Later studies, however, were unclear as to the effectiveness of release on recognizance, with some finding a no-show rate as high as 12%.[13]

Property Bonds **Property bonds** substitute other items of value in place of cash. Land, houses, automobiles, stocks, and so on may be consigned to the court as collateral against pretrial flight.

Deposit Bail Deposit bail is an alternative form of cash bond available in some jurisdictions. Deposit bail places the court in the role of the bondsman, allowing the defendant to post a percentage of the full bail with the court. Unlike private bail bondsmen, court-run deposit bail programs usually return the amount of the deposit except for a small administrative fee (perhaps 1%). If the defendant fails to appear for court, the entire amount of court-ordered bail is forfeited.

Conditional Release **Conditional release** imposes requirements on the defendant, such as participating in a drug-treatment program; staying away from specified others, such as potential witnesses; and working at a regular job. *Release under supervision* is similar to conditional release but adds the stipulation that defendants report to an officer of the court or to a police officer at designated times.

release on recognizance (ROR)

The pretrial release of a criminal defendant on his or her written promise to appear in court as required. No cash or property bond is required.

property bond

The setting of bail in the form of land, houses, stocks, or other tangible property. In the event that the defendant absconds prior to trial, the bond becomes the property of the court.

conditional release

The release by executive decision of a prisoner from a federal or state correctional facility who has not served his or her full sentence and whose freedom is contingent on obeying specified rules of behavior.

Bounty hunter Duane "Dog" Chapman, owner of Bounty Hunter International, who calls himself the "greatest bounty hunter in the world." Bounty hunters collect fees from bail bondsmen, who otherwise stand to forfeit money they have posted for clients who do not appear in court. Chapman, an ex-con born-again Christian, makes a living pursuing felons who fail to appear for their court dates after posting bail through a bondsman. He has more than 6,000 captures to his credit. Read more about him at http://www.dogthebounty-hunter.com. Would you want to be a bounty hunter?

Jim Ruymen/REUTERS/Corbis/Bettmann

Third-Party Custody   Third-party custody is a bail bond alternative that assigns custody of the defendant to an individual or agency that promises to ensure his or her later appearance in court.[14] Some pretrial release programs allow attorneys to assume responsibility for their clients in this fashion. If a defendant fails to appear, the attorney's privilege to participate in the program may be ended.

Unsecured Bonds   Unsecured bonds are based on a court-determined dollar amount of bail. Like a credit contract, it requires no monetary deposit with the court. The defendant agrees in writing that failure to appear will result in forfeiture of the entire amount of the bond, which might then be taken in the seizure of land, personal property, bank accounts, and so on.

Signature Bonds   Signature bonds allow release based on the defendant's written promise to appear. Signature bonds involve no particular assessment of the defendant's dangerousness or likelihood of later appearance in court. They are used only in cases of minor offenses like traffic-law violations and some petty drug-law violations. Signature bonds may be issued by the arresting officer acting on behalf of the court.

PRETRIAL RELEASE AND PUBLIC SAFETY

Pretrial release is common practice. Approximately 62% of all state-level felony criminal defendants[15] and 66% of all federal felony defendants[16] are released before trial (Figure 10–1). A growing movement, arguing that defendants released before trial may be dangerous to themselves or to others, seeks to reduce the number of defendants released under any conditions. Advocates of this conservative policy cite a number of studies documenting crimes committed by defendants released on bond. One study found that 16% of defendants released before trial were rearrested; of those, 30% were arrested more than once.[17] Another study determined that as many as 41% of those released before trial for serious crimes, such as rape and robbery, were rearrested before their trial date.[18] Not surprisingly, such studies generally find that the longer the time spent free on bail prior to trial, the greater the likelihood of misconduct.

In response to findings like these, some states have enacted **danger laws**, which limit the right to bail to certain kinds of offenders.[19] Other states, including Arizona, California, Colorado, Florida, and Illinois, have approved constitutional amendments restricting the use of bail.[20] Most such provisions exclude defendants charged with certain crimes from being eligible for bail and demand that other defendants being considered for bail meet stringent conditions. Some states combine these strictures with tough release conditions designed to keep close control over defendants before trial.

The 1984 federal Bail Reform Act allows federal judges to assess the danger of an accused to the community and to deny bail to defendants who are thought to be dangerous. In the words of the act, a suspect held in pretrial custody on federal criminal charges must be detained if "after a hearing . . . he is found to pose a risk of flight and a danger to others or the community and if no condition of release can give reasonable assurances against these contingencies."[21] Defendants

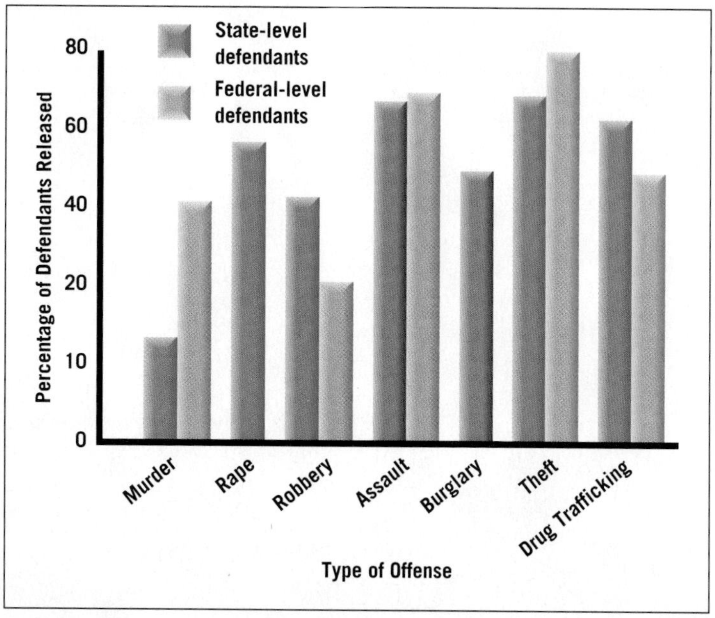

I have tried to minimize what I feel is one of the less desirable aspects of the job . . . that judges can become isolated from the people whose lives their decisions affect.

—U.S. Supreme Court Justice
Stephen Breyer

danger law

A law intended to prevent the pretrial release of criminal defendants judged to represent a danger to others in the community.

FIGURE 10–1

Proportion of state and federal felony defendants released before trial.

Note: Federal pretrial release statistics are not available for the crimes of rape and burglary.

Source: Thomas A. Cohen and Brian A. Reaves, *Felony Defendants in Large Urban Counties, 2002* (Washington, DC: Bureau of Justice Statistics, 2006); and John Scalia, *Federal Pretrial Release and Detention, 1996* (Washington, DC: Bureau of Justice Statistics, 1999).

seeking bail must demonstrate a high likelihood of later court appearance. The act also requires that a defendant have a speedy first appearance and, if he or she is to be detained, that a *detention hearing* be held together with the initial appearance.

In the 1990 case of *U.S.* v. *Montalvo-Murillo*,[22] however, a defendant who was not provided with a detention hearing at the time of his first appearance and was subsequently released by an appeals court was found to have no "right" to freedom because of this "minor" statutory violation. The Supreme Court held that "unless it has a substantial influence on the outcome of the proceedings . . . failure to comply with the Act's prompt hearing provision does not require release of a person who should otherwise be detained" because "[a]utomatic release contravenes the statutory purpose of providing fair bail procedures while protecting the public's safety and assuring a defendant's appearance at trial."[23]

Court challenges to the constitutionality of pretrial detention legislation have not met with much success. The U.S. Supreme Court case of *U.S.* v. *Hazzard* (1984),[24] decided only a few months after enactment of federal bail reform, held that Congress was justified in providing for denial of bail to offenders who represent a danger to the community. Later cases have supported the presumption of flight, which federal law presupposes for certain types of defendants.[25]

The Grand Jury

The federal government and about half of the states use grand juries as part of the pretrial process. Grand juries comprise private citizens (often 23 in number) who hear evidence presented by the prosecution. Grand juries serve primarily as filters to eliminate cases for which there is not sufficient evidence for further processing.

In early times, grand juries served a far different purpose. The grand jury system began in England in 1166 as a way of identifying law violators. Lacking a law enforcement agency with investigative authority, the government looked to the grand jury as a source of information on criminal activity in the community. Even today, grand juries in most jurisdictions may initiate prosecution independently of the prosecutor, although they rarely do.

Grand jury hearings are held in secret, and the defendant is generally not afforded the opportunity to appear.[26] Similarly, the defense has no opportunity to cross-examine prosecution witnesses. Grand juries have the power to subpoena witnesses and to mandate a review of books, records, and other documents crucial to their investigation.

After hearing the evidence, the grand jury votes on the indictment presented to it by the prosecution. The indictment is a formal listing of proposed charges. If the majority of grand jury members agree to forward the indictment to the trial court, it becomes a "true bill" on which further prosecution will turn.

A grand jury in action. Grand jury proceedings are generally very informal, as this picture shows. What is the grand jury's job?

David Young-Wolff/Getty Images, Inc.–Stone Allstock

CJ Today Exhibit 10–1

Nonjudicial Pretrial Release Decisions

In most American jurisdictions, judicial officers decide whether an arrested person will be detained or released. Some jurisdictions, however, allow others to make that decision. Some observers argue that the critical issue is not whether the decision maker is a judge, but whether there are clear and appropriate criteria for making the decision, whether the decision maker has adequate information, and whether he or she has been well trained in pretrial release/detention decision making.

Nonjudicial decision makers and release/detention mechanisms include the following:

- *Police officers and desk appearance tickets.* Desk appearance tickets, or citations, are summonses given to defendants at the police station, usually for petty offenses or misdemeanor charges. The tickets can greatly reduce the use of pretrial detention and can save the court system a great deal of time by avoiding initial pretrial release or bail hearings in minor cases. However, because they are typically based only on the current charge (and sometimes on a computer search to check for outstanding warrants), high-risk defendants could be released without supervision or monitoring. As computerized access to criminal history information becomes more readily available, enabling rapid identification of individuals with prior records who pose a risk to the community, desk appearance tickets may be more widely used.

- *Jail administrators.* In many jurisdictions, jail officials have the authority to release (or to refuse to book into jail) arrestees who meet certain criteria. In some localities, jail officials exercise this authority pursuant to a court order that specifies priorities with respect to the categories of defendants who can be admitted to the jail and those who are to be released when the jail population exceeds a court-imposed ceiling. The "automatic release" approach helps minimize jail crowding, but it does so at the risk of releasing some defendants who pose a high risk of becoming fugitives or committing criminal acts. To help minimize these risks, some sheriffs and jail administrators have developed their own pretrial services or "release on recognizance" units with staff who conduct risk assessments based on interviews with arrestees, information from references, and criminal history checks.

- *Bail schedules.* These predetermined schedules set levels of bail (from release on recognizance to amounts of surety bond) based solely on the offense charged. Depending on local practices, release pursuant to a bail schedule may take place at a police station, at the local jail, or at court. This practice saves time for judicial officers and allows rapid release of defendants who can afford to post the bail amount. However, release determinations based solely on the current charge are of dubious value because there is no proven relationship between a particular charge and risk of flight or subsequent crime. Release pursuant to a bail schedule depends simply on the defendant's ability to post the amount of the bond. Moreover, when a defendant is released by posting bond, there is generally no procedure for supervision to minimize the risks of nonappearance and subsequent crime.

- *Bail bondsmen.* When a judicial officer sets the amount of bond that a defendant must produce to be released, or when bond is set mechanically on the basis of a bail schedule, the real decision makers are often the surety bail bondsmen. If no bondsman will offer bond, the defendant without other sources of money will remain in jail. The defendant's ability to pay a bondsman the 10% fee (and sometimes to post collateral) bears no relationship to his or her risk of flight or danger to the community.

- *Pretrial service agencies.* In some jurisdictions, pretrial service agencies have the authority to release certain categories of defendants. The authority is usually limited to relatively minor cases, although agencies in a few jurisdictions can release some categories of felony defendants. Because the pretrial service agency can obtain information about the defendant's prior record, community ties, and other pending charges, its decision to release or detain is based on more extensive information and criteria than when the decision is based on a bail schedule. However, because these programs lack the independence that judicial officers are allowed, they are susceptible to political and public pressure.

Reference: Adapted from Barry Mahoney et al., *Pretrial Services Programs: Responsibilities and Potential* (Washington, DC: National Institute of Justice, 2001).

The Preliminary Hearing

States that do not use grand juries rely instead on a preliminary hearing "for charging defendants in a fashion that is less cumbersome and arguably more protective of the innocent."[27] In these jurisdictions, the prosecutor files an accusatory document called an *information*, or complaint, against the accused. A preliminary hearing is then held to determine whether there is probable cause to hold the defendant for trial. A few states, notably Tennessee and Georgia, use both the grand jury mechanism and a preliminary hearing as a "double check against the possibility of unwarranted prosecution."[28]

Although the preliminary hearing is not nearly as elaborate as a criminal trial, it has many of the same characteristics. The defendant is taken before a lower-court judge who summarizes the charges and reviews the rights to which all criminal defendants are entitled. The prosecution may present witnesses and will offer evidence in support of the complaint. The defendant is afforded the right to testify and may also call witnesses.

The primary purpose of the preliminary hearing is to give the defendant an opportunity to challenge the legal basis for his or her detention. At this point, defendants who appear to be or claim to be mentally incompetent may be ordered to undergo further evaluation to determine whether they are **competent to stand trial**. Competence to stand trial, which was briefly discussed in Chapter 4, may become an issue when a defendant appears to be incapable of understanding the proceedings or is unable to assist in his or her own defense due to mental disease or defect.

In 2003, the U.S. Supreme Court placed strict limits on the government's power to forcibly medicate some mentally ill defendants to make them competent to stand trial.[29] In the case of *Sell* v. *U.S.*,[30] the Court ruled that the use of antipsychotic drugs on a nonviolent pretrial defendant who does not represent a danger while institutionalized must be in the defendant's best medical interest and must be "substantially unlikely" to cause side effects that might compromise the fairness of the trial.

Barring a finding of mental incompetence, all that is required for the wheels of justice to move forward is a demonstration "sufficient to justify a prudent man's belief that the suspect has committed or was committing an offense" within the jurisdiction of the court.[31] If the magistrate finds enough evidence to justify a trial, the defendant is bound over to the grand jury. In states that do not require grand jury review, the defendant is sent directly to the trial court. If the complaint against the defendant cannot be substantiated, he or she is released. A release is not a bar to further prosecution, however, and the defendant may be rearrested if further evidence comes to light.

competent to stand trial

A finding by a court that the defendant has sufficient present ability to consult with his or her attorney with a reasonable degree of rational understanding and that the defendant has a rational as well as factual understanding of the proceedings against him or her.

Arraignment and the Plea

Once an indictment has been returned or an information has been filed, the accused will be formally arraigned. Arraignment is "the first appearance of the defendant before the court that has the authority to conduct a trial."[32] Arraignment is generally a brief process with two purposes: (1) to once again inform the defendant of the specific charges against him or her and (2) to allow the defendant to enter a **plea**. The Federal Rules of Criminal Procedure allow for one of three types of pleas to be entered: guilty, not guilty, and *nolo contendere*. A **nolo contendere** (no-contest) plea is much the same as a guilty plea. A defendant who pleads "no contest" is immediately convicted and may be sentenced just as though he or she had pleaded guilty. A no-contest plea, however, is not an admission of guilt and provides one major advantage to defendants: It may not be used later as a basis for civil proceedings that seek monetary or other damages against the defendant.

Some defendants refuse to enter any plea and are said to "stand mute." Standing mute is a defense strategy that is rarely employed. Defendants who choose this alternative simply do not answer the request for a plea. However, for procedural purposes, a defendant who stands mute is considered to have entered a plea of not guilty.

plea

In criminal proceedings, the defendant's formal answer in court to the charge contained in a complaint, information, or indictment that he or she is guilty of the offense charged, is not guilty of the offense charged, or does not contest the charge.

nolo contendere

A plea of "no contest." A no-contest plea is used when the defendant does not wish to contest conviction. Because the plea does not admit guilt, however, it cannot provide the basis for later civil suits that might follow a criminal conviction.

Plea Bargaining

Guilty pleas are often not straightforward and are typically arrived at only after complex negotiations known as *plea bargaining*. **Plea bargaining** is a process of negotiation that usually involves the defendant, the prosecutor, and the defense counsel. It is founded on the mutual interests of all involved. Defense attorneys and their clients will agree to a plea of guilty when they are unsure of their ability to win acquittal at trial. Prosecutors may be willing to bargain because the evidence they have against the defendant is weaker than they would like it to be. Plea bargaining offers prosecutors the additional advantage of a quick conviction without the need to commit the time and resources necessary for trial. Benefits to the accused include the possibility of reduced or combined charges, lower defense costs, and a shorter sentence than might otherwise be anticipated.

The U.S. Supreme Court has held that a guilty plea constitutes conviction.[33] To validate the conviction, negotiated pleas require judicial consent. Judges often accept pleas that are the result of a bargaining process because such pleas reduce the court's workload. Although few judges are willing to guarantee a sentence before a plea is entered, most prosecutors and criminal trial lawyers know what sentences to expect from typical pleas.

Bargained pleas are commonplace. Surveys have found that 90% of all criminal cases prepared for trial are eventually resolved through a negotiated plea.[34] In a study of 37 big-city prosecutors, the Bureau of Justice Statistics found that for every 100 adults arrested on a felony charge, half were eventually convicted of either a felony or a misdemeanor.[35] Of all convictions, fully 94% were the result of a plea. Only 6% of convictions were the result of a criminal trial.

plea bargaining

The process of negotiating an agreement among the defendant, the prosecutor, and the court as to an appropriate plea and associated sentence in a given case. Plea bargaining circumvents the trial process and dramatically reduces the time required for the resolution of a criminal case.

After a guilty plea has been entered, it may be withdrawn with the consent of the court. In the case of *Henderson* v. *Morgan* (1976),[36] for example, the U.S. Supreme Court permitted a defendant to withdraw a plea of guilty nine years after it had been given. In that case, the defendant had originally entered a plea of guilty to second-degree murder but had attempted to withdraw it before trial. Reasons for wanting to withdraw the plea included the defendant's belief that he had not been completely advised as to the nature of the charge or the sentence he might receive as a result of the plea.

Some Supreme Court decisions, however, have enhanced the prosecutor's authority in the bargaining process by declaring that defendants cannot capriciously withdraw negotiated pleas.[37] Other rulings have supported discretionary actions by prosecutors in which sentencing recommendations were retracted even after bargains had been struck.[38] Some lower-court cases have upheld the government's authority to withdraw from a negotiated plea when the defendant fails to live up to certain conditions.[39] These conditions may include requiring the defendant to provide information on other criminals, criminal cartels, and smuggling activities.

While it is generally agreed that bargained pleas should relate in some way to the original charge, they do not always relate. Entered pleas may be chosen for the punishments likely to be associated with them rather than for their accuracy in describing the criminal offense in which the defendant was involved.[40] This is especially true when the defendant wants to minimize the socially stigmatizing impact of the offense. A charge of indecent liberties, for example, in which the defendant is accused of sexual misconduct, may be pleaded out as assault. Such a plea, which takes advantage of the fact that indecent liberties can be considered a form of sexual assault, would effectively disguise the true nature of the offense.

Even though the Supreme Court has endorsed plea bargaining, the public sometimes views it suspiciously. Law-and-order advocates, who generally favor harsh punishments and long jail terms, claim that plea bargaining results in unjustifiably light sentences. As a consequence, prosecutors who regularly engage in the practice rarely advertise it. Plea bargaining can be a powerful prosecutorial tool, but this power carries with it the potential for misuse. Because they circumvent the trial process, plea bargains can be abused by prosecutors and defense attorneys who are more interested in the speedy resolution of cases than they are in seeing justice done. Carried to the extreme, plea

Convicted bomber Eric Rudolph, shown here in a police mug shot. Rudolph pleaded guilty in 2005 to the deadly 1996 Atlanta Olympic Park bombing, a fatal 1998 abortion clinic blast in Birmingham, and two other Atlanta-area bombings. Rudolph's deal with prosecutors spared him a possible death sentence, although he received four consecutive life prison terms. A follower of a white supremacist religion that is antiabortion, antigay, and anti-Semitic, Rudolph was on the FBI's Ten Most Wanted List for more than five years as he hid in the mountains of North Carolina. He was finally apprehended by a lone officer as he scavenged for food in a garbage bin. What might the defendant gain from a plea bargain? Why would prosecutors engage in plea bargaining?
AP Wide World Photos

bargaining may result in defendants being convicted of crimes they did not commit. Although it is rare, innocent defendants (especially those with prior criminal records) who think a jury will convict them—for whatever reason—may plead guilty to reduced charges to avoid a trial. In an effort to protect defendants against hastily arranged pleas, the Federal Rules of Criminal Procedure require judges to (1) inform the defendant of the various rights he or she is surrendering by pleading guilty, (2) determine that the plea is voluntary, (3) require disclosure of any plea agreements, and (4) make sufficient inquiry to ensure there is a factual basis for the plea.[41]

Bargained pleas can take many forms and can be quite inventive. The case of Jeffrey Morse illustrates an unusual attempt at a bargained plea. In 1998, Morse, a convicted sex offender, petitioned courts in Illinois for permission to leave jail prior to sentencing for sexual assaults on two young girls so that he could undergo surgical castration. A judge agreed, and he was surgically castrated in a 45-minute outpatient procedure. Morse's mother noted that the surgery was done in an effort to avoid a long prison sentence. "He will cut whatever bodily part he has to be able to reduce his sentence," she said.[42] Two months later, however, Kane County Judge Donald C. Hudson refused to show leniency for Morse. Instead, Hudson sentenced Morse to 26 years in prison, saying that he wouldn't "place a seal of approval on trading body parts for a lesser sentence."[43]

The Criminal Trial

From arrest through sentencing, the criminal justice process is carefully choreographed. Arresting officers must follow proper procedure when gathering evidence and arresting and questioning suspects. Magistrates, prosecutors, jailers, and prison officials are all subject to their own strictures. Nowhere, however, is the criminal justice process more closely circumscribed than it is at the criminal trial.

rules of evidence

Court rules that govern the admissibility of evidence at criminal hearings and trials.

Procedures in a modern courtroom are highly formalized. **Rules of evidence**, which govern the admissibility of evidence, and other procedural guidelines determine the course of a criminal hearing and trial. While rules of evidence are partially based on tradition, all U.S. jurisdictions have formalized, written rules of evidence. Criminal trials at the federal level generally adhere to the requirements of the Federal Rules of Evidence.

Trials are also circumscribed by informal rules and professional expectations. An important component of law school education is the teaching of rules that structure and define appropriate courtroom demeanor. In addition to statutory rules, law students are thoroughly exposed to the ethical standards of their profession, as found in the American Bar Association standards and other writings.

Nature and Purpose of the Criminal Trial

In the remainder of this chapter, we will describe the chronology of a criminal trial and will explore some of the widely accepted rules of criminal procedure. Before we begin, however, it is good to keep two points in mind. One is that the primary purpose of any criminal trial is the determination of the defendant's guilt or innocence. In this regard, it is important to recognize the crucial distinction that scholars make between factual guilt and legal guilt. Factual guilt deals with the issue of whether the defendant is actually responsible for the crime of which he or she stands accused. If the defendant did it, then he or she is, in fact, guilty. Legal guilt is not as clear. Legal guilt is established only when the prosecutor presents sufficient evidence to convince the judge (where the judge determines the verdict) or the jury that the defendant is guilty as charged. The distinction between factual guilt and legal guilt is crucial because it points to the fact that the burden of proof rests with the prosecution, and it indicates the possibility that guilty defendants may, nonetheless, be found "not guilty."

adversarial system

The two-sided structure under which American criminal trial courts operate. The adversarial system pits the prosecution against the defense. In theory, justice is done when the most effective adversary is able to convince the judge or jury that his or her perspective on the case is the correct one.

The second point to remember is that criminal trials under our system of justice are built around an **adversarial system** and that central to this system is the advocacy model. Participating in the adversarial system are advocates for the state (the prosecutor or the district attorney) and for the defendant (the defense counsel, the public defender, and so on). The philosophy behind the adversarial system is that the greatest number of just resolutions in criminal trials will occur when both sides are allowed to argue their cases effectively and vociferously before a fair and impartial jury. The system requires that advocates for both sides do their utmost, within the boundaries set by law and professional ethics, to protect and advance the interests of their clients (that is, the defendant and the state). The advocacy model makes clear that it is not the job of the defense attorney or the prosecution to decide the guilt of any defendant. Hence, even defense attorneys who are convinced that their clients are guilty are still exhorted to offer the best possible defense and to counsel their clients as effectively as possible.

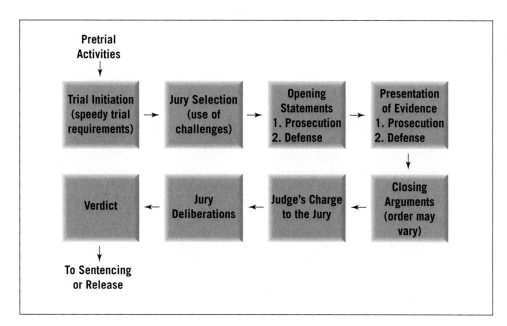

FIGURE 10–2

Stages in a criminal trial.

The adversarial system has been criticized by some thinkers who point to fundamental differences between law and science in the way the search for truth is conducted.[44] While proponents of traditional legal procedure accept the belief that truth can best be uncovered through an adversarial process, scientists adhere to a painstaking process of research and replication to acquire knowledge. Most of us would agree that scientific advances in recent years may have made factual issues less difficult to ascertain. For example, some of the new scientific techniques in evidence analysis, such as DNA fingerprinting, can now unequivocally link a suspect to criminal activity or even show that someone who was once thought guilty is actually innocent. At least 328 convictions have been overturned using DNA evidence since 1989, when Gary Dotson of Illinois became the first person exonerated through such evidence. (Read about Dotson's case in "The Rape That Wasn't" at Library Extra 10–2 at cjtoday.com.) According to Samuel Gross and colleagues at the University of Michigan Law School, who published a comprehensive study of exonerations in 2004, those 328 people "had spent more than 3400 years in prison for crimes for which they never should have been convicted."[45] Exonerations occur more frequently in cases where DNA evidence is relatively easy to acquire, such as rape and murder cases. False conviction rates for other crimes, such as robbery, are much more difficult to assess using DNA. Hence, according to Gross, "The clearest and most important lesson from the recent spike in rape exonerations is that false convictions that come to light are the tip of the iceberg."[46]

Whether scientific findings should continue to serve a subservient role to the adversarial process is a question widely discussed. The answer will be determined by the results the two processes are able to produce. If the adversarial model results in the acquittal of too many demonstrably guilty people because of legal "technicalities," or if the scientific approach identifies too many suspects inaccurately, either could be restricted.

There is no such thing as justice—in or out of court.

—Clarence Darrow (1857–1938)[j]

LIBRARY
Extra

Stages of a Criminal Trial

We turn now to a discussion of the steps in a criminal trial. As Figure 10–2 shows, trial chronology consists of eight stages:

1. Trial initiation
2. Jury selection
3. Opening statements
4. Presentation of evidence
5. Closing arguments
6. Judge's charge to the jury
7. Jury deliberations
8. Verdict

Jury deliberations and the verdict are discussed jointly. If the defendant is found guilty, a sentence is imposed by the judge at the conclusion of the trial. Sentencing is discussed in the next chapter.

Trial Initiation: The Speedy Trial Act

In 2005, a Louisiana state appeals court threw out murder charges against James Thomas and ordered him released. Thomas, an impoverished day laborer, had been arrested in 1996 and had spent eight and a half years in jail waiting for a trial that never came. The ruling by the appeals court was widely seen as an indictment of Louisiana's understaffed and underfunded public defender system; the public defenders had simply been too busy to work on Thomas's case. A private attorney managed to get Thomas set free after his mother scraped together $500 to pay his fee.

The U.S. Constitution contains a speedy trial provision in its Sixth Amendment, which guarantees that "[i]n all criminal prosecutions, the accused shall enjoy the right to a speedy and public trial." Clogged court calendars, limited judicial resources, and general inefficiency, however, often combine to produce what appears to many to be unreasonable delays in trial initiation. The attention of the U.S. Supreme Court was brought to bear on trial delays in three precedent-setting cases: *Klopfer* v. *North Carolina* (1967),[47] *Barker* v. *Wingo* (1972),[48] and *Strunk* v. *U.S.* (1973).[49] The *Klopfer* case involved a Duke University professor who had engaged in civil disobedience to protest segregated facilities. In ruling on Klopfer's long-delayed trial, the Court asserted that the right to a speedy trial is a fundamental guarantee of the Constitution. In the *Barker* case, the Court held that Sixth Amendment guarantees to a quick trial could be illegally violated even in cases where the accused did not explicitly object to delays. In *Strunk*, it found that the denial of a speedy trial should result in the dismissal of all charges.

In 1974, against the advice of the Justice Department, the U.S. Congress passed the federal **Speedy Trial Act**.[50] The act, which was phased in gradually and became fully effective in 1980, allows for the dismissal of federal criminal charges in cases in which the prosecution does not seek an indictment or information within 30 days of arrest (a 30-day extension is granted when the grand jury is not in session) or where a trial does not begin within 70 working days after indictment for defendants who plead "not guilty." If a defendant is not available for trial, or if witnesses cannot be called within the 70-day limit, the period may be extended up to 180 days. Delays brought about by the defendant, through requests for a continuance or because of escape, are not counted in the specified time periods.

In an important 1988 decision, *U.S.* v. *Taylor*,[51] the U.S. Supreme Court applied the requirements of the Speedy Trial Act to the case of a drug defendant who had escaped following arrest. The Court made it clear that trial delays that derive from the willful actions of the defendant do not apply to the 70-day period. The Court also held that trial delays, even when they result from government action, do not necessarily provide grounds for dismissal if they occur "without prejudice." Delays without prejudice are those that are due to circumstances beyond the control of criminal justice agencies.

In 1993, an Indiana prisoner, William Fex, appealed a Michigan conviction on armed robbery and attempted murder charges, claiming that he had to wait 196 days after submitting a request to Indiana prison authorities for his Michigan trial to commence. In *Fex* v. *Michigan* (1993),[52] the U.S. Supreme Court ruled that "common sense compel[s] the conclusion that the 180-day period does not commence until the prisoner's disposition request has actually been delivered to the court and prosecutor of the jurisdiction that lodged the detainer against him." In Fex's case, Indiana authorities had taken 22 days to forward his request to Michigan.

However, in a 1992 case, *Doggett* v. *U.S.*,[53] the Court held that a delay of eight and a half years violated speedy trial provisions because it resulted from government negligence. In *Doggett*, the defendant was indicted on a drug charge in 1980 but left the country for Panama, where he lived until 1982, when he reentered the United States. He lived openly in the United States until 1988, when a credit check revealed him to authorities. He was arrested, tried, and convicted of federal drug charges stemming from his 1980 indictment. In overturning his conviction, the U.S. Supreme Court ruled, "[E]ven delay occasioned by the Government's negligence creates prejudice that compounds over time, and at some point, as here, becomes intolerable."[54]

In 2006, the Court refused to hear an appeal by dirty bomb conspiracy suspect Jose Padilla, letting stand a lower court's decision that said the president could order a U.S. citizen who was arrested in this country for suspected ties to terrorism to be held indefinitely without charges and without going to trial.[55] Padilla, who was arrested in 2002, had been held for four years in a Navy brig without being charged with a crime. Shortly before Padilla's case was to come before the

James Thomas, who was charged with murder in 1996 and was freed in April 2005 after spending eight and a half years in a Louisiana jail waiting for his case to go to trial. A Louisiana state appeals court ruled that the state had taken too long to try him. Why does our system of justice require speedy trials?

Bill Feig/AP Wide World Photos

Court, however, he was transferred from military custody to a civilian jail, indicted on terrorism charges, and scheduled to go to trial—rendering his appeal moot. Although there was no official ruling in the case, Justice Anthony Kennedy, writing for himself, Justice John Paul Stevens, and Chief Justice John Roberts, observed that the federal district court scheduled to hear the case would now "be obliged to afford him the protection, including the right to a speedy trial, guaranteed to all federal criminal defendants."[56]

The federal Speedy Trial Act is applicable only to federal courts. However, the *Klopfer* case effectively made constitutional guarantees of a speedy trial applicable to state courts. In keeping with the trend toward reduced delays, many states have since enacted their own speedy trial legislation. Most state legislation sets a limit of 90 or 120 days as a reasonable period of time for a trial to commence.

Jury Selection

The Sixth Amendment guarantees the right to an impartial jury. An impartial jury is not necessarily an ignorant one. In other words, potential jurors will not always be excused from service on a jury if they have some knowledge of the case before them.[57] However, candidates who have already formed an opinion as to the guilt or innocence of the defendant are likely to be excused.

Some prospective jurors *try* to get excused, whereas others who would like to serve are excused because they are not judged to be suitable. Prosecution and defense attorneys use challenges to ensure the impartiality of the jury being impaneled. Three types of challenges are recognized in criminal courts: (1) challenges to the array, (2) challenges for cause, and (3) **peremptory challenges**.

Challenges to the array signify the belief, generally by the defense attorney, that the pool from which potential jurors are to be selected is not representative of the community or is biased in some significant way. A challenge to the array is argued before the hearing judge before **jury selection** begins.

During jury selection, both prosecution and defense attorneys question potential jurors in a process known as *voir dire* examination. Jurors are expected to be unbiased and free of preconceived notions of guilt or innocence. Challenges for cause, which may arise during *voir dire* examination, make the claim that an individual juror cannot be fair or impartial. A special issue of juror objectivity that has concerned the U.S. Supreme Court is whether jurors with philosophical opposition to the death penalty should be excluded from juries whose decisions might result in the imposition of capital punishment. In the case of *Witherspoon* v. *Illinois* (1968),[58] the Court ruled that a juror opposed to the death penalty could be excluded from such juries if it were shown that (1) the juror would automatically vote against conviction without regard to the evidence or (2) the juror's philosophical orientation would prevent an objective consideration of the evidence. The *Witherspoon* case left a number of issues unresolved, among them the concern that

peremptory challenge

The right to challenge a potential juror without disclosing the reason for the challenge. Prosecutors and defense attorneys routinely use peremptory challenges to eliminate from juries individuals who, although they express no obvious bias, are thought to be capable of swaying the jury in an undesirable direction.

jury selection

The process whereby, according to law and precedent, members of a trial jury are chosen.

it is difficult to demonstrate how a juror would automatically vote, a fact that might not even be known to the juror before trial begins.

Another area of concern that the Supreme Court has addressed involves the potential that jurors could be influenced by pretrial news stories. In 1991, for example, the Court decided the case of *Mu'Min* v. *Virginia* (1991).[59] Dawud Majud Mu'Min was a Virginia inmate who was serving time for first-degree murder. While accompanying a work detail outside the prison, he committed another murder. At the ensuing trial, 8 of the 12 jurors who were seated admitted that they had heard or read something about the case, although none indicated that he or she had formed an opinion in advance as to Mu'Min's guilt or innocence. Following his conviction, Mu'Min appealed to the Supreme Court, claiming that his right to a fair trial had been denied due to pretrial publicity. The Court disagreed and upheld his conviction, citing the jurors' claim not to be biased.

The third kind of challenge, the peremptory challenge, allows attorneys to remove potential jurors without having to give a reason. Peremptory challenges, used by both the prosecution and the defense, are limited in number. Federal courts allow each side up to 20 peremptory challenges in capital cases and as few as 3 in minor criminal cases.[60] States vary as to the number of peremptory challenges they permit.

A developing field that seeks to take advantage of peremptory challenges is **scientific jury selection**. Scientific jury selection uses correlational techniques from the social sciences to gauge the likelihood that a potential juror will vote for conviction or acquittal. It makes predictions based on the economic, ethnic, and other personal and social characteristics of each member of the juror pool. Such techniques generally remove potential jurors who have any knowledge or opinions about the case to be tried. Also removed are people who have been trained in the law or in criminal justice. Anyone working for a criminal justice agency or anyone who has a family member working for such an agency or for a defense attorney will likely be dismissed through peremptory challenges on the chance that they may be biased in favor of one side or the other. Additionally, scientific jury selection techniques may result in the dismissal of highly educated or professionally successful individuals to eliminate the possibility of such individuals exercising undue control over jury deliberations.

Critics of the jury-selection process charge that the end result is a jury composed of people who are uneducated, uninformed, and generally inexperienced at making any type of well-considered decision. Some jurors may not understand the charges against the defendant or may not comprehend what is required for a finding of guilt or innocence. Likewise, some may not even possess the attention span needed to hear all the testimony that will be offered in a case. As a consequence, critics say, decisions rendered by such a jury may be based more on emotion than on findings of fact.

Another emerging technique is the use of "shadow juries" to assess the impact of a defense attorney's arguments. Shadow jurors are hired court observers who sit in the courtroom and listen to what both sides in a criminal trial have to say. They hear evidence as it is presented and listen as witnesses are examined and cross-examined. Unlike professional legal experts, shadow jurors are laypeople who are expected to give defense attorneys a feel for what the "real" jurors are thinking and feeling as a case progresses, allowing for ongoing modifications in defense strategy.[61]

After wrangling over jury selection has run its course, the jury is sworn in, and alternate jurors are selected. Alternates may be called to replace jurors taken ill or dismissed from the jury because they don't conform to the requirements of jury service once trial has begun. At this point, the judge will decide whether the jury is to be sequestered during the trial. Members of **sequestered juries**, like those in the O. J. Simpson criminal trial, are not permitted to have contact with the public and are often housed in a motel or hotel until the trial ends. Anyone who attempts to contact a sequestered jury or to influence members of a nonsequestered jury may be held accountable for jury tampering. Following jury selection, the stage is set for opening arguments[62] to begin.

JURY SELECTION AND RACE

Race alone cannot provide the basis for jury selection, and juries many not be intentionally selected for racial balance. As long ago as 1880, the U.S. Supreme Court held that "a statute barring blacks from service on grand or petit juries denied equal protection of the laws to a black man convicted of murder by an all-white jury."[63] Even so, peremptory challenges continued to be used to strike racial imbalance on juries. In 1965, for example, a black defendant in Alabama was convicted of rape by an all-white jury. The local prosecutor had used his peremptory challenges to exclude blacks from the jury. The case eventually reached the Supreme Court, where the conviction was upheld.[64] At that time, the Court refused to limit the practice of peremptory challenges, reasoning that to do so would place these challenges under the same judicial scrutiny as challenges for cause.

---

scientific jury selection

The use of correlational techniques from the social sciences to gauge the likelihood that potential jurors will vote for conviction or for acquittal.

sequestered jury

A jury that is isolated from the public during the course of a trial and throughout the deliberation process.

CJ Today Exhibit 10–2

Peremptory Challenges and Race

A "peremptory challenge to a juror means that one side in a trial has been given the right to throw out a certain number of possible jurors before the trial without giving any reasons."[1] As this definition—borrowed from a legal dictionary—indicates, attorneys were once able to remove unwanted potential jurors from a criminal case through the use of a limited number of peremptory challenges without having to provide any reason whatsoever for the choices they made. (Challenges for cause, on the other hand, although not limited in number, require an acceptable rationale for juror removal.) The understanding of peremptory challenges was changed by the 1991 landmark U.S. Supreme Court case of *Powers* v. *Ohio*.[2] The *Powers* case dealt with a white defendant's desire to ensure a racially balanced jury. In *Powers*, the Supreme Court identified three reasons why peremptory challenges may not be issued if based on race:[3]

> First, the discriminatory use of peremptory challenges causes the defendant cognizable injury, and he or she has a concrete interest in challenging the practice, because racial discrimination in jury selection casts doubt on the integrity of the judicial process and places the fairness of the criminal proceeding in doubt.
>
> Second, the relationship between the defendant and the excluded jurors is such that . . . both have a common interest in eliminating racial discrimination from the courtroom. . . .
>
> Third, it is unlikely that a juror dismissed because of race will possess sufficient incentive to set in motion the arduous process needed to vindicate his or her own rights.

The Court continued:

> The very fact that [members of a particular race] are singled out and expressly denied . . . all right to participate in the administration of the law, as jurors, because of their color, though they are citizens, and may be in other respects fully qualified, is practically a brand upon them, affixed by the law, an assertion of their infe-

riority, and a stimulant to that race prejudice which is an impediment to securing to individuals of that race equal justice which the law aims to secure to all others.

Near the end of its 1991 term, in a move that surprised many observers, the Supreme Court extended to civil cases its ban on racially motivated peremptory challenges. In *Edmonson* v. *Leesville Concrete Co., Inc.*,[4] the Court ruled,

> The harms we recognized in *Powers* are not limited to the criminal sphere. A civil proceeding often implicates significant rights and interests. Civil juries, no less than their criminal counterparts, must follow the law and act as impartial fact-finders. And, as we have observed, their verdicts, no less than those of their criminal counterparts, become binding judgments of the court. Racial discrimination has no place in the courtroom, whether the proceeding is civil or criminal.

Following *Powers* and *Edmonson*, it is clear that neither prosecuting nor civil attorneys will be able to exclude minority jurors consistently unless they are able to articulate clearly credible race-neutral rationales for their actions.

Even so, some dissenting opinions indicate that considerable sentiment may exist among the justices that could lead to the return of a broader use of peremptory challenges. In a dissenting opinion in *J.E.B.* v. *Alabama* (1994),[5] for example, Justices Antonin Scalia, William H. Rehnquist, and Clarence Thomas wrote, "[T]he core of the Court's reasoning [banning peremptory challenges based on gender] is that peremptory challenges on the basis of any group characteristic subject to heightened scrutiny are inconsistent with the guarantee of the Equal Protection Clause. . . . Since all groups are subject to the peremptory challenge . . . it is hard to see how any group is denied equal protection."

Read **Library Extra 10–3** at cjtoday.com to learn more about the role of race in America's courtrooms today.

LIBRARY
Extra
▪▪▪▪

[1] Daniel Oran, *Oran's Dictionary of the Law* (St. Paul, MN: West, 1983), p. 312.
[2] *Powers* v. *Ohio*, 499 U.S. 400 (1991).
[3] Ibid.
[4] *Edmonson* v. *Leesville Concrete Co., Inc.*, 500 U.S. 614, 111 S.Ct. 2077, 114 L.Ed.2d 660 (1991).
[5] *J.E.B.* v. *Alabama*, 114 S.Ct. 1419, 128 L.Ed.2d 89 (1994).

However, in the 1986 case of *Batson* v. *Kentucky*,[65] following what many claimed was widespread abuse of peremptory challenges by prosecution and defense alike, the Supreme Court was forced to overrule its earlier decision. Batson, an African American man, had been convicted of second-degree burglary and other offenses by an all-white jury. The prosecutor had used his peremptory challenges to remove all blacks from jury service at the trial. The Court agreed that the use of peremptory challenges for purposeful discrimination constitutes a violation of the defendant's right to an impartial jury.

The *Batson* decision laid out the requirements that defendants must prove when seeking to establish the discriminatory use of peremptory challenges. They include the need to prove that the defendant is a member of a recognized racial group that was intentionally excluded from the jury and the need to raise a reasonable suspicion that the prosecutor used peremptory challenges in a discriminatory manner. Justice Thurgood Marshall, writing a concurring opinion in *Batson*, presaged what was to come: "The inherent potential of peremptory challenges to destroy the jury process by permitting the exclusion of jurors on racial grounds should ideally lead the Court to ban them entirely from the criminal justice system."

A few years later, in *Ford* v. *Georgia* (1991),[66] the Court moved much closer to Justice Marshall's position when it remanded a case for a new trial because the prosecutor had misused peremptory challenges. The prosecutor had used nine of the ten peremptory challenges available under Georgia law to eliminate black prospective jurors. Following his conviction on charges of kidnapping, raping, and murdering a white woman, the African American defendant, James Ford, argued that the prosecutor had demonstrated a systematic racial bias in other cases as well as his own. Specifically, Ford argued that his Sixth Amendment right to an impartial jury had been violated by the prosecutor's racially based method of jury selection. His appeal to the Supreme Court claimed that "the exclusion of members of the black race in the jury when a black accused is being tried is done in order that the accused will receive excessive punishment if found guilty, or to inject racial prejudice into the fact finding process of the jury."[67] While the Court did not find a basis for such a Sixth Amendment claim, it did determine that the civil rights of the jurors themselves had been violated under the Fourteenth Amendment due to a pattern of discrimination based on race.

In another 1991 case, *Powers* v. *Ohio*[68] (see CJ Today Exhibit 10–2), the Court found in favor of a white defendant who claimed that his constitutional rights had been violated by the intentional exclusion of blacks from his jury through the use of peremptory challenges. In *Powers*, the Court held that "[a]lthough an individual juror does not have the right to sit on any particular petit jury, he or she does possess the right not to be excluded from one on account of race."

In *Edmonson* v. *Leesville Concrete Co., Inc.* (1991),[69] a civil case with significance for the criminal justice system, the Court held that peremptory challenges in *civil* suits were not acceptable if based on race. Justice Anthony Kennedy, writing for the majority, said that race-based juror exclusions are forbidden in civil lawsuits because jury selection is a "unique governmental function delegated to private litigants" in a public courtroom.

In the 1992 case of *Georgia* v. *McCollum*,[70] the Court barred *criminal* defendants and their attorneys from using peremptory challenges to exclude potential jurors on the basis of race. In *McCollum*, Justice Harry Blackmun, writing for the majority, said, "Be it at the hands of the state or defense, if a court allows jurors to be excluded because of group bias, it is a willing participant in a scheme that could only undermine the very foundation of our system of justice—our citizens' confidence in it."

Soon thereafter, peremptory challenges based on gender were similarly restricted (*J.E.B.* v. *Alabama*, 1994[71]), although at the time of this writing the Court has refused to ban peremptory challenges that exclude jurors because of religious or sexual orientation.[72] Also, in 1996, the Court refused to review "whether potential jurors can be stricken from a trial panel because they are too fat."[73] The case involved Luis Santiago-Martinez, a drug defendant whose lawyer objected to the prosecution's use of peremptory challenges "because the government," he said, "had used such strikes to discriminate against the handicapped, specifically the obese." The attorney, who was himself obese, claimed that thin jurors might have been unfairly biased against his arguments.

In the 1998 case of *Campbell* v. *Louisiana*,[74] the Court held that a white criminal defendant can raise equal protection and due process objections to discrimination against blacks in the selection of grand jurors. Attorneys for Terry Campbell, who was white, objected to an apparent pattern of discrimination in the selection of grand jury foremen. The foreman of the Evangeline Parish, Louisiana, grand jury that heard second-degree murder charges against him (in the killing of another white man) was white, as had been all such foremen for the last 16 years. The Supreme Court reasoned that "regardless of skin color, an accused suffers a significant 'injury in fact' when the grand jury's composition is tainted by racial discrimination." The Court also said, "The integrity of the body's decisions depends on the integrity of the process used to select the grand jurors."

Finally, in the 2003 case of *Miller-El* v. *Cockrell*,[75] the Court found that a convicted capital defendant's constitutional rights had been violated by Dallas County, Texas, prosecutors who engaged in intentional efforts to remove eligible blacks from the pool of potential jurors. Ten out of 11 eligible blacks were excluded through the use of peremptory strikes. The Court said, "In this case, debate as to whether the prosecution acted with a race-based reason when striking prospective jurors was raised by the statistical evidence demonstrating that 91% of the eligible African Americans were excluded . . . ; and by the fact that three of the State's proffered race-neutral rationales for striking African Americans—ambivalence about the death penalty, hesitancy to vote to execute defendants capable of being rehabilitated, and the jurors' own family history of criminality—pertained just as well to some white jurors who were not challenged and who did serve on the jury."[76] The decision was reaffirmed in the 2005 U.S. Supreme Court case of *Miller-El* v. *Dretke*.[77]

Opening Statements

The presentation of information to the jury begins with **opening statements** made by the prosecution and the defense. The purpose of opening statements is to advise the jury of what the attorneys intend to prove and to describe how such proof will be offered. Evidence is not offered during opening statements. Eventually, however, the jury will have to weigh the evidence presented during the trial and decide which side made the more effective arguments. When a defendant has little evidence to present, the main job of the defense attorney will be to dispute the veracity of the prosecution's version of the facts. Under such circumstances, defense attorneys may choose not to present any evidence or testimony at all, focusing instead on the burden-of-proof requirement facing the prosecution. Such plans will generally be made clear during opening statements. At this time, the defense attorney is also likely to stress the human qualities of the defendant and to remind jurors of the awesome significance of their task.

Lawyers for both sides are bound by a "good-faith" ethical requirement in their opening statements. Attorneys may mention only the evidence that they believe actually can and will be presented as the trial progresses. Allusions to evidence that an attorney has no intention of offering are regarded as unprofessional and have been defined by the U.S. Supreme Court as "professional misconduct."[78] When material alluded to in an opening statement cannot, for whatever reason, later be presented in court, opposing counsel gains an opportunity to discredit the other side.

opening statement

The initial statement of the prosecutor or the defense attorney, made in a court of law to a judge or jury, describing the facts that he or she intends to present during trial to prove the case.

The Presentation of Evidence

The crux of the criminal trial is the presentation of evidence. First, the state is given the opportunity to present evidence intended to prove the defendant's guilt. After prosecutors have rested their case, the defense is afforded the opportunity to provide evidence favorable to the defendant.

TYPES OF EVIDENCE

Evidence can be either direct or circumstantial. **Direct evidence**, if believed, proves a fact without requiring the judge or jury to draw inferences. For example, direct evidence may consist of the information contained in a photograph or a videotape. It might also consist of testimonial evidence provided by a witness on the stand. A straightforward statement by a witness ("I saw him do it!") is a form of direct evidence.

Circumstantial evidence is indirect. It requires the judge or jury to make inferences and to draw conclusions. At a murder trial, for example, a person who heard gunshots and moments later saw someone run by with a smoking gun in hand might testify to those facts. Even without an eyewitness to the actual homicide, the jury might conclude that the person seen with the gun was the one who pulled the trigger and committed the crime. Circumstantial evidence is sufficient to produce a conviction in a criminal trial. In fact, some prosecuting attorneys prefer to work entirely with circumstantial evidence, weaving a tapestry of the criminal act into their arguments to the jury.

Real evidence, which may be either direct or circumstantial, consists of physical material or traces of physical activity. Weapons, tire tracks, ransom notes, and fingerprints all fall into the category of real evidence. Real evidence, sometimes called *physical evidence*, is introduced in the trial by means of exhibits. *Exhibits* are objects or displays that, after having been formally accepted as evidence by the judge, may be shown to members of the jury. *Documentary evidence*, one type of real evidence, includes written evidence like business records, journals, written confessions, and letters. Documentary evidence can extend beyond paper and ink to include stored computer data and video and audio recordings.

evidence

Anything useful to a judge or jury in deciding the facts of a case. Evidence may take the form of witness testimony, written documents, videotapes, magnetic media, photographs, physical objects, and so on.

direct evidence

Evidence that, if believed, directly proves a fact. Eyewitness testimony and videotaped documentation account for the majority of all direct evidence heard in the criminal courtroom.

circumstantial evidence

Evidence that requires interpretation or that requires a judge or jury to reach a conclusion based on what the evidence indicates. From the proximity of the defendant to a smoking gun, for example, the jury might conclude that he or she pulled the trigger.

real evidence

Evidence that consists of physical material or traces of physical activity.

THE EVALUATION OF EVIDENCE

One of the most significant decisions a trial court judge makes is which evidence can be presented to the jury. To make this determination, judges examine the relevance of the evidence to the case at hand. Relevant evidence has a bearing on the facts at issue. For example, decades ago, it was not unusual for a woman's sexual history to be brought out in rape trials. Under "rape shield statutes," most states today will not allow this practice, recognizing that these details have no bearing on the case. Rape shield statutes have been strengthened by recent U.S. Supreme Court decisions, including the 1991 case of *Michigan* v. *Lucas*.[79]

Colorado's rape shield law played a prominent role in the 2004 case of Kobe Bryant, a basketball superstar who was accused of sexually assaulting a 19-year-old Vail-area resort employee. Bryant admitted to having a sexual encounter with the woman but claimed it was consensual. Defense attorneys sought to have the Colorado law declared unconstitutional in an effort to show that injuries to the woman were the result of her having had sexual intercourse with multiple partners before and

CJ Today Exhibit 10–3

Pretrial and Post-Trial Motions

A *motion* is "an oral or written request made to a court at any time before, during, or after court proceedings, asking the court to make a specified finding, decision, or order."[1] Written motions are called *petitions*. This exhibit lists the most common motions made by both sides in a criminal case before and after trial.

MOTION FOR DISCOVERY

A motion for discovery, filed by the defense, asks the court to allow the defendant's lawyers to view the evidence that the prosecution intends to present at trial. Physical evidence, lists of witnesses, documents, photographs, and so on that the prosecution plans to introduce in court are usually made available to the defense as a result of a motion for discovery.

MOTION TO SUPPRESS EVIDENCE

The defense may file a motion to suppress evidence if it learns, in the preliminary hearing or through pretrial discovery, of evidence that it believes to have been unlawfully acquired.

MOTION TO DISMISS CHARGES

A variety of circumstances may result in the filing of a motion to dismiss charges. They include (1) an opinion, by defense counsel, that the indictment or information is not sound; (2) violations of speedy trial legislation; (3) a plea bargain with the defendant, which may require testimony against codefendants; (4) the death of an important witness or the destruction or disappearance of necessary evidence; (5) the confession, by a supposed victim, that the facts in the case were fabricated; and (6) the success of a motion to suppress evidence that effectively eliminates the prosecution's case.

MOTION FOR CONTINUANCE

This motion seeks a delay in the start of the trial. Defense motions for continuance are often based on an inability to locate important witnesses, the illness of the defendant, or a change in defense counsel immediately prior to trial.

MOTION FOR CHANGE OF VENUE

In well-known cases, pretrial publicity may lessen the opportunity for a case to be tried before an unbiased jury. A motion for a change in venue asks that the trial be moved to some other area where prejudice against the defendant is less likely to exist.

MOTION FOR SEVERANCE OF OFFENSES

Defendants charged with a number of crimes may ask to be tried separately on all or some of the charges. Although consolidating charges for trial saves time and money, some defendants believe that it is more likely to make them appear guilty.

MOTION FOR SEVERANCE OF DEFENDANTS

This request asks the court to try the accused separately from any codefendants. Motions for severance are likely to be filed when the defendant believes that the jury may be prejudiced against him or her by evidence applicable only to other defendants.

MOTION TO DETERMINE PRESENT SANITY

A lack of "present sanity," even though it may be no defense against the criminal charge, can delay trial. A person cannot be tried, sentenced, or punished while insane. If a defendant is insane at the time a trial is to begin, this motion may halt the proceedings until treatment can be arranged.

MOTION FOR A BILL OF PARTICULARS

This motion asks the court to order the prosecutor to provide detailed information about the charges that the defendant will be facing in court. Defendants charged with a number of offenses, or with a number of counts of the same offense, may make such a motion. They may, for example, seek to learn which alleged instances of an offense will become the basis for prosecution or which specific items of contraband allegedly found in their possession are held to violate the law.

MOTION FOR A MISTRIAL

A mistrial may be declared at any time, and a motion for a mistrial may be made by either side. Mistrials are likely to be declared in cases in which highly prejudicial comments are made by either attorney. Defense motions for a mistrial do not provide grounds for a later claim of double jeopardy.

MOTION FOR ARREST OF JUDGMENT

After the verdict of the jury has been announced, but before sentencing, the defense may make a motion for arrest of judgment. With this motion, the defense asserts that some legally acceptable reason exists as to why sentencing should not occur. Defendants who are seriously ill, who are hospitalized, or who have gone insane prior to judgment being imposed may file such a motion.

MOTION FOR A NEW TRIAL

After a jury has returned a guilty verdict, the court may entertain a defense motion for a new trial. Acceptance of such a motion is usually based on the discovery of new evidence that is of significant benefit to the defense and that will set aside the conviction.

[1]U.S. Department of Justice, *Dictionary of Criminal Justice Data Terminology*, 2nd ed. (Washington, DC: U.S. Government Printing Office, 1982).

after her encounter with Bryant. The woman later dropped the criminal case against Bryant and settled a civil suit against him in 2005.[80] The terms of the suit were not disclosed.

In evaluating evidence, judges must also weigh the **probative value** of an item of evidence against its potential inflammatory or prejudicial qualities. Evidence has probative value when it is useful and relevant, but even useful evidence may unduly bias a jury if it is exceptionally gruesome or is presented in such a way as to imply guilt. For example, gory color photographs may be withheld from the jury's eyes. In one recent case, a new trial was ordered when photos of the crime scene were projected on a wall over the head of the defendant as he sat in the courtroom. An appellate court found the presentation to have prejudiced the jury.

Sometimes evidence is found to have only limited admissibility. This means that the evidence can be used for a specific purpose but that it might not be accurate in other details. Photographs, for example, may be admitted as evidence for the narrow purpose of showing spatial relationships between objects under discussion, even if the photographs were taken under conditions that did not exist when the offense was committed (such as daylight).

When judges allow the use of evidence that may have been illegally or unconstitutionally gathered, there may be grounds for a later appeal if the trial concludes with a "guilty" verdict. Even when evidence is improperly introduced at trial, however, a number of Supreme Court decisions[81] have held that there may be no grounds for an effective appeal unless such introduction "had substantial and injurious effect or influence in determining the jury's verdict."[82] Called the *harmless error rule*, this standard places the burden on the prosecution to show that the jury's decision would most likely have been the same even in the absence of the inappropriate evidence. The rule is not applicable when a defendant's constitutional guarantees are violated by "structural defects in the constitution of the trial mechanism" itself[83]—as when a judge gives constitutionally improper instructions to a jury. (We'll discuss those instructions later in this chapter.)

THE TESTIMONY OF WITNESSES

Witness **testimony** is generally the chief means by which evidence is introduced at trial. Witnesses may include victims, police officers, the defendant, specialists in recognized fields, and others with useful information to provide. Some of these witnesses may have been present during the commission of the offense, while most will have had only a later opportunity to investigate the situation or to analyze evidence.

Before a witness is allowed to testify to any fact, the questioning attorney must establish the person's competence. Competence to testify requires that witnesses have personal knowledge of the information they will discuss and that they understand their duty to tell the truth.

One of the defense attorney's most critical decisions is whether to put the defendant on the stand. Defendants have a Fifth Amendment right to remain silent and to refuse to testify. In the precedent-setting case of *Griffin* v. *California* (1965),[84] the U.S. Supreme Court declared that if a defendant refuses to testify, prosecutors and judges are enjoined from even commenting on this fact, although the judge should instruct the jury that such a failure cannot be held to indicate guilt. In the 2001 case of *Ohio* v. *Reiner*,[85] the U.S. Supreme Court extended Fifth Amendment protections to witnesses who deny any and all guilt in association with a crime for which another person is being prosecuted.

Direct examination of a witness takes place when a witness is first called to the stand. If the prosecutor calls the witness, the witness is referred to as a *witness for the prosecution*. If the direct examiner is a defense attorney, the witness is a *witness for the defense*.

The direct examiner may ask questions that require a "yes" or "no" answer or may ask narrative questions that allow the witness to tell a story in his or her own words. During direct examination, courts generally prohibit the use of leading questions or those that suggest answers to the witness.[86]

Cross-examination is the questioning of a witness by someone other than the direct examiner. Anyone who offers testimony in a criminal court has the duty to submit to cross-examination.[87] The purpose of cross-examination is to test the credibility and the memory of the witness.

Most states and the federal government restrict the scope of cross-examination to material covered during direct examination. Questions about other matters, even though they may relate to the case before the court, are not allowed in most states, although a few states allow the cross-examiner to raise any issue as long as the court deems it relevant. Leading questions, generally disallowed in direct examination, are regarded as the mainstay of cross-examination. Such questions allow for a concise restatement of testimony that has already been offered and serve to focus efficiently on potential problems that the cross-examiner seeks to address.

Some witnesses commit **perjury**—that is, they make statements that they know are untrue. Reasons for perjured testimony vary, but most witnesses who lie on the stand do so in an effort

probative value

The degree to which a particular item of evidence is useful in, and relevant to, proving something important in a trial.

testimony

Oral evidence offered by a sworn witness on the witness stand during a criminal trial.

perjury

The intentional making of a false statement as part of the testimony by a sworn witness in a judicial proceeding on a matter relevant to the case at hand.

Michael Jackson fans reading copies of a special edition of the *Santa Maria Times* outside Jackson's Neverland Ranch in Los Olivos, California. The 46-year-old singer was found not guilty of child molestation and other charges in a 2005 trial that lasted almost four months and involved testimony from 140 witnesses. What is the primary purpose of a criminal trial?

Ethan Miller/Getty Images

to help friends accused of crimes. Witnesses who perjure themselves are subject to impeachment, in which either the defense or the prosecution demonstrates that a witness has intentionally offered false testimony. For example, previous statements made by the witness may be shown to be at odds with more recent declarations. When it can be demonstrated that a witness has offered inaccurate or false testimony, the witness has been effectively impeached. Perjury is a serious offense in its own right, and dishonest witnesses may face fines or jail time.

At the conclusion of the cross-examination, the direct examiner may again question the witness. This procedure is called *redirect examination* and may be followed by a recross-examination and so on, until both sides are satisfied that they have exhausted fruitful lines of questioning.

CHILDREN AS WITNESSES

An area of special concern is the use of children as witnesses in a criminal trial, especially when the children are also victims. Currently, in an effort to avoid what may be traumatizing direct confrontations between child witnesses and the accused, 37 states allow the use of videotaped testimony in criminal courtrooms, and 32 permit the use of closed-circuit television, which allows the child to testify out of the presence of the defendant. In 1988, however, in the case of *Coy* v. *Iowa*,[88] the U.S. Supreme Court ruled that a courtroom screen, used to shield child witnesses from visual confrontation with a defendant in a child sex-abuse case, had violated the confrontation clause of the Constitution (found in the Sixth Amendment).

On the other hand, in the 1990 case of *Maryland* v. *Craig*,[89] the Court upheld the use of closed-circuit television to shield children who testify in criminal courts. The Court's decision was partially based on the realization that "a significant majority of States have enacted statutes to protect child witnesses from the trauma of giving testimony in child-abuse cases . . . [which] attests to the widespread belief in the importance of such a policy."

Although a face-to-face confrontation with a child victim may not be necessary in the courtroom, until 1992 the Supreme Court had been reluctant to allow into evidence descriptions of abuse and other statements made by children, even to child-care professionals, when those statements were made outside the courtroom. In *Idaho* v. *Wright* (1990),[90] the Court reasoned that such "statements [are] fraught with the dangers of unreliability which the Confrontation Clause is designed to highlight and obviate."

However, in *White* v. *Illinois* (1992),[91] the Court reversed its stance, ruling that in-court testimony provided by a medical provider and the child's baby-sitter, which repeated what the child had said to them concerning White's sexually abusive behavior, was permissible. The Court rejected White's claim that out-of-court statements should be admissible only when the witness is unavailable to testify at trial, saying instead, "A finding of unavailability of an out-of-court declarant is necessary only if the out-of-court statement was made at a prior judicial proceeding." Placing *White* within the context of generally established exceptions, the Court declared, "A statement that has been offered in a moment of excitement—without the opportunity to reflect on the consequences of one's exclamation—may justifiably carry more weight with a trier of fact than a similar statement offered in the relative calm of the courtroom. Similarly, a statement made in the course of procuring medical services, where the declarant knows that a false statement may cause misdiagnosis or mistreatment, carries special guarantees of credibility that a trier of fact may not think replicated by courtroom testimony."

THE HEARSAY RULE

Hearsay is anything not based on the personal knowledge of a witness. A witness may say, for example, "John told me that Fred did it!" Such a witness becomes a hearsay declarant, and following a likely objection by counsel, the trial judge will have to decide whether the witness's statement will be allowed to stand as evidence. In most cases, the judge will instruct the jury to disregard the witness's comment, thereby enforcing the **hearsay rule**, which prohibits the use of "secondhand evidence."

Exceptions to the hearsay rule have been established by both precedent and tradition. One exception is the dying declaration. A dying declaration is a statement made by a person who is about to die. When heard by a second party, it may usually be repeated in court, provided that certain conditions have been met. A dying declaration is generally a valid exception to the hearsay rule when it is made by someone who knows that he or she is about to die and when the statement made relates to the cause and circumstances of the impending death.

Spontaneous statements provide another exception to the hearsay rule. A statement is considered spontaneous when it is made in the heat of excitement before the person has had time to make it up. For example, a defendant who was injured and is just regaining consciousness following a crime may say something that could later be repeated in court by those who heard it.

Out-of-court statements, especially if they were recorded during a time of great excitement or while a person was under considerable stress, may also become exceptions to the hearsay rule. Many states, for example, permit juries to hear 9-1-1 tape recordings or to read police transcripts of victim interviews without requiring that the people who made them appear in court. In two recent cases, however, the U.S. Supreme Court barred admission of tape-recorded 9-1-1 calls when the people making them were alive and in good health but not available for cross-examination. In *Crawford* v. *Washington*,[92] a 2004 case, the Court disallowed a woman's tape-recorded eyewitness account of a fight in which her husband stabbed another man, holding that the Constitution bars admission of testimonial statements of a witness who did not appear at trial unless he was unable to testify and the defendant had a prior opportunity for cross-examination. In *Davis* v. *Washington*,[93] decided in 2006, the Court held that a 9-1-1 call made by a woman who said that her former boyfriend was beating her had been improperly introduced as testimonial evidence. The woman had been subpoenaed but failed to appear in court. The keyword in both cases is *testimonial*, and the Court indicated that "statements are nontestimonial when made in the course of police interrogation under circumstances objectively indicating that the primary purpose of interrogation is to enable police assistance to meet an ongoing emergency."[94]

The use of other out-of-court statements, such as writings or routine video or audio recordings, usually requires the witness to testify that the statements or depictions were accurate at the time they were made. Witnesses who so testify may be subject to cross-examination by the defendant's attorney. Nonetheless, this "past recollection recorded" exception to the hearsay rule is especially useful in drawn-out court proceedings that occur long after the crime. Under such circumstances, witnesses may no longer remember the details of an event. Their earlier statements to authorities, however, can be introduced into evidence as past recollection recorded.

Closing Arguments

At the conclusion of a criminal trial, both sides have the opportunity for a final narrative presentation to the jury in the form of a **closing argument**. This summation provides a review and analysis of the evidence. Its purpose is to persuade the jury to draw a conclusion favorable to the presenter. Testimony can be quoted, exhibits referred to, and attention drawn to inconsistencies in the evidence presented by the other side.

States vary as to the order of closing arguments. Nearly all allow the defense attorney to speak to the jury before the prosecution makes its final points. A few permit the prosecutor the first opportunity for summation. Some jurisdictions and the Federal Rules of Criminal Procedure[95] authorize a defense rebuttal. A rebuttal is a response to the closing argument of the other side.

Some specific issues may need to be addressed during summation. If, for example, the defendant has not taken the stand during the trial, the defense attorney's closing argument will

hearsay

Something that is not based on the personal knowledge of a witness. Witnesses who testify about something they have heard, for example, are offering hearsay by repeating information about a matter of which they have no direct knowledge.

hearsay rule

The long-standing precedent that hearsay cannot be used in American courtrooms. Rather than accepting testimony based on hearsay, the court will ask that the person who was the original source of the hearsay information be brought in to be questioned and cross-examined. Exceptions to the hearsay rule may occur when the person with direct knowledge is dead or is otherwise unable to testify.

closing argument

An oral summation of a case presented to a judge, or to a judge and jury, by the prosecution or by the defense in a criminal trial.

inevitably stress that this failure to testify cannot be regarded as indicating guilt. Where the prosecution's case rests entirely on circumstantial evidence, the defense can be expected to stress the lack of any direct proof, and the prosecutor is likely to argue that circumstantial evidence can be stronger than direct evidence, since it is not as easily affected by human error or false testimony.

The Judge's Charge to the Jury

After closing arguments, the judge charges the jury to "retire," select one of its number as a foreman, and deliberate on the evidence that has been presented until it has reached a verdict. The words of the judge's "charge" vary somewhat between jurisdictions and among judges, but all judges will remind members of the jury of their duty to consider objectively only the evidence that has been presented and of the need for impartiality. Most judges also remind jury members of the statutory elements of the alleged offense, of the burden of proof that rests on the prosecution, and of the need for the prosecution to have proved the defendant's guilt beyond a reasonable doubt before the jury can return a guilty verdict.

In their charge, many judges also provide a summary of the evidence presented, usually from notes they took during the trial, as a means of refreshing the jurors' memories of events. About half of all the states allow judges the freedom to express their own views as to the credibility of witnesses and the significance of evidence. Other states only permit judges to summarize the evidence in an objective and impartial manner.

Following the charge, the jury is removed from the courtroom and is permitted to begin its deliberations. In the absence of the jury, defense attorneys may choose to challenge portions of the judge's charge. If they feel that some oversight has occurred in the original charge, they may ask the judge to provide the jury with additional instructions or information. Such objections, if denied by the judge, often become the basis for an appeal when a conviction is returned.

Jury Deliberations and the Verdict

verdict

The decision of the jury in a jury trial or of a judicial officer in a nonjury trial.

In cases in which the evidence is either very clear or very weak, jury deliberations may be brief, lasting only a matter of hours or even minutes. Some juries, however, deliberate days or sometimes weeks, carefully weighing all the nuances of the evidence they have seen and heard. Many jurisdictions require that juries reach a unanimous **verdict**, although the U.S. Supreme Court has ruled that unanimous verdicts are not required in noncapital cases.[96] Even so, some juries are unable to agree on any verdict. When a jury is deadlocked, it is said to be a *hung jury*. When a unanimous decision is required, juries may be deadlocked by the strong opposition of several members or of only one member to a verdict agreed on by all the others.

In some states, judges are allowed to add a boost to nearly hung juries by recharging them under a set of instructions that the Supreme Court put forth in the 1896 case of *Allen* v. *U.S.*[97] The *Allen* charge, as it is known, urges the jury to vigorous deliberations and suggests to obstinate jurors that their objections may be ill founded if they make no impression on the other jurors.

PROBLEMS WITH THE JURY SYSTEM

Judge Harold J. Rothwax, a well-known critic of today's jury system, tells the tale of a rather startling 1991 case over which he presided. The case involved a murder defendant, a handsome young man who had been fired by a New York company that serviced ATMs. After being fired, the defendant intentionally caused a machine in a remote area to malfunction. When two former colleagues arrived to fix it, he robbed them, stole the money inside the ATM, and shot both men repeatedly. One of the men survived long enough to identify his former coworker as the shooter. The man was arrested, and a trial ensued, but after three weeks of hearing the case, the jury deadlocked. Judge Rothwax later learned that the jury had voted 11 to 1 to convict the defendant, but the one holdout just couldn't believe that "someone so good-looking could . . . commit such a crime."[98]

Many routine cases as well as some highly publicized cases, like the murder trial of O. J. Simpson, have called into question the ability of the American jury system to do its job—that is, to sort through the evidence and to accurately determine the defendant's guilt or innocence.

In a televised 1995 trial, Simpson was acquitted of the charge that he murdered his ex-wife Nicole Brown and her friend Ronald Goldman outside Brown's home in 1994. Many people believed that strong evidence tied Simpson to the crimes, and the criminal trial left many people feeling unsatisfied with the criminal justice system and with the criminal trial process. Later, a civil jury ordered Simpson to pay $33.5 million to the Goldman family and to Nicole Brown's estate.

Because jurors are drawn from all walks of life, many cannot be expected to understand modern legal complexities and to appreciate all the nuances of trial court practice. It is likely that even the best-intentioned jurors cannot understand and rarely observe some jury instructions.[99] In highly charged cases, emotions are often difficult to separate from fact, and during deliberations, some juries are dominated by one or two members with forceful personalities.

Jurors may be less than effective in cases where they fear personal retaliation. In the state-level trial of the police officers accused in the infamous Rodney King beating, for example, jurors reported being afraid for their lives due to the riots in Los Angeles that broke out after their not-guilty verdict was announced. Some slept with weapons by their side, and others sent their children away to safe locations.[100] Because of the potential for harm that jurors faced in the 1993 federal trial of the same officers, U.S. District Judge John G. Davies ruled that the names of the jurors be forever kept secret. Members of the press called the secrecy order "an unprecedented infringement of the public's right of access to the justice system."[101] Similarly, in the 1993 trial of three black men charged with the beating of white truck driver Reginald Denny during the Los Angeles riots that followed the Rodney King verdict, Los Angeles Superior Court Judge John Ouderkirk ordered that the identities of the jurors not be released.

Opponents of the jury system have argued that it should be replaced by a panel of judges who would both render a verdict and impose sentence. Regardless of how well considered such a suggestion may be, such a change could not occur without modification of the Constitution's Sixth Amendment right to trial by jury.

An alternative suggestion for improving the process of trial by jury has been the call for professional jurors. Professional jurors would be paid by the government, as are judges, prosecutors, and public defenders. They would be expected to have the expertise to sit on any jury. Professional jurors would be trained to listen objectively and would be taught the kinds of decision-making skills they would need to function effectively within an adversarial context. They would hear one case after another, perhaps moving between jurisdictions in cases of highly publicized crimes.

A professional jury system offers these advantages:

1. *Dependability.* Professional jurors could be expected to report to the courtroom in a timely fashion and to be good listeners, since both would be required by the nature of the job.

2. *Knowledge.* Professional jurors would be trained in the law, would understand what a finding of guilt requires, and would know what to expect from the other professionals in the courtroom.

3. *Equity.* Professional jurors would understand the requirements of due process and would be less likely to be swayed by the emotional content of a case, having been schooled in the need to separate matters of fact from personal feelings.

A professional jury system would not be without difficulties. Jurors under such a system might become jaded, deciding cases out of hand as routines lead to boredom. They might categorize defendants according to whether they "fit the type" for guilt or innocence based on the jurors' previous experiences. Job requirements for professional jurors would be difficult to establish without infringing on the jurors' freedom to decide cases as they understand them. For the same reason, any evaluation of the job performance of professional jurors would be a difficult call. Finally, professional jurors might not truly be peer jurors, since their social characteristics might be skewed by education, residence, and politics.

Improving the Adjudication Process

Courts today are coming under increasing scrutiny, and well-publicized trials, like those of Michael Jackson, Andrea Yates, Martha Stewart, Scott Peterson, O. J. Simpson, and John Allen Muhammad, have heightened awareness of problems with the American court system. One of today's most important issues is reducing the number of jurisdictions by unifying courts. The current multiplicity of jurisdictions frequently leads to what many critics believe are avoidable conflicts and overlaps in the handling of criminal defendants. In some states, problems are exacerbated by the lack of any centralized judicial authority that might resolve jurisdictional and

In suits at common law, . . . the right of trial by jury shall be preserved, and no fact tried by a jury, shall be otherwise reexamined in any Court of the United States, than according to the rules of the common law.

—Seventh Amendment to the U.S. Constitution

CJ Futures

Courtrooms of the Future

In the mid-1990s, the College of William and Mary, in conjunction with the National Center for State Courts (NCSC), unveiled Courtroom 21. At the time, it was the most technologically advanced courtroom in the United States. Courtroom 21, located in the McGlothlin Courtroom of the College of William and Mary, offers a glimpse at what American courtrooms might be like in the mid-twenty-first century. Courtroom 21 includes the following integrated capabilities:

1. *Automatic video recording of the proceedings, using ceiling-mounted cameras with voice-initiated switching.* A sophisticated voice-activation system directs cameras to record the person speaking and to record evidence as it is being presented.

2. *Recorded and televised evidence display with optical disk storage.* Documentary or real evidence can be presented to the judge and the jury through the use of a video "presenter," which also makes a video record of the evidence as it is being presented, so it can be used later.

3. *Remote two-way television.* The two-way television arrangement allows video and audio signals to be sent from the judge's bench to areas throughout the courtroom, including the jury box.

4. *Text-, graphics-, and video-capable jury computers.* Courtroom 21's jury box contains computers for information display and animation so that jury members can easily view documents, live or prerecorded video, and graphics, such as charts, diagrams, and pictures. Video-capable jury computers also allow for the remote appearance of witnesses—that is, for questioning witnesses who are unable or unwilling to appear in the courtroom—and for the display of crime-scene reenactments via computer animation.

5. *Access to online legal research databases for the judge and for counsel on both sides.* Available databases contain an extensive selection of state and federal statutes, case law, and other precedent, allowing the judge and the lawyers to find answers to unanticipated legal questions that arise during trial.

6. *Built-in video playback facilities for out-of-court testimony.* Because an increasing number of depositions are being videotaped by attorneys in preparation for trial, Courtroom 21 has capabilities for video playback. Video depositions can be played on courtroom monitors to present expert witness testimony or to impeach a witness.

7. *Information storage with software search capabilities.* Integrated software programs provide text-searching capabilities for courtroom participants. Previously transcribed testimony and precedent-setting cases from other courts can be searched and reviewed.

8. *Concurrent (real-time) court reporter transcription.* A court reporter uses a self-contained computerized writing machine for the real-time capture of testimony in the courtroom. While the reporter writes, the computer translates strokes into English transcripts, which are immediately distributed to the judge and counsel via their personal computers. Using this technology, the judge and attorneys can mark an individual copy of the day's testimony and take it with them on their laptop computer or on a floppy disk for later review and trial preparation.

Fred Lederer, director of Courtroom 21 at the College of William and Mary Law School in Williamsburg, Virginia, acting as a bailiff as he swears in a witness via the Internet. The witness, Hugh Selby from the University of Canberra in Australia, was participating in a mock terrorism trial. The demonstration trial depended heavily on computer technology and the Internet to bring together attorneys, witnesses, defendants, jurors, and a judge. What limits do you think might be applied to "virtual courtrooms" of the future?

Gary C. Knapp/AP Wide World Photos

CJ Futures (continued)

The technology demonstrated in Courtroom 21 suggests many possibilities. For one thing, attorneys could use court video equipment for filing remote motions and for other types of hearings. As one of Courtroom 21's designers puts it, "Imagine the productivity gains if lawyers no longer need to travel across a city or county for a ten-minute appearance."

Courtroom 21's designers also suggest that the innovative use of audio and video technology can preserve far more evidence and trial detail than written records, making a comprehensive review of cases easier for appellate judges. One study that has already been conducted by the NCSC showed that when a video record is available, an appellate court is less likely to reverse the original determination of the trial court. Video court records, analysts say, "might also improve the performance of attorneys and judges. By preserving matters not now apparent on a written record, such as facial expressions, voice inflections, body gestures, and the like, video records may cause trial participants to be more circumspect in their behavior than at present."

Advanced technology can also be expected to have a considerable impact on the trial itself. The technology built into Courtroom 21 facilitates computer animations and crime-scene reenactments. As one of the designers of Courtroom 21 says, "*Jurassic Park* quality computer reenactment may have enormous psychological impact" on jurors.

While Courtroom 21 shows what a typical courtroom of the near future may be like, it also raises questions about the appropriate use of innovative courtroom technologies. As Fred Lederer, one of Courtroom 21's designers, points out, "Modern technology holds enormous promise for our courts. We must recognize, however, that technology's utility often depends upon how people will use it. Although we must continue to improve our courts via technology, we must be sensitive to technology's impact and work to recognize and minimize any negative consequences it might have on our system of justice."

An even more intriguing vision of courtrooms of the future is offered by the Technology of Justice Task Force in its draft report to the Pennsylvania Futures Commission. The task force predicted that by the year 2020, "there will be 'virtual courtrooms,' where appropriate, to provide hearings without the need for people to come to a physical courthouse." The task force envisions trials via teleconferencing, public Internet access to many court documents, and payment of fines by credit card.

Visit Courtroom 21 on the Web at http://www.courtroom21.net, and take a virtual tour of its facilities at http://www.courtroom21.net/ctrm21_hires.ipx.

DISCUSSION QUESTIONS

1. Do you think that technologies like those discussed in this box might affect the outcome of criminal trials? Explain.

2. Are there any types of criminal trials in which the use of high-technology courtrooms might not be appropriate? If so, describe them.

References: National Center for State Courts website, http://www.ncsc.us (accessed October 11, 2007), from which some of the material in this box is taken; and Courtroom 21 website, http://www.courtroom21.net (accessed October 11, 2007).

procedural disputes.[102] Proponents of unification suggest eliminating overlapping jurisdictions, creating special-purpose courts, and establishing administrative offices to achieve economies of scale.[103]

The number of court-watch citizens' groups is also rapidly growing. Such organizations focus on the trial court level, but they are part of a general movement seeking greater openness in government decision making at all levels.[104] Court-watch groups regularly monitor court proceedings and attempt to document and often publicize inadequacies. They frequently focus on the handling of indigents, fairness in the scheduling of cases for trial, unnecessary court delays, the reduction of waiting time, the treatment of witnesses and jurors, and the adequacy of rights advisements for defendants throughout judicial proceedings.

The statistical measurement of court performance is another area that is receiving increased attention. Research has looked at the efficiency with which prosecutors schedule cases for trial, the speed with which judges resolve issues, the amount of time judges spend on the bench, and the economic and other costs to defendants, witnesses, and communities involved in the judicial process.[105] Statistical studies of this type often attempt to measure elements of court performance as diverse as sentence variation, charging accuracy, fairness in plea bargaining, evenhandedness, delays, and attitudes toward the court by lay participants. Visit Library Extra 10–4 at cjtoday.com for more information on standards and measures in court performance.

LIBRARY
Extra
■ ■ ■ ■

Multiculturalism and Diversity

The Bilingual Courtroom

One of the central multicultural issues facing the criminal justice system today is the need for clear communication with recent immigrants and subcultural groups that have not been fully acculturated. Many such groups hold to traditions and values that differ from those held by the majority of Americans. Such differences influence the interpretation of things seen and heard. Even more basic, however, are language differences that might prevent effective communication with criminal justice system personnel.

Techniques that law enforcement officers can use in overcoming language differences were discussed in Chapter 8. This box focuses on the use of courtroom interpreters to facilitate effective and accurate communication. The role of the courtroom interpreter is to present neutral verbatim, or word-for-word, translations. Interpreters must provide true, accurate, and complete interpretation of the exact statements made by non-English-speaking defendants, victims, and witnesses—whether on the stand, in writing, or in court-related conferences. The Court Interpreters and Translators Association also requires, through its code of professional ethics, that translators remember their "absolute responsibility to keep all oral and written information gained completely confidential."

Although most court interpreters are actually present in the courtroom at the time of the trial, telephone interpreting provides an alternative for courts that have trouble locating qualified interpreters. Today, state court administrative offices in Florida, Idaho, New Jersey, and Washington sponsor programs through which qualified interpreters in metropolitan counties are made available to courts in rural counties by telephone.

The federal Court Interpreters Act of 1978[1] specifically provides for the use of interpreters in federal courts. It applies to both criminal and civil trials and hearings. The act reads, in part, as follows:[2]

> The presiding judicial officers . . . shall utilize [an interpreter] . . . in judicial proceedings instituted by the United States, if the presiding judicial officer determines on such officer's own motion or on the motion of a party that such party (including the defendant in a criminal case), or a witness who may present testimony in such judicial proceedings—
> (A) speaks only or primarily a language other than English; or
> (B) suffers from a hearing impairment . . . so as to inhibit such party's comprehension of the proceedings or communication

with counsel or the presiding officer, or so as to inhibit such witness's comprehension of questions and the presentation of such testimony.

As this extract from the statute shows, translators are also required for individuals with hearing impairments who communicate primarily through American Sign Language. The act does not require that an interpreter be appointed when a person has a speech impairment that is not accompanied by a hearing impairment. A court is not prohibited, however, from providing assistance to that person if it will aid in the efficient administration of justice.

Because it is a federal law, the Court Interpreters Act does not apply to state courts. Nonetheless, most states have enacted similar legislation. A few states are starting to introduce high-standard testing for court interpreters, although most states currently conduct little or no interpreter screening. The federal government and states with high standards for court interpreters generally require interpreter certification. To become certified, an interpreter must pass an oral examination, such as the federal court interpreter's examination or an examination administered by a state court or by a recognized international agency, such as the United Nations.

There is growing recognition among professional court interpreters of the need for standardized interstate testing and certification programs. To meet that need, the National Center for State Courts created the Consortium for State Court Interpreter Certification. The consortium works to pool state resources for developing and administering court interpreter testing and training programs. The consortium's founding states were Minnesota, New Jersey, Oregon, and Washington, and many other states have since joined.

Because certified interpreters are not always available, even by telephone, most states have created a special category of "language-skilled interpreters." To qualify as a language-skilled interpreter, a person must demonstrate to the court's satisfaction his or her ability to interpret court proceedings from English to a designated language and from that language to English. Many states require sign language interpreters to hold a Legal Specialist Certificate, or its equivalent, from the Registry of Interpreters for the Deaf, showing that they are certified in American Sign Language. Learn more about language interpretation in the courts from the National Association of Judiciary Interpreters and Translators via **Web Extra 10–3** at cjtoday.com.

[1]U.S. Code, Title 28, Section 1827.
[2]Ibid., at Section 1827(d)(1).

References: The National Association of Judiciary Interpreters and Translators website, http://www.najit.org (accessed October 11, 2007); Madelynn Herman and Anne Endress Skove, "State Court Rules for Language Interpreters," memorandum number IS 99.1242, National Center for State Courts, Knowledge Management Office, September 8, 1999; Madelynn Herman and Dot Bryant, "Language Interpreting in the Courts," National Center for State Courts, http://www.ncsc.dni.us/KMO/Projects/Trends/99-00/articles/CtInterpreters.htm (accessed October 11, 2007); and National Crime Prevention Council, *Building and Crossing Bridges: Refugees and Law Enforcement Working Together* (Washington, DC: NCPC, 1994).

SUMMARY

- This chapter describes the criminal trial process and the court-related activities that take place before the trial begins. Pretrial activities include the first appearance, which involves appointment of counsel for indigent defendants and consideration of pretrial release; the preliminary hearing to determine whether there is probable cause to hold the defendant; the filing of an information by the prosecutor or the return of an indictment by the grand jury; and arraignment, at which the defendant may enter a plea. This chapter points out that guilty pleas, when they are made, are often not as straightforward as they might seem and are typically arrived at only after complex negotiations known as plea bargaining.

- The criminal trial involves an adversarial process that pits the prosecution against the defense. Trials are peer-based fact-finding processes intended to protect the rights of the accused while disputed issues of guilt or innocence are resolved. The primary purpose of a criminal trial is to determine whether a defendant, through his or her behavior, violated the criminal law of the jurisdiction in which the court has authority.

- A criminal trial has eight stages: trial initiation, jury selection, opening statements, the presentation of evidence, closing arguments, the judge's charge to the jury, jury deliberations, and the verdict. Each is described in detail in this chapter. At least a few experts have suggested the training and use of a cadre of professional jurors, versed in the law and in trial practice, who could insulate themselves from media portrayals of famous defendants and who would resolve questions of guilt or innocence more on the basis of reason than emotion.

- The American court system has been called into question by some well-publicized trials of the last two decades, which have demonstrated apparent weaknesses in the trial process. Some people suggest that court unification might help address a number of today's problems by reducing the number of jurisdictions—resulting in more uniform procedures.

KEY TERMS

adversarial system, 360

bail bond, 353

circumstantial evidence, 367

closing argument, 371

competent to stand trial, 358

conditional release, 354

danger law, 355

direct evidence, 367

evidence, 367

first appearance, 351

hearsay, 371

hearsay rule, 371

jury selection, 363

nolo contendere, 358

opening statement, 367

peremptory challenge, 363

perjury, 369

plea, 358

plea bargaining, 358

pretrial release, 352

probative value, 369

property bond, 354

real evidence, 367

release on recognizance (ROR), 354

rules of evidence, 360

scientific jury selection, 364

sequestered jury, 364

Speedy Trial Act, 362

testimony, 369

verdict, 372

KEY CASES

County of Riverside v. *McLaughlin*, 351

Coy v. *Iowa*, 370

Doggett v. *U.S.*, 362

Edmonson v. *Leesville Concrete Co., Inc.*, 366

Fex v. *Michigan*, 362

Georgia v. *McCollum*, 366

Idaho v. *Wright*, 370

Maryland v. *Craig*, 370

McNabb v. *U.S.*, 351

Michigan v. *Lucas*, 367

Miller-El v. *Cockrell*, 366

Mu'Min v. *Virginia*, 364

Powers v. *Ohio*, 366

U.S. v. *Montalvo-Murillo*, 356

White v. *Illinois*, 370

QUESTIONS FOR REVIEW

1. What steps are typically taken during pretrial activities (that is, before the start of a criminal trial)?

2. What is the purpose of a criminal trial? What is the difference between factual guilt and legal guilt? What do we mean by the term *adversarial system*?

3. What are the various stages of a criminal trial? Describe each one.

4. How might the adjudication process be improved?

QUESTIONS FOR REFLECTION

1. Before trial, courts may act to shield the accused from the punitive power of the state through the use of pretrial release. In doing so, how can they balance the rights of the defendant against the potential for future harm that he or she may represent?

2. A significant issue facing pretrial decision makers is how to ensure that all defendants, rich and poor, black and white, male and female, are afforded the same degree of protection from unfair processing by the criminal justice system. How can that be achieved?

3. What is plea bargaining, and what is its function? To what kinds of cases is it most suited?

4. What purpose does plea bargaining serve for the defense? For the prosecution? Given the criticisms leveled against plea bargaining, do you believe that it's an acceptable practice? Explain.

5. Might recent advances in technology, such as DNA fingerprinting, possibly supplant the role of advocacy in the fact-finding process that is today regarded as central to criminal trials? If so, how? If not, why not?

6. What exceptions to the hearsay rule have courts recognized? Describe the reasoning behind these exceptions.

7. Do you think the present jury system is outmoded? Why? How might a professional jury system be more effective than the present system of peer jurors?

Discuss your answers to these questions and other issues on the CJ Today e-mail discussion list (join the list at cjtoday.com).

WEB QUEST

Visit Court TV on the Web by going to http://www.courttv.com. Once there, click on "Trial Coverage" and then on "Trials." Browse through some of the recent criminal cases displayed on the site. Which of the cases listed there do you find the most interesting? What aspects of the cases are most compelling? Write down your answers, along with a description of each of the cases you've chosen, and submit what you've written to your instructor if asked to do so.

To complete this Web Quest online, go to the Web Quest module in Chapter 10 of the *Criminal Justice Today* Companion Website at cjtoday.com.

CHAPTER 11

Sentencing

LEARNING OBJECTIVES

After reading this chapter, you should be able to

- Describe the five goals of contemporary criminal sentencing.
- Describe the nature of indeterminate sentencing and explain its purpose.
- Describe the nature of structured sentencing and describe the different types of structured sentencing models in use today.
- Identify alternative sanctions and assess recent sentencing innovations.
- Describe the nature and importance of the presentence investigation report.
- Describe the history of victims' rights and services and discuss the growing role of the victim in criminal justice proceedings today.
- List the four traditional sentencing options.
- Outline the arguments for and against capital punishment.

OUTLINE

In sentencing, we have gone through determinate, indeterminate and back and forth in the last century. But in our time, life moves much faster. It took a hundred years from the peak of indeterminate sentencing, or the full realization of indeterminate sentencing values in the late 1870s to 1900 to wash away by the mid-1970s. . . . Is it possible that, with things happening so much faster, in just twenty or twenty-five years the cycle might once again be changing back in a different direction?

—*Michael Tonry, Director, Institute of Criminology, Cambridge University*[1]

Developing a sentencing system that provides appropriate types and lengths of sentences for all offenders is a challenging task.

—*National Conference of State Legislatures*

Hear the author discuss
this chapter at
cjtoday.com

Introduction

On July 30, 2002, in what appeared to be an incident of vigilante justice, a small angry mob dragged two men from a crashed rental van and beat them to death with bricks and stones in a South Side Chicago neighborhood. The van had veered out of control and struck the front porch of a home, injuring three young women, one of them critically.[2] Witnesses said the vehicle appeared to accelerate wildly before hitting the women. "It all happened so fast, it seemed like he floored it or something," said witness Taquita Mixon, who saw the incident from her apartment window.[3] A bystander told reporters that one of the young men involved in the killings was the boyfriend of the critically injured woman.

While some in the neighborhood were ready to forgive the killers, others wanted them brought to trial. "It was an accident," one woman said of the beating. "I think emotions just got out of hand."[4] Another person disagreed, calling for those who participated in the killings to be arrested. "It's not going to bring them back, but it'll let them know you can't take the law in your own hands," she said.

In vigilante justice, a mob typically decides the fate of suspects before they can be fairly tried and formally sentenced. Under an organized system of criminal justice, **sentencing** is the imposition of a penalty on a person convicted of a crime. Sentencing follows an impartial judicial proceeding during which criminal responsibility is ascertained. Most sentencing decisions are made by judges, although in some cases, especially where a death sentence is possible, juries may be involved in a special sentencing phase of courtroom proceedings. The sentencing decision is one of the most difficult made by any judge or jury. Not only does it affect the future of the defendant—and at times it is a decision about his or her life or death—but society looks to sentencing to achieve a diversity of goals, some of which are not fully compatible with others.

This chapter examines sentencing in terms of both philosophy and practice. We will describe the goals of sentencing as well as the historical development of various sentencing models in the United States. This chapter also contains a detailed overview of victimization and victims' rights in general, especially as they relate to courtroom procedure and to sentencing practice. Federal sentencing guidelines and the significance of presentence investigations are also described. For an overview of sentencing issues, visit the Sentencing Project via Web Extra 11–1 at cjtoday.com. Resources on sentencing and sentencing law are available at Web Extra 11–2.

sentencing

The imposition of a criminal sanction by a judicial authority.

WEB
Extra
▪▪▪▪

If you want a small prison population, make punishment certain. If you want a large prison population, make punishment uncertain.

—*Former House Speaker Newt Gingrich*

The Philosophy and Goals of Criminal Sentencing

Traditional sentencing options have included imprisonment, fines, probation, and—for very serious offenses—death. Limits on the range of options available to sentencing authorities are generally specified by law. Historically, those limits have shifted as understanding of crime and the goals of sentencing have changed. Sentencing philosophies, or the justifications on which various sentencing strategies are based, are manifestly intertwined with issues of religion, morals, values, and emotions.[5] Philosophies that gained ascendancy at a particular point in history usually reflected more deeply held social values. Centuries ago, for example, it was thought that crime was due to sin and that suffering was the culprit's due. Judges were expected to be harsh. Capital punishment, torture, and painful physical penalties served this view of criminal behavior.

An emphasis on equitable punishments became prevalent around the time of the American and French Revolutions, brought about in part by Enlightenment philosophies. Offenders came to be seen as highly rational beings who intentionally and somewhat carefully chose their course of action. Sentencing philosophies of the period stressed the need for sanctions that outweighed the benefits to be derived from criminal activity. The severity of punishment became less important than quick and certain penalties.

Recent thinking has emphasized the need to limit offenders' potential for future harm by separating them from society. We also still believe that offenders deserve to be punished, and we have not entirely abandoned hope for their rehabilitation. Modern sentencing practices are influenced by five goals, which weave their way through widely disseminated professional and legal models, continuing public calls for sentencing reform, and everyday sentencing practice. Each goal represents a quasi-independent sentencing philosophy, since each makes distinctive assumptions about human nature and holds implications for sentencing practice. These are the five goals of contemporary sentencing:

- Retribution
- Incapacitation
- Deterrence
- Rehabilitation
- Restoration

Retribution

Retribution is a call for punishment based on a perceived need for vengeance. Retribution is the earliest known rationale for punishment. Most early societies punished all offenders who were caught. Early punishments were immediate—often without the benefit of a hearing—and they were often extreme, with little thought given to whether the punishment "fit" the crime. Death and exile, for

As a society we have at least in part created what we fear—a mass of convicts running loose through our society but unintegrated, hopeless, and hell-bent for reinstitutionalization, due in part to our focus on unrelenting lifelong punishment.

—Bernard H. Levin, Blue Ridge Community College[i]

retribution

The act of taking revenge on a criminal perpetrator.

A courtroom drawing showing Rosemary Dillard, whose husband was killed on September 11, 2001, speaking to Zacarias Moussaoui, as family members of 9/11 victims listen. The scene took place in U.S. District Court in Alexandria, Virginia, during the sentencing hearing for the convicted al-Qaeda conspirator. On May 4, 2006, federal judge Leonie M. Brinkema sentenced Moussaoui to life in prison with no possibility of release. What was Moussaoui's crime? Do you think that his sentence was just and fair? Might it deter other would be terrorists?

Dana Verkouteren/AP Wide World Photos

example, were commonly imposed, even for relatively minor offenses. The Old Testament dictum of "an eye for an eye, a tooth for a tooth"—often cited as an ancient justification for retribution—was actually intended to reduce the severity of punishment for relatively minor crimes.

Today, retribution corresponds to the **just deserts** model of sentencing, which holds that offenders are responsible for their crimes. When they are convicted and punished, they are said to have gotten their "just deserts." Retribution sees punishment as deserved, justified, and even required[6] by the offender's behavior. The primary sentencing tool of the just deserts model is imprisonment, but in extreme cases capital punishment (that is, death) becomes the ultimate retribution.

In both the public's view and in political policy making, retribution is still a primary goal of criminal sentencing. During the 1990s, as the public-order perspective with its emphasis on individual responsibility became dominant, public demands for retribution-based criminal punishments grew loud and clear. In the mid-1990s, for example, the Mississippi legislature, encouraged by then-Governor Kirk Fordice, voted to ban prison air-conditioning, remove privately owned television sets from prison cells and dormitories, and prohibit weight lifting by inmates. Governor Fordice sent a "get tough" proposal to the legislature, which was quickly dubbed the "Clint Eastwood Hang 'Em High Bill"[7] and which required inmates to wear striped uniforms with the word *CONVICT* stamped on the back. State Representative Mac McInnis explained the state's retribution-inspired fervor this way: "We want a prisoner to look like a prisoner, to smell like a prisoner."[8] As critics note, however, none of these measures are likely to deter crime, but that is beside the point. The goal of retribution, after all, is not deterrence, but satisfaction.[9]

Incapacitation

Incapacitation, the second goal of criminal sentencing, seeks to protect innocent members of society from offenders who might harm them if not prevented from doing so. In ancient times, mutilation and amputation of the extremities were sometimes used to prevent offenders from repeating their crimes. Modern incapacitation strategies separate offenders from the community to reduce opportunities for further criminality. Incapacitation, sometimes called the "lock 'em up approach," forms the basis for the modern movement toward prison "warehousing."

Unlike retribution, incapacitation requires only restraint—and not punishment. Hence, advocates of the incapacitation philosophy of sentencing are sometimes also active prison reformers, who want to humanize correctional institutions. Innovations in confinement offer new ways to achieve the goal of incapacitation without imprisonment. Remote location monitoring (discussed in Chapter 12) and biomedical intervention (such as "chemical castration") may offer alternatives to imprisonment.

Deterrence

Deterrence uses the example or threat of punishment to convince people that criminal activity is not worthwhile. Its overall goal is crime prevention. **Specific deterrence** seeks to reduce the likelihood of recidivism (repeat offenses) by convicted offenders, while **general deterrence** strives to influence the future behavior of people who have not yet been arrested and who may be tempted to turn to crime.

Deterrence is one of the more "rational" goals of sentencing because it is an easily articulated goal and because it is possible to investigate objectively the amount of punishment required to deter. It is generally agreed today that harsh punishments can virtually eliminate many minor forms of criminality.[10] Few traffic tickets would have to be written, for example, if minor driving offenses were punishable by death. A free society like our own, of course, is not willing to impose extreme punishments on petty offenders, and even harsh punishments are not demonstrably effective in reducing the incidence of serious crimes, such as murder and drug running.

Deterrence is compatible with the goal of incapacitation, since at least specific deterrence can be achieved through incapacitating offenders. Tufts University Professor Hugo Adam Bedau, however, points to significant differences between retribution and deterrence.[11] Retribution is oriented toward the past, says Bedau. It seeks to redress wrongs already committed. Deterrence, in contrast, is a strategy for the future. It aims to prevent new crimes. But as legal philosopher H. L. A. Hart observed, retribution can be the means through which deterrence is achieved.[12] By serving as an example of what might happen to others, punishment may have an inhibiting effect.

Rehabilitation

Rehabilitation seeks to bring about fundamental changes in offenders and their behavior. As in the case of deterrence, the ultimate goal of rehabilitation is a reduction in the number of criminal offenses. Whereas deterrence depends on a fear of the consequences of violating the law, rehabilitation generally works through education and psychological treatment to reduce the likelihood of future criminality.

The term *rehabilitation*, however, is a misnomer for the kinds of changes that its supporters seek. Rehabilitation literally means to return a person to his or her previous condition, just as medical rehabilitation programs seek to restore functioning to atrophied limbs, to rejuvenate injured organs, and to mend shattered minds. In the case of criminal offenders, however, it is likely that in most cases restoring criminals to their previous state will result in nothing but a more youthful type of criminality.

In the late 1970s, the rehabilitative goal in sentencing fell victim to the "nothing-works doctrine." The nothing-works doctrine was based on studies of recidivism rates that consistently showed that rehabilitation was more an ideal than a reality.[13] With as many as 90% of former convicted offenders returning to lives of crime following release from prison-based treatment programs, public sentiments in favor of incapacitation grew. Although the rehabilitation ideal has clearly suffered in the public arena, emerging evidence has begun to suggest that effective treatment programs do exist and may be growing in number.[14] See Library Extra 11–1 at cjtoday.com to read more about treatment programs that work.

rehabilitation

The attempt to reform a criminal offender. Also, the state in which a reformed offender is said to be.

Nobody gets rehabilitated. Well, I shouldn't say no one; some of them die.

—Former Los Angeles Police Chief
Daryl Gates

LIBRARY
Extra
▪▪▪▪

Restoration

Victims of crime and their families are frequently traumatized by their experiences. Some victims are killed, and others receive lasting physical or emotional injuries. For many, the world is never the same. The victimized may live in constant fear, be reduced in personal vigor, and be unable to form trusting relationships. **Restoration** is a sentencing goal that seeks to address this damage by making the victim and the community "whole again."

A U.S. Department of Justice report explains restoration this way: "Crime was once defined as a 'violation of the State.' This remains the case today, but we now recognize that crime is far more. It is—among other things—a violation of one person by another. While retributive justice

restoration

A goal of criminal sentencing that attempts to make the victim "whole again."

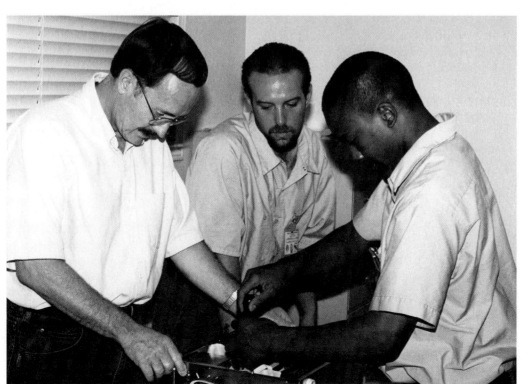

Inmates in a California prison learning how to repair computer equipment. Skills acquired through such prison programs might translate into productive, noncriminal careers for ex-convicts. Rehabilitation is an important, but infrequently voiced, goal of modern sentencing practices. What are some other sentencing goals identified in this chapter?
Courtesy of Robert W. Winslow

may address the first type of violation adequately, restorative justice is required to effectively address the latter. . . . Thus [through restorative justice] we seek to attain a balance between the legitimate needs of the community, the . . . offender, and the victim."[15] The "healing" of all parties has many aspects, ranging from victim assistance initiatives to legislation supporting victims' compensation.

restorative justice (RJ)

A sentencing model that builds on restitution and community participation in an attempt to make the victim "whole again."

Restorative justice (RJ) is also referred to as *balanced and restorative justice*. Conceptually, "balance" is achieved by giving equal consideration to community safety and offender accountability. Restorative justice focuses on "crime as harm, and justice as repairing the harm."[16] The community safety dimension of the RJ philosophy recognizes that the justice system has a responsibility to protect the public from crime and from offenders.[17] It also recognizes that the community can participate in ensuring its own safety. The accountability element defines criminal conduct in terms of obligations incurred by the offender, both to the victim and to the community.[18] RJ also has what some describe as a competency development element, which holds that offenders who enter the justice system should leave it more capable of participating successfully in the wider society than when they entered. In essence, RJ is community-focused; its primary goal is improving the quality of life for all members of the community. See Table 11–1 for a comparison of retributive and restorative justice.

Sentencing options that seek to restore the victim have focused primarily on restitution payments that offenders are ordered to make, either to their victims or to a general fund, which may then go to reimburse victims for suffering, lost wages, and medical expenses. In support of these goals, the 1984 Federal Comprehensive Crime Control Act specifically requires that "[i]f sentenced to probation, the defendant must also be ordered to pay a fine, make restitution, and/or work in community service."[19]

The root of revenge is in the weakness of the Soul; the most abject and timorous are the most addicted to it.

—Akhenaton (circa 1375 B.C.)

Vermont began a new Sentencing Options Program in 1995 built around the concept of reparative probation. According to state officials, the Vermont reparative options program, which "requires the offender to make reparations to the victim and to the community, marks the first time in the United States that the Restorative Justice model has been embraced by a state department of corrections and implemented on a statewide scale."[20] Vermont's reparative program builds on "community reparative boards" consisting of five or six citizens from the community where

TABLE 11–1 Differences between Retributive and Restorative Justice	
Retributive Justice	**Restorative Justice**
Crime is an act against the state, a violation of a law, an abstract idea.	Crime is an act against another person or the community.
The criminal justice system controls crime.	Crime control lies primarily with the community.
Offender accountability is defined as taking punishment.	Offender accountability is defined as assuming responsibility and taking action to repair harm.
Crime is an individual act with individual responsibility.	Crime has both individual and social dimensions of responsibility.
Victims are peripheral to the process of resolving a crime.	Victims are central to the process of resolving a crime.
The offender is defined by deficits.	The offender is defined by the capacity to make reparation.
The emphasis is on adversarial relationships.	The emphasis is on dialogue and negotiation.
Pain is imposed to punish, deter, and prevent.	Restitution is a means of restoring both parties; the goal is reconciliation.
The community is on the sidelines, represented abstractly by the state.	The community is the facilitator in the restorative process.
The response is focused on the offender's past behavior.	The response is focused on harmful consequences of the offender's behavior; the emphasis is on the future and on reparation.
There is dependence on proxy professionals.	There is direct involvement by both the offender and the victim.

Source: Adapted from Gordon Bazemore and Mark S. Umbreit, *Balanced and Restorative Justice: Program Summary* (Washington, DC: Office of Juvenile Justice and Delinquency Prevention, 1994), p. 7.

the crime was committed. It requires face-to-face public meetings between the offender and board representatives. Keeping in mind the program's avowed goals of "making the victim(s) whole again" and having the offender "make amends to the community," board members determine the specifics of the offender's sentence. Options are restitution, community service work, victim–offender mediation, victim empathy programs, driver improvement courses, and the like.

Some advocates of the restoration philosophy of sentencing point out that restitution payments and work programs that benefit the victim can also have the added benefit of rehabilitating the offender. The hope is that such sentences will teach offenders personal responsibility through structured financial obligations, job requirements, and regularly scheduled payments. Learn more about restorative justice by visiting Library Extras 11–2 and 11–3 and Web Extra 11–3 at cjtoday.com.

> *Putting people in prison is the single most important thing we've done [to decrease crime].*
>
> *—James Q. Wilson, Professor Emeritus, University of California at Los Angeles[ii]*

LIBRARY
Extra

WEB
Extra

Indeterminate Sentencing

While the *philosophy* of criminal sentencing is reflected in the goals of sentencing we have just discussed, different sentencing *practices* have been linked to each goal. During most of the twentieth century, for example, the rehabilitation goal was influential. Since rehabilitation requires that individual offenders' personal characteristics be closely considered in defining effective treatment strategies, judges were generally permitted wide discretion in choosing from among sentencing options. Although incapacitation is increasingly becoming the sentencing strategy of choice today, many state criminal codes still allow judges to impose fines, probation, or widely varying prison terms, all for the same offense. These sentencing practices, characterized primarily by vast judicial choice, constitute an **indeterminate sentencing** model.

Indeterminate sentencing has both a historical and a philosophical basis in the belief that convicted offenders are more likely to participate in their own rehabilitation if participation will reduce the amount of time they have to spend in prison. Inmates exhibiting good behavior will be released early, while recalcitrant inmates will remain in prison until the end of their terms. For that reason, parole generally plays a significant role in states that employ the indeterminate sentencing model.

Indeterminate sentencing relies heavily on judges' discretion to choose among types of sanctions and to set upper and lower limits on the length of prison stays. Indeterminate sentences are typically imposed with wording like this: "The defendant shall serve not less than five and not more than twenty-five years in the state's prison, under the supervision of the state department of correction." Judicial discretion under the indeterminate model also extends to the imposition of concurrent or consecutive sentences when the offender is convicted on more than one charge. Consecutive sentences are served one after the other, while concurrent sentences expire simultaneously.

The indeterminate model was also created to take into consideration detailed differences in degrees of guilt. Under this model, judges can weigh minute differences among cases, situations, and offenders. All of the following can be considered before sentence is passed: (1) whether the offender committed the crime out of a need for money, for the thrill it afforded, out of a desire for revenge, or "just for the hell of it"; (2) how much harm the offender intended; (3) how much the victim contributed to his or her own victimization; (4) the extent of the damages inflicted; (5) the mental state of the offender; (6) the likelihood of successful rehabilitation; and (7) the degree of the offender's cooperation with authorities. Under the indeterminate sentencing model, the inmate's behavior while incarcerated is the primary determinant of the amount of time served. State parole boards wield great discretion under this model, acting as the final arbiters of the actual sentence served.

A few states employ a partially indeterminate sentencing model. They allow judges to specify only the maximum amount of time to be served. Some minimum is generally implied by law but is not under the control of the sentencing authority. General practice is to set one year as a minimum for all felonies, although a few jurisdictions assume no minimum time at all, making offenders eligible for immediate parole.

indeterminate sentencing

A model of criminal punishment that encourages rehabilitation through the use of general and relatively unspecific sentences (such as a term of imprisonment of from one to ten years).

Critiques of Indeterminate Sentencing

Indeterminate sentencing is still the rule in many jurisdictions, including Georgia, Hawaii, Iowa, Kentucky, Massachusetts, Michigan, Nevada, New York, North Dakota, Oklahoma, Rhode Island, South Carolina, South Dakota, Texas, Utah, Vermont, West Virginia, and Wyoming.[21] Since the 1970s, however, the model has come under fire for contributing to inequality in sentencing. Critics claim that the indeterminate model allows judges' personalities and personal philosophies to produce too wide a range of sentencing practices, from very lenient to very strict. The indeterminate model is also criticized for perpetuating a system under which offenders might be sentenced, at least by some judges, more on the basis of personal and social characteristics, such as race, gender, and social class, than on culpability.

Because of the personal nature of judicial decisions under the indeterminate model, offenders often depend on the advice and ploys of their attorneys to appear before a judge who is thought to be a good sentencing risk. Requests for delays are a common defense strategy in indeterminate sentencing states, where they are used to try to manipulate the selection of the judge involved in the sentencing decision.

Another charge leveled against indeterminate sentencing is that it tends to produce "dishonesty" in sentencing. Because of sentence cutbacks for good behavior and involvement in work and study programs, time served in prison is generally far less than sentences would seem to indicate. An inmate sentenced to five to ten years, for example, might actually be released in a couple of years after all **gain time**, **good time**, and other special allowances have been calculated. (Some of the same charges can be leveled against determinate sentencing schemes under which corrections officials can administratively reduce the time served by an inmate.) A recent survey by the Bureau of Justice Statistics found that even violent offenders released from state prisons during the study period served, on average, only 51% of the sentences they originally received.[22] Nonviolent offenders served even smaller portions of their sentences. Table 11–2 shows the percentage of an imposed sentence that an offender sentenced to state prison in 1996 could expect to serve.

To ensure long prison terms in indeterminate jurisdictions, some court officials have gone to extremes. In 1994, for example, Oklahoma Judge Dan Owens sentenced convicted child molester Charles Scott Robinson to 30,000 years in prison.[23] Judge Owens, complying with the jury's efforts to ensure that Robinson would spend the rest of his life behind bars, sentenced him to serve six consecutive 5,000-year sentences. Robinson had 14 previous felony convictions.

Structured Sentencing

Until the 1970s, all 50 states used some form of indeterminate (or partially indeterminate) sentencing. Eventually, however, calls for equity and proportionality in sentencing, heightened by claims of racial disparity in the sentencing practices of some judges,[24] led many states to move toward greater control over their sentencing systems.

Critics of the indeterminate model called for the recognition of three fundamental sentencing principles: **proportionality**, **equity**, and **social debt**. Proportionality refers to the belief that the severity of sanctions should bear a direct relationship to the seriousness of the crime committed. Equity means that similar crimes should be punished with the same degree of severity, regardless of the social or personal characteristics of offenders. According to the principle of equity, for example, two bank robbers in different parts of the country, who use the same techniques and weapons, with the same degree of implied threat, should receive roughly the same sentence even though they are tried under separate circumstances and in different jurisdictions. The equity principle needs to be balanced, however, against the notion of social debt. In the case of the bank robbers, the offender who has a prior criminal record can be said to have a higher level of social

gain time

The amount of time deducted from time to be served in prison on a given sentence as a consequence of participation in special projects or programs.

good time

The amount of time deducted from time to be served in prison on a given sentence as a consequence of good behavior.

proportionality

A sentencing principle that holds that the severity of sanctions should bear a direct relationship to the seriousness of the crime committed.

equity

A sentencing principle, based on concerns with social equality, that holds that similar crimes should be punished with the same degree of severity, regardless of the social or personal characteristics of the offenders.

social debt

A sentencing principle that holds that an offender's criminal history should objectively be taken into account in sentencing decisions.

TABLE 11–2 Percentage of Sentence Likely to Be Served, by New Court Commitments to State Prison	
Offense Type	**Percentage**
Violent	51
Property	46
Drug	46
Public-order	49
Average for all felonies	49

Source: Paula M. Ditton and Doris James Wilson, *Truth in Sentencing in State Prisons* (Washington, DC: Bureau of Justice Statistics, 1999).

debt than the first-time robber, where all else is equal. Greater social debt, of course, suggests a more severe punishment or a greater need for treatment.

Beginning in the 1970s, a number of states addressed these concerns by developing a different model of sentencing, known as **structured sentencing**. One form of structured sentencing, called **determinate sentencing**, requires that a convicted offender be sentenced to a fixed term that may be reduced by good time (time off for good behavior) or earned time (time off in recognition of special efforts on the part of the inmate). Determinate sentencing states eliminated the use of parole and created explicit standards to specify the amount of punishment appropriate for a given offense. Determinate sentencing practices also specify an anticipated release date for each sentenced offender.

In a 1996 report that traced the historical development of determinate sentencing, the National Council on Crime and Delinquency (NCCD) observed that "the term 'determinate sentencing' is generally used to refer to the sentencing reforms of the late 1970s." At that time, the legislatures of California, Illinois, Indiana, and Maine abolished the parole release decision and replaced indeterminate penalties with fixed (or flat) sentences that could be reduced by good-time provisions. In response to the then-growing determinate sentencing movement, a few states developed **voluntary/advisory sentencing guidelines** during the 1980s. These guidelines consist of recommended sentencing policies that are not required by law and serve as guides to judges. Voluntary/advisory sentencing guidelines are usually based on past sentencing practices and may build on either determinate or indeterminate sentencing structures. Florida, Maryland, Massachusetts, Michigan, Rhode Island, Utah, and Wisconsin all experimented with voluntary/advisory guidelines during the 1980s. Voluntary/advisory guidelines constitute a second form of structured sentencing.

A third model of structured sentencing employs what NCCD calls "commission-based presumptive sentencing guidelines." **Presumptive sentencing** became common in the 1980s as states began to experiment with sentencing guidelines developed by sentencing commissions. These models differed from both determinate and voluntary/advisory guidelines in three respects. First, presumptive sentencing guidelines were not developed by the state legislature but by a sentencing commission that often represented a diverse array of criminal justice and sometimes private interests. Second, presumptive sentencing guidelines were explicit and highly structured, typically relying on a quantitative scoring instrument to classify the offense for which a person was to be sentenced. Third, the guidelines were not voluntary in that judges had to adhere to the sentencing system or provide a written rationale for departing from it.

By 2006, the federal government and 16 states had established commission-created sentencing guidelines. Ten of the 16 states used presumptive sentencing guidelines. The remaining six relied on voluntary/advisory guidelines. As a consequence, with the advent of the twenty-first century, sentencing guidelines authored by legislatively created sentencing commissions had become the most popular form of structured sentencing. Learn more about the history of sentencing reform via Library Extras 11–4 and 11–5 at cjtoday.com.

Guideline jurisdictions, which specified a presumptive sentence for a given offense, generally allowed for "aggravating" or "mitigating" circumstances—indicating a greater or lesser degree of culpability—which judges could take into consideration when imposing a sentence somewhat at variance from the presumptive term. **Aggravating circumstances** call for a tougher sentence and may include especially heinous behavior, cruelty, injury to more than one person, and so on. **Mitigating circumstances**, which indicate that a lesser sentence is called for, are generally similar to legal defenses, although in this case they only reduce criminal responsibility, not eliminate it. Mitigating circumstances include such things as cooperation with the investigating authority, surrender, and good character. Common aggravating and mitigating circumstances are listed in CJ Today Exhibit 11–1.

Federal Sentencing Guidelines

In 1984, with the passage of the Comprehensive Crime Control Act, the federal government adopted presumptive sentencing for nearly all federal offenders.[25] The act also addressed the issue of **truth in sentencing**. Under the old federal system, on average, good-time credits and parole reduced time served to about one-third of the actual sentence.[26] At the time, the sentencing practices of most states reflected the federal model. While sentence reductions may have benefited offenders, they often outraged victims, who felt betrayed by the sentencing process. The 1984 act nearly eliminated good-time credits[27] and began the process of phasing out federal parole and eliminating the U.S. Parole Commission (read more about the commission in Chapter 12).[28] The emphasis on truth in sentencing created, in effect, a sentencing environment of "what

---

structured sentencing

A model of criminal punishment that includes determinate and commission-created presumptive sentencing schemes, as well as voluntary/advisory sentencing guidelines.

determinate sentencing

A model of criminal punishment in which an offender is given a fixed term of imprisonment that may be reduced by good time or gain time. Under the model, for example, all offenders convicted of the same degree of burglary would be sentenced to the same length of time behind bars.

voluntary/advisory sentencing guidelines

Recommended sentencing policies that are not required by law.

presumptive sentencing

A model of criminal punishment that meets the following conditions: (1) The appropriate sentence for an offender convicted of a specific charge is presumed to fall within a range of sentences authorized by sentencing guidelines that are adopted by a legislatively created sentencing body, usually a sentencing commission. (2) Sentencing judges are expected to sentence within the range or to provide written justification for failing to do so. (3) There is a mechanism for review, usually appellate, of any departure from the guidelines.

LIBRARY
Extra
■ ■ ■ ■

aggravating circumstances

Circumstances relating to the commission of a crime that make it more grave than the average instance of that crime.

mitigating circumstances

Circumstances relating to the commission of a crime that may be considered to reduce the blameworthiness of the defendant.

truth in sentencing

A close correspondence between the sentence imposed on an offender and the time actually served in prison.[iii]

CJ Today Exhibit 11–1

Aggravating and Mitigating Circumstances

Listed here are typical aggravating and mitigating circumstances that judges may consider in arriving at sentencing decisions in presumptive sentencing jurisdictions.

AGGRAVATING CIRCUMSTANCES

- The defendant induced others to participate in the commission of the offense.
- The offense was especially heinous, atrocious, or cruel.
- The defendant was armed with or used a deadly weapon during the crime.
- The defendant committed the offense to avoid or prevent a lawful arrest or to escape from custody.
- The offense was committed for hire.
- The offense was committed against a current or former law enforcement or corrections officer while engaged in the performance of official duties or because of the past exercise of official duties.
- The defendant took advantage of a position of trust or confidence to commit the offense.

MITIGATING CIRCUMSTANCES

- The defendant has no record of criminal convictions punishable by more than 60 days of imprisonment.
- The defendant has made substantial or full restitution.
- The defendant has been a person of good character or has had a good reputation in the community.
- The defendant aided in the apprehension of another felon or testified truthfully on behalf of the prosecution.
- The defendant acted under strong provocation, or the victim was a voluntary participant in the criminal activity or otherwise consented to it.
- The offense was committed under duress, coercion, threat, or compulsion that was insufficient to constitute a defense but that significantly reduced the defendant's culpability.
- At the time of the offense, the defendant was suffering from a mental or physical condition that was insufficient to constitute a defense but that significantly reduced the defendant's culpability.

Note: Recent U.S. Supreme Court rulings have held that facts influencing sentencing enhancements, other than prior record or admissions made by a defendant, must be determined by a jury, not by a judge.

you get is what you serve." Truth in sentencing, described as "a close correspondence between the sentence imposed upon those sent to prison and the time actually served prior to prison release,"[29] has become an important policy focus of many state legislatures and the U.S. Congress. The Violent Crime Control and Law Enforcement Act of 1994 set aside $4 billion in federal prison construction funds (called Truth in Sentencing Incentive Funds) for states that adopt truth-in-sentencing laws and are able to guarantee that certain violent offenders will serve 85% of their sentences.

Title II of the Comprehensive Crime Control Act, called the Sentencing Reform Act of 1984,[30] established the nine-member U.S. Sentencing Commission. The commission, which continues to function today, comprises presidential appointees, including three federal judges. The Sentencing Reform Act limited the discretion of federal judges by mandating the creation of federal sentencing guidelines, which federal judges were required to follow. The sentencing commission was given the task of developing structured sentencing guidelines to reduce disparity, promote consistency and uniformity, and increase fairness and equity in sentencing.

The guidelines established by the commission took effect in November 1987 but quickly became embroiled in a series of legal disputes, some of which challenged Congress's authority to form the Sentencing Commission. In January 1989, in the case of *Mistretta* v. *U.S.*,[31] the U.S. Supreme Court held that Congress had acted appropriately in establishing the Sentencing Commission and that the guidelines developed by the commission could be applied in federal cases nationwide. The federal Sentencing Commission continues to meet at least once a year to review the effectiveness of the guidelines it created. Visit the U.S. Sentencing Commission via Web Extra 11–4 at cjtoday.com.

WEB Extra

FEDERAL GUIDELINE PROVISIONS

As originally established, federal sentencing guidelines specified a sentencing range from which judges had to choose. If a particular case had "atypical features," judges were allowed to depart from the guidelines. Departures were generally expected only in the presence of aggravating or mitigating circumstances—a number of which are specified in the guidelines.[32] Aggravating circumstances may include the possession of a weapon during the commission of a crime, the degree of criminal involvement (whether the defendant was a leader or a follower in the criminal activity), and extreme psychological injury to the victim. Punishments also increase when a defendant violates a position of public or private trust, uses special skills to commit or conceal offenses, or has a criminal history. Defendants who express remorse, cooperate with authorities, or willingly make restitution may have their sentences reduced under the guidelines. Any departure from the guidelines may, however, become the basis for appellate review concerning the reasonableness of the sentence imposed, and judges who deviate from the guidelines were originally required to provide written reasons for doing so.

Federal sentencing guidelines are built around a table containing 43 rows, each corresponding to one offense level. The penalties associated with each level overlap those of the levels above and below to discourage unnecessary litigation. A person convicted of a crime involving $11,000, for example, and sentenced under the guidelines, is unlikely to receive a penalty substantially greater than if the amount had been somewhat less than $10,000. A change of six levels roughly doubles the sentence imposed under the guidelines, regardless of the level at which one starts. Because of their matrix-like quality, federal sentencing provisions have been referred to as *structured*. The federal sentencing table is available at Web Extra 11–5 at cjtoday.com.

The sentencing table also contains six rows corresponding to the criminal history category into which an offender falls. Criminal history categories are determined on a point basis. Offenders earn points for previous convictions. Each prior sentence of imprisonment for more than one year and one month counts as three points. Two points are assigned for each prior prison sentence over six months or if the defendant committed the offense while on probation, parole, or work release. The system also assigns points for other types of previous convictions and for offenses committed less than two years after release from imprisonment. Points are added to determine the criminal history category into which an offender falls. Thirteen points or more are required for the highest category. At each offense level, sentences in the highest criminal history category are generally two to three times as severe as for the lowest category.

Defendants may also move into the highest criminal history category by virtue of being designated a career offender. Under the sentencing guidelines, a defendant is a career offender if "(1) the defendant was at least 18 years old at the time of the . . . offense, (2) the . . . offense is a crime of violence or trafficking in a controlled substance, and (3) the defendant has at least two prior felony convictions of either a crime of violence or a controlled substance offense."[33]

According to the U.S. Supreme Court, an offender may be adjudged a career offender in a single hearing, even when previous convictions are lacking. In *Deal* v. *U.S.* (1993),[34] the defendant, Thomas Lee Deal, was convicted in a single proceeding of six counts of carrying and using a firearm during a series of bank robberies in the Houston, Texas, area. A federal district court sentenced him to 105 years in prison as a career offender—5 years for the first count and 20 years for each of the five other counts, with sentences to run consecutively. In the words of the Supreme Court, "We see no reason why [the defendant should not receive such a sentence], simply because he managed to evade detection, prosecution, and conviction for the first five offenses and was ultimately tried on all six in a single proceeding."

PLEA BARGAINING UNDER THE GUIDELINES

Plea bargaining plays a major role in the federal judicial system. Approximately 90% of all federal sentences are the result of guilty pleas,[35] and the large majority of those stem from plea negotiations. In the words of former Sentencing Commission Chairman William W. Wilkins, Jr., "With respect to plea bargaining, the Commission has proceeded cautiously. . . . The Commission did not believe it wise to stand the federal criminal justice system on its head by making too drastic and too sudden a change in these practices."[36]

Although the commission allowed plea bargaining to continue, it required that the agreement (1) be fully disclosed in the record of the court (unless there is an overriding and demonstrable reason why it should not be) and (2) detail the actual conduct of the offense. Under these requirements, defendants are unable to hide the actual nature of their offense behind a substitute plea. Information on the decision-making process itself is available to victims, the media, and the public.

In 1996, in the case of *Melendez* v. *U.S.*,[37] the U.S. Supreme Court held that a government motion requesting that a trial judge deviate from the federal sentencing guidelines as part of a cooperative plea agreement does not permit imposition of a sentence below a statutory minimum specified by law. In other words, under *Melendez*, while federal judges could depart from the guidelines, they could not accept plea bargains that would have resulted in sentences lower than the minimum required by law for a particular type of offense. Visit Library Extra 11–6 at cjtoday.com to read more about presumptive sentencing.

African-American men comprise less than 6% of the U.S. population and almost one-half of its criminal prisoners.

—Bureau of Justice Statistics

WEB
Extra
▪▪▪▪

LIBRARY
Extra
▪▪▪▪

CJ News

Vast DNA Bank Pits Policing versus Privacy

Brimming with the genetic patterns of more than 3 million Americans, the nation's databank of DNA "fingerprints" is growing by more than 80,000 people every month, giving police an unprecedented crime-fighting tool but prompting warnings that the expansion threatens constitutional privacy protections.

With little public debate, state and federal rules for cataloging DNA have broadened in recent years to include not only violent felons, as was originally the case, but also perpetrators of minor crimes and even people who have been arrested but not convicted.

Now some in law enforcement are calling for a national registry of every American's DNA profile, against which police could instantly compare crime-scene specimens. Advocates say the system would dissuade many would-be criminals and help capture the rest.

"This is the single best way to catch bad guys and keep them off the street," said Chris Asplen, a lawyer with the Washington firm Smith Alling Lane and former executive director of the National Commission on the Future of DNA Evidence. "When it's applied to everybody, it is fair, and frankly you wouldn't even know it was going on."

But opponents say that the growing use of DNA scans is making suspects out of many law-abiding Americans and turning the "innocent until proven guilty" maxim on its head.

"These databases are starting to look more like a surveillance tool than a tool for criminal investigation," said Tania Simoncelli of the American Civil Liberties Union in New York.

The debate is part of a larger, post-Sept. 11 tug of war between public safety and personal privacy that has intensified amid recent revelations that the government has been collecting information on personal phone calls. In particular, it is about the limits of the Fourth Amendment, which protects people from being swept into criminal investigations unless there is good reason to suspect they have broken the law.

Once someone's DNA code is in the federal database, critics say, that person is effectively treated as a suspect every time a match with a crime-scene specimen is sought—even though there is no reason to believe that the person committed the crime.

At issue is not only how many people's DNA is on file but also how the material is being used. In recent years, for example, crime fighters have initiated "DNA dragnets" in which hundreds or even thousands of people were asked to submit blood or tissue samples to help prove their innocence.

Also stirring unease is the growing use of "familial searches," in which police find crime-scene DNA that is similar to the DNA of a known criminal and then pursue that criminal's family members, reasoning that only a relative could have such a similar pattern. Critics say that makes suspects out of people just for being related to a convict.

Such concerns are amplified by fears that, in time, authorities will try to obtain information from stored DNA beyond the unique personal identifiers.

"Genetic material is a very powerful identifier, but it also happens to carry a heck of a lot of information about you," said Jim Harper, di-

A cotton swab that was used to collect a DNA sample being prepared to be sent to a lab in New Jersey. Five states allow testing of arrestees, but more are set to follow, meaning that the number of DNA profiles in government databases could soar. How might individual-rights and public-order advocates assess this issue?

Getty Images, Inc.

rector of information policy at the Cato Institute, a libertarian think tank in Washington concerned about DNA database trends.

Law enforcement officials say they have no interest in reading people's genetic secrets. The U.S. profiling system focuses on just 13 small regions of the DNA molecule—regions that do not code for any known biological or behavioral traits but vary enough to give everyone who is not an identical twin a unique 52-digit number.

"It's like a Social Security number, but not assigned by the government," said Michael Smith, a University of Wisconsin law professor who favors a national database of every American's genetic ID with certain restrictions.

Still, the blood, semen or cheek-swab specimen that yields that DNA, and which authorities almost always save, contains additional genetic information that is sensitive, including disease susceptibilities that could affect employment and health insurance prospects and, in some cases, surprises about who a child's father is.

"We don't know all the potential uses of DNA, but once the state has your sample and there are not limits on how it can be used, then the potential civil liberty violations are as vast as the uses themselves," said Carol Rose, executive director of the ACLU of Massachusetts.

She and others want samples destroyed once the identifying profile has been extracted, but the FBI favors preserving them.

Sometimes authorities need access to those samples to make sure an old analysis was done correctly, said Thomas Callaghan, who oversees the FBI database. The agency also wants to be able to use new DNA identification methods on older samples as the science improves.

Without that option, Callaghan said, "you'd be freezing the database to today's technology."

CJ News (continued)

CRIME-FIGHTING USES

Over the past dozen years, the FBI-managed national database has made more than 30,000 "cold hits," or exact matches to a known person's DNA, showing its crime-fighting potential.

In a recent case, a Canadian woman flew home the day after she was sexually assaulted in Mexico. Canadian authorities performed a semen DNA profile and, after finding no domestic matches, consulted the FBI database. The pattern matched that of a California man on probation, who was promptly found in the Mexican town where the woman had been staying and was charged by local authorities.

Congress authorized the FBI database precisely for cases like that, on the rationale that sexual predators and other violent felons tend to be repeat offenders and are likely to leave DNA behind. In recent years, however, Congress and state legislators have vastly extended the system's reach.

At least 38 states now have laws to collect DNA from people found guilty of misdemeanors, in some cases for such crimes as shoplifting and fortune-telling. At least 28 now collect from juvenile offenders, too, according to information presented last month at a Boston symposium on DNA and civil liberties, organized by the American Society of Law, Medicine and Ethics.

The federal government and five states, including Virginia, go further, allowing DNA scans of people arrested. At least four other states plan[ed] to do so [in 2006], and California will start in 2009.

Opponents of the growing inclusion of people arrested note that a large proportion of charges (fully half for felony assaults) are eventually dismissed. Blood specimens are not destroyed automatically when charges are dropped, they note, and the procedures for getting them expunged are not simple.

Even more controversial are DNA dragnets, which snare many people for whom there is no evidence of guilt. Given questions about whether such sweeps can be truly voluntary—"You know that whoever doesn't participate is going to become a 'person of interest,'" said Rose of the ACLU—some think they violate the Fourth Amendment.

Civil liberties issues aside, the sweeps rarely pay off, according to a September 2004 study by Samuel Walker, a criminology professor at the University of Nebraska. Of the 18 U.S. DNA dragnets he documented since 1990, including one in which police tested 2,300 people, only one identified the offender. And that one was limited to 25 men known to have had access to the victim, who was attacked while incapacitated in a nursing home.

Dragnets, Walker concluded, "are highly unproductive" and "possibly unconstitutional."

Familial searches of the blood relatives of known offenders raise similar issues. The method can work: In a recent British case, police retrieved DNA from a brick that was thrown from an overpass and smashed through a windshield, killing the driver. A near-match of that DNA with someone in Britain's criminal database led police to investigate that offender's relatives, one of whom confessed when confronted with the evidence.

Not investigating such leads "would be like getting a partial license plate number on a getaway car and saying, 'Well, you didn't get the whole plate so we're not going to investigate the crime,'" said Frederick Bieber, a Harvard geneticist who studies familial profiling.

But such profiling stands to exacerbate already serious racial inequities in the U.S. criminal justice system, said Troy Duster, a sociologist at New York University.

"Incarceration rates are eight times higher for blacks than they are for whites," he said, so any technique that focuses on relatives of people in the FBI database will just expand that trend.

A UNIVERSAL DATABASE?

That's a concern that many in law enforcement raise, too—as an argument in favor of creating a universal DNA database of all Americans. The system would make everyone a suspect of sorts in every crime, they acknowledge. But every criminal, regardless of race, would be equally likely to get caught.

Opponents cite a litany of potential problems, including the billions it would cost to profile so many people and the lack of lab capacity to handle the specimens.

Backlogs are already severe, they note. The National Institute of Justice estimated in 2003 that more than 350,000 DNA samples from rape and homicide cases were waiting to be processed nationwide. As of the end of [2005], more than 250,000 samples were backlogged in California alone.

And delays can matter. In 2004, police in Indiana arrested a man after his DNA matched samples from dozens of rapes—the last 13 of which were committed during the two years it took for the sample to get through the backlog.

A big increase in tests would also generate more mistakes, said William C. Thompson, a professor of criminology, law and society at the University of California at Irvine, whose studies have found DNA lab accuracy to be "very uneven."

In one of many errors documented by Thompson, a years-old crime-scene specimen was found to match the DNA from a juvenile offender, leading police to suspect the teenager until they realized he was a baby at the time of the crime. The teenager's blood, it turned out, had been processed in the lab the same day as an older specimen was being analyzed, and one contaminated the other.

"A universal database will bring us more wrongful arrests and possibly more wrongful convictions," said Simoncelli of the ACLU.

But Asplen of Smith Alling Lane said Congress has been helping states streamline and improve their DNA processing. And he does not think a national database would violate the Constitution.

"We already take blood from every newborn to perform government-mandated tests . . . so the right to take a sample has already been decided," Asplen said. "And we have a precedent for the government to maintain an identifying number of a person."

For the latest in crime and justice news, visit the Talk Justice news feed at http://www.crimenews.info.

Source: Rick Weiss, "Vast DNA Bank Pits Policing vs. Privacy," *Washington Post*, June 3, 2006, p. A01. © 2006, The *Washington Post*.

The Legal Environment of Structured Sentencing

A crucial critique of aggravating factors and their use in presumptive sentencing schemes was offered by the U.S. Supreme Court in 2000 in the case of *Apprendi* v. *New Jersey*.[38] In *Apprendi*, the Court questioned the fact-finding authority of judges in making sentencing decisions, ruling that other than the fact of a prior conviction, any fact that increases the penalty for a crime beyond the prescribed statutory maximum is, in effect, an element of the crime, which must be submitted to a jury and proved beyond a reasonable doubt. The case involved Charles Apprendi, a New Jersey defendant who pleaded guilty to unlawfully possessing a firearm—an offense that carried a prison term of five to ten years under state law. Before sentence was imposed, however, the judge found that Apprendi had fired a number of shots into the home of an African American family living in his neighborhood and concluded that he had done so to frighten the family and convince them to move. The judge held that statements made by Apprendi allowed the offense to be classified as a hate crime, which required a longer prison term under the sentencing enhancement provision of New Jersey's hate-crime statute than did the weapons offense to which Apprendi had confessed. The Supreme Court, in overturning the judge's finding and sentence, took issue with the fact that after Apprendi pleaded guilty, an enhanced sentence was imposed without the benefit of a jury-based fact-finding process. The high court ruled that "under the Due Process Clause of the Fifth Amendment and the notice and jury trial guarantees of the Sixth Amendment, any fact (other than prior conviction) that increases the maximum penalty for a crime must be charged in an indictment, submitted to a jury, and proven beyond a reasonable doubt."

The *Apprendi* case essentially says that requiring sentencing judges to consider facts not proven to a jury violates the federal Constitution. It raised the question of whether judges anywhere could legitimately deviate from established sentencing guidelines or apply sentence enhancements based solely on judicial determinations of aggravating factors—especially when such determinations involve findings of fact that might otherwise be made by a jury.[39]

In 2004, in the important case of *Blakely* v. *Washington*,[40] the U.S. Supreme Court effectively invalidated any state sentencing schema that allow judges rather than juries to determine any factor that increases a criminal sentence, except for prior convictions. The Court found that because the facts supporting Blakely's increased sentence were neither admitted by the defendant himself nor found by a jury, the sentence violated the Sixth Amendment right to trial by jury. The *Blakely* decision required that the sentencing laws of eight states be rewritten. Washington state legislators responded quickly and created a model law for other legislatures to emulate. The Washington law mandates that "the facts supporting aggravating circumstances shall be proved to a jury beyond a reasonable doubt," or, "if a jury is waived, proof shall be to the court beyond a reasonable doubt." The Washington law can be read at Library Extra 11–7 at cjtoday.com.

LIBRARY
Extra
■ ■ ■ ■

In 2007, in the case of *Cunningham* v. *California*,[41] the Supreme Court applied its reasoning in *Blakely* to California's determinate sentencing law, finding the law invalid because it placed sentence-elevating fact-finding within the judge's purview. As in *Blakely*, the California law was found to violate a defendant's Sixth Amendment right to trial by jury.

In 2005, in the combined cases of *U.S.* v. *Booker*[42] and *U.S.* v. *Fanfan*,[43] attention turned to the constitutionality of federal sentencing practices that relied on extra-verdict determinations of fact in the application of sentencing enhancements. In *Booker*, the U.S. Supreme Court issued what some have called an "extraordinary opinion,"[44] which actually encompasses two separate decisions. The combined cases brought two issues before the Court: (1) whether fact-finding done by judges under federal sentencing guidelines violates the Sixth Amendment right to trial by jury; and (2) if so, whether the guidelines are themselves unconstitutional. As in the preceding cases discussed in this section, the Court found that, on the first question, defendant Freddie Booker's drug-trafficking sentence had been improperly enhanced under the guidelines on the basis of facts found solely by a judge. In the view of the Court, the Sixth Amendment right to trial by jury is violated where, under a mandatory guidelines system, a sentence is increased because of an enhancement based on facts found by the judge that were not found by a jury nor admitted by the defendant.[45] Consequently, Booker's sentence was ruled unconstitutional and invalidated. On the second question, the Court reached a compromise and did not strike down the federal guidelines as many thought it would. Instead, it held that the guidelines could be *considered* by federal judges during sentencing but that they were no longer mandatory. In effect, the decision in *Booker* and *Fanfan* turned the federal sentencing guidelines on their head, making them merely advisory and giving federal judges wide latitude in imposing punishments. While federal judges must still take the guidelines into consideration in reaching sentencing decisions, they do not have to follow them.

In 2007, however, in the case of *Rita* v. *U.S.*,[46] the Supreme Court ruled that federal appeals courts that hear challenges from defendants that challenge the defendants' prison time may presume that federal criminal sentences are reasonable if they fall within U.S. Sentencing Guidelines. The Court held that "even if the presumption increases the likelihood that the judge, not the jury, will find 'sentencing facts,' it does not violate the Sixth Amendment." The Justices reasoned that "a nonbinding appellate reasonableness presumption for Guidelines sentences does not *require* the sentencing judge to impose a Guidelines sentence."

A recent survey by the U.S. Sentencing Commission found that 61.2% of all federal sentences handed down in the year following *Booker* and *Fanfan* were within ranges specified under federal sentencing guidelines.[47] In comparison, in the year prior to *Blakely*, 72.2% were within guideline ranges.[48] In light of the Court's decisions, it is now up to Congress to reconsider federal sentencing law in light of *Booker*—a process that is under way as this book goes to press.[49] In the meantime, some expect the federal courts to be flooded with inmates appealing their sentences.

Mandatory Sentencing

Mandatory sentencing, another form of structured sentencing, deserves special mention.[50] Mandatory sentencing is just what its name implies: a structured sentencing scheme that mandates clearly enumerated punishments for specific offenses or for habitual offenders convicted of a series of crimes. Mandatory sentencing, because it is truly *mandatory*, differs from presumptive sentencing, which allows at least a limited amount of judicial discretion within ranges established by published guidelines. Some mandatory sentencing laws require only modest mandatory prison terms (for example, three years for armed robbery), while others are much more far-reaching.

Typical of far-reaching mandatory sentencing schemes are "three-strikes" laws, discussed in CJ Today Exhibit 11–2. Three-strikes laws (and, in some jurisdictions, two-strikes laws) require mandatory sentences (sometimes life in prison without the possibility of parole) for offenders convicted of a third (or second) serious felony. Such mandatory sentencing enhancements are aimed at deterring known and potentially violent offenders and are intended to incapacitate convicted criminals through long-term incarceration.

Three-strikes laws impose longer prison terms than most earlier mandatory minimum sentencing laws. California's three-strikes law, for example, requires that offenders who are convicted of a violent crime and who have had two prior convictions serve a minimum of 25 years in prison. The law doubled prison terms for offenders convicted of a second violent felony.[51]

mandatory sentencing

A structured sentencing scheme that allows no leeway in the nature of the sentence required and under which clearly enumerated punishments are mandated for specific offenses or for habitual offenders convicted of a series of crimes.

Singer Courtney Love being escorted into the Beverly Hills, California, courthouse by a Los Angeles County bailiff. In 2005, Love was sentenced to three years probation and ordered to undergo anger-management counseling, pay fines, submit to random drug tests, and perform 100 hours of community service after she pleaded "no contest" to assault charges. The charges were related to an incident at the home of an ex-boyfriend. Love also pleaded guilty to a drug charge stemming from an earlier break-in at the same residence. Should Love have gone to prison?

Nick Ut/AP Wide World Photos

CJ Today Exhibit 11–2

Three Strikes and You're Out: A Brief History of the "Get Tough on Crime" Movement

In the spring of 1994, California legislators passed the state's now-famous "three strikes and you're out" bill. Amid much fanfare, Governor Pete Wilson signed the "three-strikes" measure into law, calling it "the toughest and most sweeping crime bill in California history."[1]

California's law, which is retroactive in that it counts offenses committed before the date the legislation was signed, requires a sentence of 25 years to life for three-time felons with convictions for two or more serious or violent prior offenses. Criminal offenders facing a "second strike" can receive up to double the normal sentence for their most recent offense. Parole consideration is not available until at least 80% of the sentence has been served.

Today, about half of the states have passed three-strikes legislation, and other states may be considering it. At the federal level, the Violent Crime Control and Law Enforcement Act of 1994 contains a three-strikes provision that mandates life imprisonment for federal criminals convicted of three violent felonies or drug offenses.

Questions remain, however, about the effectiveness of three-strikes legislation, and many are concerned about its impact on the justice system. One year after it was signed into law, the California three-strikes initiative was evaluated by the RAND Corporation.[2] RAND researchers found that in the first year, more than 5,000 defendants were convicted and sentenced under the law's provisions. The large majority of those sentenced, however, had committed nonviolent crimes, causing critics of the law to argue that it is too broad. Eighty-four percent of two-strikes convictions and nearly 77% of three-strikes convictions resulted from nonviolent drug or property crimes. A similar 1997 study of three-strikes laws in 22 states, conducted by the Campaign for an Effective Crime Policy (CECP), concluded that such legislation results in clogged court systems and crowded correctional facilities while encouraging two-time felons to take dramatic risks to avoid capture for a third offense.[3] A 1998 study found that only California and Georgia were making widespread use of three-strikes laws.[4] Other states, the study found, have narrowly written laws that are applicable to repeat offenders only in rare circumstances.

A 2001 study of the original California legislation and its consequences concluded that three-strikes laws are overrated.[5] According to the study, which was conducted by the Washington, D.C.–based Sentencing Project, "California's three-strikes law has increased the number and severity of sentences for nonviolent offenders—and contributed to the aging of the prison population—but has had no significant effect on the state's decline in crime." The study found that declines in California crime rates that are often attributed to the legislation are consistent with nationwide declines in the rate of crime and would mostly have occurred without the law. "Crime had been declining for several years prior to the enactment of the three-strikes law, and what's happening in California is very consistent with what's been happening nationally, including in states with no three-strikes law," said Marc Mauer, an author of the study.

Supporters of three-strikes laws argue that those convicted under them are career criminals who will be denied the opportunity to commit more violent crimes. "The real story here is the girl somewhere that did not get raped," said Mike Reynolds, a Fresno, California, photographer whose 18-year-old daughter was killed by a paroled felon. "The real story is the robbery that did not happen," he added.[6]

Practically speaking, California's three-strikes law has had a dramatic impact on the state's criminal justice system. By 1999, more than 40,000 people had been sentenced under the law. But the law has its critics. "'Three strikes and you're out' sounds great to a lot of people," says Alan Schuman, president of the American Probation and Parole Association. "But no one will cop a plea when it gets to the third time around. We will have more trials, and this whole country works on plea bargaining and pleading guilty, not jury trials," Schuman said at a meeting of the association.[7] According to RAND, full enforcement of the law could cost as much as $5.5 billion annually—or $300 per California taxpayer.

Researchers at RAND conclude that while California's sweeping three-strikes legislation could cut serious adult crime by as much as one-third throughout the state, the high cost of enforcing the law may keep it from ever being fully implemented. In 1996, the California three-strikes controversy became even more complicated following a decision by the state supreme court (in *People* v. *Superior Court of San Diego—Romero*[8]) that California judges retain the discretion to reduce three-strikes sentences and to refuse to count previous convictions at sentencing "in furtherance of justice."

In 2003, however, in two separate cases, the U.S. Supreme Court upheld the three-strikes California convictions of Gary Ewing and Leandro Andrade in California.[9] Ewing, who had four prior felony convictions, had received a 25-year-to-life sentence following his conviction for felony grand theft of three golf clubs. Andrade, who also had a long record, was sentenced to 50 years in prison for two petty theft convictions.[10] In writing for the Court in the *Ewing* case, Justice Sandra Day O'Connor noted that states should be able to decide when repeat offenders "must be isolated from society . . . to protect the public safety," even when nonserious crimes trigger the lengthy sentence. In deciding these two cases, both of which were based on Eighth Amendment claims, the Court found that it is *not* cruel and unusual punishment to impose a possible life term for a nonviolent felony when the defendant has a history of serious or violent convictions.

In 2004, Californians voted down Proposition 66, a ballot initiative that would have changed the state's three-strikes law so that only specified serious or violent crimes could be counted as third

CJ Today Exhibit 11–2 (continued)

strikes. Passage of the proposition would also have meant that only previous convictions for violent or serious felonies, brought and tried separately, would have qualified for second- and third-strike sentence increases.

California's three-strikes law remains firmly in place. In its current form, it punishes anyone who commits a third felony, regardless of its severity, with a mandatory sentence of 25 years to life if the first two felonies were violent or serious.

[1]Michael Miller, "California Gets 'Three Strikes' Anti-Crime Bill," Reuters, March 7, 1994.

[2]Dion Nissenbaum, "Three-Strikes First Year Debated," United Press International, northern edition, March 6, 1995.

[3]Campaign for an Effective Crime Policy, *The Impact of Three Strikes and You're Out Laws: What Have We Learned?* (Washington, DC: CECP, 1997).

[4]Walter Dickey and Pam Stiebs Hollenhorst, "Three-Strikes Laws: Massive Impact in California and Georgia, Little Elsewhere," *Overcrowded Times*, Vol. 9, No. 6 (December 1998), pp. 2–8.

[5]Tamar Lewin, "Three-Strikes Law Is Overrated in California, Study Finds," *New York Times*, August 23, 2001.

[6]Bruce Smith, "Crime Solutions," Associated Press, January 11, 1995.

[7]Ryan S. King and Marc Mauer, *Aging behind Bars: "Three Strikes" Seven Years Later* (Washington, DC: Sentencing Project, August 2001).

[8]*People* v. *Superior Court of San Diego—Romero*, 13 Cal. 4th 497, 917 P.2d 628 (1996).

[9]*Ewing* v. *California*, 538 U.S. 11 (2003); and *Lockyer* v. *Andrade*, 538 U.S. 63 (2003).

[10]Under California law, a person who commits petty theft can be charged with a felony if he or she has prior felony convictions. The charge is known as "petty theft with prior convictions." Andrade's actual sentence was two 25-year prison terms to be served consecutively.

Three-strikes laws also vary in breadth. The laws of some jurisdictions stipulate that both of the prior convictions and the current one be for violent felonies; others require only that the prior convictions be for violent felonies. Some three-strikes laws count only prior adult convictions, while others permit consideration of juvenile crimes.

By passing mandatory sentencing laws, legislators convey the message that certain crimes are deemed especially grave and that people who commit them deserve, and should expect, harsh sanctions. These laws are sometimes passed in response to public outcries following heinous or well-publicized crimes.

Research findings on the impact of mandatory sentencing laws on the criminal justice system have been summarized by British criminologist Michael Tonry.[52] Tonry found that under mandatory sentencing, officials tend to make earlier and more selective arrest, charging, and **diversion** decisions. They also tend to bargain less and to bring more cases to trial. Specifically, Tonry found the following: (1) Criminal justice officials and practitioners (police, lawyers, and judges) exercise discretion to avoid the application of laws they consider unduly harsh. (2) Arrest rates for target crimes tend to decline soon after mandatory sentencing laws take effect. (3) Dismissal and diversion rates increase during the early stages of case processing after mandatory sentencing laws become effective. (4) For defendants whose cases are not dismissed, plea bargain rates decline and trial rates increase. (5) For convicted defendants, sentencing delays increase. (6) When the effects of declining arrests, indictments, and convictions are taken into account, the enactment of mandatory sentencing laws has little impact on the probability that offenders will be imprisoned. (7) Sentences become longer and more severe. Mandatory sentencing laws may also occasionally result in unduly harsh punishments for marginal offenders who nonetheless meet the minimum requirements for sentencing under such laws.

In an analysis of federal sentencing guidelines, other researchers found that blacks receive longer sentences than whites, not because of differential treatment by judges but because they constitute the large majority of those convicted of trafficking in crack cocaine (versus powdered cocaine),[53] a crime Congress has singled out for especially harsh mandatory penalties. This pattern can be seen as constituting a "disparity in results," and partly for this reason, in 1999 the U.S. Sentencing Commission recommended to Congress that it eliminate the legal distinction between crack and regular cocaine for purposes of sentencing (a recommendation that Congress rejected). Recent indications, however, are that the heightened discretion available to federal judges in the wake of *Booker* and *Fanfan* is resulting in sentences that are similar for all types of cocaine trafficking and that vary more by the amount of cocaine involved, and not the type.[54]

diversion

The official suspension of criminal or juvenile proceedings against an alleged offender at any point after a recorded justice system intake, but before the entering of a judgment, and referral of that person to a treatment or care program administered by a nonjustice or private agency. Also, release without referral.

Punishment, that is justice for the unjust.

—*Saint Augustine* (A.D. 354–430)

Sherelle Purnell, 18, of Salisbury, Maryland, walking along the street in front of a Tiger Mart gas station wearing a sign declaring her offense. On July 30, 2004, Purnell drove away from the station without paying for 2.78 gallons of fuel. Innovative judges sometimes make use of creative sentences in an attempt to deter offenders from future law violations. How effective do you think Purnell's sentence will be as a general deterrent, and whom is it most likely to deter?

Salisbury Daily Times/*Todd Dudek/AP Wide World Photos*

Innovations in Sentencing

We will not punish a man because he hath offended, but that he may offend no more; nor does punishment ever look to the past, but to the future; for it is not the result of passion, but that the same thing be guarded against in time to come.

—*Seneca (4 B.C.–A.D. 65)*

alternative sentencing

The use of court-ordered community service, home detention, day reporting, drug treatment, psychological counseling, victim–offender programming, or intensive supervision in lieu of other, more traditional sanctions, such as imprisonment and fines.

In an ever-growing number of cases, innovative judges in certain jurisdictions have begun to use discretionary sentencing to impose truly unique punishments. In 2004, for example, 18-year-old Sherelle Purnell was ordered by county judge D. William Simpson to spend three hours walking along the grassy strip between a convenience store and a busy highway in Salisbury, Maryland, wearing a sign that read "I was caught stealing gas."[55] The theft was recorded by a video surveillance device as Purnell drove away without paying for 2.78 gallons of gas from a Tiger Mart. In Memphis, Tennessee, Judge Joe Brown escorted burglary victims to thieves' homes, inviting them to take whatever they wanted.[56] An Arkansas judge made shoplifters walk in front of the stores they stole from, carrying signs describing their crimes. And in California, a purse snatcher was ordered to wear noisy tap dancing shoes whenever he went out in public.[57]

Faced with prison overcrowding, high incarceration costs, and public calls for retribution, other judges have used shaming strategies to deter wrongdoers. At least one Florida court ordered those convicted of drunk driving to put a "Convicted DUI" sticker on their license plates. In 2001, Coshocton County (Ohio) municipal judge David Hostetler ordered two men to parade down the main street of their hometown dressed as women. The men, Jason Householder, 23, and John Stockum, 21, had been convicted of criminal damage for throwing beer bottles at a woman. The judge told the men that they could either comply with his order or go to jail for 60 days. He also fined them $250 each. Similarly, a few years ago Boston courts began ordering men convicted of sexual solicitation to spend time sweeping streets in Chinatown, an area known for prostitution. The public was invited to watch men sentenced to the city's "John Sweep" program clean up streets and alleyways littered with used condoms and sexual paraphernalia.

There is considerable support in criminal justice literature for shaming as a crime-reduction strategy. Australian criminologist John Braithwaite, for example, found shaming to be a particularly effective strategy because, he said, it holds the potential to enhance moral awareness among offenders, thereby building conscience and increasing inner control.[58] Dan Kahan, a professor at the University of Chicago Law School, points out that "shame supplies the main motive why people obey the law, not so much because they're afraid of formal sanctions, but because they care what people think about them."[59]

Whether public shaming will continue to grow in popularity as an **alternative sentencing** strategy is unclear. What is clear, however, is that the American public and an ever-growing number of judicial officials are now looking for workable alternatives to traditional sentencing options.

CJ Futures

Is Chemical Castration a Valid Sentencing Option?

In 2000, convicted Florida sex offender Shannon Coleman circumvented a 21-year prison term by agreeing to undergo chemical castration. Coleman, a self-described sex addict, had used the Internet to contact two Florida girls, ages 12 and 15. He admitted to visiting the 12-year-old at her house, where he fondled her and then masturbated. He had sex with the 15-year-old after she invited him to her house. Coleman and his lawyer asked the judge handling the case to exercise his discretion under Florida's 1997 sex-offender law, which gives judges the discretion to order people convicted of sexual battery to undergo drug treatment to stop or reduce testosterone production.

The first chemical castration law in the United States was enacted in California in 1996, signed into law by then-Governor Pete Wilson. The California statute requires regular hormone injections for twice-convicted child molesters (where the victim is under 13 years of age) upon their release from prison. Under the law, judges can also mandate injections for first offenders. Treatment is to continue until state authorities determine that it is no longer necessary.

Most chemical castration laws require convicted offenders to receive weekly injections of synthetic female hormones known as Depo-Provera (medroxy-progesterone acetate) and Depo-Lupron. The laboratory-manufactured chemicals reduce blood levels of the sex hormone testosterone and are believed to lower the male sex drive.

To date, California, Florida, Georgia, Texas, and Montana have chemical castration legislation in place, and some other states are considering enacting chemical castration laws. If chemical castration survives continuing court challenges, it may establish itself in the mid-twenty-first century as a widely used form of alternative sentencing. Opposition to chemical castration laws, however, is plentiful. After the California law was enacted, for example, a spokeswoman for the American Civil Liberties Union (ACLU) claimed that the legislation mandates an unproven remedy for child molestation and is therefore a violation of civil rights. "There is no evidence, absolutely no evidence, that chemical castration will alleviate the problem," said Ann Bradley, a Los Angeles ACLU spokeswoman. "We see this as a violation of prisoners' civil liberties," she said.

Proponents of the legislation, on the other hand, cite studies in Canada and Europe in which repeat offender rates of more than 80% were reduced to less than 4% among criminals treated with Depo-Provera. "I would have to say to the ACLU that there is no right to molest a child," Governor Wilson replied.

References: Kevin Giordano, "The Chemical Knife," Salon.com, March 1, 2002, http://dir.salon.com/health/feature/2002/03/01/castration/index.html (accessed July 5, 2005); "Castration, 1998–2001," http://members.aol.com/USCCCN/FAQ-castration.index.html (accessed July 5, 2005); and Dave Lesher, "Molester Castration Measure Signed: California Becomes the First State to Require That Offenders Get Periodic Injections to Suppress Sex Drive," *Los Angeles Times*, September 18, 1996.

Questions about Alternative Sanctions

Alternative sanctions include the use of court-ordered community service, home detention, day reporting, drug treatment, psychological counseling, victim–offender programming, or intensive supervision in lieu of other, more traditional, sanctions, such as imprisonment and fines. Many of these strategies are discussed in more detail in the next chapter.

As prison populations continue to rise, alternative sentencing strategies are likely to become increasingly attractive. A number of questions must be answered, however, before most alternative sanctions can be employed with confidence. These questions were succinctly stated in a RAND Corporation study authored by Joan Petersilia.[60] Unfortunately, although the questions can be listed, few definitive answers are available yet. Here are some of the questions Petersilia poses:

To make punishments efficacious, two things are necessary. They must never be disproportioned to the offense, and they must be certain.

—William Sims (1806–1870)

- Do alternative sentencing programs threaten public safety?
- How should program participants be selected?
- What are the long-term effects of community sanctions on people assigned to these programs?
- Are alternative sanctions cost-effective?
- Who should pay the bill for alternative sanctions?
- Who should manage stringent community-based sanctions?
- How should program outcomes be judged?
- What kinds of offenders benefit most from alternative sanctions?

presentence investigation (PSI)

The examination of a convicted offender's background prior to sentencing. Presentence examinations are generally conducted by probation or parole officers and are submitted to sentencing authorities.

The Presentence Investigation

Before imposing sentence, a judge may request information on the background of a convicted defendant. This is especially true in indeterminate sentencing jurisdictions, where judges retain considerable discretion in selecting sanctions. Traditional wisdom has held that certain factors increase the likelihood of rehabilitation and reduce the need for lengthy prison terms. These factors include a good job record, satisfactory educational attainment, strong family ties, church attendance, no prior arrests for violent offenses, and psychological stability.

Information about a defendant's background often comes to the judge in the form of a **presentence investigation (PSI)** report. The task of preparing presentence reports usually falls to the probation or parole office. Presentence reports take one of three forms: (1) a detailed written report on the defendant's personal and criminal history, including an assessment of present conditions in the defendant's life (often called the *long form*); (2) an abbreviated written report summarizing the information most likely to be useful in a sentencing decision (the *short form*); and (3) a verbal report to the court made by the investigating officer based on field notes but structured according to established categories. A presentence report is much like a résumé, except that it focuses on what might be regarded as negative as well as positive life experiences.

The data on which a presentence report is based come from a variety of sources. The Federal Bureau of Investigation's National Crime Information Center (NCIC), begun in 1967, contains computerized information on people wanted for criminal offenses throughout the United States. Individual jurisdictions also maintain criminal records repositories that can provide comprehensive files on the criminal history of those who have been processed by the justice system.

Sometimes the defendant provides much of the information in the presentence report. In this case, efforts must be made to corroborate the defendant's information. Unconfirmed data are generally marked on the report as "defendant-supplied data" or simply "unconfirmed."

In a presentence report, almost all third-party data are subject to ethical and legal considerations. The official records of almost all agencies and organizations, though often an ideal source of information, are protected by state and federal privacy requirements. In particular, the federal Privacy Act of 1974[61] may limit access to these records. Investigators must first check on the legal availability of all records before requesting them and must receive in writing the defendant's permission to access the records. Other public laws, among them the federal Freedom of Information Act,[62] may make the presentence report available to the defendant, although courts and court officers have generally been held to be exempt from the provision of such statutes.

The final section of a presentence report is usually devoted to the investigating officer's recommendations. A recommendation may be made in favor of probation, split sentencing, a term of imprisonment, or any other sentencing option available in the jurisdiction. Participation in community service programs or in drug or substance abuse programs may be recommended for probationers. Most judges are willing to accept the report writer's recommendation because they recognize the professionalism of the presentence investigator and because they know that the investigator may be assigned to supervise the defendant if he or she is sentenced to a community alternative.

Jurisdictions vary in their use of presentence reports. Federal law mandates presentence reports in federal criminal courts and specifies 15 topical areas that each report must cover. The 1984 federal Determinate Sentencing Act directs report writers to include information on the classification of the offense and of the defendant under the offense-level and criminal history categories established by the statute. Some states require presentence reports only in felony cases, and others require them in cases where the defendant faces the possibility of incarceration for six months or more. Other states have no requirement for presentence reports beyond those ordered by a judge.

Report writing, rarely anyone's favorite task, may seriously tax the limited resources of probation agencies. In September 2004, officers from the New York City Department of Probation wrote 2,414 presentence investigation reports for adult offenders and 461 reports for juvenile offenders, averaging about 10 reports per probation officer per month.[63] Learn more about the sentencing environment at Library Extra 11–8 at cjtoday.com.

LIBRARY
Extra
■ ■ ■ ■

The Victim—Forgotten No Longer

Thanks to a grassroots resurgence of concern for the plight of victims that began in this country in the early 1970s, the sentencing process now frequently includes consideration of the needs of victims and their survivors.[64] In times past, although victims might testify at trial, the criminal justice system frequently downplayed a victim's experience, including the psychological trauma

Demonstrators in Washington, D.C., supporting a victims' rights amendment to the U.S. Constitution. What rights would such an amendment be likely to protect?

Maryland Crime Victims' Resource Center, Inc.

engendered both by having been a victim and by having to endure the criminal proceedings that bring the criminal to justice. That changed in 1982, when the President's Task Force on Victims of Crime gave focus to a burgeoning victims' rights movement and urged the widespread expansion of victims' assistance programs during what was then their formative period.[65] Victims' assistance programs today offer services in the areas of crisis intervention and follow-up counseling and help victims secure their rights under the law.[66] Following successful prosecution, some victims' assistance programs also advise victims in the filing of civil suits to recoup financial losses directly from the offender. In the mid-1990s, the National Institute of Justice (NIJ) conducted a survey of 319 full-service victims' assistance programs based in law enforcement agencies and prosecutors' offices.[67] The survey found that "the majority of individuals seeking assistance were victims of domestic assault and the most common assistance they received was information about legal rights." Other common forms of assistance included help in applying for state victims' compensation aid and referrals to social service agencies.

About the same time, voters in California approved Proposition 8, a resolution that called for changes in the state's constitution to reflect concern for victims. A continuing goal of victims' advocacy groups is an amendment to the U.S. Constitution, which such groups say is needed to provide the same kind of fairness to victims that is routinely accorded to defendants. In the past, for example, the National Victims' Constitutional Amendment Project (NVCAP), for example, has sought to add a phrase to the Sixth Amendment: "likewise, the victim, in every criminal prosecution, shall have the right to be present and to be heard at all critical stages of judicial proceedings." NVCAP now advocates the addition of a new amendment to the U.S. Constitution. Visit NVCAP via **Web Extra 11–6** at cjtoday.com.

In September 1996, a victims' rights constitutional amendment—Senate Joint Resolution 65— was proposed by a bipartisan committee in the U.S. Congress,[68] but problems of wording and terminology prevented its passage. A revised amendment was proposed in 1998,[69] but its wording was too restrictive for it to gain endorsement from victims' organizations.[70] In 1999, a new amendment was proposed by the Senate Judiciary Committee's Subcommittee on the Constitution, Federalism, and Property, but it did not make it to the Senate floor. The U.S. Department of Justice, which had previously supported the measure, reversed its position due to a provision in the proposed amendment that gives crime victims the right to be notified of any state or federal grant of clemency. The U.S. attorney general apparently believed that the provision would impede the power of the president. The legislation also lacked the support of President Bill Clinton and was officially withdrawn by its sponsors in 2000. The amendment may still have a future, however, as President George W. Bush expressed support for the measure in 2002,[71] and 39 state attorneys general have publicly endorsed its adoption.[72] The text of the proposed amendment, known as Senate Joint Resolution 3, is reproduced in CJ Today Exhibit 11–3.

Although a victims' rights amendment to the federal Constitution may not yet be a reality, more than 30 states have passed their own victims' rights amendments,[73] and significant federal legislation has already been adopted. The 1982 Victim and Witness Protection Act (VWPA),[74] for example, requires judges to consider victim-impact statements at federal sentencing hearings and

WEB
Extra
▪▪▪▪

When our criminal justice system treats victims as irrelevant bystanders, they are victimized for a second time. And because Americans are justifiably proud of our system and expect it to treat us fairly, the second violation of our rights can be traumatic.

—President George W. Bush[vi]

CJ Today Exhibit 11–3

The Call for a Victims' Rights Amendment

In 2002, President George W. Bush announced his support for a constitutional amendment for victims of violent crime. Bush said, "In the year 2000, Americans were victims of millions of crimes. Behind each of these numbers is a terrible trauma, a story of suffering and a story of lost security. Yet the needs of victims are often an afterthought in our criminal justice system. It's not just, it's not fair, and it must change. As we protect the rights of criminals, we must take equal care to protect the rights of the victims."

The president's remarks were made in support of a Senate Joint Resolution offered by Senators Jon Kyl of Arizona and Dianne Feinstein of California. The bill, which has been repeatedly introduced in the past, did not receive the support of President Bill Clinton during his eight years in office. The text of the Kyl–Feinstein resolution follows.

Proposing an amendment to the Constitution of the United States to protect the rights of crime victims:

Resolved by the Senate and the House of Representatives of the United States of America in Congress assembled (two-thirds of each House concurring therein), That the following article is proposed as an amendment to the Constitution of the United States, which shall be valid for all intents and purposes as part of the Constitution when ratified by the legislatures of three-fourths of the several States within seven years from the date of its submission by the Congress:

ARTICLE

Section 1. A victim of a crime of violence, as these terms may be defined by law, shall have the rights:

- to reasonable notice of, and not to be excluded from, any public proceedings relating to the crime;
- to be heard, if present, and to submit a statement at all such proceedings to determine a conditional release from custody, an acceptance of a negotiated plea, or a sentence;

- to the foregoing rights at a parole proceeding that is not public, to the extent those rights are afforded to the convicted offender;
- to reasonable notice of a release or escape from custody relating to the crime;
- to consideration of the interest of the victim that any trial be free from unreasonable delay;
- to an order of restitution from the convicted offender;
- to consideration for the safety of the victim in determining any conditional release from custody relating to the crime; and
- to reasonable notice of the rights established by this article.

Section 2. Only the victim or the victim's lawful representative shall have standing to assert the rights established by this article. Nothing in this article shall provide grounds to stay or continue any trial, reopen any proceeding or invalidate any ruling, except with respect to conditional release or restitution or to provide rights guaranteed by this article in future proceedings, without staying or continuing a trial. Nothing in this article shall give rise to or authorize the creation of a claim for damages against the United States, a State, a political subdivision, or a public officer or employee.

Section 3. The Congress shall have the power to enforce this article by appropriate legislation. Exceptions to the rights established by this article may be created only when necessary to achieve a compelling interest.

Section 4. This article shall take effect on the 180th day after the ratification of this article. The right to an order of restitution established by this article shall not apply to crimes committed before the effective date of this article.

Section 5. The rights and immunities established by this article shall apply in Federal and State proceedings, including military proceedings to the extent that the Congress may provide by law, juvenile justice proceedings, and proceedings in the District of Columbia and any commonwealth, territory, or possession of the United States.

Source: Senate Joint Resolution 3, 106th Congress.

[Unless the Constitution is amended] we will never correct the existing imbalance in this country between [a] defendant's irreducible constitutional rights and the current haphazard patchwork of victims' rights.

—Former U.S. Attorney General Janet Reno

places responsibility for their creation on federal probation officers. In 1984, the federal Victims of Crime Act (VOCA) was enacted with substantial bipartisan support. VOCA authorized federal funding to help states establish victims' assistance and victims' compensation programs. Under VOCA, the U.S. Department of Justice's Office for Victims of Crime provides a significant source of both funding and information for victims' assistance programs. The rights of victims were further strengthened under the Violent Crime Control and Law Enforcement Act of 1994, which created a federal right of allocution, or right to speak, for victims of violent and sex crimes. This gave victims the right to speak at the sentencing of their assailants. The 1994 law also requires sex offenders and child molesters convicted under federal law to pay restitution to their victims and prohibits the diversion of federal victims' funds to other programs. Other provisions of the 1994 law provide civil rights remedies for victims of felonies motivated by gender bias and extend "rape shield law" protections to civil cases and to all criminal cases, prohibiting inquiries into a victim's sexual history. A significant feature of the 1994 law can be found in a subsection titled the Violence against Women Act (VAWA). VAWA, which provides financial support for police, prosecutors, and victims' services in cases involving sexual violence or domestic abuse, is discussed in greater detail in Chapter 2.

Much of the philosophical basis of today's victims' movement can be found in the restorative justice model, which was discussed briefly earlier in this chapter. Restorative justice emphasizes offender accountability and victim reparation. Restorative justice also provides the basis for victims' compensation programs, which are another means of recognizing the needs of crime victims. Today, all 50 states have passed legislation providing for monetary payments to victims of crime. Such payments are primarily designed to compensate victims for medical expenses and lost wages. All existing programs require that applicants meet certain eligibility criteria, and most set limits on the maximum amount of compensation that can be received. Generally disallowed are claims from victims who are significantly responsible for their own victimization, such as those who end up being the losers in fights they provoke. In 2002, California's victims' compensation program, the largest in the nation, provided $117 million to more than 50,000 victims for crime-related expenses. A comprehensive California proposal to improve victim's services, with applicability to victim's service programs throughout the nation, can be read at Library Extra 11–9 at cjtoday.com.

In 2001, the USA PATRIOT Act amended the Victims of Crime Act of 1984 to make victims of terrorism and their families eligible for victims' compensation payments.[75] It also created an antiterrorism emergency reserve fund to help provide compensation to victims of terrorism. A year earlier, in November 2000, the federal Office for Victims of Crime (OVC) created the Terrorism and International Victims Unit (TIVU) to develop and manage programs and initiatives that help victims of domestic and international terrorism, mass violence, and crimes that have transnational dimensions.[76]

On October 9, 2004, the U.S. Senate passed the Crime Victims' Rights Act[77] as part of the Justice for All Act of 2004. Some saw the legislation as at least a partial statutory alternative to a constitutional crime victims' rights amendment. The Crime Victims' Rights Act establishes statutory rights for victims of federal crimes and gives them the necessary legal authority to assert those rights in federal court. The Crime Victims' Rights Act grants the following rights to victims of federal crimes:[78]

1. The right to be reasonably protected from the accused

2. The right to reasonable, accurate, and timely notice of any public proceeding involving the crime or of any release or escape of the accused

3. The right to be included in any such public proceeding

4. The right to be reasonably heard at any public proceeding involving release, plea, or sentencing

5. The right to confer with the federal prosecutor handling the case

6. The right to full and timely restitution as provided by law

7. The right to proceedings free from unreasonable delay

8. The right to be treated with fairness and with respect for the victim's dignity and privacy

In addition to establishing these rights, the legislation expressly requires federal courts to ensure that they are afforded to victims. In like manner, federal law enforcement officials are required to make their "best efforts to see that crime victims are notified of, and accorded," these rights. To teach citizens about the rights of victims of crime, the federal government created crimevictims.gov, which you can access on the Internet via Web Extra 11–7 at cjtoday.com. The resource includes an online directory of crime victims' services, which can be searched locally, nationally, and internationally.

Victim-Impact Statements

Another consequence of the national victims' rights movement has been a call for the use of **victim-impact statements** before sentencing. A victim-impact statement is generally a written document describing the losses, suffering, and trauma experienced by the crime victim or by the victim's survivors. Judges are expected to consider such statements in arriving at an appropriate sanction for the offender.

The drive to mandate inclusion of victim-impact statements in sentencing decisions, already required in federal courts by the 1982 Victim and Witness Protection Act, was substantially enhanced by the "right of allocution" provision of the Violent Crime Control and Law Enforcement Act of 1994. Victim-impact statements played a prominent role in the sentencing of Timothy McVeigh, who was convicted of the 1995 bombing of the Murrah Federal Building in Oklahoma

Of all the initiatives that this Congress could undertake, few will touch the heart of Americans as dearly as the measure seeking to ensure that the judicial process is just and fair for the victims of crime.

—Senator Orrin Hatch

LIBRARY
Extra
■ ■ ■ ■

WEB
Extra
■ ■ ■ ■

victim-impact statement

The in-court use of victim- or survivor-supplied information by sentencing authorities seeking to make an informed sentencing decision.

City and was executed in 2001. Some states, however, have gone further than the federal government. In 1984, the state of California, for example, passed legislation giving victims a right to attend and participate in sentencing and parole hearings.[79] Approximately 20 states now have laws requiring citizen involvement in sentencing, and all 50 states and the District of Columbia "allow for some form of submission of a victim-impact statement either at the time of sentencing or to be contained in the presentence investigation reports" made by court officers.[80] Where written victim-impact statements are not available, courts may invite the victim to testify directly at sentencing. An alternative to written impact statements and to the appearance of victims at sentencing hearings is the victim-impact video.

One study of the efficacy of victim-impact statements found that sentencing decisions are rarely affected by them. In the words of the study, "These statements did not produce sentencing decisions that reflected more clearly the effects of crime on victims. Nor did we find much evidence that—with or without impact statements—sentencing decisions were influenced by our measures of the effects of crime on victims, once the charge and the defendant's prior record were taken into account."[81] The authors concluded that victim-impact statements have little effect on courts because judges and other officials "have established ways of making decisions which do not call for explicit information about the impact of crime on victims." Learn more about the rights of crime victims and the history of the victims' movement at **Web Extra 11–8** at cjtoday.com, and read about the constitutionality of victim-impact statements at Library Extra 11–10 at cjtoday.com.

WEB   **LIBRARY**
Extra   Extra
■■■■   ■■■■

Modern Sentencing Options

Sentencing is fundamentally a risk-management strategy designed to protect the public while serving the ends of retribution, incapacitation, deterrence, rehabilitation, and restoration. Because the goals of sentencing are difficult to agree on, so too are sanctions. Lengthy prison terms do little for rehabilitation, while community-release programs can hardly protect the innocent from offenders bent on continuing criminality.

Assorted sentencing philosophies continue to permeate state-level judicial systems. Each state has its own sentencing laws, and frequent revisions of those statutes are not uncommon. Because of huge variation from one state to another in the laws and procedures that control the imposition of criminal sanctions, sentencing has been called "the most diversified part of the Nation's criminal justice process."[82]

There is at least one common ground, however. It can be found in the four traditional sanctions that continue to dominate the thinking of most legislators and judges—fines, probation, imprisonment, and death. Fines and the death penalty are discussed in this chapter, while probation is described in Chapter 12, and imprisonment is covered in Chapters 13 and 14.

In jurisdictions that employ indeterminate sentencing, fines, probation, and imprisonment are widely available to judges. The option selected generally depends on the severity of the offense and the judge's best guess as to the likelihood of the defendant's future criminal involvement. Sometimes two or more options are combined, such as when an offender is fined and sentenced to prison or placed on probation and fined in support of restitution payments.

Jurisdictions that operate under presumptive sentencing guidelines generally limit the judge's choice to only one option and often specify the extent to which that option can be applied. Dollar amounts of fines, for example, are rigidly set, and prison terms are specified for each type of offense. The death penalty remains an option in a fair number of jurisdictions, but only for a highly select group of offenders.

A recent report by the Bureau of Justice Statistics on the sentencing practices of trial courts found that state courts convicted 1,079,000 felons in 2004.[83] Another 66,518 felony convictions occurred in federal courts. The report also found the following for offenders convicted of felonies in state courts (Figure 11–1):

See our Sentencing Law and Policy blogs.

- Forty percent were sentenced to active prison terms.

- The average sentence length for those sent to state prisons has decreased since 1990 (from six years to four years and nine months).

- Felons sentenced in 2004 were likely to serve more of their sentence before release (50%) than those sentenced in 1990 (33%).

- Thirty percent received jail sentences, usually involving less than a year's confinement.

- Those sent to jail received an average sentence of six months.

- Twenty-eight percent were sentenced to probation, with no jail or prison time to serve.

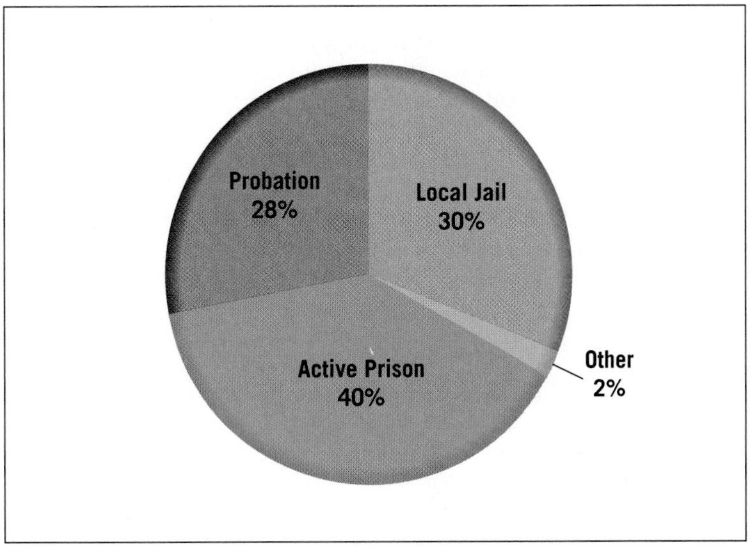

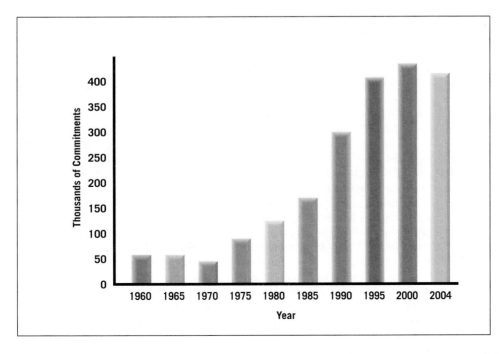

FIGURE 11–1

The sentencing of convicted felons in state courts, by type of sentence.

Source: Data from Matthew R. Durose and Patrick A. Langan, *Felony Sentences in State Courts, 2004* (Washington, DC: Bureau of Justice Statistics, 2007).

- The average probation sentence was 41 months.
- Fines were imposed on 33% of convicted felons, and restitution was ordered in 18% of cases.

Although the percentage of felons who receive active sentences may seem low, the number of criminal defendants receiving active prison time has increased dramatically. Figure 11–2 shows that the number of court-ordered prison commitments has increased nearly eightfold in the past 40 years.

Fines

While the fine is one of the oldest forms of punishment, the use of fines as criminal sanctions suffers from built-in inequities and a widespread failure to collect them. Inequities arise when offenders with vastly different financial resources are fined similar amounts. A fine of $100, for example, can place a painful economic burden on a poor defendant but is negligible when imposed on a wealthy offender.

FIGURE 11–2

Court-ordered prison commitments, 1960–2004.

Source: Data from Matthew R. Durose and Patrick A. Langan, *Felony Sentences in State Courts, 2004* (Washington, DC: Bureau of Justice Statistics, 2007), and other years.

Nonetheless, fines are once again receiving attention as a serious sentencing alternative. One reason for the renewed interest is the stress placed on state resources by burgeoning prison populations. The extensive imposition of fines not only results in less crowded prisons but can contribute to state and local coffers and can lower the tax burden of law-abiding citizens. There are other advantages:

- Fines can deprive offenders of the proceeds of criminal activity.
- Fines can promote rehabilitation by enforcing economic responsibility.
- Fines can be collected by existing criminal justice agencies and are relatively inexpensive to administer.
- Fines can be made proportionate to both the severity of the offense and the ability of the offender to pay.

A National Institute of Justice (NIJ) survey found that an average of 86% of convicted defendants in courts of limited jurisdiction receive fines as sentences, some in combination with another penalty.[84] Fines are also widely used in courts of general jurisdiction, where the NIJ study found judges imposing fines in 42% of all cases that came before them for sentencing. Some studies estimate that more than $1 billion in fines are collected nationwide each year.[85]

Fines are often imposed for relatively minor law violations, such as driving while intoxicated, reckless driving, disturbing the peace, disorderly conduct, public drunkenness, and vandalism. Judges in many courts, however, report the use of fines for relatively serious violations of the law, including assault, auto theft, embezzlement, fraud, and the sale and possession of various controlled substances. Fines are most likely to be imposed where the offender has both a clean record and the ability to pay.[86]

Opposition to the use of fines is based on the following arguments:

- Fines allow the release of convicted offenders into the community but do not impose stringent controls on their behavior.
- Fines are a relatively mild form of punishment and are not consistent with the "just deserts" philosophy.
- Fines discriminate against the poor and favor the wealthy. Indigent offenders are especially subject to discrimination since they lack the financial resources with which to pay fines.
- Fines are difficult to collect.

A number of these objections can be answered by procedures that make available to judges complete financial information on defendants. Studies have found, however, that courts of limited jurisdiction, which are the most likely to impose fines, are also the least likely to have adequate information on offenders' financial status.[87] Perhaps as a consequence, judges are sometimes reluctant to impose fines. Two of the most widely cited objections by judges to the use of fines are (1) that fines allow more affluent offenders to "buy their way out" and (2) that poor offenders cannot pay fines.[88]

A solution to both objections can be found in the Scandinavian system of day fines. The day-fine system is based on the idea that fines should be proportionate to the severity of the offense but also need to take into account the financial resources of the offender. Day fines are computed by first assessing the seriousness of the offense, the defendant's degree of culpability, and his or her prior record as measured in "days." The use of days as a benchmark of seriousness is related to the fact that, without fines, the offender could be sentenced to a number of days (or months or years) in jail or prison. The number of days an offender is assessed is then multiplied by the daily wages that person earns. Hence, if two people are sentenced to a five-day fine, but one earns only $20 per day and the other $200 per day, the first would pay a $100 fine and the second $1,000.

In 2004, one of Finland's richest men, 27-year-old Jussi Salonoja, was fined a record 170,000 euros ($217,000) for speeding through the center of Helsinki. Salonoja, heir to his family's international sausage business, was caught driving 80 kilometers per hour (kph) in a 40-kph zone. The fine was based on Salonoja's 2002 earnings, which were estimated at close to 7 million euros.

In the early 1990s, the NIJ reported on experimental day-fine programs conducted by the Richmond County Criminal Court in Staten Island, New York, and by the Milwaukee Municipal Court.[89] Both studies concluded that "the day fine can play a major . . . role as an intermediate sanction"[90] and that "the day-fine concept could be implemented in a typical American limited-jurisdiction court."[91] Those conclusions were supported by a 1996 RAND Corporation report that examined ongoing day-fine demonstration projects in Maricopa County, Arizona; Des Moines, Iowa; Bridgeport, Connecticut; and four counties in Oregon.[92]

We've never had a doubt about the guilt of Timothy McVeigh. But, we needed more than a guilty defendant. We needed an innocent system.

—Former U.S. Attorney General John Ashcroft[vii]

Death: The Ultimate Sanction

Some crimes are especially heinous and seem to cry out for extreme punishment. In 2006, for example, in an especially atrocious murder, a 26-year-old grocery store stock clerk named Kevin Ray Underwood was arrested and charged with first-degree murder in the killing of a ten-year-old girl in what authorities said was an elaborate plan to cannibalize the girl's flesh.[93] Underwood had been the girl's neighbor in Purcell, Oklahoma, and her mutilated body was discovered in his apartment covered with deep saw marks. Investigators told reporters that Underwood had sexually assaulted the little girl and planned to eat her corpse using the meat tenderizer and barbecue skewers that they confiscated from his kitchen. "In my 24 years as a prosecutor this ranks as one of the most heinous and atrocious cases I've ever been involved with," said McClain County Prosecutor Tim Kuykendall.

Many states today have statutory provisions that provide for a sentence of **capital punishment** for especially repugnant crimes (known as **capital offenses**). Estimates are that more than 18,800 legal executions have been carried out in the United States since 1608, when records began to be kept on capital punishment.[94] Although capital punishment was widely used throughout the eighteenth and nineteenth centuries, the mid-twentieth century offered a brief respite in the number of offenders legally executed in this country. Between 1930 and 1967, the year when the U.S. Supreme Court ordered a nationwide stay of pending executions, nearly 3,800 people were put to death. The peak years were 1935 and 1936, with nearly 200 legal killings each year. Executions declined substantially every year thereafter. Between 1967 and 1977, a *de facto* moratorium existed, with no executions carried out in any U.S. jurisdiction. Following the lifting of the moratorium, executions resumed (Figure 11–3). In 1983, only 5 offenders were put to death, while 65 were executed nationwide in 2003. A modern record for executions was set in 1999, with 98 executions—35 in Texas alone. Substantially fewer offenders (60) were executed in 2005.

Today, the federal government and 38 of the 50 states[95] permit execution for first-degree murder, while treason, kidnapping, aggravated rape, the murder of a police or corrections officer, and murder while under a life sentence are punishable by death in selected jurisdictions.[96]

The list of crimes punishable by death under federal jurisdiction increased dramatically with passage of the Violent Crime Control and Law Enforcement Act of 1994 and was expanded still further by the 2001 USA PATRIOT Act. The list now includes a total of about 60 offenses. State legislators have also worked to expand the types of crimes for which a death sentence can be imposed. In 1997, for example, the Louisiana Supreme Court upheld the state's year-old child rape

capital punishment

The death penalty. Capital punishment is the most extreme of all sentencing options.

capital offense

A criminal offense punishable by death.

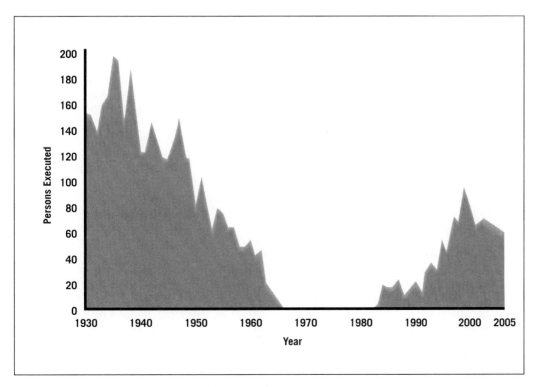

FIGURE 11–3

Court-ordered executions carried out in the United States, 1930–2005.

Note: Excludes executions ordered by military authority.

Source: Tracy L. Snell, *Capital Punishment, 2005* (Washington, DC: Bureau of Justice Statistics, 2006).

statute, which allows for the imposition of a capital sentence when the victim is younger than 12 years of age. The case involved an AIDS-infected father who raped his three daughters, ages five, eight, and nine. In upholding the father's death sentence, the Louisiana court ruled that child rape is "like no other crime."[97]

A total of 3,370 offenders were under sentence of death throughout the United States on April 1, 2006.[98] The latest statistics show that 98% of those on death row are male, approximately 45% are white, 11% are Hispanic, 42% are African American, and 2% are of other races (mostly Native American and Pacific Islander).[99]

Methods of imposing death vary by state. The majority of death-penalty states authorize execution through lethal injection. Electrocution is the second most common means, while hanging, the gas chamber, and firing squads have survived, at least as options available to the condemned, in a few states. For the most current statistical information on capital punishment, visit the Death Penalty Information Center via Web Extra 11–9 at cjtoday.com. Learn more about the history of capital punishment at Library Extra 11–11 at cjtoday.com.

WEB Extra **LIBRARY Extra**

Habeas Corpus Review

The legal process through which a capital sentence is carried to conclusion is fraught with problems. One serious difficulty centers on the fact that automatic review of all death sentences by appellate courts and constant legal maneuvering by defense counsel often lead to a dramatic delay between the time the sentence is handed down and the time it is carried out. Today, an average of ten years and eight months passes between the imposition of a death sentence and execution.[100] Such lengthy delays, compounded by uncertainty over whether an execution will ever occur, directly contravene the generally accepted notion that punishment should be swift and certain.

Even death-row inmates can undergo life-altering changes. When that happens, long-delayed executions can become highly questionable events. The case of Stanley "Tookie" Williams, who was executed at California's San Quentin Prison in 2005 at age 51, is illustrative.[101] Williams, self-described cofounder of the infamous Crips street gang in the early 1970s, was sentenced to die for the brutal shotgun murders of four people during a robbery 26 years earlier. In 1993, however, he experienced what he called a "reawakening" and began working from prison as an antigang crusader. Williams found a sympathetic publisher and wrote a series of children's books titled *Tookie Speaks Out against Gang Violence.* The series was intended to help urban youth reject the lure of gang membership and embrace traditional values. He also wrote *Life in Prison*, an autobiography describing the isolation and despair experienced by death-row inmates. In his final years, Williams worked with his editor, Barbara Cottman Becnel, to create the Internet Project for Street Peace, a demonstration project linking teens from the rough-and-tumble streets of Richmond, California, to peers in Switzerland in an effort to help them avoid street violence. In 2001, Williams was nominated for the Nobel Peace Prize by a member of the Swiss Parliament and for the Nobel Prize in Literature by a number of college professors. Pleas to spare his life, which came from Jesse Jackson, anti–death penalty activist Sister Helen Prejean, the National Association for the Advancement of Colored People (NAACP), and others, were rejected by Governor Arnold Schwarzenegger who said that "there is no reason to second-guess the jury's decision of guilt or raise significant doubts or serious reservations about Williams' convictions and death sentence."[102]

In a speech before the American Bar Association (ABA) in 1989, then-Chief Justice William Rehnquist called for reforms of the federal *habeas corpus* system, which, at the time, allowed condemned prisoners virtually limitless opportunities for appeal. **Writs of *habeas corpus*** (Latin for "you have the body"), which require that a prisoner be brought into court to determine if he or she is being legally held, form the basis for many federal appeals made by prisoners on state death rows. In 1968, Chief Justice Earl Warren called the right to file *habeas* petitions, as guaranteed under the U.S. Constitution, the "symbol and guardian of individual liberty." Twenty years later, however, Rehnquist claimed that writs of *habeas corpus* were being used indiscriminately by death-row inmates seeking to delay executions even where grounds for delay did not exist. "The capital defendant does not need to prevail on the merits in order to accomplish his purpose," said Rehnquist. "He wins temporary victories by postponing a final adjudication."[103]

In a move to reduce delays in the conduct of executions, the U.S. Supreme Court, in the case of *McCleskey* v. *Zant* (1991),[104] limited the number of appeals a condemned person may lodge with the courts. Saying that repeated filing for the sole purpose of delay promotes "disrespect for the finality of convictions" and "disparages the entire criminal justice system," the Court established a two-pronged criterion for future appeals. According to *McCleskey*, in any petition beyond the first filed with the federal court, a capital defendant must (1) demonstrate good cause why the claim now being made was not included in the first filing and (2) explain how the ab-

writ of *habeas corpus*

A writ that directs the person detaining a prisoner to bring him or her before a judicial officer to determine the lawfulness of the imprisonment.

sence of that claim may have harmed the petitioner's ability to mount an effective defense. Two months later, the Court reinforced *McCleskey* when it ruled, in *Coleman* v. *Thompson* (1991),[105] that state prisoners could not cite "procedural default," such as a defense attorney's failure to meet a state's filing deadline for appeals, as the basis for an appeal to federal court.

In 1995, in the case of *Schlup* v. *Delo*,[106] the Court continued to define standards for further appeals from death-row inmates, ruling that before appeals based on claims of new evidence could be heard, "a petitioner must show that, in light of the new evidence, it is more likely than not that no reasonable juror would have found him guilty beyond a reasonable doubt." A "reasonable juror" was defined as one who "would consider fairly all of the evidence presented and would conscientiously obey the trial court's instructions requiring proof beyond a reasonable doubt."

Opportunities for federal appeals by death-row inmates were further limited by the Antiterrorism and Effective Death Penalty Act (AEDPA) of 1996,[107] which sets a one-year postconviction deadline for state inmates filing federal *habeas corpus* appeals. The deadline is six months for state death-row inmates who were provided a lawyer for *habeas* appeals at the state level. The act also requires federal courts to presume that the factual findings of state courts are correct, does not permit the claim of state court misinterpretations of the U.S. Constitution as a basis for *habeas* relief unless those misinterpretations are "unreasonable," and requires that all petitioners must show, prior to obtaining a hearing, facts sufficient to establish by clear and convincing evidence that but for constitutional error, no reasonable fact-finder would have found the petitioner guilty. The act also requires approval by a three-judge panel before an inmate can file a second federal appeal raising newly discovered evidence of innocence. In 1996, in the case of *Felker* v. *Turpin*,[108] the U.S. Supreme Court ruled that limitations on the authority of federal courts to consider successive *habeas corpus* petitions imposed by AEDPA are permissible since they do not deprive the U.S. Supreme Court of its original jurisdiction over such petitions.

Some recent statements by Supreme Court justices have indicated that long delays caused by the government in carrying out executions may render the punishment unconstitutionally cruel and unusual. One example comes from the 1998 case of *Elledge* v. *Florida*,[109] where the execution of William D. Elledge had been delayed for 23 years. Although the full Court refused to hear the case, Justice Stephen Breyer observed that "[t]wenty-three years under sentence of death is unusual—whether one takes as a measuring rod current practice or the practice in this country and in England at the time our Constitution was written." Moreover, wrote Breyer, execution after such a long delay could be considered cruel because Elledge "has experienced that delay because of the State's own faulty procedures and not because of frivolous appeals on his own part." Elledge remains on death row at the Union Correctional Institution in Florida. He has been under sentence of death for 33 years.

Opposition to Capital Punishment

Thirty years ago, David Magris, who was celebrating his twenty-first birthday with a crime spree, shot Dennis Tapp in the back during a holdup, leaving Tapp a paraplegic. Tapp had been working a late-night shift, tending his father's quick-serve gas station. Magris went on to commit more robberies that night, killing 20-year-old Steven Tompkins in a similar crime. Although Magris was sentenced to death by a California court, the U.S. Supreme Court overturned the state's death-penalty law in 1972, opening the door for Magris to be paroled in 1985. Long before Magris was freed from prison, however, Tapp had already forgiven him. A few minutes after the shooting happened, Tapp regained consciousness, dragged himself to a telephone, and called for help. The next thing he did was ask "God to forgive the man who did this to me."[110] Today, the men—both staunch death-penalty opponents—are friends, and Magris is president of the Northern California Coalition to Abolish the Death Penalty. "Don't get me wrong," says Tapp, "What [David] did was wrong. . . . He did something stupid and he paid for it."[111]

Because for many the death penalty is such an emotional issue, attempts have been made to abolish capital punishment since the founding of the United States. The first recorded effort to eliminate the death penalty occurred at the home of Benjamin Franklin in 1787.[112] At a meeting there on March 9 of that year, Dr. Benjamin Rush, a signer of the Declaration of Independence and a leading medical pioneer, read a paper against capital punishment to a small but influential audience. Although his immediate efforts came to naught, his arguments laid the groundwork for many debates that followed. Michigan, widely regarded as the first abolitionist state, joined the Union in 1837 without a death penalty. A number of other states, including Alaska, Hawaii, Massachusetts, Minnesota, West Virginia, and Wisconsin, have since spurned death as a possible sanction for criminal acts. As noted earlier, it remains a viable sentencing option in 38 of the states and in all federal jurisdictions, so arguments continue to rage over its value.

I think this country would be much better off if we did not have capital punishment. . . . We cannot ignore the fact that in recent years a disturbing number of inmates on death row have been exonerated.

—U.S. Supreme Court Justice John Paul Stevens[viii]

There can be no doubt that the taking of the life of the President creates much more societal harm than the taking of the life of a homeless person.

—Tennessee Attorney General Charles Burson, arguing before the U.S. Supreme Court in Payne v. Tennessee[ix]

What Are the Limits of Genetic Privacy?

In 2005, police in Truro, Massachusetts, charged Christopher M. McCowen, a garbageman with a long rap sheet, with the murder of 46-year-old Christa Worthington, a fashion writer who had been raped and stabbed to death in the kitchen of her isolated home in 2002. The case, which had baffled authorities for three years, drew national interest when Truro authorities asked the town's 790 male residents to voluntarily submit saliva-swab DNA samples for analysis. Investigators were hoping to use genetic testing to match semen recovered from the murder scene to the killer. "We're trying to find the person who has something to hide," said Sergeant David Perry of the Truro Police Department. Although McCowen voluntarily submitted a DNA sample from a cheek swab in early 2004, it took the state crime lab more than a year to analyze it.

As the Massachusetts case shows, DNA profiling can be a powerful forensic tool, although it has been used in criminal investigations for only 20 years. The first well-known DNA forensic analysis occurred in 1986, when British police sought the help of Alec Jeffreys, a geneticist at the University of Leicester who is widely regarded as the father of "DNA fingerprinting." The police were trying to solve the vicious rape and murder of two young schoolgirls. At the center of their investigation was a young man who worked at a mental institution close to where the girls' bodies had been found. Soon after he was questioned, the man confessed to the crimes and was arrested, but police were uncertain of the suspect's state of mind and wanted to be sure that they had the right person.

Jeffreys compared the suspect's DNA to DNA taken from semen samples found on the victims. The samples did not match, leading to a wider police investigation. Lacking any clear leads, the authorities requested that all males living in the area of the killings voluntarily submit to DNA testing so that they might be excluded as suspects. By the fall of 1987, the number of men tested had exceeded 4,500, but the murderer still hadn't been found. Then, however, investigators received an unexpected tip. They learned that a local baker named Colin Pitchfork had convinced another man to provide a DNA sample in his place. Pitchfork was picked up and questioned. He soon confessed, providing details about the crime that only the perpetrator could know. Pitchfork became the 4,583rd man to undergo DNA testing, and his DNA proved a perfect match with that of the killer.

In the last 20 years, the use of DNA testing by police departments has come a long way. Today, the FBI's Combined DNA Index System (CODIS) database makes use of computerized records to match the DNA of individuals previously convicted of certain crimes with forensic samples gathered at crime scenes across the country.

Advocates of genetic privacy, however, question whether anyone—even those convicted of crimes—should be sampled against their wishes and have their genetic profiles added to government databases. The Truro case, in which the American Civil Liberties Union (ACLU) sent letters to the town's police chief and Cape Cod prosecutor calling for an end to the "DNA dragnet," highlights what many fear—especially when local police announced that they would pay close attention to those who refused to cooperate. One commentator noted that it's "a very old trap" to say, "If you have nothing to hide, then why not cooperate?"

YOU DECIDE

What degree of "genetic privacy" should an individual be entitled to? Should the government require routine genetic testing of nonoffenders for identification purposes? How might such information be used in the event of a terrorist attack?

References: "Man Charged with 2002 Murder of Cape Cod Writer," *USA Today*, April 15, 2005, http://www.usatoday.com/news/nation/2005-04-15-cape-cod-murder_x.htm (accessed July 4, 2006); "ACLU Slams Mass DNA Collection," CBSNews.com, January 10, 2005, http://www.cbsnews.com/stories/2005/01/10/national/main665938.shtml (accessed July 4, 2006); and Howard C. Coleman and Eric D. Swenson, *DNA in the Courtroom: A Trial Watcher's Guide* (Seattle: Genelex Corporation, 2000), http://www.genelex.com/paternitytesting/paternitybook.html (accessed July 4, 2006).

Today, six main rationales for abolishing capital punishment are heard:

1. The death penalty can be and has been inflicted on innocent people.
2. The death penalty is not an effective deterrent.
3. The imposition of the death penalty is, by the nature of our legal system, arbitrary.
4. The death penalty discriminates against certain ethnic and racial groups.
5. The death penalty is far too expensive to justify its use.
6. Human life is sacred, and killing at the hands of the state is not a righteous act but rather one that is on the same moral level as the crimes committed by the condemned.

Life is sacred. It's about the only sacred thing on earth—and no one has a right to do away with it.

—Aldona DeVetsco, mother of a murder victim, commenting on the execution of her son's killer

The first five abolitionist claims are pragmatic, that is, they can be measured and verified or disproved by looking at the facts. The last claim is primarily philosophical and therefore not amenable to scientific investigation. Hence, we shall briefly examine only the first five.

Former Illinois Governor George Ryan posing with former death-row inmates Laurence Hayes (left), David Keaton (seated), and Gary Gauger (right) at a film festival. While governor, Ryan declared a moratorium on executions in Illinois and appointed a commission to review the capital punishment system in that state. What was the reason for Ryan's actions? If you had been governor, would you have done the same thing?

Douglas C. Pizac/AP Wide World Photos

The Death Penalty Information Center claims that 124 people in 25 states were freed from death row between 1973 and 2007 after it was determined that they were innocent of the capital crime of which they had been convicted.[113] One study of felony convictions that used analysis of DNA to provide postconviction evidence of guilt or innocence found 28 cases in which defendants had been wrongly convicted and sentenced to lengthy prison terms. The study, *Convicted by Juries, Exonerated by Science*, effectively demonstrated that the judicial process can be flawed.[114] DNA testing can play a critical role in identifying wrongful convictions because, as Barry Scheck and Peter Neufeld, cofounders of the Innocence Project at the Benjamin N. Cardozo School of Law, point out, "Unlike witnesses who disappear or whose recollections fade over time, DNA in biological samples can be reliably extracted decades after the commission of the crime. The results of such testing have invariably been found to have a scientific certainty that easily outweighs the eyewitness identification testimony or other direct or circumstantial proof that led to the original conviction."[115] "Very simply," say Scheck and Neufeld, "DNA testing has demonstrated that far more wrongful convictions occur than even the most cynical and jaded scholars had suspected."[116]

In 2006, for example, Floridian Alan Crotzer, 45, was freed from prison after spending almost 24 years behind bars for two rapes that DNA tests later showed he didn't commit.[117] Crotzer had been convicted in 1982 of raping a 12-year-old girl and kidnapping, raping, and robbing a Tampa woman. Five eyewitnesses identified him as the shotgun-wielding leader of a gang of robbers who invaded a Tampa, Florida, home and assaulted the people inside. Crotzer was also convicted of aggravated assault, burglary, robbery, and attempted robbery and was sentenced to 130 years in prison. Although DNA testing was not readily available at the time he was tried, DNA tests performed in 2005 on rape kit evidence stored in a Florida Department of Law Enforcement locker since the crime proved Crotzer's innocence. The test's findings were supported by the admission of another man, Douglas James, one of the original suspects, that he had committed the crimes along with his brother and a childhood friend.[118] Shortly after learning of the test results, prosecutors asked Tampa Judge J. Rogers Padgett to set aside Crotzer's conviction and set him free. "The motion is granted. You are a free man," Padgett told Crotzer in a courtroom crowded with members of the press and Crotzer's family. Asked whether he would seek compensation from the state for the years he spent behind bars, Crotzer told reporters, "There ain't no compensation for what they done to me; but I'm not bitter."[119]

A 2000 study by Columbia Law School Professor James Liebman and colleagues examined 4,578 death-penalty cases in state and federal courts from 1973 to 1995.[120] They found that appellate courts overturned the conviction or reduced the sentence in 68% of the cases examined. In 82% of the successful appeals, defendants were found to be deserving of a lesser sentence,

Alan Crotzer hugging his sister, Wanda Sanders, following his release from a Florida prison in 2006. Crotzer spent 25 years behind bars but was released after DNA tests proved that he did not take part in a brutal 1982 rape and robbery in Tampa, Florida. Should similar tests be provided to all convicted felons at government expense where DNA evidence is available?

Chris O'Meara/AP Wide World Photos

LIBRARY
Extra

while convictions were overturned in 7% of such appeals. According to the study's authors, "Our 23 years worth of findings reveal a capital punishment system collapsing under the weight of its own mistakes." You can read the Liebman report in its entirety at **Library Extra 11–12** at cjtoday.com.

Claims of innocence are being partially addressed today by recently passed state laws that mandate DNA testing of all death-row inmates in situations where DNA testing might help establish guilt or innocence (that is, in cases where blood or semen from the perpetrator is available for testing).[121] In 2000, Illinois Governor George Ryan announced that he was suspending all executions in his state indefinitely. Ryan's proclamation came after DNA testing showed that 13 Illinois death-row prisoners could not have committed the capital crimes of which they were convicted. In 2006, the New Jersey legislature voted to suspend use of the death penalty until a state task force made its report on whether capital punishment is fairly imposed.[122] In a sad footnote to the Illinois proclamation,[123] former Governor Ryan, who drew international praise for his stance against the death penalty and who had been nominated for the Nobel Prize, was found guilty in 2006 of racketeering and fraud in a corruption scandal that ended his political career.[124]

In 2004, in recognition of the potential of DNA testing to exonerate the innocent, President George W. Bush signed the Innocence Protection Act[125] into law. The Innocence Protection Act provides federal funds to eliminate the backlog of unanalyzed DNA samples in the nation's crime laboratories[126] and sets aside money to improve the capacity of federal, state, and local crime laboratories to conduct DNA analyses.[127] The act also facilitates access to postconviction DNA testing for those serving time in state[128] or federal prisons or on death row and sets forth conditions under which a federal prisoner asserting innocence may obtain postconviction DNA testing of specific evidence. Similarly, the legislation requires the preservation of biological evidence by federal law enforcement agencies for any defendant under a sentence of imprisonment or death.

Not all claims of innocence are supported by DNA tests, however. In 2006, for example, DNA test results confirmed the guilt of Roger Keith Coleman, a Virginia coal miner who had steadfastly maintained his innocence until he was executed in 1992. Coleman, executed for the 1981 rape and murder of his sister-in-law, Wanda McCoy, died declaring his innocence and proclaiming that he would one day be exonerated. His case became a cause célèbre for death-penalty opponents, who convinced Virginia Governor Mark Warner to order DNA tests on surviving evidence. Coleman's supporters claimed that the tests would provide the first scientific proof that an innocent man had been executed in the United States. Results from the tests, however, conclusively showed that

 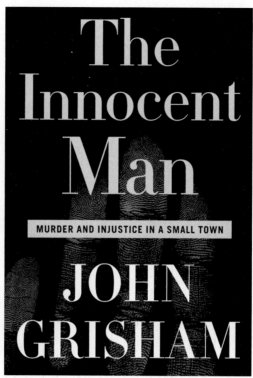

Author John Grisham, shown with his new book, *The Innocent Man.* Grisham wrote the book, his first nonfiction work, to bring attention to the plight of the wrongfully convicted. How can it happen that innocent people are convicted of crimes or even sentenced to death? How can it be prevented?

© *Deborah Feingold/CORBIS. All Rights Reserved. Jacket cover from* The Innocent Man: Murder and Injustice in a Small Town *by John Grisham. Used by permission of Doubleday, a division of Random House, Inc.*

blood and semen found at the crime scene had come from Coleman. After the test results were announced, James McCloskey, director of a New Jersey prison ministry and one of the leaders in the effort to clear Coleman's name, told reporters, "We who seek the truth must live or die by the sword of DNA, [but] this particular truth feels like a kick in the stomach." Learn more about DNA testing and how it can help determine guilt or innocence from the President's DNA Initiative via Web Extra 11–10 at cjtoday.com.

WEB
Extra

During the 1970s and 1980s, the deterrent effect of the death penalty became a favorite subject for debate in academic circles.[129] Studies of states that had eliminated the death penalty failed to show any increase in homicide rates.[130] Similar studies of neighboring states, in which jurisdictions retaining capital punishment were compared with those that had abandoned it, also failed to demonstrate any significant differences.[131] Although death-penalty advocates remain numerous, few still argue for the penalty based on its deterrent effects. One study that has found support for use of the death penalty as a deterrent was reported in 2001 by Hashem Dezhbakhsh and his colleagues at Emory University.[132] According to the researchers, "Our results suggest that capital punishment has a strong deterrent effect. . . . In particular, each execution results, on average, in 18 fewer murders."[133] They note that most other studies in the area have not only been methodologically flawed but have failed to consider the fact that a number of states sentence select offenders to death but do not carry out executions. They write, "If criminals know that the justice system issues many death sentences but the executions are not carried out, then they may not be deterred by an increase in probability of a death sentence."[134]

The third abolitionist claim, that the death penalty is arbitrary, is based on the belief that access to effective representation and to the courts themselves is differentially available to people with varying financial and other resources. The notion of arbitrariness also builds on beliefs that differences in jury composition, judges' personal dispositions and backgrounds, varying laws and procedures, and jurisdictional social characteristics may lead to varying sentences and could mean that a person who might be sentenced to die in one place might receive a lesser sentence elsewhere.

Access to the courts, which some see as more dependent on a changing legal environment than on fair standards of due process, is another area in which arbitrariness can play a role. In recent years, access to appellate courts has been restricted by a number of new state and federal laws (discussed in greater detail in Chapter 14). Such restrictions led the American Bar Association (ABA) House of Delegates in 1997 to cite what it called "an erosion of legal rights of death row inmates" and to urge an immediate halt to executions in the United States until the judicial

CJ News

DNA Tests Confirm Executed Man Was Guilty

DNA test results announced recently confirmed the guilt of Roger Coleman, a Virginia coal miner executed in 1992 for the rape and murder of his sister-in-law.

Coleman died declaring his innocence in Wanda McCoy's slaying in 1981 and predicting that one day he would be exonerated. His case became a cause célèbre for death penalty opponents, who lobbied Virginia Gov. Mark Warner to order DNA tests that had not yet been perfected at the time of Coleman's death. Warner recently agreed to the tests.

Coleman's supporters, led by James McCloskey, director of a New Jersey–based prison ministry, said they were certain the DNA tests would be the first scientific proof that an innocent man had been executed in the USA. They said Virginia courts had barred Coleman from presenting evidence that a neighbor committed the crime.

Instead, the police lab in Ontario, Canada, that performed the test found only a 1-in-19-million chance that the blood and semen found at the crime scene was not Coleman's.

"We who seek the truth must live or die by the sword of DNA," McCloskey said. "This particular truth feels like a kick in the stomach."

Michael McGlothlin, a Grundy, Va., lawyer who prosecuted the case, said McCloskey and other death penalty opponents minimized the "overwhelming evidence" against Coleman.

They convinced some media organizations that the boyish, charming Coleman had been "unfairly convicted" by a vengeful small-town jury, McGlothlin said. "The people of Grundy are owed an apology," he said.

Peter Neufeld, co-founder of the Innocence Project, which uses DNA to undo wrongful convictions, said the Coleman case shows there is "no harm" in testing cases in which an executed man claimed innocence. "Whichever way it goes, you get to the truth," Neufeld said.

Roger Keith Coleman waiting for an interview on death row in the Greensville Correctional Center in Jarratt, Virginia, in 1992. Coleman was executed while maintaining his innocence—a claim later disproved by DNA evidence. What does his case say about claims of wrongful conviction?

Steve Helber/AP Wide World Photos

He asked governors to study the 1,004 executions that have taken place since the Supreme Court restored the death penalty in 1976 for possible DNA testing.

Joshua Marquis, vice president of the National District Attorneys Association, said Coleman's guilt "gives the lie to the urban myth that there is an epidemic of wrongful convictions."

For the latest in crime and justice news, visit the Talk Justice news feed at http://www.crimenews.info.

Source: Richard Willing, "DNA Tests Confirm Man Executed in 1992 Was Guilty," USA TODAY, January 12, 2006. Reprinted by permission.

process could be overhauled.[135] ABA delegates were expressing concerns that during the past decade, Congress and the states have unfairly limited death-row appeals through restrictive legislation. The ABA resolution also called for a halt to executions of people under 18 years of age and of those who are mentally retarded.[136]

The claim that the death penalty is discriminatory is harder to investigate. Although past evidence suggests that blacks and other minorities in the United States have been disproportionately sentenced to death,[137] more recent evidence is not as clear. At first glance, disproportionality seems apparent: 45 of the 98 prisoners executed between January 1977 and May 1988 were African American or Hispanic, and 84 of the 98 had been convicted of killing whites.[138] A 1996 Kentucky study found that blacks accused of killing whites in that state between 1976 and 1991 had a higher-than-average probability of being charged with a capital crime and of being sentenced to die than did homicide offenders of other races.[139] For an accurate appraisal to be made,

Death-penalty opponent Mark Bherand sitting outside San Quentin Prison holding a sign as he awaits the execution of convicted killer Stanley "Tookie" Williams on December 13, 2005. Williams, reputed cofounder of the Crips street gang, had been convicted of four murders that occurred in 1979. He was denied clemency by California Governor Arnold Schwartzenegger. What is your position on capital punishment?

Justin Sullivan/Getty Images

however, any claims of disproportionality must go beyond simple comparisons with racial representation in the larger population and must somehow measure both frequency and seriousness of capital crimes between and within racial groups. Following that line of reasoning, the Supreme Court, in the 1987 case of *McCleskey* v. *Kemp*,[140] held that a simple showing of racial discrepancies in the application of the death penalty does not constitute a constitutional violation. A 2001 study of racial and ethnic fairness in federal capital punishment sentences attempted to go beyond mere percentages in its analysis of the role played by race and ethnicity in capital punishment sentencing decisions.[141] Although the study, which closely reviewed 950 capital punishment cases, found that approximately 80% of federal death-row inmates are African American, researchers found "no intentional racial or ethnic bias in how capital punishment was administered in federal cases."[142] Underrepresented groups were more likely to be sentenced to death, "but only because they are more likely to be arrested on facts that could support a capital charge, not because the justice system acts in a discriminatory fashion," the report said.[143] Read the entire report at Library Extra 11–13 at cjtoday.com.

Another 2001 study, this one by New Jersey Supreme Court Special Master David Baime, found no evidence of bias against African American defendants in capital cases in New Jersey during the period studied (August 1982 through May 2000). The study concluded, "Simply stated, we discern no sound basis from the statistical evidence to conclude that the race or ethnicity of the defendant is a factor in determining which cases advance to a penalty trial and which defendants are ultimately sentenced to death. The statistical evidence abounds the other way—it strongly suggests that there are no racial or ethnic disparities in capital murder prosecution and death sentencing rates."[144]

Evidence of socioeconomic discrimination in the imposition of the death penalty in Nebraska between 1973 and 1999 was found in a 2001 study of more than 700 homicide cases in that state. The study, which had been mandated by the state legislature, found that while race did not appear to influence death-penalty decisions, killers of victims with high socioeconomic status received the death penalty four times as often as would otherwise be expected. According to the study, "The data document significant statewide disparities in charging and sentencing outcomes based on the socio-economic status of the victim."[145]

The fifth claim, that the death penalty is too expensive, is difficult to explore. Although the "official" costs associated with capital punishment are high, many death-penalty supporters argue that no cost is *too* high if it achieves justice. Death-penalty opponents, on the other hand, point to the huge costs associated with judicial appeals and with the executions themselves. According to

There is no evidence of racial bias in the administration of the federal death penalty.

—*Former U.S. Attorney General John Ashcroft*[x]

LIBRARY
Extra
■ ■ ■ ■

When I walked out of that execution chamber that night, I felt like I had been given my life back. It could not bring Cary back, but it gave us our life back.

—*Charlotte Stout, the mother of an eight-year-old murder victim, after witnessing the killer's execution in 2000*[xi]

the Death Penalty Information Center (DPIC), which maintains information on state-by-state estimates of such costs, "The death penalty costs North Carolina $2.16 million per execution *over* the costs of a non-death penalty murder case with a sentence of imprisonment for life."[146] The DPIC also says that some states spend far more on executions because of jurisdiction-specific litigation over such things as methods used. According to research cited by DPIC Director Richard C. Dieter, Florida spends $24 million for each execution that it carries out, and the death penalty costs California more than $100 million per event.[147] At those rates, a single execution costs many times what it would cost to imprison someone in a single cell at the highest security level for 40 years.[148] The death penalty can be expensive even in states where no executions have occurred. One 2005 New Jersey study, for example, found that the death penalty has cost state taxpayers more than $253 million in prosecution and other costs since 1992, even though no one has been executed in New Jersey since 1963.[149] Learn more about the costs of capital punishment at Library Extra 11–14 at cjtoday.com.

LIBRARY
Extra

Justifications for Capital Punishment

Meminerimus etiam adversus infimos justitiam esse servandam. [Let us remember that justice must be observed even to the lowest.]

—*Cicero (Marcus Tullius Cicero)*, De Natura Deorum *(III, 15)*

On February 11, 2004, 47-year-old Edward Lewis Lagrone was executed by lethal injection in Huntsville, Texas, for the murder of three people in their home. Earlier, Lagrone had molested and impregnated one of the victims, a 10-year-old child, whom he shot in the head as she was trying to protect her 19-month-old sister.[150] Lagrone also killed two of the child's great-aunts who were in the house at the time of the attack. One of the women, 76-year-old Caola Lloyd, was deaf, blind, and bedridden with cancer. Prior to the killings, Lagrone had served seven years of a 20-year prison sentence for another murder and was on parole. "He's a poster child to justify the death penalty," said David Montague, the Tarrant County assistant district attorney who prosecuted Lagrone.

Like many others today, Prosecutor Montague feels that "cold-blooded murder" justifies a sentence of death. Justifications for the death penalty are collectively referred to as the *retentionist position*. The three retentionist arguments are (1) revenge, (2) just deserts, and (3) protection. Those who justify capital punishment as revenge attempt to appeal to the idea that survivors, victims, and the state are entitled to "closure." Only after execution of the criminal perpetrator, they say, can the psychological and social wounds engendered by the offense begin to heal.

The just deserts argument makes the simple and straightforward claim that some people deserve to die for what they have done. Death is justly deserved; anything less cannot suffice as a sanction for the most heinous crimes. As U.S. Supreme Court Justice Potter Stewart once wrote, "The decision that capital punishment may be the appropriate sanction in extreme cases is an expression of the community's belief that certain crimes are themselves so grievous an affront to humanity that the only adequate response may be the penalty of death."[151]

The third retentionist claim, that of protection, asserts that offenders, once executed, can commit no further crimes. Clearly the least emotional of the retentionist claims, the protectionist argument may also be the weakest, since societal interests in protection can also be met in other ways, such as incarceration. In addition, various studies have shown that there is little likelihood of repeat offenses among people convicted of murder and later released.[152] One reason for such results, however, may be that murderers generally serve lengthy prison sentences prior to release and may have lost whatever youthful propensity for criminality they previously possessed. For an intriguing dialogue between two U.S. Supreme Court justices over the constitutionality of the death penalty, see Web Extra 11–11 at cjtoday.com.

WEB
Extra

The Courts and the Death Penalty

The U.S. Supreme Court has for some time served as a sounding board for issues surrounding the death penalty. One of the Court's earliest cases in this area was *Wilkerson* v. *Utah* (1878),[153] which questioned shooting as a method of execution and raised Eighth Amendment claims that firing squads constituted a form of cruel and unusual punishment. The Court disagreed, however, contrasting the relatively civilized nature of firing squads with the various forms of torture often associated with capital punishment around the time the Bill of Rights was written.

Similarly, the Court supported electrocution as a permissible form of execution in *In re Kemmler* (1890).[154] In *Kemmler*, the Court defined cruel and unusual methods of execution as follows: "Punishments are cruel when they involve torture or a lingering death; but the punishment of death is not cruel, within the meaning of that word as used in the Constitution. It implies there is something inhuman and barbarous, something more than the mere extinguishing of life."[155] Almost 60 years later, the Court ruled that a second attempt at the electrocution of a convicted person, when the first did not work, did not violate the Eighth Amendment.[156] The Court reasoned that the initial failure was the consequence of accident or unforeseen circumstances and not the result of an effort on the part of executioners to be intentionally cruel.

It was not until 1972, however, in the landmark case of *Furman* v. *Georgia*,[157] that the Court recognized "evolving standards of decency"[158] that might necessitate a reconsideration of Eighth Amendment guarantees. In a 5-4 ruling, the *Furman* decision invalidated Georgia's death penalty statute on the basis that it allowed a jury unguided discretion in the imposition of a capital sentence. The majority of justices concluded that the Georgia statute, which permitted a jury to decide issues of guilt or innocence while it weighed sentencing options, allowed for an arbitrary and capricious application of the death penalty.

Many other states with statutes similar to Georgia's were affected by the *Furman* ruling but moved quickly to modify their procedures. What evolved was the two-step procedure used today in capital cases. In the first stage, guilt or innocence is decided. If the defendant is convicted of a crime for which execution is possible, or if he pleads guilty to such an offense, a second, or penalty, phase ensues. The penalty phase, a kind of minitrial, generally permits the introduction of new evidence that may have been irrelevant to the question of guilt but that may be relevant to punishment, such as drug use or childhood abuse. In most death-penalty jurisdictions, juries determine the punishment. However, in Arizona, Idaho, Montana, and Nebraska, the trial judge sets the sentence in the second phase of capital murder trials, and Alabama, Delaware, Florida, and Indiana allow juries only to recommend a sentence to the judge. One of the most widely followed penalty hearings took place in 2006, in the case of al-Qaeda conspirator Zacarias Moussaoui. After a six-week trial and seven days of deliberations, a federal jury of nine men and three women decided that Moussaoui should spend the rest of his life in prison rather than be executed for his part in the 9/11 attacks.[159]

The Supreme Court formally approved the two-step trial procedure in *Gregg* v. *Georgia* (1976).[160] In *Gregg*, the Court upheld the two-stage procedural requirements of Georgia's new capital punishment law as necessary for ensuring the separation of the highly personal information needed in a sentencing decision from the kinds of information reasonably permissible in a jury trial where issues of guilt or innocence alone are being decided. In the opinion written for the majority, the Court for the first time recognized the significance of public opinion in deciding on the legitimacy of questionable sanctions.[161] Its opinion cited the strong showing of public support for the death penalty following *Furman* to mean that death was still a socially and culturally acceptable penalty.

Post-*Gregg* decisions set limits on the use of death as a penalty for all but the most severe crimes. In 1977, in the case of *Coker* v. *Georgia*,[162] the Court struck down a Georgia law imposing the death penalty for the rape of an adult woman. The Court concluded that capital punishment under such circumstances would be "grossly disproportionate" to the crime. A year earlier, in the 1976 case of *Woodson* v. *North Carolina*,[163] a law requiring mandatory application of the death penalty for specific crimes was overturned.

In two 1990 rulings, *Blystone* v. *Pennsylvania*[164] and *Boyde* v. *California*,[165] the Court upheld state statutes dictating that death penalties must be imposed where juries find a lack of mitigating factors that could offset obvious aggravating circumstances. In the 1990 case of R. Gene Simmons, an Arkansas mass murderer convicted of killing 16 relatives during a 1987 shooting rampage, the Court granted inmates under sentence of death the right to waive appeals.[166] Prior to the *Simmons* case, any interested party could file a brief on behalf of the condemned—with or without their consent.

In 2005, in the case of *Deck* v. *Missouri*,[167] the Court forbade the use of visible shackles during the penalty phase of capital trials, unless special circumstances justify their use. Although the Court meant to maintain the dignity and decorum of trial proceedings by not forcing a person to plead for his or her life in shackles, the justices also recognized that judges may order the use of restraints when they are necessary to protect themselves and their courtrooms and to reduce the risk of escape for offenders who are especially likely to flee.

Recently, death-row inmates, and those who file cases on their behalf to test the boundaries of statutory acceptability, have been busy challenging state capital punishment laws. Most such challenges focus on the procedures involved in sentencing decisions. In 1994, for example, a challenge to the constitutionality of California's capital sentencing law, which requires the jury to consider details such as the circumstances of the offense, prior violent crimes by the defendant, and the defendant's age, was rejected in *Tuilaepa* v. *California*.[168]

Excessive bail shall not be required, nor excessive fines imposed, nor cruel and unusual punishments inflicted.

—Eighth Amendment to the U.S. Constitution

Timothy Ring, the Arizona death-row inmate who won a 2002 U.S. Supreme Court case that could potentially invalidate the death sentences of at least 150 other prisoners. In that case, *Ring* v. *Arizona*, the Court held that defendants have a Sixth Amendment right to have a jury, and not just a judge, determine the existence of aggravating factors justifying the death penalty. What other decisions, made by the Court since then, have further refined the *Ring* ruling?

Matt York/AP Wide World Photos

Following *Apprendi* v. *New Jersey* (discussed earlier in this chapter), attorneys for an Arizona death-row inmate successfully challenged that state's practice of allowing judges, sitting without a jury, to make factual determinations necessary for imposition of the death penalty. In *Ring* v. *Arizona* (2002),[169] a jury had found Timothy Stuart Ring guilty of felony murder occurring in the course of an armed robbery for the killing of an armored car driver in 1994, but it deadlocked on the charge of premeditated murder. Under Arizona law, Ring could not be sentenced to death, the statutory maximum penalty for first-degree murder, unless a judge made further findings in a separate sentencing hearing. The death penalty could be imposed only if the judge found the existence of at least one aggravating circumstance specified by law that was not offset by mitigating circumstances. During such a hearing, the judge listened to an accomplice who said that Ring planned the robbery and shot the guard. The judge then determined that Ring was the actual killer and found that the killing was committed for financial gain (an aggravating factor). Following the hearing, Ring was sentenced to death. His attorneys appealed, claiming that, by the standards set forth in *Apprendi*, Arizona's sentencing scheme violated the Sixth Amendment's guarantee of a jury trial because it entrusted a judge with fact-finding powers that allowed Ring's sentence to be raised above what would otherwise have been the statutory maximum. The U.S. Supreme Court agreed and overturned Ring's sentence, finding that "Arizona's enumerated aggravating factors operate as the functional equivalent of an element of a greater offense." *Ring* established that juries, not judges, must decide the facts that lead to a death sentence. The *Ring* ruling called into question at least 150 judge-imposed death sentences[170] in at least five states (Arizona, Colorado, Idaho, Montana, and Nebraska).[171]

In 2003, in the case of *Summerlin* v. *Stewart*,[172] the U.S. Court of Appeals for the Ninth Circuit retroactively applied the *Ring* decision and vacated the death sentences of 100 prisoners in three states that fall within its jurisdiction. The court found that inmates in Arizona, Idaho, and Montana had been sent to death row by judges rather than juries in violation of *Ring* and ordered that their sentences be commuted to life in prison. Those sentences were reinstated, however, by the U.S. Supreme Court in the 2004 case of *Schriro* v. *Summerlin*,[173] in which the retroactivity analysis of the Ninth Circuit Court was invalidated. The rule established in *Apprendi* and *Ring*, said the Court, could not be applied to sentences that had already been imposed because it was merely a new procedural rule and not a substantive change. Only substantive changes, said the Court, are watershed events retroactively applicable to sentences that have already been finalized. Soon after *Ring* was decided, however, the affected states began the process of amending their death-penalty laws to bring them into line with the Court's new requirements.

Although questions may arise about sentencing practices, the majority of justices on today's high court seem largely convinced of the fundamental constitutionality of a sentence of death. Open to debate, however, is the constitutionality of *methods* for execution. In a 1993 hearing, *Poyner* v. *Murray*,[174] the U.S. Supreme Court hinted at the possibility of revisiting questions first raised in *Kemmler*. The case challenged Virginia's use of the electric chair, calling it a form of cruel and unusual punishment. Syvasky Lafayette Poyner, who originally brought the case before the Court, lost his bid for a stay of execution and was electrocuted in March 1993. Nonetheless, in *Poyner*, Justices David H. Souter, Harry A. Blackmun, and John Paul Stevens wrote, "The Court has not spoken squarely on the underlying issue since *In re Kemmler* . . . and the holding of that case does not constitute a dispositive response to litigation of the issue in light of modern knowledge about the method of execution in question."

In a still more recent ruling, members of the Court questioned the constitutionality of hanging, suggesting that it too may be a form of cruel and unusual punishment. In that case, *Campbell* v. *Wood* (1994),[175] the defendant, Charles Campbell, raped a woman, was released from prison at the completion of his sentence, and then went back and murdered her. His request for a stay of execution was denied since the law of Washington State, where the murder occurred, offered Campbell a choice of various methods of execution and, therefore, an alternative to hanging. Similarly, in 1996, the Court upheld California's death-penalty statute, which provides for lethal injection as the primary method of capital punishment in that state.[176] The constitutionality of the statute had been challenged by two death-row inmates who claimed that a provision in the law that permitted condemned prisoners the choice of lethal gas in lieu of injection brought the statute within the realm of allowing cruel and unusual punishments.

Questions about the constitutionality of electrocution as a means of execution again came to the fore in 1997, when flames shot from the head and the leather mask covering the face of Pedro Medina during his Florida execution. Similarly, in 1999, blood poured from behind the mask covering Allen Lee "Tiny" Davis's face as he was put to death in Florida's electric chair. State officials claimed that the 344-pound Davis suffered a nosebleed brought on by hypertension and the blood-thinning medication that he had been taking. Photographs of Davis taken during and immediately after the execution showed him grimacing while bleeding profusely onto his chest and neck. In 2001, the Georgia Supreme Court declared electrocution to be unconstitutional, ending its use in that state.[177] The Georgia court cited testimony from lower court records showing that electrocution may not result in a quick death or in an immediate cessation of consciousness. By the time of the court's decision, however, the Georgia legislature had already passed a law establishing lethal injection as the state's sole method of punishment for capital crimes. Today, only one state, Nebraska, still uses electrocution as its sole method of execution.[178]

In 2006, questions were raised about lethal injections as constituting cruel and unusual punishment. Those questions originated with eyewitness accounts, postmortem blood testing, and execution logs that seemed to show that some of those executed remained conscious but paralyzed and experienced excruciating pain before dying.[179] Such claims focused on the composition of the chemical cocktail used in executions, which contains one drug (sodium thiopental, a short-acting barbiturate) to induce sleep, another (pancuronium bromide) to paralyze the muscles (but which does not cause unconsciousness), and a third (potassium chloride) to stop the heart. If the first chemical is improperly administered, the condemned person remains conscious, and the procedure can cause severe pain. Complicating matters is the fact that the ethical codes of most professional medical organizations forbid medical practitioners to take life—meaning that, although the codes are not legally binding, medical professionals are largely excluded from taking part in executions, other than to verify the fact that death has occurred. To counter fears that lethal injections cause pain, some states have begun using medical monitoring devices that show brain activity and that can ensure that the person is unconscious.[180]

The U.S. Supreme Court has ruled that certain personal characteristics of the perpetrator, such as age and mental inability, can be a bar to execution. In 2001, for example, in the case of *Penry* v. *Johnson*,[181] the U.S. Supreme Court found that a state trial court in Texas had failed to allow a jury to properly consider a murder defendant's low IQ and childhood abuse as mitigating factors when it found that his crime warranted the death penalty rather than life in prison. This was the second time that the Court had ordered a new sentencing hearing for Johnny Paul Penry, who was first convicted of brutally raping and murdering Pamela Carpenter on October 25, 1979, and had twice been sentenced to die.[182] In both cases, the Court found fault with Texas jury instructions and the system for their implementation, which restricted jurors from effectively weighing Penry's mental retardation as a mitigating circumstance in their sentencing decision. However, shortly after the Court's decision, Texas Governor Rick Perry vetoed legislation that would have banned the execution of mentally retarded death-row inmates throughout the state.[183]

At bottom, then, the Cruel and Unusual Punishments Clause prohibits the infliction of uncivilized and inhuman punishments. The State, even as it punishes, must treat its members with respect for their intrinsic worth as human beings. A punishment is "cruel and unusual," therefore, if it does not comport with human dignity.

—Former U.S. Supreme Court Justice William Brennan, concurring in Furman v. Georgia[xii]

When a juvenile commits a heinous crime, the State can exact forfeiture of some of the most basic liberties, but the State cannot extinguish his life and his potential to attain a mature understanding of his own humanity.

—Roper *v.* Simmons *(2005)*

Following *Penry*, the U.S. Supreme Court ruled in the case of *Atkins* v. *Virginia* (2002)[184] that executing mentally retarded people violates the Constitution's ban on cruel and unusual punishments. The Court, following the lead of the federal government and the 18 states that had already banned such executions, noted that "a national consensus has developed against it." According to the Court, the standards by which the practice and imposition of capital punishment are to be judged today are not those that prevailed at the time the Bill of Rights was authored. They are, rather, "the evolving standards of decency that mark the progress of a maturing society."[185] Atkins, whose IQ was measured at 59 (100 is "average"), had been convicted of murdering a man during a robbery when he was 18.

In what some thought an unusual turn of events, Johnny Paul Penry, whose case sparked national interest in the execution of mentally retarded offenders, was sentenced to death for a third time only 10 days after the *Atkins* ruling. The Texas jury that sentenced him rejected his claims of mental inadequacy.[186] Nonetheless, *Atkins* called into question the standing of a substantial number of death-row inmates across the country, many of whom are expected to appeal their convictions. The case also ushered in a national debate on how mental retardation should be measured. Finally, some people questioned the Court's wisdom in keeping mentally retarded offenders from facing the death penalty, saying that capital crimes involve moral judgments, not intellectual ones, and that even people of low intelligence should be expected to act morally.[187]

Although people with very low IQs may not be executed, serious mental illness is *not* a bar to execution unless it affects the condemned inmate's mind such that he doesn't know why he's on death row or doesn't understand the punishment he faces. In 2004, for example, Texas Governor Rick Perry rejected a recommendation by the Texas Board of Pardons and Paroles as well as a humanitarian request by the president of the European Union that he commute the sentence of mentally ill killer Kelsey Patterson to life imprisonment.[188] Patterson, who apparently suffered from a particularly severe form of paranoid schizophrenia, frequently spoke of "remote control devices" and "implants" that controlled him and said that he committed acts involuntarily.[189] Patterson was executed shortly after the governor denied clemency. Patterson had been on death row since 1992 for the shooting death of a secretary and her boss at an oil company office in Palestine, Texas.

Finally, in 2007, a closely divided U.S. Supreme Court stayed the execution of Texas murderer Scott Panetti who suffers from an especially severe form of schizophrenia. Panetti had killed his parents-in-law in 1992 by shooting them at close range inside their Texas home while his terrified wife and daughter watched. In preventing Panetti's execution, the Court held that "gross delusions stemming from a severe mental disorder may put an awareness of a link between a crime and its punishment in a context so far removed from reality that the punishment can serve no proper purpose."[190] Because the *Panetti* ruling focused narrowly on Panetti's particular form of mental illness, it is not expected to prevent the execution of other mentally ill death-row inmates.

Age *is* a bar to execution when the offender committed the crime when he was younger than 18, a standard announced in the 2005 U.S. Supreme Court case of *Roper* v. *Simmons*.[191] The majority opinion in the case, based on what the Court considered to be evolving standards of decency, was rendered after the justices heard evidence that juveniles are generally impetuous, immature, and vulnerable to negative peer pressure. The ruling, which is also discussed in Chapter 15, invalidated the capital sentences of 72 death-row inmates in 12 states. Among the 962 people put to death between January 1976 and January 2004, 22 had committed their crimes as juveniles.[192]

Although there is as yet no *upper* age limit on executions, some have made the argument that a person may be too old and infirm to die at the hands of the state. Just such an argument was advanced in the case of San Quentin State Prison inmate Clarence Ray Allen before his January 17, 2006, execution by lawyers who said that the 76-year-old Allen, sentenced to die for a triple murder that he ordered from behind bars, was too old and too sick to be put to death. Executing someone like Allen—who had had two heart attacks and a stroke and was legally blind, nearly deaf, diabetic, and confined to a wheelchair—"is beyond the borders of civilized behavior," said his attorney, Michael Satris.[193]

The Future of the Death Penalty

Evolving standards of human decency will finally lead to the abolition of the death penalty in this country.

—Former U.S. Supreme Court Justice William Brennan

Support for the death penalty varies considerably from state to state and from one region of the country to another. Short of renewed Supreme Court intervention, the future of capital punishment may depend more on popular opinion than it does on arguments pro or con. A Gallup poll taken in May 2003 found 79% of those polled in favor of the death penalty under certain circumstances. A similar poll by the same organization found that although most respondents voiced support for the death penalty, that support dropped to 53% when respondents were offered an al-

CJ News

Wider Use of the Death Penalty Being Sought

At least a half-dozen states are considering broadening the death penalty, countering a national trend toward scaling back its use.

Lawmakers have proposed legislation that would increase the range of crimes eligible for execution. In Texas and Tennessee, for example, legislators want to include certain child molesters who did not murder their victims.

"The hope is that these monsters will see that Texas is serious about protecting children," says Rich Parsons, spokesman for Lt. Gov. David Dewhurst. Dewhurst, a Republican, is working with state senators to draft legislation that would make repeat offenders subject to capital punishment in some cases. "If they understand they could face the ultimate punishment," they might "think twice," Parsons says.

Virginia is considering bills that would make accomplices to murder, as well as killers of judges and court witnesses, eligible for the death penalty.

"I'm a believer in the deterrent effect of the death penalty," says Republican Delegate Todd Gilbert, a state prosecutor who sponsored two of the measures. "I know a number of states are reconsidering their position on the death penalty. . . . I feel confident Virginia's system is set up to work."

Lawmakers or courts have temporarily halted all executions in 11 states in the past year, most of them over concerns that lethal injection is cruel and unusual punishment, says Richard Dieter of the Death Penalty Information Center, which he says takes no position on the death penalty but has been critical of how it is applied.

In December, a convicted killer in Florida took 34 minutes to die and had chemical burns on his arms after a lethal injection procedure. After the execution, then-governor Jeb Bush created a commission to study possible improvements and halted executions until the commission releases its report.

Other states with proposals to expand the death penalty:

- Missouri. Gov. Matt Blunt said in his State of the State address [in January 2007] that he wants a mandatory death penalty for the murder of law enforcement officers. Blunt, a Republican, says the state must protect its public servants and the death penalty would be a deterrent. "This is the type of crime that calls for the death penalty," he says.

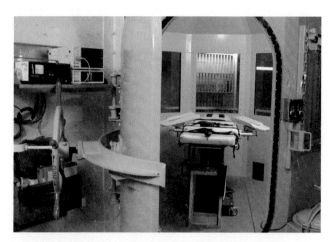

The execution chamber at San Quentin State Prison. What arguments can be made in favor of and against capital punishment? Which arguments do you find most compelling?
California Department of Corrections and Rehabilitation

Robert Blecker, a law professor at New York Law School who specializes in the death penalty, says the Supreme Court has found mandatory death sentences unconstitutional because they don't allow defendants to present mitigating evidence. Blunt says his measure will take that into account.

- Georgia. GOP state Rep. Barry Fleming has introduced a bill to allow a judge to impose the death sentence if at least nine of 12 jurors—not all 12, as now—voted for it.

- Utah. The House passed a bill Tuesday making murder of a child under 14 subject to execution.

State Rep. Paul Ray, a Republican, introduced a bill to allow the death penalty for killing a child during abuse, sexual assault or kidnapping, even if prosecutors cannot prove intent to kill. He expects the House to vote later this week.

"We're going to send a message that if you kill our kids in Utah, we're going to kill you," he says. "In Utah, I don't think we use the death penalty enough."

For the latest in crime and justice news, visit the Talk Justice news feed at http://www.crimenews.info.

Source: Emily Bazar, "Wider Death Penalty Sought," USA TODAY, February 7, 2007, p. 1A. Reprinted by permission.

ternative sentence of life without parole.[194] Pollsters also learned that the percentage of Americans supporting capital punishment appeared to increase substantially following the events of September 11, 2001.[195]

Ultimately, public opinion about the death penalty may turn on the issue of whether innocent people have been executed. According to one 2005 study, Americans from all walks of life are less likely to support capital punishment if they believe that innocent people have been put to death

*So justice, while she winks
at crimes, stumbles on
innocence sometimes.*

—Samuel Butler, Hudibras *(canto II, pt.
II, l. 1177)*

at the hands of the justice system or if they think that the death penalty is being applied unfairly.[196] The study's authors note that support for the death penalty among Americans varies by race, with African Americans less likely to support capital punishment than whites. They found that much of the difference, however, is explained by differing beliefs between the races about the number of executed innocents and perceived fairness in application of capital sanctions. Consequently, execution of the innocent is at the center of today's debate concerning the legitimacy of capital punishment, and it is likely to determine the future of the death penalty in individual states as local legislatures move to mandate procedural enhancements meant to guarantee fairness.

In 2002, a special commission appointed by Governor George Ryan to examine the imposition of capital punishment in Illinois made its report, saying that the system through which capital sentences are imposed should be modified to encompass a number of procedural safeguards. Safeguards that were recommended included (1) tighter controls on how the police investigate cases, including a requirement that investigators "continue to pursue all reasonable lines of inquiry, whether these point toward or away from the suspect"; (2) controls on the potential fallibility of eyewitness testimony, including lineups where the person in charge is not aware of which person in the lineup is the suspect (to preclude him or her from unconsciously identifying the suspect); and (3) statutory reform so that the death penalty cannot be applied based solely on the testimony of any single accomplice or eyewitness without further corroboration.[197] In April 2003, incoming Illinois Governor Rod R. Blagojevich said that because of his concerns over executing innocent people, he would not lift his state's ban on executions even if the state's legislature passed a bill aimed at improving the system.[198]

SUMMARY

- The goals of criminal sentencing include retribution, incapacitation, deterrence, rehabilitation, and restoration. Retribution corresponds to the just deserts model of sentencing, which holds that offenders are responsible for their crimes. Incapacitation seeks to protect innocent members of society from offenders who might harm them if not prevented from doing so. The goal of deterrence is to prevent future criminal activity through the example or threat of punishment. Rehabilitation seeks to bring about fundamental changes in offenders and their behavior to reduce the likelihood of future criminality. Restoration seeks to address the damage done by crime by making the victim and the community "whole again."

- The indeterminate sentencing model is characterized primarily by vast judicial choice. It builds on the belief that convicted offenders are more likely to participate in their own rehabilitation if such participation will reduce the amount of time that they have to spend in prison.

- Structured sentencing is largely a child of the just deserts philosophy. It grew out of concerns with proportionality, equity, and social debt—all of which this chapter discusses. A number of different types of structured sentencing models have been created, including determinate sentencing, which requires that a convicted offender be sentenced to a fixed term that may be reduced by good time or gain time, and a voluntary/advisory sentencing model under which guidelines consist of recommended sentencing policies that are not required by law, are usually based on past sentencing practices, and are meant to serve as guides to judges. Mandatory sentencing, another form of structured sentencing, mandates clearly enumerated punishments for specific offenses or for habitual offenders convicted of a series of crimes. The applicability of structured sentencing guidelines has been called into question by recent U.S. Supreme Court decisions.

- Alternative sanctions include the use of court-ordered community service, home detention, day reporting, drug treatment, psychological counseling, victim–offender mediation, and intensive supervision in lieu of other, more traditional, sanctions, such as imprisonment and fines. A number of questions have been raised about alternative sentences, including questions about their impact on public safety, the cost-effectiveness of such sanctions, and the long-term effects of community sanctions on people assigned to alternative programs.

- Probation and parole officers routinely conduct background investigations to provide information that judges may use in deciding on the appropriate kind or length of sentence for convicted offenders.

- Historically, criminal courts have often allowed victims to testify at trial but have otherwise downplayed the experience of victimization and the suffering it causes. A new interest in the rights experience of victims, beginning in the 1970s in this country, has led to a greater legal recognition of victims' rights, including a right to allocution (the right to be heard during criminal proceedings). Many states have passed victims' rights amendments to their constitutions, although a federal victims' rights amendment has yet to be enacted. The Crime Victims' Rights Act of 2004 established statutory rights for victims of federal crimes and gives them the necessary legal authority to assert those rights in federal court.

- The four traditional sentencing options identified in this chapter are fines, probation, imprisonment, and—in cases of especially horrific offenses—death. The appropriateness of each sentencing option for various kinds of crimes was dis-cussed, and the pros and cons of each were examined.

- Arguments for capital punishment identified in this chapter include revenge, just deserts, and the protection of society. The revenge argument builds upon the need for personal and communal closure. The just deserts argument makes the straightforward claim that some people deserve to die for what they have done. Societal protection is couched in terms of deterrence, since those who are executed cannot commit future crimes, and execution serves as an example to other would-be wrongdoers. Arguments against capital punishment include findings that a death sentence has been imposed on innocent people, that the death penalty has not been found to be an effective deterrent, that it is often arbitrarily imposed, that it tends to discriminate against powerless groups and individuals, and that it is very expensive because of the numerous court appeals involved. Opponents also argue that the state should recognize the sanctity of human life.

KEY TERMS

aggravating circumstances, 389

alternative sentencing, 398

capital offense, 407

capital punishment, 407

determinate sentencing, 389

deterrence, 384

diversion, 397

equity, 388

gain time, 388

general deterrence, 384

good time, 388

incapacitation, 384

indeterminate sentencing, 387

just deserts, 384

mandatory sentencing, 395

mitigating circumstances, 389

presentence investigation (PSI), 400

presumptive sentencing, 389

proportionality, 388

rehabilitation, 385

restoration, 385

restorative justice (RJ), 386

retribution, 383

sentencing, 382

social debt, 388

specific deterrence, 384

structured sentencing, 389

truth in sentencing, 389

victim-impact statement, 403

voluntary/advisory sentencing guidelines, 389

writ of *habeas corpus*, 408

KEY CASES

Apprendi v. *New Jersey,* 394

Atkins v. *Virginia,* 420

Blakely v. *Washington,* 394

Coker v. *Georgia,* 417

Coleman v. *Thompson,* 409

Deal v. *U.S.* 391

QUESTIONS FOR REVIEW

1. Describe the five goals of contemporary criminal sentencing discussed in this chapter. Which of these goals do you think ought to be the primary goal of sentencing? How might your choice vary with the type of offense? In what circumstances might your choice be less acceptable?

2. Illustrate the nature of indeterminate sentencing, and explain its positive aspects. What led some states to abandon indeterminate sentencing?

3. What is structured sentencing? What structured sentencing models are in use today? Which model holds the best promise for long-term crime reduction? Why?

4. What are alternative sanctions? Give some examples of alternative sanctions, and offer an assessment of how effective they might be.

5. What is a presentence investigation? How do presentence investigations contribute to the contents of presentence reports? How are presentence reports used?

6. Describe the history of victims' rights and services in this country. What role does the victim play in criminal justice proceedings today?

7. What are the four traditional sentencing options? Under what circumstances might each be appropriate?

8. Do you support or oppose capital punishment? Outline the arguments on both sides of the issue.

QUESTIONS FOR REFLECTION

1. Of the different kinds of sentencing practices described in this chapter, which do you think make the most sense? Why?

2. If you could set sentencing practices in your state and had to choose between a determinate and an indeterminate scheme, which would you select? Why?

3. What is truth in sentencing? Do you agree that it is an important concept? Why or why not?

4. Explain the development of federal sentencing guidelines. What have recent court decisions said about the applicability of those guidelines?

5. In your opinion, is the return to just deserts consistent with structured sentencing? Explain.

WEB QUEST

Visit the U.S. Sentencing Commission (USSC) on the Web at http://www.ussc.gov. Review the most recent publications and reports to Congress available at that site, and identify the current issues in federal sentencing. List and describe these issues. Also view the USSC employment opportunities listed at the site, and read the information about the Judicial Fellows Program.

Now visit the Sentencing Project at http://www.sentencingproject.org. (You can use the Prentice Hall Cybrary to find sites that have moved since this book was published.) What is the mission of the Sentencing Project? How does that mission coincide with the interests of the National Association of Sentencing Advocates? (A link to this organization can be found on the Sentencing Project home page, or you can find it through the Cybrary.) Summarize what you have learned, and submit your findings to your instructor if asked to do so.

To complete this Web Quest online, go to the Web Quest module in Chapter 11 of the *Criminal Justice Today* Companion Website at cjtoday.com.

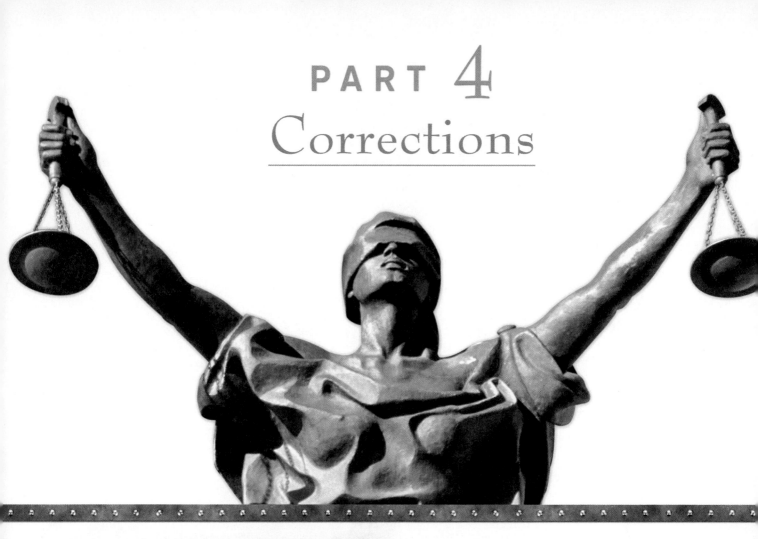

PART 4
Corrections

RIGHTS OF THE CONVICTED AND IMPRISONED

The convicted and imprisoned have these common law, constitutional, statutory, and humanitarian rights

- A right against cruel or unusual punishment

- A right to protection from physical harm

- A right to sanitary and healthy conditions of confinement

- A limited right to legal assistance while imprisoned

- A limited right to religious freedom while imprisoned

- A limited right to freedom of speech while imprisoned

- A limited right to due process prior to denial of privileges

These individual rights must be effectively balanced against these public-order concerns

- Punishment of the guilty

- Safe communities

- The reduction of recidivism

- Secure prisons

- Control over convicts

- The prevention of escape

- Rehabilitation

- Affordable prisons

How does our system of justice work toward balance?

12

Probation, Parole, and Community Corrections

13

Prisons and Jails

14

Prison Life

Punishment—Justice for the Unjust?

The great Christian writer C. S. Lewis (1898–1963) once remarked that if satisfying justice is to be the ultimate goal of Western criminal justice, then the fate of offenders cannot be dictated merely by practical considerations. "The concept of just desert is the only connecting link between punishment and justice," Lewis wrote. "It is only as deserved or undeserved that a sentence can be just or unjust," he concluded.

Once a person has been arrested, tried, and sentenced, the correctional process begins. Unlike Lewis's exhortation, however, the contemporary American correctional system—which includes probation, parole, jails, prisons, capital punishment, and a variety of innovative alternatives to traditional sentences—is tasked with far more than merely carrying out sentences. We also ask of our correctional system that it ensure the safety of law-abiding citizens, that it select the best alternative from among the many available for handling each offender, that it protect those under its charge, and that it guarantee fairness in the handling of all with whom it comes into contact.

This section of *Criminal Justice Today* details the development of probation, parole, community corrections, and imprisonment as corrections philosophies; describes the nuances of prison and jail life; discusses special issues in contemporary corrections (including AIDS, geriatric offenders, and female inmates); and summarizes the legal environment that both surrounds and infuses the modern-day practice of corrections. Characteristic of today's corrections emphasis is a society-wide push for harsher punishments. The culmination of that strategy, however, is significantly overcrowded correctional institutions, the problems of which are also described. As you read through this section, encountering descriptions of various kinds of criminal sanctions, you might ask yourself, "When would a punishment of this sort be deserved?" In doing so, remember to couple that thought with another question: "What are the ultimate consequences (for society and for the offender) of the kind of correctional program we are discussing here?" Unlike Lewis, you may also want to ask, "Can we afford it?"

CHAPTER 12

Probation, Parole, and Community Corrections

LEARNING OBJECTIVES

After reading this chapter, you should be able to

- Explain the history, nature, and purposes of probation.

- Explain the history, nature, and purposes of parole.

- Describe the advantages and disadvantages of probation and parole.

- Describe the legal environment surrounding the use of probation and parole, and know the names of significant court cases.

- Explain the nature of the job of probation and parole officers.

- Explain what intermediate sanctions are, and list the advantages of intermediate sanctions over more traditional forms of sentencing.

- Describe the likely future of probation and parole.

There is ample evidence that well-designed reentry programs reduce recidivism.

—Senate Judiciary Committee Chairman Arlen Specter[1]

Community corrections is an integral part of the criminal justice system and should be fully implemented and promoted in order to save expensive and scarce jail and prison space for violent and serious offenders.

—National Association of Counties, Justice and Public Safety Steering Committee[2]

Hear the author discuss this chapter at cjtoday.com

Introduction

On May 27, 2006, parolee Richard Davis and his girlfriend Dena Riley were arrested after their pickup truck spun out of control and crashed into a ditch on a dirt road in southwestern Missouri.[3] The arrest ended a multistate search for the Independence, Missouri, couple, who were accused of videotaping the rape of a woman in their bedroom and then killing her. Davis, 41, and Riley, 39, were charged with first-degree murder, first-degree assault, kidnapping, forcible rape, and two counts of forcible sodomy in the death of 41-year-old Marsha Spicer, whose naked body had been found in a shallow grave 12 days earlier. Davis had spent nearly 18 years in prison for a 1987 rape and sodomy conviction and was still on parole at the time of his arrest. The videotape of the assault on Spicer was said to be so disturbing that authorities were reported to be offering counseling to investigators who had viewed it.

In yet another sad story, 11-year-old Floridian Carlie Brucia was abducted in 2004 as she took a shortcut to her home from a slumber party at a friend's house. Video footage of Carlie's abduction was captured by an unattended car wash security camera, which showed the girl being grabbed by an unidentified man and led away.[4] Carlie's body was discovered days later in a church parking lot a few miles from her home. Shortly after her abduction, authorities arrested Joseph P. Smith, a 37-year-old auto mechanic and father of three who had a lengthy criminal record. It was soon learned that Smith had been arrested at least 13 times in Florida in the 11 years before Carlie's abduction and had previously been charged with kidnapping and false imprisonment. Only a month before Carlie's murder, a probation officer had asked a Florida judge to declare Smith a probation violator because of unpaid fines and court costs that he had been ordered to pay. The probation officer's request had been denied, and Smith remained free. Smith was convicted of first-degree murder and rape by a Florida jury in 2005, and he was sentenced to death by state Judge Andrew Owens in March 2006.[5]

Stories with victims like Spicer and Brucia appear all too frequently in the media and cast a harsh light on the early release and poor supervision of criminal offenders. This chapter takes a close look at the realities behind the practice of what we call **community corrections**. Community corrections, also termed *community-based corrections*, is a sentencing style that depends less on traditional confinement options and more on correctional resources available in the community. Community corrections includes a wide variety of sentencing options, such as probation, parole, home confinement, the electronic monitoring of offenders, and other new and developing programs—all of which are covered in this chapter. Learn more about community corrections by visiting the International Community Corrections Association via Web Extra 12–1 at cjtoday.com.

community corrections

The use of a variety of officially ordered program-based sanctions that permit convicted offenders to remain in the community under conditional supervision as an alternative to an active prison sentence.

WEB
Extra

What Is Probation?

probation

A sentence of imprisonment that is suspended. Also, the conditional freedom granted by a judicial officer to a convicted offender, as long as the person meets certain conditions of behavior.

Probation, one aspect of community corrections, is "a sentence served while under supervision in the community."[6] Like other sentencing options, probation is a court-ordered sanction. Its goal is to retain some control over criminal offenders while using community programs to help rehabilitate them. Most of the alternative sanctions discussed later in this chapter are, in fact, predicated on probationary sentences in which the offender is ordered to abide by certain conditions—such as participation in a specified program—while remaining free in the community. Although the court in many jurisdictions can impose probation directly, most probationers are sentenced first to confinement but then immediately have their sentences suspended and are remanded into the custody of an officer of the court—the probation officer.

Two frames from a car wash surveillance camera in Sarasota, Florida, showing 11-year-old Carlie Brucia being abducted in 2004. Brucia's body was later discovered at a church three miles from the abduction site. Police quickly arrested Joseph P. Smith, 37, a chronic drug abuser with a long arrest record, and charged him with kidnapping and murder. Court records showed that Smith had violated the conditions of his probation and should have been imprisoned at the time of the abduction. In 2005, Smith was tried and convicted of kidnapping, raping, and strangling Brucia. How can such crimes be prevented?

© David Kadlubowski/Sarasota County Sheriff's Office/CORBIS/All Rights Reserved and Sarasota County Sheriff's Office/AP Wide World Photos

Probation has a long history. By the fourteenth century, English courts had established the practice of "binding over for good behavior,"[7] in which offenders could be entrusted into the custody of willing citizens. American John Augustus (1784–1859) is generally recognized as the world's first probation officer. Augustus, a Boston shoemaker, attended sessions of criminal court in the 1850s and offered to take carefully selected offenders into his home as an alternative to imprisonment.[8] At first, he supervised only drunkards, but by 1857 Augustus was accepting many kinds of offenders and was devoting all his time to the service of the court.[9] Augustus died in 1859, having bailed out more than 2,000 convicts. In 1878, the Massachusetts legislature enacted a statute that authorized the city of Boston to hire a salaried probation officer. Missouri followed suit in 1897, along with Vermont (1898) and Rhode Island (1899).[10] Before the end of the nineteenth century, probation had become an accepted and widely used form of community-based supervision. By 1925, all 48 states had adopted probation legislation. In that same year, the federal government enacted legislation enabling federal district court judges to appoint paid probation officers and to impose probationary terms.[11]

Accepting released offenders into the community without a period of supervised release is morally unsatisfying; they have not yet earned their place at our table.

—Jeremy Travis, President, John Jay College of Criminal Justice[i]

The Extent of Probation

Today, probation is the most common form of criminal sentencing in the United States. Between 20% and 60% of those found guilty of crimes are sentenced to some form of probation. Figure 12–1 shows that 59% of all offenders under correctional supervision in the United States as of January 1, 2006, were on probation. Not shown is that the number of offenders supervised yearly on probation has increased from slightly more than 1 million in 1980 to over 4 million today—almost a 300% increase.[12]

Even violent offenders stand about a one in five chance of receiving a probationary term. A Bureau of Justice Statistics study of felony sentences found that 5% of people convicted of homicide were placed on probation, as were 21% of convicted sex offenders.[13] Twelve percent of convicted robbers and 30% of those committing aggravated assault were similarly sentenced to probation rather than active prison time. In one example, 47-year-old Carrie Mote of Vernon, Connecticut, was sentenced to probation for shooting her fiancé in the chest with a .38-caliber handgun after he called off their wedding.[14] Mote, who faced a maximum of 20 years in prison, claimed to be suffering from diminished psychological capacity at the time of the shooting because of the emotional stress brought on by the canceled wedding.

At the beginning of 2007, a total of 4,237,023 adults were on probation throughout the nation.[15] Individual states, however, make greater or lesser use of probation. North Dakota authorities, with

Offenders under correctional supervision in the United States, by type of supervision.

Source: Bureau of Justice Statistics, Correctional Surveys.

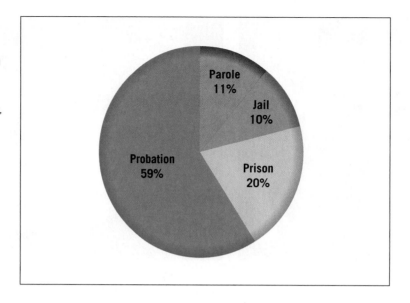

the smallest probationary population, supervise only 4,085 people, while Texas reports 430,301 offenders on probation. On a per capita basis, New Hampshire has the lowest rate of probation (450 for every 100,000 residents), while Georgia has the highest (6,059 for every 100,000 residents). The national average is 1,868 for every 100,000 residents. Fifty-seven percent of the more than 2.2 million adults discharged from probation in 2006 had successfully met the conditions of their supervision. Approximately 13% of those discharged from supervision, however, were incarcerated because of a rule violation or because they committed a new offense. Another 4% absconded, and 12% had their probation sentence revoked without being ordered to serve time.[16] See more statistics describing community corrections at Library Extra 12–1 at cjtoday.com.

LIBRARY
Extra
■■■■

Probation Conditions

probation revocation

A court order taking away a convicted offender's probationary status and usually withdrawing the conditional freedom associated with that status in response to a violation of the conditions of probation.

Those sentenced to probation must agree to abide by court-mandated conditions of probation. A violation of conditions can lead to **probation revocation**. Conditions are of two types: general and specific. General conditions apply to all probationers in a given jurisdiction and usually require that the probationer obey all laws, maintain employment, remain within the jurisdiction of the court, possess no firearms, allow the probation officer to visit at home or at work, and so forth. As a general condition of probation, many probationers are also required to pay a fine to the court, usually in a series of installments. The fine is designed to reimburse victims for damages and to pay lawyers' fees and other court costs.

Special conditions may be mandated by a judge who feels that the probationer is in need of particular guidance or control. Depending on the nature of the offense, a judge may require that the offender surrender his or her driver's license; submit at reasonable times to warrantless and unannounced searches by a probation officer; supply breath, urine, or blood samples as needed for drug or alcohol testing; complete a specified number of hours of community service; or pass the general equivalency diploma (GED) test within a specified time. The judge may also dictate special conditions tailored to the probationer's situation. Such individualized conditions may prohibit the offender from associating with named others (a codefendant, for example), they may require that the probationer be at home after dark, or they may demand that the offender complete a particular treatment program within a set time.

Federal Probation

The federal probation system is more than 80 years old.[17] In 1916, in the *Killets* case,[18] the U.S. Supreme Court ruled that federal judges did not have the authority to suspend sentences and to order probation. After a vigorous campaign by the National Probation Association, Congress passed the National Probation Act in 1925, authorizing the use of probation in federal courts. The bill came just in time to save a burgeoning federal prison system from serious overcrowding. The prostitution-fighting Mann Act, Prohibition legislation, and the growth of organized crime all led

CJ News

More Sex Offenders Tracked by Satellite

Hundreds of convicted sex offenders will have to wear a two-piece electronic tracking device for the rest of their lives under a new Wisconsin law.

Ankle bracelets and a pager-sized unit, often attached to a belt, will use Global Positioning System (GPS) technology to follow their every step. If they enter restricted areas, such as schools, officials will be alerted.

GPS programs will track 285 offenders the first year, beginning July 2007, and up to 400 by the second year, says Dan Leistikow, spokesman for Wisconsin Gov. Jim Doyle.

In May 2006, Wisconsin joined a rapidly rising number of states using GPS to monitor convicted sex offenders. At least 23 states are doing so, according to a survey in February by the Pennsylvania Board of Probation and Parole. Others have since begun or expanded GPS programs.

"In the last several months, it's been exponential growth," says Steve Chapin, president of Pro-Tech, a Florida-based firm that provides GPS services to 27 statewide agencies. He says his business has doubled in the past three months.

As of January 2006, 13 states had laws requiring or allowing GPS tracking, says the National Conference of State Legislatures.

Aside from Wisconsin, governors in at least six states (Arkansas, Georgia, Kansas, Virginia, Washington and Michigan) have signed such bills this year [2006]. New Hampshire Gov. John Lynch plans to do so soon. Similar bills are pending elsewhere.

"It's the law you can't vote against," says Chapin.

Several of the laws are named after Jessica Lunsford, a 9-year-old Florida girl who was kidnapped, raped and killed in February 2005. The man charged with killing her was a convicted sex offender who hadn't reported that he lived across the street from her family. After he fled, it took almost a month to find him.

Even states without specific GPS laws, including Minnesota and Texas, are testing the technology and expanding its use.

Congress may accelerate such efforts. The House and Senate have each passed sex offender bills this year that approve funding for GPS tracking. They need to craft a final bill.

MORE ACCURATE TECHNOLOGY

The surge in GPS use coincides with the technology's dramatic advancements. The devices have become smaller and more accurate, often pinpointing a person's position within 30 feet. They are more precise than older devices that use radio frequencies and detect only when the wearer leaves a certain area, such as home if under house arrest.

GPS units can be programmed to have "exclusion zones" where offenders are not allowed and "inclusion zones" where they should be.

States are spending $5 to $10 daily to track each sex offender. Some require offenders, unless indigent, to pay the tab. They can choose the costlier "active" tracking, which gives real-time reports, or "passive" monitoring, which sends one report daily that lists where the offender went that day.

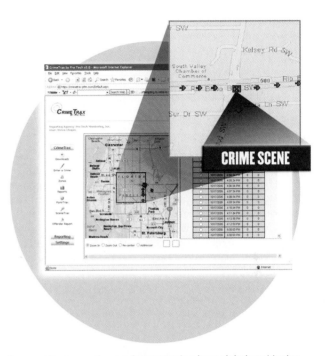

A computer screen image demonstrating how global positioning systems allow parole officers to track the movements of supervised offenders. What do you see as the advantages and disadvantages of this technology? How would individual-rights and public-safety advocates see this technology?

Courtesy of Pro Tech Monitoring

States have tried both:

- California uses GPS to track 430 sex offenders and has funds to follow 2,500 offenders by 2009, says Elaine Jennings of the California Department of Corrections and Rehabilitation.

  Since the program began in July 2005, 45 offenders have been arrested for violating parole and no new crimes have been committed, she says.

  "It's an excellent supervision tool" but doesn't supplant human supervision, says Jennings.

- Massachusetts has issued eight arrest warrants for violations by the 192 high-risk offenders it has tracked since its "active" GPS program began in May 2005, says Paul Lucci, one of the state's deputy probation commissioners. The state has officers who constantly watch a computer screen recording offenders' whereabouts and who can respond immediately.

- Michigan finished three pilot programs in 2003 and plans this summer [2006] to begin tracking up to 1,000 sex offenders, says Steve Bock of the Michigan Department of Corrections' Electronic Monitoring Center.

(continued)

CJ News (continued)

Bock says the state will use "passive" monitoring, because "active" GPS is too labor-intensive. He says real-time tracking generates "a ton of messages" that necessitate a 24/7 response team. He says it's problematic if offenders are barred from many areas, because GPS allows only a certain number of exclusion zones. "It can become a nightmare to enforce," Bock says.

OPPOSITION TO GPS TRACKING

Jake Goldenflame, 68, a convicted sex offender released 15 years ago, opposes lifetime GPS tracking. "If a man is so dangerous he needs it, he shouldn't be released," he says. Goldenflame says such monitoring may provide a "false sense of security," because it tells where the offender is, not what he's doing.

"It is not an effective way to prevent sexual assaults," says Richard Wright, a professor of criminal justice at Bridgewater State College. He says many serious sex offenders evade police by failing to register and others may re-offend regardless of tracking. He says no definitive study proves GPS deters crime.

Chapin says GPS reduces recidivism because offenders can't get away as easily. He says a December 2004 analysis by the Florida Department of Corrections found 3.8% of offenders tracked with GPS committed a new felony within two years compared to 7.7% of those supervised without it.

Offenders tracked by GPS were 90% less likely to abscond or re-offend than those not electronically monitored, says a February [2006] study by Florida State University of 75,661 offenders placed on home confinement. GPS did about as well as radio frequency, which costs four times less. "It's not a cost-free device," says Mark Carey, president of the American Probation and Parole Association. "It's an augmentation of what we do. It's not a replacement."

For the latest in crime and justice news, visit the Talk Justice news feed at http://www.crimenews.info.

Source: Wendy Koch, "More Sex Offenders Tracked by Satellite," USA TODAY, June 6, 2006. Reprinted by permission.

Texas has one of the toughest parole policies in the country with the most violent offenders serving 50 percent of their sentences in actual time and capital offenders sentenced to life serving 40 years of actual time before parole consideration.

—Tony Fabelo, Executive Director of the Texas Criminal Justice Policy Council

parole

The status of a convicted offender who has been conditionally released from prison by a paroling authority before the expiration of his or her sentence, is placed under the supervision of a parole agency, and is required to observe the conditions of parole.

reentry

The managed return to the community of an individual released from prison. Also, the successful transitioning of a released inmate back into the community.

to increased arrests and a dramatic growth in the number of federal probationers in the early years of the system.

Although the 1925 act authorized one probation officer per federal judge, it allocated only $25,000 for officers' salaries. As a consequence, only eight officers were hired to serve 132 judges, and the system came to rely heavily on voluntary probation officers. Some sources indicate that as many as 40,000 probationers were under the supervision of volunteers at the peak of the system.[19] By 1930, however, Congress provided adequate funding, and a corps of salaried professionals began to provide probation services to the U.S. courts. Today, approximately 7,750 federal probation officers (also known as *community corrections officers*), whose services are administered through the Administrative Office of the U.S. Courts, serve the 94 federal judicial districts in more than 500 locations across the country.[20] At any given time, they supervise approximately 151,000 offenders—a number that has increased annually throughout the past decade.

Federal probation and pretrial services officers are federal law enforcement officers. They have statutory authority to arrest or detain individuals suspected or convicted of federal offenses, as well as the authority to arrest probationers for a violation of the conditions of probation. Under existing policy, however, they are encouraged to obtain an arrest warrant from a court, and the warrant is to be executed by the U.S. Marshals Service. Most federal probation officers may carry a firearm for defensive purposes while on duty. Before doing so, however, they must complete rigorous training and certification requirements, provide objective justification for doing so, and be approved to do so on an individual basis. Some federal districts do not allow any probation officers to carry firearms in the performance of their official duties; these include the Eastern and Western districts of Wisconsin, Eastern Virginia, Eastern Virgin Islands, Middle Tennessee, Massachusetts, Connecticut, and Central California.[21]

What Is Parole?

Parole is the supervised early release of inmates from correctional confinement. It is a prisoner **reentry** strategy that differs from probation in both purpose and implementation. Whereas probationers generally avoid serving time in prison, parolees have already been incarcerated. Whereas probation is a sentencing option available to a judge who determines the form probation

Hotel heiress Paris Hilton arriving for a birthday party for namesake celebrity gossip blogger Perez Hilton in West Hollywood, California, on March 23, 2007. Only two months earlier, Paris had pleaded no contest to an alcohol-related reckless driving offense in Los Angeles and was sentenced to three years' probation. She was also fined $1,500 plus court costs and ordered to participate in an alcohol-education program. Stopped for driving with her lights out not long afterward, she was ordered to spend time in jail—a sentence completed in June 2007. Why wasn't probation enough to deter Paris? What do you think that she learned from her experience?

Francis Specker/Landov LLC

will take, parole results from an administrative decision by a legally designated paroling authority. Whereas probation is a sentencing strategy, parole is a corrections strategy whose primary purpose is to return offenders gradually to productive lives. By making early release possible, parole can also act as a stimulus for positive behavioral change.

States differ as to the type of parole decision-making mechanism they use, as well as the level at which it operates. Two major models prevail: (1) **Parole boards** grant parole based on their judgment and assessment. The parole board's decisions are termed *discretionary parole.* (2) Statutory decrees produce *mandatory parole*, with release dates usually set near the completion of the inmate's prison sentence, minus time off for good behavior and other special considerations. Fifteen states have entirely abolished **discretionary release** from prison by a parole board for all offenders. Another five states have abolished discretionary parole for certain violent offenses or other crimes against a person. As a result of the movement away from release by parole boards, statutory release, usually involving a brief mandatory period of postrelease supervision, has become the most common method of release from prison.[22]

States that do not utilize discretionary parole can still have a substantial reentry population, and everyone who is released from prison faces the challenges of reentering society. California, for example, one of the states that no longer uses parole boards for release decisions, has the largest reentry population in the country.[23] Although it does not have a parole board, California does have a Board of Prison Terms, which determines when the state's most serious offenders are ready for release from prison. These offenders, however, make up only a very small percentage of the state's prison population. Alabama, which has abandoned traditional parole, continues to make use of parole boards with the authority to revoke the postrelease supervision status of offenders who violate release conditions and to order them returned to custody.

Parole was a much-heralded tool of nineteenth-century corrections. Its advocates had been looking for a behavioral incentive to motivate youthful offenders to reform. Parole, through its promise of earned early release, seemed the ideal innovation. The use of parole in this country began with New York's Elmira Reformatory in 1876. Indeterminate sentences were then a key part of the rehabilitation philosophy, and they remain so today.

parole board

A state paroling authority. Most states have parole boards that decide when an incarcerated offender is ready for conditional release. Some boards also function as revocation hearing panels.

discretionary release

The release of an inmate from prison to supervision that is decided by a parole board or other authority.

Multiculturalism and Diversity

Culturally Skilled Probation Officers

A recent article by Robert Shearer and Patricia King in the journal *Federal Probation* describes the characteristics of "good therapeutic relationships" in probation work and says that "one of the major impediments to building an effective relationship may be found in cross-cultural barriers."

According to Shearer and King, probation officers who work with immigrants or with those whose cultures differ substantially from that of mainstream America must realize that a client's culture has to be taken into consideration. Doing so can make officers far more effective as both counselors and supervisors.

That's because differences in culture can lead to difficulties in developing the rapport that is necessary to build a helping relationship between an offender and a probation officer. Consequently, effective probation officers work to understand the values, norms, lifestyles, roles, and methods of communicating that characterize their clients.

Culturally skilled probation officers, say the authors, are aware of and sensitive to their own cultural heritage, and they value and respect differences as long as they do not lead to continued law violation. Culturally skilled officers are also aware of their own preconceived notions, biases, prejudicial attitudes, feelings, and beliefs. They avoid stereotyping and labeling. Skilled officers are comfortable with the cultural differences that exist between themselves and their clients, and they willingly refer clients to someone who may be better qualified to help.

Developing multicultural awareness is the first step to becoming culturally skilled, say Shearer and King. Developing awareness is an ongoing process that culminates in cultural empathy—the ability to understand a client's worldview.

According to the authors, developing cultural empathy involves six steps:

- The counselor must understand and accept the context of family and community for clients from different cultural backgrounds. This is especially important when working with Hispanic clients, who highly value relationships within the extended family.

- Counselors should incorporate indigenous healing practices from the client's culture whenever they can. For example, this might be possible when working with Native Americans.

- Counselors must become knowledgeable about the historical and sociopolitical background of clients, especially when clients have fled from repressive regimes in their home countries and might still fear authority figures.

- They must become knowledgeable of the psychosocial adjustment that must be made by clients who have moved from one environment to another. This includes the sense of loneliness and separation that some immigrants feel on arrival in their adopted country.

- They must be sensitive to the oppression, discrimination, and racism previously encountered by many clients, such as the Kurdish people who suffered discrimination and experienced genocide under Saddam Hussein.

- Counselors must facilitate empowerment for those clients who feel underprivileged and devalued (for example, immigrants who may feel forced to accept menial jobs even though they worked in prestigious occupations in their native countries).

Shearer and King conclude that developing cultural awareness provides the probation officer with an effective approach that actively draws the probationer into the therapeutic relationship and that increases the likelihood of a successful outcome.

Reference: Robert A. Shearer and Patricia Ann King, "Multicultural Competencies in Probation: Issues and Challenges," *Federal Probation*, Vol. 68, No. 1 (June 2004).

The Extent of Parole

Parolees make up one of the smallest of the correctional categories shown in Figure 12–1. The growing reluctance to use parole today seems to be due to the realization that correctional routines have generally been ineffective at producing any substantial reformation among many offenders before their release back into the community. The abandonment of the rehabilitation goal, combined with a return to determinate sentencing in many jurisdictions—including the federal judicial system—has substantially reduced the amount of time the average corrections client spends on supervised parole.

Although discretionary parole releases are far less common than they used to be, about 25% of inmates who are freed from prison are still paroled by a paroling authority, such as a parole board.[24] States operating under determinate sentencing guidelines, however, often require that inmates serve a short period of time, such as 90 days, on what some jurisdictions term *reentry parole*—a form of supervised **mandatory release**. Mandatory parole releases have increased 91% since 1990,[25] even though they typically involve either a very small amount of time on parole or no time at all. As a result, determinate sentencing schemes have changed the face of parole in America, resulting in a dramatic reduction in the average time spent under postprison supervision. They have, however, had little or no impact on the actual number of offenders released from prison.

mandatory release

The release of an inmate from prison that is determined by statute or sentencing guidelines and is not decided by a parole board or other authority.

At the beginning of 2006, approximately 798,200 people were under parole supervision throughout the United States.[26] As with probation, states vary considerably in the use they make of parole, influenced as they are by the legislative requirements of sentencing schemes. For example, on January 1, 2006, Maine, a state that is phasing out parole, reported only 34 people under parole supervision (the lowest of all the states), and North Dakota had only 302. California (the highest of all) had a parole population in excess of 111,000, and Texas officials were busy supervising 102,000 parolees. The per capita rate at which parole is used varies, as well. Only three out of every 100,000 Maine residents are on parole, whereas 1,158 out of every 100,000 District of Columbia residents are on parole. The national average is 352 per 100,000.[27]

Nationwide, approximately 44% of parolees successfully complete parole, while about 26% are returned to prison for **parole violations**, and another 11% go back to prison for new offenses during their parole period. (Others may be transferred to new jurisdictions, may abscond and not be caught, or may die—bringing the total to 100%.)[28] Learn more about trends in parole via Library Extra 12–2 at cjtoday.com.

Parole Conditions

In those jurisdictions that retain discretionary parole, the **conditions of parole** remain very similar to the conditions agreed to by probationers. General conditions of parole usually include agreement not to leave the state as well as to obey extradition requests from other jurisdictions. Parolees must also periodically report to parole officers, and parole officers may visit parolees at their homes and places of business, often arriving unannounced.

The successful and continued employment of parolees is one of the major concerns of parole boards and their officers, and studies have found that successful employment is a major factor in reducing the likelihood of repeat offenses.[29] Hence, the importance of continued employment is typically stressed on parole agreement forms, with the condition that failure to find employment within 30 days may result in **parole revocation**. As with probationers, parolees who are working can be ordered to pay fines and penalties. A provision for making **restitution** payments is also frequently included as a condition of parole.

As with probation, special parole conditions may be added by the judge and might require the parolee to pay a "parole supervisory fee" (often around $15 to $20 per month). This relatively new innovation shifts some of the expense of community corrections to the offender.

Federal Parole

Federal parole decisions are made by the U.S. Parole Commission, which employs hearing examiners to visit federal prisons. Examiners typically ask inmates to describe why, in their opinion, they are ready for parole. The inmate's job readiness, home plans, past record, accomplishments while in prison, good behavior, and previous experiences on probation or parole form the basis for the examiners' report to the parole commission. The 1984 Comprehensive Crime Control Act, which mandated federal fixed sentencing and abolished parole for offenses committed after November 1, 1978, began a planned phaseout of the U.S. Parole Commission. Under the act, the commission was to be abolished by 1992. Various federal legislation has since extended the life of the commission. Visit the commission's website via Web Extra 12–2 at cjtoday.com. Read a detailed history of the federal parole system at Library Extra 12–3 at cjtoday.com.

Probation and Parole: The Pluses and Minuses

Probation is used to meet the needs of offenders who require some correctional supervision short of imprisonment while providing a reasonable degree of security to the community. Parole, which is essentially a reentry program, fulfills a similar purpose for offenders released from prison.

Advantages of Probation and Parole

Both probation and parole provide a number of advantages over imprisonment, including these:

- *Lower cost.* Imprisonment is expensive. Incarcerating a single offender in Georgia, for example, costs approximately $39,501 per year, while the cost of intensive probation is as little as $1,321 per probationer.[30] The expense of imprisonment in some other states may be more than three times as high as it is in Georgia.

---

parole (probation) violation

An act or a failure to act by a parolee (or a probationer) that does not conform to the conditions of his or her parole (or probation).

LIBRARY
Extra

conditions of parole (probation)

The general and special limits imposed on an offender who is released on parole (or probation). General conditions tend to be fixed by state statute, while special conditions are mandated by the sentencing authority (court or board) and take into consideration the background of the offender and the circumstances of the offense.

parole revocation

The administrative action of a paroling authority removing a person from parole status in response to a violation of lawfully required conditions of parole, including the prohibition against committing a new offense. Parole revocation usually results in the offender's return to prison.

WEB   **LIBRARY**
Extra   Extra

restitution

A court requirement that an accused or convicted offender pay money or provide services to the victim of the crime or provide services to the community.

- *Increased employment.* Few people in prison have the opportunity for productive employment. Work-release programs, correctional industries, and inmate labor programs operate in most states, but they usually provide only low-paying jobs and require few skills. At best, such programs include only a small portion of the inmates in any given facility. Probation and parole, on the other hand, make it possible for offenders under correctional supervision to work full-time at jobs in the "free" economy. Offenders can contribute to their own and their families' support, stimulate the local economy by spending their wages, and support the government through the taxes they pay.

- *Restitution.* Offenders who are able to work are candidates for court-ordered restitution. Society's interest in restitution may be better served by a probationary sentence or parole than by imprisonment. Restitution payments to victims may help restore their standard of living and personal confidence while teaching the offender responsibility.

- *Community support.* The decision to release a prisoner on parole or to sentence a convicted offender to probation is often partially based on considerations of family and other social ties. Such decisions are made in the belief that offenders will be more subject to control in the community if they participate in a web of positive social relationships. An advantage of both probation and parole is that they allow the offender to continue personal and social relationships. Probation avoids splitting up families, while parole may reunite family members separated from each other by a prison sentence.

- *Reduced risk of criminal socialization.* Criminal values permeate prisons; prison has been called a "school in crime." Probation insulates adjudicated offenders, at least to some degree, from these kinds of values. Parole, by virtue of the fact that it follows time served in prison, is less successful than probation in reducing the risk of criminal socialization.

- *Increased use of community services.* Probationers and parolees can take advantage of services offered through the community, including psychological therapy, substance-abuse counseling, financial services, support groups, church outreach programs, and social services. While a few similar opportunities may be available in prison, the community environment itself can enhance the effectiveness of treatment programs by reducing the stigmatization of the offender and by allowing the offender to participate in a more "normal" environment.

- *Increased opportunity for rehabilitation.* Probation and parole can both be useful behavioral management tools. They reward cooperative offenders with freedom and allow for the opportunity to shape the behavior of offenders who may be difficult to reach through other programs.

Disadvantages of Probation and Parole

Any honest appraisal of probation and parole must recognize that they share a number of strategic drawbacks, including these:

- *Relative lack of punishment.* The just deserts model of criminal sentencing insists that punishment should be a central theme of the justice process. While rehabilitation and treatment are recognized as worthwhile goals, the model suggests that punishment serves both society's need for protection and the victim's need for revenge. Many view probation, however, as practically no punishment at all, and it is coming under increasing criticism as a sentencing strategy. Parole is likewise accused of unhinging the scales of justice because (1) it releases some offenders early, even when they have been convicted of serious crimes, while some relatively minor offenders remain in prison, and (2) it is dishonest because it does not require completion of the offender's entire sentence behind bars.

- *Increased risk to the community.* Probation and parole are strategies designed to deal with convicted criminal offenders. The release into the community of such offenders increases the risk that they will commit additional offenses. Community supervision can never be so complete as to eliminate such a possibility, and evaluations of parole have pointed out that an accurate assessment of offender dangerousness is beyond our present capability.[31]

- *Increased social costs.* Some offenders placed on probation and parole will effectively and responsibly discharge their obligations. Others, however, will become social liabilities. In addition to the increased risk of new crimes, probation and parole increase the chance that added expenses will accrue to the community in the form of child support, welfare costs, housing expenses, legal aid, indigent health care, and the like.

- *Discriminatory and unequal effects.* Some experts argue that reentry programs are unfair to women because female inmates undergoing the reentry experience find themselves qualitatively disadvantaged in their search for jobs and shelter, in reobtaining custody of their children, and in successfully finding programs to help them abstain from drugs, and so on.[32] Some say, for example, that a man leaving prison, "has better opportunities for securing a sufficient income-producing and legal job by virtue of his gender alone."[33]

The Legal Environment

Ten especially significant U.S. Supreme Court decisions provide the legal framework for probation and parole supervision. Among those cases, that of *Griffin* v. *Wisconsin* (1987)[34] may be the most significant. In *Griffin*, the Supreme Court ruled that probation officers may conduct searches of a probationer's residence without either a search warrant or probable cause. According to the Court, "A probationer's home, like anyone else's, is protected by the Fourth Amendment's requirement that searches be 'reasonable.' " However, "[a] State's operation of a probation system . . . presents 'special needs' beyond normal law enforcement that may justify departures from the usual warrant and probable cause requirements." Probation, the Court concluded, is similar to imprisonment because it is a "form of criminal sanction imposed upon an offender after a determination of guilt."

Similarly, in the 1998 case of *Pennsylvania Board of Probation and Parole* v. *Scott*,[35] the Court declined to extend the exclusionary rule to apply to searches by parole officers, even where such searches yield evidence of parole violations. In the words of the Court, "[T]he Court has repeatedly declined to extend the [exclusionary] rule to proceedings other than criminal trials. . . . The social costs of allowing convicted criminals who violate their parole to remain at large are particularly high . . . and are compounded by the fact that parolees . . . are more likely to commit future crimes than are average citizens."

In 2001, the case of *U.S.* v. *Knights*[36] expanded the search authority normally reserved for probation and parole officers to police officers under certain circumstances. Mark James Knights was a California probationer who had signed a standard state probation form agreeing to waive his constitutional protection against warrantless searches as a condition of his probation. The form did not limit such searches to probation officers but instead required that Knights submit to a search at any time, with or without a search or arrest warrant or reasonable cause, by any probation or law enforcement officer. When Knights came under suspicion of setting a fire that caused $1.5 million in damages, police officers searched his home without a warrant. The search uncovered evidence that implicated Knights in the arson. A federal district court granted a motion by Knights's attorneys to suppress the evidence because the search was for police investigatory purposes, rather than for probationary purposes. The Ninth Circuit Court affirmed the lower court's decision. The U.S. Supreme Court disagreed, however, and held that the warrantless search of Knights's residence "supported by reasonable suspicion and authorized by a probation condition, satisfied the Fourth Amendment . . . as nothing in Knights' probation condition limits searches to those with a 'probationary purpose.' "

Similarly, in 2006, the U.S. Supreme Court found that the Fourth Amendment does not prohibit police officers from conducting a warrantless search of a person who is subject to a parole search condition, even when there is no suspicion of criminal wrongdoing and the sole reason for the search is because the person is on parole. The case, *Samson* v. *California*,[37] involved a parolee who was searched by a San Bruno, California, police officer who later admitted that he stopped and searched Samson only because he knew that he was on parole. The search yielded methamphetamine, and Sampson was convicted of drug possession. Relevant to the case, the California legislature had adopted a provision in 1996 requiring that every prisoner eligible for release on state parole "shall agree in writing to be subject to search or seizure by a parole officer or other peace officer at any time of the day or night, with or without a search warrant and with or without cause."[38] Sampson claimed that the California legislative requirement conferred "unfettered discretion on law enforcement officers to conduct searches of parolees" and unjustly diminished the Fourth Amendment's guarantee of personal privacy—an argument that the Court rejected.

Other court cases focus on the conduct of parole or probation **revocation hearings**. Revocation is a common procedure. Annually, about 26% of adults on parole and 25% of those on probation throughout the United States have their conditional release revoked.[39] The supervising officer may request that probation or parole be revoked if a client has violated the conditions of community release or has committed a new crime. The most frequent violations for which revocation occurs are (1) failure to report as required to a probation or parole officer, (2) failure to participate in a stipulated treatment program, and (3) alcohol or drug abuse while under supervision.[40] Revocation hearings may result in an order that a probationer's suspended sentence be made "active" or that a parolee return to prison to complete his sentence in confinement.

revocation hearing

A hearing held before a legally constituted hearing body (such as a parole board) to determine whether a parolee or probationer has violated the conditions and requirements of his or her parole or probation.

We in law enforcement need to recognize that when we locked these guys up, they didn't go away forever. Now, they're coming back, released from prisons and jail systems that our elected officials can't afford to grow anymore. We have to find a way to make sure these people succeed while maintaining the decline in violent crime.

—Chief Dean Esserman, Providence (Rhode Island) Police Department[ii]

In a 1935 decision (*Escoe* v. *Zerbst*[41]) that has since been greatly modified, the U.S. Supreme Court held that probation "comes as an act of grace to one convicted of a crime" and that the revocation of probation without hearing or notice to the probationer is acceptable practice. In 1967, however, in the case of *Mempa* v. *Rhay*,[42] the Warren Court changed direction and declared that both notice and a hearing were required. The Court also held that the probationer should have the opportunity for representation by counsel before a deferred prison sentence could be imposed.[43]

Two of the most widely cited cases affecting parolees and probationers are *Morrissey* v. *Brewer* (1972)[44] and *Gagnon* v. *Scarpelli* (1973).[45] In *Morrissey*, the Court declared a need for procedural safeguards in revocation hearings involving parolees. After *Morrissey*, revocation proceedings would require that (1) the parolee be given written notice specifying the alleged violation; (2) evidence of the violation be disclosed; (3) a neutral and detached body constitute the hearing authority; (4) the parolee have the chance to appear and offer a defense, including testimony, documents, and witnesses; (5) the parolee have the right to cross-examine witnesses; and (6) a written statement be provided to the parolee at the conclusion of the hearing that includes the hearing body's decision, the testimony considered, and reasons for revoking parole, if such occurs.[46]

In 1973, the Court extended the procedural safeguards of *Morrissey* to probationers in *Gagnon* v. *Scarpelli*. Citing its own decision a year earlier in *Morrissey*, the Supreme Court ruled that probationers, because they face a substantial loss of liberty, were entitled to two hearings: (1) a preliminary hearing to determine whether there is "probable cause to believe that he has committed a violation of his parole" and (2) "a somewhat more comprehensive hearing prior to the making of the final revocation decision." The Court also ruled that probation revocation hearings were to be held "under the conditions specified in *Morrissey* v. *Brewer*."

In *Gagnon* and later cases, however, the Court reasserted that probation and parole revocation hearings were not a stage in the criminal prosecution process, but a simple adjunct to it, even though they might result in substantial loss of liberty. The difference is a crucial one, for it permits hearing boards and judicial review officers to function, at least to some degree, outside the adversarial context of the trial court and with lessened attention to the constitutional rights of the accused.

In 1997, the U.S. Supreme Court extended the rationale found in *Morrissey* and *Gagnon* to inmates set free from prison under early-release programs. In a unanimous decision, the Court held that "an inmate who has been released under a program to relieve prison crowding cannot be reincarcerated without getting a chance to show at a hearing that he has met the conditions of the program and is entitled to remain free."[47]

In 1979, the case of *Greenholtz* v. *Nebraska Penal Inmates*[48] established that parole boards do not have to specify the evidence used in deciding to deny parole. The *Greenholtz* case focused on a Nebraska statute that required that inmates denied parole be provided with reasons for the denial. The Court held that reasons for parole denial might be provided in the interest of helping inmates prepare themselves for future review but that to require the disclosure of evidence used in the review hearing would turn the process into an adversarial proceeding.

The 1983 Supreme Court case of *Bearden* v. *Georgia*[49] established that probation could not be revoked for failure to pay a fine and make restitution if it could not be shown that the defendant

Angel Coronado, 20, rushing through the door of the Huntsville (Texas) Prison Unit after being released due to overcrowding. Coronado, who has been in trouble nearly half his life, spent nearly two years in a six- by ten-foot cell by himself. The U.S. Supreme Court has held that "an inmate who has been released under a program to relieve prison crowding cannot be reincarcerated without getting a chance to show at a hearing that he has met the conditions [of his release] and is entitled to remain free." How likely are ex-convicts to commit new crimes?

Todd Bigelow Photography

HUNTSVILLE UNIT

Georgia probation officers preparing to excavate a site at the Tri-State Crematory in Noble, Georgia, in 2002. Officials found the remains of hundreds of corpses on the crematory's 16-acre grounds. The crematory's operator, Ray Brent Marsh, was charged with 787 felony counts including theft by deception, abuse of a corpse, and burial service fraud. He was also charged with 47 counts of making false statements to authorities. Convicted on many of the charges, he was sentenced to 12 years in prison in 2005. A probation officer's job can involve a wide variety of duties. What are the usual duties of a probation officer?

Mark Humphrey/AP Wide World Photos

was responsible for the failure. The Court also held that alternative forms of punishment must be considered by the hearing authority and must be shown to be inadequate before the defendant can be incarcerated. The Supreme Court decision stated that "[i]f the State determines a fine or restitution to be the appropriate and adequate penalty for the crime, it may not thereafter imprison a person solely because he lacked the resources to pay it."[50] The Court held that if a defendant lacks the capacity to pay a fine or make restitution, then the hearing authority must consider any viable alternatives to incarceration before imposing a prison sentence.

Finally, a probationer's incriminating statements to a probation officer may be used as evidence if the probationer does not specifically claim a right against self-incrimination, according to *Minnesota* v. *Murphy* (1984).[51] According to the Court, the burden of invoking the Fifth Amendment privilege against self-incrimination lies with the probationer.

An important legal issue today surrounds the potential liability of probation officers and parole boards for the criminal actions of offenders they supervise or whom they have released. Some courts have held that officers are generally immune from suit because they are performing a judicial function on behalf of the state.[52] Other courts, however, have indicated that parole board members who do not carefully consider mandated criteria for judging parole eligibility could be liable for injurious actions committed by parolees.[53] In general, however, most experts agree that parole board members cannot be successfully sued unless release decisions are made in a grossly negligent or wantonly reckless manner.[54] Discretionary decisions of individual probation and parole officers that result in harm to members of the public, however, may be more actionable under civil law, especially where their decisions were not reviewed by judicial authority.[55]

The Job of Probation and Parole Officers

The tasks performed by probation and parole officers are often quite similar. Some jurisdictions combine the roles of both into one job. This section describes the duties of probation and parole officers, whether separate or performed by the same individuals. Probation/parole work consists primarily of four functions: (1) presentence investigations, (2) other intake procedures, (3) diagnosis and needs assessment, and (4) client supervision.

A critical assessment of probation must begin by placing its ailments within the more encompassing and deeper crisis of legitimacy affecting the entire system of justice.

—Reinventing Probation Council

Where probation is a possibility, intake procedures may include a presentence investigation, which examines the offender's background to provide the sentencing judge with facts needed to make an informed sentencing decision. Intake procedures may also involve a dispute-settlement process during which the probation officer works with the defendant and the victim to resolve the complaint before sentencing. Intake duties tend to be more common for juvenile offenders than they are for adults, but all officers may eventually have to recommend to the judge the best sentencing alternative for a particular case.

Diagnosis, the psychological inventorying of the probation or parole client, may be done either formally with written tests administered by certified psychologists or through informal arrangements, which typically depend on the observational skills of the officer. Needs assessment, another area of officer responsibility, extends beyond the psychological needs of the client to a cataloging of the services necessary for a successful experience on probation or parole. Supervision of sentenced probationers or released parolees is the most active stage of the probation/parole process, involving months (and sometimes years) of periodic meetings between the officer and the client and an ongoing assessment of the success of the probation/parole endeavor in each case.

All probation and parole officers must keep confidential the details of the presentence investigation, including psychological tests, needs assessment, conversations between the officer and the client, and so on. On the other hand, courts have generally held that communications between the officer and the client are not privileged, as they might be between a doctor and a patient or between a social worker and his or her client.[56] Hence, officers can share with the appropriate authorities any incriminating evidence that a client relates.

The Challenges of the Job

One of the biggest challenges that probation and parole officers face is the need to balance two conflicting sets of duties—one of which is to provide quasi-social work services and the other is to handle custodial responsibilities. In effect, two inconsistent models of the officer's role coexist. The social work model stresses an officer's service role and views probationers and parolees as clients. In this model, officers are caregivers whose goals are to accurately assess the needs of their clients and to match clients with community resources, such as job placement, indigent medical care, family therapy, and psychological and substance-abuse counseling. The social work model depicts probation/parole as a "helping profession" wherein officers assist their clients in meeting the conditions imposed on them by their sentence. The other model for officers is correctional. In this model, probation and parole clients are "wards" whom officers are expected to control. This model emphasizes community protection, which officers are supposed to achieve through careful and close supervision. Custodial supervision means that officers will periodically visit their charges at work and at home, often arriving unannounced. It also means that they must be willing to report clients for new offenses and for violations of the conditions of their release.

Most officers, by virtue of their personalities and experiences, identify more with one model than with the other. They consider themselves primarily caregivers or corrections officers. Regardless of the emphasis that each individual officer chooses, however, the demands of the job are bound to generate role conflict at one time or another.

caseload

The number of probation or parole clients assigned to one probation or parole officer for supervision.

A second challenge of probation and parole work is large **caseloads**. Back in 1973, the President's Commission on Law Enforcement and Administration of Justice recommended that probation and parole caseloads average around 35 clients per officer.[57] However, caseloads of 250 clients are common in some jurisdictions today. Large caseloads combined with limited training and the time constraints imposed by administrative demands culminate in stopgap supervisory measures. "Postcard probation," in which clients mail in a letter or card once a month to report on their whereabouts and circumstances, is an example of one stopgap measure that harried agencies with large caseloads use to keep track of their wards.

Another difficulty with probation and parole work is the frequent lack of opportunity for career mobility within the profession. Probation and parole officers are generally assigned to small agencies serving limited geographic areas, under the leadership of one or two chief probation officers. Unless retirement or death claims a supervisor, there is little chance for other officers to advance.

A 2005 report by the National Institute of Justice (NIJ) found that, like law enforcement officers, probation and parole officers experienced a lot of stress.[58] The major sources of stress for probation and parole officers were found to be high caseloads, excess paperwork, and pressures associated with deadlines. Stress levels have also increased in recent years because offenders who are sentenced to probation and released on parole today have committed more serious crimes than in the past, and more offenders have serious drug-abuse histories and show less hes-

CJ Careers

Probation Officer

Name: Jesse J. Gomes

Position: U.S. Probation Officer

City: Boston, Massachusetts

College Attended: Northeastern University

Year Hired: 2000

"I chose a career in probation because it puts me in a position to address issues from both law enforcement and human service perspectives. To work in probation is to quite literally 'serve and protect' by serving a population that requires positive intervention while protecting the public from those individuals who choose not to comply.

"Working for U.S. Probation was the culmination of seven years of case management and offender supervision experience. I started my career as a case manager at a prerelease and intermediate sanctions program in Boston and was then hired as a probation officer for the state of Massachusetts. Federal probation was the next logical step in my career path.

"U.S. probation officers must remain informed and flexible because the nature of the work is ever changing. In general, officers must have strong written and oral skills, be tied into a comprehensive network of treatment and service providers, be able to communicate effectively with a wide array of people, and have a working understanding of applicable laws. Because treatment methodologies, crime, and the laws themselves are all fluid to some extent, officers must be willing and able to implement these changes or anticipate their effects on probationers.

"When you do your job well, people's lives are actually improved. That may mean helping an addict establish sobriety, obtaining housing for a homeless person, or ensuring that a dangerous offender is adequately supervised or, if necessary, removed from the community. Much is said about improving people's lives, but in reality that's rarer and more difficult than we would like it to be. But when actual change does occur, it makes up for the many disappointments."

TYPICAL POSITIONS

A U.S. probation officer has a wide range of duties and responsibilities, including supervising offenders, conducting presentence investigations, and preparing presentence reports. Tasks involve interviewing offenders and their families, investigating offenses, determining prior record and financial status of offenders, and contacting law enforcement agencies, attorneys, and victims of crimes.

EMPLOYMENT REQUIREMENTS

To qualify for the position of probation officer at the GS-5 level, an applicant must possess a bachelor's degree from an accredited college or university and must have a minimum of two years of general work experience. General experience must have been acquired after obtaining the bachelor's degree and cannot include experience as a police, custodial, or security officer unless the work involved criminal

investigative experience. In lieu of general experience, a bachelor's degree from an accredited college or university in an accepted field of study (including criminology, criminal justice, penology, correctional administration, social work, sociology, public administration, or psychology) will qualify an applicant for immediate employment at the GS-5 level, provided that at least 32 semester hours or 48 quarter hours were taken in one or more of the accepted fields of study. One year of graduate study qualifies applicants for appointment at the GS-7 level, while a master's degree in an appropriate field or a law degree may qualify the applicant for advanced placement.

OTHER REQUIREMENTS

Applicants must be younger than 37 years of age at the time of hiring and must be in excellent physical health. A full field background investigation by the Federal Bureau of Investigation and preemployment drug testing are also required.

(continued)

CJ Careers (continued)

SALARY

Appointees are typically hired at federal pay grade GS-5 or GS-7, depending on education and prior work history.

BENEFITS

U.S. probation and pretrial services officers are included in the federal hazardous-duty law enforcement classification and are covered by liberal federal health and life insurance programs. A comprehensive retirement program is available to all federal employees.

Source: Administrative Office of the U.S. Courts.

DIRECT INQUIRIES TO:

Administrative Office of the U.S. Courts
Personnel Office
Washington, D.C. 20544

Phone: 202-273-1297

Website: http://www.uscourts.gov

For more information on the rapidly expanding criminal justice careers area, read *Where the Jobs Are: Mission Critical Opportunities for America,* available on the Web at http://www.justicestudies.com/jobs.htm.

---

itation in using violence.[59] The NIJ study found that officers typically cope by requesting transfers, retiring early, or taking "mental health days" off from work. The report says, however, that "physical exercise is the method of choice for coping with the stress."[60]

Learn more about working as a probation or parole officer at the American Probation and Parole Association's website via **Web Extra 12–3** at cjtoday.com.

WEB Extra

Intermediate Sanctions

intermediate sanctions

The use of split sentencing, shock probation or parole, shock incarceration, community service, intensive supervision, or home confinement in lieu of other, more traditional, sanctions, such as imprisonment and fines.

As noted in Chapter 11, significant new alternative sentencing options have become available to judges during the past few decades. Many such options are called **intermediate sanctions** because they employ sentencing alternatives that fall somewhere between outright imprisonment and simple probationary release back into the community. They are also sometimes termed *alternative sentencing strategies*. Michael J. Russell, former director of the National Institute of Justice, says that "intermediate punishments are intended to provide prosecutors, judges, and corrections officials with sentencing options that permit them to apply appropriate punishments to convicted offenders while not being constrained by the traditional choice between prison and probation. Rather than substituting for prison or probation, however, these sanctions, which include intensive supervision, house arrest with electronic monitoring (also referred to as *remote location monitoring*), and shock incarceration—programs that stress a highly structured and regimented routine, considerable physical work and exercise, and at times intensive substance abuse treatment—bridge the gap between those options and provide innovative ways to ensure swift and certain punishment."[61]

A number of citizen groups and special-interest organizations are working to widen the use of sentencing alternatives. One organization of special note is the Sentencing Project. The organization, based in Washington, D.C., is dedicated to promoting a greater use of alternatives to incarceration. It provides technical assistance to public defenders, court officials, and other community organizations.

The Sentencing Project and other groups like it have contributed to the development of more than 100 locally based alternative sentencing service programs. Most alternative sentencing services work in conjunction with defense attorneys to develop written sentencing plans. Such plans are basically well-considered citizen suggestions as to appropriate sentencing in a given instance. Plans are often quite detailed and may include letters of support from employers, family members, the defendant, and even victims. Sentencing plans may be used in plea bargaining sessions or may be presented to judges following trial and conviction. More than a decade ago, for example, lawyers for country-and-western singer Willie Nelson successfully proposed to tax court officials an alternative option that allowed the singer to pay huge past tax liabilities by performing in concerts for that purpose. Lacking such an alternative, the tax court might have seized Nelson's property or even ordered the singer to be confined to a federal facility. More recently, NBA player DeShawn Stevenson was sentenced to two years of probation in 2002 and was ordered to perform 100 hours of community service for the statutory rape of a 14-year-old girl whom he had plied with brandy.[62] Stevenson, who played for the Utah Jazz at the time of the offense, fulfilled the terms of his sentence by delivering motivational speeches at boys' clubs in California and New York.

The basic philosophy behind intermediate sanctions is this: When judges are offered well-planned alternatives to imprisonment for offenders who appear to represent little or no continuing threat to the community, the likelihood of a prison sentence is reduced. An analysis of alternative sentencing plans like those sponsored by the Sentencing Project shows that judges accept them in up to 80% of the cases in which they are recommended and that as many as two-thirds of offenders who receive intermediate sentences successfully complete them.[63]

Intermediate sanctions have three distinct advantages: (1) They are less expensive to operate per offender than imprisonment; (2) they are "socially cost-effective" because they keep the offender in the community, thus avoiding both the breakup of the family and the stigmatization that accompanies imprisonment; and (3) they provide flexibility in terms of resources, time of involvement, and place of service.[64] Some of these new sentencing options are described in the paragraphs that follow.

Split Sentencing

In jurisdictions where **split sentences** are an option, judges may impose a combination of a brief period of imprisonment and probation. Defendants who are given split sentences are often ordered to serve time in a local jail rather than in a long-term confinement facility. Ninety days in jail, followed by two years of supervised probation, is a typical split sentence. Split sentences are frequently given to minor drug offenders and serve notice that continued law violations may result in imprisonment for much longer periods.

split sentence

A sentence explicitly requiring the convicted offender to serve a period of confinement in a local, state, or federal facility, followed by a period of probation.

Shock Probation and Shock Parole

Shock probation strongly resembles split sentencing. The offender serves a relatively short period of time in custody (usually in a prison rather than a jail) and is released on probation by court order. The difference is that shock probation clients must *apply* for probationary release from confinement and cannot be certain of the judge's decision. In shock probation, the court in effect makes a resentencing decision. Probation is only a statutory possibility and often little more than an aspiration for the offender as imprisonment begins. If probationary release is ordered, it may well come as a "shock" to the offender. The hope is that the unexpected reprieve will cause the offender to steer clear of future criminal involvement. Shock probation was begun in Ohio in 1965[65] and is used today in about half of the United States.[66] Shock probation lowers the cost of confinement, maintains community and family ties, and may be an effective rehabilitative tool.[67]

Shock parole is similar to shock probation. Whereas shock probation is ordered by judicial authority, shock parole is an administrative decision made by a paroling authority. Parole boards or their representatives may order an inmate's early release, hoping that the brief exposure to prison has reoriented the offender's life in a positive direction.

shock probation

The practice of sentencing offenders to prison, allowing them to apply for probationary release, and surprisingly permitting such release. Offenders who receive shock probation may not be aware that they will be released on probation and may expect to spend a much longer time behind bars.

Shock Incarceration

Shock incarceration programs, which became popular during the 1990s, utilize military-style "boot camp" prison settings to provide highly regimented environments involving strict discipline, physical training, and hard labor.[68] Shock incarceration programs are designed primarily for young first offenders and are of short duration, generally lasting for only 90 to 180 days. Offenders who successfully complete these programs are typically returned to the community under some form of supervision. Program "failures" may be moved into the general prison population for longer terms of confinement.

Georgia established the first shock incarceration program in 1983.[69] Following Georgia's lead, more than 30 other states began their own programs.[70] About half of the states provide for voluntary entry into the program. A few allow inmates to decide when and whether they want to quit. Although most states allow judges to place offenders into these programs, some delegate that authority to corrections officials. Two states, Louisiana and Texas, give judges and corrections personnel joint authority in the decision-making process.[71] Some states, including Massachusetts,

shock incarceration

A sentencing option that makes use of "boot camp"–type prisons to impress on convicted offenders the realities of prison life.

A New Mexico boot camp staff member conducting a push-up drill with young offenders. Boot camps use military-style discipline in an attempt to lessen the likelihood of recidivism among young and first-time offenders. How successful have boot camps been in reducing recidivism?

Vladimir Chaloupka/Las Cruces Sun-News/AP Wide World Photos

accept female inmates into boot camp settings. The Massachusetts program, which first accepted women in 1993, requires inmates to spend nearly four months undergoing the rigors of training.

One of the most comprehensive studies to date of boot camp prison programs focused on eight states: Florida, Georgia, Illinois, Louisiana, New York, Oklahoma, South Carolina, and Texas. The report found that boot camp programs have been popular because "they are . . . perceived as being tough on crime" and "have been enthusiastically embraced as a viable correctional option."[72] The report concluded, however, that "the impact of boot camp programs on offender recidivism is at best negligible."

More limited studies, such as one that focused on shock incarceration in New York State, have found that boot camp programs can be effective money savers. The research indicates that such programs save money in two ways: "first by reducing expenditures for care and custody" (since the intense programs reduce time spent in custody, and participation in them is the only way New York inmates can be released from prison before their minimum parole eligibility dates) and "second, by avoiding capital costs for new prison construction."[73] A 1995 study of Oregon's Summit boot camp program reached a similar conclusion. Although they did not study recidivism, the Oregon researchers found that "the Summit boot camp program is a cost-effective means of reducing prison overcrowding by treating and releasing specially selected inmates earlier than their court-determined minimum period of incarceration."[74]

Mixed Sentencing and Community Service

mixed sentence

A sentence that requires that a convicted offender serve weekends (or other specified periods of time) in a confinement facility (usually a jail) while undergoing probationary supervision in the community.

Some **mixed sentences** require that offenders serve weekends in jail and receive probation supervision during the week. Other types of mixed sentencing require offenders to participate in treatment or community service programs while on probation. Community service programs began in Minnesota in 1972 with the Minnesota Restitution Program, which gave property offenders the opportunity to work and turn over part of their pay as restitution to their victims.[75] Courts throughout the nation quickly adopted the idea and began to build restitution orders into suspended-sentence agreements.

Supermodel Naomi Campbell showing off a safety vest and boots at the Manhattan Sanitation Depot after being ordered by a judge to perform community service following an assault on a domestic worker at her residence. Campbell pleaded guilty to hitting her housekeeper on the head with a cell phone after she couldn't find a pair of her jeans. Was Campbell's sentence appropriate?

Kevin Mazur/WireImage.com

Community service is more an adjunct to, rather than a type of, correctional sentence. Community service is compatible with most other forms of innovation in probation and parole. Even with home confinement (discussed below), offenders can be sentenced to community service activities that are performed in the home or at a job site during the hours they are permitted to be away from their homes. Washing police cars, cleaning school buses, refurbishing public facilities, and assisting in local government offices are typical forms of community service. Some authors have linked the development of community service sentences to the notion that work and service to others are good for the spirit.[76] Community service participants are usually minor criminals, drunk drivers, and youthful offenders.

One problem with community service sentences is that authorities rarely agree on what they are supposed to accomplish. Most people admit that offenders who work in the community are able to reduce the costs of their own supervision. There is little agreement, however, on whether such sentences reduce recidivism, act as a deterrent, or serve to rehabilitate offenders.

community service

A sentencing alternative that requires offenders to spend at least part of their time working for a community agency.

Intensive Supervision

Intensive probation supervision (IPS) has been described as the "strictest form of probation for adults in the United States."[77] IPS is designed to achieve control in a community setting over offenders who would otherwise go to prison. Some states have extended intensive supervision to parolees, allowing the early release of some who would otherwise serve longer prison terms.

Georgia was the first state to implement IPS, beginning its program in 1982. The Georgia program involves a minimum of five face-to-face contacts between the probationer and the supervising officer per week, mandatory curfew, required employment, a weekly check of local arrest records, routine and unannounced alcohol and drug testing, 132 hours of community service, and automatic notification of probation officers via the State Crime Information Network when an IPS client is arrested.[78] The caseloads of probation officers involved in IPS are much lower than the national average. Georgia officers work as a team, with one probation officer and two surveillance officers supervising about 40 probationers.[79]

A study published in 2000 shows that IPS programs can be effective at reducing recidivism, especially if the programs are well planned and fully implemented.[80] The study, which examined

intensive probation supervision (IPS)

A form of probation supervision involving frequent face-to-face contact between the probationer and the probation officer.

Ethics and Professionalism

American Probation and Parole Association Code of Ethics

- I will render professional service to the justice system and the community at large in effecting the social adjustment of the offender.

- I will uphold the law with dignity, displaying an awareness of my responsibility to offenders while recognizing the right of the public to be safeguarded from criminal activity.

- I will strive to be objective in the performance of my duties, recognizing the inalienable right of all persons, appreciating the inherent worth of the individual, and respecting those confidences which can be reposed in me.

- I will conduct my personal life with decorum, neither accepting nor granting favors in connection with my office.

- I will cooperate with my co-workers and related agencies and will continually strive to improve my professional competence through the seeking and sharing of knowledge and understanding.

Source: American Probation and Parole Association. Reprinted with permission.

- I will distinguish clearly, in public, between my statements and actions as an individual and as a representative of my profession.

- I will encourage policy, procedures and personnel practices, which will enable others to conduct themselves in accordance with the values, goals and objectives of the American Probation and Parole Association.

- I recognize my office as a symbol of public faith and I accept it as a public trust to be held as long as I am true to the ethics of the American Probation and Parole Association.

- I will constantly strive to achieve these objectives and ideals, dedicating myself to my chosen profession.

THINKING ABOUT ETHICS

1. Which of the ethical principles enumerated here might also apply to corrections officers working in prisons and jails?
2. Which might apply to law enforcement officers?
3. Which might apply to prosecutors and criminal defense attorneys?

---

programs in California's Contra Costa and Ventura Counties, found that the programs worked because, among other things, they used team approaches in their supervision activities and had clear missions and goals.

Home Confinement and Remote Location Monitoring

home confinement

House arrest. Individuals ordered confined to their homes are sometimes monitored electronically to ensure they do not leave during the hours of confinement. Absence from the home during working hours is often permitted.

remote location monitoring

A supervision strategy that uses electronic technology to track offenders who have been sentenced to house arrest or who have been ordered to limit their movements while completing a sentence involving probation or parole.

Home confinement, also referred to as *house arrest*, can be defined as "a sentence imposed by the court in which offenders are legally ordered to remain confined in their own residences."[81] Home confinement usually makes use of a system of **remote location monitoring**. Remote location monitoring is typically performed via a computerized system of electronic bracelets. Participants wear a waterproof, shock-resistant transmitting device around the ankle 24 hours a day. The transmitter continuously emits a radio-frequency signal, which is detected by a receiving unit connected to the home telephone. Older systems use random telephone calls that require the offender to insert a computer chip worn in a wristband into a specially installed modem in the home, verifying his or her presence. Some use voice recognition technology and require the offender to verify his or her presence in the home by answering computerized calls. Modern electronic monitoring systems alert the officer when a participant leaves a specific location or tampers with the electronic monitoring equipment, and some systems even make it possible to record the time a supervised person enters or leaves the home.

Much of the electronic monitoring equipment in use today only indicates when participants enter or leave the equipment's range—not where they have gone or how far they have traveled. Newer satellite-supported systems, however, are capable of continuously monitoring the location of offenders and tracking them as they move from place to place (Figure 12–2). Satellite-based systems can alert the officer when participants venture into geographically excluded locations or when they fail to present themselves at required locations at specific times.[82]

Most remotely monitored offenders on home confinement may leave home only to go to their jobs, attend to medical emergencies, or buy household essentials. Because of the strict limits it imposes on offender movements, house arrest has been cited as offering a valuable alternative to prison for offenders with special needs. Pregnant women, geriatric convicts, offenders with spe-

FIGURE 12–2

How remote location monitoring works.

Source: iSECUREtrac Corporation, 5022 South 114th Street, Omaha, NE 68137; phone: 866-537-0022. Copyright © 2005 iSECUREtrac Corporation. All rights reserved. Used with permission.

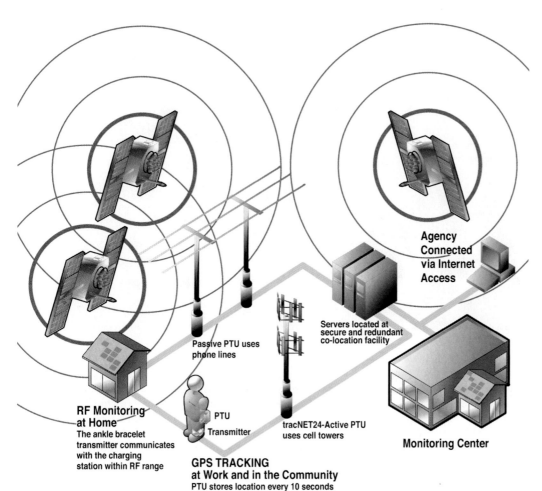

Agency Connected via Internet Access

Servers located at secure and redundant co-location facility

Monitoring Center

RF Monitoring at Home
The ankle bracelet transmitter communicates with the charging station within RF range

PTU
Transmitter

Passive PTU uses phone lines

tracNET24-Active PTU uses cell towers

GPS TRACKING at Work and in the Community
PTU stores location every 10 seconds

cial handicaps, seriously or terminally ill offenders, and mentally retarded people may all be better supervised through home confinement than through traditional incarceration.

One of the best-known people to be placed recently under house arrest using a remote location monitoring system was 63-year-old Martha Stewart, former CEO of Martha Stewart Living Omnimedia, Inc. Stewart served five months in prison for insider stock transactions and was ordered to serve an additional five months under house arrest at her Bedford, New York, estate.[83] She was allowed daily commutes totaling 48 hours weekly to her office in New York City, 40 miles away.[84]

The Community Justice Assistance Division of the Texas Department of Criminal Justice runs one of the most ambitious home confinement programs in the country. In 1997, 89,095 adults (3.5% of the state's probationers) were being electronically monitored on probation.[85] By 2002, parole offices throughout the state adopted electronic monitoring, and 700 electronic monitoring units were available for parolees.[86]

The electronic monitoring of offenders has increased across the nation. A survey by the National Institute of Justice in 1987, as the use of electronic monitoring was just beginning, showed only 826 offenders being monitored electronically nationwide.[87] By 2000, however, more than 16,000 defendants and offenders under the supervision of U.S. probation and pretrial services officers were on home confinement—most under electronic monitoring programs.[88]

In 1999, South Carolina's Probation and Parole Department began using satellites to track felons recently freed from state prisons. The satellite-tracking plan, which makes use of 21 satellites in the Global Positioning System (GPS), allows the agency's officers to track every move made by convicts wearing electronic bracelets.[89] The system, which also notifies law enforcement officers when a bracelet-wearing offender leaves his assigned area, can electronically alert anyone holding a restraining order whenever the offender comes within two miles of them.

The home confinement program in the federal court system has three components, or levels of restriction.[90] *Curfew* requires program participants to remain at home every day during certain

The number of people under criminal justice supervision in this country has reached a record high. As a result, the sentencing policies driving that number, and the field of corrections, where the consequences are felt, have acquired an unprecedented salience. It is a salience defined more by issues of magnitude, complexity, and expense than by any consensus about future directions.

—Julie E. Samuels, Acting Director, National Institute of Justice[iii]

Electronic supervision in action. Boxing's most notorious middleweight, 38-year-old Tony "El Torito" Ayala, conceals an electronic ankle bracelet under his left sock as he spars during a workout at the Zarzamore Street Gym in San Antonio, Texas, before a scheduled fight. In 2001, the fighter pleaded guilty to burglary and was sentenced to 90 days in jail and ten years' probation. Ayala had previously served 16 years in a New Jersey prison on a 1983 rape conviction. What kinds of offenders are most likely to benefit from remote location monitoring?

AP Wide World Photos

Probation and parole services are characteristically poorly staffed and often poorly administered.

—President's Commission on Law Enforcement and Administration of Justice

times, usually in the evening. With *home detention*, the participant remains at home at all times except for preapproved and scheduled absences, such as for work, school, treatment, church, attorney's appointments, court appearances, and other court-ordered obligations. *Home incarceration*, the highest level of restriction, calls for 24-hour-a-day "lockdown" at home, except for medical appointments, court appearances, and other activities that the court specifically approves.

Many states and the federal government view house arrest as a cost-effective response to the high cost of imprisonment. Georgia, for example, estimates that home confinement costs approximately $1,130 per year per supervised probationer and $2,190 per supervised parolee.[91] Incarceration costs are much higher, running around $18,100 per year per Georgia inmate, with another $43,756 needed to build each cell.[92] Advocates of house arrest argue that it is also socially cost-effective[93] because it substantially decreases the opportunity for the kinds of negative socialization that occur in prison. Opponents, however, have pointed out that house arrest may endanger the public and that it may provide little or no actual punishment. Critics of Martha Stewart's home confinement, for example, complained that the sentence was more of a reward than a punishment. Stewart's home, a 153-acre multimillion-dollar mansion with guest quarters, lacks few amenities, and the conditions imposed on Stewart allowed her to entertain colleagues, neighbors, friends, and relatives—as long as they didn't have criminal records.

The Future of Probation and Parole

Probation and parole have essentially shifted from legitimate correctional options in their own right to temporary diversionary strategies that we are using while we are trying to figure out how to get tough on crime, [pay] no new taxes, and not pay for any prisons at all, or to pay as little as we can, or pass it off to another generation.

—Dr. Charles M. Friel, Sam Houston State University

Parole was widely criticized during the 1980s and 1990s by citizen groups who claimed that it unfairly reduces prison sentences imposed on serious offenders. Official attacks on parole came from some powerful corners. Senator Edward Kennedy called for the abolition of parole, as did former Attorney General Griffin Bell and former U.S. Bureau of Prisons Director Norman Carlson.[94] Academics chimed in, alleging that parole programs provide no assurance that criminals will not commit further crimes. The media joined the fray, condemning parole for its failure to curb recidivism and highlighting the so-called revolving prison door as representative of the failure of parole. These criticisms are not without value. In 2003, for example, more than 625,000 former prisoners—about 1,700 per day—were released from state and federal prisons and returned to society, most of them on some form of supervised release.[95] Although statistics on the 2003 cohort are not yet available, estimates are that just over half of them will have been reincarcerated within three years (and some of them will have successfully completed parole prior to their return to prison).[96] Parole violators account for more than half of prison admissions in California (67%), Utah (55%), and Montana and Louisiana (both 53%). Seventy percent of parole violators in prison were arrested or were convicted of a new offense *while* on parole.[97] Many of these offenses involved drugs. Critics say that numbers like these are indicative of poor reintegration of prisoners into the community and are associated with wide-ranging social costs, including decreased public safety and weakened family and community ties.[98]

Even prisoners have also challenged the fairness of parole, saying it is sometimes arbitrarily granted, which creates an undue amount of uncertainty and frustration for inmates. Parolees have complained about the unpredictable nature of the parole experience, citing their powerlessness in the parole contract.

Against the pressure of attacks like these, parole advocates struggled to clarify and communicate the value of supervised release in the corrections process. As more and more states moved toward the elimination of parole, advocates called for moderation. A 1995 report by the American Probation and Parole Association (APPA), for example, concluded that states that have eliminated parole "have jeopardized public safety and wasted tax dollars." The researchers wrote, "Getting rid of parole dismantles an accountable system of releasing prisoners back into the community and replaces it with a system that bases release decisions solely on whether a prison term has been completed."[99]

Reinventing Reentry

By the close of the twentieth century, criticisms of parole had begun to wane, and a number of recent reports have supported well-considered offender reentry and postrelease supervision programs. In 2005, for example, the Re-entry Policy Council, a bipartisan assembly of almost 100 leading elected officials, policymakers, corrections leaders, and practitioners from community-based organizations around the country, released a report on offender reentry entitled *Charting the Safe and Successful Return of Prisoners to the Community*. The 500-page report pointed out that virtually every person incarcerated in a jail in this country, as well as 97% of those incarcerated in prisons, will eventually be released back into society. This, said the report, results in nearly 650,000 people being released from prisons, and more than 7 million individuals being released from jails throughout the United States each year—many of them without any form of postrelease supervision.[100]

As the report pointed out, almost two out of every three people released from prison are rearrested within three years of their release.[101] Report authors noted that while the number of people reentering society has increased fourfold in the past 20 years, and spending on corrections has increased nearly sevenfold during that time, the likelihood of a former prisoner succeeding in the community upon release has not improved.

A host of complex issues create barriers to successful reentry. Three-quarters of those released from prison and jail, for example, have a history of substance abuse; two-thirds have no high school diploma; nearly half of those leaving jail earned less than $600 per month immediately prior to their incarceration; and they leave jail with significantly diminished opportunities for employment. Moreover, said the report, more than a third of jail inmates are saddled with a physical or mental disability, and the rate of serious mental illness among released inmates is at least three times higher than the rate of mental illness among the general population.[102]

According to the report, "the multi-faceted—and costly—needs of people returning to their families and communities require a re-inventing of reentry akin to the reinvention of welfare in the 90s." It requires, the report continued, "a multi-system, collaborative approach that takes into account all aspects of [the] problem." In other words, "the problems faced by re-entering adults are not merely the problems of corrections or community corrections, but also of public health workers, housing providers, state legislators, workforce development staff, and others."

To guide states and local jurisdictions in the creation of successful offender reentry programs, the report provides 35 policy statements, each of which is supported by a series of research highlights. The report can be read in its entirety at Library Extra 12–4 at cjtoday.com. A 24-page summary is available at Library Extra 12–5.

In 2003, the U.S. Department of Justice, in conjunction with other federal agencies, initiated funding for 89 reentry sites across the country under the Serious and Violent Offender Reentry Initiative (SVORI).[103] SVORI programs are geared toward serious and violent offenders, particularly adults released from prison, as well as juveniles released from correctional facilities.[104] The goal of the SVORI initiative is to reduce the likelihood of reincarceration by providing tailored supervision and services to improve the odds for a successful transition to the community. SVORI services include employment assistance, education and skills training, substance-abuse counseling, and help with postrelease housing. SVORI programs also try to reduce criminality by closely monitoring participant noncompliance, reoffending, rearrest, reconviction, and reincarceration.[105] The initiative's priorities include providing services to those adults and juveniles who are most likely to pose a risk to the community upon release and to those who face multiple challenges

By writing parole boards out of the release decision, our sentencing reforms over the past 25 years have eliminated a valuable role they played, namely overseeing the process of preparing prisoners for reentry.

—Jeremy Travis, President, John Jay College of Criminal Justice[iv]

LIBRARY
Extra
■■■■

FIGURE 12–3

The SVORI program model.

Source: Laura Winterfield and Susan Brumbaugh, *The Multi-site Evaluation of the Serious and Violent Offender Reentry Initiative* (RTI International and the Urban Institute, 2006). Reprinted with permission.

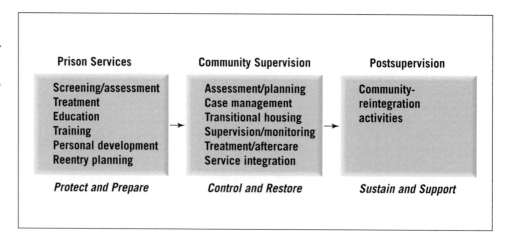

upon returning to the community. SVORI funding supports the creation of a three-phase continuum of services (Figure 12–3) that begins in prison, moves to a structured reentry phase before and during the early months of release, and continues for several years as released prisoners take on increasingly productive roles in the community. These phases have been described in SVORI-related publications as follows:[106]

- *Phase 1—protect and prepare: institution-based programs*. Phase 1 programs are designed to prepare offenders to reenter society. Services include education, mental health and substance-abuse treatment, job training, mentoring, and full diagnostic and risk assessment.

- *Phase 2—control and restore: community-based transition programs*. Phase 2 programs work with offenders prior to and immediately following their release from correctional institutions. Services provided in this phase include, as appropriate, education, monitoring, mentoring, life skills training, assessment, job skills development, and mental health and substance-abuse treatment.

- *Phase 3—sustain and support: community-based long-term support programs*. Phase 3 programs connect individuals who have left the supervision of the justice system with a network of social services agencies and community-based organizations to provide ongoing services and mentoring relationships.

Although evaluation of SVORI programs is ongoing, a recent review identified several reentry strategies that appear to work. In particular, vocational and work-release programs were found to improve job skills and to reduce recidivism, and some prerelease SVORI-sponsored drug-treatment programs were found to be successful. SVORI evaluators also found that program participants who stayed in halfway houses committed less severe and fewer crimes than those who lived elsewhere, and a number of educational programs were found to be capable of increasing achievement scores among reentry program participants.

One innovative approach to managing former prisoners who are returning to their communities is the use of reentry courts. Reentry courts are based on the drug-court model, begun in Miami in 1989, which functions to rapidly place drug-affected defendants into appropriate treatment programs with close supervision by a single judge familiar with both the treatment and the offenders.[107] Similarly, under the reentry court concept, reentry court judges oversee an offender's supervised release into the community.[108] The Indiana Department of Corrections, for example, operates an SVORI-funded reentry court program.[109] Under the program, participants are brought to Allen County Community Corrections (ACCC) in Fort Wayne, Indiana, when released and are given in-depth risk assessments. A remote location monitoring system keeps track of each offender after release. On the first Friday after release, offenders appear before the reentry court judge for their first reentry court hearing. At the hearing, they learn about the program and its goals and are told what's expected of them. Two weeks later, offenders meet with the judge individually, and a reintegration plan is imposed by the court. Successful adherence to the plan is a condition for continued freedom. Participants continue to appear before the court every two to five weeks to review progress and to assess any problems that have arisen. The reentry court offers an array of reintegration services to which participants can be referred and provides continual oversight using a preestablished set of graduated sanctions and rewards. The court also has a strong relationship with the faith-based community, and local pastors attend court hearings and offer mentoring services. Throughout the program, ACCC provides ongoing offender supervision for up to two years, and a reentry case-management team makes continual recommendations to the judge.

Faith-based organizations in the SVORI program generally provide services like emergency aid (e.g., clothing, food), mentoring, pastoral counseling, employment, transportation, and housing; conduct pre- and postrelease needs assessments for program participants; coordinate family and community support for individual offenders; provide guidance to the program through participation in the program's steering committee or advisory board; and serve as community advocates for the SVORI program. Learn more about the SVORI initiative and the individual programs that comprise it at Library Extra 12–6 at cjtoday.com. Reports about ongoing SVORI-related research can be read online via Web Extra 12–4 at cjtoday.com. Web Extra 12–5 links to the e-book *Venturing Beyond the Gates* which is published by the Prisoner Reentry Initiative at John Jay College.

LIBRARY Extra ∎∎∎∎

WEB Extra ∎∎∎∎

Reinventing Probation

Although probation has generally fared better than parole, it too has its critics. The primary purpose of probation has always been rehabilitation. Probation is a powerful rehabilitative tool because, at least in theory, it allows the resources of a community to be focused on the offender. Unfortunately for advocates of probation, however, the rehabilitative ideal is far less popular today than it has been in the past. The contemporary demand for just deserts appears to have reduced society's tolerance for even relatively minor offenders. Also, because it has been too frequently and inappropriately used with repeat or relatively serious offenders, the image of probation has been tarnished. Probation advocates have been forced to admit that it is not a very powerful deterrent because it is far less punishing than a term of imprisonment.

In a series of reports issued in 1999 and 2000, the Reinventing Probation Council, a project of New York's Manhattan Institute, called for the "reinvention of probation."[110] Probation is currently in the midst of a crisis, said the council, because probationers are not being held to even simple standards of behavior and because the field of probation lacks leadership. According to the council, "probation will be reinvented when the probation profession places public safety first, and works with and in the community." Read the council's full reports at Library Extras 12–7 and 12–8 at cjtoday.com.

In an intriguing American Society of Criminology task force report on community corrections, Joan Petersilia notes that the "get tough on criminals" attitude that swept the nation during the 1990s resulted in increased funding for prisons but left in its wake stagnating budgetary allotments for probation and parole services.[111] This result has been especially unfortunate, Petersilia says, because "it has been continually shown that there is a 'highly significant statistical relationship between the extent to which probationers received needed services and the success of probation.' . . . As services have dwindled," she says, "recidivism rates have

Probation will change when those who run probation departments are held accountable for achieving— or failing to achieve— specific outcomes.

—Reinventing Probation Council

LIBRARY Extra ∎∎∎∎

David Duke, the former Ku Klux Klan leader whose case raised eyebrows when he was released on federal parole in 2004. Duke, who served a year in federal prison on fraud charges, was released to a halfway house in Baton Rouge, Louisiana, and met the work requirements of his release by performing duties for the "white civil rights group" that he heads. Might a more suitable placement have been found for Duke?

Burt Steel/AP Wide World Photos

CJ Futures

Probation Kiosks: High-Tech Supervision

In 1997, probation authorities in New York City began experimenting with the use of "probation kiosks" designed to lower probation officer caseloads. Fifteen electronic kiosks, similar in design to ATMs, were soon scattered throughout the city. They allow probationers to check in with probation officers by placing their palms on a specially designed surface and by answering questions presented on a flashing screen.

The kiosks identify probationers by the shape and size of their hands, which were previously scanned into the system. Probationers are then prompted to press "yes" or "no" in response to questions like these: "Have you moved recently?" "Have you been arrested again?" "Do you need to see a probation officer?" Meetings with officers can be scheduled directly from the kiosk. Probation officers use a computer to monitor data sent from the kiosks and can zero in on individual probationers who are having problems, prompting more personal attention. By the time the system is fully operational, as many as 30,000 "low-risk" probationers—about one-third of New York City's total—will report through kiosks.

Kiosks have already yielded positive results, according to New York City probation officer Genée Bogans. Before the kiosks, says Bogans, she was swamped by the administrative details required to track the 250 offenders in her caseload. Kiosks allow her to track older nonviolent offenders with a minimum of time and effort, and she now focuses most of her attention on the relatively few violent youths who are also part of her caseload, meeting with them and their families twice weekly in small-group sessions. Bogans even goes to family funerals and graduations, making youthful offenders feel like they are getting special attention. "But it can be done only when you have 30 cases as opposed to 200," says Bogans.

New York's use of kiosks is being watched closely by other probation and parole agencies around the country as they face swelling caseloads and shrinking budgets. Some jurisdictions, like Marion County, Indiana, have installed similar machines. Under its Expedited Caseload Program, Marion County (home to the city of Indianapolis) reports lowering the number of hours required of its probation officers for caseload supervision. "Since its inception," say county officials, the Expedited Caseload Program (which accepts offenders convicted of nonviolent and less serious crimes) "has taken more than 650 cases that would have otherwise gone to the regular probation caseloads. This is a savings of between 15 and 20 cases per casework officer over a two-month period." The most recent statistics available show that about 4 million probationers were monitored through kiosks in 2001.

Other jurisdictions have taken different steps to automate their probation systems. Denver and Seattle, for example, are using 900-numbers through which probationers can report.

Some cities may have been too quick to jump on the kiosk bandwagon. In 2005, for example, Dallas, Texas, temporarily suspended the use of kiosks after finding that not all program participants had been properly screened. Although participation in the program required an assessment for readiness through face-to-face meetings with probation officers, some participants had undetected problems, including drug dependence and mental illness. As one critic of the Dallas program pointed out, "Inappropriate use of probation automation risks saving money in the short run while increasing long-term costs through higher recidivism rates."

Other critics charge that without personal supervision, probationers are more likely to reoffend—an assertion that is essentially untested. Other opponents say kiosks, 900-numbers, and similar reporting initiatives are far removed from meaningful "punishment" and that offenders deserve stricter treatment. Supporters, on the other hand, say that kiosks and 900-numbers will soon become more commonplace. "New York City had no choice; it had to do something like that," says Todd Clear, professor of criminal justice at New York's John Jay College. Clear assisted the city in restructuring its probation program. "No one wants probationers reporting to kiosks, but the alternative was even more unthinkable—a system in which nobody receives quality service," said Clear.

References: Marc A. Levin, "Salvation in Probation Automation?" *Conservative Voice*, September 27, 2005, http://www.theconservativevoice.com/articles/article.html?id=8585 (accessed May 1, 2007); Marion Superior Court Probation Department, "Operation: Probationer Accountability," http://www.indygov.org/probation/report/1998/4gh. htm (accessed May 1, 2005; Isabelle de Pommereau, "N.Y.C. Probation Officers to Get High-Tech Helper," *Christian Science Monitor*, February 8, 1997; Deborah J. Myers, "Take Your Order? Check Probation? Kiosk Use Grows," *Boulder County Business Report*, http://www.bcbr.com/display.phtml?VI5P2101&Section5News&Page52 (accessed May 5, 2006); and the Rice County (Minnesota) website, http://www.co.rice.mn.us (accessed May 7, 2007).

climbed." Some jurisdictions spend only a few hundred dollars per year on each probation or parole client, even though successful treatment in therapeutic settings is generally acknowledged to cost nearly $15,000 per person per year. The investment of such sums in the treatment of corrections clients, argues Petersilia, is potentially worthwhile because diverting probationers and parolees from lives of continued crime will save society even more money in terms of the costs of crime and the expenses associated with eventual imprisonment. The solution to the crisis that now exists in community corrections, says Petersilia, is to "first regain the public's trust that probation and parole can be meaningful, credible sanctions." She concludes, "Once we have that in place, we need to create a public climate to support a reinvestment in community corrections. Good community corrections cost money, and we should be honest about that."[112]

SUMMARY

- Probation, simply put, is a sentence of imprisonment that is suspended. Its goal is to retain some control over criminal offenders while using community programs to help rehabilitate them. Probation, a court-ordered sanction, is one form of community corrections (also termed *community-based corrections*)—that is, a sentencing style that depends less on traditional confinement options and more on correctional resources available in the community. John Augustus, a Boston shoemaker, is generally recognized as the world's first probation officer. By 1925, all 48 states had adopted probation legislation. In that same year, the federal government enacted legislation enabling federal district court judges to appoint paid probation officers and to impose probationary terms.

- Parole is the conditional early release of a convicted offender from prison. It is a corrections strategy whose primary purpose is to return offenders gradually to productive lives. Parole differs from probation in that parolees, unlike probationers, have been incarcerated. Parole supported the concept of indeterminate sentencing, which held that a prisoner could earn early release through good behavior and self-improvement.

- Both probation and parole provide opportunities for the reintegration of offenders into the community through the use of resources not readily available in institutional settings. They are far less expensive than imprisonment, lead to increased employment among program participants, make possible restitution payments, and increase opportunities for rehabilitation. Unfortunately, however, increased freedom for criminal offenders also means some degree of increased risk for other members of society and increased social costs. Until and unless we solve the problems of inaccurate risk assessment, increased recidivism, and inadequate supervision, probation and parole will continue to be viewed with suspicion by a public that has become intolerant of crime and criminal offenders.

- Ten especially significant U.S. Supreme Court decisions, each of which was discussed in this chapter, provide the legal framework for probation and parole supervision. The 1987 case of *Griffin* v. *Wisconsin* may be the most significant. In *Griffin*, the Supreme Court ruled that probation officers may conduct searches of a probationer's residence without either a search warrant or probable cause. Other important court decisions include the 1998 case of *Pennsylvania Board of Probation and Parole* v. *Scott*, in which the Court declined to extend the exclusionary rule to apply to searches by parole officers, and the 2001 case of *U.S.* v. *Knights*, which expanded the search authority normally reserved for probation and parole officers to police officers under certain circumstances.

- Probation/parole work consists primarily of four functions: (1) presentence investigations, (2) other intake procedures, (3) diagnosis and needs assessment, and (4) client supervision. The tasks performed by probation and parole officers are often quite similar, and some jurisdictions combine the roles of both into one job.

- Intermediate sanctions, which are sometimes termed *alternative sentencing strategies*, employ sentencing alternatives that fall somewhere between outright imprisonment and simple probationary release back into the community. These sanctions include shock incarceration, intensive supervision, and home confinement with electronic monitoring (also referred to as *remote location monitoring*). Intermediate sanctions have three distinct advantages: (1) They are less expensive than imprisonment; (2) they are "socially cost-effective" because they keep the offender in the community; and (3) they provide flexibility in terms of resources, time of involvement, and place of service.

- In recent years, parole and sometimes probation have been criticized for increasing the risk of community victimization by known offenders. In response, many states have eliminated or significantly curtailed parole opportunities. The future of parole may lie in an emerging concept of reentry that envisions successfully transitioning released inmates into the community using a variety of resources, including institutional and community programs.

KEY TERMS

caseload, 442

community corrections, 430

community service, 447

conditions of parole (probation), 437

discretionary release, 435

home confinement, 448

intensive probation supervision (IPS), 447

intermediate sanctions, 444

mandatory release, 436

mixed sentence, 446

parole, 434

parole board, 435

parole (probation) violation, 437

parole revocation, 437

probation, 430

probation revocation, 432

reentry, 434

remote location monitoring, 448

restitution, 437

revocation hearing, 439

shock incarceration, 445

shock probation, 445

split sentence, 445

KEY CASES

Bearden v. *Georgia,* 440

Escoe v. *Zerbst,* 440

Gagnon v. *Scarpelli,* 440

Greenholtz v. *Nebraska Penal Inmates,* 440

Griffin v. *Wisconsin,* 439

Mempa v. *Rhay,* 440

Minnesota v. *Murphy,* 441

Morrissey v. *Brewer,* 440

Pennsylvania Board of Probation and Parole v. *Scott,* 439

Samson v. *California,* 439

U.S. v. *Knights,* 439

QUESTIONS FOR REVIEW

1. What is probation? How did it develop? What purpose does it serve?

2. What is parole? How do probation and parole differ? How are they alike?

3. List and explain the advantages and disadvantages of probation and parole.

4. Describe significant court cases that have had an impact on the practice of probation and parole.

5. What do probation and parole officers do? What role do probation officers play in the sentencing of convicted offenders?

6. What are intermediate sanctions? How do they differ from more traditional forms of sentencing? What advantages do they offer?

7. How are probation and parole changing? What does the future hold for them?

QUESTIONS FOR REFLECTION

1. What significance does the contemporary concept of prisoner reentry hold for today's corrections administrators? For society? How do the terms *reentry* and *parole* differ?

2. What corrections philosophy originally supported the idea of indeterminate sentencing and parole? Does that philosophy still have merit today? Why or why not?

3. Do you believe, as some do, that traditional parole has been a failure? Explain.

Discuss your answers to these questions and other issues on the CJ Today e-mail discussion list (join the list at cjtoday.com).

WEB QUEST

Use the Cybrary (http://www.cybrary.info) to search the Web to learn as much as you can about the future of probation and parole. In particular, you might want to focus on the use of satellite technology to monitor offenders placed on probation, the use of home confinement, or public and media attitudes toward probation and parole. Also, gather studies on the future of probation and parole. Group your findings under headings (for example, "Innovative Options," "Alternative Sanctions," "Probation in My Home State," and "The Future of Probation and Parole").

Also visit the American Probation and Parole Association at http://www.appa-net.org. (The organization is listed in the Cybrary.) What is the mission of the APPA? What are its goals and objectives? What organizations are affiliated with it? How many of them have websites? Submit your findings to your instructor if asked to do so.

To complete this Web Quest online, go to the Web Quest module in Chapter 12 of the *Criminal Justice Today* Companion Website at cjtoday.com.

CHAPTER 13

Prisons and Jails

LEARNING OBJECTIVES

After reading this chapter, you should be able to

- Describe the nature and history of early punishments and discuss their impact on the modern philosophy of corrections.
- Outline the historical development of prisons.
- Discuss the major characteristics and purpose of today's prisons.
- Explain the role that jails play in American corrections and discuss the issues that jail administrators currently face.
- Describe the role of private prisons today and assess their future.

OUTLINE

> *To put people behind walls and bars and do little or nothing to change them is to win a battle but lose a war. It is wrong. It is expensive. It is stupid.*
>
> —Chief Justice Warren E. Burger (1907–1995)[1]

> *Infinite are the nine steps of a prison cell, and endless is the march of him who walks between the yellow brick wall and the red iron gate, thinking things that cannot be chained and cannot be locked.*
>
> —Arturo Giovannitti (1884–1959)

Hear the author discuss this chapter at cjtoday.com

prison

A state or federal confinement facility that has custodial authority over adults sentenced to confinement.

Introduction

In the history of criminal justice, the two decades that have just passed may be remembered as a time of mass imprisonment. In the 1980s, as concerns with community protection reached a near crescendo, and as stiff drug laws and strict repeat offender statutes put more and more people behind bars, rates of imprisonment reached previously unheralded levels. By the early 2000s, prison populations approached the breaking point, requiring the construction of many new facilities. Yet the use of **prisons** as places where convicted offenders serve time as punishment for breaking the law is a relatively new development in the handling of offenders. In fact, the emphasis on *time served* as the essence of criminal punishment is scarcely 200 years old.

Early Punishments

Before the development of prisons, early punishments were often cruel and torturous. An example is the graphic and unsettling description of a man broken on the rack in 1721, which is provided by Camden Pelham in his *Chronicles of Crime*.[2] The offender, Nathaniel Hawes, a domestic servant in the household of a wealthy nobleman, had stolen a sheep. When the overseer of the household discovered the offense, Hawes "shot him dead." This is Pelham's description of what happened next: "For these offences, of course, he was sentenced to be broken alive upon the rack, without the benefit of the *coup de grâce*, or mercy-stroke. Informed of the dreadful sentence, he composedly laid himself down upon his back on a strong cross, on which, with his arms and legs extended, he was fastened by ropes. The executioner, having by now with a hatchet chopped off his left hand, next took up a heavy iron bar, with which, by repeated blows, he broke his bones to shivers, till the marrow, blood, and splinters flew about the field; but the prisoner never uttered a groan nor a sigh! The ropes being next unlashed, I imagined him dead . . . till . . . he writhed himself from the cross. When he fell on the grass . . . he rested his head on part of the timbar, and asked the by-standers for a pipe of tobacco, which was infamously answered by kicking and spitting on him. He then begged his head might be chopped off, but to no purpose." Pelham goes on to relate how the condemned man then engaged in conversation with onlookers, recounting details of his trial. At one point he asked one of those present to repay money he had loaned him, saying, "Don't you perceive, I am to be kept alive." After six hours, Pelham says, Hawes was put out of his misery by a soldier assigned to guard the proceedings. "He was knocked on the head by the . . . sentinel; and having been raised upon a gallows, the vultures were busy picking out the eyes of the mangled corpse, in the skull of which was clearly discernible the mark of the soldier's musket."

This gruesome tale may seem foreign to modern readers—as though it describes an event that happened in a barbarous time long ago or in a place far away. However, a mere 200 years ago, before the emergence of imprisonment, convicted offenders were routinely subjected to physical punishment that often resulted in death. While fines were sometimes levied, corporal punishments were the most common form of criminal punishment and generally fit the doctrine of **lex talionis** (the law of retaliation). Under *lex talionis*, the convicted offender was sentenced to suffer a punishment that closely approximated the original injury. This rule of "an eye for an eye, a tooth for a tooth," generally duplicated the offense. Hence, if a person blinded another, he was blinded in return. Murderers were executed, sometimes in a way tailored to approximate the method they had used in committing the crime.

lex talionis

The law of retaliation, often expressed as "an eye for an eye" or "like for like."

Flogging

Historically, the most widely used of physical punishment was flogging.[3] The Bible mentions instances of whipping, and Christ himself was scourged. Whipping was widely used in England throughout the Middle Ages, and some offenders were said to have been beaten as they ran through the streets, hands tied behind their backs. American colonists carried the practice of flogging with them to the New World.

The last officially sanctioned flogging of a criminal offender in the United States was in Delaware on June 16, 1952, when a burglar received 20 lashes,[4] but the practice of whipping continues in other parts of the world. Amnesty International reports its use in various countries for political and other prisoners. In 1994, the flogging in Singapore of Michael Fay, an American teenager convicted of spray-painting parked cars, caused an international outcry from opponents of corporal punishment. But in parts of the United States some people reacted in just the opposite way. After the Fay flogging (called caning in Singapore because it was carried out with a bamboo rod), eight states entertained legislation to endorse whipping or paddling as a criminal sanction. For example, Mississippi legislators proposed paddling graffitists and petty thieves; Tennessee lawmakers considered punishing vandals and burglars by public caning on courthouse steps; and Louisiana looked into the possibility of ordering parents (or a corrections officer if the parents refused) to spank their children in judicial chambers.[5] None of the proposals made it into law.

Mutilation

While flogging is a painful punishment whose memory might deter repeat offenses, mutilation is primarily a strategy of specific deterrence that makes it difficult or impossible for individuals to commit future crimes. Throughout history, various societies have amputated the hands of thieves and robbers, blinded spies, and castrated rapists. Blasphemers had their tongues ripped out, and pickpockets suffered broken fingers. Extensive mutilation, which included cutting off the ears and ripping out the tongue, was instituted in eleventh-century Britain and imposed on hunters who poached on royal lands.[6]

Today, some countries in the Arab world, including Iran and Saudi Arabia, still rely on a limited use of mutilation as a penalty to incapacitate selected offenders. Mutilation also creates a general deterrent by providing potential offenders with walking examples of the consequences of crime.

Branding

Before modern technology and the advent of mechanized record keeping, branding was used to readily identify convicted offenders and to warn others with whom they might come in contact of their dangerous potential.

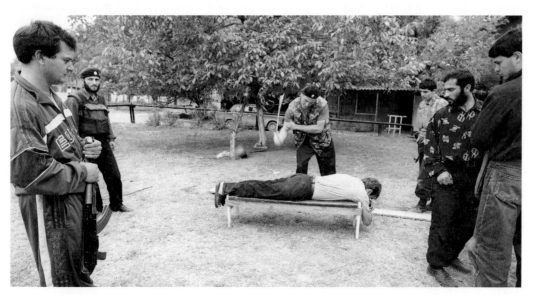

A man undergoing public punishment for a transgression of the Islamic code in Grozny, Chechnya. Other than the death penalty, corporal punishment for crime has been abolished in the United States, but it remains common in some Muslim nations. Might similar corporal punishments ever again have a place in Western criminal justice? Why or why not?

AP Wide World Photos

The Romans, Greeks, French, British, and many others have all used branding at one time or another. Harry Barnes and Negley Teeters, early writers on the history of the criminal justice system, report that branding in the American colonies was customary for certain crimes, with first offenders being branded on the hand and repeat offenders receiving an identifying mark on the forehead.[7] Women were rarely marked physically, although they may have been shamed and forced to wear marked clothing. Nathaniel Hawthorne's *The Scarlet Letter* is a report on that practice, where the central figure is required to wear a red letter A embroidered on her dress, signifying adultery.

Public Humiliation

A number of early punishments were designed to humiliate offenders in public and to allow members of the community an opportunity for vengeance. The stocks and pillory were two such punishments. The pillory closed over the head and hands and held the offender in a standing position, while the stocks kept the person sitting with the head free. A few hundred years ago, each European town had its stocks or pillory, usually located in some central square or alongside a major thoroughfare.

Offenders sent to the stocks or pillory could expect to be heckled and spit on by passersby. Other citizens might gather to throw tomatoes or rotten eggs. On occasion, citizens who were particularly outraged by the magnitude or nature of the offense would throw rocks at the offender, ending his life. Retribution remained a community prerogative, and citizens wielded the power of final sentencing. The pillory was still used in Delaware as late as 1905.[8]

The ducking stool, used in colonial times to punish gossips, provided another form of public humiliation. The offender was tied to it and lowered into a river or lake, turning nearly upside down like a duck searching for food underwater.

Workhouses

Sixteenth-century Europe suffered severe economic upheaval, caused partly by wars and partly by the approach of the Industrial Revolution, which was soon to sweep the continent. By 1550, thousands of unemployed and vagrant people were scouring towns and villages seeking food and shelter. It was not long before they depleted the economic reserves of churches, which were the primary social relief agencies of the time.

workhouse

An early form of imprisonment whose purpose was to instill habits of industry in the idle.

In the belief that poverty was caused by laziness, governments were quick to create **workhouses** designed to instill "habits of industry" in the unemployed. The first workhouse in Europe opened in 1557 and taught work habits, not specific skills. Inmates were made to fashion their own furniture, build additions to the facility, and raise gardens. When the number of inmates exceeded the volume of useful work to be done, make-work projects, including treadmills and cranks, were invented to keep them busy.

Workhouses were judged successful, if only because they were constantly filled. By 1576, Parliament decreed that every county in England should build a workhouse. Although workhouses were forerunners of our modern prisons, they did not incarcerate criminal offenders—only vagrants and the destitute. Nor were they designed to punish, but served instead to reinforce the value of hard work.

Exile

Many societies have banished criminals. The French sent criminal offenders to Devil's Island, and the Russians used Siberia for centuries for the same purpose. England sent convicts to the American colonies beginning in 1618. The British program of exile, known as *transportation*, served the dual purpose of providing a captive labor force for development of the colonies while assuaging growing English sentiments opposing corporal punishments. In 1776, however, the American Revolution forced the practice to end, and British penology shifted to the use of aging ships, called *hulks*, as temporary prisons. Hulks were anchored in harbors throughout England and served as floating confinement facilities even after transportation (to other parts of the globe) resumed.

In 1787, only 17 years after Captain Cook had discovered the continent, Australia became the new port of call for English prisoners. The name of Captain William Bligh, governor of the New South Wales penal colony, survives today as a symbol of the difficult conditions and the rough men and women of those times.

The Emergence of Prisons

The identity of the world's first true prison is unknown, but at some point, penalties for crime came to include incarceration. During the Middle Ages, "punitive imprisonment appears to have been introduced into Europe . . . by the Christian Church in the incarceration of certain offenders against canon law."[9] Similarly, debtors' prisons existed throughout Europe during the fifteenth and sixteenth centuries, although they housed inmates who had violated the civil law rather than criminals. John Howard, an early prison reformer, mentions prisons housing criminal offenders in Hamburg, Germany; Bern, Switzerland; and Florence, Italy, in his 1777 book, *State of Prisons*.[10] Early efforts to imprison offenders led to the founding of the Hospice of San Michele, a papal prison that opened in 1704, and the Maison de Force, begun at Ghent, Belgium, in 1773. The Hospice was actually a residential school for delinquent boys and housed 60 youngsters at its opening. Both facilities stressed reformation over punishment and became early alternatives to the use of physical and public punishments.

Near the end of the eighteenth century, the concept of imprisonment as punishment for crime reached its fullest expression in the United States. Imprisonment *as* punishment differs significantly from the concept of imprisonment *for* punishment, and embodiment of this concept in American penal institutions represented the beginning of a new chapter in corrections reform. Soon after they opened, U.S. prisons came to serve as models for European reformers searching for ways to humanize criminal punishment. For that reason, and to better appreciate how today's prisons operate, it is important to understand the historical development of the prison movement in the United States. Figure 13–1 depicts the stages through which American prisons progressed following the introduction around 1790 of the concept of incarceration as a punishment for crime. Each historical era is discussed in the pages that follow. For an online history of early prison development in England, see Web Extra 13–1 at cjtoday.com.

WEB
Extra
▪ ▪ ▪ ▪

The Penitentiary Era (1790–1825)

In 1790, Philadelphia's Walnut Street Jail was converted into a penitentiary by the Pennsylvania Quakers. The Quakers viewed incarceration as an opportunity for penance and saw prisons as places wherein offenders might make amends with society and accept responsibility for their misdeeds. The philosophy of imprisonment begun by the Quakers, heavily imbued with elements of rehabilitation and deterrence, carries over to the present day.[11]

Inmates of the Philadelphia Penitentiary were expected to wrestle alone with the evils they harbored. Penance was the primary vehicle through which rehabilitation was anticipated, and a study of the Bible was strongly encouraged. Solitary confinement was the rule, and the penitentiary was architecturally designed to minimize contact between inmates and between inmates and staff. Exercise was allowed in small high-walled yards attached to each cell. Eventually, handicrafts were introduced into the prison setting, permitting prisoners to work in their cells.

The Walnut Street Jail, America's first "true" prison, circa 1800. What philosophical principles were behind the Quaker penitentiary concept?

Culver Pictures, Inc.

Prison Era

Year	The Penitentiary Era 1790	The Mass (Congregate) Prison Era 1825	The Reformatory Era 1876	The Industrial Era 1890	The Punitive Era 1935	The Treatment Era 1945	The Community-based (Decarceration) Era 1967	The Warehousing Era 1980	The Just Deserts Era 1995
Philosophy	Rehabilitation, Deterrence	Incapacitation, Deterrence	Rehabilitation	Incapacitation, Restoration	Retribution	Rehabilitation	Restoration, Rehabilitation	Incapacitation	Retribution, Incapacitation, Deterrence
Representative Institutions	Philadelphia Penitentiary Eastern Penitentiary (Cherry Hill, PA) Western Penitentiary (Pittsburgh)	New York State Prison (Auburn, NY)	Elmira Reformatory (Elmira, NY)	Auburn (NY) Sing Sing (NY) Stateville (IL) San Quentin (CA) Attica (NY)	Alcatraz (CA)	Marion (IL)	Massachusetts Youth Services Halfway Houses	Most Major Prisons	Characteristic of Many Prisons Today

FIGURE 13–1

Stages of prison development in the United States.

Fashioned after the Philadelphia model, the Western Penitentiary opened in Pittsburgh in 1826, and the Eastern Penitentiary opened in Cherry Hill, Pennsylvania, three years later. Solitary confinement and individual cells, supported by a massive physical structure with impenetrable walls, became synonymous with the Pennsylvania system of imprisonment. Supporters heralded the **Pennsylvania system** as one that was humane and provided inmates with the opportunity for rehabilitation. Many well-known figures of the day spoke out in support of the Pennsylvania system, among them Benjamin Franklin and Benjamin Rush—both of whom were influential members of the Philadelphia Society for Alleviating the Miseries of Public Prisons.[12]

The Mass Prison Era (1825–1876)

Vermont, Massachusetts, Maryland, and New York all built institutions modeled after Pennsylvania's penitentiaries. As prison populations began to grow, however, solitary confinement became prohibitively expensive. One of the first large prisons to abandon the Pennsylvania model was the New York State Prison at Auburn. Auburn introduced the congregate but silent system, under which inmates lived, ate, and worked together in enforced silence. This style of imprisonment, which came to be known as the **Auburn system**, featured group workshops rather than solitary handicrafts and reintroduced corporal punishments into the handling of offenders. Whereas isolation and enforced idleness were inherent punishments under the early Pennsylvania system, Auburn depended on whipping and hard labor to maintain the rule of silence.[13]

The Auburn prison was the site of an experiment in solitary confinement, which was the basis of the Pennsylvania system. Eighty-three men were placed in small solitary cells on Christmas Day of 1821 and were released in 1823 and 1824. Five of the 83 died, one went insane, another attempted suicide, and the others became "seriously demoralized."[14] Although the Auburn experiment did not accurately simulate the conditions in Pennsylvania (it allowed for no exercise, placed prisoners in tiny cells, and shunned handicrafts—which had been introduced into Pennsylvania's prisons by the time the experiment began), it did provide an effective basis for condemnation of the Pennsylvania system. Partly as a result of the experiment, the Reverend Louis Dwight, an influential prison reformer of the time and the leader of the prestigious Prison Discipline Society of Boston, became an advocate of the Auburn system, citing its lower cost[15] and

Pennsylvania system

A form of imprisonment developed by the Pennsylvania Quakers around 1790 as an alternative to corporal punishments. This style of imprisonment made use of solitary confinement and encouraged rehabilitation.

Auburn system

A form of imprisonment developed in New York State around 1820 that depended on mass prisons, where prisoners were held in congregate fashion and required to remain silent. This style of imprisonment was a primary competitor with the Pennsylvania system.

Eastern State Penitentiary in Philadelphia. Built in the 1820s, construction costs totaled $780,000, making it the most expensive public building at that time. Although the penitentiary building today serves only as a tourist attraction, it's early-nineteenth-century builders hoped that just the sight of its 30-foot-high, 12-foot-thick walls would be enough to instill fear in the hearts of would-be lawbreakers. Did they achieve their goal?

Albert Vecerka/Courtesy of Eastern State Penitentiary Historic Site, Philadelphia, Pennsylvania.

more humane conditions.[16] The lower cost resulted from the simpler facilities required by mass imprisonment and from group workshops that provided economies of scale unachievable under solitary confinement. Dwight also believed that the Pennsylvania style of imprisonment was unconscionable and inhumane. As a consequence of criticisms fielded by Dwight and others, most American prisons built after 1825 followed the Auburn architectural style and system of prison discipline.

About the same time, however, a number of European governments sent representatives to study the virtues of the two American systems. Interestingly, most concluded that the Pennsylvania system was more conducive to reformation than the Auburn system, and many European prisons adopted a strict separation of inmates. Two French visitors, Gustave de Beaumont and Alexis de Tocqueville, stressed the dangers of what they called "contamination," whereby prisoners housed in Auburn-like prisons could negatively influence one another.[17]

The Reformatory Era (1876–1890)

With the tension between the Auburn and Pennsylvania systems, American penology existed in an unsettled state for a half century. That tension was resolved in 1876 with the emergence of the **reformatory style**, which grew out of practices innovated by two especially noteworthy corrections leaders of the mid-1880s: Captain Alexander Maconochie and Sir Walter Crofton.

reformatory style

A late-nineteenth-century correctional model based on the use of the indeterminate sentence and the belief in the possibility of rehabilitation, especially for youthful offenders. The reformatory concept faded with the emergence of industrial prisons around the start of the twentieth century.

CAPTAIN ALEXANDER MACONOCHIE AND NORFOLK ISLAND

During the early 1840s, Captain Alexander Maconochie served as the warden of Norfolk Island, a prison off the coast of Australia for "doubly condemned" inmates. English prisoners sent to Australia who committed other crimes while there were taken to Norfolk to be segregated from less recalcitrant offenders. Prior to Maconochie's arrival, conditions at Norfolk had been atrocious. Disease and unsanitary conditions were rampant on the island, fights among inmates left many dead and more injured, and the physical facilities were not conducive to good supervision. Maconochie immediately set out to reform the island prison by providing incentives for prisoners to participate in their own reformation.

Maconochie developed a system of marks through which prisoners could earn enough credits to buy their freedom. Bad behavior removed marks from the inmate's ledger, while acceptable behavior added marks. The mark system made possible early release and led to a recognition of the indeterminate sentence as a useful tool in the reformation of offenders. Before Maconochie, inmates had been sentenced to determinate sentences specifying a fixed number of years they had

CJ Today Exhibit 13–1

Chaplain James Finley's Letter from the Ohio Penitentiary, 1850

It is true, there are yet two systems of prison discipline still in use, but both claim to have the two parties—the criminal and society—equally in view. The congregate system, going on the supposition that habits of labor and moral character are the chief desiderata among this class of men, set them to work at those trades for which their physical and mental powers, together with the consideration of their former occupations, may more especially adapt them; religious instruction is also given them by men appointed expressly for the purpose; and they are permitted to labor in large communities, where they can see but not converse with each other, as the friends of this system imagine that social inter-course, of some kind and to some extent, is almost as necessary to man as food. The separate system, on the other hand, looking upon all intercourse between criminals as only evil in its tendency, by which one rogue becomes the instructor or accomplice of another, secludes the convicts from each other but, to atone for this defect, it encourages the visits of good men to the cells of the prisoners; and the officers of these prisons make it a particular point of duty to visit the inmates very frequently themselves. The physical habits of the imprisoned are provided for by such trades as can be carried on by individual industry; a teacher is employed to lead them on in the study of useful branches of education; while the Gospel is regularly taught them, not only by sermons on the Sabbath, but by private efforts of the chaplain in his daily rounds.

Source: James Finley, *Memorials of Prison Life* (Cincinnati, OH: Swormstedt and Poe, 1855).

CJ Today Exhibit 13–2

An Early Texas Prison

In 1860, an unknown writer described conditions in the Texas Penitentiary at Huntsville as follows:

> By a special enactment of the Legislature, the front of the cell of any prisoner sentenced to solitary confinement for life, is painted black, and his name and sentence distinctly marked thereon. The object would seem to be to infuse a salutary dread into the minds of the other prisoners. Upon the only black-painted cell in the prison was the following inscription, in distinct white letters: William Brown, aged twenty-four years, convicted for murder in Grimes County, spring term, 1858, for which he is now suffering solitary confinement for life. Brown himself, however, was in fact at work in the factory with the other convicts! He entered the Penitentiary in May, 1859, and had been kept in close confinement in his cell, without labor, never being permitted to leave it for any purpose, until about the first of October, when his health was found to have suffered so much that, to preserve his life, he was, under a discretionary power vested in the Directors, released from the rigor of his sentence, and subjected to only the ordinary confinement of the prison. His health has since greatly improved. It is not to be wondered at that his health should decline under the strict enforcement of such a sentence. The cell in which he was confined was the same as to size, ventilation, and light as the rest; and being one of the lower tier of cells, the top of the doorway was some feet below the lower edge of the window upon the opposite side of the corridor in the outside wall. He had even less chance for fresh air than if his cell had been in almost any other location. It is the sight and knowledge of such instances of solitary unemployed confinement as this, and a willful neglect or refusal to inform themselves upon, and recognize, the very wide distinction between the terms separate and solitary, that renders many persons so violently prejudiced against, and opposed to the "Separate System."

Source: The Journal of Prison Discipline and Philanthropy, Vol. 15, No. 1 (January 1860), pp. 7–17.

to serve before release. The mark system placed responsibility for winning an early release squarely on the inmate. Because of the system's similarity to the later practice of parole, it won for Maconochie the title "father of parole."

Opinion leaders in England, however, saw Maconochie's methods as too lenient. Many pointed out that the indeterminate sentence made possible new lives for criminals in a world of vast opportunity (the Australian continent) at the expense of the British Empire. Amid charges that he coddled inmates, Maconochie was relieved of his duties as warden in 1844.

SIR WALTER CROFTON AND THE IRISH SYSTEM

Maconochie's innovations soon came to the attention of Sir Walter Crofton, head of the Irish prison system. Crofton adapted the idea of early release to his program of progressive stages. Inmates who entered Irish prisons had to work their way through four stages. The first, or entry level, involved solitary confinement and dull work. Most prisoners in the first level were housed at Mountjoy Prison in Dublin. The second stage assigned prisoners to Spike Island, where they worked on fortifications. The third stage placed prisoners in field units, which worked directly in the community on public-service projects. Unarmed guards supervised the prisoners. The fourth stage depended on what Crofton called the "ticket of leave." The ticket of leave allowed prisoners to live and work in the community under the occasional supervision of a "moral instructor." It could be revoked at any time up until the expiration of the offender's original sentence.

Crofton was convinced that convicts could not be rehabilitated without successful reintegration into the community. His innovations were closely watched by reformers across Europe. But in 1862, a wave of violent robberies swept England and led to the passage of the 1863 Garotters Act, which mandated whipping for robberies involving violence and longer prison sentences for many other crimes, effectively rolling back the clock on Crofton's innovations, at least in Europe.

THE ELMIRA REFORMATORY AND THE BIRTH OF PAROLE IN THE UNITED STATES

In 1865, Gaylord B. Hubbell, warden of Sing Sing Prison in New York, visited Great Britain and studied prisons there. He returned to the United States greatly impressed by the Irish system and recommended that indeterminate sentences be used in American prisons. The New York Prison

Association supported Hubbell and called for the creation of a "reformatory" based on the concept of an earned early release if the inmate reformed himself.

When the new National Prison Association held its first conference in 1870 in Cincinnati, it adopted a 37-paragraph Declaration of Principles that called for reformation to replace punishment as the goal of imprisonment. The most significant result of the conference, however, was the move to embody those principles in a reformatory built on American soil.

In 1876, the Elmira Reformatory opened in Elmira, New York, under the direction of Zebulon Brockway, a leading advocate of indeterminate sentencing and the former superintendent of the Detroit House of Correction. The state of New York had passed an indeterminate sentencing bill that made possible early release for inmates who earned it. However, because reformation was thought most likely among younger people, the Elmira Reformatory accepted only first offenders between the ages of 16 and 30. A system of graded stages required inmates to meet educational, behavioral, and other goals. Schooling was mandatory, and trade training was available in telegraphy, tailoring, plumbing, carpentry, and other areas.

Unfortunately, the reformatory "proved a relative failure and disappointment."[18] Many inmates reentered lives of crime following their release, which called the success of the reformatory ideal into question. Some authors attributed the failure of the reformatory to "the ever-present jailing psychosis"[19] of the prison staff or to an overemphasis on confinement and institutional security rather than reformation, which made it difficult to implement many of the ideals on which the reformatory had been based.

Even though the reformatory was not a success, the principles it established remain important today. Thus, indeterminate sentencing, parole, trade training, education, and primacy of reformation over punishment all serve as a foundation for ongoing debates about the purpose of imprisonment.

The Industrial Era (1890–1935)

With the failure of the reformatory style of prison, concerns over security and discipline became dominant in American prisons. Inmate populations rose, costs soared, and states began to study practical alternatives. An especially attractive option was found in the potential profitability of inmate labor, and the era of the **industrial prison** in America was born.

industrial prison

A correctional model intended to capitalize on the labor of convicts sentenced to confinement.

Industrial prisons in the northern United States were characterized by thick, high walls, stone or brick buildings, guard towers, and smokestacks rising from within the walls. These prisons smelted steel, manufactured cabinets, molded tires, and turned out many other goods for the open market. Prisons in the South, which had been devastated by the Civil War, tended more toward farm labor and public-works projects. The South, with its labor-intensive agricultural practices, used inmates to replace slaves who had been freed during the war.

The following six systems of inmate labor were in use by the early twentieth century:[20]

- *Contract system.* Private businesses paid to use inmate labor. They provided the raw materials and supervised the manufacturing process inside prison facilities.
- *Piece-price system.* Goods were produced for private businesses under the supervision of prison authorities. Prisons were paid according to the number and quality of the goods manufactured.
- *Lease system.* Prisoners were taken to the work site under the supervision of armed guards. Once there, they were turned over to the private contractor, who employed them and maintained discipline.
- *Public-account system.* This system eliminated the use of private contractors. Industries were entirely prison owned, and prison authorities managed the manufacturing process from beginning to end. Goods were sold on the free market.
- **State-use system**. Prisoners manufactured only goods that could be sold by or to other state offices, or they provided labor to assist other state agencies.
- *Public-works system.* Prisoners maintained roads and highways, cleaned public parks and recreational facilities, and maintained and restored public buildings.

state-use system

A form of inmate labor in which items produced by inmates may only be sold by or to state offices. Items that only the state can sell include such things as license plates and hunting licenses, while items sold only to state offices include furniture and cleaning supplies.

Large prisons that were built or converted to industrialization included San Quentin in California, Sing Sing and Auburn in New York, and the Illinois State Penitentiary at Statesville. Many prison industries were quite profitable and contributed significantly to state treasuries. Reports from 1932 show that 82,276 prisoners were involved in various forms of prison labor that year, producing products with a total value of $75,369,471—a huge amount considering the worth of the dollar 70 years ago.[21] Beginning as early as the 1830s, however, workers began to complain of

Church services in Sing Sing Prison in 1906. Note the "ushers" with shotguns. How is security maintained in today's correctional facilities?

Ossining, New York/Underwood Photo Archives

being forced to compete with cheap prison labor. In 1834, mechanics in New York filed a petition with the state legislature asking that prison industries paying extremely low wages be eliminated. Labor unions became very well organized and powerful by the early part of the twentieth century, and the Great Depression of the 1930s, during which jobs were scarce, brought with it a call for an end to prison industries.

In 1929, union influence led Congress to pass the Hawes-Cooper Act, which required prison-made goods to conform to the regulations of the states through which they were shipped. Hence, states that outlawed the manufacture of free-market goods in their own prisons were effectively protected from prison-made goods that might be imported from other states. The death blow to prison industries, however, came in 1935 with the passage of the **Ashurst-Sumners Act**, which specifically prohibited the interstate transportation and sale of prison goods where state laws forbade them. In consort with the Ashurst-Sumners legislation, and because of economic pressures brought on by the Depression, most states soon passed statutes that curtailed prison manufacturing within their borders, and the industrial era in American corrections came to a close.

Ashurst-Sumners Act

Federal legislation of 1935 that effectively ended the industrial prison era by restricting interstate commerce in prison-made goods.

PRISON INDUSTRIES TODAY

Although still hampered by some federal and state laws, prison industries have begun making a comeback. Under the state-use philosophy, most states still permit the prison manufacture of goods that will be used exclusively by the prison system itself or by other state agencies or that only the state can legitimately sell on the open market. An example of the latter is license plates, the sale of which is a state monopoly. North Carolina provides a good example of a modern state-use system. Its Correction Enterprises operates around 20 inmate-staffed businesses, each of which is self-supporting. North Carolina inmates manufacture prison clothing; raise vegetables and farm animals to feed inmates throughout the state; operate an oil refinery, a forestry service, and a cannery; and manufacture soap, license plates, and some office furniture. All manufactured goods other than license plates are for use within the prison system or by other state agencies. North Carolina's Correction Enterprises pays 5% of its profits to the state's crime victims' compensation fund.[22]

The federal government also operates a kind of state-use system in its institutions through a government-owned corporation called Federal Prison Industries, Inc. (also called UNICOR).[23] The corporation was established in 1934 to retain some employment programs for federal inmates in anticipation of the elimination of free-market prison industries. Critics of UNICOR charge that inmates are paid very low wages and are trained for jobs that do not exist in the free economy.[24] Even so, a long-term study published in 1994 found that federal inmates who participated in UNICOR "showed better adjustment, were less likely to be revoked at the end of their first year

Incarceration is a crash course in extortion and criminal behavior.

—Vincent Schiraldi, Executive Director, Justice Policy Institute

back in the community, and were more likely to find employment in the halfway house and community."[25] The study also found that inmates "earned slightly more money in the community than inmates who had similar background characteristics, but who did not participate in work and vocational training programs."

Free-market moneymaking prison industries are also staging a comeback, some funded by private-sector investment. In 1981, under the Prison Rehabilitative Industries and Diversified Enterprises, Inc., legislation, commonly called the PRIDE Act, Florida became the first state to experiment with the wholesale transfer of its correctional industry program from public to private control.[26] PRIDE industries include sugarcane processing, construction, and automotive repair. Other states have since followed suit.

Today, the Prison Industry Enhancement Certification Program (PIECP),[27] administered by the Bureau of Justice Assistance (BJA), exempts certified state and local departments of corrections from normal federal restrictions on the sale of inmate-made goods in interstate commerce.[28] In addition, the program lifts restrictions on certified corrections departments, permitting them to sell inmate-made goods to the federal government in amounts exceeding the $10,000 maximum normally imposed on such transactions. The PIECP also allows private industry to establish joint ventures with state and local correctional agencies to produce goods using inmate labor. As of March 2004, 38 jurisdictions were certified to operate under the PIECP. Learn more about the history of federal prison industries at Library Extra 13–1 at cjtoday.com. Visit the National Correctional Industries Association at Web Extra 13–2 at cjtoday.com to see additional information about the PIECP.

LIBRARY Extra ∎∎∎∎   **WEB** Extra ∎∎∎∎

The Punitive Era (1935–1945)

The moratorium on free-market prison industries initiated by the Ashurst-Sumners Act was to last for more than half a century. Prison administrators, left with few ready alternatives, seized on custody and institutional security as the long-lost central purposes of the correctional enterprise. The punitive era that resulted was characterized by the belief that prisoners owed a debt to society that only a rigorous period of confinement could repay. Writers of the period termed such beliefs the *convict bogey* and the *lock psychosis*,[29] referring to the fact that convicts were to be both shunned and securely locked away from society. Large maximum-security institutions flourished, and the prisoner's daily routine became one of monotony and frustration. The punitive era was a lackluster time in American corrections. Innovations were rare, and an "out of sight, out of mind" philosophy characterized American attitudes toward inmates. The term *stir-crazy* grew out of the experience of many prisoners with the punitive era's lack of educational, treatment, and work programs. In response, inmates created their own diversions, frequently attempting to escape or inciting riots. One especially secure and still notorious facility of the punitive era was the federal penitentiary on Alcatraz Island, which is described in some detail at Web Extra 13–3 at cjtoday.com.

WEB Extra ∎∎∎∎

Alcatraz Federal Penitentiary. The island prison closed in 1963, a victim of changing attitudes toward corrections. It survives today as a San Francisco tourist attraction. What security levels characterize most American prisons today?

Paul S. Howell/Getty Images, Inc.– Liaison

The Treatment Era (1945–1967)

In the late 1940s, the mood of the nation was euphoric. Memories of World War II were dimming, industries were productive beyond the best hopes of most economic forecasters, and America's position of world leadership was fundamentally unchallenged. Nothing seemed impossible. Amid the bounty of a postwar boom economy, politicians and the public accorded themselves the luxury of restructuring the nation's prisons. A new interest in "corrections" and reformation, combined with the latest in behavioral techniques, ushered in a new era. The treatment era was based on a **medical model** of corrections—one that implied that the offender was sick and that rehabilitation was only a matter of finding the right treatment. Inmates came to be seen more as "clients" or "patients" than as offenders, and terms like *resident* and *group member* replaced *inmate*.

Therapy during the period took a number of forms, many of which are still used today. Most therapeutic models assumed that inmates needed help to mature psychologically and had to be taught to assume responsibility for their lives. Prisons built their programs around both individual treatment and group therapy approaches. In individual treatment, the offender and the therapist develop a face-to-face relationship. Group therapy relies on the sharing of insights, gleaned by members of the therapeutic group, to facilitate the growth process, often by first making clear to offenders the emotional basis of their criminal behavior. Other forms of therapy used in prisons have included behavior therapy, drug therapy, neurosurgery, sensory deprivation, and aversion therapy.

Inmates have not always been happy with the treatment model. In 1972, a group of prisoners at the Marion, Illinois, federal prison joined together and demanded a right to refuse treatment.[30] The National Prison Project of the American Civil Liberties Union (ACLU) supported the inmates' right to refuse personality-altering treatment techniques.[31] Other suits followed. Worried about potential liability, the Law Enforcement Assistance Administration (LEAA) banned the expenditure of LEAA funds to support any prison programs utilizing psychosurgery, medical research, chemotherapy, or behavior modification.[32]

The treatment era also suffered from attacks on the medical model on which it was based. Academics and legal scholars pointed to a lack of evidence in support of the model[33] and began to stress individual responsibility rather than treatment in the handling of offenders. Indeterminate sentencing statutes, designed to reward inmates for improved behavior, fell before the swelling drive to replace treatment with punishment.

Any honest evaluation of the treatment era would conclude that, in practice, treatment was more an ideal than a reality. Many treatment programs existed, some of them quite intensive. Unfortunately, the correctional system in America was never capable of providing any consistent or widespread treatment because the majority of its guards and administrators were oriented primarily toward custody and were not trained to provide treatment. However, although we have identified 1967 as the end of the treatment era, many correctional rehabilitation programs survive to the present day, and new ones are continually being developed.

The Community-Based Era (1967–1980)

Beginning in the 1960s, the realities of prison overcrowding combined with a renewed faith in humanity and the treatment era's belief in the possibility of behavioral change to inspire a movement away from institutionalized corrections and toward the creation of opportunities for reformation within local communities. The transition to community corrections (also called *deinstitutionalization*, *diversion*, and *decarceration*) was based on the premise that rehabilitation could not occur in isolation from the free social world to which inmates must eventually return.[34] Advocates of community corrections portrayed prisons as dehumanizing, claiming that they further victimized offenders who had already been negatively labeled by society. Some states strongly embraced the movement toward decarceration. In 1972, for example, Massachusetts drew national attention when it closed all of its reform schools and replaced them with group homes.[35]

Decarceration, which built on many of the intermediate sanctions discussed in the previous chapter, used a variety of programs to keep offenders in contact with the community and out of prison. Among them were halfway houses, work-release programs, and open institutions. Halfway houses have sometimes been called *halfway-in* or *halfway-out houses*, depending on whether offenders were being given a second chance before incarceration or were in the process of gradual release from prison. Boston had halfway houses as early as the 1920s, but they operated for only a few years.[36] It was not until 1961 that the Federal Bureau of Prisons (BOP) opened a few experimental residential centers in support of its new prerelease programs focusing on

medical model

A therapeutic perspective on correctional treatment that applies the diagnostic perspective of medical science to the handling of criminal offenders.

What we have learned from years of practice and the results of hundreds of studies, is that reducing recidivism is a very complex task that requires serious work on multiple fronts.

—Jeff Beard, Secretary, Pennsylvania Department of Corrections[i]

The central aim of a true prison system is the protection of society against crime, not the punishment of criminals.

—Zebulon R. Brockway[ii]

work release

A prison program through which inmates are temporarily released into the community to meet job responsibilities.

juveniles and youthful offenders. Called *prerelease guidance centers*, the first of these facilities were based in Los Angeles and Chicago.[37]

Although the era of community corrections is now in decline, halfway houses and work-release programs still operate in many parts of the country. A typical residential treatment facility today houses 15 to 20 residents and operates under the supervision of a director, supported by a handful of counselors. The environment is nonthreatening, and residents are generally free to come and go during the workday. The building looks more like a motel or a house than it does a prison. Fences and walls are nonexistent. Transportation is provided to and from work or educational sites, and the facility retains a portion of the resident's wages to pay the costs of room and board. Residents are expected to return to the facility after work, and some group therapy may be provided.

Today's work-release programs house offenders in traditional correctional environments—usually minimum-security prisons—but permit them to work at jobs in the community during the day and to return to the prison at night. Inmates are usually required to pay a token amount for their room and board in the institution. The first work-release law was passed by Wisconsin in 1913, but it was not until 1957 that a comprehensive program created by North Carolina spurred the development of work-release programs nationwide.[38] **Work release** for federal prisoners was authorized by the federal Prisoner Rehabilitation Act of 1965.[39] As work-release programs grew, study release—whereby inmates attend local colleges and technical schools—was initiated in most jurisdictions as an adjunct to work release.

Work-release programs are still very much a part of modern corrections. Almost all states have them, and many inmates work in the community as they approach the end of their sentence. Unfortunately, work-release programs are not without their social costs. Some inmates commit new crimes while in the community, and others use the opportunity to escape.

The community-based format led to innovations in the use of volunteers and to the extension of inmate privileges. "Open institutions" routinely provided inmates with a number of opportunities for community involvement and encouraged the community to participate in the prison environment. Some open institutions allowed weekend passes or extended visits by family members and friends, while a few experimented with conjugal visiting and with prisons that housed both men and women ("coeducational incarceration"). In 1968, the California Correctional Institute at Tehachapi initiated conjugal visits, in which inmates who were about to begin parole were permitted to live with their families for three days per month in apartments on the prison grounds. By the late 1960s, conjugal visitation was under consideration in many other states, and the National Advisory Commission on Criminal Justice Standards and Goals recommended that correctional authorities should make "provisions for family visits in private surroundings conducive to maintaining and strengthening family ties."[40] In 1995, however, California, which then allowed about 26,000 conjugal visits a year, eliminated this privilege for those sentenced to death or to life without parole and for those without a parole date. Rapists, sex offenders, and recently disciplined inmates were also denied conjugal privileges.

The Warehousing Era (1980–1995)

During the late 1970s and into the 1980s, public disappointment bred of high recidivism[41] rates, coupled with dramatic media stories of inmates who committed gruesome crimes while on release in the community, led many legislatures to curtail the most liberal aspects of educational and work-release programs. Media descriptions of institutions where inmates lounged in relative luxury, enjoyed regular visits from spouses and lovers, and took frequent weekend passes created the image of "prison country clubs." The failure of the rehabilitative ideal in community-based corrections, however, was due as much to changes in the individual sentencing decisions of judges as it was to citizen outrage and restrictive legislative action. Evidence shows that many judges came to regard rehabilitation programs as failures and decided to implement the just deserts model[42] of criminal sentencing. The just deserts model, which we talked about earlier, built on a renewed belief that offenders should "get what's coming to them." It quickly led to a policy of **warehousing** serious offenders for the avowed purpose of protecting society—and led also to a rapid decline of the decarceration initiative.

warehousing

An imprisonment strategy that is based on the desire to prevent recurrent crime and that has abandoned all hope of rehabilitation.

Recidivism rates were widely quoted in support of the drive to warehouse offenders. One study, for example, showed that nearly 70% of young adults paroled from prison in 22 states during 1978 were rearrested for serious crimes one or more times within six years of their release.[43] The study group was estimated to have committed 36,000 new felonies within the six years following their release, including 324 murders, 231 rapes, 2,291 robberies, and 3,053 violent assaults.[44] Worse still, observed the study's authors, was the fact that 46% of recidivists would have been in prison at the time of their readmission to prison if they had served the maximum term to which they had originally been sentenced.[45]

The failure of the rehabilitative model in corrections had already been proclaimed emphatically by Robert Martinson in 1974.[46] Martinson and his colleagues had surveyed 231 research studies conducted to evaluate correctional treatments between 1945 and 1967. They were unable to identify any treatment program that substantially reduced recidivism. Although Martinson argued for fixed sentences, a portion of which would be served in the community, his findings were often interpreted to mean that lengthy prison terms were necessary to incapacitate offenders who could not be reformed. About the same time, the prestigious National Academy of Sciences released a report in support of Martinson, saying, "We do not now know of any program or method of rehabilitation that could be guaranteed to reduce the criminal activity of released offenders."[47] This combined attack on the treatment model led to the **nothing-works doctrine**, which, beginning in the late 1970s, cast a pall of doubt over the previously dominant treatment philosophy.

The nothing-works philosophy contributed to new sentencing schemes, such as mandatory minimum sentencing provisions and truth-in-sentencing requirements. Together with the growing popularity of "three strikes and you're out" laws, these sentencing rules affected prison populations by substantially increasing the average time served by offenders before release. In the 1990s, prison populations continued to grow substantially because of a rise in the number of parole violators returned to prison; a drop in the annual release rates of inmates; a small number of inmates who would serve long terms or who would never be released; and enhanced punishments for drug offenders.[48] Average time served continues to increase. In 1990, for example, murderers served, on average, 92 months before release. Today, a person convicted of murder can expect to serve 106 months in prison before being released—a 15% increase. During the same period, actual time served in prison for the crime of rape increased 27%, while drug offenders spent 35% more time behind bars.[49]

American prison populations grew dramatically during the warehousing era (Figure 13–2)—and continue to increase. Between 1980 and 2007, state and federal prison populations more than quadrupled, from 329,000 inmates to more than 1.5 million.[50] Much of the rise in prison populations can be attributed directly to changes in sentencing laws aimed at taking drug offenders off the streets and to the resulting rapid growth in the number of incarcerated drug felons. A warehousing era report by the American Bar Association, for example, directly attributed the huge growth in the number of inmates to what it saw as a system-wide overemphasis on drug-related offenses—an emphasis that tended to imprison mostly poor, undereducated African American

nothing-works doctrine

The belief, popularized by Robert Martinson in the 1970s, that correctional treatment programs have had little success in rehabilitating offenders.

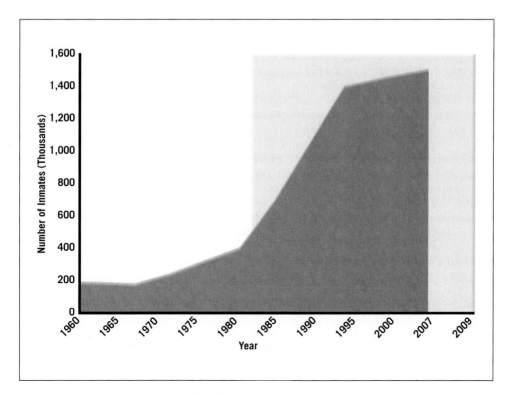

FIGURE 13–2

U.S. prison population, 1960–2007.

Source: Bureau of Justice Statistics.

youths who were rarely dangerous.[51] The report pointed out that while the per capita *rate of reported crime* dropped 2.2% across the nation during the 1980s, "the *incarceration rate* increased more than 110 percent."[52]

Warehousing also contributed to numerous administrative difficulties, many of which continue to affect prison systems throughout the nation today. By 1992, when the warehousing era was in full swing, institutions in 40 states and the District of Columbia were operating under court orders to alleviate overcrowding.[53] Entire prison systems in nine states—Alaska, Florida, Kansas, Louisiana, Mississippi, Nevada, Rhode Island, South Carolina, and Texas—had come under court control because overcrowded conditions made it impossible for prison administrators to meet court-supported constitutional requirements related to inmate safety. Today, even more state corrections systems have become subject to federal oversight or are operating under federal consent decrees.[54]

To meet the housing needs of burgeoning prison populations during the 1980s and 1990s, some states constructed "temporary" tent cities within prison yards. Others moved more beds into already packed dormitories, often stacking prisoners three high in triple bunk beds. A few states declared a policy of early release for less dangerous inmates and instituted mandatory diversion programs for first-time nonviolent offenders. Others used sentence rollbacks to reduce the sentences of selected inmates by a fixed amount, usually 90 days. Early parole was similarly employed by numerous states to reduce overcrowded conditions. Most states shifted some of their correctional burden to local jails, and by 2000, 34 states, the District of Columbia, and the federal government were sending prisoners to other jails because of overcrowding at their own long-term institutions.[55]

The Just Deserts Era (1995–Present)

Warehousing and prison overcrowding were primarily the result of both public and official frustration with rehabilitative efforts. In a sense, however, they were also consequences of a strategy without a clear-cut philosophy. Because rehabilitation didn't seem to work, early advocates of warehousing—not knowing what else to do—assumed a pragmatic stance and advocated separating criminals from society by keeping them locked up for as long as possible. Their avowed goal was the protection of law-abiding citizens.

justice model

A contemporary model of imprisonment based on the principle of just deserts.

Since the end of the warehousing era, however, a new philosophy based on the second prong of the **justice model**—that is, an emphasis on individual responsibility—has become the operative principle underlying many correctional initiatives. This new philosophy is grounded squarely on the concept of just deserts, in which imprisonment is seen as a fully deserved and proper consequence of criminal and irresponsible behavior rather than just the end result of a bankrupt system unable to reform its charges. Unlike previous correctional eras, which layered other purposes on the correctional experience (the reformatory era, for example, was concerned with reformation, and the industrial era sought economic gain), the current era of just deserts represents a kind of return to the root purpose of incarceration: punishment.

At the start of the just deserts era, state legislatures, encouraged in large part by their constituencies, scrambled to limit inmate privileges and to increase the pains of imprisonment. As with any other era, the exact beginning of the just deserts era is difficult to pinpoint. Noted corrections expert Jeanne Stinchcomb says, "The justice model gained momentum throughout the 1980s and 1990s, fueled by political conservatism, media sensationalism, an all-out 'war on drugs,' and public attitudes expressed in 'zero-tolerance' terms."[56] It is safe to say, however, that the just deserts model of criminal punishments was firmly in place by 1995. In that year, Alabama became the first state in modern times to reestablish chain gangs.[57] Under the Alabama system, shotgun-armed guards oversaw prisoners who were chained together by the ankles while they worked the state's roadsides—picking up trash, clearing brush, and filling ditches. The system, intended primarily for parole violators, was tough and unforgiving. Inmates served up to 90 days on chain gangs, during which they worked 12-hour shifts and remained chained even while using portable toilet facilities.

A few months later, Arizona became the second state to field prison chain gangs. Florida jumped on the chain gang bandwagon soon afterward.[58] Alabama chain gangs, which had expanded to include female prisoners, were discontinued in 1996 following a lawsuit against the state. The Florida Department of Corrections continues to use restricted labor squads (its name for chain gangs) at seven correctional institutions. Florida chain gang inmates are shackled at the ankles but are not connected to each other in any way.[59]

Nationally, chain gang proponents, though dwindling in number, continue to be adamant about the purpose this punishment serves. "If a person knows they're going to be out on the highway in chains, they are going to think twice about committing a crime," says former Georgia Prison Commissioner Ron Jones.[60] Opponents of the chain gang, however, like ACLU National Prison Project spokeswoman Jenni Gainsborough, call it "a giant step backward" and "a return to the dark ages."[61]

In another example of the move toward greater punishment indicative of the just deserts era, Virginia abolished parole in 1995, increased sentences for certain violent crimes by as much as 700%, and announced that it would build a dozen new prisons.[62] Changes in Virginia law were intended to move the state further in the direction of truth in sentencing and to appease the state's voters, who—reflecting public opinion nationwide—demanded a "get tough" stance toward criminals.

"Get tough" initiatives can be seen in the "three strikes and you're out" laws that swept through state legislatures in the late 1990s.[63] Three-strikes legislation, which is discussed in more detail in CJ Exhibit 11–2 in Chapter 11, mandates lengthy prison terms for criminal offenders convicted of a third violent crime or felony. Three-strikes laws have been enacted in almost 30 states and by the federal government. Critics of such laws, however, say that they do not prevent crime.[64] Jerome Skolnick, of the University of California at Berkeley, for example, criticizes three-strikes legislation because, he says, such practices almost certainly do not reduce the risk of victimization—especially the risk of becoming a victim of random violence. That is so, says Skolnick, because most violent crimes are committed by young men between the ages of 13 and 23. "It follows," according to Skolnick, "that if we jail them for life after their third conviction, we will get them in the twilight of their careers, and other young offenders will take their place."[65] Three-strikes programs, says Skolnick, are leading to the creation of "the most expensive, taxpayer-supported middle-age and old-age entitlement program in the history of the world," which will provide housing and medical care to older, burned-out law violators. Another author puts it this way: "The question . . . is whether it makes sense to continue to incarcerate aged prisoners beyond the time they would have served under ordinary sentences. This is unnecessary from the standpoint of public safety, and it is expensive."[66]

Criticisms of three-strikes laws fail to appreciate the sentiments underlying the current correctional era. Proponents of "get tough" policies, while no doubt interested in personal safety, lower crime rates, and balanced state and federal budgets, are keenly focused on retribution. And where retribution fuels a correctional policy, deterrence, reformation, and economic considerations play only secondary roles. As more and more states have enacted three-strikes and other "get tough" legislation, prison populations across the nation have continued to swell, eclipsing those of the warehousing era. The just deserts era of correctional philosophy now provides what has become for many an acceptable rationale for continued prison expansion. Some, however, fear that the prevailing retribution-based "lock 'em up" philosophy bodes ill for the future of American corrections. "I am worried there is going to be a disaster in our prisons," says J. Michael Quinlan, who was director of the Federal Bureau of Prisons under Presidents Ronald Reagan and

If you don't like the place, don't come here.

—Maricopa County (Arizona) Sheriff Joe Arpaio, offering advice to inmates housed in his desert tent city[iii]

Prison and jail populations have skyrocketed during the past two decades, spurring new construction and often generating crowded conditions in our institutions and facilities. Substance abuse is directly and indirectly responsible for a large portion of this population increase.

—James A. Gondles, Jr., Executive Director, American Correctional Association[iv]

An Alabama chain gang setting out to work on the roads. In 1995, reflecting a renewed society-wide emphasis on punishment, Alabama became the first state in modern times to revive the use of prison chain gangs. Following a lawsuit, however, the state later abandoned the concept. How do you feel about chain gangs for prisoners?

AP Wide World Photos

LIBRARY
Extra

George Bush.[67] The combination of burgeoning prison populations and restrictions on inmate privileges could have a catastrophic and disastrous effect—leading to riots, more prison violence, work stoppages, an increased number of inmate suicides, and other forms of prison disorder—says Quinlan.[68] Learn more about the impact of the just deserts model on corrections via Library Extra 13–2 at cjtoday.com.

Prisons Today

There are approximately 1,325 state prisons and 84 federal prisons in operation across the country today.[69] More are being built as both the states and the federal government continue to fund and construct new facilities. America's prison population has more than quadrupled since 1980, although the growth rate has recently been slowing. On January 1, 2007, the nation's state and federal prisons held 1,570,861 inmates.[70] Seven percent (or 112,498) of those imprisoned were women.[71] A special report released by the Public Safety Performance Project of the Pew Charitable Trusts in 2007 predicts that the nation's prison population will rise to more than 1.72 million by 2011.[72]

The incarceration rate for state and federal prisoners sentenced to more than a year has reached a record 501 prisoners for every 100,000 U.S. residents. One out of every 108 men and one out of every 1,538 women were sentenced prisoners under the jurisdiction of state or federal authorities in early 2007.[73] Even if today's incarceration rates remain unchanged, 6.6% of U.S. residents born in 2001 will go to prison at some time during their lifetime.[74]

Most people sentenced to state prisons are convicted of violent crimes (50.5%), while property crimes (20.4%) and drug crimes (21.4%) are nearly tied as the second most common type of offenses for which offenders are imprisoned.[75] In contrast, prisoners sentenced for drug-law violations are the single largest group of federal inmates (55%), and the increase in the imprisonment of drug offenders accounts for more than three-quarters of the total growth in the number of federal inmates since 1980.[76]

An examination of imprisonment statistics by race highlights the huge disparity between blacks and whites in prison. While only an estimated 1,172 white men are imprisoned in the United States for every 100,000 white men in their late 20s, the latest figures show an incarceration rate of 8,367 black men for every 100,000 black men of the same age—seven times greater than the figure for whites.[77] Worse, the imprisonment rate of blacks increased dramatically during the past ten years, while the rate of white imprisonment grew far less. Almost 17% of adult black men in the United States have served time in prison—a rate over twice as high as that for adult Hispanic males (7.7%) and over six times as high as that for adult white males (2.6%).[78] According to the Bureau of Justice Statistics (BJS), a black male living in America today has a 32.3% lifetime chance of going to prison, and a black female has a 5.6% lifetime chance of imprisonment. That contrasts sharply with the lifetime chances of imprisonment for white males (5.9%) and white females (0.9%).[79]

The use of imprisonment varies considerably between states. While the average rate of imprisonment in the United States at the start of 2007 was 501 per every 100,000 people in the population,[80] some state rates were nearly double that figure.[81] Louisiana, for example, was holding 846 out of every 100,000 of its citizens in prison on January 1, 2007, while Mississippi was a close second with an incarceration rate of 658. Texas, a state with traditionally high rates of imprisonment, held 683 prisoners per every 100,000 people. Maine had the lowest rate of imprisonment of all the states (151), while other states with low rates were Rhode Island (202), North Dakota (214), and New Hampshire (207). More statistics are available via Library Extra 13–3 at cjtoday.com.

LIBRARY
Extra

A recent study by David Greenberg and Valerie West identified factors that contribute to variation in incarceration rates between states.[82] Greenberg and West found that a state's violent crime rate was a significant determinant of its incarceration rate but was not the only factor involved. Also important were the political leanings of the state's population (more politically conservative states made greater use of imprisonment), the amount of money available to build and maintain prisons (more money led to more imprisonment), the employment rate (unemployment contributed to higher rates of imprisonment), the percentage of African American men in the state's population (the higher the percentage, the higher the rate of imprisonment), and the level of welfare support available to the poor (higher welfare payments meant less imprisonment). The authors also found that income inequality was not a predictor of imprisonment rates and that the degree of urbanization in a state had no effect on imprisonment.

The size of prison facilities varies greatly. One out of every four state institutions is a large maximum-security prison, with a population approaching 1,000 inmates. A few exceed that figure, but the typical state prison is small, with an inmate population of less than 500. Community-based facilities average around 50 residents. The typical prison system in relatively populous states consists of[83]

- One high-security prison for long-term, high-risk offenders
- One or more medium-security institutions for offenders who are not high risks
- One institution for adult women
- One or two institutions for young adults (generally under age 25)
- One or two specialized mental hospital–type security prisons for mentally ill prisoners
- One or more open-type institutions for low-risk, nonviolent inmates

Incarceration costs average around $62 per inmate per day at both the state and federal levels when all types of adult correctional facilities are averaged together.[84] Prison systems across the nation face spiraling costs as the number of inmates grows and as the age of the inmate population increases. The cost of running the nation's correctional facilities and related programs approached $67 billion in 2003.[85]

Overcrowding

The just deserts philosophy has led to substantial and continued increases in the American prison population even as crime rates have been dropping. In 1990, for example, the U.S. rate of imprisonment stood at 292 prisoners per every 100,000 residents. By 1995, it had reached 399, and on January 1, 2007, it was 501. While the rate of growth has been slowing, it is still inching higher.[86] The Pew Charitable Trust study, cited earlier in this chapter, predicts that the rate of imprisonment will reach 562 per 100,000 by 2011.[87]

At the same time, crime rates have been falling. As noted in Chapter 2, between 1991 and 2006, the official rate of crime in the United States dropped from 5,897 to 3,835 offenses per every 100,000 residents—a level that had not been seen since 1975.[88] Hence, a 36% *decrease* in the national crime rate over a ten-year period was accompanied by a 62% *increase* in the rate of imprisonment. Just deserts advocates, of course, argue that increased rates of incarceration are at least partially responsible for reduced crime rates, since incarceration removes those who are likely to reoffend from the community.

Even though many new prisons have been built throughout the nation during the past 20 years to accommodate the growing number of inmates, prison overcrowding is still very much a reality

> *Prisons are no longer a response to increasing crime, and crime does not respond to increasing prisons. The prison system just grows like a weed in the yard.*
>
> —Vincent Schiraldi, Executive Director, Justice Policy Institute

Inmates making collect phone calls at the Davidson County Prison in Tennessee. There are approximately 1,500 state prisons and 84 federal prisons in operation across the country today. Together they hold almost 1.5 million inmates. The prison shown here is run by Corrections Corporation of America. Are we likely to see a greater use of privately run correctional facilities in the future? Why or why not?

A. Ramey/PhotoEdit Inc.

in many jurisdictions (Figure 13–3). Prison overcrowding can be measured along a number of dimensions, including these:[89]

- Space available per inmate (such as square feet of floor space)
- How long inmates are confined in cells or housing units (versus time spent on recreation and other activities)
- Living arrangements (for example, single versus double bunks)
- Type of housing (use of segregation facilities, tents, and so on in place of general housing)

Further complicating the picture is the fact that prison officials have developed three definitions of **prison capacity**. **Rated capacity** refers to the size of the inmate population that a facility can handle according to the judgment of experts. **Operational capacity** is the number of inmates that a facility can effectively accommodate based on an appraisal of the institution's staff, programs, and services. **Design capacity** refers to the inmate population that the institution was originally built to handle. Rated capacity estimates usually yield the largest inmate capacities, while design capacity (on which observations in this chapter are based) typically shows the highest amount of overcrowding.

Overcrowding by itself is not cruel and unusual punishment, according to the U.S. Supreme Court in *Rhodes* v. *Chapman* (1981),[90] which considered the issue of double bunking along with other alleged forms of "deprivation" at the Southern Ohio Correctional Facility. The Court, reasoning that overcrowding is not necessarily dangerous if other prison services are adequate, held that prison housing conditions may be "restrictive and even harsh," for they are part of the penalty that offenders pay for their crimes.

However, overcrowding combined with other negative conditions may lead to a finding against the prison system. The American Correctional Association (ACA) believes that such a totality-of-conditions approach requires courts to assess the overall quality of prison life while viewing overcrowded conditions in combination with

- The prison's meeting of basic human needs
- The adequacy of the facility's staff
- The program opportunities available to inmates
- The quality and strength of the prison management

prison capacity

The size of the correctional population an institution can effectively hold.[v] There are three types of prison capacity: rated, operational, and design.

rated capacity

The number of inmates a prison can handle according to the judgment of experts.

operational capacity

The number of inmates a prison can effectively accommodate based on management considerations.

design capacity

The number of inmates a prison was intended to hold when it was built or modified.

FIGURE 13–3

State prison populations, inmates versus capacity, 1980–2006.

Source: Bureau of Justice Statistics, *Correctional Populations in the United States* (Washington, DC: Bureau of Justice Statistics, various years).

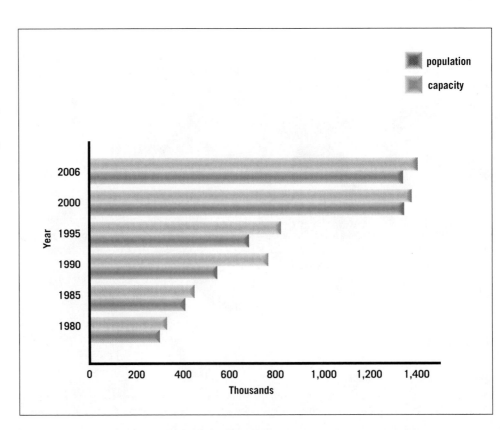

Learn more about *Rhodes* v. *Chapman*, including the background of the case, at Library Extra 13–4 at cjtoday.com.

LIBRARY
Extra

SELECTIVE INCAPACITATION: A STRATEGY TO REDUCE PRISON POPULATIONS

Some authors have identified the central issue of imprisonment as one of selective versus collective incapacitation.[91] Collective incapacitation, a strategy that would imprison almost all serious offenders, is still found today in states that rely on predetermined, or fixed, sentences for given offenses or for a series of specified kinds of offenses (as in the case of three-strikes legislation). Collective incapacitation is, however, prohibitively expensive as well as unnecessary, in the opinion of many experts. Not all offenders need to be imprisoned because not all represent a continuing threat to society, but those who do are difficult to identify.[92]

In most jurisdictions where the just deserts model holds sway, selective incapacitation has become the rule. Selective incapacitation seeks to identify the most dangerous criminals, with the goal of removing them from society. Repeat offenders with records of serious and violent crimes are the most likely candidates for incapacitation—as are those who will probably commit violent crimes in the future, even though they have no records. But potentially violent offenders cannot be readily identified, and those thought likely to commit crimes cannot be sentenced to lengthy prison terms for things they have not yet done.

In support of selective incapacitation, many states have enacted career offender statutes that attempt to identify potentially dangerous offenders out of known criminal populations. Selective incapacitation efforts, however, have been criticized for yielding a rate of "false positives" of over 60%,[93] and some authors have called selective incapacitation a "strategy of failure."[94] Nevertheless, in an analysis of recidivism studies, Canadians Paul Gendreau, Tracy Little, and Claire Goggin found that criminal history, a history of preadult antisocial behavior, and "criminogenic needs"—which were defined as measurable antisocial thoughts, values, and behaviors—were all dependable predictors of recidivism.[95] The article, subtitled "What Works!" was intended as a response to Martinson's nothing-works doctrine, mentioned earlier.

Some state programs designed to reduce prison overcrowding, however, have run afoul of selective incarceration principles. In 1997, for example, the U.S. Supreme Court ordered Florida to release as many as 2,500 inmates—many of whom had been convicted of violent crimes—under a "gain time" program set up by the state in 1983.[96] Provisions of the program allowed inmates to earn as much as two months off their sentences for every month served. Although the program was originally intended to relieve overcrowding, a change in public sentiment led Florida Attorney General Bob Butterworth to revoke gain time that had already been earned. In ordering the inmates' release, however, the U.S. Supreme Court unanimously ruled that Florida had violated constitutional guarantees against *ex post facto* laws and required officials to be bound by the program's original conditions. The release of hundreds of murderers, rapists, robbers, and other felons caused a statewide uproar and media furor.

The Florida experience and others like it have caused states to tighten restrictions on early-release programs. As the just deserts model continues to take center stage, it is likely that we will see the continued sentencing of violent criminals to lengthy prison stays with little possibility of release and the increased use of alternative sanctions for minor offenders.

Today, with an unprecedented number of people behind bars, we are no safer than before. We are, however, much less free.

—American Civil Liberties Union website

Security Levels

Maximum-custody (or maximum-security) prisons tend to be massive old buildings with large inmate populations. However, some, like Central Prison in Raleigh, North Carolina, are much newer and incorporate advances in prison architecture to provide tight security without sacrificing building aesthetics. Such institutions provide a high level of security characterized by high fences, thick walls, secure cells, gun towers, and armed prison guards. Maximum-custody prisons tend to locate cells and other inmate living facilities at the center of the institution and place a variety of barriers between the living area and the institution's outer perimeter. Technological innovations, such as electric perimeters, laser motion detectors, electronic and pneumatic locking systems, metal detectors, X-ray machines, television surveillance, radio communications, and computer information systems, are frequently used today to reinforce the more traditional maximum-security strategies. These technologies have helped to lower the cost of new prison construction. However, some people argue that prisons may rely too heavily on electronic detection devices that have not yet been adequately tested.[97] Death-row inmates are all maximum-security prisoners, although the level of security on death row exceeds even that experienced by

Inmates flashing gang signs for the camera. If you were a warden, what changes would you make to improve the management of a prison like this one?

Damian Dovarganes/AP Wide World Photos

most prisoners held in maximum custody. Prisoners on death row must spend much of the day in single cells and are often permitted a brief shower only once a week under close supervision.

Most states today have one large, centrally located maximum-security institution. Some of these prisons combine more than one custody level and may be both maximum- and medium-security facilities. Medium security is a custody level that in many ways resembles maximum security. Medium-security prisoners are generally permitted more freedom to associate with one another and can go to the prison yard, exercise room, library, and shower and bathroom facilities under less intense supervision. An important security tool in medium-security prisons is the count, which is a head count of inmates taken at regular intervals. Counts may be taken four times a day and usually require inmates to report to designated areas to be counted. Until the count has been "cleared," all other inmate activity must cease. Medium-security prisons tend to be smaller than maximum-security institutions and often have barbed-wire-topped chain-link fences instead of the more secure stone or concrete block walls found in many of the older maximum-security facilities. Cells and living quarters tend to have more windows and are often located closer to the perimeter of the institution than in maximum-security facilities. Dormitory-style housing, where prisoners live together in wardlike arrangements, is sometimes found in medium-security facilities. There are generally more opportunities for inmates to participate in recreational and other prison programs than in maximum-custody facilities.

In minimum-security institutions, inmates are generally housed in dormitory-like settings and are free to walk the yard and to visit most of the prison facilities. Some newer prisons provide minimum-security inmates with private rooms, which they can decorate (within limits) according to their tastes. Inmates usually have free access to a canteen that sells items like cigarettes, toothpaste, and candy bars. Minimum-security inmates often wear uniforms of a different color from those of inmates in higher custody levels, and in some institutions they may wear civilian clothes. They work under only general supervision and usually have access to recreational, educational, and skills-training programs on the prison grounds. Guards are unarmed, gun towers do not exist, and fences, if they are present at all, are usually low and gates are sometimes even unlocked. Many minimum-security prisoners participate in some sort of work- or study-release program, and some have extensive visitation and furlough privileges. Counts may be taken, although most minimum-security institutions keep track of inmates through daily administrative work schedules. The primary "force" holding inmates in minimum-security institutions is their own restraint. Inmates live with the knowledge that minimum-security institutions are one step removed from close correctional supervision and that if they fail to meet the expectations of administrators, they will be transferred into more secure institutions, which will probably delay their release. Inmates returning from assignments in the community may be frisked for contraband, but body-cavity searches are rare in minimum custody, being reserved primarily for inmates suspected of smuggling.

The typical American prison today is medium or minimum custody. Some states have as many as 80 or 90 small institutions, which may originally have been located in every county to serve the needs of public works and highway maintenance. Medium- and minimum-security institutions house the bulk of the country's prison population and offer a number of programs and services designed to assist with the rehabilitation of offenders and to create the conditions necessary for a successful reentry of the inmate into society. Most prisons offer psychiatric services, academic education, vocational education, substance-abuse treatment, health care, counseling, recreation, library services, religious programs, and industrial and agricultural training.[98] Learn more about all aspects of contemporary prisons from the Corrections Connection via Web Extra 13–4 at cjtoday.com.

WEB
Extra
▪▪▪▪

Prison Classification Systems

Most states use a **classification system** to assign new prisoners to initial custody levels based on their perceived dangerousness, escape risk, and type of offense. A prisoner might be assigned to a minimum-, medium-, or maximum-custody institution. Inmates move through custody levels according to the progress they are judged to have made in self-control and demonstrated responsibility. Serious violent criminals who begin their prison careers with lengthy sentences in maximum custody have the opportunity in most states to work their way up to minimum security, although the process usually takes a number of years. Those who represent continual disciplinary problems are returned to closer custody levels. Minimum-security prisons, as a result, house inmates convicted of all types of criminal offenses.

Once an inmate has been assigned to a custody level, he or she may be reassessed for living and work assignments within the institution. Just as initial (or external) custody classification systems determine security levels, internal classification systems are designed to help determine appropriate housing plans and program interventions within a particular facility for inmates who share a common custody level. In short, initial classification determines the institution in which an inmate is placed, and internal classification determines placement and program assignment within that institution.[99] An overview of the external and internal classification process is shown in Figure 13–4. Learn more about internal prison classification systems at Library Extra 13–5 at cjtoday.com.

Objective prison classification systems were adopted by many states in the 1980s, but it wasn't until the late 1990s that such systems were refined and validated. Fueled by litigation and overcrowding, classification systems are now viewed as the principal management tool for allocating scarce prison resources efficiently and for minimizing the potential for violence or escape. Classification systems are also expected to provide greater accountability and to forecast future prison bed-space needs. A properly functioning classification system is the "brain" of prison management, governing and influencing many important decisions, including such fiscal matters as staffing levels, bed space, and programming.[100]

One of the best-known internal classification systems in use today is the adult internal management system (AIMS). AIMS was developed more than 20 years ago to reduce institutional predatory behavior by identifying potential predators and separating them from vulnerable inmates. AIMS assesses an inmate's predatory potential by quantifying aspects of his or her (1) record of misconduct, (2) ability to follow staff directions, and (3) level of aggression toward other inmates.

Before concluding this discussion of classification, it is important to recognize that the criteria used to classify prisoners must be relevant to the legitimate security needs of the institution. In 2005, for example, the U.S. Supreme Court, in the case of *Johnson* v. *California*,[101] invalidated the California Department of Corrections and Rehabilitation's (CDCR) unwritten policy of racially segregating prisoners in double cells for up to 60 days each time they entered a new correctional facility. The policy had been based on a claim that it prevented violence caused by racial gangs. The Court, however, held that the California policy was "immediately suspect" as an "express racial classification" and found that the CDCR was unable to demonstrate that the practice served a compelling state interest.

classification system

A system used by prison administrators to assign inmates to custody levels based on offense history, assessed dangerousness, perceived risk of escape, and other factors.

LIBRARY
Extra
▪▪▪▪

We spend $60,000 building a prison cell, another $35,000 a year to keep that inmate. They have central heating and air conditioning. At the same time we spend less than $4,000 on each school student. And many of them don't have air-conditioned or centrally heated schools. Let's put the money in education. That's the only answer to crime.

—*Louisiana Congressman Cleo Fields*

FIGURE 13–4

The flow of activities in prison classification systems.

Source: Adapted from Patricia L. Hardyman et al., *Internal Prison Classification Systems: Case Studies in Their Development and Implementation* (Washington, DC: National Institute of Corrections, 2002), p. 3.

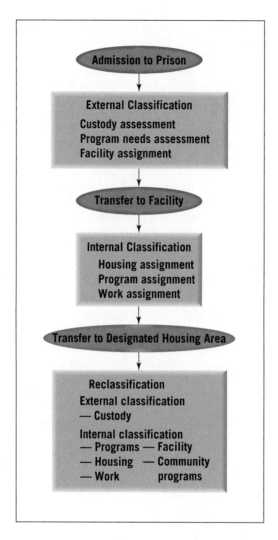

The Federal Prison System

We are the prisoners of the prisoners we have taken.

—*Jennifer Clegg*

In 1895, the federal government opened a prison at Leavenworth, Kansas, for civilians convicted of violating federal law. Leavenworth had been a military prison, and control over the facility was transferred from the Department of the Army to the Department of Justice. By 1906, the Leavenworth facility had been expanded to a capacity of 1,200 inmates, and another federal prison—in Atlanta, Georgia—was built. McNeil Island Prison in Washington State was also functioning by the early 1900s. The first federal prison for women opened in 1927 in Alderson, West Virginia. With the increasing complexity of the federal criminal code, the number of federal prisoners grew.[102]

On May 14, 1930, the Federal Bureau of Prisons (BOP) was created under the direction of Sanford Bates. The BOP was charged with providing progressive and humane care for federal inmates, professionalizing the federal prison service, and ensuring consistent and centralized administration of the 11 federal prisons in operation at the time.[103] The bureau inherited a system that was dramatically overcrowded. Many federal prisoners were among the most notorious criminals in the nation, and ideals of humane treatment and rehabilitation were all but lacking in the facilities of the 1920s. Bates began a program of improvements to relieve overcrowding and to increase the treatment capacity of the system. In 1933, the Medical Center for Federal Prisoners opened in Springfield, Missouri, with a capacity of around 1,000 inmates. Alcatraz Island began operations in 1934.

Most of the federal prison system's growth since the mid-1980s has been the result of the Sentencing Reform Act of 1984 (which established determinate sentencing, abolished parole, and reduced good time) and federal mandatory minimum sentences enacted in 1986, 1988, and 1990. From 1980 to 1989, the federal inmate population more than doubled, from just over 24,000 to almost 58,000. During the 1990s, the population more than doubled again, and it continued to grow

The federal Bureau of Prisons ADMAX facility in Florence, Colorado, which opened in 1995. It is the only ultra-high-security institution in the federal system. What kinds of inmates are held here?

Bob Daemmrich/Agence France Presse/Getty Images

throughout the early years of the twenty-first century, reaching approximately 173,500 prisoners (or 37% over capacity) at the start of 2007.[104]

Today, the federal prison system consists of 103 institutions, six regional offices, the Central Office (headquarters), two staff-training centers, and 28 community corrections offices.[105] The regional offices and the Central Office provide administrative oversight and support to the institutions and to the community corrections offices, which oversee community corrections centers and home-confinement programs. The federal correctional workforce is one of the fastest growing in the country, and at the start of 2006, the Federal Bureau of Prisons (BOP) employed more than 35,000 people.[106]

The BOP classifies its institutions according to five security levels: (1) administrative maximum (**ADMAX**), (2) high security, (3) medium security, (4) low security, and (5) minimum security. High-security facilities are called *U.S. penitentiaries* (USPs); medium- and low-security institutions are both called *federal correctional institutions* (FCIs); and minimum-security prisons are termed *federal prison camps* (FPCs).[107] Minimum-security facilities (like Eglin Air Force Base, Florida, and Maxwell Air Force Base, Alabama) are essentially honor-type camps with barracks-type housing and no fencing. Low-security facilities in the federal prison system are surrounded by double chain-link fencing and employ vehicle patrols around their perimeters to enhance security. Medium-security facilities (like those in Terminal Island, California; Lompoc, California; and Seagoville, Texas) make use of similar fencing and patrols but supplement them with electronic monitoring of the grounds and perimeter areas. High-security facilities (USPs like those in Atlanta, Georgia; Lewisburg, Pennsylvania; Terre Haute, Indiana; and Leavenworth, Kansas) are architecturally designed to prevent escapes and to contain disturbances. They also make use of armed patrols and intense electronic surveillance.

A separate federal prison category is that of administrative facilities, consisting of institutions with special missions that are designed to house all types of inmates. Most administrative facilities are metropolitan detention centers (MDCs). MDCs, which are generally located in large cities close to federal courthouses, are the jails of the federal correctional system and hold defendants awaiting trial in federal court. Another five administrative facilities, medical centers for federal prisoners (MCFPs), function as hospitals.

Federal correctional facilities exist either as single institutions or as federal correctional complexes—that is, sites consisting of more than one type of correctional institution (Figure 13–5). The federal correctional complex at Allenwood, Pennsylvania, for example, consists of a U.S. penitentiary, a federal prison camp, and two federal correctional institutions (one low and one medium security), each with its own warden. Federal institutions can be classified by type as follows: 55 are federal prison camps (holding 35% of all federal prisoners), 17 are low-security facilities (28%), 26 are medium-security facilities (23%), eight are high-security prisons (13%), and one is an ADMAX facility (1%).

ADMAX

Administrative maximum. The term is used by the federal government to denote ultra-high-security prisons.

With the huge expansion of prisons starting in the 1980s, most prison systems gave up believing they had any responsibility for changing offenders or [for] what happened after offenders were released. The objective became that prisons should be just for punishment, and politicians competed to see who could make prisons more unpleasant.

—Todd Clear, John Jay College of Criminal Justice

FIGURE 13–5

Locations of long-term confinement facilities in the federal correctional system, 2007.

Note: Does not include Bureau of Prisons offices or community corrections management offices.

Source: Federal Bureau of Prisons.

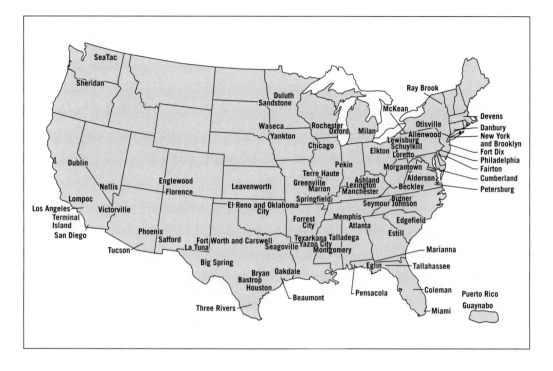

The federal system's only ADMAX unit, the $60 million ultra-high-security prison at Florence, Colorado, is a relatively recent addition to the federal system. Dubbed "the Alcatraz of the Rockies," the 575-bed facility was designed to be the most secure prison ever built by the government.[108] Opened in 1995, it holds mob bosses, spies, terrorists, murderers, and escape artists. Dangerous inmates are confined to their cells 23 hours per day and are not allowed to see or associate with other inmates. Electronically controlled doors throughout the institution channel inmates to individual exercise sessions, and educational courses, religious services, and administrative matters are conducted via closed-circuit television piped directly into the prisoners' cells. Remote-controlled heavy steel doors within the prison allow correctional staff to section off the institution in the event of rioting, and the system can be controlled from outside if the entire prison is compromised.

In an effort to combat rising expenses associated with a rapidly growing federal prison population, the U.S. Congress passed legislation in 1992 that imposes a "user fee" on federal inmates who are able to pay the costs associated with their incarceration.[109] Under the law, inmates may be assessed a dollar amount up to the cost of a year's incarceration—currently around $22,600.[110] The statute, which was designed so as not to impose hardships on poor offenders or their dependents, directs that collected funds, estimated to total $48 million per year, are to be used to improve alcohol- and drug-abuse programs within federal prisons. To learn more about the Federal Bureau of Prisons, visit Web Extra 13–5 or read Library Extras 13–6 and 13–7 at cjtoday.com.

WEB
Extra
■■■■

LIBRARY
Extra
■■■■

Recent Improvements

In the midst of frequent lawsuits, court-ordered changes in prison administration, and overcrowded conditions, outstanding prison facilities are being recognized through the American Correctional Association's (ACA's) accreditation program. The ACA Commission on Accreditation has developed a set of standards that correctional institutions can use for conducting self-evaluations. Institutions that meet the standards can apply for accreditation under the program.

Another avenue toward improvement of the nation's prisons can be found in the National Academy of Corrections, the training arm of the National Institute of Corrections. The academy, located in Boulder, Colorado, offers seminars, videoconferencing, and training sessions for state and local corrections managers, trainers, personnel directors, sheriffs, and state legislators.[111] Issues covered include strategies to control overcrowding, community corrections program management, prison programs, gangs and disturbances, security, and public and media relations.[112]

CJ Careers

Federal Bureau of Prisons

Name: Don Drennon Gala, Ph.D.

Position: Correctional Treatment Specialist (Senior Case Manager)/Federal Officer

City: Atlanta, Georgia

Colleges Attended: University of Rochester, University of Central Oklahoma, Rochester Institute of Technology, Monroe Community College

Year Hired: 1983

"The more education I attained, the more open I became to other positions within the law enforcement field. The field of law enforcement is continually evolving as a profession. This is true in federal corrections as well. Today, many federal correctional officers have at least a bachelor's degree and many hold a master's degree. The professionalism of BOP staff is viewed as improving on a daily basis, with all professional personnel holding college or university degrees. Through Unit Management, of which I am a part, a team of professionals provides services that have an impact on inmates' lives following release—and on the general public. This work is anything but boring; it demands professionalism and constant attention."

TYPICAL POSITIONS

Case managers engage in multiple tasks within and outside the institution. They perform correctional casework and interview inmates for multiple agency needs, such as detecting violations of regulations and law and determining inmate needs in terms of safety and possible central inmate monitoring assignments. They prepare reports for the special investigative agent, addressing violations of regulations and laws as well as possible gang activity. They also develop, evaluate, and analyze program needs and assess inmate need; evaluate the progress of individual offenders in the institution; prepare progress reports periodically for transfers, special programs, and release; coordinate and integrate inmate training programs; develop social histories and prepare written reports; evaluate positive and negative aspects in each case situation as part of the assessment process; advise new inmates about available programs; conduct program reviews; conduct individual and group counseling of inmates about their previous lifestyle and problem-solving skills; provide case reports to the U.S. Parole Commission and U.S. Probation; work with inmates, their families, and other interested people in developing parole and release plans; work with the U.S. Probation Officers and other agencies in developing and implementing release plans or programs for inmates; set up and coordinate the release of inmates to halfway houses, supervised release through U.S. Probation, and any other court-ordered action to be taken; and enforce criminal statutes and judicial sanctions, including investigative, arrest, and detention authority. A case manager also screens new inmates and prepares written reports of the information obtained and conducts physical and electronic surveillance of inmates and visitors, using a variety of audio, video, and photographic equipment.

EMPLOYMENT REQUIREMENTS

General employment requirements include (1) an age between 23 and 37; (2) excellent physical health; (3) good vision, 20/20 corrected; (4) good hearing; (5) U.S. citizenship; (6) a valid driver's license; (7) successful completion of a comprehensive field background investigation; (8) passing a urinalysis; (9) a formal interview; and (10) successful completion of the academy at the Federal Law Enforcement Training Center at Glynco, Georgia.

OTHER REQUIREMENTS

Positions as a psychologist or attorney require the appropriate professional degrees and licenses. The case manager position requires a bachelor's degree from an accredited college or university, including 24 semester hours in the social sciences. Entry-level positions in information technology require a bachelor's degree in computer science or a closely related field. The Bureau of Prisons (BOP) values education and emphasizes college or university degrees when hiring personnel for most positions above the entry-level correctional officer positions.

SALARY

Correctional officers enter the BOP at the GS-5 or GS-6 level with a bachelor's degree or one year of pertinent experience. Case managers enter at GS-9, and after successfully completing one year in this position, they are eligible to be promoted to GS-11. BOP employees can advance to GS-12 as a first-line supervisor and to GS-14 as a middle manager. Positions are available at the GS-15 level and senior executive service.

(continued)

CJ Careers (continued)

BENEFITS

Benefits include (1) 13 days of sick leave per year; (2) two and a half to five weeks of paid vacation each year based on length of service; (3) ten paid federal holidays; (4) federal health and life insurance; and (5) participation in the Federal Employees' Retirement System.

DIRECT INQUIRES TO:

Human Resource Management Division–Staffing
U.S. Department of Justice
Federal Bureau of Prisons

320 First St., N.W.
Room 700
Washington, DC 20534
Phone: 202-307-3177
Website: http://www.bop.gov or http://www.usajobs.gov

For more information on the rapidly expanding criminal justice careers area, read *Where the Jobs Are: Mission Critical Opportunities for America,* available on the Web at http://www.justicestudies.com/jobs.htm.

Note: The views expressed in this profile do not necessarily represent the views of the Federal Bureau of Prisons, the U.S. Department of Justice, or the United States.

Jails

jail

A confinement facility administered by an agency of local government, typically a law enforcement agency, intended for adults but sometimes also containing juveniles, which holds people detained pending adjudication or committed after adjudication, usually those sentenced to a year or less.

Jails are locally operated short-term confinement facilities originally built to hold suspects following arrest and pending trial. Today's jails also serve these purposes:[113]

- They receive individuals pending arraignment and hold them awaiting trial, conviction, or sentencing.
- They readmit probation, parole, and bail-bond violators and absconders.
- They temporarily detain juveniles, the mentally ill, and others pending transfer to appropriate facilities.
- They hold individuals for the military, for protective custody, for contempt, and for the courts as witnesses.
- They release convicted inmates to the community upon completion of their sentence.
- They transfer inmates to federal, state, or other authorities.
- They house inmates for federal, state, or other authorities because of overcrowding in their facilities.
- They operate community-based programs with day reporting, home detention, electronic monitoring, or other types of supervision.
- They hold inmates sentenced to short terms (generally less than one year).

A 2007 report by the Bureau of Justice Statistics (BJS) found that the nation's jails held 766,010 inmates—12.9% of whom were women.[114] Juveniles held in local jails numbered 4,836.[115] More than half of jail inmates have been convicted of a crime; a quarter are being detained while awaiting arraignment or trial; and a sixth are being held on a prior sentence but are also awaiting arraignment or trial on a new charge.[116] Jail authorities also supervised an additional 60,222 men and women in the community under programs that included the following: electronic monitoring (10,999), home detention without electronic monitoring (807), day reporting (4,841), community service (14,667), and weekender programs (11,421).[117]

A total of 3,365 jails operate throughout the United States, staffed by approximately 207,600 jail employees—the equivalent of about one employee for every three jail inmates.[118] Overall, the nation's jail budget is huge, and facilities are overflowing. State and local governments spend $10 billion every year to operate the nation's jails,[119] with more than $1 billion in additional monies earmarked for new jail construction and for renovation. On average, the housing of one jail inmate costs more than $14,500 per year.[120]

Approximately 20 million people are admitted (or readmitted) to the nation's jails each year. Some jail inmates stay for as little as one day, while others serve extended periods of time. Sig-

Los Angeles County's Men's Central Jail. The $373 million jail, officially known as the Twin Towers Correctional Facility, opened in 1997 and is one of the world's largest jails. What are the differences between a prison and a jail?

A. Ramey/PhotoEdit Inc.

nificantly, one of the fastest-growing sectors of today's jail population consists of sentenced offenders serving time in local jails because overcrowded prisons cannot accept them.

Most people processed through the country's jails are members of minority groups (56%), with 38.6% of jail inmates classifying themselves as African American, 15.6% as Hispanic, and 1.8% as other minorities. Less than 1% report being of more than one race, and 44% of jail inmates classify themselves as white. Slightly more than 87% are male, and 7.8% are noncitizens.[121] The typical jail inmate is an unmarried black male between 25 and 34 years of age who reports having had some high school education. Typical charges include drug trafficking (12.1%), assault (11.7%), drug possession (10.8%), and larceny (7%).[122]

According to the BJS, about 6% of jail facilities house more than half of all jail inmates in the nation.[123] So, although most jails are small—many were built to house 50 or fewer inmates—most people who spend time in jail do so in larger institutions. Across the country, a handful of "mega-jails" house thousands of inmates each. The largest such facilities are in Los Angeles; New York City; Cook County, Illinois; Harris County, Texas; and Maricopa County, Arizona. Los Angeles County's 4,000-bed Twin Towers Correctional Facility cost $373 million to build and opened in 1997.[124] The largest employer among these huge jails is Cook County's, with more than 1,200 personnel on its payroll.[125] In 2006, the nation's 50 largest jail jurisdictions held 29.5% of all jail inmates. The two jurisdictions with the most jail inmates, Los Angeles County and New York City, together held approximately 32,700 inmates, or 4.3% of the national total.[126] More jail statistics are available at Library Extra 13–8 at cjtoday.com.

LIBRARY
Extra
∎∎∎∎

Women and Jail

Although women number only 12.9% of the country's jail population, they are the largest growth group in jails nationwide.[127] Jailed women face a number of special problems. Only 25.7% of the nation's jails report having a classification system specifically designed to evaluate female inmates,[128] and although many jurisdictions have plans "to build facilities geared to the female offender,"[129] not all jurisdictions today even provide separate housing areas for women. Educational levels are very low among jailed women, and fewer than half are high school graduates.[130] Drug abuse is another significant source of difficulty for jailed women. More than 30% of women who are admitted to jail have a substance-abuse problem at the time of admission, and in some parts of the country, that figure may be as high as 70%.[131]

Pregnancy is another problem. Nationally, 4% of female inmates are pregnant when they enter jail,[132] but in urban areas, as much as 10% of the female jail population is reported to be pregnant on any given day.[133] As a consequence, a few hundred children are born in jails each year. However, substantive medical programs for female inmates, such as obstetrics and gynecological care, are often lacking. In planning future medical services for female inmates, some writers have advised jail administrators to expect to see an increasingly common kind of inmate: "an opiate-addicted female who is pregnant with no prior prenatal care having one or more sexually transmitted diseases, and fitting a high-risk category for AIDS (prostitution, IV drug use)."[134]

Not only are jailed mothers separated from their children, but they may have to pay for their support. Twelve percent of all jails in one study reported requiring employed female inmates to contribute to the support of their dependent children.

When we consider women and jails, female inmates are only half the story. Women who work in corrections are the other half. In one study, Linda Zupan, a member of a new generation of outstanding jail scholars, found that women made up 22% of the corrections officer force in jails across the nation.[135] The deployment of female personnel, however, was disproportionately skewed toward jobs in the lower ranks. Although 60% of all support staff (secretaries, cooks, and janitors) were women, only one in every ten chief administrators was female. Even so, Zupan did find that female corrections employees were significantly committed to their careers and that the attitudes of male workers toward female coworkers in jails were generally positive. Zupan's study uncovered 626 jails in which over 50% of the corrections officer force consisted of women. However, 954 of the nation's 3,316 jails operating at the time of the study had no female officers.[136] Zupan noted that "an obvious problem associated with the lack of female officers in jails housing females concerns the potential for abuse and exploitation of women inmates by male staff."[137]

Jails that do hire women generally accord them equal footing with male staffers. Although cross-gender privacy is a potential area of legal liability, in three-quarters of the jails studied by Zupan, female officers were assigned to supervise male housing areas. Only one in four jails that employed women restricted their access to unscreened shower and toilet facilities used by men or to other areas, such as sex-offender units.

The first two decades of the [twenty-first] century, at least, will see a major growth in prison populations. We have an opportunity now to start doing a better job of handling the responsibilities of the criminal justice system as well as of society.

I hope we take both more seriously in the future than we do currently.

—Dr. Alfred Blumstein, Dean of the School of Urban and Public Affairs, Carnegie-Mellon University

The Growth of Jails

Jails have been called the "shame of the criminal justice system." Many are old, poorly funded, scantily staffed by underpaid and poorly trained employees, and given low priority in local budgets. By the end of the 1980s, many of our nation's jails had become seriously overcrowded, and court-ordered caps were sometimes placed on jail populations. One of the first such caps was imposed on the Harris County Jail in Houston, Texas, in 1990. In that year, the jail was forced to release 250 inmates after missing a deadline for reducing its resident population of 6,100 people.[138] A nationwide survey by the Bureau of Justice Statistics, undertaken around the same time, found that 46% of all jails had been built more than 25 years earlier, and of that percentage, over half were more than 50 years old.[139]

A 1983 national census revealed that jails were operating at 85% of their rated capacity (Table 13–1).[140] In 1990, however, the nation's jails were running at 104% of capacity, and new jails could be found on drawing boards and under construction across the country. By 2006, jail capacity had increased substantially, and overall jail occupancy was reported at 94% of rated capacity. Some individual facilities, however, were still desperately overcrowded.[141] Jail jurisdictions with the largest average daily populations also reported the highest occupancy rates.

TABLE 13–1 Jail Facts

	1983	1988	1993	2000	2006
Number of jails	3,338	3,316	3,304	3,365	3,360*
Number of jail inmates	223,551	343,569	459,804	621,149	766,010
Rated capacity of jails	261,556	339,949	475,224	677,787	810,863
Percentage of capacity occupied	85%	101%	97%	92%	94%

*Estimate based on earlier data.

Source: William J. Sabol, Todd D. Minton, and Paige M. Harrison, *Prison and Jail Inmates at Midyear 2006* (Washington, DC: Bureau of Justice Statistics, 2007), and other years.

At midyear 2006, occupancy was 97% of rated capacity in jail jurisdictions with an average daily population of 1,000 or more inmates, compared to 64% in those with fewer than 50 inmates.[142]

Although jail overcrowding is not the issue it was a decade ago, it is still a problem. Overcrowded prisons have taken a toll on jails. In 2004, for example, approximately 74,378 inmates were being held in local jails because of overcrowding in state and federal prisons.[143] Also, the practice of giving jail sentences to offenders who are unable or unwilling to make restitution, alimony, or child-support payments has added to jail occupancy and has made the local lockup, at least partially, a debtors' prison. Symptomatic of problems brought on by huge jail populations, 314 suicides were reported in jails across the nation during a recent year.[144] Jail deaths from all causes total about 980 annually. Other factors conspire to keep jail populations high. They include the following:[145]

- The inability of jail inmates to make bond due to institutionalized bail-bond practices and lack of funding sources for indigent defendants
- Unnecessary delays between arrest and final case disposition
- Unnecessarily limited access to vital information about defendants that could be useful in facilitating court-ordered pretrial release
- The limited ability of the criminal justice system to handle cases expeditiously due to a lack of needed resources (judges, assistant prosecuting attorneys, and so on)
- Inappropriate attorney delays in moving cases through court
- Unproductive statutes requiring that specified nonviolent offenders be jailed (including mandatory pretrial jailing of those caught driving while intoxicated, minor drug offenders, second-offense shoplifters, and so on)

Some innovative jurisdictions have successfully contained the growth of jail populations by diverting arrestees to community-based programs. San Diego, California, for example, uses a privately operated detoxification reception program to divert many inebriates from the "drunk tank."[146] Officials in Galveston County, Texas, routinely divert mentally ill arrestees directly to a mental health facility.[147] Other areas use pretrial services and magistrates' offices, which are open 24 hours a day, for setting bail, making release possible. Learn more about jail overcrowding by reading Library Extra 13–9 at cjtoday.com.

LIBRARY
Extra
▪▪▪▪

Direct-Supervision Jails

Some suggest that the problems found in many jails stem from "mismanagement, lack of fiscal support, heterogeneous inmate populations, overuse and misuse of detention, overemphasis on custodial goals, and political and public apathy."[148] Others propose that environmental and organizational aspects of traditional jail architecture and staffing have led to many difficulties.[149] Traditional jails, say these observers, were built on the assumption that inmates are inherently violent and potentially destructive. Through the use of thick walls, bars, and other architectural barriers, jails were constructed to give staff maximum control and to restrict inmates' movements. Such institutions, however, also limit the correctional staff's visibility and access to confinement areas. As a consequence, they tend to encourage just the kinds of inmate behavior that jails were meant to control. Today, efficient hallway patrols and expensive video technology help in overcoming the limits that old jail architecture places on supervision.

In an effort to solve many of the problems that dogged jails in the past, a new jail-management strategy emerged during the 1970s. Called **direct-supervision jail**, or podular/direct-supervision (PDS) jail, this approach joined "podular/unit architecture with a participative, proactive management philosophy."[150] Often built in a system of "pods," or modular self-contained housing areas linked to one another, direct-supervision jails helped eliminate the old physical barriers that separated staff and inmates. Gone were the bars and the isolated, secure observation areas for officers. They were replaced by an open environment in which inmates and correctional personnel could mingle with relative freedom. In a number of such "new-generation" jails, large reinforced Plexiglas panels supplanted walls and served to separate activity areas, such as classrooms and dining halls, from one another. Soft furniture is the rule throughout such institutions, and individual rooms take the place of cells, allowing inmates at least a modicum of personal privacy. In today's direct-supervision jails, 16 to 46 inmates typically live in one pod, with correctional staffers present among the inmate population around the clock.

Direct-supervision jails have been touted for their tendency to reduce inmate dissatisfaction and for their ability to deter rape and violence among the inmate population. By eliminating architectural barriers to staff–inmate interaction, direct-supervision facilities are said to place officers back

direct-supervision jail

A temporary confinement facility that eliminates many of the traditional barriers between inmates and correctional staff. Physical barriers in direct-supervision jails are far less common than in traditional jails, allowing staff members the opportunity for greater interaction with, and control over, residents.

in control of institutions. A number of studies have demonstrated the success of such jails at reducing the likelihood of inmate victimization. One such study also found that staff morale in direct-supervision jails was far higher than in traditional institutions, that inmates reported reduced stress levels, and that fewer inmate-on-inmate and inmate-on-staff assaults occurred.[151] Similarly, sexual assault, jail rape, suicide, and escape have all been found to occur far less frequently in direct-supervision facilities than in traditional institutions.[152] Significantly, new-generation jails appear to be substantially less susceptible to lawsuits brought by inmates and to adverse court-ordered judgments against jail administrators.

While the number of direct-supervision jails has grown rapidly, such facilities are not without their problems. In 1993, for example, the 238-bed Rensselaer County PDS jail in Troy, New York, experienced a disturbance that resulted in "a total loss of control," the removal of officers from the pods, and the escape of two inmates.[153] Somewhat later, the 700-bed San Joaquin County Jail in Stockton, California, experienced numerous problems, including the escape of seven inmates.

Some authors have recognized that new-generation jails are too frequently run by old-style managers and that correctional personnel sometimes lack the training needed to make the transition to the direct style of supervision.[154] Others have suggested that managers of direct-supervision jails, especially mid-level managers, could benefit from clearer job descriptions and additional training.[155] In the words of one direct-supervision advocate, "Training becomes particularly critical in direct supervision jails where relationships are more immediate and are more complex."[156] Finally, those tasked with hiring have recommended psychological screening and intensive use of preemployment interviews to determine the suitability of applicants for corrections officer positions in direct-supervision jails.[157] Learn more about the history of direct-supervision jails via Library Extra 13–10 at cjtoday.com.

LIBRARY
Extra
■■■■

Jails and the Future

In contrast to more visible issues confronting the justice system—such as the death penalty, gun control, the war on drugs, terrorism, and big-city gangs—jails have received relatively little attention from the media and have generally escaped close public scrutiny.[158] National efforts are under way, however, to improve the quality of jail life. Some changes involve adding crucial programs for inmates. An American Jail Association (AJA) study of drug-treatment programs in jails, for example, found that "a small fraction (perhaps fewer than 10%) of inmates needing drug treatment actually receive these services."[159]

Jail industries are another growing programmatic area. The best of them serve the community while training inmates in marketable skills.[160] In an exemplary effort to humanize its megajails, for example, the Los Angeles County Sheriff's Department opened an inmate telephone-answering

Inmates playing cards at the Los Angeles North County Correctional Facility in Saugus, California. The Los Angeles County jail system is the largest in the world, housing more than 20,000 inmates on a given day. What are direct-supervision jails?

Damian Dovarganes/AP Wide World Photos

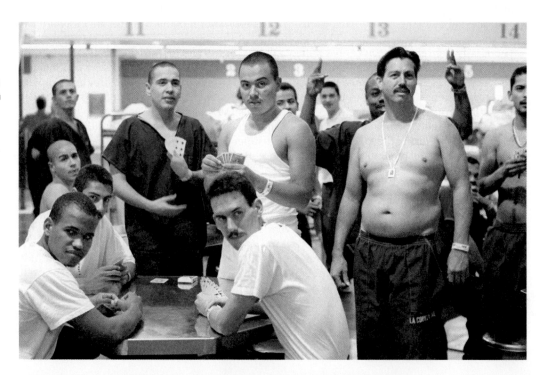

service.[161] Many callers contact the sheriff's department daily, requesting information about the county's 22,000 jail inmates. These requests for information were becoming increasingly difficult to handle due to the growing fiscal constraints facing local government. To handle the huge number of calls effectively without tying up sworn law enforcement personnel, the department began using inmates specially trained to handle incoming calls. Eighty inmates were assigned to the project, with groups of different sizes covering shifts throughout the day. Each inmate staffer went through a training program to learn proper telephone procedures and how to run computer terminals containing routine data on the department's inmates. The new system now handles 4,000 telephone inquiries a day. The time needed to answer a call and to begin to provide information has dropped from 30 minutes under the old system to a remarkable 10 seconds today.

Jail "boot camps," like the one run by the Harris County, Texas, probation department, are also popular. Jail boot camps give offenders who are sentenced to probationary terms a taste of confinement and the rigors of life behind bars. The Harris County Courts Regimented Intensive Probation Program (CRIPP) facility began operation in 1991 and is located in Humble, Texas. Separate CRIPPs are run for about 400 male and 50 female probationers.[162] The most recent comprehensive study of jail boot camps found only ten such jail-based programs in the country,[163] but current numbers are probably higher.

Capturing much recent attention are **regional jails**—that is, jails that are built and run using the combined resources of a variety of local jurisdictions. Regional jails have begun to replace smaller and often antiquated local jails in at least a few locations. One example of a regional jail is the Western Tidewater Regional Jail, serving the cities of Suffolk and Franklin and the county of Isle of Wright in Virginia.[164] Regional jails, which are just beginning to come into their own, may develop quickly in Virginia, where the state, recognizing the economies of consolidation, offers to reimburse localities up to 50% of the cost of building regional jails.

One final element in the unfolding saga of jail development should be mentioned: the emergence of state jail standards. Thirty-two states have set standards for municipal and county jails.[165] In 25 states, those standards are mandatory. The purpose of jail standards is to identify basic minimum conditions necessary for inmate health and safety. On the national level, the Commission on Accreditation for Corrections, operated jointly by the American Correctional Association and the federal government, has developed its own set of jail standards,[166] as has the National Sheriff's Association. Both sets of standards are designed to ensure a minimal level of comfort and safety in local lockups. Increased standards, though, are costly. Local jurisdictions, already hard-pressed to meet other budgetary demands, will probably be slow to upgrade their jails to meet such external guidelines unless forced to do so. In a study of 61 jails that was designed to test compliance with National Sheriff's Association guidelines, Ken Kerle discovered that in many standards areas—especially those of tool control, armory planning, community resources, release preparation, and riot planning—the majority of jails were badly out of compliance.[167] Lack of a written plan was the most commonly cited reason for failing to meet the standards. Learn more about jails by visiting the American Jail Association via **Web Extra 13–6** at cjtoday.com.

Private Prisons

State-run prison systems have always contracted with private industries for food, psychological testing, training, and recreational and other services, and it is estimated that more than three dozen states today rely on private businesses to serve a variety of correctional needs. It follows, then, that states have now turned to private industry for the provision of prison space. The **privatization** movement, which began in the early 1980s, was slow to catch on, but it has since grown at a rapid pace. In 1986, only 2,620 prisoners could be found in privately run confinement facilities.[168] But by 2007, privately operated correctional facilities serving as prisons and jails held over 113,790 state and federal prisoners across 32 states and the District of Columbia.[169] **Private prisons** held 6.2% of all state prisoners and 14.4% of federal prisoners at the start of 2007. One source says that the growth rate of the private prison industry has been around 35% annually[170]—comparable to the highest growth rates anywhere in the corporate sector.

Privately run prisons are operated by Cornell Corrections, Corrections Corporation of America (CCA), Correctional Services Corporation (CSC), Wackenhut Corrections Corporation, and numerous other smaller companies. Most states that use private firms to supplement their prison resources contract with such companies to provide a full range of custodial and other correctional services. State corrections administrators use private companies to reduce overcrowding, lower operating expenses, and avoid lawsuits targeted at state officials and employees.[171] But some

regional jail

A jail that is built and run using the combined resources of a variety of local jurisdictions.

WEB
Extra
■ ■ ■ ■

privatization

The movement toward the wider use of private prisons.

private prison

A correctional institution operated by a private firm on behalf of a local or state government.

Ethics and Professionalism

American Jail Association Code of Ethics for Jail Officers

As an officer employed in a detention/correctional capacity, I swear (or affirm) to be a good citizen and a credit to my community, state, and nation at all times. I will abstain from all questionable behavior which might bring disrepute to the agency for which I work, my family, my community, and my associates. My lifestyle will be above and beyond reproach and I will constantly strive to set an example of a professional who performs his/her duties according to the laws of our country, state, and community and the policies, procedures, written and verbal orders, and regulations of the agency for which I work.

On the job I promise to:

Keep | The institution secure so as to safeguard my community and the lives of the staff, inmates, and visitors on the premises.

Work | With each individual firmly and fairly without regard to rank, status, or condition.

Maintain | A positive demeanor when confronted with stressful situations of scorn, ridicule, danger, and/or chaos.

Report | Either in writing or by word of mouth to the proper authorities those things which should be reported, and keep silent about matters which are to remain confidential according to the laws and rules of the agency and government.

Manage | And supervise the inmates in an evenhanded and courteous manner.

Refrain | At all times from becoming personally involved in the lives of the inmates and their families.

Treat | All visitors to the jail with politeness and respect and do my utmost to ensure that they observe the jail regulations.

Take | Advantage of all education and training opportunities designed to assist me to become a more competent officer.

Communicate | With people in or outside of the jail, whether by phone, written word, or word of mouth, in such a way so as not to reflect in a negative manner upon my agency.

Contribute | To a jail environment which will keep the inmate involved in activities designed to improve his/her attitude and character.

Support | All activities of a professional nature through membership and participation that will continue to elevate the status of those who operate our nation's jails. Do my best through word and deed to present an image to the public at large of a jail professional, committed to progress for an improved and enlightened criminal justice system.

THINKING ABOUT ETHICS

1. Why does this code of ethics require jail officers to "Take advantage of all education and training opportunities designed to assist [them] to become a more competent officer"? What does education have to do with ethics?

2. Are there any elements that you might add to this code? Are there any that you might delete?

Source: American Jail Association, *Code of Ethics for Jail Officers*, adopted January 10, 1991. Revised May 19, 1993. Reprinted with permission.

studies have shown that private prisons may not bring the kinds of cost savings that had been anticipated.[172] A 1996 study by the U.S. General Accounting Office,[173] for example, found "neither cost savings nor substantial differences in the quality of services" between private and publicly run prisons.[174] Similar findings emerged in a 2001 report by the Bureau of Justice Assistance. That report, entitled *Emerging Issues on Privatized Prisons*, found that "private prisons offer only modest cost savings, which are basically a result of moderate reductions in staffing patterns, fringe benefits, and other labor-related costs."[175]

Many hurdles remain before the privatization movement can effectively provide large-scale custodial supervision. Among the most significant barriers to privatization are old state laws that prohibit private involvement in correctional management. Other practical hurdles exist as well. States that do contract with private firms may face the specter of strikes by corrections officers who do not come under state laws restricting the ability of public employees to strike. Moreover, since responsibility for the protection of inmate rights still lies with the state, their liability will not transfer to private corrections.[176] In today's legal climate, it is unclear whether a state can shield itself or its employees through private prison contracting, but it appears that the courts are unlikely to recognize such shielding. To limit their own liability, states will probably have to

CJ Futures

Jails and the Future

A number of trends are beginning to emerge as America's jails meet the needs of the twenty-first century. Among them are these:

- A shift away from traditional publicly run facilities to jails that are operated by private corporations under contract with local governments. More information on the privatization of prisons and jails is provided in this chapter.

- An increase in the proportion of inmates who are expected to pay for at least a portion of the expenses associated with their incarceration. In 1996, for example, pretrial inmates in the Broward County, Florida, jail system began paying a $2 per day fee for housing and meals. Charges are deducted from inmates' commissary funds, which are contributed by the inmates themselves or by family members. Inmates who feel they are unable to pay the fee are required to petition jail administrators and to demonstrate why they should not be required to pay.

- The growing use of computer-based inmate information systems that are integrated with networks used for the administration of court schedules, for docket monitoring, and for coordination with other criminal justice agencies. One jail consultant has gone so far as to claim that as a result of efficient and integrated information management systems, "paperwork will [soon] be a thing of the past."[1]

- A movement toward the improvement of jail facilities, made possible through growing opportunities for accreditation. Accreditation programs, such as those offered through the American Correctional Association, the Commission on Accreditation for Law Enforcement Agencies, and the National Commission on Correctional Health Care, are already helping shield jail administrators and local governments from the threat of lawsuits by demonstrating adherence to professional standards.

- A movement toward the increased professionalization of jail personnel, made possible by certification programs like the Jail Manager Certification Program operated by the American Jail Association. Certified Jail Manager status has been available since 1997.

- A changing public climate that may soon shift away from the "get tough" policies of the past decade toward a more pragmatic emphasis on the needs of both inmates and administrators. Inmate needs in the areas of mental health counseling, suicide prevention, and opportunities for meaningful employment will be met in an effort to facilitate institutional administration.

- A greater use of direct-supervision jails, resulting in fewer internal problems and easier administration. The increased use of direct-supervision jails will heighten both inmate and staff morale in most locations.

- A growing use of inmate labor, as counties, communities, the nonprofit sector, and corporations begin to more fully recognize the advantages to be gained from the meaningful employment of inmates. As a consequence, more inmates will work, and those who do will be involved in an ever-widening sphere of activities. The increase in inmate labor will lead to a widening of partnerships among jails, their administrators, and other community groups. Corporate employers, for example, will begin to operate more and more training programs in jails with the goal of increasing workforce efficiency.

- A greater use of research in the field of jail operations, which will lead to better informed and more effective programs and strategies. Research showing that a greater number of female officers means fewer assaults overall, for example, should lead to the hiring of more women in the corrections field.

[1]Ron Carroll, "Jails and the Criminal Justice System in the Twenty-first Century," *American Jails* (March/April 1997), p. 31.
References: Ron Carroll, "Jails and the Criminal Justice System in the Twenty-First Century," *American Jails* (March/April 1997), pp. 26–31; Susan W. McCampbell, "The Paying Prisoner," *American Jails* (March/April 1997), pp. 37–43; Cindy Malm, "AJA Jail Manager Certification Program," *American Jails* (March/April 1997), p. 99; Rod Miller, "Inmate Labor in the Twenty-First Century," *American Jails* (March/April 1997), pp. 45–49; and Joseph R. Rowan, "Corrections in the Twenty-First Century," *American Jails* (March/April 1997), pp. 32–36.

oversee private operations as well as set standards for training and custody. In 1997, in the case of *Richardson* v. *McKnight*,[177] the U.S. Supreme Court made it clear that corrections officers employed by a private firm are not entitled to qualified immunity from suits by prisoners charging a violation of Section 1983 of Title 42 of the U.S. Code. (See Chapter 8 for more information on Section 1983 lawsuits.) In 2001, however, in the case of *Correctional Services Corporation* v. *Malesko*,[178] the Court found that private corporations acting under color of federal law cannot be held responsible in a *Bivens* action because the purpose of *Bivens* (which was discussed in Chapter 8) "is to deter individual federal officers from committing Constitutional violations."[179]

Perhaps the most serious legal issues confront states that contract to hold inmates outside of their own jurisdiction. In 1996, for example, two inmates escaped from a 240-man sex-offender unit run by Corrections Corporation of America under contract with the state of Oregon. Problems

CJ Today Exhibit 13–3

Arguments for and against the Privatization of Prisons

REASONS TO PRIVATIZE

1. Private operators can provide construction financing options that allow the government to pay only for capacity as needed in lieu of assuming long-term debt.

2. Private companies offer state-of-the-art correctional facility designs that are efficient to operate and that are based on cost–benefit considerations.

3. Private operators typically design and construct a new correctional facility in half the time it takes to build a comparable government project.

4. Private companies provide government with the convenience and accountability of one entity for all compliance issues.

5. Private companies can mobilize rapidly and specialize in unique facility missions.

6. Private companies provide economic development opportunities by hiring and purchasing locally.

7. Government can reduce or share its liability exposure by contracting with private corrections companies.

8. Government can retain flexibility by limiting the contract's duration and by specifying the facility's mission.

9. The addition of alternative service providers injects competition among both public and private organizations.

REASONS NOT TO PRIVATIZE

1. There are certain responsibilities that only the government should meet, such as public safety. The government has legal, political, and moral obligations to provide incarceration. Constitutional issues underlie both public and private corrections and involve deprivation of liberty, discipline, and preservation of the rights of inmates. Related issues include use of force, equitable hiring practices, and segregation.

2. Few private companies are available from which to choose.

3. Private operators may be inexperienced with key corrections issues.

4. A private operator may become a monopoly through political ingratiation, favoritism, and so on.

5. Government may, over time, lose the capability to perform the corrections function.

6. The profit motive will inhibit the proper performance of corrections duties. Private companies have financial incentives to cut corners.

7. The procurement process is slow, inefficient, and open to risks.

8. Creating a good, clear contract is a daunting task.

9. The lack of enforcement remedies in contracts leaves only termination or lawsuits as recourse.

Source: Dennis Cunningham, "Public Strategies for Private Prisons," paper presented at the Private Prison Workshop at the Institute on Criminal Justice, University of Minnesota Law School, January 29–30, 1999.

immediately arose because the CCA unit was located near Houston, Texas—not in Oregon, where the men had originally been sentenced to confinement. Following the escape, Texas officials were unsure whether they even had arrest power over the former prisoners, since their escape was not a crime in Texas. While prison escape *is* a crime under Texas law, the law only applies to state-run facilities, not to private facilities where correctional personnel are not employed by the state or empowered in any official capacity by state law. Harris County (Texas) Prosecutor John Holmes explained the situation this way: "They have not committed the offense of escape under Texas law . . . and the only reason at all that they're subject to being arrested and were arrested was because during their leaving the facility, they assaulted a guard and took his motor vehicle. That we can charge them with and have."[180]

Opponents of the movement toward privatization cite these and many other issues. They claim that, aside from legal concerns, cost reductions via the use of private facilities can only be achieved by lowering standards. They fear a return to the inhumane conditions of early jails, as private firms seek to turn prisons into profit-making operations. For states that do choose to contract with private firms, the National Institute of Justice (NIJ) recommends a "regular and systematic sampling" of former inmates to appraise prison conditions, as well as annual on-site inspections of each privately run institution. State personnel serving as monitors should be stationed in large facilities, says NIJ, and a "meticulous review" of all services should be conducted before the contract renewal date.[181] You can learn more about prison privatization at Library Extras 13–11 and 13–12 and via Web Extra 13–7 at cjtoday.com.

 LIBRARY Extra

 WEB Extra

The 2,300-bed California City Correctional Center in the Mojave Desert town of California City. The facility, which opened in December 1999, was built by the Corrections Corporation of America (CCA) to provide medium-security correctional services under a contract with the federal Bureau of Prisons. Nashville-based CCA says that it can run prisons as efficiently as the government, and its supporters claim that private prisons are the way of the future. Do you agree? Why or why not?

Reed Saxon/AP Wide World Photos

SUMMARY

- Before the development of prisons in the late eighteenth and early nineteenth centuries, early criminal punishments were frequently cruel and torturous. Flogging, mutilation, branding, and public humiliation were some of the physical punishments imposed on offenders before the development of prisons.

- In an important historical development, around the year 1800, imprisonment *as* punishment replaced the notion of imprisonment *for* punishment. The state of today's prisons is largely the result of historical efforts to humanize the treatment of offenders, coupled with recent attempts to have the prison experience reflect prevailing social attitudes toward crime and punishment. Early workhouses, which flourished in Europe a few hundred years ago and housed the noncriminal poor and destitute, provided a model for efforts to institutionalize those whom society perceived as burdensome. Imprisonment in the United States began with the penitentiary philosophy of the Pennsylvania Quakers, who believed that solitary confinement and meditation on one's transgressions could lead to reformation. Soon, however, the mass prison philosophy, represented by prisons like Auburn Prison in New York, won the day, and the contemporary system of imprisonment—in which relatively large numbers of people are confined together and often allowed to interact closely—emerged.

- Prisons today are largely classified according to security level, such as maximum, medium, and minimum security. Most contemporary American correctional facilities are medium and minimum security. Although the goals of recidivism and deterrence are still important in the minds of corrections administrators, today's prisons tend to warehouse inmates awaiting release. Public disappointment with high rates of recidivism has produced a prison system today that is focused on the concept of just deserts and that is only beginning to emerge from the strong influence of the nothing-works doctrine discussed in this chapter. Overcrowded facilities are still the norm in many jurisdictions, although a prison building boom over the last decade has alleviated some of the extremely overcrowded conditions that had previously existed.

- In contrast to prisons, which are long-time confinement facilities designed to hold those who have been sentenced to serve time for committing crime, jails are short-term confinement facilities whose traditional purpose has been to hold those awaiting trial or sentencing. Inmates who have been tried and sentenced may also be held at jails until their transfer to a prison facility, and today's jails sometimes hold inmates serving short sentences of confinement. Recently, the emergence of direct-supervision jails, in which traditional barriers between inmates and staff have been mostly eliminated, seems to have reduced the incidence of jail violence and can be credited with improving the conditions of jailed inmates in jurisdictions where such facilities operate.

- Privately run correctional facilities, or private prisons, have grown in number over the past few decades as the movement toward the privatization of correctional facilities has gained steam. Private prisons, operated by for-profit corporations, hold inmates on behalf of state governments or the federal government and provide for their care and security. A number of questions remain as to the role such facilities will play in the future, including whether they can be cost-effective and whether they can somehow reduce the legal liability of state governments and government employees that is often associated with confinement.

KEY TERMS

ADMAX, 483

Ashurst-Sumners Act, 469

Auburn system, 465

classification system, 481

design capacity, 478

direct-supervision jail, 489

industrial prison, 468

jail, 486

justice model, 474

lex talionis, 460

medical model, 471

nothing-works doctrine, 473

operational capacity, 478

Pennsylvania system, 465

prison, 460

prison capacity, 478

private prison, 491

privatization, 491

rated capacity, 478

reformatory style, 466

regional jail, 491

state-use system, 468

warehousing, 472

workhouse, 462

work release, 472

KEY NAMES

Zebulon Brockway, 468

Sir Walter Crofton, 467

Alexander Maconochie, 466

Robert Martinson, 473

Alexis de Tocqueville, 466

QUESTIONS FOR REVIEW

1. What types of criminal punishments were used before the advent of imprisonment as a criminal sanction? How have early punishments influenced modern correctional philosophy?

2. Trace the historical development of prisons in the United States, beginning with the Pennsylvania system. How has correctional practice in America changed over time? What changes do you predict for the future?

3. What are today's prisons like? What purposes do they serve?

4. What role do jails play in American corrections? What are some of the issues that jail administrators currently face?

5. What is the role of private prisons today?

QUESTIONS FOR REFLECTION

1. What are the demographics (social characteristics) of today's prisoners? What gender and racial disparities, if any, exist in today's prison population?

2. What is the just deserts model of corrections? Explain the pros and cons of this model. How has it led to an increased use of imprisonment and to prison overcrowding?

3. What is the relationship, if any, between changes in the rate of criminal offending and changes in the rate of imprisonment in America during the last decade? What is the reason for that relationship?

4. What will be the state of private prisons two or three decades from now?

Discuss your answers to these questions and other issues on the CJ Today e-mail discussion list (join the list at cjtoday.com).

WEB QUEST

Visit the Corrections Connection at http://www.corrections.com. What are some of the many features available at this site? Explore the Legal Issues bulletin board at the Corrections Connection site to learn about the latest legal issues of concern to corrections professionals. Then participate in a Corrections Connections chat room conversation. (The "Corrections Lobby" is often a good place to find an ongoing chat.) What topics are being discussed? If no one is in the chat room when you enter, visit the Listserve message boards and list the most recent topics being discussed. Submit this information to your instructor if asked to do so.

To complete this Web Quest online, go to the Web Quest module in Chapter 13 of the *Criminal Justice Today* Companion Website at cjtoday.com.

CHAPTER 14

Prison Life

LEARNING OBJECTIVES

After reading this chapter, you should be able to

- Describe the realities of prison life and prison subculture from the inmate's point of view.

- Illustrate the significant differences between men's prisons and women's prisons.

- Describe the realities of prison life from the corrections officer's point of view.

- Describe the causes of prison riots and list the stages through which most riots progress.

- Discuss the legal aspects of prisoners' rights and explain the consequences of precedent-setting U.S. Supreme Court cases in the area of prisoners' rights.

- Describe the major problems and issues that prisons face today.

OUTLINE

Mass incarceration seems to have made the streets safer. The vast increase in the prison and jail population from about 380,000 in 1975 to 2.2 million today overlaps with equally stunning declines in crime. . . . Many critics of incarceration argue (a bit too quickly) that crime would have fallen without the prison boom. Perhaps. Still the value of safer neighborhoods is immediate, while the costs of excessive imprisonment are theoretical and vague.

—Jason DeParle[1]

Jurisdictions should develop, with the assistance of prosecutors and others, community supervision programs that allow all but the most serious to avoid incarceration and a conviction record.

—American Bar Association, Criminal Justice Section[2]

Hear the author discuss this chapter at cjtoday.com

Introduction

On the FOX TV show *Prison Break*, Wentworth Miller plays the role of an engineer named Michael Scofield who holds up a bank so that he can join his brother in the fictional Fox River State Penitentiary. Scofield's brother, Lincoln (Dominic Purcell), has been convicted of a sensational murder and is housed on the prison's death row. The show, which centers around Michael's elaborate plan to break Lincoln out and to prove that he's innocent, draws a large weekly audience and demonstrates the fascination that the American public has with prison life.

For many years, prisons and prison life could be described by the phrase "out of sight, out of mind." Very few citizens cared about prison conditions, and those unfortunate enough to be locked away were regarded as lost to the world. By the mid-twentieth century, however, this attitude started to change. Concerned citizens began to offer their services to prison administrations, neighborhoods began accepting work-release prisoners and halfway houses, and social scientists initiated a serious study of prison life. Today, as shows like *Prison Break* make clear,

Dominic Purcell (left) and Wentworth Miller, stars of the hit FOX TV show, *Prison Break*. Why do so many TV viewers find prison life intriguing?

John Zich/Corbis/Bettmann

prisons and prison life have entered the American mainstream. Part of the reason for this is because prisons today hold more people than ever before, and incarceration impacts not only those imprisoned but family members, friends, and victims on the outside.

This chapter describes the realities of prison life today, including prisoner lifestyles, prison subcultures, sexuality in prison, prison violence, and prisoners' rights and grievance procedures. We will discuss both the inmate world and the staff world. A separate section on women in prison details the social structure of women's prisons, daily life in those facilities, and the various types of female inmates. We begin with a brief overview of early research on prison life.

Research on Prison Life—Total Institutions

In 1935, Hans Reimer, who was then chairman of the Department of Sociology at Indiana University, set the tone for studies of prison life when he voluntarily served three months in prison as an incognito participant-observer.[3] Reimer reported the results of his studies to the American Prison Association, stimulating many other, albeit less spectacular, efforts to examine prison life. Other early studies include Donald Clemmer's *The Prison Community* (1940),[4] Gresham Sykes's *The Society of Captives* (1958),[5] Richard Cloward and Donald Cressey's *Theoretical Studies in Social Organization of the Prison* (1960),[6] and Cressey's edited volume, *The Prison* (1961).[7]

These studies and others focused primarily on maximum-security prisons for men. They treated correctional institutions as formal or complex organizations and employed the analytic techniques of organizational sociology, industrial psychology, and administrative science.[8] As modern writers on prisons have observed, "The prison was compared to a primitive society, isolated from the outside world, functionally integrated by a delicate system of mechanisms, which kept it precariously balanced between anarchy and accommodation."[9]

Another approach to the study of prison life was developed by Erving Goffman, who coined the term **total institution** in a 1961 study of prisons and mental hospitals.[10] Goffman described total institutions as places where the same people work, recreate, worship, eat, and sleep together daily. Such places include prisons, concentration camps, mental hospitals, seminaries, and other facilities in which residents are cut off from the larger society either forcibly or willingly. Total institutions are small societies. They evolve their own distinctive values and styles of life and pressure residents to fulfill rigidly prescribed behavioral roles.

Generally speaking, the work of prison researchers built on findings of other social scientists who discovered that any group with similar characteristics confined in the same place at the same time develops its own subculture. Prison subcultures, described in the next section, also provide the medium through which prison values are communicated and expectations are made known. Learn more about prison research via Library Extra 14–1 at cjtoday.com.

total institution

An enclosed facility separated from society both socially and physically, where the inhabitants share all aspects of their daily lives.

LIBRARY
Extra
▪▪▪▪

A notice posted on a prison wall. Custody and control remain the primary concerns of prison staffers throughout the country—a fact reinforced by this notice. Is the emphasis on custody and control justified?
Mike Fiala/Agence France Presse/Getty Images

The Male Inmate's World

Two social realities coexist in prison settings. One is the official structure of rules and procedures put in place by the wider society and enforced by prison staff. The other is the more informal but decidedly more powerful inmate world.[11] The inmate world, best described by how closely it touches the lives of inmates, is controlled by **prison subculture**. The realities of prison life—including a large and often densely packed inmate population that must look to the prison environment for all its needs—mean that prison subculture develops independently of the plans of prison administrators and is not easily subjected to the control of prison authorities.

Inmates entering prison discover a whole new social world in which they must participate or face consequences ranging from dangerous ostracism to physical violence and homicide.[12] The socialization of new inmates into the prison subculture has been described as a process of **prisonization**[13]—the new prisoner's learning of convict values, attitudes, roles, and even language. By the time this process is complete, new inmates have become "cons." Gresham Sykes and Sheldon Messinger recognized five elements of the prison code in 1960:[14]

1. Don't interfere with the interests of other inmates. Never rat on a con.
2. Don't lose your head. Play it cool and do your own time.
3. Don't exploit inmates. Don't steal. Don't break your word. Be right.
4. Don't whine. Be a man.
5. Don't be a sucker. Don't trust the guards or staff.

Some criminologists have suggested that the prison code is simply a reflection of general criminal values. If so, these values are brought to the institution rather than created there. Either way, the power and pervasiveness of the prison code require convicts to conform to the worldview held by the majority of prisoners.

Stanton Wheeler, Ford Foundation Professor of Law and Social Sciences at the University of Washington, closely examined the concept of prisonization in an early study of the Washington State Reformatory.[15] Wheeler found that the degree of prisonization experienced by inmates tends to vary over time. He described changing levels of inmate commitment to prison norms and values by way of a U-shaped curve. When an inmate first enters prison, Wheeler said, the conventional values of outside society are of paramount importance. As time passes, inmates adopt the lifestyle of the prison. However, within the half year prior to release, most inmates begin to demonstrate a renewed appreciation of conventional values. Learn more about both the positive and negative impacts of imprisonment at Library Extra 14–2 at cjtoday.com.

Different prisons share aspects of a common inmate culture.[16] **Prison argot**, or language, provides one example of how widespread prison subculture can be. The terms used to describe inmate roles in one institution are generally understood in others. The word *rat*, for example, is prison slang for an informer. Popularized by crime movies of the 1950s, the term is understood today by members of the wider society. Other words common to prison argot are shown in CJ Today Exhibit 14–1. View an online prisoner's dictionary via Web Extra 14–1 at cjtoday.com.

Prison Subcultures

Prison subcultures, like all subcultures, evolve to reflect the concerns and experiences of the wider culture. John Irwin's 1970 classic study, *The Felon*,[17] recognized that the prison subcultures of the time had begun to reflect the cultural changes sweeping America. A decade later, other investigators of prison subcultures were able to write, "It was no longer meaningful to speak of a single inmate culture or even subculture. By the time we began our field research . . . it was clear that the unified, oppositional convict culture, found in the sociological literature on prisons, no longer existed."[18] Changes in the larger society again affected prison subculture in the 1980s, when the AIDS epidemic brought about changes in prison sexual behavior, at least for a segment of the inmate population.

Charles Stastny and Gabrielle Tyrnauer, describing prison life at Washington State Penitentiary in 1982, discovered four clearly distinguishable subcultures: (1) official, (2) traditional, (3) reform, and (4) revolutionary.[19] Official culture was promoted by the staff and by the administrative rules of the institution. Enthusiastic participants in official culture were mostly corrections officers and other staff members, although inmates were also well aware of the normative expectations that official culture imposed on them. Official culture affected the lives of inmates primarily through the creation of a prisoner hierarchy based on sentence length, prison jobs, and the "perks" that cooperation with the dictates of official culture could produce. Traditional prison

---

prison subculture

The values and behavioral patterns characteristic of prison inmates. Prison subculture has been found to be surprisingly consistent across the country.

prisonization

The process whereby newly institutionalized offenders come to accept prison lifestyles and criminal values. Although many inmates begin their prison experience with only a few values that support criminal behavior, the socialization experience they undergo while incarcerated leads to a much greater acceptance of such values.

prison argot

The slang characteristic of prison subcultures and prison life.

LIBRARY
Extra
■ ■ ■ ■

WEB
Extra
■ ■ ■ ■

CJ Today Exhibit 14–1

Prison Argot: The Language of Confinement

Writers who have studied prison life often comment on prisoners' use of a special language or slang termed *prison argot*. This language generally describes prison activities and the roles assigned by prison culture to types of inmates. This box lists a few of the many words and phrases identified in studies by different authors. The first group includes words that are characteristic of men's prisons; the second group includes words used in women's prisons.

MEN'S PRISON SLANG

Ace duce: A best friend

Badge (or bull, hack, the man, or screw): A corrections officer

Banger (or burner, shank, or sticker): A knife

Billy: A white man

Boneyard: The conjugal visiting area

Cat-J (or J-cat): A prisoner in need of psychological or psychiatric therapy or medication

Cellie: A cell mate

Chester: A child molester

Dog: A homeboy or friend

Fag: A male inmate who is believed to be a "natural" or "born" homosexual

Featherwood: A white prisoner's woman

Fish: A newly arrived inmate

Gorilla: An inmate who uses force to take what he wants from others

Homeboy: A prisoner from one's hometown or neighborhood

Ink: Tattoos

Lemon squeezer: An inmate who masturbates frequently

Man walking: A phrase used to signal that a guard is coming

Merchant (or peddler): One who sells when he should give

Peckerwood (or wood): A white prisoner

Punk: A male inmate who is forced into a submissive role during homosexual relations

Rat (or snitch): An inmate who squeals (provides information about other inmates to the prison administration)

Schooled: Knowledgeable in the ways of prison life

Shakedown: A search of a cell or of a work area

Tree jumper: A rapist

Turn out: To rape or make into a punk

Wolf: A male inmate who assumes the dominant role during homosexual relations

WOMEN'S PRISON SLANG

Cherry (or cherrie): A female inmate who has not yet been introduced to lesbian activities

Fay broad: A white female inmate

Femme (or mommy): A female inmate who plays the female role during lesbian relations

Safe: The vagina, especially when used for hiding contraband

Stud broad (or daddy): A female inmate who assumes the male role during lesbian relations

References: Gresham Sykes, *The Society of Captives* (Princeton, NJ: Princeton University Press, 1958); Rose Giallombardo, *Society of Women: A Study of a Woman's Prison* (New York: John Wiley, 1966); and Richard A. Cloward et al., *Theoretical Studies in Social Organization of the Prison* (New York: Social Science Research Council, 1960). For a more contemporary listing of prison slang terms, see Reinhold Aman, *Hillary Clinton's Pen Pal: A Guide to Life and Lingo in Federal Prison* (Santa Rosa, CA: Maledicta Press, 1996); Jerome Washington, *Iron House: Stories from the Yard* (Ann Arbor, MI: QED Press, 1994); Morrie Camhi, *The Prison Experience* (Boston: Charles Tuttle, 1989); and Harold Long, *Survival in Prison* (Port Townsend, WA: Loompanics, 1990).

culture, described by early writers on the subject, still existed, but its participants spent much of their time lamenting the decline of the convict code among younger prisoners. Reform culture was unique at Washington State Penitentiary. It was the result of a brief experiment with inmate self-government during the early 1970s. Some elements of prison life that evolved during the experimental period survived the termination of self-government and were eventually institutionalized in what Stastny and Tyrnauer called "reform culture." They included inmate participation in civic-style clubs, citizen involvement in the daily activities of the prison, banquets, and inmate speaking tours. Revolutionary culture built on the radical political rhetoric of the disenfranchised and found a ready audience among minority prisoners who saw themselves as victims of society's basic unfairness. Although they did not participate in it, revolutionary inmates understood traditional prison culture and generally avoided running afoul of its rules.

The Functions of Prison Subcultures

*It is better to prevent crimes
than to punish them.*

—*Cesare Beccaria (1738-1794)*

How do social scientists and criminologists explain the existence of prison subcultures? Although people around the world live in groups and create their own cultures, in few cases does the intensity of human interaction approach the level found in prisons. As we discussed in Chapter 13, many of today's prisons are densely crowded places where inmates can find no retreat from the constant demands of staff and the pressures of fellow prisoners. Prison subcultures, according to some authors, are fundamentally an adaptation to deprivation and confinement. In *The Society of Captives*, Sykes called these deprivations the "pains of imprisonment."[20] The pains of imprisonment—the frustrations induced by the rigors of confinement—form the nexus of a deprivation model of prison subculture. Sykes said that prisoners are deprived of (1) liberty, (2) goods and services, (3) heterosexual relationships, (4) autonomy, and (5) personal security—and that these deprivations lead to the development of subcultures intended to ameliorate the personal pains that accompany deprivation.

In contrast to the deprivation model, the importation model of prison subculture suggests that inmates bring with them values, roles, and behavior patterns from the outside world. Such external values, second nature as they are to career offenders, depend substantially on the criminal worldview. When offenders are confined, these external elements shape the social world of inmates.

The social structure of the prison—the accepted and relatively permanent social arrangements—is another element that shapes prison subculture. Clemmer's early prison study recognized nine structural dimensions of inmate society. He said that prison society could be described in terms of[21]

- Prisoner–staff dichotomy
- Three general classes of prisoners
- Work gangs and cell-house groups
- Racial groups
- Type of offense
- Power of inmate "politicians"
- Degree of sexual abnormality
- Record of repeat offenses
- Personality differences due to preprison socialization

Clemmer's nine structural dimensions still describe prison life today. When applied to individuals, they designate an inmate's position in the prison "pecking order" and create expectations of the appropriate role for that person. Prison roles serve to satisfy the needs of inmates for power, sexual performance, material possessions, individuality, and personal pleasure and to define the status of one prisoner relative to another. For example, inmate leaders, sometimes referred to as "real men" or "toughs" by prisoners in early studies, offer protection to those who live by the rules. They also provide for a redistribution of wealth inside prison and see to it that the rules of the complex prison-derived economic system—based on barter, gambling, and sexual favors—are observed. For an intimate multimedia portrait of life behind bars, visit Web Extra 14–2 at cjtoday.com.

WEB
Extra
■ ■ ■ ■

Prison Lifestyles and Inmate Types

Prison society is strict and often unforgiving. Even so, inmates are able to express some individuality through the choice of a prison lifestyle. John Irwin viewed these lifestyles (like the subcultures of which they are a part) as adaptations to the prison environment.[22] Other writers have since elaborated on these coping mechanisms. Listed below are some of the types of prisoners that researchers have described.

- *The mean dude.* Some inmates adjust to prison by being violent. Other inmates know that these prisoners are best left alone. The mean dude is frequently written up and spends much time in solitary confinement. This role is most common in male institutions and in maximum-security prisons. For some prisoners, the role of mean dude in prison is similar to the role they played in their life prior to being incarcerated. Certain personality types, such as the psychopath, may feel a natural attraction to this role. Prison culture supports violence in two ways: (1) by expecting inmates to be tough and (2) through the prevalence of the idea that only the strong survive inside prison.

- *The hedonist.* Some inmates build their lives around the limited pleasures available within the confines of prison. The smuggling of contraband, homosexuality, gambling, drug running,

A male inmate dressing as a female in the protective custody wing of the Ferguson Unit in Midway, Texas. Homosexuality is common in both men's and women's prisons. How does it differ between the two?

© Andrew Lichtenstein/Corbis Sygma

and other officially condemned activities provide the center of interest for prison hedonists. Hedonists generally have an abbreviated view of the future, living only for the "now."

- *The opportunist.* The opportunist takes advantage of the positive experiences prison has to offer. Schooling, trade training, counseling, and other self-improvement activities are the focal points of the opportunist's life in prison. Opportunists are generally well liked by prison staff, but other prisoners shun and mistrust them because they come closest to accepting the role that the staff defines as "model prisoner."

- *The retreatist.* Prison life is rigorous and demanding. Badgering by the staff and actual or feared assaults by other inmates may cause some prisoners to attempt psychological retreat from the realities of imprisonment. Such inmates may experience neurotic or psychotic episodes, become heavily involved in drug and alcohol abuse through the illicit prison economy, or even attempt suicide. Depression and mental illness are the hallmarks of the retreatist personality in prison.

- *The legalist.* The legalist is the "jailhouse lawyer." Convicts facing long sentences, with little possibility for early release through the correctional system, are most likely to turn to the courts in their battle against confinement.

- *The radical.* Radical inmates view themselves as political prisoners. They see society and the successful conformists who populate it as oppressors who have forced criminality on many "good people" through the creation of a system that distributes wealth and power inequitably. The inmate who takes on the radical role is unlikely to receive much sympathy from prison staff.

- *The colonizer.* Some inmates think of prison as their home and don't look forward to leaving. They "know the ropes," have many "friends" inside, and may feel more comfortable institutionalized than on the streets. They typically hold positions of power or respect among the inmate population. Once released, some colonizers commit new crimes to return to prison.

- *The religious.* Some prisoners profess a strong religious faith. They may be "born-again" Christians, committed Muslims, or even satanists or witches. Religious inmates frequently attend services, may form prayer groups, and sometimes ask the prison administration to allocate meeting facilities or to create special diets to accommodate their claimed spiritual needs. While it is certainly true that some inmates have a strong religious faith, staff members are apt to be suspicious of the overly religious prisoner.

- *The gang-banger.* Gang-bangers are affiliated with prison gangs and depend upon the gang for defense and protection. They display gang signs, sport gang-related tattoos, and use their gang membership as a channel for the procurement of desired goods and services both inside and outside of prison.

Whilst we have prisons it matters little which of us occupies the cells.

−George Bernard Shaw (1856–1950)

- *The realist.* The realist sees confinement as a natural consequence of criminal activity and as an unfortunate cost of doing business. This stoic attitude toward incarceration generally leads the realist to "pull his (or her) own time" and to make the best of it. Realists tend to know the inmate code, are able to avoid trouble, and continue in lives of crime once released.

Homosexuality in Prison

Homosexual behavior inside prisons is both constrained and encouraged by prison subculture. One Houston woman, whose son is serving time in a Texas prison, explained the path to prison homosexuality this way: "Within a matter of days, if not hours, an unofficial prison welcome wagon sorts new arrivals into those who will fight, those who will pay extortion cash of up to $60 every two weeks, and those who will be servants or slaves. 'You're jumped on by two or three prisoners to see if you'll fight,' said the woman. 'If you don't fight, you become someone's girl, until they're tired of you and they sell you to someone else.'"[23]

Sykes's early study of prison argot found many words describing homosexual activity. Among them were the terms *wolf*, *punk*, and *fag*. Wolves were aggressive men who assumed the masculine role in homosexual relations. Punks were forced into submitting to the female role. The term *fag* described a special category of men who had a natural proclivity toward homosexual activity and effeminate mannerisms. While both wolves and punks were fiercely committed to their heterosexual identity and participated in homosexuality only because of prison conditions, fags generally engaged in homosexual lifestyles before their entry into prison and continued to emulate feminine mannerisms and styles of dress once incarcerated.

Prison homosexuality depends to a considerable degree on the naiveté of young inmates experiencing prison for the first time. Even when newly arrived inmates are protected from fights, older prisoners looking for homosexual liaisons may ingratiate themselves by offering cigarettes, money, drugs, food, or protection. At some future time, these "loans" will be called in, with payoffs demanded in sexual favors. Because the inmate code requires the repayment of favors, the "fish" who tries to resist may quickly find himself face-to-face with the brute force of inmate society.

Prison rape represents a special category of homosexual behavior behind bars. In 2003, Congress mandated the collection of statistics on prison rape as part of the Prison Rape Elimination Act (PREA).[24] The purposes of the PREA are to[25]

- Establish a zero-tolerance standard for prison rape
- Make prison rape prevention a top priority in correctional facilities and systems
- Develop and implement national standards for the detection, prevention, reduction, and punishment of prison rape
- Increase the availability of information on the incidence and prevalence of prison rape
- Increase the accountability of corrections officials with regard to the issue of sexual violence in U.S. prisons

The PREA requires the Bureau of Justice Statistics (BJS) to collect data in federal and state prisons, county and city jails, and juvenile institutions, with the U.S. Census Bureau acting as the official repository for collected data. The first national survey under PREA auspices was completed in 2005 and covered 2,700 correctional facilities and 1,754,000 inmates—or 79% of all adults and juveniles in custody at the time.[26] Based on 5,528 reported allegations of sexual violence, surveyors estimated that 8,210 incidents of sexual violence took place nationwide in correctional facilities in 2004. Of the total, 42% of the allegations involved sexual misconduct by staff (including "consensual" acts); 37% involved inmate-on-inmate nonconsensual sexual acts; 11% were incidents of sexual harassment of inmates by correctional facility employees; and 10% were classified as abusive sexual contact in which one inmate touches another inmate inappropriately.[27] Male inmates comprised 90% of both victims and perpetrators in instances of inmate-on-inmate nonconsensual sexual activity. Somewhat surprisingly, survey results showed that 69% of victims of staff sexual misconduct in state prisons were male, while 67% of perpetrators were female. The 2005 survey is only a first step in understanding and eliminating prison rape. As BJS notes, "Due to fear of reprisal from perpetrators, a code of silence among inmates, personal embarrassment, and lack of trust in staff, victims are often reluctant to report incidents to correctional authorities."[28] Learn more about the PREA and read new survey results as they become available via Web Extra 14–3 at cjtoday.com.

WEB
Extra
■ ■ ■ ■

An earlier but comprehensive review of rape inside male prisons was published in 2001 by Human Rights Watch. Entitled *No Escape: Male Rape in U.S. Prisons*,[29] the 378-page report examined three years of research and interviews with more than 200 prisoners in 34 states. Perpetrators of prison rape were found to be young (generally 20 to 30 years old), larger or stronger than their victims, and "generally more assertive, physically aggressive, and more at home in the prison environment" than their victims. Rapists were also found to be "street smart" and were frequently gang members who were well established in the inmate hierarchy and who had been convicted of violent crimes. A large proportion of sexual aggressors are characterized by low education and poverty, having grown up in a broken home headed by the mother, and having a record of violent offenses.[30] Lee H. Bowker, summarizing studies of sexual violence in prison, provides the following observations:[31]

- Most sexual aggressors do not consider themselves homosexuals.
- Sexual release is not the primary motivation for sexual attack.
- Many aggressors must continue to participate in gang rapes to avoid becoming victims themselves.
- The aggressors have themselves suffered much damage to their masculinity in the past.

As in cases of heterosexual rape, sexual assaults in prison are likely to leave psychological scars on the victim long after the physical event is over.[32] Victims of prison rape live in fear, may feel constantly threatened, and can turn to self-destructive activities.[33] Many victims question their masculinity and undergo a personal devaluation. Some victims of prison sexual assault become violent, attacking and sometimes killing the person who raped them. The Human Rights Watch researchers found that prisoners "fitting any part of the following description" are more likely to become rape victims: "young, small in size, physically weak, white, gay, first offender, possessing 'feminine' characteristics such as long hair or a high voice; being unassertive, unaggressive, shy, intellectual, not street-smart, or 'passive'; or having been convicted of a sexual offense against a minor." The researchers also noted that "prisoners with several overlapping characteristics are much more likely than other prisoners to be targeted for abuse."

The report concluded that to reduce the incidence of prison rape, "prison officials should take considerably more care in matching cell mates, and that, as a general rule, double-celling should be avoided." Learn more about male rape in U.S. prisons at Library Extra 14–3 at cjtoday.com.

LIBRARY
Extra
■ ■ ■ ■

The Female Inmate's World

As Chapter 13 showed, more than 112,000 women were imprisoned in state and federal correctional institutions throughout the United States at the start of 2007, accounting for 7% of all prison inmates.[34] Texas had the largest number of female prisoners (13,799), exceeding even the federal government.[35] Figure 14–1 provides a breakdown of the total American prison population by gender and ethnicity. While there are still far more men imprisoned across the nation than women (approximately 14 men for every woman), the number of female inmates is rising.[36] In 1981, women made up only 4% of the nation's overall prison population, but the number of female inmates nearly tripled during the 1980s and is continuing to grow at a rate greater than that of male inmates.

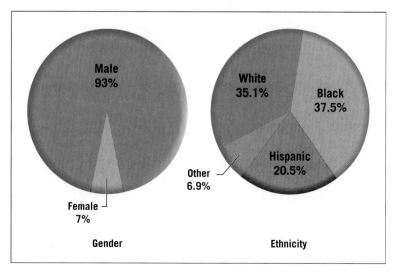

FIGURE 14–1

Prison inmates by gender and ethnicity in state and federal prisons.

Source: William J. Sabol, Heather Couture, and Paige M. Harrison, *Prisoners in 2006* (Washington, DC: Bureau of Justice Statistics, 2007).

In 2003, the National Institute of Corrections (NIC) published the results of its three-year project on female offenders in adult correctional settings.[37] Findings from the study produced the national profile of incarcerated women that is shown in Table 14–1.

NIC says that "women involved in the criminal justice system represent a population marginalized by race, class, and gender."[38] Black women, for example, are overrepresented in correctional populations. While they constitute only 13% of women in the United States, nearly 50% of women in prison are black, and black women are eight times more likely than white women to be incarcerated.

Study authors found that most female offenders are nonviolent and that their crimes are typically less threatening to community safety than those of male offenders. Female offenders, according to the study, are disproportionately low-income women of color who are undereducated and unskilled, with sporadic employment histories. They are less likely than men to have committed violent offenses and are more likely to have been convicted of crimes involving drugs or property. Often, their property offenses are economically driven, motivated by poverty and by the abuse of alcohol or other drugs. The majority of offenses committed by women who are in prisons and jails are nonviolent drug and property crimes.

According to NIC, women face life circumstances that tend to be specific to their gender, such as sexual abuse, sexual assault, domestic violence, and the responsibility of being the primary caregiver for dependent children. Research shows that female offenders differ significantly from their male counterparts regarding personal histories and pathways to crime.[39] A female offender, for example, is more likely to have been the primary caretaker of young children at the time of her arrest, more likely to have experienced physical and/or sexual abuse, and more likely to have distinctive physical and mental health needs.

The most common pathways to crime for women, according to NIC, involve survival strategies that result from physical and sexual abuse, poverty, and substance abuse. Consequently, the first life circumstance that the NIC study examined closely was physical and sexual abuse. "Not all women who suffer abuse commit crimes, but one of the things most women in prison share is a background of victimization," says Harvard University researcher Angel Browne. Supporting data come from BJS findings showing that about half (48%) of women in jail (but only 13% of men) and half (48%) of women in state and federal prisons (but only 12% of men) had been physically or sexually abused before incarceration.[40] Women in prison are three times more likely to have a history of abuse than men in prison.[41] Approximately 37% of women in state prison, 23% of women in federal prison, 37% of women in jail, and 28% of women on probation reported physical or sexual abuse before the age of 18.[42]

Other studies show a much higher rate of abuse than the BJS data. One study, for example, found that 80% of a sample of incarcerated women in California had been physically and/or sexually abused prior to incarceration.[43] A later study found that more than 80% of the women incarcerated in North Carolina's state prisons had been physically and/or sexually abused.[44] In interviews with women at a New York maximum-security prison, Browne found that 70% of incarcerated women reported physical violence, and nearly 60% reported sexual abuse.[45]

I beseech you all to think about these women—to encourage the American people to ask for reforms, both in sentencing guidelines, in length of incarceration for nonviolent first-time offenders, and for those involved in drug-taking. They would be much better served in a true rehabilitation center than in prison where there is no real help, no real programs to rehabilitate, no programs to educate, no way to be prepared for life "out there" where each person will ultimately find herself, many with no skills and no preparation for living.

—*Martha Stewart*

TABLE 14–1   National Profile of Female Offenders

A profile based on national data for female offenders reveals the following characteristics:

- Disproportionately women of color
- In their early to mid-30s
- Most likely to have been convicted of a drug-related offense
- From fragmented families that include other family members who have been involved with the criminal justice system
- Survivors of physical and/or sexual abuse as children and adults
- Individuals with significant substance-abuse problems
- Individuals with multiple physical and mental health problems
- Unmarried mothers of minor children
- Individuals with a high school or general equivalency diploma (GED) but limited vocational training and sporadic work histories

Source: Barbara Bloom, Barbara Owen, and Stephanie Covington, *Gender-Responsive Strategies: Research, Practice, and Guiding Principles for Women Offenders* (Washington, DC: National Institute of Corrections, 2003).

The link between female criminality and substance abuse is very strong, and it was the second life circumstance that the NIC study examined. Research shows that women are more likely to be involved in crime if they are drug users.[46] Approximately 80% of women in state prisons have substance-abuse problems.[47] About half of the female offenders in state prisons had been using alcohol, drugs, or both at the time of their offense. Nearly one in three women serving time in state prisons reported committing the offense to obtain money to support a drug habit. About half described themselves as daily users.[48] To put these statistics into perspective, it is helpful to compare them to statistics on substance abuse among women in the general population. The Substance Abuse and Mental Health Services Administration reports that 2.1% of females in the United States age 12 and older had engaged in heavy alcohol use within the 30 days preceding the survey, 4.1% had used an illicit drug, and 1.2% had used a psychotherapeutic drug for a nonmedical purpose.[49] By contrast, the National Center on Addiction and Substance Abuse found that 54% of female offenders in state prisons had used an illicit drug during the month before they committed their crimes, and 48% were under the influence of either alcohol or another drug when they committed their crimes.[50] Among female offenders in federal prisons, 27% had used an illicit drug in the month before they committed their crimes, and 20% were under the influence when they committed their crimes.

Some complain that many women are being unfairly sent to prison by current federal drug policies for playing only minor roles in drug-related offenses. "We've gone from being a nation of latchkey kids to a nation of locked-up moms, where women are the invisible prisoners of drug laws, serving hard time for someone else's crime,"[51] says Lenora Lapidus, coauthor of the 2005 report *Caught in the Net: The Impact of Drug Policies on Women and Families*.[52] "Even when they have minimal or no involvement whatsoever in the drug trade," the report claims, "women are increasingly caught in the ever-widening net cast by current drug laws." *Caught in the Net* is available at Library Extra 14–4 at cjtoday.com.

The third life circumstance that the NIC study examined was physical health. Female inmates face health issues, including pregnancy, that differ from those of men. Women frequently enter jails and prisons in poor health, and they experience more serious health problems than do their male counterparts. Their poor health is often due to poverty, poor nutrition, inadequate health care, and substance abuse.[53] It is estimated that 20% to 35% of women attend prison sick call daily, compared with 7% to 10% of men. Women also have more medical problems related to their reproductive systems than do men. About 5% of women enter prison while pregnant, and most of these pregnancies are considered high risk due to a history of inadequate medical care, abuse, and substance abuse.

Sexually transmitted diseases are also a problem among female offenders. Approximately 3.5% of women in prison are HIV-positive, and female prisoners are 50% more likely than male prisoners to be HIV-positive. The number of women infected with HIV has increased 69% since 1991, while the number of infected male offenders has decreased by 22%.[54] Female offenders are also at greater risk than nonincarcerated women for breast, lung, and cervical cancer. One study, for example, found that incarcerated women who reported sexual abuse before the age of 17 were six times more likely than those who did not experience this abuse to exhibit precancerous cervical lesions.[55]

Women in prison have a higher incidence of mental disorders than do women in the community, and mental health was the fourth focus of the NIC study. One-quarter of women in state prisons have been identified as suffering from mental illness.[56] The major diagnoses of mental illness are depression, post-traumatic stress disorder (PTSD), and substance abuse. Female offenders have histories of abuse that are associated with psychological trauma, and PTSD is a psychiatric condition often seen in women who have experienced sexual abuse and other trauma. Symptoms of PTSD include depression, low self-esteem, insomnia, panic, nightmares, and flashbacks. Approximately 75% of women who have serious mental illness also suffer from substance-abuse disorders, and about one-quarter of all women in state prisons are receiving medication for psychological disorders. A total of 22.3% of women in jail have been diagnosed with PTSD, 13.7% have been diagnosed with a current episode of depression, and about 17% are receiving medication for psychological disorders.[57] Women with serious mental illness and co-occurring disorders experience significant difficulties in jail and prison settings, and the lack of appropriate assessment of and treatment for women with mental health issues is an ongoing problem in correctional settings.[58]

Children and marital status were identified as a fifth important life circumstance by the NIC study. Eighty percent of women entering prison are mothers, and 85% of those women had custody of their children at the time of admission. Approximately 70% of all women under correctional supervision have at least one child younger than age 18. Two-thirds of incarcerated women have minor children; about two-thirds of women in state prisons and half of women in federal prisons had lived with their young children before entering prison. One out of four women entering prison has either recently given birth or is pregnant. Pregnant inmates, many of whom are drug users, malnourished, or sick, often receive little prenatal care—a situation that risks additional complications.

We must remember always that the doors of prisons swing both ways.

—Mary Belle Harris, the first federal female warden

LIBRARY
Extra
▪▪▪▪

It is estimated that 1.3 million minor children have a mother who is under correctional supervision, and more than 250,000 minor children have mothers in jail or prison.[59] Separation from their children is a significant deprivation for many women. Although husbands or boyfriends may assume responsibility for the children of their imprisoned partners, this outcome is the exception to the rule. Eventually, many children of imprisoned mothers are placed into foster care or are put up for adoption.

Some states do offer parenting classes for female inmates with children. In a national survey of prisons for women, 36 states responded that they provide parenting programs that deal with caretaking, reducing violence toward children, visitation problems, and related issues.[60] Some offer play areas furnished with toys, while others attempt to alleviate difficulties attending mother–child visits. The typical program studied meets for two hours per week and lasts from four to nine weeks.

Of children whose fathers are incarcerated, approximately 90% live with their mothers; only 25% of the children of female offenders live with their fathers. Grandparents are most likely to be the caregivers of the children of female offenders. Approximately 10% of these children are in foster care or group homes. More than half of the children of female prisoners never visit their mothers during the period of incarceration.[61] The lack of visits is due primarily to the remote location of prisons, a lack of transportation, and the inability of caregivers to arrange visitation.

Women under criminal justice supervision are more likely than the general population never to have been married. In one survey, nearly half of the women in jail and prison reported that they had never been married.[62] Forty-two percent of women on probation reported that they had never been married, and about 31% of women in prison reported that they were either separated or divorced.

Education and employment were the final life circumstances that the NIC study examined. An estimated 55% of women in local jails, 56% of women in state prisons, and 73% of women in federal prisons have a high school diploma.[63] Approximately 40% of the women in state prisons report that they were employed full-time at the time of their arrest. This compares with almost 60% of males.[64] About 37% of women and 28% of men had incomes of less than $600 per month prior to arrest. Most of the jobs held by women were low-skill entry-level jobs with low pay. Two-thirds of the women reported they had never held a job that paid more than $6.50 per hour. Women are less likely than men to have engaged in vocational training before incarceration. Those who did receive vocational training in the community tended to focus on traditional women's jobs, such as cosmetology, clerical work, and food service.

Gender Responsiveness

Critics have long charged that female inmates face a prison system designed for male inmates and run by men. Consequently, meaningful prison programs for women are often lacking, and the ones that are in place were originally based on models adapted from men's prisons or were based on traditional views of female roles that leave little room for employment opportunities in the contemporary world. Many trade-training programs still emphasize low-paying jobs, such as cook, beautician, or laundry machine operator, and classes in homemaking are not uncommon.

A central purpose of the NIC report on the female offender was to identify effective gender-responsive approaches for managing female prisoners. The study defined gender responsiveness as "creating an environment . . . that reflects an understanding of the realities of women's lives and addresses the issues of women."[65] The NIC report concluded with a call for recognition of the behavioral and social differences between female and male offenders—especially those that have specific implications for gender-responsive policies and practices. Among the report's recommendations are the following:

- The creation of an effective system for female offenders that is structured differently from a system for male offenders
- The development of gender-responsive policies and practices targeting women's pathways to criminality in order to provide effective interventions that address the intersecting issues of substance abuse, trauma, mental health needs, and economic marginality
- The modification of criminal justice sanctions and interventions to recognize the low risk to public safety represented by the typical female offender
- The consideration of women's relationships, especially those with their children, and women's roles in the community in deciding appropriate correctional sanctions

The NIC study concluded that gender-responsive correctional practices can improve outcomes for female offenders by considering their histories, behaviors, and life circumstances. It also suggested that investments in gender-responsive policy and procedures will likely produce long-term dividends for the criminal justice system and the community as well as for female offenders and their families. Read the entire NIC report at Library Extra 14–5 at cjtoday.com.

LIBRARY
Extra

Institutions for Women

Most female inmates are housed in centralized state facilities known as women's prisons, which are dedicated exclusively to incarcerating female felons. Some states, however, particularly those with small populations, continue to keep female prisoners in special wings of what are otherwise institutions for men. Although there is not a typical prison for women, the American Correctional Association's (ACAs) 1990 report by the Task Force on the Female Offender found that the institutions that house female inmates could be generally described as follows:[66]

- Most prisons for women are located in towns with fewer than 25,000 inhabitants.
- A significant number of facilities were not designed to house female inmates.
- Some facilities that house female inmates also house men.
- Few facilities for women have programs especially designed for female offenders.
- Few major disturbances or escapes are reported among female inmates.
- Substance abuse among female inmates is very high.
- Few work assignments are available to female inmates.

Social Structure in Women's Prisons

"Aside from sharing the experience of being incarcerated," says Professor Marsha Clowers of the John Jay College of Criminal Justice, "female prisoners have much in common."[67] Because so many female inmates share social characteristics such as lack of education and a history of abuse, they often also share similar values and behaviors. Early prison researchers found that many female inmates construct organized pseudofamilies. Typical of such studies are D. Ward and G. Kassebaum's *Women's Prison* (1966),[68] Esther Heffernan's *Making It in Prison* (1972),[69] and Rose Giallombardo's *Society of Women* (1966).[70]

A female inmate housed in the segregation unit of a Rhode Island correctional facility because of disciplinary problems. The number of women in prison is growing steadily. Why?

Richard Falco/Black Star

Giallombardo, for example, examined the Federal Reformatory for Women at Alderson, West Virginia, spending a year gathering data in the early 1960s. Focusing closely on the social formation of families among female inmates, she entitled one of her chapters "The Homosexual Alliance as a Marriage Unit." In it, she described in great detail the sexual identities assumed by women at Alderson and the symbols they chose to communicate those roles. Hairstyle, dress, language, and mannerisms were all used to signify "maleness" or "femaleness." Giallombardo detailed "the anatomy of the marriage relationship from courtship to 'fall out,' that is, from inception to the parting of the ways, or divorce."[71] Romantic love at Alderson was of central importance to any relationship between inmates, and all homosexual relationships were described as voluntary. Through marriage, the "stud broad" became the husband and the "femme" the wife.

Studies attempting to document how many inmates are part of prison "families" have produced varying results. Some found as many as 71% of female prisoners involved in the phenomenon, while others found none.[72] The kinship systems described by Giallombardo and others, however, extend beyond simple "family" ties to the formation of large, intricately related groups that include many nonsexual relationships. In these groups, the roles of "children," "in-laws," "grandparents," and so on may be explicitly recognized. Even "birth order" within a family can become an issue for kinship groups.[73] Kinship groups sometimes occupy a common household—usually a prison cottage or a dormitory area. The descriptions of women's prisons provided by authors like Giallombardo show a closed society in which all aspects of social interaction—including expectations, normative forms of behavior, and emotional ties—are regulated by an inventive system of artificial relationships that mirror those of the outside world.

Recent studies provide additional details about the nature of sexual behavior in women's prisons. A 1998 study of the Central California Women's Facility, for example, found that most of the staff and inmates alike claimed that "everybody was involved" in homosexual behavior. When inmates were interviewed individually, however, and asked to provide some details about the extent of their involvement in such behavior, many denied any lesbian activity.

A 2001 study of a women's correctional facility in the southeastern United States found that female inmates asked about their preincarceration sexual orientation gave answers that were quite different than when they were asked about their sexual orientation while incarcerated.[74] In general, before being incarcerated, 64% of inmates interviewed reported being exclusively heterosexual, 28% said they were bisexual, and 8% said that they were lesbians. In contrast, while incarcerated these same women reported sexual orientations of 55% heterosexual, 31% bisexual, and 13% lesbian. Researchers found that same-sex sexual behavior within the institution was more likely to occur in the lives of young inmates who had had such experiences before entering prison. The study also found that female inmates tended to take part in lesbian behavior the longer they were incarcerated.

Finally, a significant aspect of sexual activity far more commonly found in women's prisons than in men's prisons is sexual misconduct between staff and inmates. While a fair amount of such behavior is attributed to the exploitation of female inmates by male corrections officers acting from positions of power, some studies suggest that female inmates may sometimes attempt to manipulate unsuspecting male officers into illicit relationships in order to gain favors.[75]

Types of Female Inmates

As in institutions for men, the subculture of women's prisons is multidimensional. Esther Heffernan, for example, found that three terms used by the female prisoners she studied—the *square*, the *cool*, and the *life*—were indicative of three styles of adaptation to prison life.[76] Square inmates had few early experiences with criminal lifestyles and tended to sympathize with the values and attitudes of conventional society. Cool prisoners were more likely to be career offenders. They tended to keep to themselves and generally supported inmate values. Women who participated in the life subculture were quite familiar with lives of crime. Many had been arrested repeatedly for prostitution, drug use, theft, and so on. They were full participants in the economic, social, and familial arrangements of the prison. Heffernan believed that the life offered an alternative lifestyle to women who had experienced early consistent rejection by conventional society. Within the life, women could establish relationships, achieve status, and find meaning in their lives. The square, the cool, and the life represented subcultures to Heffernan because individuals with similar adaptive choices tended to relate closely to one another and to support the lifestyle characteristic of that type.

Recently, the social structure of women's prisons has been altered by the arrival of "crack kids," as they are called in prison argot. Crack kids, whose existence highlights generational differences among female offenders, are streetwise young women with little respect for traditional prison values, for their elders, or even for their own children. Known for frequent fights and for their lack of even simple domestic skills, these young women quickly estrange many older inmates, some of whom call them "animalescents."

Violence in Women's Prisons

Some authors suggest that violence in women's prisons is less frequent than it is in institutions for men. Lee Bowker observes that "except for the behavior of a few 'guerrillas,' it appears that violence is only used in women's prisons to settle questions of dominance and subordination when other manipulative strategies fail to achieve the desired effect."[77] It appears that few homosexual liaisons are forced, perhaps representing a general aversion among women to such victimization in wider society. At least one study, however, has shown the use of sexual violence in women's prisons as a form of revenge against inmates who are overly vocal in their condemnation of lesbian practices among other prisoners.[78]

Not all abuse occurs at the hands of inmates. In 1992, 14 corrections officers, ten men and four women, were indicted for the alleged abuse of female inmates at the 900-bed Women's Correctional Institute in Hardwick, Georgia. The charges resulted from affidavits filed by 90 female inmates alleging "rape, sexual abuse, prostitution, coerced abortions, sex for favors, and retaliation for refusal to participate" in such activities.[79] One inmate who was forced to have an abortion after becoming pregnant by a male staff member said, "As an inmate, I simply felt powerless to avoid the sexual advances of staff and to refuse to have an abortion."[80]

To address the problems of imprisoned women, including violence, the Task Force on the Female Offender recommended a number of changes in the administration of prisons for women.[81] Among those recommendations were these:

- Substance-abuse programs should be available to female inmates.
- Female inmates need to acquire greater literacy skills, and literacy programs should form the basis on which other programs are built.
- Female offenders should be housed in buildings without male inmates.
- Institutions for women should develop programs for keeping children in the facility in order to "fortify the bond between mother and child."
- To ensure equal access to assistance, institutions should be built to accommodate programs for female offenders.

Learn more about women in prison and their special needs via Library Extras 14–6 and 14–7 at cjtoday.com.

LIBRARY Extra

Female inmates in Sheriff Joe Arpaio's "equal opportunity jail" in Maricopa County, Arizona, being inspected by a corrections officer before leaving for chain-gang duty. Not all states make use of chain gangs, and only a few use female inmates on chain gangs. Should jail chain gangs be more widely used?
Jack Kurtz/The Image Works

The Staff World

The flip side of inmate society can be found in the world of the prison staff, which includes many people working in various professions. Staff roles encompass those of warden, psychologist, counselor, area supervisor, program director, instructor, corrections officer, and—in some large prisons—physician and therapist.

According to the American Correctional Association (ACA), approximately 350,000 people are employed in corrections,[82] with the majority performing direct custodial tasks in state institutions. On a per capita basis, the District of Columbia has the most state and local corrections employees (53.3 per every 10,000 residents), followed by Texas (43.8).[83] Across the nation, 70% of corrections officers are white, 22% are black, and slightly over 5% are Hispanic.[84] Women account for 20% of all corrections officers, with the proportion of female officers increasing at around 19% per year.[85] The ACA encourages correctional agencies to "ensure that recruitment, selection, and promotion opportunities are open to women."

Corrections officers, generally considered to be at the bottom of the staff hierarchy, may be divided into cell-block guards and tower guards; others are assigned to administrative offices, where they perform clerical tasks. The inmate-to-staff ratio in state prisons averages around 4.1 inmates for each corrections officer.[86]

Like prisoners, corrections officers undergo a socialization process that helps them function by the official and unofficial rules of staff society. In a classic study, Lucien Lombardo described the process by which officers are socialized into the prison work world.[87] Lombardo interviewed 359 corrections personnel at New York's Auburn Prison and found that rookie officers quickly had to abandon preconceptions of both inmates and other staff members. According to Lombardo, new officers learn that inmates are not the "monsters" much of the public make them out to be. On the other hand, rookies may be seriously disappointed in their experienced colleagues when they realize that the ideals of professionalism, often emphasized during early training, rarely translate into reality. The pressures of the institutional work environment, however, soon force most corrections personnel to adopt a united front when relating to inmates.

One of the leading formative influences on staff culture is the potential threat that inmates pose. Inmates far outnumber corrections personnel in every institution, and the hostility they feel for guards is only barely hidden even at the best of times. Corrections personnel know that however friendly inmates may appear, a sudden change in the institutional climate—from a simple

Actor Tom Hanks playing the role of a corrections officer in the movie *The Green Mile*. The job of a corrections officer centers largely on the custody and control of inmates, but growing professionalism is enhancing both personal opportunities and job satisfaction among officers. Why is professionalism important to job satisfaction?

Photofest

FREEDOM OR SAFETY?
You Decide

Dress Codes and Public Safety

On July 1, 2004, the New York City Commission on Human Rights ordered reinstatement of a New York Police Department (NYPD) officer who had quit the force in 2002 because supervisors would not allow him to wear a turban while working. Jasjit Jaggi is a Sikh whose religion mandates the wearing of turbans and beards by adult males as a sign of their faith. The order, compelling the police department to grant a Sikh employee a religious accommodation, was the first such ruling in the nation issued to a law enforcement agency.

Although turbaned corrections officers are a rarity, some observers have pointed to the possibility of similar lawsuits in the corrections arena. One way for agencies and businesses to avoid legal action comes from the resolution of a religious bias claim brought against United Airlines by a turban-wearing Sikh employee in 2001. Although airline regulations banned the wearing of headgear by employees while indoors, company officials were able to avoid civil liability by offering the man six alternative jobs where he could wear a turban.

YOU DECIDE

How might dress codes relate to public safety? Should agencies have the authority to enforce dress codes without fear of civil liability if those codes enhance public safety? What if they merely enforce uniformity of appearance? How do these ideas apply to correctional agencies?

Jasjit Jaggi directing traffic headed toward the Brooklyn Bridge in New York City in 2004. Jaggi, a devout Sikh, quit the New York Police Department in 2002 because his supervisors would not allow him to wear a turban on the job. He was reinstated by the New York City Commission on Human Rights. Jaggi's experience highlights the clash of cultures for all justice system workers, including corrections officers. What limits, if any, should corrections administrators set on faith-based personal displays? How might such limits relate to the security needs of correctional facilities?

Todd Maisel/New York Daily News

References: New York City Commission on Human Rights, "Sikh Traffic Enforcement Agent Returns to Work in Landmark Case," *NYC Commission on Human Rights Newsletter*, summer/fall 2004, p. 1; Sikh Coalition, Office of Community Relations, "Petition to Mayor Bloomberg: Allow Turbaned Sikhs to Serve as Officers in the NYPD," http://www.petitiononline.com/SikhNYPD/petition.html (accessed July 30, 2006); and Bureau of National Affairs, Inc., "Religious Bias, Indoor Head-Gear Ban, Offering Six Other Jobs to Turban-Wearing Sikh Sufficient Accommodation," *Employment Discrimination Report*, Vol. 18, p. 469, http://www.bna.com/current/edr/topa.htm (accessed July 30, 2006).

disturbance on the yard to a full-blown riot—can quickly and violently unmask deep-rooted feelings of mistrust and hatred.

As in years past, prison staffers are still most concerned with custody and control. Society, especially under the just deserts philosophy of criminal sentencing, expects corrections staff to keep inmates in custody; this is the basic prerequisite of successful job performance. Custody is necessary before any other correctional activities, such as instruction or counseling, can be undertaken.

Control, the other major staff concern, ensures order, and an orderly prison is thought to be safe and secure. In routine daily activities, control over almost all aspects of inmate behavior becomes paramount in the minds of most corrections officers. It is the twin interests of custody and control that lead to institutionalized procedures for ensuring security in most facilities. The enforcement of strict rules; body and cell searches; counts; unannounced shakedowns; the control of dangerous items, materials, and contraband; and the extensive use of bars, locks, fencing, cameras, and alarms all support the staff's vigilance in maintaining security.

The Professionalization of Corrections Officers

Corrections officers have generally been accorded low occupational status. Historically, the role of prison guard required minimal formal education and held few opportunities for professional growth and career advancement. Such jobs were typically low paying, frustrating, and often boring. Growing problems in our nation's prisons, including emerging issues of legal liability, however, increasingly require a well-trained and adequately equipped force of professionals. As corrections personnel have become better trained and more proficient, the old concept of guard has been supplanted by that of corrections officer.

Many states and a growing number of large-city correctional systems try to eliminate individuals with potentially harmful personality characteristics from corrections officer applicant pools. New Jersey, New York, Ohio, Pennsylvania, and Rhode Island, for example, have all used some form of psychological screening in assessing candidates for prison jobs.[88]

Although only a few states utilize psychological screening, all have training programs intended to prepare successful applicants for prison work. New York, for example, requires trainees to complete six weeks of classroom-based instruction, 40 hours of rifle range practice, and six weeks of on-the-job training. Training days begin around 5 A.M. with a mile run and conclude after dark with study halls for students who need extra help. To keep pace with rising inmate populations, the state has often had to run a number of simultaneous training academies.[89]

Prison Riots

In 2004, a disturbance took place at the medium- to high-security Arizona State Prison complex–Lewis. Two corrections officers and a staff member were injured in a ruckus that broke out during breakfast preparations, and two other officers were captured and held hostage for 15 days in a watchtower. The episode, which was followed by the major national news services, may have begun as an escape attempt. Officials were able to keep disorder from spreading to the rest of the fa-

The Arizona State Prison Complex at Lewis, where two inmates held two corrections officers hostage in a watchtower in 2004. One officer, a female, was raped. On April 30, 2004, inmate Steven Coy was sentenced to seven consecutive life sentences for his part in the hostage crisis. How can the safety of corrections workers be improved?

Tom Hood/AP Wide World Photos

Ethics and Professionalism

American Correctional Association Code of Ethics

PREAMBLE

The American Correctional Association expects of its members unfailing honesty, respect for the dignity and individuality of human beings and a commitment to professional and compassionate service. To this end, we subscribe to the following principles:

- Members shall respect and protect the civil and legal rights of all individuals.
- Members shall treat every professional situation with concern for the welfare of the individuals involved and with no intent to personal gain.
- Members shall maintain relationships with colleagues to promote mutual respect within the profession and improve the quality of service.
- Members shall make public criticisms of their colleagues or their agencies only when warranted, verifiable, and constructive.
- Members shall respect the importance of all disciplines within the criminal justice system and work to improve cooperation with each segment.
- Members shall honor the public's right to information and share information with the public to the extent permitted by law subject to individuals' right to privacy.
- Members shall respect and protect the right of the public to be safeguarded from criminal activity.
- Members shall refrain from using their positions to secure personal privileges or advantages.
- Members shall refrain from allowing personal interest to impair objectivity in the performance of duty while acting in an official capacity.
- Members shall refrain from entering into any formal or informal activity or agreement which presents a conflict of interest or is inconsistent with the conscientious performance of duties.

- Members shall refrain from accepting any gifts, service, or favor that is or appears to be improper or implies an obligation inconsistent with the free and objective exercise of professional duties.
- Members shall clearly differentiate between personal views/statements and views/statements/positions made on behalf of the agency or association.
- Members shall report to appropriate authorities any corrupt or unethical behaviors in which there is sufficient evidence to justify review.
- Members shall refrain from discriminating against any individual because of race, gender, creed, national origin, religious affiliation, age, disability, or any other type of prohibited discrimination.
- Members shall preserve the integrity of private information; they shall refrain from seeking information on individuals beyond that which is necessary to implement responsibilities and perform their duties; members shall refrain from revealing nonpublic information unless expressly authorized to do so.
- Members shall make all appointments, promotions, and dismissals in accordance with established civil service rules, applicable contract agreements, and individual merit, and not in furtherance of partisan interests.
- Members shall respect, promote, and contribute to a workplace that is safe, healthy, and free of harassment in any form.

Adopted August 1975 at the 105th Congress of Correction. Revised August 1990 at the 120th Congress of Correction. Revised August 1994 at the 124th Congress of Correction.

THINKING ABOUT ETHICS

1. How does the American Correctional Association's Code of Ethics differ from the American Jail Association's Code of Ethics found in Chapter 13? How is it similar?

2. Do you think that one code of ethics should cover corrections officers working in both jails and prisons? Why or why not?

Source: American Correctional Association. Reprinted with permission. Visit the American Correctional Association at http://www.corrections.com/aca.

---

cility, and the incident ended when inmates released the officers and surrendered. "It could have been a lot worse," said Joe Masella, president of the Arizona Correctional Peace Officers' Association. "Once these inmates get a taste of blood, so to speak, there's no telling what they can do."[90]

Although today's prisons are relatively calm, the ten years between 1970 and 1980 have been called the "explosive decade" of prison riots.[91] The decade began with a massive uprising at Attica Prison in New York State in September 1971, in which 43 deaths occurred and more than 80 men were wounded. The decade ended in 1980 in Santa Fe, New Mexico. There, in a riot at the New Mexico Penitentiary, 33 inmates died, the victims of vengeful prisoners out to eliminate rats and informants. Many of the deaths involved mutilation and torture. More than 200 other inmates were beaten and sexually assaulted, and the prison was virtually destroyed.

While the number of prison riots decreased after the 1970s, they did continue. For 11 days in 1987, the federal penitentiary in Atlanta, Georgia, was under the control of inmates. The institution was heavily damaged, and inmates had to be temporarily relocated while it was rebuilt. The

Atlanta riot followed on the heels of a similar, but less intense, disturbance at the federal detention center in Oakdale, Louisiana. Both outbreaks were attributed to the dissatisfaction of Cuban inmates, most of whom had arrived in the mass exodus known as the *Mariel boat lift*.[92]

Easter Sunday 1993 marked the beginning of an 11-day rebellion at the 1,800-inmate Southern Ohio Correctional Facility in Lucasville, Ohio—one of the country's toughest maximum-security prisons. When the riot ended, nine inmates and one corrections officer were dead. The officer had been hung. The end of the riot—involving a parade of 450 inmates—was televised as prisoners had demanded. Among other demands were (1) no retaliation by officials, (2) review of medical staffing and care, (3) review of mail and visitation rules, (4) review of commissary prices, and (5) better enforcement against what the inmates called "inappropriate supervision."[93]

Riots related to inmate grievances over perceived disparities in federal drug-sentencing policies and the possible loss of weight-lifting equipment occurred throughout the federal prison system in October 1995. Within a few days, the unrest led to a nationwide lockdown of 73 federal prisons. Although fires were set and a number of inmates and guards were injured, no deaths resulted. In February 2000, a riot between 200 black and Hispanic prisoners in California's Pelican Bay State Prison resulted in the death of one inmate. Fifteen other inmates were wounded. Then, in November 2000, 32 inmates took a dozen corrections officers hostage at the privately run Torrance County Detention Facility in Estancia, New Mexico. Two of the officers were stabbed and seriously injured, while another eight were beaten. The riot was finally quelled after an emergency-response team threw tear-gas canisters into the area where the prisoners had barricaded themselves.[94]

In 2005, 42 inmates were injured when a fight broke out during breakfast between Hispanic and white prisoners at California's San Quentin State Prison. The riot occurred in a section of the prison housing about 900 inmates who were under lockdown because of previous fighting between the groups.[95] In 2007, a two-hour disturbance at the medium-security New Castle Correctional Facility, about 45 miles east of Indianapolis, injured two staff members and resulted in a number of fires at the facility. The prison, built to house 2,200 inmates, held about 1,000 at the time of the disturbance but will soon house up to 1,260 Arizona inmates being sent there under an interstate agreement.[96]

Causes of Riots

Researchers have suggested a variety of causes for prison riots.[97] Among them are these:

- An insensitive prison administration that neglects inmates' demands. Calls for "fairness" in disciplinary hearings, better food, more recreational opportunities, and the like may lead to riots when ignored.

- The lifestyles most inmates are familiar with on the streets. It should be no surprise that prisoners use organized violence when many of them are violent people.

- Dehumanizing prison conditions. Overcrowded facilities, the lack of opportunity for individual expression, and other aspects of total institutions culminate in explosive situations, including riots.

- A desire to regulate inmate society and redistribute power balances among inmate groups. Riots provide the opportunity to "cleanse" the prison population of informers and rats and to resolve struggles among power brokers and ethnic groups within the institution.

- "Power vacuums" created by changes in prison administration, the transfer of influential inmates, or court-ordered injunctions that significantly alter the informal social control mechanisms of the institution.

Although riots are difficult to predict in specific institutions, some state prison systems appear ripe for disorder. The Texas prison system, for example, is home to a number of gangs—referred to by corrections personnel as **security threat groups (STGs)**—among whom turf violations can easily lead to widespread disorder. Gang membership among inmates in the Texas prison system, practically nonexistent in 1983, was estimated at over 1,200 in 1992.[98] The Texas Syndicate, the Aryan Brotherhood of Texas, and the Mexican Mafia (sometimes known as *La Eme*, Spanish for the letter *M*) are thought to be the largest gangs functioning in the Texas prison system. Each has around 300 members.[99] Other gangs known to operate in some Texas prisons include Aryan Warriors, Black Gangster Disciples (mostly in midwestern Texas), the Black Guerrilla Family, the Confederate Knights of America, and Nuestra Familia, an organization of Hispanic prisoners.

Gangs in Texas grew rapidly in part because of the power vacuum created when a court ruling ended the "building tender" system.[100] Building tenders were tough inmates who were given almost free rein by prison administrators in keeping other inmates in line, especially in many of the state's worst prisons. The end of the building tender system dramatically increased demands

security threat group (STG)

An inmate group, gang, or organization whose members act together to pose a threat to the safety of correctional staff or the public, who prey upon other inmates, or who threaten the secure and orderly operation of a correctional institution.

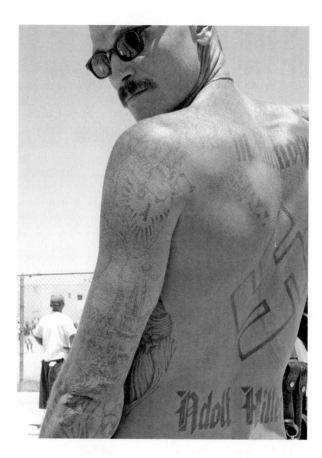

A California inmate with Aryan Brotherhood ties showing off his tattoos in a sensitive-needs housing facility at Calipatria State Prison. What are security threat groups? Can you name some?

© *Mark Allen Johnson/ZUMA Press*

on the Texas Department of Criminal Justice for increased abilities and professionalism among its guards and other prison staff.

The real reasons for any riot are specific to the institution and do not allow for easy generalization. However, a clue to prison unrest is provided when we consider that the "explosive decade" of prison riots coincided with the growth of a revolutionary prisoner subculture. As the old convict code gave way to an emerging perception of social victimization among inmates, it was only a matter of time until those perceptions sparked militancy.

Stages in Riots and Riot Control

Most prison riots are spontaneous and are typically the result of some relatively minor precipitating event. Generally, riots evolve through five phases: (1) explosion, (2) organization into inmate-led groups, (3) confrontation with authority, (4) termination through negotiation or physical confrontation, and (5) reaction and explanation, usually by investigative commissions.[101] Donald Cressey points out that the early explosive stages of a riot often involve "binges" during which inmates exult in their newfound freedom with virtual orgies of alcohol and drug use or sexual activity.[102] It is during this phase that buildings are burned, facilities are wrecked, and old grudges between individual inmates and inmate groups are settled, often through violence. After this initial explosive stage, leadership changes occur. New leaders emerge who, at least for a time, may effectively organize inmates into a force that can confront and resist officials' attempts to regain control of the institution. Bargaining strategies then develop, and the process of negotiation begins.

In the past, many correctional facilities depended on informal procedures to quell disturbances, often drawing on the expertise of seasoned corrections officers who were veterans of past skirmishes and riots. Given the large size of many of today's institutions, the changing composition of inmate and staff populations, and increasing tensions caused by overcrowding and reduced inmate privileges, the "old guard" system can no longer be depended on to quell disturbances. Hence, most modern facilities have incident-management procedures and systems in place in case a disturbance occurs. Such systems remove the burden of riot control from the individual officer, depending instead on a systematic and deliberate approach developed to deal with a wide variety of correctional incidents.

Prisoners' Rights

In May 1995, Limestone Prison inmate Larry Hope was handcuffed to a hitching post after arguing with another inmate while working on a chain gang near an interstate highway in Alabama.[103] Hope was released two hours later, after a supervising officer determined that Hope had not instigated the altercation. During the two hours that he was coupled to the post, Hope was periodically offered drinking water and bathroom breaks, and his responses to those offers were recorded on an activity log. Because of the height of the hitching post, however, his arms grew tired, and it was later determined that whenever he tried moving his arms to improve his circulation, the handcuffs cut into his wrists, causing pain.

One month later, Hope was punished more severely after he had taken a nap during the morning bus ride to the chain gang's work site. When the bus arrived, he was slow in responding to an order to exit the vehicle. A shouting match soon led to a scuffle with an officer, and four other guards intervened and subdued Hope, handcuffing him and placing him in leg irons for transportation back to the prison. When he arrived at the facility, officers made him take off his shirt and again put him on the hitching post. He stood in the sun for approximately seven hours, sustaining a sunburn. Hope was given water only once or twice during that time and was provided with no bathroom breaks. At one point, an officer taunted him about his thirst. According to Hope: "[The guard] first gave water to some dogs, then brought the water cooler closer to me, removed its lid, and kicked the cooler over, spilling the water onto the ground."

Eventually, Hope filed a civil suit against three officers, claiming that he experienced "unnecessary pain" and that the "wanton infliction of pain . . . constitutes cruel and unusual punishment forbidden by the Eighth Amendment." His case eventually reached the U.S. Supreme Court, and on June 27, 2002, the Court found that Hope's treatment was "totally without penological justification" and constituted an Eighth Amendment violation. The Court ruled, "Despite the clear lack of emergency, respondents knowingly subjected [Hope] to a substantial risk of physical harm, unnecessary pain, unnecessary exposure to the sun, prolonged thirst and taunting, and a deprivation of bathroom breaks that created a risk of particular discomfort and humiliation."

In deciding the *Hope* case, the Court built on almost 40 years of precedent-setting decisions in the area of prisoners' rights. Before the 1960s, American courts had taken a neutral approach—commonly called the **hands-off doctrine**—toward the running of prisons. Judges assumed that prison administrators were sufficiently professional in the performance of their duties to balance institutional needs with humane considerations. The hands-off doctrine rested on the belief that defendants lost most of their rights upon conviction, suffering a kind of **civil death**. Many states defined the concept of civil death through legislation that denied inmates the right to vote, to hold public office, and even to marry. Some states made incarceration for a felony a basis for uncontested divorce at the request of the noncriminal spouse. Aspects of the old notion of civil death are still a reality in a number of jurisdictions today, and the Sentencing Project says that 3.9 million American citizens across the nation are barred from voting because of previous felony convictions.[104]

Although the concept of civil death has not entirely disappeared, the hands-off doctrine ended in 1970, when a federal court declared the entire Arkansas prison system to be unconstitutional after hearing arguments that it represented a form of cruel and unusual punishment.[105] The court's decision resulted from what it judged to be pervasive overcrowding and primitive living conditions. Longtime inmates claimed that over the years, a number of inmates had been beaten or shot to death by guards and buried in unmarked graves on prison property. An investigation did unearth some skeletons in old graves, but their origin was never determined.

Detailed media coverage of the Arkansas prison system gave rise to suspicions about correctional institutions everywhere. Within a few years, federal courts intervened in the running of prisons in Florida, Louisiana, Mississippi, New York City, and Virginia.[106] In 1975, in a precedent-setting decision, U.S. District Court Judge Frank M. Johnson issued an order banning the Alabama Board of Corrections from accepting any more inmates. Citing a population that was more than double the capacity of the state's system, Judge Johnson enumerated 44 standards to be met before additional inmates could be admitted to prison. Included in the requirements were specific guidelines on living space, staff-to-inmate ratios, visiting privileges, the racial makeup of staff, and food service modifications.[107]

hands-off doctrine

A policy of nonintervention with regard to prison management that U.S. courts tended to follow until the late 1960s. For the past 40 years, the doctrine has languished as judicial intervention in prison administration dramatically increased, although there is now some evidence that a new hands-off era is approaching.

civil death

The legal status of prisoners in some jurisdictions who are denied the opportunity to vote, hold public office, marry, or enter into contracts by virtue of their status as incarcerated felons. While civil death is primarily of historical interest, some jurisdictions still limit the contractual opportunities available to inmates.

The Legal Basis of Prisoners' Rights

In 1974, the U.S. Supreme Court case of *Pell* v. *Procunier*[108] established a "balancing test" that, although originally addressing only First Amendment rights, eventually served as a general guideline for all prison operations. In *Pell*, the Court ruled that the "prison inmate retains those

First Amendment rights that are not inconsistent with his status as a prisoner or with the legitimate penological objectives of the corrections system."[109] In other words, inmates have rights, much the same as people who are not incarcerated, provided that the legitimate needs of the prison for security, custody, and safety are not compromised. Other courts have declared that order maintenance, security, and rehabilitation are all legitimate concerns of prison administration but that financial exigency and convenience are not. As the **balancing test** makes clear, we see reflected in prisoners' rights a microcosm of the "individual rights versus public order" dilemma found in wider society.

Further enforcing the legal rights of prisoners is the Civil Rights of Institutionalized Persons Act (CRIPA) of 1980.[110] The law, which has been amended over time, applies to all adult and juvenile state and local jails, detention centers, prisons, mental hospitals, and other care facilities (such as those operated by a state, county, or city for the physically challenged or chronically ill). Section 1997a of the act, entitled "Initiation of Civil Actions," reads as follows:

> Whenever the Attorney General has reasonable cause to believe that any State, political subdivision of a State, official, employee, or agent thereof, or other person acting on behalf of a State or political subdivision of a State is subjecting persons residing in or confined to an institution . . . to egregious or flagrant conditions which deprive such persons of any rights, privileges, or immunities secured or protected by the Constitution or laws of the United States . . . and that such deprivation is pursuant to a pattern or practice of resistance to the full enjoyment of such rights, privileges, or immunities, the Attorney General, for or in the name of the United States, may institute a civil action in any appropriate United States district court against such party for such equitable relief as may be appropriate.

Significantly, the most recent version of CRIPA also states:[111]

> No action shall be brought with respect to prison conditions under section 1983 of this title, or any other Federal law, by a prisoner confined in any jail, prison, or other correctional facility until such administrative remedies as are available are exhausted.

Prisoners' rights, because they are constrained by the legitimate needs of imprisonment, can be thought of as conditional rights rather than absolute rights. The Second Amendment to the U.S. Constitution, for example, grants citizens the right to bear arms. The right to arms is, however, necessarily compromised by the need for order and security in prison, and we would not expect a court to rule that inmates have a right to weapons. Prisoner rights must be balanced against the security, order-maintenance, and treatment needs of correctional institutions.

Conditional rights, because they are subject to the exigencies of imprisonment, bear a strong resemblance to privileges, which is not surprising since "privileges" were all that inmates officially had until the modern era. The practical difference between a privilege and a conditional right is that privileges exist only at the convenience of granting institutions and can be revoked at any time for any reason. The rights of prisoners, on the other hand, have a basis in the Constitution and in law external to the institution. Although the institution may restrict such rights for legitimate correctional reasons, those rights may not be infringed without cause that can be demonstrated in a court of law. Mere institutional convenience does not provide a sufficient legal basis for the denial of rights.

The past few decades have seen many lawsuits brought by prisoners challenging the constitutionality of some aspect of confinement. As mentioned in Chapter 11, suits filed by prisoners with the courts are generally called writs of *habeas corpus* and formally request that the person detaining a prisoner bring him or her before a judicial officer to determine the lawfulness of the imprisonment. The American Correctional Association says that most prisoner lawsuits are based on "1. the Eighth Amendment prohibition against cruel and unusual punishment; 2. the Fourteenth Amendment prohibition against the taking of life, liberty, or property without due process of law; and 3. the Fourteenth Amendment provision requiring equal protection of the laws."[112] Aside from appeals by inmates that question the propriety of their convictions and sentences, such constitutional challenges represent the bulk of legal action initiated by the imprisoned. State statutes and federal legislation, however, including Section 1983 of the Civil Rights Act of 1871, provide other bases for challenges to the legality of specific prison conditions and procedures.

balancing test

A principle, developed by the courts and applied to the corrections arena by *Pell* v. *Procunier* (1974), that attempts to weigh the rights of an individual, as guaranteed by the Constitution, against the authority of states to make laws or to otherwise restrict a person's freedom in order to protect the state's interests and its citizens.

The person of a prisoner sentenced to imprisonment in the State prison is under the protection of the law, and any injury to his person, not authorized by law, is punishable in the same manner as if he were not convicted or sentenced.

—Section 2650 of the California Penal Code

Precedents in Prisoners' Rights

The U.S. Supreme Court has not yet spoken with finality on many questions of prisoners' rights. Nonetheless, high court decisions of the last few decades and a number of lower-court findings can be interpreted to identify the existing conditional rights of prisoners, as shown in Table 14–2. A number of especially significant Supreme Court decisions are discussed in the pages that follow.

TABLE 14–2 The Conditional Rights of Inmates[1]

Communications and Visitation

A right to receive publications directly from the publisher
A right to meet with members of the press[2]
A right to communicate with nonprisoners

Religious Freedom

A right of assembly for religious services and groups
A right to attend services of other religious groups
A right to receive visits from ministers
A right to correspond with religious leaders
A right to observe religious dietary laws
A right to wear religious insignia

Access to the Courts and Legal Assistance

A right to have access to the courts[3]
A right to visits from attorneys
A right to have mail communications with lawyers[4]
A right to communicate with legal assistance organizations
A right to consult jailhouse lawyers[5]
A right to assistance in filing legal papers, which should include one of the following:
- Access to an adequate law library
- Paid attorneys
- Paralegal personnel or law students

Medical Care

A right to sanitary and healthy conditions
A right to medical attention for serious physical problems
A right to required medications
A right to treatment in accordance with "doctor's orders"

Protection from Harm

A right to food, water, and shelter
A right to protection from foreseeable attack
A right to protection from predictable sexual abuse
A right to protection against suicide

Institutional Punishment and Discipline

An absolute right against corporal punishments (unless sentenced to such punishments)
A limited right to due process before punishment, including the following:
- A notice of charges
- A fair and impartial hearing
- An opportunity for defense
- A right to present witnesses
- A written decision

[1]All "rights" listed are provisional in that they may be constrained by the legitimate needs of imprisonment.
[2]But not beyond the opportunities afforded for inmates to meet with members of the general public.
[3]As restricted by the Prison Litigation Reform Act of 1996.
[4]Mail communications are generally designated as privileged or nonprivileged. Privileged communications include those between inmates and their lawyers or court officials and cannot legitimately be read by prison officials. Nonprivileged communications include most other written communications.
[5]Jailhouse lawyers are inmates with experience in the law, usually gained from filing legal briefs on their own behalf or on the behalf of others. Consultation with jailhouse lawyers was ruled permissible in the Supreme Court case of Johnson v. Avery, 393 U.S. 483 (1968), unless inmates are provided with paid legal assistance.

Inmates Thomas Casey (left) and Robert McCabe reviewing statutes in the law library of the Huttonsville Correctional Center in West Virginia. Casey and McCabe are known to others in the institution as jailhouse lawyers. They help other inmates prepare legal writs and represent them in in-house disciplinary actions. Why are jailhouse lawyers important to today's prisons?

Courtesy Huttonsville Correctional Center

COMMUNICATIONS AND VISITATION

First Amendment guarantees of freedom of speech are applicable to prisoners' rights in three important areas: (1) the receipt of mail, (2) communications with others, especially those on the outside, and (3) visitation.

Courts have generally not allowed restrictions on the receipt of published mail, especially magazines and newspapers that do not threaten prison security.

In 2006, in the case of *Beard* v. *Banks*,[113] however, the U.S. Supreme Court held that prison officials in Pennsylvania could prohibit the state's most violent inmates from receiving magazines, photographs, and newspapers sent to them in the mail. Pennsylvania Department of Corrections rules prohibit all inmates classified as disruptive and problematic and who are housed at the Long-Term Segregation Unit (LTSU) in LaBelle, Pennsylvania, from receiving newspapers or magazines from all sources, including publishers and the prison library. LTSU inmates are kept alone in their cells for 23 hours a day and are not permitted access to television or radio, although they are allowed to have and read religious literature. Visits from friends and family members are limited to one per month. Prison officials argued that the restrictions on print materials placed on LTSU inmates served legitimate penological interests by controlling materials that could be used to start fires and by providing incentives for improved inmate behavior. The Court agreed, holding that "prison officials have imposed the deprivation only upon those with serious prison-behavior problems; and those officials, relying on their professional judgment, reached an experience-based conclusion that the policies help to further legitimate prison objectives."

In the case of *Procunier* v. *Martinez* (1974),[114] the Supreme Court ruled that a prisoner's incoming and outgoing mail may be censored if necessary for security purposes. In *McNamara* v. *Moody* (1979),[115] however, a federal court upheld the right of an inmate to write vulgar letters to his girlfriend in which he made disparaging comments about the prison staff. The court reasoned that the letters may have been embarrassing to prison officials but that they did not affect the security or order of the institution. However, libelous materials have generally not been accorded First Amendment protection in or out of institutional contexts.

Concerning publications produced by inmates, legal precedent holds that prisoners have no inherent right to publish newspapers or newsletters for use by other prisoners, although many institutions do permit and finance such periodicals.[116] Publications originating from outside of prison, such as newspapers, magazines, and special-interest tracts, are generally protected when mailed directly from the publisher, although magazines that depict deviant sexual behavior can be banned, according to *Mallery* v. *Lewis* (1983)[117] and other precedents. Nudity by itself is not necessarily obscene, and federal courts have held that prisons cannot ban nude pictures of inmates' wives or girlfriends.[118]

Visitation and access to the news media are other areas that have come under court scrutiny. Maximum-security institutions rarely permit "contact" visits, and some have on occasion suspended all visitation privileges. In the case of *Block* v. *Rutherford* (1984),[119] the U.S. Supreme Court upheld the policy of the Los Angeles County Central Jail, which prohibited all visits from friends and relatives. The Court agreed that the large jail population and the conditions under which visits might take place could combine to threaten the security of the jail.

In the 2003 case of *Overton* v. *Bazzetta*,[120] the Court held that new visitation restrictions imposed by the Michigan Department of Corrections (DOC) in an effort to counter prison security problems caused by an increasing number of visitors and by substance abuse among inmates were acceptable. The regulations allow routine visits for most inmates but state that prisoners who commit two substance-abuse violations while incarcerated may receive visits only from clergy and attorneys. Family members are prohibited from visiting, although substance-abusing inmates can apply for reinstatement of visitation privileges after two years. In upholding the Michigan DOC's visitation regulations, the Court found that "the fact that the regulations bear a rational relation to legitimate penological interests suffices to sustain them."

In *Pell* v. *Procunier* (1974),[121] discussed earlier in regard to the balancing test, the Court found in favor of a California law that denied prisoners the opportunity to hold special meetings with members of the press. The Court reasoned that media interviews could be conducted through regular visitation arrangements and that most of the information desired by the media could be conveyed through correspondence. In *Pell*, the Court also held that any reasonable policy of media access was acceptable so long as it was administered fairly and without bias.

In a later case, the Court ruled that news personnel cannot be denied correspondence with inmates but also ruled that they have no constitutional right to interview inmates or to inspect correctional facilities beyond the visitation opportunities available to the public.[122] This equal-access policy was set forth in *Houchins* v. *KQED, Inc.* (1978) by Justice Potter Stewart, who wrote, "The Constitution does no more than assure the public and the press equal access once government has opened its doors."[123]

RELIGIOUS FREEDOM

The First and Fourteenth Amendments provide the basis for claims of prisoners' rights in the area of religious freedoms. The U.S. Supreme Court case of *Cruz* v. *Beto* (1972)[124] established that inmates must be given a "reasonable opportunity" to pursue their faith, even if it differs from traditional forms of worship. Meeting facilities must be provided for religious use when those same facilities are made available to other groups of prisoners for other purposes,[125] but no group can claim exclusive use of a prison area for religious reasons.[126] The right to assemble for religious purposes, however, can be denied to inmates who use such meetings to plan escapes or who take

Inmate Antonio Ferreria participating in a Catholic worship service at Florida's Everglades Correctional Institution. Florida has established what are called "faith-based" programs at nine of its correctional facilities. Faith-based programs are sponsored by religious organizations and supplement government-sponsored training and rehabilitation programs. What special roles might such programs play?

© Deborah Coleman/Palm Beach Post

the opportunity to dispense contraband. Similarly, prisoners in segregation can be denied the opportunity to attend group religious services.[127]

Although prisoners cannot be made to attend religious services,[128] records of religious activity can be maintained to administratively determine dietary needs and eligibility for passes to religious services outside of the institution.[129] In *Dettmer* v. *Landon* (1985),[130] a federal district court held that an inmate who claimed to practice witchcraft must be provided with the artifacts necessary for his worship services. Included were items such as sea salt, sulfur, a quartz clock, incense, candles, and a white robe without a hood. The district court's opinion was later partially overturned by the U.S. Court of Appeals for the Fourth Circuit. The appellate court recognized the Church of Wicca as a valid religion but held that concerns over prison security could preclude inmates' possession of dangerous items of worship.[131]

Drugs and dangerous substances have not been considered permissible even when inmates claimed they were a necessary part of their religious services.[132] Prison regulations prohibiting the wearing of beards, even those grown for religious reasons, were held acceptable for security reasons in the 1985 federal court case of *Hill* v. *Blackwell*.[133]

A federal law passed in 2000, the Religious Land Use and Institutionalized Persons Act (RLUIPA), has particular relevance to prison programs and activities that are at least partially supported with federal monies. RLUIPA says, "No government shall impose a substantial burden on the religious exercise of a person residing in or confined to an institution even if the burden results from a rule of general applicability, unless the government demonstrates that imposition of the burden on that person (1) is in furtherance of a compelling governmental interest; and (2) is the least restrictive means of furthering that compelling governmental interest." In 2005, in the case of *Benning* v. *State*,[134] the Eleventh Circuit U.S. Court of Appeals found in favor of a Georgia inmate who claimed that RLUIPA supported his right as a "Torah observant Jew" to eat only kosher food and wear a yarmulke at all times.

Also in 2005, in the case of *Cutter* v. *Wilkinson*,[135] the U.S. Supreme Court found in favor of past and present inmates of Ohio's correctional system who claimed that the system failed to accommodate their nonmainstream religious practices. Perhaps the most important aspect of the *Cutter* ruling, however, was the Court's finding that RLUIPA does *not* improperly advance religion in violation of the constitutional requirement of separation of church and state.

ACCESS TO THE COURTS AND LEGAL ASSISTANCE

Access to the courts[136] and to legal assistance is a well-established right of prisoners. The right of prisoners to petition the court was recognized in *Bounds* v. *Smith* (1977),[137] which was a far-reaching Supreme Court decision at the time. While attempting to define "access," the Court in *Bounds* imposed on the states the duty of assisting inmates in the preparation and filing of legal papers. Assistance could be provided through trained personnel knowledgeable in the law or via law libraries in each institution, which all states have since built. In 1996, however, in the case of *Lewis* v. *Casey*,[138] the U.S. Supreme Court repudiated part of the *Bounds* decision, saying, "[S]tatements in *Bounds* suggesting that prison authorities must also enable the prisoner to discover grievances, and to litigate effectively once in court . . . have no antecedent in this Court's pre-*Bounds* cases, and are now disclaimed." In *Lewis*, the Court overturned earlier decisions by a federal district court and by the Ninth Circuit Court of Appeals. Both lower courts had found in favor of Arizona inmates who had complained that state prison law libraries provided inadequate legal research facilities, thereby depriving them of their right of legal access to the courts, as established by *Bounds*. In turning back portions of *Bounds*, the majority in *Lewis* wrote that inmates raising such claims need to demonstrate "widespread actual injury" to their ability to access the courts, not merely "isolated instances of actual injury." "Moreover," wrote the justices, "*Bounds* does not guarantee inmates the wherewithal to file any and every type of legal claim, but requires only that they be provided with the tools to attack their sentences . . . and to challenge the conditions of their confinement."

In an earlier case, *Johnson* v. *Avery* (1968),[139] the Court had ruled that prisoners under correctional supervision have a right to consult "jailhouse lawyers" for advice when assistance from trained professionals is not available. Other court decisions have established that inmates have a right to correspond with their attorneys[140] and with legal assistance organizations. Such letters, however, can be opened and inspected for contraband[141] (but not read) by prison authorities in the presence of the inmate. The right to meet with hired counsel for reasonable lengths of time has also been upheld.[142] Indigent defendants must be provided with stamps for the purpose of legal correspondence,[143] and inmates cannot be disciplined for communicating with lawyers or for requesting legal help. Conversations between inmates and their lawyers can be monitored, although any evidence thus obtained cannot be used in court.[144] Inmates do not, however, have the right to an appointed lawyer, even when indigent, if no judicial proceedings have been initiated against them.[145]

CJ Today Exhibit 14–2

Federal Oversight of the Texas Prison System: A Timeline

1972: Inmate David Ruiz and several other prisoners file a handwritten civil rights suit (*Ruiz* v. *Estelle*) against the Texas Department of Corrections (now called the Texas Department of Criminal Justice), alleging various constitutional violations.

October 2, 1978–September 20, 1979: The *Ruiz* case is tried in Houston.

December 10, 1980: U.S. District Court Judge William Wayne Justice finds that confinement in the Texas prison system constitutes cruel and unusual punishment. He cites overcrowding, understaffing, brutality by guards and inmate-guards known as *building tenders*, substandard medical care, and uncontrolled physical abuse among inmates.

January 12, 1981: The judge orders improvements to be made to the system and sets deadlines.

April 19, 1981: Judge Justice appoints a special master to supervise compliance with his order.

April 1982: The state agrees to halt the building tender system and to hire additional corrections officers.

January–June 1983: The Texas legislature passes laws intended to reduce the prison population.

November 1987: Texas voters authorize $500 million in bonds for prison construction.

March 31, 1990: The special master's office is closed.

November 1990: Texas voters approve $672 million in bonds to build 25,300 prison beds and 12,000 drug- and alcohol-treatment beds.

February 1992: Inmates' attorneys and the Texas Board of Criminal Justice reach a settlement agreement. Texas Attorney General Dan Morales rejects it.

May 1, 1992: Morales offers a settlement proposal.

July 14, 1992: Inmates' attorneys accept the proposal.

December 11, 1992: Judge Justice signs the settlement.

January 21, 1999: Judge Justice begins a hearing to determine whether Texas prisons should be freed of federal court oversight.

March 1, 1999: Judge Justice decides to maintain oversight of the prison system.

March 20, 2001: The 5th U.S. Circuit Court of Appeals reverses Judge Justice's ruling, ending oversight but giving him 90 days to review the matter.

June 18, 2001: Judge Justice says that the Texas prison system has improved but that oversight is still needed in the areas of "conditions of confinement in administrative segregation, the failure to provide reasonable safety to inmates against assault and abuse, and the excessive use of force by correctional officers." Judge Justice discontinues federal oversight of other aspects of the prison system, including health services and staffing.

June 17, 2002: Judge Justice orders an end to federal judicial oversight. The National Institute of Corrections, an arm of the U.S. Department of Justice, is asked to provide further recommendations to the Texas Department of Criminal Justice for a period of two years.

Source: Adapted from Ed Timms, "Judge to Lessen Oversight of Texas Prisons," *Dallas Morning News,* June 19, 2001, http://www.dallasnews.com/archive (accessed March 2, 2006). Reprinted with permission of the *Dallas Morning News.*

MEDICAL CARE

deliberate indifference

A wanton disregard by corrections personnel for the well-being of inmates. Deliberate indifference requires both actual knowledge that a harm is occurring and disregard of the risk of harm. A prison official may be held liable under the Eighth Amendment for acting with deliberate indifference to inmate health or safety only if he or she knows that inmates face a substantial risk of serious harm and disregards that risk by failing to take reasonable measures to abate it.

The historic Supreme Court case of *Estelle* v. *Gamble* (1976)[146] specified prison officials' duty to provide for inmates' medical care. In *Estelle,* the Court concerned itself with **deliberate indifference** on the part of the staff toward a prisoner's need for serious medical attention. "Deliberate indifference" can mean a wanton disregard for the health of inmates. Hence, while poor treatment, misdiagnosis, and the like may constitute medical malpractice, they do not necessarily constitute deliberate indifference.[147] In 1992, in *Hudson* v. *McMillan,*[148] the Court clarified the concept of "deliberate indifference" by holding that it requires both actual knowledge and disregard of risk of harm.

Two other cases, *Ruiz* v. *Estelle* (1980)[149] and *Newman* v. *Alabama* (1972),[150] have had a substantial impact on the rights of prisoners to medical attention. In *Ruiz,* the Texas Department of Criminal Justice was found lacking in its correctional medical treatment programs. The court ordered an improvement in record keeping, physical facilities, and general medical care while it continued to monitor the progress of the department. In *Newman,* Alabama's prison medical services were found to be so inadequate as to be "shocking to the conscience."

Part of the issue of medical treatment is the question of whether inmates can be forced to take medication. A 1984 state court held that inmates could be medicated against their will in an emergency.[151] The court did recognize that unwanted medications designed to produce only

CJ News

Inmates Go to Court for Right to Use the Internet

When a friend sent Georgia inmate Danny Williams some legal research that had been downloaded from the Internet . . . , state prison guards confiscated the package.

Prison officials said the material was prohibited under a 5-year-old regulation that, according to state Department of Corrections Commissioner James Donald, bars inmates from receiving any printed material downloaded from the Internet. The policy is designed to prevent inmates from gaining access to material on the Internet that could compromise security—bombmaking instructions, for example.

Now, Williams is challenging the policy in federal court, the latest in a series of cases in which inmates are seeking changes in prison regulations or state law to try to use the Internet to do research or communicate with the outside world.

State and federal inmates do not have direct access to computers. However, some have used written correspondence with friends or family members to set up and maintain websites and e-mail accounts to air grievances, solicit legal assistance and express political views. Legal challenges such as Williams'—along with recent reports that several death-row inmates in Texas have posted personal profiles on the social networking site MySpace.com—have ignited a national debate over speech rights and how much contact prisoners should be allowed with the public in the Internet age.

John Boston, a prisoners' rights advocate in New York, says inmates' use of the Internet—albeit indirectly—represents a matter of simple free speech that should be protected.

However, Andy Kahan, director of Houston's crime victims office, says some of that speech, potentially viewable around the world, could reinjure victims.

"It's like getting (harmed) all over again," Kahan says.

In some states, crime victims and prison officials have launched legal and informal campaigns to block all access to the Internet by inmates. Those strategies, however, have been largely unsuccessful:

- In a case similar to Williams' challenge in Georgia, a federal appeals court in California two years ago sided with an inmate who was barred under state prison regulations from receiving printed copies of Internet-generated documents through regular mail. Prison authorities feared that the materials could contain coded messages.

- In Arizona, prisoners' rights groups successfully challenged a state law that once banned inmates from exchanging written mail with Internet service providers or establishing profiles on websites through outside contacts.

The Arizona law, overturned in 2003, called for additional disciplinary sanctions against inmates if they were found to have corresponded with Internet providers or requested that "any person access a provider's website."

The Arizona Department of Corrections, according to court documents, had imposed sanctions against at least five inmates "because their names appeared on Internet websites."

A similar issue surfaced this month in Texas, when Kahan discovered that 30 death-row inmates had profiles on MySpace.com.

"Is it (MySpace's) policy to give killers a platform for all the world to see?" Kahan says. "I'm asking MySpace to take a stand.

Texas death-row inmate Randy Halprin, who was convicted of the murder of a law enforcement officer in a Dallas suburb. Halprin has a personal profile on MySpace.com featuring photos and a personal diary. Should inmates be allowed Internet access? If so, what limits, if any, should be set?
Brett Coomer/AP Wide World Photos

Do they want convicted killers to infiltrate a system geared to young people?"

Among the most notorious inmates featured on the site is Randy Halprin, 29. He was a member of the "Texas 7," a group of inmates who escaped from the state prison system in 2000 and went on a murderous rampage.

The group was involved in the fatal shooting of a police officer during a botched robbery near Dallas. Halprin was sentenced to death for his role in the slaying.

On MySpace, Halprin established a profile, which included a gallery of photographs chronicling his life from childhood to a current photo of a smiling Halprin on death row. The page is no longer accessible to the public.

Texas Department of Criminal Justice spokeswoman Michelle Lyons says that for years, death row inmates have been using relatives and others to post information on their behalves. "We cannot police the Internet for what outsiders are posting," she says.

MySpace spokesman Jeff Berman says the site is reviewing profiles posted on behalf of inmates and says it will "remove any that violate our terms of service, such as hate speech, advocating violence and threatening conduct.

"Unless you violate the terms of service or break the law, we don't step in the middle of free expression," Berman says. "There's a lot on our site we don't approve of in terms of taste or ideas, but it's not our role to be censors."

Jayne Hawkins says she believes MySpace should do more to discourage inmate profiles. Her son, Aubrey Hawkins, was the police officer killed in the robbery that involved Halprin.

"Websites that allow criminals are helping them turn into romantic figures; that is so detrimental to our children," Hawkins says.

"This kind of thing dishonors Aubrey. What should happen on death row is that these people should sit behind a locked door, and we should be allowed to forget about them."

For the latest in crime and justice news, visit the Talk Justice news feed at http://www.crimenews.info.

Source: Kevin Johnson, "Inmates Go to Court to Seek Right to Use the Internet," USA TODAY, November 24, 2006, p. 5A. Reprinted with permission.

psychological effects, such as tranquilizers, might be refused more readily than life-sustaining drugs.[152] In the 1984 federal court case of *Bee* v. *Greaves*,[153] the Tenth Circuit Court of Appeals ruled that "less restrictive alternatives" should be considered before the administration of antipsychotic drugs to in-custody pretrial detainees. In 1990, in the case of *Washington* v. *Harper*,[154] the U.S. Supreme Court held that prisoners can refuse the involuntary administration of antipsychotic drugs unless government officials can demonstrate an "overriding justification" as to why administration of the drugs is necessary. Under *Washington*, an inmate in a correctional institution "may be treated involuntarily with antipsychotic drugs where there is a determination that the inmate is dangerous to himself or others and the treatment is in the inmate's medical interest."

In 1998, in the case of *Pennsylvania Department of Corrections* v. *Yeskey*,[155] the Supreme Court held that the Americans with Disabilities Act (ADA) of 1990[156] applies to prisons and to prison inmates. In May 1994, Ronald Yeskey was sentenced to serve 18 to 36 months in a Pennsylvania correctional facility. The sentencing court recommended that he be placed in Pennsylvania's Motivational Boot Camp for first-time offenders, the successful completion of which would have led to his release on parole in just six months. When Yeskey was refused admission because of his medical history of hypertension, he sued the Pennsylvania Department of Corrections and several state officials, alleging that his exclusion violated Title II of the ADA, which prohibits a "public entity" from discriminating against a "qualified individual with a disability" on account of that disability. Lawyers for the state of Pennsylvania argued that state prisoners are not covered by the ADA. The Supreme Court ruled, however, that "state prisons fall squarely within Title II's statutory definition of 'public entity,' which includes 'any . . . instrumentality of a State . . . or local government.'"

Similarly, in the 2006 case of *U.S.* v. *Georgia*,[157] the U.S. Supreme Court ruled in favor of Georgia inmate Tony Goodman, holding that a state's claim of sovereign immunity could not bar suits brought under the Americans with Disabilities Act. Goodman, a paraplegic who filed a Section 1983 lawsuit, was able to show that his constitutional rights were violated by prison officials who failed to accommodate his disability. Goodman had been confined for more than 23 hours per day in a cell too narrow for him to turn his wheelchair, making it impossible for him to reach the toilet.

PROTECTION FROM HARM

Claims that inmates have a right to expect prisons to meet their fundamental human needs for food, water, shelter, and reasonable protection from physical and other harm (including potential harm from corrections personnel, other inmates, and themselves) are largely based on Eighth Amendment protection against cruel and unusual punishment. One well-known court decision in this area is the federal district court case of *Holt* v. *Sarver*,[158] in which conditions at two Arkansas state prison farms were found to constitute punishment disproportionate to any offense. Among other things, the court found that inmates have "the right to be fed, housed, and clothed

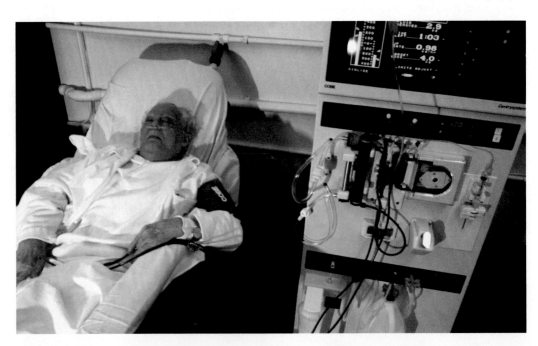

Inmate Santos Pagon undergoing kidney dialysis at Laurel Highlands Prison in Pennsylvania. Court decisions over the years have established a firm set of inmate rights. Among them is the right to necessary health care. What other rights do inmates have?

Mark Peterson/Corbis/SABA Press Photos, Inc.

so as not to be subjected to loss of health or life, . . . the right to be free from the abuses of fellow prisoners in all aspects of daily life," and "the right to be free from the brutality of being guarded by fellow inmates." In *Holt*, Arkansas was ordered to correct defects in the conditions of confinement throughout its prisons.

In the case of *Farmer* v. *Brennan* (1994),[159] the U.S. Supreme Court provided substantial protections to prison administration and staff when it found that even when a prisoner is harmed, and even when prison officials knew that a risk of harm existed, they cannot be held liable for that harm if they took appropriate steps to mitigate the risk. The case involved Dee Farmer, a pre-operative transsexual with obvious feminine characteristics who had been incarcerated with other males in the federal prison system. While mixing with other inmates, Farmer was beaten and raped by a fellow prisoner. Subsequently, he sued corrections officials, claiming that they had acted with deliberate indifference to his safety because they knew that the penitentiary had a violent environment as well as a history of inmate assaults and because they should have known that Farmer would be particularly vulnerable to sexual attack. Although both a federal district court and the U.S. Court of Appeals for the Seventh Circuit agreed with Farmer, the U.S. Supreme Court sent Farmer's case back to a lower court for rehearing after clarifying what it said was necessary to establish deliberate indifference. "Prison officials," wrote the justices, "have a duty under the Eighth Amendment to provide humane conditions of confinement. They must ensure that inmates receive adequate food, clothing, shelter, and medical care and must protect prisoners from violence at the hands of other prisoners. However, a constitutional violation occurs only where . . . the official has acted with 'deliberate indifference' to inmate health or safety." The Court continued, "A prison official may be held liable under the Eighth Amendment for acting with 'deliberate indifference' to inmate health or safety only if he knows that inmates face a substantial risk of serious harm and disregards that risk by failing to take reasonable measures to abate it."[160]

In 1993, the U.S. Supreme Court indicated that environmental conditions of prison life that pose a threat to inmate health may have to be corrected. In *Helling* v. *McKinney*,[161] Nevada inmate William McKinney claimed that exposure to secondary cigarette smoke circulating in his cell was threatening his health, in violation of the Eighth Amendment's prohibition against cruel and unusual punishment. The Court, in ordering that a federal district court provide McKinney with the opportunity to prove his allegations, held that "an injunction cannot be denied to inmates who plainly prove an unsafe, life-threatening condition on the ground that nothing yet has happened to them." In effect, the *Helling* case gave notice to prison officials that they are responsible not only for "inmates' current serious health problems" but also for maintaining environmental conditions under which health problems might be prevented from developing.

PRIVACY

The Fourth Amendment to the U.S. Constitution guarantees free citizens the right against unreasonable searches and seizures. Courts, however, have not extended this right to prisoners. Many court decisions, including the Tenth Circuit case of *U.S.* v. *Ready* (1978)[162] and the U.S. Supreme Court decisions of *Katz* v. *U.S.* (1967)[163] and *Hudson* v. *Palmer* (1984),[164] have held that inmates do not have a reasonable expectation to privacy while incarcerated. Palmer, an inmate in Virginia, claimed that Hudson, a prison guard, had unreasonably destroyed some of his personal (noncontraband) property during a cell search. Palmer's complaint centered on the lack of due process that accompanied the destruction. The Court disagreed, saying that the need for prison officials to conduct thorough and unannounced searches precludes inmate privacy in personal possessions. In *Block* v. *Rutherford* (1984),[165] mentioned earlier, the Court established that prisoners do not have a right to be present during a search of their cells.

Some lower courts, however, have begun to indicate that body-cavity searches may be unreasonable unless based on a demonstrable suspicion or conducted after prior warning has been given to the inmate.[166] They have also indicated that searches conducted simply to "harass or humiliate" inmates are illegitimate.[167] These cases may be an indication that the Supreme Court will eventually recognize a limited degree of privacy in prison-cell searches, especially those that uncover and remove legal documents and personal papers prepared by the prisoner or such documents prepared on his or her behalf.

INSTITUTIONAL PUNISHMENT AND DISCIPLINE

A major area of inmate concern is the hearing of grievances. Complaints may arise in areas as diverse as food service (quality of food or special diets for religious purposes or health regimens), interpersonal relations between inmates and staff, denial of privileges, and alleged misconduct of an inmate or a guard.

CJ Today Exhibit 14–3

The Commission on Safety and Abuse in America's Prisons

On June 8, 2006, the Commission on Safety and Abuse in America's Prisons released its much-anticipated final report.[1] The commission was formed in 2005 with support from the Vera Institute of Justice following the widely publicized scandals at Abu Ghraib prison in Iraq. The commission's avowed purpose was to explore the most serious problems inside U.S. correctional facilities and to assess their impact on the incarcerated, corrections personnel, and society at large.[2] "As President Bush was calling the abuse at Abu Ghraib 'un-American,'" said the commission's website, "many Americans raised questions about the treatment of prisoners here at home."

The commission's 21-member nonpartisan panel was co-chaired by former U.S. Attorney General Nicholas Katzenbach and the Honorable John J. Gibbons, former chief judge of the U.S. Third Circuit Court of Appeals.

During much of 2005 and into 2006, the commission held public hearings across the country and interviewed corrections professionals, legislators, and interested parties to explore the most serious problems facing correctional facilities today, including violence, sexual abuse, the degradation of prisoners, overcrowding, treatment for the mentally ill, and the working conditions of corrections officers. Interim reports were released following each hearing.

The commission's final report was built around practical recommendations intended to be useful to local, state, and federal policymakers seeking to improve conditions in prisons and jails in their jurisdictions. Recommendations were made in the areas of violence reduction, health care, high-security segregation, corrections leadership and professionalism, oversight and accountability, and the development, collection and use of standardized data helpful in the creation of public policy about prisons and jails.

Following are the commission's recommendations in the area of correctional leadership:

1. *Promote a culture of mutual respect.* Create a positive culture in jails and prisons grounded in an ethic of respectful behavior and interpersonal communication that benefits prisoners and staff.

2. *Recruit and retain a qualified corps of officers.* Enact changes at the state and local levels to advance the recruitment and retention of a high-quality diverse workforce and otherwise further the professionalism of the workforce.

3. *Support today's leaders and cultivate the next generation.* Governors and local executives must hire the most qualified leaders and support them politically and professionally, and corrections administrators must, in turn, use their positions to promote healthy and safe prisons and jails. Equally important is developing the skills and capacities of middle-level managers, who play a large role in running safe facilities and are poised to become the next generation of senior leaders.

To obtain more information about the commission and to read the commission's final report, visit www.prisoncommission.org.

[1]Commission on Safety and Abuse in America's Prisons, *Confronting Confinement: A Report of the Commission on Safety and Abuse in America's Prisons* (New York: Vera Institute of Justice, 2006).
[2]Vera Institute of Justice, "National Commission to Examine U.S. Prison Conditions: Post–Abu Ghraib, Panel to Study U.S. Prisons and Their Impact on Prisoners, Corrections Officers and Society at Large," press release, March 1, 2005.

In 1972, the National Council on Crime and Delinquency developed a Model Act for the Protection of Rights of Prisoners, which included the opportunity for grievances to be heard. The 1973 National Advisory Commission on Criminal Justice Standards and Goals called for the establishment of responsible practices for the hearing of inmate grievances. Finally, in 1977, in the case of *Jones* v. *North Carolina Prisoners' Labor Union*,[168] the Supreme Court held that prisons must establish some formal opportunity for the airing of inmate grievances. Soon, formal grievance plans were established in prisons in an attempt to divert inmate grievances away from the courts.

grievance procedure

A formalized arrangement, usually involving a neutral hearing board, whereby institutionalized individuals have the opportunity to register complaints about the conditions of their confinement.

Today, all sizable prisons have established **grievance procedures** whereby an inmate files a complaint with local authorities and receives a mandated response. Modern grievance procedures range from the use of a hearing board composed of staff members and inmates to a single staff appointee charged with the resolution of complaints. Inmates who are dissatisfied with the handling of their grievance can generally appeal beyond the local prison.

Disciplinary actions by prison authorities may also require a formalized hearing process, especially when staff members bring charges of rule violations against inmates that might result in some form of punishment being imposed on them. In a precedent-setting decision in the case of *Wolff* v. *McDonnell* (1974),[169] the Supreme Court decided that sanctions could not be levied against inmates without appropriate due process. The *Wolff* case involved an inmate who had been deprived of previously earned good-time credits because of misbehavior. The Court established that good-time credits were a form of "state-created right(s)," which, once created, could not be "arbitrarily abrogated."[170] *Wolff* was especially significant because it began an era of court scrutiny into what came to be called *state-created liberty interests.* State-created liberty interests were based on the language used in published prison regulations and were held, in effect, to confer due process guarantees on prisoners. Hence, if a prison regulation said that a disciplinary hearing should be held before a prisoner could be sent to solitary confinement and that the hearing should permit a discussion of the evidence for and against the prisoner, courts interpreted that regulation to mean that the prisoner had a state-created right to a hearing and that sending him or her to solitary confinement in violation of the regulation was a violation of a state-created liberty interest. In later court decisions, state-created rights and privileges were called *protected liberties* and were interpreted to include any significant change in a prisoner's status.

In the interest of due process, and especially where written prison regulations governing the hearing process exist, courts have generally held that inmates going before disciplinary hearing boards are entitled to (1) a notice of the charges brought against them, (2) the chance to organize a defense, (3) an impartial hearing, and (4) the opportunity to present witnesses and evidence in their behalf. A written statement of the hearing board's conclusions should be provided to the inmate.[171] In the case of *Ponte* v. *Real* (1985),[172] the Supreme Court held that prison officials must provide an explanation to inmates who are denied the opportunity to have a desired witness at their hearing. The case of *Vitek* v. *Jones* (1980)[173] extended the requirement of due process to inmates about to be transferred from prisons to mental hospitals.

So that inmates will know what is expected of them as they enter prison, the American Correctional Association recommends that "a rulebook that contains all chargeable offenses, ranges of penalties and disciplinary procedures [be] posted in a conspicuous and accessible area; [and] a copy . . . given to each inmate and staff member."[174]

A Return to the Hands-Off Doctrine?

Many state-created rights and protected liberties may soon be a thing of the past. In June 1991, an increasingly conservative U.S. Supreme Court signaled what seemed like the beginning of a new hands-off era. The case, *Wilson* v. *Seiter et al.*,[175] involved a 1983 suit brought against Richard P. Seiter, director of the Ohio Department of Rehabilitation and Correction, and Carl Humphreys, warden of the Hocking Correctional Facility (HCF) in Nelsonville, Ohio. In the suit, Pearly L. Wilson, a felon incarcerated at HCF, alleged that a number of the conditions of his confinement constituted cruel and unusual punishment in violation of the Eighth and Fourteenth Amendments. Specifically, Wilson cited overcrowding, excessive noise, insufficient locker storage space, inadequate heating and cooling, improper ventilation, unclean and inadequate restrooms, unsanitary dining facilities and food preparation, and housing with mentally and physically ill inmates. Wilson asked for a change in prison conditions and sought $900,000 from prison officials in compensatory and punitive damages.

Both the federal district court in which Wilson first filed affidavits and the Sixth Circuit Court of Appeals held that no constitutional violations existed because the conditions cited by Wilson were not the result of malicious intent on the part of officials. The U.S. Supreme Court agreed, noting that the "deliberate indifference" standard applied in *Estelle* v. *Gamble* (1976)[176] to claims involving medical care is similarly applicable to other cases in which prisoners challenge the conditions of their confinement. In effect, the Court created a standard that effectively means that all future challenges to prison conditions by inmates, which are brought under the Eighth Amendment, must show "deliberate indifference" by the officials responsible for the existence of those conditions before the Court will hear the complaint.

The written opinion of the Court in *Wilson* v. *Seiter* is telling. Writing for the majority, Justice Antonin Scalia observed that "if a prison boiler malfunctions accidentally during a cold winter, an inmate would have no basis for an Eighth Amendment claim, even if he suffers objectively significant harm. If a guard accidentally stepped on a prisoner's toe and broke it, this would not be punishment in anything remotely like the accepted meaning of the word." At the time that the *Wilson* decision was handed down, critics voiced concerns that the decision could effectively excuse prison authorities from the need to improve living conditions within institutions on the basis of simple budgetary constraints.

In the 1995 case of *Sandin* v. *Conner*,[177] the U.S. Supreme Court took a much more definitive stance in favor of a new type of hands-off doctrine and voted 5 to 4 to reject the argument that any state action taken for a punitive reason encroaches on a prisoner's constitutional due process right to be free from the deprivation of liberty. In *Sandin*, Demont Conner, an inmate at the Halawa Correctional Facility in Hawaii, was serving an indeterminate sentence of 30 years to life for numerous crimes, including murder, kidnapping, robbery, and burglary. In a lawsuit in federal court, Conner alleged that prison officials had deprived him of procedural due process when a hearing

See our Corrections blogs.

committee refused to allow him to present witnesses during a disciplinary hearing and then sentenced him to segregation for alleged misconduct. An appellate court agreed with Conner, concluding that an existing prison regulation that instructed the hearing committee to find guilt in cases where a misconduct charge is supported by substantial evidence meant that the committee could not impose segregation if it did not look at all the evidence available to it.

The Supreme Court, however, reversed the decision of the appellate court, holding that while "such a conclusion may be entirely sensible in the ordinary task of construing a statute defining rights and remedies available to the general public, [i]t is a good deal less sensible in the case of a prison regulation primarily designed to guide correctional officials in the administration of a prison." The Court concluded that "such regulations [are] not designed to confer rights on inmates" but are meant only to provide guidelines to prison staff members.

In *Sandin*, the Court effectively set aside substantial portions of earlier decisions, such as *Wolff* v. *McDonnell* (1974)[178] and *Hewitt* v. *Helms* (1983),[179] which, wrote the justices, focused more on procedural issues than on those of "real substance." As a consequence, the majority opinion held, past cases like these have "impermissibly shifted the focus" away from the nature of a due process deprivation to one based on the language of a particular state or prison regulation. "The *Hewitt* approach," wrote the majority in *Sandin*, "has run counter to the view expressed in several of our cases that federal courts ought to afford appropriate deference and flexibility to state officials trying to manage a volatile environment. . . . The time has come," said the Court, "to return to those due process principles that were correctly established and applied" in earlier times. In short, *Sandin* made it much more difficult for inmates to effectively challenge the administrative regulations and procedures imposed on them by prison officials, even when stated procedures are not explicitly followed.

THE PRISON LITIGATION REFORM ACT OF 1996

Only about 2,000 petitions per year concerning inmate problems were filed with the courts in 1961, but by 1975 the number of filings had increased to around 17,000, and in 1996 prisoners filed 68,235 civil rights lawsuits in federal courts nationwide.[180] Some inmate-originated suits seemed patently ludicrous and became the subject of much media coverage in the mid-1990s.[181] One such suit involved Robert Procup, a Florida State Prison inmate serving time for the murder of his business partner. Procup repeatedly sued Florida prison officials—once because he got only one roll with his dinner; again because he didn't get a luncheon salad; a third time because prison-provided TV dinners didn't come with a drink; and a fourth time because his cell had no television. Two other well-publicized cases involved an inmate who went to court asking to be allowed to exercise religious freedom by attending prison chapel services in the nude and an inmate who, thinking he could become pregnant via homosexual relations, sued prison doctors who wouldn't provide him with birth-control pills. An infamous example of seemingly frivolous inmate lawsuits was one brought by inmates claiming religious freedoms and demanding that members of the Church of the New Song, or CONS, be provided steak and Harvey's Bristol Cream every Friday in order to celebrate communion. The CONS suit stayed in various courts for ten years before finally being thrown out.[182]

The huge number of inmate-originated lawsuits in the mid-1990s created a backlog of cases in many federal courts and was targeted by the media and by some citizens' groups as an unnecessary waste of taxpayers' money. The National Association of Attorneys General, which supports efforts to restrict frivolous inmate lawsuits, estimated that lawsuits filed by prisoners cost states more than $81 million a year in legal fees alone.[183]

In 1996, the federal Prison Litigation Reform Act (PLRA) became law.[184] The PLRA was a legislative effort to restrict inmate filings to worthwhile cases and to reduce the number of suits brought by state prisoners in federal courts. The PLRA

- Requires inmates to exhaust their prison's grievance procedure before filing a lawsuit
- Requires judges to screen all inmate complaints against the federal government and to immediately dismiss those deemed frivolous or without merit
- Prohibits prisoners from filing a lawsuit for mental or emotional injury unless they can also show there has been physical injury
- Requires inmates to pay court filing fees. Prisoners who don't have the needed funds can pay the filing fee over a period of time through deductions to their prison commissary accounts.
- Limits the award of attorneys' fees in successful lawsuits brought by inmates
- Revokes the credits earned by federal prisoners toward early release if they file a malicious lawsuit

- Mandates that court orders affecting prison administration cannot go any further than necessary to correct a violation of a particular inmate's civil rights
- Makes it possible for state officials to have court orders lifted after two years unless there is a new finding of a continuing violation of federally guaranteed civil rights
- Mandates that any court order requiring the release of prisoners due to overcrowding be approved by a three-member court before it can become effective

The U.S. Supreme Court has upheld provisions of the PLRA on a number of occasions. In 1997, for example, in the case of *Edwards* v. *Balisok*,[185] the Supreme Court made it harder to successfully challenge prison disciplinary convictions, holding that, under the PLRA, prisoners cannot sue for damages under Title 42, Section 1983, of the U.S. Code for loss of good-time credits until they sue in state court and get their disciplinary conviction set aside.[186] In *Booth* v. *Churner* (2001),[187] the U.S. Supreme Court held that under the PLRA, "an inmate seeking only [monetary] damages must complete any prison administrative process capable of addressing the inmate's complaint and providing some form of relief [before filing his or her grievance with a federal court], even if the process does not make specific provision for monetary relief." Similarly, in the case of *Porter* v. *Nussle* (2002),[188] the U.S. Supreme Court held that a Connecticut inmate had inappropriately brought a Section 1983 complaint directly to federal district court without first having filed an inmate grievance as required by Connecticut Department of Correction procedures. In *Porter*, the Court held that the PLRA's exhaustion requirement applies to all inmate suits about prison life, whether they involve general circumstances or particular episodes and whether they allege excessive force or some other wrong.

Finally, in the 2006 case of *Woodford* v. *Ngo*,[189] the Supreme Court found that the PLRA requires *proper* exhaustion of administrative remedies before a prisoner can use the federal courts to challenge conditions of imprisonment. Proper exhaustion, the Court said, "means using all steps that the agency holds out, and doing so properly." The *Woodford* case involved an inmate seeking to file a federal suit after prison grievance procedures were no longer available to him because he had failed to follow the administrative steps outlined by the prison within the time allotted for such steps to be taken.

According to a 2002 BJS study, the PLRA has been effective in reducing the number of frivolous lawsuits filed by inmates alleging unconstitutional prison conditions.[190] The study found that the filing rate of inmates' civil rights petitions in federal courts had been cut in half four years after passage of the act. A similar study by the National Center for State Courts, whose results were published in 2004, found that the act "produced a statistically significant decrease in both the volume and trend of lawsuits . . . nationally and in every [federal court] circuit."[191]

Opponents of the PLRA fear that it might stifle the filing of meritorious suits by inmates facing real deprivations. According to the American Civil Liberties Union (ACLU), for example, "The Prison Litigation Reform Act . . . attempts to slam the courthouse door on society's most vulnerable members. It seeks to strip the federal courts of much of their power to correct even the most egregious prison conditions by altering the basic rules which have always governed prison reform litigation. The PLRA also makes it difficult to settle prison cases by consent decree, and limits the life span of any court judgment."[192] The ACLU is leading a nationwide effort to have many provisions of the PLRA overturned. So far, however, the effort has borne little fruit.

> *To return to society discharged prisoners unreformed is to poison it with the worst elements possible.*
>
> *—Zebulon R. Brockway*[i]

Issues Facing Prisons Today

Prisons are society's answer to a number of social problems. They house outcasts, misfits, and some highly dangerous people. While prisons provide a part of the answer to the question of crime control, they also face problems of their own. A few of those special problems are described here.

> *The degree of civilization in a society can be judged by entering its prisons.*
>
> *—Fyodor Dostoyevsky*

AIDS

Chapter 8 discussed the steps that police agencies are taking to deal with health threats from acquired immunodeficiency syndrome (AIDS). In 2007, the Justice Department reported finding that 22,480 state and federal inmates were infected with HIV (human immunodeficiency virus), the virus that causes AIDS.[193] At the time of the survey, 2.4% of all female state prison inmates tested positive for HIV infection, as did 1.8% of male prisoners. Some states have especially high rates of HIV infection among their prisoners. About 7% of New York prison inmates, for example, are HIV-positive.

The incidence of HIV infection among the general population stands at 140 cases per 100,000, according to a recent report by the Centers for Disease Control and Prevention. Among inmates, however, best estimates place the reported HIV-infection rate at 510 cases per 100,000[194]—more than three times as great. Some years ago, AIDS was the leading cause of death among prison inmates.[195] Today, however, the number of inmates who die from AIDS (or, more precisely, from AIDS-related complications like pneumonia or Kaposi's sarcoma) is much lower. The introduction of drugs like protease inhibitors and useful combinations of antiretroviral therapies have reduced inmate deaths from AIDS by 75% since 1995.[196]

Most infected inmates brought the HIV virus into prison with them, and one study found that fewer than 10% of HIV-positive inmates acquired the virus while in prison.[197] Nonetheless, the virus can be spread behind bars through homosexual activity (including rape), intravenous drug use, and the sharing of tainted tattoo and hypodermic needles. Inmates who were infected before entering prison are likely to have had histories of high-risk behavior, especially intravenous drug use.

A report by the National Institute of Justice (NIJ) suggests that corrections administrators can use two types of strategies to reduce the transmission of AIDS.[198] One strategy relies on medical technology to identify seropositive inmates and to segregate them from the rest of the prison population. Mass screening and inmate segregation, however, may be prohibitively expensive. They may also be illegal. Some states specifically prohibit HIV-antibody testing without the informed consent of the person tested.[199] The related issue of confidentiality may be difficult to manage, especially when the purpose of testing is to segregate infected inmates from others. In addition, civil liability may result if inmates are falsely labeled as infected or if inmates known to be infected are not prevented from spreading the disease. Only Alabama and South Carolina still segregate all known HIV-infected inmates,[200] but more limited forms of separation are practiced elsewhere. Many state prison systems have denied HIV-positive inmates jobs, educational opportunities, visitation privileges, conjugal visits, and home furloughs, causing some researchers to conclude that "inmates with HIV and AIDS are routinely discriminated against and denied equal treatment in ways that have no accepted medical basis."[201] In 1994, for example, a federal appeals court upheld a California prison policy that bars inmates who are HIV-positive from working in food-service jobs.[202] In contrast, in 2001, the Mississippi Department of Correction ended its policy of segregating HIV-positive prisoners from other inmates in educational and vocational programs.

The second strategy is prevention through education. Educational programs teach both inmates and staff members about the dangers of high-risk behavior and suggest ways to avoid HIV infection. An NIJ model program recommends the use of simple, straightforward messages presented by knowledgeable and approachable trainers.[203] Alarmism, says the NIJ, should be avoided. One survey found that 98% of state and federal prisons provide some form of AIDS/HIV education and that 90% of jails do as well—although most such training is oriented toward corrections staff rather than inmates.[204] Learn more about HIV in prisons and jails at Library Extra 14–8 at cjtoday.com. Inmate medical problems in general are discussed in Library Extra 14–9.

LIBRARY
Extra
■ ■ ■ ■

Geriatric Offenders

In 2003, Eugene Guevara of El Monte, California, shot a physician at Kaiser Permanente's Baldwin Park Medical Center.[205] Surveillance cameras filmed Guevara, who was in his late 70s, fleeing the scene using his walker. Guevara later shot and killed himself outside a fast-food restaurant.

Elderly inmates inside the geriatric unit of Texas's Estelle Prison. Geriatric inmates are becoming an increasingly large part of the inmate population. Why is the proportion of geriatric inmates increasing?

Andrew Lichtenstein/The Image Works

CJ Careers

U.S. Customs and Border Protection

Name: Jeffrey D. Adami

Position: Customs and Border Protection Inspector

City: Jamaica, New York

College Attended: State University of New York at Brockport

Year Hired: 1999

"Customs and Border Protection has given me an excellent working knowledge of the federal justice system, along with endless opportunities for advancement."

TYPICAL POSITIONS

Border Patrol agent, immigration inspector, immigration officer, immigration agent, deportation officer, detention enforcement officer, and criminal investigator. The primary mission of U.S. Customs and Border Protection is to detect and prevent the smuggling and unlawful entry of undocumented aliens into the United States. It also acts as the primary drug-interdicting agency along U.S. land borders. Entry-level Border Patrol agents are stationed in Texas, New Mexico, Arizona, and California along the U.S.–Mexico border. Immigration inspector and criminal investigator positions are available nationwide.

EMPLOYMENT REQUIREMENTS

Applicants for the position of Border Patrol agent must meet the general requirements for a federal law enforcement officer and must (1) be a U.S. citizen, (2) pass a background investigation, (3) pass a drug-screening test and a medical exam, (4) hold a valid driver's license, (5) be under age 37 at time of appointment, (6) have one year of qualifying experience or a bachelor's degree, and (7) pass the U.S. Customs and Border Protection entrance exam.

OTHER REQUIREMENTS

Border Patrol agents must demonstrate proficiency in the Spanish language.

Source: U.S. Office of Personnel Management and http://www.cbp.gov.

SALARY

New agents are hired at the GS-5 or GS-7 level, depending on education and experience, and are paid at the special salary rate for federal law enforcement personnel.

BENEFITS

Benefits include paid annual vacation, sick leave, life and health insurance, and a liberal retirement plan.

DIRECT INQUIRIES TO:

U.S. Customs and Border Protection

Twin Cities Hiring Center

One Federal Dr., Room 400

Fort Snelling, MN 55111-4055

Website: http://www.cbp.gov

For more information on the rapidly expanding criminal justice careers area, read *Where the Jobs Are: Mission Critical Opportunities for America,* available on the Web at http://www.justicestudies.com/jobs.htm.

Crimes committed by the elderly, especially violent crimes, have recently been on the decline. Nonetheless, the significant expansion of America's retiree population has led to an increase in the number of elderly people who are behind bars. In fact, crimes of violence are what bring most older people into the correctional system. According to one early study, 52% of inmates who were over the age of 50 when they entered prison had committed violent crimes, compared with 41% of younger inmates.[206] On January 1, 2007, 76,500 inmates age 55 or older were housed in state and federal prisons. The number of prisoners older than 55 increased more than 400% between 1990 and 2007.[207] Similarly, the per capita rate of incarceration for inmates age 55 and over now stands at 231 per 100,000 residents of like age and, until very recently, had steadily increased.

Not all of today's elderly inmates were old when they entered prison. Because of harsh sentencing laws passed throughout the country in the 1990s, a small but growing number of inmates (10%) will serve 20 years or more in prison, and 5% will never be released.[208] This means that many inmates who enter prison when they are young will grow old behind bars. The "graying"

Prison walls do not form a barrier separating prison inmates from the protections of the Constitution.

—Turner v. Safley, 482 U.S. 78 (1987)

of America's prison population has a number of causes: "(1) the general aging of the American population, which is reflected inside prisons; (2) new sentencing policies such as 'three strikes,' 'truth in sentencing,' and 'mandatory minimum' laws that send more criminals to prison for longer stretches; (3) a massive prison building boom that took place in the 1980s and 1990s, and which has provided space for more inmates, reducing the need to release prisoners to alleviate overcrowding; and (4) significant changes in parole philosophies and practices,"[209] with state and federal authorities phasing out or cancelling parole programs, thereby forcing jailers to hold inmates with life sentences until they die.

Long-termers and geriatric inmates have special needs. They tend to suffer from handicaps, physical impairments, and illnesses not generally encountered among their more youthful counterparts. Unfortunately, few prisons are equipped to deal adequately with the medical needs of aging offenders. Some large facilities have begun to set aside special sections to care for elderly inmates with "typical" disorders, such as Alzheimer's disease, cancer, or heart disease. Unfortunately, such efforts have barely kept pace with the problems that geriatric offenders present. The number of inmates requiring round-the-clock care is expected to increase dramatically during the next two decades.[210]

The idea of rehabilitation takes on a new meaning where geriatric offenders are concerned. What kinds of programs are most useful in providing the older inmate with the tools needed for success on the outside? Which counseling strategies hold the greatest promise for introducing socially acceptable behavior patterns into the long-established lifestyles of elderly offenders about to be released? There are few answers to these questions. Learn about some of the oldest prisoners in America via Web Extra 14–4 at cjtoday.com.

WEB
Extra

Mentally Ill and Mentally Deficient Inmates

Mentally ill inmates make up another group with special needs. Some mentally ill inmates are neurotic or have personality problems, which increase tensions in prison. Others have serious psychological disorders that may have escaped diagnosis at trial or that did not provide a legal basis for the reduction of criminal responsibility. A fair number of offenders develop psychiatric symptoms while in prison.

Inmates suffering from significant mental illnesses account for a substantial number of those imprisoned. A 2002 lawsuit brought by a New York advocacy group on behalf of mentally ill prisoners in New York's penal institutions put the number of inmates suffering from psychiatric illnesses at 16,000 (out of a total state prison population of 67,000). The suit alleges that problem inmates with psychiatric illnesses are often isolated, exacerbating their condition and resulting in a "cycle of torment" for inmates unable to conform to prison regimens.[211]

In contrast to the allegations made by the lawsuit, a 2000 Bureau of Justice Statistics survey of public and private state-level adult correctional facilities (excluding jails) found that 51% of such institutions provide 24-hour mental health care, while 71% provide therapy and counseling by trained mental health professionals as needed.[212] A large majority of prisons distribute psychotropic medications (when such medications are ordered by a physician), and 66% have programs to help released inmates obtain community mental health services. According to BJS, 13% of state prisoners were receiving some type of mental health therapy at the time of the survey, and 10% were receiving psychotropic medications, including antidepressants, stimulants, sedatives, and tranquilizers.

Unfortunately, few state-run correctional institutions have any substantial capacity for the in-depth psychiatric treatment of inmates who are seriously mentally disturbed. A number of states, however, do operate facilities that specialize in psychiatric confinement of convicted criminals. The BJS reports that state governments throughout the nation operate 12 facilities devoted exclusively to the care of mentally ill inmates and that another 143 prisons report psychiatric confinement as one specialty among other functions that they perform.

As mentioned previously, the U.S. Supreme Court has ruled that mentally ill inmates can be required to take antipsychotic drugs, even against their wishes.[213] A 1999 study by the BJS found that the nation's prisons and jails hold an estimated 283,800 mentally ill inmates (16% of those confined) and that 547,800 such offenders are on probation.[214] The government study also found that 40% of mentally ill inmates receive no treatment at all. For more details about the report, visit Web Extra 14–5 at cjtoday.com.

WEB
Extra

Mentally deficient inmates constitute still another group with special needs. Some studies estimate the proportion of mentally deficient inmates at about 10%.[215] Inmates with low IQs are less likely than other inmates to complete training and rehabilitative programs successfully. They also evidence difficulty in adjusting to the routines of prison life. As a consequence, they are likely to exceed the averages in proportion of sentence served.[216] Only seven states report special facilities or programs for retarded inmates.[217] Other state systems "mainstream" such inmates, making them participate in regular activities with other inmates.

CJ Futures

Technocorrections

The technological forces that have made cell phones ubiquitous are beginning to converge with the forces of law and order to create what some have called *technocorrections.* Members of the correctional establishment—the managers of the jail, prison, probation, and parole systems and their sponsors in elected office—are seeking more cost-effective ways to increase public safety as the number of people under correctional supervision continues to grow. Technocorrections is being defined by a correctional establishment that seeks to take advantage of all the potential offered by the new technologies to reduce the costs of supervising criminal offenders and to minimize the risk they pose to society.

Emerging technologies in three areas will soon be central elements of technocorrections: electronic tracking and location systems, pharmacological treatments, and genetic and neurobiological risk assessments. While these technologies may significantly increase public safety, we must also be mindful of the threats they pose to democratic principles. The critical challenge will be to learn how to take advantage of new technological opportunities applicable to the corrections field while minimizing their threats.

TRACKING AND LOCATION SYSTEMS

Electronic tracking and location systems are the technology that is perhaps most familiar to correctional practitioners today. Most states use electronic monitoring—either with the older bracelets that communicate through a device connected to telephone lines or with more modern versions based on cellular or satellite tracking. With such technology, corrections officials can continuously track offenders' locations and use that information to supervise their movements. As this technology expands, it will enable corrections officials to define geographic areas from which offenders are prohibited and to furnish tracking devices to potential victims (such as battered spouses). The devices will set "safe zones" that trigger alarms or warning notices when the offender approaches.

Tiny cameras might also be integrated into tracking devices to provide live video of offenders' locations and activities. Miniature electronic devices implanted in the body to signal the location of offenders at all times, to create unique identifiers that trigger alarms, and to monitor key bodily functions that affect unwanted behaviors are under development and are close to becoming reality.[1]

PHARMACOLOGICAL TREATMENTS

Pharmacological breakthroughs—new "wonder drugs" being developed to control behavior in correctional and noncorrectional settings—will also be a part of technocorrections. Corrections officials are already familiar with some of these drugs, which are currently used to treat mentally ill offenders. Yet these drugs could also be used to control mental conditions affecting undesirable behaviors even for offenders who are not mentally ill. Research into the relationship between levels of the neurotransmitter serotonin and violent behavior continues to be refined. Findings to date seem to indicate that people who have low levels of serotonin are more prone than others to impulsive violent acts, especially when they abuse alcohol.[2]

Not long ago, the National Academy of Sciences (NAS) recommended a new emphasis in biomedical research on violence as a means to understand the biological roots of violent behavior.[3] The NAS reports that research findings from animal and human studies "point to several features of the nervous system as promising sites" for discovering reliable biological "markers" for violent behavior and designing preventive therapies.[4]

It is only a matter of time before research findings in this area lead to the development of drugs to control neurobiological processes. These drugs could become correctional tools to manage violent offenders and perhaps even to prevent violence. Such advances are related to the third area of technology that will affect corrections: genetic and neurobiological risk-assessment technologies.

RISK-ASSESSMENT TECHNOLOGIES

Corrections officials today are familiar with the DNA profiling of offenders, particularly sex offenders. This is just the beginning of the correctional application of gene-related technologies, however. The Human Genome Project, supported by the National Institutes of Health and the Department of Energy, began in 1990 and was completed in 2003. The goal of the Human Genome Project was to create a map of the 3 billion chemical bases that make up human DNA. The map was constructed by high-powered "sequencer" machines that can analyze human DNA faster than any human researcher can.[5] Emerging as a powerhouse of the high-tech economy, the biotechnology industry will drive developments in DNA-based risk assessment.

Gene "management" technologies are already widely used in agriculture and are increasingly used in medicine. The progression is likely to continue with applications in psychiatric and behavioral management. Researchers are investigating the genetic—or inherited—basis of behavior, including antisocial and criminal behavior. Studies of twins, for example, have revealed similarities in behavior attributable to a genetic effect.[6] Eventually, the genetic roots of human behavior could be profiled.

Neurobiological research is taking the same path, although thus far no neurobiological patterns specific enough to be reliable biological markers for violent behavior have been uncovered. Is it possible that breakthroughs in these areas will lead to the development of risk-assessment tools that use genetic or neurobiological profiles to identify children who have a propensity toward addiction or violence? Might they also be capable of identifying individuals with a propensity for becoming sex offenders? We may soon be able to link genetic and neurobiological traits with social and environmental factors to reliably predict who is at risk for addiction, sex offending, violent behavior, or crime in general.

Attempts will surely be made to develop genetic or neurobiological tests for assessing risks posed by individuals. This is already done for the risk of contracting certain diseases. Demand for risk assessments of individuals will come from corrections officials under pressure to prevent violent recidivism. Once under correctional control, specific offenders could be identified, on the basis of such testing and risk assessment, as likely violent recidivists. The group so classified could be placed under closer surveillance or declared a

(continued)

CJ Futures (continued)

danger to themselves and society and be civilly committed to special facilities for indeterminate periods. In other words, incarceration could assume a more preventive role.

"Preventive incarceration" is already a reality for some convicted sex offenders. More than a dozen states commit certain sex offenders to special "civil commitment" facilities after they have served their prison sentences because of a behavioral or mental abnormality that makes them dangerous.[7] This happens today with no clear understanding of the nature of the abnormality. It is not difficult to imagine what might be done to justify preventive incarceration if this "abnormal" or criminal behavior could be explained and predicted by genetic or neurobiological profiling.

[1]"Microchip Implants Closer to Reality," *Futurist,* Vol. 33, No. 8 (October 1999), p. 9.

[2]Sheryl Stolberg, "Scientific Studies Are Generating Controversy," *Austin American-Statesman*, January 16, 1994.

[3]Albert J. Reiss, Jr., and Jeffrey A. Roth, eds., *Understanding and Preventing Violence* (Washington, DC: National Academy Press, 1993). Reiss and Roth call for "systematic searches for neurobiologic markers for persons with elevated potentials for violent behavior" (p. 24).

[4]Ibid., p. 12. Reiss and Roth caution, however, that "the generalizability of experimental findings from other animal species to humans is not always straightforward" (p. 116).

[5]Walter Isaacson, "The Biotech Century," *Time,* January 11, 1999, p. 42; and Michael D. Lemonick and Dick Thompson, "Racing to Map Our DNA," *Time,* January 11, 1999, p. 44.

[6]G. Carey and D. Goldman, "The Genetics of Antisocial Behavior," in D. M. Stoff et al., eds., *Handbook of Antisocial Behavior* (New York: John Wiley, 1997), pp. 243–254.

[7]See *Kansas* v. *Hendricks,* 521 U.S. 346 (1997), in which the Court approved such a practice. In the case of *Kansas* v. *Crane* (122 S.Ct. 867 [2002]), however, the U.S. Supreme Court ruled that the Constitution does not permit commitment of certain types of dangerous sexual offenders without a "lack-of-control determination."

Source: Adapted from Tony Fabelo, *"Technocorrections": The Promises, the Uncertain Threats* (Washington, DC: National Institute of Justice, 2000); and U.S. Department of Energy, "Human Genome Project Information," http://www.ornl.gov/TechResources/Human_Genome/home.html (accessed July 30, 2007).

Texas, one state that does provide special services for retarded inmates, began the Mentally Retarded Offender Program (MROP) in 1984. Inmates in Texas are given a battery of tests that measure intellectual and social adaptability skills, and prisoners who are identified as retarded are housed in special satellite correctional units. The Texas MROP provides individual and group counseling, along with training in adult life skills.

Terrorism

Today's antiterrorism efforts have brought to light the important role that corrections personnel can play in preventing future attacks against America and in averting crises that could arise in correctional institutions as a result of terrorist action. In 2005, former New York City Police Commissioner Bernard B. Kerik told participants at the American Correctional Association's winter conference that corrections officers can help in the fight against terrorism through effective intelligence gathering and intelligence sharing. "Intelligence—that's the key to the success of this battle," Kerik said.[218] "You have to be part of that, because when we take the people off the streets in this country that go to jail, they communicate and they talk, they work with other criminals, organized gangs, organized units. You've got to collect that information, you have to get it back to the authorities that need it."

Jess Maghan, director of the Forum for Comparative Corrections and professor of criminal justice at the University of Illinois at Chicago, points to the critical role that intelligence gathering and analysis by correctional agencies can play in providing critical information to prevent terrorist attacks. According to Maghan, "the interaction of all people in a prison (staff, officers, and inmates) can become important intelligence sources."[219] Moreover, says Maghan, the flow of information between inmates and the outside world must be monitored to detect attack plans, especially when prisons house known terrorist leaders or group members. Vital intelligence, according to Maghan, can be passed through legal visits (where people conveying information may have no idea of its significance), sub-rosa communications networks in prisons that can support communications between inmates and the outside world, and prison transportation systems.

The security problems presented by potential information leaks were demonstrated in 2003 at the U.S. Navy's Guantánamo Bay Naval Station prison in Cuba when a translator working with

FREEDOM OR SAFETY?
You Decide

Censoring Prison Communications

On February 28, 2005, NBC News announced that it had learned that Arab terrorists in federal maximum-security prisons had been sending letters to extremists on the outside, exhorting them to attack Western interests. The terrorists included Mohammed Salameh, a follower of radical sheik Omar Abdel-Rahman. Salameh had been sentenced to more than 100 years in prison for his part in the 1993 bombing attack on New York's World Trade Center. That attack, which killed six and injured more than 1,000, blew a huge hole in the basement parking garage of one of the towers but failed to topple the buildings.

The men are being held in the federal ADMAX facility in Florence, Colorado—the country's most secure federal prison. While there, NBC News revealed, they sent at least 14 letters to a Spanish terror cell, praised Osama bin Laden in Arabic newspapers, and advocated additional terror attacks. In July 2002, Salameh, a Palestinian with a degree in Islamic law from a Jordanian university, sent a letter to the Al-Quds Arabic daily newspaper, proclaiming that "Osama Bin Laden is my hero of this generation."

Andy McCarthy, a former federal prosecutor who worked to send the terrorists to prison, said that Salameh's letters were "exhorting acts of terrorism and helping recruit would-be terrorists for the *Jihad*." Michael Macko, who lost his father in the Trade Center bombing, posed this question: "If they are encouraging acts of terrorism internationally, how do we know they're not encouraging acts of terrorism right here on U.S. soil?"

Prison officials told reporters that communications involving the imprisoned bombers had not been closely censored because the men hadn't been considered very dangerous. The letters didn't contain any plans for attacks, nor did they name any specific targets. One Justice Department official said that Salameh was "a low level guy" who was not under any special restrictions and that his letters were seen as "generic stuff" and "no cause for concern."

Rights advocates suggested that inmates should have the right to free speech—even those imprisoned for acts of terrorism—and that advocating terrorism is not the same thing as planning it or carrying it out. After all, they said, calls for a holy war, however repugnant they may be in the current international context, are merely political statements—and politics is not against the law.

YOU DECIDE

What kinds of prison communications, if any, should be monitored or restricted (letters, telephone calls, e-mail)? Do you believe that communications containing statements like those described here should be confiscated? What kinds of political statements, if any, should be permitted?

References: Lisa Myers, "Imprisoned Terrorists Still Advocating Terror," NBC Nightly News, February 28, 2005, http://www.msnbc.msn.com/id/7046691 (accessed August 28, 2005); and Lisa Myers, "Bureau of Prisons under Fire for Jihad Letters," MSNBC.com, March 1, 2005, http://www.msnbc.msn.com/id/7053165 (accessed August 28, 2005).

Arab internees was accused of having unlawful possession of classified information, including diagrams of the prison layout and names of the prisoners. Prison administrators responsible for the incarceration of suspected al-Qaeda and Taliban members, like those at Guantánamo, face especially delicate situations as opponents of the government's policies challenge the propriety of using military assets in what they argue is a "law enforcement" role.

Prison administrators must also be concerned about the potential impact of outside terrorist activity on their facility's inmate and staff populations. Of particular concern to today's prison administrators is the possibility of bioterrorism. A concentrated population like that of a prison or jail is highly susceptible to the rapid transmission of biological agents.[220]

The threat of a terrorist act being undertaken by inmates within a prison or jail can be an important consideration in facility planning and management, especially because inmates may be particularly vulnerable to recruitment by terrorist organizations. According to Chip Ellis, research and program coordinator for the National Memorial Institute for the Prevention of Terrorism, "Prisoners are a captive audience, and they usually have a diminished sense of self or a need for identity and protection. They're usually a disenchanted or disenfranchised group of people, [and] terrorists can sometimes capitalize on that situation."[221] Inmates can be radicalized in many ways, including exposure to other radical inmates, the distribution of extremist literature, and anti-U.S. sermons heard during religious services.

Officials of the Federal Bureau of Investigation (FBI) say al-Qaeda continues to actively recruit members from U.S. prisons and looks especially to the 9,600 Muslims held in the federal prison system. "These terrorists seek to exploit our freedom to exercise religion to their advantage by using radical forms of Islam to recruit operatives," says FBI Counterterrorism Chief John Pistole. "Unfortunately, U.S. correctional institutions are a viable venue for such radicalization and

CJ News

Feds Target Terrorist Recruiting in Prisons

The federal government is working with prisons in dozens of states to improve intelligence gathering and monitoring of inmates in a stepped-up campaign to curb homegrown terrorism behind bars.

The FBI and Homeland Security Department are urging prison officials to do more extensive background checks on workers and volunteers who meet with inmates. And members of Congress are looking at possible reforms in prison security as a way to combat the spread of extremist Islamic beliefs.

Chief among the concerns is that radical Muslim clerics could have access to prisoners and coerce them with terrorist literature.

"It's a concern because we know that violent extremist groups will target people in prisons," said Donald Van Duyn, the FBI's counterterrorism director. "We're working to improve monitoring, improve training and increase awareness."

The intensified surveillance follows the recent arrests of people alleged to be home-grown terrorism suspects in London and Canada, which have raised concerns that the United States may be vulnerable to terrorism at the hands of its own citizens. British authorities said in August [2006] that they broke up a conspiracy to blow up U.S.-bound airliners with liquid bombs, and Canadian officials charged 17 people in June [2006] with an al-Qaeda-inspired plot to possess 3 tons of bombmaking materials.

Homeland Security officials, who are sending investigators to prisons around the country to gather intelligence on inmate radicalization, are worried that similar plots could be hatched in U.S. prisons. "Prisons can be a breeding ground," says Charles Allen, Homeland Security's top intelligence officer.

Among the steps that the FBI and Homeland Security are urging prisons to take:

- Develop more informants and set up more intelligence units in state prison systems. The FBI is encouraging prison systems to set up their own intelligence units and to work with local agents to share information. The bureau won't say whether it has undercover agents in the nation's prisons.

- Train more prison staff to recognize signs that prisoners are turning to extremist propaganda, sharing radical views, and attempting to convert other inmates.

- Conduct background checks on volunteers and workers to ensure extremist Muslim clerics don't have access to prisoners.

Muslim inmate Christopher McCullon, with his prayer rug draped over his shoulder, talking with Muslim corrections officer Umar Abddullah after weekly worship in a room used as a mosque at Rikers Island Correctional Institution, located in New York City. How might corrections officers help in the nation's fight against terrorism?

Stephan Savoia/AP Wide World Photo

"Our concern is not with prison inmates converting to Islam," says Sen. Susan Collins, R-Maine, chairwoman of the Senate Homeland Security Committee. "For many converts, this religion brings the direction and purpose their lives previously lacked."

A case in California shows how some U.S. prisons have spawned converts to radical forms of Islam.

Members of an extremist group robbed a dozen Los Angeles gas stations in 2005 to raise money to finance terrorist attacks on the United States.

The group's founder, Kevin James, is alleged by the FBI to have recruited members from prison. Four members of the group are awaiting trial on charges including conspiracy to levy war against the U.S. government.

"We have to wonder how many other such conspiracies are taking shape under the radar in other prisons," Collins says.

For the latest in crime and justice news, visit the Talk Justice news feed at http://www.crimenews.info.

Source: Mimi Hall, "Feds Target Terrorist Recruiting in Prisons," USA TODAY, November 7, 2006, p. 1A. Reprinted with permission.

recruitment."[222] In 2005, the Institute for the Study of Violent Groups, located at Sam Houston State University, charged that the most radical form of Islam, Wahhabism, was being spread in American prisons by clerics approved by the Islamic Society of North America (ISNA), one of two organizations chosen by the federal Bureau of Prisons (BOP) to select prison chaplains.[223] "Proselytizing in prisons," said the institute, "can produce new recruits with American citizenship." An example might be Jose Padilla, aka Abdullah al-Mujahir, a Chicago thug who converted to Islam after being exposed to radical Islam while serving time in a Florida jail. According to authorities, Padilla, who was arrested in Chicago, intended to contaminate a U.S. city with a radiological dirty bomb. Likewise, British citizen Richard Reid, convicted for attempting to blow up an American Airlines flight from Paris to Miami with explosives in his shoes, had converted to radical Islam in an English prison.[224]

In 2004, the Office of the Inspector General of the U.S. Department of Justice released its review of the BOP's practices in selecting Muslim clergy to minister to inmates in BOP facilities. The report concluded that the primary threat of radicalization comes from inmates, not chaplains, contractors, or volunteers. In the words of the report, "inmates from foreign countries politicize Islam and radicalize inmates, who in turn radicalize more inmates when they transfer to other prisons."[225] The report also identified a form of Islam unique to the prison environment called "Prison Islam."[226] Prison Islam, the report said, is a form of Islam that adapts itself to prison values and is used by gangs and radical inmates to further unlawful goals. It was found to be especially common in institutions where religious services are led by lay *mullahs* (spiritual leaders)—a practice made necessary by a lack of Muslim chaplains. The report concluded with a number of recommendations, including one that the BOP should provide staff training on Islam so that corrections officers can recognize radical Islamist messages. The report also recommended that "the BOP can and should improve its process for selecting, screening, and supervising Muslim religious services providers. We recommend," said the report, that "the BOP take steps to examine all chaplains', religious contractors', and religious volunteers' doctrinal beliefs to screen out anyone who poses a threat to security."

In response, the BOP implemented a number of new practices, and today it coordinates with other federal agencies to share intelligence information about suspected or known terrorists in its inmate population. The bureau closely tracks inmates with known or suspected terrorist ties and monitors their correspondence and other communications. The bureau also trains staff members to recognize terrorist-related activity and to effectively manage convicted terrorists within the correctional environment. A BOP program to counter radicalization efforts among inmates has been in place for the past few years.[227]

The incarceration of convicted terrorists presents new challenges for corrections administrators at both the state and federal levels. Sheik Omar Abdel-Rahman, a blind Muslim cleric and spiritual leader for many Islamic terrorists, including Osama bin Laden, is currently serving a life sentence in a U.S. federal penitentiary for conspiring to assassinate Egyptian President Hosni Mubarak and to blow up five New York City landmarks in the 1990s. Speculation that the sheik continues to motivate terrorist acts against the United States gained credibility when his attorney and three others were indicted in April 2002 for allegedly passing illegal communications between Abdel-Rahman and an Egyptian-based terrorist organization known as the Islamic Group.[228]

The current world situation, and the environment in which correctional agencies operate, is likely to ensure that the issues identified here will take on ever-increasing significance for prison administrators in the future. Learn more about prison issues of all kinds from the Prison Policy Initiative via **Web Extra 14–6** at cjtoday.com. Read about concerns over Muslim religious services in correctional institutions at Library Extra 14–10 at cjtoday.com.

Mass incarceration is a major cause of modern inequality, with large and uncounted collateral effects. Imprisonment does more than reflect the divides of race and class. It deepens those divides—walling off the disadvantaged, especially unskilled black men, from the promise of American life.

—Jason DeParle[iii]

WEB Extra

LIBRARY Extra

SUMMARY

- Prisons are small self-contained societies that are sometimes described as *total institutions*. Studies of prison life have detailed the existence of prison subcultures, or inmate worlds, replete with inmate values, social roles, and lifestyles. New inmates who are socialized into prison subculture are said to undergo the process of prisonization. Prison subcultures are very influential, and both inmates and staff must reckon with them. Today's prisons are miniature societies, reflecting the problems and challenges that exist in the larger society of which they are a part.

- Female inmates represent a small but growing proportion of the nation's prison population. Many female inmates have histories of physical and sexual abuse. Although they are likely to have dependent children, their parenting skills may be limited. Most female inmates are housed in centralized state facilities known as women's prisons, which are dedicated exclusively to incarcerating female felons. Some states, however, particularly those with small populations, continue to keep female prisoners in special wings of what are otherwise institutions for men. Few facilities for women have programs especially designed for female offenders.

- Like prisoners, corrections officers undergo a socialization process that helps them function by the official and unofficial rules of staff society. Prison staffers are most concerned with custody and control. The enforcement of strict rules; body and cell searches; counts; unannounced shakedowns; the control of dangerous items, materials, and contraband; and the extensive use of bars, locks, fencing, cameras, and alarms all support the staff's vigilance in maintaining security. Although concerns with security still command center stage, professionalism is playing an increasing role in corrections today, and today's corrections personnel are better trained and more proficient than ever before.

- As this chapter discusses, the causes of prison riots are diverse. They include (1) unmet inmate needs, (2) the violent tendencies of some inmates, (3) the dehumanizing conditions of imprisonment, (4) a desire to regulate inmate society and redistribute power, and (5) power vacuums created by changes in prison administration, the transfer of influential inmates, or court-ordered injunctions. Riots, when they do occur, typically pass through five phases: (1) explosion, (2) organization into inmate-led groups, (3) confrontation with authority, (4) termination through negotiation or physical confrontation, and (5) reaction and explanation, usually by investigative commissions.

- For many years, courts throughout the nation assumed a hands-off approach to prisons, rarely intervening in the day-to-day administration of prison facilities. That changed in the late 1960s, when the U.S. Supreme Court began to identify inmates' rights mandated by the Constitution. Rights identified by the Court include the right to physical integrity, an absolute right to be free

from unwarranted corporal punishments, certain religious rights, and procedural rights, such as those involving access to attorneys and to the courts. The conditional rights of prisoners, which have repeatedly been supported by the Court, mandate professionalism among prison administrators and require vigilance in the provision of correctional services. High court decisions have generally established that prison inmates retain those constitutional rights that are not inconsistent with their status as prisoners or with the legitimate penological objectives of the correctional system. In other words, inmates have rights, much the same as people who are not incarcerated, provided that the legitimate needs of the prison for security, custody, and safety are not compromised. The era of prisoners' rights was sharply curtailed in 1996 with the passage of the Prison Litigation Reform Act, spurred on by a growing recognition of the legal morass resulting from unregulated access to federal courts by inmates across the nation.

- The major problems and issues facing prisons today include (1) threats from infectious diseases, including AIDS, (2) the need to deal with a growing geriatric offender population, which is the result of longer sentences and the aging of the American population, (3) a sizable number of mentally ill and mentally deficient inmates, and (4) a concern over inmates with terrorist leanings and those who have been incarcerated for terrorism-related crimes.

KEY TERMS

balancing test, 521

civil death, 520

deliberate indifference, 526

grievance procedure, 530

hands-off doctrine, 520

prison argot, 502

prisonization, 502

prison subculture, 502

security threat group (STG), 518

total institution, 501

KEY CASES

Block v. *Rutherford*, 524

Bounds v. *Smith*, 525

Cruz v. *Beto*, 524

Estelle v. *Gamble*, 526

Helling v. *McKinney*, 529

Houchins v. *KQED, Inc.*, 524

Hudson v. *Palmer*, 529

Johnson v. *Avery*, 525

Jones v. *North Carolina Prisoners' Labor Union*, 530

Katz v. *U.S.*, 529

Overton v. *Bazzetta*, 524

Pell v. *Procunier*, 520

Pennsylvania Department of Corrections v. *Yeskey*, 528

Ruiz v. *Estelle*, 526

Sandin v. *Conner*, 531

Wolff v. *McDonnell*, 530

QUESTIONS FOR REVIEW

1. What are prison subcultures, and how do they influence prison life? How do they develop, and what purpose do they serve?

2. How do women's prisons differ from men's? Why have women's prisons been studied less often than institutions for men?

3. What are the primary concerns of prison staff? What other goals do staff members focus on?

4. What causes prison riots? Through what stages do most riots progress? How might riots be prevented?

5. What are the commonly accepted rights of prisoners in the United States today? Where do these rights come from? What U.S. Supreme Court cases are especially significant in the area of prisoners' rights?

6. What are some of the major issues that prisons face today? What new issues might the future bring?

QUESTIONS FOR REFLECTION

1. What does *prisonization* mean? Describe the U-shaped curve developed by Stanton Wheeler to illustrate the concept of prisonization. How can an understanding of Wheeler's U-shaped curve help to prevent recidivism?

2. What is the hands-off doctrine? What is the status of that doctrine today? What is its likely future?

3. Explain the balancing test established by the Supreme Court in deciding issues of prisoners' rights. How might such a test apply to the emerging area of inmate privacy?

4. What does the term *state-created rights* mean within the context of corrections? What do you predict for the future of state-created rights?

Discuss your answers to these questions and other issues on the CJ Today e-mail discussion list (join the list at ctoday.com).

WEB QUEST

Visit the Cybrary, and search for "jobs," "careers," and "employment." What criminal justice–related employment sites can you find? Explore some of the sites you find, and consider the possibility of a career in corrections. Document the sources you used, and list the URLs and the date you accessed each. Then answer these questions:[229]

1. What is the difference between a job and a career?
2. What career opportunities are available in corrections?
3. Why is career planning important? How can you develop an effective career plan?
4. What is the difference between education and training?
5. Why are education and training important to building a career in corrections?
6. What role might professionalism play in building your career?
7. What traits must you have to achieve your goals and to be successful in a career in corrections?

E-mail your answers to your instructor if asked to do so.

To complete this Web Quest online, go to the Web Quest module in Chapter 14 of the *Criminal Justice Today* Companion Website at cjtoday.com.

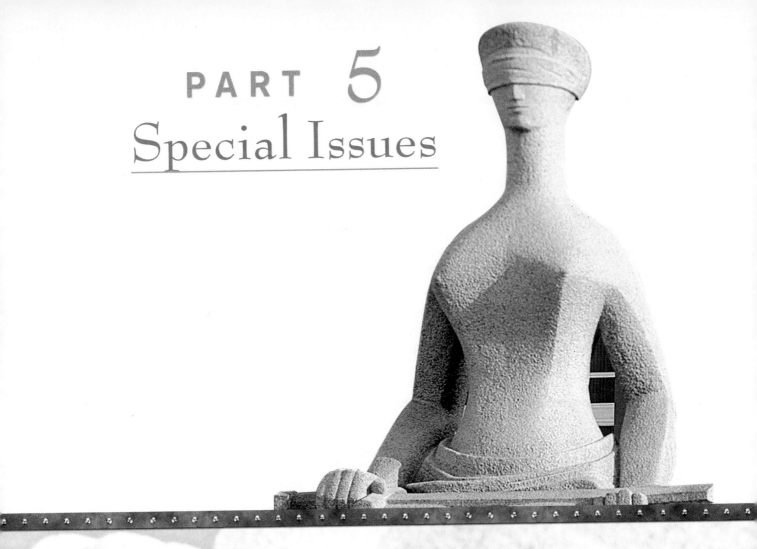

PART 5
Special Issues

ISSUES FOR THE FUTURE

The accused has these common law, constitutional, statutory, and humanitarian rights that may be threatened by technological advances and other developments

- A right to privacy
- A right to be assumed innocent
- A right against self-incrimination
- A right to equal protection of the laws
- A right against cruel and unusual punishment

These individual rights must be effectively balanced against these present and emerging community concerns

- Widespread drug abuse among youth
- The threat of juvenile crime
- Urban gang violence
- High-technology, computer, and Internet crime (cybercrime)
- Terrorism and narcoterrorism
- Occupational and white-collar crime

How does our system of justice work toward balance?

15

Juvenile Justice

16

Drugs and Crime

17

Terrorism and Multinational Criminal Justice

18

The Future of Criminal Justice

The Future Comes One Day at a Time

No one can truly say what the future holds. Will the supporters of individual rights or the advocates of public order ultimately claim the day? We cannot say for sure. This much is certain, however: Things change. The future system of American criminal justice will not be quite the same system we know today. Many of the coming changes, however, are now discernible—and hints of what is to come appear on the horizon with increasing frequency and growing clarity. Some of the more obvious of the coming changes are already upon us. They include (1) a restructuring of the juvenile justice system in the face of growing concerns about violent juvenile crime and spreading youth gang warfare; (2) the increased bankruptcy of a war against drugs whose promises seem increasingly hollow; (3) a growing recognition of America's international role as both victim and purveyor of worldwide criminal activity; (4) the war on terrorism, including its substantial potential consequences for individual rights in America; and (5) the quickly unfolding potential of cybercrimes, those that both employ high technology in their commission and target the fruits of such technology.

This last part of *Criminal Justice Today* discusses each of these issues in the chapters that follow. It also draws your attention back to the bedrock underlying the American system of justice: the Constitution, the Bill of Rights, and the demands of due process, all of which will continue to structure the American justice system well into the future.

CHAPTER 15

Juvenile Justice

LEARNING OBJECTIVES

After reading this chapter, you should be able to

- Describe the history and evolution of the juvenile justice system in the Western world.
- Name the important U.S. Supreme Court decisions relating to juvenile justice and describe their impact on the handling of juveniles by the system.
- Explain the similarities and differences between the juvenile and adult systems of justice.
- Identify possible future directions in juvenile justice.

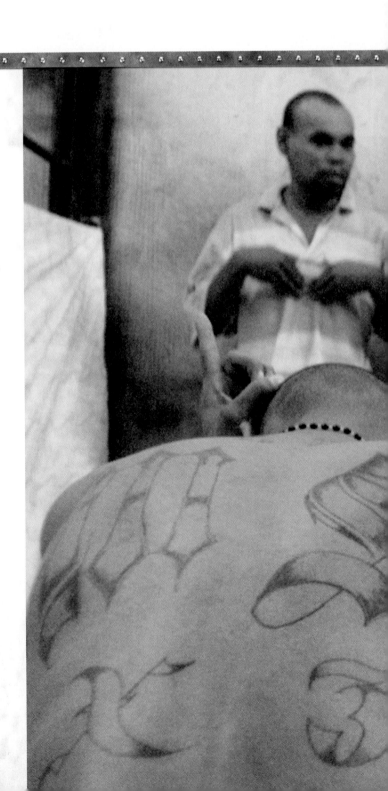

We fight for our children, that they may enjoy the promise of America. We fight for their innocence and their dreams. It is a fight for our future.

—*Former U.S. Attorney General Alberto R. Gonzales*

Our society's fearful of our kids. I think we don't know how to set limits on them. They begin to behave in severely outrageous ways, and nobody stops them.

—*David York, cofounder of Toughlove International[1]*

Hear the author discuss
this chapter at
cjtoday.com

Introduction

A few years ago, 13-year-old Tavaris Knight was convicted by a criminal court jury in Tampa, Florida, of kidnapping and raping a 43-year-old woman. Prosecutors proved that Knight, who was 12 at the time of the offense, had used a silver toy gun to force the woman away from her four young children at a playground and into the surrounding woods. Knight raped the woman twice and beat her with the gun, which he left behind.[2] Knight's case had been transferred to adult criminal court because of the serious nature of his crimes. In closing arguments, prosecutor Michael Sinacore pointed to Knight, saying, "That young man is not a child. He stopped being a child when he forced [his victim] into the woods and raped her."[3] Following conviction, Knight was sentenced to 15 years in prison by Florida Circuit Judge Jack Espinosa, Jr. Knight will likely be held at a youth facility for sexual offenders until he is 21, at which time he could be transferred to another youth offender facility until the age of 25, followed by adult prison.[4]

Crimes committed by preteens are not that unusual. In 2005, for example, a 9-year-old girl, identified only as Shanice K., admitted that she fatally stabbed her 11-year-old Brooklyn, New York, playmate in the heart with a steak knife during an argument over a rubber ball.[5] The killing occurred in the midst of a Memorial Day barbecue that was being held at Shanice's home. In another example, two 12-year-old St. Lucie County, Florida, girls were charged in 2001 with trying to drown a classmate in a lake near her home. The victim, 12-year-old Nicole Maines, had refused to surrender her swimming mask and flippers—leading the other girls to jump into the water, grab her gear, and beat her.[6] When the attackers shoved Maines's head underwater, a bystander, 16-year-old Hosea Rivers, jumped into the lake and pulled the girls apart. A police report noted that Maines suffered cuts and bruises all over her body.

A key finding of the Office of Juvenile Justice and Delinquency Prevention's (OJJDP's) Study Group on Serious and Violent Juvenile Offenders is that most chronic juvenile offenders begin their delinquency careers before age 12, and some as early as age 10.[7] The most recent national data show that in 2006 police arrested about 111,600 children ages 12 and younger.[8] These very young offenders (known as *child delinquents*) represent almost 10% of the total number of juvenile arrestees (those up to age 18).

Although states vary as to the age at which a person legally enters adulthood, statistics on crime make it clear that young people are disproportionately involved in certain offenses. A recent report, for example, found that nearly 16% of all violent crimes and 26% of all property crimes are committed by people younger than 18, though this age group makes up only 26% of the population of the United States.[9] On average, about 17% of all arrests in any year are of juveniles,[10] and people younger than 18 have a higher likelihood of being arrested for robbery and other property crimes than do people in any other age group. Figure 15–1 shows Uniform Crime Report/NIBRS statistics on juvenile arrests for selected offense categories.

OJJDP is a primary source of information on juvenile justice in the United States. A sweeping OJJDP overview of juvenile crime and the juvenile justice system in America reveals the following:[11]

- About 1.6 million juveniles (under 18) are arrested annually in America.
- Violent crime by juveniles is decreasing.
- Younger juveniles account for a substantial proportion of juvenile arrests and the juvenile court caseload.
- Female delinquency has grown substantially, increasing 76% in the last ten years.
- The number of juveniles held in public facilities has increased sharply.

There was nothing to do.

—*Terrance Wade, 15, on why he and his friends allegedly raped, stomped, stabbed, and ultimately murdered a Boston woman*

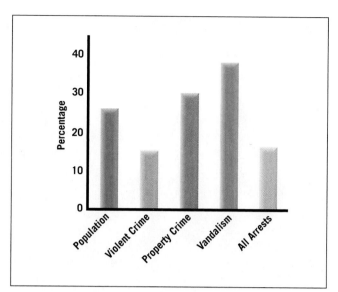

FIGURE 15–1

Juvenile involvement in crime versus system totals, 2006.

Note: The term *juvenile* refers to people younger than 18 years of age.

Source: Federal Bureau of Investigation, *Crime in the United States, 2006* (Washington, DC: U.S. Dept. of Justice, 2007).

- Minority juveniles are greatly overrepresented in the custody population.

- Crowding is a serious problem in juvenile facilities.

Learn more about OJJDP via Web Extra 15–1 at cjtoday.com

This chapter has four purposes. First, we will briefly look at the history of the **juvenile justice system**. The juvenile justice system has its roots in the adult system. In the juvenile system, however, we find a more uniform philosophical base and a generally clear agreement about the system's purpose. These differences may be due to the system's relative newness and to the fact that society generally agrees that young people who have gone wrong are worth salvaging. However, the philosophy that underlies the juvenile justice system in America is increasingly being questioned by "get tough" advocates of law and order, many of whom are fed up with violent juvenile crime.

Our second purpose is to compare the juvenile and adult systems as they currently operate. The reasoning behind the juvenile justice system has led to administrative and other procedures that, in many jurisdictions, are not found in the adult system. The juvenile justice process, for example, is frequently not as open as the adult system. Hearings may be held in secret, the names of offenders are not published, and records of juvenile proceedings may later be destroyed.[12]

Our third purpose is to describe the agencies, processes, and problems of the juvenile justice system itself. Although each state may have variations, they all share a common system structure.

Near the end of this chapter, we will turn to our fourth focus and will consider some of the issues raised by critics of the current system. As conservative attitudes began to bring changes in the adult criminal justice system during the last few decades, the juvenile justice system remained relatively unchanged. Based on premises quite different from those of the adult system, juvenile justice has long been a separate decision-making arena in which the best interests of the child have been accorded great importance. As we will see, substantial changes are now afoot.

WEB Extra

juvenile justice system

The aggregate of the government agencies that function to investigate, supervise, adjudicate, care for, or confine youthful offenders and other children subject to the jurisdiction of the juvenile court.

Juvenile Justice throughout History

Before the modern era, children who committed crimes in the Western world received no preferential treatment because of their youth. They were adjudicated and punished alongside adults, and a number of recorded cases have come down through history of children as young as six being hung or burned at the stake. Children were also imprisoned alongside adults; no segregated juvenile facilities existed.

Earliest Times

Neither the development of gaols (an old English word for "jails") in the thirteenth century nor the early English prisons provided any leniency on the basis of age.[13] Similarly, little distinction was made between criminality and **delinquency** or other kinds of undesirable behavior. Problems like epilepsy, insanity, retardation, and poverty were seen in the same light as crime,[14] and people suffering from these conditions were shut away in facilities shared by juvenile and adult offenders.

delinquency

In the broadest usage, juvenile actions or conduct in violation of criminal law, juvenile status offenses, and other juvenile misbehavior.

Columbine (Colorado) High School shooters Eric Harris (left) and Dylan Klebold examining a sawed-off shotgun in a still image taken from a videotape made at a makeshift shooting range in 1999. About six weeks after the video was made, Klebold (17) and Harris (18) shot and killed 15 people and injured 20 more at the school. How might such disasters be averted in the future?

Getty Images, Inc.

parens patriae

A common law principle that allows the state to assume a parental role and to take custody of a child when he or she becomes delinquent, is abandoned, or is in need of care that the natural parents are unable or unwilling to provide.

Early court philosophy in dealing with juveniles derived from an early Roman principle called *patria postestas*. Under Roman law (circa 753 B.C.), children were members of their family, but the father had absolute control over children, and they in turn had an absolute responsibility to obey his wishes. Roman understanding of the social role of children strongly influenced English culture and eventually led to the development of the legal principle of **parens patriae**. *Parens patriae* allowed the king, or the English state, to take the place of parents in dealing with children who broke the law. *Parens patriae* held that the king was father of the country and thus had parental rights over all his citizens.

By the Middle Ages, social conceptions of children had become strongly influenced by Christian churches. Church doctrine held that children under the age of seven had not yet reached the age of reason and could not be held liable for spiritual transgressions. In adopting the perspective of the Church, English law of the period excepted children under the age of seven from criminal responsibility. Juveniles ages 7 to 14 were accorded a special status, being tried as adults only if it could be demonstrated that they fully understood the nature of their criminal acts.[15] Adulthood was considered to begin at age 14, when marriage was also allowed.[16]

Early English institutions placed a large burden of responsibility on the family and especially on the father, who, as head of the household, was held accountable for the behavior of all family members, even his wife. When the father failed in his responsibility to control family members, the king, through the concept of *parens patriae*, could intervene.

The inexorable power of the king, often marked by his personal and unpredictable whims, combined with a widespread fear of the dismal conditions in English institutions made many families hide their problem kin. The retarded, insane, and epileptic were kept in attics or basements, sometimes for their entire lives. Delinquent children were confined to the home or, if their families were wealthy enough, were sent overseas to escape the conditions of asylums and gaols.

Juveniles in Early America

Early American solutions to the problems of delinquency were much like those of the English. Puritan influence in the colonies, with its heavy emphasis on obedience and discipline, led to frequent use of jails and prisons for both juveniles and adults. Legislation reflected the Ten Commandments and often provided harsh punishments for transgressors of almost any age. For example, one seventeenth-century Massachusetts law provided, in part, that[17]

> if a man have a stubborn or rebellious son of sufficient years of understanding, viz. sixteen, which will not obey the voice of his father or the voice of his mother, and that when they have chastened him will not harken to them, then shall his father and mother, being his natural parents, lay hold on him and bring him to the magistrates assembled in Court, and testify to them by sufficient evidence

that this their son is stubborn and rebellious and will not obey their voice and chastisement, but lives in sundry notorious crime. Such a son shall be put to death.

Severe punishment was consistent with the Puritan belief that unacknowledged social evils might bring the wrath of God down upon the entire colony. In short, disobedient children had no place in a social group committed to a spiritual salvation understood as strict obedience to the wishes of the Divine.

By the end of the eighteenth century, social conditions in Europe and America began to change. The Enlightenment, a highly significant intellectual and social movement, focused on human potential. It was accompanied by the growth of an industrialized economy, with a corresponding move away from farming. English poor laws (which preceded welfare legislation), lower infant death rates, and social innovations born of the Enlightenment led to a reassessment of the place of children in society. In this new age, children were recognized as the only true heirs to the future, and society became increasingly concerned about their well-being.

The Institutional Era

The nineteenth century was a time of rapid social change in the United States. The population was growing dramatically, cities were burgeoning, and the industrial era was in full swing. Industrial tycoons, the new rich, and frontier-bound settlers lived elbow to elbow with immigrants eking out a living in the sweatshops of the new mercantile centers. In this environment, children took on new value as a source of cheap labor. They fueled assembly lines and proved invaluable to shop owners who could not or would not pay fair wages. Parents were gratified by the income-producing opportunities available to their offspring. On the frontier, settlers and farm families put their children to work clearing land and seeding crops.

Unfortunately, economic opportunities and the luck of the draw were not equally favorable to all. Some immigrant families became victims of the cities that drew them, settling in squalor in hastily formed ghettos. Many families, seeing only the economic opportunities represented by their children, neglected to provide them with anything but a rudimentary education. Children who did work labored for long hours and had little time for family closeness. Other children, abandoned by families that were unable to support them, were forced into lives on the streets, where they formed tattered gangs—surviving off the refuse of the cities.

THE HOUSE OF REFUGE

An 1823 report by the Society for the Prevention of Pauperism in the city of New York called for the development of "houses of refuge" to save children from lives of crime and poverty. The society also cited the problems caused by locking up children with mature criminals. Houses of refuge were to be places of care and education where children could learn positive attitudes about work.

In 1824, the first house of refuge opened in New York City.[18] The New York House of Refuge was intended only for those children who could still be "rescued," and it sheltered mostly young thieves, vagrants, and runaways. Other children, especially those with more severe delinquency problems, were placed in adult prisons and jails. Houses of refuge became popular in New York, and other cities quickly copied them. It was not long before overcrowding developed and living conditions deteriorated.

The 1838 case of *Ex parte Crouse* clarified the power that states had in committing children to institutions.[19] The case involved Mary Ann Crouse, who had been committed to the Philadelphia House of Refuge by a lower court over the objections of her father. The commitment was based on allegations made by the girl's mother that she was incorrigible—that is, beyond the control of her parents. Mary Ann's father petitioned the court to release his daughter on the grounds that she had been denied the right to trial by jury.

The decision by the appeals court upheld the legality of Mary Ann's commitment. It pointed to the state's interest in assisting children and denied that punishment or retribution played any part in her treatment. The court also focused on parental responsibilities in general and stressed the need for state intervention to provide for the moral development of children whose parents had failed them. Most important of all, the court built its decision around the doctrine of *parens patriae*, taking what had previously been an English judicial concept and applying it to the American scene.[20]

THE CHICAGO REFORM SCHOOL

Around the middle of the nineteenth century, the child-savers movement began. Child savers espoused a philosophy of productivity and eschewed idleness and unprincipled behavior. Anthony Platt, a modern writer who recognizes the significance of the child-savers movement, suggests that the mid-nineteenth century provided an ideological framework combining Christian principles with a strong emphasis on the worth of the individual.[21] It was a social perspective that held that children were to be guided and protected.

One product of the child-savers movement was the reform school—a place for delinquent juveniles that embodied the atmosphere of a Christian home. By the middle of the nineteenth century, the reform school approach to handling juveniles was well under way. The Chicago Reform School, which opened in the 1860s, provided an early model for the reform school movement. The movement focused primarily on predelinquent youths who showed tendencies toward more serious criminal involvement. Reform schools attempted to emulate wholesome family environments to provide the security and affection thought necessary in building moral character.

The reform school movement also emphasized traditional values and the worth of hard work, idealizing country living. Some early reform schools were built in rural settings, and many were farms. A few programs even tried to relocate problem children to the vast open expanses of the western states.

The reform school movement was not without its critics. As Platt writes, "If institutions sought to replicate families, would it not have been better to place the predelinquents directly in real families?"[22] As with houses of refuge, reform schools soon became overcrowded. What began as a meaningful attempt to help children ended in routinized institutional procedures devoid of the reformers' original zeal.

In 1870, the Illinois Supreme Court handed down a decision that practically ended the reform school movement. The case of *People ex rel. O'Connell* v. *Turner*[23] centered on Daniel O'Connell, who had been committed to the Chicago Reform School under an Illinois law that permitted confinement for "misfortune." Youngsters classified as "misfortunate" had not necessarily committed any offense. They were, rather, ordered to reform school because their families were unable to care for them or because they were seen as social misfits. Because O'Connell had not been convicted of a crime, the Illinois Supreme Court ordered him released. The court reasoned that the power of the state under *parens patriae* could not exceed the power of the natural parents except in punishing crime. The *O'Connell* case is remembered today for the lasting distinction it made between criminal and noncriminal acts committed by juveniles.

The Juvenile Court Era

In 1870, an expanding recognition of children's needs led the state of Massachusetts to enact legislation that required separate hearings for juveniles.[24] New York followed with a similar law in 1877,[25] which also prohibited contact between juvenile and adult offenders. Rhode Island enacted juvenile court legislation in 1898, and in 1899 the Colorado School Law became the first comprehensive legislation designed to address the adjudication of problem children.[26] It was, however, the 1899 codification of Illinois juvenile law that became the model for juvenile court statutes throughout the nation.

The Illinois Juvenile Court Act created a juvenile court, separate in form and function from adult criminal courts. To avoid the lasting stigma of criminality, the law applied the term *delinquent* rather than *criminal* to young adjudicated offenders. The act specified that the best interests of the child were to guide juvenile court judges in their deliberations. In effect, judges were to serve as advocates for juveniles, guiding their development. Determining guilt or innocence took second place to the betterment of the child. The law abandoned a strict adherence to the due process requirements of adult prosecutions, allowing informal procedures designed to scrutinize the child's situation. By sheltering the juvenile from the punishment philosophy of the adult system, the Illinois Juvenile Court emphasized reformation in place of retribution.[27]

In 1938, the federal government passed the Juvenile Court Act, which embodied many of the features of the Illinois statute. By 1945, every state had enacted special legislation focusing on the handling of juveniles, and the juvenile court movement became well established.[28]

The juvenile court movement was based on five philosophical principles that can be summarized as follows:[29]

- The state is the "higher or ultimate parent" of all the children within its borders.
- Children are worth saving, and nonpunitive procedures should be used to save the child.
- Children should be nurtured. While the nurturing process is under way, they should be protected from the stigmatizing impact of formal adjudicatory procedures.
- To accomplish the goal of reformation, justice needs to be individualized, that is, each child is different, and the needs, aspirations, living conditions, and so on of each child must be known in their individual particulars if the court is to be helpful.

status offender

A child who commits an act that is contrary to the law by virtue of the offender's status as a child. Purchasing cigarettes, buying alcohol, and being truant are examples of such behavior.

status offense

An act or conduct that is declared by statute to be an offense, but only when committed by or engaged in by a juvenile, and that can be adjudicated only by a juvenile court.

- Noncriminal procedures are necessary to give primary consideration to the needs of the child. The denial of due process can be justified in the face of constitutional challenges because the court acts not to punish, but to help.

Learn more about the history of juvenile justice and the juvenile court at Library Extra 15–1 at cjtoday.com.

LIBRARY
Extra
∎ ∎ ∎ ∎

Categories of Children in the Juvenile Justice System

By the time of the Great Depression, most states had expanded juvenile statutes to include the following six categories of children. These categories are still used today in most jurisdictions to describe the variety of children subject to juvenile court jurisdiction.

- **Delinquent children** are those who violate the criminal law. If they were adults, the word *criminal* would be applied to them.

- **Undisciplined children** are said to be beyond parental control, as evidenced by their refusal to obey legitimate authorities, such as school officials and teachers. They need state protection.

- **Dependent children** typically have no parents or guardians to care for them. Their parents are deceased, they were placed for adoption, or they were abandoned in violation of the law.

- **Neglected children** are those who do not receive proper care from their parents or guardians. They may suffer from malnutrition or may not be provided with adequate shelter.

- **Abused children** are those who suffer physical abuse at the hands of their custodians. This category was later expanded to include emotional and sexual abuse.

- **Status offender** is a special category that embraces children who violate laws written only for them. In some states, status offenders are referred to as persons in need of supervision (PINS).

Status offenses include behavior such as truancy, vagrancy, running away from home, and incorrigibility. The youthful "status" of juveniles is a necessary element in such offenses. Adults, for example, may "run away from home" and not violate any law. Runaway children, however, are subject to apprehension and juvenile court processing because state laws require that they be subject to parental control.

Status offenses were a natural outgrowth of juvenile court philosophy. As a consequence, however, juveniles in need of help often faced procedural dispositions that treated them as though they were delinquent. Rather than lowering the rate of juvenile incarceration, the juvenile court movement led to its increase. Critics of the juvenile court movement quickly focused on the abandonment of due process rights, especially in the case of status offenders, as a major source of problems. Detention and incarceration, they argued, were inappropriate options where children had not committed crimes.

delinquent child

A child who has engaged in activity that would be considered a crime if the child were an adult. The term *delinquent* is used to avoid the stigma associated with the term *criminal*.

undisciplined child

A child who is beyond parental control, as evidenced by his or her refusal to obey legitimate authorities, such as school officials and teachers.

dependent child

A child who has no parents or whose parents are unable to care for him or her.

neglected child

A child who is not receiving the proper level of physical or psychological care from his or her parents or guardians or who has been placed up for adoption in violation of the law.

abused child

A child who has been physically, sexually, or mentally abused. Most states also consider a child who is forced into delinquent activity by a parent or guardian to be abused.

Young people spending time together. American juveniles have many opportunities but also face numerous challenges. What are the six categories of children that state juvenile justice statutes usually describe as being subject to juvenile court jurisdiction?

Michael Newman/PhotoEdit Inc.

CJ News

Mean Streets Once Again: Gang Activity Surging

A decade after police crackdowns on drug gangs helped lead to historically low crime rates in cities across the nation, gangs suddenly are re-emerging in waves of violence that have jolted officials in Tulsa, the Virginia suburbs of Washington, D.C., and many other communities well beyond the groups' traditional big-city bases.

The resurgence of gangs whose names became symbols of the turf wars over crack cocaine during the 1980s—the Crips, the Bloods, the Mexican Mafia, the Gangster Disciples and others—is helping to lift homicide rates in several cities at a time when overall crime rates remain low.

Some police officials—including those in Tulsa, where federal, state and local authorities now keep an intelligence database on suspected gang members—say they can trace the recent violence to the releases of senior gang members from prison. Others note that the violence has flared as police agencies, facing budget cuts and increased concerns about terrorism, gradually have dismantled anti-gang units. Now, officials from Durham, N.C., to Los Angeles are scrambling to assign more cops and prosecutors to deal with gangs. "We had a chance to pull the weeds out of our communities for good a few years ago," says Tim Twining, director of gang prosecutions in Denver, where budget cuts forced the elimination of the district attorney's anti-gang unit in 2002 before it was re-established last year. "We didn't do it; we got distracted. Now, the weeds are back."

Nationwide, gang-related homicides jumped by 50% from 1999 to 2002, according to a report commissioned by Fight Crime: Invest in Kids, a coalition of big-city police chiefs. In 2002, the most recent year analyzed in the study by Northeastern University professor James Alan Fox, 1,034 of the 16,204 homicides across the nation were linked to gangs—the most since 1995, when there were 1,237 gang-related slayings.

A separate Justice Department review [in 2004] found that 42% of the 2,182 cities that responded to the 2002 National Youth Gang Survey reported that gang activity was "getting worse," up from 27% the previous year. In the same survey, 87% of U.S. cities with populations of at least 100,000 reported problems with gangs.

Recently, the U.S. House of Representatives responded to increased reports of gang violence by approving the creation of a National Gang Intelligence Center. If approved by the Senate, the center would provide additional federal agents and prosecutors to track gang members involved in crimes.

Authorities say that in many cases, gangs have branched out from their traditional homes in Los Angeles, Chicago and New York City because they have found new drug markets—and less scrutiny from police—in smaller communities. In a few instances, authorities say, youths from troubled urban neighborhoods who were sent to live with relatives in safer, smaller towns have wound up starting new criminal groups.

CLAMPING DOWN ON GANGS

Gangs have operated in Tulsa since the late 1980s. Like many other cities, Tulsa was slow to respond to them. But during the early 1990s, Tulsa police formed a squad to clamp down on gang turf wars and illegal drug sales.

Nearly a dozen officers were assigned to the unit at its peak during the late 1990s. As crime declined, several officers were reas-

Los Angeles gang members displaying signs of membership in front of a street mural. The National Youth Gang Survey found that 42% of cities surveyed say that gang activity is getting worse. What is the attraction of gangs for young people?

A. Reininger/Woodfin Camp & Associates

signed to more pressing priorities. That all began to change [in 2003], when Tulsa had a record 70 slayings, 17 of which police linked to gangs. Then came a flurry of violence late last spring [2004], after a local gang leader was released from prison.

"We knew he was coming back," says police Capt. Walter Busby, who asked that the gang leader not be identified because he is a focus of several pending investigations. "When he did, (violence) started to spike significantly."

Tulsa authorities now suspect that the gang leader has been involved in as many as a half-dozen killings since his release from prison in late March [2004]. Meanwhile, police in this city of 393,049 estimate that more than 3,300 residents have at least some tie to a gang, and that the number is rising by about 200 people a year.

Tulsa's murder rate is down this year [2004]; there have been 24 slayings. But police have linked about one-third of the killings to gangs, a higher percentage than last year.

For many Tulsa residents, the escalating danger posed by gangs became vivid in late February, when police were called to the modest, North Side home of Ples and Shelly Vann. The couple had been executed, apparently because their sons had been involved in a dispute with Crips members, police say. Philip Summers, a suspected Crips member, was charged in the slayings and is awaiting trial.

CJ News (continued)

The Vann slayings shocked the city and reinvigorated Tulsa's anti-gang efforts. Police Major Mark McCrory says the brutality of the slayings was "an eye-opener" that led city officials to put unprecedented pressure on gangs and to conduct almost-daily raids on suspected safe houses.

A new police team of a dozen officers has joined Tulsa's existing anti-gang unit on 92 raids. Authorities routinely have recovered drugs and bundles of cash and guns, including several assault weapons. More than 100 people, most of them alleged gang members, have been arrested.

"HITTING THEM AS HARD AS WE CAN"

McCrory, a burly officer who oversees the raid teams in the manner of an enthusiastic football coach, says he believes the aggressive tactics by police have helped to slow the violence. "We're hitting them as hard as we can," he says. "Our goal is to make life as miserable as possible for these people."

In Tulsa, a coalition of local, state and federal law enforcement agencies has been formed to chart gang membership. Each week, representatives of the FBI, the federal Bureau of Alcohol, Tobacco, Firearms and Explosives, the Tulsa police, Oklahoma's state prison system and the Tulsa County Sheriff's Office meet to examine the spread of gang membership in the area.

The officials keep track of gang members with a database that includes information from patrol officers, informants and other sources. The idea is to learn who is joining gangs and to find out more about gangs' crime networks.

Tulsa's process of designating people as possible gang members is based on a range of factors, officials say. Those in the database—about 3,300 residents—might have criminal records or tattoos or brands on their skin that claim an allegiance to specific gangs. Or they might be frequent associates of known gang members.

Tulsa officials say that to avoid violating privacy rights, the intelligence files are restricted to suspected gang members and do not include information on others.

[In 2002], Denver police dropped a broader database effort after residents accused the department of compiling "spy files" against innocent people. The Denver database included information about thousands of residents, including some who had been involved in lawful protests or demonstrations. Denver officials disbanded the database and issued public apologies.

In Tulsa, McCrory says, authorities have used the database to track gang members' movements through the community and state prisons. [In June 2004], some of the intelligence led McCrory's officers to the brick home of a 27-year-old admitted Crips member and suspected cocaine dealer. The man had been released from prison two months earlier after serving 18 months for a drug conviction.

Police say that when they broke through the man's door, the last of his cocaine supply was swirling down the toilet. Police salvaged some of the evidence when an officer yanked the toilet from its foundation and fought through a gusher of water to retrieve a small amount of crack.

Police hope the seizure will give investigators enough leverage to turn the suspect into an informant.

BUSY WITH ANTITERRORISM EFFORTS

Since the September 11, 2001, attacks, U.S. authorities have been consumed by the threat of terrorism. But [in 2004], a spate of violence in the Virginia suburbs of Washington, D.C., that involved suspected members of the Mara Salvatrucha (MS-13) gang caught the attention of U.S. Attorney General John Ashcroft.

In a . . . meeting with Paul McNulty, the U.S. attorney in Alexandria, Va., Ashcroft expressed concern that gangs were threatening several communities a short drive from the nation's capital.

In a follow-up memo, McNulty called the gang threat "serious" and "growing" and said U.S. authorities had begun to help local police deal with an estimated 2,700 gang members and their associates in northern Virginia's mostly affluent suburbs. A string of recent attacks has underscored the increasing gang activity there.

In May [2004], a suspected MS-13 member was charged in a machete attack on a 16-year-old boy in Alexandria. . . . U.S. authorities who are investigating MS-13 announced charges against four of the gang's members in the slaying of a pregnant, 17-year-old member who had become a government informant.

Meanwhile, gang violence has exploded in Durham, N.C., where police Sgt. Howard Alexander says there were three gang-related slayings and "too many shootings to count" [in one] week. The city of 187,035 had a record low 22 homicides [in 2003]. Already there have been 18 this year, and more than half have been linked to gangs, Alexander says.

"We've got murders, armed robberies, home invasions and witness intimidation," says Alexander, who says Durham's gang wars, like those elsewhere, are rooted in disputes over turf and the local market for illegal drugs.

The violence has led Durham police to increase the city's anti-gang unit from seven to 20 officers.

The resurgence of gangs, some law enforcement analysts say, can be traced to police departments' post-9/11 emphasis

"This (gang) problem has been around for a long time, but we've taken our eye off the ball since 9/11," said John Moore, director of the National Youth Gang Center. Funded by the Justice Department, the center monitors gang activity across the nation.

As gang violence spreads, it also is surging in places where it has long been a problem. In southern California, authorities estimate that there are 100,000 gang members in Los Angeles County, home to about 9.8 million people. Gang membership has been stable during the past two years, but Los Angeles Police Chief William Bratton says gang-related killings have contributed to a 5% increase in homicides in the city this year [2004].

"This thing is growing, but it has been masked to a great extent by reports about how overall crime has been coming down," Bratton says. "Not a lot of people are paying attention to this. But the way it's going, it has the potential to explode as it did in the early '90s."

For the latest in crime and justice news, visit the Talk Justice news feed at http://www.crimenews.info.

Source: Kevin Johnson, "Mean Streets Once Again: Gang Activity Surging," USA TODAY, July 21, 2004. Reprinted with permission.

The Legal Environment

Throughout the first half of the twentieth century, the U.S. Supreme Court followed a hands-off approach to juvenile justice, much like its early approach to prisons (see Chapter 14). The adjudication and further processing of juveniles by the system were left mostly to specialized juvenile courts or to local appeals courts. Although one or two early Supreme Court decisions[30] dealt with issues of juvenile justice, it was not until the 1960s that the Court began close legal scrutiny of the principles underlying the system itself. In the pages that follow, we will discuss some of the most important U.S. Supreme Court cases relating to juvenile justice (Figure 15–2).

Kent v. U.S. (1966)

The U.S. Supreme Court case that ended the hands-off era in juvenile justice was *Kent* v. *U.S.*,[31] decided in 1966. The *Kent* case, which focused on the long-accepted concept of *parens patriae*, signaled the beginning of the Court's systematic review of all lower-court practices involving delinquency hearings.

Morris Kent, Jr., age 14, was apprehended in the District of Columbia in 1959 and was charged with several house burglaries and an attempted purse snatching. Kent was placed on juvenile probation and was released into the custody of his mother. In 1961, an intruder entered a woman's apartment, took her wallet, and raped her. At the scene, police found fingerprints that matched those on file belonging to Morris Kent. At the time, Kent was 16 years old and, according to the laws of the District of Columbia, was still under the exclusive jurisdiction of the juvenile court.

Kent was taken into custody and interrogated. He volunteered information about the crime and spoke about other offenses involving burglary, robbery, and rape. Following interrogation, his mother retained counsel on his behalf. Kent was kept in custody for another week, during which time psychological and psychiatric evaluations were conducted. The professionals conducting the evaluations concluded that Kent was a "victim of severe psychopathology." Without conferring with Kent, his parents, or his lawyers, the juvenile court judge ruled that Kent should be remanded to the authority of the adult court system. He was eventually tried in U.S. District Court for the District of Columbia. The judge gave no reasons for assigning Kent to the adult court.

Kent was indicted in criminal court on eight counts of burglary, robbery, and rape. Citing the psychological evaluations performed earlier, Kent's lawyers argued that his behavior was the product of mental disease or defect. Their defense proved fruitless, and Kent was found guilty on six counts of burglary and robbery. He was sentenced to 5 to 15 years in prison on each count. Kent's lawyers ultimately appealed to the U.S. Supreme Court. They argued that Kent should have been entitled to an adequate hearing at the level of the juvenile court and that, lacking such a hearing, his transfer to adult jurisdiction was unfair.

The Supreme Court, reflecting the Warren Court ideologies of the times, agreed with Kent's attorneys, reversed the decision of the district court, and ordered adequate hearings for juveniles being considered for transfer to adult court. At these hearings, the Court ruled, juveniles are entitled to representation by attorneys who must have access to their records.

Although it focused only on a narrow issue, the *Kent* decision was especially important because for the first time it recognized the need for at least minimal due process in juvenile court hearings. The *Kent* decision set the stage for what was to come, but it was the *Gault* decision, which we look at next, that turned the juvenile justice system upside down.

In re Gault (1967)

In 1964, Gerald Gault and a friend, Ronald Lewis, were taken into custody by the sheriff of Gila County, Arizona, on the basis of a neighbor's complaint that the boys had telephoned her and made lewd remarks. At the time, Gault was on probation for having been in the company of another boy who had stolen a wallet.

When Gault was apprehended, his parents were both at work. No notice was posted at their house to indicate that their son had been taken into custody, a fact that they later learned from Lewis's parents. The authorities gave Gault's parents little information. Although they were notified when their son's initial hearing would be held, the Gaults were not told the nature of the complaint against him or the identity of the complainant, who was not present at the hearing.

At the hearing, the only evidence presented was statements made by young Gault and testimony given by the juvenile officer as to what the complainant had alleged. Gault was not

Established in the 1960s, status offender systems were created to help parents, schools, and communities get disobedient, but not delinquent, children back on track by providing treatment, counseling, and supervision. Yet despite their good intentions, many status offender systems across the country have had the opposite effect.

—Vera Institute of Justice[i]

There are no illegitimate children—only illegitimate parents.

—U.S. District Court Judge Leon R. Yankwich, in Zipkin v. Mozon (1928)

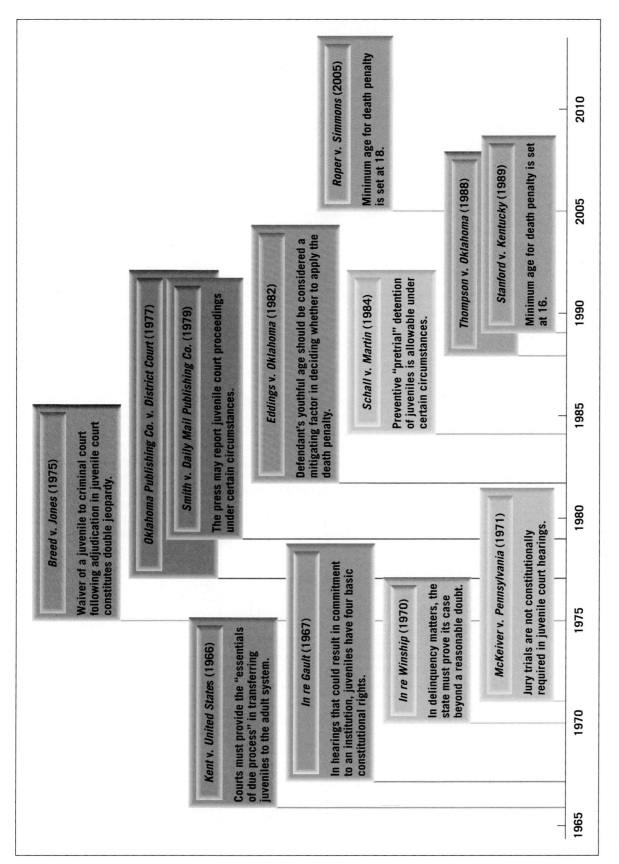

FIGURE 15–2

U.S. Supreme Court decisions of special relevance to juvenile justice.

Source: Adapted from Office of Juvenile Justice and Delinquency Prevention, *Juvenile Offenders and Victims: 2006 National Report* (Washington, DC: OJJDP, 2006), p. 101.

represented by counsel. He admitted to having made the phone call but stated that after dialing the number he had turned the phone over to his friend, Lewis. After hearing the testimony, Judge McGhee ordered a second hearing, to be held a week later. At the second hearing, Mrs. Gault requested that the complainant be present so that she could identify the voice of the person making the lewd call. Judge McGhee ruled against her request. Finally, young Gault was adjudicated delinquent and remanded to the State Industrial School until his twenty-first birthday.

On appeal, eventually to the U.S. Supreme Court, Gault's attorney argued that his constitutional rights were violated because he had been denied due process. The appeal focused specifically on six areas:

- *Notice of charges.* Gault was not given enough notice to prepare a reasonable defense to the charges against him.
- *Right to counsel.* Gault was not notified of his right to an attorney or allowed to have one at his hearing.
- *Right to confront and to cross-examine witnesses.* The court did not require the complainant to appear at the hearing.
- *Protection against self-incrimination.* Gault was never advised that he had the right to remain silent, nor was he informed that his testimony could be used against him.
- *Right to a transcript.* In preparing for the appeal, Gault's attorney was not provided a transcript of the adjudicatory hearing.
- *Right to appeal.* At the time, the state of Arizona did not give juveniles the right to appeal.

The Supreme Court ruled in Gault's favor on four of the six issues raised by his attorneys. The majority opinion read, in part, as follows:[32]

> In *Kent* v. *United States*, we stated that the Juvenile Court Judge's exercise of the power of the state as *parens patriae* was not unlimited. . . . Notice, to comply with due process requirements, must be given sufficiently in advance of scheduled court proceedings so that reasonable opportunity to prepare will be afforded. . . . The probation officer cannot act as counsel for the child. His role in the adjudicatory hearing, by statute and in fact, is as arresting officer and witness against the child. There is no material difference in this respect between adult and juvenile proceedings of the sort here involved. . . . A proceeding where the issue is whether the child will be found to be "delinquent" and subjected to the loss of his liberty for years is comparable in seriousness to a felony prosecution. The juvenile needs the assistance of counsel to cope with the problems of law, to make skilled inquiry into the facts, to insist upon regularity of the proceedings, and to ascertain whether he has a defense and to prepare and submit it.

The Court did not agree with the contention of Gault's lawyers relative to appeal or with their arguments in favor of transcripts. Right to appeal, where it exists, is usually granted by statute or by state constitution—not by the U.S. Constitution. Similarly, the Court did not require a transcript because (1) there is no constitutional right to a transcript, and (2) no transcripts are produced in the trials of most adult misdemeanants.

Today, the impact of *Gault* is widely felt in the juvenile justice system. Juveniles are now guaranteed many of the same procedural rights as adults. Most precedent-setting Supreme Court decisions that followed *Gault* further clarified the rights of juveniles, focusing primarily on those few issues of due process that it had not explicitly addressed.

Under our Constitution, the condition of being a boy does not justify a kangaroo court.

—In re Gault, *387 U.S. 1 (1967)*

In re Winship (1970)

At the close of the 1960s, a New York Family Court judge found a 12-year-old boy named Samuel Winship delinquent on the basis of a petition that alleged that he had illegally entered a locker and stolen $112 from a pocketbook. The judge acknowledged to those present at the hearing that the evidence in the case might not be sufficient to establish Winship's guilt beyond a reasonable doubt. Statutory authority, however, in the form of the New York Family Court Act, required a determination of facts based only on a preponderance of the evidence—the same standard required in civil suits. Winship was sent to a training school for 18 months, subject to extensions until his eighteenth birthday.

Winship's appeal to the U.S. Supreme Court centered on the lower court's standard of evidence. His attorney argued that Winship's guilt should have been proved beyond a reasonable doubt—the evidentiary standard of adult criminal trials. The Court agreed, ruling that[33] the constitutional safeguard of proof beyond a reasonable doubt is as much required during the adjudicatory stage of a delinquency proceeding as are those constitutional guards applied in *Gault*. . . . We therefore hold . . . that where a 12 year old child is charged with an act of stealing which renders him liable to confinement for as long as six years, then, as a matter of due process . . . the case against him must be proved beyond a reasonable doubt.

As a consequence of *Winship*, allegations of delinquency today must be established beyond a reasonable doubt. The Court allowed, however, the continued use of the lower evidentiary standard in adjudicating juveniles charged with status offenses. Even though both standards continue to exist, most jurisdictions have chosen to use the stricter burden-of-proof requirement for all delinquency proceedings.

McKeiver v. *Pennsylvania* (1971)

Cases like *Winship* and *Gault* have not extended all adult procedural rights to juveniles charged with delinquency. For example, juveniles do not have the constitutional right to trial by a jury of their peers. The case of *McKeiver* v. *Pennsylvania* (1971)[34] reiterated what earlier decisions had established and legitimized some generally accepted practices of juvenile courts.

Joseph McKeiver, age 16, was charged with robbery, larceny, and receiving stolen property, all felonies in Pennsylvania. McKeiver had been involved with 20 to 30 other juveniles who chased three teenage boys and took 25 cents from them. He had no previous arrests and was able to demonstrate a record of gainful employment. McKeiver's attorney requested that his client be allowed a jury trial. The request was denied. McKeiver was adjudicated delinquent and committed to a youth development center. McKeiver's attorney pursued a series of appeals and was finally granted a hearing before the U.S. Supreme Court. There he argued that his client, even though a juvenile, should have been allowed a jury trial as guaranteed by the Sixth and Fourteenth Amendments to the Constitution.

The Court, although recognizing existent problems in the administration of juvenile justice, held to the belief that the Constitution did not mandate jury trials for juveniles. In the opinion of the Court,

> [t]he imposition of the jury trial on the juvenile court system would not strengthen greatly, if at all, the fact-finding function, and would contrarily, provide an attrition of the juvenile court's assumed ability to function in a unique manner. It would not remedy the defects of the system. . . . If the jury trial were to be injected into the juvenile court system as a matter of right, it would bring with it into that system the traditional delay, the formality, and the clamor of the adversary system and, possibly, the public trial. . . . If the formalities of the criminal adjudicative process are to be superimposed upon the juvenile court system, there is little need for its separate existence.

McKeiver v. *Pennsylvania* did not set any new standards. Rather, it reinforced the long-accepted practice of conducting juvenile adjudicatory hearings in the absence of certain due process considerations, particularly those pertaining to trial by jury. It is important to note, however, that the *McKeiver* decision did not specifically prohibit jury trials for juveniles. As a consequence, approximately 12 states today allow the option of jury trials for juveniles.

Breed v. *Jones* (1975)

In 1971, a delinquency complaint was filed against Jones, age 17, alleging that he committed robbery while armed with a deadly weapon. At the adjudicatory hearing, Jones was declared delinquent. A later dispositional hearing determined that Jones was "unfit for treatment as a juvenile," and he was transferred to superior court for trial as an adult. The superior court found Jones guilty of robbery in the first degree and committed him to the custody of the California Youth Authority.

In an appeal eventually heard by the U.S. Supreme Court, Jones alleged that his transfer to adult court, and the trial that ensued, placed him in double jeopardy because he had already been adjudicated in juvenile court. Double jeopardy is prohibited by the Fifth and Fourteenth Amendments. The state of California argued that the superior court trial was only a natural continuation of the juvenile justice process and, as a consequence, did not fall under the rubric of double jeopardy. The state further suggested that double jeopardy existed only where an individual ran the risk of being punished more than once. In the case of Jones, no punishment had been imposed by the juvenile court.

The U.S. Supreme Court did not agree that the possibility of only one punishment negated double jeopardy.[35] The Court pointed to the fact that the double jeopardy clause speaks in terms of "potential risk of trial and conviction—not punishment" and concluded that two separate adjudicatory processes were sufficient to warrant a finding of double jeopardy. Jones's conviction was vacated, clearing the way for him to be returned to juvenile court. However, by the time the litigation had been completed, Jones was beyond the age of juvenile court jurisdiction, and he was released from custody.

The *Jones* case severely restricted the conditions under which transfers from juvenile to adult courts may occur. In effect, the high court mandated that such transfers as do occur must be made before an adjudicatory hearing in juvenile court.

Schall v. *Martin* (1984)

Gregory Martin, age 14, was arrested in New York City, charged with robbery and weapons possession, and detained in a secure detention facility for more than two weeks until his hearing. The detention order drew its authority from a New York preventive detention law that allowed for the jailing of juveniles thought to represent a high risk of continued delinquency.

Martin was adjudicated delinquent. His case eventually reached the U.S. Supreme Court, where his lawyer argued that the New York detention law had effectively denied Martin's freedom before conviction and that it was therefore in violation of the Fourteenth Amendment to the U.S. Constitution.

The Supreme Court, however, upheld the constitutionality of the New York statute, ruling that pretrial detention of juveniles based on "serious risk" does not violate the principle of fundamental fairness required by due process.[36] In so holding, the Court recognized that states have a legitimate interest in preventing future delinquency by juveniles thought to be dangerous. Preventive detention, the Court reasoned, is nonpunitive in its intent and is therefore not a "punishment."

While the *Schall* decision upheld the practice of preventive detention, it seized on the opportunity provided by the case to impose procedural requirements on the detaining authority. Consequently, preventive detention today cannot be imposed without (1) prior notice, (2) an equitable detention hearing, and (3) a statement by the judge setting forth the reason or reasons for detention.

Roper v. *Simmons* (2005)

In 1988, in the case of *Thompson* v. *Oklahoma*,[37] the U.S. Supreme Court determined that national standards of decency did not permit the execution of any offender who was under age 16 at the time of the crime. The next year, in *Stanford* v. *Kentucky*,[38] the Court considered whether the imposition of capital punishment on offenders ages 16 to 18 violates evolving standards of decency and decided that it does not. In its ruling, the Court said that it looked "not to its own subjective conceptions, but, rather, to the conceptions of modern American society as reflected by objective evidence." The most useful and reliable evidence of a national consensus, said the justices, was "the pattern of federal and state laws" which, at the time, found that 22 of 37 death-penalty states permitted capital punishment for those 16 and older, and 25 permitted it for 17-year-olds. "This does not," said the Court, "establish the degree of national agreement this Court has previously thought sufficient to label a punishment cruel and unusual."[39] Consequently, the Court ruled that the decision of whether to subject 16- or 17-year-olds to capital punishment must be made by the states and could not be categorically denounced as cruel and unusual punishment.

In 2005, however, in the case of *Roper* v. *Simmons*,[40] the Court set a new standard when it ruled that age *is* a bar to execution when the offender commits a capital crime when younger than 18. The *Roper* case (which was briefly mentioned in Chapter 9) involved Christopher Simmons, a high school junior who, at 17, planned and committed a callous capital murder of a woman whom he bound with duct tape and electrical wire, terrorized, and threw off a bridge. About nine months later, after he had turned 18, he was tried and sentenced to death. Regardless of the heinous nature of Simmons's crime, the justices reasoned that "juveniles' susceptibility to immature and irresponsible behavior means their irresponsible conduct is not as morally reprehensible as that of an adult . . . [and] their own vulnerability and comparative lack of control over their immediate surroundings mean juveniles have a greater claim than adults to be forgiven for failing to escape negative influences in their whole environment." The fact, said the Court, "that juveniles still struggle to define their identity means it is less supportable to conclude that even a heinous crime committed by a juvenile is evidence of irretrievably depraved character." The *Roper* ruling invalidated the capital sentences of 72 death-row inmates in 12 states. Among the 962 people put to death between January 1976 and January 2004, 22 had committed their crimes as juveniles.[41]

Legislation Concerning Juveniles and Justice

In response to the rapidly increasing crime rates of the late 1960s, Congress passed the Omnibus Crime Control and Safe Streets Act of 1968. The act provided money and technical assistance for states and municipalities seeking to modernize their justice systems. The Safe Streets Act provided funding for youth services bureaus, which had been recommended by the 1967 presidential commission report *The Challenge of Crime in a Free Society*. These bureaus were available to police, juvenile courts, and probation departments and acted as a centralized community resource for handling delinquents and status offenders. Youth services bureaus also handled juveniles referred by schools and young people who referred themselves. Unfortunately, within a decade after their establishment, most youth services bureaus succumbed to a lack of continued federal funding.

In 1974, recognizing the special needs of juveniles, Congress passed the Juvenile Justice and Delinquency Prevention (JJDP) Act. Employing much the same strategy as the 1968 law, the JJDP Act provided federal grants to states and cities seeking to improve their handling and disposition of delinquents and status offenders. Nearly all the states chose to accept federal funds through the JJDP Act. Participating states had to meet two conditions within five years:

- They had to agree to a "sight and sound separation mandate," under which juveniles would not be held in institutions where they might come into regular contact with adult prisoners.

- Status offenders had to be deinstitutionalized, with most being released into the community or placed in foster homes.

Within a few years, institutional populations were cut by more than half, and community alternatives to juvenile institutionalization were rapidly being developed. Jailed juveniles were housed in separate wings of adult facilities or were removed from adult jails entirely.

When the JJDP Act was reauthorized for funding in 1980, the separation mandate was expanded to require that separate juvenile jails be constructed by the states. Studies supporting reauthorization of the JJDP Act in 1984 and 1988, however, found that nearly half the states had failed to come into "substantial compliance" with the new jail and lockup mandate. As a consequence, Congress modified the requirements of the act, continuing funding for states making "meaningful progress" toward removing juveniles from adult jails.[42] The 1988 reauthorizing legislation added a "disproportionate minority confinement" (DMC) requirement under which states seeking federal monies in support of their juvenile justice systems had to agree to ameliorate conditions leading to the disproportionate confinement of minority juveniles.[43]

In 1996, in the face of pressures toward punishment and away from treatment for violent juvenile offenders, the Office of Juvenile Justice and Delinquency Prevention proposed new rules for jailing juveniles. The new rules allow an adjudicated delinquent to be detained for up to 12 hours in an adult jail before a court appearance and make it easier for states to house juveniles in separate wings of adult jails.[44] The most recent JJDP reauthorization occurred in 2002[45] and expanded the DMC concept to include all aspects of the juvenile justice process. Consequently, DMC has come to mean "disproportionate minority contact" under today's law.[46] By 2005, 56 of 57 eligible states and U.S. territories had agreed to all of the act's requirements and were receiving federal funding under the legislation.[47]

In 2003, Congress passed child-protection legislation in what is commonly called the "Amber Alert" law. Officially known as the PROTECT Act of 2003 (Prosecutorial Remedies and Other Tools to End the Exploitation of Children Today), the law provides federal funding to the states to ensure the creation of a national Amber network (America's Missing: Broadcast Emergency Response) to facilitate rapid law enforcement and community response to kidnapped or abducted children. The law also established the position of a federal Amber Alert coordinator and set uniform standards for the use of Amber Alerts across our country. The federal government's Amber Alert website can be accessed via Web Extra 15–2 at cjtoday.com.

WEB
Extra
■■■■

The Legal Rights of Juveniles

Most jurisdictions today have statutes designed to extend the *Miranda* provisions to juveniles. Many police officers routinely offer *Miranda* warnings to juveniles in their custody before questioning them. It is unclear, however, whether juveniles can legally waive their *Miranda* rights. A 1979 U.S. Supreme Court ruling held that juveniles should be accorded the opportunity for a knowing waiver when they are old enough and sufficiently educated to understand the consequences of a waiver.[48] A later high court ruling upheld the murder conviction of a juvenile who had been advised of his rights and waived them in the presence of his mother.[49]

Today we are living with a juvenile justice system that was created around the time of the silent film.

—Former Attorney General John Ashcroft

One important area of juvenile rights centers on investigative procedures. In 1985, for example, the U.S. Supreme Court ruled in *New Jersey* v. *T.L.O.*[50] that schoolchildren have a reasonable expectation of privacy in their personal property. The case involved a 14-year-old girl who was accused of violating school rules by smoking in a high school bathroom. A vice principal searched the girl's purse and found evidence of marijuana use. Juvenile officers were called, and the girl was eventually adjudicated in juvenile court and found delinquent.

On appeal to the New Jersey Supreme Court, the girl's lawyers were successful in having her conviction reversed on the grounds that the search of her purse, as an item of personal property, had been unreasonable. The state's appeal to the U.S. Supreme Court resulted in a ruling that prohibited school officials from engaging in unreasonable searches of students or their property. A reading of the Court's decision leads to the conclusion that a search could be considered reasonable if it (1) is based on a logical suspicion of rule-breaking actions; (2) is required to maintain order, discipline, and safety among students; and (3) does not exceed the scope of the original suspicion.

The Juvenile Justice Process Today

Juvenile court jurisdiction rests on the offender's age and conduct. The majority of states today define a child subject to juvenile court jurisdiction as a person who has not yet turned 18. A few states set the age at 16, and several use 17. Figure 15–3 shows the upper ages of children subject to juvenile court jurisdiction in delinquency matters, by state. When they reach their eighteenth birthday, children in most states become subject to the jurisdiction of adult criminal courts.

In 2005, OJJDP reported that U.S. courts with juvenile jurisdiction annually handle slightly more than 1.6 million delinquency cases.[51] Depending on the laws of the state and the behavior involved, the jurisdiction of the juvenile court may be exclusive. Exclusive jurisdiction applies when the juvenile court is the only court that has statutory authority to deal with children for specified infractions. For example, status offenses like truancy normally fall within the exclusive jurisdiction of juvenile courts. Delinquency, which involves violation of the criminal law, however, is often not within the juvenile court's exclusive jurisdiction. All 50 states, the District of Columbia, and the federal government have provisions that allow juveniles who commit serious crimes to be bound over to criminal court. Forty-six states give juvenile court judges the power to waive jurisdiction over cases involving juveniles so that they can be transferred to criminal court.[52] Fifteen states have "direct file" provisions that authorize the prosecutor to decide whether to file certain kinds of cases in juvenile or criminal court.

FIGURE 15–3

Limit of juvenile court jurisdiction over young offenders, by state.

Source: Office of Juvenile Justice and Delinquency Prevention.

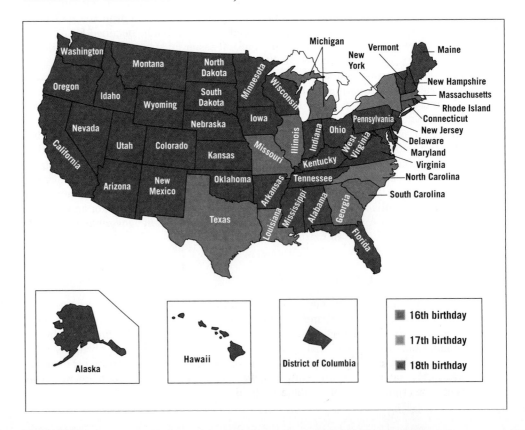

Juveniles who commit violent crimes or who have prior records are among the most likely to be transferred to adult courts.[53] In a case that made national headlines about eight years ago, for example, Lionel Tate, who was 12 years old when he killed a 6-year-old playmate while imitating wrestling moves he had seen on TV, was tried as an adult in Fort Lauderdale, Florida; he was found guilty of first-degree murder and sentenced to life in prison without the possibility of parole. At the time, he was touted as the youngest person in modern American history to be sentenced to life in prison. Three years later, after intense public debate, Tate was released from prison and ordered to serve 11 years on probation, to receive counseling, and to perform 1,000 hours of community service. In 2005, however, 18-year-old Tate was again arrested and charged with pulling a gun on a pizza delivery man at a friend's apartment and assaulting his friend.[54] When he was arrested, officers found a knife in his pocket. On March 1, 2006, Tate pleaded guilty to armed robbery in a plea arrangement intended to spare him a life sentence for violating probation.[55] A few days later, however, he attempted to withdraw his plea over the objections of his attorney, who resigned. Broward County Circuit Judge Joel T. Lazarus allowed Tate to withdraw the armed robbery plea but later sentenced him to 30 years in prison for violating probation. In the courtroom, the judge told Tate, whose mother is a Florida Highway Patrol trooper,[56] that he had shown "disdain and disrespect" for the law and had "run out of second chances."[57]

Where juvenile court authority is not exclusive, the jurisdiction of the court may be original or concurrent. Original jurisdiction means that a particular offense must originate, or begin, with juvenile court authorities. Juvenile courts have original jurisdiction over most delinquency petitions and all status offenses. Concurrent jurisdiction exists where other courts have equal statutory authority to originate proceedings. If a juvenile has committed a homicide, rape, or other serious crime, for example, an arrest warrant may be issued by the adult court.

Some states specify that juvenile courts have no jurisdiction over certain excluded offenses. Delaware, Louisiana, and Nevada, for example, allow no juvenile court jurisdiction over children charged with first-degree murder. Twenty-nine states have statutes that exclude certain serious, violent, or repeat offenders from the juvenile court's jurisdiction.

CJ Today Exhibit 15–1

The Juvenile Justice System versus Criminal Case Processing

CRIMINAL PROCEEDINGS	JUVENILE PROCEEDINGS
Focus on criminality	Focus on delinquency and a special category of "status offenses"
Comprehensive rights against unreasonable searches of person, home, and possessions	Limited rights against unreasonable searches
A right against self-incrimination; a knowing waiver is possible	A right against self-incrimination; waivers are questionable
Assumed innocent until proven guilty	Guilt and innocence are not primary issues; the system focuses on the interests of the child
Adversarial setting	Helping context
Arrest warrants form the basis for most arrests	Petitions or complaints legitimize apprehension
Right to an attorney	Right to an attorney
Public trial	Closed hearing; no right to a jury trial
System goals are punishment and reformation	System goals are protection and treatment
No right to treatment	Specific right to treatment
Possibility of bail or release on recognizance	Release into parental custody
Public record of trial and judgment	Sealed records; sometimes destroyed by a specified age
Possible incarceration in adult correctional facility	Separate facilities at all levels

Adult and Juvenile Justice Compared

The court cases of relevance to the juvenile justice system that we've discussed in this chapter have two common characteristics. They all turn on due process guarantees specified by the Bill of Rights, and they all make the claim that adult due process should serve as a model for juvenile proceedings. Due process guarantees, as interpreted by the U.S. Supreme Court, are clearly designed to ensure that juvenile proceedings are fair and that the interests of juveniles are protected. However, the Court's interpretations do not offer any pretense of providing juveniles with the same kinds of protections guaranteed to adult defendants. While the high court has tended to agree that juveniles are entitled to due process protection, it has refrained from declaring that juveniles have a right to all the aspects of due process afforded adult defendants.

Juvenile court philosophy brings with it other differences from the adult system. Among them are (1) a reduced concern with legal issues of guilt or innocence and an emphasis on the child's best interests; (2) an emphasis on treatment rather than punishment; (3) privacy and protection from public scrutiny through the use of sealed records, laws against publishing the names of juvenile offenders, and so forth; (4) the use of the techniques of social science in dispositional decision making rather than sentences determined by a perceived need for punishment; (5) no long-term confinement, with most juveniles being released from institutions by their twenty-first birthday, regardless of offense; (6) separate facilities for juveniles; and (7) broad discretionary alternatives at all points in the process.[58] This combination of court philosophy and due process requirements has created a unique justice system for juveniles that takes into consideration the special needs of young people while attempting to offer reasonable protection to society. The juvenile justice process is diagrammed in Figure 15–4.

How the System Works

The juvenile justice system can be viewed as a process that, when carried to completion, moves through four stages: intake, adjudication, disposition, and postadjudicatory review. Though organizationally similar to the adult criminal justice process, the juvenile system is far more likely to maximize the use of discretion and to employ diversion from further formal processing at every point in the process. Each stage is discussed in the pages that follow.

INTAKE AND DETENTION HEARINGS

juvenile petition

A document filed in juvenile court alleging that a juvenile is a delinquent, a status offender, or a dependent and asking that the court assume jurisdiction over the juvenile or that an alleged delinquent be transferred to a criminal court for prosecution as an adult.

Delinquent juveniles may come to the attention of the police or juvenile court authorities either through arrest or through the filing of a **juvenile petition** by an aggrieved party. Juvenile petitions are much like criminal complaints in that they allege illegal behavior. They are most often filed by teachers, school administrators, neighbors, store managers, or others who have frequent contact with juveniles. Parents who are unable to control the behavior of their teenage children are the source of many other petitions. Crimes in progress bring other juveniles to the attention of the police; three-quarters of all referrals to juvenile court come directly from law enforcement authorities.[59]

Many police departments have juvenile officers who are specially trained in dealing with juveniles. Because of the emphasis on rehabilitation that characterizes the juvenile justice process, juvenile officers can usually choose from a number of discretionary alternatives in the form of special programs, especially in the handling of nonviolent offenders. In Delaware County, Pennsylvania, for example, police departments participate in "youth aid panels." These panels are composed of private citizens who volunteer their services to provide an alternative to the formal juvenile court process. Youngsters who are referred to a panel and agree to abide by the decision of the group are diverted from the juvenile court.

Real justice conferencing (RJC) is another example of a diversionary program. Started in Bethlehem, Pennsylvania, in 1995, RJC is said to be a cost-effective approach to juvenile crime, school misconduct, and violence prevention. The Bethlehem program has served as a model for programs in other cities. It makes use of family group conferences (sometimes called *community conferences*) in lieu of school disciplinary or judicial processes or as a supplement to them. The family group conference, built around a restorative justice model, allows young offenders to tell what they did, to hear from those they affected, and to help decide how to repair the harm their actions caused. Successful RJC participants avoid the more formal mechanisms of the juvenile justice process.

However, even youth who are eventually diverted from the system may spend some time in custody. One juvenile case in five involves detention before adjudication.[60] Unlike the adult system, where jail is seen as the primary custodial alternative for people awaiting a first appearance, the use of secure detention for juveniles is acceptable only as a last resort. Detention hearings investigate whether candidates for confinement represent a "clear and immediate danger to themselves and/or

THE JUVENILE JUSTICE SYSTEM

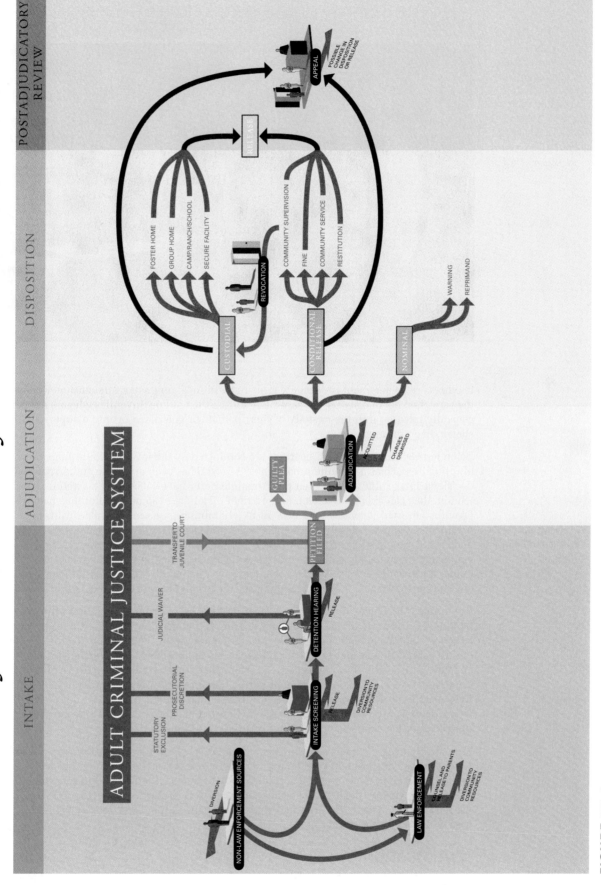

FIGURE 15-4

The juvenile justice system.

Juvenile court in action. Juvenile courts are expected to act in the best interests of the children who come before them. Should that rule apply to all juveniles who come before the court—no matter what their offense might be?

Billy Barnes/Stock Boston

to others." This judgment is normally rendered within 24 hours of apprehension. Runaways, since they are often not dangerous, are especially difficult to confine. Juveniles who are not detained are generally released into the custody of their parents or guardians or into a supervised temporary shelter, like a group home.

Detention Hearing   Detention hearings are conducted by the juvenile court judge or by an officer of the court, such as a juvenile probation officer who has been given the authority to make **intake** decisions. Intake officers, like their police counterparts, have substantial discretion. Along with detention, they can choose diversion and outright dismissal of some or all of the charges against the juvenile. Diverted juveniles may be sent to job-training programs, mental health facilities, drug-treatment programs, educational counseling, or other community service agencies. When caring parents are present who can afford private counseling or therapy, intake officers may release the juvenile into their custody with the understanding that they will provide for treatment. The National Center for Juvenile Justice estimates that more than half of all juvenile cases disposed of at intake are handled informally, without a petition, and are dismissed or diverted to a social service agency.[61]

Preliminary Hearing   A preliminary hearing may be held in conjunction with the detention hearing. The purpose of the preliminary hearing is to determine whether there is probable cause to believe that the juvenile committed the alleged act. At the hearing, the juvenile, along with the child's parents or guardians, will be advised of his or her rights as established by state legislation and court precedent. If probable cause is established, the juvenile may still be offered diversionary options, such as an "improvement period" or "probation with adjudication." These alternatives usually provide a one-year period during which the juvenile must avoid legal difficulties, attend school, and obey his or her parents. Charges may be dropped at the end of this informal probationary period if the juvenile has met the conditions specified.

Transfer Hearing   When a serious offense is involved, statutory provisions may allow for transfer of the case to adult court at the prosecuting attorney's request. Transfer hearings are held in juvenile court and focus on (1) the applicability of transfer statutes to the case under consideration and (2) whether the juvenile is amenable to treatment through the resources available to the juvenile justice system. Exceptions exist where statutes mandate transfer (as is sometimes the case with first-degree murder).

ADJUDICATION

Adjudicatory hearings for juveniles are similar to adult trials, with some notable exceptions. Similarities derive from the fact that the due process rights of children and adults are essentially the same. Differences include the following:

- *Emphasis on privacy.* An important distinctive characteristic of the juvenile system is its concern with privacy. Juvenile hearings are not open to the public or to the media. Witnesses are

intake

The first step in decision making regarding a juvenile whose behavior or alleged behavior is in violation of the law or could otherwise cause a juvenile court to assume jurisdiction.

adjudicatory hearing

The fact-finding process by which the juvenile court determines whether there is sufficient evidence to sustain the allegations in a petition.

CJ Today Exhibit 15–2

Juvenile Courts versus Adult Courts

The language used in juvenile courts is less harsh than that used in adult courts. For example, juvenile courts

- Accept "petitions of delinquency" rather than criminal complaints.

- Conduct "hearings," not trials
- "Adjudicate" juveniles to be "delinquent" rather than find them guilty of a crime
- Order one of a number of available "dispositions" rather than sentences

---

permitted to be present only to offer testimony and may not stay for the rest of the hearing. No transcript of the proceedings is created. One purpose of the emphasis on privacy is to prevent juveniles from being negatively labeled by the community.

- *Informality.* Whereas the adult criminal trial is highly structured, the juvenile hearing is more informal and less adversarial. The juvenile court judge takes an active role in the fact-finding process rather than serving as arbitrator between prosecution and defense.

- *Speed.* Informality, the lack of a jury, and the absence of an adversarial environment promote speed. While the adult trial may run into weeks or even months, the juvenile hearing is normally completed in a matter of hours or days.

- *Evidentiary standard.* On completion of the hearing, the juvenile court judge must weigh the evidence. If the charge involves a status offense, the judge may adjudicate the juvenile as a status offender upon finding that a preponderance of the evidence supports this finding. A preponderance of the evidence exists when evidence of an offense is more convincing than evidence offered to the contrary. If the charge involves a criminal-type offense, the evidentiary standard rises to the level of reasonable doubt.

- *Philosophy of the court.* Even in the face of strong evidence pointing to the offender's guilt, the judge may decide that it is not in the juvenile's best interests to be adjudicated delinquent. The judge also has the power, even after the evidence is presented, to divert the juvenile from the system. Juvenile court statistics indicate that only about half of all cases disposed of by juvenile courts are processed formally.[62] Formal processing involves the filing of a petition requesting an adjudicatory or transfer hearing. Informal cases, on the other hand, are handled without a petition. Among informally handled (nonpetitioned) delinquency cases, almost half were dismissed by the court. Most of the remainder resulted in voluntary probation (33%) or other dispositions (27%), but a small number (less than 1%) involved voluntary out-of-home placements.[63] Residential treatment was ordered 24% of the time in cases where the youth was adjudicated delinquent.[64]

- *No right to trial by jury.* As we discussed in our review of the U.S. Supreme Court case of *McKeiver* v. *Pennsylvania*,[65] juveniles do not have a constitutional right to trial by jury, and most states do not provide juveniles with a statutory opportunity for jury trial.[66]

Some jurisdictions, however, allow juveniles to be tried by their peers. The juvenile court in Columbus County, Georgia, for example, began experimenting with peer juries in 1980.[67] In Georgia, peer juries are composed of youths under the age of 17 who receive special training by the court. Jurors are required to be successful in school and may not be under the supervision of the court or have juvenile petitions pending against them. Training consists of classroom exposure to the philosophy of the juvenile court system, Georgia's juvenile code, and Supreme Court decisions affecting juvenile justice.[68] The county's youthful jurors are used only in the dispositional (or sentencing) stage of the court process, and then only when adjudicated youths volunteer to go before the jury.

Today, hundreds of **teen court** programs are in operation across the country. OJJDP notes that teen courts are "an effective intervention in many jurisdictions where enforcement of misdemeanor charges is sometimes given low priority because of heavy caseloads and the need to focus on more serious offenders."[69] Teen courts, says OJJDP, "present communities with opportunities to teach young people valuable life and coping skills and promote positive peer influence for youth who are defendants and for volunteer youth who play a variety of roles in the teen court process." Learn more about teen courts via Web Extra 15–3 at cjtoday.com.

Eventually, the justice system may need to adapt to a new environment in which all criminal matters are referred to a single system, regardless of the offender's age.

—Jeffrey Butts and Ojmarrh Mitchell[ii]

teen court

An alternative approach to juvenile justice in which alleged offenders are judged and sentenced by a jury of their peers.

WEB
Extra

DISPOSITION

dispositional hearing

The final stage in the processing of adjudicated juveniles in which a decision is made on the form of treatment or penalty that should be imposed on the child.

juvenile disposition

The decision of a juvenile court, concluding a dispositional hearing, that an adjudicated juvenile be committed to a juvenile correctional facility; be placed in a juvenile residence, shelter, or care or treatment program; be required to meet certain standards of conduct; or be released.

Once a juvenile has been found delinquent, the judge will set a **dispositional hearing**, which is similar to an adult sentencing hearing. Dispositional hearings are used to decide what action the court should take relative to the juvenile. As in adult courts, the judge may order a presentence investigation before making a dispositional decision. These investigations are conducted by special court personnel, sometimes called *juvenile court counselors*, who are, in effect, juvenile probation officers. Attorneys on both sides of the issue will also have the opportunity to make recommendations concerning dispositional alternatives.

The juvenile justice system typically gives the judge a much wider range of sentencing alternatives than does the adult system. Two major classes of **juvenile disposition** exist: to confine or not to confine. Because rehabilitation is still the primary objective of the juvenile court, the judge is likely to select the least restrictive alternative that meets the needs of the juvenile while recognizing the legitimate concerns of society for protection.

Most judges decide not to confine juveniles. Statistics indicate that in nearly two-thirds (62%) of all adjudicated delinquency cases, juveniles are placed on formal probation.[70] Probationary disposition usually means that juveniles will be released into the custody of a parent or guardian and ordered to undergo some form of training, education, or counseling. As in the adult system, juveniles placed on probation may be ordered to pay fines or to make restitution. In 11% of adjudicated delinquency cases, courts order juveniles to pay restitution or a fine, to participate in some form of community service, or to enter a treatment or counseling program—dispositions that require minimal continuing supervision by probation staff.[71] Because juveniles rarely have financial resources or jobs, most economic sanctions take the form of court-ordered work programs, as in refurbishing schools or cleaning school buses.

The Lehigh County (Pennsylvania) Juvenile Probation Office runs an innovative probation program that places juvenile probation officers in public schools. The officers function much like school counselors, paying special attention to the needs of their charges in areas like tutoring, attendance, and grades. In-school probation officers work at addressing problems as diverse as getting students to school on time (by developing personal schedules), raising grades (through improving study skills, tutoring, and sitting in on classes), and successful involvement in extracurricular activities. The program, which began more than a decade ago, has since been expanded through a federal grant to 29 other Pennsylvania counties.[72]

Of course, not all juveniles who are adjudicated delinquent receive probation. Nearly one-quarter (24%) of adjudicated cases in 1999 resulted in the youth being placed outside the home in a residential facility. In a relatively small number of cases (4%), the juvenile was adjudicated delinquent, but the case was then dismissed or the youth was otherwise released.[73]

Secure Institutions for Juveniles　Juveniles who demonstrate the potential for serious new offenses may be ordered to participate in rehabilitative programs within a secure environment, such as a youth center or a training school. As of January 2003, approximately 104,400 young people were being held under custodial supervision in the United States.[74] Of these, 25% were being held for personal crimes like murder, rape, or robbery; 29% were being held for property crimes; 9% were locked up for drug offenses; 23% were held for public-order offenses (including weapons offenses); and 4% were held for status offenses. Probation and parole violations accounted for another 14% of those confined.[75]

Most confined juveniles are held in semisecure facilities designed to look less like prisons and more like residential high school campuses. Most states, however, operate at least one secure facility for juveniles that is intended as a home for the most recalcitrant youthful offenders. Halfway houses, "boot camps,"[76] ranches, forestry camps, wilderness programs, group homes, and state-hired private facilities also hold some of the juveniles reported to be under confinement. Children placed in group homes continue to attend school and live in a family-like environment in the company of other adjudicated children, shepherded by "house parents." Learn more about the juvenile justice systems of each state from the National Center for Juvenile Justice's State Juvenile Justice Profiles via Web Extra 15–4 at cjtoday.com.

The operative philosophy of custodial programs for juveniles focuses squarely on the rehabilitative ideal. Juveniles are usually committed to secure facilities for indeterminate periods of time, with the typical stay being less than one year. Release is often timed to coincide with the beginning or the end of the school year.

Most juvenile facilities are small, with 80% designed to hold 40 residents or fewer.[77] Many institutionalized juveniles are held in the thousand or so homelike facilities across the nation that are limited to ten residents or fewer.[78] At the other end of the scale are the nation's 70 large juvenile institutions, each designed to hold more than 200 hard-core delinquents.[79] Residential facilities for juveniles are intensively staffed. One study found that staff members out-

WEB
Extra
■■■■

number residents ten to nine on the average in state-run institutions, and by an even greater ratio in privately run facilities.[80]

Jurisdictions vary widely in their use of secure detention for juveniles. In 2001, juvenile custody populations ranged from a low of 62 in Vermont to a high of 18,145 in California.[81] This variance reflects population differences as well as economic realities and philosophical beliefs. Some jurisdictions, like California, expect rehabilitative costs to be borne by the state rather than by families or local government agencies. Hence, California shows a higher rate of institutionalization than many other states. Similarly, some states have more firmly embraced the reformation ideal and are more likely to use diversionary options for juveniles.

Characteristics of Juveniles in Confinement Institutionalized juveniles are a small but special category of young people with serious problems. A recent report on institutionalized youth by the Bureau of Justice Statistics found five striking characteristics:[82]

- 85.5% were male.
- 38.9% were black, 39.4% were white, and 17.3% were Hispanic.
- 6.5% were institutionalized for having committed a status offense, such as being truant, running away, or violating curfew.
- 42.4% were in residential facilities for a serious personal or property offense.
- 1% were charged with homicide.

Overcrowding in Juvenile Facilities As in adult prisons, overcrowding exists in many juvenile institutions. In a recent survey, half of all states reported overcrowding in juvenile facilities, and 22 states were operating facilities at more than 50% over capacity.[83]

A national study of the conditions of confinement in juvenile detention facilities conducted by OJJDP found that "there are several areas in which problems in juvenile facilities are substantial and widespread—most notably living space, health care, security, and control of suicidal behavior."[84] Using a variety of evaluative criteria, the study found that 47% of juveniles were confined in facilities whose populations exceeded their reported design capacity and that 33% of residents had to sleep "in rooms that were smaller than required by nationally recognized standards." To address the problem, the authors of the study recommended the use of alternative placement options so that only juveniles judged to be the most dangerous to their communities would be confined in secure facilities. Similarly, because it found that injuries to residents were most likely to occur within large dormitory-like settings, the OJJDP study recommended that "large dormitories be eliminated from juvenile facilities." Finally, the study recommended that "all juveniles be screened for risk of suicidal behavior immediately upon their admission to confinement" and that initial health screenings be "carried out promptly at admission." Other problems that OJJDP found "still important enough to warrant attention" included education and treatment services. Further study of both areas is needed, OJJDP said.

A number of states use private facilities. A survey found that 13 states contract with 328 private facilities—most of which were classified as halfway houses—for the custody of adjudicated juveniles.[85] In the past few years, admissions to private facilities (comprised primarily of halfway houses, group homes, shelters, ranches, camps, and farms) have increased by more than 100%, compared with an increase of only about 10% for public facilities (mostly detention centers and training schools).[86] The fastest-growing category of detained juveniles includes drug and alcohol offenders. Approximately 12% of all juvenile detainees are being held because of alcohol- and drug-related offenses.[87] Reflecting widespread socioeconomic disparities, an OJJDP report found that "a juvenile held in a public facility . . . was most likely to be black, male, between 14 and 17 years of age, and held for a delinquent offense such as a property crime or a crime against a person. On the other hand, a juvenile held in custody in a private facility . . . was most likely to be white, male, 14 to 17 years of age, and held for a nondelinquent offense such as running away, truancy, or incorrigibility."[88] The report also noted that "juvenile corrections has become increasingly privatized."

POSTADJUDICATORY REVIEW

The detrimental effects of institutionalization on young offenders may make the opportunity for appellate review more critical for juveniles than it is for adults. However, federal court precedents have yet to establish a clear right to appeal from juvenile court. Even so, most states do have statutory provisions that make such appeals possible.[89]

From a practical point of view, however, juvenile appeals may not be as consequential as are appeals of adult criminal convictions. Most juvenile complaints are handled informally, while only a relatively small proportion of adjudicated delinquents are placed outside the family. Moreover,

Recent arrivals at a California "boot camp" for juvenile offenders listening to what will be expected of them. Although institutionalized juveniles are housed separately from adult offenders, juvenile institutions share many of the problems of adult facilities. What changes have recently occurred in the handling of juvenile offenders?

Tony Savino/JB Pictures, Ltd./The Image Works

because sentence lengths are short for most confined juveniles, appellate courts hardly have time to complete the review process before the juvenile is released.

The Post–Juvenile Court Era

Three decades of reform have largely dissolved the traditional juvenile court, and the system that remains is rapidly losing political viability. Policy makers may soon need to devise an entirely new process for handling young offenders.

—Jeffrey Butts and Adele Harrell[iii]

In August 2005, Mitchell Johnson was released from a federal facility for youthful offenders.[90] Mitchell, whose release was mandated by law on his twenty-first birthday, was 13 years old in 1998 when he and an 11-year-old friend, Andrew Golden, murdered four children and a teacher at Westside Middle School in Jonesboro, Arkansas, with hunting rifles they had taken from Golden's grandfather. At the time of the killings, laws in Arkansas and many other states allowed juveniles to be confined only until they reached their eighteenth birthday—no matter how serious their offense. It was only Johnson's conviction on federal gun charges that had kept him locked up for an additional three years.

Cases like Johnson's, combined with extensive media coverage of violent juvenile crime across the United States, fueled public perceptions that violence committed by teenagers had reached epidemic proportions and that no community was immune to random acts of youth violence. At the same time, the apparent "professionalization" of delinquency, the hallmark of which is the repeated and often violent criminal involvement of juveniles in drug-related gang activity, came to be viewed as a major challenge to the idealism of the juvenile justice system. Consequently, by the turn of the twenty-first century, the issue of youth violence was at or near the top of nearly every state's agenda. Most states took some form of legislative or executive action to stem what was seen as an escalating level of dangerous crime by juveniles. As OJJDP observed, "This level of [legislative and executive] activity has occurred only three other times in our nation's history: at the outset of the juvenile court movement at the turn of the [twentieth] century; following the U.S. Supreme Court's *Gault* decision in 1967; and with the enactment of the Juvenile Justice and Delinquency Prevention Act in 1974."[91] OJJDP has identified five significant developments that have taken place in many states over the past decade:[92]

- *Transfer provisions.* Laws that make it easier to transfer juvenile offenders from the juvenile justice system to the criminal justice system.
- *Sentencing authority.* Laws that give criminal and juvenile courts expanded sentencing options, such as **blended sentences**, in cases involving juveniles.
- *Confidentiality changes.* Modifications to laws containing court confidentiality provisions in order to make juvenile records and proceedings more open.
- *Victims' rights.* New laws that increase the role of victims of juvenile crime in the juvenile justice process.
- *Correctional programming.* The development of new programs in adult and juvenile facilities to handle juveniles sentenced as adults or as violent juvenile offenders.

blended sentence

A juvenile court disposition that imposes both a juvenile sanction and an adult criminal sentence upon an adjudicated delinquent. The adult sentence is suspended if the juvenile offender successfully completes the term of the juvenile disposition and refrains from committing any new offense.[iv]

Jeffrey Butts and Ojmarrh Mitchell, members of the Program on Law and Behavior at the Urban Institute in Washington, D.C., and experts on juvenile justice, say that today, "policymakers throughout the United States have greatly dissolved the border between juvenile and criminal justice. Young people who violate the law are no longer guaranteed special consideration from the legal system. Some form of juvenile court still exists in every state, but the purposes and procedures of juvenile courts are becoming indistinguishable from those of criminal courts."[93] Butts and Mitchell also claim that "changes in juvenile law and juvenile court procedure are slowly dismantling the jurisdictional border between juvenile and criminal justice."[94] As evidence, they note that juvenile courts across the United States are becoming increasingly similar to criminal courts in the methods they use to reach conclusions and to process cases, as well as in the general atmosphere that characterizes them.

As a result of ongoing changes, some say that many states have substantially "criminalized" juvenile courts. In March 2000, for example, California voters endorsed sweeping changes in the state's juvenile justice system by passing Proposition 21, the Gang Violence and Juvenile Crime Prevention Act. The law reduces confidentiality in the juvenile court, limits the use of probation for young offenders, and increases the power of prosecutors to send juveniles to adult court and to put them in adult prisons. Public support for the measure was undiminished by projections that it would increase operational costs in the California juvenile justice system by $500 million annually.[95] Because laws like California's Proposition 21 are being passed at a growing rate throughout the country, a leading expert on juvenile justice notes that "the similarities of juvenile and adult courts are becoming greater than the differences between them."[96]

Cindy Lederman, presiding judge of the Miami-Dade Juvenile Court, refers to the changes as the "adultification" of the juvenile justice system.[97] The juvenile court, says Lederman, has undergone significant change since it was created. In the early twentieth century, the juvenile court focused on social welfare and was primarily concerned with acting in a child's best interest. By the mid-twentieth century, it had seized on the issue of children's due process rights as an important guiding principle. The court today, says Lederman, has turned its focus to accountability and punishment.

Proposals for further change abound. In 2001, the Task Force on Juvenile Justice Reform (TFJJR) of the American Academy of Child and Adolescent Psychiatry issued a report on juvenile justice reform. The report covered many areas, including competence to stand trial, forensic evaluations of children and adolescents, recommended standards for juvenile detention and confinement facilities, health care in the juvenile justice system, female youth in the juvenile justice system, disproportionate minority confinement, the educational needs of youth in juvenile justice facilities, and the transfer of juvenile cases to criminal courts. Read the entire report at Library Extra 15–2 at cjtoday.com.

LIBRARY
Extra
■■■■

The Department of Justice Authorization Act for Fiscal Year 2003[98] set dramatic new accountability standards for federally funded programs for juveniles who violate the law.[99] The law built on the premise that young people who violate criminal laws should be held accountable for their offenses through the swift and consistent application of sanctions that are proportionate to the offense.[100] Lawmakers made it clear that it was their belief that enhanced accountability and swift sanctions were both a matter of basic justice and a way to combat delinquency and improve the quality of life in our nation's communities.

The flood of new federal and state legislation, mandated by surging public demand for greater responsibility among adolescents, is leading to significant changes in the American juvenile justice system. Hence, the juvenile justice system of the mid-twenty-first century may in many respects be quite different than the one we have known for the past hundred years. Learn more about likely changes to the juvenile justice system at Library Extra 15–3 at cjtoday.com. For an overview of the issues being debated, see Web Extra 15–5 at cjtoday.com.

LIBRARY   **WEB**
Extra   Extra
■■■■   ■■■■

Children are the living messages we send to a time we will not see.

–John Whitehead[v]

SUMMARY

- Under today's laws, children occupy a special status that is tied closely to cultural advances that occurred in the Western world during the past 200 years. Before the modern era, children who committed crimes received no preferential treatment. They were adjudicated, punished, and imprisoned alongside adults. Beginning a few hundred years ago, England, from which we derive many of our legal traditions, adapted the principle of *parens patriae*. That principle allowed the government to take the place of parents in dealing with children who broke the law. Around the middle of the nineteenth century, the child-savers movement began in the United States. Child savers espoused a philosophy of productivity and eschewed idleness and unprincipled behavior. Not long afterward, the 1899 codification of Illinois juvenile law became the model for juvenile court statutes throughout the United States. It created a juvenile court separate in form and function from adult criminal courts and based on the principle of *parens patriae*. To avoid the lasting stigma of criminality, the term *delinquent*, rather than *criminal*, began to be applied to young adjudicated offenders. Soon, juvenile courts across the country focused primarily on the best interests of the child as a guide in their deliberations.

- Important U.S. Supreme Court decisions of special relevance to the handling of juveniles by the justice system include (1) *Kent* v. *U.S.* (1966), which established minimal due process standards for juvenile hearings; (2) *In re Gault* (1967), in which the Court found that a child has many of the same due process rights as an adult; (3) *In re Winship*, which held that the constitutional safeguard of proof beyond a reasonable doubt is required during the adjudicatory stage of a delinquency proceeding; (4) *McKeiver* v. *Pennsylvania* (1971), which held that jury trials were not required in delinquency cases; (5) *Breed* v. *Jones* (1975), which restricted the conditions under which transfers from juvenile to adult court may occur; (6) *Schall* v. *Martin* (1984), in which the Court held that pretrial detention of juveniles based on "serious risk" does not violate due process, although prior notice, an equitable detention hearing, and a statement by the juvenile court judge explaining the reasons for detention are required; and (7) *Roper* v. *Simmons* (2005), which held that age *is* a bar to capital punishment when the offender commits a capital crime when he or she is younger than 18.

- Due process guarantees, as interpreted by the U.S. Supreme Court, are designed to ensure that juvenile proceedings are fair and that the interests of juveniles are protected. Although the Court has established that juveniles are entitled to fundamental due process protections, it has refrained from declaring that juveniles have a right to all aspects of due process afforded adult defendants. The juvenile justice system differs in other ways from the adult system. For example, the juvenile system (1) is less concerned with legal issues of guilt or innocence and focuses on the child's best interests; (2) emphasizes treatment rather than punishment; (3) ensures privacy and protection from public scrutiny through the use of sealed records and laws against publishing the names of juvenile offenders; (4) uses the techniques of social science in dispositional decision making rather than sentences determined by a perceived need for punishment; (5) does not order long-term confinement, with most juveniles being released from institutions by their twenty-first birthday; (6) has separate facilities for juveniles; and (7) allows broad discretionary alternatives at all points in the process.

- The juvenile justice system's commitment to a philosophy of protection and restoration, expressed in the juvenile court movement of the late nineteenth and early twentieth centuries, has begun to dissipate. The present juvenile system, for the most part, still differs substantially from the adult system in the multitude of opportunities it provides for diversion and in the emphasis it places on rehabilitation rather than punishment. The "professionalization" of delinquency, however, the hallmark of which is the repeated and often violent criminal involvement of juveniles in drug-related gang activity, represents a major challenge to the idealism of the juvenile justice system. Efforts to address that challenge are starting to result in what some have called the "adultification" of the juvenile justice system.

KEY TERMS

abused child, 553

adjudicatory hearing, 566

blended sentence, 570

delinquency, 549

delinquent child, 553

dependent child, 553

dispositional hearing, 568

intake, 566

juvenile disposition, 568

juvenile justice system, 549

juvenile petition, 564

neglected child, 553

parens patriae, 550

status offender, 552

status offense, 552

teen court, 567

undisciplined child, 553

KEY CASES

Breed v. *Jones,* 559

In re Gault, 556

In re Winship, 558

Kent v. *U.S.,* 556

McKeiver v. *Pennsylvania,* 559

Roper v. *Simmons,* 560

Schall v. *Martin,* 560

QUESTIONS FOR REVIEW

1. Describe the history and evolution of the juvenile justice system in the Western world, and list the six categories of children recognized by the laws of most states.

2. What was the impact of the *Gault* decision on juvenile justice in America? What adult rights were not accorded to juveniles by *Gault*? What other U.S. Supreme Court decisions have had a substantial impact on the handling of juvenile offenders by the justice system?

3. What are the major similarities and differences between the juvenile and adult justice systems?

4. In your opinion, should juveniles continue to receive what many regard as preferential treatment from the courts? Why or why not?

QUESTIONS FOR REFLECTION

1. This chapter pointed out that substantial changes are now afoot in the area of juvenile justice. What are some of those changes? With which of those changes do you agree? Are there any with which you don't agree? Explain.

2. This chapter discussed California's Proposition 21, which voters in that state passed in 2000. What was the intent of Proposition 21? Were the changes that it brought about needed, or do you think that the state would have been better off if the proposition had failed to pass? Why?

3. What is meant by the "adultification" of the juvenile justice system? Is adultification a good idea? Explain.

Discuss your answers to these questions and other issues on the CJ Today e-mail discussion list (join the list at cjtoday.com).

WEB QUEST

Visit the National Council on Crime and Delinquency (NCCD) at http://www.nccd-crc.org. What are some of the areas in which NCCD is working to prevent and understand delinquency? What other areas do you think it should be exploring?

Use the Cybrary to identify other juvenile justice research and delinquency-prevention sites on the Web. Which sites contain information about school shootings? What, if anything, do they suggest can be done to reduce the incidence of these crimes? Submit your findings to your instructor if asked to do so.

To complete this Web Quest online, go to the Web Quest module in Chapter 15 of the *Criminal Justice Today* Companion Website at cjtoday.com.

CHAPTER 16

Drugs and Crime

LEARNING OBJECTIVES

After reading this chapter, you should be able to

- Explain the nature of illegal drugs and the role that social convention plays in deciding what constitutes an illegal drug.

- Discuss the history of drug abuse and of antidrug legislation in America.

- Identify the different types of drugs that are illegally used in this country, as well as the effects and legal classifications of each.

- Explain the link between drugs and other social problems, including different forms of criminal activity.

- Describe the various efforts to respond to the drug problem and assess the effectiveness of each.

OUTLINE

As the Republican governor of New Mexico, I'm neither soft on crime nor pro-drugs in any sense. I believe a person who harms another person should be punished. But as a successful businessman, I also believe that locking up more and more people who are nonviolent drug offenders, people whose real problem is that they are addicted to drugs, is simply a waste of money and human resources.

—Former Governor Gary Johnson[1]

The myth that anti-drug efforts do not work is refuted by the tireless, everyday efforts of our partners in this struggle: parents, teachers, coaches, and community leaders throughout the nation. They are a tribute to what works and what has kept these levels from skyrocketing.

—"Drug Czar" John P. Walters[2]

Hear the author discuss this chapter at cjtoday.com

drug abuse

Illicit drug use that results in social, economic, psychological, or legal problems for the user.[i]

Introduction

Drug abuse is pervasive in American society. A recent Police Foundation survey of 300 police chiefs across the country found that drug abuse is the most serious law enforcement problem facing communities today.[3] Sixty-three percent of the chiefs, who represented cities and towns of all sizes, cited drug abuse as an "extremely serious" or "very serious" problem. Other serious problems that the chiefs identified were domestic violence (50%), property crime (48%), violent crime (18%), and the threat of terrorism (17%). As the chiefs knew well, the last four decades have seen a dramatic increase in drug-related crime relative to other offenses, and a corresponding expansion of both drug laws and efforts at enforcement.

The resulting impact on the criminal justice system has been nothing less than phenomenal. In some parts of the country, court dockets have become so clogged with drug cases that criminal case processing has almost ground to a halt. Prison populations also reflect the huge increase in drug crimes (Figure 16–1). Today, three-quarters of the growth in the number of federal prison inmates is due to drug crimes,[4] and about 70% of all first offenders in the federal prisons are serving drug sentences. This is also true of 85% of the noncitizens and 66% of women who are imprisoned. And drug offenders are rarely violent. More than half (55.7%) of federal prisoners

FIGURE 16–1

Percentage of federal prisoners sentenced for drug offenses, 1970–2006.

Source: Sourcebook of Criminal Justice Statistics Online.

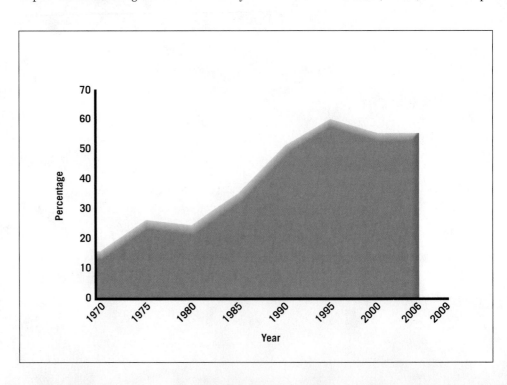

sentenced for a drug offense fall into the lowest criminal history category of the federal sentencing guidelines, and in 87% of cases no weapon is involved.[5] Although drug crimes account for only about 20% of state prison populations, the number of men held in state prisons as a result of drug crimes has increased by almost 50% since 1990, while the number of women incarcerated for drug crimes has risen by 108%.[6] Even though we are incarcerating more drug offenders than ever before, a strong majority of the chiefs who were surveyed in 2004 said that today's drug problem is greater than it was in the mid-1990s.[7] Only 1% of the surveyed chiefs scored the police response to drug abuse as "very successful."[8]

Drug Abuse: More Than an Individual Choice

While in many textbooks drug-related crime is looked at briefly as one of several social-order or victimless crimes, in this book we will take an in-depth look at drug crime because of its pervasive and far-reaching impact, not only on the criminal justice system but on all aspects of society. Drug abuse accounts for a large proportion of present-day law violations. It contributes to other types of criminal activity, such as smuggling, theft, robbery, and murder, and leads to a huge number of arrests, clogged courtrooms, and overcrowded prisons. As a consequence, drug abuse places tremendous strain on the criminal justice system, and the fight against it is one of the most expensive activities ever undertaken by federal, state, and local governments.

Because drug abuse is one of a great number of social-order offenses, it shares a number of characteristics with "victimless" crimes, like prostitution and gambling. A hallmark of such crimes is that they involve willing participants. In the case of drug-law violations, buyers, sellers, and users willingly purchase, sell, and consume illegal drugs. They do not complain to the authorities of criminal injuries to themselves or to others resulting from the illegal use of drugs. Few so-called victimless crimes, however, are truly without an injured party. Even where the criminal participant does not perceive an immediate or personal injury, the behavior frequently affects the legitimate interests of nonparticipants. In many so-called victimless crimes, it is society that is the ultimate victim. Prostitution, for example, lowers property values in areas where it regularly occurs, degrades the status of women, and may victimize the customers and their families through the spread of AIDS and other venereal diseases.

Drug abuse has many of its own destructive consequences, including lost productivity, an inequitable distribution of economic resources among the poorest members of society, disease, wasted human potential, fragmented families, violence, and other crimes. Some evidence has even linked drug trafficking to international terrorism and to efforts to overthrow the democratic governments of the West. Each of these consequences will be discussed in some detail in this chapter. We begin now with an analysis of what constitutes a drug, explore the history of drug abuse in America, and then describe the various categories of major **controlled substances**. Finally, we will

controlled substance

A specifically defined bioactive or psychoactive chemical substance proscribed by law.

Former Playboy Playmate and billionaire's widow Anna Nicole Smith posing with her son, Daniel Wayne Smith, and her baby girl, Dannie Lynn Hope, on September 9, 2006, at Doctors Hospital in the Bahamas. Daniel died one day after this photo was taken—apparently from a fatal mixture of prescription drugs, including the heroin antagonist methadone. Smith died in 2007 in a Florida hotel room from what the medical examiner's office indicated was combined drug intoxication, produced by ingesting a number of prescription medicines in what may have been relatively large quantities simultaneously. Might their deaths have been prevented? If so, how?

Getty Images, Inc.

WEB
Extra

look at the link between drugs and other forms of crime and will describe possible solutions to the problem of drug abuse. See Web Extra 16–1 at cjtoday.com to learn more about drugs and crime.

What Is a Drug?

drug

Any chemical substance defined by social convention as bioactive or psychoactive.

Before we begin any comprehensive discussion of drugs, we must first grapple with the concept of what a drug is. In common usage, a **drug** may be any ingestible substance that has a noticeable effect on the mind or body. Drugs may enter the body via injection, inhalation, swallowing, or even direct absorption through the skin or mucous membranes. Some drugs, like penicillin and tranquilizers, are useful in medical treatment, while others, like heroin and cocaine, are attractive only to **recreational drug users**[9] or to those who are addicted to them.

recreational drug user

A person who uses drugs relatively infrequently and primarily with friends and in social contexts that define drug use as pleasurable. Most addicts begin as recreational users.

In determining which substances should be called "drugs," it is important to recognize the role that social definitions of any phenomenon play in our understanding of it. Hence, what Americans today consider to be a drug depends more on social convention or agreed-on definitions than it does on any inherent property of the substance itself. The history of marijuana provides a case in point. Before the early twentieth century, marijuana was freely available in the United States. Although alcohol was the recreational drug of choice at the time, marijuana found a following among some artists and musicians. Marijuana was also occasionally used for medical purposes to "calm the nerves" and to treat hysteria. Howard Becker, in his classic study of the early Federal Bureau of Narcotics (forerunner of the Drug Enforcement Administration, or DEA), demonstrates how federal agencies worked to outlaw marijuana in order to increase their power.[10] Federally funded publications voiced calls for laws against the substance, and movies like *Reefer Madness* led the drive toward classifying marijuana as a dangerous drug. The 1939 Marijuana Tax Act was the result, and marijuana has been thought of as a drug worthy of federal and local enforcement efforts ever since.

Both the law and social convention make strong distinctions between drugs that are socially acceptable and those that are not. Some substances with profound effects on the mind and body are not even thought of as drugs. Gasoline fumes, chemical vapors of many kinds, perfumes, certain vitamins, sugar-rich foods, and toxic chemicals may all have profound effects. Even so, most people do not think of these substances as drugs, and they are rarely regulated by the criminal law.

Recent social awareness has reclassified alcohol, caffeine, and nicotine as "drugs," although before the 1960s it is doubtful that most Americans would have applied that word to these three substances. Even today, alcohol, caffeine, and nicotine are readily available throughout the country, with only minimal controls on their manufacture and distribution. As a result, these three drugs continue to enjoy favored status in both our law and culture. Nonetheless, alcohol abuse and addiction are commonplace in American society, and anyone who has tried to quit smoking knows the power that nicotine can wield.

Occupying a middle ground on the continuum between acceptability and illegality are substances that have a legitimate medical use and are usually available only with a prescription. Antibiotics, diet pills, and, in particular, tranquilizers, stimulants, and mood-altering chemicals (like the popular drug Prozac) are culturally acceptable but typically can be attained legally only with a physician's prescription. The majority of Americans clearly recognize these substances as drugs, albeit useful ones.

psychoactive substance

A chemical substance that affects cognition, feeling, or awareness.

Powerful drugs, those with the ability to produce substantially altered states of consciousness and with a high potential for addiction, occupy the forefront in social and legal condemnation. Among them are **psychoactive substances** like heroin, peyote, mescaline, LSD, and cocaine. Even here, however, legitimate uses for such drugs may exist. Cocaine is used in the treatment of certain medical conditions and can be applied as a topical anesthetic during medical interventions. LSD has been employed experimentally to investigate the nature of human consciousness, and peyote and mescaline may be used legally by members of the Native American Church in religious services. Even heroin has been advocated as beneficial in relieving the suffering associated with some forms of terminal illness. Hence, answers to the question of "What is a drug?" depend to a large extent on the social definitions and conventions operating at a given time and in a given place. Some of the clearest definitional statements relating to controlled substances can be found in the law, although informal strictures and definitions guide much of everyday drug use.

Alcohol Abuse

Although the abuse of alcohol is rarely described in the same terms as the illegal use of controlled substances, alcohol misuse can lead to serious problems with grim consequences. Ten years ago, for example, a pickup truck driven by Gallardo Bermudes, 35, rear-ended a car carrying 11 people—two adults and nine children—near Beaumont, California.[11] Most of the children in the car were the sons and daughters of Jose Luis Rodriquez and Mercedes Diaz. Eight of the children burned to death when the car flipped and caught fire after being hit. Bermudes, who fled from the scene, had been convicted of drunk driving on three previous occasions. He later told police investigators that he had consumed 10 to 15 beers before the crash.

Most states define a blood-alcohol level of 0.08% to 0.10% or more as intoxication and hold that anyone who drives with that amount of alcohol in his or her blood is driving under the influence (DUI) of alcohol.[12] In October 2000, however, an amendment to a federal highway construction bill[13] required that states lower their blood-alcohol limits for drunk driving to 0.08% by the year 2004 or lose a substantial percentage of the federal highway construction funds allocated to them.[14] Any state that adopts the new standard by 2007 will be permitted to recover any previously forfeited highway funds.

Drunk driving has been a major social concern for some time. Groups like Mothers against Drunk Driving (MADD) and Remove Intoxicated Drivers (RID) have given impetus to enforcement efforts to curb drunk drivers. Today, approximately 1.5 million drunk-driving arrests are made annually—more than for any offense other than drug abuse.[15] The average driver arrested for DUI is substantially impaired. Studies show that he or she has consumed an average of six ounces of pure alcohol (the equivalent of a dozen bottles of beer) in the four hours preceding arrest.[16] Twenty-six percent of arrestees have consumed nearly twice that amount. Approximately 40% of all vehicle crashes resulting in death are alcohol related.[17] The National Highway Traffic Safety Administration estimates that alcohol caused 17,013 traffic fatalities in 2003—the first year since 1999 that showed a decline from the previous year in alcohol-related fatalities.[18] (Visit MADD via Web Extra 16–2 at cjtoday.com.)

Another offense directly related to alcohol consumption is public drunkenness. During the late 1960s and early 1970s, some groups fought to decriminalize drunkenness and to treat it as a health problem. Although the number of arrests for public drunkenness reached 553,188 in 2006,[19] law enforcement officers retain a great deal of discretion in handling these offenders. Many people who are drunk in public, unless they are assaultive or involved in other crimes, are likely to receive an "official escort" home rather than face arrest.

The use of alcohol may also lead to the commission of other, very serious crimes. Some experts have found that alcohol use lowers inhibitions and increases the likelihood of aggression.[20] A report by the National Institute of Justice (NIJ) concluded that "of all psychoactive substances, alcohol is the only one whose consumption has been shown to commonly increase aggression."[21] As Figure 16–2 shows, approximately 37% of offenders consume alcohol immediately before committing a crime.[22] In cases of violent crime, the percentage of offenders under the influence of alcohol at the time of the crime jumps to 42%—and is highest for murder (44.6%).[23]

Lawmakers appear willing to deal with the problems caused by alcohol only indirectly. The American experience with Prohibition is not one that legislators are anxious to repeat. In all likelihood, future efforts to reduce the damaging effects of alcohol will continue to take the form of educational programs, legislation to raise the drinking age, and enforcement efforts designed to deter the most visible forms of abuse. Struggles in other areas may also have some impact. For example, lawsuits claiming civil damages are now being brought against some liquor companies and taverns on behalf of accident victims, cirrhosis patients, and others. We can anticipate, however, that while concern over alcohol abuse will continue, few sweeping changes in either law or social custom will occur anytime soon.

A History of Drug Abuse in America

Alcohol is but one example of the many conflicting images of drug use prevalent in contemporary American society. The "war on drugs," initiated during the latter part of the twentieth century, portrayed an America fighting for its very existence against the scourge of drug abuse. While many of the negative images of drugs that emanated from the "war" period may be correct, they have not always been a part of the American worldview.

Opium and its derivatives, for example, were widely available in patent medicines of the nineteenth and early twentieth centuries. Corner drugstores stocked mixtures of opium and alcohol, and traveling road shows extolled the virtues of these magical curatives. These elixirs, purported to offer relief from almost every malady, did indeed bring about feelings of well-being in most users. Although no one is certain just how widespread opium use was in the United States a hundred years ago, some authors have observed that baby formulas containing opium were fed to infants born to addicted mothers.[24]

WEB
Extra

The drug problem did not develop overnight; it took years and years to get to this point as a result of misguided attitudes and a mindset that drug usage, at least using cocaine and marijuana, was all right. Dealing with the drug problem involves changing attitudes, and that takes time.

—Judge Reggie B. Walton

FIGURE 16–2

Percentage of state prisoners admitting drug use immediately before crime commission, by type of drug.

Source: Christopher J. Mumola, *Substance Abuse and Treatment, State and Federal Prisoners, 1997* (Washington, DC: Bureau of Justice Statistics, 1999).

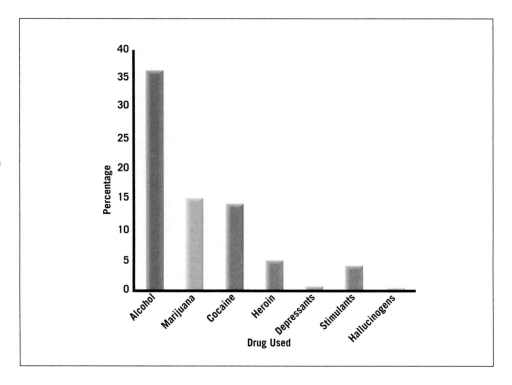

I keep in my house a letter from Bill O'Dwyer, who once was the mayor of New York, and who wrote to me, "There is no power on earth to match the power of the poor, who, just by sitting in their hopelessness, can bring the rest of us down." It always sounded right, but I never saw it happen until crack came along. And with it, there are no more rules in American crime. The implied agreements on which we were raised are gone. You now shoot women and children. A news reporter is safe as long as he is not there. A cop in his uniform means nothing.

—Jimmy Breslin[ii]

Opium was also widely used by Chinese immigrants who came to the West Coast in the nineteenth century, often to work on the railroads. Opium dens—in which the drug was smoked—flourished, and the use of opium quickly spread to other ethnic groups throughout the West. Some of the more affluent denizens of West Coast cities ate the substance, and avant-garde poetry was written extolling the virtues of the drug.

Morphine, an opium derivative, has a similar history. Although it was legally available in this country almost since its invention, its use as a painkiller on the battlefields of the Civil War dramatically heightened public awareness of the drug.[25] In the late nineteenth century, morphine was widely prescribed by physicians and dentists, many of whom abused the substance themselves. By 1896, per capita morphine consumption peaked, and addiction to the substance throughout the United States was apparently widespread.[26]

Heroin, the most potent derivative of opium ever created, was invented as a substitute for morphine in 1874. It was commercially marketed as a new pain remedy and cough suppressant beginning in 1898.[27] When it was first introduced, heroin's addictive properties were unknown, and it was said to be useful in treating morphine addiction.[28]

Marijuana, which is considerably less potent than heroin, has a relatively short history in this country. Imported by Mexican immigrants around the turn of the twentieth century, the drug quickly became associated with nonmainstream groups. By 1930, most of the states in the Southwest had passed legislation outlawing marijuana, and some authors have suggested that antimarijuana laws were primarily targeted at Spanish-speaking immigrants who were beginning to challenge whites in the economic sector.[29] As mentioned earlier, other writers have suggested that the rapidly growing use of marijuana throughout the 1920s and 1930s provided a rationale for the development of drug legislation and the concomitant expansion of drug-enforcement agencies.[30] By the 1960s, public attitudes regarding marijuana had begun to change. The hippie generation popularized the drug, touting its "mellowing" effects on users. In a short time, marijuana use became epidemic across the country, and books on marijuana cultivation and preparation flourished.

Another drug that found adherents among some youthful idealists of the 1960s and 1970s was LSD. LSD, whose chemical name is lysergic acid diethylamide, was first synthesized in Switzerland in 1938 and was used occasionally in this country in the 1950s for the treatment of psychiatric disorders.

Many drugs, when first "discovered," were touted for their powerful analgesic or therapeutic effects. Cocaine was one of them. An early leading proponent of cocaine use, for example, was

A Mexican federal policeman guarding a shipment of high-grade cocaine seized near Mexico City. Drug abuse is one of the most significant problems facing the criminal justice system and society today. What other kinds of crime are linked to drug crime?

Miguel Castillo/MIC Photo Press/Corbis/Sygma

Sigmund Freud, who prescribed it for a variety of psychological disorders. Freud was himself a user and wrote a book, *The Cocaine Papers*, describing the many benefits of the drug. The cocaine bandwagon reached the United States in the late nineteenth century, and various medicines and beverages containing cocaine were offered to the American public. Prominent among them was Coca-Cola, which combined seltzer water, sugar, and cocaine in a new soft drink advertised as providing a real "pick-me-up." Cocaine was removed from Coca-Cola in 1910 but continued to be used by jazz musicians and artists. Beginning in the 1970s, cocaine became associated with exclusive parties, the well-to-do, and the jet set. It was not long before an extensive drug underworld developed, catering to the demands of affluent users. Crack cocaine, a derivative of powdered cocaine that is smoked, became popular in the 1980s and is sold today in the form of "rocks," "cookies," or "biscuits" (large pieces of crack).

Drug Use and Social Awareness

Although drugs have long been a part of American society, there have been dramatic changes during the last century in the form drug use takes and in the social consequences associated with drug involvement. Specifically, six elements have emerged that today cast drug use in a far different light than in the past:

- The conceptualization of addiction as a physical condition
- The understanding that drug use is associated with other kinds of criminal activity
- Generally widespread social condemnation of drug use as a waste of economic resources and human lives
- Comprehensive and detailed federal and state laws regulating the use or availability of drugs
- A large and perhaps still growing involvement with illicit drugs among the urban poor and the socially disenfranchised, both as an escape from the conditions of life and as a path to monetary gain
- The view that drug abuse is a law enforcement issue rather than primarily a medical problem

An early advertisement for cocaine-laced wine. Cocaine, a controlled substance today, was commonly found in late-nineteenth-century medicines and consumer products. Why did the federal government enact legislation outlawing the use of psychoactive substances like marijuana and cocaine?

Corbis/Bettmann

In an insightful work that clarifies the ideational basis of modern antidrug sentiments, criminologists Franklin Zimring and Gordon Hawkins examine three schools of thought that, they say, form the basis for current drug policy in the United States.[31] The first is "public health generalism," a perspective that holds that all controlled substances are potentially harmful and that drug abusers are victimized by the disease of addiction. This approach views drugs as medically harmful and argues that effective drug control is necessary as a matter of public health. The second approach, "cost–benefit specifism," proposes that drug policy be built around a balancing of the social costs of drug abuse (crime, broken families, drug-related killings, and so on) with the costs of enforcement. The third approach, the "legalist," suggests that drug-control policies are necessary to prevent the collapse of public order and of society itself. Advocates of the legalist perspective say that drug use is "defiance of lawful authority that threatens the social fabric."[32] According to Zimring and Hawkins, all recent and contemporary antidrug policies have been based on one of these three schools of thought. Unfortunately, say these authors, it may not be possible to base successful antidrug policy on such beliefs since they do not necessarily recognize the everyday realities of drug use. Nonetheless, antidrug legislation and activities undertaken in the United States today are accorded political and ideational legitimacy via all three perspectives.

Antidrug Legislation

Antidrug legislation in the United States dates back to around 1875, when the city of San Francisco enacted a statute prohibiting the smoking of opium.[33] A number of western states were quick to follow the city's lead. The San Francisco law and many that followed it, however, clearly targeted Chinese immigrants and were rarely applied to other ethnic groups involved in the practice.

The first major piece of federal antidrug legislation came in 1914, with the enactment of the **Harrison Narcotics Act**. The Harrison Act required anyone dealing in opium, morphine, heroin, cocaine, and specified derivatives of these drugs to register with the federal government and to pay a tax of $1 per year. The only people permitted to register were physicians, pharmacists, and members of the medical profession. Nonregistered drug traffickers faced a maximum fine of $2,000 and up to five years in prison.

Because the Harrison Act allowed physicians to prescribe controlled drugs for the purpose of medical treatment, heroin addicts and other drug users could still legally purchase the drugs they needed. All the law required was a physician's prescription. By 1920, however, court rulings had established that drug "maintenance" only prolonged addiction and did not qualify as "treatment."[34] The era of legally available heroin had ended.

Marijuana was not included in the Harrison Act because it was not considered a dangerous drug.[35] By the 1930s, however, government attention became riveted on marijuana. At the urging of the Federal Bureau of Narcotics, Congress passed the Marijuana Tax Act in 1937. As the title of the law indicates, the act simply placed a tax of $100 per ounce on cannabis. Those who did not pay the tax were subject to prosecution. With the passage of the Boggs Act in 1951, however, marijuana, along with a number of other drugs, entered the class of federally prohibited controlled substances. The Boggs Act also removed heroin from the list of medically useful substances and required the removal, within 120 days, of any medicines containing heroin from pharmacies across the country.[36]

The Narcotic Control Act of 1956 increased penalties for drug trafficking and possession and made the sale of heroin to anyone under age 18 a capital offense. However, on the eve of the massive explosion in drug use that was to begin in the mid-1960s, the Kennedy administration began a shift in emphasis from the strict punishment of drug traffickers and users to rehabilitation. A 1963 presidential commission recommended the elimination of the Federal Bureau of Narcotics, recommended shorter prison terms for drug offenders, and stressed the need for research and social programs in dealing with the drug problem.[37]

THE COMPREHENSIVE DRUG ABUSE PREVENTION AND CONTROL ACT OF 1970

By 1970, America's drug problem was clear, and legislators were anxious to return to a more punitive approach to controlling drug abuse. Under President Richard Nixon, legislation designed to encompass all aspects of drug abuse and to permit federal intervention at all levels of use was enacted. Termed the Comprehensive Drug Abuse Prevention and Control Act of 1970, the legislation still forms the basis of federal enforcement efforts today. Title II of the law is the **Controlled Substances Act (CSA)**. The CSA sets up five schedules that classify psychoactive drugs according to their degree of psychoactivity and abuse potential:[38]

- Schedule I controlled substances have no established medical usage, cannot be used safely, and have great potential for abuse.[39] Federal law requires that any research employing Schedule I substances be fully documented and that the substances themselves be stored in secure vaults. Included under this category are heroin, LSD, mescaline, peyote, methaqualone (Quaaludes), psilocybin, marijuana,[40] and hashish, as well as other specified hallucinogens. Penalties for first-offense possession and sale of Schedule I controlled substances under the federal Narcotic Penalties and Enforcement Act of 1986 include up to life imprisonment and a $10 million fine. Penalties increase for subsequent offenses.

- Schedule II controlled substances are drugs with high abuse potential for which there is a currently accepted pharmacological or medical use. Most Schedule II substances are also considered to be addictive.[41] Drugs that fall into this category include opium, morphine, codeine, cocaine, phencyclidine (PCP), and their derivatives. Certain other stimulants, such as methylphenidate (Ritalin) and phenmetrazine (Preludin), and a few barbiturates with high abuse potential also come under Schedule II. Legal access to Schedule II substances requires written nonrefillable prescriptions, vault storage, and thorough record keeping by vendors. Penalties for first-offense possession and sale of Schedule II controlled substances include up to 20 years' imprisonment and a $5 million fine under the federal Narcotic Penalties and Enforcement Act. Penalties increase for subsequent offenses.

- Schedule III controlled substances have lower abuse potential than do those in Schedules I and II. They are drugs with an accepted medical use but that may lead to a high level of **psychological dependence** or to moderate or low **physical dependence**.[42] Schedule III substances include many of the drugs found in Schedule II but in derivative or diluted form. Common low-dosage antidiarrheals, such as opium-containing paregoric, and cold medicines and pain relievers with low concentrations of codeine fall into this category. Anabolic steroids,

---

Harrison Narcotics Act

The first major piece of federal antidrug legislation, passed in 1914.

Controlled Substances Act (CSA)

Title II of the Comprehensive Drug Abuse Prevention and Control Act of 1970, which established schedules classifying psychoactive drugs according to their degree of psychoactivity.

psychological dependence

A craving for a specific drug that results from long-term substance abuse. Psychological dependence on drugs is marked by the belief that drugs are needed to achieve a feeling of well-being.[iii]

physical dependence

A biologically based craving for a specific drug that results from frequent use of the substance. Physical dependence on drugs is marked by a growing tolerance of a drug's effects, so that increased amounts of the drug are needed to obtain the desired effect, and by the onset of withdrawal symptoms over periods of prolonged abstinence.[iv]

Baseball player Mark McGwire, formerly of the Oakland Athletics and the St. Louis Cardinals, being sworn in before testifying at a hearing on Capitol Hill on the use of steroids in major league baseball in March 2005. Sammy Sosa, now with the Texas Rangers, is at the far left; Rafael Palmeiro, who last played for the Baltimore Orioles in 2005, is to the right of McGwire, and Curt Schilling of the Boston Red Sox is at far right. Anabolic steroids were added to the list of Schedule III controlled substances in 1991. Why did the federal government outlaw the nonmedical use of most steroidal compounds?

Gerald Herbert/AP Wide World Photos

whose abuse by professional athletes has been subject to scrutiny, were added to the list of Schedule III controlled substances in 1991. Legitimate access to Schedule III drugs is through a doctor's prescription (written or oral), with refills authorized in the same manner. Maximum penalties associated with first-offense possession and sale of Schedule III controlled substances under federal law include five years' imprisonment and fines of up to $1 million.

- Schedule IV controlled substances have a relatively low potential for abuse (when compared to higher schedules), are useful in established medical treatments, and involve only a limited risk of psychological or physical dependence.[43] Depressants and minor tranquilizers such as Valium, Librium, and Equanil fall into this category, as do some stimulants. Schedule IV substances are medically available in the same fashion as Schedule III drugs. Maximum penalties associated with first-offense possession and sale of Schedule IV substances under federal law include three years in prison and fines of up to $1 million.

- Schedule V controlled substances are prescription drugs with a low potential for abuse and with only a very limited possibility of psychological or physical dependence.[44] Cough medicines (antitussives) and antidiarrheals containing small amounts of opium, morphine, or codeine are found in Schedule V. A number of Schedule V medicines may be purchased through retail vendors with only minimal controls or upon the signature of the buyer (with some form of identification required). Maximum federal penalties for first-offense possession and sale of Schedule V substances include one year in prison and a $250,000 fine.

Pharmacologists, chemists, and botanists regularly create new drugs. Likewise, street-corner "chemists" in clandestine laboratories churn out inexpensive *designer drugs*—laboratory-created psychoactive substances with widely varying effects and abuse potential. Designer drugs include substances with names like Ecstasy (MDMA), GHB (gamma-hydroxybutyrate), ketamine, and methamphetamine (meth), which will be discussed in greater detail later in this chapter. The Controlled Substances Act includes provisions for determining which new drugs should be controlled and into which schedule they should be placed. Under the CSA, criteria for assigning a new drug to one of the existing schedules include (1) the drug's actual or relative potential for abuse; (2) scientific evidence of the drug's pharmacological effects; (3) the state of current scientific knowledge regarding the substance; (4) its history and current pattern of abuse; (5) the scope, duration, and significance of abuse; (6) risk, if any, to the public health; (7) the drug's psychic or physiological dependence liability; and (8) whether the substance is an immediate precursor of a substance already controlled.[45] Proceedings to add a new chemical substance to the list of those controlled by law or to delete or change the schedule of an existing drug may be initiated by the chief administrator of the Drug Enforcement Administration, by the Department of Health and Human Services, or by a petition from any interested party, including manufacturers, medical societies, or public-interest groups.[46] Read the text of the CSA at Library Extra 16–1 at cjtoday.com.

LIBRARY
Extra
▪▪▪▪

CJ Careers

Drug Enforcement Administration

Name: James L. Capra

Position: Chief of Domestic Operations

City: Arlington, Virginia

Colleges Attended: Marist College and Seton Hall University

Year Hired: 1987

"Although I was influenced by my father, a retired New York City police officer, I didn't choose this career; it chose me. I truly believe that individuals who seek out careers as law enforcement professionals are answering a calling in their lives. They have a desire to serve others, and they embody the finest attributes of what it means to be a public servant. . . . One of the greatest challenges I have is ensuring that DEA uses every resource available to disrupt and dismantle those drug-trafficking organizations that impact the United States. What raises the stakes on this challenge is that there are now terrorist organizations that rely on drug proceeds to finance their terrorist activity against our nation and its citizens. . . . DEA is a single-mission agency; it takes drugs off the street and puts bad guys in jail, and we do this very creatively, with great distinction and honor. One of the greatest rewards is witnessing the incredible impact we have in making our towns, cities, states, and, for that matter, our nation a safer place to live, work, and play."

TYPICAL POSITIONS

Special agent, criminal investigator, chemist, diversion investigator, and intelligence research specialist. Special agents conduct clandestine surveillance, infiltrate drug-trafficking organizations, conduct investigations, arrest violators, confiscate controlled substances, collect and prepare evidence, and testify in criminal court cases.

EMPLOYMENT REQUIREMENTS

Applicants for the GS-5 level must (1) be a U.S. citizen, (2) be between the ages of 21 and 36 at time of hiring, (3) hold a four-year college degree, (4) be in good health, (5) pass a comprehensive background investigation, (6) hold a valid driver's license, (7) possess effective oral and written communications skills, and (8) have three years of general job experience. Applicants for the GS-7 level must also demonstrate *one* of the following: (1) a 2.95 overall college grade point average, (2) a 3.5 grade point average in the applicant's major field of study, (3) a standing in the upper one-third of the applicant's graduating class, (4) membership in a national honorary scholastic society, (5) one year of successful graduate study, or (6) one year of specialized experience (defined as "progressively responsible investigative experience").

OTHER REQUIREMENTS

Applicants must (1) be willing to travel frequently, (2) submit to a urinalysis test designed to detect the presence of controlled substances, and (3) successfully complete a two-month formal training program at the FBI's Training Center in Quantico, Virginia. Special-agent applicants must be in excellent physical condition, possess sharp hearing, and have uncorrected vision of at least 20/200 and corrected vision of 20/20 in one eye and at least 20/40 in the other. (Radial keratotomy is disqualifying.) They must also possess normal color vision and be capable of heavy lifting (including carrying 45 pounds or more).

SALARY

Entry-level positions for individuals with four-year college degrees begin at GS-7. Appointments are made at higher pay grades for individuals possessing additional education and experience.

BENEFITS

Benefits include (1) 13 days of sick leave annually, (2) two and a half to five weeks of paid vacation and ten paid federal holidays each year, (3) federal health and life insurance, and (4) a comprehensive retirement program.

DIRECT INQUIRIES TO:

Drug Enforcement Administration
Special Agent Recruitment Unit
Office of Personnel
700 Army Navy Dr.
Alexandria, VA 22202

Phone: 800-DEA-4288

Website: http://www.dea.gov

For more information on the rapidly expanding criminal justice careers area, read *Where the Jobs Are: Mission Critical Opportunities for America*, available on the Web at http://www.justicestudies.com/jobs.htm.

Source: Drug Enforcement Administration.

THE ANTI-DRUG ABUSE ACT OF 1988

Wake up, America. The drug war is over. We lost.

—*David Nyhan*, Boston Globe *columnist*

In 1988, the country's Republican leadership, under President Ronald Reagan, capitalized on the public's frustration with rampant drug abuse and stepped up the "war on drugs." The president created a new cabinet-level post, naming a "drug czar" who would be in charge of federal drug-fighting initiatives through the Office of National Drug Control Policy (ONDCP). William Bennett, a former secretary of education, was appointed to fill the post. At the same time, Congress passed the Anti-Drug Abuse Act. The overly optimistic tenor of the act is clear from its preamble, which reads, "It is the declared policy of the United States Government to create a Drug-Free America by 1995."[47] That goal, which reflected far more political rhetoric than realistic planning, was incredibly naïve.

Even so, the Anti-Drug Abuse Act of 1988 carries much weight. Under the law, penalties for "recreational" drug users increased substantially,[48] and weapons purchases by suspected drug dealers became more difficult. The law also denies federal benefits, ranging from loans (including student loans) to contracts and licenses, to convicted drug offenders.[49] Earned benefits, such as Social Security, retirement, and health and disability benefits, are not affected by the legislation, nor are welfare payments or existing public-housing arrangements (although separate legislation does provide for termination of public-housing tenancy for drug offenses[50]). Under the law, civil penalties of up to $10,000 may be assessed against convicted "recreational" users for possession of even small amounts of drugs.

The legislation also allows capital punishment for drug-related murders. The killing of a police officer by an offender seeking to avoid apprehension or prosecution is specifically cited as carrying a possible sentence of death, although other murders by major drug dealers also fall under the capital punishment provision.[51] In May 1991, 37-year-old David Chandler, an Alabama marijuana kingpin, became the first person to be sentenced to die under the law.[52] Chandler was convicted of ordering the murder of a police informant in 1990.

drug czar

The popular name for the head of the Office of National Drug Control Policy (ONDCP), a federal cabinet-level position that was created during the Reagan presidency to organize federal drug-fighting efforts.

One especially interesting aspect of the Anti-Drug Abuse Act is its provision for designating selected areas as high-intensity drug-trafficking areas (HIDTAs), making them eligible for federal drug-fighting assistance so that joint interagency operations can be implemented to reduce drug problems. Using the law, former **drug czar** William Bennett declared Washington, D.C., a "drug zone" in 1989. His designation was based in part on what was then the city's reputation as the murder capital of the country. At the time of the declaration, more than 60% of Washington's murders were said to be drug related,[53] and legislators and tourists were clamoring for action. Bennett's plan called for more federal investigators and prosecutors and for specially built prisons to handle convicted drug dealers. Visit ONDCP via Web Extra 16–3, and learn more about HIDTAs via Web Extra 16–4 at cjtoday.com.

WEB Extra

OTHER FEDERAL ANTIDRUG LEGISLATION

Other significant federal antidrug legislation exists in the form of the Crime Control Act of 1990, the Violent Crime Control and Law Enforcement Act of 1994, the Drug-Free Communities Act of 1997, and reauthorization of the USA PATRIOT Act in 2006.[54] The Crime Control Act of 1990 (1) doubled the appropriations authorized for drug-law enforcement grants to states and local communities; (2) enhanced drug-control and drug-education programs aimed at the nation's schools; (3) expanded specific drug-enforcement assistance to rural states; (4) expanded regulation of precursor chemicals used in the manufacture of illegal drugs; (5) sanctioned anabolic steroids under the Controlled Substances Act; (6) included provisions to enhance control over international money laundering; (7) created "drug-free school zones" by enhancing penalties for drug offenses occurring in proximity to schools; and (8) enhanced the ability of federal agents to seize property used in drug transactions or purchased with drug proceeds.

The Violent Crime Control and Law Enforcement Act of 1994 provided $245 million for rural anticrime and antidrug efforts; set aside $1.6 billion for direct funding to localities around the country for anticrime efforts, including drug-treatment programs; budgeted $383 million for drug-treatment programs for state and federal prisoners; created a treatment schedule for all drug-addicted federal prisoners; required postconviction drug testing of all federal prisoners upon release; allocated $1 billion for drug-court programs for nonviolent offenders with substance-abuse problems; and mandated new stiff penalties for drug crimes committed by gangs. The act also tripled penalties for using children to deal drugs and enhanced penalties for drug dealing in drug-free zones near playgrounds, school yards, video arcades, and youth centers. Finally, the law also expanded the federal death penalty to cover offenders involved in large-scale drug trafficking and mandated life imprisonment for criminals convicted of three violent felonies or drug offenses.

The Drug-Free Communities Act of 1997 provided support to local communities to reduce substance abuse among youth. It helped enhance broad-based community antidrug coalitions, which were previously shown to be successful at driving down casual drug use. Under the law, neighborhoods with successful antidrug programs became eligible to apply for federal grants to assist in their continued development.

More recently, the congressional reauthorization of the USA PATRIOT Act in 2006 led to enactment of a provision in that legislation known as the Combat Methamphetamine Epidemic Act. That legislation makes it harder to obtain pseudoephedrine, ephedrine, and phenylpropanolamine—ingredients in some over-the-counter cold medicines that can be used in the manufacture of methamphetamine.[55] The legislation requires medicines containing these chemicals to be kept behind store counters or in locked cabinets and limits the amount of those substances that a person can purchase to 3.6 grams per day, or up to 9 grams per month. Under the legislation, customers purchasing pseudoephedrine, ephedrine, or phenylpropanolamine are required to show photo identification and to sign a store log. The PATRIOT Act renewal also authorized $99 million per year through 2010 for the federal Meth Hot Spots program intended to train state and local law enforcement officers in how to investigate methamphetamine offenses and to provide personnel and equipment for enforcement and prosecution.

The Investigation of Drug Abuse and Manufacturing

Investigation of the illegal production, transportation, sale, and use of controlled substances is a major police activity. Investigation of drug-manufacturing activities has given rise to an area of case law that supplements the plain-view doctrine discussed in Chapter 7. Two legal concepts, abandonment and curtilage, have taken on special significance in drug investigations.

Abandonment refers to the fact that property, once it has been clearly thrown away or discarded, ceases to fall under Fourth Amendment protections against unreasonable search and seizure. The U.S. Supreme Court case of *California* v. *Greenwood* (1988)[56] began when Officer Jenny Stracner of the Laguna Beach (California) Police Department arranged with a neighborhood trash collector to receive garbage collected at a suspect's residence. The refuse was later found to include items "indicative of narcotics use."[57] Based on this evidence, Stracner applied for a search warrant, which was used in a search of the defendant's home. The search uncovered controlled substances, including cocaine and hashish. The defendant, Billy Greenwood, was arrested. Upon conviction, Greenwood appealed, arguing that the trash had been placed in opaque bags and could reasonably be expected to remain unopened until it was collected and disposed of. His appeal emphasized his right to privacy with respect to his trash.

The Supreme Court disagreed, saying that "[a]n expectation of privacy does not give rise to Fourth Amendment protection unless society is prepared to accept that expectation as objectively reasonable. . . . [I]t is common knowledge that plastic garbage bags left on or at the side of a public street are readily accessible to animals, children, scavengers, snoops, and other members of the public." Hence, the Court concluded, the property in question had been abandoned, and no reasonable expectation of privacy can attach to trash left for collection "in an area accessible to the public." The concept of abandonment extends beyond trash that is actively discarded. In *Abel* v. *U.S.* (1960),[58] for example, the Court found that the warrantless search of a motel room by an FBI agent immediately after it had been vacated was acceptable.

Curtilage, a concept that the Supreme Court clearly recognized in the case of *Oliver* v. *U.S.* (1984),[59] refers to the fact that household activity generally extends beyond the walls of a residence. People living in a house, for example, spend some of their time in their yard. Property within the curtilage of a residence has generally been accorded the same Fourth Amendment guarantees against search and seizure as areas within the walls of a house or an apartment. But just how far does the curtilage of a residence extend? Does it vary according to the type or location of the residence? Is it necessary for an area to be fenced for it to fall within residential curtilage?

A collateral area of concern is that of activity conducted in fields. The open fields doctrine began with the case of *Hester* v. *U.S.* (1924),[60] in which the Supreme Court held that law enforcement officers could search an open field without a warrant. The *Oliver* case extended that authority to include secluded and fenced fields posted with *No Trespassing* signs.

In *U.S.* v. *Dunn* (1987),[61] the U.S. Supreme Court considered a Houston-area defendant's claim that the space surrounding a barn, which was located approximately 50 yards from the edge of a fence surrounding a farmhouse, was protected against intrusion by the Fourth Amendment. The Court rejected the defendant's arguments and concluded that even though an area may be fenced, it is not within the curtilage of a residence if it is sufficiently distant from the area of household activity that attends the residence.

Other related decisions have supported seizures based on warrantless aerial observation of marijuana plants growing in the backyard of a defendant's home[62] and those based on naked-eye

If I were king, I would find a civil way to allow citizens to sue the drug dealer for selling drugs to their children.

—Samuel F. Saxton, Director, Prince George's County (Maryland) Department of Corrections

curtilage

In legal usage, the area surrounding a residence that can reasonably be said to be a part of the residence for Fourth Amendment purposes.

FREEDOM OR SAFETY?
You Decide

Drug-Related Criminal Activity and Public Housing

Seventy-nine-year-old Herman Walker lives in a public-housing development in Oakland, California. Walker, who suffers from severe arthritis and complications from a stroke he suffered five years ago, is facing eviction from his apartment because federal housing authority officials determined that his full-time caretaker had hidden crack pipes in his home. Authorities admit that Walker likely had no knowledge of his caretaker's illegal actions, but they say that Walker's eviction will serve notice to other residents that they must carefully oversee the activities of people who live with them.

Walker's problems stem from federal law[1] and from a rule based on that law that was adopted by the Department of Housing and Urban Development (HUD) in 1991. Both the law and the HUD rule were upheld by a unanimous U.S. Supreme Court decision in 2002.[2] The rule provides that "any drug-related criminal activity on or off [federally assisted low-income housing] premises, engaged in by a public housing tenant, any member of the tenant's household, or any guest or other person under the tenant's control, shall be cause for termination of tenancy." The decision opened the door for the eviction of poor, elderly, and sick public-housing residents for drug use of which they had no personal knowledge. Tenants' rights advocates condemned the ruling, saying that it allows harsh punishments to be imposed on the innocent. Supporters of the Court's decision saw it as an affirmation of their belief that drug-free public housing is an important priority.

In a related issue, the U.S. Supreme Court upheld a Richmond, Virginia, public-housing trespass law in 2003.[3] The law makes it illegal for nonresidents to be on public-housing premises without a legitimate reason. The case grew out of efforts by the Richmond Redevelopment and Housing Authority (RRHA) to combat "rampant crime and drug dealing" at its Whitcomb Court development, where "open-air drug markets" had been commonplace.

RRHA closed the streets of the development to nonresidents and posted "No Trespassing" signs, warning that "unauthorized persons will be subject to arrest and prosecution." Police were authorized to arrest any nonresidents who refused to leave or who returned after being warned that they were trespassing. Critics charged that housing authority streets were public avenues and that members of the public should have access to them.[4]

YOU DECIDE

In your opinion, does the goal of reducing drug-related criminal activity in public housing justify evicting residents who have no knowledge of such activities in their homes? Does it justify restricting access to public housing and criminalizing the acts of nonresident trespassers?

[1] U.S. Code, Title 42, Section 1437d(l)(6).
[2] *Department of Housing and Urban Development* v. *Rucker*, 122 S.Ct. 1230, 152 L.Ed.2d 258 (2002).
[3] *Virginia* v. *Hicks*, 539 U.S. 113 (2003).
[4] The argument before the Court was actually more complex. RRHA, which had assumed control of the Whitcomb Court development from the city of Richmond some years previously, is not regarded as a public agency. Lawyers representing nonresidents argued that the area's streets had served as a "traditional public forum," although from a strict legal viewpoint they may no longer be public.
References: Evelyn Nieves, "Drug Ruling Worries Some in Public Housing," *New York Times,* March 28, 2002; Tom Schoenberg, "Supremes Examine Trespassing Policy," Law.com, May 1, 2003; and "U.S. Supreme Court Upholds Public Housing Trespass Law," *Criminal Justice Newsletter,* July 1, 2003, p. 4.

The 11th Commandment: Thou shalt not end the war on drugs.

—Anonymous

sightings from helicopters of the contents of a greenhouse.[63] The Court's reasoning in such cases is that flights within navigable airspace are common. Where no comprehensive efforts to secure privacy have been made, there can be no reasonable expectation of privacy—even within areas that might normally be considered curtilage. Were sophisticated surveillance techniques to be employed by law enforcement authorities, however—such as the use of drone aircraft, satellite, or infrared photography—the Court's decision would be in doubt because such devices extend beyond the realm of "normal flight."

The Most Common Drugs—
And Who Is Using Them

The 2006 *National Survey on Drug Use and Health* (NSDUH), an annual publication of the federal Substance Abuse and Mental Health Services Administration (SAMHSA), estimates that 20.4 million Americans age 12 and older are "current" users of illegal drugs—defined as those who

CJ Today Exhibit 16–1

Drugs: What's in a Name?

Drug names have been a source of confusion for many people who have attempted to grapple with the drug problem. A single drug may have a dozen or more names. Drugs may be identified according to brand name, generic name, street name, or psychoactive category.

BRAND NAME

The name given to a chemical substance by its manufacturer is the *brand name*. Brand names are registered and are often associated with trademarks. They identify a drug in the pharmaceutical marketplace and may not be used by other manufacturers. Psychoactive substances with no known medical application or experimental use are not produced by legitimate companies and have no brand name.

GENERIC NAME

The chemical or other identifying name of a drug is the *generic name*. Generic names are often used by physicians in writing prescriptions because generic drugs are often less costly than brand-name drugs. Generic names are also used in most drug-abuse legislation at the federal and state levels to specify controlled substances. Generic names are sometimes applicable only to the psychoactive chemical substances in drugs and not to the drugs themselves. With marijuana, for example, the chemical tetrahydrocannabinol, or THC, is the active substance.

STREET NAME

Street names are slang terms. Many of them originated with the pop culture of the 1960s, and others continue to be produced by modern-day drug subculture. For example, street names for cocaine include coke, flake, and snow; heroin is known as horse, smack, or H. Learn more about street names currently in use via **Web Extra 16–5** at cjtoday.com. **WEB Extra**

PSYCHOACTIVE CATEGORY

Psychoactive drugs are categorized according to the effects they produce on the human mind. Narcotics, stimulants, depressants, and hallucinogens are typical psychoactive categories.

AN EXAMPLE

PCP and angel dust are the street names for a veterinary anesthetic marketed under the brand name Sernylan. Sernylan contains the psychoactive chemical phencyclidine, which is classified as a depressant under the Controlled Substances Act.

---

have used an illicit drug in the month preceding the survey[64] (Table 16–1). Nearly 15 million people were estimated to be using marijuana, and 5 million of those were thought to be "frequent" marijuana users (defined as those who used the drug on 20 or more days during the past month). An estimated 2.4 million people (1%) were current cocaine users, 702,000 of whom used crack during the same time period. Hallucinogens were used by more than 1 million people, including 528,000 users of Ecstasy. There were an estimated 731,000 current methamphetamine users and 338,000 current heroin users. An estimated 7 million Americans were current nonmedical users of prescription-type psychotherapeutic drugs. This includes 5.2 million using pain relievers, 1.8 million using tranquilizers, 1.2 million using stimulants, and nearly 400,000 using sedatives. In 2006, approximately 4.1 million people age 12 or older had used the painkiller OxyContin nonmedically at least once in their lives.

These figures represent a considerable decline from 1979, the year in which the highest levels of drug abuse in the United States were reported, although figures for recent years have shown a gradual increase in drug use (especially "occasional use"). As the Office of National Drug Control Policy points out, however, federal studies typically underestimate the number of hard-core drug abusers in the country because they fail to survey the homeless, prisoners, people living at colleges, active-duty military personnel, and those in mental and other institutions. ONDCP estimates that there are 2.1 million hard-core cocaine addicts and up to 1 million heroin addicts in the country[65]—figures well above those reported by the survey.

Rates of drug use show substantial variation by age. In 2005, for example, 3.8 percent of American youths age 12 or 13 reported current illicit drug use compared with 8.9 percent of youths age 14 or 15 and 17 percent of youths age 16 or 17 (Figure 16–3). As in other years, illicit drug use in 2005 tended to increase with age among young people, peaking among 18- to 20-year-olds (22.3 percent) and declining steadily after that point with increasing age. Current employment status is also highly correlated with rates of current illicit drug use. An estimated 18.2% of unemployed adults age 18 or older were current illicit drug users in the United States in 2005, compared with 7.9% of those employed full-time and 10.7% of those employed part-time. Although the rate of drug use was higher among the unemployed compared with those from other employment groups, most drug users were employed. Of the 16.7 million illicit drug users age 18 or older in 2005, 12.4 million (74.3%) were employed either full- or part-time. The use of drugs is also more

We cannot define what victory is. We cannot tell you which objectives to look at. We can only try to have policymakers at all levels of government working together to do what is right for this nation: reduce the impact of drug abuse and increase the strength of our families and communities. If we do that, we may still have a drug use issue, but we will have a healthier nation that can absorb that issue, that will reduce the harm of drug abuse.

—Ross Deck, Assistant Deputy Director, Office of National Drug Control Policy

TABLE 16–1   Estimates of Drug Use by the U.S. Population Age 12 and Older in Lifetime, Past Year, and Past Month, 2006

	Lifetime	Past Year	Past Month
ILLICIT DRUGS (Total)[1]	111,774,000	35,775,000	20,357,000
Marijuana and Hashish	97,825,000	25,378,000	14,813,000
Cocaine	35,298,000	6,069,000	2,421,000
Crack	8,554,000	1,479,000	702,000
Heroin	3,785,000	560,000	338,000
Hallucinogens	35,281,000	3,956,000	1,006,000
LSD	23,346,000	666,000	130,000
PCP	6,618,000	187,000	30,000
Ecstasy	12,262,000	2,130,000	528,000
Inhalants	22,879,000	2,218,000	761,000
Nonmedical Use of Psychotherapeutics[2]	49,842,000	16,287,000	6,991,000
Pain Relievers	33,472,000	12,649,000	5,220,000
OxyContin	4,098,000	1,323,000	276,000
Tranquilizers	21,303,000	5,058,000	1,766,000
Stimulants	20,118,000	3,394,000	1,191,000
Sedatives	8,822,000	966,000	385,000

[1]Includes those using multiple drugs.

[2]Nonmedical use of prescription-type psychotherapeutics includes the nonmedical use of pain relievers, tranquilizers, stimulants, or sedatives and does not include over-the-counter drugs.

Source: Substance Abuse and Mental Health Services Administration, Office of Applied Studies, *National Survey on Drug Use and Health, 2006.*

LIBRARY
Extra

prevalent in some parts of the country than in others (Figure 16–4). Read a summary of the latest findings from the National Survey on Drug Use and Health at Library Extra 16–2 at cjtoday.com.

Drug Trafficking

A number of agencies report on the amount and types of illicit drugs that enter the country or are produced here. One such group, the National Drug Intelligence Center (NDIC) based in Johnstown, Pennsylvania, was established in 1993 and is a component of the U.S. Department of Jus-

FIGURE 16–3

Past-month illicit drug use by age in the United States, 2006.

Source: Department of Health and Human Services, Substance Abuse and Mental Health Services Administration, *Overview of Findings from the 2006 National Survey on Drug Use and Health* (Washington, DC: SAMHSA, 2007).

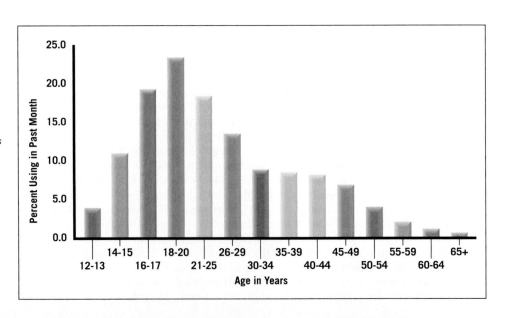

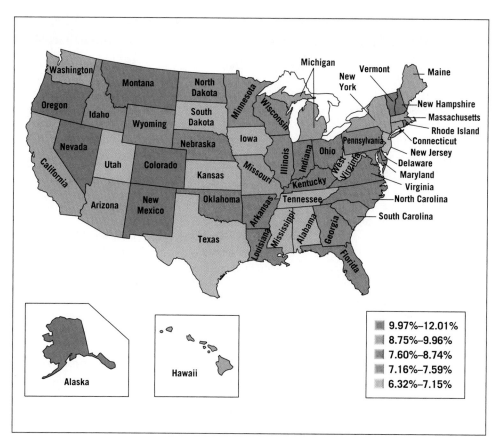

FIGURE 16–4

Prevalence of illicit drug use by state.

Source: Originally appeared in Donna Leinwand, "Extensive New Study Details States' Drug, Alcohol Use: Binge Drinking Is Big Problem," *USA Today*, February 14, 2005, p. 1A. Copyright © *USA Today*. Reprinted with permission.

Legend:
- 9.97%–12.01%
- 8.75%–9.96%
- 7.60%–8.74%
- 7.16%–7.59%
- 6.32%–7.15%

tice and a member of the national intelligence community. The federal General Counterdrug Intelligence Plan,[66] implemented in February 2000, designated NDIC as the nation's principal center for strategic domestic counterdrug intelligence and planning.[67] Each year, the NDIC publishes the *National Drug Threat Assessment*, a comprehensive report on **drug trafficking** and abuse trends within the United States. The assessment identifies the most serious drug threats, monitors fluctuations in national consumption levels, tracks drug availability by geographic area, and analyzes trafficking and distribution patterns. The report also includes the most current information on illicit drug availability, demand, production, cultivation, transportation, and distribution, as well as the effects of particular drugs on abusers and society as a whole. NDIC and DEA data for each of the major drug categories are described in the paragraphs that follow. Learn more about the DEA via Web Extra 16–6 at cjtoday.com. You can reach the NDIC via Web Extra 16–7. The latest *National Drug Threat Assessment*, which contains detailed trafficking information, can be read in its entirety at Library Extra 16–3 at cjtoday.com. The entire General Counterdrug Intelligence Plan is available at Library Extra 16–4.

drug trafficking

Trading or dealing in controlled substances, including the transporting, storage, importing, exporting, or sale of a controlled substance.

WEB Extra

LIBRARY Extra

Marijuana

Marijuana, whose botanical name is *Cannabis sativa L.*, grows wild throughout most of the tropic and temperate regions of the world.[68] Marijuana commonly comes in loose form, as the ground leaves and seeds of the hemp plant. Also available to street-level users are stronger forms of the drug, such as sinsemilla (the flowers and the leaves of the female cannabis plant), hashish (the resinous secretions of the hemp plant), and hash oil (a chemically concentrated form of delta-9-tetrahydrocannabinol, or THC, the psychotropic agent in marijuana).

Marijuana is usually smoked, although it may be eaten or made into a "tea." Low doses of marijuana create restlessness and an increasing sense of well-being, followed by dreamy relaxation and a frequent craving for sweets. Sensory perceptions may be heightened by the drug, while memory and rational thought are impaired (see Table 16–2). Marijuana's effects begin within a few minutes following use and may last for two to three hours.

Although marijuana has no officially sanctioned medical use, it may sometimes serve as a supplemental medication in cases of ongoing chemotherapy (where it often reduces nausea), glaucoma (where it may reduce pressure within the eye), anorexia and "AIDS wasting" (where it may

Antidrug strategies must be supported by knowledge gained from research.

—The National Drug Control Strategy

TABLE 16–2   Major Controlled Substances: Their Uses and Effects

Substance	Legitimate Use	Street Use
Narcotics, including opium, morphine, heroin, codeine, Dilaudid	Pain relief, antidiarrheal, cough suppressant	To produce pleasure, euphoria, lack of concern, general feeling of well-being
Stimulants, including amphetamines, such as Dexedrine and Benzedrine, and other drugs like cocaine, crack, crank, methamphetamine, ice	Increased alertness, reduced fatigue, weight control	To produce excitability, feelings of competence and power
General depressants, including sedatives and tranquilizers, such as Nembutal, Seconal, phenobarbital, Quaalude, sopor, Valium, Librium Thorazine, Equanil	Release from anxiety, mood elevation, treatment of psychological problems	In high doses to produce intoxication; also used to counter the effects of other drugs or in the self-treatment of withdrawal
Marijuana, including hashish, cannabis, sinsemilla, hashish oil	None fully recognized; possible use in treating nausea from chemotherapy	To produce euphoria, relaxation, intoxication, time distortion, memory alteration, focused awareness
Hallucinogens, including LSD, mescaline, psilocybin, peyote, MDMA	None recognized	To produce hallucinations and distortions of reality
Inhalants, including nitrous oxide, gasoline, toluene, amyl nitrite, butyl nitrite	Some are used as medical sedatives	To produce a "rush" or sense of light-headedness
Anabolic steroids, including nandrolone, oxandrolone, oxymetholone, stanozolol	Weight gain; treatment of anemia, breast cancer, angioedema	To build muscle mass and increase strength (in weight lifters, professional athletes, others)

Note: Each drug may have a variety of effects or may produce different effects on individual users. Drugs used in combination may have unpredictable effects.

Source: Adapted from Drug Enforcement Administration, *Drugs of Abuse* (Washington, DC: U.S. Dept. of Justice, 1999) and U.S. Pharmacopeial Convention, *USP DI Drug Information for the Healthcare Professional*, 23rd ed. (Greenwood Village, CO: Thomson Micromedex, 2003).

increase appetite and lead to weight gain), and sleep disorders.[69] To support such use, voters in California and Arizona passed ballot initiatives in 1996 legalizing the use of marijuana for medical purposes when approved or prescribed by a doctor. California's medical marijuana law was overturned, however, by a unanimous U.S. Supreme Court in the 2001 case of *U.S.* v. *Oakland Cannabis Buyers' Cooperative*.[70] In that case, the Court found that the activities of the Oakland (California) Cannabis Buyers' Cooperative, which distributed marijuana to qualified patients for medical purposes, were in violation of the U.S. Controlled Substances Act—regardless of what state law said. The Court also held that there is no medical necessity exception to the federal act's prohibitions on manufacturing and distributing marijuana.[71] In 2005, in the case of *Gonzales* v. *Raich*,[72] the Court reinforced its earlier holding, ruling that Congress holds the final authority, under the Commerce Clause of the U.S. Constitution, to prohibit the cultivation and use of marijuana.

Most illicit marijuana users, however, do not use cannabis for medical purposes. The majority of users are young people, many younger than 20 years old. In 2005, for example, the U.S. Department of Health and Human Services reported that past-year use of marijuana was 11.8% for eighth graders, 27.5% for tenth graders, and 34.3% for twelfth graders.[73]

Intelligence shows that domestic production accounts for about 19% of all marijuana in the United States. Most marijuana brought into the United States comes from Mexico, Jamaica, and

Michael Sullivan, left, and David Shull of San Francisco sharing a pipe of marijuana in a smoking lounge. Both men have AIDS, and smoking pot eases their discomfort. In 1996, voters in California and Arizona passed ballot initiatives legalizing the use of marijuana for medical purposes when approved or prescribed by a doctor. In 2001 and again in 2005, however, the U.S. Supreme Court effectively invalidated California's Compassionate Use Act when it held that Congress has the authority to prohibit all marijuana cultivation and use. What is the current legal status of medical marijuana in the United States?

Fred Mertz

Colombia.[74] Of all the marijuana entering the country or produced domestically, approximately one-quarter, or 4,000 metric tons, is seized or lost in transit.[75]

Cocaine

Cocaine (cocaine hydrochloride [HCL]) is the most potent central nervous system stimulant of natural origin.[76] Cocaine is extracted from the leaves of the coca plant (whose botanical name is *Erythroxylon coca*). Since ancient times, the drug has been used by native Indians throughout the highlands of Central and South America, who chew the leaves of the coca plant to overcome altitude sickness and to sustain the high levels of physical energy needed for strenuous mountain farming.

Cocaine has some medical value as a topical anesthetic for use on sensitive tissues, such as the eyes and mucous membranes. Throughout the early twentieth century, physicians valued cocaine for its ability to anesthetize tissue while simultaneously constricting blood vessels and reducing bleeding. Recently, more effective products have replaced cocaine in many medical applications.

A report by ONDCP classifies cocaine users into three groups: "(1) the younger, often minority crack user; (2) the older injector who is combining cocaine HCL with heroin in a speedball; and (3) the older, more affluent user who is snorting cocaine HCL."[77] Cocaine generally reaches the United States in the form of a much-processed white crystalline powder. It is often diluted with a variety of other ingredients, including sugar and anesthetics like lidocaine. Dilution allows sellers to reap high profits from small amounts of the drug.

Cocaine produces intense psychological effects, including a sense of exhilaration, superabundant energy, hyperactivity, and extended wakefulness.[78] Irritability and apprehension may be unwanted side effects. Excessive doses may cause seizures and death from heart failure, cerebral hemorrhage, and respiratory collapse. Some studies show that repeated use of cocaine may heighten sensitivity to these toxic side effects of the drug.[79]

National Narcotics Intelligence Consumers Committee (NNICC) data indicate that cocaine has become the country's most dangerous commonly used drug. During a recent year, nearly 100,000 hospital emergencies involving cocaine abuse were reported across the country.[80] In 1998, at the time of the NNICC report, cocaine was available in all major American metropolitan areas and in most small communities. The cocaine derivative crack, manufactured by numerous street-level laboratories, was available primarily in large urban areas. A DEA survey in the mid-1990s, however, found that "crack dealers are expanding their markets to target potential users in small towns and rural areas across the United States" because "crack distribution and use appear to have reached the saturation point in large urban areas."[81] The Federal Drug Seizure System reports the seizure of around 300,000 pounds of cocaine throughout the United States annually.[82]

We cannot go into tomorrow with the same formulas that are failing today. We must not blindly add to the body count and the terrible cost of the War on Drugs, only to learn . . . 30 years from now, that what we've been doing is wrong, terribly wrong.

—Walter Cronkite

Most cocaine enters the United States from Peru, Bolivia, or Colombia. Together, these three countries have an estimated annual production capability of around 555 tons of pure cocaine.[83] During the 1980s, most cocaine coming into the United States was controlled by the Medellín Cartel, based in Medellín, Colombia. Multinational counterdrug efforts had crippled the cartel by the start of the 1990s, however, and the Cali Cartel (based in Cali, Colombia), a loose organization of five semi-independent trafficking organizations, took over as the major illegal supplier of cocaine to this country. Arrests of the Cali Cartel's top leaders, Gilberto Rodriguez and his brother, Miguel, however, are said to have sounded the death knell for what may have been the world's most successful drug-trafficking organization ever.[84]

Heroin

Classified as a narcotic, heroin is a derivative of opium—itself the product of the milky fluid found in the flowering poppy plant (*Papaver somniferum*). Opium poppies have been grown in the Mediterranean region since 300 B.C.[85] and are now produced in many other parts of the world as well. Although heroin is not used medicinally in this country, many of the substances to which it is chemically related—such as morphine, codeine, hydrocodone, naloxone, and oxymorphone—do have important medical uses as pain relievers.

Heroin is a highly seductive and addictive drug that produces euphoria when smoked, injected underneath the skin ("skin popping"), or shot directly into the bloodstream ("mainlining").Because tolerance for the drug increases with use, larger and larger doses of heroin must be taken to achieve the pleasurable effects desired by addicts. Heroin deprivation causes withdrawal symptoms that initially include watery eyes, runny nose, yawning, and perspiration. Further deprivation results in restlessness, irritability, insomnia, tremors, nausea, and vomiting. Stomach cramps, diarrhea, chills, and other flulike symptoms are also common. Most withdrawal symptoms disappear within seven to ten days[86] or when the drug is readministered.

Street-level heroin varies widely in purity. It is often cut with powdered milk, food coloring, cocoa, or brown sugar. Most heroin sold in the United States is only 5% pure.[87] Because of dosage uncertainties, overdosing is common. Mild overdoses produce lethargy and stupor, while larger doses may cause convulsions, coma, and death. Other risks, including infectious hepatitis and AIDS, are associated with using contaminated needles from other users. The Centers for Disease Control and Prevention (CDC) estimates that almost one-third of AIDS cases are associated with intravenous drug use.[88]

Heroin abuse has remained fairly constant during the past few decades. Some indicators point to an increased availability of heroin in the last few years.[89] Street-level heroin prices have de-

Sayed Mohammed checking his poppy field at a village in Bagh-e-Afghan, about 70 miles northwest of Kabul, Afghanistan. Despite U.S. efforts to curtail poppy cultivation in the country, Afghanistan remains the world's largest producer of heroin. Much of the money that Mohammed earns comes from the United States—where the sale of illicit drugs constitutes a multibillion-dollar industry. Why haven't U.S. efforts to stop poppy cultivation worked?

© Ahmad Sear/Reuters/Corbis

CJ News

Always on Guard in Nuevo Laredo

Police Cmdr. Carlos Moreno and a weary squad of local officers stopped for a quick lunch near the downtown financial district [in Nuevo Laredo, Mexico,] one day [in May 2006]. But no one ate until Officer Adrian Lopez, cradling his AR-15 rifle, was posted at the cafe door.

In the shadow of the U.S. border, lunch has become a life-threatening proposition for Nuevo Laredo police. They increasingly are being targeted in an unprecedented surge of violence between warring drug cartels that has redefined life here and in Laredo, Texas, just across the muddy Rio Grande.

Two weeks [earlier], five Nuevo Laredo police officers were wounded when masked gunmen attacked a seafood restaurant. A few weeks earlier, four Mexican federal agents were assassinated on a busy downtown street here.

Besides making this one of the deadliest places in North America, such brazen killings—and the inescapable sense that violence could break out at any moment—have underscored the challenge the U.S. government faces in trying to improve border security and limit the flow of illegal immigrants and drugs into the USA.

The instability in this city of about 330,000 has made the USA increasingly attractive not just for Mexicans seeking a better life, but also for marijuana, cocaine and heroin traffickers who have begun to set up safe houses and makeshift weapons manufacturing sites on the U.S. side of the border, says Elias Bazan, the top agent in Laredo for the U.S. Bureau of Alcohol, Tobacco, Firearms and Explosives (ATF).

The chaos in Mexico has "started to spill over here," says Bazan, whose agency formed an unusual working relationship with Mexican law enforcement and military authorities [in fall 2005] to try to curb violence and weapons trafficking.

As President Bush aims to put up to 6,000 National Guard troops on the Southwest border to deter illegal immigration, the disorder here—near one of the USA's busiest entry points—touches virtually every aspect of border security:

- The battle between the "Gulf" and "Sinaloa" drug cartels is threatening to disrupt one of the major commerce routes into the USA. The cartels have sought to piggyback loads of drugs and even illegal immigrants onto some of the 6,000 to 7,000 trucks that carry a wide range of merchandise into the USA from Nuevo Laredo each day, says Rick Flores, the sheriff in Webb County, Texas, where Laredo is the county seat.

- Drug seizures and detentions of illegal immigrants on the U.S. side of the border are continuing to rise, according to Flores' department and U.S. Customs and Border Protection (CBP). Local deputies have seized $6.4 million worth of narcotics [as of May 2006], Flores says, up from $4.4 million at the same time last year.

  Meanwhile, arrests of illegal immigrants in the Laredo area are on pace to top the 75,330 caught in 2005, according to the CBP.

  Flores isn't optimistic that Bush's plan to post thousands of National Guard troops along the border will do much to help authorities overwhelmed by the flow of immigrants and by increasing concerns about security. "What are they gonna do when they get here?" he says. "They have no law enforcement powers."

Mexican police officers Enoch Albores (center) and Mario Rodriguez eating lunch while fellow officer Adrian Lopez keeps a watch on the streets in the city of Nuevo Laredo, Mexico. Why do some fear that Mexican drug violence is spilling into the United States?

Photo by Jack Gruber. © 2006 USA Today. Reprinted with permission.

- Long a destination for tourists from across Texas, the Laredo border area has seen its popularity decline amid the violence. Convention business is down 25% this year [2006] compared with 2005, and the number of weekend visitors is off by at least 30%, says Ramon Hernandez of the Convention and Visitors Bureau in Laredo, a blue-collar city of 203,000.

On the grittier Mexican side of the border, the landmark Victoria restaurant has closed its doors. Señor Frog's, once a popular hangout for American visitors, is shuttered, as are many other gift and curiosity shops along Guerrero Street.

Flores says he no longer travels to the Mexican side, where he has many relatives. "I fear for my life" in Nuevo Laredo, he says. Drug cartels "have no respect for law enforcement. They don't care about life."

There have been 110 slayings [as of May 2006] in Nuevo Laredo, a homicide rate far above those of major U.S. cities and ahead of Nuevo Laredo's record pace of 2005, when there were 176 slayings, Flores says. Laredo has had 10 homicides this year.

In Nuevo Laredo, "there is a war" going on, city police Lt. Mario Espino Rodriguez says. "Nobody can control it."

Guillermo Marquez, Nuevo Laredo's assistant police chief, was meeting with Laredo Police Chief Agustin Dovalina on the U.S. side of the border [in May 2006] when Marquez's cellphone chirped with an urgent message: Five Nuevo Laredo officers had been shot during an ambush at the Titanic seafood restaurant.

Marquez, who was in Laredo on behalf of his underfunded squad to seek donations of police supplies—body armor, gun belts and uniforms—rushed back to Mexico. The officers survived the shooting, but it marked an escalation of violence that included six slayings on May 8, a day the *Laredo Morning Times* dubbed "Deadly Monday."

The first slayings that day occurred at a pharmacy near Santo Nio, the city's landmark Catholic church, and just two blocks from the International Bridge. Gunmen stormed the pharmacy and killed

(continued)

CJ News (continued)

the 14-year-old son of the owner and another person, in what Dovalina says was a dispute over local drug sales involving the cartels.

"These people are ruthless," Dovalina says, adding that violence in Nuevo Laredo has escalated as the cartels have enlisted violent gang members as enforcers.

He says the Sinaloa cartel is being aided by Mara Salvatrucha (MS-13), a Central American gang that has a reputation for brutality and is a growing presence in the USA. The Gulf group has been aided by the Zetas, a well-armed Mexican militia, Dovalina says.

Beyond a lack of equipment and training in Mexican police units, border security efforts have been complicated by corruption within Nuevo Laredo's department, Flores says. Drug cartels have used cash and intimidation to get protection from local cops, he says.

[In 2005], new Nuevo Laredo Police Chief Alejandro Dominguez vowed to fight corruption. He was assassinated hours after taking office. Dominguez's successor, Omar Pimental, resigned in March after the entire 800-officer force was suspended temporarily because of corruption concerns voiced by Mexico's federal government.

A force of about 300 officers was reinstated this spring [2006] while a search for a permanent chief continues by the city and federal governments. Nuevo Laredo Mayor Daniel Pea says through a spokesman that an appointment could take several weeks.

Until then, Cmdr. Moreno and Lt. Espino will try to protect interim Chief Guillermo Landa and Assistant Chief Marquez with patrols around their homes.

The violence in the Laredo border area has long been confined largely to the Mexican side, but there are signs that Mexico's problem is increasingly becoming the United States' problem.

In January [2006], Laredo police and federal agents with U.S. Immigration and Customs Enforcement (ICE) and the ATF made a startling discovery when they raided a local home: a small assembly line for building improvised explosive devices (IEDs).

Agents recovered two IEDs and materials to build about 33 more, the ICE and ATF reported. In a separate raid just south of downtown Laredo, ATF agents seized several machine guns in a home that was used to make automatic weapons.

The ATF's Bazan says the raids and other evidence have led authorities in the USA to believe that drug cartel leaders have begun using Laredo as a safe haven from the fighting on the Mexican side.

Donnie Carter, who as the ATF's top agent in Houston oversees the Justice Department's project with Mexican authorities, says ATF officials meet with Mexican law enforcement and military officials each month to discuss ways to combat drug and weapons trafficking. The effort helped prompt the weapons raids.

Carter says it's clear that the drug cartels are well funded and well armed. Because of the widespread corruption on the Mexican side, Bazan says, it is "difficult to trust anyone" in forming strategies to improve security.

"One thing you'll notice (about shootings in Mexico) is that it seems nobody is ever arrested," Bazan says. "The level of fear is very serious and very high."

His family's new El Rancho restaurant and bar in north Laredo is doing well, but Sol Manzilla's thoughts often drift to his family's original El Rancho, which opened in Nuevo Laredo in 1970 and became a local landmark.

Largely because of the relentless violence, business at the original El Rancho is down 40% . . . , Manzilla says. His family is struggling to keep it afloat.

"I try to avoid talking about it," Manzilla says, his eyes misting with tears. "The morale of the people is down. People are afraid to say anything because they fear they could be targeted."

He says he has seen several businesses that catered to tourism in Nuevo Laredo close or move to a safer spot on the U.S. side. "I'd like to invite people to go back," he says. "But how can I?"

For the latest in crime and justice news, visit the Talk Justice news feed at http://www.crimenews.info.

Source: Kevin Johnson, "Always on Guard in Nuevo Laredo," USA TODAY, May 18, 2006. Reprinted with permission.

---

clined in recent years, while nationwide heroin-related emergency room admissions have reached almost 40,000 per year.

Most heroin in the United States comes from South America, Southwest Asia (Afghanistan, Pakistan, and Iran), Southeast Asia (Burma, Laos, and Thailand), and Mexico. According to data from the Heroin Signature Program (HSP), which uses chemical analysis of the trace elements in heroin supplies to identify source countries, 65% of all heroin entering the United States comes from South America.[90] The Federal Drug Seizure System reports the seizure of approximately 2,500 pounds of heroin throughout the United States annually.[91]

Evidence indicates that the heroin abuse picture is changing. Although older users still dominate heroin markets in all parts of the country,[92] increasing numbers of non-inner-city young users (under 30 years of age) are turning to the drug. Additionally, because high-purity powdered heroin is widely available in most parts of the country, new users seem to be experimenting with heroin inhalation, which often appears to lead to injection as addiction progresses. Treatment programs report that the typical heroin user is male, is over 30 years old, and has been in treatment previously.[93] Alcohol, cocaine, and marijuana remain concurrent problems for heroin users in treatment. Learn more about heroin, including statistics on use, production, and trafficking, at Library Extra 16–5 at cjtoday.com.

LIBRARY
Extra
■■■■

Methamphetamine

Known on the street as *speed*, *chalk*, *meth*, *ice*, *crystal*, and *glass*, methamphetamine is a stimulant drug chemically related to other amphetamines (like MDMA) but with stronger effects on the central nervous system. Methamphetamine is taken in pill form or is used in powdered form by snorting or injecting.[94] Crystallized methamphetamine (known as *ice*, *crystal*, or *glass*) is a smokable and still more powerful form of the drug. Effects of methamphetamine use include increased heart rate and blood pressure, increased wakefulness, insomnia, increased physical activity, decreased appetite, and anxiety, paranoia, or violent behavior. The drug is easily made in simple home "laboratories" ("meth labs") from readily available chemicals, and recipes describing how to produce the substance circulate on the Internet. Methamphetamine appeals to the abuser because it increases the body's metabolism, produces euphoria and alertness, and gives the user a sense of increased energy. An increasingly popular drug at raves, it is not physically addictive but can be psychologically addictive. High doses or chronic use of the drug increases nervousness, irritability, and paranoia.

Methamphetamine use increases the release of very high levels of the neurotransmitter dopamine, which stimulates brain cells, enhancing mood and body movement.[95] Chronic methamphetamine abuse significantly changes how the brain functions. Animal research going back more than 30 years shows that high doses of methamphetamine can damage neuron cell endings. Dopamine- and serotonin-containing neurons do not die after methamphetamine use, but their nerve endings ("terminals") are stunted, and regrowth appears to be limited. Noninvasive human brain imaging studies have shown alterations in the activity of the dopamine system with regular methamphetamine use. These alterations are associated with reduced motor speed and impaired verbal learning. Recent studies in chronic methamphetamine abusers have also revealed significant structural and functional changes in areas of the brain associated with emotion and memory, which may account for many of the emotional and cognitive problems observed in chronic methamphetamine abusers.

In 2007 the DEA reported the emergence of candy-flavored methamphetamine around the country, leading to fears that methamphetamine manufacturers were targeting especially young users. Police departments in Nevada, California, Washington, Idaho, Texas, and New Mexico reported finding bags of what users term "Strawberry Quick"—a flavored form of methamphetamine meant to be snorted or sold illegally as a powerful energy drink.[96]

Club Drugs

In 1997, DEA officials recommended that the "date rape drug" Rohypnol (also discussed in Chapters 2 and 4) be added to the list of Schedule I controlled substances. Rohypnol is a powerful sedative manufactured by Hoffmann-LaRoche Pharmaceuticals.[97] Rohypnol is among the new "club drugs" that became popular in the mid to late 1990s. **Club drug** is a general term used to refer primarily to synthetic psychoactive substances often found at nightclubs, bars, and "raves" (all-night dance parties). In addition to Rohypnol, club drugs include GHB, GBL (gamma-butyrolactone), MDMA (Ecstasy), methamphetamine (meth), ketamine, and PCP. According to the Drug Enforcement Administration, the use of club drugs is increasing rapidly (Figure 16–5).

A few years ago, the growing use of Rohypnol at fraternity parties, raves, bars, and dance clubs gave rise to the phrase *chemically assisted date rape*, a term now applied to rapes in which sexual predators use drugs to incapacitate unsuspecting victims. Rohypnol (a brand name for flunitrazepam) is a member of the benzodiazepine family of depressants and is legally prescribed in 64 countries for insomnia and as a preoperative anesthetic. Seven to 10 times more powerful than Valium, Rohypnol has become popular with some college students and with "young men [who] put doses of Rohypnol in women's drinks without their consent in order to lower their inhibitions."[98] Available on the black market, it dissolves easily in drinks and can leave anyone who unknowingly consumes it unconscious for hours, making them vulnerable to sexual assault. The drug is variously known as *roples*, *roche*, *ruffles*, *roofies*, and *rophies* on the street.

Penalties for trafficking in flunitrazepam were increased under the Drug-Induced Rape Prevention and Punishment Act of 1996,[99] effectively placing it into a Schedule I category for sentencing purposes. Under the act, it is a crime to give someone a controlled substance without the person's knowledge and with intent to commit a violent crime.

club drug

A synthetic psychoactive substance often found at nightclubs, bars, "raves," and dance parties. Club drugs include MDMA (Ecstasy), ketamine, methamphetamine (meth), GBL, PCP, GHB, and Rohypnol.

FIGURE 16–5

Club drugs involved in hospital emergency department visits in 2005.

Source: Drug Abuse Warning Network (DAWN).

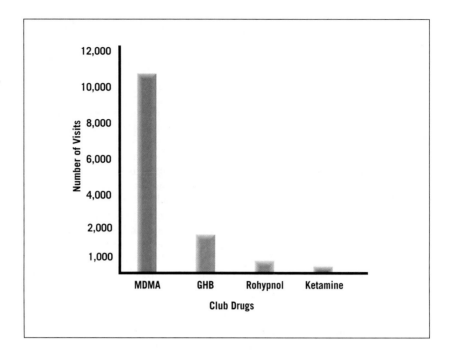

GHB, another "date rape drug," has effects similar to those of Rohypnol. GHB, a central nervous system depressant, is now designated as a Schedule I drug but was once sold in health food stores as a performance enhancer for use by bodybuilders. Rumors that GHB stimulates muscle growth were never proven. The intoxicating effects of GHB, however, soon became obvious. In 1990, the Food and Drug Administration (FDA) banned the use of GHB except under the supervision of a physician. In 2001, federal sentencing guideline changes removed the upper limit, or cap, on GHB sentences in cases where large amounts of the drug were sold or distributed.[100]

GBL is a chemical used in many industrial cleaners and is the precursor chemical for the manufacture of GHB. Several Internet businesses offer kits that contain GBL and the proper amount of sodium hydroxide or potassium hydroxide, along with litmus paper and directions for the manufacture of GHB. The process is quite simple and does not require complex laboratory equipment. Like GHB, GBL can be added to water and is nearly undetectable. GBL is synthesized by the body to produce GHB. As a consequence, some users drink small quantities of unmodified GBL. This often causes a severe physical reaction, usually vomiting. GBL increases the effects of alcohol and can cause respiratory distress, seizure, coma, and death.

MDMA (Ecstasy), the most popular of the club drugs, is primarily manufactured in and trafficked from Europe. DEA reports indicate widespread abuse of this drug within virtually every city in the United States. Estimates from the Drug Abuse Warning Network (DAWN) show that hospital emergency department mentions for MDMA quadrupled over three years, from 1,143 in 1998 to 4,511 in 2000.[101] A redesigned DAWN survey, known as the *New DAWN*, found that 10,752 MDMA-related emergency department visits were reported in 2005.[102] Although it is primarily found in urban settings, abuse of this substance has also been noted in rural communities. Prices in the United States generally range from $20 to $30 per dosage unit; however, prices as high as $50 per dosage unit have been reported in Miami. MDMA (3, 4-methylenedioxymethamphetamine) is a synthetic psychoactive substance possessing stimulant and mild hallucinogenic properties. Known as the "hug drug" or the "feel good drug," it reduces inhibitions, produces feelings of empathy for others, eliminates anxiety, and produces extreme relaxation. In addition to chemical stimulation, the drug reportedly suppresses the need to eat, drink, or sleep. This enables club goers to endure all-night and sometimes two- to three-day parties. MDMA is taken orally, usually in tablet form, and its effects last approximately four to six hours. Often taken in conjunction with alcohol, the drug destroys both dopamine and serotonin cells in the brain. When taken at raves, the drug often leads to severe dehydration and heatstroke, since it has the effect of "short-circuiting" the body's temperature signals to the brain. An MDMA overdose is characterized by a rapid heartbeat, high blood pressure, faintness, muscle cramping, panic attacks, and, in more severe cases, seizures or loss of consciousness. Side effects of the drug are jaw muscle tension and teeth grinding. As a consequence, MDMA users will often use pacifiers to help relieve the tension. The most critical life-threatening response to MDMA is hyperthermia, or ex-

A fire juggler lighting up the night at a rave attended by thousands in the French village of Paule. Raves typically involve abundant drugs, particularly the designer drug Ecstasy. What are some other club drugs?

AP Wide World Photos

cessive body heat. Many rave clubs now have cooling centers or cold showers designed to allow participants to lower their body temperatures. MDMA is a Schedule I drug under the Controlled Substances Act.

The Ecstasy Anti-Proliferation Act of 2000[103] directed the U.S. Sentencing Commission to increase penalties for the manufacture, importation, exportation, and trafficking of MDMA. Under resulting emergency amendments to the U.S. Sentencing Guidelines, MDMA trafficking became a crime with serious consequences. As a result of this penalty enhancement, which became permanent in 2001, a violator convicted of trafficking 200 grams of MDMA (approximately 800 tablets) can receive a five-year prison sentence.

Ketamine (known as *K*, *special K*, and *cat valium*) produces effects that include mild intoxication, hallucinations, delirium, catatonia, and amnesia. Low doses of the drug create an experience called *K-Land*, a mellow, colorful "wonder world." Higher doses produce an effect referred to as *K-Hole*, an "out-of-body" or "near-death" experience. Use of the drug can cause delirium, amnesia, depression, long-term memory and cognitive difficulties, and fatal respiratory problems.[104]

Marketed as a dissociative general anesthetic for human and veterinary use, the only known street source of ketamine is **pharmaceutical diversion**. A significant number of veterinary clinics have been robbed specifically for their ketamine stock. Ketamine liquid can be injected, applied to smokable material, or consumed in drinks. The powdered form is made by allowing the solvent to evaporate, leaving a white or slightly off-white powder that, once pulverized, looks very similar to cocaine. The powder can be put into drinks, smoked, or injected. Pharmaceutical diversion and illicit Internet pharmacies are major sources of supply for *pharming parties*, which have been called "the newest venue for teenage prescription-drug abuse."[105]

Learn more about club drugs via Web Extra 16–8, and discover more about drug abuse among young people at Library Extra 16–6 at cjtoday.com.

pharmaceutical diversion

The transfer of prescription medicines controlled by the Controlled Substances Act by theft, deception, and/or fraudulent means for other than their intended legitimate therapeutic purposes.

WEB Extra

LIBRARY Extra

Costs of Abuse

The societal costs of drug abuse can be categorized as direct and indirect. *Direct costs* are those costs immediately associated with drug crimes themselves, such as the dollar losses incurred by a homeowner from a burglary committed to support a drug habit. The value of stolen property, damage to the dwelling, and the costs of cleanup and repair figure into any calculation of direct costs. *Indirect costs*, which are harder to measure, include such things as the homeowner's lost wages from time off at work needed to deal with the burglary's aftermath, the value of time spent filling out police reports, going to court, and so on. Other indirect costs, such as the mental stress and feelings of violation and personal insecurity that often linger in the wake of criminal victimization are much harder to measure.

The Indirect Costs of Abuse

A December 2004 report by the Office of National Drug Control Policy entitled *The Economic Costs of Drug Abuse in the United States*[106] placed the annual national cost of illicit drug use in the United States at a staggering $180.9 billion. That total includes costs from three areas: (1) lost productivity, (2) health care, and (3) justice system and social welfare expenditures needed to prevent drug abuse and to deal with its consequences.

The ONDCP says that the largest proportion of indirect costs, or $128.6 billion, comes from lost worker productivity. In contrast to the other indirect costs of drug abuse (which entail expenditures for goods and services), this value reflects a loss of potential—specifically, lost work in the labor market and in household production that was never performed but could reasonably be expected to have been performed in the absence of drug abuse. The greatest share of productivity loss comes from drug-related criminal activities that directly lead to the incarceration of approximately 660,000 offenders each year. The ONDCP study also includes the impact that an estimated 23,500 annual drug use–related accidental deaths have on productivity. Estimates of lost worker productivity based on premature death from drug use, lost time at work due to criminal victimization, and institutionalization for drug treatment and dependence also enter the totals. The study found that the legitimate U.S. economy loses about 1 million person years of effort every 12 months as the result of drug-related crimes.

Annual health-related costs associated with illicit drug use are estimated to total $15.8 billion and include costs associated with emergency room care, ongoing medical treatment for drug abuse–related illnesses and dependence, institutionalization, and hospitalization. A major component of health-care costs related to drug abuse consists of spending on care for HIV/AIDS patients whose infections are directly attributable to drug-related activities (for example, the sharing of needles). Also included are expenses stemming from the annual estimated 23,500 drug-related deaths from overdose, poisoning, homicide, HIV, and hepatitis B and C.

The third major indirect drug cost is justice system–related expenses, which ONDCP estimates total about $36.4 billion annually, $14.2 billion of which is spent incarcerating drug offenders. Another $9.8 billion is spent on state and local drug abuse–related police protection, followed by $6.2 billion for federal supply-reduction initiatives. Additional money is spent on jails, for the adjudication of drug offenders ($2.3 billion), for the cost of private legal defense attributable to drug abuse ($647 million), and for the administration of those components of the social welfare system that are forced to compensate for worker productivity lost to drugs. Federal justice system expenditures on drug-control activities stood at $12.96 billion in fiscal year 2008 and were expected to increase during the next few years.[107]

Drug-Related Crime

The direct costs of drug-related crime have at least three dimensions: (1) economic losses from crimes committed by drug users to obtain money for drugs or from crimes committed by users whose judgment is altered by drugs; (2) the costs associated with drug transactions themselves (for example, what people spend to buy drugs); and (3) economic losses due to organized criminal activities in support of the drug trade (including money laundering).

ONDCP says that about 382,000 individuals suffer drug abuse–attributable violent crimes every year and that about 5.2% of all homicides are related to narcotic drug-law violations.[108] Additionally, an estimated 5 million property offenses are committed annually in order to pay for illicit drugs. ONDCP estimates that more than a quarter of the total number of property offenses in any given year are directly attributable to drug abuse.[109] Other crimes committed by those seeking to pay for drugs include prostitution, identity theft, fraud, and robbery.

As Figure 16–6 shows, almost 1.9 million people were arrested for drug-law violations (excluding alcohol) in the United States in 2006.[110] Eighty-two percent of all arrests nationally were for possession of controlled substances; most of the remainder were for sale or manufacture.[111] Arrests for heroin or cocaine possession accounted for 23% of all possession arrests, while 39% of such arrests were for marijuana possession.[112] Possession of PCP, LSD, amphetamines, and tranquilizers accounted for only a relatively small number of arrests.

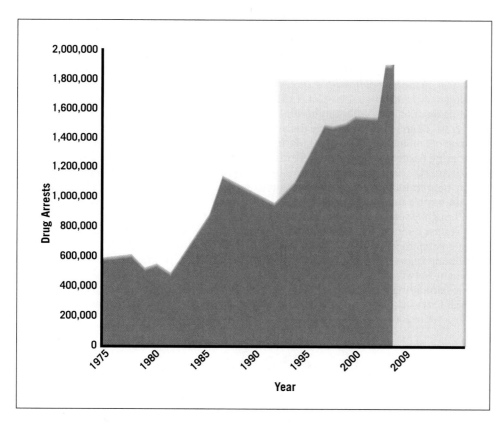

FIGURE 16–6

Drug arrests in the United States, 1975–2006.

Source: Federal Bureau of Investigation, *Crime in the United States*, various years.

Crimes committed by drug-dependent offenders can run the gamut from serious to relatively minor. A National Institute of Justice study of 201 heroin users in Central and East Harlem (New York City), for example, found that each daily user committed on average about 1,400 crimes per year. Of these offenses, 1,116 were directly drug related, involving primarily drug sales and use.[113] Another 75 were relatively minor crimes, such as shoplifting, but the remaining 209 offenses committed by each user involved relatively serious violations of the law, such as robbery, burglary, theft, forgery, fraud, and the fencing of stolen goods. Another study, which examined the daily activities of 354 Baltimore heroin addicts over a nine-year period, found that they had committed a total of nearly 750,000 criminal offenses.[114] Learn more about the dynamics of the drug–crime relationship at Library Extra 16–7 at cjtoday.com.

The sale of illegal drugs is a $57 billion industry in the United States, and that's the amount that ONDCP estimates that Americans spend annually on illicit drugs.[115] Some perspective on this figure can be gained by recognizing that each year Americans spend approximately $44 billion on alcohol products and another $37 billion on tobacco products.[116]

Organized criminal activities in support of the drug trade represent a third area of indirect costs. Cash can flow into the hands of dealers in such huge amounts that it can be difficult for them to spend it. Few people buy houses, cars, and other big-ticket items with cash, and cash transactions arouse suspicion. **Money laundering** is the name given to the process used by drug dealers to hide the source of their revenues, to avoid taxes, and to disguise the financial evidence of drug dealing. Drug profits are laundered by converting them into other assets, such as real estate, stocks and bonds, racehorses, jewels, gold, and other valuables. The Bureau of Justice Statistics says that many millions of dollars in drug money are laundered through commercial banks and other financial institutions each year.[117] Under the federal Money Laundering Strategy Act of 1998,[118] particular regions have been designated as high-intensity financial crimes areas (HIFCAs). HIFCAs can be found in Chicago, New York, New Jersey, San Juan, Los Angeles, San Francisco, and the southwestern border region, including Arizona and Texas. During 2001, 1,477 defendants were charged in U.S. district courts with money laundering as their most serious offense.[119]

In an effort to catch money launderers, U.S. banking law requires financial institutions to report deposits in excess of $10,000.[120] Traffickers attempt to avoid the law through two techniques known as *smurfing* and *structuring*.[121] Smurfers repeatedly purchase bank checks in denominations of less than $10,000, which are then sent to accomplices in other parts of the country, who deposit them in existing accounts. Once the checks have cleared, the funds are transferred to other banks or moved out of the country. Structuring is very similar and involves cash deposits

LIBRARY
Extra

money laundering

The process by which criminals or criminal organizations seek to disguise the illicit nature of their proceeds by introducing them into the stream of legitimate commerce and finance.[v]

to bank accounts in amounts of less than $10,000 at a time. After accounts are established, the money is withdrawn and deposited in increments elsewhere, making it difficult to trace. Countries that have secrecy laws protecting depositors are favorites for drug traffickers. Among them are Switzerland, Panama, Hong Kong, the United Arab Emirates, and the Bahamas.[122]

In 1994, in the case of *Ratzlaf* v. *U.S.*,[123] the U.S. Supreme Court made the task of catching money launderers more difficult. The Court ruled that no one can be convicted of trying to evade bank-reporting requirements unless authorities can prove that offenders knew they were violating the law.

In 2001, in an effort to enhance the amount of information received by federal regulators from banks about potential money-laundering activities, Congress passed the International Money Laundering Abatement and Anti-Terrorist Financing Act of 2001, which is Title III of the USA PATRIOT Act.[124] The law requires banks to make considerable effort in determining the source of money held in individual overseas accounts and provides for sanctions to be placed on nations that hinder this reporting.

Although federal law prohibits the laundering of money, relatively few states have had strict laws against the practice. As a consequence, many local enforcement agencies were reluctant to investigate money-laundering activities in their jurisdictions. To counteract this reluctance and to facilitate interagency cooperation, the federal government created the Financial Crimes Enforcement Network (FINCEN). Partially as a result of FINCEN leadership, 36 states have adopted money-laundering legislation and more are likely to do so.[125] You can access the FINCEN website via Web Extra 16–9 at cjtoday.com. Learn more about money laundering and efforts to combat it at Library Extra 16–8 at cjtoday.com.

WEB Extra

LIBRARY Extra

Solving the Drug Problem

American drug-control strategies seem caught in a kind of limbo between conservative approaches, advocating supply reduction through strict enforcement and interdiction, and innovative strategies, proposing demand reduction through education, treatment, and counseling. In 2007, the Office of National Drug Control Policy released another *National Drug Control Strategy*,[126] a yearly publication outlining the current drug-abuse situation in the United States and detailing a strategy intended to guide the nation's criminal justice agencies in the continuing battle against drugs. The 2007 *National Drug Control Strategy* set as its first priority "stopping drug use before it starts."[127] The strategy said that it is critical to teach young people how to avoid drug use because of the damage drugs can inflict on their health and on their future. A major portion of the strategy was built on the $2 billion five-year National Youth Anti-Drug Media Campaign, which the *Strategy* claims "has had an impact on improving youth anti-drug attitudes and intentions."[128] The campaign is an integrated effort that combines media advertising with public communications outreach. It uses television and newspaper advertisements intended to coach parents in monitoring teen behavior and to promote quick parental intervention against signs of early drug use.

Although the federal strategy's primary focus is on education and prevention, the White House report maintains that no single solution can suffice to deal with the multifaceted challenge that drug abuse represents. Hence, the strategy also views law enforcement as essential to reducing drug use in the United States and sees policing as the first line of defense against drug trafficking. The strategy stresses the need to protect borders from drug incursion and to cut drug supply more effectively in domestic communities, seeks to curtail illegal drug trafficking via the interdiction of illicit drugs, focuses on supply-reduction operations at the source, and supports international efforts to curtail drug production and trafficking. Read the latest *National Drug Control Strategy* in its entirety at Library Extra 16–9 at cjtoday.com.

LIBRARY Extra

Politics aside, six general types of strategies can be identified among the many methods proposed for attacking the drug problem: (1) strict law enforcement, (2) asset forfeiture, (3) interdiction, (4) domestic and international crop control, (5) prevention and treatment, and (6) legalization and decriminalization. Each of these strategies is discussed in the following pages.

Strict Law Enforcement

Trafficking in controlled substances is, of course, an illegal activity in the United States—and has been for a long time. Conservative politicians generally opt for a strict program of antidrug law enforcement and costly drug sentences, with the goal of removing dealers from the streets, disrupting supply lines, and eliminating sources of supply. Unfortunately, legal prohibitions appear to have done little to discourage widespread drug abuse. Those who look to strict law enforce-

Sergeant Jeff Yurkiewicz of the Pennsylvania State Police K-9 Unit leading his dog, Jake, through a search for drugs and contraband at the Allegheny County Jail in Pittsburgh. More than 20 dogs were brought in to search the entire jail for drugs. Strict enforcement of antidrug laws is one of six strategies discussed in this chapter for attacking the drug problem. What are the other five?

AP Wide World Photos

ment as a primary drug-control strategy usually stress the need for secure borders, drug testing to identify users, and stiff penalties to discourage others from drug involvement. The U.S. Coast Guard policy of "zero tolerance," for example, which was highly touted in the late 1980s, led to widely publicized seizures of multimillion-dollar vessels when even small amounts of drugs (probably carried aboard by members of the crew) were found.

But strict enforcement measures may be only a stopgap strategy and may eventually lead to greater long-term problems. As James Q. Wilson observes, "It is not clear that enforcing the laws against drug use would reduce crime. On the contrary, crime may be caused by such enforcement because it keeps drug prices higher than they would otherwise be."[129]

Some U.S. enforcement strategies attempt to enlist the help of foreign officials. However, because drug exports represent extremely lucrative sources of revenue and may even be thought of as valuable "foreign trade" by the governments of some nations, effective international antidrug cooperation is hard to come by. In 1991, for example, partly in response to pressures from cocaine-producing cartels within the country, Colombia outlawed the extradition of Colombian citizens for any purpose—making the extradition and trial of Colombian cocaine kingpins impossible.

A number of international drug-control treaties do, however, exist. In 2005, in actions supported by such treaties, the DEA announced that its Operation Cyber Chase, which had targeted Internet traffickers who used more than 200 websites to illicitly distribute pharmaceutical controlled substances, had led to more than 20 arrests in the United States, Australia, Costa Rica, and India.[130] Among the substances being sold by the cybertraffickers through illegal pharmaceutical websites were the drugs Vicodin, Xanax, and OxyContin. International cooperation resulted in the forfeiture of 41 bank accounts that were linked to the storefronts and worth over $6 million.[131] One important group concerned with ensuring compliance with United Nations drug-control conventions is the International Narcotics Control Board (INCB). Visit the INCB via Web Extra 16–10 at cjtoday.com.

forfeiture

The authorized seizure of money, negotiable instruments, securities, or other things of value. Under federal antidrug laws, judicial representatives are authorized to seize all cash, negotiable instruments, securities, or other things of value furnished or intended to be furnished by any person in exchange for a controlled substance, as well as all proceeds traceable to such an exchange.

WEB
Extra

Asset Forfeiture

Forfeiture, an enforcement strategy that federal statutes and some state laws support, bears special mention. Antidrug forfeiture statutes authorize judges to seize "all monies, negotiable instruments, securities, or other things of value furnished or intended to be furnished by any person in exchange for a controlled substance . . . [and] all proceeds traceable to such an exchange."[132] Forfeiture statutes are based on the relation-back doctrine. This doctrine assumes that because the government's right to illicit proceeds relates back to the time they are generated, anything acquired through the expenditure of those proceeds also belongs to the government.[133]

The first federal laws to authorize forfeiture as a criminal sanction were passed in 1970. They were the Continuing Criminal Enterprise (CCE) statute and the Organized Crime Control Act. A section of the Organized Crime Control Act known as the **Racketeer Influenced and Corrupt Organizations (RICO)** statute was designed to prevent criminal infiltration of legitimate businesses and has been extensively applied in federal drug-smuggling cases. In 1978, Congress authorized civil forfeiture of any assets acquired through narcotics trafficking in violation of federal law. Many states modeled their own legislation after federal law and now have similar statutes.

Racketeer Influenced and Corrupt Organizations (RICO)

A federal statute that allows for the federal seizure of assets derived from illegal enterprise.

The newer civil statutes have the advantage of being relatively easy to enforce. Civil forfeiture requires proof only by a preponderance of the evidence, rather than proof beyond a reasonable doubt, as in criminal prosecution. In civil proceedings based on federal statutes, there is no need to trace the proceeds in question to a particular narcotics transaction. It is enough to link them to narcotics trafficking generally.[134]

Forfeiture amounts can be huge. In one 15-month period, for example, the South Florida–Caribbean Task Force, composed of police agencies from the federal, state, and local levels, seized $47 million in airplanes, vehicles, weapons, cash, and real estate.[135] In a single investigation involving two brothers convicted of heroin smuggling, the federal government seized a shopping center, three gasoline stations, and seven homes worth more than $20 million in New York City.[136]

Although almost all states now have forfeiture statutes, prosecutions built on them have met with less success than prosecutions based on federal law. The Police Executive Research Forum attributes the difference to three causes: (1) the fact that federal law is more favorable to prosecutors than most state laws are, (2) the greater resources of the federal government, and (3) the difficulties imposed by statutory requirements that illegal proceeds be traced to narcotics trafficking.[137]

In 1993, in *U.S.* v. *92 Buena Vista Ave.*,[138] the U.S. Supreme Court established an "innocent owner defense" in forfeiture cases, whereby the government is prohibited from seizing drug-transaction assets that were later acquired by a new and innocent owner. In the same year, in the case of *Austin* v. *U.S.*,[139] the Court placed limits on the government's authority to use forfeiture laws against drug criminals, finding that seizures of property must not be excessive when compared to the seriousness of the offense charged. Otherwise, the justices wrote, the Eighth Amendment's ban on excessive fines could be contravened. The justices, however, refused to establish a rule by which excessive fines could be judged. The *Austin* ruling was supported by two other 1993 cases, *Alexander* v. *U.S.* and *U.S.* v. *James Daniel Good Real Property.*[140] In *Alexander*, the Court found that forfeitures under the RICO statute must be limited according to the rules established in *Austin*, while in *Good*, the Court held that "absent exigent circumstances, the Due Process Clause requires the Government to afford notice and a meaningful opportunity to be heard before seizing real property subject to civil forfeiture."

In 1996, the U.S. Supreme Court upheld the seizure of private property used in the commission of a crime, even though the property belonged to an innocent owner not involved in the crime. The case, *Bennis* v. *Michigan*,[141] involved the government's taking of a car that had been used by the owner's husband when procuring the services of a prostitute. In effect, the justices ruled, an innocent owner is not protected from property forfeiture related to criminal conviction.

Also in 1996, in the case of *U.S.* v. *Ursery*,[142] the Supreme Court rejected claims that civil forfeiture laws constitute a form of double jeopardy. In *Ursery*, the defendant's house had been seized by federal officials who claimed that it had been used to facilitate drug transactions. The government later seized other personal items owned by Guy Jerome Ursery, saying that they had been purchased with the proceeds of drug sales and that Ursery had engaged in money-laundering activities to hide the source of his illegal income. The court of appeals, however, reversed Ursery's drug conviction and the forfeiture judgment, holding that the double jeopardy clause of the U.S. Constitution prohibits the government from both punishing a defendant for a criminal offense and forfeiting his property for that same offense in a separate civil proceeding. In reaffirming Ursery's conviction, however, the U.S. Supreme Court concluded that "civil forfeitures are neither 'punishment' nor criminal for purposes of the Double Jeopardy Clause." In distinguishing civil forfeitures and criminal punishments, the majority opinion held that "Congress has long authorized the Government to bring parallel criminal actions and . . . civil forfeiture proceedings based upon the same underlying events . . . , and this Court consistently has concluded that the Double Jeopardy Clause does not apply to such forfeitures because they do not impose punishment."

Civil forfeiture laws have come under considerable fire recently as being fundamentally unfair. More than 200 forfeiture laws have been enacted across the country in recent years, many requiring only mere suspicion before items of value can be seized by government agents. Once property has been seized, getting it back can be a nightmare, even when no crime was committed. A few years ago, U.S. Representative Henry Hyde of Illinois reported that 80% of people whose property was seized by the federal government under drug laws were never formally charged with any crime.[143]

To address problems with federal forfeiture provisions, Congress passed the Civil Asset Forfeiture Reform Act of 2000. Under the law, federal prosecutors must meet a new burden-of-proof standard in forfeiture cases. They are required to establish by a *preponderance of the evidence* that the property in question was subject to forfeiture. The property owner has five years in which to make a claim on the property after the government has claimed it, but a claimant's status as a fugitive from justice is grounds for dismissal of the case contesting the forfeiture of the property. Under the new law, it is a crime to remove or destroy property to prevent seizure for forfeiture.

Interdiction

Annual seizures of cocaine in the United States total about 140 tons. In 2007, however, officials were surprised at the amount of cocaine seized when the U.S. Coast Guard cutter *Sherman* stopped the Panamanian cargo ship *Gatun* about 20 miles off the California coast.[144] Twenty tons of cocaine, with an estimated street value of $600 million, were discovered and transported to the Coast Guard facility in Alameda to be destroyed. The 14 crew members aboard the *Gatun* were Panamanians and Mexicans who were not armed and offered no resistance when stopped. It was not immediately clear if any of them knew what cargo they were carrying. Prior to the 2007 Coast Guard seizure, other large caches had vied for size records, including nine tons of cocaine found in a house in Harlingen, Texas; six tons discovered on a ship in the Gulf of Mexico; and more than five tons hidden in barrels of lye in New York City.[145] A 2001 seizure by the Coast Guard of 13 tons of cocaine aboard a Belize-registered fishing boat south of San Diego, California, had held the previous record as the biggest cocaine seizure in U.S. maritime history.[146]

A key response to drug use and drug trafficking is an aggressive and coordinated law enforcement effort. Americans have the right to feel safe in their homes and secure in their communities.

—The National Drug Control Strategy

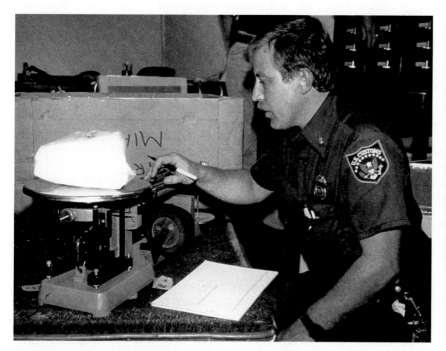

U.S. Customs officers with seized cocaine. Officer Rick Dallent (right) shows how four tons of packaged cocaine were hidden in hardwood boards designed for picnic tables and shipped from Honduras to Florida. The officer on the left is shown weighing seized cocaine. Some drug seizures—like the ones pictured above—involve huge amounts of drugs. Where does most cocaine come from?

Bob Sherman/Carolyn Sherman and UPI/Corbis/Bettmann

Customs inspectors James McDermott and Jessica Quiles searching travelers' belongings at Newark International Airport in New Jersey. Drug interdiction, which involves efforts aimed at stopping drugs from entering a country, is an international strategy. Are U.S. interdiction efforts working?

Todd Plitt

interdiction

The interception of drug traffic at the nation's borders. Interdiction is one of the many strategies used to stem the flow of illegal drugs into the United States.

Interdiction involves efforts aimed at stopping drugs from entering the United States. The Coast Guard, the Border Patrol, and Customs agents have played the most visible roles in interdiction efforts during the last few decades. Interdiction strategies in the fight against drugs, however, are almost doomed to failure by the sheer size of the task. Although most enforcement efforts are focused on international airports and major harbors, the international boundary of the United States extends over 12,000 miles. Rough coastline, sparsely populated desert, and dense forests provide natural barriers to easy observation and make detection of controlled substances entering the country very difficult. Add to this the fact that over 420 billion tons of goods and more than 270 million people cross over the American border annually, and the job of interdiction becomes more complicated still.[147] Because most drugs can be highly potent in even minute quantities, the interdiction strategy suffers from the proverbial "needle in the haystack" predicament.

Crop Control

One of the most promising means of reducing the supply of drugs is a strong source country strategy.

—The National Drug Control Strategy

Crop control strategies attempt to limit the amount of drugs available for the illicit market by targeting foreign producers. Crop control in source countries generally takes one of two forms. In the first, government subsidies (often with U.S. support) are made available to farmers to induce them to grow other kinds of crops. Sometimes illegal crops are bought and destroyed. The second form of control involves aerial spraying or ground-level crop destruction.

Source country crop control suffers from two major drawbacks.[148] First, the potentially large profits that can be made from illegal acreage encourage farmers in unaffected areas to take up the production of crops that have been destroyed elsewhere. Second, it can be difficult to get foreign governments to cooperate in eradication efforts. In some parts of the world, opium and coca are major cash crops, and local governments are reluctant to undertake any action directed against them.

Prevention and Treatment

As the population of incarcerated drug offenders swelled, some state legislatures began to question the necessity of imprisoning nonviolent substance abusers who were not involved in drug sale or distribution. In 1996, as a consequence of such thinking, Arizona voters approved Proposition 200, the Drug Medicalization, Prevention, and Control Act. A central purpose of the act was to expand drug-treatment and education services for drug offenders and to utilize probation for nonviolent drug offenders, thereby potentially diverting many arrested drug abusers from prison.

To fund the program, the Arizona law established the state's Drug Treatment and Education Fund, administered by Arizona's Office of the Courts; the fund draws revenues from the state's luxury tax on liquor.

A study by Arizona's Administrative Office of the Courts concluded that the Arizona law is "resulting in safer communities and more substance abusing probationers in recovery."[149] Moreover, said the report, the law has saved the state millions of dollars and has helped more than 75% of program participants to remain drug free.[150] In 2000, the state of California followed Arizona's lead when voters approved Proposition 36 (the California Substance Abuse and Crime Prevention Act of 2000), a sweeping initiative requiring treatment instead of imprisonment for nonviolent drug users throughout the state.[151] Similar legislation became law in Kansas in 2003 when Governor Sebelius signed Senate Bill 123, the First Time Non-Violent Drug Offenders Act. The law requires Kansas judges to place nonviolent offenders convicted of nothing more than drug possession in community-based or faith-based drug-treatment programs for up to 18 months.[152]

Many different kinds of prevention and treatment programs are available for drug offenders. Michael Goodstadt of the Addiction Research Foundation groups drug-prevention and drug-treatment programs into three categories: (1) those that provide factual information about drugs; (2) those that address feelings, values, and attitudes; and (3) those that focus directly on behavior.[153] Most modern programs contain elements of all three approaches, and most experts agree that drug-prevention programs, if they are to be successful, must include a wide array of components, including components for individuals, families, schools, the media, health-care providers, law enforcement officials, and other community agencies and organizations.[154]

Antidrug education programs can be found in schools, churches, and youth groups and may be provided by police departments, social service agencies, hospitals, and private citizens' groups. Project DARE (the Drug Abuse Resistance Education program) falls into Goodstadt's second category. DARE, the nation's most visible school-based antidrug education program, began as a cooperative effort between the Los Angeles Police Department and the Los Angeles Unified School District in 1983. Using uniformed law enforcement officers to conduct classes in elementary schools, the program focuses on decision-making skills, peer pressure, and alternatives to drug use.

A 1994 study cast the effectiveness of the DARE program into doubt, and officials in the Clinton administration were charged with refusing to recognize the study's results. The study, published in the *American Journal of Public Health*, reviewed DARE programs in six states and British Columbia and found that "the popular drug prevention program does not work well and is less effective than other drug prevention efforts targeted at students."[155] Defending the DARE program, Justice Department officials questioned the study's methodology and published their own version of the study's results, which showed that "user satisfaction" with the DARE program is high. The study, according to Justice Department interpreters, found substantial grassroots support for the DARE program and led to the conclusion that DARE "has been extremely successful at placing substance abuse education in the nation's schools."[156]

Later studies again questioned Project DARE's effectiveness. A 1997 review of numerous DARE studies concluded that the program's "effects on drug use, except for tobacco use, are nonsignificant."[157] Finally, a 1999 University of Kentucky study tracked more than 1,000 Midwestern students who participated in Project DARE in the sixth grade in order to see if the level of drug abuse among them differed from those who had not been exposed to the program.[158] The study found no difference in actual drug use immediately following exposure to the program or ten years later, when most of the former students were 20 years old.

Other studies also show that there is little evidence to support the belief that school-based antisubstance-abuse education will produce the desired effect on problem drug users or those at risk of beginning drug use.[159] Studies analyzing state-by-state spending on school-based drug education, for example, show little relationship between the amount of money spent on drug education and the number of hard-core cocaine users.[160] To be effective, programs will probably have to acknowledge the perceived positive aspects of the drug experience, as well as cultural messages that encourage drug use.[161] Until they do, many participants in today's antidrug programs may discount them as conflicting with personal experience. Read more about the debate over DARE via Web Extra 16–11 at cjtoday.com.

Other kinds of drug-education programs may be effective, however. A recent study by the RAND Corporation's Drug Policy Research Center (DPRC), for example, found education to be the most efficacious alternative for dealing with drug abuse.[162] DPRC researchers focused on the use of alternative strategies for reducing cocaine abuse. Visit RAND's DPRC via Web Extra 16–12 at cjtoday.com.

WEB
Extra
▪▪▪▪

WEB
Extra
▪▪▪▪

A young woman shooting up with help from friends. Drug abuse extends to all social groups and can be found among all ages. Why does illicit drug use persist in the United States after decades of efforts to curtail it?

Dennis MacDonald/PhotoEdit Inc.

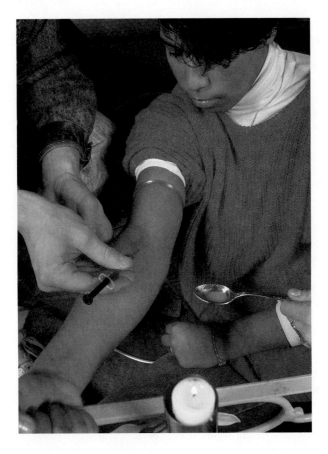

DRUG COURTS

drug court

A special state, county, or municipal court that offers first-time substance-abuse offenders judicially mandated and court-supervised treatment alternatives to prison.

One of the most widely accepted antidrug programs operating today is the **drug court**. Drug courts focus on promoting public safety and employ a nonadversarial approach that provides defendants with easy access to a range of alcohol, drug, and other related treatment and rehabilitation services. Drug courts also monitor abstinence from the use of drugs on an individual basis through frequent alcohol and other drug testing. Failing to comply with court-ordered treatment, or returning to drug use, results in harsher punishments, including imprisonment.

Modern drug courts are modeled after a Dade County, Florida, innovation that became known as the *Miami Drug Court model.* An early evaluation of Miami's drug court found a high rate of success: Few clients were rearrested, incarceration rates were lowered, and the burden on the criminal justice system was lessened.[163] The success of the drug-court model led to $1 billion worth of funding under the Violent Crime Control and Law Enforcement Act of 1994 for the establishment of similar courts throughout the nation. Since then, the growth in the number of drug courts serving the nation has been huge. In 2005, the National Association of Drug Court Professionals (NADCP) reported that nearly 1,500 drug courts were in existence or were being planned.[164] The federal budget for fiscal year 2006 included $70.1 million in continuation funding for such courts, although state and local governments also contribute to the support of drug courts.[165] The Congress of State Drug Courts, part of the NADCP, is working to support and nurture drug-court leadership at local levels in anticipation of the day when federal funding for drug courts runs out.

There are special drug courts for juveniles and for drunk drivers (sometimes called DUI courts). The National Drug Court Institute, in conjunction with the NADCP, provides training for judges and professional courtroom staff interested in today's drug-court movement.[166] Learn more about drug courts via **Web Extra 16–13** and **Library Extras 16–10** and **16–11** at cjtoday.com.

WEB Extra

LIBRARY Extra

Legalization and Decriminalization

Some years ago at an annual conference on controversies in criminal justice, Ross Deck, senior policy analyst at the Office of National Drug Control Policy, opened his remarks to a yearly conference on controversies in criminal justice with these words: "First of all, we are not fighting a

Cher Fisher (left) of England and Henny Fou of Holland posing before the start of the sixth annual beauty pageant for inmates at the Santa Monica Women's Prison in Lima, Peru. Most women incarcerated at the Peruvian penitentiary worked as drug "mules" and were caught trying to smuggle cocaine out of Peru. How can we solve the drug problem?

Jaime Razuri/Agence France Presse/Getty Images

drug war anymore. To have a war you must have enemies. In this situation, we are our own enemy."[167] Such realizations have led a number of well-meaning people to question the wisdom of current laws and to seek alternatives to existing U.S. drug-control policies. For them, it has become clear that the fight against drug abuse through the application of strict criminal justice sanctions is bound to fail. Arrest, incarceration, and a national prison system filled with drug-law violators do not seem to hold the answer to winning the drug-control battle.

More than one-third (37%) of the police chiefs who participated in the survey mentioned at the start of this chapter state that our nation's drug policy needs a fundamental overhaul, and 47% think that it needs major changes. Only 2% of responding chiefs said that they would maintain the status quo.[168]

In 2006, reflecting such sentiments, Mexican lawmakers passed a sweeping new law intended to legalize the possession of small quantities of illegal drugs for personal use—including marijuana, Ecstasy, LSD, cocaine, and heroin. The law, which President Vincente Fox indicated he would sign, also would have mandated drug treatment for people found to be drug addicts. When the legislation reached President Fox's desk, however, he refused to sign it into law; some people said that he had given in to pressure from Washington not to turn Mexico into a center for drug tourism.[169]

Often regarded as the most "radical" approach to solving the drug problem, legalization and decriminalization have been proposed repeatedly, and in recent years, these ideas have seemed to be gaining at least a modicum of respectability. Although the words *legalization* and *decriminalization* are often used interchangeably, there is a significant difference. **Legalization** refers to the removal of all legal strictures from the use or possession of the drug in question. Manufacture and distribution might still be regulated. **Decriminalization**, on the other hand, substantially reduces penalties associated with drug use but may not eliminate them entirely. States like Oregon, which have decriminalized marijuana possession, for example, treat simple possession of small amounts of the substance as a ticketable offense similar to jaywalking or improper parking.[170] Hence, decriminalization of a controlled substance might mean that the drug "would remain illegal but the offense of possession would be treated like a traffic violation, with no loss of liberty involved for the transgressor."[171]

The following arguments have been offered in support of both legalization and decriminalization:[172]

- Legal drugs would be easy to track and control. The involvement of organized criminal cartels in the drug-distribution network could be substantially curtailed.

- Legal drug sales could be taxed, generating huge revenues.

- Legal drugs would be cheap, significantly reducing the number of drug-related crimes committed to feed expensive drug habits.

- Since some people are attracted to anything taboo, legalization could, in fact, reduce the demand for drugs.

- The current "war on drugs" is already a failure and will be remembered as one of history's follies.[173] Prohibiting drugs is too expensive in terms of tax dollars, sacrificed civil liberties, and political turmoil.

legalization

Elimination of the laws and associated criminal penalties associated with certain behaviors—usually the production, sale, distribution, and possession of a controlled substance.

decriminalization

The redefinition of certain previously criminal behaviors into regulated activities that become "ticketable" rather than "arrestable."

- Drug dealers and users care little about criminal justice sanctions. They will continue their illegal activities no matter what the penalties.
- Drug use should ultimately be a matter of personal choice.

Advocates of legalization are primarily motivated by cost–benefit considerations, weighing the social costs of prohibition against its results.[174] The results, they say, have been meager at best, while the costs have been almost more than society can bear.

Opponents of legalization argue from both a moral and a practical stance. Some, like former New York City Mayor Rudolph Giuliani, believe that legalization would only condone a behavior that is fundamentally immoral.[175] Others argue that under legalization, drug use would increase, causing more widespread drug-related social problems than exist today. Robert DuPont, former head of the National Institute on Drug Abuse, for example, estimates that up to ten times the number of people who now use cocaine would turn to the substance if it were legal.[176]

A compromise approach has been suggested in what some writers call the *limitation model.* The limitation model "would make drugs legally available, but with clearly defined limits as to which institutions and professions could distribute the drugs."[177] Hence, under such a model, doctors, pharmacists, and perhaps licensed drug counselors could prescribe controlled substances under appropriate circumstances, and the drugs themselves might be taxed. Some claim that a more extreme form of the limitation model might be workable. Under that model, drugs would be sold through designated "drugstores" with distribution systems structured much like those of liquor stores today. Controlled substances would be sold to those of suitable age but taxed substantially, and the use of such substances under certain circumstances (when driving, for example) might still be illegal. The regulation and taxation of controlled substances would correspond to today's handling of alcoholic beverages.

Another example of the limitation model, already tried in some countries, is the two-market system.[178] The two-market approach would allow inexpensive and legitimate access to controlled substances for registered addicts. Only maintenance amounts (the amounts needed to forestall symptoms of drug withdrawal) of the needed drugs, however, would be available. The two-market approach would purportedly reduce the massive profits available to criminal drug cartels while simultaneously discouraging new drug use among those who are not addicted. Great Britain provides an example of the two-market system. During the 1960s and 1970s, British heroin addicts who registered with the government received prescriptions for limited amounts of heroin, which was dispensed through medical clinics. Because of concern about system abuses, clinics in the late 1970s began to dispense reduced amounts of heroin, hoping to wean addicts away from the drug.[179] By 1980, heroin was replaced by methadone,[180] a synthetic drug designed to prevent the physical symptoms of heroin withdrawal. Methadone, in amounts sufficient to prevent withdrawal, does not produce a heroin-like high. Recent studies, however, show that methadone, a drug implicated in the death of Daniel Wayne Smith who was pictured earlier in this chapter, can build up in the body to a toxic level if taken too often.[181]

It is doubtful that the two-market system will be adopted in the United States anytime soon. American cultural condemnation of major mind-altering drugs has created a reluctance to accept the legitimacy of drug treatment using controlled substances. In addition, cocaine is much more of a problem in the United States than heroin is. The large number of drug abusers in the country, combined with the difficulty of defining and measuring addiction to drugs like cocaine, would make any maintenance program impractical.

One group advocating for a change in current drug laws, including the possible decriminalization of some controlled substances, is Law Enforcement against Prohibition (LEAP). LEAP members are current and former law enforcement officers, and the group describes itself as "an organization made up of former drug warriors speaking out about the excesses and abuses of current drug policy and the utter failure of the war on drugs." The group originated with Peter Christ, a retired police captain living in New York City. Christ believed that an organization modeled after Vietnam Veterans against the War would catch the attention of the media and appeal to other law enforcement officers. Visit LEAP on the Web at Web Extra 16–14 at cjtoday.com. Read the DEA's perspective on the possibility of legalization via Web Extra 16–15.

WEB
Extra
∎∎∎∎

SUMMARY

- In determining which substances should be called *drugs*, it is important to recognize the role of social convention. Hence, what Americans today consider to be a drug depends more on agreed-on understandings than it does on any inherent property of the chemical substance itself. Powerful drugs, those with the ability to produce substantially altered states of consciousness and with a high potential for addiction, occupy the forefront in social and legal condemnation. Among them are psychoactive substances like heroin, peyote, mescaline, LSD, and cocaine. Changes in thinking that took place during the 1960s and 1970s led to the inclusion of far less powerful substances, such as alcohol and nicotine, in the "drug" category.

- Many of today's controlled substances were once unregulated by law. Even heroin, cocaine, opium, and marijuana were once freely available and contained in widely used medicines. The first major piece of federal antidrug legislation was the Harrison Narcotics Act of 1914. It required anyone dealing in opium, morphine, heroin, cocaine, and specified derivatives of these drugs to register with the federal government and to pay a tax. In 1937, Congress passed the Marijuana Tax Act, which simply placed a tax on cannabis; those who did not pay the tax were subject to prosecution. The passage of the Boggs Act in 1951 made marijuana, along with a number of other drugs, a federally prohibited controlled substance. The Narcotic Control Act of 1956 increased penalties for drug trafficking and possession and made the sale of heroin to anyone under age 18 a capital offense. The Comprehensive Drug Abuse Prevention and Control Act, passed in 1970, is the basis of federal enforcement efforts today. Title II of the law is the Controlled Substances Act. The CSA sets up five schedules that classify psychoactive drugs according to their degree of psychoactivity and abuse potential. The Anti-Drug Abuse Act of 1988 increased penalties for "recreational" drug users and made weapons purchases by suspected drug dealers more difficult. The law also denies federal benefits, ranging from loans to contracts and licenses, to convicted drug offenders and allows capital punishment for drug-related murders.

- The use of illicit drugs is fairly widespread in the United States. One of the best sources of data on the use of illegal drugs and the characteristics of drug users is the federal *National Survey on Drug Use and Health* (NSDUH). NSDUH is an annual publication of the Substance Abuse and Mental Health Services Administration (SAMHSA). NSDUH data for 2005 showed that 19.7 million Americans age 12 and older were "current" users of illegal drugs. Nearly 15 million people were estimated to be using marijuana, and an estimated 2.4 million people were current cocaine users. An estimated 6.4 million Americans were current nonmedical users of prescription-type psychotherapeutic drugs. Although the numbers may seem large, these figures represent a considerable decline from 1979, the year in which the highest levels of drug abuse in the United States were reported. Nonetheless, figures for recent years show a gradual increase in drug use (especially "occasional use"). As this chapter points out, rates of drug use vary considerably by age, and adolescents and people in their twenties tend to show the highest rates of illicit drug use.

- Drug crimes and drug-related crimes account for a substantial proportion of all crimes committed in this country. While the manufacture, importation, sale, and use of illegal drugs account for many law violations, many others are also linked to drug use. Among them are thefts of all kinds, burglary, assault, and murder. Similarly, many criminal enterprises are supported by the street-level demand for drugs. The high cost of drugs forces many users, some of whom have little legitimate income, to commit property crimes to make money to continue their drug habit. On the other hand, users of illicit drugs who have substantial legitimate incomes may indirectly shift the cost of drug use to society through lowered job productivity, psychological or family problems, and medical expenses.

- Six general types of strategies were identified in this chapter as being among the many methods proposed for attacking the drug problem: (1) strict law enforcement, (2) asset forfeiture, (3) interdiction, (4) crop control, (5) prevention and treatment, and (6) legalization and decriminalization.

KEY TERMS

club drug, 597

controlled substance, 577

Controlled Substances Act (CSA), 583

curtilage, 587

decriminalization, 609

drug, 578

drug abuse, 576

drug court, 608

drug czar, 586

drug trafficking, 591

forfeiture, 603

Harrison Narcotics Act, 583

interdiction, 606

legalization, 609

money laundering, 601

pharmaceutical diversion, 599

physical dependence, 583

psychoactive substance, 578

psychological dependence, 583

Racketeer Influenced and Corrupt Organizations (RICO), 604

recreational drug user, 578

KEY CASES

Alexander v. *U.S.*, 604

Austin v. *U.S.*, 604

California v. *Greenwood*, 587

Oliver v. *U.S.*, 587

Ratzlaf v. *U.S.*, 602

U.S. v. *Dunn*, 587

U.S. v. *92 Buena Vista Ave.*, 604

U.S. v. *Oakland Cannabis Buyers' Cooperative*, 592

U.S. v. *Ursery*, 604

QUESTIONS FOR REVIEW

1. What constitutes a drug for purposes of the criminal law? What role does social convention play in deciding what constitutes a controlled substance?

2. How long have substances that today would be considered illicit been used in the United States? For what purposes? List and describe some of the most important pieces of federal drug-control legislation.

3. What are the major types of drugs that are illegally used in this country? Describe the effects and legal classification of each.

4. What is the relationship between drug use and other social problems? What kinds of crimes might be linked to drug use?

5. What strategies have been used or suggested as ways of responding to the drug problem? Which of these strategies seem to hold the most potential?

QUESTIONS FOR REFLECTION

1. How successful have government efforts to curtail illicit drug use been? Why haven't they met with greater success?

2. What is meant by the decriminalization of illicit drugs? How does decriminalization differ from legalization?

3. Would you be in favor of the decriminalization of any drugs that are currently considered to be federally controlled substances? If so, which ones and why?

Discuss your answers to these questions and other issues on the CJ Today e-mail discussion list (join the list at cjtoday.com).

WEB QUEST

Research drug and alcohol abuse using the Cybrary (http://www.cybrary.info) as a starting point. Search the Cybrary listings to find sites that contain suggestions and ideas on how to solve the drug problems facing this country.

What sources did you find? (Don't forget the *National Drug Control Strategy* available from ONDCP.) Describe the various strategies you've found. Which do you think are the most useful? Why? Submit your findings to your instructor if asked to do so.

To complete this Web Quest online, go to the Web Quest module in Chapter 16 of the *Criminal Justice Today* Companion Website at cjtoday.com.

CHAPTER 17

Terrorism and Multinational Criminal Justice

LEARNING OBJECTIVES

After reading this chapter, you should be able to

- Describe the principles that form the basis of Islamic law.
- Identify important international criminal justice organizations and explain their role in fighting international crime.
- Explain globalization and explicate its possible relationship to crime and terrorism.
- Define *terrorism,* and identify two major types of terrorism.

OUTLINE

- Introduction
- Islamic Criminal Justice

- International Criminal Justice Organizations
- Globalization and Crime
- Terrorism

America's response to globalization in the criminal justice arena will necessitate major changes in both law and policy, placing greater emphasis on the education and training of practitioners at all levels of government. In addition to culture and language, tomorrow's criminal justice practitioner must have a broader understanding of the legal systems of other countries and respect for the customs and practices of immigrants, as well as an increasing number of international visitors.

—Richard Ward, Dean and Director, Criminal Justice Center, Sam Houston State University[1]

In the 21st century, Americans have come to appreciate that they are part of a global society and that criminal transgressions within and beyond our Nation's borders have worldwide ramifications.

—Office for Victims of Crime[2]

Hear the author discuss this chapter at cjtoday.com

Introduction

On May 8, 2007, federal agents arrested a reputed Islamic terrorist who lived in Cherry Hill, New Jersey, and who went by the unlikely name of Elvis. Eljjvir Duka, 23, was one of six aspiring Islamic holy warriors who, the government said, were planning to attack the U.S. Army base at Fort Dix, which is near Cookstown, New Jersey.[3] The men apparently had trained out of a rented house in Pennsylvania's Pocono Mountains. They were arrested after a 15-month investigation that began when a store clerk saw them firing automatic weapons and shouting "God is great!" in Arabic on a videotape that they had asked to have transferred to DVD. The men were taken into custody after meeting with an undercover agent to purchase automatic weapons that they planned to use in the attack. The group had been infiltrated by Federal Bureau of Investigation (FBI) agents, and some of their conversations had been secretly recorded—including one in which the group's leader regretted having missed an opportunity to launch an attack at the Army-Navy football game in Philadelphia in 2006. Three of the men taken into custody are ethnic Albanian brothers who were born in the former Yugoslavia and were living in the United States illegally. One is a naturalized American citizen from Jordan, and another is a legal permanent resident from Turkey. The sixth is a legal permanent resident born in Yugoslavia. All are Muslim and in their mid-twenties, and one worked as a pizza delivery person with easy access to the targeted base.

The six men, some of whom had been living in the United States since childhood and had attended public schools here, held jobs ranging from roofer to cabdriver and seemed to have had no clear motivation other than a shared desire to kill U.S. soldiers in the name of Islam. Although they were not directly affiliated with any other known terrorist organization, the group had watched al-Qaeda videos posted on foreign websites and were apparently inspired by the idea of a worldwide Jihad, or holy war. "This is a new brand of terrorism where a small cell of people can bring enormous devastation," said Christopher J. Christie, the U.S. attorney for New Jersey.[4]

Although the link between small, independently organized terrorist groups, like the New Jersey cell, and larger, more formal organizations like al-Qaeda may be mostly ideological, it can still provide a powerful motivation for destructive criminal activities. Hence, it has become vitally important for American criminal justice and other government organizations to appreciate the ideology, culture, and means of communications linking criminal and terrorist groups in this country to those overseas and around the world.

Criminologists who study crime and criminal justice on a cross-national level are referred to as **comparative criminologists**, and their field is called *comparative criminal justice, comparative criminology,* or *cross-national criminal justice.* Comparative criminal justice is becoming increasingly valued for the insights it provides. By contrasting native institutions of justice with similar institutions in other countries, procedures and problems in one system can be reevaluated in the light of world experience. As technological advances effectively "shrink" the world,

comparative criminologist

One who studies crime and criminal justice on a cross-national level.

we are able to learn firsthand about the criminal justice systems of other countries and to use that information to improve our own.

This chapter explains the value of comparative criminal justice, points to the problems that arise in comparing data from different nations, and explains international terrorism within the context of cross-national crime. By way of example, this chapter also briefly examines criminal justice systems based on Islamic principles. International police agencies are described, and the role of the United Nations (UN) in the worldwide fight against crime and terrorism is discussed. Additional information on the justice systems of many countries can be found in the *World Factbook of Criminal Justice Systems,* available at Library Extra 17–1 at cjtoday.com. Another place to visit for international criminal justice information is the National Institute of Justice's (NIJ) International Center, which is accessible via Web Extra 17–1 at cjtoday.com.

LIBRARY Extra

WEB Extra

Ethnocentrism and the Study of Criminal Justice

The study of criminal justice in the United States has been largely **ethnocentric.** Because people are socialized from birth into a particular culture, they tend to prefer their own culture's way of doing things over that of any other. Native patterns of behavior are seen as somehow "natural" and therefore better than foreign ones. The same is true for values, beliefs, and customs. People tend to think that their religion holds a spiritual edge over other religions, that their values and ethical sense are superior to those of others, and that the fashions they wear, the language they speak, and the rituals of daily life in which they participate are somehow better than comparable practices elsewhere. Ethnocentric individuals do not consider that people elsewhere in the world cling to their own values, beliefs, and standards of behavior with just as much fervor as they do.

ethnocentric

Holding a belief in the superiority of one's own social or ethnic group and culture.

Only in recent years have American students of criminal justice begun to examine the justice systems of other cultures. Unfortunately, not all societies are equally open, and it is not always easy to explore them. In some societies, even the *study* of criminal justice is taboo. As a result, data-gathering strategies taken for granted in Western societies may not be well received elsewhere. One author, for example, has observed that in China, "the seeking of criminal justice information through face-to-face questioning takes on a different meaning in Chinese officialdom than it does generally in the Western world. While we accept this method of inquiry because we prize thinking on our feet and quick answers, it is rather offensive in China because it shows lack of respect and appreciation for the information given through the preferred means of prepared questions and formal briefings."[5] Hence, most of the information available about Chinese criminal justice comes by way of bureaucracy, and routine Western social science practices like door-to-door interviews, participant observation, and random surveys would produce substantial problems for researchers who attempt to use these techniques in China.

Problems with Data

Similar difficulties arise in the comparison of crime rates from one country to another. The crime rates of different nations are difficult to compare because of (1) differences in the way a specific crime is defined, (2) diverse crime-reporting practices, and (3) political and other influences on the reporting of statistics to international agencies.[6]

Definitional differences create what may be the biggest problem. For cross-national comparisons of crime data to be meaningful, it is essential that the reported data share conceptual similarities. Unfortunately, that is rarely the case. Nations report offenses according to the legal criteria by which arrests are made and under which prosecution can occur. Switzerland, for example, includes bicycle thefts in its reported data on what we call "auto theft" because Swiss data gathering focuses more on the concept of personal transportation than it does on the type of vehicle stolen. The Netherlands has no crime category for robberies, counting them as thefts. Japan classifies an assault that results in death as an assault or an aggravated assault, not as a homicide. Greek rape statistics include crimes of sodomy, "lewdness," seduction of a child, incest, and prostitution. China reports only robberies and thefts that involve the property of citizens; crimes against state-owned property fall into a separate category.

Social, cultural, and economic differences among countries compound these difficulties. Auto theft statistics, for example, when compared between countries like the United States and China, need to be placed in an economic as well as demographic context. While the United States has two automobiles for every three people, China has only one car per every 100 of its citizens. For the Chinese auto theft rate to equal that of the United States, every automobile in the country would have to be stolen nearly twice each year!

Reporting practices vary substantially between nations. The International Criminal Police Organization (Interpol) and the United Nations are the only international organizations that regularly collect crime statistics from a large number of countries.[7] Both agencies can only request data and have no way of checking on the accuracy of the data reported to them. Many countries do not disclose the requested information, and those that do often make only partial reports. In general, small countries are more likely to report than are large ones, and nonsocialist countries are more likely to report than are socialist countries.[8]

International reports of crime are often delayed. Complete up-to-date data are rare since the information made available to agencies like the United Nations and Interpol is reported at different times and according to schedules that vary from nation to nation. In addition, official United Nations world crime surveys are conducted infrequently. To date, only ten such surveys have been undertaken.[9]

Crime statistics also reflect political biases and national values. Some nations do not accurately admit to the frequency of certain kinds of culturally reprehensible crimes. Communist countries, for example, appear loathe to report crimes like theft, burglary, and robbery because the very existence of such offenses demonstrates felt inequities within the Communist system. After the breakup of the Soviet Union, Alexander Larin, a criminal justice scholar who worked as a Russian investigator during the 1950s and 1960s, revealed that "inside the state security bureaucracy, where statistics were collected and circulated, falsification of crime figures was the rule, not the exception. The practice was self-perpetuating," said Larin. "Supervisors in the provinces were under pressure to provide Moscow with declining crime rates. And no self-respecting investigator wanted to look worse than his neighbor. . . . From the top to the bottom, the bosses depended on their employees not to make them look bad with high crime statistics."[10]

On the other hand, observers in democratic societies showed similar biases in their interpretation of statistics following the end of the cold war. Some Western analysts, for example, reporting on declines in the prison populations of Eastern and Central Europe during that period, attributed the decline to lessened frustration and lowered crime rates brought about by democratization. In one country, Hungary, prison populations declined from 240 inmates per 100,000 residents in 1986 to 130 per 100,000 in 1993, with similar decreases in other nations.[11] The more likely explanation, however, is the wholesale post-Soviet release of political dissidents from prisons formerly run by Communist regimes. Learn more about world crime via the UN's *Global Report on Crime and Justice,* which is available at Library Extra 17–2 at cjtoday.com. View data from the UN Survey on Crime Trends via Web Extra 17–2, and access the *European Sourcebook of Crime and Criminal Justice Statistics* at Library Extra 17–3.

LIBRARY
Extra

WEB
Extra

An Iraqi man holding a picture of top Shiite cleric Ayatollah Ali Sistani during a protest in support of an Islamic constitution. The traditions and legal systems of many Middle Eastern countries are strongly influenced by Islamic law, which is based on the teachings of the Koran and the sayings of the Prophet Muhammad. How does Islamic law differ from the laws of most Western nations?

Karim Kadim/AP Wide World Photos

Islamic Criminal Justice

Islamic law has been the subject of much discussion in the United States since the September 11, 2001, terrorist attacks on the World Trade Center and the Pentagon. It is important for American students of criminal justice to recognize, however, that Islamic law refers to legal ideas (and sometimes entire legal systems) based on the teachings of Islam and that it bears no intrinsic relationship to acts of terrorism committed by misguided zealots with Islamic backgrounds. Similarly, Islamic law is by no means the same thing as Jihad (Islamic holy war) or Islamic fundamentalism. Although Americans are now much better informed about the concept of Islamic law than they were in the past, some may not be aware that various interpretations of Islam still form the basis of laws in many countries and that the entire legal systems of some nations are based on Islamic principles. Islamic law holds considerable sway in a large number of countries, including Syria, Iran, Iraq (where a new constitution was voted on and approved in 2005), Pakistan, Afghanistan, Yemen, Saudi Arabia, Kuwait, the United Arab Emirates, Bahrain, Algeria, Jordan, Lebanon, Libya, Ethiopia, Gambia, Nigeria, Oman, Qatar, Senegal, Tunisia, Tajikistan, Uzbekistan, and Turkey (which practices official separation of church and state).

Islamic law descends directly from the teachings of the Prophet Muhammad, whom the *Cambridge Encyclopedia of Islam* describes as a "prophet-lawyer."[12] Muhammad rose to fame in the city of Mecca (in what is now Saudi Arabia) as a religious reformer. Later, however, he traveled to Medina, where he became the ruler and lawgiver of a newly formed religious society. In his role as lawgiver, Muhammad enacted legislation whose aim was to teach men what to do and how to behave in order to achieve salvation. As a consequence, Islamic law today is a system of duties and rituals founded on legal and moral obligations—all of which are ultimately sanctioned by the authority of a religious leader (or leaders) who may issue commands (known as *fatwas* or *fatwahs*) that the faithful are bound to obey.

Criminal justice professor Sam Souryal and his coauthors describe four aspects of justice in Arab philosophy and religion. Islamic justice, they say, means the following:[13]

- A sacred trust, a duty imposed on humans to be discharged sincerely and honestly. As such, these authors say, "justice is the quality of being morally responsible and merciful in giving everyone his or her due."

- A mutual respect of one human being by another. From this perspective, a just society is one that offers equal respect for individuals through social arrangements made in the common interest of all members.

- An aspect of the social bond that holds society together and transforms it into a brotherhood in which everyone becomes a keeper of everyone else and each is held accountable for the welfare of all.

- A command from God. Whoever violates God's commands should be subject to strict punishments according to Islamic tradition and belief.

As Souryal and his coauthors observe, "The third and fourth meanings of justice are probably the ones most commonly invoked in Islamic jurisprudence" and form the basis of criminal justice practice in many Middle Eastern countries.

The *Hudud* Crimes

Islamic law (or *Shari'ah* in Arabic, which means "path of God") forms the basis of theocratic judicial systems in Kuwait, Saudi Arabia, the Sudan, Iran, and Algeria. Other Arabic nations, such as Egypt, Jordan, and Iraq, recognize substantial elements of Islamic law in their criminal justice systems but also make wide use of Western and nontheocratic legal principles. Islamic law is based on four sources. In order of importance, these sources are (1) the Koran (also spelled *Quran* and *Qur'an*), or Holy Book of Islam, which Muslims believe is the word of God, or Allah; (2) the teachings of the Prophet Muhammad; (3) a consensus of the clergy in cases where neither the Koran nor the prophet directly addresses an issue; and (4) reason or logic, which should be used when no solution can be found in the other three sources.[14]

Islamic law recognizes seven ***Hudud* crimes**—or crimes based on religious strictures. *Hudud* (sometimes called *Hodood* or *Huddud*) crimes are essentially violations of "natural law" as interpreted by Arab culture. Divine displeasure is thought to be the basis of crimes defined as *Hudud,* and *Hudud* crimes are often said to be crimes against God (or, more specifically, God's rights). The Koran specifies punishments for four of the seven *Hudud* crimes: (1) making war on

It may be only a matter of time before al-Qaeda or other groups attempt to use chemical, biological, radiological or nuclear weapons. We must focus on that.

—CIA Director Porter Goss[i]

Islamic law

A system of laws, operative in some Arab countries, based on the Muslim religion and especially the holy book of Islam, the Koran.

***Hudud* crime**

A serious violation of Islamic law that is regarded as an offense against God. *Hudud* crimes include such behavior as theft, adultery, sodomy, alcohol consumption, and robbery.

Iraqi Shiite Muslims flagellating themselves during a procession in Karbala, Iraq, on March 20, 2006. Islamic law, which is based on the teachings of Islam, underpins the legal systems of many nations in the Middle East and elsewhere. What kinds of offenses does it prohibit? What punishments does it specify?

Hadi Misban/AP Wide World Photos

With criminals' ability to cross international borders in a few hours, and the advances of our modern age, such as the Internet and telecommunications, crime can no longer be viewed as just a national issue.

—Assistant U.S. Attorney General Laurie Robinson

Allah and His messengers, (2) theft, (3) adultery or fornication, and (4) false accusation of fornication or adultery. The three other *Hudud* offenses are mentioned by the Koran, but no punishment is specified: (1) "corruption on earth," (2) drinking alcohol, and (3) highway robbery—and the punishments for these crimes are determined by tradition.[15] The *Hudud* offenses and associated typical punishments are shown in Table 17–1. "Corruption on earth" is a general category of religious offense, not well understood in the West, which includes activities like embezzlement, revolution against lawful authority, fraud, and "weakening the society of God." In 2004, for example, Mehdi Hassan, a 36-year-old Pakistani was sentenced to life in prison by a court in Lahore for burning a copy of the Koran. Hassan was convicted and sentenced under Pakistan's laws covering offenses against Islam.[16]

Islamic law mandates strict punishment of moral failure. Sexual offenders, even those who engage in what would be considered essentially victimless crimes in Western societies, are subject to especially harsh treatment. The Islamic penalty for sexual intercourse outside of marriage, for example, is 100 lashes. Men are stripped to the waist, women have their clothes bound tightly, and flogging is carried out with a leather whip. Adultery carries a much more severe penalty: flogging and stoning to death.

TABLE 17–1   Crime and Punishment in Islamic Law: The Iranian Example

Islamic law looks to the Koran and to the teachings of the Prophet Muhammad to determine which acts should be classified as crimes. The Koran and tradition specify punishments to be applied to designated offenses, as the following verse from the Koran demonstrates: "The only reward of those who make war upon Allah and His messenger and strive after corruption in the land will be that they will be killed or crucified, or have their hands and feet on alternate sides cut off, or will be expelled out of the land" (*Surah* V, Verse 33). Other crimes and punishments include the following:

Offense	Punishment
Theft	Amputation of the hand
Adultery	Stoning to death
Fornication	One hundred lashes
False accusation (of fornication or adultery)	Eighty lashes
Corruption on earth	Death by the sword or by burning
Drinking alcohol	Eighty lashes; death if repeated three times
Robbery	Cutting off of hands and feet on alternate sides, exile, or execution

Note: For more information, see Sam S. Souryal, Dennis W. Potts, and Abdullah I. Alobied, "The Penalty of Hand Amputation for Theft in Islamic Justice," *Journal of Criminal Justice*, Vol. 22, No. 3 (1994), pp. 249–265; and Parviz Saney, "Iran," in Elmer H. Johnson, ed., *International Handbook of Contemporary Developments in Criminology* (Westport, CT: Greenwood Press, 1983), pp. 356–369.

Under Islamic law, even property crimes are firmly punished. Thieves who are undeterred by less serious punishments may eventually suffer amputation of the right hand. In a reputedly humane move, Iranian officials recently began to use an electric guillotine, specially made for the purpose, which can sever a hand at the wrist in one-tenth of a second. For amputation to be imposed, the item stolen must have value in Islam. Pork and alcohol, for example, are regarded as being without value, and their theft is not subject to punishment. Islamic legal codes also establish a minimum value for stolen items that could result in a sentence of amputation. Likewise, offenders who have stolen because they are hungry or are in need are exempt from the punishment of amputation and receive fines or prison terms.

Slander and the consumption of alcohol are both punished by 80 lashes. Legal codes in strict Islamic nations also specify whipping for the crimes of pimping, lesbianism, kissing by an unmarried couple, cursing, and failure of a woman to wear a veil. Islamic law provides for the execution, sometimes through crucifixion, of robbers. Laws stipulate that anyone who survives three days on the cross may be spared. Depending on the circumstances of the robbery, however, the offender may suffer the amputation of opposite hands and feet or may be exiled.

Rebellion, or revolt against a legitimate political leader or established economic order, which is considered an aspect of "corruption on earth," is punishable by death. The offender may be killed outright in a military or police action or, later, by sentence of the court. The last of the *Hudud* crimes is rejection of Islam. The penalty, once again, is death and can be imposed for denying the existence of God or angels, denying any of the prophets of Islam, or rejecting any part of the Koran.

Souryal and coauthors observe that *Hudud* crimes can be severely punished because "punishment serves a three-tiered obligation: (1) the fulfillment of worship, (2) the purification of society, and (3) the redemption of the individual." However, they add, the interests of the individual are the least valuable component of this triad and may have to be sacrificed "for the wholesomeness and integrity of the encompassing justice system."[17]

The *Tazir* Crimes

All crimes other than *Hudud* crimes fall into an offense category called *tazirat*. **Tazir crimes** are regarded as any actions not considered acceptable in a spiritual society. They include crimes against society and against individuals, but not against God. *Tazir* crimes may call for *quesas* (retribution) or *diya* (compensation or fines). Crimes requiring *quesas* are based on the Arabic principle of "an eye for an eye" and generally require physical punishments up to and including death. *Quesas* offenses may include murder, manslaughter, assault, and maiming. Under Islamic law, such crimes may require the victim or his representative to serve as prosecutor. The state plays a role only in providing the forum for the trial and in imposing punishment. Sometimes victims' representatives dole out punishment. In 1997, for example, 28-year-old taxi driver Ali Reza Khoshruy, nicknamed "The Vampire" because he stalked, raped, and killed women at night after picking them up in his cab, was hung from a yellow crane in the middle of Tehran, the Iranian capital.[18] Before the hanging, prison officials and male relatives of the victims cursed Khoshruy and whipped him with thick leather belts as he lay tied to a metal bed. The whipping was part of a 214-lash sentence.

Tazir crime

A minor violation of Islamic law that is regarded as an offense against society, not God.

Islamic Courts

Islamic courts typically exist on three levels.[19] The first level hears cases involving the potential for serious punishments, including death, amputation, and exile. The second level deals with relatively minor matters, such as traffic offenses and violations of city ordinances. Special courts, especially in Iran, may hear cases involving crimes against the government, narcotics offenses, state security, and corruption. Appeals within the Islamic court system are only possible under rare circumstances and are by no means routine. A decision rendered by second-level courts will generally stand without intervention by higher judicial authorities.

Under Islamic law, men and women are treated very differently. Testimony provided by a man, for example, can be heard in court. The same evidence, however, can only be provided by two virtuous women; one female witness is not sufficient.

While Islamic law may seem archaic or even barbaric to many Westerners, Islamic officials defend their system by pointing to low crime rates at home and by pointing to what they consider near anarchy in Western nations. An early criticism of Islamic law was offered by Max Weber at the start of the twentieth century.[20] Weber said that Islamic justice is based more on the moral conceptions of individual judges than on any rational and predictable code of laws. He found that the personality of each judge, what he called "charisma," was more important in reaching a final legal result than was the written law. Weber's conclusion was that a modern society could not develop under Islamic law because enforcement of the law was too unpredictable. Complex social organizations, he argued, could only be based on a rational and codified law that is relatively unchanging from place to place and over time.[21]

More recent observers have agreed that "Islamic justice is based on philosophical principles that are considered alien, if not unconscionable, to the Western observer." However, these same writers note, strict punishments such as hand amputation "may not be inconsistent with the fundamentals of natural law or Judeo-Christian doctrine. The imposition of the penalty in specific cases and under rigorous rules of evidence—as the principle requires—may be indeed justifiable, and even necessary, in the Islamic context of sustaining a spiritual . . . society."[22]

International Criminal Justice Organizations

At the beginning of the third millennium, the criminal phenomenon not only does not care about borders, but it also participates in globalization.

—Andre Bossard, former Secretary General of Interpol[ii]

The first international conference on criminology and criminal justice met in London in 1872.[23] It evolved out of emerging humanitarian concerns about the treatment of prisoners. Human rights, the elimination of corporal punishment, and debates over capital punishment occupied the conference participants. Although other meetings were held from time to time, little agreement could be reached among the international community on criminal etiology, justice paradigms, or the philosophical and practical bases for criminal punishment and rehabilitation. Finally, in 1938, the International Society for Criminology (ISC) was formed to bring together people from diverse cultural backgrounds who shared an interest in social policies relating to crime and justice. In its early years, membership in the ISC consisted mostly of national officials and academics with close government ties.[24] As a consequence, many of the first conferences (called *international congresses*) sponsored by the ISC strongly supported the status quo and were devoid of any significant recommendations for change or growth.

Throughout the 1960s and 1970s, the ISC was strongly influenced by a growing worldwide awareness of human rights. About the same time, a number of international organizations began to press for an understanding of the political and legal processes through which deviance and crime come to be defined. Among them were the Scandinavian Research Council for Criminology (formed in 1962), the Criminological Research Council (created in 1962 by the Council of Europe), and other regional associations concerned with justice issues.

A number of contemporary organizations and publications continue to focus world attention on criminal justice issues. Perhaps the best-known modern center for the academic study of cross-national criminal justice is the International Center of Comparative Criminology at the University of Montreal. Established in 1969, the center serves as a locus of study for criminal justice professionals from around the world and maintains an excellent library of international criminal justice information. The International Police Executive Symposium (IPES) was founded in 1994 to bring international police researchers and practitioners together and to facilitate cross-cultural and international exchanges between criminal justice experts around the world. IPES, which is associated with the Human Rights and Law Enforcement Institute (HRALEI) at the State University of New York at Plattsburg, publishes *Police Practice and Research: An International Journal*. The Office of International Criminal Justice (OICJ), with offices in Illinois, Indiana, and Texas, has also become a well-known contributor to the study of comparative criminal justice. In conjunction with Sam Houston State University's Criminal Justice Center (in Huntsville, Texas), OICJ publishes the magazine *Crime and Justice International* and sponsors study tours of various nations. Visit OICJ via Web Extra 17–3 at cjtoday.com.

In 1995, Mitre Corporation in McLean, Virginia, began an Internet service that provides information about the UN Crime Prevention Branch. The UN Crime and Justice Information Network (UNCJIN) holds much promise as an online provider of international criminal justice information. Visit UNCJIN via Web Extra 17–4 at cjtoday.com. Similarly, the World Justice Information Network (WJIN), sponsored by the National Institute of Justice and the U.S. Department of State, provides a members-only forum for the discussion of justice issues around the globe. Apply for membership in WJIN via Web Extra 17–5. Finally, the UN Center for International Crime Prevention, in conjunction with the World Society of Victimology, sponsors the International Victimology website, available via Web Extra 17–6.

WEB
Extra
■ ■ ■ ■

The Role of the United Nations in Criminal Justice

The United Nations, composed of 185 member states and based in New York City, is the largest and most inclusive international body in the world. From its inception in 1945, the United Nations has been very interested in international crime prevention and world criminal justice systems. A UN resolution entitled the International Bill of Human Rights supports the rights and dignity of everyone who comes into contact with a criminal justice system.

One of the best-known specific UN recommendations on criminal justice is its Standard Minimum Rules for the Treatment of Prisoners. The rules call for the fair treatment of prisoners, including recognition of the basic humanity of all inmates, and set specific standards for housing, nutrition, exercise, and medical care. Follow-up surveys conducted by the United Nations have shown that the rules have had a considerable influence on national legislation and prison regulations throughout the world.[25] Although the rules do not have the weight of law unless adopted and enacted into local legislation, they carry the strong weight of tradition, and at least one expert claims that "there are indeed those who argue that the rules have entered the *corpus* of generally customary human rights law, or that they are binding . . . as an authoritative interpretation of the human rights provisions of the UN charter."[26]

A more recent and potentially significant set of recommendations can be found in the UN Code of Conduct for Law Enforcement Officials. The code calls on law enforcement officers throughout the world to be cognizant of human rights in the performance of their duties. It specifically proscribes the use of torture and other abuses.

The UN World Crime Surveys, which report official crime statistics from nearly 100 countries, provide a global portrait of criminal activity. Seen historically, the surveys have shown that crimes against property are most characteristic of nations with developed economies (where they constitute approximately 82% of all reported crime), while crimes against the person occur much more frequently in developing countries (where they account for 43% of all crime).[27] Complementing the official statistics of the World Crime Surveys are data from the International Victim Survey (IVS), which is conducted in approximately 50 countries. To date, three surveys have been conducted—in 1989, 1992, and 1996–1997.

Through its Office for Drug Control and Crime Prevention (ODCCP), the United Nations continues to advance the cause of crime prevention and to disseminate useful criminal justice information. The program provides forums for ongoing discussions of justice practices around the world. It has regional links throughout the world, sponsored by supportive national governments that have agreed to fund the program's work. The European Institute for Crime Prevention and Control (HEUNI), for example, provides the program's regional European link in a network of institutes operating throughout the world. Other network components include the UN Interregional Crime and Justice Research Institute (UNICRI) in Rome; an Asian regional institute (UNAFEI) in Tokyo; ILANUE, based in San Jose, Costa Rica, which focuses on crime problems in Latin America and the Caribbean; an African institute (UNAFRI) in Kampala, Uganda; Australia's AIC in Canberra; an Arabic institute (ASSTC) in Riyadh, Saudi Arabia; and other centers in Siracusa, Italy, and in Vancouver and Montreal, Canada.[28] Visit the UN Office for Drug Control and Crime Prevention via Web Extra 17–7 at cjtoday.com.

In 1995, the United States signed an agreement with the UN Crime Prevention and Criminal Justice Branch that is intended to facilitate the international sharing of information and research findings.[29] Under the agreement, the National Institute of Justice joined 11 other criminal justice research organizations throughout the world as an associate UN institute.

Continuing a tradition begun in 1885 by the former International Penal and Penitentiary Commission, the United Nations holds an international congress on crime every five years. The first UN crime congress, the 1955 Congress on the Prevention of Crime and the Treatment of Offenders, met in Geneva, Switzerland. Crime congresses provide a forum through which member states can exchange information and experiences, compare criminal justice practices between countries, find solutions to crime, and take action at an international level. The Tenth UN crime congress was held in Vienna, Austria, in 2000. Topics discussed at the meeting included (1) promoting the rule of law and strengthening the criminal justice systems of various nations, (2) the need for international cooperation in combating transnational crime, and (3) the need for a fair, ethical, and effective system of criminal justice in the promotion of economic and social development. CJ Today Exhibit 17–1 contains the UN declaration on crime and justice that resulted from the Vienna meeting.

The meeting also led to passage of the 2000 UN Protocol to Prevent, Suppress and Punish Trafficking in Persons, Especially Women and Children, which supplements the UN Convention against Transnational Organized Crime.[30] Nations that are parties to the protocol must criminalize the offense of human trafficking, prevent trafficking, protect and assist victims of trafficking,

WEB
Extra
■■■■

CJ Today Exhibit 17–1

Vienna Declaration on Crime and Justice

We the Member States of the United Nations,

Concerned about the impact on our societies of the commission of serious crimes of a global nature and convinced of the need for bilateral, regional and international cooperation in crime prevention and criminal justice,

Concerned in particular about transnational organized crime and the relationships between its various forms,

Convinced that adequate prevention and rehabilitation programmes are fundamental to an effective crime control strategy, and that such programmes should take into account social and economic factors which may make people more vulnerable to, and likely to engage in criminal behaviour,

Stressing that a fair, responsible, ethical and efficient criminal justice system is an important factor in the promotion of economic and social development and of security,

Aware of the promise of restorative approaches to justice that aim to reduce and promote the healing of victims, offenders and communities,

Having assembled at the Tenth United Nations Congress on the Prevention of Crime and the Treatment of Offenders in Vienna from 10 to 17 April 2000 to decide to take effective concerted action, in a spirit of cooperation, to combat the world crime problem,

Declare as follows:

- We emphasize the responsibility of each State to establish and maintain a fair, responsible, ethical and efficient criminal justice system.
- We recognize the necessity of closer coordination and cooperation among States in combating the world crime problem, bearing in mind that action against it is a common and shared responsibility. . . .
- We undertake to strengthen international cooperation in order to create a conducive environment for the fight against organized crime, promoting growth and sustainable development and eradicating poverty and unemployment.
- We also commit ourselves to the development of action-oriented policy recommendations based on the special needs of women as criminal justice practitioners, victims, prisoners and offenders.
- We commit ourselves to the development of more effective ways of collaborating with one another with a view to eradicating the scourge of trafficking in persons, especially women and children, and the smuggling of migrants. . . .
- We also commit ourselves to the enhancement of international cooperation and mutual legal assistance to curb illicit manufacturing of and trafficking in firearms, their parts and components and ammunition, and we establish 2005 as the target year for achieving a significant decrease in their incidence worldwide.
- We reaffirm that combating money-laundering and the criminal economy constitutes a major element of the strategies against organized crime. . . .

- We decide to develop action-oriented policy recommendations on the prevention and control of computer-related crime. . . . We also commit ourselves to working towards enhancing our ability to prevent, investigate and prosecute high-technology and computer-related crime.
- We note that acts of violence and terrorism continue to be of grave concern. In conformity with the Charter of the United Nations and taking into account all the relevant General Assembly resolutions, we will together, in conjunction with our other efforts to prevent and to combat terrorism, take effective, resolute and speedy measures with respect to preventing and combating criminal activities carried out for the purpose of furthering terrorism in all its forms and manifestations. . . .
- We also note that racial discrimination, xenophobia and related forms of intolerance continue and we recognize the importance of taking steps to incorporate into international crime prevention strategies and norms measures to prevent and combat crime associated with racism, racial discrimination, xenophobia and related forms of intolerance.
- We affirm our determination to combat violence stemming from intolerance on the basis of ethnicity and resolve to make a strong contribution, in the area of crime prevention and criminal justice. . . .
- We also recognize the importance of prison reform, the independence of the judiciary and the prosecution authorities, and the International Code of Conduct for Public Officials. . . .
- We shall endeavour, as appropriate, to use and apply the United Nations standards and norms in crime prevention and criminal justice in national law and practice. . . .
- We further recognize with great concern that juveniles in difficult circumstances are often at risk of becoming delinquent or easy candidates for recruitment by criminal groups, including groups involved in transnational organized crime, and we commit ourselves to undertaking countermeasures to prevent this growing phenomenon. . . .
- We recognize that comprehensive crime prevention strategies at the international, national, regional and local levels must address the root causes and risk factors related to crime and victimization through social, economic, health, educational and justice policies. . . .
- We commit ourselves to according priority to containing the growth and overcrowding of pre-trial and detention prison populations, as appropriate, by promoting safe and effective alternatives to incarceration.
- We decide to introduce, where appropriate, national, regional and international action plans in support of victims of crime, such as mechanisms for mediation and restorative justice. . . .
- We encourage the development of restorative justice policies, procedures and programmes that are respectful of the rights, needs and interests of victims, offenders, communities and all other parties. . . .

Source: Excerpted from the Tenth United Nations Congress on the Prevention of Crime and the Treatment of Offenders,
Vienna Declaration on Crime and Justice: Meeting the Challenges of the Twenty-First Century, Vienna, April 10–17, 2000.

Young girls working in a brothel in Thailand. The 2003 federal Trafficking Victims Protection Reauthorization Act focuses on the illegal practice of sex trafficking and on the illegal "obtaining of a person for labor services." How common is human trafficking? In what parts of the world is it most prevalent?

© Way Gary/Corbis Sygma

and promote international cooperation to combat the problem of trafficking.[31] Learn more about the crime of human trafficking via the Protection Project at Web Extra 17–8 at cjtoday.com, and read the U.S. Department of State's 2003 *Trafficking in Persons Report* at Library Extra 17–4 at cjtoday.com.

WEB
Extra
■ ■ ■ ■

LIBRARY
Extra
■ ■ ■ ■

Interpol and Europol

The **International Criminal Police Organization (Interpol)**, headquartered in Lyons, France, traces its origins back to the first International Criminal Police Congress of 1914, which met in Monaco.[32] The theme of that meeting was international cooperation in the investigation of crimes and the apprehension of fugitives. Interpol, however, did not officially begin operations until 1946, when the end of World War II brought about a new spirit of international harmony.

Today, 182 nations belong to Interpol.[33] The U.S. Interpol unit is called the U.S. National Central Bureau (USNCB) and is a separate agency within the U.S. Department of Justice. USNCB is staffed with personnel from 12 federal agencies, including the Drug Enforcement Administration, the Secret Service, and the Federal Bureau of Investigation. Through USNCB, Interpol is linked to all major U.S. computerized criminal records repositories, including the FBI's National Crime Information Index, the State Department's Advanced Visa Lookout System, and the Department of Homeland Security's Master Index.

Interpol's primary purpose is to act as a clearinghouse for information on offenses and suspects who are believed to operate across national boundaries. The organization is committed to promoting "the widest possible mutual assistance between all criminal police authorities within the limits of laws existing in . . . different countries and in the spirit of the Universal Declaration of Human Rights."[34] Historically, Interpol pledged itself not to intervene in religious, political, military, or racial disagreements in participant nations. As a consequence, a number of bombings and hostage situations that were related to these types of disagreements were not officially investigated until 1984, when Interpol officially entered the fight against international terrorism.

In late 2001, Interpol's Seventieth General Assembly unanimously adopted the Budapest Anti-Terrorism Resolution. The resolution calls for greater police cooperation in fighting international terrorism. In 2005, delegates attending Interpol's first Global Conference on Preventing Bio-Terrorism met in Lyon, France, and agreed on a series of measures aimed at preventing or effectively responding to bioterror attacks.[35] As this book goes to press, Interpol continues to expand its activities. It is in the process of developing a centralized international forensic DNA database and is creating an international framework for disaster victim identification.[36]

Interpol does not have its own field investigators. The agency has no powers of arrest or of search and seizure in member countries. Instead, Interpol's purpose is to facilitate, coordinate, and encourage police cooperation as a means of combating international crime. It draws on the willingness of local and national police forces to lend support to its activities. The headquarters

International Criminal Police Organization (Interpol)

An international law enforcement support organization that began operations in 1946 and today has 182 member nations.

WEB
Extra

LIBRARY
Extra

European Police Office (Europol)

The integrated police–intelligence gathering and dissemination arm of the member nations of the European Union.

staff of Interpol consists of about 250 individuals, many with prior police experience, who direct data-gathering efforts around the world and who serve to alert law enforcement organizations to the movement of suspected offenders within their jurisdiction. Visit Interpol headquarters via Web Extra 17–9, and read the organization's latest annual activity report at Library Extra 17–5 at cjtoday.com.

The members of the European Union (EU) agreed to the establishment of the **European Police Office (Europol)** in the Maastricht Treaty of February 7, 1992. Based in The Hague, the Netherlands, Europol started limited operations in 1994 in the form of the Europol Drugs Unit. Over time, other important law enforcement activities were added to the Europol agenda. The Europol Convention was ratified by all member states in 1998, and Europol commenced full operations the next year. Europol's mission is to improve the effectiveness and cooperation of law enforcement agencies within the member states of the European Union with the ultimate goal of preventing and combating terrorism, illegal drug trafficking, illicit trafficking in radioactive and nuclear substances, illegal money laundering, trafficking in human beings, and other serious forms of international organized crime. Europol is sometimes described as the "European Union police clearing house."[37] Following the July 2005 London underground and bus bombings, in which more than 50 people died and hundreds were injured, German Interior Minister Otto Schilly asked his European Union counterparts meeting in Brussels to give Europol executive powers to conduct EU-wide investigations.[38]

Europol and Interpol work together to develop information on international terrorism, drug trafficking, and trafficking in human beings.[39] Learn more about Europol via Web Extra 17–10 at cjtoday.com.

WEB
Extra

The International Criminal Court

Unfortunately, the world is not yet ready for a transnational criminal justice system.

–Andre Bossard, former Secretary General of Interpol[iii]

On April 12, 2000, the International Criminal Court (ICC) was created under the auspices of the United Nations. The ICC, whose operations are only now beginning, is intended to be a permanent criminal court for trying individuals (not countries) who commit the most serious crimes of concern to the international community, such as genocide, war crimes, and crimes against humanity—including the wholesale murder of civilians, torture, and mass rape. The ICC intends to be a global judicial institution with international jurisdiction complementing national legal systems around the world. Support for the ICC was developed through the United Nations, where more than 90 countries approved the court's creation by ratifying what is known as the Rome Statute of the International Criminal Court. The ICC's first prosecutor, Luis Moreno Ocampo of Argentina, was elected in April 2003.[40]

The ICC initiative began after World War II, with unsuccessful efforts to establish an international tribunal to try individuals accused of genocide and other war crimes.[41] In lieu of such a court, military tribunals were held in Nuremberg, Germany, and Tokyo, Japan, to try those accused of war crimes. The 1948 UN Genocide Convention[42] called for the creation of an international criminal court to punish genocide-related offenses and identified the crimes (1) genocide, (2) conspiracy to commit genocide, (3) direct and public incitement to commit genocide, (4) attempt to commit genocide, and (5) complicity in genocide.

In December 1948, the UN General Assembly adopted the Universal Declaration of Human Rights and the Convention on the Prevention and Punishment of the Crime of Genocide. It also called for criminals to be tried "by such international penal tribunals as may have jurisdiction." A number of member states soon asked the United Nation's International Law Commission (ILC) to study the possibility of establishing an ICC.

Development of an ICC was delayed by the cold war that took place between the world's superpowers, who were not willing to subject their military personnel or commanders to international criminal jurisdiction in the event of a "hot" war. In 1981, however, the UN General Assembly asked the International Law Commission to consider creating an international Code of Crimes.

The 1992 war in Bosnia-Herzegovina, which involved clear violations of the Genocide and Geneva Conventions, heightened world interest in the establishment of a permanent ICC. A few years later, 160 countries participated in the Conference of Plenipotentiaries on the Establishment of an International Criminal Court,[43] which was held in Rome. At the end of that conference, member states voted overwhelmingly in favor of the Rome Statute,[44] calling for establishment of an ICC. Effective July 1, 2002, the Rome Statute criminalized trafficking in persons, categorizing it as a crime against humanity.

A few years ago, in what became a stumbling block on the road to the court's creation, the United States expressed concern about the ICC, saying that members of the American military could become subject to ICC jurisdiction. That concern led to U.S. efforts to delay the court's cre-

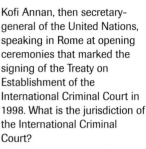

Kofi Annan, then secretary-general of the United Nations, speaking in Rome at opening ceremonies that marked the signing of the Treaty on Establishment of the International Criminal Court in 1998. What is the jurisdiction of the International Criminal Court?

UN/DPI/E. Schneider

ation. The issue was resolved in 2002 when the UN Security Council voted to exempt members of the American military from prosecution by the court's War Crimes Tribunal.[45] The Security Council resolution, however, must be renewed annually if it is to remain in force.[46]

In 2005, in one of the court's first official actions, a panel of ICC judges decided to allow independent Dutch investigators to carry out forensic tests in the Democratic Republic of Congo (DRC) as part of an ongoing investigation into the deaths of thousands of people in genocidal violence throughout central Africa.[47] In 2007, the court announced that it would hold its first trial; Thomas Lubanga is charged with kidnapping and forcibly recruiting child soldiers during the DRC civil war in violation of international law. Prosecutors claim that Lubanga kidnapped children as young as ten and forced them to fight—leaving many dead or injured.[48] Learn more about this case and other activities of the ICC by visiting the Coalition for an International Criminal Court via Web Extra 17–11 at cjtoday.com.

Before the ICC came into existence, Belgium made its courts available to the rest of the world for the prosecution of alleged crimes against humanity.[49] The country's legal system, in essence, took on the role of global prosecutor for these kinds of crimes. Under a 1993 Belgian law, which is regarded by many as the world's most expansive statute against genocide and other crimes against humanity, Belgian justices were called on to enforce substantial portions of the country's criminal laws on a global scale. Belgian courts also focused on enforcing the 1949 Geneva Convention governing the conduct of war and the treatment of refugees. Belgian law specifically provides for the criminal prosecution of individuals who are not Belgian citizens, and it provides no immunity to prosecution for foreign leaders. In 2001, for example, a Brussels jury convicted four people, including two Catholic nuns, of contributing to ethnic violence in the central African nation of Rwanda in 1994.

Belgian authorities have investigated more than a dozen complaints involving current and former state officials, including Ariel Sharon (prime minister of Israel), Saddam Hussein (former Iraqi leader), Hissene Habre (former dictator of Chad), Hashemi Rafsanjani (former president of Iran), Driss Basri (former interior minister of Morocco), Denis Sassou Nguesso (president of Congo-Brazzaville), and Fidel Castro (leader of Cuba). In the case of the Cuban leader, Cuban exiles charged Castro in Brussels's criminal court in October 2001 with false imprisonment, murder, torture, and other crimes against humanity. As a result of such investigations, Belgium has experienced strained relationships with a number of countries, and some in the nation have questioned the wisdom of charging sitting heads of state with violations of the criminal law.

WEB
Extra
■ ■ ■ ■

The effects of globalization have created a growing phenomenon of globalized crime that is threatening the stability and values of the entire world community.

—Daniel Mabrey, Sam Houston State University[iv]

Globalization and Crime

Globalization refers to the internationalization of trade, services, investments, information, and other forms of human social activity, including crime. The process of globalization is fed by modern systems of transportation and communication, including air travel, television, and the Internet. Globalization contributes to growing similarities in the way people do things and in the beliefs and values that they hold. The lessening of differences brought about by globalization is highlighted by a definition from one authoritative source, which says that globalization is "a process of social homogenization by which the experiences of everyday life, marked by the diffusion of commodities and ideas, can foster a standardization of cultural expressions around the

globalization

The internationalization of trade, services, investment, information, and other forms of human social activity.

Globalization has given us cheap Chinese T-shirts and Indian software; it has also brought the international trade in atomic weapons design and al-Qaeda websites.

—Philip Stephens, in the Financial Times

world."[50] The adoption of English as the *de facto* standard language on the Internet and of the global software community, for example, has exposed many around the world to literature and ideas that they might not otherwise have encountered and has influenced the way they think. Consequently, globalization is opposed in many parts of the world by those who would hold to traditional ways of thinking and acting. Instead of inevitably uniting humanity, as some had hoped, globalization has also made people aware of differences—and has led many people to reject cultures and ideas dissimilar to their own.

The first steps toward globalization occurred long before the modern era and were taken by nation-states seeking to expand their spheres of influence. The banner of globalization today is carried by multinational corporations whose operations span the globe. The synergistic effects of rapid travel, instantaneous communication, and national economies that are tied closely to one another have led to an increasingly rapid pace of the globalization process, which some refer to as *hyperglobalization*. Criminal entrepreneurs and terrorists are among those with a global vision, and at least some of them think and plan like the CEOs of multinational businesses. Today's international criminal community consists of terrorists, drug traffickers, pornography peddlers, identity thieves, copyright violators, and those who traffic in human beings, body parts, genetic material, and military weapons.

Transnational Crime

In 2006, Cheng Chui Ping, known to her associates as the Snakehead Queen, was sentenced in U.S. District Court to 35 years in prison for having smuggled as many as 3,000 illegal immigrants into the United States from her native China. "Snakeheads" are human smugglers, and prior to her arrest Ping may have been the most active human trafficker in New York City. Her fees, which were partially determined by an immigrant's ability to pay, ranged up to $40,000 per person, and the FBI says that her illegal transnational activities may have netted her as much as $40 million.[51]

transnational crime

Unlawful activity undertaken and supported by organized criminal groups operating across national boundaries.

Transnational crime and the internationally organized criminal groups that support it are partly the result of an ongoing process of globalization. Transnational crime is unlawful activity undertaken and supported by organized criminal groups operating across national boundaries, and it promises to become one of the most pressing challenges of the twenty-first century for criminal justice professionals. In a recent conference in Seoul, Korea, Assistant U.S. Attorney General Laurie Robinson addressed the issue of transnational crime, saying, "The United States recognizes that we cannot confront crime in isolation. . . . It is clear crime does not respect international boundaries. It is clear crime is global. As recent economic trends demonstrate, what happens in one part of the world impacts all the rest. And crime problems and trends are no different."[52]

According to the United Nations, an offense can be considered transnational in nature if any of the following conditions are met:[53]

1. It is committed in more than one country.

2. It is committed in one country but a substantial part of its preparation, planning, direction, or control takes place in another country.

3. It is committed in one country but involves an organized criminal group that engages in criminal activities in more than one country.

4. It is committed in one country but has substantial effects in another country.

The post–cold war world is more dangerous and less stable than when power was balanced among superpowers. The power vacuum created in many parts of the world by the fall of the Soviet Union and the growing instability in the Middle East has led to a number of new threats. According to Robert Gelbard, U.S. assistant secretary for international narcotics and law enforcement affairs, "The main threat now is transnational organized crime. It comes in many forms: drug trafficking, money laundering, terrorism, alien smuggling, trafficking in weapons of mass destruction, [human trafficking, often involving forced prostitution], fraud and other forms of corruption. These problems all have one critical element in common," says Gelbard. "They threaten the national security of all states and governments—from our closest allies to those that we find most repugnant. No country is safe. International criminal organizations all seek to establish pliant governments that can be manipulated through bribery and intimidation. They respect no national boundaries and already act with virtual impunity in many parts of the world."[54]

According to the National Institute of Justice, transnational crime groups have profited more from globalization than have legitimate businesses, which are subject to domestic and host country laws and regulations. NIJ points out that transnational crime syndicates and networks, abetted by official corruption, blackmail, and intimidation, can use open markets and open societies to their full advantage.[55]

Worse still, entire nations may become rogue countries, or quasi-criminal regimes where criminal activity runs rampant and wields considerable influence over the national government. Russia, for example, appears to be approaching this status through an intertwining of the goals of organized criminal groups and official interests that run to the top levels of government. The number of organized criminal groups operating in Russia is estimated to be more than 12,000.[56] Emilio Viano, professor of criminology at American University and an expert on Russian organized crime, notes that "what we have is an immense country practically controlled by organized crime. These groups are getting stronger and stronger and using Russia as a base for their global ventures—taking over everything from drugs and prostitution to currency exchange and stealing World Bank and IMF [International Monetary Fund] loans."[57] In late 2006, for example, Russian organized crime hitmen shot and killed Andrei Kozlov, the top deputy chairman of the Russian Central Bank.[58] Kozlov, who was gunned down as he left a soccer match in Moscow, had worked for four years to fight criminality and money laundering in Russia's banking system in an effort to draw foreign investments into the country.

The recent globalization of crime and terrorism, which is sometimes termed the *globalization of insecurity,* has necessitated enhanced coordination of law enforcement efforts in different parts of the world as well as the expansion of American law enforcement activities beyond national borders. In 2003, for example, the U.S. Congress passed the Trafficking Victims Protection Reauthorization Act (TVPA)[59] to further protect victims of human trafficking, regardless of their country of origin. Trafficking offenses under the law, which is aimed primarily at international offenders, include (1) sex trafficking, in which a commercial sex act is induced by force, fraud, or coercion or in which the person induced to perform such act has not attained 18 years of age,[60] and (2) the recruitment, harboring, transportation, provision, or obtaining of a person for labor services, through the use of force, fraud, or coercion, for the purpose of subjection to involuntary servitude, peonage, debt bondage, or slavery. The TVPA also provides funds for training U.S. law enforcement personnel at international police academies, and U.S. police agencies routinely send agents to assist law enforcement officers in other countries who are involved in transnational investigations.

Another tool in the fight against transnational crime is **extradition**. Not all countries, however, are willing to extradite suspects wanted in the United States. Consequently, as Kevin Ryan of Vermont's Norwich University observes, "The globalization of United States law enforcement policy has also entailed the abduction of fugitives from abroad to stand trial when an asylum nation refuses an extradition request."[61] While certainly not a common practice, the forcible removal of criminal suspects from foreign jurisdictions appears more likely with suspected terrorists than with other types of criminals. A 2007 special report on transnational organized crime and its impact on the United States is available at Library Extra 17–6 at cjtoday.com. For additional information on transnational organized crime and the globalization phenomenon, see Web Extra 17–12 at cjtoday.com.

extradition

The surrender by one state or jurisdiction to another of an individual accused or convicted of an offense in the second state or jurisdiction.

LIBRARY **WEB**
Extra Extra

Terrorism

Terrorism as a criminal activity and the prevention of further acts of terrorism became primary concerns of American political leaders and justice system officials following the September 11, 2001, terrorist attacks on the United States. There is, however, no single uniformly accepted definition of terrorism that is applicable to all places and all circumstances. Some definitions are statutory in nature, while others were created for such practical purposes as gauging success in the fight against terrorism. Still others relate to specific forms of terrorism, such as cyberterrorism (discussed later in this section), and many legislative sources speak only of "acts of terrorism" or "terrorist activity" rather than terrorism itself because the nature of Western jurisprudence is to legislate against acts rather than against concepts.

The federal Foreign Relations Authorization Act[62] defines *terrorism* in terms of four primary elements. The act says that terrorism is (1) premeditated, (2) politically motivated (3) violence (4) committed against noncombatant targets.[63] The FBI offers a nonstatutory working definition of terrorism as "a violent act or an act dangerous to human life in violation of the criminal laws of the United States or of any state to intimidate or coerce a government, the civilian population, or any segment thereof, in furtherance of political or social objectives."[64] Among the laws that define certain forms of human *activity* as terrorism, the Immigration and Nationality Act provides one of the most comprehensive and widely used definitions. That definition is shown in CJ Today Exhibit 17–2.

terrorism

A violent act or an act dangerous to human life, in violation of the criminal laws of the United States or of any state, that is committed to intimidate or coerce a government, the civilian population, or any segment thereof, in furtherance of political or social objectives.[v]

CJ Today Exhibit 17–2

What Is Terrorist Activity?

Federal law enforcement efforts directed against agents of foreign terrorist organizations derive their primary authority from the Immigration and Nationality Act, found in Title 8 of the U.S. Code. The act defines *terrorist activity* as follows:

(ii) "Terrorist activity" defined

As used in this chapter, the term "terrorist activity" means any activity which is unlawful under the laws of the place where it is committed (or which, if committed in the United States, would be unlawful under the laws of the United States or any State) and which involves any of the following:

(I) The hijacking or sabotage of any conveyance (including an aircraft, vessel, or vehicle).

(II) The seizing or detaining, and threatening to kill, injure, or continue to detain, another individual in order to compel a third person (including a governmental organization) to do or abstain from doing any act as an explicit or implicit condition for the release of the individual seized or detained.

(III) A violent attack upon an internationally protected person (as defined in section 1116(b)(4) of title 18) or upon the liberty of such a person.

(IV) An assassination.

(V) The use of any—

(a) biological agent, chemical agent, or nuclear weapon or device, or

(b) explosive or firearm (other than for mere personal monetary gain), with intent to endanger, directly or indirectly, the safety of one or more individuals or to cause substantial damage to property.

(VI) A threat, attempt, or conspiracy to do any of the foregoing.

(iii) "Engage in terrorist activity" defined

As used in this chapter, the term "engage in terrorist activity" means to commit, in an individual capacity or as a member of an organization, an act of terrorist activity or an act which the actor knows, or reasonably should know, affords material support to any individual, organization, or government in conducting a terrorist activity at any time, including any of the following acts:

(I) The preparation or planning of a terrorist activity.

(II) The gathering of information on potential targets for terrorist activity.

(III) The providing of any type of material support, including a safe house, transportation, communications, funds, false documentation or identification, weapons, explosives, or training, to any individual the actor knows or has reason to believe has committed or plans to commit a terrorist activity.

(IV) The soliciting of funds or other things of value for terrorist activity or for any terrorist organization.

(V) The solicitation of any individual for membership in a terrorist organization, terrorist government, or to engage in a terrorist activity.

According to criminologist Gwynn Nettler, all forms of terrorism share six characteristics:[65]

- *No rules.* There are no moral limitations on the type or degree of violence that terrorists can use.

- *No innocents.* No distinctions are made between soldiers and civilians. Children can be killed as well as adults.

- *Economy.* Kill one, frighten 10,000.

- *Publicity.* Terrorists seek publicity, and publicity encourages terrorism.

- *Meaning.* Terrorist acts give meaning and significance to the lives of terrorists.

- *No clarity.* Beyond the immediate aim of destructive acts, the long-term goals of terrorists are likely to be poorly conceived or impossible to implement.

Moreover, notes Nettler, "Terrorism that succeeds escalates."[66]

Types of Terrorism

It is important to distinguish between two major forms of terrorism: domestic and international. Distinctions between the two forms are made in terms of the origin, base of operations, and objectives of a terrorist organization. In the United States, **domestic terrorism** refers to the unlawful use of force or violence by an individual or a group that is based and operates entirely within this country and its territories without foreign direction and whose acts are directed against elements of the U.S. government or population.[67] **International terrorism,** in contrast, is the unlawful use of force or violence by an individual or a group that has some connection to a foreign power, or whose activities transcend national boundaries, against people or property in order to intimidate or coerce a government, the civilian population, or any segment thereof, in furtherance of political or social objectives.[68] International terrorism is sometimes mistakenly called *foreign*

domestic terrorism

The unlawful use of force or violence by an individual or a group that is based and operates entirely within the United States and its territories, acts without foreign direction, and directs its activities against elements of the U.S. government or population.[vi]

international terrorism

The unlawful use of force or violence by an individual or a group that has some connection to a foreign power, or whose activities transcend national boundaries, against people or property in order to intimidate or coerce a government, the civilian population, or any segment thereof, in furtherance of political or social objectives.[vii]

terrorism, a term that, strictly speaking, refers only to acts of terrorism that occur outside of the United States.

DOMESTIC TERRORISM

Throughout the 1960s and 1970s, domestic terrorism in the United States required the expenditure of considerable criminal justice resources. The Weathermen, Students for a Democratic Society, the Symbionese Liberation Army, the Black Panthers, and other radical groups routinely challenged the authority of federal and local governments. Bombings, kidnappings, and shootouts peppered the national scene. As overt acts of domestic terrorism declined in frequency in the 1980s, international terrorism took their place. The war in Lebanon; terrorism in Israel; bombings in France, Italy, and Germany; and the many violent offshoots of the Iran-Iraq war and the first Gulf War occupied the attention of the media and of much of the rest of the world. Vigilance by the FBI, the Central Intelligence Agency (CIA), and other agencies largely prevented the spread of terrorism to the United States.

Worrisome today are domestic underground survivalist and separatist groups and potentially violent special-interest groups, each with its own vision of a future America. In 1993, for example, a confrontation between David Koresh's Branch Davidian followers and federal agents left 72 Davidians (including Koresh) and four federal agents dead in Waco, Texas.

Exactly two years to the day after the Davidian standoff ended in a horrific fire that destroyed the compound, a powerful truck bomb devastated the Alfred P. Murrah Federal Building in downtown Oklahoma City. One hundred sixty-eight people died, and hundreds more were wounded. The targeted nine-story building had housed offices of the Social Security Administration; the Drug Enforcement Administration; the Secret Service; the Bureau of Alcohol, Tobacco, Firearms, and Explosives; and a day-care center called America's Kids. The fertilizer-and-diesel-fuel device used in the terrorist attack was estimated to have weighed about 1,200 pounds and had been left in a rental truck on the Fifth Street side of the building. The blast, which left a crater 30 feet wide and 8 feet deep and spread debris over a ten-block area, demonstrated just how vulnerable the United States is to terrorist attack.

In 1997, a federal jury found 29-year-old Timothy McVeigh guilty of 11 counts, ranging from conspiracy to first-degree murder, in the Oklahoma City bombing. Jurors concluded that McVeigh had conspired with Terry Nichols, a friend he had met in the Army, and with unknown others to destroy the Murrah Building. Prosecutors made clear their belief that the attack was intended to revenge the 1993 assault on the Branch Davidian compound. McVeigh was sentenced to death and was executed by lethal injection at the U.S. penitentiary in Terre Haute, Indiana, in 2001.[69] McVeigh was the first person under federal jurisdiction to be put to death since 1963. In 2004, Terry Nichols was convicted of 161 counts of first-degree murder by an Oklahoma jury and was sentenced to 161 life terms for his role in the bombings.[70] He had previously been convicted of various federal charges.

Some experts believe that the Oklahoma City attack was modeled after a similar bombing described in the *Turner Diaries,* a novel used by extremist groups to map their rise to power.[71] Just as Hitler's biography *Mein Kampf* served as a call to arms for Nazis in Europe during the 1930s, the *Turner Diaries* describes an Aryan revolution that occurs in the United States during the 1990s in which Jews, blacks, and other minorities are removed from positions of influence in government and society.

No group or nation should mistake America's intentions: We will not rest until terrorist groups of global reach have been found, have been stopped, and have been defeated.

—President George W. Bush

Sport utility vehicles destroyed in a New Year's Day fire at a Ford Lincoln Mercury dealership in Girard, Pennsylvania. The Earth Liberation Front (ELF), a domestic terrorist organization, claimed responsibility for the fire. What are the goals of the ELF?

AP Wide World Photos

CJ News

Domestic Terrorism: New Trouble at Home

Since 9/11, the nation's attention has been focused on possible threats from Islamic terrorists. But home-grown terrorists have been steadily plotting and carrying out attacks in unrelated incidents across the nation, according to federal authorities and two organizations that monitor hate groups.

None of the incidents over the past few years matched the devastation of 9/11 or even the 1995 bombing of the Oklahoma City federal building, which killed 168 and remains the deadliest act of terrorism against the nation by a U.S. citizen.

But some of the alleged domestic terrorists who have been arrested had ambitious plans. The people and groups range from white supremacists, anti-government types and militia members to eco-terrorists and people who hate corporations. They include violent anti-abortionists and black and brown nationalists who envision a separate state for blacks and Latinos. And they have been busy.

"Not a lot of attention is being paid to this, because everybody is concerned about the guy in a turban. But there are still plenty of angry, Midwestern white guys out there," says U.S. Marshals Service chief inspector Geoff Shank.

Shank, who is based in the Chicago area, says the concerns about domestic terrorism range from anti-abortion extremists who threaten to attack clinics and doctors to some violent biker gangs that may be involved in organized crime. And the FBI said in June [2004] that eco-terrorism—acts of violence, sabotage or property damage motivated by concern for animals or the environment—was the nation's top domestic terrorism threat. The bureau said then that eco-terrorists had committed more than 1,100 criminal acts and caused property damage estimated [to be] at least $110 million since 1976.

Alleged terrorist plots by U.S. citizens are not new, but many of the recent conspiracies were overshadowed by 9/11 and the hunt for terrorists abroad. Most of the foiled plots didn't get very far. And few got much publicity. But there were some potentially close calls, such as the scheme by William Krar, an east Texas man who stockpiled enough sodium cyanide to gas everyone in a building the size of a high school basketball gymnasium before he was arrested in 2002.

Shank, whose unit mainly searches for fugitives, including some wanted on domestic terror-related charges, led the manhunt for Clayton Lee Waagner, 48, of Kennerdell, Pa. Waagner was convicted in December [2003] of mailing hundreds of threat letters containing bogus anthrax to abortion clinics in 24 states. During his trial in Philadelphia, prosecutors documented Waagner's ties to the Army of God, an extremist group that believes violence against abortion providers is an acceptable way to end abortion.

"There's been a very, very heavy focus nationally on foreign terrorism since 9/11," says Mark Potok of the Southern Poverty Law Center in Montgomery, Ala., which has tracked hate groups since 1971. "The reality is that, meanwhile, domestic terrorism has hummed along at quite a steady clip. It . . . still poses a very serious threat."

William Krar, 63, left, and his common-law wife, Judith Bruey, 55, being escorted by authorities following their sentencing at the U.S. courthouse in Tyler, Texas, on May 4, 2004, after pleading guilty to illegally stockpiling an array of dangerous chemical weapons and conspiracy to possess illegal chemical weapons. Krar received a sentence of 11 years in prison, while Bruey was ordered to serve five years. How can we protect ourselves against domestic terrorists?

Tyler Morning Telegraph, *D.J. Peters/AP Wide World Photos*

Among the incidents since 9/11:

- In Tennessee, the FBI recently arrested a man who agents say hated the federal government and was attempting to acquire chemical weapons and explosives to blow up a government building. Demetrius "Van" Crocker, 39, of McKenzie, Tenn., pleaded not guilty on November 5, 2004. His attorney, public defender Stephen Shankman, did not return calls.

- In May [2004], Krar, 63, of Noonday, Texas, was sentenced to more than 11 years in prison after he stockpiled enough sodium cyanide to kill everyone inside a 30,000-square-foot building. Krar, described by federal prosecutors as a white supremacist, also had nine machine guns, 67 sticks of explosives and more than 100,000 rounds of ammunition. Investigators and the federal prosecutor said they didn't know what Krar intended to do with the potentially deadly chemicals. Krar's common-law wife, Judith Bruey, 55, pleaded guilty to conspiracy to possess illegal weapons and was sentenced to nearly five years.

- In 2004, two Utah men described by the U.S. attorney there as "domestic terrorists" pleaded guilty to setting separate arson fires related to eco-terrorism. Justus Ireland, 23, admitted start-

CJ News (continued)

ing a fire that caused $1.5 million damage at a West Jordan lumber company and spray-painting "ELF" at the site. The Earth Liberation Front has been connected to dozens of acts of vandalism and arson around the country since 1996. Joshua Demmitt, 18, of Provo, pleaded guilty to starting a fire at Brigham Young University's Ellsworth Farm, where animal experiments are conducted, in the name of the Animal Liberation Front. A third man, Harrison Burrows, 18, also of Provo, pleaded guilty earlier.

- In May 2004, the FBI's domestic terrorism unit charged seven members of an animal rights group with terrorism after investigating what they said was a marked increase in crimes to stop the use of animals for product testing. The activists, arrested in New York, New Jersey, California and Washington state, are members of Stop Huntingdon Animal Cruelty. The group seeks to shut down Huntingdon Life Sciences, a New Jersey product-testing company.

  Prosecutors allege that the activists set fire to Huntingdon employees' cars, vandalized shareholders' homes and threatened their families. They are charged with conspiring to commit terrorism against an enterprise that uses animals for research and could face up to three years in prison if convicted.

- In mid-2004, a Brookfield, Wisconsin, man labeled a domestic terrorist by federal prosecutors received an eight-year prison sentence for interfering with Madison police radio frequencies. Rajib Mitra, 26, had blocked police radio signals and later broadcast sex sounds over police radios. His attorney argued that the transmissions were an accident.

Mitra was one of the first defendants sentenced under guidelines changed after the Sept. 11 terrorist attacks. The changes, effective November 5, 2003, impose stiffer penalties for domestic terrorism. Under the previous sentencing guidelines, Mitra probably would have been sentenced to 18 to 24 months.

Mitra's attorney, Chris Van Wagner, says his client was not a terrorist and should have received a lesser punishment. "It's clear that (the guidelines) were put in place to punish those who seek to subvert our government and not intended to increase the punishment for people who simply engage in criminal mischief but had no terrorist angle or connection whatsoever," Van Wagner says. "He was just a dolphin caught in a tuna net."

Mitra was charged under provisions of the USA PATRIOT Act that make it a crime to cause such public-safety problems, even if there were no monetary damages. "This is a vivid example of how the PATRIOT Act has been used in cases that clearly have nothing to do with terrorism and that are far removed from what Congress was concerned about when it passed the PATRIOT Act," says Timothy Edgar of the American Civil Liberties Union.

During the 1990s, anti-government groups sprang up all over the country, according to the Southern Poverty Law Center and the Anti-Defamation League, which was founded in 1913 to combat anti-

Semitism and now monitors hate groups. Many formed militias to prepare for large-scale resistance to the government, which the groups blamed for the Randy Weaver siege at Ruby Ridge, Idaho, in 1992 and the Branch Davidian confrontation in Waco, Texas, in 1993.

Many of these group members believed the federal government was secretly setting up concentration camps for dissident Americans and was planning a takeover of the United States by United Nations troops as part of a "new world order." Many also said that mysterious black helicopters were conducting surveillance in the West, according to the ADL.

"The 'black helicopter' crowd is still out there," says Wisconsin federal prosecutor Tim O'Shea, referring to extremists who distrust and abhor the federal government.

Potok says the Southern Poverty Law Center identified 751 hate groups last year, a 6% increase over the 708 such organizations it counted in 2002.

Potok, director of the center's Intelligence Project, which monitors hate groups, says, "I don't mean to minimize the work of groups with ties to al-Qaeda. Obviously, there's a huge external threat as well. But there's a tendency to want to externalize the threat and say the people who want to hurt us don't look like us, they don't worship the same god and don't have the same skin color."

In 2004, the National District Attorneys Association, which has about 7,000 members, held a first-ever conference on domestic terrorism in Washington, D.C., to help local prosecutors identify potential terrorist groups.

"It was very well received," says the association's vice president, Robert Honecker, a prosecutor in Monmouth County, N.J. "They were appreciative of getting the information and the knowledge so they would be prepared should something happen in their jurisdiction."

Some of the alleged efforts by domestic terrorists are chilling.

According to an FBI affidavit in the Tennessee case, Crocker had inquired last spring about where he could obtain nuclear waste or nuclear materials. An informant told the FBI that Crocker, who had "absolute hatred" for the government, wanted "to build a bomb to be detonated at a government building, particularly a courthouse, either federal or state."

In September 2004, according to the affidavit, Crocker told an undercover FBI agent "it would be a good thing if somebody could detonate some sort of weapon of mass destruction in Washington, D.C.," while both houses of Congress "were in session." Crocker allegedly told the agent he admired Adolf Hitler and the Nazi Party. He said "establishing a concentration camp for Jewish insurance executives would be a desirable endeavor."

Crocker later bought what he thought was Sarin nerve gas and a block of C-4 explosive from the undercover agent, the affidavit says.

Authorities arrested Crocker in 2004.

For the latest in crime and justice news, visit the Talk Justice news feed at http://www.crimenews.info.

Source: Larry Copeland, "Domestic Terrorism: New Trouble at Home," USA TODAY, November 15, 2004. Reprinted with permission.

*Those who employ terrorism
. . . strive to subvert the rule
of law and effect change
through violence and fear.*

—National Strategy for Combating
Terrorism, 2003

In 2005, 38-year-old Eric Robert Rudolph pleaded guilty to a string of bombing attacks in Alabama and Georgia, including a blast at Atlanta's Centennial Park during the 1996 Olympics in which one person died and 111 were injured.[72] Rudolph, an antiabortion and antigay extremist, was sentenced to life in prison without the possibility of parole after having eluded law enforcement officers for years.

Active fringe groups include those espousing a nationwide "common law movement," under which the legitimacy of elected government officials is not recognized. An example is the Republic of Texas separatists who took neighbors hostage near Fort Davis, Texas, in 1997 to draw attention to their claims that Texas was illegally annexed by the United States in 1845. While not necessarily bent on terrorism, such special-interest groups may turn to violence if thwarted in attempts to reach their goals.

Sometimes individuals can be as dangerous as organized groups. In 1996, for example, 52-year-old Theodore Kaczynski, a Lincoln, Montana, antitechnology recluse, was arrested and charged in the Unabomber case. The Unabomber (so called because the bomber's original targets were universities and airlines) had led police and FBI agents on a 17-year-long manhunt through a series of incidents that involved as many as 16 bombings, resulting in three deaths and 23 injuries. Kaczynski pleaded guilty to federal charges in 1998 and was sentenced to life in prison without possibility of parole.

INTERNATIONAL TERRORISM

In 1988, Pan American's London–New York Flight 103 was destroyed over Scotland by a powerful two-stage bomb as it reached its cruising altitude of 30,000 feet, killing all of the 259 passengers and crew members aboard. Another 11 people on the ground were killed and many others injured as flaming debris from the airplane crashed down on the Scottish town of Lockerbie. It was the first time Americans were undeniably the target of international terrorism. Any doubts that terrorists were targeting U.S. citizens were dispelled by the 1996 truck bomb attack on U.S. military barracks in Dhahran, Saudi Arabia. Nineteen U.S. Air Force personnel were killed and more than 250 others were injured in the blast, which destroyed the Khobar Towers housing complex.

The 1993 bombing of the World Trade Center in New York City and the 1995 conviction of Sheik Omar Abdel-Rahman and eight other Islamic fundamentalists on charges of plotting to start a holy war and of conspiring to commit assassinations and bomb the United Nations[73] indicated to many that the threat of international terrorism could soon become a part of daily life in America. According to some terrorism experts, the 1993 explosion at the World Trade Center, which killed four people and created a 100-foot hole through four subfloors of concrete, ushered in an era of international terrorist activity in the United States. In 1999, the Second U.S. Circuit Court of Appeals upheld the convictions of the sheik and his coconspirators. They remain in federal prison.

In 2001, Islamic terrorist Osama bin Laden showed the world how terrorists can successfully strike at American interests on U.S. soil when members of his organization allegedly attacked the World Trade Center and the Pentagon using commandeered airliners, killing approximately 3,000 people. Earlier, in 1998, bin Laden's agents struck American embassies in Nairobi, Kenya, and Dares Salaam, Tanzania, killing 257 people, including 12 Americans. In 2003, a coordinated attack by Islamic extremists on a residential compound for foreigners in Riyadh, Saudi Arabia, killed 34 people (nine attackers died), including eight Americans, and wounded many more.[74] Similar attacks are continuing in the Middle East and elsewhere.

Some believe that the wars in Afghanistan and Iraq, as well as a coordinated international effort against al-Qaeda, may have substantially weakened that organization's ability to carry out future strikes outside of the Middle East. Those who study international terrorism, however, note that Jihadism, or the Islamic holy war movement, survives independent of any one organization and appears to be gaining strength around the world.[75] Jihadist principles continue to serve as the organizing rationale for extremist groups in much of the Muslim world. Learn more about the global threat from Islamic fundamentalism at Library Extra 17–7 at cjtoday.com.

LIBRARY
Extra
■ ■ ■ ■

CYBERTERRORISM

cyberterrorism

A form of terrorism that makes use of high technology, especially computers and the Internet, in the planning and carrying out of terrorist attacks.

A new kind of terrorism, called **cyberterrorism**, makes use of high technology, especially computers and the Internet, in the planning and carrying out of terrorist attacks. The term was coined in the 1980s by Barry Collin, a senior research fellow at the Institute for Security and Intelligence in California, who used it to refer to the convergence of cyberspace and terrorism.[76] It was later popularized by a 1996 RAND report that warned of an emerging "new terrorism" distinguished by how terrorist groups organize and by how they use technology. The report warned of a coming "netwar" or "infowar" consisting of coordinated cyberattacks on our nation's economic, busi-

A still frame taken from a security video camera that recorded the detonation of a bomb in Atocha railway station in Madrid, Spain, on March 11, 2004. The bomb was one in a series of terrorist explosions that went off within seconds of one other on Madrid's trains, killing 191 people. Hundreds more were injured by the blasts, which were blamed on Muslim extremists linked to al-Qaeda who were operating in Spain. Could such attacks happen here in the United States?

© Reuters/Corbis

ness, and military **infrastructure.**[77] A year later, FBI agent Mark Pollitt offered a working definition of *cyberterrorism,* saying that it is "the premeditated, politically motivated attack against information, computer systems, computer programs, and data which results in violence against noncombatant targets by subnational groups or clandestine agents."[78]

Scenarios describing cyberterrorism possibilities are imaginative and diverse. Some have suggested that a successful cyberterrorist attack on the nation's air traffic control system might cause airplanes to collide in midair or that an attack on food- and cereal-processing plants that drastically altered the levels of certain nutritional supplements might sicken or kill a large number of our nation's children. Other such attacks might cause the country's power grid to collapse or could muddle the records and transactions of banks and stock exchanges. Possible targets in such attacks are almost endless.

In 1998, the Critical Infrastructure Assurance Office (CIAO) was created by a presidential directive to coordinate the federal government's initiatives on critical infrastructure protection and to provide a national focus for cyberspace security. In 2001, the White House formed the President's Critical Infrastructure Protection Board (PCIPB) and tasked it with recommending policies in support of critical infrastructure protection.[79] In September 2002, the PCIPB released an important document entitled *The National Strategy to Secure Cyberspace,*[80] which is available at Library Extra 17–8 at cjtoday.com. In 2003, CIAO functions were transferred to the National Cyber Security Division (NCSD) of the Directorate of Information Analysis and Infrastructure Protection within the Department of Homeland Security. According to DHS, the creation of NCSD improved protection of critical cyberassets by "maximizing and leveraging the resources" of previously separate offices.[81] NCSD coordinates its activities with the U.S. Computer Emergency Response Team (US-CERT), which runs a National Cyber Alert System. Visit US-CERT, which is also a part of the Department of Homeland Security, at Web Extra 17–13 at cjtoday.com. Another group, the Secret Service National Threat Assessment Center (NTAC), is developing its Critical Systems Protection Initiative and will soon offer advanced cybersecurity prevention and response capabilities to the nation's business community. Visit NTAC at Web Extra 17–14 at cjtoday.com.

infrastructure

The basic facilities, services, and installations that a country needs to function. Transportation and communications systems, water and power lines, and institutions that serve the public, including banks, schools, post offices, and prisons, are all part of a country's infrastructure.[viii]

LIBRARY
Extra
■ ■ ■ ■

WEB
Extra
■ ■ ■ ■

WEB
Extra
■ ■ ■ ■

NARCOTERRORISM

Some authors have identified a link between major drug traffickers and terrorist groups.[82] In mid-2005, for example, Afghan drug lord Bashir Noorzai was arrested in New York and held without bond on charges that he tried to smuggle more than $50 million worth of heroin into the United

narcoterrorism

A political alliance between terrorist organizations and drug-supplying cartels. The cartels provide financing for the terrorists, who in turn provide quasi-military protection to the drug dealers.

States.[83] Noorzai, who was on the Drug Enforcement Administration's list of most wanted drug kingpins, had apparently operated with impunity under the protection of the Taliban between 1990 and 2004. According to the DEA, Noorzai's organization "provided demolitions, weapons and manpower to the Taliban." In exchange, the Taliban were said to have protected Noorzai's opium crops and transit routes through Afghanistan and Pakistan.

The link between drug traffickers and insurgents has been termed **narcoterrorism.**[84] Narcoterrorism, simply defined, is the involvement of terrorist organizations and insurgent groups in the trafficking of narcotics.[85] The relationship that exists between terrorist organizations and drug traffickers is mutually beneficial. Insurgents derive financial benefits from their supporting role in drug trafficking, while the traffickers receive protection and benefit from the use of terrorist tactics against foes and competitors.

The first documented instance of an insurgent force financed at least in part with drug money came to light during an investigation of the virulent anti-Castro Omega 7 group in the early 1980s.[86] Clear-cut evidence of modern narcoterrorism, however, is difficult to obtain. Contemporary insurgent organizations with links to drug dealers probably include the 19th of April Movement (M-19) operating in Colombia, Sendero Luminoso (Shining Path) of Peru, the Revolutionary Armed Forces of Colombia, and the large Farabundo Marti National Liberation Front, which has long sought to overthrow the elected government of El Salvador.[87]

Narcoterrorism raises a number of questions. Drug researcher James Inciardi summarizes them as follows:[88]

- What is the full threat posed by narcoterrorism?
- How should narcoterrorism be dealt with?
- Is narcoterrorism a law enforcement problem or a military one?
- How might narcoterrorism be affected by changes in official U.S. policy toward drugs and drug use?
- Is the international drug trade being used as a tool by anti-U.S. and other interests to undermine Western democracies in a calculated way?

Unfortunately, in the opinion of some experts, the United States is ill prepared to combat this type of international organized crime. Testifying before the Senate's Foreign Relations Subcommittee on Terrorism, Narcotics, and International Operations, William J. Olson, a senior fellow at the National Strategy Information Center, told Congress that more than $1 trillion (equivalent to one-sixth of the U.S. gross national product) is generated yearly by organized criminal activities like those associated with narcoterrorism. "We must recognize that the rules of the crime game have changed," said Olson. "International criminal organizations are challenging governments, permeating societies. They're running roughshod over weak institutions and exploiting gaps in the U.S. and international response. They have the upper hand at the moment and they know it," he said.[89] Other experts testified that a comprehensive national strategy—one that goes far beyond law enforcement and criminal prosecution to include diplomacy and organized international efforts—is needed to combat international organized criminal enterprises before they can co-opt global markets and worldwide financial institutions.[90]

Even more potentially damaging are efforts being made by some criminal groups to wrest control of political institutions in various parts of the world. As transnational organized crime expert Emilio C. Viano points out, "powerful drug constituencies influence the electoral process more and more, seeking to gain actual political representation and consequently weaken the rule of law in a number of countries."[91]

Causes of Terrorism

According to the U.S. government,[92] international terrorist organizations build on a process shown in Figure 17–1. The federal government's *National Strategy for Combating Terrorism,*[93] from which this figure is derived, says that the *underlying conditions* that lead to terrorism include poverty, political corruption, religious and ideational conflict, and ethnic strife. Such conditions provide terrorists with the opportunity to legitimize their cause and to justify their actions. Feeding on the social disorganization fostered by these conditions, terrorists position themselves to demand political change.

The second level in Figure 17–1, the *international environment,* refers to the geopolitical boundaries within which terrorist organizations form and through which they operate. If international borders are free and open, then terrorist groups can readily establish safe havens, hone their capabilities, practice their techniques, and provide support and funding to distant members

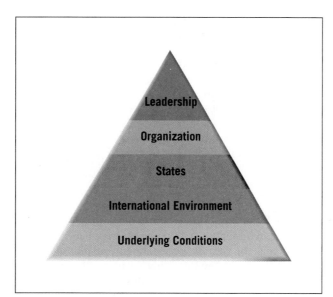

FIGURE 17–1

International terrorist organizations: the building process.

Source: National Strategy for Combating Terrorism (Washington, DC: The White House, 2003), p. 6.

The pyramid, from bottom to top, reads:
Underlying Conditions
International Environment
States
Organization
Leadership

and collaborators. Either knowingly or unwittingly, nations (*states*) can provide the physical assets and bases needed for the terrorist *organization* to grow and function. Finally, the terrorist *leadership,* at the top of the pyramid, provides the overall direction and strategy that give life to the organization's terror campaign.

Combating Terrorism

Terrorism represents a difficult challenge to all societies. The open societies of the Western world, however, are potentially more vulnerable than are totalitarian regimes like dictatorships. Western democratic ideals restrict police surveillance of likely terrorist groups and curtail luggage, vehicle, and airport searches. Press coverage of acts of terrorism encourage copycat activities by other fringe groups and communicate information on workable techniques. Laws designed to limit terrorist access to technology, information, and physical locations are stopgap measures at best. The federal Terrorist Firearms Detection Act of 1988 is an example. Designed to prevent the development of plastic firearms by requiring handguns to contain at least 3.7 ounces of detectable metal,[94] it applies only to weapons manufactured within U.S. borders.

In 1996, the Antiterrorism and Effective Death Penalty Act (AEDPA) became law. The act includes a number of provisions. It

- Bans fund-raising and financial support within the United States for international terrorist organizations
- Provides $1 billion for enhanced terrorism-fighting measures by federal and state authorities
- Allows foreign terrorism suspects to be deported or to be kept out of the United States without the disclosure of classified evidence against them
- Permits a death sentence to be imposed on anyone committing an international terrorist attack in the United States in which a death occurs
- Makes it a federal crime to use the United States as a base for planning terrorist attacks overseas
- Orders identifying chemical markers known as *taggants* to be added to plastic explosives during manufacture
- Orders a feasibility study on marking other explosives (except gunpowder)

More than a year before the events of September 11, 2001, the National Commission on Terrorism released a report titled *Countering the Changing Threat of International Terrorism.*[95] The commission, created by House and Senate leaders in 1998 in response to the bombings of the U.S. embassies in Kenya and Tanzania, was led by former U.S. Ambassador-at-Large for Counter-Terrorism L. Paul Bremer. The commission's report, which we now see presaged the 2001 attacks on the World Trade Center and the Pentagon, began with these words: "International terrorism poses an increasingly dangerous and difficult threat to America." The report identified Afghanistan, Iran, Iraq, Sudan, and Syria as among state sponsors of terrorism and concluded

Powerful international criminal groups now work outside national or international law. They include traffickers in drugs, money laundering, the illegal trade in arms—including trade in nuclear materials—and the smuggling of precious metals and other commodities. These criminal elements exploit both the new liberal international economic order and the different approaches and practices of States. They command vast sums of money, which they use to suborn State officials. Some criminal "empires" are richer than many poorer States. These problems demand a concerted, global response.

—Former United Nations Secretary-General Boutros Boutros-Ghali[ix]

that "the government must immediately take steps to reinvigorate the collection of intelligence about terrorists' plans, use all available legal avenues to disrupt and prosecute terrorist activities and private sources of support, convince other nations to cease all support for terrorists, and ensure that federal, state, and local officials are prepared for attacks that may result in mass casualties." A number of the commission's recommendations were implemented only *after* the terrorist attacks of 2001.

Following the 2001 attacks, Congress enacted, and the president signed, the USA PATRIOT Act. The act, which is discussed in detail in other chapters and which was reauthorized in 2006 with some amendments, created a number of new crimes, such as terrorist attacks against mass transportation and harboring or concealing terrorists. Those crimes were set forth in Title VIII of the act, titled "Strengthening the Criminal Laws against Terrorism." Excerpts from Title VIII can be found in CJ Today Exhibit 17–3.

ANTITERRORISM COMMITTEES AND REPORTS

A number of important antiterrorism reports and studies have been released during the last seven or eight years by various groups, including the Advisory Panel to Assess Domestic Response Capabilities for Terrorism Involving Weapons of Mass Destruction (also known as the Gilmore Commission), the National Commission on Terrorism, the U.S. Commission on National Security in the Twenty-First Century, the New York–based Council on Foreign Relations (CFR), and the National Commission on Terrorist Attacks upon the United States (aka the 9/11 Commission).

Some pre–September 11, 2001, reports offered valuable suggestions that, if followed, might have helped prevent the events that took place on that day. Some of the subsequent reports have been voices of reason in the rush to strengthen the nation's antiterrorism defenses at potentially high costs to individual freedoms. The 2002 CFR report, for example, notes that "systems such as those used in the aviation sector, which start from the assumption that every passenger and every bag of luggage poses an equal risk, must give way to more intelligence-driven and layered security approaches that emphasize prescreening and monitoring based on risk criteria."

The report of the 9/11 Commission, released on July 22, 2004, which many saw as especially valuable, said that the September 11, 2001, attacks should have come as no surprise because the U.S. government had received clear warnings that Islamic terrorists were planning to strike at targets within the United States (see CJ Today Exhibit 17–4). The report also said that the United States is still not properly prepared to deal adequately with terrorist threats and called for the creation of a new federal intelligence-gathering center to unify the more than a dozen federal agencies currently gathering terrorism-related intelligence at home and abroad. In December 2005, members of the 9/11 Commission held a final news conference in which they lambasted the lack of progress made by federal officials charged with implementing safeguards to prevent future terrorist attacks

Palestinian boys holding toy rifles as a girl displays a poster of Osama bin Laden in Gaza City during a demonstration at Al Azhar University to honor suicide bombers. The school was organized by members of the Islamic Jihad. The 9/11 Commission report, released in 2004, pointed to the radical ideology underpinning international Islamic terrorism today and bemoaned the fact that too many Middle Eastern children are being socialized into a culture of terrorism. How can radical ideologies be combated?

AP Wide World Photos

CJ Today Exhibit 17–3

The USA PATRIOT Act of 2001 (as Amended and Reauthorized in 2006)

Title VIII of the USA PATRIOT Act created two new federal crimes of terrorist activity: (1) terrorist attacks against mass transportation systems and (2) harboring or concealing terrorists. The following excerpts from the act describe these offenses.

TITLE VIII—STRENGTHENING THE CRIMINAL LAWS AGAINST TERRORISM

Sec. 801. Terrorist Attacks and Other Acts of Violence against Mass Transportation Systems.

Chapter 97 of title 18, United States Code, is amended by adding at the end the following:

§ 1993. Terrorist attacks and other acts of violence against mass transportation systems

(a) GENERAL PROHIBITIONS.—Whoever willfully—

(1) wrecks, derails, sets fire to, or disables a mass transportation vehicle or ferry;

(2) places or causes to be placed any biological agent or toxin for use as a weapon, destructive substance, or destructive device in, upon, or near a mass transportation vehicle or ferry, without previously obtaining the permission of the mass transportation provider, and with intent to endanger the safety of any passenger or employee of the mass transportation provider, or with a reckless disregard for the safety of human life;

(3) sets fire to, or places any biological agent or toxin for use as a weapon, destructive substance, or destructive device in, upon, or near any garage, terminal, structure, supply, or facility used in the operation of, or in support of the operation of, a mass transportation vehicle or ferry, without previously obtaining the permission of the mass transportation provider, and knowing or having reason to know such activity would likely derail, disable, or wreck a mass transportation vehicle or ferry used, operated, or employed by the mass transportation provider;

(4) removes appurtenances from, damages, or otherwise impairs the operation of a mass transportation signal system, including a train control system, centralized dispatching system, or rail grade crossing warning signal without authorization from the mass transportation provider;

(5) interferes with, disables, or incapacitates any dispatcher, driver, captain, or person while they are employed in dispatching, operating, or maintaining a mass transportation vehicle or ferry, with intent to endanger the safety of any passenger or employee of the mass transportation provider, or with a reckless disregard for the safety of human life;

(6) commits an act, including the use of a dangerous weapon, with the intent to cause death or serious bodily injury to an employee or passenger of a mass transportation provider or any other person

while any of the foregoing are on the property of a mass transportation provider;

(7) conveys or causes to be conveyed false information, knowing the information to be false, concerning an attempt or alleged attempt being made or to be made, to do any act which would be a crime prohibited by this subsection; or

(8) attempts, threatens, or conspires to do any of the aforesaid acts,

shall be fined under this title or imprisoned not more than twenty years, or both, if such act is committed, or in the case of a threat or conspiracy such act would be committed, on, against, or affecting a mass transportation provider engaged in or affecting interstate or foreign commerce, or if in the course of committing such act, that person travels or communicates across a State line in order to commit such act, or transports materials across a State line in aid of the commission of such act.

(b) AGGRAVATED OFFENSE.—Whoever commits an offense under subsection (a) in a circumstance in which—

(1) the mass transportation vehicle or ferry was carrying a passenger at the time of the offense; or

(2) the offense has resulted in the death of any person, shall be guilty of an aggravated form of the offense and shall be fined under this title or imprisoned for a term of years or for life, or both.

Sec. 803. Prohibition against Harboring Terrorists.

(a) In General.—Chapter 113B of title 18, United States Code, is amended by adding after section 2338 the following new section:

§ 2339. Harboring or concealing terrorists

(a) Whoever harbors or conceals any person who he knows, or has reasonable grounds to believe, has committed, or is about to commit, an offense under section 32 (relating to destruction of aircraft or aircraft facilities), section 175 (relating to biological weapons), section 229 (relating to chemical weapons), section 831 (relating to nuclear materials), paragraph (2) or (3) of section 844(f) (relating to arson and bombing of government property risking or causing injury or death), section 1366(a) (relating to the destruction of an energy facility), section 2280 (relating to violence against maritime navigation), section 2332a (relating to weapons of mass destruction), or section 2332b (relating to acts of terrorism transcending national boundaries) of this title, section 236(a) (relating to sabotage of nuclear facilities or fuel) of the Atomic Energy Act of 1954 (42 U.S.C. 2284(a)), or section 46502 (relating to aircraft piracy) of title 49, shall be fined under this title or imprisoned not more than ten years, or both.

(b) A violation of this section may be prosecuted in any Federal judicial district in which the underlying offense was committed, or in any other Federal judicial district as provided by law.

(b) TECHNICAL AMENDMENT.—The chapter analysis for chapter 113B of title 18, United States Code, is amended by inserting after the item for section 2338 the following: "2339. Harboring or concealing terrorists."

Note: The USA PATRIOT Act was reauthorized by Congress in March 2006.

within the United States. Former Commission Chairman Thomas Kean called it "shocking" that the nation remains so vulnerable. "We shouldn't need another wake-up call," said Kean. "We believe that the terrorists will strike again."[96] While it is impossible to discuss each of the reports mentioned here in detail in this textbook, they are available in their entirety at Library Extras 17–9 through 17–18 at cjtoday.com.

THE DEPARTMENT OF HOMELAND SECURITY

The Homeland Security Act of 2002, enacted to protect America against terrorism, created the federal Department of Homeland Security, which is charged with protecting the nation's critical infrastructure against terrorist attack. The new department began operations on March 1, 2003, with former Pennsylvania Governor Tom Ridge as its first director. The director, whose official title is secretary of homeland security, is a member of the cabinet. In 2005, Michael Chertoff became the new secretary of homeland security. A former federal prosecutor, Chertoff previously served as assistant attorney general for the Criminal Division at the U.S. Department of Justice and helped trace the 9/11 terrorist attacks to the al-Qaeda network.

Experts say that the creation of DHS is the most significant transformation of the U.S. government since 1947, when President Harry S. Truman merged the various branches of the armed forces into the Department of Defense in an effort to better coordinate the nation's defense against military threats.[97] DHS coordinates the activities of 22 disparate domestic agencies by placing administration of those agencies under five "directorates," or departmental divisions:

1. *Border and Transportation Security (BTS).* BTS is responsible for maintaining security of the nation's borders and transportation systems. The largest of the directorates, it is home to the Transportation Security Administration, the U.S. Customs Service, the border security functions of the former Immigration and Naturalization Service,[98] the Animal and Plant Health Inspection Service, and the Federal Law Enforcement Training Center.

2. *Emergency Preparedness and Response (EPR).* EPR works to ensure that the nation is prepared for, and able to recover from, terrorist attacks and natural disasters.

3. *Science and Technology (S&T).* This directorate coordinates the department's efforts in research and development, including preparing for and responding to the full range of terrorist threats involving weapons of mass destruction.

4. *Information Analysis and Infrastructure Protection (IAIP).* IAIP merges under one roof the functions of identifying and assessing a broad range of intelligence information concerning threats to the homeland, issuing timely warnings, and taking appropriate preventive and protective actions.

5. *Management.* The Management Directorate is responsible for budgetary, managerial, and personnel issues within DHS.

The members of the National Commission on Terrorist Attacks upon the United States (aka the 9/11 Commission), from left: Thomas H. Kean, Lee H. Hamilton, Fred F. Fielding, Bob Kerrey, John F. Lehman, and Richard Ben-Veniste. The commission's report, released on July 22, 2004, called for a major overhaul of U.S. intelligence agencies and for a realignment of federal expenditures on homeland security. What else did the report say?

Doug Mills/The New York Times

CJ Today Exhibit 17–4

The Report of the National Commission on Terrorist Attacks upon the United States

On July 22, 2004, the National Commission on Terrorist Attacks upon the United States (better known as the 9/11 Commission) released its report. The commission was created by President George W. Bush and the Congress on November 27, 2002, and was charged with investigating the "facts and circumstances relating to the terrorist attacks of September 11, 2001, including those relating to intelligence agencies, law enforcement agencies, diplomacy, immigration issues and border control, the flow of assets to terrorist organizations, commercial aviation, the role of congressional oversight and resource allocation, and other areas determined relevant by the Commission."

In preparing their report, commission members reviewed more than 2.5 million pages of documents and interviewed more than 1,200 people in ten countries. The final 585-page report touched on a variety of topics. Central to the report, however, is a "global strategy" to defeat terrorism.

"The enemy is not just 'terrorism,' some generic evil," the commission wrote. A generic response to "terrorism" would blur the need for a focused U.S. antiterrorism response. "The catastrophic threat at this moment in history is more specific. It is the threat posed by *Islamist* terrorism—especially the al Qaeda network, its affiliates, and its ideology."

The commission noted that Islam is not the enemy and that Islam is not synonymous with terror. "Nor does Islam teach terror," said the Commission. "America and its friends oppose a perversion of Islam, not the great world faith itself."

The following paragraphs, taken directly from the commission's report, identify the radical ideology underpinning much of international terrorism today and lay out an important long-term strategy for dealing with the continuing terrorist threat.

> Osama Bin Ladin and other Islamist terrorist leaders, draw on a long tradition of extreme intolerance within one stream of Islam (a minority tradition). . . . That stream is motivated by religion and does not distinguish politics from religion, thus distorting both. It is further fed by grievances stressed by Bin Ladin and widely felt throughout the Muslim world—against the U.S. military presence

in the Middle East, policies perceived as anti-Arab and anti-Muslim, and support of Israel. Bin Ladin and Islamist terrorists mean exactly what they say: to them America is the fount of all evil, the "head of the snake," and it must be converted or destroyed.

It is not a position with which Americans can bargain or negotiate. With it there is no common ground—not even respect for life—on which to begin a dialogue. It can only be destroyed or utterly isolated.

Because the Muslim world has fallen behind the West politically, economically, and militarily for the past three centuries, and because few tolerant or secular Muslim democracies provide alternative models for the future, Bin Ladin's message finds receptive ears. It has attracted active support from thousands of disaffected young Muslims and resonates powerfully with a far larger number who do not actively support his methods. The resentment of America and the West is deep, even among leaders of relatively successful Muslim states. Tolerance, the rule of law, political and economic openness, the extension of greater opportunities to women—these cures must come from within Muslim societies themselves. The United States must support such developments.

But this process is likely to be measured in decades, not years. It is a process that will be violently opposed by Islamist terrorist organizations, both inside Muslim countries and in attacks on the United States and other Western nations. The United States finds itself caught up in a clash *within* a civilization. That clash arises from particular conditions in the Muslim world, conditions that spill over into expatriate Muslim communities in non-Muslim countries.

Our enemy is twofold: al Qaeda, a stateless network of terrorists that struck us on 9/11; and a radical ideological movement in the Islamic world, inspired in part by al Qaeda, which has spawned terrorist groups and violence across the globe. The first enemy is weakened, but continues to pose a grave threat. The second enemy is gathering, and will menace Americans and American interests long after Osama Bin Ladin and his cohorts are killed or captured. Thus our strategy must match our means to two ends: dismantling the al Qaeda network and prevailing in the longer term over the ideology that gives rise to Islamist terrorism.

Source: National Commission on Terrorist Attacks upon the United States, *The 9/11 Commission Report: Final Report of the National Commission on Terrorist Attacks on the United States* (Washington, DC: U.S. Government Printing Office, 2004), pp. 362–363.

Several other critical agencies have been folded into the new department or have been created under the five directorates:[99]

- *U.S. Coast Guard.* The commandant of the Coast Guard reports directly to the secretary of DHS. However, the Coast Guard also works closely with the undersecretary of BTS and maintains its existing identity as an independent military service. Upon declaration of war or when the president so directs, the Coast Guard will operate as an element of the Department of Defense, consistent with existing law.

- *U.S. Secret Service.* The primary mission of the Secret Service is the protection of the president and other government leaders, as well as security for designated national events. The Secret Service is also the primary agency responsible for protecting U.S. currency from counterfeiters and safeguarding Americans from credit card fraud.

- *Bureau of Citizenship and Immigration Services (CIS).* A new agency, CIS (also known as U.S. Citizenship and Immigration Services, or USCIS) dedicates its energies to providing efficient immigration services and easing the transition to American citizenship.

- *Bureau of Customs and Border Protection (CBP).* CBP, the unified border control agency of the United States, has as its mission the protection of our country's borders and the American people.

- *Bureau of Immigration and Customs Enforcement (ICE).* Also known as U.S. Immigration and Customs Enforcement, ICE (along with CIS) has roots in the now-defunct U.S. Immigration and Naturalization Service. ICE, the largest investigative arm of the Department of Homeland Security, is responsible for identifying and eliminating vulnerabilities in the nation's border, economic, transportation, and infrastructure security.

- *Office of State and Local Government Coordination.* This office ensures close coordination between local, state, and federal governments to ensure an effective terrorism-prevention effort and to provide quick responses to terrorist incidents.

- *Office of Private Sector Liaison.* The Office of Private Sector Liaison provides the business community with a direct line of communication to DHS. The office works directly with individual businesses and through trade associations and other nongovernmental organizations to foster dialogue between the private sector and DHS on the full range of issues and challenges that America's businesses face today.

- *Office of Inspector General.* The Office of Inspector General serves as an independent and objective inspection, audit, and investigative body to promote effectiveness, efficiency, and economy in DHS's programs and operations and to prevent and detect fraud, abuse, mismanagement, and waste.

All of the agencies described here can be found in the Cybrary at http://www.cybrary.info. You can visit DHS on the Web via **Web Extra 17–15** at cjtoday.com. Learn what DHS is doing to keep America safe at **Web Extra 17–16**.

WEB
Extra

THE NATIONAL STRATEGY FOR COMBATING TERRORISM

In 2003, the White House released its official *National Strategy for Combating Terrorism.*[100] The strategy includes a multipronged initiative aimed at reducing both the threat severity and international reach of international terrorist organizations. The avowed goals of the *National Strategy* are as follows:

- Defeat terrorists and their organizations by identifying, locating, and destroying them.

- Deny sponsorship, support, and sanctuary to terrorists by helping other nations fulfill their responsibilities and obligations to combat terrorism.

- Diminish the underlying conditions that terrorists seek to exploit by resolving regional disputes; by fostering economic, social, and political development; by encouraging market-based economies; by supporting good governance and the rule of law; and by "winning the war of ideas" to ensure that ideologies that promote terrorism do not find fertile ground in any nation.

- Defend U.S. citizens and interests at home and abroad by implementing strong and effective security measures and by enhancing measures intended to ensure the integrity, reliability, and availability of critical physical and information-based infrastructures (including transportation and information systems).

Figure 17–2, which is taken from the *National Strategy,* shows the assessed threat severity and geopolitical reach of two terrorist groups at the time of the report. The figure illustrates the federal government's two-pronged strategy of reducing the scope and the capability of such organizations.

The July 2004 report of the 9/11 Commission proposed sweeping changes within the U.S. intelligence community, including the creation of the position of national intelligence director (NID). Soon afterward, the Intelligence Reform and Terrorism Prevention Act of 2004 facilitated the creation of the National Counterterrorism Center (NCTC) under the newly created position of NID.[101] The NID acts as the principal adviser to the president, the National Security Council, and the Homeland Security Council for intelligence matters related to national security. The NCTC

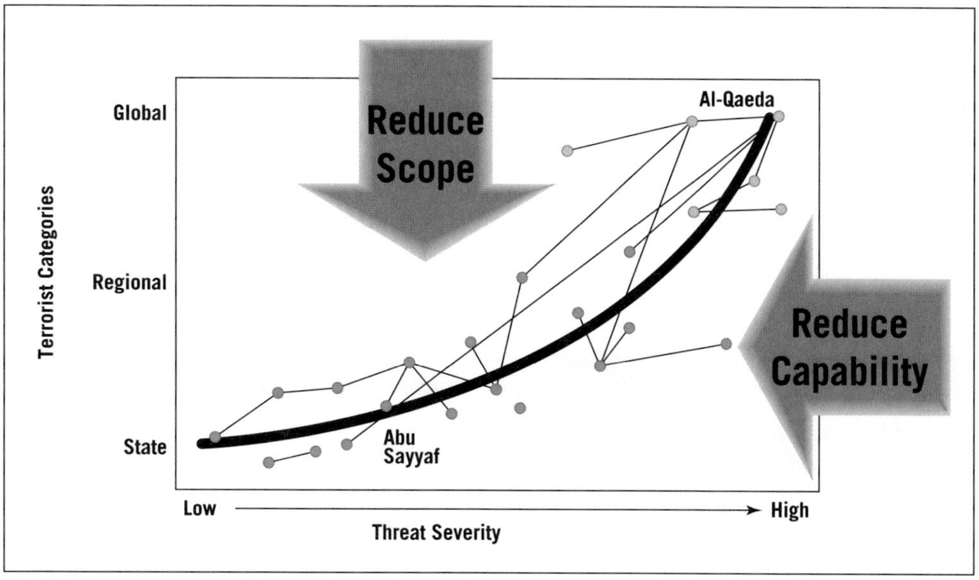

FIGURE 17–2

Reducing the scope and capability of terrorist organizations.

Source: National Strategy for Combating Terrorism (Washington, DC: The White House, 2003), p. 13.

[Figure 17-2: A graph with "Terrorist Categories" on the vertical axis (State, Regional, Global) and "Threat Severity" on the horizontal axis (Low to High). A curve rises from State/Low to Global/High, with Al-Qaeda at the top right and Abu Sayyaf near the bottom. Two large arrows labeled "Reduce Scope" (pointing down) and "Reduce Capability" (pointing left) are shown.]

serves as the primary organization in the U.S. government for integrating and analyzing all intelligence pertaining to terrorism and counterterrorism and for conducting strategic counterterrorism operational planning. Today's NCTC intelligence analysts have access to dozens of networks and information systems from across the intelligence, law enforcement, military, and homeland security communities. These systems provide foreign and domestic information pertaining to international terrorism and sensitive law enforcement activities.[102] Learn more about countering terrorist threats at Library Extra 17–19 at cjtoday.com. The *National Strategy* is available in its entirety at Library Extra 17–20. Visit the National Counterterrorism Center at Web Extra 17–17.

Foreign Terrorist Organizations

The Immigration and Nationality Act[103] and the Intelligence Reform and Terrorism Prevention Act of 2004[104] provide the U.S. Department of State with the authority to designate any group outside the United States as a **foreign terrorist organization (FTO)**. The process involves an exhaustive interagency review process in which all evidence of a group's activity, from both classified and open sources, is scrutinized. The State Department, working closely with the Justice and

LIBRARY Extra

WEB Extra

foreign terrorist organization (FTO)

A foreign organization that engages in terrorist activity that threatens the security of U.S. nationals or the national security of the United States and that is so designated by the U.S. secretary of state.

Air travelers being screened by Transportation Security Administration employees in Chicago's O'Hare International Airport. The hijackings of four airplanes by Islamic terrorists on September 11, 2001, led to tightened security controls over air travel nationwide and abroad. How did the hijackings reduce freedoms that Americans had previously taken for granted?

Sue Ogrocki/Corbis/Bettman

Treasury Departments and the intelligence community, prepares a detailed "administrative record" that documents the organization's terrorist activity.

Federal law requires that any organization considered for FTO designation must meet three criteria: (1) It must be foreign; (2) it must engage in terrorist activity as defined in Section 212 (a)(3)(B) of the Immigration and Nationality Act;[105] and (3) the organization's activities must threaten the security of U.S. nationals or the national security (national defense, foreign relations, or economic interests) of the United States. Table 17–2 lists 40 FTOs, as designated by the U.S. Department of State. For more detailed descriptions of these organizations, see the State Depart-

---

TABLE 17–2 Designated Foreign Terrorist Organizations

1. Abu Nidal Organization (ANO)
2. Abu Sayyaf Group
3. Al-Aqsa Martyrs' Brigade
4. Ansar al-Islam
5. Armed Islamic Group (GIA)
6. Asbat al-Ansar
7. Aum Shinrikyo
8. Basque Fatherland and Liberty (ETA)
9. Communist Party of the Philippines/New People's Army (CPP/NPA)
10. Continuity Irish Republican Army
11. Gama'a al-Islamiyya (Islamic Group)
12. Hamas (Islamic Resistance Movement)
13. Harakat ul-Mujahidin (HUM)
14. Hizballah (Party of God)
15. Islamic Movement of Uzbekistan (IMU)
16. Jaish-e-Mohammed (JEM) (Army of Mohammed)
17. Jemaah Islamiya (JI)
18. al-Jihad (Egyptian Islamic Jihad)
19. Kahane Chai (Kach)
20. Kongra-Gel (KGK) (formerly Kurdistan Workers' Party, PKK, KADEK)
21. Lashkar-e Tayyiba (LT) (Army of the Righteous)
22. Lashkar i Jhangvi
23. Liberation Tigers of Tamil Eelam (LTTE)
24. Libyan Islamic Fighting Group (LIFG)
25. Mujahedin-e Khalq Organization (MEK)
26. National Liberation Army (ELN)
27. Palestine Liberation Front (PLF)
28. Palestinian Islamic Jihad (PIJ)
29. Popular Front for the Liberation of Palestine (PFLP)
30. Popular Front for the Liberation of Palestine–General Command (PFLP–GC)
31. al-Qaeda
32. Real IRA
33. Revolutionary Armed Forces of Colombia (FARC)
34. Revolutionary Nuclei (formerly ELA)
35. Revolutionary Organization 17 November
36. Revolutionary People's Liberation Party/Front (DHKP/C)
37. Salafist Group for Call and Combat (GSPC)
38. Shining Path (Sendero Luminoso, SL)
39. Tanzim Qa'idat al-Jihad fi Bilad al-Rafidayn (QJBR) (al-Qaeda in Iraq; formerly Jama'at al-Tawhid wa'al-Jihad, JTJ, al-Zarqawi Network)
40. United Self-Defense Forces of Colombia (AUC)

Source: U.S. Department of State. Current as of October 1, 2007.

ment publication *Patterns of Global Terrorism,* which can be accessed at Library Extra 17–21 at cjtoday.com. The insignia of various terrorist organizations are shown in Figure 17–3.

LIBRARY Extra

Under federal law, FTO designations are subject to judicial review. In the event of a challenge to a group's FTO designation in federal court, the U.S. government relies on the administrative record to defend the designation decision. These administrative records contain intelligence information and are therefore classified. FTO designations expire in two years unless renewed.

Once an organization has been designated as an FTO, a number of legal consequences follow. First, it becomes unlawful for a person in the United States or subject to the jurisdiction of the United States to provide funds or other material support to a designated FTO. Second, representatives and certain members of a designated FTO, if they are aliens, can be denied visas or kept from entering the United States. Finally, U.S. financial institutions must block funds of designated FTOs and their agents and must report the blockage to the Office of Foreign Assets Control within the U.S. Department of the Treasury.

The State Department also has the authority to designate selected foreign governments as state sponsors of international terrorism. As of mid-2007, Cuba, Iran, North Korea, Sudan, and

17N
17 November
Abu Nidal Organization (ANO)
Al-Aqsa Martyrs' Brigade
Al-Jihad
Al-Qa'ida
宗教団体・アレフ
Aum Shinrikyo A.K.A. Aum Supreme Truth
Democratic Front for the Liberation of Palestine (DFLP)
EUSKADI TA ASKATASUNA
E.T.A.
Euzkadi Ta Askatasuna (ETA)
FARC-EP
FARC Revolutionary Armed Forces of Colombia
First of October Anti-Fascist Resistance Group
HAMAS
HIZB UT-TAHRIR
Hizb Ut-Tahrir
Hizballah (Party of God)
Lashkar-e-Tayyiba (LT or LeT) Army of the Righteous
Kahane Chai (KACH)
Kurdistan Worker's Party (PKK)

FIGURE 17–3

Terrorist organization insignias.

Source: Office of the Director of National Intelligence, National Counterterrorism Center, *Counterterrorism 2007* (Washington, DC: NCTC, 2007), pp. 116–117.

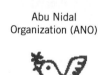

Liberation Tigers of Tamil
Eelam (LTTE)

Loyalist Volunteer Force
(LVF)

Mujahedin-e Khalq
Organization (MEK)

National Liberation Army
(ELN)

New People's Army
(NPA)

Orange Volunteers
(OV)

Palestine Islamic
Jihad
(PIJ)

People against
Gangsterism and Drugs
(PAGAD)

Popular Front for the
Liberation of Palestine
(PFLP)

Popular Front for the
Liberation of Palestine-
General Command
(PFLP-GC)

Revolutionary People's
Liberation Party/Front

Shining Path
(Sendero Luminoso)

Tupac Amaru
Revolutionary Movement
(MRTA)

Ulster Defense Association
(UDA)

FIGURE 17–3

Terrorist organization insignias. (continued)

Syria were designated as state sponsors of international terrorism. According to the State Department, Iran remains the most active state sponsor of terrorism.[106] The State Department says that the Iranian government provides continuing support to numerous terrorist groups, including the Lebanese Hizballah, Hamas, and the Palestinian Islamic Jihad, all of which seek to undermine the Middle East peace process through the use of terrorism. Syria provides safe haven and support to several terrorist groups, some of which oppose Middle East peace negotiations. The State Department notes, however, that Libya is attempting to mend its international image following its surrender in 1999 of two Libyan suspects for trial in the bombing of Pan Am Flight 103. In early 2001, one of those suspects was convicted of murder, and judges in the case found that he had acted "in furtherance of the purposes of . . . Libyan Intelligence Services." Also in 2003, Libya agreed to foreswear its well-developed nuclear arms program in an effort to attract foreign investment. Cuba, however, continues to provide safe haven to several terrorists and U.S. fugitives and maintains ties to other state sponsors of terrorism and to Latin American insurgents. North Korea harbored several hijackers of a Japanese Airlines flight to North Korea in the 1970s and maintains links to terrorist groups. It also continues to sell ballistic missile technology to countries designated by the United States as state sponsors of terrorism, including Syria and Libya. Finally, Sudan continues to provide a safe haven for members of various terrorist groups, including the Lebanese Hizballah, Gama'a al-Islamiyya, Egyptian Islamic Jihad, the Palestinian Islamic Jihad, and Hamas, although it has been engaged in a counterterrorism dialogue with the United States since mid-2000. Learn more about terrorism from the Terrorism Research Center via Web Extra 17–18 at cjtoday.com. Visit the State Department's Counterterrorism Office via Web Extra 17–19.

WEB
Extra
▪ ▪ ▪ ▪

The Future of International Terrorism

Terrorist groups are active throughout the world (Figure 17–4), and the United States is not their only target. Terrorist groups operate in South America, Africa, the Middle East, Latin America, the Philippines, Japan, India, England, Nepal, and some of the now independent states of the former Soviet Union. The Central Intelligence Agency reports that "between now and 2015 terrorist tactics will become increasingly sophisticated and designed to achieve mass casualties."[107] The CIA also notes that nations "with poor governance; ethnic, cultural, or religious tensions; weak economies; and porous borders will be prime breeding grounds for terrorism."[108] In the area of Islamic terrorism, the CIA expects that "by 2020 Al-Qaeda will have been superseded by similarly inspired but more diffuse Islamic extremist groups."[109] Read two CIA reports on the global trends that are likely to increase the risk of terrorism at Library Extras 17–22 and 17–23 at cjtoday.com.

LIBRARY
Extra
■ ■ ■ ■

The current situation leads many observers to conclude that the American justice system is not fully prepared to deal with the threat represented by domestic and international terrorism. Prior intelligence-gathering efforts that focused on such groups have largely failed or were not quickly acted on, leading to military intervention in places like Afghanistan and Iraq. Intelligence failures are at least partially understandable, given that many terrorist organizations are tight-knit and very difficult for intelligence operatives to penetrate.

SUMMARY

- Islamic law descends directly from the teachings of the Prophet Muhammad and looks to the Koran to determine which acts should be classified as crimes. Today's Islamic law is a system of duties and rituals founded on legal and moral obligations—all of which are ultimately sanctioned by the authority of religious leaders who may issue commands known as *fatwas*. Islamic law recognizes seven *Hudud* crimes—or crimes based on religious strictures. In Middle Eastern countries today, punishments for *Hudud* offenses are often physical and may include lashing, flogging, or even stoning. All other crimes fall into an offense category called *tazirat*. *Tazir* crimes are regarded as any actions not considered acceptable in a spiritual society. They include crimes against society and against individuals, but not those against God.

- The United Nations (UN) is the largest and most inclusive international body in the world. Since its inception in 1945, it has concerned itself with international crime prevention and world criminal justice systems, as illustrated by a number of important resolutions and documents, including the International Bill of Human Rights, which supports the rights and dignity of everyone who comes into contact with a criminal justice system; the Standard Minimum Rules for the Treatment of Prisoners; and the UN Code of Conduct for Law Enforcement Officials, which calls on law enforcement officers throughout the world to be cognizant of human rights in the perfor-

mance of their duties. The World Crime Surveys, which report official crime statistics from nearly 100 countries, provide a periodic global portrait of criminal activity. Other significant international criminal justice organizations are the International Criminal Police Organization (Interpol), which acts as a clearinghouse for information on offenses and suspects who are believed to operate across national boundaries, and the European Police Office (Europol), which aims to improve the effectiveness and cooperation of law enforcement agencies within the member states of the European Union. Finally, the International Criminal Court (ICC) was created in 2000 under the auspices of the United Nations. The ICC, whose operations are only now beginning, is intended to be a permanent criminal court for trying individuals who commit the most serious crimes of concern to the international community, such as genocide, war crimes, and crimes against humanity—including the wholesale murder of civilians, torture, and mass rape.

- Globalization, or the internationalization of trade, services, investment, information, and other forms of human social activity, has been occurring for a long time but has recently increased in pace due largely to advances in technology, such as new modes of transportation and communication. Transnational crime, which may be one of the most significant challenges of the twenty-first century, is a negative consequence of globalization. Transnational

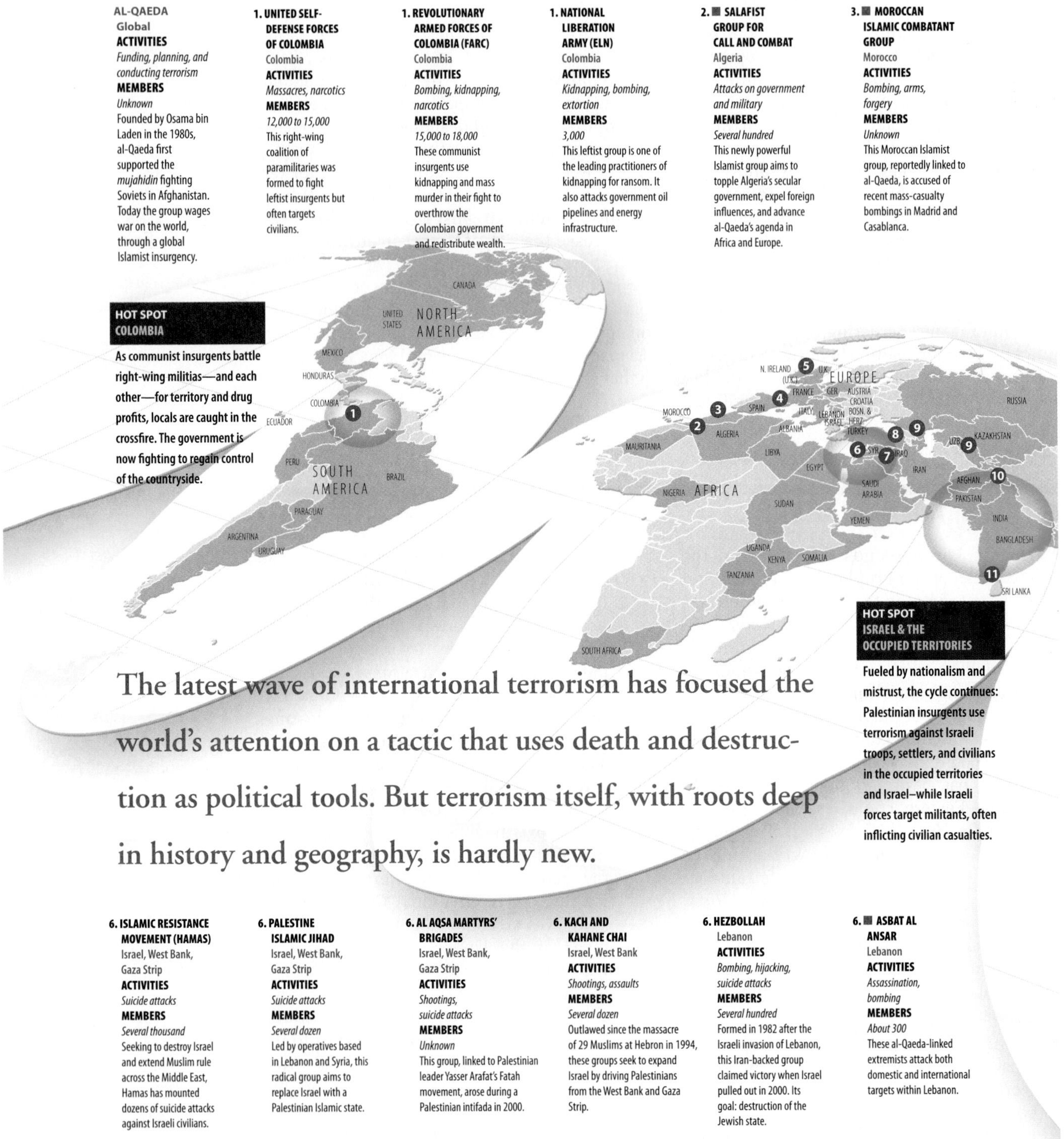
AL-QAEDA
Global
ACTIVITIES
Funding, planning, and conducting terrorism
MEMBERS
Unknown
Founded by Osama bin Laden in the 1980s, al-Qaeda first supported the mujahidin fighting Soviets in Afghanistan. Today the group wages war on the world, through a global Islamist insurgency.
1. UNITED SELF-DEFENSE FORCES OF COLOMBIA
Colombia
ACTIVITIES
Massacres, narcotics
MEMBERS
12,000 to 15,000
This right-wing coalition of paramilitaries was formed to fight leftist insurgents but often targets civilians.
1. REVOLUTIONARY ARMED FORCES OF COLOMBIA (FARC)
Colombia
ACTIVITIES
Bombing, kidnapping, narcotics
MEMBERS
15,000 to 18,000
These communist insurgents use kidnapping and mass murder in their fight to overthrow the Colombian government and redistribute wealth.
1. NATIONAL LIBERATION ARMY (ELN)
Colombia
ACTIVITIES
Kidnapping, bombing, extortion
MEMBERS
3,000
This leftist group is one of the leading practitioners of kidnapping for ransom. It also attacks government oil pipelines and energy infrastructure.
2. ■ SALAFIST GROUP FOR CALL AND COMBAT
Algeria
ACTIVITIES
Attacks on government and military
MEMBERS
Several hundred
This newly powerful Islamist group aims to topple Algeria's secular government, expel foreign influences, and advance al-Qaeda's agenda in Africa and Europe.
3. ■ MOROCCAN ISLAMIC COMBATANT GROUP
Morocco
ACTIVITIES
Bombing, arms, forgery
MEMBERS
Unknown
This Moroccan Islamist group, reportedly linked to al-Qaeda, is accused of recent mass-casualty bombings in Madrid and Casablanca.
HOT SPOT
COLOMBIA
As communist insurgents battle right-wing militias—and each other—for territory and drug profits, locals are caught in the crossfire. The government is now fighting to regain control of the countryside.
CANADA
UNITED STATES
NORTH AMERICA
MEXICO
HONDURAS
COLOMBIA
ECUADOR
PERU
SOUTH AMERICA
BRAZIL
PARAGUAY
ARGENTINA
URUGUAY
N. IRELAND (U.K.)
U.K.
EUROPE
FRANCE
GER.
AUSTRIA
CROATIA
BOSN. & HERZ.
SPAIN
ITALY
ALBANIA
LEBANON
ISRAEL
TURKEY
MOROCCO
ALGERIA
LIBYA
EGYPT
MAURITANIA
NIGERIA
AFRICA
SUDAN
SYR.
IRAQ
IRAN
SAUDI ARABIA
YEMEN
RUSSIA
UZB.
KAZAKHSTAN
AFGHAN.
PAKISTAN
INDIA
BANGLADESH
SRI LANKA
UGANDA
KENYA
SOMALIA
TANZANIA
SOUTH AFRICA
HOT SPOT
ISRAEL & THE OCCUPIED TERRITORIES
Fueled by nationalism and mistrust, the cycle continues: Palestinian insurgents use terrorism against Israeli troops, settlers, and civilians in the occupied territories and Israel—while Israeli forces target militants, often inflicting civilian casualties.
The latest wave of international terrorism has focused the world's attention on a tactic that uses death and destruction as political tools. But terrorism itself, with roots deep in history and geography, is hardly new.
6. ISLAMIC RESISTANCE MOVEMENT (HAMAS)
Israel, West Bank, Gaza Strip
ACTIVITIES
Suicide attacks
MEMBERS
Several thousand
Seeking to destroy Israel and extend Muslim rule across the Middle East, Hamas has mounted dozens of suicide attacks against Israeli civilians.
6. PALESTINE ISLAMIC JIHAD
Israel, West Bank, Gaza Strip
ACTIVITIES
Suicide attacks
MEMBERS
Several dozen
Led by operatives based in Lebanon and Syria, this radical group aims to replace Israel with a Palestinian Islamic state.
6. AL AQSA MARTYRS' BRIGADES
Israel, West Bank, Gaza Strip
ACTIVITIES
Shootings, suicide attacks
MEMBERS
Unknown
This group, linked to Palestinian leader Yasser Arafat's Fatah movement, arose during a Palestinian intifada in 2000.
6. KACH AND KAHANE CHAI
Israel, West Bank
ACTIVITIES
Shootings, assaults
MEMBERS
Several dozen
Outlawed since the massacre of 29 Muslims at Hebron in 1994, these groups seek to expand Israel by driving Palestinians from the West Bank and Gaza Strip.
6. HEZBOLLAH
Lebanon
ACTIVITIES
Bombing, hijacking, suicide attacks
MEMBERS
Several hundred
Formed in 1982 after the Israeli invasion of Lebanon, this Iran-backed group claimed victory when Israel pulled out in 2000. Its goal: destruction of the Jewish state.
6. ■ ASBAT AL ANSAR
Lebanon
ACTIVITIES
Assassination, bombing
MEMBERS
About 300
These al-Qaeda-linked extremists attack both domestic and international targets within Lebanon.

FIGURE 17–4

International terrorist groups and areas of operation.

Source: Walter Laqueur, "World of Terror" (National Geographic Maps), *National Geographic*, November 2004, pp. 72–74.

4. BASQUE FATHERLAND AND LIBERTY (ETA)
Spain, France
ACTIVITIES
Assassination, bombing, extortion
MEMBERS
Dozens
Founded in 1959, this group has targeted Spanish officials and security forces in its fight for an independent Basque state in northern Spain and southwestern France.

5. REAL IRA
Northern Ireland
ACTIVITIES
Assassination, bombing, robbery
MEMBERS
100 to 200
An offshoot that formed after the Irish Republican Army declared a cease-fire in 1997, the RIRA has killed dozens in its fight for a united Ireland, free from British

WHERE THEY ARE

This map shows a sample of the many groups that use terror to achieve their goals, attracting an array of nationalists, political ideologues, and religious zealots. Some groups are multifaceted, incorporating politics and social programs along with violence; others are purely brutal. Today one type of group—related to a movement called Islamism—has earned an especially high profile for its drive to impose theocracy on Muslim lands and excise "impure" Western influences. According to the CIA, the deadliest of these groups—al-Qaeda—operates in 68 countries worldwide.

HOT SPOT
INDIA & PAKISTAN

Nuclear rivals India and Pakistan duel over the region of Kashmir, a flash point for conflict between Indian troops and Pakistan-based terrorist groups. Attacks against the pro-U.S. government of Pakistan are also on the rise.

ASIA

MALAYSIA
12 PHILIPPINES
INDONESIA

AUSTRALIA

HOT SPOT
INDONESIA & PHILIPPINES

Recent acts of terrorism have claimed hundreds of lives in Indonesia, prime target for indigenous groups like Jemaah Islamiyah that are now affiliated with al-Qaeda. In the Philippines, Muslim and Marxist rebels are an ongoing threat to stability.

5. ULSTER DEFENCE ASSOCIATION
Northern Ireland
ACTIVITIES
Bombing, narcotics, shootings, intimidation
MEMBERS
Several hundred
Largest of the Protestant paramilitary groups that favor retaining British rule. Though bound by a cease-fire, the group often engages in violence against Catholics.

8. KURDISTAN WORKERS' PARTY (PKK)
Turkey
ACTIVITIES
Assassination, bombing
MEMBERS
More than 5,000
Also known as Kongra-Gel, this separatist group operates from northern Iraq and targets Turkish security forces and civilians in its fight for an independent Kurdish state.

9. ■ CHECHEN SEPARATISTS
Russia
ACTIVITIES
Bombing, kidnapping, murder
MEMBERS
Several thousand
Seeking independence from Russia, rebels have killed Moscow-backed Chechen officials, including Chechnya's president, and killed and kidnapped Russian civilians.

9. ■ ISLAMIC MOVEMENT OF UZBEKISTAN
Central Asia
ACTIVITIES
Bombing, kidnapping
MEMBERS
More than 1,000
This homegrown Islamist coalition seeks to replace Uzbekistan's secular regime and advance the regional goals of al-Qaeda.

10. ■ LASHKAR E-JHANGVI
Pakistan
ACTIVITIES
Massacres, bombing
MEMBERS
Fewer than a hundred
A small but brutally effective Sunni group, LEJ has attacked Shiite mosques and foreigners in a bid to destabilize Pakistan. Also linked to the 2002 murder of journalist Daniel Pearl.

10. ■ JAISH-E-MOHAMMED
Pakistan
ACTIVITIES
Massacres, bombing
MEMBERS
Several hundred
This Islamist group is blamed for the bombing of an Indian state legislature in Kashmir that killed 38. Now split into two factions, this group, like others, fights to make predominantly Muslim Kashmir part of Pakistan.

10. LASHKAR E-TAIBA
Pakistan
ACTIVITIES
Massacres, bombing
MEMBERS
Several hundred
With training camps in Afghanistan, LET specializes in daredevil missions with devastating results, directed mainly against Indian troops and civilians in Kashmir.

11. LIBERATION TIGERS OF TAMIL EELAM
Sri Lanka
ACTIVITIES
Assassination, bombing
MEMBERS
10,000 to 15,000
Favoring suicide attacks, members seek an independent Tamil state in Sri Lanka. A precarious cease-fire is now in place.

12. ■ JEMAAH ISLAMIYAH
Southeast Asia
ACTIVITIES
Bombing
MEMBERS
Unknown
Responsible for a series of deadly bombings across Southeast Asia—including the Bali night-club attacks in 2002—al-Qaeda's local partner seeks an Islamic superstate spanning the region.

7. TAWHID W' AL JIHAD
Iraq
ACTIVITIES
Kidnapping, bombing
MEMBERS
Unknown
Jordanian Abu Musab al Zarqawi leads this loose network of jihadists, most of whom are Iraqi. Their common goal: to expel U.S. forces and create a Sunni Islamic state in Iraq. Many of its fighters are veterans of an older group, Ansar al Islam.

12. ABU SAYYAF
Philippines
ACTIVITIES
Kidnapping, bombing, piracy
MEMBERS
300 to 500
High-profile kidnappings of foreigners for ransom keep this group well financed—though the profit motive may be clouding Abu Sayyaf's founding vision of an Islamic state in the southern Philippines.

12. ■ MORO ISLAMIC LIBERATION FRONT
Philippines
ACTIVITIES
Bombing
MEMBERS
Around 12,000
Though it officially disavows terrorism, this insurgent group is linked to attacks on Philippine cities through its support for Jemaah Islamiyah. Now in peace talks with the government, the MILF aims for ethnic autonomy.

LEGEND

■ **Countries where al-Qaeda cells are known to be operating**
■ **Countries where al-Qaeda cells may be operating**
■ **Group affiliated with al-Qaeda**

crime is unlawful activity undertaken and supported by organized criminal groups operating across national boundaries. Criminal opportunities for transnational groups have come about in part by globalization of the world's economy and by advances in communications, transportation, and other technologies. Today's organized international criminal cartels recognize no boundaries and engage in activities like drug trafficking, money laundering, human trafficking, counterfeiting of branded goods, and weapons smuggling.

- This chapter defines *terrorism* as a violent act or an act dangerous to human life, in violation of the criminal laws of the United States or of any state, that is committed to intimidate or coerce a government, the civilian population, or any segment thereof, in furtherance of political or social objec-

tives. Terrorism, which today is the focus of significant criminal justice activity, brings with it the threat of massive destruction and large numbers of casualties. Domestic and international terrorism are the two main forms of terrorism with which law enforcement organizations concern themselves today. Specific forms of terrorist activity, such as cyberterrorism and attacks on information-management segments of our nation's critical infrastructure, could theoretically shut down or disable important infrastructure services like electricity, food processing, military activity, and even state and federal governments. The vigilance required to prevent terrorism, both domestic and international, consumes a significant number of law enforcement resources and has resulted in new laws that restrict a number of freedoms that many Americans have previously taken for granted.

KEY TERMS

comparative criminologist, 616

cyberterrorism, 634

domestic terrorism, 630

ethnocentric, 617

European Police Office (Europol), 626

extradition, 629

foreign terrorist organization (FTO), 643

globalization, 627

Hudud crime, 619

infrastructure, 635

International Criminal Police Organization (Interpol), 625

international terrorism, 630

Islamic law, 619

narcoterrorism, 636

Tazir crime, 621

terrorism, 629

transnational crime, 628

QUESTIONS FOR REVIEW

1. What are the principles that inform Islamic law? How do these principles contribute to the structure and activities of the criminal justice systems of Muslim nations that follow Islamic law?

2. What important international criminal justice organizations does this chapter discuss? Describe the role of each in fighting international crime.

3. What is globalization, and how does it relate to transnational crime? What relationships might exist between transnational crime and terrorism?

4. What is terrorism? What are the two major types of terrorism discussed in this chapter?

QUESTIONS FOR REFLECTION

1. Why is terrorism a law enforcement concern? How is terrorism a crime? What can the American criminal justice system do to better prepare for future terrorist crimes?

2. What are the causes of terrorism? What efforts is the U.S. government making to prevent and control the spread of domestic terrorism? Of international terrorism?

3. What are the benefits of studying criminal justice systems in other countries? What problems are inherent in such study?

Discuss your answers to these questions and other issues on the CJ Today e-mail discussion list (join the list at cjtoday.com).

WEB QUEST

Use the Cybrary (http://www.cybrary.info) to identify countries other than the United States that make information on their criminal justice system available on the Web. (You might want to begin by clicking on the "International" category.) List the sites that you find, and describe the justice system of each nation.

Then use the Cybrary to identify countries other than the United States that make crime statistics available on the Web. List the statistics sites that you find for each country, and include a summary of the statistics available for each. Submit your findings to your instructor if asked to do so.

To complete this Web Quest online, go to the Web Quest module in Chapter 17 of the *Criminal Justice Today* Companion Website at cjtoday.com.

CHAPTER 18

The Future of Criminal Justice

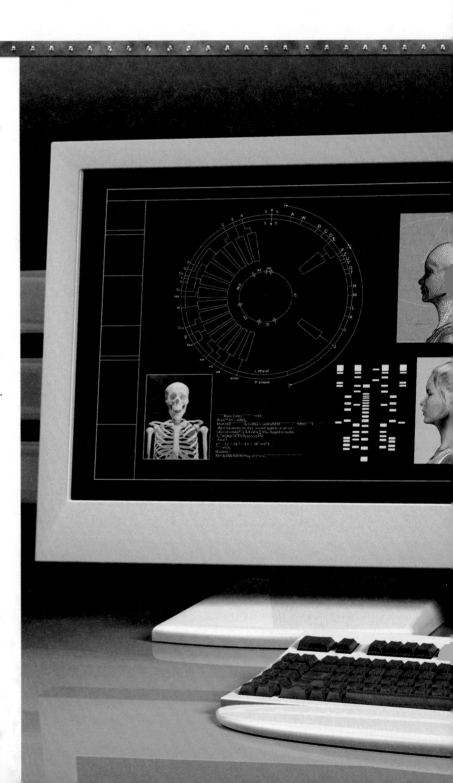

LEARNING OBJECTIVES

After reading this chapter, you should be able to

- Describe the historical relationship between technological advances and criminal activity.

- Explain the important role that technology has played, and will continue to play, in the fight against crime and the quest for justice.

- Provide an overview of criminalistics and explain how evolving technology contributes to advances in that field.

- Identify the threats to individual rights inherent in the ever-increasing use of advanced crime-fighting technologies.

OUTLINE

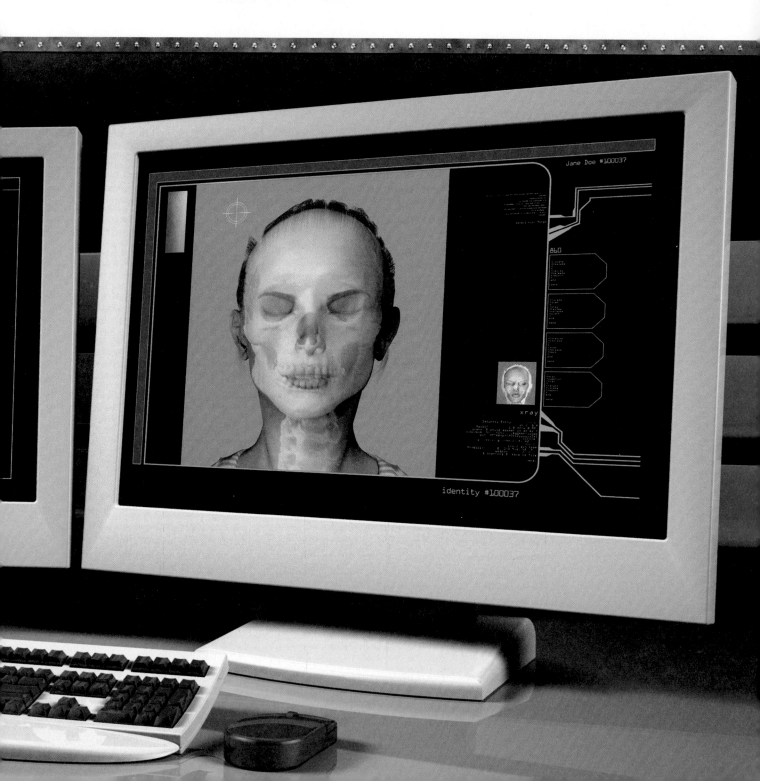

At some point, we can do away with cybercrime laws because most crimes will involve computers in some way, and all crime will be cybercrime.

—*Cybercrime expert Donn Parker[1]*

The rise of a new kind of America requires a new kind of law enforcement system.

—*Alvin Toffler*

He that will not apply new remedies must expect new evils; for time is the greatest innovator.

—*Sir Francis Bacon, 1601*

Introduction

Hear the author discuss this chapter at cjtoday.com

At 9 P.M. on October 24, 2004, Secret Service Assistant Director Brian K. Nagel issued a "go" order for the arrest of suspected members of the ShadowCrew, an international gang of computer hackers adept at pillaging bank accounts, stealing identities, and laundering money over the Internet.[2] The arrests, which netted 28 cybercriminals in eight states and a dozen countries, were the culminating step in Operation Firewall, a month-long international effort involving federal, state, and local law enforcement agencies, along with Britain's National High-Tech Crimes Unit, the Royal Canadian Mounted Police, and the Bulgarian Interior Ministry. Agents in participating countries struck simultaneously in a coordinated effort to prevent gang members from warning one another. By the time the raid ended, investigators had confiscated 1.7 million stolen credit card numbers, 18 million pilfered e-mail addresses and passwords, and identity data for thousands of people in the United States and abroad.

The ring leaders, Andrew Mantovani, 23, a part-time community college student from Arizona, and David Appleyard, 45, a former New Jersey mortgage broker, ran a website called ShadowCrew.com, which served as an international clearinghouse for stolen credit card numbers and identity information. Affidavits filed by the Secret Service said that the ShadowCrew website served the nefarious needs of 4,000 gang members who used it to buy and sell stolen information and merchandise. Dozens of companies were targeted by the cyberoffenders, including companies operated by Bank of America and MasterCard, Inc. The ShadowCrew site, which director Nagel called a "criminal bazaar," also posted tips on how to avoid arrest, including pages of information about how to use stolen credit cards and fake IDs at large retail stores and online shopping services. In 2006, Mantovani was sentenced to 32 months in federal prison for his role in the online scheme. Other ShadowCrew members and participants eventually pleaded guilty to various charges, including conspiracy to defraud.[3] According to Howard Cox, an attorney with the U.S. Department of Justice's Computer Crime and Intellectual Property Section, there are plenty more ShadowCrew-like operations out there. "We're not scratching the surface," Cox said at a recent security conference in San Jose, California. "We're seeing Internet crime without borders."[4]

New technologies can make life easier for those who use them. They can also provide novel criminal opportunities to those looking for ill-gotten gains. The tools of the trade used by cybercriminals like the ShadowCrew members, for example, did not exist a mere generation ago. Because technology is one of the most important instruments of change in the modern world, this chapter focuses on the opportunities and threats that contemporary technology represents to the justice system. Learn more about technology and its role in social change via Library Extra 18–1 at cjtoday.com.

LIBRARY Extra ▪▪▪▪

Technology and Crime

technocrime

A criminal offense that employs advanced or emerging technology in its commission.

Rapid advances in the biological sciences and electronic technologies during the past few decades, including genetic mapping, nanotechnology, computer networking, the Internet, wireless services of all kinds, artificial intelligence (AI), and geopositioning devices, have ushered in a wealth of new criminal opportunities. Crimes that employ advanced or emerging technologies in their commission are referred to as **technocrimes**.

A Muslim traveler arriving in Saudi Arabia for the annual Hajj, or pilgrimage to Mecca, undergoing an iris scan to authenticate his identity. Technology is an important tool in the worldwide fight against identity manipulation and terrorism. Does the use of such technology impinge on individual rights? If so, how?

Nicole Bengiveno/The New York Times

New York State Police Captain and law enforcement visionary Thomas Cowper says that "it is important for police officers and their agencies to understand emerging technologies" for three reasons:[5] (1) to anticipate their use by terrorists and criminals and thereby thwart their use against our nation and citizens, (2) to incorporate their use into police operations when necessary, and (3) to deal effectively with the social changes and cultural impact that inevitably result from technological advances. According to Cowper, "Continued police apathy and ignorance of nanotech, biotech and AI, and the potential changes they will bring to our communities and way of life, will only add to the turmoil, making law enforcement a part of the problem and not part of the solution."[6]

Computers can be broken into. If they're on the Internet, [they] might as well have a welcome mat.

—Kevin Mitnick

Biocrime

In 2005, the World Health Organization raised alarms when it said that some samples of a potentially dangerous influenza virus that had been sent to thousands of laboratories in 18 countries had been lost and could not be located. Bio-kits containing the influenza A (H2N2) virus, which caused the flu pandemic of 1957–1958, were sent to 4,614 laboratories for use in testing the labs' ability to identify flu viruses. Meridian Bioscience Inc. of Cleveland, Ohio, sent the kits on behalf of the College of American Pathologists and three other U.S. organizations that set testing standards for laboratories. Although most of the laboratories were in the United States, some were in Latin America, and a few were in the Arab world—raising fears that Islamic terrorists might use the viral material, against which most people living today have no immunity, to create a pandemic. The H2N2 scare ended on May 2, 2005, when the U.S. Centers for Disease Control and Prevention (CDC) issued a press release saying that the last remaining sample of the virus outside the United States had been found and destroyed at the American University of Beirut in Lebanon.[7] The Lebanese sample had been misplaced by a local delivery service but was discovered in a warehouse at the Beirut airport. Although the incident came to a successful conclusion, it heightened concerns about the spread of highly pathogenic avian influenza viruses and the possible appropriation by criminals of reverse-genetics research on the 1918 pandemic flu virus that killed millions worldwide.

Biological crime, or **biocrime**, is a criminal offense perpetrated through the use of biologically active substances, including chemicals and toxins, disease-causing organisms, altered genetic material, and organic tissues and organs. Biocrimes unlawfully affect the metabolic, biochemical, genetic, physiological, or anatomical status of living organisms. A major change in such status can, of course, produce death.

Biocrimes can be committed with simple poisons, but the biocrimes of special concern today involve technologically sophisticated delivery and dispersal systems and include the use of substances that have been bioengineered to produce the desired effect. Biocrime becomes a high-technology offense when it involves the use of purposefully altered genetic material or advanced bioscientific techniques.

biocrime

A criminal offense perpetrated through the use of biologically active substances, including chemicals and toxins, disease-causing organisms, altered genetic material, and organic tissues and organs. Biocrimes unlawfully affect the metabolic, biochemical, genetic, physiological, or anatomical status of living organisms.

Although many people are aware of the dangers of terrorist-related biocrimes, including biological attacks on agricultural plants and animals (agroterrorism) and on human beings, many other kinds of potential biocrimes lurk on the horizon. They include the illegal harvesting of human organs for medical transplantation, human cloning, and the direct alteration of the DNA of living beings to produce a mixing of traits between species. Stem cell harvesting, another area that faces possible criminalization, is currently the subject of hot debate. As this book goes to press, the situation in the United States with regard to stem cell harvesting is one of funding restrictions, not legal or criminal restrictions. Although the federal government has yet to enact comprehensive legislation curtailing, regulating, or forbidding many of the kinds of activities mentioned here, there are indications that legislative action may soon come.

In 2004, Korean scientists became the first to announce that they had successfully cloned a human embryo and had extracted embryonic stem cells from it.[8] In 2005, those same scientists used the process to make stem cells tailored to match an individual patient, meaning that medical treatments for diseases like diabetes might be possible without fear of cellular rejection. Similarly, in 2005, British scientists working at Newcastle University in England disclosed that they had created a cloned human embryo. Cloning is a cellular reproductive process that does not require the joining of a sperm and an egg; it occurs when the nucleus of an egg is replaced with the nucleus of another cell.

President George W. Bush favored a ban on all research into human cloning in the United States[9] and threatened to veto proposed federal legislation in 2005 that would have provided federal support for cloning research.[10] Similarly, in 2003, the U.S. House of Representatives voted to criminalize all human cloning activities and research.[11] The proposed legislation, known as the Human Cloning Research Prohibition Act, would have made it a crime to transfer the nucleus of an ordinary human cell into an unfertilized human egg whose own nucleus had been removed.[12] It also would have made it a crime to "receive or import a cloned human embryo or any product derived from a cloned human embryo." The scientific technique targeted by the bill, known as *nuclear transfer,* is the process that was used to clone Dolly the sheep in 1996.[13] A similar bill, known as the Human Cloning Prohibition Act of 2005, was introduced by Senator Sam Brownback, a Republican from Kansas.[14] If passed, the bill would have prohibited both reproductive cloning and the use of cloning technology to derive stem cells. In other words, the legislation aimed to thwart not just reproductive cloning, in which a copy of a living organism might be made, but also therapeutic cloning.[15] Therapeutic cloning is a healing technique in which a person's own cells are used to grow a new organ, such as a heart, liver, or lungs, to replace a diseased or damaged organ. Opponents feared that the proposed legislation, which specified punishments of up to a $1 million fine and ten years in prison, would have significantly retarded biomedical progress in the United States, relegating America to a kind of technological backwater in the world's burgeoning biotechnology industry.[16]

Cybercrime

The dark side of new technologies, as far as the justice system is concerned, is the potential they create for committing old crimes in new ways or for committing new crimes never before imagined. In 2003, for example, technologically savvy scam artists replicated the website of the Massachusetts State Lottery Commission.[17] The scammers, believed to be operating out of Nigeria, sent thousands of e-mails and cell phone text messages telling people that they had won $30,000 in the Massachusetts State Lottery. People who received the messages were told to sign on to an official-looking website to claim their prize. The site required that users enter their Social Security and credit card numbers and pay a $100 processing fee before the winnings could be distributed.

A person's online activities occur in a virtual world comprised of bits and bytes. That's why we said in Chapter 2 that "true" computer criminals engage in behavior that goes beyond the theft of hardware. Cybercrime, or computer crime, focuses on the information stored in electronic media, which is why it is sometimes referred to as *information technology crime* or *infocrime.* A decade ago, for example, the activities of computer expert Kevin Mitnick, then known as the Federal Bureau of Investigation's (FBI's) "most wanted **hacker**,"[18] alarmed security experts because of the potential for harm that Mitnick's electronic intrusions represented. The 31-year-old Mitnick broke into an Internet service provider's computer system and stole more than 20,000 credit card numbers. Tsutoma Shimomura, whose home computer Mitnick had also attacked, helped FBI experts track Mitnick through telephone lines and computer networks to the computer in his Raleigh, North Carolina, apartment, where he was arrested. In March 1999, Mitnick pleaded guilty to seven federal counts of computer and wire fraud. He was sentenced to 46 months in

hacker

A computer hobbyist or professional, generally with advanced programming skills. Today, the term *hacker* has taken on a sinister connotation, referring to hobbyists who are bent on illegally accessing the computers of others or who attempt to demonstrate their technological prowess through computerized acts of vandalism.

prison but was released on parole in January 2000. Under the terms of his release, Mitnick was barred from access to computer hardware and software and from any form of wireless communication for a period of three years.[19] In an interview after his release, Mitnick pointed out that "malicious hackers don't need to use stealth computer techniques to break into a network. . . . Often they just trick someone into giving them passwords and other information."[20] According to Mitnick, "People are the weakest link. . . . You can have the best technology, firewalls, intrusion-detection systems, biometric devices . . . and somebody can call an unsuspecting employee . . . [and] they [get] everything."

Neil Barrett, a digital crime expert at International Risk Management, a London-based security consultancy, agrees. "The most likely way for bad guys to break into the system is through **social engineering**. This involves persuading administrators or telephonists to give details of passwords or other things by pretending to be staff, suppliers or trusted individuals—even police officers. They could be even masquerading as a computer repair man to get access to the premises."[21] Social engineering is a devastating security threat, says Barrett, because it targets and exploits a computer network's most vulnerable aspect—people.

TRANSNATIONAL CYBERCRIME

As the story that opened this chapter showed, an especially important characteristic of cybercrime is that it can easily be cross-jurisdictional or transnational. A cybercriminal sitting at a keyboard in Australia, for example, can steal money from a bank in Russia and then transfer the digital cash to an account in Chile. For investigators, the question may be "What laws were broken?" Complicating matters is the fact that Australia and Chile have fragmented cybercrime laws, and Russia[22] has laws that are particularly ineffective.

According to researchers at McConnell International, a consulting firm based in Washington, D.C., of 52 developing countries surveyed in 2000, only the Philippines had effective cybercrime legislation in effect.[23] The Philippines enacted new cybercrime laws in 2000 after the creator of the highly damaging "Love Bug" computer virus, a 23-year-old Filipino student named Onel de Guzman, could not be prosecuted under the country's existing cybercrime laws.[24] De Guzman was finally charged with theft and violation of a law that had been enacted to deter credit card fraud. The country's new cybercrime law could not be applied to him retroactively.

In an effort to enhance similarities in the cybercrime laws of different countries and to provide a model for national law-making bodies concerned with controlling cybercrimes, the 43-nation Council of Europe approved a cybercrime treaty in November 2001.[25] The treaty outlaws specific online activities, including fraud and child pornography, and outlines what law enforcement officials in member nations may and may not do in enforcing cybercrime laws. The goal of the treaty is to standardize both legal understandings of cybercrime and cybercrime laws in member nations. It also allows police officers to detain suspects wanted in other countries for cybercrimes and facilitates the gathering of information on such crimes across national borders. In addition to the council's member states, the treaty was also signed by the United States, Canada, Japan, and South Africa.[26] Visit the Council of Europe's Treaty Office via Web Extra 18–1 at cjtoday.com, and click on "New Treaties" to find the full text of the council's cybercrime treaty. Learn more about cybercrime from the President's Working Group on Unlawful Conduct on the Internet at Library Extra 18–2 at cjtoday.com.

TYPES OF CYBERCRIME

In 2005, a novel form of cybercrime made its appearance in the form of computer ransomware that installs itself on users' computers through an unsecure Internet connection and then encrypts the users' data files.[27] When the machines' owners try to access their own information, they are presented with a message telling them to provide their charge card number to a remote server, which then sends them an unlock code. According to the FBI, this high-tech form of extortion is still rare but on the rise. Particularly targeted are financial institutions and other businesses that stand to lose large amounts of money if their data is corrupted or unretrievable.[28]

Although a generally accepted comprehensive typology of cybercrime has yet to be developed,[29] Peter Grabosky of the Australian Institute of Criminology suggests that most such crimes fall into one of the following broad categories:[30] (1) theft of services, such as telephone or long-distance access; (2) communications in furtherance of criminal conspiracies—for example, the e-mail communications said to have taken place between members of Osama bin Laden's al-Qaeda terrorist network;[31] (3) information piracy and forgery—that is, the stealing of trade secrets or copyrighted information; (4) the dissemination of offensive materials like child pornography, high volumes of unwanted commercial material like bulk e-mail (spam), or extortion threats like those made against financial institutions by hackers claiming the ability to destroy a company's

The future comes one day at a time.

—Dean Acheson

social engineering

A nontechnical kind of cyberintrusion that relies heavily on human interaction and often involves tricking people into breaking normal security procedures.

WEB Extra

LIBRARY Extra

CJ News

Cybercrime Flourishes in Online Hacker Forums

Criminals covet your identity data like never before. What's more, they've perfected more ways to access your bank accounts, grab your Social Security number and manipulate your identity than you can imagine.

Want proof? Just visit any of a dozen or so thriving cybercrime forums, websites that mirror the services of Amazon.com and the efficiencies of eBay. Criminal buyers and sellers convene at these virtual emporiums to wheel and deal in all things related to cyberattacks—and in the fruit of cyberintrusions: pilfered credit and debit card numbers, hijacked bank accounts and stolen personal data.

The cybercrime forums gird a criminal economy that robs U.S. businesses of $67.2 billion a year, according to an FBI projection. Over the past two years, U.S. consumers lost more than $8 billion to viruses, spyware and online fraud schemes, *Consumer Reports* says.

In 2004, a crackdown by the FBI and U.S. Secret Service briefly disrupted growth of the forums. But they soon regrouped, more robust than ever. Today, they are maturing—and consolidating—just like any other fast-rising business sector, security experts and law enforcement officials say. In fact, [in the summer of 2006] a prominent forum leader who calls himself Iceman staged a hostile takeover of four top-tier rivals, creating a megaforum.

Security firms CardCops, of Malibu, Calif., and RSA Security, a division of Hopkinton, Mass.–based EMC, and volunteer watchdog group Shadowserver observed the forced mergers, as well, and compiled dozens of takeover-related screen shots. "It's like he created the Wal-Mart of the underground," says Dan Clements, CEO of CardCops, an identity-theft-prevention company. "Anything you need to commit your crimes, you can get in his forum."

The Secret Service and FBI declined to comment on Iceman or the takeovers. Even so, the activities of this mystery figure illustrate the rising threat that cybercrime's relentless expansion—enabled in large part by the existence of forums—poses for us all.

In the spy vs. spy world of cybercrime, where trust is ephemeral and credibility hard won, CardersMarket's expansion represents the latest advance of a criminal business segment that began to take shape with the formation of the pioneering Shadowcrew forum.

Shadowcrew, which peaked at about 4,000 members in 2004, arose in 2002. It established the standard for cybercrime forums—set up on well-designed, interactive Web pages and run much like a well-organized co-op. Communication took place methodically, via the exchange of messages posted in topic areas. Members could also exchange private messages.

Shadowcrew gave hackers and online scammers a place to congregate, collaborate and build their reputations, says Scott Christie, a former assistant U.S. Attorney in New Jersey who helped prosecute some of its members.

In the October 2004 dragnet, called Operation Firewall, federal agents arrested 22 forum members in several states, including co-founder Andrew Mantovani, 24, aka ThankYouPleaseDie. At the time, Mantovani was a community college student in Scottsdale, Ariz. In August, he began serving a 32-month federal sentence for credit card fraud and identification theft.

Teenagers playing the video game "Counterstrike" at the Cyber Zone in Sacramento, California. Although these boys are just having fun, they represent the demographic group from which most computer hackers come. What kinds of computer mischief should be punished with imprisonment?

Sacramento Bee Photo/Paul Kitagaki Jr./ZUMA Press

Shadowcrew's takedown became the catalyst for the emergence of forums as they operate today. With billions to be made, new forums have reformed like amoebas, splintering into 15 to 20 smaller-scale co-ops. "They learned that it's best to disperse," says Yohai Einav, director of RSA Security's Tel Aviv-based fraud intelligence team.

Forum leaders have become increasingly selective about accepting new members. "Vouching" for new members is now the norm, requiring a member in good standing to extend an invitation to new recruits. Some forums charge an initiation fee; others limit the power to invite new members to the forum leaders.

Veteran vendors and buyers typically do business in multiple forums simultaneously, in case any particular forum shuts down.

"If criminals get caught one way, they modify their behavior," says Kevin O'Dowd, an assistant U.S. Attorney in New Jersey who prosecuted the Shadowcrew case.

Some forums have become known for their specialties, such as offering free research tools to do things such as confirming the validity of a stolen credit card number or learning about security weaknesses at specific banks. A few offer escrow services, handling the details of complex deals for a fee.

The better-run forums invest in tech-security measures that have become the norm in the corporate world, such as use of encrypted Web pages. All forums run aggressive campaigns to identify and sweep out rippers—the con artists who gain membership and instigate deals, only to renege on their part of the bargain.

From this post-Shadowcrew milieu, Iceman has emerged as a forum leader to watch.

RSA Security has tracked Iceman's postings on CardersMarket since October 2005; CardCops has compiled an archive of hundreds of postings on several forums by someone using the nickname Iceman since January 2006.

In the boastful world of cybercrime, nicknames, or nics, are sacrosanct. It's not unusual for a hacker or cyberthief to go by two

CJ News (continued)

or three different nics, but unthinkable for two or three people to knowingly share the same nic, says RSA Security's Einav. "I believe we're talking about one guy and not a group hiding behind his name," he says.

Clearly enterprising and given to posting rambling messages explaining his strategic thinking, Iceman grew CardersMarket's membership to 1,500. On Aug. 16, [2006,] he hacked into four rival forums' databases, electronically extracted their combined 4,500 members, and in one stroke quadrupled CardersMarket's membership to 6,000, according to security experts who monitored the takeovers.

The four hijacked forums—DarkMarket, TalkCash, Scandinavian-Carding and TheVouched—became inaccessible to their respective members. Shortly thereafter, all of the historical postings from each of those forums turned up integrated into the CardersMarket website.

To make that happen, Iceman had to gain access to each forum's underlying database, tech-security experts say. Iceman boasted in online postings that he took advantage of security flaws lazily left unpatched. CardCops' Clements says he probably cracked weak database passwords. "Somehow he got through to those servers to grab the historical postings and move them to CardersMarket," he says.

Iceman lost no time touting his business rationale and hyping the benefits. In a posting on CardersMarket shortly after completing the takeovers he wrote: "basically, (sic) this was long overdue . . . why (sic) have five different forums each with the same content, splitting users and vendors, and a mish mash of poor security and sometimes poor administration?"

He dispatched an upbeat e-mail to new members heralding CardersMarket's superior security safeguards. The linchpin: a recent move of the forum's host computer server to Iran, putting it far beyond the reach of U.S. authorities. He described Iran as "possibly the most politically distant country to the united states (sic) in the world today."

At *USA Today's* request, CardCops traced CardersMarket's point of origin and confirmed that it is registered to a computer server in Iran.

If Iceman succeeds in establishing CardersMarket as the Wal-Mart of forums, its routing through an Iranian server will make an already complex law enforcement challenge that much more difficult, security experts say.

"Chasing these carding fraudsters is like chasing terrorists in Afghanistan," says RSA Security's Einav. "You know they are somewhere out there, but finding their caves, their underground bunkers, is almost impossible."

The U.S. Secret Service declined to answer questions about Iceman and CardersMarket. It would not acknowledge whether they are under investigation as part of Operation Rolling Stone, the most intensive federal probe of cybercrime since Operation Firewall. This year, 35 suspects have been arrested. No names were initially released, but a few have surfaced after indictments were unsealed.

Suspects include Binyamin Schwartz, 28, of Oak Park, Mich., indicted in July in Nashville for allegedly trafficking more than 100,000 Social Security numbers, and Paulius Kalpokas, 23, of Lithuania, whose extradition to Nashville on charges of trafficking stolen credit card data has been requested.

Schwartz "got caught up in something on the Internet but did not profit from it," says Sanford Schulman, Schwartz's attorney. "He in-

quired about acquiring information online without criminal intent, nor was he involved in a sophisticated enterprise."

Secret Service spokesman Thomas Mazur says Operation Rolling Stone is designed to "disrupt and dismantle any of these carding forums," but he declined to say which forums or how many are being investigated.

Security experts worry that CardersMarket's emergence as a model for setting up hypersafe forums could translate into a spike of activity by the best and brightest cybercrooks.

"It's called bulletproofing," says CardCops' Clements. "Guys will now migrate to CardersMarket because they really are untouchable there."

Iceman's masterstroke rattled his rivals and raised suspicions among his peers.

In the tech industry, companies routinely spread what they call FUD—fear, uncertainty and doubt—about a competitor's business model. Shortly after Iceman swept up TalkCash's 2,600 members onto CardersMarket's website, TalkCash's leader, nicknamed Unknown Killer, e-mailed a shrill warning to TalkCash members: "I've talked to a number of guys and all say that they didn't merge a (expletive) with that site . . . so please beware as they can be feds."

Speculation abounds on the Internet that the FBI helped install Iceman as head of a dominant forum set up to lure kingpin cybercrooks into capture.

In busting up Shadowcrew, law enforcement had used a high-ranking member of Shadowcrew as an inside informant, beginning in August 2003, according to court records. Security experts say it's possible, though unlikely, Iceman could be an informant. While not commenting directly about Iceman, FBI spokesman Paul Bresson says, "The FBI is not in the business of exposing Americans to fraud."

Instead of being admired by his peers, Iceman found himself scrambling to deal with an intensifying backlash. A forum member, nicknamed Silo, posted this public comment on CardersMarket: "How Can we TRUST you and this boards admin? You breached our community's security. Stole the Databases of other forums . . . you've breached what little trust exist's (sic) in the community."

Ten days after the forced mergers, the deposed leaders of DarkMarket and ScandinavianCarding managed to reconstitute forums under those names. And CardersMarket appeared to be under assault, with some of the features on its website functioning sporadically, according to RSA Security's Einav.

Security experts expect the infighting to run its course. They say Iceman's attack prompted forum leaders to beef up database passwords and patch other security holes, making both hostile takeovers and law enforcement investigations more difficult. Most experts expect the activity level of the forums to rise, because many consumers and businesses are uninformed or apathetic.

Consumers continue to exhibit lax attitudes, even as Internet intrusions and scams rise in frequency and sophistication. John Thompson, CEO of anti-virus giant Symantec, contends Internet users must adopt the same "sixth sense about security" they use when they get in their cars or leave home.

Meanwhile, the commercial sector has been slow to ask consumers to take other steps, such as using a smartcard or fingerprint reader—along with typing a log-on and password—to prove they are who they say online.

(continued)

CJ News (continued)

Thomas Harkins spent two decades as operations director for MasterCard International's fraud division, gaining an insider's view of cybercrime's breakneck rise. Now COO of security firm Edentify, based in Bethlehem, Pa., Harkins says identity theft is poised to increase by a factor of 20 over the next two years.

"There's so many stolen identities in criminals' hands that (identity theft) could easily rise 20 times," Harkins says. "The criminals are still trying to figure out what to do with all the data."

Meanwhile, stories such as Kevin Munro's will continue to pile up. In late August [2006], the name, Social Security number and other data of the 51-year-old Warsaw, N.Y., building inspector turned up for sale on a forum monitored by CardCops. Munro re-

calls changing checking accounts after a thief tried to cash several bad checks in 2002. Since then, his personal data have persisted in circulation.

Cybercrooks have used it online to order magazines, purchase three Dell computers and attempt to take out a real estate loan. Recently, MasterCard notified Munro that an account he's had for 20 years and uses infrequently was being canceled.

"I work for a living," Munro says. "I do everything on the up-and-up, and some lowlife comes by and takes it away."

For the latest in crime and justice news, visit the Talk Justice news feed at http://www.crimenews.info.

Source: Byron Acohido and Jon Swartz, "Cybercrime Flourishes in Online Hacker Forums," USA TODAY, October 12, 2006. Reprinted with permission.

electronic records; (5) electronic money laundering and tax evasion (through electronic funds transfers that conceal the origin of financial proceeds); (6) electronic vandalism and terrorism, including computer viruses, worms, Trojan horses, and cyberterrorism (see Chapter 17); (7) telemarketing fraud (including investment frauds and illegitimate electronic auctions); (8) illegal interception of telecommunications—that is, illegal eavesdropping; and (9) electronic funds–transfer fraud (specifically, the illegal interception and diversion of legitimate transactions).

The 2006 Computer Crime and Security Survey, conducted annually by the Computer Security Institute (CSI) and the FBI, found that 52% of the large businesses, medical institutions, universities, and government agencies participating in the survey reported detecting security-related breaches of their computer networks in 2006.[32] The survey also found that only about half of all reported breaches originated outside of the organization. Other researchers have determined that some of the most serious corporate computer security threats come from employees, including 70% of all incidents involving unauthorized access to information systems and 95% of all network intrusions that result in significant financial loss.[33] The CSI/FBI report found that the highest average annual computer security expenditure per employee ($608) in 2006 was reported by organizations in the transportation sector. The federal government reported spending $261 annually per federal employee to secure its computers, and the telecommunications industry reported annual computer security expenditures averaging $209 per employee.[34] Small companies spent the most on computer security, according to the survey, and those with annual revenue of under $10 million reported spending over $1,300 per employee on information security, including costs for information security awareness training.[35]

In 2004, the Bureau of Justice Statistics (BJS) released initial results from its 2001 Computer Security Survey (CSS), which had been conducted in collaboration with the U.S. Census Bureau.[36] The 2004 report summarized findings from a pilot survey of 500 companies nationwide. Nearly three-fourths of businesses surveyed reported detecting at least one computer security incident during the previous 12-month period. Computer viruses were the most common type of incident reported (65%), followed by denial-of-service attacks (25%) and vandalism or sabotage of computer equipment or computer networks (19%). Other crimes, such as fraud, theft of proprietary information, and embezzlement, were also reported. Not surprisingly, the largest companies experienced the greatest number of incidents. When fully implemented, the CSS will provide the first official national statistics on the extent and consequences of cybercrime against the nation's 5.3 million businesses. You may access the initial BJS report in its entirety at Library Extra 18–3 at cjtoday.com. The Computer Crime and Security Survey can be found online at Library Extra 18–4.

Computer Viruses, Worms, and Trojan Horses Computer viruses are a special concern of computer users everywhere. Computer viruses were first brought to public attention in 1988, when the Pakistani virus (or Pakistani brain virus) became widespread in personal and office comput-

LIBRARY
Extra
■■■■

computer virus

A computer program designed to secretly invade systems and either modify the way in which they operate or alter the information they store. Viruses are destructive software programs that may effectively vandalize computers of all types and sizes.

Tennis superstar Anna Kournikova. Kournikova served as inspiration for Jan de Wit, 20, of Sneek, Netherlands, creator of the Kournikova computer virus. In 2001, Wit was convicted of violating Holland's law against spreading data into a computer network with the intention of causing damage. He was sentenced to 150 hours of community service. What kinds of problems can computer viruses cause? Should Wit have gone to prison?

AP Wide World Photos

ers across the United States.[37] The Pakistani virus was created by Amjad Farooq Alvi and his brother, Basit Farooq Alvi, two cut-rate computer software dealers in Lahore, Pakistan. The Alvi brothers made copies of costly software products and sold them at low prices, mostly to Western shoppers looking for a bargain. Motivated by convoluted logic, the brothers hid a virus on each disk they sold to punish buyers for seeking to evade copyright laws.

A more serious virus incident later that year affected sensitive machines in the National Aeronautics and Space Administration (NASA) nuclear weapons labs, federal research centers, and universities across the United States.[38] The virus did not destroy data. Instead, it made copies of itself and multiplied so rapidly that it clogged and effectively shut down computers within hours after invading them. Robert Morris, creator of the virus, was sentenced in 1990 to 400 hours of community service, three years' probation, and a fine of $10,000.[39] Since then, many other virus attacks have made headlines, including the infamous Michelangelo virus in 1992; the intentional distribution of infected software on an AIDS-related research CD-ROM distributed about the same time; the Kournikova virus in 2000; and the Sircam, Nimda, W32, NastyBrew, Berbew, Mydoom, and Code Red worms—all of which made their appearance or were substantially modified by their creators between 2001 and 2005.

Technically speaking, most of today's malicious software falls under the category of worms or Trojan horses—called **malware** by technophiles. Malware (also called *crimeware*) has become increasingly sophisticated. Although early viruses were relatively easy to detect with hardware or software scanning devices that looked for virus "signatures," new malicious software using stealth and polymorphic computer codes changes form with each new "infection" and is much more difficult to locate and remove. Moreover, while older viruses infected only executable programs, or those that could be run, newer malware (such as the Word for Windows Macro virus, also called the Concept virus) attaches itself to word-processing documents and to computer codes that are routinely distributed via the World Wide Web (including Java and Active-X components used by Web browsers). In 1998, the world's first HTML virus was discovered. The virus, named HTML.Internal, infects computers whose users are merely viewing Web pages.[40] Later that year, the first JAVA-based malware, named Strange Brew, made its appearance,[41] and in 2004 malware capable of infecting digital images using the Joint Photographic Experts Group (JPEG format) was discovered.[42] Evolving forms of malware are even able to infect cellular phones (Figure 18–1) and other wireless-enabled handheld devices.

malware

Malicious computer programs like viruses, worms, and Trojan horses.

Phishing   One form of cybercrime that relies primarily on social engineering to succeed is *phishing* (pronounced "fishing"). Phishing is a relatively new form of high-technology fraud that uses official-looking e-mail messages to elicit responses from victims, directing them to phony websites. Microsoft Corporation says that phishing is "the fastest-growing form of online fraud in the world today."[43] Phishing e-mails typically instruct recipients to validate or update account information before their accounts are canceled. Phishing schemes, which have targeted most major

Our "can-do" spirit as Americans generates tremendous fascination with technology and what it can do for us [as a society]. But at the same time we have an innate and healthy skepticism, perhaps even a fear, of what technology can do to us as individuals.

—Mark H. Gitenstein, Executive Director, Foundation for Change

FIGURE 18–1

The great cell phone robbery.

Source: blanddesigns.co.uk. Originally published in *Wired Magazine,* December 2004, p. 94. Reprinted with permission.

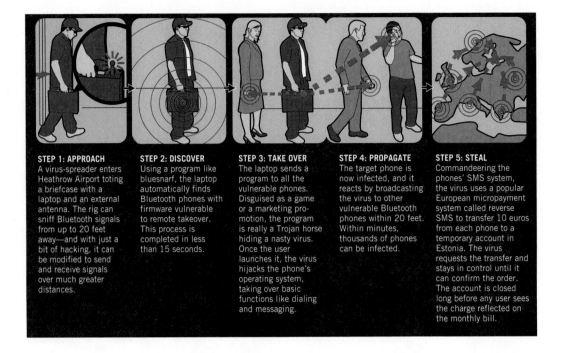

STEP 1: APPROACH
A virus-spreader enters Heathrow Airport toting a briefcase with a laptop and an external antenna. The rig can sniff Bluetooth signals from up to 20 feet away—and with just a bit of hacking, it can be modified to send and receive signals over much greater distances.

STEP 2: DISCOVER
Using a program like bluesnarf, the laptop automatically finds Bluetooth phones with firmware vulnerable to remote takeover. This process is completed in less than 15 seconds.

STEP 3: TAKE OVER
The laptop sends a program to all the vulnerable phones. Disguised as a game or a marketing promotion, the program is really a Trojan horse hiding a nasty virus. Once the user launches it, the virus hijacks the phone's operating system, taking over basic functions like dialing and messaging.

STEP 4: PROPAGATE
The target phone is now infected, and it reacts by broadcasting the virus to other vulnerable Bluetooth phones within 20 feet. Within minutes, thousands of phones can be infected.

STEP 5: STEAL
Commandeering the phones' SMS system, the virus uses a popular European micropayment system called reverse SMS to transfer 10 euros from each phone to a temporary account in Estonia. The virus requests the transfer and stays in control until it can confirm the order. The account is closed long before any user sees the charge reflected on the monthly bill.

banks, the Federal Deposit Insurance Corporation, IBM, eBay, PayPal, and some major health-care providers, are designed to steal valuable information like credit card numbers, Social Security numbers, user IDs, and passwords. In 2004, Gartner Inc., a leading provider of research and analysis on the global information technology industry, released a report estimating that some 57 million adult Americans received phishing e-mails during the spring of 2004 and that 11 million recipients clicked on the link contained in the messages.[44] Gartner estimated that 1.78 million recipients actually provided personal information to the thieves behind the phishing schemes.

software piracy

The unauthorized duplication of software or the illegal transfer of data from one storage medium to another. Software piracy is one of the most prevalent cybercrimes in the world.

Software Piracy   Another form of cybercrime, the unauthorized copying of software programs, also called **software piracy**, appears to be rampant. According to the Software and Information Industry Association (SIIA), global losses from software piracy total nearly $12.2 billion annually.[45] The SIIA says that 38% of all software in use in the world today has been copied illegally. Some countries have especially high rates of illegal use. Of all the computer software in use in Vietnam, for example, SIIA estimates that 97% has been illegally copied, while 95% of the software used in China and 92% of the software used in Russia are thought to be pirated—resulting in a substantial loss in manufacturers' revenue.

Software pirates seem to be especially adept at evading today's copy-protection schemes, including those that involve software "keys" and Internet authentication. Similar to software piracy, peer-to-peer Internet file-sharing services (which directly connect users' computers with one another via the Internet) have been criticized for allowing users to download copyright-protected e-music and digital video files free of charge. Lawsuits involving the music-sharing service Napster resulted in the site's near closure, and similar websites, such as KaZaA, Morpheus, and Grokster, are the targets of ongoing music industry lawsuits. In 2003, however, a U.S. district court in New York held that many music-swapping services and their operators could not be held accountable for the actions of their users, although individual users who download copyrighted materials *can* be held liable for copyright infringements.[46] That same year, a federal judge in Los Angeles ruled that peer-to-peer network software providers Grokster and StreamCast Networks could not be held liable for the copyright infringements of their users.[47] In 2004, the 9th U.S. Circuit Court of Appeals upheld that ruling,[48] but in 2005, in the landmark case of *MGM* v. *Grokster,*[49] the U.S. Supreme Court found that online file-sharing services may be held liable for copyright infringement if they promote their services explicitly as a way for users to download copyrighted music and other content. The *Grokster* decision contrasts with the 1984 case of *Sony Corporation of America* v. *Universal City Studios, Inc.,* in which the Court held that a distributor/operator of a copying tool cannot be held liable for users' copyright infringements so long as the tool in question is capable of substantial noninfringing uses.[50]

spam

Unsolicited commercial bulk e-mail (UCBE), whose primary purpose is the advertisement or promotion of a commercial product or service.

Spam   A few years ago, federal legislators acted to criminalize the sending of unsolicited commercial e-mail, or **spam**. The federal CAN-SPAM Act (Controlling the Assault of Non-Solicited Pornography and Marketing), which took effect on January 1, 2004, regulates the sending of "commercial electronic mail messages."[51] The law, which applies equally to mass mailings and to individual e-mail messages, defines commercial electronic mail messages as electronic mail whose *primary purpose* is the "commercial advertisement or promotion of a commercial product or service." The CAN-SPAM law requires that a commercial e-mail message include the following three features: (1) a clear and conspicuous identification that the message is an advertisement or solicitation, (2) an opt-out feature, allowing recipients to opt out of future mailings, and (3) a valid physical address identifying the sender.

Some experts estimate that 80% of all e-mail today is spam,[52] and a number of states have enacted their own antispam laws. Virginia's 2003 antispam statute,[53] for example, imposes criminal penalties of from one to five years for anyone convicted of falsifying electronic mail transmission information or other routing information during the sending of unsolicited commercial bulk e-mail (UCBE). The law applies to anyone sending more than 10,000 UCBEs in a 24-hour period and to anyone who generates more than $1,000 in revenue from a UCBE transmission. The law also applies to anyone who uses fraudulent practices to send bulk e-mail to or from Virginia, a state that is home to a number of large Internet service providers, including America Online. In 2005, in the nation's first felony prosecution of a spammer, Jeremy Jaynes, 30, one of the world's most active spammers, received a nine-year prison sentence under Virginia's law after he was convicted of using false Internet addresses and aliases to send mass e-mailings to America Online subscribers. Prosecutors were able to prove that Jaynes, a Raleigh, North Carolina, resident, earned as much as $750,000 a month by sending as many as 10 million illegal messages a day using computers operating in Virginia.[54] Learn more about cybercrime and efforts to combat it at **Web Extra 18–2** at cjtoday.com.

WEB
Extra
▪▪▪▪

Terrorism and Technology

The technological sophistication of state-sponsored terrorist organizations is rapidly increasing. Handguns and even larger weapons are now being manufactured out of plastic polymers and ceramics. Capable of firing Teflon-coated armor-piercing hardened ceramic bullets, such weapons are extremely powerful and impossible to uncover with metal detectors. Evidence points to the black market availability of other sinister items, including liquid metal embrittlement (LME), a chemical that slowly weakens any metal it contacts. LME could easily be applied with a felt-tipped pen to fuselage components in domestic aircraft, causing delayed structural failure.[55] Backpack-type electromagnetic pulse generators may soon be available to terrorists. Such devices could be carried into major cities, set up next to important computer installations, and activated to wipe out billions of items of financial, military, or other information now stored on magnetic media. International terrorists, along with the general public, have easy access to maps and other information that could be used to cripple the nation. The approximately 500 extremely high-voltage (EHV) transformers on which the nation's electric grid depends, for example, are largely undefended and until recently were specified with extreme accuracy on easily available Web-based power network maps.

It is now clear that at least some terrorist organizations are seeking to obtain **weapons of mass destruction (WMDs)**, involving possible chemical, biological, radiological, and nuclear threats. A Central Intelligence Agency (CIA) report recently made public warned that al-Qaeda's "end goal" is to use WMDs. The CIA noted that the group had "openly expressed its desire to produce nuclear weapons" and that sketches and documents recovered from an al-Qaeda facility in Afghanistan contained plans for a crude nuclear device.[56]

The collapse of the Soviet Union in the late 1980s led to very loose internal control over nuclear weapons and weapons-grade fissionable materials held in the former Soviet republics. Evidence of this continues to surface. In 2003, for example, a cab driver in the Eastern European nation of Georgia was arrested while transporting containers of cesium-137 and strontium-90, materials that could be used to make a "dirty" bomb (a radiological dispersal device, or RDD[57]) that would use conventional explosives to spread nuclear contamination over a wide area.[58] A month later, officials arrested a traveler in Bangkok, Thailand, who had a canister of cesium-137 in his possession. Although the Thai traveler told police that he had acquired the cesium in Laos, scientists were able to determine that it had originated in Russia.

A study by Harvard University researchers found that the United States and other countries are moving too slowly in efforts to help Russia and other former Soviet-bloc nations destroy poorly protected nuclear material and warheads left over from the cold war.[59] The study also warned that most civilian nuclear reactors in Eastern Europe are "dangerously insecure." Experts say the amount of plutonium needed to make one bomb can be smuggled out of a supposedly secure area in a briefcase or even in the pocket of an overcoat.

weapon of mass destruction (WMD)

A chemical, biological, or nuclear weapon that has the potential to cause mass casualties.

CJ News

Growing Unarmed al-Qaeda Battalion Using the Internet

On the fifth anniversary of the Sept. 11 attacks, Abu Omar received the call to jihad. Literally.

"There's a present for you," a voice on the other end of the phone said that morning, he recalled. It was a common code whenever his friends and colleagues wanted to share a new broadcast or communiqué from al-Qaeda over the Internet, he said.

Abu Omar, speaking on the condition that only his nickname be used, said he soon went to one of the Internet cafes he frequents in Amman and began distributing the latest video by al-Qaeda, alerting friends and occasionally adding commentary.

"We are the energy behind the path to jihad," Abu Omar said proudly. "Just like the jihadis reached their target on Sept. 11, we will reach ours through the Internet."

Abu Omar, 28, is part of an increasingly sophisticated network of contributors and discussion leaders helping to wage al-Qaeda's battle for Muslim hearts and minds. A self-described Qaeda sympathizer who defends the Sept. 11 attacks and continues to find inspiration in Osama bin Laden's call for jihad, Abu Omar is part of a growing army of young men who may not seek to take violent action, but who help spread jihadist philosophy, shape its message and hope to inspire others to their cause.

Though he does not appear to be directly connected to al-Qaeda, Abu Omar does seem to be on a direct e-mail list for groups sympathetic to al-Qaeda, making him a link in a chain that spreads the organization's propaganda using code and special software to circumvent official scrutiny of their Internet activity.

As al-Qaeda gradually transforms itself from a terrorist organization carrying out its own attacks into an ideological umbrella that encourages local movements to take action, its increased reliance on various forms of media have made Web-savvy sympathizers like Abu Omar ever more important.

For example, this past Sept. 11, [2006,] Abu Omar said, a link sent to a jihadist e-mail list took him to a general interest Islamic Web site, which led him to a password-protected Web site, then onto yet another site containing the latest release from al-Qaeda: a lecture by its No. 2 man, Ayman al-Zawahri, threatening attacks on Israel and the Persian Gulf. Abu Omar said he then passed the video to friends and confidants, acting as a local distributor to other sympathizers.

In recent years, al-Qaeda has formed a special media production division called Al Sahab to produce videos about leaders like Mr. bin Laden and Mr. Zawahri, terrorism experts say. The group largely once relied on Arab television channels like Al Jazeera to broadcast its videos and taped messages.

Al Sahab, whose name means the cloud, has continued to draw on a video library featuring everything from taped suicide messages by the Sept. 11 hijackers to images of gun battles and bombings spearheaded by al-Qaeda and others, said Marwan Shehadeh, an expert on Islamist movements with the Vision Research Institute in Amman who has close ties to jihadists in Jordan and Syria.

But this year Al Sahab has released many more recordings than in previous years, said Chris Heffelfinger, a specialist in jihadi ideol-

Islamist expert Marwan Shehadeh of the Vision Research Institute in Amman. He believes that the Jihadists are using American technology to their advantage. How can we use technology to counter the efforts of the Jihadists?

Bryan Denton/The New York Times

ogy at the Combating Terrorism Center at West Point, in what many analysts see as a new offensive focusing on the Muslim mainstream. Jihadi Web sites, meanwhile, have continued sprouting on the Internet, serving as a conduit for al-Qaeda's propaganda.

Mr. Shehadeh describes Al Sahab as an informal group with video camcorders and laptops. Some news reports have described it as an organization with a mobile production unit that navigates the Pakistani provinces. "The jihadis have successfully used American technology to show the U.S. as a loser," Mr. Shehadeh said. "This is an open-ended war, and they use media as part of their jihad against Western and Arab regimes."

Just days before the fifth anniversary of the Sept. 11 attacks, Al Sahab released a barrage of videos, including images of Mr. bin Laden seated with some of the Sept. 11 suicide bombers; a documentary that some have described as a "making of Sept. 11" feature, with testaments by two of the bombers; and the lecture by Mr. Zawahri that Abu Omar said he received that morning.

What is most striking about the messages is their tone, terrorism analysts say. In the past, the group's leaders were generally depicted as soldiers in battle, often filmed outdoors with weapons in the background. But the more recent communiqués show al-Qaeda's leaders in the comfort of a living room or office, set against bookshelves with religious texts. The group has also taken to quoting Western authors and famous speeches, in what seems to be an effort to reach those with Western sensibilities.

"It's a clear message: when there's a gun in the background, they're saying, 'I'm a fighter like you'; when there are books in the background, it means, 'I am a scholar and deserve authority,'" said Fares bin Hizam, a journalist who reports on militant groups for the Arab satellite news channel Al Arabiya. "It is a message that resonates well with an impressionable young man who is 17 or 18."

CJ News (continued)

One result, terrorism analysts say, is a militant group in transition, seeking to push ideology over direct action, franchising its name and principles to smaller groups acting more independently.

"al-Qaeda has been turning itself from an active organization into a propaganda organization," said Mr. Heffelfinger. "They now appear to be focused on putting out disinformation and projecting the strength of the mujahedeen [holy warriors]. They're no longer the group that is organizing the mujahedeen. Instead, they are giving guidance to all the movements."

Men like Abu Omar have become integral to that transformation. Mr. Shehadeh, who introduced Abu Omar to this reporter, says he has known Abu Omar ever since he was a teenager and has observed his gradual embrace of jihadist ideology. He says he has seen Abu Omar's contributions on numerous chat boards and notes that while Abu Omar is probably not a Qaeda member, he regularly relays news and spreads the group's message to friends and colleagues.

In Amman's more conservative neighborhoods, Abu Omar and several analysts said, one or two jihadists tend to be the organizers, distributing messages and content to volunteers, and controlling membership in jihadist e-mail lists.

"We are typically observers, but when we see something on the Net, our job is to share it," Abu Omar said. He no longer trusts news reports on television, he said. He even cast doubt on Al Jazeera, which typically broadcasts al-Qaeda's videos but is, he said, still beholden to Arab governments. "We become like journalists ourselves."

Abu Omar, who owns a computer store in one of Amman's refugee camps, said he became involved in jihadi movements about six years ago, driven in part by his anger over the death of his father,

who he said was a fighter with the Palestinian faction Fatah when Israel invaded Lebanon in 1982. "On the Net, you can see all the pictures of Palestine and the Muslim world being attacked, and then you see the planes crashing into one of the towers and you think, 'I can understand it,'" he said.

He goes to an Internet cafe several times a week. In recent years, Jordan's Internet cafes have begun taking increased security measures, like registering users' identification cards, he said, but jihadists in Amman alternate among a network of sympathetic cafe owners who allow them to surf anonymously.

He never uses his own computer to search for jihadi content, and he limits his time online to about 30 minutes—not long enough for the authorities to locate him, he figures.

In 2005, Jordanian authorities arrested an 18-year-old man, Murad al-Assaydeh, accusing him of using the Internet to threaten attacks on intelligence officials. Abu Omar said several of his friends and comrades had been arrested by the General Information Department in Jordan in connection with Mr. Assaydeh's case and in subsequent dragnets. Abu Omar said he was once called in for questioning but was released the same day.

He now changes his e-mail address frequently, he said, and he typically carries software that can delete details of his actions from a computer. "In the beginning, I thought maybe I would go for jihad in Iraq, but it was very difficult to get there," he said. "Now I realize it's better to work on the Net and get the message out."

For the latest in crime and justice news, visit the Talk Justice news feed at http://www.crimenews.info.

Source: Hassan M. Fattah, "Growing Unarmed Battalion in Qaeda Army Is Using Internet to Get the Message Out," *New York Times,* September 30, 2006.

Biological weapons were banned by the 1975 international Biological Weapons Convention,[60] but biological terrorism (or bioterrorism), which seeks to disperse destructive or disease-producing biologically active agents among civilian or military populations, is of considerable concern today. **Bioterrorism**, one form of biocrime, is defined by the Centers for Disease Control and Prevention as the "intentional or threatened use of viruses, bacteria, fungi, or toxins from living organisms to produce death or disease in humans, animals, or plants."[61] The infamous anthrax letters mailed to at least four people in the United States in 2001 provide an example of a bioterrorism incident intended to create widespread fear among Americans. Five people, including mail handlers, died, and 23 others were infected.[62] Other possible bioterror agents include botulism toxin, brucellosis, cholera, glanders, plague, ricin, smallpox, tularemia Q fever, and a number of viral agents capable of producing diseases such as viral hemorrhagic fever and severe acute respiratory syndrome (SARS). As mentioned earlier, experts fear that technologically savvy terrorists could create their own novel bioweapons through bioengineering, a process that uses snippets of made-to-order DNA, the molecular code on which life is based.[63] Learn more about biological agents at the CDC website via Web Extra 18–3, and visit the Center for the Study of Bioterrorism via Web Extra 18–4 at cjtoday.com. Read the CDC's overview of bioterrorism at Library Extra 18–5 at cjtoday.com.

bioterrorism

The intentional or threatened use of viruses, bacteria, fungi, or toxins from living organisms to produce death or disease in humans, animals, or plants.[iii]

WEB
Extra
■ ■ ■ ■

LIBRARY
Extra
■ ■ ■ ■

Technology and Crime Control

The crucial component of effective policing in a rapidly changing world is the ability to think creatively about emerging technologies and how they can be used successfully within the constitutional limits of a free society.

—Thomas J. Cowper, New York State Police[iv]

Technology, while it has increased criminal opportunity, has also been a boon to police investigators and other justice system personnel. We will now look at technology's impact on the arsenal of crime-fighting and administrative techniques available to criminal justice practitioners.

Law enforcement access to high-technology investigative tools has produced enormous amounts of information on crimes and suspects, and the use of innovative investigative tools like DNA fingerprinting, keystroke captures, laser and night-vision technologies, digital imaging, and thermography are beginning to shape many of the practical aspects of the twenty-first-century criminal justice system (Table 18–1). Today, some laptop computers and vehicles are programmed to contact police when they are stolen and provide satellite-based tracking information so authorities can determine their whereabouts. A number of rental car companies, for example, now have cars equipped with systems that can receive instructions from a central location. These instructions can be used to prevent the car from starting and thus being stolen. The system can also track the car as it moves. Likewise, some police departments are using high-technology "bait cars" to catch auto thieves.[64] Bait cars can signal when stolen, send digitized images of perpetrators to investigators, radio their position to officers, be remotely immobilized, and lock their doors on command, trapping thieves inside.

Another crime-fighting technology making headway in the identification of stolen vehicles is automatic plate recognition (APR) technology. In December 2004, for example, the Ohio State Highway Patrol completed a four-month evaluation of an APR system using infrared cameras mounted at strategic points along the state's highways and connected to computers to alert troopers to the possible presence of stolen vehicles or wanted persons. During the four-month test period, the system led to the apprehension of 23 criminal suspects and the recovery of 24 stolen vehicles.[65]

Car thieves, however, have made some technological advances of their own, including the "laundering" of vehicle identification numbers (VINs), which allows stolen cars to be sold as legitimate vehicles. In mid-2005, for example, the National Insurance Crime Bureau reported that about 600 luxury cars and SUVs had been seized during the previous 12 months whose VINs had been removed and replaced with numbers copied from nonstolen vehicles.[66] Stolen cars with "cloned" VINs are usually not discovered until an insurance claim is filed and investiga-

---

TABLE 18–1   Special Technologies Used by Local Police Departments, by Size of Population Served, 2003

Percentage of Agencies Using

Population Served	Night Vision/Electro-Optic			Vehicle Stopping/Tracking			Digital Imaging			
	Infrared (Thermal) Imagers	Image Intensifiers	Laser Range Finders	Tire Deflation Spikes	Stolen Vehicle Tracking	Electrical/ Engine Disruption	Mug Shots	Finger- prints	Suspect Composites	Facial Recognition
All sizes	23%	10%	8%	31%	7%	—%[a]	48%	26%	20%	4%
1,000,000 or more	69	25	44	50	69	6	88	81	44	19
500,000–999,999	76	30	24	54	68	8	87	67	59	5
250,000–499,999	54	17	17	66	56	7	88	85	59	10
100,000–249,999	53	25	26	60	42	5	85	81	62	6
50,000–99,999	55	19	31	57	31	—	83	71	55	9
25,000–49,999	43	18	21	61	21	1	80	55	55	9
10,000–24,999	34	16	12	43	10	1	73	29	37	7
2,500–9,999	20	10	7	33	4	0	55	22	17	3
Under 2,500	13	5	1	16	1	—	24	18	6	2

[a]— = less than 0.5%.

Source: Matthew J. Hickman and Brian A. Reaves, *Local Police Departments, 2003* (Washington, DC: Bureau of Justice Statistics, 2006), p. 29.

Police officers in Ottawa, Canada, arresting a car thief snared in a bait car program, while news cameras roll. Bait cars, now in use in more than 100 cities across the United States and in some other countries, demonstrate how advancing technology can serve law enforcement needs. Could these types of programs be extended to things like laptops or cellular phones? Would doing so be fair?

Michael Houston/Ottawa Police Service

tors learn that there are two or more vehicles registered with the same VIN to people in different locations.

As these stories indicate, the future will no doubt see a race between technologically sophisticated offenders and law enforcement authorities to determine who can wield the most advanced technical skills in the age-old battle between crime and justice.[67]

Leading Technological Organizations in Criminal Justice

The National Law Enforcement and Corrections Technology Center (NLECTC) performs yearly assessments of key technological needs and opportunities facing the justice system. The center is responsible for helping to identify, develop, manufacture, and adopt new products and technologies designed for law enforcement, corrections, and other criminal justice applications.[68] NLECTC concentrates on four areas of advancing technology: (1) communications and electronics, (2) forensic science, (3) transportation and weapons, and (4) protective equipment.[69] Once NLECTC researchers have identified opportunities for improvement in any area, they make referrals to the Law Enforcement Standards Laboratory—a part of the National Bureau of Standards—for the testing of available hardware. The Justice Technology Information Network (JUSTNET), a service of NLECTC, acts as an information gateway for law enforcement, corrections, and criminal justice technology and notifies the justice community of the latest technological advances. JUSTNET, accessible on the Web, lists the websites of technology providers and makes them easy to access.

Another important organization is the Society of Police Futurists International (PFI). PFI members are a highly select group of forward-thinking international police professionals. The group employs prediction techniques developed by other futures researchers to make reasonable forecasts about the likely role of the criminal justice system in the future. Recently, PFI and the Federal Bureau of Investigation collaborated to form a futures working group (FWG) to examine and promote innovation in policing. Consisting of approximately 15 members from PFI and staff members from the FBI Academy, the FWG has implemented a variety of projects in collaboration with other organizations and academic institutions engaged in futures research. The group intends to continue to pursue opportunities for further cooperative efforts between American and international law enforcement agencies and organizations like the Foresight Institute (a British-based futures think tank).

While justice technology assessment programs concentrate primarily on facilitating suspect apprehension and the protection of enforcement personnel, some authors have pointed to the potential of emerging technologies in the area of offender treatment. Some have suggested, for example, that novel forms of biomedical intervention, building on the earlier practices of castration, psychosurgery, and drug treatment, will continue to be adapted from advances in the biological sciences and will serve as innovative treatment modalities.[70] Chemical substances to reform the offender, drugs to enhance the memories of witnesses and victims, recombinant DNA behavioral therapy, and microchip extensions of the personality all appear to be on the horizon.[71]

Keep abreast of technological, cultural, and other changes affecting justice systems worldwide by visiting the Society of Police Futurists International via Web Extra 18–5 and the Foresight Institute via Web Extra 18–6 at cjtoday.com.

WEB Extra ▪▪▪▪

Criminalistics: Past, Present, and Future

Technological advances throughout history have signaled both threats and opportunities for the justice field. By the turn of the twentieth century, for example, police call boxes were standard features in many cities, utilizing the new technology of telephonic communications to pass along information on crimes in progress or to describe suspects and their activities. A few years later, police departments across the nation adapted to the rapid growth in the number of private automobiles and the laws governing their use. Over the years, motorized patrol, VASCAR speed-measuring devices, radar, laser speed detectors, and police helicopters and aircraft were all called into service to meet the need for a rapid response to criminal activity. Today's citizens band radios, often monitored by local police and highway patrol agencies, and cell phones with direct numbers to police dispatchers are continuing the trend of adapting advances in communications technology to police purposes. In-field computers (that is, laptop or handheld computers typically found in police vehicles) are commonplace, and many local police departments provide their officers with access to computer databases from the field.

The use of technology in the service of criminal investigation is a subfield of criminal justice referred to as **criminalistics**. Criminalistics applies scientific techniques to the detection and evaluation of criminal evidence. Police crime-scene analysts and laboratory personnel who use these techniques are referred to as **criminalists**. Modern criminalistics began with the need for the certain identification of individuals. Early methods of personal identification were notoriously inaccurate. In the nineteenth century, for instance, one day of the week was generally dedicated to a "parade" of newly arrested offenders; experienced investigators from distant jurisdictions would scrutinize the convicts, looking for recognizable faces.[72] By the 1840s, the Quetelet system of anthropometry was gaining in popularity.[73] The Quetelet system depended on precise measurements of various parts of the body to give an overall "picture" of a person for use in later identification.

The first "modern" system of personal identification was created by Alphonse Bertillon.[74] Bertillon was the director of the Bureau of Criminal Identification of the Paris Police Department during the late nineteenth century. The Bertillon system of identification was based on the idea that certain physical characteristics, such as eye color, skeletal size and shape, and ear form, did not change substantially after physical maturity. The system combined physical measurements with the emerging technology of photography. Although photography had been used previously in criminal identification, Bertillon standardized the technique by positioning measuring guides beside suspects so that their physical dimensions could be calculated from their photographs and by taking both front views and profiles.

Fingerprints, produced by contact with the ridge patterns in the skin on the fingertips, became the subject of intense scientific study in the mid-1840s. While their importance in criminal investigation today seems obvious, it was not until the 1880s that scientists began to realize that each person's fingerprints are unique and unchangeable over a lifetime. Both discoveries appear to have come from the Englishmen William Herschel and Henry Faulds, who were working in Asia.[75] Some writers, observing that Asian lore about finger ridges and their significance extends back to antiquity, suggest that Herschel and Faulds must have been privy to such information.[76] As early as the Tang Dynasty (A.D. 618–906), inked fingerprints were being used in China as personal seals on important documents, and there is some evidence that the Chinese had classified patterns of the loops and whorls found in fingerprints and were using them for the identification of criminals as far back as 1,000 years ago.[77]

The use of fingerprints in identifying offenders was popularized by Sir Francis Galton[78] and was officially adopted by Scotland Yard in 1901. By the 1920s, fingerprint identification was being used in police departments everywhere, having quickly replaced Bertillon's anthropometric system. Suspects were fingerprinted, and their prints were compared with those lifted from a crime scene. Those comparisons typically required a great deal of time and a bit of luck to produce a match.

criminalistics

The use of technology in the service of criminal investigation; the application of scientific techniques to the detection and evaluation of criminal evidence.

criminalist

A police crime-scene analyst or laboratory worker versed in criminalistics.

Over time, as fingerprint inventories in the United States grew huge, including those of everyone in the armed services and in certain branches of federal employment, researchers looked for a rapid and efficient way to compare large numbers of prints. Until the 1980s, most effective comparison schemes depended on manual classification methods that automatically eliminated large numbers of prints from consideration. As late as 1974, one author lamented, "Considering present levels of technology in other sciences . . . [the] classification of fingerprints has profited little by technological advancements, particularly in the computer sciences. [Fingerprint comparisons are] limited by the laborious inspection by skilled technicians required to accurately classify and interpret prints. Automation of the classification and comparison process would open up fingerprinting to its fullest potential."[79]

Within a decade, advances in computer hardware and software made possible CAL-ID, the automated fingerprint identification system (AFIS) of the California Department of Justice. The system used optical scanning and software pattern matching to compare suspects' fingerprints. Such computerized systems have grown rapidly in capability, and links between systems operated by different agencies are now routine. Modern technology employs proprietary electro-optical scanning systems that digitize live fingerprints, eliminating the need for traditional inking and rolling techniques.[80] Other advances in fingerprint identification and matching are also being made. The use of lasers in fingerprint lifting, for example, allowed the FBI to detect a 50-year-old fingerprint of a Nazi war criminal on a postcard.[81] Other advances now make it possible, in at least some cases, to lift latent fingerprints from the skin of crime victims and even from bodies that have been submerged underwater for considerable periods of time.[82]

Computerization and digitization have improved accuracy and reduced the incidence of "false positives" in fingerprint comparisons.[83] The Los Angeles Police Department (LAPD), which uses an automated fingerprint identification system, estimates that fingerprint comparisons that in the past would have taken as long as 60 years can now be performed in a single day or less.[84] Computerized fingerprint identification systems took a giant step forward in 1986 with the introduction of a new electronic standard for fingerprint data exchange.[85] This standard makes it possible to exchange data between different automated fingerprint identification systems. Before its invention, the comparison of fingerprint data among AFISs was often difficult or impossible. Using the standard, cities across the nation can share and compare fingerprint information over the Internet or over secure networks linking their AFISs (see Table 18–2).[86] Recently, the FBI has developed the Integrated Automated Fingerprint Identification System (IAFIS) as part of the National Crime Information Center (NCIC) (see Chapter 5). IAFIS will integrate state fingerprint databases and automate search requests from police agencies throughout the country.

Fingerprinting provides an example of an early form of biometric technology used to positively identify individuals. Modern **biometrics** typically employs hardware and software to provide

biometrics

The science of recognizing people by physical characteristics and personal traits.

TABLE 18–2	**Use of Automated Fingerprint Identification Systems (AFISs) in Local Police Departments, by Size of Population Served, 2003**

| | **Percentage of Agencies with AFIS Access** | | |
Population Served	**Total with Access**	**Exclusive or Shared Ownership**	**Remote Terminal Access Only**
All sizes	62%	8%	4%
1,000,000 or more	100	87	19
500,000–999,999	100	65	19
250,000–499,999	98	59	32
100,000–249,999	97	54	25
50,000–99,999	95	38	16
25,000–49,999	87	27	14
10,000–24,999	74	10	8
2,500–9,999	64	2	2
Under 2,500	47	2	1

Source: Adapted from Matthew J. Hickman and Brian A. Reaves, *Local Police Departments, 2003* (Washington, DC: Bureau of Justice Statistics, 2006), p. 44.

identity verification for specific purposes. Today's biometric devices include retinal and iris scanners, facial recognition systems, keyboard rhythm recognition units, voice authentication systems, hand geometry and digital fingerprint readers, facial thermography, and body odor sniffers. Some universities are now using hand geometry units to allow resident access to secure dormitories. In a significant adaptation of biometric technology, the Liberian International Ship and Corporate Registry, one of the largest shipping registries in the world, announced in 2003 that it was implementing a digital fingerprint recognition system to prevent known terrorists from infiltrating the cargo ship industry.[87] Multimodal biometric systems utilize more than one physiological or behavioral characteristic for identification (preventing, for example, the use of a severed finger to gain access to a controlled area). Learn more about security-related biometrics via **Web Extra 18–7** at cjtoday.com.

Modern criminalistics also depends heavily on **ballistics** to analyze weapons, ammunition, and projectiles; medical pathology to determine the cause of injury or death; **forensic anthropology** to reconstruct the likeness of a decomposed or dismembered body; **forensic entomology** to determine issues such as the time of death; forensic dentistry to help identify deceased victims and offenders; the photography of crime scenes (now often done with video or digital cameras); plaster and polymer castings of tire tracks, boot prints, and marks made by implements; polygraph (the "lie detector") and voiceprint identification (used by the Central Intelligence Agency and the National Security Agency to authenticate voice recordings made by known terrorists); as well as a plethora of other techniques. Many criminal investigative practices have been thoroughly tested and are now accepted by most courts for the evidence they offer. Polygraph[88] and voiceprint identification techniques are still being refined, however, and have not won the wide acceptance of the other techniques mentioned.

New Technologies in Criminalistics

Law enforcement practitioners of the future will be aided in their work by a number of technologies, some of which are still in their infancy. These technologies include the following:

- DNA profiling and new serological/tissue identification techniques, many of which have already received widespread acceptability
- Online databases for the sharing of in-depth and timely criminal justice information
- Computer-aided investigations
- Computer-based training

WEB
Extra
▪ ▪ ▪ ▪

ballistics

The analysis of firearms, ammunition, projectiles, bombs, and explosives.

forensic anthropology

The use of anthropological principles and techniques in criminal investigation.

forensic entomology

The study of insects to determine such matters as a person's time of death.

Forensic anthropologist Frank Bender explaining how he makes forensic models at his studio in Philadelphia. Bender, who describes himself as "the recomposer of the decomposed," has helped police identify dozens of murder victims and, in some cases, find their killers. Would you consider working as a forensic anthropologist?

AP Wide World Photos

CJ Careers

California Department of Justice Criminalist

Name: J. Sippa Pardo-Hastings

Position: Senior Criminalist

City: Richmond, California

College Attended: University of California, Berkeley

Year Hired: 1994

"After studying ballet from childhood through my twenties, I felt the need to pursue my very early love of all things scientific. I returned to my early fictional role models, Nancy Drew and Sherlock Holmes, and realized that what interested me most was using science to solve mysteries—specifically, to solve crimes. After graduation I assumed a criminalist position with the San Francisco City and County Crime Laboratory, a full-service forensic lab where I gained my initial professional experience. This included crime-scene processing (recognition and collection of potential evidence samples), serology (analysis of biological evidence), controlled substance analysis, as well as trial testimony in these same areas. Working with detectives and attorneys was especially compelling, as was learning about the "big picture" with respect to the criminal justice system and the role of the criminalist within this context. I then accepted a position as a criminalist with the California Department of Justice DNA lab, which was located in Berkeley. It was at this lab that I became immersed in forensic DNA analysis, a subsection of both serology and trace evidence. After several years of performing forensic DNA analyses, which often included court testimony throughout the state, I was promoted to the position of senior criminalist."

TYPICAL POSITIONS

Criminalist, forensic analyst, missing and unidentified persons specialist, and DNA databank/CODIS analyst. The criminalist is called on to render scientific opinions in writing as well as in court testimony. The criminalist may also visit violent crime scenes to collect potential evidence. Senior criminalists perform the most complex types of evidence examination and analyses of physical evidence associated with complex criminal investigations. The senior criminalist generally performs casework and/or research in areas of criminalistics, such as crime-scene investigation, biological evidence, firearms and toolmark examinations, and trace evidence.

EMPLOYMENT REQUIREMENTS

Education equivalent to graduation from college with a major in one of the physical or biological sciences, including the equivalent of eight semester hours of general chemistry and three semester hours of quantitative analysis; or four years of professional experience in a physical or biological science laboratory performing independent research related to forensic science. (Possession of a master's degree in a physical or biological science may be substituted for one year of experience, and possession of a Ph.D. in a physical or biological science for two years of the required experience.) Successful completion of criminalist examination and completion of a successful interview are also required. Senior criminalist positions require two years of experience in the California state service performing the duties of a criminalist or four years of professional experience beyond the trainee level in a physical or biological science laboratory setting performing the duties of a chemist, biochemist, or a related position.

OTHER REQUIREMENTS

Personal qualities of successful applicants include attention to detail, meticulous work habits, ability to focus, integrity, analytic ability, keenness of observation, patience, tact, ability to work independently, openness of mind, creative thinking, and good communication skills. The senior criminalist should be able to independently devise experiments and conduct research to address complex forensic science questions. Candidates must possess a state of health consistent with the ability to perform the assigned duties. A medical examination may be required. California Department of Justice regulations require pre-employment investigations consisting of fingerprinting; inquiry to local, state, and national files to disclose criminal records; verification of minimum qualifications (college transcripts); examination of financial status; previous employment background checks; and personal interviews to determine applicant's suitability for employment.

SALARY

Range A: $2,674–$3,132; Range B: $3,499–$4,320; Range C: $4,215–$5,208; senior criminalist: $4,857–$6,012 monthly.

(continued)

CJ Careers (continued)

BENEFITS

Benefits include (1) participation in the California Public Employee's Retirement System (CALPERS), (2) participation in the state health insurance and vision programs, (3) availability of dental insurance, and (4) earned vacation and sick leave.

DIRECT INQUIRIES TO:

California Department of Justice
Testing and Selection Unit

Source: State of California, Department of Justice.

1300 "I" St., 7th Floor
Sacramento, CA 95815
Attn: Criminalist Exam

Phone: 916-324-5039

For more information on the rapidly expanding criminal justice careers area, read *Where the Jobs Are: Mission Critical Opportunities for America,* available on the Web at http://www.justicestudies.com/jobs.htm.

That's what happens in a free society. With rights come responsibilities.

—U.S. Representative J. D. Hayworth[v]

Brief descriptions of these technologies, including their current state of development and the implications they hold for the future, are provided in the paragraphs that follow.

DNA PROFILING

In March 2000, a man known only by his genetic makeup was indicted and charged with a series of sexual assaults in Manhattan.[89] Authorities said that it was the first indictment based solely on a DNA profile. The man, dubbed the "East Side Rapist" and named in the indictment as "John Doe, an unidentified male," followed by his DNA profile, was charged with two sexual assaults in 1995 and one in 1997. He is alleged to have sexually attacked 16 women since 1994. No arrest has yet been made.

Three years later, New York City Mayor Michael Bloomberg announced that his city would begin using DNA to seek hundreds of indictments in unsolved sexual attacks.[90] Bloomberg said that the DNA-based indictments would effectively "stop the clock" on the state's ten-year statute of limitations, which bars prosecution of even known felons if they have not been charged with the crime within ten years of its commission.

DNA analysis (also discussed in Chapter 11) is nearly infallible from a scientific point of view and is increasingly preferred by criminal justice experts as a method of identification. It can prove innocence as well as demonstrate guilt. In December 2001, for example, Marvin Lamond Anderson, a Virginia parolee, was cleared of rape charges stemming from a 1982 crime for which he had served 15 years in prison.[91] Anderson received assistance from the Innocence Project, a volunteer organization specializing in the use of DNA technology to investigate and challenge what it regards as dubious convictions. A Virginia law passed in 2000, which allows felons to seek exoneration and expungement of their convictions on the basis of modern DNA testing, helped Anderson prove that he could not have committed the crime of which he had been convicted. DNA taken from a 19-year-old cotton swab was compared to the state's DNA database of more than 100,000 convicted felons and conclusively demonstrated that Anderson had not committed the crime. Learn more about the Innocence Project via Web Extra 18–8 at cjtoday.com.

The U.S. Department of Justice notes that "DNA evidence is playing a larger role than ever before in criminal cases throughout the country, both to convict the guilty and to exonerate those wrongly accused or convicted."[92] **DNA profiling**, also termed *DNA fingerprinting,* makes use of human DNA for purposes of identification. DNA (deoxyribonucleic acid) is a nucleic acid found in the center of cells. It is the principal component of chromosomes, the structures that transmit hereditary characteristics between generations. Each DNA molecule is a long two-stranded chain made up of subunits called *nucleotides,* coiled in the form of a double helix. Because genetic material is unique to each individual (except in the case of identical twins or clones), it can provide a highly reliable source of suspect identification. DNA profiling was originally used as a test for determining paternity.

DNA profiling requires only a few human cells for comparison. One drop of blood, a few hairs, a small amount of skin, or a trace of semen usually provides sufficient genetic material. Because

WEB
Extra

DNA profiling

The use of biological residue, found at the scene of a crime, for genetic comparisons in aiding in the identification of criminal suspects.

FIGURE 18–2

The DNA fingerprinting process.

Source: Cellmark Diagnostics. Reprinted with permission.

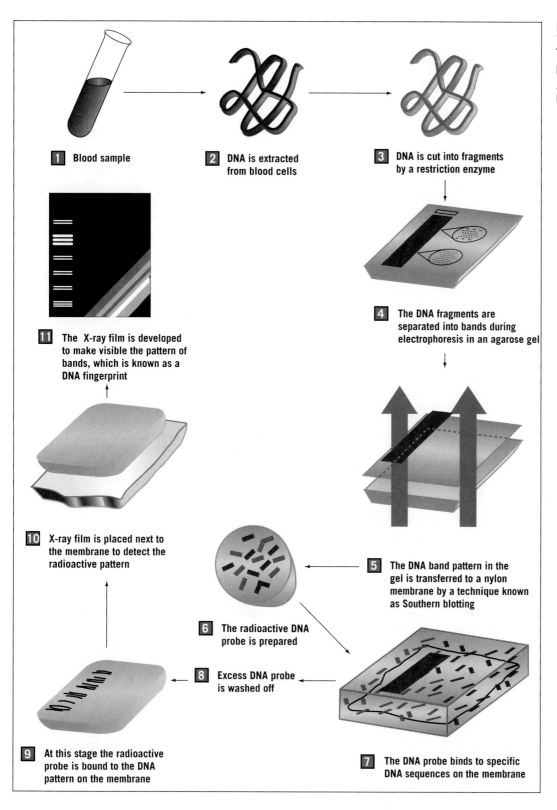

1 Blood sample

2 DNA is extracted from blood cells

3 DNA is cut into fragments by a restriction enzyme

4 The DNA fragments are separated into bands during electrophoresis in an agarose gel

5 The DNA band pattern in the gel is transferred to a nylon membrane by a technique known as Southern blotting

6 The radioactive DNA probe is prepared

7 The DNA probe binds to specific DNA sequences on the membrane

8 Excess DNA probe is washed off

9 At this stage the radioactive probe is bound to the DNA pattern on the membrane

10 X-ray film is placed next to the membrane to detect the radioactive pattern

11 The X-ray film is developed to make visible the pattern of bands, which is known as a DNA fingerprint

the DNA molecule is very stable, genetic tests can be conducted on evidence taken from crime scenes long after fingerprints have disappeared. The process, diagrammed in Figure 18–2, involves the use of a highly technical procedure called electrophoresis. As of mid-2004, most states were building forensic DNA databases, and 32 states and the federal government required the collection of DNA samples from all convicted felons.[93]

Forensic use of DNA technology in criminal cases began in 1986 when British police asked Dr. Alec Jeffreys (who coined the term *DNA fingerprint*[94]) of Leicester University to verify a suspect's confession that he was responsible for two rape-murders in the English Midlands. DNA tests proved that the suspect could not have committed the crimes. Police then began obtaining blood samples from several thousand male inhabitants in the area in an attempt to identify a new suspect.[95]

In another British case the next year, 32-year-old Robert Melias became the first person ever convicted of a crime on the basis of DNA evidence.[96] Melias was convicted of raping a 43-year-old disabled woman, and the conviction came after genetic tests of semen left on the woman's clothes positively identified him as the perpetrator.[97]

In the civil case of *Daubert* v. *Merrell Dow Pharmaceuticals, Inc.* (1993),[98] the Supreme Court revised the criteria for the admissibility of scientific evidence by rejecting a previous admissibility standard established in the 1923 case of *Frye* v. *U.S.*[99] The *Daubert* Court ruled that the older *Frye* standard requiring "general acceptance" of a test or procedure by the relevant scientific community "is not a necessary precondition to the admissibility of scientific evidence." The baseline rule for the admissibility of scientific evidence, said the Court, is established by Rule 402 of the Federal Rules of Evidence, which was published after *Frye* and supersedes it. Rule 402 says that in a trial, "all relevant evidence is admissible, except as otherwise provided by the Constitution of the United States, by Act of Congress, by these Rules, or by other rules prescribed by the Supreme Court pursuant to statutory authority." The Court went on to say that although "the Frye test was displaced by the Rules of Evidence, [that] does not mean . . . that the Rules themselves place no limits on the admissibility of purportedly scientific evidence. Nor is the trial judge disabled from screening such evidence. To the contrary, under the Rules the trial judge must ensure that any and all scientific testimony or evidence admitted is not only relevant, but reliable." The real test for the admissibility of scientific expert testimony, said the Court, is for the trial judge to decide "at the outset . . . whether the expert is proposing to testify to (1) scientific knowledge that (2) will assist the trier of fact to understand or determine a fact in issue." The Court concluded that the task of the trial judge is one of "ensuring that an expert's testimony both rests on a reliable foundation and is relevant to the task at hand. Pertinent evidence based on scientifically valid principles," said the Court, "will satisfy those demands."

The plaintiffs in *Daubert* did not argue the merits of DNA testing but claimed, instead, that the drug Bendectin caused birth defects. Nonetheless, the **Daubert** standard eased the criteria for the introduction of scientific evidence at both civil and criminal trials, effectively clearing the way for the use of DNA evidence in the courtroom.[100] Specifically, the *Daubert* Court found that the following factors may be used to determine whether any form of scientific evidence is reliable:[101]

Daubert standard

A test of scientific acceptability applicable to the gathering of evidence in criminal cases.

- Whether it has been subject to testing
- Whether it has been subject to peer review
- Known or potential rates of error
- The existence of standards controlling application of the techniques involved

In 1994, the DNA Identification Act[102] provided substantial funding to improve the quality and availability of DNA analyses for law enforcement identification. The act also provided for the establishment of the Combined DNA Index for law enforcement purposes (see Chapter 5 for more information). The index, which held 1 million profiles by mid-2002,[103] allows investigators to produce quick matches with DNA samples already on file. The law limits accessibility of DNA samples to investigators, court officials, and personnel authorized to evaluate such samples for the purposes of criminal prosecution and defense.

In 1996, the most comprehensive report to date on the applicability of DNA testing to criminal case processing was released by the National Institute of Justice (NIJ). The report, entitled *Convicted by Juries, Exonerated by Science,*[104] called DNA testing "the most important technological breakthrough of twentieth-century forensic science" and provided a detailed review of 28 cases in which postconviction DNA evidence exonerated defendants who had been sentenced to lengthy prison terms. The cases were selected on the basis of a detailed examination of records that indicated that the convicted defendants might have actually been innocent. The men in the study had served, on average, seven years in prison, and most had been tried and sentenced before the widespread availability of reliable DNA testing.

In each of the cases, which involved 14 states and the District of Columbia, the imprisoned defendant obtained, through an attorney, case evidence for DNA testing and consented to a comparison to his own DNA sample. In each case, the results conclusively showed the lack of matching DNA, and the defendant was ultimately set free. Sexual assault was the most frequent crime for which the defendants had been sentenced. In six of the cases, the victims had also been murdered. All but one case involved a jury trial.[105] Of the cases where the time required for jury deliberations was known, most verdicts had been returned in less than a day.

The 28 wrongful conviction cases shared several common themes in the evidence presented during and after trial, including (1) eyewitness identification—all cases, except for homicides, involved identification by the victim both prior to and at trial; (2) an alibi defense—most defendants had presented an alibi defense, frequently corroborated by family or friends; (3) the use of forensic evidence other than DNA testing, including the examination of nonvictim specimens of blood, semen, or hair at the crime scene; (4) the testimony of prosecution experts who explained the reliability and scientific strength of non-DNA evidence to the jury; and (5) alleged government malfeasance or misconduct, including perjured testimony at trial, police and prosecutors who intentionally kept exculpatory evidence from the defense, and intentionally erroneous laboratory tests and expert testimony admitted at trial as evidence.

One provocative finding of the NIJ report was that "every year since 1989, in about 25% of the sexual assault cases referred to the FBI where results could be obtained (primarily by State and local law enforcement), the primary suspect has been excluded by forensic DNA testing. . . . The fact that these percentages have remained constant for seven years, and that the National Institute of Justice's informal survey of private laboratories reveals a strikingly similar 26% exclusion rate, strongly suggests that postarrest and postconviction DNA exonerations are tied to some strong, underlying systemic problems that generate erroneous accusations and convictions."

As standards develop, DNA identification techniques continue to evolve. Notably, the amount of DNA needed for accurate identification continues to grow smaller. In 1997, for example, Australian forensic scientists reported success in obtaining useful amounts of DNA from the surface of objects that people touched for as little as five seconds as long ago as one year. In their tests, researchers at the Victoria Forensic Science Center in Victoria, Australia, used swabs to recover DNA-laden material from partial fingerprints found on gloves, glasses, mugs, pens, car keys, briefcases, knives, locker handles, and telephone handsets. Moreover, in one in four cases, they also were able to recover DNA that was transferred from one person to another while shaking hands. The technique developed by Australian forensic scientists uses "naked DNA," such as that found on the surface of skin, rather than the DNA found inside cells.[106]

In 1998, in an effort to enhance the use of DNA evidence as a law enforcement tool, the U.S. attorney general established the National Commission on the Future of DNA Evidence. The task of the commission was to submit recommendations to the U.S. Department of Justice to help ensure more effective use of DNA as a crime-fighting tool and to foster its use throughout the criminal justice system. The commission addressed issues in five specific areas: (1) the use of DNA in postconviction relief cases; (2) legal concerns, including *Daubert* challenges and the scope of discovery in DNA cases; (3) criteria for training and technical assistance for criminal justice professionals involved in the identification, collection, and preservation of DNA evidence at the crime scene; (4) essential laboratory capabilities in the face of emerging technologies; and (5) the impact of future technological developments on the use of DNA in the criminal justice system. Each topic became the focus of in-depth analysis by separate working groups comprised of prominent professionals. The work of the commission culminated in the National Law Enforcement Summit on DNA Technology, held in Washington, D.C., on July 27–28, 2000. The proceedings of the summit, as well as transcripts of commission meetings, are available via Web Extra 18–9 at cjtoday.com.

WEB
Extra
▪ ▪ ▪ ▪

The commission's work led the White House to sponsor an *Advancing Justice through DNA Technology* initiative. The initiative culminated in passage of federal legislation designed to take advantage of the opportunities offered by DNA testing. That legislation, the DNA Sexual Assault Justice Act of 2004 and the Innocence Protection Act of 2004 (also discussed in Chapter 11)—both of which are parts of the Justice for All Act of 2004[107]—was signed into law by President George W. Bush on October 30, 2004. The Innocence Protection Act established new procedures for applications for DNA testing by inmates in the federal prison system. Those new procedures require a court to order DNA testing if (1) the inmate applicant asserts that he or she is actually innocent of a qualifying offense, (2) the proposed DNA testing would produce new material evidence that would support such an assertion, and (3) it would create a reasonable probability that the applicant did not commit the offense. The court must grant the applicant's motion for a new trial or resentencing if DNA testing indicates that a new trial would likely result in acquittal. The act also seeks to preserve DNA evidence by prohibiting the destruction of biological evidence in a federal criminal case while a defendant remains incarcerated. The law established the Kirk Bloodsworth Post-Conviction DNA Testing Program, which provides millions of dollars in grants to states for postconviction DNA testing. It also provided money for states to train prosecutors in the appropriate use of DNA evidence and to train defense counsel to ensure effective representation in capital cases. A provision of the Innocence Protection Act increased the maximum amount of damages an individual may be awarded for being wrongfully imprisoned in the federal system from $5,000 to $50,000 per year in noncapital cases and $100,000 per year in capital cases.

The DNA Sexual Assault Justice Act authorized (1) $10 million per year for five years for grants to states and local governments to eliminate forensic science backlogs; (2) $12.5 million per year for five years to provide grants for training and education relating to the identification, collection, preservation, and analysis of DNA evidence for law enforcement officers, correctional personnel, and court officers; (3) $42.1 million in additional funds for the FBI to enhance its DNA programs, including the Combined DNA Index System; (4) $30 million per year for five years to create a grant program to provide training, technical assistance, education, equipment, and information to medical personnel relating to the identification, collection, preservation, analysis, and use of DNA evidence; and (5) $15 million per year for five years to establish a National Forensic Science Commission to be appointed by the attorney general to provide recommendations for maximizing the use of forensic science technology in the criminal justice system.

Finally, the Justice for All Act also amended the federal statute of limitations[108] by adding the following words to existing law: "In a case in which DNA testing implicates an identified person in the commission of a felony . . . no statute of limitations that would otherwise preclude prosecution of the offense shall preclude such prosecution until a period of time following the implication of the person by DNA testing has elapsed that is equal to the otherwise applicable limitation period." The wording allows for prosecutions where DNA analysis reveals the identity of "cold case" perpetrators in investigations that might have otherwise been abandoned. Learn more about the impact of forensic DNA on American criminal justice at Library Extra 18–6 at cjtoday.com.

LIBRARY
Extra
■■■■

ONLINE DATABASES

Computerized information systems and the personnel who operate them are an integral part of most police departments today. Police department computers assist with such routine tasks as word processing, filing, record keeping, report printing, and personnel, equipment, and facilities scheduling. Computers that serve as investigative tools, however, have the greatest potential to affect criminal justice in the near future. The automated fingerprint technology discussed earlier is but one example of information-based systems designed to help in identifying offenders and solving crimes. Others include the nationwide National Crime Information Center and the Violent Criminal Apprehension Program (ViCAP) databases; state-operated police identification networks; specialized services like METAPOL, an information-sharing network run by the Police Executive Research Forum; and the FBI's Combined DNA Index System (CODIS), which allows law enforcement agencies to compare DNA profiles in their possession with other DNA profiles that have been entered into local, state, and national databases in order to identify a suspect or to link serial crimes. NCIC and police information networks furnish a 24-hour channel with information on suspects, stolen vehicles, and other data that can be accessed through computers installed in patrol cars.

Increasingly, law enforcement agencies are making criminal database information available to the public via the Internet. Among the most common forms of information available are sex-offender registries, although the FBI's Most Wanted list and the Most Wanted lists of various states can also be viewed online. In 1998, Texas became the first state to make its entire criminal convictions database available on the Internet.[109] View the sex-offender registries for a number of states via Web Extra 18–10 at cjtoday.com, and see the FBI's Most Wanted list via Web Extra 18–11.

WEB
Extra
■■■■

COMPUTER-AIDED INVESTIGATIONS

Some police agencies use large computer databases that can cross-reference specific information about crimes to determine patterns and to identify suspects. One of the earliest of these programs was HITMAN, developed by the Hollywood (California) Police Department in 1985. HITMAN has since evolved into a department-wide database that helps detectives in the Los Angeles Police Department solve violent crimes. The LAPD uses a similar computer program to track a target population of approximately 60,000 gang members.[110]

The developing field of artificial intelligence uses computers to make inferences based on available information and to draw conclusions or to make recommendations to the system's operators. **Expert systems**, as these computer models are often called, depend on three components: (1) a user interface or terminal, (2) a knowledge base containing information on what is already known in the area of investigation, and (3) a computer program known as an *inference engine* that compares user input and stored information according to established decision-making rules.

A number of expert systems exist today. One is used by the FBI's National Center for the Analysis of Violent Crime (NCAVC) in a project designed to profile violent serial criminals. The NCAVC system depends on computer models of criminal profiling to provide a theoretical basis for the development of investigative strategies. A number of other systems have been developed, in-

expert system

Computer hardware and software that attempt to duplicate the decision-making processes used by skilled investigators in the analysis of evidence and in the recognition of patterns that such evidence might represent.

cluding some that focus on serological (blood serum) analysis, narcotics interdiction, serial murder and rape, and counterterrorism.[111]

Similar to expert systems are relational databases, which permit fast and easy sorting of large numbers of records. Perhaps the best known early criminal justice database of this sort was called Big Floyd. It was developed in the 1980s by the FBI in conjunction with the Institute for Defense Analyses. Big Floyd was designed to access the more than 3 million records in the FBI's Organized Crime Information System and to allow investigators to decide which federal statutes apply in a given situation and whether investigators have enough evidence for a successful prosecution.[112] In the years since Big Floyd, other "bad-guy" relational databases targeting malfeasants of various types have been created, including computer systems to track deadbeat parents and quack physicians. In 1996, President Bill Clinton ordered the Department of Justice to create a computerized national registry of sex offenders.[113] The national sex-offender registry, developed as part of an overhaul of the FBI's computer systems, went online in 1999.

Some systems are even more problem specific. For example, ImAger, a product of Face Software, Inc., uses computer technology to artificially age photographs of missing children. The program has been used successfully to identify and recover a number of children. One of them was only six months old when he disappeared and was found after ImAger created a photo of what the child would look like at age five. The child was recognized by viewers who called police after the image was broadcast on television.[114] Another composite-imaging program, Compusketch by Visatex Corporation, is used by police artists to create simulated photographs of criminal suspects.[115]

The most advanced computer-aided investigation systems are being touted by agencies like NASA and the Defense Advanced Research Projects Agency (DARPA) as having the ability to prevent crime. DARPA, for example, announced its new Total Information Awareness (TIA) Program in 2003.[116] The five-year development project used information-sorting and pattern-matching software to sift through vast numbers of existing business and government databases in an effort to identify possible terror threats. The software attempted to detect suspicious patterns of activity, identify the people involved, and locate them so that investigations could be conducted. Suspected insurgents might be identified with similar software when it detects a series of credit card, bank, and official transactions that form a pattern that resembles preparations for an insurgency attack. The process, which is known as *data mining,* generates computer models in an attempt to predict terrorists' actions. Privacy advocates have raised concerns about the DARPA software, but the agency has tried to defuse concerns by assuring the public that the project "is not an attempt

And say, finally, whether peace is best preserved by giving energy to the government, or information to the people—this last is the most certain, and the most legitimate engine of government. Educate and inform the whole mass of the people.

—Thomas Jefferson (quote inscribed on the wall of the FBI National Academy)

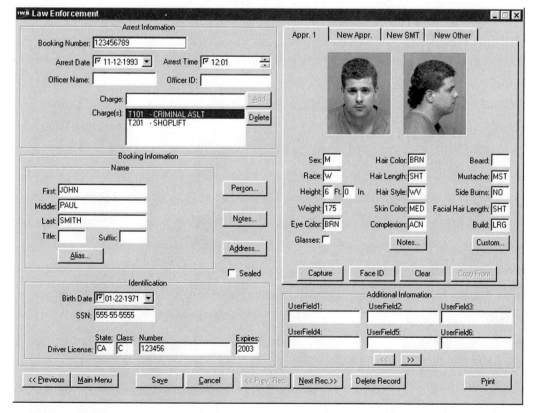

A screen shot of ImageWare Systems' digital mug book software. The software, which can store snapshots and detailed demographic information on criminal suspects, can also be used to scan mug shot databases for likely matches. What other kinds of advanced technology do today's police departments use?

Image courtesy of ImageWare Systems, Inc.

to build a supercomputer to snoop into the private lives or track the everyday activities of American citizens." The agency claims that "all TIA research complies with all privacy laws, without exception."

Another DARPA project that could meet the needs of American law enforcement agencies but is currently being developed for military use overseas is called Combat Zones That See (CZTS).[117] The CZTS program will build a huge surveillance system by networking existing cameras from department stores, subway platforms, banks, airports, parking lots, and other points of surveillance and by feeding images to supercomputer-like processors capable of recognizing suspects by face, gait, and mannerisms as they move from one place to another. The data can be fed via satellite to remote locations across the globe, allowing the agency to track suspects on the move—either within cities or between countries. Vehicles could also be tracked. CZTS is being introduced gradually in selected locations, beginning with areas in and around American military bases. Future implementations of CZTS may involve nanocameras equipped with microminiaturized transmitters that can be spread over a city like grains of dust but which have the power to communicate relatively detailed information to local cellular-like installations for entry into the CZTS network. The civil rights implications of local adaptations of DARPA's TIA and CZTS technology within the United States must be explored by any law enforcement agency considering the use of similar kinds of technologies.

COMPUTER-BASED TRAINING

Computers provide an ideal training medium for criminal justice agencies. They allow users to work at their own pace, and they can be made available around the clock to provide off-site instruction to personnel whose job requirements make other kinds of training difficult to implement. Computer-based training (CBT) is already well established as a management training tool and is used extensively in law enforcement. CBT has the added advantage of familiarizing personnel with computers so that they will be better able to use them in other tasks.

Some of the more widely used computer-training programs include shoot/no-shoot decision-based software and police-pursuit driving simulators. The Atari Mobile Operations Simulator, firearms training simulation, and Robbec's JUST (Judgment Under Stress Training) are just a few of the products available to police-training divisions. Recent innovations in the field of virtual reality (a kind of high-tech-based illusion) have led to the creation of realistic computer-based virtual environments in which law enforcement agents can test their skills.[118]

We have looked at just some of the most prominent uses of technology in criminal justice. Laser fingerprint-lifting devices, space age photography, video camera–equipped patrol cars, satellite and computerized mapping,[119] advanced chemical analysis techniques, chemical sniffers, and hair and fiber identification are all contemporary crime-fighting techniques based on new and emerging technologies. Field test kits for drug analysis, chemical sobriety checkers, and handheld ticket-issuing computers have also made the transition from costly high technology to

Some people fail to understand that security is designed to secure something, and what we are securing are the rights of individuals.

—Former U.S. Attorney General
John Ashcroft

A "radar flashlight" in use. With this new technology, police officers can "see" through walls—even those made of concrete. As technological advances provide additional criminal opportunity, technologies that serve the justice system will improve as well. What kinds of privacy issues might arise as a result?

Gary Meek/Georgia Institute of Technology

widespread and relatively inexpensive use. As one expert has observed, "Police agencies throughout the world are entering an era in which high technology is not only desirable but necessary in order to combat crime effectively."[120] Learn more about information technology innovations in criminal justice at Library Extra 18–7 and Web Extra 18–12 at cjtoday.com.

LIBRARY
Extra
▪▪▪▪

WEB
Extra
▪▪▪▪

On the Horizon

In late 2006, the Department of Homeland Security (DHS) submitted its eighth semiannual report to Congress.[121] The report, which is available in its entirety at Library Extra 18–8, provides insight into some of the intrusion-detection technologies being used to help secure the nation's borders.

LIBRARY
Extra
▪▪▪▪

The latest DHS report, like those that preceded it, recognizes existing concerns that weapons of mass destruction and other contraband of use to terrorists might enter the country through our nation's seaports. Shipping containers are too numerous for each to be opened and visually inspected. Millions of such containers enter the country every year from ports around the world. DHS notes that shipping containers are "highly vulnerable to exploitation by terrorists" and has begun to focus on the need to enhance container-inspection efforts.

Since the terrorist attacks of September 11, 2001, border security has expanded to include the use of high-technology equipment to search for radioactive materials, explosives, toxic chemicals, and dangerous biological materials. These pieces of equipment—which include various vehicle and rail X-ray systems, radiation-detection units, trace-detection devices, video systems, and the like—permit officers to inspect cargo and conveyances for contraband without having to perform the costly and time-consuming process of unloading cargo or drilling through or dismantling containers.

Trace-detection technology, which focuses on cargo, luggage, packages, containers, and vehicles, gathers and analyzes the minute amounts of vapors given off and the microscopic particles left behind when narcotics and explosives contraband are packaged and handled. Current technology provides security screeners with nonintrusive search capabilities.

Radiation-detection equipment is used at the nation's ports and border crossings to detect attempts to smuggle radioactive materials into the United States. Detection devices range from personal radiation detectors, which are somewhat limited in capability and not very costly, to more sophisticated, capable, and expensive portable radiation-detection systems.

Passengers, cargo handlers, seamen, and flight crews must also be screened to determine the level of risk they represent. The 2006 DHS report notes that Customs and Border Protection routinely processes more than 1.1 million arriving passengers for entry into the United States at 324 air, land, and sea ports every day. The Advance Passenger Information System (APIS) is a border enforcement tool used at our nation's airports to identify and detain high-risk travelers on flights bound for the United States. The system is intended to collect biographical information such as name, date of birth, and country of residence from international airline passengers and crew members entering the United States at airports around the country. Before arrival, travelers are matched against law enforcement databases to identify people who should be detained and examined for violation of U.S. law. All airlines serving the United States are required to provide APIS information to the Department of Homeland Security.

The Remote Video Inspection System (RVIS) used at border crossings is designed to expedite the clearance of low-risk travelers and to enhance security at remote border areas, including parts of the U.S.-Canadian border. RVIS transmits images of a driver, vehicle, documents, and passengers to an inspector located miles away at a main port of entry that is monitored 24 hours a day.

Other security technologies now being employed sound like science fiction. Recently, for example, officials at NASA told security specialists that the agency is developing "noninvasive neuro-electric sensors," or brain-monitoring devices, that can receive and analyze brain-wave and heartbeat patterns from a distance.[122] The data are fed into a computer, which scrutinizes it in order to "detect passengers who potentially might pose a threat."[123]

Especially intriguing technological advances can be found in the field of **augmented reality (AR)**.[124] Whereas virtual-reality systems generate audio and visual stimuli predicated on fictional scenarios and usually experienced by relatively passive viewers in situations not requiring interpersonal interaction, AR technology provides users with real-time fact-based information that can be accessed in the midst of real-world activity. Wearable AR systems, like those being developed by the U.S. military under the name Battlefield Augmented Reality System, provide visual, audio, and tactile overlays that can give the user critical information about the people he or she is facing and the situation in which he or she is involved. AR systems supply the user with data presented in a fashion similar to the science fiction visual readouts shown in *Terminator* films. There, the main character's computer-like brain automatically and continuously computes threat

augmented reality (AR)

The real-time and accurate overlay of digital information on a user's real-world experience, through visual, aural, and/or tactile interfaces.[vi] The computer readouts superimposed on the visual fields of the fictional cyborgs in the various *Robocop* and *Terminator* movies provide an example.

The X-45A Unmanned Combat Air Vehicle (UCAV) in flight during a test at Edwards Air Force Base, California. Miniaturized unmanned aerial vehicles (UAVs)—offshoots of military technology—can be used to gather law enforcement intelligence, follow suspects, and patrol borders. UAVs frequently offer long-range capabilities and transmit aerial images back to controllers. Guided by the Global Positioning System and ground controllers, some UAVs are less than six inches in size. Does their use raise any privacy concerns? Why or why not?
Jim Ross/NASA/Dryden Flight Research Center

assessments by accessing stored databases and displays them in the character's visual field as easy-to-read schematics that are overlaid on the immediate surroundings. It is predicted that AR systems will soon be available that will provide "wired" officers with capabilities like these:

- Real-time intelligence about crime and criminals in the surrounding area
- Facial, voiceprint, and other biometric recognition data of known criminals, allowing for instantaneous identification
- Automated scans for chemical, biological, and explosive threats in the immediate area
- Real-time language translation to assist interaction with non-English-speaking people
- Three-dimensional maps, complete with building floor plans, sewer system schematics, and possible access and escape routes
- Advanced optics, including digital zoom and audio amplification for seeing and hearing at a distance
- Identification Friend or Foe technology to allow immediate recognition of "good guys"
- Coordinated deployment of robots and unmanned aerial vehicles (UAVs), including the ability to "see" and "hear" what the robots or UAVs encounter

Augmented-reality systems incorporating at least some of the features mentioned here are already a reality in police work. Xybernaut Corporation, for example, a leading provider of wearable computers, has teamed up with ZNQ3, a company that specializes in secure communications and dynamic identification, to provide wearable computers that enhance tactical awareness. According to Jeffrey Stutzman, founder and CEO of ZNQ3, "The secure communications and point-of-task computing power afforded by the joint Xybernaut/ZNQ3 solution allow first responders complete access to information providing critical situational awareness during a crisis."[125]

Thomas Cowper, whom we mentioned earlier in this chapter, poses some important questions about the practicality of augmented-reality applications in police work. How would "wired" officers be accepted by the public, given that their appearance would differ substantially from that of other officers? How cost-effective would AR technology be in police work? Who will pay for such systems, especially in smaller agencies? How can the accuracy of AR databases be ensured? What legal issues might arise?

Nanotechnology, or engineering and creating useful products on a molecular level, is another cutting-edge technology whose application to policing and the justice system is still largely in the realm of science fiction. Nonetheless, the National Science Foundation predicts that the field could potentially grow into a $1 trillion industry annually by 2015. Nanotechnology may produce practical investigative applications in the near future. Microscopic cameras, motors, solar cells, recording devices, and high-frequency transmitters built with nanotechnology may have already resulted in the production of classified spy hardware like a maneuverable mechanical mosquito able to fly into buildings and vehicles, providing its controllers with "fly on the wall" observation capabilities.[126] Super sensors on such ultraminiaturized devices are said to be able to literally read over a person's shoulder and transmit visual, audio, Global Positioning System (GPS), infrared, and other data to remote recording and viewing devices, all the while remaining nearly invisible to those being targeted. The Institute of Nanotechnology says that miniaturized machines will soon be used to enhance tamper-prevention devices; bolster anticounterfeiting efforts; provide labs on a chip (sometimes called *dipstick technology*) for drug, food, explosives, and DNA testing; permit easy product tracking; and contribute to futuristic intruder-detection and intruder-identification systems.[127]

Recently, the Japanese news agency Kyodo reported that Hitachi Corporation is involved in talks with the European Central Bank to control counterfeiting and money laundering by embedding radio tags much smaller than a grain of sand in European bank notes (Euros).[128] Radio-frequency identification (RFID) tags built with nanotechnology cannot be seen with the naked eye nor felt by fingertips. The devices, called Mu-Chips, can authenticate bank notes that carry them and can even record details about the transactions in which they have been involved. RFID devices, which act much like digital watermarks, are queried by radio and use the energy of the incoming signal to generate a reply. Applicability of the technology was demonstrated at Japan's 2005 International Expo—an event that used RFID-tagged admission tickets. The Expo, which ran for five months, involved participants from 125 countries and drew nearly 15 million visitors.[129]

Problems in Implementing New Technologies

Technological innovations are not always easy to integrate into standard systems. First, the speed with which justice agencies successfully adapt to the opportunities offered by technology may be limited. Some writers have observed that "law enforcement has been slow to utilize new technology,"[130] and an early study by the International Association of Chiefs of Police found that only 10% of police departments were innovative in their use of computers.[131] Line staff and decision makers within police departments may lack the personal experience and knowledge to use technology effectively. Equally significant, the future legal acceptability and social applicability of specific technologies are uncertain.[132]

A second area of concern arises from the "supersleuth" capabilities of some high-technology items. As high-tech gadgetry becomes more commonplace in criminal justice agencies, we can be sure that the courts will watch for potential violations of individual rights. The use of photographic techniques developed for the space program, for example, which permit enlargement of details never before thought possible, and the use of supersensitive listening devices, like those now used to isolate and amplify the voices of referees and quarterbacks on televised football games, may extend investigative capabilities beyond previous understandings of limited search and seizure.

The industry that most lags in the distribution of computing is government, and the most needy is probably the criminal justice system.

—Dr. Alfred Blumstein, Dean of the School of Urban and Public Affairs, Carnegie-Mellon University

Criminal defense lawyer Jennifer Granick in her San Francisco office. Granick specializes in defending computer hackers and crackers. Tougher cybercrime laws are keeping her busy, and her desk is cluttered with software piracy and unauthorized access cases. She also directs the public-interest law and technology clinic at Stanford University Law School's Center for Internet and Society in Stanford, California. Why is cybercrime so common today? What are its attractions?

Douglas Adesko/Douglas Adesko Photography

PROSECUTION OF CYBERCRIME AND HIGH-TECHNOLOGY CRIME

A generation ago, cybercrimes were virtually unheard of, and as recently as a decade ago, few states had cybercrime laws. People who committed crimes using computer technology had to be prosecuted, if at all, under laws intended for other purposes. Burglary laws sometimes served to prosecute illegal entry into computer systems, laws against theft were applied to the stealing of digitized information, and embezzlement statutes were applied to illegal electronic funds transfers. Forty years ago, for example, an employee of Texas Instruments Corporation who stole more than 50 typewritten copies of software programs was convicted of theft under Texas law.[133] Had the software been stolen in electronic form or through the use of a modem, prosecution under the state larceny statute would have been much more difficult. In another early case, Wisconsin authorities found themselves at a loss as to how to prosecute the "414 gang"—a group of teenage computer hackers based in Milwaukee who had infiltrated the computers of 60 businesses and other organizations, including government computer systems, the Los Alamos National Laboratory, the Sloan-Kettering Cancer Center, and the Security Pacific National Bank in Los Angeles.[134] At the time of the offense (1983), neither Wisconsin nor the federal government had specific legislation applicable to the hackers' activity, and they had to be arraigned under a law pertaining to telephone mischief.

Because existing laws were often not adequate in the prosecution of cybercrimes, most states and the federal government moved rapidly to create cybercrime and high-technology crime statutes. In 1984, the first federal cybercrime law was enacted.[135] The Computer Fraud and Abuse Act (CFAA) criminalized unauthorized access to government computers or to computers containing information protected under the Federal Privacy Act.[136] It also made unauthorized interstate entry into any computer illegal. In 1986, Congress modified the CFAA,[137] expanding the penalty for illegal access to federal-interest computers—or those that represent a "unique federal interest." (The term *federal-interest computer* has since been replaced by the term **protected computer**.) Under the CFAA, which has been revised a number of times since it was first enacted, convicted offenders face penalties of up to ten years' imprisonment and fines of up to twice the amount of any "unlawful gain."

Today, high-tech criminals may be prosecuted under a variety of other federal statutes. In addition to the CFAA, applicable federal statutes include the Computer Abuse Amendments Act of 1994 (a part of the Violent Crime Control and Law Enforcement Act); the Cyber Security Enhancement Act of 2002[138] (part of the Homeland Security Act); aspects of the Electronic Communications Privacy Act of 1986; the National Stolen Property Act;[139] the Federally Protected Property Act;[140] the federal Trade Secrets Act;[141] the amended Copyright Act of 1980;[142] the No Electronic Theft Act of 1997;[143] the Digital Millennium Copyright Act of 1998;[144] the Digital Theft Deterrence and Copyright Damages Improvement Act of 1999;[145] the federal Wiretap Act of 1968;[146] and various federal wire, mail, and bank fraud statutes.[147] All can support prosecutions of high-tech offenders.

protected computer

Under federal law, (1) a computer used exclusively by a financial institution or the U.S. government, (2) a computer used by or for a financial institution or the U.S. government, or (3) a computer used in interstate or foreign commerce or communication.

FREEDOM OR SAFETY?
You Decide

Religion and Public Safety

In 2003, Orange County (Florida) Circuit Court Judge Janet Thorpe ruled that a Muslim woman could not wear a veil while being photographed for a state driver's license. The woman, Sultaana Freeman, claimed that her religious rights were violated when the state department of motor vehicles required that she reveal her face for the photograph. She offered to show her eyes, but not the rest of her face, to the camera.

Judge Thorpe said, however, that a "compelling interest in protecting the public from criminal activities and security threats" did not place an undue burden on Freeman's ability to practice her religion.

After the hearing, Freeman's husband, Abdul-Maalik Freeman, told reporters, "This is a religious principle; this is a principle that's imbedded in us as believers. So, she's not going to do that. We'll take the next step, and this is what we call the American way." Howard Marks, the Freemans' attorney, said that he would file an appeal in a higher court.

YOU DECIDE

Do the demands of public safety justify the kind of restriction on religious practice described here? Should photo IDs, such as driver's licenses, be replaced with other forms of identification (such as an individual's stored DNA profile) in order to accommodate the beliefs of individuals like the Freemans?

Reference: "Judge: No Veil in Driver's License Photo," Associated Press, June 6, 2003.

In December 2000, the Computer Crime Enforcement Act was signed into law. The act established a grant program within the U.S. Department of Justice to help state and local law enforcement officers and prosecutors improve education, training, enforcement, and prosecution of computer crimes. The funds could be used to assist state and local law enforcement agencies enforce laws relating to computer crime; educate and train law enforcement officers and prosecutors to conduct investigations, forensic analyses of evidence, and prosecutions of computer crime; acquire computers and other equipment to conduct investigations and forensic analysis of evidence of computer crimes; and facilitate and promote the sharing of federal law enforcement expertise and information about the investigation, analysis, and prosecution of computer crimes with state and local law enforcement officers and prosecutors, including the use of multijurisdictional task forces.

Following the lead of the federal government, most states developed their own cybercrime laws. New York's Computer Crime Act is an example of such legislation.[148] Enacted in 1986, it created six crime categories involving software and computer misuse. The law specifically prohibits the duplication of copyrighted software and makes the possession of illegally duplicated software a felony. Other activities defined as illegal under the law include the unauthorized use of a computer, computer trespass, and theft of computer services. The New York law also created sweeping amendments to existing laws. Theft laws were modified to specifically include "computer program" and "computer data" under the definition of "property," and computer terminology was incorporated into forgery laws. Most state cybercrime laws impose punishments proportional to the damage done, although California bases penalties on the number of violations.

Secure Identity Management

As noted in Chapter 2, one of the fastest growing crimes in the United States is identity theft. According to the Federal Trade Commission, identity theft directly affects as many as 10 million victims annually, although most do not report the crime[149]—and the number is rising at a breathtaking rate. Most identity thieves seek personal gain, using stolen identities to acquire charge cards, purchase personal items, and so on. They hunt for discarded credit card receipts, steal personal identification numbers, and purchase Social Security cards from purse snatchers and robbers.

The theft and manipulation of identities, however, can take on a far more sinister character when committed by terrorists or by those who use assumed identities or identity deception to hide from security and enforcement officials. In October 2001, for example, Luis Martinez-Flores, an illegal immigrant from El Salvador, was arraigned in federal court and charged with identity fraud for allegedly helping some of the September 11 hijackers procure Virginia driver's licenses just six weeks before the hijackings.[150] About the same time, Kenys Galicia, a legal secretary and notary public, was arrested and charged with notarizing falsified documents for the hijackers. Apparently, neither was aware that the men they were dealing with were terrorists.

The need for secure **identity management** and for a comprehensive and workable identity-management system is more apparent today than ever before. The crux of any such system is accurate and dependable identity authentication or verification. A number of foreign countries have moved toward the adoption of national identification cards—an idea that, at least to date, has proved unpopular in the United States. Citizens and visitors can carry the identification cards in lieu of other documents, such as driver's licenses, visas, passports, and birth certificates. One of the most interesting techniques for effective and secure identity management is the smart card. **Smart cards** are technologically advanced credit card–like devices that can store a considerable amount of unalterable information about the cardholder. Smart cards were developed independently in Germany in 1967, in Japan in 1970, in the United States in 1972, and in France in 1974.[151] The term *smart card* was not coined, however, until 1980, when France initiated a major campaign to export smart card technology.

Smart cards can be used for a variety of purposes. They can store detailed records of a person's medical history or banking transactions. They can enable the holder to purchase goods and services, to enter restricted areas (both real and virtual), or to perform other operations. Smart cards can even be designed so that they can be tracked from orbiting satellites, which can report a card's location to within ten feet anywhere on the earth's surface. Most of today's smart cards are tailored for a variety of limited uses, however. A number of universities, for example, have adopted modified versions of smart cards for use as student identification cards. Credit card companies have also begun to make use of at least certain aspects of smart card technology. One of the most widely carried smart cards today is Blue, an "intelligent" credit card available through American Express.

Today's smart cards may feature a tamper-resistant hologram of the intended bearer, along with a miniature computer memory chip containing unalterable digitized information, such as name, home address, Social Security number, birth date, gender, ethnicity, telephone number, e-mail ad-

I learned that the concept of individual rights is far, far from self-evident, that most of the world does not grasp it, that the United States grasped it only for a brief historical moment and is now in the process of losing the memory.

—Ayn Rand[vii]

identity management

The comprehensive management and administration of a user's individual profile information, permissions, and privileges across a variety of social settings.[viii]

smart card

A plastic card or similar device containing a computer chip and other sources of nonalterable information (such as a hologram or a laser-encoded memory strip) that is used to provide highly secure personal identification.

Smart cards and smart card readers. These bank cards contain microchips allowing for enhanced security and ease of use. The chips in these cards keep track of how much money is available in the holder's account and permit a wide variety of secure transactions tied to that account. Smart cards are being developed for many different purposes. They can store details of a person's medical history, allow the holder access to restricted areas (both real and virtual), authenticate the holder's identity (through embedded DNA code, stored and unalterable retinal images, and so on), or be tracked from orbiting satellites, which can report a card's location to within a few feet anywhere on the earth's surface. Most of today's smart cards, however, are tailored for more limited uses. What's the next step in this kind of technology likely to be?

AP Wide World Photos

WEB Extra

dress, office address, frequent flyer numbers, or bank account and credit card numbers. Some cards also include a plastic strip encoded with read-only laser-imprinted information that may contain something as complex as the intended bearer's DNA code. None of today's smart cards hold all of the information described here, although cards capable of doing so can readily be made. Currently being tested by the U.S. military and by governments in Italy and Singapore, smart cards are already used in some industries to enhance access security in the workplace.[152] See a visual presentation of smart card technology via Web Extra 18–13 at cjtoday.com.

Technology and Individual Rights

The Office of Technology Assessment of the U.S. Congress notes that "what is judicially permissible and socially acceptable at one time has often been challenged when technology changes."[153] Barring global war or world catastrophe, advances in technology will continue to occur. When agencies of the justice system use cutting-edge technology, it inevitably provokes fears of a future in which citizens' rights are abrogated in favor of advancing technology. Individual rights, equal treatment under the law, and due process issues all require constant reinterpretation as technology improves.

In 1996, for example, amidst fierce debate, the U.S. Congress passed and President Clinton signed a law intended to control the availability of obscene materials on the Internet. Entitled the Communications Decency Act (CDA),[154] the new law was part of the Telecommunications Act of 1996. The CDA made it a federal offense for anyone to distribute "indecent" or "patently offensive" material to minors (anyone under 18 years of age) over computer networks like the Internet or commercial online services. The law provided for prison terms of up to two years and a $250,000 fine for breaking the law. Opponents of the law claimed that it unconstitutionally restricted free speech because it is not technologically possible for providers of access or content on the Internet to prevent minors from obtaining indecent materials intended for adults. A federal court agreed and soon found portions of the CDA unconstitutional. In 1997, the U.S. Supreme Court upheld the lower court's decision in the landmark case of *Reno* v. *ACLU*.[155] In 2003, however, a split Supreme Court upheld a federal law that denied federal funds to libraries that refused to install pornography filters on computers that provide patrons with Internet access.[156] Emily Sheketoff, executive director of the American Library Association, decried the ruling, saying that it "forces libraries to choose between federal funding and censorship."[157]

The Second Amendment to the U.S. Constitution reads, "A well regulated Militia, being necessary to the security of a free State, the right of the people to keep and bear Arms, shall not be infringed." Many interpret the words of this amendment as a complete and total ban on gun control by the federal government. Gun-control advocates, however, are now suggesting the adoption

The correct question is not "What rights does the Constitution give to the American people?" but rather "What powers does the Constitution grant to the government?"

—Jacob Hornberger

FREEDOM OR SAFETY?
You Decide

A National ID: An Idea Whose Time Has Come?

In 2005, the National Institute of Standards and Technology announced a new Federal Information Processing Standard (FIPS) intended to improve the procedures used to authenticate the identity of federal employees and contractors seeking access to federal facilities and federal information systems.

The new FIPS came in response to a Homeland Security Presidential Directive issued by the White House calling for a secure and reliable government-wide personal identification standard.

U.S. government offices nationwide and overseas have mandated the use of the new identification system, which is based on a credit card–sized Personal Identification Verification (PIV) smart card containing integrated circuit chips. The chips store an identification number, personal information, and biometric data, including two digitized fingerprints and a photograph.

Critics of the system see the PIV card as the first step toward a mandatory national ID. In fact, with plans already in place for the use of digital photographs stored in enhanced state driver's licenses and federal passports, the future of biometric recognition technology appears to be quickly growing.

The Intelligence Reform and Terrorism Prevention Act of 2004, which set national standards for driver's licenses, Social Security cards, and birth certificates, may be another step in this direction.

Under the law, state-issued driver's licenses will soon have to conform to federal requirements or will not be accepted for certain federally mandated identification requirements, such as the screening of airline passengers.

One aspect of biometric technology, facial-recognition systems, has already been used to scan crowds at Super Bowls, and camera-equipped taxicabs and public transportation facilities are making it easier to identify suspected terrorists and wanted criminals. Passive scanning of PIV cards can be used to conduct clandestine identity verification without the bearer's knowledge.

What many fear is the creation of a national identification system that would require anyone living in this country to carry some form of electronic biometric identification with them at all times. Supporters say that such a system would provide for far greater security on public transportation systems, in public buildings, on highways, and at border crossings than is available today.

Critics say that under such a system, personal privacy would quickly become a thing of the past and that government intrusion into the lives of individuals could be overwhelming.

YOU DECIDE

Do you think that the creation of a mandatory national ID, such as a smart card, is a good idea? Why or why not? Under what circumstances should citizens and others living in the United States be required to present identification for inspection by enforcement authorities?

References: Alan Beckley, "The Future of Privacy in Law Enforcement," *FBI Law Enforcement Bulletin,* September 2004, pp. 16–23; Duncan Graham-Rowe, "ID Row Is Bad News for Transatlantic Travelers," *New Scientist,* April 16, 2005, pp. 23–24; "Commerce Secretary Announces New ID Standard for Federal Agencies," NIST news release, February 25, 2005; and NIST PIV Project website, http://csrc.nist.gov/piv-project/index.html (accessed August 10, 2007).

---

of international treaties requiring gun manufacturers to embed special transponder chips in each weapon made for civilian use so that it can be tracked anywhere in the world. Such miniaturized computer chips, which draw their energy from background electromagnetic radiation (like passing radio or TV signals), would be detectable by a variety of high-tech means, as well as through a network of geosynchronous satellites circling the earth, which could pinpoint the location of a specific weapon to within ten feet. Tampering with embedded transponders might carry penalties similar to those now imposed for altering or removing a weapon's serial number.

The Fourth Amendment to the U.S. Constitution guarantees "[t]he right of the people to be secure in their persons, houses, papers, and effects, against unreasonable searches and seizures." Given the electronic network that permeates contemporary society, today's "houses" are far less secure from prying eyes than were those of the eighteenth century. Modern dwellings are linked to the outside world through phone lines, modems, fax machines, electronic mail, broadband connections, and even direct radio and television communications. Wireless computer networks can also provide anyone who knows how to "listen" with substantial insight into what is occurring within the home. One highly significant question centers on where the "security" of the home ends and the public realm begins.

Complicating matters still further are today's "supersnoop" technologies, which provide investigators with the ability to literally hear through walls (using vibration detectors), listen to conversations over tremendous distances (with parabolic audio receivers), record voices in distant rooms (via laser readings of windowpane vibrations), and even look through walls using forward-looking infrared (FLIR) devices, which can detect temperature differences of as little as two-tenths of one degree. (The use of FLIR for certain kinds of investigative purposes was discussed in Chapter 7.)

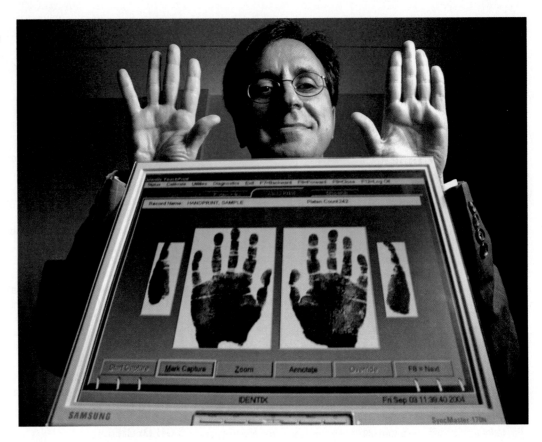

Identix Corporation's CEO Joseph Atick demonstrating the use of a digital handprint scanner. As personal identification technologies continue to develop, some people are concerned that terrorism and other criminal threats have seriously eroded personal liberties. How much liberty are you willing to sacrifice in order to be safe?

Steve Woit

Another question concerns the Fourth Amendment's guarantee of secure "papers and effects." The phrase "papers and effects" takes on a much wider meaning when we enter the world of modern technology. Although the framers of the Constitution could not envision electronic documents and databases, their admonition would seem to apply to such records. Electronic tax listings, records of draft registrants, Social Security rolls, health reports, criminal histories, credit bureau ratings, and government and bank logs all contain billions of items of information on almost every man, woman, and child in the country. Most agree that official access to such information should be limited. A separate question centers on the privacy of various kinds of information, the proper legal steps to be used in acquiring information for investigative purposes, and the types of information that can appropriately be stored in criminal justice data repositories (and for how long). In a 2003 civil case that may prove prophetic, the New Hampshire Supreme Court ruled that the family of a young woman who was killed by an obsessed stalker could sue the Internet data broker that he hired to locate his victim.[158]

Finally, Section One of the Fourteenth Amendment concludes with the phrase, "No State shall . . . deny to any person within its jurisdiction the equal protection of the laws." Modern technology, because it is expensive and often experimental, is not always equally available. Criminal justice programs that depend on technology that is limited in its availability may contravene this Fourteenth Amendment provision. Court-ordered confinement, for example, which utilizes electronic monitoring and house arrest, is an alternative to imprisonment that offenders greatly prefer. The technology supporting this kind of confinement is expensive, however, which dramatically limits its availability. Although the Supreme Court has yet to address this particular topic, it has ruled that programs that require the offender to bear a portion of the cost of confinement are unconstitutional when their availability is restricted to only those offenders who can afford them.[159]

Criminal Justice in 2040

At a recent NIJ-sponsored symposium, three experts offered their views of what American criminal justice will look like in 2040.[160] The three were Bryan J. Vila, former chief of the NIJ's Crime Control and Prevention Research Division; Christopher E. Stone, professor of the practice of criminal justice at Harvard University's John F. Kennedy School of Government; and David Weisburd, professor of criminology at the University of Maryland.

Vila said that he believes that future crime fighters will need to more accurately understand what he calls the *coevolution* of crime commission and crime fighting. Technological advances, he says, will have a great influence on crime fighting. Developments in surveillance, biometrics, DNA analysis and radio frequency identification microchips will enhance crime prevention and crime solving. Increasingly sophisticated intelligence databases will likely be used not only by police officers and analysts but by the general public—as is now common with sex-offender registries. The future, says Vila, will also bring improvements in systems that allow officials to talk electronically to one another, particularly during emergencies. He concludes that better connections among people and agencies will lead to a decrease in criminal opportunities.

Stone pointed to what he sees as an emerging professional culture around the globe that will influence the world's criminal justice systems in the decades to come. He believes that a new culture is spreading professionalism through justice systems worldwide in these areas:

- The bilateral transfer of information between countries
- The global dissemination of justice products, such as court management computer systems, consulting services, and prison design
- Comparative empirical evidence about what works, what doesn't, and why

Weisburd says that the nature of criminal justice in 2040 will depend in large part on the primary research methodology that we employ between now and then. Is the criminal justice community better served, he asks, by relying on the experiences and opinions of practitioners (which he calls the *clinical experience model*) or by research that tests programs and measures outcomes (the *evidence-based model*)?

The clinical experience model is currently the research path most frequently followed, Weisburd says. As a consequence, today's policies and technologies are based primarily on reports from practitioners about what they have found to work or not work. The drawback to this model, says Weisburd, is that a program may be widely adopted before scientific research demonstrates its efficacy in more than one place. In contrast, under the evidence-based model a new program undergoes systematic research and evaluation before it is widely adopted. But the evidence-based model also has shortcomings, says Weisburd. Effective research requires a large investment of time and money, and many practitioners would rather spend resources implementing an innovation than wait for confirming research. Weisburd, a proponent of the evidence-based model, proposes making the evidence-based model "more realistic." He believes this can be done by streamlining the process of developing evidence and conducting evaluations and by building an infrastructure to ensure that studies do not reinvent the wheel.

All three experts emphasized the need to find new ways to work with practitioners around the globe. Ultimately, Vila, Stone, and Weisburd agreed that the world of criminal justice in 2040 will have a more shared culture due to trends like globalization, mobility, and integrated communications. Within this context, they say, the priority over the next three decades should be to develop policies and technologies that will help policymakers and citizens realize a criminal justice system that is fair, equitable, and respectful for all.

Although the crimes it faces may change, the American criminal justice system of the future will likely remain recognizable through its backbone of subsystems: the police, the courts, and corrections. It will continue to rest on constitutional mandates and be responsive to court precedent. New issues will arise, but most of them will be resolved within the context of the question that has guided American criminal justice since its inception: How do we ensure public order and safety while guaranteeing individual rights and social justice in a free society? Learn more about what the American criminal justice system of the future may be like at Library Extra 18–9 at cjtoday.com. Future crimes are discussed in the IBM podcast available at Web Extra 18–14 at cjtoday.com.

LIBRARY Extra

WEB Extra

SUMMARY

- Old concepts of crime and criminality have undergone significant revision as a result of emerging technologies. Science fiction–like products that are now readily available either legally or on the black market have brought with them a plethora of possibilities for new high-stakes crimes. The well-equipped, technologically advanced offender in tomorrow's world will be capable of attempting crimes involving dollar amounts undreamed of only a few decades ago, and the potential for crime-caused human suffering will rise astronomically. Some of these crimes, like the theft of funds from electronic repositories or the ready availability of illegal goods and services, are much like traditional offenses, except that they make use of new communications technologies in their commission. The relentless advance of globalization is now combining with powerful emerging technologies to produce a new world of challenges for criminal justice agencies. Domestic and international terrorism, highly organized transnational criminal cartels, and changing social values are having a synergistic effect that is creating a complex tangle of legal, technological, and social issues.

- In response to new forms of crime and new technologies of crime commission, the crime-fighting abilities of police agencies will need to be substantially enhanced by cutting-edge surveillance and enforcement technologies and by international and interagency cooperation. A massive infusion of funds will be needed to support the adoption of new crime-fighting technologies such as laser and night-vision technologies, digital imaging, wearable computers, and thermography. Similarly, sophisticated personnel capable of operating in multicultural environments must be hired and trained to allow tomorrow's enforcement agencies to compete with the global reach of technologically adept criminals.

- Criminalistics refers to the use of technology in the service of criminal investigation and the application of scientific techniques to the detection and evaluation of criminal evidence. Law enforcement practitioners of the future will be aided in their work by a number of technologies, some of which are still in their infancy. These technologies include (1) DNA profiling and new serological/tissue identification techniques, many of which have already received widespread acceptability; (2) online databases for sharing digitized criminal justice information; (3) computer-aided investigations; and (4) computer-based training.

- When agencies of the justice system use cutting-edge technology, it inevitably provokes fears of a future in which citizens' rights are abrogated in favor of advancing technology. Individual rights, equal treatment under the law, and due process issues all require constant reinterpretation as technology improves. Complicating matters are today's "supersnoop" technologies, which provide investigators with the ability to literally hear and see through walls and listen to conversations over tremendous distances.

KEY TERMS

augmented reality (AR), 679

ballistics, 670

biocrime, 655

biometrics, 669

bioterrorism, 665

computer virus, 660

criminalist, 668

criminalistics, 668

Daubert standard, 674

DNA profiling, 672

expert system, 676

forensic anthropology, 670

forensic entomology, 670

hacker, 656

identity management, 683

malware, 661

protected computer, 682

smart card, 683

social engineering, 657

software piracy, 662

spam, 662

technocrime, 654

weapon of mass destruction (WMD), 663

KEY CASES

Daubert v. *Merrell Dow Pharmaceuticals, Inc.*, 674

Frye v. *U.S.*, 674

Reno v. *ACLU*, 684

QUESTIONS FOR REVIEW

1. Historically speaking, how have advances in technology affected society and criminal activity? What new kinds of crimes have technological advances made possible? Distinguish between new types of crimes produced by advancing technology and new ways of committing "old crimes" that have been facilitated by emerging technologies.

2. What role does technology play in the fight against crime? What new crime-fighting technologies hold the most promise for combating high-technology crimes?

3. What is criminalistics? Explain the interplay between advancing technology and methods used to gather evidence in the fight against crime.

4. What threats to individual rights might advanced technology create? Will our standards as to what constitutes admissible evidence, what is reasonable privacy, and so on undergo a significant reevaluation as a result of emerging technologies?

QUESTIONS FOR REFLECTION

1. How has technology affected the practice of criminal justice in America during the past century? How has it affected the criminal law?

2. Why do criminal laws have to change to keep up with changes in technology? What modifications in current laws defining criminal activity might soon be necessary to meet the criminal possibilities inherent in new technologies?

Discuss your answers to these questions and other issues on the CJ Today e-mail discussion list (join the list at cjtoday.com).

WEB QUEST

Use the Cybrary (http://www.cybrary.info) to learn about cybercrimes and high-technology crimes and their link to international terrorism. Specifically, answer the following questions:

1. How can terrorists use computer technology to attack the United States?

2. How likely is such an attack?

3. What might be the potential consequences of a cyberterrorism attack? (See Chapter 17 for more information.)

4. How well prepared is the United States to defend itself against cyberterrorism?

5. What other forms of cybercrime might international organized criminal groups engage in?

Summarize the information you've found, and submit it to your instructor if asked to do so.

To complete this Web Quest online, go to the Web Quest module in Chapter 18 of the *Criminal Justice Today* Companion Website at cjtoday.com.

LIST OF ACRONYMS

AACAP	American Academy of Child and Adolescent Psychiatry
ABA	American Bar Association
ACA	American Correctional Association
ACJS	Academy of Criminal Justice Sciences
ACLU	American Civil Liberties Union
ADA	Americans with Disabilities Act
ADAM	Arrestee Drug Abuse Monitoring
ADD	attention deficit disorder
ADMAX	administrative maximum
AEDPA	Antiterrorism and Effective Death Penalty Act (1996)
AFDA	Association of Federal Defense Attorneys
AFIS	automated fingerprint identification system
AI	artificial intelligence
AIDS	acquired immunodeficiency syndrome
AIMS	adult internal management system
AJA	American Jail Association
ALI	American Law Institute
ANS	autonomic nervous system
AOUSC	Administrative Office of the United States Courts
APIS	Advance Passenger Information System
APPA	American Probation and Parole Association
AR	augmented reality
ASC	American Society of Criminology
ASIS	ASIS International (formerly the American Society for Industrial Security)
ASLET	American Society for Law Enforcement Training
ATF	Bureau of Alcohol, Tobacco, Firearms, and Explosives
AWDWWITK	assault with a deadly weapon with intent to kill
BCS	British Crime Survey
BJA	Bureau of Justice Assistance
BJS	Bureau of Justice Statistics
BOP	Bureau of Prisons
BTS	Border and Transportation Security
BWS	battered women's syndrome
CAD	computer-assisted dispatch
CAFA	Class Action Fairness Act
CALEA	Commission on Accreditation for Law Enforcement Agencies
CAN-SPAM	Controlling the Assault of Non-Solicited Pornography and Marketing
CAPRA	clients, acquired/analyzed, partnerships, respond, assess
CAPS	Chicago's Alternative Policing Strategy
CAT	computer-aided transcription
CBT	computer-based training
CCA	Corrections Corporation of America
CCE	Continuing Criminal Enterprise (statute)
CCIPS	Computer Crime and Intellectual Property Section (FBI)
CCJJDP	Coordinating Council on Juvenile Justice and Delinquency Prevention

CDA	Communications Decency Act (1996)
CDC	Centers for Disease Control and Prevention
CFAA	Computer Fraud and Abuse Act (1986)
CFR	Council on Foreign Relations
CIA	Central Intelligence Agency
CIAO	Critical Infrastructure Assurance Office
CIC	children in custody
CJA	Criminal Justice Act (England)
CJIS	Criminal Justice Information Services (FBI)
CLET	Certified Law Enforcement Trainer
CODIS	Combined DNA Index System (FBI)
COPE	Citizen Oriented Police Enforcement
COPS	Community Oriented Policing Services
CPO	certified protection officer
CPOP	Community Police Officer Program (New York City)
CPP	Certified Protection Professional
CPTED	crime prevention through environmental design
CRIPA	Civil Rights of Institutionalized Persons Act
CRIPP	Courts Regimented Intensive Probation Program (Texas)
CSA	Controlled Substances Act (1970)
CSC	Correctional Services Corporation
CSE	child sexual exploitation
CSO	chief security officer
CZTS	Combat Zones That See
DARE	Drug Abuse Resistance Education
DARPA	Defense Advanced Research Projects Agency
DART	Directed Area Responsibility Teams (Houston)
DAWN	Drug Abuse Warning Network
DCA	district court of appeals
DCCTAP	Drug Court Clearinghouse and Technical Assistance Project (American University)
DEA	Drug Enforcement Administration
DES	data encryption standard
DHS	Department of Homeland Security
DIRPPA	Drug-Induced Rape Prevention and Punishment Act (1996)
DNA	deoxyribonucleic acid
DOJ	United States Department of Justice
DPIC	Death Penalty Information Center
DPRC	Drug Policy Research Center (RAND Corporation)
DUF	Drug Use Forecasting
DUI	driving under the influence (of alcohol or drugs)
DWI	driving while intoxicated
EBP	evidence-based policing
ECPA	Electronic Communications Privacy Act (1986)
EPR	Emergency Preparedness and Response
Europol	European Police Office
FACTS	Factual Analysis Criminal Threat Solution (software application)
FBI	Federal Bureau of Investigation

FCC	federal correctional complex	LME	liquid metal embrittlement
FCI	federal correctional institution	M-19	19th of April Movement
FDA	Food and Drug Administration	MADD	Mothers Against Drunk Driving
FDSS	Federal-wide Drug Seizure System	MATRIX	Multistate Anti-Terrorism Information Exchange
FGC	family group conference		
FINCEN	Financial Crimes Enforcement Network	MCFP	medical center for federal prisoners
FLETC	Federal Law Enforcement Training Center	MDC	metropolitan detention center
FLIR	forward-looking infrared	MPC	Model Penal Code
FOP	Fraternal Order of Police	MROP	Mentally Retarded Offender Program (Texas)
FPC	federal prison camp	MSBP	Munchausen syndrome by proxy
FSB	Federal Security Service (Russia)	MTF	Monitoring the Future (survey)
FTCA	Federal Tort Claims Act	NAACP	National Association for the Advancement of Colored People
FTO	foreign terrorist organization		
FWG	futures working group	NACDL	National Association of Criminal Defense Lawyers
GBL	gamma-butyrolactone		
GBMI	guilty but mentally ill	NADCP	National Association of Drug Court Professionals
GED	general equivalency diploma		
GGI	guided group interaction	NADDIS	Narcotics and Dangerous Drugs Information System
GHB	gamma-hydroxybutyrate		
HCL	hydrochloride	NAP	National Assessment Program
HEUNI	European Institute for Crime Prevention and Control	NCAVC	National Center for the Analysis of Violent Crime (FBI)
HIDTA	high-intensity drug-trafficking area	NCCD	National Council on Crime and Delinquency
HIFCA	high-intensity financial crimes area		
HIV	human immunodeficiency virus	NCCS	National Computer Crime Squad (FBI)
HRALEI	Human Rights and Law Enforcement Institute	NCEA	National Center on Elder Abuse
		NCIC	National Crime Information Center (FBI)
HSP	Heroin Signature Program	NCIC 2000	National Crime Information Center 2000 (FBI)
IACP	International Association of Chiefs of Police	NCIS	National Criminal Intelligence Service (England)
IAD	internal affairs division		
IAFIS	Integrated Automated Fingerprint Identification System (FBI)	NCISP	National Criminal Intelligence Sharing Plan
		NCJC	National Criminal Justice Commission
IAIP	Information Analysis and Infrastructure Protection	NCJRS	National Criminal Justice Reference Service
		NCSC	National Center for State Courts
ICC	International Criminal Court	NCTC	National Counterterrorism Center
ICE	Immigration and Customs Enforcement	NCTP	National Cybercrime Training Partnership
IDRA	Insanity Defense Reform Act (1984)	NCVS	National Crime Victimization Survey
ILC	International Law Commission	NCWP	National Center for Women and Policing
ILEA	International Law Enforcement Academy	NDAA	National District Attorneys Association
ILP	intelligence-led policing	NDIC	National Drug Intelligence Center
INCB	International Narcotics Control Board	NDIS	National DNA Index System (FBI)
Interpol	International Criminal Police Organization	NETA	No Electronic Theft Act (1997)
IPES	International Police Executive Symposium	NGCRC	National Gang Crime Research Center
IPS	intensive probation supervision	NIBRS	National Incident-Based Reporting System (FBI)
IRTPA	Intelligence Reform and Terrorism Prevention Act (2004)		
		NIDA	National Institute on Drug Abuse
ISC	International Society for Criminology	NIJ	National Institute of Justice
IVS	International Victim Survey (UN)	NIPC	National Infrastructure Protection Center
JCPT	Joint Community Police Training	NISMART	National Incidence Study of Missing, Abducted, Runaway, and Thrownaway Children
JIC	Justice Information Center		
JJDP	Juvenile Justice and Delinquency Prevention Act (1974)		
		NLADA	National Legal Aid and Defender Association
JTTF	Joint Terrorism Task Force	NLECTC	National Law Enforcement and Corrections Technology Center
JUST	Judgment Under Stress Training		
JUSTNET	Justice Technology Information Network	NLETS	International Justice and Public Safety Information Sharing Network
LAPD	Los Angeles Police Department		
LASD	Los Angeles County Sheriff's Department	NNICC	National Narcotics Intelligence Consumers Committee
LEAA	Law Enforcement Assistance Administration		
LEAP	law enforcement availability pay	NOBLE	National Organization of Black Law Enforcement Executives
LEEP	Law Enforcement Education Program		
LESL	Law Enforcement Standards Laboratory	NRA	National Rifle Association
LESTN	Law Enforcement Satellite Training Network	NSA	National Sheriffs' Association

NSDUH	National Survey on Drug Use and Health	ROR	release on recognizance
NVAWS	National Violence against Women Survey	RTTF	Regional Terrorism Task Force
NVC	National Victims Center	RVIS	Remote Video Inspection System
NVCAN	National Victims' Constitutional Amendment Network	SAMHSA	Substance Abuse and Mental Health Services Administration
NW3C	National White Collar Crime Center	SARA	scanning, analysis, response, and assessment
NYGC	National Youth Gang Center	SARS	severe acute respiratory syndrome
NYPD	New York City Police Department	SBI	State Bureau of Investigation
OBTS	offender-based transaction statistics	SCU	Street Crimes Unit (New York City)
ODCCP	Office for Drug Control and Crime Prevention (UN)	SEARCH	National Consortium for Justice Information and Statistics
OICJ	Office of International Criminal Justice	SIIA	Software and Information Industry Association
OIG	Office of the Inspector General (Department of Justice)	SLATT	State and Local Anti-Terrorism Training Program
OJARS	Office of Justice Assistance, Research, and Statistics	SPECDA	School Program to Educate and Control Drug Abuse
OJJDP	Office of Juvenile Justice and Delinquency Prevention	STG	security threat group
OLES	Office of Law Enforcement Standards	SVORI	Serious and Violent Offender Reentry Initiative
OLETC	Office of Law Enforcement Technology Commercialization	SWAT	special weapons and tactics
ONDCP	Office of National Drug Control Policy	TFJJR	Task Force on Juvenile Justice Reform
OSCA	Office of the State Courts Administrator	TIA	Total Information Awareness
PCC	Police Cadet Corps (New York City)	TIVU	Terrorism and International Victims Unit (Office for Victims of Crime)
PCCIP	President's Commission on Critical Infrastructure Protection	TVPA	Trafficking Victims Protection Reauthorization Act
PCIPB	President's Critical Infrastructure Protection Board	TWGECSI	Technical Working Group for Electronic Crime Scene Investigation
PCP	phencyclidine	TWGEDE	Technical Working Group for the Examination of Digital Evidence
PCR	police–community relations		
PDS	podular/direct supervision	UAV	unmanned aerial vehicle
PERF	Police Executive Research Forum	UCBE	unsolicited commercial bulk e-mail
PFI	Police Futurists International	UCR	Uniform Crime Reports
PHDCN	Project on Human Development in Chicago Neighborhoods	UN	United Nations
		UNCJIN	United Nations Crime and Justice Information Network
PIJ	Palestine Islamic Jihad	UNICRI	United Nations Interregional Crime and Justice Research Institute
PINS	persons in need of supervision (status offenders)		
PLRA	Prison Litigation Reform Act (1996)	UNOJUST	United Nations Online Justice Information System
PMS	premenstrual syndrome		
PORAC	Peace Officer's Research Association of California	USBP	United States Border Patrol
		U.S.C.	United States Code
POST	peace officer standards and training	USCG	United States Coast Guard
PPS	personal protection specialist	USCIS	United States Citizenship and Immigration Services
PRC	People's Republic of China		
PREA	Prison Rape Elimination Act (2003)	USNCB	United States National Central Bureau (Interpol)
PSI	presentence investigation		
RAS	reticular-activating system	USP	United States penitentiary
RCMP	Royal Canadian Mounted Police	USSC	United States Sentencing Commission
RESTTA	Restitution Education, Specialized Training, and Technical Assistance (program)	VAWA	Violence against Women Act (1994)
		VCAN	Victims' Constitutional Amendment Network
RFID	radio-frequency identification	VCF	virtual case file
RICO	Racketeer Influenced and Corrupt Organizations (statute)	ViCAP	Violent Criminal Apprehension Program (FBI)
RID	Remove Intoxicated Drivers	VOCA	Victims of Crime Act (1984)
RISE	Reintegrative Shaming Experiments (Australian Institute of Criminology)	VWPA	Victim and Witness Protection Act (1982)
		WAR	White Aryan Resistance
RISS-ATIX	Regional Information Sharing Systems Anti-Terrorism Information Exchange Program	WJIN	World Justice Information Network
		WMD	weapon of mass destruction
RJC	real justice conferencing (Pennsylvania)	WTC	World Trade Center
RLUIPA	Religious Land Use and Institutionalized Persons Act (2000)	WWW	World Wide Web

THE BILL OF RIGHTS

The first ten amendments to the U.S. Constitution are known as the Bill of Rights. These amendments, ratified in 1791, have special relevance to criminal justice and are reproduced here. The entire U.S. Constitution can be found online at this book's Companion Website (http://www.cjtoday.com). You can save the file to your desktop or easily print it.

Amendment I Congress shall make no law respecting an establishment of religion, or prohibiting the free exercise thereof; or abridging the freedom of speech, or of the press; or the right of the people peaceably to assemble, and to petition the Government for a redress of grievances.

Amendment II A well regulated Militia, being necessary to the security of a free State, the right of the people to keep and bear Arms, shall not be infringed.

Amendment III No Soldier shall, in time of peace be quartered in any house, without the consent of the Owner, nor in time of war, but in a manner to be prescribed by law.

Amendment IV The right of the people to be secure in their persons, houses, papers, and effects, against unreasonable searches and seizures, shall not be violated, and no Warrants shall issue, but upon probable cause, supported by Oath or affirmation, and particularly describing the place to be searched, and the persons or things to be seized.

Amendment V No person shall be held to answer for a capital, or otherwise infamous crime, unless on a presentment or indictment of a Grand Jury, except in cases arising in the land or naval forces, or in the Militia, when in actual service in time of War or public danger; nor shall any person be subject for the same offence to be twice put in jeopardy of life or limb; nor shall be compelled in any criminal case to be a witness against himself, nor be deprived of life, liberty, or property, without due process of law; nor shall private property be taken for public use, without just compensation.

Amendment VI In all criminal prosecutions, the accused shall enjoy the right to a speedy and public trial, by an impartial jury of the State and district wherein the crime shall have been committed, which district shall have been previously ascertained by law, and to be informed of the nature and cause of the accusation; to be confronted with the witnesses against him; to have compulsory process for obtaining witnesses in his favor, and to have the Assistance of Counsel for his defence.

Amendment VII In suits of common law, where the value in controversy shall exceed twenty dollars, the right of trial by jury shall be preserved, and no fact tried by a jury, shall be otherwise reexamined in any court of the United States, than according to the rules of the common law.

Amendment VIII Excessive bail shall not be required, nor excessive fines imposed, nor cruel and unusual punishments inflicted.

Amendment IX The enumeration in the Constitution, of certain rights, shall not be construed to deny or disparage others retained by the people.

Amendment X The powers not delegated to the United States by the Constitution, nor prohibited by it to the States, are reserved to the States respectively, or to the people.

GLOSSARY

The 18 chapters of *Criminal Justice Today* contain hundreds of terms commonly used in the field of criminal justice. This glossary contains many more. Wherever they appear in the book, all concepts are explained whenever possible according to definitions provided by the Bureau of Justice Statistics under a mandate of the Justice System Improvement Act. That mandate was to create a consistent terminology set for use by criminal justice students, practitioners, and planners. It found its most complete expression in the *Dictionary of Criminal Justice Data Terminology*,[1] the second edition of which provides many of our definitions. Others (especially those in Chapter 2) are derived from the FBI's Uniform Crime Reporting Program and are taken from the most recent edition of the agency's *Uniform Crime Reporting Handbook*.[2]

Standardization of terminology is important because American criminal justice agencies, justice practitioners, and involved citizens now routinely communicate between and among themselves, often over considerable distances, about the criminal justice system and about justice-related issues. For communications to be meaningful and efficient, a shared terminology is necessary. Standardization, however desirable, is not easy to achieve—sometimes because of legal and technical distinctions between jurisdictions or because of variations in customary usage. In the words of the Bureau of Justice Statistics, "It is not possible to construct a single national standard criminal justice data terminology where every term always means the same thing in all of its appearances. However, it is possible and necessary to standardize the language that represents basic categorical distinctions."[3] Although this glossary should be especially valuable to the student who will one day work in the criminal justice system, it should also prove beneficial to anyone seeking a greater insight into that system.

1983 lawsuit A civil suit brought under Title 42, Section 1983, of the U.S. Code against anyone who denies others their constitutional right to life, liberty, or property without due process of law.

abused child A child who has been physically, sexually, or mentally abused. Most states also consider a child who is forced into delinquent activity by a parent or guardian to be abused.

acquittal The judgment of a court, based on a verdict of a jury or a judicial officer, that the defendant is not guilty of the offense or offenses for which he or she was tried.

actus reus An act in violation of the law. Also, a guilty act.

adjudication The process by which a court arrives at a decision regarding a case. Also, the resultant decision.

adjudicatory hearing The fact-finding process by which the juvenile court determines whether there is sufficient evidence to sustain the allegations in a petition.

ADMAX Administrative maximum. The term is used by the federal government to denote ultra-high-security prisons.

administration of justice The performance of any of the following activities: detection, apprehension, detention, pretrial release, post-trial release, prosecution, adjudication, correctional supervision, or rehabilitation of accused persons or criminal offenders.[4]

admission In corrections, the entry of an offender into the legal jurisdiction of a correctional agency or into the physical custody of a correctional facility.

adult A person who is within the original jurisdiction of a criminal court, rather than a juvenile court, because his or her age at the time of an alleged criminal act was above a statutorily specified limit.

adversarial system The two-sided structure under which American criminal trial courts operate. The adversarial system pits the prosecution against the defense. In theory, justice is done when the most effective adversary is able to convince the judge or jury that his or her perspective on the case is the correct one.

aftercare In juvenile justice usage, the status or program membership of a juvenile who has been committed to a treatment or confinement facility, conditionally released from the facility, and placed in a supervisory or treatment program.

aggravated assault (UCR/NIBRS) The unlawful, intentional inflicting, or attempted or threatened inflicting, of serious injury upon the person of another. While *aggravated assault* and *simple assault* are standard terms for reporting purposes, most state penal codes use labels like *first-degree* and *second-degree* to make such distinctions.

aggravating circumstances Circumstances relating to the commission of a crime that make it more grave than the average instance of that crime. See also **mitigating circumstances**.

alias Any name used for an official purpose that is different from a person's legal name.

alibi A statement or contention by an individual charged with a crime that he or she was so distant when the crime was committed, or so engaged in other provable activities, that his or her participation in the commission of that crime was impossible.

alter ego rule   In some jurisdictions, a rule of law that holds that a person can only defend a third party under circumstances and only to the degree that the third party could legally act on his or her own behalf.

alternative sanctions   See **intermediate sanctions**.

alternative sentencing   The use of court-ordered community service, home detention, day reporting, drug treatment, psychological counseling, victim–offender programming, or intensive supervision in lieu of other, more traditional sanctions, such as imprisonment and fines.

anomie   A socially pervasive condition of normlessness. Also, a disjunction between approved goals and means.

anticipatory warrants   Search warrants issued on the basis of probable cause to believe that evidence of a crime, while not presently at the place described, will likely be there when the warrant is executed.

Antiterrorism Act   See **USA PATRIOT Act.**

appeal   Generally, the request that a court with appellate jurisdiction review the judgment, decision, or order of a lower court and set it aside (reverse it) or modify it.

appearance (court)   The act of coming into a court and submitting to its authority.

appellant   The person who contests the correctness of a court order, judgment, or other decision and who seeks review and relief in a court having appellate jurisdiction. Also, the person on whose behalf this is done.

appellate court   A court whose primary function is to review the judgments of other courts and of administrative agencies.

appellate jurisdiction   The lawful authority of a court to review a decision made by a lower court.

arraignment   Strictly, the hearing before a court having jurisdiction in a criminal case, in which the identity of the defendant is established, the defendant is informed of the charge and of his or her rights, and the defendant is required to enter a plea. Also, in some usages, any appearance in criminal court before trial.

arrest   The act of taking an adult or juvenile into physical custody by authority of law for the purpose of charging the person with a criminal offense, a delinquent act, or a status offense, terminating with the recording of a specific offense. Technically, an arrest occurs whenever a law enforcement officer curtails a person's freedom to leave.

arrest (UCR/NIBRS)   Each separate instance in which a person is taken into physical custody or is notified or cited by a law enforcement officer or agency, except those incidents relating to minor traffic violations.

arrest rate   The number of arrests reported for each unit of population.

arrest warrant   A document issued by a judicial officer that directs a law enforcement officer to arrest an identified person who has been accused of a specific offense.

arson (UCR/NIBRS)   Any willful or malicious burning or attempting to burn, with or without the intent to defraud, a dwelling house, public building, motor vehicle or aircraft, personal property of another, and so on. Some instances of arson result from malicious mischief, some involve attempts to claim insurance money, and some are committed in an effort to disguise other crimes, such as murder, burglary, or larceny.

Ashurst-Sumners Act   Federal legislation of 1935 that effectively ended the industrial prison era by restricting interstate commerce in prison-made goods.

assault (UCR/NIBRS)   An unlawful attack by one person upon another. Historically, *assault* meant only the attempt to inflict injury on another person; a completed act constituted the separate offense of battery. Under modern statistical usage, however, attempted and completed acts are grouped together under the generic term *assault.*

assault on a law enforcement officer   A simple or aggravated assault in which the victim is a law enforcement officer engaged in the performance of his or her duties.

atavism   A condition characterized by the existence of features thought to be common in earlier stages of human evolution.

attendant circumstances   The facts surrounding an event.

attorney   A person trained in the law, admitted to practice before the bar of a given jurisdiction, and authorized to advise, represent, and act for others in legal proceedings. Also called *lawyer; legal counsel.*

Auburn system   A form of imprisonment developed in New York State around 1820 that depended on mass prisons, where prisoners were held in congregate fashion and required to remain silent. This style of imprisonment was a primary competitor with the Pennsylvania system.

augmented reality (AR)   The real-time and accurate overlay of digital information on a user's real-world experience, through visual, aural, and/or tactile interfaces.[5] The computer readouts superimposed on the visual fields of the fictional cyborgs in the various *Robocop* and *Terminator* movies provide an example.

backlog (court)   The number of cases awaiting disposition in a court that exceeds the court's capacity for disposing of them within the period of time considered appropriate.

bail   The money or property pledged to the court or actually deposited with the court to effect the release of a person from legal custody.

bail bond   A document guaranteeing the appearance of a defendant in court as required and recording the pledge of money or property to be paid to the court if he or she does not appear, which is signed by the person to be released and anyone else acting on his or her behalf.

bail bondsman   A person, usually licensed, whose business it is to effect release on bail for people charged with offenses and held in custody, by pledging to pay a sum of money if the defendant fails to appear in court as required.

bailiff   The court officer whose duties are to keep order in the courtroom and to maintain physical custody of the jury.

bail revocation A court decision withdrawing the status of release on bail that was previously conferred on a defendant.

balancing test A principle, developed by the courts and applied to the corrections arena by *Pell* v. *Procunier* (1974), that attempts to weigh the rights of an individual, as guaranteed by the Constitution, against the authority of states to make laws or to otherwise restrict a person's freedom in order to protect the state's interests and its citizens.

ballistics The analysis of firearms, ammunition, projectiles, bombs, and explosives.

battered women's syndrome (BWS) 1. A series of common characteristics that appear in women who are abused physically and psychologically over an extended period of time by the dominant male figure in their lives. 2. A pattern of psychological symptoms that develops after somebody has lived in a battering relationship. 3. A pattern of responses and perceptions presumed to be characteristic of women who have been subjected to continuous physical abuse by their mates.[6]

behavioral conditioning A psychological principle that holds that the frequency of any behavior can be increased or decreased through reward, punishment, and association with other stimuli.

bench warrant A document issued by a court directing that a law enforcement officer bring a specified person before the court. A bench warrant is usually issued for a person who has failed to obey a court order or a notice to appear.

bias crime See **hate crime**.

Bill of Rights The popular name given to the first ten amendments to the U.S. Constitution, which are considered especially important in the processing of criminal defendants.

bind over To require by judicial authority that a person promise to appear for trial, appear in court as a witness, or keep the peace. Also, the decision by a court of limited jurisdiction requiring that a person charged with a felony appear for trial on that charge in a court of general jurisdiction, as the result of a finding of probable cause at a preliminary hearing held in the court of limited jurisdiction.

biocrime A criminal offense perpetrated through the use of biologically active substances, including chemicals and toxins, disease-causing organisms, altered genetic material, and organic tissues and organs. Biocrimes unlawfully affect the metabolic, biochemical, genetic, physiological, or anatomical status of living organisms.

Biological School A perspective on criminological thought that holds that criminal behavior has a physiological basis.

biological weapon A biological agent used to threaten human life (for example, anthrax, smallpox, or any infectious disease).[7]

biometrics The science of recognizing people by physical characteristics and personal traits.

bioterrorism The intentional or threatened use of viruses, bacteria, fungi, or toxins from living organisms to produce death or disease in humans, animals, or plants.[8]

***Bivens* action** A civil suit, based on the case of *Bivens* v. *Six Unknown Federal Agents*, brought against federal government officials for denying the constitutional rights of others.

blended sentence A juvenile court disposition that imposes both a juvenile sanction and an adult criminal sentence upon an adjudicated delinquent. The adult sentence is suspended if the juvenile offender successfully completes the term of the juvenile disposition and refrains from committing any new offense.[9]

bobbies The popular British name given to members of Sir Robert (Bob) Peel's Metropolitan Police Force.

booking A law enforcement or correctional administrative process officially recording an entry into detention after arrest and identifying the person, the place, the time, the reason for the arrest, and the arresting authority.

Bow Street Runners An early English police unit formed under the leadership of Henry Fielding, magistrate of the Bow Street region of London.

broken windows thesis A perspective on crime causation that holds that the physical deterioration of an area leads to higher crime rates and an increased concern for personal safety among residents.

Bureau of Justice Statistics (BJS) A U.S. Department of Justice agency responsible for the collection of criminal justice data, including the annual National Crime Victimization Survey.

burglary By the narrowest and oldest definition, the trespassory breaking and entering of the dwelling house of another in the nighttime with the intent to commit a felony.

burglary (UCR/NIBRS) The unlawful entry of a structure to commit a felony or a theft (excludes tents, trailers, and other mobile units used for recreational purposes). For the UCR/NIBRS Program, the crime of burglary can be reported if (1) an unlawful entry of an unlocked structure has occurred, (2) a breaking and entering (of a secured structure) has taken place, or (3) a burglary has been attempted.

capacity (legal) The legal ability of a person to commit a criminal act. Also, the mental and physical ability to act with purpose and to be aware of the certain, probable, or possible results of one's conduct.

capacity (prison) See **prison capacity**.

capital offense A criminal offense punishable by death.

capital punishment The death penalty. Capital punishment is the most extreme of all sentencing options.

career criminal In prosecutorial and law enforcement usage, a person who has a past record of multiple arrests or convictions for serious crimes or who has an unusually large number of arrests or convictions for crimes of varying degrees of seriousness. Also called *professional criminal*.

carnal knowledge Sexual intercourse, coitus, sexual copulation. Carnal knowledge is accomplished "if there is the slightest penetration of the sexual organ of the female by the sexual organ of the male."[10]

case law The body of judicial precedent, historically built on legal reasoning and past interpretations of statutory laws, that serves as a guide to decision making, especially in the courts.

caseload The number of probation or parole clients assigned to one probation or parole officer for supervision.

caseload (corrections) The total number of clients registered with a correctional agency or agent on a given date or during a specified time period, often divided into active supervisory cases and inactive cases, thus distinguishing between clients with whom contact is regular and those with whom it is not. Also, the number of probation or parole clients assigned to one probation or parole officer for supervision.

caseload (court) The number of cases requiring judicial action at a certain time. Also, the number of cases acted on in a given court during a given period.

certiorari See **writ of** *certiorari.*

chain of command The unbroken line of authority that extends through all levels of an organization, from the highest to the lowest.

change of venue The movement of a trial or lawsuit from one jurisdiction to another or from one location to another within the same jurisdiction. A change of venue may be made in a criminal case to ensure that the defendant receives a fair trial.

charge An allegation that a specified person has committed a specific offense, recorded in a functional document such as a record of an arrest, a complaint, an information or indictment, or a judgment of conviction. Also called *count.*

Chicago School A sociological approach that emphasizes demographics (the characteristics of population groups) and geographics (the mapped location of such groups relative to one another) and that sees the social disorganization that characterizes delinquency areas as a major cause of criminality and victimization.

child abuse The illegal physical, emotional, or sexual mistreatment of a child by his or her parent or guardian.

child neglect The illegal failure by a parent or guardian to provide proper nourishment or care to a child.

circumstantial evidence Evidence that requires interpretation or that requires a judge or jury to reach a conclusion based on what the evidence indicates. From the proximity of the defendant to a smoking gun, for example, the jury might conclude that he or she pulled the trigger.

citation (to appear) A written order issued by a law enforcement officer directing an alleged offender to appear in a specific court at a specified time to answer a criminal charge and not permitting forfeit of bail as an alternative to court appearance.

citizen's arrest The taking of a person into physical custody by a witness to a crime other than a law enforcement officer for the purpose of delivering him or her to the physical custody of a law enforcement officer or agency.

civil death The legal status of prisoners in some jurisdictions who are denied the opportunity to vote, hold public office, marry, or enter into contracts by virtue of their status as incarcerated felons. While civil death is primarily of historical interest, some jurisdictions still limit the contractual opportunities available to inmates.

civil justice The civil law, the law of civil procedure, and the array of procedures and activities having to do with private rights and remedies sought by civil action. Civil justice cannot be separated from social justice because the justice enacted in our nation's civil courts reflects basic American understandings of right and wrong.

civil law The branch of modern law that governs relationships between parties.

civil liability Potential responsibility for payment of damages or other court-ordered enforcement as a result of a ruling in a lawsuit. Civil liability is not the same as criminal liability, which means "open to punishment for a crime."[11]

class-action lawsuit A lawsuit filed by one or more people on behalf of themselves and a larger group of people "who are similarly situated."[12]

Classical School An eighteenth-century approach to crime causation and criminal responsibility that grew out of the Enlightenment and that emphasized the role of free will and reasonable punishments. Classical thinkers believed that punishment, if it is to be an effective deterrent, has to outweigh the potential pleasure derived from criminal behavior.

classification system A system used by prison administrators to assign inmates to custody levels based on offense history, assessed dangerousness, perceived risk of escape, and other factors.

clearance (UCR/NIBRS) The event in which a known occurrence of a Part I offense is followed by an arrest or another decision that indicates that the crime has been solved.

clearance rate A traditional measure of investigative effectiveness that compares the number of crimes reported or discovered to the number of crimes solved through arrest or other means (such as the death of the suspect).

clemency An executive or legislative action in which the severity of punishment of a single person or a group of people is reduced, the punishment is stopped, or the person or group is exempted from prosecution for certain actions.

closing argument An oral summation of a case presented to a judge, or to a judge and jury, by the prosecution or by the defense in a criminal trial.

club drug A synthetic psychoactive substance often found at nightclubs, bars, raves, and dance parties. Club drugs include MDMA (Ecstasy), ketamine, methamphetamine (meth), GBL, PCP, GHB, and Rohypnol.

codification The act or process of rendering laws in written form.

cohort A group of individuals sharing similarities of age, place of birth, and residence. Cohort analysis is a social science technique that tracks cohorts over time to identify the unique and observable behavioral traits that characterize them.

comes stabuli A nonuniformed mounted law enforcement officer of medieval England. Early police forces were small and relatively unorganized but made effective use of local resources in the formation of posses, the pursuit of offenders, and the like.

commitment The action of a judicial officer in ordering that a person subject to judicial proceedings be placed in a particular kind of confinement or residential facility for a specific reason authorized by law. Also, the result of the action—that is, the admission to the facility.

common law Law originating from usage and custom rather than from written statutes. The term refers to an unwritten body of judicial opinion, originally developed by English courts, that is based on nonstatutory customs, traditions, and precedents that help guide judicial decision making.

community-based corrections See **community corrections**.

community corrections The use of a variety of officially ordered program-based sanctions that permit convicted offenders to remain in the community under conditional supervision as an alternative to an active prison sentence. Also called *community-based corrections*.

community court A low-level court that focuses on quality-of-life crimes that erode a neighborhood's morale. Community courts emphasize problem solving rather than punishment and build on restorative principles like community service and restitution.

community policing "A collaborative effort between the police and the community that identifies problems of crime and disorder and involves all elements of the community in the search for solutions to these problems."[13]

community service A sentencing alternative that requires offenders to spend at least part of their time working for a community agency.

comparative criminologist One who studies crime and criminal justice on a cross-national level.

compelling interest A legal concept that provides a basis for suspicionless searches when public safety is at stake. (Urinalysis tests of train engineers are an example.) It is the concept on which the U.S. Supreme Court cases of *Skinner* v. *Railway Labor Executives' Association* (1989) and *National Treasury Employees Union* v. *Von Raab* (1989) turned. In those cases, the Court held that public safety may sometimes provide a sufficiently compelling interest to justify limiting an individual's right to privacy.

compensatory damages Damages recovered in payment for an actual injury or economic loss.

competent to stand trial A finding by a court that the defendant has sufficient present ability to consult with his or her attorney with a reasonable degree of rational understanding and that the de-

fendant has a rational as well as factual understanding of the proceedings against him or her.

complaint Generally, any accusation that a person has committed an offense, received by or originating from a law enforcement or prosecutorial agency or received by a court. Also, in judicial process usage, a formal document submitted to the court by a prosecutor, law enforcement officer, or other person, alleging that a specified person has committed a specific offense and requesting prosecution.

CompStat A crime-analysis and police-management process, built on crime mapping, that was developed by the New York City Police Department in the mid-1990s.

computer crime See **cybercrime**.

computer virus A computer program designed to secretly invade systems and either modify the way in which they operate or alter the information they store. Viruses are destructive software programs that may effectively vandalize computers of all types and sizes.

concurrence The coexistence of (1) an act in violation of the law and (2) a culpable mental state.

concurrent sentence One of two or more sentences imposed at the same time, after conviction for more than one offense, and served at the same time. Also, a new sentence for a new conviction, imposed upon a person already under sentence for a previous offense, served at the same time as the previous sentence.

concurring opinion An opinion written by a judge who agrees with the conclusion reached by the majority of judges hearing a case but whose reasons for reaching that conclusion differ. Concurring opinions, which typically stem from an appellate review, are written to identify issues of precedent, logic, or emphasis that are important to the concurring judge but that were not identified by the court's majority opinion.

conditional release The release by executive decision of a prisoner from a federal or state correctional facility who has not served his or her full sentence and whose freedom is contingent on obeying specified rules of behavior.

conditions of parole (probation) The general and special limits imposed on an offender who is released on parole (or probation). General conditions tend to be fixed by state statute, while special conditions are mandated by the sentencing authority (court or board) and take into consideration the background of the offender and the circumstances of the offense.

confinement In corrections, the physical restriction of a person to a clearly defined area from which he or she is lawfully forbidden to depart and from which departure is usually constrained by architectural barriers, guards or other custodians, or both.

conflict model A criminal justice perspective that assumes that the system's components function primarily to serve their own interests. According to this theoretical framework, justice is more a product of conflicts among agencies within the system than it is the result of cooperation among component agencies.

conflict perspective A theoretical approach that holds that crime is the natural consequence of economic and other social inequities. Conflict theorists highlight the stresses that arise among and within social groups as they compete with one another for resources and for survival. The social forces that result are viewed as major determinants of group and individual behavior, including crime.

consecutive sentence One of two or more sentences imposed at the same time, after conviction for more than one offense, and served in sequence with the other sentence. Also, a new sentence for a new conviction, imposed upon a person already under sentence for a previous offense, which is added to the previous sentence, thus increasing the maximum time the offender may be confined or under supervision.

consensus model A criminal justice perspective that assumes that the system's components work together harmoniously to achieve the social product we call *justice*.

constitutive criminology The study of the process by which human beings create an ideology of crime that sustains the notion of crime as a concrete reality.

containment The aspects of the social bond and of the personality that act to prevent individuals from committing crimes and engaging in deviance.

contempt of court Intentionally obstructing a court in the administration of justice, acting in a way calculated to lessen the court's authority or dignity, or failing to obey the court's lawful orders.

controlled substance A specifically defined bioactive or psychoactive chemical substance proscribed by law.

Controlled Substances Act (CSA) Title II of the Comprehensive Drug Abuse Prevention and Control Act of 1970, which established schedules classifying psychoactive drugs according to their degree of psychoactivity.

conviction The judgment of a court, based on the verdict of a jury or judicial officer or on the guilty plea or *nolo contendere* plea of the defendant, that the defendant is guilty of the offense with which he or she has been charged.

corporate crime A violation of a criminal statute by a corporate entity or by its executives, employees, or agents acting on behalf of and for the benefit of the corporation, partnership, or other form of business entity.[14]

corpus delicti The facts that show that a crime has occurred. The term literally means "the body of the crime."

correctional agency A federal, state, or local criminal or juvenile justice agency, under a single administrative authority, whose principal functions are the intake screening, supervision, custody, confinement, treatment, or presentencing or predisposition investigation of alleged or adjudicated adult offenders, youthful offenders, delinquents, or status offenders.

corrections A generic term that includes all government agencies, facilities, programs, procedures, personnel, and techniques concerned with the intake, custody, confinement, supervision, treatment, and presentencing and predisposition investigation of alleged or adjudicated adult offenders, youthful offenders, delinquents, and status offenders.

corruption See **police corruption**.

Cosa Nostra A secret criminal organization of Sicilian origin. Also called *Mafia*.

counsel (legal) See **attorney**.

count (offense) See **charge**.

court An agency or unit of the judicial branch of government, authorized or established by statute or constitution and consisting of one or more judicial officers, which has the authority to decide cases, controversies in law, and disputed matters of fact brought before it.

court calendar The court schedule; the list of events comprising the daily or weekly work of a court, including the assignment of the time and place for each hearing or other item of business or the list of matters that will be taken up in a given court term. Also called *docket*.

court clerk An elected or appointed court officer responsible for maintaining the written records of the court and for supervising or performing the clerical tasks necessary for conducting judicial business. Also, any employee of a court whose principal duties are to assist the court clerk in performing the clerical tasks necessary for conducting judicial business.

court disposition 1. For statistical reporting purposes, generally, the judicial decision terminating proceedings in a case before judgment is reached. 2. The judgment. 3. The outcome of judicial proceedings and the manner in which the outcome was arrived at.

court-martial A military court convened by senior commanders under the authority of the Uniform Code of Military Justice for the purpose of trying a member of the armed forces accused of a violation of the code.

court of last resort The court authorized by law to hear the final appeal on a matter.

court of record A court in which a complete and permanent record of all proceedings or specified types of proceedings is kept.

court order A mandate, command, or direction issued by a judicial officer in the exercise of his or her judicial authority.

court probation A criminal court requirement that an offender fulfill specified conditions of behavior in lieu of a sentence to confinement, but without assignment to a probation agency's supervisory caseload.

court reporter A person present during judicial proceedings who records all testimony and other oral statements made during the proceedings.

courtroom work group The professional courtroom actors, including judges, prosecuting attorneys, defense attorneys, public defenders, and others who earn a living serving the court.

credit card fraud The use or attempted use of a credit card to obtain goods or services with the intent to avoid payment.

crime Conduct in violation of the criminal laws of a state, the federal government, or a local jurisdiction, for which there is no legally acceptable justification or excuse.

crime-control model A criminal justice perspective that emphasizes the efficient arrest and conviction of criminal offenders.

Crime Index A now defunct but once inclusive measure of the UCR Program's violent and property crime categories, or what are called *Part I offenses*. The Crime Index, long featured in the FBI's publication *Crime in the United States*, was discontinued in 2004. The index had been intended as a tool for geographic (state-to-state) and historical (year-to-year) comparisons via the use of crime rates (the number of crimes per unit of population). However, criticism that the index was misleading arose after researchers found that the largest of the index's crime categories, larceny-theft, carried undue weight and led to an underappreciation of changes in the rates of more violent and serious crimes.

crime prevention The anticipation, recognition, and appraisal of a crime risk and the initiation of action to eliminate or reduce it.

crime rate The number of offenses reported for each unit of population.

crime scene The physical area in which a crime is thought to have occurred and in which evidence of the crime is thought to reside.

crime-scene investigator An expert trained in the use of forensics techniques, such as gathering DNA evidence, collecting fingerprints, photographing the scene, sketching, and interviewing witnesses.

crime typology A classification of crimes along a particular dimension, such as legal categories, offender motivation, victim behavior, or the characteristics of individual offenders.

criminal homicide (UCR/NIBRS) The act of causing the death of another person without legal justification or excuse.

criminal incident In National Crime Victimization Survey terminology, a criminal event involving one or more victims and one or more offenders.

criminal intelligence Information compiled, analyzed, or disseminated in an effort to anticipate, prevent, or monitor criminal activity.[15]

criminal investigation "The process of discovering, collecting, preparing, identifying, and presenting evidence to determine *what happened and who is responsible*"[16] when a crime has occurred.

criminalist A police crime-scene analyst or laboratory worker versed in criminalistics.

criminalistics The use of technology in the service of criminal investigation; the application of scientific techniques to the detection and evaluation of criminal evidence.

criminal justice In the strictest sense, the criminal (penal) law, the law of criminal procedure, and the array of procedures and activities having to do with the enforcement of this body of law. Criminal justice cannot be separated from social justice because the justice enacted in our nation's criminal courts reflects basic American understandings of right and wrong.

criminal justice system The aggregate of all operating and administrative or technical support agencies that perform criminal justice functions. The basic divisions of the operational aspects of criminal justice are law enforcement, courts, and corrections.

criminal law The body of rules and regulations that define and specify the nature of and punishments for offenses of a public nature or for wrongs committed against the state or society. Also called *penal law.*

criminal negligence Behavior in which a person fails to reasonably perceive substantial and unjustifiable risks of dangerous consequences.

criminology The scientific study of the causes and prevention of crime and the rehabilitation and punishment of offenders.

criminal proceedings The regular and orderly steps, as directed or authorized by statute or a court of law, taken to determine whether an adult accused of a crime is guilty or not guilty.

cruel and unusual punishment Punishment involving torture or a lingering death or the infliction of unnecessary and wanton pain.

culpability Blameworthiness; responsibility in some sense for an event or situation deserving of moral blame. Also, in Model Penal Code usage, a state of mind on the part of one who is committing an act that makes him or her potentially subject to prosecution for that act.

cultural defense A defense to a criminal charge in which the defendant's culture is taken into account in judging his or her culpability.

cultural pluralism See **multiculturalism**.

curtilage In legal usage, the area surrounding a residence that can reasonably be said to be a part of the residence for Fourth Amendment purposes.

custody The legal or physical control of a person or a thing. Also, the legal, supervisory, or physical responsibility for a person or a thing.

cybercrime Any crime perpetrated through the use of computer technology. Also, any violation of a federal or state cybercrime statute. Also called *computer crime.*

cyberstalking The use of the Internet, e-mail, and other electronic communication technologies to stalk another person.[17]

cyberterrorism A form of terrorism that makes use of high technology, especially computers and the Internet, in the planning and carrying out of terrorist attacks.

danger law A law intended to prevent the pretrial release of criminal defendants judged to represent a danger to others in the community.

dangerousness The likelihood that a given individual will later harm society or others. Dangerousness is often measured in terms of recidivism, or the likelihood that an individual will commit an additional crime within five years following arrest or release from confinement.

dark figure of crime Crime that is not reported to the police and that remains unknown to officials.

data encryption The encoding of computerized information.

date rape Unlawful forced sexual intercourse with a female against her will that occurs within the context of a dating relationship. Date rape, or acquaintance rape, is a subcategory of rape that is of special concern today.

***Daubert* standard** A test of scientific acceptability applicable to the gathering of evidence in criminal cases.

deadly force Force likely to cause death or great bodily harm. Also, "the intentional use of a firearm or other instrument resulting in a high probability of death."[18]

deadly weapon An instrument that is designed to inflict serious bodily injury or death or that is capable of being used for such a purpose.

deconstructionist theory One of the emerging approaches that challenges existing criminological perspectives to debunk them and that works toward replacing them with concepts more applicable to the postmodern era.

decriminalization The redefinition of certain previously criminal behaviors into regulated activities that become "ticketable" rather than "arrestable."

defendant A person formally accused of an offense by the filing in court of a charging document.

defense (to a criminal charge) Evidence and arguments offered by a defendant and his or her attorney to show why the defendant should not be held liable for a criminal charge.

defense attorney See **defense counsel**.

defense counsel A licensed trial lawyer hired or appointed to conduct the legal defense of a person accused of a crime and to represent him or her before a court of law. Also called *defense attorney.*

defensible space theory The belief that an area's physical features may be modified and structured so as to reduce crime rates in that area and to lower the fear of victimization that residents experience.

deliberate indifference   A wanton disregard by correctional personnel for the well-being of inmates. Deliberate indifference requires both actual knowledge that a harm is occurring and disregard of the risk of harm. A prison official may be held liable under the Eighth Amendment for acting with deliberate indifference to inmate health or safety only if he or she knows that inmates face a substantial risk of serious harm and disregards that risk by failing to take reasonable measures to abate it.

delinquency   In the broadest usage, juvenile actions or conduct in violation of criminal law, juvenile status offenses, and other juvenile misbehavior.

delinquent   A juvenile who has been adjudged by a judicial officer of a juvenile court to have committed a delinquent act.

delinquent act   An act committed by a juvenile for which an adult could be prosecuted in a criminal court but for which a juvenile can be adjudicated in a juvenile court or prosecuted in a court having criminal jurisdiction if the juvenile court transfers jurisdiction. Generally, a felony- or misdemeanor-level offense in states employing those terms.

delinquent child   A child who has engaged in activity that would be considered a crime if the child were an adult. The term *delinquent* is used to avoid the stigma associated with the term *criminal*.

dependent child   A child who has no parents or whose parents are unable to care for him or her.

design capacity   The number of inmates a prison was intended to hold when it was built or modified. Also called *bed capacity*.

detainee   Usually, a person held in local short-term confinement while awaiting consideration for pretrial release or a first appearance for arraignment.

detention   The legally authorized confinement of a person subject to criminal or juvenile court proceedings, until the point of commitment to a correctional facility or until release.

detention hearing   In juvenile justice usage, a hearing by a judicial officer of a juvenile court to determine whether a juvenile is to be detained, is to continue to be detained, or is to be released while juvenile proceedings are pending.

determinate sentencing   A model of criminal punishment in which an offender is given a fixed term of imprisonment that may be reduced by good time or gain time. Under the model, for example, all offenders convicted of the same degree of burglary would be sentenced to the same length of time behind bars. Also called *fixed sentencing*.

deterrence   A goal of criminal sentencing that seeks to inhibit criminal behavior through the fear of punishment.

deviance   A violation of social norms defining appropriate or proper behavior under a particular set of circumstances. Deviance often includes criminal acts. Also called *deviant behavior*.

digital criminal forensics   The lawful seizure, acquisition, analysis, reporting, and safeguarding of data from digital devices that may contain information of evidentiary value to the trier of fact in criminal events.[19]

diminished capacity   A defense based on claims of a mental condition that may be insufficient to exonerate the defendant of guilt but that may be relevant to specific mental elements of certain crimes or degrees of crime. Also called *diminished responsibility*.

directed patrol   A police-management strategy designed to increase the productivity of patrol officers through the scientific analysis and evaluation of patrol techniques.

direct evidence   Evidence that, if believed, directly proves a fact. Eyewitness testimony and videotaped documentation account for the majority of all direct evidence heard in the criminal courtroom.

direct-supervision jail   A temporary confinement facility that eliminates many of the traditional barriers between inmates and correctional staff. Physical barriers in direct-supervision jails are far less common than in traditional jails, allowing staff members the opportunity for greater interaction with, and control over, residents. Also called *new-generation jail; podular direct jail*.

discharge   To release from confinement or supervision or to release from a legal status imposing an obligation upon the subject person.

discretion   See **police discretion**.

discretionary release   The release of an inmate from prison to supervision that is decided by a parole board or other authority.

disposition   The action by a criminal or juvenile justice agency that signifies that a portion of the justice process is complete and that jurisdiction is terminated or transferred to another agency or that signifies that a decision has been reached on one aspect of a case and a different aspect comes under consideration, requiring a different kind of decision.

dispositional hearing   The final stage in the processing of adjudicated juveniles in which a decision is made on the form of treatment or penalty that should be imposed on the child.

dispute-resolution center   An informal hearing place designed to mediate interpersonal disputes without resorting to the more formal arrangements of a criminal trial court.

district attorney (DA)   See **prosecutor**.

diversion   The official suspension of criminal or juvenile proceedings against an alleged offender at any point after a recorded justice system intake, but before the entering of a judgment, and referral of that person to a treatment or care program administered by a nonjustice or private agency. Also, release without referral.

DNA profiling   The use of biological residue, found at the scene of a crime, for genetic comparisons in aiding in the identification of criminal suspects.

docket   See **court calendar**.

domestic terrorism   The unlawful use of force or violence by an individual or a group that is based and operates entirely within the United States and its territories, acts without foreign direction, and directs its activities against elements of the U.S. government or population.[20]

double jeopardy   A common law and constitutional prohibition against a second trial for the same offense.

drug Any chemical substance defined by social convention as bioactive or psychoactive.

drug abuse Illicit drug use that results in social, economic, psychological, or legal problems for the user.[21]

drug court A special state, county, or municipal court that offers first-time substance-abuse offenders judicially mandated and court-supervised treatment alternatives to prison.

drug czar The popular name for the head of the Office of National Drug Control Policy (ONDCP), a federal cabinet-level position that was created during the Reagan presidency to organize federal drug-fighting efforts.

drug-law violation The unlawful sale, purchase, distribution, manufacture, cultivation, transport, possession, or use of a controlled or prohibited drug. Also, the attempt to commit one of these acts.

drug trafficking Trading or dealing in controlled substances, including the transporting, storage, importing, exporting, or sale of a controlled substance.

due process A right guaranteed by the Fifth, Sixth, and Fourteenth Amendments of the U.S. Constitution and generally understood, in legal contexts, to mean the due course of legal proceedings according to the rules and forms established for the protection of individual rights. In criminal proceedings, due process of law is generally understood to include the following basic elements: a law creating and defining the offense, an impartial tribunal having jurisdictional authority over the case, accusation in proper form, notice and opportunity to defend, trial according to established procedure, and discharge from all restraints or obligations unless convicted.

due process model A criminal justice perspective that emphasizes individual rights at all stages of justice system processing.

Electronic Communications Privacy Act (ECPA) A law passed by Congress in 1986 establishing the due process requirements that law enforcement officers must meet in order to legally intercept wire communications.

electronic evidence Information and data of investigative value that are stored in or transmitted by an electronic device.[22]

element (of a crime) In a specific crime, one of the essential features of that crime, as specified by law or statute.

embezzlement The misappropriation, or illegal disposal, of legally entrusted property by the person to whom it was entrusted, with the intent to defraud the legal owner or the intended beneficiary.

emergency search A search conducted by the police without a warrant, which is justified on the basis of some immediate and overriding need, such as public safety, the likely escape of a dangerous suspect, or the removal or destruction of evidence.

entrapment An improper or illegal inducement to crime by agents of law enforcement. Also, a defense that may be raised when such inducements have occurred.

equity A sentencing principle, based on concerns with social equality, that holds that similar crimes should be punished with the same degree of severity, regardless of the social or personal characteristics of the offenders.

espionage The "gathering, transmitting, or losing"[23] of information related to the national defense in such a manner that the information becomes available to enemies of the United States and may be used to their advantage.

ethnocentric Holding a belief in the superiority of one's own social or ethnic group and culture.

ethnocentrism The phenomenon of "culture-centeredness" by which one uses one's own culture as a benchmark against which to judge all other patterns of behavior.

European Police Office (Europol) The integrated police–intelligence gathering and dissemination arm of the member nations of the European Union.

evidence Anything useful to a judge or jury in deciding the facts of a case. Evidence may take the form of witness testimony, written documents, videotapes, magnetic media, photographs, physical objects, and so on.

evidence-based policing (EBP) The use of the best available research on the outcomes of police work to implement guidelines and evaluate agencies, units, and officers.[24]

excessive force The application of an amount and/or frequency of force greater than that required to compel compliance from a willing or unwilling subject.[25]

exclusionary rule The understanding, based on U.S. Supreme Court precedent, that incriminating information must be seized according to constitutional specifications of due process or it will not be allowed as evidence in a criminal trial.

excuse A legal defense in which the defendant claims that some personal condition or circumstance at the time of the act was such that he or she should not be held accountable under the criminal law.

exemplary damages See **punitive damages**.

Exemplary Projects Program An initiative, sponsored by the Law Enforcement Assistance Administration, designed to recognize outstanding innovative efforts to combat crime and to provide assistance to crime victims.

expert system Computer hardware and software that attempt to duplicate the decision-making processes used by skilled investigators in the analysis of evidence and in the recognition of patterns that such evidence might represent.

expert witness A person who has special knowledge and skills recognized by the court as relevant to the determination of guilt or innocence. Unlike lay witnesses, expert witnesses may express opinions or draw conclusions in their testimony.

ex post facto Latin for "after the fact." The Constitution prohibits the enactment of *ex post facto* laws, which make acts committed before the laws in question were passed punishable as crimes.

extradition The surrender by one state or jurisdiction to another of an individual accused or convicted of an offense in the second state or jurisdiction.

federal court system The three-tiered structure of federal courts, comprising U.S. district courts, U.S. courts of appeal, and the U.S. Supreme Court.

federal law enforcement agency A U.S. government agency or office whose primary functional responsibility is to enforce federal criminal laws.

felony A criminal offense punishable by death or by incarceration in a prison facility for at least one year.

feminist criminology A developing intellectual approach that emphasizes gender issues in criminology.

filing The initiation of a criminal case by formal submission to the court of a charging document, alleging that a named person has committed a specified criminal offense.

fine The penalty imposed on a convicted person by a court, requiring that he or she pay a specified sum of money to the court.

first appearance An appearance before a magistrate during which the legality of the defendant's arrest is initially assessed and the defendant is informed of the charges on which he or she is being held. At this stage in the criminal justice process, bail may be set or pretrial release arranged. Also called *initial appearance*.

first plea See **initial plea**.

fixed sentencing See **determinate sentencing**.

fleeting-targets exception An exception to the exclusionary rule that permits law enforcement officers to search a motor vehicle based on probable cause and without a warrant. The fleeting-targets exception is predicated on the fact that vehicles can quickly leave the jurisdiction of a law enforcement agency.

force See **police use of force**.

forcible rape (UCR/NIBRS) The carnal knowledge of a female, forcibly and against her will. For statistical reporting purposes, the FBI defines *forcible rape* as "unlawful sexual intercourse with a female, by force and against her will, or without legal or factual consent." Statutory rape differs from forcible rape in that it generally involves nonforcible sexual intercourse with a minor. See also **carnal knowledge; rape**.

foreign terrorist organization (FTO) A foreign organization that engages in terrorist activity that threatens the security of U.S. nationals or the national security of the United States and that is

so designated by the U.S. secretary of state.

forensic anthropology The use of anthropological principles and techniques in criminal investigation.

forensic entomology The study of insects to determine such matters as a person's time of death.

forfeiture The authorized seizure of money, negotiable instruments, securities, or other things of value. Under federal antidrug laws, judicial representatives are authorized to seize all cash, negotiable instruments, securities, or other things of value furnished or intended to be furnished by any person in exchange for a controlled substance, as well as all proceeds traceable to such an exchange. Also called *asset forfeiture*.

forgery The creation or alteration of a written or printed document, which if validly executed would constitute a record of a legally binding transaction, with the intent to defraud by affirming it to be the act of an unknowing second person. Also, the creation of an art object with intent to misrepresent the identity of the creator.

fraud An offense involving deceit or intentional misrepresentation of fact, with the intent of unlawfully depriving a person of his or her property or legal rights.

frivolous suit A lawsuit with no foundation in fact. Frivolous suits are generally brought by lawyers and plaintiffs for reasons of publicity, politics, or other non-law-related issues and may result in fines against plaintiffs and their counsel.

fruit of the poisonous tree doctrine A legal principle that excludes from introduction at trial any evidence later developed as a result of an illegal search or seizure.

gain time The amount of time deducted from time to be served in prison on a given sentence as a consequence of participation in special projects or programs.

general deterrence A goal of criminal sentencing that seeks to prevent others from committing crimes similar to the one for which a particular offender is being sentenced by making an example of the person sentenced.

globalization The internationalization of trade, services, investment, information, and other forms of human social activity. Also, a process of social homogenization by which the experiences of everyday life, marked by the diffusion of commodities and ideas, can foster a standardization of cultural expressions around the world.[26]

good-faith exception An exception to the exclusionary rule. Law enforcement officers who conduct a search or who seize evidence on the basis of good faith (that is, when they believe they are operating according to the dictates of the law) and who later discover that a mistake was made (perhaps in the format of the application for a search warrant) may still provide evidence that can be used in court.

good time The amount of time deducted from time to be served in prison on a given sentence as a consequence of good behavior.

grand jury A group of jurors who have been selected according to law and have been sworn to hear the evidence and to determine whether there is sufficient evidence to bring the accused person to trial, to investigate criminal activity generally, or to investigate the conduct of a public agency or official.

grievance procedure A formalized arrangement, usually involving a neutral hearing board, whereby institutionalized individuals have the opportunity to register complaints about the conditions of their confinement.

gross negligence The intentional failure to perform a manifest duty in reckless disregard of the consequences as affecting the life or property of another.[27]

guilty but mentally ill (GBMI) A verdict, equivalent to a finding of "guilty," that establishes that the defendant, although mentally ill, was in sufficient possession of his or her faculties to be morally blameworthy for his or her acts.

guilty plea A defendant's formal answer in court to the charge or charges contained in a complaint, information, or indictment, claiming that he or she did commit the offense or offenses listed.

guilty verdict See **verdict**.

habeas corpus   See **writ of *habeas corpus***.

habitual offender   A person sentenced under the provisions of a statute declaring that people convicted of a given offense and shown to have previously been convicted of another specified offense shall receive a more severe penalty than that for the current offense alone.

hacker   A computer hobbyist or professional, generally with advanced programming skills. Today, the term *hacker* has taken on a sinister connotation, referring to hobbyists who are bent on illegally accessing the computers of others or who attempt to demonstrate their technological prowess through computerized acts of vandalism.

hands-off doctrine   A policy of nonintervention with regard to prison management that U.S. courts tended to follow until the late 1960s. For the past 40 years, the doctrine has languished as judicial intervention in prison administration dramatically increased, although there is now some evidence that a new hands-off era is approaching.

Harrison Narcotics Act   The first major piece of federal antidrug legislation, passed in 1914.

hate crime (UCR/NIBRS)   A criminal offense committed against a person, property, or society that is motivated, in whole or in part, by the offender's bias against a race, religion, disability, sexual orientation, or ethnicity/national origin. Also called *bias crime*.

hearing   A proceeding in which arguments, witnesses, or evidence is heard by a judicial officer or an administrative body.

hearsay   Something that is not based on the personal knowledge of a witness. Witnesses who testify about something they have heard, for example, are offering hearsay by repeating information about a matter of which they have no direct knowledge.

hearsay rule   The long-standing precedent that hearsay cannot be used in American courtrooms. Rather than accepting testimony based on hearsay, the court will ask that the person who was the original source of the hearsay information be brought in to be questioned and cross-examined. Exceptions to the hearsay rule may occur when the person with direct knowledge is dead or is otherwise unable to testify.

hierarchy rule   A pre-NIBRS Uniform Crime Reporting Program scoring practice in which only the most serious offense was counted in a multiple-offense incident.

high-technology crime   Violations of the criminal law whose commission depends on, makes use of, and often targets sophisticated and advanced technology. See also **cybercrime**.

home confinement   House arrest. Individuals ordered confined to their homes are sometimes monitored electronically to ensure they do not leave during the hours of confinement. Absence from the home during working hours is often permitted.

homicide   See **criminal homicide**.

Hudud **crime**   A serious violation of Islamic law that is regarded as an offense against God. *Hudud* crimes include such behavior as theft, adultery, sodomy, alcohol consumption, and robbery.

hung jury   A jury that, after long deliberation, is so irreconcilably divided in opinion that it is unable to reach any verdict.

hypothesis   An explanation that accounts for a set of facts and that can be tested by further investigation. Also, something that is taken to be true for the purpose of argument or investigation.[28]

identity management   The comprehensive management and administration of a user's individual profile information, permissions, and privileges across a variety of social settings.[29]

identity theft   A crime in which an impostor obtains key pieces of information, such as Social Security and driver's license numbers, to obtain credit, merchandise, and services in the name of the victim. The victim is often left with a ruined credit history and the time-consuming and complicated task of repairing the financial damage.[30]

illegally seized evidence   Evidence seized without regard to the principles of due process as described by the Bill of Rights. Most illegally seized evidence is the result of police searches conducted without a proper warrant or of improperly conducted interrogations.

illegal search and seizure   An act in violation of the Fourth Amendment of the U.S. Constitution, which reads, "The right of the people to be secure in their persons, houses, papers, and effects, against unreasonable searches and seizures, shall not be violated, and no Warrants shall issue, but upon probable cause, supported by Oath or affirmation, and particularly describing the place to be searched, and the persons or things to be seized."

incapacitation   The use of imprisonment or other means to reduce the likelihood that an offender will commit future offenses.

inchoate offense   An offense not yet completed. Also, an offense that consists of an action or conduct that is a step toward the intended commission of another offense.

incident-based reporting   Compared with summary reporting, a less restrictive and more expansive method of collecting crime data in which all of the analytical elements associated with an offense or arrest are compiled by a central collection agency on an incident-by-incident basis.

included offense   An offense that is made up of elements that are a subset of the elements of another offense having a greater statutory penalty, the occurrence of which is established by the same evidence or by some portion of the evidence that has been offered to establish the occurrence of the greater offense.

incompetent to stand trial   In criminal proceedings, a finding by a court that, as a result of mental illness, defect, or disability, a defendant is incapable of understanding the nature of the charges and proceedings against him or her, of consulting with an attorney, and of aiding in his or her own defense.

indeterminate sentence   A type of sentence imposed on a convicted criminal that is meant to encourage rehabilitation through the use of relatively unspecific punishments (such as a term of imprisonment of from one to ten years).

indeterminate sentencing   A model of criminal punishment that encourages rehabilitation through the use of general and relatively unspecific sentences (such as a term of imprisonment of from one to ten years).

index crime   See **Crime Index**.

indictment   A formal, written accusation submitted to the court by a grand jury, alleging that a specified person has committed a specified offense, usually a felony.

individual rights   The rights guaranteed to all members of American society by the U.S. Constitution (especially those found in the first ten amendments to the Constitution, known as the *Bill of Rights*). These rights are particularly important to criminal defendants facing formal processing by the criminal justice system.

individual-rights advocate   One who seeks to protect personal freedoms within the process of criminal justice.

industrial prison   A correctional model intended to capitalize on the labor of convicts sentenced to confinement.

information   A formal, written accusation submitted to the court by a prosecutor, alleging that a specified person has committed a specific offense.

infraction   A minor violation of state statute or local ordinance punishable by a fine or other penalty or by a specified, usually limited, term of incarceration.

infrastructure   The basic facilities, services, and installations that a country needs to function. Transportation and communications systems, water and power lines, and institutions that serve the public, including banks, schools, post offices, and prisons, are all part of a country's infrastructure.[31]

inherent coercion   The tactics used by police interviewers that fall short of physical abuse but that nonetheless pressure suspects to divulge information.

initial appearance   See **first appearance**.

initial plea   The first plea to a given charge entered in the court record by or for the defendant. The acceptance of an initial plea by the court unambiguously indicates that the arraignment process has been completed. Also called *first plea.*

insanity defense   A legal defense based on claims of mental illness or mental incapacity.

institutional capacity   The official number of inmates that a confinement or residential facility is housing or was intended to house.

intake   The first step in decision making regarding a juvenile whose behavior or alleged behavior is in violation of the law or could otherwise cause a juvenile court to assume jurisdiction.

intelligence-led policing (ILP)   The collection and analysis of information to produce an intelligence end product designed to inform police decision making at both the tactical and strategic levels.[32]

intensive probation supervision (IPS)   A form of probation supervision involving frequent face-to-face contact between the probationer and the probation officer.

intent   The state of mind or attitude with which an act is carried out. Also, the design, resolve, or determination with which a person acts to achieve a certain result.

interdiction   The interception of drug traffic at the nation's borders. Interdiction is one of the many strategies used to stem the flow of illegal drugs into the United States.

interdisciplinary theory   An approach that integrates a variety of theoretical viewpoints in an attempt to explain something, such as crime and violence.

intermediate appellate court   An appellate court whose primary function is to review the judgments of trial courts and the decisions of administrative agencies and whose decisions are, in turn, usually reviewable by a higher appellate court in the same state.

intermediate sanctions   The use of split sentencing, shock probation or parole, shock incarceration, community service, intensive supervision, or home confinement in lieu of other, more traditional, sanctions, such as imprisonment and fines. Also called *alternative sanctions.*

internal affairs   The branch of a police organization tasked with investigating charges of wrongdoing involving members of the department.

International Criminal Police Organization (Interpol)   An international law enforcement support organization that began operations in 1946 and today has 182 member nations.

international terrorism   The unlawful use of force or violence by an individual or a group that has some connection to a foreign power, or whose activities transcend national boundaries, against people or property in order to intimidate or coerce a government, the civilian population, or any segment thereof, in furtherance of political or social objectives.[33]

interrogation   The information-gathering activity of police officers that involves the direct questioning of suspects.

Islamic law   A system of laws, operative in some Arab countries, based on the Muslim religion and especially the holy book of Islam, the Koran.

jail   A confinement facility administered by an agency of local government, typically a law enforcement agency, intended for adults but sometimes also containing juveniles, which holds people detained pending adjudication or committed after adjudication, usually those sentenced to a year or less.

jail commitment   A sentence of commitment to the jurisdiction of a confinement facility system for adults that is administered by an agency of local government and whose custodial authority is usually limited to people sentenced to a year or less of confinement.

judge   An elected or appointed public official who presides over a court of law and who is authorized to hear and sometimes to decide cases and to conduct trials.

judgment   The statement of the decision of a court that the defendant is acquitted or convicted of the offense or offenses charged.

judgment suspending sentence   A court-ordered sentencing alternative that results in the convicted offender being placed on probation.

judicial officer   Any person authorized by statute, constitutional provision, or court rule to exercise the powers reserved to the judicial branch of government.

judicial review   The power of a court to review actions and decisions made by other agencies of government.

jural postulates   Propositions developed by the famous jurist Roscoe Pound that hold that the law reflects shared needs without which members of society could not coexist. Pound's jural postulates are often linked to the idea that the law can be used to engineer the social structure to ensure certain kinds of outcomes. In capitalist societies, for example, the law of theft protects property rights.

jurisdiction The territory, subject matter, or people over which a court or other justice agency may exercise lawful authority, as determined by statute or constitution. See also **venue**.

jurisprudence The philosophy of law. Also, the science and study of the law.

juror A member of a trial or grand jury who has been selected for jury duty and is required to serve as an arbiter of the facts in a court of law. Jurors are expected to render verdicts of "guilty" or "not guilty" as to the charges brought against the accused, although they sometimes fail to do so (as in the case of a hung jury).

jury panel The group of people summoned to appear in court as potential jurors for a particular trial. Also, the people selected from the group of potential jurors to sit in the jury box, from which those acceptable to the prosecution and the defense are finally chosen as the jury.

jury selection The process whereby, according to law and precedent, members of a trial jury are chosen.

just deserts A model of criminal sentencing that holds that criminal offenders deserve the punishment they receive at the hands of the law and that punishments should be appropriate to the type and severity of the crime committed.

justice The principle of fairness; the ideal of moral equity.

justice model A contemporary model of imprisonment based on the principle of just deserts.

justification A legal defense in which the defendant admits to committing the act in question but claims it was necessary in order to avoid some greater evil.

juvenile A person subject to juvenile court proceedings because a statutorily defined event or condition caused by or affecting that person was alleged to have occurred while his or her age was below the statutorily specified age limit of original jurisdiction of a juvenile court.

juvenile court A court that has, as all or part of its authority, original jurisdiction over matters concerning people statutorily defined as juveniles.

juvenile court judgment The juvenile court decision, terminating an adjudicatory hearing, that the juvenile is a delinquent, a status offender, or a dependent or that the allegations in the petition are not sustained.

juvenile disposition The decision of a juvenile court, concluding a dispositional hearing, that an adjudicated juvenile be committed to a juvenile correctional facility; be placed in a juvenile residence, shelter, or care or treatment program; be required to meet certain standards of conduct; or be released.

juvenile justice The policies and activities of law enforcement and the courts in handling law violations by youths under the age of criminal jurisdiction.[34]

juvenile justice agency A government agency, or subunit thereof, whose functions are the investigation, supervision, adjudication, care, or confinement of juvenile offenders and nonoffenders subject to the jurisdiction of a juvenile court. Also, in some usages, a private agency providing care and treatment.

juvenile justice system The aggregate of the government agencies that function to investigate, supervise, adjudicate, care for, or confine youthful offenders and other children subject to the jurisdiction of the juvenile court.

juvenile petition A document filed in juvenile court alleging that a juvenile is a delinquent, a status offender, or a dependent and asking that the court assume jurisdiction over the juvenile or that an alleged delinquent be transferred to a criminal court for prosecution as an adult.

Kansas City experiment The first large-scale scientific study of law enforcement practices. Sponsored by the Police Foundation, it focused on the practice of preventive patrol.

kidnapping The transportation or confinement of a person without authority of law and without his or her consent or without the consent of his or her guardian, if a minor.

Knapp Commission A committee that investigated police corruption in New York City in the early 1970s.

labeling theory A social process perspective that sees continued crime as a consequence of the limited opportunities for acceptable behavior that follow from the negative responses of society to those defined as offenders.

landmark case A precedent-setting court decision that produces substantial changes in both the understanding of the requirements of due process and in the practical day-to-day operations of the justice system.

larceny-theft (UCR/NIBRS) The unlawful taking or attempted taking, carrying, leading, or riding away of property, from the possession or constructive possession of another. Motor vehicles are excluded. Larceny is the most common of the eight major offenses, although probably only a small percentage of all larcenies are actually reported to the police because of the small dollar amounts involved.

latent evidence Evidence of relevance to a criminal investigation that is not readily seen by the unaided eye.

law A rule of conduct, generally found enacted in the form of a statute, that proscribes or mandates certain forms of behavior. Statutory law is often the result of moral enterprise by interest groups that, through the exercise of political power, are successful in seeing their valued perspectives enacted into law.

law enforcement The generic name for the activities of the agencies responsible for maintaining public order and enforcing the law, particularly the activities of preventing, detecting, and investigating crime and apprehending criminals.

law enforcement agency A federal, state, or local criminal justice agency or identifiable subunit whose principal functions are the prevention, detection, and investigation of crime and the apprehension of alleged offenders.

Law Enforcement Assistance Administration (LEAA) A now-defunct federal agency established under Title I of the Omnibus Crime Control and Safe

Streets Act of 1968 to funnel federal funding to state and local law enforcement agencies.

law enforcement intelligence See **criminal intelligence**.

law enforcement officer An officer employed by a law enforcement agency who is sworn to carry out law enforcement duties.

lawyer See **attorney**.

lay witness An eyewitness, character witness, or other person called on to testify who is not considered an expert. Lay witnesses must testify to facts only and may not draw conclusions or express opinions.

learning organization "An organization skilled at creating, acquiring, and transferring knowledge and at modifying its behavior to reflect new knowledge and insights."[35]

legal cause A legally recognizable cause. A legal cause must be demonstrated in court in order to hold an individual criminally liable for causing harm.

legal counsel See **attorney**.

legalistic style A style of policing marked by a strict concern with enforcing the precise letter of the law. Legalistic departments may take a hands-off approach to disruptive or problematic behavior that does not violate the criminal law.

legalization Elimination of the laws and associated criminal penalties associated with certain behaviors—usually the production, sale, distribution, and possession of a controlled substance.

less-lethal weapon A weapon that is designed to disable, capture, or immobilize—but not kill—a suspect. Occasional deaths do result from the use of such weapons, however.

lex talionis The law of retaliation, often expressed as "an eye for an eye" or "like for like."

life course perspective An approach to explaining crime and deviance that investigates developments and turning points in the course of a person's life.

line operations In police organizations, the field activities or supervisory activities directly related to day-to-day police work.

Mafia See **Cosa Nostra**.

major crimes See **Part I offenses**.

mala in se Acts that are regarded, by tradition and convention, as wrong in themselves.

mala prohibita Acts that are considered wrong only because there is a law against them.

malware Malicious computer programs like viruses, worms, and Trojan horses.

mandatory release The release of an inmate from prison that is determined by statute or sentencing guidelines and is not decided by a parole board or other authority.

mandatory sentence A statutorily required penalty that must be set and carried out in all cases upon conviction for a specified offense or series of offenses.

mandatory sentencing A structured sentencing scheme that allows no leeway in the nature of the sentence required and under which clearly enumerated punishments are mandated for specific offenses or for habitual offenders convicted of a series of crimes.

MATRIX An acronym for the Multistate Anti-Terrorism Information Exchange, an Internet-based proof-of-concept pilot program funded by the Department of Justice and the Department of Homeland Security to increase and enhance the exchange of sensitive information about terrorism and other criminal activity between enforcement agencies at the local, state, and federal levels.

maximum sentence In legal usage, the maximum penalty provided by law for a given criminal offense, usually stated as a maximum term of imprisonment or a maximum fine. Also, in corrections usage in relation to a given offender, any of several quantities (expressed in days, months, or years) that vary according to whether calculated at the point of sentencing or at a later point in the correctional process and according to whether the time period referred to is the term of confinement or the total period under correctional jurisdiction.

medical model A therapeutic perspective on correctional treatment that applies the diagnostic perspective of medical science to the handling of criminal offenders.

mens rea The state of mind that accompanies a criminal act. Also, a guilty mind.

Miranda **rights** The set of rights that a person accused or suspected of having committed a specific offense has during interrogation and of which he or she must be informed prior to questioning, as stated by the U.S. Supreme Court in deciding *Miranda* v. *Arizona* (1966) and related cases.

Miranda **triggers** The dual principles of custody and interrogation, both of which are necessary before an advisement of rights is required.

Miranda **warnings** The advisement of rights due criminal suspects by the police before questioning begins. *Miranda* warnings were first set forth by the U.S. Supreme Court in the 1966 case of *Miranda* v. *Arizona*.

misdemeanor An offense punishable by incarceration, usually in a local confinement facility, for a period whose upper limit is prescribed by statute in a given jurisdiction, typically one year or less.

mistrial A trial that has been terminated and declared invalid by the court because of some circumstance that created a substantial and uncorrectable prejudice to the conduct of a fair trial or that made it impossible to continue the trial in accordance with prescribed procedures.

mitigating circumstances Circumstances relating to the commission of a crime that may be considered to reduce the blameworthiness of the defendant. See also **aggravating circumstances**.

mixed sentence A sentence that requires that a convicted offender serve weekends (or other specified periods of time) in a confinement facility (usually a jail) while undergoing probationary supervision in the community.

M'Naghten rule A rule for determining insanity, which asks whether the defendant knew what he or she was doing or whether the defendant knew that what he or she was doing was wrong.

Model Penal Code (MPC) A generalized modern codification considered basic to criminal law, published by the American Law Institute in 1962.

money laundering The process by which criminals or criminal organizations seek to disguise the illicit nature of their proceeds by introducing them into the stream of legitimate commerce and finance.[36]

moral enterprise The process undertaken by an advocacy group to have its values legitimated and embodied in law.

motion An oral or written request made to a court at any time before, during, or after court proceedings, asking the court to make a specified finding, decision, or order.

motive A person's reason for committing a crime.

motor vehicle theft (UCR/NIBRS) The theft or attempted theft of a motor vehicle. *Motor vehicle* is defined as a self-propelled road vehicle that runs on land surface and not on rails. The stealing of trains, planes, boats, construction equipment, and most farm machinery is classified as larceny under the UCR/NIBRS Program, not as motor vehicle theft.

multiculturalism The existence within one society of diverse groups that maintain unique cultural identities while frequently accepting and participating in the larger society's legal and political systems.[37] *Multiculturalism* is often used in conjunction with the term *diversity* to identify many distinctions of social significance. Also called *cultural pluralism*.

municipal police department A city- or town-based law enforcement agency. Also known as *local police*.

murder The unlawful killing of a human being. *Murder* is a generic term that in common usage may include first- and second-degree murder, manslaughter, involuntary manslaughter, and other similar offenses.

murder and nonnegligent manslaughter (UCR/NIBRS) Intentionally causing the death of another without legal justification or excuse. Also, causing the death of another while committing or attempting to commit another crime.

narcoterrorism A political alliance between terrorist organizations and drug-supplying cartels. The cartels provide financing for the terrorists, who in turn provide quasi-military protection to the drug dealers.

National Crime Victimization Survey (NCVS) An annual survey of selected American households conducted by the Bureau of Justice Statistics to determine the extent of criminal victimization—especially unreported victimization—in the United States.

National Incident-Based Reporting System (NIBRS) An incident-based reporting system that collects data on every single crime occurrence. NIBRS data will soon supersede the kinds of summary data that has traditionally been provided by the FBI's Uniform Crime Reporting Program.

natural law Rules of conduct inherent in human nature and in the natural order that are thought to be knowable through intuition, inspiration, and the exercise of reason, without the need for reference to created laws.

NCVS See **National Crime Victimization Survey**.

neglected child A child who is not receiving the proper level of physical or psychological care from his or her parents or guardians or who has been placed up for adoption in violation of the law.

negligence In legal usage, generally, a state of mind accompanying a person's conduct such that he or she is not aware, though a reasonable person should be aware, that there is a risk that the conduct might cause a particular harmful result.

negligent manslaughter (UCR/NIBRS) Causing the death of another by recklessness or gross negligence.

neoclassical criminology A contemporary version of classical criminology that emphasizes deterrence and retribution and that holds that human beings are essentially free to make choices in favor of crime and deviance or conformity to the law.

new police A police force formed in 1829 under the command of Sir Robert Peel. It became the model for modern-day police forces throughout the Western world. Also called *Metropolitan Police Force*.

night watch An early form of police patrol in English cities and towns.

nolle prosequi A formal entry in the record of the court indicating that the prosecutor declares that he or she will proceed no further in the action. The prosecutor's decision not to pursue the case requires the approval of the court in some jurisdictions.

nolo contendere A plea of "no contest." A no-contest plea is used when the defendant does not wish to contest conviction. Because the plea does not admit guilt, however, it cannot provide the basis for later civil suits that might follow a criminal conviction.

not guilty by reason of insanity The plea of a defendant or the verdict of a jury or judge in a criminal proceeding that the defendant is not guilty of the offense charged because at the time the crime was committed, the defendant did not have the mental capacity to be held criminally responsible for his or her actions.

nothing-works doctrine The belief, popularized by Robert Martinson in the 1970s, that correctional treatment programs have had little success in rehabilitating offenders.

no true bill The decision by a grand jury that it will not return an indictment against the person accused of a crime on the basis of the allegations and evidence presented by the prosecutor.

occupational crime Any act punishable by law that is committed through opportunity created in the course of a legitimate occupation.

offender An adult who has been convicted of a criminal offense.

offense A violation of the criminal law. Also, in some jurisdictions, a minor crime, such as jaywalking, that is sometimes described as *ticketable*.

offenses known to police (UCR/NIBRS) Reported occurrences of offenses that have been verified at the police level.

opening statement The initial statement of the prosecutor or the defense attorney, made in a court of law to a judge or jury, describing the facts that he or she intends to present during trial to prove the case.

operational capacity The number of inmates a prison can effectively accommodate based on management considerations.

opinion The official announcement of a decision of a court, together with the reasons for that decision.

opportunity theory A perspective that sees delinquency as the result of limited legitimate opportunities for success available to most lower-class youth.

organized crime The unlawful activities of the members of a highly organized, disciplined association engaged in supplying illegal goods or services, including gambling, prostitution, loan-sharking, narcotics, and labor racketeering, and in other unlawful activities.[38]

original jurisdiction The lawful authority of a court to hear or to act on a case from its beginning and to pass judgment on the law and the facts. The authority may be over a specific geographic area or over particular types of cases.

parens patriae A common law principle that allows the state to assume a parental role and to take custody of a child when he or she becomes delinquent, is abandoned, or is in need of care that the natural parents are unable or unwilling to provide.

Parliament The British legislature, the highest law-making body of the United Kingdom.

parole The status of a convicted offender who has been conditionally released from prison by a paroling authority before the expiration of his or her sentence, is placed under the supervision of a parole agency, and is required to observe the conditions of parole.

parole board A state paroling authority. Most states have parole boards that decide when an incarcerated offender is ready for conditional release. Some boards also function as revocation hearing panels. Also called *parole commission*.

parolee A person who has been conditionally released by a paroling authority from a prison prior to the expiration of his or her sentence, is placed under the supervision of a parole agency, and is required to observe conditions of parole.

parole (probation) violation An act or a failure to act by a parolee (or a probationer) that does not conform to the conditions of his or her parole (or probation).

parole revocation The administrative action of a paroling authority removing a person from parole status in response to a violation of lawfully required conditions of parole, including the prohibition against committing a new offense.

Parole revocation usually results in the offender's return to prison.

parole supervision Guidance, treatment, or regulation of the behavior of a convicted adult who is obligated to fulfill conditions of parole or conditional release. Parole supervision is authorized and required by statute, is performed by a parole agency, and occurs after a period of prison confinement.

parole supervisory caseload The total number of clients registered with a parole agency or officer on a given date or during a specified time period.

paroling authority A board or commission that has the authority to release on parole adults committed to prison, to revoke parole or other conditional release, and to discharge from parole or other conditional release status.

Part I offenses A UCR/NIBRS offense group used to report murder, rape, robbery, aggravated assault, burglary, larceny-theft, motor vehicle theft, and arson, as defined under the FBI's UCR/NIBRS Program. Also called *major crimes*.

Part II offenses A UCR/NIBRS offense group used to report arrests for less serious offenses. Agencies are limited to reporting only arrest information for Part II offenses, with the exception of simple assault.

PATRIOT Act See **USA PATRIOT Act**.

peacemaking criminology A perspective that holds that crime-control agencies and the citizens they serve should work together to alleviate social problems and human suffering and thus reduce crime.

peace officer standards and training (POST) program The official program of a state or legislative jurisdiction that sets standards for the training of law enforcement officers. All states set such standards, although not all use the term *POST*.

penal code The written, organized, and compiled form of the criminal laws of a jurisdiction.

penal law See **criminal law**.

penitentiary A prison. See also **Pennsylvania system**.

Pennsylvania system A form of imprisonment developed by the Pennsyl-

vania Quakers around 1790 as an alternative to corporal punishments. This style of imprisonment made use of solitary confinement and encouraged rehabilitation.

peremptory challenge The right to challenge a potential juror without disclosing the reason for the challenge. Prosecutors and defense attorneys routinely use peremptory challenges to eliminate from juries individuals who, although they express no obvious bias, are thought to be capable of swaying the jury in an undesirable direction.

perjury The intentional making of a false statement as part of the testimony by a sworn witness in a judicial proceeding on a matter relevant to the case at hand.

perpetrator The chief actor in the commission of a crime; that is, the person who directly commits the criminal act.

petition A written request made to a court asking for the exercise of its judicial powers or asking for permission to perform some act that requires the authorization of a court.

petit jury See **trial jury**.

pharmaceutical diversion The transfer of prescription medicines controlled by the Controlled Substance Act by theft, deception, and or fraudulent means for other than their intended legitimate therapeutic purposes.

phrenology The study of the shape of the head to determine anatomical correlates of human behavior.

physical dependence A biologically based craving for a specific drug that results from frequent use of the substance. Physical dependence on drugs is marked by a growing tolerance of a drug's effects, so that increased amounts of the drug are needed to obtain the desired effect, and by the onset of withdrawal symptoms over periods of prolonged abstinence.[39] Also called *physical addiction*.

piracy See **software piracy**.

plaintiff A person who initiates a court action.

plain view A legal term describing the ready visibility of objects that might be seized as evidence during a search by police in the absence of a search warrant specifying the seizure of those objects. To lawfully seize evidence in plain view, officers must have a legal right to be in the viewing area and must have cause to believe that the evidence is somehow associated with criminal activity.

plea In criminal proceedings, the defendant's formal answer in court to the charge contained in a complaint, information, or indictment that he or she is guilty of the offense charged, is not guilty of the offense charged, or does not contest the charge.

plea bargaining The process of negotiating an agreement among the defendant, the prosecutor, and the court as to an appropriate plea and associated sentence in a given case. Plea bargaining circumvents the trial process and dramatically reduces the time required for the resolution of a criminal case.

police–community relations (PCR) An area of police activity that recognizes the need for the community and the police to work together effectively. PCR is based on the notion that the police derive their legitimacy from the community they serve. Many police agencies began to explore PCR in the 1960s and 1970s.

police corruption The abuse of police authority for personal or organizational gain.[40]

police discretion The opportunity of law enforcement officers to exercise choice in their daily activities.

police ethics The special responsibility to adhere to moral duty and obligation that is inherent in police work.

police management The administrative activities of controlling, directing, and coordinating police personnel, resources, and activities in the service of preventing crime, apprehending criminals, recovering stolen property, and performing regulatory and helping services.[41]

police professionalism The increasing formalization of police work and the accompanying rise in public acceptance of the police.

police subculture A particular set of values, beliefs, and acceptable forms of behavior characteristic of American police. Socialization into the police subculture begins with recruit training and continues thereafter. Also called *police culture*.

police use of force The use of physical restraint by a police officer when dealing with a member of the public.[42]

police working personality All aspects of the traditional values and patterns of behavior evidenced by police officers who have been effectively socialized into the police subculture. Characteristics of the police personality often extend to the personal lives of law enforcement personnel.

political defense An innovative defense to a criminal charge that claims that the defendant's actions stemmed from adherence to a set of political beliefs and standards significantly different from those on which the American style of government is based. A political defense questions the legitimacy and purpose of all criminal proceedings against the defendant.

Positivist School An approach to criminal justice theory that stresses the application of scientific techniques to the study of crime and criminals.

POST See **peace officer standards and training (POST) program**.

postconviction remedy The procedure or set of procedures by which a person who has been convicted of a crime can challenge in court the lawfulness of a judgment of conviction, a penalty, or a correctional agency action and thus obtain relief in situations where this cannot be done by a direct appeal.

postmodern criminology A branch of criminology that developed after World War II and that builds on the tenets of postmodern social thought.

precedent A legal principle that ensures that previous judicial decisions are authoritatively considered and incorporated into future cases.

preliminary hearing A proceeding before a judicial officer in which three matters must be decided: (1) whether a crime was committed, (2) whether the crime occurred within the territorial jurisdiction of the court, and (3) whether there are reasonable grounds to believe that the defendant committed the crime.

preliminary investigation All of the activities undertaken by a police officer who responds to the scene of a crime, including determining whether a crime has occurred, securing the crime scene, and preserving evidence.

presentence investigation (PSI) The examination of a convicted offender's background prior to sentencing. Presentence examinations are generally conducted by probation or parole officers and are submitted to sentencing authorities.

presentment Historically, unsolicited written notice of an offense provided to a court by a grand jury from their own knowledge or observation. In current usage, any of several presentations of alleged facts and charges to a court or a grand jury by a prosecutor.

presumptive sentencing A model of criminal punishment that meets the following conditions: (1) The appropriate sentence for an offender convicted of a specific charge is presumed to fall within a range of sentences authorized by sentencing guidelines that are adopted by a legislatively created sentencing body, usually a sentencing commission. (2) Sentencing judges are expected to sentence within the range or to provide written justification for failure to do so. (3) There is a mechanism for review, usually appellate, of any departure from the guidelines.

pretrial detention Confinement occurring between the time of arrest or of being held to answer a charge and the conclusion of prosecution.[43]

pretrial discovery In criminal proceedings, disclosure by the prosecution or the defense prior to trial of evidence or other information that is intended to be used in the trial.

pretrial release The release of an accused person from custody, for all or part of the time before or during prosecution, on his or her promise to appear in court when required.

prison A state or federal confinement facility that has custodial authority over adults sentenced to confinement.

prison argot The slang characteristic of prison subcultures and prison life.

prison capacity The size of the correctional population an institution can effectively hold.[44] There are three types of prison capacity: rated, operational, and design.

prison commitment A sentence of commitment to the jurisdiction of a state or federal confinement facility system for adults whose custodial authority extends to offenders sentenced to more than a year of confinement, to a term expressed in years or for life, or to await execution of a death sentence.

prisoner A person in physical custody in a state or federal confinement facility or in the personal physical custody of a criminal justice official while being transported to or between confinement facilities.

prisoner reentry See **reentry**.

prisonization The process whereby newly institutionalized offenders come to accept prison lifestyles and criminal values. Although many inmates begin their prison experience with only a few values that support criminal behavior, the socialization experience they undergo while incarcerated leads to a much greater acceptance of such values.

prison subculture The values and behavioral patterns characteristic of prison inmates. Prison subculture has been found to be surprisingly consistent across the country.

private prison A correctional institution operated by a private firm on behalf of a local or state government.

private protective service An independent or proprietary commercial organization that provides protective services to employers on a contractual basis.

private security Self-employed individuals and privately funded business entities and organizations that provide security-related services to specific clientele for a fee, for the individual or entity that retains or employs them or for themselves, in order to protect people, private property, or interests from various hazards.[45]

private security agency See **private protective service**.

privatization The movement toward the wider use of private prisons.

probable cause A set of facts and circumstances that would induce a reasonably intelligent and prudent person to believe that a specified person has committed a specified crime. Also, reasonable grounds to make or believe an accusation. Probable cause refers to the necessary level of belief that would allow for police seizures (arrests) of individuals and full searches of dwellings, vehicles, and possessions.

probation A sentence of imprisonment that is suspended. Also, the conditional freedom granted by a judicial officer to a convicted offender, as long as the person meets certain conditions of behavior.

probation revocation A court order taking away a convicted offender's probationary status and usually withdrawing the conditional freedom associated with that status in response to a violation of the conditions of probation.

probation termination The ending of the probation status of a given person by routine expiration of the probationary period, by special early termination by the court, or by revocation of probation.

probation violation An act or a failure to act by a probationer that does not conform to the conditions of his or her probation.

probation workload The total set of activities required to carry out the probation agency functions of intake screening of juvenile cases, referral of cases to other service agencies, investigation of juveniles and adults for the purpose of preparing predisposition or presentence reports, supervision or treatment of juveniles and adults granted probation, assistance in the enforcement of court orders concerning family problems, such as abandonment and nonsupport cases, and other such functions assigned by statute or court order.

probative value The degree to which a particular item of evidence is useful in, and relevant to, proving something important in a trial.

problem police officer A law enforcement officer who exhibits problem behavior, as indicated by high rates of citizen complaints and use-of-force incidents and by other evidence.[46]

problem-solving policing A type of policing that assumes that crimes can be controlled by uncovering and effectively addressing the underlying social problems that cause crime. Problem-solving policing makes use of community resources, such as counseling centers, welfare programs, and job-training facilities. It also attempts to involve citizens in crime prevention through education, negotiation, and conflict management. Also called *problem-oriented policing*.

procedural defense A defense that claims that the defendant was in some significant way discriminated against in the justice process or that some important aspect of official procedure was not properly followed in the investigation or prosecution of the crime charged.

procedural law The part of the law that specifies the methods to be used in enforcing substantive law.

profession An organized undertaking characterized by a body of specialized knowledge acquired through extensive education and by a well-considered set of internal standards and ethical guidelines that hold members of the profession accountable to one another and to society.

professional criminal See **career criminal**.

property bond The setting of bail in the form of land, houses, stocks, or other tangible property. In the event that the defendant absconds prior to trial, the bond becomes the property of the court.

property crime A UCR/NIBRS summary offense category that includes burglary, larceny-theft, motor vehicle theft, and arson.

proportionality A sentencing principle that holds that the severity of sanctions should bear a direct relationship to the seriousness of the crime committed.

prosecution agency A federal, state, or local criminal justice agency or subunit whose principal function is the prosecution of alleged offenders.

prosecutor An attorney whose official duty is to conduct criminal proceedings on behalf of the state or the people against those accused of having committed criminal offenses. Also called *county attorney; district attorney (DA); state's attorney; U.S. attorney*.

prosecutorial discretion The decision-making power of prosecutors, based on the wide range of choices available to them, in the handling of criminal defendants, the scheduling of cases for trial, the acceptance of negotiated pleas, and so on. The most important form of prosecutorial discretion lies in the power to charge, or not to charge, a person with an offense.

prostitution The act of offering or agreeing to engage in, or engaging in, a sex act with another in return for a fee.

protected computer Under federal law, (1) a computer used exclusively by a financial institution or the U.S. government, (2) a computer used by or for a financial institution or the U.S. government, or (3) a computer used in interstate or foreign commerce or communication.

psychoactive substance A chemical substance that affects cognition, feeling, or awareness.

psychoanalysis A theory of human behavior, based on the writings of Sigmund Freud, that sees personality as a complex composite of interacting mental entities.

psychological dependence A craving for a specific drug that results from long-term substance abuse. Psychological dependence on drugs is marked by the belief that drugs are needed to achieve a feeling of well-being.[47] Also called *psychological addiction.*

psychological manipulation Manipulative actions by police interviewers that are designed to pressure suspects to divulge information and that are based on subtle forms of intimidation and control.

psychological profiling The attempt to categorize, understand, and predict the behavior of certain types of offenders based on behavioral clues they provide.

Psychological School A perspective on criminological thought that views offensive and deviant behavior as the product of dysfunctional personality. Psychological thinkers identify the conscious, and especially the subconscious, contents of the human psyche as major determinants of behavior.

psychopath A person with a personality disorder, especially one manifested in aggressively antisocial behavior, which is often said to be the result of a poorly developed superego. Also called *sociopath.*

psychopathology The study of pathological mental conditions—that is, mental illness.

psychosis A form of mental illness in which sufferers are said to be out of touch with reality.

public defender An attorney employed by a government agency or subagency, or by a private organization under contract to a government body, for the purpose of providing defense services to indigents, or an attorney who has volunteered such service.

public-defender agency A federal, state, or local criminal justice agency or subunit whose principal function is to represent in court people accused or convicted of a crime who are unable to hire private counsel.

public-order advocate One who believes that under certain circumstances involving a criminal threat to public safety, the interests of society should take precedence over individual rights.

public-safety department A state or local agency that incorporates various law enforcement and emergency service functions.

punitive damages Damages requested or awarded in a civil lawsuit when the defendant's willful acts were malicious, violent, oppressive, fraudulent, wanton, or grossly reckless.[48] Also called *exemplary damages.*

quality-of-life offense A minor violation of the law (sometimes called a *petty crime*) that demoralizes community residents and businesspeople. Quality-of-life offenses involve acts that create physical disorder (for example, excessive noise or vandalism) or that reflect social decay (for example, panhandling and prostitution).

racial profiling "Any police-initiated action that relies on the race, ethnicity, or national origin rather than [1] the behavior of an individual, or [2] . . . information that leads the police to a particular individual who has been identified as being, or having been, engaged in criminal activity."[49]

Racketeer Influenced and Corrupt Organizations (RICO) A federal statute that allows for the federal seizure of assets derived from illegal enterprise.

radical criminology A conflict perspective that sees crime as engendered by the unequal distribution of wealth, power, and other resources, which adherents believe is especially characteristic of capitalist societies. Also called *critical criminology; Marxist criminology.*

rape Unlawful sexual intercourse, achieved through force and without consent. Broadly speaking, the term *rape* has been applied to a wide variety of sexual attacks and may include same-sex rape and the rape of a male by a female. Some jurisdictions refer to same-sex rape as *sexual battery*. See also **forcible rape; sexual battery**.

rated capacity The number of inmates a prison can handle according to the judgment of experts.

rational choice theory A perspective on crime causation that holds that criminality is the result of conscious choice. Rational choice theory predicts that individuals will choose to commit crime when the benefits of doing so outweigh the costs of disobeying the law.

reaction formation The process whereby a person openly rejects that which he or she wants or aspires to but cannot obtain or achieve.

real evidence Evidence that consists of physical material or traces of physical activity.

reasonable doubt In legal proceedings, an actual and substantial doubt arising from the evidence, from the facts or circumstances shown by the evidence, or from the lack of evidence.[50] Also, the state of a case such that, after the comparison and consideration of all the evidence, jurors cannot say they feel an abiding conviction of the truth of the charge.[51]

reasonable doubt standard The standard of proof necessary for conviction in criminal trials.

reasonable force A degree of force that is appropriate in a given situation and is not excessive. Also, the minimum degree of force necessary to protect oneself, one's property, a third party, or the property of another in the face of a substantial threat.

reasonable suspicion The level of suspicion that would justify an officer in making further inquiry or in conducting further investigation. Reasonable suspicion may permit stopping a person for questioning or for a simple pat-down search. Also, a belief, based on a consideration of the facts at hand and on reasonable inferences drawn from those facts, that would induce an ordinarily prudent and cautious person under the same circumstances to conclude that criminal activity is taking place or that criminal activity has recently occurred. Reasonable suspicion is a *general* and reasonable belief that a crime is in progress or has occurred, whereas probable cause is a reasonable belief that a *particular* person has committed a *specific* crime. See also **probable cause**.

recidivism The repetition of criminal behavior. In statistical practice, a recidivism rate may be any of a number of possible counts or instances of arrest, conviction, correctional commitment, or correctional status change related to repetitions of these events within a given period of time.

recidivist A person who has been convicted of one or more crimes and who is alleged or found to have subsequently committed another crime or series of crimes.

reckless behavior Activity that increases the risk of harm.

recreational drug user A person who uses drugs relatively infrequently and primarily with friends and in social contexts that define drug use as pleasurable. Most addicts begin as recreational users.

reentry The managed return to the community of an individual released from prison. Also, the successful transitioning of a released inmate back into the community. Also called *prisoner reentry*.

reformatory style A late-nineteenth-century correctional model based on the use of the indeterminate sentence and the belief in the possibility of rehabilitation, especially for youthful offenders. The reformatory concept faded with the emergence of industrial prisons around the start of the twentieth century.

regional jail A jail that is built and run using the combined resources of a variety of local jurisdictions.

rehabilitation The attempt to reform a criminal offender. Also, the state in which a reformed offender is said to be.

release on recognizance (ROR) The pretrial release of a criminal defendant on his or her written promise to appear in court as required. No cash or property bond is required.

remote location monitoring A supervision strategy that uses electronic technology to track offenders who have been sentenced to house arrest or who have been ordered to limit their movements while completing a sentence involving probation or parole.

reprieve An executive act temporarily suspending the execution of a sentence, usually a death sentence. A reprieve differs from other suspensions of sentence not only in that it almost always applies to the temporary withdrawing of a death sentence, but also in that it is usually an act of clemency intended to provide the prisoner with time to secure amelioration of the sentence.

research The use of standardized, systematic procedures in the search for knowledge.

resident A person required, by official action or by his or her acceptance of placement, to reside in a public or private facility established for purposes of confinement, supervision, or care.

residential commitment A sentence of commitment to a correctional facility for adults in which the offender is required to reside at night but from which he or she is regularly permitted to depart during the day, unaccompanied by any official.

response time A measure of the time that it takes for police officers to respond to calls for service.

restitution A court requirement that an accused or convicted offender pay money or provide services to the victim of the crime or provide services to the community.

restoration A goal of criminal sentencing that attempts to make the victim "whole again."

restorative justice (RJ) A sentencing model that builds on restitution and community participation in an attempt to make the victim "whole again."

retribution The act of taking revenge on a criminal perpetrator.

revocation hearing A hearing held before a legally constituted hearing body (such as a parole board) to determine whether a parolee or probationer has violated the conditions and requirements of his or her parole or probation.

rights of defendant The powers and privileges that are constitutionally guaranteed to every defendant.

robbery (UCR/NIBRS) The unlawful taking or attempted taking of property that is in the immediate possession of another by force or violence and/or by putting the victim in fear. Armed robbery differs from unarmed, or strong-arm, robbery in that it involves a weapon. Contrary to popular conceptions, highway robbery does not necessarily occur on a street—and rarely in a vehicle. The term *highway robbery* applies to any form of robbery that occurs outdoors in a public place.

routine activities theory A neoclassical perspective that suggests that lifestyles contribute significantly to both the amount and the type of crime found in any society.

rule of law The maxim that an orderly society must be governed by established principles and known codes that are applied uniformly and fairly to all of its members.

rules of evidence Court rules that govern the admissibility of evidence at criminal hearings and trials.

runaway A juvenile who has been adjudicated by a judicial officer of juvenile court as having committed the status offense of leaving the custody and home of his or her parents, guardians, or custodians without permission and of failing to return within a reasonable length of time.

schizophrenic A mentally ill individual who suffers from disjointed thinking and possibly from delusions and hallucinations.

scientific jury selection The use of correlational techniques from the social sciences to gauge the likelihood that potential jurors will vote for conviction or for acquittal.

scientific police management The application of social science techniques to the study of police administration for the purpose of increasing effectiveness, reducing the frequency of citizen complaints, and enhancing the efficient use of available resources.

search incident to an arrest A warrantless search of an arrested individual conducted to ensure the safety of the arresting officer. Because individuals placed under arrest may be in possession of weapons, courts have recognized the need for arresting officers to protect themselves by conducting an immediate search of arrestees without obtaining a warrant.

search warrant A document issued by a judicial officer that directs a law enforcement officer to conduct a search at a specific location for specified property or person relating to a crime, to seize the property or person if found, and to account for the results of the search to the issuing judicial officer.

security The restriction of inmate movement within a correctional facility, usually divided into maximum, medium, and minimum levels.

security threat group (STG) An inmate group, gang, or organization whose members act together to pose a threat to the safety of correctional staff or the public, who prey upon other inmates, or who threaten the secure and orderly operation of a correctional institution.

self-defense The protection of oneself or of one's property from unlawful injury or from the immediate risk of unlawful injury. Also, the justification that the person who committed an act that would otherwise constitute an offense reasonably believed that the act was necessary to protect self or property from immediate danger.

sentence 1. The penalty imposed by a court on a person convicted of a crime. 2. The court judgment specifying the penalty imposed on a person convicted of a crime. 3. Any disposition of a defendant resulting from a conviction, including the court decision to suspend execution of a sentence.

sentencing The imposition of a criminal sanction by a judicial authority.

sentencing disposition 1. A court disposition of a defendant after a judgment of conviction, expressed as a penalty, such as imprisonment or payment of a fine. 2. Any of a number of alternatives to actually executed penalties, such as a suspended sentence, a grant of probation, or an order to perform restitution. 3. Various combinations of the foregoing.

sentencing hearing In criminal proceedings, a hearing during which the court or jury considers relevant information, such as evidence concerning aggravating or mitigating circumstances, for the purpose of determining a sentencing disposition for a person convicted of an offense.

sequestered jury A jury that is isolated from the public during the course of a trial and throughout the deliberation process.

service style A style of policing marked by a concern with helping rather than strict enforcement. Service-oriented police agencies are more likely to use community resources, such as drug-treatment programs, to supplement traditional law enforcement activities than are other types of agencies.

sex offense In current statistical usage, any of a broad category of varying offenses, usually consisting of all offenses having a sexual element except forcible rape and commercial sex offenses. The category includes all unlawful sexual intercourse, unlawful sexual contact, and other unlawful behavior intended to result in sexual gratification or profit from sexual activity.

sex offense (UCR/NIBRS) Any of various "offenses against chastity, common decency, morals, and the like," except forcible rape, prostitution, and commercialized vice.

sexual battery Intentional and wrongful physical contact with a person, without his or her consent, that entails a sexual component or purpose.

sheriff The elected chief officer of a county law enforcement agency. The sheriff is usually responsible for law enforcement in unincorporated areas and for the operation of the county jail.

sheriff's department A local law enforcement agency, directed by a sheriff, that exercises its law enforcement functions at the county level, usually within unincorporated areas, and that operates the county jail in most jurisdictions.

shock incarceration A sentencing option that makes use of "boot camp"–type prisons to impress on convicted offenders the realities of prison life.

shock probation The practice of sentencing offenders to prison, allowing them to apply for probationary release, and surprisingly permitting such release. Offenders who receive shock probation may not be aware that they will be released on probation and may expect to spend a much longer time behind bars.

simple assault (UCR/NIBRS) The unlawful threatening, attempted inflicting, or inflicting of less-than-serious bodily injury, without a deadly weapon.

smart card A plastic card or similar device containing a computer chip and other sources of nonalterable information (such as a hologram or a laser-encoded memory strip) that is used to provide highly secure personal identification.

smuggling The unlawful movement of goods across a national frontier or state boundary or into or out of a correctional facility.

sneak and peek search A search that occurs in the suspect's absence and without his or her prior knowledge. Also known as *delayed notification search*.

social control The use of sanctions and rewards within a group to influence and shape the behavior of individual members of that group. Social control is a primary concern of social groups and communities, and it is their interest in the exercise of social control that leads to the creation of both criminal and civil statutes.

social debt A sentencing principle that holds that an offender's criminal history should objectively be taken into account in sentencing decisions.

social development theory An integrated view of human development that points to the process of interaction among and between individuals and society as the root cause of criminal behavior.

social disorganization A condition said to exist when a group is faced with social change, uneven development of culture, maladaptiveness, disharmony, conflict, and lack of consensus.

social ecology A criminological approach that focuses on the misbehavior of lower-class youth and sees delinquency primarily as the result of social disorganization.

social engineering A nontechnical kind of cyberintrusion that relies heavily on human interaction and often involves tricking people into breaking normal security procedures.

social justice An ideal that embraces all aspects of civilized life and that is linked to fundamental notions of fairness and to cultural beliefs about right and wrong.

social learning theory A psychological perspective that says that people learn how to behave by modeling themselves after others whom they have the opportunity to observe.

social order The condition of a society characterized by social integration, consensus, smooth functioning, and lack of interpersonal and institutional conflict. Also, a lack of social disorganization.

social process theory A perspective on criminological thought that highlights the process of interaction between individuals and society. Most social process theories highlight the role of social learning.

social-psychological theory A perspective on criminological thought that highlights the role played in crime causation by weakened self-esteem and meaningless social roles. Social-psychological thinkers stress the relationship of the individual to the social group as the underlying cause of behavior.

sociopath See **psychopath**.

software piracy The unauthorized duplication of software or the illegal transfer of data from one storage medium to another. Software piracy is one of the most prevalent cybercrimes in the world.

solvability factor Information about a crime that forms the basis for determining the perpetrator's identity.

somatotyping The classification of human beings into types according to body build and other physical characteristics.

spam Unsolicited commercial bulk e-mail (UCBE), whose primary purpose is the advertisement or promotion of a commercial product or service.

span of control The number of police personnel or the number of units supervised by a particular commander.

specific deterrence A goal of criminal sentencing that seeks to prevent a particular offender from engaging in repeat criminality.

speedy trial A trial that is held in a timely manner. The right of a defendant to have a prompt trial is guaranteed by the Sixth Amendment of the U.S. Constitution, which begins, "In all criminal prosecutions, the accused shall enjoy the right to a speedy and public trial."

Speedy Trial Act A 1974 federal law requiring that proceedings against a defendant in a federal criminal case begin within a specified period of time, such as 70 working days after indictment. Some states also have speedy trial requirements.

split sentence A sentence explicitly requiring the convicted offender to serve a period of confinement in a local, state, or federal facility, followed by a period of probation.

staff operations In police organizations, activities (such as administration and training) that provide support for line operations.

stalking Repeated harassing and threatening behavior by one individual against another, aspects of which may be planned or carried out in secret. Stalking might involve following a person, appearing at a person's home or place of business, making harassing phone calls, leaving written messages or objects, or vandalizing a person's property. Most stalking laws require that the perpetrator make a credible threat of violence against the victim or members of the victim's immediate family.

stare decisis A legal principle that requires that, in subsequent cases on similar issues of law and fact, courts be bound by their own earlier decisions and by those of higher courts having jurisdiction over them. The term literally means "standing by decided matters."

state-action doctrine The traditional legal principle that only government officials or their representatives in the criminal justice process can be held accountable for the violation of an individual's constitutional civil rights.

state court administrator A coordinator who assists with case-flow management, operating funds budgeting, and court docket administration.

state court system A state judicial structure. Most states have at least three court levels: trial courts, appellate courts, and a state supreme court.

state highway patrol A state law enforcement agency whose principal functions are preventing, detecting, and investigating motor vehicle offenses and apprehending traffic offenders.

state police A state law enforcement agency whose principal functions usually include maintaining statewide police communications, aiding local police in criminal investigations, training police, and guarding state property. The state police may include the highway patrol.

state-use system A form of inmate labor in which items produced by inmates may only be sold by or to state offices. Items that only the state can sell include such things as license plates and hunting licenses, while items sold only to state offices include furniture and cleaning supplies.

status offender A child who commits an act that is contrary to the law by virtue of the offender's status as a child. Purchasing cigarettes, buying alcohol, and being truant are examples of such behavior.

status offense An act or conduct that is declared by statute to be an offense, but only when committed by or engaged in by a juvenile, and that can be adjudicated only by a juvenile court.

Statute of Winchester A law, written in 1285, that created a watch and ward system in English cities and towns and that codified early police practices.

statutory law Written or codified law; the "law on the books," as enacted by a government body or agency having the power to make laws.

statutory rape Sexual intercourse with a person who is under the legal age of consent.

stay of execution The stopping by a court of the implementation of a judgment—that is, of a court order previously issued.

stolen property offense The unlawful receiving, buying, distributing, selling, transporting, concealing, or possessing of the property of another by a person who knows that the property has been unlawfully obtained from the owner or other lawful possessor.

stop and frisk The detaining of a person by a law enforcement officer for the purpose of investigation, accompanied by a superficial examination by the officer of the person's body surface or clothing to discover weapons, contraband, or other objects relating to criminal activity.

stranger violence Seemingly random violence perpetrated by assailants who were previously unknown to their victims. Stranger violence often results from rage, opportunity, or insanity.

strategic policing A type of policing that retains the traditional police goal of professional crime fighting but enlarges the enforcement target to include nontraditional kinds of criminals, such as serial offenders, gangs and criminal associations, drug-distribution networks, and sophisticated white-collar and computer criminals. Strategic policing generally makes use of innovative enforcement techniques, including intelligence operations, undercover stings, electronic surveillance, and sophisticated forensic methods.

street crime A class of offenses, sometimes defined with some degree of formality as those that occur in public locations and are visible and assaultive, which are a special risk to the public and a special target of law enforcement preventive efforts and prosecutorial attention.

strict liability Liability without fault or intention. Strict liability offenses do not require *mens rea*.

structured sentencing A model of criminal punishment that includes determinate and commission-created presumptive sentencing schemes, as well as voluntary/advisory sentencing guidelines.

subculture of violence A cultural setting in which violence is a traditional and often accepted method of dispute resolution.

subpoena A written order issued by a judicial officer or grand jury requiring an individual to appear in court and to give testimony or to bring material to be used as evidence. Some subpoenas mandate that books, papers, and other items be surrendered to the court.

substantive criminal law The part of the law that defines crimes and specifies punishments.

supermale A human male displaying the XYY chromosome structure.

superpredator A juvenile who is coming of age in actual and "moral poverty" without the benefits of parents, teachers, coaches, and clergy to teach right from wrong[52] and who turns to criminal activity. The term is often applied to inner-city youths, socialized in violent settings without the benefit of wholesome life experiences, who hold considerable potential for violence.

supervised probation Guidance, treatment, or regulation by a probation agency of the behavior of a person who is subject to adjudication or who has been convicted of an offense, resulting from a formal court order or a probation agency decision.

suspect An adult or a juvenile who has not been arrested or charged but whom a criminal justice agency believes may be the person responsible for a specific criminal offense.

suspended sentence The court decision to delay imposing or executing a penalty for a specified or unspecified period. Also, a court disposition of a convicted person pronouncing a penalty of a fine or a commitment to confinement but unconditionally discharging the defendant or holding execution of the penalty in abeyance upon good behavior. Also called *sentence withheld.*

suspicionless search A search conducted by law enforcement personnel without a warrant and without suspicion. Suspicionless searches are permissible only if based on an overriding concern for public safety.

sworn officer A law enforcement officer who is trained and empowered to perform full police duties, such as making arrests, conducting investigations, and carrying firearms.[53]

Tazir crime A minor violation of Islamic law that is regarded as an offense against society, not God.

team policing The reorganization of conventional patrol strategies into "an integrated and versatile police team assigned to a fixed district."[54]

technocrime A criminal offense that employs advanced or emerging technology in its commission.

teen court An alternative approach to juvenile justice in which alleged offenders are judged and sentenced by a jury of their peers.

TEMPEST A standard developed by the federal government that requires that electromagnetic emanations from computers designated as "secure" be below levels that would allow radio receiving equipment to "read" the data being computed.

terrorism A violent act or an act dangerous to human life, in violation of the criminal laws of the United States or of any state, that is committed to intimidate or coerce a government, the civilian population, or any segment thereof, in furtherance of political or social objectives.[55]

testimony Oral evidence offered by a sworn witness on the witness stand during a criminal trial.

theft Generally, any taking of the property of another with intent to permanently deprive the rightful owner of possession.

theory A set of interrelated propositions that attempt to describe, explain, predict, and ultimately control some class of events. A theory is strengthened by its inherent logical consistency and is "tested" by how well it describes and predicts reality.

three-strikes laws Statutes that require mandatory sentences (sometimes life in prison without the possibility of parole) for offenders convicted of a third felony. Such mandatory sentencing enhancements are aimed at deterring known and potentially violent offenders and are intended to incapacitate convicted criminals through long-term incarceration.

tort A wrongful act, damage, or injury not involving a breach of contract. Also, a private or civil wrong or injury.

total institution An enclosed facility separated from society both socially and physically, where the inhabitants share all aspects of their daily lives.

transfer to adult court The decision by a juvenile court, resulting from a transfer hearing, that jurisdiction over an alleged delinquent will be waived and that he or she should be prosecuted as an adult in a criminal court.

transnational crime Unlawful activity undertaken and supported by organized criminal groups operating across national boundaries. Also called *transnational organized crime.*

treason A U.S. citizen's actions to help a foreign government overthrow, make war against, or seriously injure the United States.[56] Also, the attempt to overthrow the government of the society of which one is a member.

trial In criminal proceedings, the examination in court of the issues of fact and relevant law in a case for the purpose of convicting or acquitting the defendant.

trial *de novo* Literally, "new trial." The term is applied to cases that are retried on appeal, as opposed to those that are simply reviewed on the record.

trial judge A judicial officer who is authorized to conduct jury and nonjury trials but who may not be authorized to hear appellate cases. Also, the judicial officer who conducts a particular trial.

trial jury A statutorily defined number of people selected according to law and sworn to determine, in accordance with the law as instructed by the court, certain matters of fact based on evidence presented in a trial and to render a verdict. Also called *petit jury*.

truth in sentencing A close correspondence between the sentence imposed on an offender and the time actually served in prison.[57]

UCR See **Uniform Crime Reporting Program (UCR)**.

unconditional release The final release of an offender from the jurisdiction of a correctional agency. Also, a final release from the jurisdiction of a court.

undisciplined child A child who is beyond parental control, as evidenced by his or her refusal to obey legitimate authorities, such as school officials and teachers.

Uniform Crime Reporting Program (UCR) A statistical reporting program run by the FBI's Criminal Justice Information Services (CJIS) division. The UCR Program publishes *Crime in the United States*, which provides an annual summation of the incidence and rate of reported crimes throughout the United States.

USA PATRIOT Act A federal law (Public Law 107–56) enacted in response to terrorist attacks on the World Trade Center and the Pentagon on September 11, 2001. The law, officially titled the Uniting and Strengthening America by Providing Appropriate Tools Required to Intercept and Obstruct Terrorism Act, substantially broadened the investigative authority of law enforcement agencies throughout America and is applicable to many crimes other than terrorism. The law was slightly revised and reauthorized by Congress in 2006. Also called *Antiterrorism Act*.

use of force See **police use of force**.

vagrancy (UCR/NIBRS) An offense related to being a suspicious person, including vagrancy, begging, loitering, and vagabondage.

vandalism (UCR/NIBRS) The destroying or damaging of public property or the property of another without the owner's consent, or the attempt to destroy or damage such property. This definition of vandalism does not include burning.

venue The particular geographic area in which a court may hear or try a case. Also, the locality within which a particular crime was committed. See also **jurisdiction**.

verdict The decision of the jury in a jury trial or of a judicial officer in a nonjury trial.

victim A person who has suffered death, physical or mental anguish, or loss of property as the result of an actual or attempted criminal offense committed by another person.

victim-assistance program An organized program that offers services to victims of crime in the areas of crisis intervention and follow-up counseling and that helps victims secure their rights under the law.

victim-impact statement The in-court use of victim- or survivor-supplied information by sentencing authorities seeking to make an informed sentencing decision.

victimization In National Crime Victimization Survey terminology, the harming of any single victim in a criminal incident.

victimology The scientific study of crime victims and the victimization process. Victimology is a subfield of criminology.

vigilantism The act of taking the law into one's own hands.

violation 1. The performance of an act forbidden by a statute or the failure to perform an act commanded by a statute. 2. An act contrary to a local government ordinance. 3. An offense punishable by a fine or other penalty but not by incarceration. 4. An act prohibited by the terms and conditions of probation or parole.

violent crime A UCR/NIBRS summary offense category that includes murder, rape, robbery, and aggravated assault.

voluntary/advisory sentencing guidelines Recommended sentencing policies that are not required by law.

warden The official in charge of the operation of a prison, the chief administrator of a prison, or the prison superintendent.

warehousing An imprisonment strategy that is based on the desire to prevent recurrent crime and that has abandoned all hope of rehabilitation.

warrant In criminal proceedings, a writ issued by a judicial officer directing a law enforcement officer to perform a specified act and affording the officer protection from damages if he or she performs it.

watchman style A style of policing marked by a concern for order maintenance. Watchman policing is characteristic of lower-class communities where police intervene informally into the lives of residents to keep the peace.

weapon of mass destruction (WMD) A chemical, biological, or nuclear weapon that has the potential to cause mass casualties.

weapons offense The unlawful sale, distribution, manufacture, alteration, transportation, possession, or use, or the attempted unlawful sale, distribution, manufacture, alteration, transportation, possession, or use, of a deadly or dangerous weapon or accessory.

white-collar crime Violations of the criminal law committed by a person of respectability and high social status in the course of his or her occupation. Also, nonviolent crime for financial gain utilizing deception and committed by anyone who has special technical or professional knowledge of business or government, irrespective of the person's occupation.

Wickersham Commission The National Commission on Law Observance and Enforcement. In 1931, the commission issued a report stating that Prohibition was unenforceable and carried a great potential for police corruption.

witness Generally, a person who has knowledge of the circumstances of a case. Also, in court usage, one who testifies as to what he or she has seen, heard, or otherwise observed or who has expert knowledge.

workhouse An early form of imprisonment whose purpose was to instill habits of industry in the idle. Also called *bridewell*.

work release A prison program through which inmates are temporarily released into the community to meet job responsibilities.

writ A document issued by a judicial officer ordering or forbidding the performance of a specified act.

writ of *certiorari* A writ issued from an appellate court for the purpose of obtaining from a lower court the record of its proceedings in a particular case. In some states, this writ is the mechanism for discretionary review. A request for review is made by petitioning for a writ of *certiorari*, and the granting of review is indicated by the issuance of the writ.

writ of *habeas corpus* A writ that directs the person detaining a prisoner to bring him or her before a judicial officer to determine the lawfulness of the imprisonment.

youthful offender A person, adjudicated in criminal court, who may be above the statutory age limit for juveniles but is below a specified upper age limit, for whom special correctional commitments and special record-sealing procedures are made available by statute.

NOTES

Chapter 1   What Is Criminal Justice?

i. ABC News, September 16, 2001.

ii. Quoted in Charles E. Silberman, *Criminal Violence, Criminal Justice* (New York: Random House, 1978), p. 12.

iii. All boldfaced terms are explained whenever possible using definitions provided by the Bureau of Justice Statistics under a mandate of the Justice System Improvement Act of 1979. That mandate found its most complete expression in the *Dictionary of Criminal Justice Data Terminology* (Washington, DC: Bureau of Justice Statistics, 1982), the second edition of which provides the wording for many definitions in this text.

iv. Quoted in *Criminal Justice Newsletter*, September 16, 1997, p. 1.

v. ABC News, September 11, 2001.

vi. Adapted from U.S. Code, Title 28, Section 20.3 (2[d]). Title 28 of the U.S. Code defines the term *administration of criminal justice*.

vii. Philip B. Kurland, "Robert H. Jackson," in Leon Friedman and Fred L. Israel, eds., *The Justices of the United States Supreme Court, 1789–1969: Their Lives and Major Opinions*, Vol. 4 (New York: Chelsea House, 1969), p. 2565.

viii. American Friends' Service Committee, *Struggle for Justice: A Report on Crime and Punishment in America* (New York: Farrar, Straus & Giroux, 1971).

ix. Adapted from Robert M. Shusta et al., *Multicultural Law Enforcement*, 2nd ed. (Upper Saddle River, NJ: Prentice Hall, 2002), p. 443.

x. Reverend Jesse L. Jackson, Sr., "Liberty and Justice for Some: Mass Incarceration Comes at a Moral Cost to Every American," July 10, 2001, http://www.motherjones.com/prisons/print_liberty. html (accessed January 2, 2007).

xi. Prepared remarks of U.S. Attorney General Alberto Gonzales, Address to the National Association of Counties Legislative Conference, Washington, DC, March 7, 2005.

---

1. American Civil Liberties Union website, http://www.aclu.org/issues/criminal/iscj.html (accessed January 22, 2007).

2. ABC News, September 11, 2001. Christopher was repeating a phrase generally attributed to former U.S. Supreme Court Justice Arthur Goldberg.

3. Sam Coates and Dan Eggen, "A City of Despair and Lawlessness," *Washington Post*, September 2, 2005, p. A1.

4. Mark Gongloff, "Anarchy in New Orleans," *Wall Street Journal*, September 1, 2005.

5. "Looters Ransack Stores in Downtown New Orleans," *Wall Street Journal*, August 31, 2005.

6. Ibid.

7. Kevin Johnson, "Officers at 'Fort Apache' Finally Get Breather," *USA Today*, September 7, 2005, p. 3A.

8. Kevin McCoy, "Fraud Mounts in Katrina Aid Program," *USA Today*, February 13, 2006, p. 1A.

9. Ibid.

10. For a thorough discussion of immigration as it relates to crime, see Ramiro Martinez, Jr., and Matthew T. Lee, "On Immigration and Crime," in National Institute of Justice, *Criminal Justice 2000*, Vol. 1: *The Nature of Crime—Continuity and Change* (Washington, DC: U.S. Dept. of Justice, Office of Justice Programs, 2000).

11. "Cries of Relief," *Time*, April 26, 1993, p. 18; and "King II: What Made the Difference?" *Newsweek*, April 26, 1993, p. 26.

12. "Inside Columbine," *Rocky Mountain News*, http://www.rockymountainnews.com/drmn/columbine (accessed July 4, 2007).

13. "Cries of Relief."

14. Public Law 107-56.

15. Laurence McQuillan, "Bush to Urge Jail for Execs Who Lie," *USA Today*, July 9, 2002, http://www.usatoday.com/news/washdc/2002/07/09/bush-business.htm (accessed July 9, 2006).

16. Sarbanes-Oxley Act of 2002 (officially known as the Public Company Accounting Reform and Investor Protection Act), Public Law 107-204, 116 Stat. 745 (July 30, 2002).

17. PricewaterhouseCoopers, "The Sarbanes-Oxley Act," http://www.pwcglobal.com/Extweb/NewCoAtWork.nsf/docid/D0D7F79003C6D64485256CF30074D66C (accessed July 8, 2007).

18. "Enron's Lay, Skilling Convicted," Associated Press, May 25, 2006.

19. Wendy Koch, "States Get Tougher with Sex Offenders," *USA Today*, May 24, 2006, p. 1A.

20. Ibid.

21. George W. Bush, "Presidential Address to the Nation," September 20, 2001.

22. *The American Heritage Dictionary on CD-ROM* (Boston: Houghton Mifflin, 1991).

23. For a good overview of the issues involved, see Judge Harold J. Rothwax, *Guilty: The Collapse of Criminal Justice* (New York: Random House, 1996).

24. For one perspective on the detention of Muslims following September 11, 2001, see the plaintiff's motion to stay proceedings on defendant's summary judgment motion pending discovery, in *Center for National Security Studies* v. *U.S. Department of Justice*, U.S. District Court for the District of Columbia (Civil Action No. 01–2500; January 2002), http://www.aclu.org/court/cnssjan22.pdf (accessed September 24, 2007).

25. The systems model of criminal justice is often attributed to the frequent use of the term *system* by the 1967 Presidential Commission in its report *The Challenge of Crime in a Free Society* (Washington, DC: U.S. Government Printing Office, 1967).

26. One of the first published works to use the nonsystem approach to criminal justice was the American Bar Association's *New Perspective on Urban Crime* (Washington, DC: ABA Special Committee on Crime Prevention and Control, 1972).

27. Jerome H. Skolnick, *Justice without Trial* (New York: John Wiley, 1966), p. 179.

28. *Miranda* v. *Arizona*, 384 U.S. 436, 16 L.Ed.2d 694, 86 S.Ct. 1602 (1966).

29. North Carolina Justice Academy, *Miranda Warning Card* (Salemburg, NC: North Carolina Justice Academy, n.d.).

30. John M. Scheb and John M. Scheb II, *American Criminal Law* (St. Paul, MN: West, 1996), p. 32.

31. Federal Rules of Criminal Procedure, 10.

32. *Blanton* v. *City of North Las Vegas*, 489 U.S. 538, 103 L.Ed.2d 550, 109 S.Ct. 1289 (1989).

33. Ibid.

34. *U.S.* v. *Nachtigal*, 122 L.Ed.2d 374, 113 S.Ct. 1072, 1073 (1993), *per curiam*.

35. Barbara Borland and Ronald Sones, *Prosecution of Felony Arrests* (Washington, DC: Bureau of Justice Statistics, 1991).

36. "The Defendants' Rights at a Criminal Trial," http://www.mycounsel.com/content/arrests/court/rights.html (accessed February 10, 2007).

37. For a complete and now-classic analysis of the impact of decisions made by the Warren Court, see Fred P. Graham, *The Due Process Revolution: The Warren Court's Impact on Criminal Law* (New York: Hayden Press, 1970).

38. *Gideon* v. *Wainwright*, 372 U.S. 353 (1963).

39. Herbert Packer, *The Limits of the Criminal Sanction* (Stanford, CA: Stanford University Press, 1968).

40. For an excellent history of policing in the United States, see Edward A. Farris, "Five Decades of American Policing, 1932–1982," *Police Chief* (November 1982), pp. 30–36.

41. Gene Edward Carte, "August Vollmer and the Origins of Police Professionalism," *Journal of Police Science and Administration*, Vol. 1, No. 1 (1973), pp. 274–281.

42. Chris Eskridge distinguishes between police *training*, which is "job-specific" and is intended to teach trainees *how* to do something (like fire a weapon), and *justice education*, whose purpose is to "develop a general spirit of inquiry." See C. W. Eskridge, "Criminal Justice Education and Its Potential Impact on the Sociopolitical-Economic Climate of Central European Nations," *Journal of Criminal Justice Education*, Vol. 14, No. 1 (spring 2003), pp. 105–118; and James O. Finckenauer, "The Quest for Quality in Criminal Justice Education," *Justice Quarterly*, Vol. 22, No. 4 (December 2005), pp. 413–426.

43. "Polygamist Wins Parole from Utah State Prison," Associated Press, August 27, 2007.

44. See Patrick O'Driscoll, "Utah Steps Up Prosecutions of Polygamists," *USA Today*, May 14, 2001, p. 5A.

45. "Polygamist Wins Parole from Utah State Prison."

46. On March 22, 1794, the U.S. Congress barred American citizens from transporting slaves from the United States to another nation or between foreign nations. On January 1, 1808, the importation of slaves into the United States became illegal, and Congress charged the U.S. Revenue Cutter Service (now known as the U.S. Coast Guard) with enforcing the law on the high seas. Although some slave ships were seized, the importation of Africans for sale as slaves apparently continued in some southern states until the early 1860s. See U.S. Coast Guard, "U.S. Coast Guard in Illegal Immigration (1794–1971)," http://www.uscg.mil/hq/g-o/g-opl/mle/amiohist.htm (accessed October 13, 2007).

47. U.S. Census Bureau website, http://www.census.gov (accessed March 22, 2006). Population statistics are estimates because race is a difficult concept to define and Census Bureau interviewers allow individuals to choose more than one race when completing census forms.

Chapter 2   The Crime Picture

i. Dan Eggen, "Maj Rise Follows Nine Years of Decline," *Washington Post*, June 23, 2002, p. A1.

ii. Ibid.

iii. Identity Theft Resource Center website, http://www.idtheftcenter.org (accessed April 24, 2007).

iv. Jonathan Turley, "Arrest Me . . . Before I Strike Again," *USA Today*, February 22, 2005, p. 13A.

v. Violence against Women Office, *Stalking and Domestic Violence: Report to Congress* (Washington, DC: U.S. Dept. of Justice, 2001), p. 5.

vi. Ibid.

vii. Andrew Backover, "Two Former WorldCom Execs Charged," *USA Today* Online, August 1, 2002, http://www.usatoday.com/money/industries/telecom/2002-08-01-worldcom-execs-surrender_x.htm (accessed August 2, 2006).

viii. Michael L. Benson, Francis T. Cullen, and William J. Maakestad, *Local Prosecutors and Corporate Crime* (Washington, DC: National Institute of Justice, 1992), p. 1.

ix. The Organized Crime Control Act of 1970.

1. James Q. Wilson, "Point of View," *Chronicle of Higher Education*, June 10, 1992, p. A40.

2. "The Programming Insider," *MediaWeek*, February 22, 2005. See also Bill Keveney, "Crime Pays for 'CSI' Franchise," *USA Today*, September 16, 2004, p. D1.

3. NBC-TV, "Law and Order: About the Show," http://www.nbc.com/Law_&_Order/about (accessed March 7, 2006).

4. Norval Morris, "Crime, the Media, and Our Public Discourse," National Institute of Justice, Perspectives on Crime and Justice video series, recorded May 13, 1997.

5. See, for example, *A Gathering Storm: Violent Crime in America* (Washington, DC: Police Executive Research Forum [PERF], 2006).

6. Police Executive Research Forum, *Violent Crime in America: 24 Months of Alarming Trends* (Washington, DC: PERF, 2007).

7. Federal Bureau of Investigation, *Crime in the United States, 1987* (Washington, DC: U.S. Dept. of Justice, 1988), p. 1.

8. Federal Bureau of Investigation, "About the UCR Program," no date, http://www.fbi.gov/ucr/05cius/about/about_ucr.html (accessed May 29, 2007).

9. See the FBI's UCR/NIBRS website at http://www.fbi.gov/hq/cjisd/ucr.htm (accessed August 27, 2005).

10. The 1990 Crime Awareness and Campus Security Act (Public Law 101-542) required college campuses to commence publishing annual security reports beginning in September 1992.

11. U.S. Dept. of Education, *Summary Campus Crime and Security Statistics, 2002–2004* (Washington, DC: U.S. Dept. of Education, 2007).

12. Katrina Baum and Patsy Klaus, *Violent Victimization of College Students, 1995–2002* (Washington, DC: Bureau of Justice Statistics, 2005).

13. Federal Bureau of Investigation, *Crime in the United States, 2006* (Washington, DC: U.S. Dept. of Justice, 2007).

14. The President's Commission on Law Enforcement and Administration of Justice, *The Challenge of Crime in a Free Society* (Washington, DC: U.S. Government Printing Office, 1967). The commission relied on Uniform Crime Reports data. The other crime statistics reported in this section come from Uniform Crime Reports for various years.

15. Frank Hagan, *Research Methods in Criminal Justice and Criminology* (New York: Macmillan, 1982).

16. U.S. Department of Justice, *Fiscal Years 2000–2005 Strategic Plan* (Washington, DC: U.S. Government Printing Office, 2000).

17. The war on drugs, and the use of that term, can be traced back to the Nixon administration. See Dan Baum, *Smoke and Mirrors: The War on Drugs and the Politics of Failure*, reprint ed. (Boston: Little, Brown, 1997).

18. John J. DiIulio, Jr., "The Question of Black Crime," *Public Interest* (fall 1994), pp. 3–12.

19. Quoted in Dan Eggen, "Major Crimes in U.S. Increase: 2001 Rise Follows Nine Years of Decline," *Washington Post*, June 23, 2002, p. A1.

20. Police Executive Research Forum, *Violent Crime in America*.

21. See, for example, James Alan Fox, *Trends in Juvenile Violence: A Report to the United States Attorney General on Current and Future Rates of Juvenile Offending* (Washington, DC: Bureau of Justice Statistics, 1996); and David G. Savage, "Urban Crime Resurges after Decade Drop," *Los Angeles Times*, November 25, 2001, in which Fox continues to predict a rise in crime.

22. That is, while crime clock data may imply that one murder occurs every half hour or so, most murders actually occur during the evening, and only a very few take place around sunrise.

23. Most offense definitions in this chapter are derived from those used by the UCR/NIBRS Program and are taken from the FBI's *Crime in the United States, 2006* or from the Bureau of Justice Statistics, *Criminal Justice Data Terminology*, 2nd ed. (Washington, DC: Bureau of Justice Statistics, 1981).

24. These and other statistics in this chapter are derived primarily from the FBI's *Crime in the United States, 2006.*

25. Bureau of Justice Statistics, *Report to the Nation on Crime and Justice*, 2nd ed. (Washington, DC: U.S. Government Printing Office, 1988), p. 4.

26. "Feds Deny Thwarting Sniper Suspect's Confession," CNN.com, October 31, 2002, http://www.cnn.com/2002/US/10/30/snipers.interrogation/index.html (accessed October 31, 2002).

27. "Sniper Malvo Given Second Life Sentence," *USA Today*, October 27, 2004, p. 3A.

28. BJS, *Report to the Nation on Crime and Justice*, p. 4.

29. Ibid.

30. For excellent coverage of serial killers, see Steven Egger, *The Killers among Us: An Examination of Serial Murder and Its Investigation* (Upper Saddle River, NJ: Prentice Hall, 1998); Steven A. Egger, *Serial Murder: An Elusive Phenomenon* (Westport, CT: Praeger, 1990); and Stephen J. Giannangelo, *The Psychopathology of Serial Murder: A Theory of Violence* (New York: Praeger, 1996).

31. "BTK" stands for "Bind, Torture, and Kill," an acronym that Rader applied to himself in letters he sent to the media during the 1970s.

32. Several years ago, Lucas recanted all of his confessions, saying that he had never killed anyone—except possibly his mother, a killing he said he didn't remember. See "Condemned Killer Admits Lying, Denies Slayings," *Washington Post*, October 1, 1995.

33. Chikatilo was executed in 1994.

34. See Mark Babineck, "Railroad Killer Gets Death Penalty," Associated Press, May 22, 2000, http://cnews.tribune.com/news/tribune/story/0,1235,tribune-nation-37649,00.html (accessed March 3, 2002).

35. Public Law 108-212.

36. FBI, *Crime in the United States, 2006.*

37. Federal Bureau of Investigation, *Uniform Crime Reporting Handbook, 2004* (Washington, DC: FBI, 2005), p. 19.

38. "Study: Rape Vastly Underreported," Associated Press, April 26, 1992.

39. Ronald Barri Flowers, *Women and Criminality: The Woman as Victim, Offender, and Practitioner* (Westport, CT: Greenwood Press, 1987), p. 36.

40. A. Nichols Groth, *Men Who Rape: The Psychology of the Offender* (New York: Plenum Press, 1979).

41. Susan Brownmiller, *Against Our Will: Men, Women, and Rape* (New York: Simon and Schuster, 1975).

42. Dennis J. Stevens, "Motives of Social Rapists," *Free Inquiry in Creative Sociology*, Vol. 23, No. 2 (November 1995), pp. 117–126.

43. BJS, *Report to the Nation on Crime and Justice*, p. 5.

44. Ibid.

45. FBI, *Crime in the United States, 2006.* For UCR reporting purposes, *minorities* are defined as African Americans, Native Americans, Asians, Pacific Islanders, and Alaskan Natives.

46. "Easter Bunny Charged with Battery for Mall Attack," Associated Press, April 18, 2006.

47. This offense is sometimes called *assault with a deadly weapon with intent to kill* (AWDWWITK).

48. FBI, *Crime in the United States, 2006.*

49. BJS, *Report to the Nation on Crime and Justice*, p. 6.

50. Ibid.

51. "Four Arrested for Stealing Moon Rocks," Associated Press, July 23, 2002; and Sheena McFarland, "U. Student Arrested for Moon Rock Theft," *Daily Utah Chronicle* online, http://www.dailyutahchronicle.com/main.cfm/include/detail/storyid/259076.html (accessed August 22, 2005).

52. "Yale Says Student Stole His Education," *USA Today*, April 12, 1995, p. 3A.

53. Steven J. Vaughan-Nichols, "Cisco Source Code Reportedly Stolen," *eWeek*, May 18, 2004, http://www.eweek.com/article2/0,1759,1593862,00.asp (accessed May 17, 2007).

54. Ibid.

55. FBI, *Uniform Crime Reporting Handbook, 2004*, p. 28.

56. Matt Stearns and Donald Bradley, "Boy's Last Moments of Life Are Frozen in Mother's Memory," *Kansas City Star*, February 23, 2000.

57. "Jury Recommends Life Term in Dragging Death Wednesday," Associated Press, October 3, 2001.

58. Patsy Klaus, *Carjacking, 1993–2002* (Washington, DC: Bureau of Justice Statistics, July 2004).

59. FBI, *Crime in the United States, 2006.*

60. As indicated in the UCR definition of *arson*. See Federal Bureau of Investigation, *Crime in the United States, 1998* (Washington, DC: U.S. Dept. of Justice, 1999).

61. FBI, *Crime in the United States, 2006.*

62. Ibid.

63. "Trends in Crime and Victimization," *Criminal Justice Research Reports*, Vol. 2, No. 6 (July/August 2001), p. 83.

64. For additional information, see Shannan M. Catalano, *Criminal Victimization, 2006* (Washington, DC: Bureau of Justice Statistics, 2007); and Patsy A. Klaus, *Crime and the Nation's Households, 2006* (Washington, DC: Bureau of Justice Statistics, 2007).

65. Klaus, *Crime and the Nation's Households, 2006.*

66. Catalano, *Criminal Victimization, 2006.*

67. Ibid., p. 1.

68. See, for example, President's Commission on Law Enforcement and Administration of Justice, *The Challenge of Crime in a Free Society*, pp. 22–23.

69. BJS, *Report to the Nation on Crime and Justice*, p. 27.

70. Hagan, *Research Methods in Criminal Justice and Criminology*, p. 89.

71. Bureau of Justice Statistics, *Criminal Victimization in the United States, 1985* (Washington, DC: U.S. Government Printing Office, 1987), p. 1.

72. FBI, *Crime in the United States, 2001*, preliminary data, http://www.fbi.gov./ucr/01prelim.pdf (accessed August 27, 2002).

73. Terance D. Miethe and Richard C. McCorkle, *Crime Profiles: The Anatomy of Dangerous Persons, Places, and Situations* (Los Angeles: Roxbury, 1998), p. 19.

74. The definition of *rape* employed by the UCR/NIBRS Program, however, automatically excludes crimes of homosexual rape such as might occur in prisons and jails. As a consequence, the rape of males is excluded from the official count for crimes of rape.

75. Catalano, *Criminal Victimization, 2006*, p. 6.

76. Thomas Simon et al., *Injuries from Violent Crime, 1992–98* (Washington, DC: Bureau of Justice Statistics, 2001), p. 5.

77. See, for example, Elizabeth Stanko, "When Precaution Is Normal: A Feminist Critique of Crime Prevention," in Loraine Gelsthorpe and Allison Morris, eds., *Feminist Perspectives in Criminology* (Philadelphia: Open University Press, 1990).

78. For more information, see Eve S. Buzawa and Carl G. Buzawa, *Domestic Violence: The Criminal Justice Response* (Thousand Oaks, CA: Sage, 1996).

79. "Battered Women Tell Their Stories to the Senate," *Charlotte (NC) Observer*, July 10, 1991, p. 3A.

80. Patricia Tjaden and Nancy Thoennes, *Full Report of the Prevalence, Incidence, and Consequences of Violence against Women: Findings from the National Violence against Women Survey* (Washington, DC: National Institute of Justice, 2000).

81. Caroline Wolf Harlow, *Female Victims of Violent Crime* (Washington, DC: Bureau of Justice Statistics, 1991).

82. Violence against Women Office, *Stalking and Domestic Violence: Report to Congress* (Washington, DC: U.S. Dept. of Justice, 2001).

83. U.S. Code, Title 18, Section 2261A.

84. As modified through VAWA 2000.

85. Violence against Women Office, *Stalking and Domestic Violence*.

86. Many of the data in this section come from Bureau of Justice Statistics, *Crimes against Persons Age 65 or Older, 1993–2002* (Rockville, MD: BJS, 2005).

87. Lamar Jordan, "Law Enforcement and the Elderly: A Concern for the Twenty-First Century," *FBI Law Enforcement Bulletin*, May 2002, pp. 20–23.

88. Public Law 101-275.

89. H.R. 4797, 102d Cong. 2d Sess. (1992).

90. FBI, *Crime in the United States, 2006*.

91. "Sept. 11 Attacks Cited in Nearly 25 Percent Increase in Florida Hate Crimes," Associated Press, August 30, 2002.

92. "Dragging Death Still Haunts Family," APB News, June 7, 1999, http://www.apbnews.com/newscenter/breakingnews/1999/06/07/byrd060701.html (accessed January 2, 2000).

93. Rita Rubin, "Justice Investigates Metabolife," *USA Today*, August 16–18, 2002, p. 1A.

94. Brooke A. Masters and Ben White, "Adelphia Founder, Son Convicted of Fraud," *Washington Post*, July 9, 2004, p. E1.

95. Dionne Searcey and Li Yuan, "Adelphia's John Rigas Gets 15 Years," *Wall Street Journal*, June 21, 2005, p. A3.

96. Samuel Maull, "Ex-Tyco Execs Convicted in Second Trial," WashingtonPost.com, June 18, 2005, http://www.washingtonpost.com/wp-dyn/content/article/2005/06/17/AR2005061700863.html (accessed May 17, 2007).

97. "Enron's Lay, Skilling Convicted," Associated Press, May 25, 2006.

98. *Andersen* v. *U.S.*, 544 U.S. 696 (2005).

99. Public Broadcasting System, "Enron: After the Collapse," http://www.pbs.org/newshour/bb/business/enron/player6.html (accessed August 27, 2005).

100. Edwin H. Sutherland, "White-Collar Criminality," *American Sociological Review* (February 1940), p. 12.

101. Scott Lindlaw, "Bush to Propose Crackdown on Corporate Abuses: President's Own Business Dealings Come under Scrutiny," Associated Press, July 9, 2002, http://www.washingtonpost.com/wp-dyn/articles/A43384-2002Jul9.html (accessed May 17, 2005).

102. Public Law 107-204.

103. R. James Woolsey, as quoted on the Transnational Threats Initiative home page of the Center for Strategic and International Studies (CSIS), http://www.csis.org/tnt/index.htm (accessed August 22, 2007).

104. These ideas were originally expressed by Assistant U.S. Attorney General Laurie Robinson in an address given at the Twelfth International Congress on Criminology, Seoul, Korea, August 28, 1998.

105. Caroline Wolf Harlow, *Firearm Use by Offenders* (Washington, DC: Bureau of Justice Statistics, 2001).

106. Ibid., p. 1.

107. U.S. Code, Title 18, Section 922(q)(1)(A).

108. Harlow, *Firearm Use by Offenders*.

109. *Firearms Purchased from Federal Firearm Licensees Using Bogus Identification* (Washington, DC: General Accounting Office, 2001).

110. Sarah Brady, "Statement on the Sniper Shootings," October 8, 2002, http://www.bradycampaign.org/press/release.asp?Record 5429 (accessed October 16, 2005).

111. J. M. Chaiken and M. R. Chaiken, *Varieties of Criminal Behavior* (Santa Monica, CA: RAND Corporation, 1982).

112. D. McBride, "Trends in Drugs and Death," paper presented at the annual meeting of the American Society of Criminology, Denver, 1983.

113. National Criminal Justice Reference Service, *The Micro Domain: Behavior and Homicide*, p. 140, http://www.ncjrs.org/pdffiles/167262-3.pdf (accessed February 23, 2007).

114. Bureau of Justice Statistics, *Substance Abuse and Treatment: State and Federal Prisoners* (Washington, DC: U.S. Dept. of Justice, January 1999).

115. Bureau of Justice Statistics, *Drug Use, Testing, and Treatment in Jails* (Washington, DC: U.S. Dept. of Justice, May 2000).

116. Information in this paragraph comes from John Scalia, *Federal Drug Offenders, 1999, with Trends, 1984–99* (Washington, DC: Bureau of Justice Statistics, 2001); and Bureau of Justice Statistics, *Federal Criminal Case Processing, 2002, with Trends, 1982–2002* (Washington, DC: BJS, 2005).

117. *Federal Criminal Case Processing, 2002*.

118. Rachel Grunwell, "Burglars Benefit from Virtual Tour," *Stuff*, August 22, 2004, http://www.stuff.co.nz/stuff/0.2106.3010824a11.00.html (accessed May 17, 2005).

119. Ibid.

120. Emergency Response and Research Institute, *Summary of Emergency Response and Research Institute Terrorism Statistics: 2000 and 2001*, http://www.emergency.com/2002/terroris00-01.pdf (accessed August 22, 2007).

121. "U.S. Plans New Secure Government Internet," Associated Press, October 11, 2001.

Chapter 3 The Search for Causes

i. *The American Heritage Dictionary and Electronic Thesaurus on CD-ROM* (Boston: Houghton Mifflin, 1987).

ii. Nicole Rafter, "Earnest A. Hooton and the Biological Tradition in American Criminology," *Criminology*, Vol. 42, No. 3 (2004), p. 735.

iii. "Gingrich Says Felons Should Be Tracked by Satellite," Reuters, March 4, 1995.

1. George W. Bush, "Remarks by the President on Project Safe Neighborhoods," Pennsylvania Convention Center, Philadelphia, May 14, 2001, http://www.whitehouse.gov/news/releases/2001/05/20010514-1.html (accessed April 28, 2007).

2. Quoted in Gwynn Nettler, *Killing One Another* (Cincinnati, OH: Anderson, 1982), p. 194.

3. "Rapper Busta Rhymes Arrested, Charged with Assault," *USA Today*, August 21, 2006, http://www.usatoday.com/life/people/2006-08-20-busta-arrest_x.htm?csp=34 (accessed January 3, 2008).

4. "Busta Rhymes Arrested, Accused of Traffic Violation in New York," *International Herald Tribune*, February 22, 2007, http://www.iht.com/articles/ap/2007/02/23/arts/NA-A-E-MUS-US-People-Busta-Rhymes.php (accessed January 3, 2008).

5. "Busta Rhymes and Manager Arrested," MTV online, December 28, 1998, http://www.mtv.com/news/articles/1426787/19981228/rhymes_busta.jhtml (accessed January 3, 2008).

6. "Busta Rhymes Arrested, Accused of Traffic Violation in New York."

7. "50 Cent," http://www.who2.com/50cent.html (accessed August 28, 2007).

8. Jason Birchmeier, "50 Cent: Bio," *All Music Guide*, http://www.mtv.com/bands/az/50_cent/bio.jhtml (accessed August 30, 2007).

9. As we will see in Chapter 4, behavior that violates the criminal law may not be "crime" if accompanied by an acceptable legal justification or excuse. Justifications and excuses that are recognized by the law may serve as defenses to a criminal charge.

10. This and many of the statistics in these opening paragraphs come from Jonathan Wright, "Media Are Mixed Blessing, Criminologists Say," Reuters, May 2, 1995.

11. See "Comments of James T. Hamilton before the Federal Communications Commission, in the Matter of Industry Proposal for Rating Video Programming," May 23, 1997, citing Suzanne Stutman, Joanne Cantor, and Victoria Duran, *What Parents Want in a Television Rating System: Results of a National Survey* (Madison: University of Wisconsin, 1996); Wes Shipley and Gary Cavender, "Murder and Mayhem at the Movies," *Journal of Criminal Justice and Popular Culture*, Vol. 9, No. 1 (2001), pp. 1–14; and Suzanne Stutman, Joanne Cantor, and Victoria Duran, "What Parents Want in a

Television Rating System: Results of a National Survey (Washington, DC: National Parent Teacher Association, 2002), http://www.pta.org/ptacommunity/tvreport.asp (accessed August 21, 2007).

12. Jeffrey Johnson, "Television Viewing and Aggressive Behavior during Adolescence and Adulthood," *Science*, Vol. 295 (2002), pp. 2468–2471.

13. Wright, "Media Are Mixed Blessing, Criminologists Say."

14. Nathan McCall, "My Rap against Rap," *Washington Post* wire service, November 14, 1993.

15. Arthur L. Cribbs, Jr., "Gangsta Rappers Sing White Racists' Tune," *USA Today*, December 27, 1993, p. 9A.

16. U.S. News/UCLA Survey on the Media and Violence, reported in "Hollywood: Right Face," *U.S. News and World Report*, May 15, 1995, p. 71.

17. See "Congress Hopes Ten Commandments Curb Violence," APB Online, June 17, 1999, http://www.apbonline.com/911/1999/06/17/congress061701.html (accessed March 1, 2000).

18. The word *scientific* is used here to refer to the application of generally accepted research strategies designed to reject explanations that rival the one under study.

19. Stephen Schafer, *Theories in Criminology* (New York: Random House, 1969), p. 109.

20. L. E. Cohen and Marcus Felson, "Social Change and Crime Rate Trends: A Routine Activity Approach," *American Sociological Review*, Vol. 44, No. 4 (August 1979), pp. 588–608. Also see Marcus Felson and L. E. Cohen, "Human Ecology and Crime: A Routine Activity Approach," *Human Ecology*, Vol. 8, No. 4 (1980), pp. 389–406; Marcus Felson, "Linking Criminal Choices, Routine Activities, Informal Control, and Criminal Outcomes," in Derek B. Cornish and Ronald V. Clarke, eds., *The Reasoning Criminal: Rational Choice Perspectives on Offending* (New York: Springer-Verlag, 1986), pp. 119–128; and Ronald V. Clarke and Marcus Felson, eds., *Advances in Criminological Theory: Routine Activity and Rational Choice* (New Brunswick, NJ: Transaction, 1993).

21. Cohen and Felson, "Social Change and Crime Rate Trends," p. 595.

22. For a test of routine activities theory as an explanation for victimization in the workplace, see John D. Wooldredge, Francis T. Cullen, and Edward J. Latessa, "Victimization in the Workplace: A Test of Routine Activities Theory," *Justice Quarterly*, Vol. 9, No. 2 (June 1992), pp. 325–335.

23. Werner Einstadter and Stuart Henry, *Criminological Theory: An Analysis of Its Underlying Assumptions* (Fort Worth, TX: Harcourt Brace, 1995), p. 70.

24. For a modern reprint of a widely read nineteenth-century work on phrenology, see Orson Squire Fowler and Lorenzo Niles Fowler, *Phrenology: A Practical Guide to Your Head* (New York: Chelsea House, 1980).

25. Schafer, *Theories in Criminology*, p. 123.

26. Richard Louis Dugdale, *The Jukes: A Study in Crime, Pauperism, Disease, and Heredity*, 3rd ed. (New York: G. P. Putnam's Sons, 1985).

27. Henry Herbert Goddard, *The Kallikak Family: A Study in the Heredity of Feeblemindedness* (New York: Macmillan, 1912).

28. For more information, see Richard Herrnstein, "Crime File: Biology and Crime," a study guide (Washington, DC: National Institute of Justice, n.d.).

29. *Buck* v. *Bell*, 274 U.S. 200, 207 (1927).

30. Patricia Jacobs et al., "Aggressive Behavior, Mental Subnormality, and the XYY Male," *Nature*, Vol. 208 (1965), pp. 1351–1352.

31. Schafer, *Theories in Criminology*, p. 193.

32. D. Hill and W. Sargent, "A Case of Matricide," *Lancet*, Vol. 244 (1943), pp. 526–527.

33. See, for example, A. R. Mawson and K. J. Jacobs, "Corn Consumption, Tryptophan, and Cross-National Homicide Rates," *Journal of Orthomolecular Psychiatry*, Vol. 7 (1978), pp. 227–230; and A. Hoffer, "The Relation of Crime to Nutrition," *Humanist in Canada*, Vol. 8 (1975), p. 8.

34. See, for example, C. Hawley and R. E. Buckley, "Food Dyes and Hyperkinetic Children," *Academy Therapy*, Vol. 10 (1974), pp. 27–32; and Alexander Schauss, *Diet, Crime, and Delinquency* (Berkeley, CA: Parker House, 1980).

35. "Special Report: Measuring Your Life with Coffee Spoons," *Tufts University Diet and Nutrition Letter*, Vol. 2, No. 2 (April 1984), pp. 3–6.

36. See, for example, "Special Report: Does What You Eat Affect Your Mood and Actions?" *Tufts University Diet and Nutrition Letter*, Vol. 2, No. 12 (February 1985), pp. 4–6.

37. See *Tufts University Diet and Nutrition Letter*, Vol. 2, No. 11 (January 1985), p. 2; and "Special Report: Why Sugar Continues to Concern Nutritionists," *Tufts University Diet and Nutrition Letter*, Vol. 3, No. 3 (May 1985), pp. 3–6.

38. Diana H. Fishbein and Susan E. Pease, "Diet, Nutrition, and Aggression," in Marc Hillbrand and Nathaniel J. Pallone, eds., *The Psychobiology of Aggression: Engines, Measurement, Control* (New York: Haworth Press, 1994), pp. 114–117.

39. A. Hoffer, "Children with Learning and Behavioral Disorders," *Journal of Orthomolecular Psychiatry*, Vol. 5 (1976), p. 229.

40. "Special Report: Does What You Eat Affect Your Mood and Actions?" p. 4.

41. See, for example, R. T. Rada, D. R. Laws, and R. Kellner, "Plasma Testosterone Levels in the Rapist," *Psychomatic Medicine*, Vol. 38 (1976), pp. 257–268.

42. Later studies, however, have been less than clear. See, for example, J. M. Dabbs, Jr., "Testosterone Measurements in Social and Clinical Psychology," *Journal of Social and Clinical Psychology*, Vol. 11 (1992), pp. 302–321.

43. "The Insanity of Steroid Abuse," *Newsweek*, May 23, 1988, p. 75.

44. E. G. Stalenheim et al., "Testosterone as a Biological Marker in Psychopathy and Alcoholism," *Psychiatry Research*, Vol. 77, No. 2 (February 1998), pp. 79–88.

45. Michelle M. Wirth and Oliver C. Schultheiss, "Basal Testosterone Moderates Responses to Anger Faces in Humans," *Physiology and Behavior*, Vol. 90 (2007), pp. 496–505.

46. For a summary of such studies, see Serena-Lynn Brown, Alexander Botsis, and Herman M. Van Praag, "Serotonin and Aggression," in Hillbrand and Pallone, eds., *The Psychobiology of Aggression,* pp. 28–39.

47. Roger D. Masters, Brian Hone, and Anil Doshi, "Environmental Pollution, Neurotoxicity, and Criminal Violence," in J. Rose, ed., *Environmental Toxicology* (London and New York: Gordon and Breach, 1997).

48. B. Bioulac et al., "Serotonergic Functions in the XYY Syndrome," *Biological Psychiatry*, Vol. 15 (1980), pp. 917–923.

49. E. G. Stalenheim, L. von Knorring, and L. Wide, "Serum Levels of Thyroid Hormones as Biological Markers in a Swedish Forensic Psychiatric Population," *Biological Psychiatry*, Vol. 43, No. 10 (May 15, 1998), pp. 755–761.

50. Sarnoff Mednick and Jan Volavka, "Biology and Crime," in Norval Morris and Michael Tonry, eds., *Crime and Justice* (Chicago: University of Chicago Press, 1980), pp. 85–159.

51. Sarnoff Mednick and S. Gloria Shaham, eds., *New Paths in Criminology* (Lexington, MA: D. C. Heath, 1979).

52. For a good survey of studies in this area, see Laurence Miller, "Traumatic Brain Injury and Aggression," in Hillbrand and Pallone, eds., *The Psychobiology of Aggression*, pp. 91–103.

53. For an excellent overview of such studies, see Shari Mills and Adrian Raine, "Neuroimaging and Aggression," in Hillbrand and Pallone, eds., *The Psychobiology of Aggression,* pp. 145–158.

54. R. B. Cattell, *The Inheritance of Personality and Ability: Research Methods and Findings* (New York: Academic Press, 1982).

55. Karl Christiansen, "A Preliminary Study of Criminality among Twins," in Sarnoff Mednick and Karl O. Christiansen, eds., *Biosocial Bases of Criminal Behavior* (New York: Gardner Press, 1977).

56. James Q. Wilson and Richard J. Herrnstein, *Crime and Human Nature* (New York: Simon and Schuster, 1985).

57. "Criminals Born and Bred," *Newsweek*, September 16, 1985, p. 69.

58. William J. Chambliss, *Exploring Criminology* (New York: Macmillan, 1988), p. 202.

59. A. Reiss and J. Roth, eds., *Understanding and Preventing Violence* (Washington, DC: National Academy Press, 1993).

60. Sigmund Freud, *A General Introduction to Psychoanalysis* (New York: Boni and Liveright, 1920).

61. Nettler, *Killing One Another*, p. 79.

62. David Abrahamsen, *Crime and the Human Mind* (reprint, Montclair, NJ: Patterson Smith, 1969), p. 23.

63. See Adrian Raine, *The Psychopathology of Crime: Criminal Behavior as a Clinical Disorder* (Orlando, FL: Academic Press, 1993).

64. Hervey M. Cleckley, *The Mask of Sanity: An Attempt to Reinterpret the So-Called Psychopathic Personality* (St. Louis, MO: Mosby, 1941).

65. Nettler, *Killing One Another*, p. 179.

66. Albert I. Rabin, "The Antisocial Personality—Psychopathy and Sociopathy," in Hans Toch, ed., *Psychology of Crime and Criminal Justice* (Prospect Heights, IL: Waveland Press, 1979), p. 330.

67. Richard L. Ault and James T. Reese, "A Psychological Assessment of Crime Profiling," *FBI Law Enforcement Bulletin* (March 1980), pp. 22–25.

68. John E. Douglas and Alan E. Burgess, "Criminal Profiling: A Viable Investigative Tool against Violent Crime," *FBI Law Enforcement Bulletin* (December 1986), pp. 9–13.

69. Robert R. Hazelwood and John E. Douglass, "The Lust Murderer," *FBI Law Enforcement Bulletin* (April 1980), pp. 18–22.

70. A. O. Rider, "The Firesetter—A Psychological Profile," *FBI Law Enforcement Bulletin* (June 1980), pp. 4–11.

71. M. Reiser, "Crime-Specific Psychological Consultation," *Police Chief* (March 1982), pp. 53–56.

72. Thomas Strentz, "A Terrorist Psychosocial Profile: Past and Present," *FBI Law Enforcement Bulletin* (April 1988), pp. 13–19.

73. Jill Peay, "Dangerousness—Ascription or Description," in M. P. Feldman, ed., *Violence*, Vol. 2 of *Developments in the Study of Criminal Behavior* (New York: John Wiley, 1982), p. 211, citing N. Walker, "Dangerous People," *International Journal of Law and Psychiatry*, Vol. 1 (1978), pp. 37–50.

74. See, for example, Michael Gottfredson and Travis Hirschi, *A General Theory of Crime* (Stanford, CA: Stanford University Press, 1990); and Travis Hirschi and Michael Gottfredson,

"Age and the Explanation of Crime," *American Journal of Sociology*, Vol. 89 (1983), pp. 552–584.

75. David F. Greenberg, "Modeling Criminal Careers," *Criminology*, Vol. 29, No. 1 (1991), p. 39.

76. Robert E. Park and Ernest Burgess, *Introduction to the Science of Sociology*, 2nd ed. (Chicago: University of Chicago Press, 1924); and Robert E. Park, ed., *The City* (Chicago: University of Chicago Press, 1925).

77. Clifford R. Shaw and Henry D. McKay, "Social Factors in Juvenile Delinquency," in *Report on the Causes of Crime*, National Commission on Law Observance and Enforcement report no. 13, Vol. 2 (Washington, DC: U.S. Government Printing Office, 1931); and Clifford R. Shaw, *Juvenile Delinquency in Urban Areas* (Chicago: University of Chicago Press, 1942).

78. Émile Durkheim, *Suicide* (reprint, New York: Free Press, 1951).

79. Robert K. Merton, "Social Structure and Anomie," *American Sociological Review*, Vol. 3 (1938), pp. 672–682.

80. Catherine E. Ross and John Mirowsky, "Normlessness, Powerlessness, and Trouble with the Law," *Criminology*, Vol. 25, No. 2 (May 1987), p. 257.

81. See Nettler, *Killing One Another*, p. 58.

82. This is not to say that all members of these groups engaged in criminal behavior, but rather that statistics indicated higher average crime rates for these groups than for certain others immediately after immigration to the United States.

83. Albert K. Cohen, *Delinquent Boys: The Culture of the Gang* (Glencoe, IL: Free Press, 1958).

84. Walter B. Miller, "Lower Class Culture as a Generating Milieu of Gang Delinquency," *Journal of Social Issues*, Vol. 14 (1958), pp. 5–19.

85. Richard Cloward and Lloyd Ohlin, *Delinquency and Opportunity: A Theory of Delinquent Gangs* (New York: Free Press, 1960).

86. Marvin Wolfgang, *Patterns in Criminal Homicide* (Philadelphia: University of Pennsylvania Press, 1958). See also Marvin Wolfgang and Franco Ferracuti, *The Subculture of Violence: Toward an Integrated Theory in Criminology* (London: Tavistock, 1967).

87. "Gang Prevention through Targeted Outreach—Boys and Girls Clubs of America," http://ojjdp.ncjrs.org/pubs/gun_violence/sect08-k.html (accessed April 10, 2007).

88. See, for example, James D. Orcutt, "Differential Association and Marijuana Use: A Closer Look at Sutherland (with a Little Help from Becker)," *Criminology*, Vol. 25, No. 2 (1987), pp. 341–358.

89. Edwin Sutherland, *Principles of Criminology*, 4th ed. (Chicago: J. B. Lippincott, 1947), p. 4.

90. John E. Conklin, *Criminology*, 3rd ed. (New York: Macmillan, 1989), p. 278.

91. Robert L. Burgess and Ronald L. Akers, "A Differential Association-Reinforcement Theory of Criminal Behavior," *Social Problems*, Vol. 14 (fall 1996), pp. 128–147.

92. Some theories are multicausal and provide explanations for criminal behavior that include a diversity of "causes."

93. For a more elaborate criticism of this sort, see Conklin, *Criminology*, p. 260.

94. Ibid.

95. Walter C. Reckless, *The Crime Problem*, 4th ed. (New York: Appleton-Century-Crofts, 1961).

96. Ibid., p. 472.

97. Travis Hirschi, *Causes of Delinquency* (Berkeley: University of California Press, 1969).

98. Ibid., p. 472.

99. Gresham Sykes and David Matza, "Techniques of Neutralization: A Theory of Delinquency," *American Sociological Review*, Vol. 22 (1957), pp. 664–670.

100. Many of the concepts used by Howard Becker in explicating his theory of labeling were, in fact, used previously not only by Frank Tannenbaum but also by Edwin M. Lemert. Lemert wrote of "societal reaction" and "primary and secondary deviance" and even used the word *labeling* in his book *Social Pathology* (New York: McGraw-Hill, 1951).

101. Frank Tannenbaum, *Crime and the Community* (Boston: Ginn, 1938), pp. 19–20.

102. Howard Becker, *Outsiders: Studies in the Sociology of Deviance* (New York: Free Press, 1963), pp. 8–9.

103. Ibid.

104. Ibid., p. 33.

105. Robert J. Sampson and John H. Laub, *Crime in the Making: Pathways and Turning Points through the Life Course* (Cambridge, MA: Harvard University Press, 1993).

106. Katharine Browning et al., "Causes and Correlates of Delinquency Program," *OJJDP Fact Sheet* (Washington, DC: U.S. Dept. of Justice, April 1999).

107. MacArthur Foundation, "The Project on Human Development in Chicago Neighborhoods," http://www.macfound.org/research/hcd/hcd_5.htm (accessed January 5, 2007).

108. Adapted from Raymond Michalowski, "Perspectives and Paradigm: Structuring Criminological Thought," in Robert F. Meier, ed., *Theory in Criminology* (Beverly Hills, CA: Sage, 1977).

109. See George B. Vold, *Theoretical Criminology* (New York: Oxford University Press, 1986).

110. Austin T. Turk, *Criminality and the Legal Order* (Chicago: Rand McNally, 1969).

111. Thorsten Sellin, *Culture Conflict and Crime* (New York: Social Science Research Council, 1938).

112. William J. Chambliss and Robert B. Seidman, *Law, Order, and Power* (Reading, MA: Addison-Wesley, 1971).

113. Richard Quinney, *The Social Reality of Crime* (Boston: Little, Brown, 1970).

114. David F. Greenberg, *Crime and Capitalism* (Palo Alto, CA: Mayfield, 1981), p. 3.

115. For examples of how this might be accomplished, see F. H. Knopp, "Community Solutions to Sexual Violence: Feminist/Abolitionist Perspectives," in Harold E. Pepinsky and Richard Quinney, eds., *Criminology as Peacemaking* (Bloomington: Indiana University Press, 1991), pp. 181–193; and S. Caringella-MacDonald and D. Humphries, "Sexual Assault, Women, and the Community: Organizing to Prevent Sexual Violence," in Pepinsky and Quinney, eds., *Criminology as Peacemaking*, pp. 98–113.

116. Richard Quinney, "Life of Crime: Criminology and Public Policy as Peacemaking," *Journal of Crime and Justice*, Vol. 16, No. 2 (1993), pp. 3–9.

117. Ram Dass and P. Gorman, *How Can I Help? Stories and Reflections on Service* (New York: Alfred A. Knopf, 1985), p. 165, as cited in Richard Quinney and John Wildeman, *The Problem of Crime: A Peace and Social Justice Perspective*, 3rd ed. (Mayfield, CA: Mountain View Press, 1991), p. 116, originally published as *The Problem of Crime: A Critical Introduction to Criminology* (New York: Bantam, 1977).

118. See, for example, Harold E. Pepinsky, "This Can't Be Peace: A Pessimist Looks at Punishment," in W. B. Groves and

G. Newman, eds., *Punishment and Privilege* (Albany, NY: Harrow and Heston, 1986); Harold E. Pepinsky, "Violence as Unresponsiveness: Toward a New Conception of Crime," *Justice Quarterly*, Vol. 5 (1988), pp. 539–563; and Pepinsky and Quinney, eds., *Criminology as Peacemaking.*

119. See, for example, Richard Quinney, "Crime, Suffering, Service: Toward a Criminology of Peacemaking," *Quest*, Vol. 1 (1988), pp. 66–75; Richard Quinney, "The Theory and Practice of Peacemaking in the Development of Radical Criminology," *Critical Criminologist*, Vol. 1, No. 5 (1989), p. 5; and Quinney and Wildeman, *The Problem of Crime.*

120. All of these themes are addressed, for example, in Pepinsky and Quinney, eds., *Criminology as Peacemaking.*

121. Michael J. Lynch and W. Byron Groves, *A Primer in Radical Criminology*, 2nd ed. (Albany, NY: Harrow and Heston, 1989), p. 128.

122. Raymond J. Michalowski, *Order, Law, and Crime: An Introduction to Criminology* (New York: Random House, 1985), p. 410.

123. Don C. Gibbons, *Talking about Crime and Criminals: Problems and Issues in Theory Development in Criminology* (Englewood Cliffs, NJ: Prentice Hall, 1994), p. 165, citing Loraine Gelsthorpe and Alison Morris, eds., *Feminist Perspectives in Criminology* (Bristol, England: Open University Press, 1990).

124. Sally S. Simpson, "Feminist Theory, Crime, and Justice," *Criminology*, Vol. 27, No. 4 (1989), p. 605.

125. For an excellent overview of feminist theory in criminology and for a comprehensive review of research regarding female offenders, see Joanne Belknap, *The Invisible Woman: Gender Crime and Justice* (Belmont, CA: Wadsworth, 1996).

126. Otto Pollak, *The Criminality of Women* (Philadelphia: University of Pennsylvania Press, 1950).

127. Freda Adler, *Sisters in Crime: The Rise of the New Female Criminal* (New York: McGraw-Hill, 1975).

128. Rita J. Simon, *Women and Crime* (Lexington, MA: Lexington Books, 1975).

129. See, for example, Darrell J. Steffensmeir, "Sex Differences in Patterns of Adult Crime, 1965–1977: A Review and Assessment," *Social Forces*, Vol. 58 (1980), pp. 1098–1099.

130. See, for example, Kathleen Daly and Meda Chesney-Lind, "Feminism and Criminology," *Justice Quarterly*, Vol. 5, No. 5 (December 1988), pp. 497–535.

131. Ibid., p. 506.

132. Ibid.

133. Ibid., p. 514.

134. Cathy Spatz Widom, "Childhood Victimization and the Derailment of Girls and Women to the Criminal Justice System," in Beth E. Richie et al., eds., *Research on Women and Girls in the Justice System* (Washington, DC: National Institute of Justice, 2000), p. iii.

135. Ibid., pp. 27–36.

136. Federal Bureau of Investigation, *Crime in the United States, 1970* (Washington, DC: U.S. Dept. of Justice, 1971); and Federal Bureau of Investigation, *Crime in the United States, 2000* (Washington, DC: U.S. Dept. of Justice, 2001).

137. Ibid.

138. Federal Bureau of Investigation, *Crime in the United States, 2000* (Washington, DC: U.S. Dept. of Justice, 2001).

139. Federal Bureau of Investigation, *Crime in the United States, 2006* (Washington, DC: U.S. Dept. of Justice, 2007).

140. Leanne Fiftal Alarid et al., "Women's Roles in Serious Offenses: A Study of Adult Felons," *Justice Quarterly*, Vol. 13, No. 3 (September 1996), pp. 432–454.

141. George Herbert Mead and Charles W. Morris, eds., *Mind, Self, and Society* (Chicago: University of Chicago Press, 1934).

142. William I. Thomas and Florian Znaneicki, *The Polish Peasant in Europe and America* (Chicago: University of Chicago Press, 1918).

143. Stuart Henry and Dragan Milovanovic, "Constitutive Criminology: The Maturation of Critical Theory," *Criminology*, Vol. 29, No. 2 (May 1991), p. 293.

144. Dragan Milovanovic, *Postmodern Criminology* (Hamden, CT: Garland, 1997).

145. See also Stuart Henry and Dragan Milovanovic, *Constitutive Criminology: Beyond Postmodernism* (London: Sage, 1996).

146. For an excellent and detailed discussion of many of these approaches, see Milovanovic, *Postmodern Criminology.*

Chapter 4   Criminal Law

i. World of Quotes, http://www.worldofquotes.com/author/Raymond-Chandler/1/index.html (accessed January 10, 2006).

ii. Daniel Oran, *Oran's Dictionary of the Law* (St. Paul, MN: West, 1983), p. 306.

iii. Henry Campbell Black, Joseph R. Nolan, and Jacqueline M. Nolan-Haley, *Black's Law Dictionary*, 6th ed. (St. Paul, MN: West, 1990), p. 24.

iv. Martin Luther King, Jr., "Letter from Birmingham Jail," in *Why We Can't Wait* (Minneapolis, MN: Econ-Clad Books, 2000), http://quotations.about.com/library/weekly/aa010103a.htm (accessed July 22, 2007).

v. The 'Lectric Law Library, http://www.lectlaw.com/ref.html (accessed July 28, 2006).

vi. "Yates Sentence Set to Be Formalized," Associated Press, March 18, 2002.

vii. Richard Cohen, "Are We Insane?" *Washington Post*, March 14, 2002, p. A27.

1. The details for this story come from Maureen Fan, "Iraqi Legal System in Transition: U.S. Occupiers Trying to Re-establish Order Even without Laws," *San Jose Mercury News*, June 7, 2003, http://www.bayarea.com/mld/mercurynews/news/world/6036097.htm (accessed June 8, 2007).

2. Ibid.

3. Henry Campbell Black, Joseph R. Nolan, and Jacqueline M. Nolan-Haley, *Black's Law Dictionary*, 6th ed. (St. Paul, MN: West, 1990), p. 884.

4. Ibid.

5. "Traficant Faces Sentencing on Corruption Charges," CNN.com, July 30, 2002, http://www.cnn.com/2002/LAW/07/30/traficant.trial.ap/index.html (accessed July 30, 2005).

6. Susan Schmidt and James V. Grimaldi, "Ney Sentenced to 30 Months in Prison for Abramoff Deals," *Washington Post*, January 20, 2007, p. A3.

7. John F. Kennedy, *Profiles in Courage* (New York: Harper and Row, 1956).

8. Fareed Zakaria, "The Enemy Within," *New York Times*, December 17, 2006.

9. American Bar Association Section of International and Comparative Law, *The Rule of Law in the United States* (Chicago: American Bar Association, 1958).

10. "'Grand Theft Auto' Led Teen to Kill, Lawyer Claims," MSNBC News online, February 15, 2005, http://www.msnbc.msn.com/id/6976676 (accessed May 22, 2007).

11. Lief H. Carter, *Reason in Law*, 4th ed. (New York: HarperCollins, 1994).

12. Florida Statutes, Title XLVII, Section 901.16.

13. U.S. Sentencing Commission, *Federal Sentencing Guidelines Manual* (St. Paul, MN: West, 1987).

14. Daniel Oran, *Oran's Dictionary of the Law* (St. Paul, MN: West, 1983), p. 306.

15. Florida Constitution, Section 20.

16. Black, Nolan, and Nolan-Haley, *Black's Law Dictionary*, p. 24.

17. Much of the information in this paragraph comes from "Hanssen Pleads Guilty to Spying for Moscow," CNN.com Law Center, July 8, 2001, http://www.cnn.com/2001/LAW/07/06/hanssen/index.html (accessed September 22, 2006).

18. Jerry Markon, "Convicted Spy Accepts Life Sentence," *Washington Post*, March 21, 2003, http://www.washingtonpost.com/wp-dyn/articles/A1276-2003Mar20.html (accessed May 14, 2005); and "Jury Pool in Espionage Trial Asked Thoughts about Death Penalty," CNN.com, January 13, 2003, http://www.cnn.com/2003/LAW/01/13/espionage.trial.ap/index.html (accessed May 14, 2005).

19. Specifically, U.S. Code, Title 21, Section 846.

20. *U.S. v. Shabani,* 510 U.S. 1108 (1994).

21. *Gordon v. State,* 52 Ala. 3008, 23 Am. Rep. 575 (1875).

22. But not for a more serious degree of homicide, since leaving a young child alone in a tub of water, even if intentional, does not necessarily mean that the person who so acts intends the child to drown.

23. O. W. Holmes, *The Common Law*, Vol. 3 (Boston: Little, Brown, 1881).

24. There is disagreement among some jurists as to whether the crime of statutory rape is a strict liability offense. Some jurisdictions treat it as such and will not accept a reasonable mistake about the victim's age. Others, however, do accept such a mistake as a defense.

25. *State v. Stiffler,* 763 P.2d 308 (Idaho App. 1988).

26. John S. Baker, Jr., et al., *Hall's Criminal Law*, 5th ed. (Charlottesville, VA: Michie, 1993), p. 138.

27. The same is not true for procedures within the criminal justice system, which can be modified even after a person has been sentenced and, hence, become retroactive. See, for example, the U.S. Supreme Court case of *California Department of Corrections* v. *Morales,* 514 U.S. 499 (1995), in which the Court allowed changes in the length of time between parole hearings, even though those changes applied to offenders who had already been sentenced.

28. Black, Nolan, and Nolan-Haley, *Black's Law Dictionary*, p. 127.

29. The statute also says, "A mother's breastfeeding of her baby does not under any circumstance violate this section."

30. Common law crimes, of course, are not based on statutory elements.

31. *People* v. *Hall—Final Analysis*, SkiSafety.com, http://www.skisafety.com/amicuscases-hall2.html (accessed August 28, 2007).

32. See *Maughs* v. *Commonwealth,* 181 Va. 117, 120, 23 S.E.2d 784, 786 (1943).

33. *State* v. *Stephenson,* Opinion No. 24403 (South Carolina, 1996). See also *State* v. *Blocker,* 205 S.C. 303, 31 S.E.2d 908 (1944).

34. *State* v. *Kindle,* 71 Mont. 58, 64, 227 (1924).

35. Black, Nolan, and Nolan-Haley, *Black's Law Dictionary*, p. 343.

36. Patrick L. McCloskey and Ronald L. Schoenberg, *Criminal Law Deskbook* (New York: Matthew Bender, 1988), Section 20.03[13].

37. The exception, of course, is that of a trespasser who trespasses in order to commit a more serious crime.

38. Sir Edward Coke, 3 *Institute,* 162.

39. *The Crown* v. *Dudly & Stephens,* 14 Q.B.D. 273, 286, 15 Cox C. C. 624, 636 (1884).

40. "The Rough-Sex Defense," *Time,* May 23, 1988, p. 55.

41. Ibid.

42. "The Preppie Killer Cops a Plea," *Time,* April 4, 1988, p. 22.

43. "Jury Convicts Condom Rapist," *USA Today,* May 14, 1993, p. 3A.

44. Black, Nolan, and Nolan-Haley, *Black's Law Dictionary*, p. 504.

45. "Girl Charged," Associated Press, northern edition, February 28, 1994.

46. *State of Tennessee* v. *Charles Arnold Ballinger,* No. E2000-01339-CCA-R3-CD (Tenn.Crim.App. 01/09/2000).

47. See, for example, *Montana v. Egelhoff,* 116 S.Ct. 2013, 135 L.Ed.2d 361 (1996).

48. "'Rophies' Reported Spreading Quickly throughout the South," *Drug Enforcement Report,* June 23, 1995, pp. 1–5.

49. Laura Parker, "Yates' Murder Conviction Tossed," *USA Today,* January 7, 2005, p. 3A.

50. Details about Yates's second trial are taken from Lisa Sweetingham, "Andrea Yates Found Not Guilty by Reason of Insanity in Children's Deaths," Court TV, July 27, 2006, http://boards.youthnoise.com/eve/forums/a/tpc/f/21510584663/m/18210091 (accessed December 1, 2007).

51. L. A. Callahan et al., "The Volume and Characteristics of Insanity Defense Pleas: An Eight-State Study," *Bulletin of the American Academy of Psychiatry and the Law,* Vol. 19, No. 4 (1991), pp. 331–338.

52. American Bar Association Standing Committee on Association Standards for Criminal Justice, *Proposed Criminal Justice Mental Health Standards* (Chicago: American Bar Association, 1984).

53. "Mrs. Bobbitt's Defense: 'Life Worth More Than Penis,'" Reuters, January 10, 1994.

54. *Durham* v. *U.S.,* 214 F.2d 867, 875 (D.C. Cir. 1954).

55. American Law Institute, *Model Penal Code: Official Draft and Explanatory Notes* (Philadelphia: American Law Institute, 1985).

56. Ibid.

57. *U.S.* v. *Brawner,* 471 F.2d 969, 973 (D.C. Cir. 1972).

58. See Joan Biskupic, "Insanity Defense: Not a Right; In Montana Case, Justices Give States Option to Prohibit Claim," *Washington Post* wire service, March 29, 1994.

59. Ibid.

60. *Ford* v. *Wainwright,* 477 U.S. 399, 106 S.Ct. 2595, 91 L.Ed.2d 335 (1986).

61. U.S. Code, Title 18, Section 401.

62. *Jones* v. *U.S.,* U.S. Sup. Ct., 33 CrL. 3233 (1983).

63. *Ake* v. *Oklahoma,* 470 U.S. 68, 105 S.Ct. 1087, 84 L.Ed.2d 53 (1985).

64. *Foucha* v. *Louisiana,* 504 U.S. 71 (1992).

65. U.S. Sentencing Commission, "Supplement to the 2002 Federal Sentencing Guidelines: Section 5K2.13. Diminished Capacity (Policy Statement)," April 30, 2003, http://www.ussc.gov/2002suppb/5K2_13.htm (accessed May 8, 2007). Italics added.

66. *U.S.* v. *Pohlot,* 827 F.2d 889 (1987).

67. Peter Arenella, "The Diminished Capacity and Diminished Responsibility Defenses: Two Children of a Doomed Marriage," *Columbia Law Review,* Vol. 77 (1977), p. 830.

68. *U.S.* v. *Brawner,* 471 F.2d 969 (1972).

69. Black, Nolan, and Nolan-Haley, *Black's Law Dictionary,* p. 458.

70. California Penal Code, Section 25(a).

71. Ibid., Section 28(b).

72. Tracy Johnson, "Charges Dropped against Mom Whose Kids Starved to Death," *Seattle Post-Intelligencer,* January 31, 2007, http://seattlepi.nwsource.com/local/ 301852_mom31ww.html (accessed June 15, 2007).

73. Natalie Singer, "Competence Issue Creates Dilemma in '04 Murder Case," *Seattle Times,* March 16, 2007, pp. 1B–2B.

74. *Time,* March 19, 1984, p. 26.

75. Ibid.

76. *U.S.* v. *Halper,* 490 U.S. 435 (1989).

77. "Dual Prosecution Can Give One Crime Two Punishments," *USA Today,* March 29, 1993, p. 10A.

78. *U.S.* v. *Felix,* 112 S.Ct. 1377 (1992).

79. "Robert Blake Found Liable for Wife's Death," Associated Press, November 18, 2005.

80. See, for example, *Hudson* v. *U.S.,* 18 S.Ct. 488 (1997); and *U.S.* v. *Ursery,* 518 U.S. 267 (1996).

81. McCloskey and Schoenberg, *Criminal Law Deskbook,* Section 20.02[4].

82. *U.S.* v. *Armstrong,* 116 S.Ct. 1480, 134 L.Ed.2d 687 (1996).

83. Speedy Trial Act, U.S.Code, Title 18, Section 3161. Significant cases involving the U.S. Speedy Trial Act are those of *U.S.* v. *Carter,* 476 U.S. 1138, 106 S.Ct. 2241, 90 L.Ed.2d 688 (1986); and *Henderson* v. *U.S.,* 476 U.S. 321, 106 S.Ct. 1871, 90 L.Ed.2d 299 (1986).

84. Peter Whoriskey, "New Orleans Justice System Besieged," *Boston Globe,* April 17, 2006, http://www.boston.com/news/ nation/articles/2006/04/17/new_orleans_justice_system_ besieged/ (accessed May 10, 2007).

85. See Jim McGee, "Judges Increasingly Question U.S. Prosecutors' Conduct," *Washington Post* wire service, November 23, 1993.

86. Francis Fukuyama, "Extreme Paranoia about Government Abounds," *USA Today,* August 24, 1995, p. 17A.

87. Lorraine Adams, "Simpson Trial Focus Shifts to Detective with Troubling Past," *Washington Post* wire service, August 22, 1995.

Chapter 5   Policing: History and Structure

i. Lawrence W. Sherman, *Evidence-Based Policing* (Washington, DC: Police Foundation, 1998), p. 3.

ii. Lawrence W. Sherman, *Evidence-Based Policing,* p. 2.

iii. From his testimony before the Committee on Intelligence of the U.S. Senate, February 16, 2005.

iv. Adapted from Darl H. Champion and Michael K. Hooper, *Introduction to American Policing* (New York: McGraw-Hill, 2003), p. 166.

v. W. C. Cunningham, *Crime and Protection in America: A Study of Private Security and Law Enforcement Resources and Relationships* (Washington, DC: National Institute of Justice, 1985).

vi. David H. Bayley and Clifford D. Shearing, *The New Structure of Policing: Description, Conceptualization, and Research Agenda* (Washington, DC: National Institute of Justice, 2001), p. 5.

1. Police Foundation, *Annual Report, 1991* (Washington, DC: Police Foundation, 1992).

2. "A Reminiscence of a Bow-Street Officer," *Harper's New Monthly Magazine,* Vol. 5, No. 28 (September 1852), p. 484.

3. For a good discussion of the development of the modern police, see Sue Titus Reid, *Criminal Justice: Procedures and Issues* (St. Paul, MN: West, 1987), pp. 110–115; and Henry M. Wrobleski and Karen M. Hess, *Introduction to Law Enforcement and Criminal Justice,* 4th ed. (St. Paul, MN: West, 1993), pp. 3–51.

4. Camdem Pelham, *Chronicles of Crime,* Vol. 1 (London: T. Miles, 1887), p. 59.

5. Gary Sykes, "Street Justice: A Moral Defense of Order Maintenance Policing," *Justice Quarterly,* Vol. 3, No. 4 (December 1986), p. 504.

6. Law Enforcement Assistance Administration, *Two Hundred Years of American Criminal Justice: An LEAA Bicentennial Study* (Washington, DC: U.S. Government Printing Office, 1976), p. 15.

7. For an excellent discussion of the history of policewomen in the United States, see Dorothy Moses Schulz, *From Social Worker to Crimefighter: Women in United States Municipal Policing* (Westport, CT: Praeger, 1995); and Dorothy Moses Schulz, "Invisible No More: A Social History of Women in U.S. Policing," in Barbara R. Price and Natalie J. Sokoloff, eds., *The Criminal Justice System and Women: Offender, Victim, Worker,* 2nd ed. (New York: McGraw Hill, 1995), pp. 372–382.

8. Schulz, *From Social Worker to Crimefighter,* p. 25.

9. Ibid., p. 27.

10. National Commission on Law Observance and Enforcement, *Wickersham Commission Reports,* 14 vols. (Washington, DC: U.S. Government Printing Office, 1931).

11. President's Commission on Law Enforcement and Administration of Justice, *The Challenge of Crime in a Free Society* (Washington, DC: U.S. Government Printing Office, 1967).

12. National Advisory Commission on Criminal Justice Standards and Goals, *A National Strategy to Reduce Crime* (Washington, DC: U.S. Government Printing Office, 1973).

13. Enacted as U.S. Code, Title 42, Chapter 136, Subchapter XII.

14. Thomas J. Deakin, "The Police Foundation: A Special Report," *FBI Law Enforcement Bulletin* (November 1986), p. 2.

15. National Institute of Justice, *The Exemplary Projects Program* (Washington, DC: U.S. Government Printing Office, 1982), p. 11.

16. George L. Kelling et al., *The Kansas City Patrol Experiment* (Washington, DC: Police Foundation, 1974).

17. Kevin Krajick, "Does Patrol Prevent Crime?" *Police Magazine* (September 1978), quoting Dr. George Kelling.

18. William Bieck and David Kessler, *Response Time Analysis* (Kansas City, MO: Board of Police Commissioners, 1977). See also J. Thomas McEwen et al., *Evaluation of the Differential Police Response Field Test: Executive Summary* (Alexandria, VA: Research Management Associates, 1984); and Lawrence Sherman, "Policing Communities: What Works?" in Michael Tonry and Norval Morris, eds., *Crime and Justice: An Annual Review of Research,* Vol. 8 (Chicago: University of Chicago Press, 1986).

19. Krajick, "Does Patrol Prevent Crime?"

20. Ibid.

21. Ibid.

22. "Evidence-Based Policing," Police Foundation press release, March 17, 1998, www.policefoundation.org/docs/evidence.html (accessed January 5, 2006).

23. Lawrence W. Sherman, *Evidence-Based Policing* (Washington, DC: Police Foundation, 1998), p. 3.

24. Much of the information in this section comes from Sherman, *Evidence-Based Policing.*

25. Carl J. Jensen III, "Consuming and Applying Research: Evidence-Based Policing," *Police Chief,* Vol. 73, No. 2 (February 2006), Accessed at http://policechiefmagazine.org/magazine/index.cfm?fuseaction=display_arch&article_id=815&issue_id=22006 (accessed May 17, 2007).

26. Ibid.

27. Government Accounting Office, "Federal Law Enforcement: Survey of Federal Civilian Law Enforcement Functions and Authorities," December 2006 (highlights of GAO-07-121).

28. U.S. Department of Justice, *A Proud History . . . a Bright Future: Careers with the FBI,* pamphlet (October 1986), p. 1.

29. Much of the information in this section comes from U.S. Department of Justice, *The FBI: The First Seventy-Five Years* (Washington, DC: U.S. Government Printing Office, 1986).

30. Some of the information in this section is adapted from Federal Bureau of Investigation, "Facts and Figures 2003," http://www.fbi.gov/priorities/priorities.htm (accessed January 5, 2008).

31. Federal Bureau of Investigation, "Life at FBI," http://www.fbijobs.gov/31.asp#1 (accessed May 20, 2007).

32. Telephone conversation with FBI officials, April 21, 1995.

33. Public Laws 98-473 and 99-474.

34. Information in this section comes from Christopher H. Asplen, "National Commission Explores Its Future," *NIJ Journal* (January 1999), pp. 17–24.

35. The DNA Identification Act is Section 210301 of the Violent Crime Control and Law Enforcement Act of 1994.

36. Federal Bureau of Investigation, "NDIS Statistics," http://www.fbi.gov/hq/lab/codis/clickmap.htm (accessed January 4, 2007).

37. Much of the information in this paragraph comes from the FBI Academy website at http://www.fbi.gov/hq/td/academy/academy.htm (accessed January 23, 2008).

38. "Attorney General Ashcroft and Deputy Attorney General Thompson Announce Reorganization and Mobilization of the Nation's Justice and Law Enforcement Resources," U.S. Department of Justice press release, November 8, 2001.

39. Testimony of Robert S. Mueller III, director of the Federal Bureau of Investigation, before the Committee on Intelligence of the U.S. Senate, February 16, 2005.

40. Henry M. Wrobleski and Karen M. Hess, *Introduction to Law Enforcement and Criminal Justice,* 4th ed. (St. Paul, MN: West, 1993), p. 34.

41. Ibid., p. 35.

42. New York City Police Department website, http://www.nyc.gov/html/nypd (accessed June 21, 2006). The *New York Times* reported only 36,450 NYPD officers as of mid-2006, although plans were said to be in place to hire another 800. See Jim Rutenberg and Sewell Chan, "In a Shift, New York Says It Will Add 800 Officers," *New York Times,* March 22, 2006, http://select.nytimes.com/mem/tnt.html?emc=tnt&tntget=2006/03/22/nyregion/22police.html (accessed June 11, 2006).

43. Brian A. Reaves and Matthew J. Hickman, *Census of State and Local Law Enforcement Agencies,* 2000 (Washington, DC: Bureau of Justice Statistics, 2002).

44. Ibid.

45. Note, however, that New York City jails may have daily populations that, on a given day, exceed those of Los Angeles County.

46. The Police Assessment Resource Center, *The Los Angeles County Sheriff's Department—19th Semiannual Report* (Los Angeles: PARC, February 2005); and telephone communication with Deputy Ethan Marquez, L.A. County Sheriff's Department, Custodial Division, January 24, 2002.

47. Matthew J. Hickman and Brian A. Reaves, *Sheriffs' Offices,* 2003 (Washington, DC: National Institute of Justice, 2006), p. 2.

48. *Private Security: Report of the Task Force on Private Security* (Washington, DC: U.S. Government Printing Office, 1976), p. 4.

49. "Olympic Committee to Review Salt Lake Security in Wake of Terror Attacks," Associated Press, September 17, 2001.

50. "Securing the Olympic Games: $142,857 Security Cost per Athlete in Greece," *Wall Street Journal,* August 22, 2004, http://www.mindfully.org/Reform/2004/Olympic-Games-Security22aug04.htm (accessed May 17, 2007).

51. The information and some of the wording in this paragraph come from the ASIS International website at http://www.asisonline.org (accessed August 5, 2007).

52. David H. Bayley and Clifford D. Shearing, *The New Structure of Policing: Description, Conceptualization, and Research Agenda* (Washington, DC: National Institute of Justice, 2001).

53. National Center for Policy Analysis, *Using the Private Sector to Deter Crime* (Washington, DC: NCPA, 2001).

54. William C. Cunningham, John J. Strauchs, and Clifford W. Van Meter, *The Hallcrest Report II: Private Security Trends, 1970–2000* (McLean, VA: Hallcrest Systems, 1990).

55. Ibid., p. 236.

56. See http://www.spyandsecuritystore.com.conex.html (accessed June 25, 2007).

57. Peter Lewis, "Companies Turn to Private Spies," *Fortune,* August 9, 2004, p. 24.

58. Ibid.

59. Bayley and Shearing, *The New Structure of Policing,* p. 15.

60. NIJ, *Crime and Protection in America,* pp. 59–72.

61. International Association of Chiefs of Police, *National Policy Summit: Building Private Security/Public Policing Partnerships to Prevent and Respond to Terrorism and Public Disorder: Vital Issues and Policy Recommendations, 2004* (Washington, DC: U.S. Dept. of Justice, 2004).

62. Ibid., p. 1.

Chapter 6   Policing: Purpose and Organization

i. Jim Hodgson, "Living the Bradley County Sheriff's Mission Statement," http://www.bradleysheriff.com/majorthoughts.htm (accessed February 22, 2007).

ii. From Michael S. Scott, *Problem-Oriented Policing: Reflections on the First 20 Years* (Washington, DC: U.S. Dept. of Justice, Office of Community Oriented Policing Services, 2000), p. 88, http://www.cops.usdoj.gov/Default.asp?Item5311 (accessed May 25, 2006).

iii. International Association of Chiefs of Police, *From Hometown Security to Homeland Security: IACP's Principles for a Locally Designed and Nationally Coordinated Homeland Security Strategy* (Alexandria, VA: IACP, 2005).

iv. Wayne W. Bennett and Karen M. Hess, *Criminal Investigation*, 6th ed. (Belmont, CA: Wadsworth, 2001), p. 3 (italics in original).

v. This definition draws on the classic work by O. W. Wilson, *Police Administration* (New York: McGraw-Hill, 1950), pp. 2–3.

vi. Sam S. Souryal, *Police Administration and Management* (St. Paul, MN: West, 1977), p. 261.

vii. Community Policing Consortium, *What Is Community Policing?* (Washington, DC: Community Policing Consortium, 1995).

viii. Matthew C. Scheider, Robert E. Chapman, and Michael F. Seelman, *Border and Transportation Security: Connecting the Dots for a Proactive Approach* (Washington, DC: U.S. Dept. of Justice, 2004), p. 162.

ix. Robert Chapman et al., *Local Law Enforcement Responds to Terrorism: Lessons in Prevention and Preparedness* (Washington, DC: U.S. Dept. of Justice, Office of Community Oriented Policing Services, 2002), p. 2.

x. Major Cities Chiefs Association, *Terrorism: The Impact on State and Local Law Enforcement*, Intelligence Commanders Conference Report, June 2002, http://www.neiassociates.org/mccintelligencereport.pdf (accessed September 30, 2007).

xi. Angus Smith, ed., *Intelligence-Led Policing* (Richmond, VA: International Association of Law Enforcement Intelligence Analysts, 1997), p. 1.

xii. Office of Justice Programs, *The National Criminal Intelligence Sharing Plan* (Washington, DC: U.S. Dept. of Justice, 2005), p. 27.

xiii. Joseph A. Schafer, ed., *Policing 2020: Exploring the Future of Crime, Communities, and Policing* (Quantico, VA: Futures Working Group, 2007), p. 387.

---

1. Major Cities Chiefs Association, *Terrorism: The Impact on State and Local Law Enforcement*, Intelligence Commanders Conference Report, June 2002, http://www.neiassociates.org/mccintelligencereport.pdf (accessed September 19, 2007).

2. "Police, Protestors Clash Near Miami Trade Talks," CNN.com, November 20, 2003, http://www.cnn.com/2003/US/South/11/20/miami.protests (accessed June 3, 2007).

3. "Demonstrators, Police Clash during Free Trade Talks," *USA Today*, November 20, 2003, http://www.usatoday.com/news/nation/2003-11-20-miami-protests_x.htm (accessed June 3, 2006).

4. Andrew P. Sutor, *Police Operations: Tactical Approaches to Crimes in Progress* (St. Paul, MN: West, 1976), p. 68, citing Peel.

5. C. D. Hale, *Police Patrol: Operations and Management* (Englewood Cliffs, NJ: Prentice Hall, 1994).

6. Victor Kappeler et al., *The Mythology of Crime and Criminal Justice* (Prospect Heights, IL: Waveland Press, 1996).

7. Darl H. Champion and Michael K. Hooper, *Introduction to American Policing* (New York: McGraw-Hill, 2003), p. 133.

8. Details for this story come from Ted Ottley, "Bad Day Dawning," Court TV's Crime Library, http://www.crimelibrary.com/serial_killers/notorious/mcveigh/dawning_1.html (accessed June 22, 2007).

9. Ibid.

10. This definition has been attributed to the National Crime Prevention Institute; see http://www.lvmpd.com/community/crmtip25.htm (accessed July 22, 2007).

11. See Steven P. Lab, *Crime Prevention at a Crossroads* (Cincinnati, OH: Anderson, 1997).

12. See the Philadelphia Police Department's Operation Identification website at http://www.ppdonline.org/ppd4_home_opid.htm (accessed July 25, 2007).

13. The term *CompStat* is sometimes interpreted to mean computer statistics, comparative statistics, or computer comparative statistics, although it is generally accorded no specific meaning.

14. Learn more about CompStat from Vincent E. Henry, *The COMPSTAT Paradigm: Management Accountability in Policing, Business, and the Public Sector* (Flushing, NY: Looseleaf Law Publications, 2002).

15. Much of the information in this section comes from the Philadelphia Police Department, "The COMPSTAT Process," http://www.ppdonline.org/ppd_compstat.htm (accessed May 28, 2006).

16. See Ned Levine, *CrimeStat: A Spatial Statistics Program for the Analysis of Crime Incident Locations*, version 2.0 (Houston, TX: Ned Levine and Associates; Washington, DC: National Institute of Justice, May 2002).

17. Robert H. Langworthy and Lawrence P. Travis III, *Policing in America: A Balance of Forces*, 2nd ed. (Upper Saddle River, NJ: Prentice Hall, 1999), p. 194.

18. Adapted from Bronx County (New York) District Attorney's Office, "Quality of Life Offenses," December 24, 2002, http://www.bronxda.net/fighting_crime/quality_of_life_offenses.html (accessed June 20, 2006).

19. Other violations may be involved, as well. On December 29, 2000, for example, Judge John S. Martin, Jr., of the Federal District Court in Manhattan, ruled that homeless people in New York City could be arrested for sleeping in cardboard boxes in public. Judge Martin held that a city Sanitation Department regulation barring people from abandoning cars or boxes on city streets could be applied to the homeless who were sleeping in boxes.

20. Norman Siegel, executive director of the New York Civil Liberties Union, as reported in "Quality of Life Offenses Targeted," *Western Queens Gazette*, November 22, 2000, http://www.qgazette.com/News/2000/1122/Editorial_pages/e01.html (accessed June 12, 2007).

21. The broken windows thesis was first suggested by George L. Kelling and James Q. Wilson in "Broken Windows: The Police and Neighborhood Safety," *Atlantic Monthly*, March 1982. The article is available online at http://www.theatlantic.com/politics/crime/windows.htm (accessed June 22, 2005).

22. For a critique of the broken windows thesis, see Bernard E. Harcourt, *Illusion of Order: The False Promise of Broken Windows Policing* (Cambridge, MA: Harvard University Press, 2001).

23. Peter Schuler, "Law Professor Harcourt Challenges Popular Policing Method, Gun Violence Interventions," *Chicago Chronicle*, Vol. 22, No. 12 (March 20, 2003).

24. George L. Kelling, Catherine M. Coles, and James Q. Wilson, *Fixing Broken Windows: Restoring Order and Reducing Crime in Our Communities* (reprint, New York: Touchstone, 1998).

25. Charles R. Swanson, Leonard Territo, and Robert W. Taylor, *Police Administration: Structures, Processes, and Behavior*, 4th ed. (Upper Saddle River, NJ: Prentice Hall, 1998), p. 1.

26. Lorraine Mazerolle et al., *Managing Citizen Calls to the Police: An Assessment of Nonemergency Call Systems* (Washington, DC: National Institute of Justice, 2001), p. 1–11.

27. The Hastings (Minnesota) Police Department Web page at http://www.ci.hastings.mn.usPolice/deptnews.htm (accessed May 24, 2006).

28. The term *operational strategies* is taken from Michael S. Scott, *Problem-Oriented Policing: Reflections on the First 20 Years* (Washington, DC: U.S. Dept. of Justice, Office of Community Oriented Policing Services, 2000), p. 85, http://www.cops.usdoj.gov/Default.asp?Item5311 (accessed May 25, 2007).

29. Ibid., from which some of the wording and much of the material in this section is adapted.

30. Ibid., p. 86.

31. Ibid., from which much of this material is adapted.

32. Ibid., p. 86.

33. New York City Mayor's Office, *Fiscal 2007 Mayor's Management Report* (New York City: Office of the Mayor, 2007).

34. Details for this story come from Kurt Streeter, "Girl, 2, Rescued from Washer," *Los Angeles Times*, May 26, 2003, http://www.latimes.com/news/local/la-me-laundry26may26,1,7334286.story (accessed May 27, 2005).

35. See Scott, *Problem-Oriented Policing*, from which much of this material is adapted.

36. Wayne W. Bennett and Karen M. Hess, *Criminal Investigation*, 6th ed. (Belmont, CA: Wadsworth, 2001), p. 3 (italics in original).

37. Chief Gordon F. Urlacher and Lieutenant Robert J. Duffy, Rochester (New York) Police Department, "The Preliminary Investigation Process," http://www.surviveall.net/preliminary_investigation_proces.htm (accessed May 27, 2007).

38. Florida Highway Patrol, "Policy Number 22.01," *Policy Manual*, February 1, 1996, http://www.fhp.state.fl.us/html/Manuals/fh22-01.pdf (accessed June 1, 2007).

39. Scott, *Problem-Oriented Policing*, p. 88.

40. Adapted from Michigan State Police, *Annual Report 2000*, p. 12.

41. This definition draws on the classic work by O. W. Wilson, *Police Administration* (New York: McGraw-Hill, 1950), pp. 2–3.

42. Charles R. Swanson, Leonard Territo, and Robert W. Taylor, *Police Administration: Structures, Processes, and Behavior* (Upper Saddle River, NJ: Prentice Hall, 1998), p. 167.

43. Los Angeles County Sheriff's Department, "About LASD," http://www.lasd.org/aboutlasd/about.html (accessed June 25, 2007).

44. For more information on the first three categories, see Francis X. Hartmann, "Debating the Evolution of American Policing," *Perspectives on Policing*, No. 5 (Washington, DC: National Institute of Justice, 1988).

45. Willard M. Oliver, "The Homeland Security Juggernaut: The End of the Community Policing Era," *Crime and Justice International*, Vol. 20, No. 79 (2004), pp. 4–10. See also Willard M. Oliver, "The Era of Homeland Security: September 11, 2001 to . . . :" *Crime and Justice International*, Vol. 21, No. 85 (2005), pp. 9–17.

46. Gene Stephens, "Policing the Future: Law Enforcement's New Challenges," *The Futurist*, March/April 2005, pp. 51–57.

47. To learn more about Wilson, see "Presidential Medal of Freedom Recipient James Q. Wilson," http://www.medaloffreedom.com/JamesQWilson.htm (accessed January 5, 2006).

48. James Q. Wilson, *Varieties of Police Behavior: The Management of Law and Order in Eight Communities* (Cambridge, MA: Harvard University Press, 1968).

49. Independent Commission on the Los Angeles Police Department, *Report of the Independent Commission on the Los Angeles Police Department* (Los Angeles: The Commission, 1991).

50. Gary W. Sykes, "Street Justice: A Moral Defense of Order Maintenance Policing," *Justice Quarterly*, Vol. 3, No. 4 (December 1986), p. 505.

51. Egon Bittner, "Community Relations," in Alvin W. Cohn and Emilio C. Viano, eds., *Police Community Relations: Images, Roles, Realities* (Philadelphia: J. B. Lippincott, 1976), pp. 77–82.

52. Paul B. Weston, *Police Organization and Management* (Pacific Palisades, CA: Goodyear, 1976), p. 159.

53. Hale, *Police Patrol*.

54. Mark H. Moore and Robert C. Trojanowicz, "Corporate Strategies for Policing," *Perspectives on Policing*, No. 6 (Washington, DC: National Institute of Justice, 1988).

55. Ibid., p. 6.

56. Community Policing Consortium, *Community Policing Is Alive and Well* (Washington, DC: Community Policing Consortium, 1995), p. 1.

57. George L. Kelling, *The Newark Foot Patrol Experiment* (Washington, DC: Police Foundation, 1981).

58. Robert C. Trojanowicz, "An Evaluation of a Neighborhood Foot Patrol Program," *Journal of Police Science and Administration*, Vol. 11 (1983).

59. Bureau of Justice Assistance, *Understanding Community Policing: A Framework for Action* (Washington, DC: Bureau of Justice Statistics, 1994), p. 10.

60. Robert C. Trojanowicz and Bonnie Bucqueroux, *Community Policing* (Cincinnati, OH: Anderson, 1990).

61. Moore and Trojanowicz, "Corporate Strategies for Policing," p. 8.

62. S. M. Hartnett and W. G. Skogan, "Community Policing: Chicago's Experience," *National Institute of Justice Journal* (April 1999), pp. 2–11.

63. Jerome H. Skolnick and David H. Bayley, *Community Policing: Issues and Practices around the World* (Washington, DC: National Institute of Justice, 1988).

64. Ibid.

65. William L. Goodbody, "What Do We Expect New-Age Cops to Do?" *Law Enforcement News*, April 30, 1995, pp. 14, 18.

66. Sam Vincent Meddis and Desda Moss, "Many 'Fed-Up' Communities Cornering Crime," *USA Today*, May 22, 1995, p. 8A.

67. Matthew J. Hickman and Brian A. Reaves, *Community Policing in Local Police Departments, 1997 and 1999*, Bureau of Justice Statistics Special Report (Washington, DC: Dept. of Justice, 2001).

68. Richard M. Daley and Matt L. Rodriguez, *Together We Can: A Strategic Plan for Reinventing the Chicago Police Department* (Chicago: Chicago Police Department, 1993), http://www.ci.chi.il.us/CommunityPolicing/Statistics/Reports/TWC.pdf (accessed March 5, 2002).

69. Bureau of Justice Assistance, *Neighborhood-Oriented Policing in Rural Communities: A Program Planning Guide* (Washington, DC: Bureau of Justice Statistics, 1994), p. 4.

70. See the COPS Office website at http://www.usdoj.gov/cops (accessed January 22, 2007).

71. Jihong Zhao, Nicholas P. Lovrich, and Quint Thurman, "The Status of Community Policing in American Cities: Facilitators and Impediments Revisited," *Policing*, Vol. 22, No. 1 (1999), p. 74.

72. For a good critique and overview of community policing, see Geoffrey P. Alpert et al., *Community Policing: Contemporary Readings* (Prospect Heights, IL: Waveland Press, 1998).

73. Jack R. Greene, "Community Policing in America: Changing the Nature, Structure, and Function of the Police," in U.S. Department of Justice, *Criminal Justice 2000*, Vol. 3 (Washington, DC: Dept. of Justice, 2000).

74. Michael D. Reisig and Roger B. Parks, "Experience, Quality of Life, and Neighborhood Context: A Hierarchical Analysis of Satisfaction with Police," *Justice Quarterly*, Vol. 17, No. 3 (2000), p. 607.

75. Mark E. Correla, "The Conceptual Ambiguity of Community in Community Policing: Filtering the Muddy Waters," *Policing*, Vol. 23, No. 2 (2000), pp. 218–233.

76. Adapted from Donald R. Fessler, *Facilitating Community Change: A Basic Guide* (San Diego, CA: San Diego State University, 1976), p. 7.

77. Daniel W. Flynn, *Defining the "Community" in Community Policing* (Washington, DC: Police Executive Research Forum, 1998).

78. Robert C. Trojanowicz and Mark H. Moore, *The Meaning of Community in Community Policing* (East Lansing: Michigan State University's National Neighborhood Foot Patrol Center, 1988).

79. Robert M. Bohm, K. Michael Reynolds, and Stephen T. Holms, "Perceptions of Neighborhood Problems and Their Solutions: Implications for Community Policing," *Policing*, Vol. 23, No. 4 (2000), p. 439.

80. Ibid., p. 442.

81. Malcolm K. Sparrow, "Implementing Community Policing," *Perspectives in Policing*, No. 9 (Washington, DC: National Institute of Justice, 1988).

82. "L.A. Police Chief: Treat People Like Customers," *USA Today*, March 29, 1993, p. 13A.

83. Robert Wasserman and Mark H. Moore, "Values in Policing," *Perspectives in Policing*, No. 8 (Washington, DC: National Institute of Justice, 1988), p. 7.

84. "New York City Mayor Sparks Debate on Community Policing," *Criminal Justice Newsletter*, Vol. 25, No. 2 (January 18, 1994), p. 1.

85. Toni Locy, "Three Men Indicted on Terror Charges," *USA Today*, April 13, 2005, p. 1A.

86. Details for this story are taken from Thor Valdmanis, "Wall Street Stays on Guard against Terror Attacks," *USA Today*, August 23, 2004, http://www.usatoday.com/money/markets/us/2004-08-03-wall-street_x.htm (accessed January 10, 2006).

87. Ibid.

88. Police Executive Research Forum, *Local Law Enforcement's Role in Preventing and Responding to Terrorism* (Washington, DC: PERF, October 2, 2001), http://www.policeforum.org/terrorismfinal.doc (accessed June 1, 2006).

89. Council on Foreign Relations, "Terrorism Questions and Answers: Police Departments," http://www.terrorismanswers.com/security/police.html (accessed April 19, 2007).

90. Ibid.

91. Michael Weissenstein, "NYPD Shifts Focus to Terrorism, Long Considered the Turf of Federal Agents," Associated Press, March 21, 2003, http://www.nj.com/newsflash/national/index.ssf?/cgi-free/getstory_ssf.cgi?a0801_BC_NYPD-Counterterror&&news&newsflash-national (accessed May 25, 2006).

92. Ibid.

93. International Association of Chiefs of Police, *From Hometown Security to Homeland Security: IACP's Principles for a Locally Designed and Nationally Coordinated Homeland Security Strategy* (Alexandria, VA: IACP, 2005).

94. Ibid.

95. Joseph G. Estey, "President's Message: Taking Command Initiative—An Update" (Washington, DC: International Association of Chiefs of Police, 2005), http://www.theiacp.org/documents/index.cfm?fuseaction5document&document_id5697 (accessed July 25, 2006).

96. Joel Leson, *Assessing and Managing the Terrorism Threat* (Washington, DC: Bureau of Justice Statistics, 2005).

97. Robert J. Jordan (FBI), Congressional Statement on Information Sharing before the U.S. Senate Committee on the Judiciary, Subcommittee on Administrative Oversight and the Courts, Washington, DC, April 17, 2002, http://www.fbi.gov/congress/congress02/jordan041702.htm (accessed April 19, 2003).

98. Suzel Spiller, "The FBI's Field Intelligence Groups and Police: Joining Forces," *FBI Law Enforcement Bulletin*, May 2006, pp. 2–6.

99. The concept of intelligence-led policing appears to have been first fully articulated in Angus Smith, ed., *Intelligence-Led Policing* (Richmond, VA: International Association of Law Enforcement Intelligence Analysts, 1997).

100. David L. Carter, *Law Enforcement Intelligence: A Guide for State, Local, and Tribal Law Enforcement Agencies* (Washington, DC: U.S. Dept. of Justice, 2004), p. 7.

101. Much of the information and some of the wording in this section is taken from Carter, *Law Enforcement Intelligence.*

102. Governor's Commission on Criminal Justice Innovation, *Final Report* (Boston: The Commission, 2004), p. 57, from which much of the wording in the rest of this paragraph is taken.

103. Lesley G. Koestner, "LEO Roars into the Future," *FBI Law Enforcement Bulletin*, September 2006, p. 9.

104. Federal Bureau of Investigation, Law Enforcement Online, http://www.fbi.gov/hq/cjisd/leo.htm (accessed September 1, 2006).

105. Bernard H. Levin, "Sharing Information: Some Open Secrets and a Glimpse at the Future," *Police Futurist*, Vol. 14, No. 1 (winter 2006), pp. 8–9.

106. The plan was an outgrowth of the IACP Criminal Intelligence Sharing Summit, held in Alexandria, VA, in March 2002. The results of the summit are documented in International Association of Chiefs of Police, *Recommendations from the IACP Intelligence Summit, Criminal Intelligence Sharing.*

107. Office of Justice Programs, *The National Criminal Intelligence Sharing Plan* (Washington, DC: U.S. Dept. of Justice, 2003).

108. Howard Cohen, "Overstepping Police Authority," *Criminal Justice Ethics* (summer/fall 1987), pp. 52–60.

109. Kenneth Culp Davis, *Police Discretion* (St. Paul, MN: West, 1975).

110. See, for example, Robert Shepard Engel, James J. Sobol, and Robert E. Worden, "Further Exploration of the Demeanor Hypothesis: The Interaction of Effects of Suspects' Characteristics and Demeanor on Police Behavior," *Justice Quarterly*, Vol. 17, No. 2 (2000), p. 235.

111. Sykes, "Street Justice," p. 505.

112. Michael Siegfried, "Notes on the Professionalization of Private Security," *Justice Professional* (spring 1989).

113. See Edward A. Farris, "Five Decades of American Policing, 1932–1982: The Path to Professionalism," *Police Chief* (November 1982), p. 34.

114. E-mail correspondence with Janice Dixon at the Commission on Accreditation for Law Enforcement Agencies, March 16, 2005. Agency estimates are from Brian A. Reaves and Matthew J. Hickman, *Census of State and Local Law Enforcement Agencies, 2000* (Washington, DC: Bureau of Justice Statistics, 2002).

115. *CALEA Update*, No. 81 (February 2003), http://www.calea. org/newweb/newsletter/No81/81index.htm (accessed May 21, 2003).

116. Brian A. Reaves and Andrew L. Goldberg, *Law Enforcement Management and Administrative Statistics, 1997: Data for Individual State and Local Law Enforcement Agencies with 100 or More Officers* (Washington, DC: Bureau of Justice Statistics, 1999).

117. California Commission on POST, "California Responds to Racial Profiling," http://www.post.ca.gov/surveys/ racialprofile.htm (accessed March 3, 2007).

118. Information in this paragraph comes from "PTO Program," COPS Office, U.S. Department of Justice, http://www.cops. usdoj.gov/print.asp?Item_461 (accessed June 3, 2007).

119. National Commission on Law Observance and Enforcement, *Report on Police* (Washington, DC: U.S. Government Printing Office, 1931).

120. President's Commission on Law Enforcement and Administration of Justice, *The Challenge of Crime in a Free Society* (Washington, DC: U.S. Government Printing Office, 1967).

121. National Advisory Commission on Criminal Justice Standards and Goals, *Report on the Police* (Washington, DC: U.S. Government Printing Office, 1973).

122. Reaves and Goldberg, *Law Enforcement Management and Administrative Statistics, 1997.*

123. Ibid.

124. Brian A. Reaves and Matthew J. Hickman, *Police Departments in Large Cities, 1990–2000* (Washington, DC: Bureau of Justice Statistics, 2002), p. 1.

125. "Dallas PD College Rule Gets Final OK," *Law Enforcement News*, July 7, 1986, pp. 1, 13.

126. *Davis v. Dallas*, 777 F.2d 205 (5th Cir. 1985).

127. David L. Carter, Allen D. Sapp, and Darrel W. Stephens, *The State of Police Education: Policy Direction for the Twenty-First Century* (Washington, DC: Police Executive Research Forum, 1989), pp. xxii–xxiii.

128. The latter two were formerly part of the Immigration and Naturalization Service until its reorganization under the Homeland Security Act of 2002.

129. National Advisory Commission on Criminal Justice Standards and Goals, *Report on the Police*, p. 238.

130. Matthew J. Hickman and Brian A. Reaves, *Local Police Departments, 2003* (Washington, DC: Bureau of Justice Statistics, 2006), p. 5.

131. Ibid., p. 270.

132. August Vollmer, *The Police and Modern Society* (Berkeley: University of California Press, 1936), p. 222.

133. O. W. Wilson and Roy Clinton McLaren, *Police Administration*, 4th ed. (New York: McGraw-Hill, 1977), p. 259.

134. *Report of the National Advisory Commission on Civil Disorders* (New York: E. P. Dutton, 1968), p. 332.

135. Hickman and Reaves, *Community Policing.*

136. R. Alan Thompson, "Black Skin-Brass Shields: Assessing the Presumed Marginalization of Black Law Enforcement Executives," *American Journal of Criminal Justice*, Vol. 30, No. 2 (2006), pp. 163–175.

137. National Center for Women and Policing, *Equality Denied: The Status of Women in Policing, 2001* (Los Angeles: NCWP, 2002), p. 2.

138. Ibid.

139. Ibid., pp. 4–5, from which some of the wording in the list is taken.

140. National Center for Women and Policing, *Recruiting and Retaining Women: A Self-Assessment Guide for Law Enforcement* (Los Angeles: NCWP, 2001), p. 22.

141. Ibid.

142. C. Lee Bennett, "Interviews with Female Police Officers in Western Massachusetts," paper presented at the annual meeting of the Academy of Criminal Justice Sciences, Nashville, TN, March 1991.

143. Ibid., p. 9.

144. Carole G. Garrison, Nancy K. Grant, and Kenneth L. J. McCormick, "Utilization of Police Women," *Police Chief*, Vol. 32, No. 7 (September 1998).

145. Susan Ehrlich Martin and Nancy C. Jurik, *Doing Justice, Doing Gender: Women in Law and Criminal Justice Occupations* (Thousand Oaks, CA: Sage, 1996).

146. Police Foundation, *On the Move: The Status of Women in Policing* (Washington, DC: Police Foundation, 1990).

147. See, for example, Pearl Jacobs, "Suggestions for the Greater Integration of Women into Policing," paper presented at the annual meeting of the Academy of Criminal Justice Sciences, Nashville, TN, March 1991; and Cynthia Fuchs Epstein, *Deceptive Distinctions: Sex, Gender, and the Social Order* (New Haven, CT: Yale University Press, 1988).

148. See Sara Roen, "The Longest Climb," *Police* (October 1996), pp. 44–46, 66.

Chapter 7 Policing: Legal Aspects

i. Quoted in Gene Stephens, "Policing the Future: Law Enforcement's New Challenges," *Futurist*, March–April 2005, p. 57.

ii. Michael O'Keefe, "Sweep Can Solve Crime," *USA Today*, January 19, 2005, p. 10A.

iii. Adapted from Technical Working Group for Electronic Crime Scene Investigation, *Electronic Crime Scene Investigation: A Guide for First Responders* (Washington, DC: National Institute of Justice, 2001), p. 2.

iv. Adapted from Larry R. Leibrock, "Overview and Impact on 21st Century Legal Practice: Digital Forensics and Electronic Discovery," http://www.courtroom21.net/FDIC.pps (accessed July 5, 2005).

1. Larry Collins and Dominique Lapierre, *The Fifth Horseman* (New York: Simon and Schuster, 1980).

2. Ellen Barry and Colin Moynihan, "Three Detectives Plead Not Guilty in 50-Shot Killing," *New York Times*, March 20, 2007.

3. Cara Buckley, "Diallo Verdict May Have Made Prosecutors Cautious," *New York Times*, March 20, 2007.

4. Marcus Baram, "How Common Is Contagious Shooting?" ABC News, November 17, 2006, http://abcnews.go.com/Politics/story?id=2681947&page=1 (accessed May 21, 2007).

5. Michael Wilson, "50 Shots Fired, and the Experts Offer a Theory," *New York Times*, November 27, 2006.

6. "Victim of Police Beating Says He Was Sober," Associated Press, October 10, 2005, http://www.msnbc.msn.com/id/9645260 (accessed July 10, 2006).

7. "New Investigation May Postpone Police Trial in Video-tape," KATC-TV, http://www.katc.com/Global/story.asp?S=4345819&nav=EyAz (accessed March 19, 2006).

8. "Police Brutality!" *Time*, March 25, 1991, p. 18.

9. "Police Charged in Beating Case Say They Feared for Their Lives," *Boston Globe*, May 22, 1991, p. 22.

10. Ibid., pp. 16–19.

11. "Cries of Relief," *Time*, April 26, 1993, p. 18.

12. "Rodney King Slams SUV into House, Breaks Pelvis," CNN.com, April 16, 2003, http://www.cnn.com/2003/US/West/04/15/rodney.king.ap/index.html (accessed August 5, 2005).

13. *Miranda* v. *Arizona*, 384 U.S. 436 (1966).

14. *Weeks* v. *U.S.*, 232 U.S. 383 (1914).

15. Roger Goldman and Steven Puro, "Decertification of Police: An Alternative to Traditional Remedies for Police Misconduct," *Hastings Constitutional Law Quarterly*, Vol. 15 (1988), pp. 45–80.

16. Hawaii police departments set their own training requirements. The Honolulu Police Department, for example, requires six and a half months of student officer training and another 14 weeks of postgraduation field training. See the Honolulu Police Department's website at http://www.honolulupd.org/main/training.htm (accessed March 29, 2007).

17. Goldman and Puro, "Decertification of Police."

18. *Silverthorne Lumber Co.* v. *U.S.*, 251 U.S. 385 (1920).

19. Ibid.

20. Clemmens Bartollas, *American Criminal Justice* (New York: Macmillan, 1988), p. 186.

21. *Mapp* v. *Ohio*, 367 U.S. 643 (1961).

22. *Wolf* v. *Colorado*, 338 U.S. 25 (1949).

23. *Chimel* v. *California*, 395 U.S. 752 (1969).

24. *U.S.* v. *Rabinowitz*, 339 U.S. 56 (1950).

25. *Katz* v. *U.S.*, 389 U.S. 347, 88 S.Ct. 507 (1967).

26. *Minnesota* v. *Olson*, 110 S.Ct. 1684 (1990).

27. *Minnesota* v. *Carter*, 525 U.S. 83 (1998).

28. *Georgia* v. *Randolph*, U.S. Supreme Court, No. 04-1067 (decided March 22, 2006).

29. The ruling left open the possibility that any evidence relating to criminal activity undertaken by the consenting party might be admissible in court. In the words of the Court, refusal by a co-occupant "renders entry and search unreasonable and invalid as to him."

30. *U.S.* v. *Leon*, 468 U.S. 897, 104 S.Ct. 3405, 82 L.Ed.2d 677, 52 U.S.L.W. 5155 (1984).

31. Judicial titles vary among jurisdictions. Many lower-level state judicial officers are called *magistrates*. Federal magistrates, however, generally have a significantly higher level of judicial authority.

32. *Massachusetts* v. *Sheppard*, 104 S.Ct. 3424 (1984).

33. *Illinois* v. *Krull*, 107 S.Ct. 1160 (1987).

34. *Maryland* v. *Garrison*, 107 S.Ct. 1013 (1987).

35. *Illinois* v. *Rodriguez*, 110 S.Ct. 2793 (1990).

36. William H. Erickson, William D. Neighbors, and B. J. George, Jr., *United States Supreme Court Cases and Comments* (New York: Matthew Bender, 1987), Section 1.13[7].

37. See *California* v. *Acevedo*, 500 U.S. 565 (1991); *Ornelas* v. *U.S.*, 517 U.S. 690 (1996); and others.

38. See *Edwards* v. *Balisok*, 520 U.S. 641 (1997); *Booth* v. *Churner*, 532 U.S. 731 (2001); and *Porter* v. *Nussle*, 534 U.S. 516 (2002).

39. See *Wilson* v. *Arkansas*, 115 S.Ct. 1914 (1995); and *Richards* v. *Wisconsin*, 117 S.Ct. 1416 (1997).

40. See *McCleskey* v. *Kemp*, 481 U.S. 279, 107 S.Ct. 1756, 95 L.Ed.2d 262 (1987); *McCleskey* v. *Zant*, 499 U.S. 467, 493–494 (1991); *Coleman* v. *Thompson*, 501 U.S. 722 (1991); *Schlup* v. *Delo*, 115 S.Ct. 851, 130 L.Ed.2d 808 (1995); *Felker* v. *Turpin, Warden*, 117 S.Ct. 30, 135 L.Ed.2d 1123 (1996); *Boyde* v. *California*, 494 U.S. 370 (1990); and others.

41. See *Ewing* v. *California*, 538 U.S. 11 (2003); and *Lockyer* v. *Andrade*, 538 U.S. 63 (2003).

42. Richard Lacayo and Viveca Novak, "How Rehnquist Changed America," *Time*, June 30, 2003, pp. 20–25.

43. *Harris* v. *U.S.*, 390 U.S. 234 (1968).

44. The legality of plain-view seizures was also confirmed in earlier cases, including *Ker* v. *California*, 374 U.S. 23, 42–43 (1963); *U.S.* v. *Lee*, 274 U.S. 559 (1927); *U.S.* v. *Lefkowitz*, 285 U.S. 452, 465 (1932); and *Hester* v. *U.S.*, 265 U.S. 57 (1924).

45. As cited in Kimberly A. Kingston, "Look but Don't Touch: The Plain View Doctrine," *FBI Law Enforcement Bulletin*, December 1987, p. 18.

46. *Horton* v. *California*, 496 U.S. 128 (1990).

47. *U.S.* v. *Irizarry*, 673 F.2d 554, 556–567 (1st Cir. 1982).

48. *Arizona* v. *Hicks*, 107 S.Ct. 1149 (1987).

49. See North Carolina Justice Academy, *Criminal Justice Today* (fall 1987), p. 24.

50. Inadvertence, as a requirement of legitimate plain-view seizures, was first cited in the U.S. Supreme Court case of *Coolidge* v. *New Hampshire*, 403 U.S. 443, 91 S.Ct. 2022 (1971).

51. *Horton* v. *California*, 496 U.S. 128 (1990).

52. Ibid.

53. *Brigham City* v. *Stuart*, U.S. Supreme Court, No. 05-502 (decided May 22, 2006).

54. John Gales Sauls, "Emergency Searches of Premises," Part 1, *FBI Law Enforcement Bulletin*, March 1987, p. 23.

55. *Warden* v. *Hayden*, 387 U.S. 294 (1967).

56. *Mincey* v. *Arizona*, 437 U.S. 385, 392 (1978).

57. Sauls, "Emergency Searches of Premises," p. 25.

58. *Maryland* v. *Buie*, 110 S.Ct. 1093 (1990).

59. *Wilson* v. *Arkansas*, 514 U.S. 927 (1995).

60. For additional information, see Michael J. Bulzomi, "Knock and Announce: A Fourth Amendment Standard," *FBI Law Enforcement Bulletin*, May 1997, pp. 27–31.

61. *Richards* v. *Wisconsin*, 117 S.Ct. 1416 (1997), syllabus.

62. *Illinois* v. *McArthur*, 531 U.S. 326, 330 (2001).

63. *U.S.* v. *Banks*, 540 U.S. 31 (2003).

64. *Hudson* v. *Michigan*, U.S. Supreme Court, No. 04-1360 (decided June 15, 2006).

65. *U.S.* v. *Grubbs*, U.S. Supreme Court, No. 04-1414 (decided March 21, 2006).

66. *U.S.* v. *Mendenhall*, 446 U.S. 544 (1980).

67. A. Louis DiPietro, "Voluntary Encounters or Fourth Amendment Seizures," *FBI Law Enforcement Bulletin*, January 1992, pp. 28–32.

68. *Stansbury* v. *California*, 114 S.Ct. 1526, 1529, 128 L.Ed.2d 293 (1994).

69. *Yarborough* v. *Alvarado*, 541 U.S. 652 (2004).

70. *Thompson* v. *Keohane*, 516 U.S. 99, 112 (1996).

71. *Atwater* v. *Lago Vista*, 532 U.S. 318 (2001).

72. In 1976, in the case of *Watson* v. *U.S.* (432 U.S. 411), the U.S. Supreme Court refused to impose a warrant requirement for felony arrests that occur in public places.

73. *Payton* v. *New York*, 445 U.S. 573, 590 (1980).

74. In 1981, in the case of *U.S.* v. *Steagald* (451 U.S. 204), the Court ruled that a search warrant is also necessary when the planned arrest involves entry into a third party's premises.

75. *Kirk* v. *Louisiana*, 122 S.Ct. 2458, 153 L.Ed.2d 599 (2002).

76. *U.S.* v. *Robinson*, 414 U.S. 218 (1973).

77. Ibid.

78. *Terry* v. *Ohio*, 392 U.S. 1 (1968).

79. *U.S.* v. *Sokolow*, 109 S.Ct. 1581 (1989).

80. The Court was quoting from *U.S.* v. *Brignoni-Ponce*, 422 U.S. 873, 878 (1975).

81. *U.S.* v. *Arvizu*, 534 U.S. 266 (2002).

82. Ibid.

83. *Minnesota* v. *Dickerson*, 113 S.Ct. 2130, 124 L.Ed.2d 334 (1993).

84. *Brown* v. *Texas*, 443 U.S. 47 (1979).

85. *Hiibel* v. *Sixth Judicial District Court of Nevada*, 542 U.S. 177 (2004).

86. *Smith* v. *Ohio*, 110 S.Ct. 1288 (1990).

87. Ibid., at 1289.

88. *California* v. *Hodari D.*, 111 S.Ct. 1547 (1991).

89. *Criminal Justice Newsletter*, May 1, 1991, p. 2.

90. *Illinois* v. *Wardlow*, 528 U.S. 119 (2000).

91. Ibid., syllabus, http://supct.law.cornell.edu/supct/html/98-1036.ZS.html (accessed April 1, 2007).

92. Ibid.

93. *Arkansas* v. *Sanders*, 442 U.S. 753 (1979).

94. Ibid.

95. *U.S.* v. *Borchardt*, 809 F.2d 1115 (5th Cir. 1987).

96. *FBI Law Enforcement Bulletin*, January 1988, p. 28.

97. *Carroll* v. *U.S.*, 267 U.S. 132 (1925).

98. *Preston* v. *U.S.*, 376 U.S. 364 (1964).

99. *South Dakota* v. *Opperman*, 428 U.S. 364 (1976).

100. *Colorado* v. *Bertine*, 479 U.S. 367, 107 S.Ct. 741 (1987).

101. *Florida* v. *Wells*, 110 S.Ct. 1632 (1990).

102. *Terry* v. *Ohio*, 392 U.S. 1 (1968).

103. *California* v. *Acevedo*, 500 U.S. 565 (1991).

104. *Ornelas* v. *U.S.*, 517 U.S. 690, 696 (1996).

105. Ibid.

106. The phrase is usually attributed to the 1991 U.S. Supreme Court case of *California* v. *Acevedo* (500 U.S. 565 [1991]). See Devallis Rutledge, "Taking an Inventory," *Police*, November 1995, pp. 8–9. See also *Pennsylvania* v. *Labron*, 518 U.S. 938 (1996), in which the Court held that if a vehicle is readily mobile and probable cause exists to believe it contains contraband, the Fourth Amendment permits police to search the vehicle, and contraband seized from such a search should not be suppressed.

107. *Florida* v. *Jimeno*, 111 S.Ct. 1801 (1991).

108. Ibid., syllabus, http://laws.findlaw.com/us/500/248.html (accessed March 2, 2007).

109. *U.S.* v. *Ross*, 456 U.S. 798 (1982).

110. Ibid.

111. *Whren* v. *U.S.*, 517 U.S. 806 (1996).

112. See *Pennsylvania* v. *Mimms*, 434 U.S. 106 (1977).

113. *Maryland* v. *Wilson*, 117 S.Ct. 882 (1997).

114. *Knowles* v. *Iowa*, 525 U.S. 113 (1998).

115. *Wyoming* v. *Houghton*, 526 U.S. 295 (1999).

116. *Thornton* v. *U.S.*, 41 U.S. 615 (2004).

117. *Illinois* v. *Caballes*, 543 U.S. 405 (2005).

118. *Michigan Dept. of State Police* v. *Sitz*, 110 S.Ct. 2481 (1990).

119. Ibid.

120. *U.S.* v. *Martinez-Fuerte*, 428 U.S. 543 (1976).

121. Ibid., syllabus.

122. *Indianapolis* v. *Edmond*, 531 U.S. 32 (2000), http://supct.law.cornell.edu/supct/html/99-1030.ZS.html (accessed April 2, 2007).

123. *Illinois* v. *Lidster*, 540 U.S. 419 (2004).

124. *U.S.* v. *Villamonte-Marquez*, 462 U.S. 579 (1983).

125. *California* v. *Carney*, 471 U.S. 386, 105 S.Ct. 2066, 85 L.Ed.2d 406, 53 U.S.L.W. 4521 (1985).

126. *U.S.* v. *Hill*, 855 F.2d 664 (10th Cir. 1988).

127. *National Treasury Employees Union* v. *Von Raab*, 489 U.S. 656 (1989).

128. *Skinner* v. *Railway Labor Executives' Association*, 489 U.S. 602 (1989).

129. *Florida* v. *Bostick*, 111 S.Ct. 2382 (1991).

130. *Bond* v. *U.S.*, 529 U.S. 334 (2000), http://supct.law.cornell.edu/supct/html/98-9349.ZS.html (accessed January 10, 2007).

131. *U.S.* v. *Drayton*, 122 S.Ct. 2105 (2002).

132. *U.S.* v. *Flores-Montano*, 541 U.S. 149 (2004).

133. *People* v. *Deutsch*, 96 C.D.O.S. 2827 (1996).

134. The thermal imager differs from infrared devices (such as night-vision goggles) in that infrared devices amplify the infrared spectrum of light, whereas thermal imagers register solely the portion of the infrared spectrum that we call *heat*.

135. *People* v. *Deutsch*, 96 C.D.O.S. 2827 (1996).

136. *Kyllo* v. *U.S.*, 533 U.S. 27 (2001).

137. Ibid.

138. *Aguilar* v. *Texas*, 378 U.S. 108 (1964).

139. *U.S.* v. *Harris*, 403 U.S. 573 (1971).

140. Ibid. at 584.

141. *Illinois* v. *Gates*, 426 U.S. 213 (1983).

142. *Alabama* v. *White*, 110 S.Ct. 2412 (1990).

143. Ibid., at 2417.

144. *Florida* v. *J. L.*, 529 U.S. 266 (2000).

145. Some of the wording in this paragraph is adapted from the *LII Bulletin*, "End of Term Wrap-Up," June 29, 2000 (e-mail bulletin of the Legal Information Institute, Cornell University School of Law).

146. *U.S. Dept. of Justice* v. *Landano*, 113 S.Ct. 2014, 124 L.Ed.2d 84 (1993).

147. Richard Willing, "Illinois Law First to Order Taping Murder Confessions," *USA Today*, July 18, 2003, p. 3A.

148. *South Dakota* v. *Neville*, 103 S.Ct. 916 (1983).

149. *Brown* v. *Mississippi*, 297 U.S. 278 (1936).

150. *Ashcraft* v. *Tennessee*, 322 U.S. 143 (1944).

151. *Chambers* v. *Florida*, 309 U.S. 227 (1940).

152. Ibid.

153. *Leyra* v. *Denno*, 347 U.S. 556 (1954).

154. Ibid.

155. *Arizona* v. *Fulminante*, 111 S.Ct. 1246 (1991).

156. *Chapman* v. *California*, 386 U.S. 18 (1967).

157. *State* v. *Fulminante*, No. CR-95-0160.

158. *Escobedo* v. *Illinois*, 378 U.S. 478 (1964).

159. *Edwards* v. *Arizona*, 451 U.S. 477, 101 S.Ct. 1880, 68 L.Ed.2d 378 (1981).

160. *Minnick* v. *Mississippi*, 498 U.S. 146 (1990).

161. *Arizona* v. *Roberson*, 486 U.S. 675, 108 S.Ct. 2093 (1988).

162. *Davis* v. *U.S.*, 114 S.Ct. 2350 (1994).

163. *Miranda* v. *Arizona*, 384 U.S. 436 (1966).

164. "Immigrants Get Civil Rights," *USA Today*, June 11, 1992, p. 1A.

165. *U.S.* v. *Dickerson*, 166 F.3d 667 (1999).

166. *Dickerson* v. *U.S.*, 530 U.S. 428 (2000), http://supct.law.cornell.edu/supct/html/99-5525.ZS.html (accessed May 10, 2007).

167. *Moran* v. *Burbine*, 475 U.S. 412, 421 (1986).

168. *Colorado* v. *Spring*, 479 U.S. 564, 107 S.Ct. 851 (1987).

169. *Brewer* v. *Williams*, 430 U.S. 387 (1977).

170. *Nix* v. *Williams*, 104 S.Ct. 2501 (1984).

171. *New York* v. *Quarles*, 104 S.Ct. 2626, 81 L.Ed.2d 550 (1984).

172. *Colorado* v. *Connelly*, 107 S.Ct. 515, 93 L.Ed.2d 473 (1986).

173. *Kuhlmann* v. *Wilson*, 477 U.S. 436 (1986).

174. *Illinois* v. *Perkins*, 495 U.S. 292 (1990).

175. *Rock* v. *Zimmerman*, 543 F.Supp. 179 (M.D. Pa. 1982).

176. Ibid.

177. See *Oregon* v. *Mathiason*, 429 U.S. 492, 97 S.Ct. 711 (1977).

178. *South Dakota* v. *Neville*, 103 S.Ct. 916 (1983).

179. *Arizona* v. *Mauro*, 107 S.Ct. 1931, 95 L.Ed.2d 458 (1987).

180. *Doyle* v. *Ohio*, 426 U.S. 610 (1976).

181. *Brecht* v. *Abrahamson*, 113 S.Ct. 1710, 123 L.Ed.2d 353 (1993).

182. Citing *Kotteakos* v. *U.S.*, 328 U.S. 750 (1946).

183. See Linda Greenhouse, "The Supreme Court: Supreme Court Roundup—Police Questioning Allowed to the Point of Coercion," *New York Times*, May 28, 2003, p. A18.

184. *Chavez* v. *Martinez*, 538 U.S. 760 (2003).

185. Ibid.

186. *Hayes* v. *Florida*, 470 U.S. 811, 105 S.Ct. 1643 (1985).

187. *Winston* v. *Lee*, 470 U.S. 753, 105 S.Ct. 1611 (1985).

188. *Schmerber* v. *California*, 384 U.S. 757 (1966).

189. "Man Coughs Up Cocaine While in Custody," *Police Magazine* online, March 4, 2005, http://www.policemag.com/t_newspick.cfm?rank574703 (accessed January 4, 2006).

190. *U.S.* v. *Montoya de Hernandez*, 473 U.S. 531, 105 S.Ct. 3304 (1985).

191. Ibid.

192. *Olmstead* v. *U.S.*, 277 U.S. 438 (1928).

193. *On Lee* v. *U.S.*, 343 U.S. 747 (1952).

194. *Lopez* v. *U.S.*, 373 U.S. 427 (1963).

195. *Berger* v. *New York*, 388 U.S. 41 (1967).

196. *Katz* v. *U.S.*, 389 U.S. 347 (1967).

197. *Lee* v. *Florida*, 392 U.S. 378 (1968).

198. Federal Communications Act of 1934, U.S. Code, Title 47, Section 151.

199. *U.S.* v. *White*, 401 U.S. 745 (1971).

200. *U.S.* v. *Karo*, 468 U.S. 705 (1984).

201. *U.S.* v. *Scott*, 436 U.S. 128 (1978).

202. For more information, see *FBI Law Enforcement Bulletin*, June 1987, p. 25.

203. Electronic Communications Privacy Act of 1986, Public Law 99-508.

204. For more information on the ECPA, see Robert A. Fiatal, "The Electronic Communications Privacy Act: Addressing Today's Technology," *FBI Law Enforcement Bulletin*, April 1988, pp. 24–30.

205. Communications Assistance for Law Enforcement Act of 1994, Public Law 103-414.

206. U.S. Department of Justice, Office of the Inspector General, *Implementation of the Communications Assistance for Law Enforcement Act by the Federal Bureau of Investigation* (Washington, DC: U.S. Dept. of Justice, 2004).

207. Administrative Office of the United States Courts, *2004 Wiretap Report*, http://www.uscourts.gov/wiretap04/contents.html (accessed January 7, 2007).

208. Telecommunications Act of 1996, Public Law 104, 110 Statute 56.

209. Title 47, U.S.C.A., Section 223(a)(1)(B)(ii) (Supp. 1997).

210. *Reno* v. *ACLU*, 117 S.Ct. 2329 (1997).

211. U.S. Code, Title 18, Section 1030.

212. Ibid., Section 202.

213. U.S. Code, Title 18, Section 2703(c).

214. Ibid.

215. Public Law 109-177.

216. Technical Working Group for Electronic Crime Scene Investigation, *Electronic Crime Scene Investigation: A Guide for First Responders* (Washington, DC: National Institute of Justice, 2001), from which much of the information in this section is taken.

217. Ibid., p. 2.

218. Computer Crime and Intellectual Property Section, U.S. Department of Justice, *Searching and Seizing Computers and Obtaining Electronic Evidence in Criminal Investigations* (Washington, DC: U.S. Dept. of Justice, 2002), http://www.usdoj.gov/criminal/cybercrime/s&smanual2002.htm (accessed August 4, 2007).

219. Technical Working Group, *Electronic Crime Scene Investigation*, p. 2.

220. *U.S.* v. *Carey*, 172 F.3d 1268 (10th Cir. 1999).

221. *U.S.* v. *Turner*, 169 F.3d 84 (1st Cir. 1999).

Chapter 8   Policing: Issues and Challenges

i. Carl B. Klockars et al., *The Measurement of Police Integrity*, National Institute of Justice Research in Brief (Washington, DC: National Institute of Justice, 2000), p. 1.

ii. Kevin Johnson, "Court Says Idaho Can Prosecute FBI Agent," *USA Today*, June 6, 2001, p. 3A.

iii. Technical Working Group on Crime Scene Investigation, *Crime Scene Investigation: A Guide for Law Enforcement* (Washington, DC: National Institute of Justice, 2000), p. 12.

iv. Jerome H. Skolnick and David H. Bayley, *The New Blue Line: Police Innovation in Six American Cities* (New York: Free Press, 1986), p. 229.

v.   National Institute of Justice, *Use of Force by Police: Overview of National and Local Data* (Washington, DC: National Institute of Justice, 1999).

vi.   International Association of Chiefs of Police, *Police Use of Force in America, 2001* (Alexandria, VA: IACP, 2001), p. 1.

vii.   Samuel Walker, Geoffrey P. Albert, and Dennis J. Kenney, *Responding to the Problem Police Officer: A National Study of Early Warning Systems* (Washington, DC: National Institute of Justice, 2000).

viii.   Sam W. Lathrop, "Reviewing Use of Force: A Systematic Approach," *FBI Law Enforcement Bulletin,* October 2000, p. 18.

ix.   Deborah Ramierz, Jack McDevitt, and Amy Farrell, *A Resource Guide on Racial Profiling Data Collection Systems: Promising Practices and Lessons Learned* (Washington, DC: U.S. Dept. of Justice, 2000), p. 3.

x.   Adapted from Gerald Hill and Kathleen Hill, *The Real Life Dictionary of the Law,* http://www.law.com (accessed June 11, 2007).

xi.   Jane Musgrave, "Charge against Officer Likely, but Conviction Not, Lawyers Say," *Palm Beach Post,* April 22, 2005.

xii.   Gene Stephens, "Policing the Future: Law Enforcement's New Challenges," *Futurist,* March/April 2005, p. 57.

1.   Lorie Fridell et al., *Racially Biased Policing: A Principled Response* (Washington, DC: Police Executive Research Forum, 2001), p. 41.

2.   Quoted in Jim Helihy, "Issues Affecting Irish Policing, 1922–1932," http://www.esatclear.ie/~garda/issues.html (accessed June 15, 2006).

3.   Janine Rauch and Etienne Marasis, "Contextualizing the Waddington Report," http://www.wits.ac.za/csvr/papers/papwadd.html (accessed January 5, 2007).

4.   Jerome H. Skolnick, *Justice without Trial: Law Enforcement in a Democratic Society* (New York: John Wiley, 1966).

5.   William A. Westley, *Violence and the Police: A Sociological Study of Law, Custom, and Morality* (Cambridge, MA: MIT Press, 1970); and William A. Westley, "Violence and the Police," *American Journal of Sociology,* Vol. 49 (1953), pp. 34–41.

6.   Arthur Niederhoffer, *Behind the Shield: The Police in Urban Society* (Garden City, NY: Anchor, 1967).

7.   Thomas Barker and David L. Carter, *Police Deviance* (Cincinnati, OH: Anderson, 1986). See also Christopher P. Wilson, *Cop Knowledge: Police Power and Cultural Narrative in Twentieth-Century America* (Chicago, IL: University of Chicago Press, 2000).

8.   Richard Bennett and Theodore Greenstein, "The Police Personality: A Test of the Predispositional Model," *Journal of Police Science and Administration,* Vol. 3 (1975), pp. 439–445.

9.   James Teevan and Bernard Dolnick, "The Values of the Police: A Reconsideration and Interpretation," *Journal of Police Science and Administration* (1973), pp. 366–369.

10.   Office of the U.S. Attorney for the Southern District of California, press release, July 28, 2006.

11.   NBC News San Diego, "Border Patrol Agent Faces Immigrant-Smuggling Charges," August 5, 2005, http://www.nbcsandiego.com/news/4816916/detail.html (accessed July 4, 2007).

12.   Alan Feuer, "2 Ex-Detectives Guilty in Killings," *New York Times,* April 7, 2006, http://www.nytimes.com/2006/04/07/nyregion/07cops.html (accessed April 7, 2006).

13.   Andy Newman, "A Juror's Question That Went Unanswered: 'How Dare You Violate That Oath?'" *New York Times,* April 7, 2006, http://www.nytimes.com/2006/04/07/nyregion/07scene.html (accessed April 7, 2006).

14.   Carl B. Klockars et al., "The Measurement of Police Integrity," National Institute of Justice Research in Brief (Washington, DC: NIJ, 2000), p. 1.

15.   Michael J. Palmiotto, ed., *Police Misconduct: A Reader for the Twenty-First Century* (Upper Saddle River, NJ: Prentice Hall, 2001), preface.

16.   Tim Prenzler and Peta Mackay, "Police Gratuities: What the Public Thinks," *Criminal Justice Ethics* (winter/spring 1995), pp. 15–25.

17.   Thomas Barker and David L. Carter, *Police Deviance* (Cincinnati, OH: Anderson, 1986). For a detailed overview of the issues involved in police corruption, see Victor E. Kappeler, Richard D. Sluder, and Geoffrey P. Alpert, *Forces of Deviance: Understanding the Dark Side of Policing,* 2nd ed. (Prospect Heights, IL: Waveland Press, 1998); Dean J. Champion, *Police Misconduct in America: A Reference Handbook* (Santa Barbara, CA: Abo-Clio, 2002); and Kim Michelle Lersch, ed., *Policing and Misconduct* (Upper Saddle River, NJ: Prentice Hall, 2002).

18.   Frank L. Perry, "Repairing Broken Windows: Preventing Corruption within Our Ranks," *FBI Law Enforcement Bulletin,* February 2001, pp. 23–26.

19.   "Nationline: NYC Cops—Excess Force Not Corruption," *USA Today,* June 16, 1995, p. 3A.

20.   *Knapp Commission Report on Police Corruption* (New York: George Braziller, 1973).

21.   Ibid.

22.   Sabrina Tavernise, "Victory for Officer Who Aided Corruption Inquiry," *New York Times,* April 3, 2004.

23.   See IMDb.com, "Notorious (2008)," http://www.imdb.com/title/tt0371115/. The movie is said to be in production as this book goes to press.

24.   See Erwin Chemerinsky, *An Independent Analysis of the Los Angeles Police Department's Board of Inquiry Report on the Rampart Scandal,* September 11, 2000, http://www.usc.edu/dept/law/faculty/chemerinsky/rampartfinalrep.html (accessed January 10, 2006).

25.   Linda Deutsch, "Appeals Court Intercedes in LAPD Corruption Trial," Associated Press, October 12, 2000, http://www.newstimes.com/archive2000/oct12/nah.htm (accessed January 20, 2006).

26.   "Three LAPD Officers Convicted," *USA Today,* November 15, 2000.

27.   "Prosecutors: LAPD Hindering Police Corruption Trial," Associated Press, October 6, 2000, http://www.newstimes.com/archive2000/oct06/nac.htm (accessed February 2, 2006).

28.   Scott Glover and Matt Lait, "LAPD Settling Abuse Scandal," *Los Angeles Times,* March 31, 2005.

29.   "Three LAPD Officers Convicted" and "This Week's Corrupt Cop Story," http://www.stopthedrugwar.org/chronicle/266/copcorruption.shtml (accessed October 2, 2003).

30.   Glover and Lait, "LAPD Settling Abuse Scandal."

31.   Ibid.

32.   Tina Daunt and Jim Newton, "Council OKs Police Reform Pact with Justice Department," *Los Angeles Times,* November 3, 2000.

33.   Scott Glover and Matt Lait, "A Tearful Perez Gets Five Years," *Los Angeles Times,* February 26, 2000.

34. Edwin H. Sutherland and Donald Cressey, *Principles of Criminology*, 8th ed. (Philadelphia: J. B. Lippincott, 1970).

35. Tim R. Jones, Compton Owens, and Melissa A. Smith, "Police Ethics Training: A Three-Tiered Approach," *FBI Law Enforcement Bulletin*, June 1995, pp. 22–26.

36. Stephen J. Gaffigan and Phyllis P. McDonald, *Police Integrity: Public Service with Honor* (Washington, DC: National Institute of Justice, 1997).

37. U.S. Department of Justice, *Principles for Promoting Police Integrity: Examples of Promising Police Practices* (Washington, DC: Dept. of Justice, 2001).

38. National Institute of Justice, *Enhancing Police Integrity* (Washington, DC: U.S. Dept. of Justice, 2005).

39. Ibid., p. ii.

40. *Carroll* v. *City of Westminster*, 4th Cir. No. 99-1556, November 17, 2000.

41. The material in this paragraph is adapted from Sharon Burrell, "Random Drug Testing of Police Officers Upheld," *Legal Views* (Office of the County Attorney, Montgomery County, Maryland), Vol. 6, No. 2 (February 2001), p. 4.

42. International Association of Chiefs of Police, *Employee Drug Testing* (St. Paul, MN: IACP, 1999).

43. *Maurice Turner* v. *Fraternal Order of Police*, 500 A.2d 1005 (D.C. 1985).

44. *Philip Caruso, President of P.B.A.* v. *Benjamin Ward, Police Commissioner*, New York State Supreme Court, Pat. 37, Index No. 12632-86, 1986.

45. *National Treasury Employees Union* v. *Von Raab*, 489 U.S. 656, 659 (1989).

46. National Law Enforcement Officers' Memorial Fund website, http://www.nleomf.com (accessed April 29, 2007).

47. Officer Down Memorial Page, "James Loyd Allen," http://www.odmp.org/officer.php?oid=17737 (accessed August 28, 2006).

48. Providence Police Department, "James L. Allen Memorial Page," http://www.providencepolice.com/jimmyallen.html (accessed August 28, 2006).

49. From the Officer Down Memorial Page, http://www.odmp.org/year.php?year=2006 (accessed September 15, 2007).

50. Ibid., http://www.odmp.org/year.php?year=2001 (accessed January 16, 2006).

51. Anthony J. Pinizzotto and Edward F. Davis, "Cop Killers and Their Victims," *FBI Law Enforcement Bulletin*, December 1992, p. 10.

52. Brian A. Reaves, *Census of State and Local Law Enforcement Agencies, 2000* (Washington, DC: Bureau of Justice Statistics, 2002); and Matthew J. Hickman and Brian A. Reaves, *Local Police Departments, 2000* (Washington, DC: Bureau of Justice Statistics, 2003).

53. Brian A. Reaves and Timothy C. Hart, *Federal Law Enforcement Officers, 2000* (Washington, DC: Bureau of Justice Statistics, 2002).

54. As reported by the Headline News Network, April 26, 1988.

55. *AIDS and Our Workplace*, New York City Police Department pamphlet, November 1987.

56. See Occupational Safety and Health Administration, OSHA Bloodborne Pathogens Act of 1991 (29 CFR 1910.1030).

57. *National Institute of Justice Reports*, No. 206 (November/December 1987).

58. "Suicides, Resignations Hit New Orleans' Thin Blue Line," *USA Today*, September 4, 2005, http://www.usatoday.com/ news/nation/2005-09-04-neworleanspolicesuicides_x.htm (accessed April 2, 2006).

59. Ibid.

60. See "On-the-Job Stress in Policing: Reducing It, Preventing It," *National Institute of Justice Journal* (January 2000), pp. 18–24.

61. "Stress on the Job," *Newsweek*, April 25, 1988, p. 43.

62. "On-the-Job Stress in Policing," p. 19.

63. Kevin Barrett, "Police Suicide: Is Anyone Listening?" *Journal of Safe Management of Disruptive and Assaultive Behavior* (spring 1997), pp. 6–9.

64. Ibid.

65. For an excellent review of coping strategies among police officers, see Robin N. Haarr and Merry Morash, "Gender, Race, and Strategies of Coping with Occupational Stress in Policing," *Justice Quarterly*, Vol. 16, No. 2 (June 1999), pp. 303–336.

66. Mark H. Anshel, "A Conceptual Model and Implications for Coping with Stressful Events in Police Work," *Criminal Justice and Behavior*, Vol. 27, No. 3 (2000), p. 375.

67. Ibid.

68. Bryan Vila, "Tired Cops: Probable Connections between Fatigue and the Performance, Health, and Safety of Patrol Officers," *American Journal of Police*, Vol. 15, No. 2 (1996), pp. 51–92.

69. Bryan Vila et al., *Evaluating the Effects of Fatigue on Police Patrol Officers: Final Report* (Washington, DC: National Institute of Justice, 2000).

70. Bryan Vila and Dennis Jay Kenney, "Tired Cops: The Prevalence and Potential Consequences of Police Fatigue," *NIJ Journal*, No. 248 (2002), p. 19.

71. Bryan Vila and Erik Y. Taiji, "Fatigue and Police Officer Performance," paper presented at the annual meeting of the American Society of Criminology, Chicago, 1996.

72. Some of the material in this section is adapted or derived from National Institute of Justice, *Use of Force by Police: Overview of National and Local Data* (Washington, DC: NIJ, 1999).

73. Matthew R. Durose, Erica L. Smith, and Patrick A. Langan, *Contacts between Police and the Public 2005* (Washington, DC: Bureau of Justice Statistics, 2007).

74. Ibid, p. 10.

75. Not all studies agree on this point, and in 2005, researchers who examined the use of force by male and female officers in the Montgomery County Police Department in Maryland found that male and female officers were relatively comparable in their use of force. See Peter B. Hoffman and Edward R. Hickey, "Use of Force by Female Police Officers," *Journal of Criminal Justice*, Vol. 33, No. 2 (2005), p. 142.

76. International Association of Chiefs of Police, *Police Use of Force in America, 2001* (Alexandria, VA: IACP, 2001), p. 1.

77. Kenneth Adams, "What We Know about Police Use of Force," in National Institute of Justice, *Use of Force by Police: Overview of National and Local Data* (Washington, DC: NIJ, 1999), p. 4.

78. Geoffrey P. Alpert and Roger G. Dunham, *The Force Factor: Measuring Police Use of Force Relative to Suspect Resistance—A Final Report* (Washington, DC: National Institute of Justice, 2001).

79. Samuel Walker, Geoffrey P. Alpert, and Dennis J. Kenney, *Responding to the Problem Police Officer: A National Study of Early Warning Systems* (Washington, DC: National Institute of Justice, 2000).

80. See Human Rights Watch, "The Christopher Commission Report," from which some of the wording in this paragraph is adapted, http://www.hrw.org/reports98/police/uspo73.htm (accessed March 30, 2007).

81. Sam W. Lathrop, "Reviewing Use of Force: A Systematic Approach," *FBI Law Enforcement Bulletin*, October 2000, p. 18.

82. Jodi M. Brown and Patrick A. Langan, *Policing and Homicide, 1976–98: Justifiable Homicide by Police, Police Officers Murdered by Felons* (Washington, DC: Bureau of Justice Statistics, 2001), p. iii.

83. *Tennessee* v. *Garner*, 471 U.S. 1 (1985).

84. *Graham* v. *Connor*, 490 U.S. 386, 396–397 (1989).

85. John C. Hall, "FBI Training on the New Federal Deadly Force Policy," *FBI Law Enforcement Bulletin*, April 1996, pp. 25–32.

86. James Fyfe, *Shots Fired: An Examination of New York City Police Firearms Discharges* (Ann Arbor, MI: University Microfilms, 1978).

87. James Fyfe, "Blind Justice? Police Shootings in Memphis," paper presented at the annual meeting of the Academy of Criminal Justice Sciences, Philadelphia, March 1981.

88. It is estimated that American police shoot *at* approximately 3,600 people every year. See William Geller, "Crime File: Deadly Force," a study guide (Washington, DC: National Institute of Justice, n.d.).

89. Anne Cohen, "I've Killed That Man Ten Thousand Times," *Police Magazine*, July 1980.

90. For more information, see Joe Auten, "When Police Shoot," *North Carolina Criminal Justice Today*, Vol. 4, No. 4 (summer 1986), pp. 9–14.

91. Details for this story come from Stephanie Slater, "Suicidal Man Killed by Police Fusillade," *Palm Beach Post*, March 11, 2005, p. 1A.

92. Rebecca Stincelli, *Suicide by Cop: Victims from Both Sides of the Badge* (Folsom, CA: Interviews and Interrogations Institute, 2004).

93. Quoted in Slater, "Suicidal Man Killed by Police Fusillade."

94. Anthony J. Pinizzotto, Edward F. Davis, and Charles E. Miller III, "Suicide by Cop: Defining a Devastating Dilemma," *FBI Law Enforcement Bulletin*, Vol. 74, No. 2 (February 2005), p. 15.

95. "Ten Percent of Police Shootings Found to Be 'Suicide by Cop,'" *Criminal Justice Newsletter*, September 1, 1998, pp. 1–2.

96. Robert J. Homant and Daniel B. Kennedy, "Suicide by Police: A Proposed Typology of Law Enforcement Officer-Assisted Suicide," *Policing: An International Journal of Police Strategies and Management*, Vol. 23, No. 3 (2000), pp. 339–355.

97. David W. Hayeslip and Alan Preszler, "NIJ Initiative on Less-Than-Lethal Weapons," National Institute of Justice Research in Brief (Washington, DC: NIJ, 1993).

98. Ibid.

99. Thomas Farragher and David Abel, "Postgame Police Projectile Kills an Emerson Student," *Boston Globe*, October 22, 2004, http://www.boston.com/sports/baseball/redsox/articles/2004/10/22/postgame_police_projectile_kills_an_emerson_student (accessed July 25, 2005).

100. Adapted from Deborah Ramirez, Jack McDevitt, and Amy Farrell, *A Resource Guide on Racial Profiling Data Collection Systems: Promising Practices and Lessons Learned* (Washington, DC: U.S. Department of Justice, 2000), p. 3.

101. David Harris, *Driving While Black: Racial Profiling on Our Nation's Highways* (Washington, DC: American Civil Liberties Union, 1999).

102. Peter Verniero and Paul Zoubek, *New Jersey Attorney General's Interim Report of the State Police Review Team Regarding Allegations of Racial Profiling* (Trenton, NJ: Office of the New Jersey Attorney General, 1999).

103. This paragraph is adapted from Ramirez, McDevitt, and Farrell, *A Resource Guide on Racial Profiling Data Collection Systems*, pp. 7–8.

104. *State of New Jersey* v. *Pedro Soto et al.*, Superior Court of New Jersey, 734 A.2d 350, 1996.

105. "Justice Department Bars Race Profiling, with Exception for Terrorism," *Criminal Justice Newsletter*, July 15, 2003, pp. 6–7.

106. "Justice Department Issues Policy Guidance to Ban Racial Profiling," U.S. Department of Justice press release (No. 355), June 17, 2003.

107. Blaine Harden and Somini Sengupta, "Some Passengers Singled Out for Exclusion by Flight Crew," *New York Times*, September 22, 2001.

108. David Cole and John Lambreth, "The Fallacy of Racial Profiling," *New York Times* Online, May 13, 2001, http://college1.nytimes.com/buests/articles/2001/05/13/846196.xml (accessed August 28, 2005).

109. Amitai Etzioni, "Another Side of Racial Profiling," *USA Today*, May 21, 2001, p. 15A.

110. Gallup Poll Organization, *Racial Profiling Is Seen as Widespread, Particularly among Young Black Men* (Princeton, NJ: Gallup Poll Organization, December 9, 1999), p. 1.

111. Christopher Stone, "Race, Crime, and the Administration of Justice," *National Institute of Justice Journal* (April 1999), p. 28.

112. Ramirez, McDevitt, and Farrell, *A Resource Guide on Racial Profiling Data Collection Systems*, p. 3.

113. Ibid., p. 55.

114. Police Executive Research Forum, *Racially Biased Policing: A Principled Response* (Washington, DC: PERF, 2001).

115. Ibid., foreword.

116. Ibid., p. 39.

117. Ibid., p. 47.

118. "Stroke Victim Sues State over Arrest," Associated Press, April 24, 1996.

119. Charles R. Swanson, Leonard Territo, and Robert W. Taylor, *Police Administration: Structures, Processes, and Behavior*, 2nd ed. (New York: Macmillan, 1988).

120. *Malley* v. *Briggs*, 475 U.S. 335, 106 S.Ct. 1092 (1986).

121. Ibid., at 4246.

122. *Biscoe* v. *Arlington County*, 238 U.S. App. D.C. 206, 738 F.2d 1352, 1362 (1984). See also 738 F.2d 1352 (D.C. Cir. 1984), cert. denied; 469 U.S. 1159; and 105 S.Ct. 909, 83 L.E.2d 923 (1985).

123. *Kaplan* v. *Lloyd's Insurance Co.*, 479 So.2d 961 (La. App. 1985).

124. John Hill, "High-Speed Police Pursuits: Dangers, Dynamics, and Risk Reduction," *FBI Law Enforcement Bulletin*, July 2002, pp. 14–18.

125. *City of Canton, Ohio* v. *Harris*, 489 U.S. 378 (1989).

126. Ibid., at 1204.

127. *Board of the County Commissioners of Bryan County, Oklahoma* v. *Brown*, 520 U.S. 397 (1997).

128. U.S. Code, Title 42, Section 1983.

129. *Bivens* v. *Six Unknown Federal Agents*, 403 U.S. 388 (1971).

130. See *F.D.I.C.* v. *Meyer*, 510 U.S. 471 (1994), in which the U.S. Supreme Court reiterated its ruling under *Bivens*, stating that only government employees and not government agencies can be sued.

131. *Wyler* v. *U.S.*, 725 F.2d 157 (2d Cir. 1983).

132. California Government Code, Section 818.

133. Federal Tort Claims Act, U.S. Code, Title 28, Section 1346(b), 2671–2680.

134. *Elder* v. *Holloway*, 114 S.Ct. 1019, 127 L.Ed.2d 344 (1994).

135. Ibid.

136. *Hunter* v. *Bryant*, 112 S.Ct. 534 (1991).

137. William U. McCormack, "Supreme Court Cases: 1991–1992 Term," *FBI Law Enforcement Bulletin*, November 1992, p. 30.

138. *Saucier* v. *Katz*, 533 U.S. 194 (2001).

139. See also *Brosseau* v. *Haugen*, 543 U.S. 194 (2004).

140. *Idaho* v. *Horiuchi*, No. 98-30149 (9th Cir. 06/05/2001).

141. For more information on police liability, see Daniel L. Schofield, "Legal Issues of Pursuit Driving," *FBI Law Enforcement Bulletin*, May 1988, pp. 23–29.

142. Michael S. Vaughn, Tab W. Cooper, and Rolando V. del Carmen, "Assessing Legal Liabilities in Law Enforcement: Police Chiefs' Views," *Crime and Delinquency*, Vol. 47, No. 1 (2001), p. 3.

Chapter 9 The Courts: Structure and Participants

i. "Fast ChatGeragos: 'I Didn't Convince 12 People,'" *Newsweek*, March 21, 2005, p. 8.

ii. Don Hardenbergh, *Trends in 2004: The Future of Court Security* (Williamsburg, VA: National Center for State Courts, 2004), http://www.ncsconline.org/wc/Publications/ KIS_CtSecu_Trends04.pdf (accessed February 6, 2007).

iii. Quoted in Richard Willing, "Courts Try to Make Jury Duty Less of Choice," *USA Today*, March 17, 2005, p. 17A.

1. Quoted in Joan Biskupic, "Courts Can't Unravel All Election Snags," *USA Today*, September 17, 2000.

2. Details for this story come from "Nichols to Make Court Appearance Today," CNN.com, March 15, 2005, http://www.cnn.com/2005/LAW/03/14/atlanta.shooting (accessed April 5, 2006).

3. Don Babwin, "Man Claims to Have Slain Judge's Family," ABC News, March 10, 2005, http://abcnews.go.com/US/ wireStory?id5568738 (accessed April 5, 2006).

4. "Police Match DNA from Lefkow Killings to Suicide Victim," cjtoday.com., March 10, 2005, http://www.channel3000. com/news/4270937/detail.html (accessed July 5, 2006).

5. Law Enforcement Assistance Administration, *Two Hundred Years of American Criminal Justice* (Washington, DC: U.S. Government Printing Office, 1976), p. 31.

6. Ibid.

7. Ibid.

8. Ibid., p. 32.

9. Ibid.

10. David B. Rottman and Shauna M. Strickland, *State Court Organization, 2004* (Washington, DC: Bureau of Justice Statistics, 2006), p. 7.

11. Thomas A. Henderson et al., *The Significance of Judicial Structure: The Effects of Unification on Trial Court Operations* (Washington, DC: National Institute of Justice, 1984).

12. Ibid.

13. In 1957, only 13 states had permanent intermediate appellate courts. Now, all but 10 states have these courts. See Rottman and Strickland, *State Court Organization, 2004*, pp. 9–10.

14. *Keeney, Superintendent, Oregon State Penitentiary* v. *Tamayo-Reyes*, 113 S.Ct. 853, 122 L.Ed.2d 203 (1992).

15. *Herrera* v. *Collins*, 113 S.Ct. 853, 122 L.Ed.2d 203 (1993).

16. H. Ted Rubin, *The Courts: Fulcrum of the Justice System* (Pacific Palisades, CA: Goodyear, 1976), p. 198.

17. Martin Wright, *Justice for Victims and Offenders* (Bristol, PA: Open University Press, 1991), p. 56.

18. "Bridging the Gap between Communities and Courts," http://www.communityjustice.org (accessed November 22, 2007).

19. M. Somjen Frazer, *The Impact of the Community Court Model on Defendant Perceptions of Fairness: A Case Study at the Red Hook Community Justice Center* (New York: Center for Court Innovation, 2006).

20. Wright, *Justice for Victims and Offenders*, pp. 104, 106.

21. Most of the information and some of the wording in this section come from Administrative Office of the U.S. Courts, *Understanding the Federal Courts*, http://www.uscourts.gov/ UFC99.pdf (accessed April 2, 2005).

22. Administrative Office of the U.S. Courts, "U.S. District Courts—Criminal Cases Commenced, Terminated, and Pending during the 12-Month Periods Ending September 30, 2003 and 2004," http://www.uscourts.gov/judbus2004/ appendices/d.pdf (accessed May 11, 2006).

23. Administrative Office of the U.S. Courts, "U.S. District Courts—Judicial Caseload Profile, during the 12-Month Periods Ending September 30, 2005 through 2006," http://www.uscourts.gov/ cgi-bin/cmsd2006.pl (accessed July 11, 2007).

24. Administrative Office of the U.S. Courts, "U.S. District Courts—Judicial Caseload Profile."

25. Administrative Office of the U.S. Courts, "Compensation Woes Threaten Recruitment and Retention in Federal Judiciary," September 20, 2006, http://www.uscourts.gov/Press_Releases/ judicialpay092006.html (accessed July 30, 2007).

26. Although the Ethics Reform Act of 1989 was supposed to allow for a cost-of-living increase in federal judicial salaries, Congress blocked the automatic increases from 1995 to 1999 because they also applied to the salaries of members of Congress and were seen as politically unpalatable.

27. Chief Justice John Roberts, "2005 Year-End Report on the Federal Judiciary," *Third Branch*, Vol. 38, No. 1 (January 2006), http://www.uscourts.gov/ttb/jan06ttb/yearend/ index.html (accessed March 30, 2007).

28. Much of the information and some of the wording in this section come from Administrative Office of the U.S. Courts, "About the Federal Courts," www.uscourts.gov/about.html (accessed October 4, 2007).

29. Stephen L. Wasby, *The Supreme Court in the Federal Judicial System*, 3rd ed. (Chicago, IL: Nelson-Hall, 1988), p. 58.

30. "Workload of the Courts: The Federal Courts' Caseload," *Third Branch*, Vol. 38, No. 1 (January 2006), appendix, http://www.uscourts.gov/ttb/jan06ttb/appendix/index.html (accessed August 28, 2006).

31. *Blakely* v. *Washington*, 542 U.S. 296 (2004).

32. *U.S.* v. *Booker*, 543 U.S. 220 (2005).

33. "Workload of the Courts: The Federal Courts' Caseload."

34. Administrative Office of the U.S. Courts, "Judicial Conference Urges Congress to Create 68 New Federal Judgeships," March 15, 2005, http://www.uscourts.gov/newsroom/ judconference68.htm (accessed May 5, 2005).

35. *The Supreme Court of the United States* (Washington, DC: U.S. Government Printing Office, no date), p. 4.

36. *Marbury* v. *Madison*, 1 Cranch 137 (1803).

37. *Mapp* v. *Ohio*, 367 U.S. 643 (1961).

38. See, for example, Jeffrey T. Ulmer, *Social Worlds of Sentencing: Court Communities under Sentencing Guidelines* (Ithaca: State University of New York Press, 1997); and Roy B. Flemming, Peter F. Nardulli, and James Eisenstein, *The Craft of Justice: Politics and Work in Criminal Court Communities* (Philadelphia: University of Pennsylvania Press, 1993).

39. See, for example, Edward J. Clynch and David W. Neubauer, "Trial Courts as Organizations," *Law and Policy Quarterly*, Vol. 3 (1981), pp. 69–94.

40. American Bar Association, *ABA Standards for Criminal Justice*, 2nd ed. (Chicago, IL: ABA, 1980).

41. In 1940, Missouri became the first state to adopt a plan for the "merit selection" of judges based on periodic public review.

42. National Judicial College, "About the NJC," http://www.judges.org/about (accessed February 2, 2007).

43. National Judicial College, "Judicial Education," http://www.judges.org/educate (accessed January 30, 2007).

44. Doris Marie Provine, *Judging Credentials: Nonlawyer Judges and the Politics of Professionalism* (Chicago, IL: University of Chicago Press, 1986).

45. Town and village justices in New York State serve part-time and may or may not be lawyers; judges of all other courts must be lawyers, whether or not they serve full-time. From New York State Commission on Judicial Conduct, *2001 Annual Report*, http://www.scjc.state.ny.us/annual.html (accessed March 10, 2002).

46. Ibid.

47. West Virginia Justice Watch, "Former Circuit Court Judge Joseph Troisi Made State and National Headlines for Biting the Nose of a Defendant (1997)," http://www.wvjusticewatch.org/ethics/bite_nose.htm (accessed July 5, 2005).

48. Details for this story come from Adam Liptak, "Issue in Two Death Sentences: Judge's Drug Use," *New York Times*, May 16, 2002, p. 1A.

49. Bureau of Justice Statistics, *Report to the Nation on Crime and Justice: The Data* (Washington, DC: U.S. Dept. of Justice, 1983).

50. For a discussion of the resource limitations that district attorneys face in combating corporate crime, see Michael L. Benson et al., "District Attorneys and Corporate Crime: Surveying the Prosecutorial Gatekeepers," *Criminology*, Vol. 26, No. 3 (August 1988), pp. 505–517.

51. Carol J. DeFrances and Greg W. Steadman, *Prosecutors in State Courts, 1996* (Washington, DC: Bureau of Justice Statistics, 1998).

52. U.S. Code, Title 28, Section 530A.

53. Some of the wording in this paragraph is adapted from Kim Murphy, "Prosecutors in Oregon Find 'Truth' Ruling a Real Hindrance," *Los Angeles Times*, August 5, 2001.

54. *In re Gatti*, S45801, Oregon Supreme Court, August 17, 2000.

55. The ruling was based on Disciplinary Rule 1-102 of the Oregon State Bar, which says, in part, that it is professional misconduct for a lawyer to "engage in conduct involving dishonesty, fraud, deceit or misrepresentation." The rule also prohibits a lawyer from violating this dishonesty provision through the acts of another. Also at issue was Disciplinary Rule 7-102, which prohibits a lawyer from "knowingly making a false statement of law or fact."

56. Most of the information and some of the wording in this section come from Administrative Office of the U.S. Courts, *Understanding the Federal Courts*, http://www.uscourts.gov/UFC99.pdf (accessed April 2, 2004).

57. "Duke Case DA's Apology Not Accepted," *USA Today*, May 13, 2007.

58. Duff Wilson, "Prosecutor Apologizes to Former Duke Players," *New York Times*, April 12, 2007.

59. Kenneth Culp Davis, *Discretionary Justice* (Baton Rouge: Louisiana State University Press, 1969), p. 190.

60. Barbara Borland, *The Prosecution of Felony Arrests* (Washington, DC: Bureau of Justice Statistics, 1983).

61. *Brady* v. *Maryland*, 373 U.S. 83 (1963).

62. *U.S.* v. *Bagley*, 473 U.S. 667 (1985).

63. *Banks* v. *Dretke*, 124 S.Ct. 1256, 1280 (2004).

64. *Imbler* v. *Pachtman*, 424 U.S. 409 (1976).

65. *Burns* v. *Reed*, 500 U.S. 478 (1991).

66. Ibid., complaint, p. 29.

67. Cassia Spohn, John Gruhl, and Susan Welch, "The Impact of the Ethnicity and Gender of Defendants on the Decision to Reject or Dismiss Felony Charges," *Criminology*, Vol. 25, No. 1 (1987), pp. 175–191.

68. American Bar Association Center for Professional Responsibility, *Model Rules of Professional Conduct* (Chicago, IL: ABA, 2003), p. 87.

69. The same is true under federal law, and in almost all of the states, of communications between defendants and members of the clergy, psychiatrists and psychologists, medical doctors, and licensed social workers in the course of psychotherapy. See, for example, *Jaffee* v. *Redmond*, 116 S.Ct. 1923 (1996).

70. *Powell* v. *Alabama*, 287 U.S. 45 (1932).

71. *Johnson* v. *Zerbst*, 304 U.S. 458 (1938).

72. *Gideon* v. *Wainwright*, 372 U.S. 335 (1963).

73. *Argersinger* v. *Hamlin*, 407 U.S. 25 (1972).

74. *In re Gault*, 387 U.S. 1 (1967).

75. *Alabama* v. *Shelton*, 535 U.S. 654 (2002).

76. Jane Fritsch, "Pataki Rethinks Promise of a Pay Raise for Lawyers to the Indigent," *New York Times*, December 24, 2001.

77. Steven K. Smith and Carol J. DeFrances, *Indigent Defense* (Washington, DC: Bureau of Justice Statistics, 1996).

78. Ibid.

79. Carol J. DeFrances, *State-Funded Indigent Defense Services, 1999* (Washington, DC: National Institute of Justice, 2001), from which the information in this paragraph is derived.

80. National Symposium on Indigent Defense, *Improving Criminal Justice Systems through Expanded Strategies and Innovative Collaborations* (Washington, DC: Office of Justice Programs, 2000).

81. National Association of Criminal Defense Lawyers, *In Defense of Public Access to Justice: An Assessment of Trial-Level Defense Services in Louisiana 40 Years after* Gideon (Washington, DC: NACDL, 2004).

82. David Exum, "Big Demand, Small Paychecks: State Struggles to Retain Public Defenders," *Jobfind* print edition, April 11, 2004.

83. DeFrances, *State-Funded Indigent Defense Services, 1999*.

84. Ibid.

85. "Nationline: McVeigh's Defense Cost Taxpayers $13.8 Million," *USA Today*, July 3, 2001, p. 3A.

86. Caroline Wolf Harlow, *Defense Counsel in Criminal Cases* (Washington, DC: Bureau of Justice Statistics, 2000); and Carol J. DeFrances and Marika F. X. Litras, *Indigent Defense Service in Large Counties, 1999* (Washington, DC: Bureau of Justice Statistics, 2000).

87. *Faretta v. California*, 422 U.S. 806 (1975).

88. Smith and DeFrances, *Indigent Defense*, pp. 2–3.

89. *Anders v. California*, 386 U.S. 738 (1967).

90. *People v. Wende*, 25 Cal.3d 436, 600 P.2d 1071 (1979).

91. *Smith v. Robbins*, 528 U.S. 259 (2000).

92. *Texas v. Cobb*, 532 U.S. 162 (2001).

93. Details for this story come from Chisun Lee, "Punishing Mmes. Stewart: The Parallel Universes of Martha and Lynne," *Village Voice*, February 15, 2005, http://www.refuseandresist.org/article-print.php?aid51757 (accessed January 5, 2006).

94. "Lawyer Convicted of Terrorist Support," *USA Today*, February 11, 2005, p. 3A.

95. Mike McKee, "California State Bar to Allow Lawyers to Break Confidentiality," *Recorder*, May 17, 2004, http://www.law.com/jsp/article.jsp?id51084316038367 (accessed August 25, 2007).

96. "ABA Eases Secrecy Rules in Lawyer-Client Relationship," *USA Today*, August 7, 2001.

97. *Nix v. Whiteside*, 475 U.S. 157 (1986).

98. Ibid.

99. "Courtroom Killings Verdict," *USA Today*, February 15, 1993, p. 3A.

100. National Center for State Courts, "Improving Security in State Courthouses: Ten Essential Elements for Court Safety," http://www.ncsconline.org/what'sNew/TenPointPlan.htm (accessed October 20, 2007).

101. President's Commission on Law Enforcement and Administration of Justice, *The Challenge of Crime in a Free Society* (Washington, DC: U.S. Government Printing Office, 1967), p. 129.

102. National Advisory Commission on Criminal Justice Standards and Goals, *Courts* (Washington, DC: U.S. Government Printing Office, 1973), Standard 9.3.

103. See, for example, Joan G. Brannon, *The Judicial System in North Carolina* (Raleigh, NC: Administrative Office of the United States Courts, 1984), p. 14.

104. Joseph L. Peterson, "Use of Forensic Evidence by the Police and Courts," National Institute of Justice Research in Brief (Washington, DC: NIJ, 1987), p. 3.

105. Ibid., p. 6.

106. Jennifer Bowles, "Simpson-Paid Experts," Associated Press, August 12, 1995.

107. *California v. Green*, 399 U.S. 149 (1970).

108. Patrick L. McCloskey and Ronald L. Schoenberg, *Criminal Law Deskbook* (New York: Matthew Bender, 1988), Section 17, p. 123.

109. Bureau of Justice Statistics, *Report to the Nation on Crime and Justice*, 2nd ed. (Washington, DC: BJS, 1988), p. 82.

110. Anna Johnson, "Jury with Oprah Winfrey Convicts Man of Murder," Associated Press, August 19, 2004.

111. *Demarest v. Manspeaker et al.*, 498 U.S. 184, 111 S.Ct. 599, 112 L.Ed.2d 608 (1991).

112. Bureau of Justice Statistics, *Report to the Nation on Crime and Justice*, p. 82.

113. Johnson, "Jury with Oprah Winfrey Convicts Man of Murder."

114. *Williams v. Florida*, 399 U.S. 78, 90 S.Ct. 1893, 26 L.Ed.2d 446 (1970).

115. *Smith v. Texas*, 311 U.S. 128 (1940). That right does not apply when the defendants are facing the possibility of a prison sentence of less than six months in length or even when the potential aggregate sentence for multiple petty offenses exceeds six months (see *Lewis v. U.S.*, 518 U.S. 322 [1996]).

116. *Thiel v. Southern Pacific Co.*, 328 U.S. 217 (1945).

117. American Bar Association, *Principles for Juries and Jury Trials* (Chicago, IL: ABA, 2005).

118. The author was himself the victim of a felony some years ago. His car was stolen in Columbus, Ohio, and recovered a year later in Cleveland. He was informed that the person who had taken it was in custody, but he never heard what happened to him, nor could he learn where or whether a trial was to be held.

119. Federal Rules of Criminal Procedure, Rule 43.

120. *Crosby v. U.S.*, 113 S.Ct. 748, 122 L.Ed.2d 25 (1993).

121. *Zafiro v. U.S.*, 113 S.Ct. 933, 122 L.Ed.2d 317 (1993).

122. *Nebraska Press Association v. Stuart*, 427 U.S. 539 (1976).

123. However, it is generally accepted that trial judges may issue limited gag orders aimed at trial participants.

124. *Press Enterprise Company v. Superior Court of California, Riverside County*, 478 U.S. 1 (1986).

125. *Caribbean International News Corporation v. Puerto Rico*, 508 U.S. 147 (1993).

126. N.Y. Civil Rights Law, Section 52.

127. Tom Perrotta, "New York Law Banning Cameras in State Courts Found Constitutional," *New York Law Journal*, May 23, 2004.

128. Charles L. Babcock et al., "Fifty-State Survey of the Law Governing Audio-Visual Coverage of Court Proceedings," http://www.jw.com/articles/details.cfm?articlenum5120 (accessed October 10, 2005).

129. See Radio-Television News Directors Association, "Summary of State Camera Coverage Rules," http://www.rtnda.org/issues/camerassummary.htm (accessed February 9, 2000).

130. *Chandler v. Florida*, 499 U.S. 560 (1981).

131. Rule 53 of the Federal Rules of Criminal Procedure reads, "The taking of photographs in the court room during the progress of judicial proceedings or radio broadcasting of judicial proceedings from the court room shall not be permitted by the court."

132. Harry F. Rosenthal, "Courts-TV," Associated Press, September 21, 1994. See also "Judicial Conference Rejects Cameras in Federal Courts," *Criminal Justice Newsletter*, September 15, 1994, p. 6.

133. Policy, U.S. Court of Appeals for the Ninth Circuit, http://www.ce9.uscourts.gov/web/OCELibra.nsf/504ca249c786e20f85256284006da7ab/ba060a3e537d2866882569760067ac8e?OpnDocument (accessed September 16, 2007).

Chapter 10 Pretrial Activities and the Criminal Trial

i. Irving Stone, *Clarence Darrow for the Defense* (New York: Doubleday, 1941).

1. D. Graham Burnett, "Anatomy of a Verdict: The View from a Juror's Chair," *New York Times* magazine, August 26, 2001.

2. *Arraignment* is another term used to describe an initial appearance, although we will reserve use of that word to describe a later court appearance following the defendant's

indictment by a grand jury or the filing of an information by the prosecutor.

3. *McNabb* v. *U.S.*, 318 U.S. 332 (1943).

4. This is the case because such arrests do not involve judicial determination of probable cause.

5. *County of Riverside* v. *McLaughlin,* 111 S.Ct. 1661 (1991).

6. *White* v. *Maryland,* 373 U.S. 59 (1963).

7. Much of the information in this section comes from Barry Mahoney et al., *Pretrial Services Programs: Responsibilities and Potential* (Washington, DC: National Institute of Justice, 2001).

8. *Taylor* v. *Taintor,* 83 U.S. 66 (1873).

9. National Advisory Commission on Criminal Justice Standards and Goals, *The Courts* (Washington, DC: U.S. Government Printing Office, 1973), p. 37.

10. C. Ares, A. Rankin, and H. Sturz, "The Manhattan Bail Project: An Interim Report on the Use of Pre-Trial Parole," *New York University Law Review,* Vol. 38 (January 1963), pp. 68–95.

11. H. Zeisel, "Bail Revisited," *American Bar Foundation Research Journal,* Vol. 4 (1979), pp. 769–789.

12. Ibid.

13. "Twelve Percent of Those Freed on Low Bail Fail to Appear," *New York Times,* December 2, 1983, p. 1.

14. Bureau of Justice Statistics, *Report to the Nation on Crime and Justice,* 2nd ed. (Washington, DC: U.S. Dept. of Justice, 1988), p. 76.

15. See Thomas H. Cohen and Brian A. Reaves, *Felony Defendants in Large Urban Counties, 2002* (Washington, DC: Bureau of Justice Statistics, 2006), p. iv.

16. John Scalia, *Federal Pretrial Release and Detention,* 1996 (Washington, DC: Bureau of Justice Statistics, 1999), p. 1, http://www.ojp.usdoj.gov/bjs/pub/pdf/fprd96.pdf (accessed January 25, 2005).

17. Donald E. Pryor and Walter F. Smith, "Significant Research Findings Concerning Pretrial Release," *Pretrial Issues,* Vol. 4, No. 1 (Washington, DC: Pretrial Services Resource Center, February 1982). See also the Pretrial Services Resource Center website at http://www.pretrial.org/mainpage.htm (accessed July 15, 2007).

18. BJS, *Report to the Nation on Crime and Justice,* p. 77.

19. According to Joseph B. Vaughn and Victor E. Kappeler, the first such legislation was the 1970 District of Columbia Court Reform and Criminal Procedure Act. See Vaughn and Kappeler, "The Denial of Bail: Pre-Trial Preventive Detention," *Criminal Justice Research Bulletin,* Vol. 3, No. 6 (Huntsville, TX: Sam Houston State University, 1987), p. 1.

20. Ibid.

21. Bail Reform Act of 1984, U.S. Code, Title 18, Section 3142(e).

22. *U.S.* v. *Montalvo-Murillo,* 495 U.S. 711 (1990).

23. Ibid., syllabus.

24. *U.S.* v. *Hazzard,* 35 CrL. 2217 (1984).

25. See, for example, *U.S.* v. *Motamedi,* 37 CrL. 2394, CA 9 (1985).

26. A few states now have laws that permit the defendant to appear before the grand jury.

27. John M. Scheb and John M. Scheb II, *American Criminal Law* (St. Paul, MN: West, 1996), p. 31.

28. Ibid.

29. The information in this paragraph is adapted from Linda Greenhouse, "Supreme Court Limits Forced Medication of Some for Trial," *New York Times,* June 16, 2003, http://www.nytimes.com/2003/06/17/politics/17DRUG.html (accessed June 17, 2005).

30. *Sell* v. *U.S.,* 539 U.S. 166 (2003).

31. Federal Rules of Criminal Procedure, 5.1(a).

32. Scheb and Scheb, *American Criminal Law,* p. 32.

33. *Kercheval* v. *U.S.,* 274 U.S. 220, 223, 47 S.Ct. 582, 583 (1927); *Boykin* v. *Alabama,* 395 U.S. 238 (1969); and *Dickerson* v. *New Banner Institute, Inc.,* 460 U.S. 103 (1983).

34. Bureau of Justice Statistics, *The Prosecution of Felony Arrests* (Washington, DC: U.S. Government Printing Office, 1983).

35. Barbara Boland et al., *The Prosecution of Felony Arrests, 1987* (Washington, DC: U.S. Government Printing Office, 1990).

36. *Henderson* v. *Morgan,* 426 U.S. 637 (1976).

37. *Santobello* v. *New York,* 404 U.S. 257 (1971).

38. *Mabry* v. *Johnson,* 467 U.S. 504 (1984).

39. *U.S.* v. *Baldacchino,* 762 F.2d 170 (1st Cir. 1985); *U.S.* v. *Reardon,* 787 F.2d 512 (10th Cir. 1986); and *U.S.* v. *Donahey,* 529 F.2d 831 (11th Cir. 1976).

40. For a classic discussion of such considerations, see David Sudnow, "Normal Crimes: Sociological Features of the Penal Code in a Public Defender Office," *Social Problems,* Vol. 123, No. 3 (winter 1965), p. 255.

41. Federal Rules of Criminal Procedure, No. 11.

42. "A Desperate Act," *Prime Time Live,* ABCNews.com, January 28, 1998, http://archive. abcnews.go.com/onair/PTL/html-files/transcripts/ptl0128c.html (accessed July 21, 2004).

43. Dan Rozek, "Castration Doesn't Gain Leniency for Pedophile," *Chicago Sun-Times,* March 4, 1998.

44. Marc G. Gertz and Edmond J. True, "Social Scientists in the Courtroom: The Frustrations of Two Expert Witnesses," in Susette M. Talarico, ed., *Courts and Criminal Justice: Emerging Issues* (Beverly Hills, CA: Sage, 1985), pp. 81–91.

45. Samuel R. Gross et al., *Exonerations in the United States, 1989 through 2003,* April 4, 2004, http://www.mindfully.org/Reform/2004/Prison-Exonerations-Gross19apr04.htm (accessed May 28, 2007).

46. Ibid.

47. *Klopfer* v. *North Carolina,* 386 U.S. 213 (1967).

48. *Barker* v. *Wingo,* 407 U.S. 514 (1972).

49. *Strunk* v. *U.S.,* 412 U.S. 434 (1973).

50. Speedy Trial Act, U.S. Code, Title 18, Section 3161 (1974).

51. *U.S.* v. *Taylor,* 487 U.S. 326, 108 S.Ct. 2413, 101 L.Ed.2d 297 (1988).

52. *Fex* v. *Michigan,* 113 S.Ct. 1085, 122 L.Ed.2d 406 (1993).

53. *Doggett* v. *U.S.,* 112 S.Ct. 2686 (1992).

54. William U. McCormack, "Supreme Court Cases: 1991–1992 Term," *FBI Law Enforcement Bulletin,* November 1992, pp. 28–29.

55. *Padilla* v. *Hanft,* No. 05-533, cert. denied.

56. Ibid.

57. See, for example, the U.S. Supreme Court's decision in the case of *Murphy* v. *Florida,* 410 U.S. 525 (1973).

58. *Witherspoon* v. *Illinois,* 391 U.S. 510 (1968).

59. *Mu'Min* v. *Virginia,* 500 U.S. 415 (1991).

60. Federal Rules of Criminal Procedure, Rule 24(6).

61. Learn more about shadow juries from Molly McDonough, "Me and My Shadow: Shadow Juries Are Helping Litigators Shape Their Cases during Trial," *National Law Journal,* May 17, 2001.

62. Although the words *argument and statement* are sometimes used interchangeably to refer to opening remarks, defense attorneys are enjoined from drawing conclusions or "arguing" to the jury at this stage in the trial. Their task, as described in the section that follows, is simply to explain to the jury how the defense will be conducted.

63. Supreme Court majority opinion in *Powers v. Ohio,* 499 U.S. 400 (1991), citing *Strauder v. West Virginia,* 100 U.S. 303 (1880).

64. *Swain v. Alabama,* 380 U.S. 202 (1965).

65. *Batson v. Kentucky,* 476 U.S. 79, 106 S.Ct. 1712 (1986).

66. *Ford v. Georgia,* 498 U.S. 411 (1991), footnote 2.

67. Ibid.

68. *Powers v. Ohio,* 499 U.S. 400 (1991).

69. *Edmonson v. Leesville Concrete Co., Inc.,* 500 U.S. 614, 111 S.Ct. 2077, 114 L.Ed.2d 660 (1991).

70. *Georgia v. McCollum,* 505 U.S. 42 (1992).

71. *J.E.B.* v. *Alabama,* 114 S.Ct. 1419 (1994).

72. See, for example, *Davis v. Minnesota,* 511 U.S. 1115 (1994).

73. Michael Kirkland, "Court Rejects Fat Jurors Case," United Press International, January 8, 1996. The case was *Santiago-Martinez v. U.S.,* No. 95-567 (1996).

74. *Campbell v. Louisiana,* 523 U.S. 392 (1998).

75. *Miller-El v. Cockrell,* 537 U.S. 322 (2003).

76. Ibid., syllabus.

77. *Miller-El v. Dretke,* 545 U.S. 231 (2005).

78. *U.S. v. Dinitz,* 424 U.S. 600, 612 (1976).

79. *Michigan v. Lucas,* 500 U.S. 145 (1991).

80. Associated Press, "Suit Settlement Ends Bryant Saga," March 3, 2005, http://msnbc.msn. com/id/7019659 (accessed July 12, 2005).

81. *Kotteakos v. U.S.,* 328 U.S. 750 (1946); *Brecht v. Abrahamson,* 113 S.Ct. 1710, 123 L.Ed.2d 353 (1993); and *Arizona v. Fulminante,* 111 S.Ct. 1246 (1991).

82. The Court, citing *Kotteakos v. U.S.* (1946), in *Brecht v. Abrahamson,* 113 S.Ct. 1710, 123 L.Ed.2d 353 (1993).

83. *Sullivan v. Louisiana,* 113 S.Ct. 2078, 124 L.Ed.2d 182 (1993).

84. *Griffin v. California,* 380 U.S. 609 (1965).

85. *Ohio v. Reiner,* 123 S.Ct. 1252, 532 U.S. 17 (2001).

86. Leading questions may, in fact, be permitted for certain purposes, including refreshing a witness's memory, impeaching a hostile witness, introducing undisputed material, and helping a witness with impaired faculties.

87. *In re Oliver,* 333 U.S. 257 (1948).

88. *Coy v. Iowa,* 487 U.S. 1012, 108 S.Ct. 2798 (1988).

89. *Maryland v. Craig,* 497 U.S. 836, 845-847 (1990).

90. *Idaho v. Wright,* 497 U.S. 805 (1990).

91. *White v. Illinois,* 112 S.Ct. 736 (1992).

92. *Crawford v. Washington,* 541 U.S. 36 (2004).

93. *Davis v. Washington,* 547 U.S. ___ (2006). See also *Hammon v. Indiana,* U.S. Supreme Court, 547 U.S. ___ (2006).

94. *Davis v. Washington,* syllabus.

95. Federal Rules of Criminal Procedure, Rule 29.1.

96. See *Johnson v. Louisiana,* 406 U.S. 356 (1972); and *Apodaca v. Oregon,* 406 U.S. 404 (1972).

97. *Allen v. U.S.,* 164 U.S. 492 (1896).

98. Judge Harold J. Rothwax, *Guilty: The Collapse of Criminal Justice* (New York: Random House, 1996).

99. Amiram Elwork, Bruce D. Sales, and James Alfini, *Making Jury Instructions Understandable* (Charlottesville, VA: Michie, 1982).

100. "King Jury Lives in Fear from Unpopular Verdict," *Fayetteville (NC) Observer-Times,* May 10, 1992, p. 7A.

101. "Los Angeles Trials Spark Debate over Anonymous Juries," *Criminal Justice Newsletter,* February 16, 1993, pp. 3–4.

102. Some states have centralized offices called Administrative Offices of the Courts or something similar. Such offices, however, are often primarily data-gathering agencies with little or no authority over the day-to-day functioning of state or local courts.

103. See, for example, Larry Berkson and Susan Carbon, *Court Unification: Its History, Politics, and Implementation* (Washington, DC: U.S. Government Printing Office, 1978); and Thomas Henderson et al., *The Significance of Judicial Structure: The Effect of Unification on Trial Court Operators* (Alexandria, VA: Institute for Economic and Policy Studies, 1984).

104. See, for example, Thomas J. Cook et al., *Basic Issues in Court Performance* (Washington, DC: National Institute of Justice, 1982).

105. See, for example, Sorrel Wildhorn et al., *Indicators of Justice: Measuring the Performance of Prosecutors, Defense, and Court Agencies Involved in Felony Proceedings* (Lexington, MA: Lexington Books, 1977).

Chapter 11   Sentencing

i. Society of Police Futurists International, e-mail communication, April 6, 2004.

ii. "The Crime Bust," *U.S. News and World Report,* May 25, 1998.

iii. Lawrence A. Greenfeld, *Prison Sentences and Time Served for Violence,* Bureau of Justice Statistics Selected Findings, No. 4 (Washington, DC: Bureau of Justice Statistics, April 1995).

iv. *Ring v. Arizona,* 122 S.Ct. 2428, 153 L.Ed.2d 556 (2002); dissent (with Chief Justice William Rehnquist).

v. "Prepared Remarks of Attorney General Alberto Gonzales," Sentencing Guidelines Speech, Washington, DC, June 21, 2005.

vi. "President Calls for Crime Victims' Rights Amendment," White House press release, April 16, 2002, http://www.whitehouse.gov/news/releases/2002/04/20020416–1.html (accessed September 13, 2002).

vii. "Judge Refuses to Delay McVeigh Execution," *New York Times,* June 6, 2001.

viii. "Fireside chat" with U.S. Supreme Court Justices John Paul Stevens and Stephen Breyer, fifty-third annual meeting of the Seventh Circuit Bar Association and Judicial Conference of the Seventh Circuit, Chicago, May 9, 2004.

ix. *Payne v. Tennessee,* 501 U.S. 808 (1991).

x. *Criminal Justice Newsletter,* Vol. 31, No. 13 (2000), p. 1.

xi. Laura Goodstein, "Death Penalty Falls from Favor as Some Lose Confidence in Its Fairness," *New York Times,* June 17, 2001.

xii. *Furman v. Georgia,* 408 U.S. 238 (1972).

1. Michael Tonry, "Implementing, Changing, and Maintaining Sentencing Guidelines in the Political Climate of the 1990's," http://students.washington.edu/ths123/state.htm (accessed January 3, 2005).

2. "Seven Charged in Chicago Beating Deaths," CNN.com, August 3, 2002, http://archives.cnn.com/2002/US/08/03/chicago.beating/index.html (accessed September 12, 2006).

3. "'Brutal Beat-Down' Kills Chicago Men; Deaths Ruled Homicides," *USA Today*, July 31, 2002.

4. Quotations in this paragraph come from John W. Fountain, "Mob Kills Two after Truck Hits Women on a Stoop," *New York Times*, August 1, 2002.

5. For a thorough discussion of the philosophy of punishment and sentencing, see David Garland, *Punishment and Modern Society: A Study in Social Theory* (Chicago: University of Chicago Press, 1990). See also Ralph D. Ellis and Carol S. Ellis, *Theories of Criminal Justice: A Critical Reappraisal* (Wolfeboro, NH: Longwood Academic, 1989); and Colin Summer, *Censure, Politics, and Criminal Justice* (Bristol, PA: Open University Press, 1990).

6. Punishment is said to be required because social order (and the laws that represent it) could not exist for long if transgressions went unsanctioned.

7. "Back to the Chain Gang," *Newsweek*, October 17, 1994, p. 87.

8. Ibid.

9. For an excellent review of the "get tough" attitudes that influenced sentencing decisions during the 1990s, see Tamasak Wicharaya, *Simple Theory, Hard Reality: The Impact of Sentencing Reforms on Courts, Prisons, and Crime* (Albany: State University of New York Press, 1995).

10. For a thorough review of the literature on deterrence, see Raymond Paternoster, "The Deterrent Effect of the Perceived Certainty and Severity of Punishment: A Review of the Evidence and Issues," *Justice Quarterly*, Vol. 4, No. 2 (June 1987), pp. 174–217.

11. Hugo Adam Bedau, "Retributivism and the Theory of Punishment," *Journal of Philosophy*, Vol. 75 (November 1978), pp. 601–620.

12. H. L. A. Hart, *Punishment and Responsibility: Essays in the Philosophy of Law* (Oxford: Clarendon Press, 1968).

13. The definitive study during this period was Douglas Lipton, Robert Martinson, and J. Woks, *The Effectiveness of Correctional Treatment: A Survey of Treatment Valuation Studies* (New York: Praeger Press, 1975).

14. See, for example, Lawrence W. Sherman et al., *Preventing Crime: What Works, What Doesn't, What's Promising* (Washington, DC: National Institute of Justice, 1997).

15. Gordon Bazemore and Mark S. Umbreit, foreword to *Balanced and Restorative Justice: Program Summary* (Washington, DC: Office of Juvenile Justice and Delinquency Prevention, 1994).

16. Shay Bilchik, *Balanced and Restorative Justice for Juveniles: A Framework for Juvenile Justice in the 21st Century* (Washington, DC: Office of Juvenile Justice and Delinquency Prevention, 1997), p. ii.

17. Ibid., p.14.

18. Ibid.

19. U.S. Code, Title 18, Section 3563(a)(2).

20. E-mail communications with the Office of Reparative Programs, Department of Corrections, State of Vermont, July 3, 1995.

21. Donna Hunzeker, "State Sentencing Systems and 'Truth in Sentencing,'" *State Legislative Report*, Vol. 20, No. 3 (Denver, CO: National Conference of State Legislatures, 1995).

22. Paula M. Ditton and Doris James Wilson, *Truth in Sentencing in State Prisons* (Washington, DC: Bureau of Justice Statistics, 1999).

23. "Oklahoma Rapist Gets 30,000 Years," United Press International, southwest edition, December 23, 1994.

24. For a historical consideration of alleged disparities, see G. Kleck, "Racial Discrimination in Criminal Sentencing: A Critical Evaluation of the Evidence with Additional Evidence on the Death Penalty," *American Sociological Review*, No. 46 (1981), pp. 783–805; and G. Kleck, "Life Support for Ailing Hypotheses: Modes of Summarizing the Evidence for Racial Discrimination in Sentencing," *Law and Human Behavior*, No. 9 (1985), pp. 271–285.

25. As discussed later in this chapter, federal sentencing guidelines did not become effective until 1987 and still had to meet many court challenges.

26. U.S. Sentencing Commission, *Federal Sentencing Guidelines Manual* (Washington, DC: U.S. Government Printing Office, 1987), p. 2.

27. Inmates can still earn a maximum of 54 days per year of good-time credit.

28. The Parole Commission Phaseout Act of 1996 requires the attorney general to report to Congress yearly as to whether it is cost-effective for the U.S. Parole Commission to remain a separate agency or whether its functions (and personnel) should be assigned elsewhere. Under the law, if the attorney general recommends assigning the commission's functions to another component of the Department of Justice, federal parole will continue as long as necessary.

29. Lawrence A. Greenfeld, *Prison Sentences and Time Served for Violence* (Washington, DC: Bureau of Justice Statistics, April 1995).

30. For an excellent review of the act and its implications, see Gregory D. Lee, "U.S. Sentencing Guidelines: Their Impact on Federal Drug Offenders," *FBI Law Enforcement Bulletin*, May 1995, pp. 17–21.

31. *Mistretta* v. *U.S.*, 488 U.S. 361, 371 (1989).

32. For an engaging overview of how mitigating factors might be applied under the guidelines, see *Koon* v. *U.S.*, 116 S.Ct. 2035, 135 L.Ed.2d 392 (1996).

33. U.S. Sentencing Commission, *Federal Sentencing Guidelines Manual*, p. 207.

34. *Deal* v. *U.S.*, 113 S.Ct. 1993, 124 L.Ed.2d 44 (1993).

35. U.S. Sentencing Commission, *Federal Sentencing Guidelines Manual*, p. 8.

36. National Institute of Justice, *Sentencing Commission Chairman Wilkins Answers Questions on the Guidelines*, National Institute of Justice Research in Action Series (Washington, DC: NIJ, 1987), p. 7.

37. *Melendez* v. *U.S.*, 117 S.Ct. 383, 136 L.Ed.2d 301 (1996).

38. *Apprendi* v. *New Jersey*, 120 S.Ct. 2348 (2000).

39. See, for example, Alexandra A. E. Shapiro and Jonathan P. Bach, "Applying 'Apprendi' to Federal Sentencing Rules," *New York Law Journal*, March 23, 2001, http://www.lw.com/pubs/articles/pdf/applyingApprendi.pdf (accessed June 30, 2006); and Freya Russell, "Limiting the Use of Acquitted and Uncharged Conduct at Sentencing: *Apprendi* v. *New Jersey* and Its Effect on the Relevant Conduct Provision of the United States Sentencing Guidelines," *California Law Review*, Vol. 89 (July 2001), p. 1199.

40. *Blakely* v. *Washington*, 542 U.S. 296 (2004).

41. *Cunningham* v. *California*, U.S. Supreme Court, No. 05-6551 (decided January 22, 2007).

42. *U.S.* v. *Booker*, 125 S.Ct. 738 (2005).

43. Combined with *U.S.* v. *Booker* (2005).

44. Stanley E. Adelman, "Supreme Court Invalidates Federal Sentencing Guidelines . . . to an Extent," *On the Line*, the Newsletter of the American Correctional Association, May 2005, p. 1.

45. See *United States* v. *Rodriguez*, 398 F.3d 1291, 1297 (11th Cir. 2005).

46. *Rita* v. *U.S.*, U.S. Supreme Court, No. 06-5754 (decided June 21, 2007).

47. "A Year after *Booker*: Most Sentences Still within Guidelines," *Third Branch*, the Newsletter of the Administrative Office of the U.S. Courts, Vol. 38, No. 2 (February 2006), p. 1.

48. Ibid.

49. Congress appears set to enact a guidelines system with mandatory minimum sentences and suggested maximum sentences. See "Congressional and Judicial Leaders at Odds over Sentencing Policy," *Criminal Justice Newsletter*, March 15, 2006, pp. 3–6.

50. Much of the material in this section is derived from Dale Parent et al., *Mandatory Sentencing*, National Institute of Justice Research in Action Series (Washington, DC: NIJ, 1997).

51. In mid-1996, the California Supreme Court ruled the state's three-strikes law an undue intrusion on judges' sentencing discretion, and California judges now use their own discretion in evaluating which offenses "fit" within the meaning of the law.

52. Michael Tonry, *Sentencing Reform Impacts* (Washington, DC: National Institute of Justice, 1987).

53. D. C. McDonald and K. E. Carlson, *Sentencing in the Courts: Does Race Matter? The Transition to Sentencing Guidelines, 1986–90* (Washington, DC: Bureau of Justice Statistics, 1993).

54. "Court Ruling Found to Reduce Crack Cocaine Prison Terms," *Corrections Journal*, February 7, 2006, p. 1.

55. "Public Humiliation," *Lawyer News*, July 31, 2004, http://www.lawyernews.com/weblog/2004/08 (accessed July 5, 2005).

56. Much of the information in this section is taken from Haya El Nasser, "Paying for Crime with Shame: Judges Say 'Scarlet Letter' Angle Works," *USA Today*, June 26, 1996, p. 1A.

57. Richard Willing, "Thief Challenges Dose of Shame as Punishment," *USA Today*, August 18, 2004, p. 3A.

58. John Braithwaite, *Crime, Shame, and Reintegration* (Cambridge, England: Cambridge University Press, 1989).

59. Such evidence does, in fact, exist. See, for example, Harold G. Grasmick, Robert J. Bursik, Jr., and Bruce J. Arneklev, "Reduction in Drunk Driving as a Response to Increased Threats of Shame, Embarrassment, and Legal Sanctions," *Criminology*, Vol. 31, No. 1 (1993), pp. 41–67.

60. Joan Petersilia, *House Arrest, A National Institute of Justice Crime File Study Guide* (Washington, DC: National Institute of Justice, 1988).

61. Privacy Act of 1974, 5 U.S.C.A. 522a, 88 Statute 1897, Public Law 93-579, December 31, 1974.

62. Freedom of Information Act, U.S. Code, Title 5, Section 522, and amendments. The status of presentence investigative reports has not yet been clarified under this act to the satisfaction of all legal scholars.

63. City of New York, Citywide Accountability Program, S.T.A.R.S. (Statistical Tracking, Analysis, and Reporting System), http://www.nyc.gov/html/prob/pdf/stars_92005.pdf (accessed May 13, 2007).

64. For a good review of the issues involved, see Robert C. Davis, Arthur J. Lurigio, and Wesley G. Skogan, *Victims of Crime*, 2nd ed. (Thousand Oaks, CA: Sage, 1997); and Leslie Sebba, *Third Parties: Victims and the Criminal Justice System* (Columbus: Ohio State University Press, 1996).

65. President's Task Force on Victims of Crime, *Final Report* (Washington, DC: U.S. Government Printing Office, 1982).

66. Peter Finn and Beverly N. W. Lee, *Establishing and Expanding Victim-Witness Assistance Programs* (Washington, DC: National Institute of Justice, 1988).

67. National Institute of Justice, *Victim Assistance Programs: Whom They Service, What They Offer* (Washington, DC: NIJ, 1995).

68. Senate Joint Resolution (SJR) 65 is a major revision of an initial proposal, SJR 52, which Senators Kyl and Feinstein introduced on April 22, 1996. Representative Henry Hyde introduced House Joint Resolution 174, a companion to SJR 52, and a similar proposal, House Joint Resolution 173, on April 22, 1996.

69. Senate Joint Resolution 44, 105th Congress.

70. See the National Center for Victims of Crime's critique of the 1998 amendment at http://www.ncvc.org/law/Ncvca.htm (accessed January 10, 2000).

71. "President Calls for Crime Victims' Rights Amendment," White House press release, April 16, 2002, http://www.whitehouse.gov/news/releases/2002/04/20020416-1.html (accessed September 13, 2005).

72. "Attorneys General Strongly Support S.J. Res. 3," National Victims' Constitutional Amendment Network, April 21, 2000, http://www.nvcan.org/news.htm (accessed January 22, 2006).

73. See the National Victims' Constitutional Amendment Network news page, http://www.nvcan.org/news.htm (accessed January 10, 2007).

74. Public Law 97-291.

75. USA PATRIOT Act of 2001, Section 624.

76. Office for Victims of Crime, *Report to the Nation 2003* (Washington, DC: OVC, 2003).

77. S.2329.

78. U.S. Senate, Republican Policy Committee, Legislative Notice No. 63, April 22, 2004.

79. Proposition 8, California's Victim's Bill of Rights.

80. National Victim Center, *Mothers against Drunk Driving, and American Prosecutors Research Institute, Impact Statements: A Victim's Right to Speak; A Nation's Responsibility to Listen* (Washington, DC: Office for Victims of Crime, July 1994).

81. Robert C. Davis and Barbara E. Smith, "The Effects of Victim Impact Statements on Sentencing Decisions: A Test in an Urban Setting," *Justice Quarterly*, Vol. 11, No. 3 (September 1994), pp. 453–469.

82. Bureau of Justice Statistics, *Report to the Nation on Crime and Justice*, 2nd ed. (Washington, DC: U.S. Government Printing Office, 1988), p. 90.

83. Matthew R. Durose and Patrick A. Langan, *Felony Sentences in State Courts, 2004* (Washington, DC: Bureau of Justice Statistics, 2006). Data for 1990 come from Matthew R. Durose, David J. Levin, and Patrick A. Langan, *Felony Sentences in State Courts, 1998* (Washington, DC: Bureau of Justice Statistics, 2001).

84. Matthew R. Durose and Patrick A. Langan, *Felony Sentences in State Courts, 2002* (Washington, DC: Bureau of Justice Statistics, 2004), p. 2.

85. Sally T. Hillsman, Joyce L. Sichel, and Barry Mahoney, *Fines in Sentencing* (New York: Vera Institute of Justice, 1983).

86. Ibid., p. 2.

87. Ibid., p. 4.

88. Ibid.

89. Douglas C. McDonald, Judith Greene, and Charles Worzella, *Day Fines in American Courts: The Staten Island and Milwaukee Experiments* (Washington, DC: National Institute of Justice, 1992).

90. Ibid., p. 56.

91. Laura A. Winterfield and Sally T. Hillsman, *The Staten Island Day-Fine Project* (Washington, DC: National Institute of Justice, 1993), p. 1.

92. S. Turner and J. Petersilia, *Day Fines in Four U.S. Jurisdictions* (Santa Monica, CA: RAND Corporation, 1996).

93. Oklahoma Man Charged with 1st-Degree Murder," *USA Today*, April 17, 2006, http://www.usatoday.com/news/nation/2006-04-17-okla-case_x.htm (accessed May 20, 2006).

94. Capital Punishment Research Project, University of Alabama Law School.

95. Death Penalty Information Center, "State-by-State Death Penalty Information," http://www.deathpenaltyinfo.org/FactSheet.pdf (accessed July 12, 2007).

96. Tracy L. Snell, *Capital Punishment, 2005* (Washington, DC: Bureau of Justice Statistics, 2006).

97. Richard Willing, "Expansion of Death Penalty to Nonmurders Faces Challenges," *USA Today*, May 14, 1997, p. 6A.

98. NAACP Legal Defense and Educational Fund, *Death Row U.S.A.: Spring 2006*, http://www.naacpldf.org/content/pdf/pubs/drusa/DRUSA_Spring_2006.pdf (accessed September 25, 2007).

99. *Capital Punishment, 2005*, p. 6.

100. Ibid.

101. Details for this story come from Jenifer Warren and Maura Dolan, "Tookie Williams Is Executed," *Los Angeles Times*, December 13, 2005, http://www.latimes.com/news/local/la-me-execution13dec13,0,799154.story?coll=la-home-headlines (accessed May 20, 2006).

102. "Warden: Williams Frustrated at End," CNN.com, December 13, 2005, http://www.cnn.com/2005/LAW/12/13/williams.execution (accessed July 2, 2006).

103. "Chief Justice Calls for Limits on Death Row Habeas Appeals," *Criminal Justice Newsletter*, February 15, 1989, pp. 6–7.

104. *McCleskey* v. *Zant*, 499 U.S. 467, 493-494 (1991).

105. *Coleman* v. *Thompson*, 501 U.S. 722 (1991).

106. *Schlup* v. *Delo*, 115 S.Ct. 851, 130 L.Ed.2d 808 (1995).

107. Public Law 103-322.

108. *Felker* v. *Turpin*, 117 S.Ct. 30, 135 L.Ed.2d 1123 (1996).

109. *Elledge* v. *Florida*, No. 98-5410 (1998).

110. Michelle Locke, "Victim Forgives," Associated Press wire service, May 19, 1996.

111. Ibid.

112. Arthur Koestler, *Reflections on Hanging* (New York: Macmillan, 1956), p. xii.

113. Death Penalty Information Center, "Innocence: List of Those Freed from Death Row," http://www.deathpenaltyinfo.org/article.php?scid=6&did=110 (accessed July 1, 2007).

114. Edward Connors et al., *Convicted by Juries, Exonerated by Science: Case Studies in the Use of DNA Evidence to Establish Innocence after Trial* (Washington, DC: National Institute of Justice, 1996).

115. Barry Scheck and Peter Neufeld, "DNA and Innocence Scholarship," in Saundra D. Westervelt and John A. Humphrey, *Wrongly Convicted: Perspectives on Failed Justice* (New Brunswick, NJ: Rutgers University Press, 2001), pp. 248–249.

116. Ibid., p. 246.

117. "DNA Test Frees Fla. Inmate after 24 Years," *USA Today*, January 24, 2006, p. 3A.

118. The Innocence Project, "Alan Crotzer," http://www.innocenceproject.org/case/display_profile.php?id=176 (accessed May 30, 2006).

119. Mitch Stacy, "DNA Exonerates Florida Man after 24 Years in Prison," Associated Press, January 23, 2006, http://www.truthinjustice.org/crotzer.htm (accessed May 30, 2006).

120. James S. Liebman, Jeffrey Fagan, and Simon H. Rifkind, *A Broken System: Error Rates in Capital Cases, 1973–1995* (New York: Columbia University School of Law, 2000), http://justice.policy. net/jpreport/finrep.PDF (accessed March 3, 2006).

121. See, for example, Jim Yardley, "Texas Retooling Criminal Justice in Wake of Furor on Death Penalty," *New York Times*, June 1, 2001.

122. "New Jersey Suspends Death Penalty Pending a Task Force Review," *Criminal Justice Newsletter*, January 17, 2006, p. 8.

123. "Jury Finds Former Ill. Gov. Ryan Guilty," *USA Today*, April 17, 2006, http://www.usatoday.com/news/nation/2006-04-17-ryan_x.htm (accessed May 10, 2006).

124. Ryan was found guilty of steering state contracts to political insiders while he was Illinois Secretary of State in the 1990s and while he was governor.

125. Title IV of the Justice for All Act of 2004.

126. At the time the legislation was enacted, Congress estimated that 300,000 rape kits remained unanalyzed in police department evidence lockers across the country.

127. The act also provides funding for the DNA Sexual Assault Justice Act (Title III of the Justice for All Act of 2004) and the Rape Kits and DNA Evidence Backlog Elimination Act of 2000 (U.S. Code, Title 42, Section 14135), authorizing more than $500 million for programs to improve the capacity of crime labs to conduct DNA analysis, reduce non-DNA backlogs, train evidence examiners, support sexual assault forensic examiner programs, and promote the use of DNA to identify missing persons.

128. In those states that accept federal monies under the legislation.

129. Studies include S. Decker and C. Kohfeld, "A Deterrence Study of the Death Penalty in Illinois: 1933–1980," *Journal of Criminal Justice*, Vol. 12, No. 4 (1984), pp. 367–379; and S. Decker and C. Kohfeld, "An Empirical Analysis of the Effect of the Death Penalty in Missouri," *Journal of Crime and Justice*, Vol. 10, No. 1 (1987), pp. 23–46.

130. See, especially, W. C. Bailey, "Deterrence and the Death Penalty for Murders in Utah: A Time Series Analysis," *Journal of Contemporary Law*, Vol. 5, No. 1 (1978), pp. 1–20; and W. C. Bailey, "An Analysis of the Deterrent Effect of the Death Penalty for Murder in California," *Southern California Law Review*, Vol. 52, No. 3 (1979), pp. 743–764.

131. B. E. Forst, "The Deterrent Effect of Capital Punishment: A Cross-State Analysis of the 1960's," *Minnesota Law Review*, Vol. 61, No. 5 (1977), pp. 743–767.

132. Hashem Dezhbakhsh, Paul Rubin, and Joanna Mehlhop Shepherd, "Does Capital Punishment Have a Deterrent Effect?

New Evidence from Post-Moratorium Panel Data," Emory University, January 2001, http://userwww.service.emory.edu/~cozden/Dezhbakhsh_01_01_paper.pdf (accessed November 13, 2001).

133. Ibid., abstract.

134. Ibid., p. 19.

135. "Attorneys Call for Halt to U.S. Executions," Reuters wire service, February 4, 1997.

136. Contrary to some popular beliefs, the term *mental retardation* is still widely used. The American Association for Mental Retardation (AAMR) defines mental retardation as "a disability characterized by significant limitations both in intellectual functioning and in adaptive behavior as expressed in conceptual, social, and practical adaptive skills." See AAMR, "Definition of Mental Retardation," http://www.aamr.org/Policies/faq_mental_retardation.shtml (accessed June 6, 2005).

137. As some of the evidence presented before the Supreme Court in *Furman v. Georgia*, 408 U.S. 238 (1972), suggested.

138. *USA Today*, April 27, 1989, p. 12A.

139. Thomas J. Keil and Gennaro F. Vito, "Race and the Death Penalty in Kentucky Murder Trials: 1976–1991," *American Journal of Criminal Justice*, Vol. 20, No. 1 (1995), pp. 17–36.

140. *McCleskey v. Kemp*, 481 U.S. 279, 107 S.Ct. 1756, 95 L.Ed.2d 262 (1987).

141. *The Federal Death Penalty System: Supplementary Data, Analysis and Revised Protocols for Capital Case Review* (Washington, DC: Department of Justice, 2001).

142. David Stout, "Attorney General Says Report Shows No Racial and Ethnic Bias in Federal Death Sentences," *New York Times*, June 7, 2001, http://college1.nytimes.com/guests/articles/2001/06/07/850513.xml (accessed May 20, 2007).

143. "Expanded Study Shows No Bias in Death Penalty, Ashcroft Says," *Criminal Justice Newsletter*, Vol. 31, No. 13 (June 18, 2001), p. 4.

144. Mary P. Gallagher, "Race Found to Have No Effect on Capital Sentencing in New Jersey," *New Jersey Law Journal* (August 21, 2001), p. 1.

145. "Nebraska Death Penalty System Given Mixed Review in a State Study," *Criminal Justice Newsletter*, Vol. 31, No. 16 (August 2001), pp. 4–5.

146. P. Cook, "The Costs of Processing Murder Cases in North Carolina," Duke University (May 1993), as cited in testimony of Richard C. Dieter before the New York State Assembly: Standing Committees on Codes, Judiciary, and Correction, January 25, 2005, p. 6, http://www. deathpenaltyinfo.org/NY-RCD-Test.pdf (accessed May 22, 2006).

147. Ibid., p. 7.

148. Ibid.

149. Mary E. Forsbert, "Money for Nothing? The Financial Cost of New Jersey's Death Penalty," New Jersey Policy Perspective, November 2005, http://www.njpp.org/rpt_moneyfornothing.html (accessed May 2, 2006).

150. Details for this story come from Michael Graczyk, "Killer of Pregnant 10-Year-Old Set to Die Tonight," Associated Press, February 10, 2004; and Texas Execution Information Center, "Edward Lagrone," http://www.txexecutions.org/reports/318.asp (accessed May 15, 2004).

151. Justice Potter Stewart, as quoted in *USA Today*, April 27, 1989, p. 12A.

152. Koestler, *Reflections on Hanging*, pp. 147–148; and Gennaro F. Vito and Deborah G. Wilson, "Back from the Dead: Tracking the Progress of Kentucky's *Furman*-Commuted Death Row Population," *Justice Quarterly*, Vol. 5, No. 1 (1988), pp. 101–111.

153. *Wilkerson* v. *Utah*, 99 U.S. 130 (1878).

154. *In re Kemmler*, 136 U.S. 436 (1890).

155. Ibid., p. 447.

156. *Louisiana ex rel. Francis* v. *Resweber*, 329 U.S. 459 (1947).

157. *Furman* v. *Georgia*, 408 U.S. 238 (1972).

158. A position first adopted in *Trop* v. *Dulles*, 356 U.S. 86 (1958).

159. "Federal Jury Spares Zacarias Moussaoui a Death Sentence," Court TV Online, May 3, 2006, http://www.courttv.com/trials/moussaoui/050306_verdict_ap.html (accessed May 30, 2006).

160. *Gregg* v. *Georgia*, 428 U.S. 153 (1976).

161. Ibid., p. 173.

162. *Coker* v. *Georgia*, 433 U.S. 584 (1977).

163. *Woodson* v. *North Carolina*, 428 U.S. 280 (1976).

164. *Blystone* v. *Pennsylvania*, 494 U.S. 310 (1990).

165. *Boyde* v. *California*, 494 U.S. 370 (1990).

166. *Simmons* v. *Arkansas*, 110 S.Ct. 1717 (1990).

167. *Deck* v. *Missouri*, 544 U.S. 622 (2005).

168. *Tuilaepa* v. *California*, 114 S.Ct. 2630, 129 L.Ed.2d 750 (1994).

169. *Ring* v. *Arizona*, 536 U.S. 584 (2002).

170. "Dozens of Death Sentences Overturned," Associated Press, June 24, 2002.

171. The ruling could also affect Florida, Alabama, Indiana, and Delaware, where juries recommend sentences in capital cases, but judges have the final say.

172. *Summerlin* v. *Stewart*, 341 F.3d 1082, 2003.

173. *Schriro* v. *Summerlin*, 542 U.S. 348 (2004).

174. *Poyner* v. *Murray*, 113 S.Ct. 1573, 123 L.Ed.2d 142 (1993).

175. *Campbell* v. *Wood*, 114 S.Ct. 1337, 127 L.Ed.2d 685 (1994).

176. *Director Gomez, et al.* v. *Fierro and Ruiz*, 117 S.Ct. 285 (1996).

177. The court issued its decision after reviewing two cases: *Dawson* v. *State* and *Moore* v. *State*.

178. "Georgia Court Finds Electrocution Unconstitutional," *Criminal Justice Newsletter*, Vol. 31, No. 18 (October 15, 2001), pp. 3–4.

179. Adam Liptak, "Judges Set Hurdles for Lethal Injection," *New York Times*, April 12, 2006.

180. "North Carolina, Using Medical Monitoring Device, Executes Killer," Associated Press, April 22, 2006.

181. *Penry* v. *Johnson*, 532 U.S. 782 (2001).

182. Penry's first death sentence was overturned in *Penry* v. *Lynaugh*, 492 U.S. 302 (1989).

183. Jim Yardley, "Two Groups Help Sway Texas Governor on Veto," *New York Times*, June 19, 2001, http://college1.nytimes.com/guests/articles/2001/06/19/852692.xml (accessed November 13, 2001).

184. *Atkins* v. *Virginia*, 122 S.Ct. 2242, 153 L.Ed.2d 335 (2002).

185. The justices were citing *Trop* v. *Dulles*, 356 U.S. 86 (1958), in which Chief Justice Earl Warren created a test that continues to govern interpretations of the cruel and unusual clause of the Eighth Amendment to this day.

186. See "Texas Jury Sentences Penry to Death Once Again," Reuters, July 3, 2002.

187. See, for example, "Letters: Ruling on Retarded Convicts Rests on 'Feeble Foundation,'" *USA Today*, June 25, 2002, p. 22A.

188. The European Union president wrote that "The EU strongly believes that the execution of persons suffering from a mental disorder is contrary to widely accepted human rights norms and in contradiction to the minimum standards of human rights set forth in several international human rights instruments." Read the EU letter to the Texas governor at http://www.internationaljusticeproject.org/pdfs/DEMAR1BPatterson.pdf (accessed October 11, 2007).

189. Details for this story come from the International Justice Project, "Kelsey Patterson," http://www.internationaljusticeproject.org/illnessKPatterson.cfm (accessed July 5, 2005).

190. *Panetti v. Quarterman*, U.S. Supreme Court, No. 06-6407 (decided June 28, 2007).

191. *Roper v. Simmons*, 543 U.S. 551 (2005).

192. Death Penalty Information Center, "Juvenile Offenders Currently on Death Row, or Executed, by State," http://www.deathpenaltyinfo.org/article.php?scid527&did5882 (accessed September 10, 2005).

193. John Ritter, "Calif. Inmate Says He's Too Old, Ill to Die," *USA Today*, January 10, 2006, p. 3A.

194. The Gallup Organization, http://www.gallup.com (accessed May 27, 2003).

195. See Janet L. Conley, "Execution Protests Wane as Opponents Shift Focus," *Fulton County Daily Report*, August 22, 2002. For the latest information on public opinion polls as they relate to capital punishment, visit the Death Penalty Information Center online at http://www.deathpenaltyinfo.org.

196. James D. Unnever and Francis T. Cullen, "Executing the Innocent and Support for Capital Punishment," *Criminology and Public Policy*, Vol. 4, No. 1 (2005), p. 3.

197. "Illinois Commission Calls for Restrictions on Death Penalty," *Criminal Justice Newsletter*, Vol. 32, No. 7 (April 2002), pp. 1–3.

198. "Death Penalty Freeze to Remain in Illinois," *USA Today*, April 25, 2003, p. 3A.

Chapter 12   Probation, Parole, and Community Corrections

i. Jeremy Travis, *But They All Come Back: Rethinking Prisoner Reentry* (Washington, DC: National Institute of Justice, 2000), p. 2.

ii. Re-entry Policy Council, *Report of the Re-entry Policy Council: Charting the Safe and Successful Return of Prisoners to the Community—Report Preview* (New York: Council of State Governments, 2005), p. 4.

iii. From the "Director's Message" in Dora Schriro, "Correcting Corrections: Missouri's Parallel Universe," *Sentencing and Corrections Issues for the 21st Century: Papers from the Executive Session on Sentencing and Corrections*, No. 8 (Washington, DC: National Institute of Justice, 2000).

iv. Jeremy Travis, "Thoughts on the Future of Parole," remarks delivered at the Vera Institute of Justice, May 22, 2002, speech transcript, p. 3.

1. Quoted in *Criminal Justice Newsletter*, January 3, 2006, p. 1.

2. Quoted in *Criminal Justice Newsletter*, January 19, 1993, p. 1.

3. Details for this story come from "Mo. Suspects in Taped Rape, Killing Nabbed," CBS News online, May 27, 2006, http://www.cbsnews.com/stories/2006/05/27/ap/national/mainD8HRVC300.shtml (accessed May 29, 2006).

4. Details for this story come from "Records: Smith Told His Brother," *Herald Tribune*, June 3, 2004.

5. "Smith Sentenced to Death for Killing Carlie Brucia," *USA Today*, March 15, 2005, http://www.usatoday.com/news/nation/2006-03-15-brucia_x.htm (accessed May 29, 2006).

6. James M. Byrne, *Probation*, National Institute of Justice Crime File Series Study Guide (Washington, DC: NIJ, 1988), p. 1.

7. Alexander B. Smith and Louis Berlin, *Introduction to Probation and Parole* (St. Paul, MN: West, 1976), p. 75.

8. John Augustus, *First Probation Officer: John Augustus' Original Report on His Labors—1852* (Montclair, NJ: Patterson-Smith, 1972).

9. Smith and Berlin, *Introduction to Probation and Parole*, p. 77.

10. Ibid., p. 80.

11. George C. Killinger, Hazel B. Kerper, and Paul F. Cromwell, Jr., *Probation and Parole in the Criminal Justice System* (St. Paul, MN: West, 1976), p. 25.

12. Lauren E. Glaze and Tomas P. Bonczar, *Probation and Parole in the United States, 2006* (Washington, DC: Bureau of Justice Statistics, December 2007).

13. Jodi M. Brown and Patrick A. Langan, *Felony Sentences in the United States, 1996* (Washington, DC: Bureau of Justice Statistics, 1999).

14. "Woman Gets Probation for Shooting Fiancé," Associated Press, April 16, 1992, p. 9A.

15. Glaze and Bonczar, *Probation and Parole in the United States, 2006*.

16. Bureau of Justice Statistics, "Probation and Parole Statistics," http://www.ojp.usdoj.gov/bjs/pandp.htm (accessed January 10, 2006).

17. This section owes much to Sanford Bates, "The Establishment and Early Years of the Federal Probation System," *Federal Probation* (June 1987), pp. 4–9.

18. *Ex parte United States*, 242 U.S. 27 (1916).

19. Bates, "The Establishment and Early Years of the Federal Probation System," p. 6.

20. U.S. Probation and Pretrial Services System, *Year-in-Review Report: Fiscal Year 2004* (Washington, DC: U.S. Probation and Pretrial Services System, 2005).

21. See Brian A. Reaves and Timothy C. Hart, *Federal Law Enforcement Officers, 2000* (Washington, DC: Bureau of Justice Statistics, 2002), p. 4, from which some of the wording in this paragraph has been adapted.

22. Adapted from Timothy A. Hughes, Doris James Wilson, and Allen J. Beck, *Trends in State Parole, 1990–2000* (Washington, DC: Bureau of Justice Statistics, 2001), p. 1.

23. Ibid.

24. Ibid.

25. Ibid.

26. Glaze and Bonczar, *Probation and Parole in the United States, 2006*, p. 1.

27. Ibid., p. 6.

28. Ibid.

29. "The Effectiveness of Felony Probation: Results from an Eastern State," *Justice Quarterly* (December 1991), pp. 525–543.

30. State of Georgia, Board of Pardons and Paroles, "Adult Offender Sanction Costs for Fiscal Year 2001," http://www.pap.state.ga.us/otisweb/corrcost.html (accessed March 1, 2004).

31. See Andrew von Hirsch and Kathleen J. Hanrahan, *Abolish Parole?* (Washington, DC: Law Enforcement Assistance Administration, 1978).

32. Theresa A. Severance, "Preparing for Re-entry: Challenges and Strategies," *Women, Girls & Criminal Justice*, Vol. 8, No. 3 (April/May 2007), p 1.

33. P. O'Brien, *Making It in the "Free World": Women in Transition from Prison* (Albany: State University of New York Press, 2001).

34. *Griffin* v. *Wisconsin*, 483 U.S. 868, 107 S.Ct. 3164 (1987).

35. *Pennsylvania Board of Probation and Parole* v. *Scott*, 524 U.S. 357 (1998).

36. *U.S.* v. *Knights*, U.S. Supreme Court, 534 U.S. 112 (2001).

37. *Samson* v. *California*, 547 U.S. ___ (2006).

38. California Penal Code, Section 3067.

39. Glaze and Bonczar, *Probation and Parole in the United States, 2005.*

40. Robyn L. Cohen, *Probation and Parole Violators in State Prison, 1991* (Washington, DC: Bureau of Justice Statistics, 1995).

41. *Escoe* v. *Zerbst*, 295 U.S. 490 (1935).

42. *Mempa* v. *Rhay*, 389 U.S. 128 (1967).

43. A deferred sentence involves postponement of the sentencing decision, which may be made at a later time following an automatic review of the defendant's behavior in the interim. A suspended sentence requires no review unless the probationer violates the law or the conditions of probation. Either type of violation may result in imprisonment.

44. *Morrissey* v. *Brewer*, 408 U.S. 471 (1972).

45. *Gagnon* v. *Scarpelli*, 411 U.S. 778 (1973).

46. Smith and Berlin, *Introduction to Probation and Parole*, p. 143.

47. See Linda Greenhouse, *New York Times* wire service, March 18, 1997 (no headline). The case is *Young* v. *Harper*, 520 U.S. 143 (1997).

48. *Greenholtz* v. *Nebraska Penal Inmates*, 442 U.S. 1 (1979).

49. *Bearden* v. *Georgia*, 461 U.S. 660, 103 S.Ct. 2064, 76 L.Ed.2d 221 (1983).

50. Ibid.

51. *Minnesota* v. *Murphy*, 465 U.S. 420 (1984).

52. *Harlow* v. *Clatterbuick*, 30 CrL. 2364 (VA S.Ct. 1986); *Santangelo* v. *State*, 426 N.Y.S.2d 931 (1980); *Welch* v. *State*, 424 N.Y.S.2d 774 (1980); and *Thompson* v. *County of Alameda*, 614 P.2d 728 (1980).

53. *Tarter* v. *State of New York*, 38 CrL. 2364 (NY S.Ct. 1986); *Grimm* v. *Arizona Board of Pardons and Paroles*, 115 Arizona 260, 564 P.2d 1227 (1977); and *Payton* v. *U.S.*, 636 F.2d 132 (5th Cir. 1981).

54. Rolando del Carmen, *Potential Liabilities of Probation and Parole Officers* (Cincinnati, OH: Anderson, 1986), p. 89.

55. See, for example, *Semler* v. *Psychiatric Institute*, 538 F.2d 121 (4th Cir. 1976).

56. *Minnesota* v. *Murphy*, 465 U.S. 420 (1984).

57. National Advisory Commission on Criminal Justice Standards and Goals, *Task Force Report: Corrections* (Washington, DC: U.S. Government Printing Office, 1973).

58. National Institute of Justice, *Stress among Probation and Parole Officers and What Can Be Done about It* (Washington, DC: NIJ, 2005).

59. Ibid., p. 1.

60. Ibid., p. ii.

61. From the introduction to James Austin, Michael Jones, and Melissa Bolyard, *The Growing Use of Jail Boot Camps: The Current State of the Art* (Washington, DC: National Institute of Justice, 1993), p. 1.

62. Michael McCarthy and Jodi Upton, "Athletes Lightly Punished after Their Day in Court," *USA Today*, May 4, 2006, p. 1A.

63. Sentencing Project, *Changing the Terms of Sentencing: Defense Counsel and Alternative Sentencing Services* (Washington, DC: Sentencing Project, no date).

64. Joan Petersilia, *Expanding Options for Criminal Sentencing* (Santa Monica, CA: RAND Corporation, 1987).

65. Ohio Revised Code, Section 2946.06.1 (July 1965).

66. Lawrence Greenfield, *Probation and Parole, 1984* (Washington, DC: U.S. Government Printing Office, 1986).

67. Harry Allen et al., *Probation and Parole in America* (New York: Free Press, 1985), p. 88.

68. For a good overview of such programs, especially as they apply to juvenile corrections, see Doris Layton MacKenzie et al., *A National Study Comparing the Environments of Boot Camps with Traditional Facilities for Juvenile Offenders* (Washington, DC: National Institute of Justice, 2001).

69. Doris Layton MacKenzie and Deanna Bellew Ballow, "Shock Incarceration Programs in State Correctional Jurisdictions—An Update," *NIJ Reports* (May/June 1989), pp. 9–10.

70. "Shock Incarceration Marks a Decade of Expansion," *Corrections Compendium* (September 1996), pp. 10–28.

71. MacKenzie and Ballow, "Shock Incarceration Programs in State Correctional Jurisdictions."

72. National Institute of Justice, *Multisite Evaluation of Shock Incarceration* (Washington, DC: NIJ, 1995).

73. Cherie L. Clark, David W. Aziz, and Doris L. MacKenzie, *Shock Incarceration in New York: Focus on Treatment* (Washington, DC: National Institute of Justice, 1994), p. 8.

74. "Oregon Boot Camp Is Saving the State Money, Study Finds," *Criminal Justice Newsletter*, May 1, 1995, pp. 5–6.

75. Douglas C. McDonald, *Restitution and Community Service*, National Institute of Justice Crime File Series Study Guide (Washington, DC: NIJ, 1988).

76. Richard J. Maher and Henry E. Dufour, "Experimenting with Community Service: A Punitive Alternative to Imprisonment," *Federal Probation* (September 1987), pp. 22–27.

77. James P. Levine, Michael C. Musheno, and Dennis J. Palumbo, *Criminal Justice in America: Law in Action* (New York: John Wiley, 1986), p. 549.

78. Billie S. Erwin and Lawrence A. Bennett, "New Dimensions in Probation: Georgia's Experience with Intensive Probation Supervision," National Institute of Justice Research in Brief (Washington, DC: NIJ, 1987).

79. Probation Division, State of Georgia, "Intensive and Specialized Probation Supervision," http://www.dcor.state.ga.us/ProbationDivision/html (accessed March 2, 2006).

80. Crystal A. Garcia, "Using Palmer's Global Approach to Evaluate Intensive Supervision Programs: Implications for Practice," *Corrections Management Quarterly*, Vol. 4, No. 4 (2000), pp. 60–69.

81. Joan Petersilia, *House Arrest*, National Institute of Justice Crime File Series Study Guide (Washington, DC: NIJ, 1988).

82. Darren Gowen, "Remote Location Monitoring: A Supervision Strategy to Enhance Risk Control," *Federal Probation*, Vol. 65, No. 2, p. 39.

83. An additional year and seven months of supervised confinement were to follow.

84. See "Martha Stewart Starts Home Confinement," Associated Press, March 3, 2005, http://moneycentral.msn.com/content/invest/extra/P111258.asp (accessed April 26, 2005).

85. *Electronic Monitoring*, TDCJ-CJAD Agency Brief (Austin: Texas Department of Criminal Justice, March 1999).

86. Texas Department of Criminal Justice, Parole Division, "Specialized Programs," http://www.tdcj.state.tx.us/parole/parole-spclpgms.htm (accessed September 20, 2007).

87. Marc Renzema and David T. Skelton, *The Use of Electronic Monitoring by Criminal Justice Agencies, 1989* (Washington, DC: National Institute of Justice, 1990).

88. U.S. Probation and Pretrial Services, *Court and Community* (Washington, DC: Administrative Office of the U.S. Courts, 2000).

89. "Satellites Tracking People on Parole," Associated Press, April 13, 1999.

90. U.S. Probation and Pretrial Services, "Home Confinement," http://www.uscourts.gov/misc/cchome.pdf (accessed March 22, 2006).

91. State of Georgia Board of Pardons and Paroles, "Adult Offender Sanction Costs for Fiscal Year 2001," http://www.pap.state.ga.us/otisweb/corrcost.html (accessed September 20, 2002).

92. Construction costs are for cells classified as "medium security."

93. *BI Home Escort: Electronic Monitoring System*, advertising brochure (Boulder, CO: BI Inc., no date).

94. James A. Inciardi, *Criminal Justice*, 2nd ed. (New York: Harcourt Brace Jovanovich, 1987), p. 664.

95. Neely Tucker, "Study Warns of Rising Tide of Released Inmates," *Washington Post*, May 21, 2003, p. A1.

96. Patrick A. Langan and David J. Levin, *National Recidivism Study of Released Prisoners: Recidivism of Prisoners Released in 1994* (Washington, DC: Bureau of Justice Statistics, 2002).

97. Bureau of Justice Statistics, "Forty-Two Percent of State Parole Discharges Were Successful," October 3, 2001, http://www.ojp.usdoj.gov/newsroom/2001/bjs01181.html (accessed July 3, 2007).

98. Urban Institute and RTI International, *National Portrait of SVORI* (Washington, DC: Urban Institute Press, 2004).

99. American Probation and Parole Association and the Association of Paroling Authorities International, *Abolishing Parole: Why the Emperor Has No Clothes* (Lexington, KY: APPA, 1995).

100. Much of this information is taken from Re-entry Policy Council, *Report of the Re-entry Policy Council: Charting the Safe and Successful Return of Prisoners to the Community—Executive Summary* (New York: Council of State Governments, 2005), http://www.reentrypolicy.org/executivesummary.html (accessed July 10, 2007).

101. Patrick A. Langan and David J. Levin, *National Recidivism Study of Released Prisoners: Recidivism of Prisoners Released in 1994* (Washington, DC: Bureau of Justice Statistics, 2002); and *Does Parole Work? Analyzing the Impact of Postprison Supervision on Rearrest Outcomes* (Washington, DC: Urban Institute, 2005).

102. Esther Griswold, Jessica Pearson, and Lanae Davis, *Testing a Modification Process for Incarcerated Parents* (Denver, CO: Center for Policy Research), pp. 11–12.

103. See Pamela K. Lattimore, "Reentry, Reintegration, Rehabilitation, Recidivism, and Redemption," *Criminologist*, Vol. 31, No. 3 (May/June 2006), pp. 1, 3–6.

104. Urban Institute and RTI International, *National Portrait of SVORI*, from which some of the wording in this section is taken.

105. See Laura Winterfield and Susan Brumbaugh, *The Multi-Site Evaluation of the Serious and Violent Offender Reentry Initiative* (Washington, DC: Urban Institute, 2005).

106. U.S. Department of Justice, Office of Justice Programs, "Learn about Reentry," http://www.reentry.gov/learn.html (accessed May 29, 2007).

107. Lane County (Oregon) Circuit Court, "Drug Court," http://www.ojd.state.or.us/lan/drugcrt/index.htm (accessed May 29, 2007).

108. See, for example, Jeremy Travis, *But They All Come Back: Facing the Challenges of Prisoner Reentry* (Washington, DC: Urban Institute Press, 2005).

109. *National Portrait of SVORI*, pp. 21, 23.

110. Reinventing Probation Council, *"Broken Windows" Probation: The Next Step in Fighting Crime* (New York: Manhattan Institute, 1999); and Reinventing Probation Council, *Transforming Probation through Leadership: The "Broken Windows" Model* (New York: Center for Civic Innovation at the Manhattan Institute, 2000), from which some of the quoted material in these paragraphs comes.

111. Joan Petersilia, "A Crime Control Rationale for Reinvesting in Community Corrections," in *Critical Criminal Justice Issues: Task Force Reports from the American Society of Criminology* (Washington, DC: National Institute of Justice, 1997).

112. For more about the future of probation and parole, see Joan Petersilia, *Reforming Probation and Parole in the Twenty-First Century* (Lanham, MD: American Correctional Association, 2002).

Chapter 13   Prisons and Jails

i. Jeff Beard, "The Complex Problem of Offender Reentry," *Corrections Today*, April 2005, p. 8.

ii. Zebulon R. Brockway, *The Ideal of a True Prison System for a State* (1865).

iii. Don Myers, "Crime: What Will It Take to Reclaim Our Country?" *USA Today*, May 26, 1995.

iv. James A. Gondles, Jr., "Who Should Be behind Bars?" *Corrections Today*, August 2002, http://www.aca.org/admin/pix/ctmagarticles/200208_whoshouldbebehindbars.pdf (accessed September 12, 2007).

v. Bureau of Justice Statistics, *Prisoners in 1998* (Washington, DC: BJS, 1999), p. 7.

---

1. Quoted in Gail S. Funke, *National Conference on Prison Industries: Discussions and Recommendations* (Washington, DC: U.S. Government Printing Office, 1986), p. 23.

2. Camden Pelham, *Chronicles of Crime: A Series of Memoirs and Anecdotes of Notorious Characters* (London: T. Miles, 1887), pp. 28–30.

3. This section owes much to Harry Elmer Barnes and Negley K. Teeters, *New Horizons in Criminology*, 3rd ed. (Englewood Cliffs, NJ: Prentice Hall, 1959).

4. Ibid., p. 290.

5. Ann O'Hanlon, "New Interest in Corporal Punishment: Several States Weigh Get-Tough Measures," *Washington Post* wire service, March 5, 1995.

6. Barnes and Teeters, *New Horizons in Criminology*, p. 292.

7. Ibid.

8. Ibid., p. 293.

9. Arthur Evans Wood and John Barker Waite, *Crime and Its Treatment: Social and Legal Aspects of Criminology* (New York: American Book Company, 1941), p. 488.

10. John Howard, *State of Prisons* (London, 1777; reprint, New York: E. P. Dutton, 1929).

11. Although some writers hold that the Quakers originated the concept of solitary confinement for prisoners, there is evidence that the practice already existed in England before 1789. John Howard, for example, described solitary confinement in use at Reading Bridewell in the 1780s.

12. Vergil L. Williams, *Dictionary of American Penology: An Introduction* (Westport, CT: Greenwood Press, 1979), p. 200.

13. Barnes and Teeters, *New Horizons in Criminology*, p. 348.

14. Williams, *Dictionary of American Penology*, p. 29.

15. With regard to cost, supporters of the Pennsylvania system argued that it was actually less expensive than the Auburn style of imprisonment because it led more quickly to reformation.

16. Williams, *Dictionary of American Penology*, p. 30.

17. Gustave de Beaumont and Alexis de Tocqueville, *On the Penitentiary System in the United States, and Its Application in France* (Philadelphia: Carey, Lea and Blanchard, 1833).

18. Barnes and Teeters, *New Horizons in Criminology*, p. 428.

19. Ibid.

20. Ibid.

21. Wood and Waite, *Crime and Its Treatment*, p. 555, citing U.S. Bureau of Labor Statistics.

22. See North Carolina Department of Corrections, Correction Enterprises website, http://www. doc.state.nc.us/eprise (accessed October 20, 2007).

23. See U.S. Department of Justice, Federal Prison Industries, Inc., website, http://www.unicor.gov.

24. Robert Mintz, "Federal Prison Industry—The Green Monster, Part One: History and Background," *Crime and Social Justice*, Vol. 6 (fall/winter 1976), pp. 41–48.

25. William G. Saylor and Gerald G. Gaes, "PREP Study Links UNICOR Work Experience with Successful Post-Release Outcome," *Corrections Compendium* (October 1994), pp. 5–6, 8.

26. Criminal Justice Associates, *Private Sector Involvement in Prison-Based Businesses: A National Assessment* (Washington, DC: U.S. Government Printing Office, 1985). See also National Institute of Justice, *Corrections and the Private Sector* (Washington, DC: U.S. Government Printing Office, 1985).

27. The PIECP was first authorized under the Justice System Improvement Act of 1979 (Public Law 96-157, Sec. 827) and later expanded under the Justice Assistance Act of 1984 (Public Law 98-473, Sec. 819). The Crime Control Act of 1990 (Public Law 101-647) authorizes continuation of the program indefinitely.

28. Domingo S. Herraiz, *Prison Industry Enhancement Certification Program* (Washington, DC: Bureau of Justice Assistance, 2004).

29. Barnes and Teeters, *New Horizons in Criminology*, p. 355.

30. Williams, *Dictionary of American Penology*, p. 225.

31. Ibid., p. 64.

32. Ibid., p. 227.

33. Donal E. J. MacNamara, "Medical Model in Corrections: Requiescat in Pace," in Fred Montanino, ed., *Incarceration:* *The Sociology of Imprisonment* (Beverly Hills, CA: Sage, 1978).

34. For a description of the community-based format in its heyday, see Andrew T. Scull, *Decarceration: Community Treatment and the Deviant—A Radical View* (Englewood Cliffs, NJ: Prentice Hall, 1977).

35. Ibid., p. 51.

36. Williams, *Dictionary of American Penology*, p. 45.

37. Ibid.

38. Clemens Bartollas, *Introduction to Corrections* (New York: Harper and Row, 1981), pp. 166–167.

39. The act also established home furloughs and community treatment centers.

40. National Advisory Commission on Criminal Justice Standards and Goals, Standard 2.17, Part 2c.

41. *Recidivism* can be defined in various ways according to the purpose the term is intended to serve in a particular study or report. Recidivism is usually defined as rearrest (versus reconviction) and generally includes a time span of five years, although some Bureau of Justice Statistics studies have used six years, and other studies one or two years, as definitional criteria.

42. Various advocates of the just deserts, or justice, model can be identified. For a detailed description of rehabilitation and just deserts, see Michael A. Pizzi, Jr., "The Medical Model and the 100 Years War," *Law Enforcement News*, July 7, 1986, pp. 8, 13; and MacNamara, "Medical Model in Corrections."

43. Bureau of Justice Statistics, *Annual Report, 1987* (Washington, DC: BJS, 1988), p. 70.

44. Ibid.

45. Ibid.

46. Robert Martinson, "What Works: Questions and Answers about Prison Reform," *Public Interest*, No. 35 (1974), pp. 22–54. See also Douglas Lipton, Robert M. Martinson, and Judith Wilkes, *The Effectiveness of Correctional Treatment: A Survey of Treatment Evaluation Studies* (New York: Praeger, 1975).

47. L. Sechrest, S. White, and E. Brown, eds., *The Rehabilitation of Criminal Offenders: Problems and Prospects* (Washington, DC: National Academy of Sciences, 1979).

48. U.S. Department of Justice, *Office of Justice Programs Fiscal Year 2000 Program Plan: Resources for the Field* (Washington, DC: Office of Juvenile Justice and Delinquency Prevention, 1999).

49. Timothy A. Hughes, Doris James Wilson, and Allen J. Beck, *Trends in State Parole, 1990–2000* (Washington, DC: Bureau of Justice Statistics, 2001).

50. Ibid.; and Paige M. Harrison and Allen J. Beck, *Prisoners in 2006* (Washington, DC: Bureau of Justice Statistics, 2007). Figures as of January 1 of each year.

51. Lynn S. Branham, *The Use of Incarceration in the United States: A Look at the Present and the Future* (Washington, DC: American Bar Association, 1992).

52. "Reliance on Prisons Is Costly but Ineffective, ABA Panel Says," *Criminal Justice Newsletter*, April 15, 1992, p. 7.

53. *Criminal Justice Newsletter*, February 3, 1992, p. 8.

54. American Correctional Association, *Vital Statistics in Corrections* (Laurel, MD: ACA, 2000).

55. Allen J. Beck and Paige M. Harrison, *Prisoners in 2000* (Washington, DC: Bureau of Justice Statistics, 2002).

56. Jeanne B. Stinchcomb, "From Rehabilitation to Retribution: Examining Public Policy Paradigms and Personnel

Education Patterns in Corrections," *American Journal of Criminal Justice*, Vol. 27, No. 1 (2002), p. 3.

57. Although many other states require inmates to work on road maintenance, and though the inmates are typically supervised by armed guards, Alabama became the first state in modern times to shackle prisoners on work crews.

58. See "Back on the Chain Gang: Florida Becomes Third State to Resurrect Forced Labor," Associated Press wire service, November 22, 1995.

59. Florida Department of Corrections, *Corrections in Florida: 1998 Opinion Survey*, http://www.dc.state.fl.us/pub/survey/index.html (accessed January 24, 2007).

60. Lori Sharn and Shannon Tangonan, "Chain Gangs Back in Alabama," *USA Today*, May 4, 1995, p. 3A.

61. Ibid.

62. See Debra L. Dailey, *Summary of the 1998 Annual Conference of the National Association of Sentencing Commissions*, http://www.ussc.gov/states/dailefsr.pdf (accessed October 30, 2006).

63. The state of Washington is generally credited with having been the first state to pass a three-strikes law by voter initiative (in 1993).

64. For a good overview of the topic, see David Shichor and Dale K. Sechrest, *Three Strikes and You're Out: Vengeance as Public Policy* (Thousand Oaks, CA: Sage, 1996).

65. David S. Broder, "When Tough Isn't Smart," *Washington Post* wire service, March 24, 1994.

66. "The Klaas Case and the Crime Bill," *Washington Post* wire service, February 21, 1994.

67. Quinlan is now president of Corrections Corporation of America.

68. David Lawsky, "Prison Wardens Decry Overcrowding, Survey Says," Reuters, December 21, 1994.

69. James J. Stephan and Jennifer C. Karberg, *Census of State and Federal Correctional Facilities, 2000* (Washington, DC: Bureau of Justice Statistics, 2003).

70. William J. Sabol, Heather Couture, and Paige M. Harrison, *Prisoners in 2006*, p. 4. This number includes state and federal prisoners held in local jails.

71. Ibid.

72. Public Safety Performance Project of the Pew Charitable Trusts, *Public Safety, Public Spending: Forecasting America's Prison Population, 2007–2011* (Philadelphia: Pew, February 2007).

73. Ibid.

74. Thomas P. Bonczar, *Prevalence of Imprisonment in the U.S. Population, 1974–2001* (Washington, DC: Bureau of Justice Statistics, 2003), p. 1.

75. William J. Sabol, Heather Couture, and Paige M. Harrison, *Prisoners in 2006*.

76. Bureau of Justice Statistics, *National Corrections Reporting Program, 1998* (Ann Arbor, MI: Interuniversity Consortium for Political and Social Research, 2001).

77. William J. Sabol, Heather Couture, and Paige M. Harrison, *Prisoners in 2006*.

78. Bonczar, *Prevalence of Imprisonment in the U.S. Population, 1974–2001*, p. 1.

79. Ibid., p. 8.

80. The number includes both state and federal prisoners.

81. Information in this paragraph comes from Sabol, Couture, and Harrison, *Prisoners in 2006*.

82. David F. Greenberg and Valerie West, "State Prison Populations and Their Growth, 1971–1991," *Criminology*, Vol. 39, No. 3 (2001), p. 615.

83. Robert M. Carter, Richard A. McGee, and E. Kim Nelson, *Corrections in America* (Philadelphia: J. B. Lippincott, 1975), pp. 122–123.

84. James J. Stephan, *State Prison Expenditures, 2001* (Washington, DC: Bureau of Justice Statistics, 2004); and e-mail correspondence with Susan Allison, Federal Bureau of Prisons, October 29, 2001.

85. Kristen A. Hughes, *Justice Expenditure and Employment in the United States, 2003* (Washington, DC: Bureau of Justice Statistics, 2006).

86. Harrison and Beck, *Prisoners in 2006*.

87. Public Safety Performance Project of the Pew Charitable Trusts, *Public Safety, Public Spending*, p. i.

88. Federal Bureau of Investigation, *Crime in the United States, 2006* (Washington, DC: U.S. Dept. of Justice, 2007), and other years.

89. Adapted from Bureau of Justice Statistics, *Report to the Nation on Crime and Justice*, 2nd ed. (Washington, DC: U.S. Government Printing Office, 1988), p. 108.

90. *Rhodes* v. *Chapman*, 452 U.S. 337 (1981).

91. D. Greenberg, "The Incapacitative Effect of Imprisonment, Some Estimates," *Law and Society Review*, Vol. 9 (1975), pp. 541–580. See also Jacqueline Cohen, "Incapacitating Criminals: Recent Research Findings," National Institute of Justice Research in Brief (Washington, DC: NIJ, December 1983).

92. For information on identifying dangerous repeat offenders, see M. Chaiken and J. Chaiken, "Selecting Career Criminals for Priority Prosecution," final report (Cambridge, MA: Abt Associates, 1987).

93. J. Monahan, *Predicting Violent Behavior: An Assessment of Clinical Techniques* (Beverly Hills, CA: Sage, 1981).

94. S. Van Dine, J. P. Conrad, and S. Dinitz, *Restraining the Wicked: The Incapacitation of the Dangerous Offender* (Lexington, MA: Lexington Books, 1979).

95. Paul Gendreau, Tracy Little, and Claire Goggin, "A Meta-analysis of the Predictors of Adult Offender Recidivism: What Works!" *Criminology*, Vol. 34, No. 4 (November 1996), pp. 575–607.

96. *Lynce* v. *Mathis*, 519 U.S. 443 (1997).

97. George Camp and Camille Camp, "Stopping Escapes: Perimeter Security," *Prison Construction Bulletin* (Washington, DC: National Institute of Justice, 1987).

98. Adapted from G. A. Grizzle and A. D. Witte, "Efficiency in Collections Agencies," in Gordon P. Whitaker and Charles D. Phillips, eds., *Evaluating the Performance of Criminal Justice Agencies* (Washington, DC: National Institute of Justice, 1983).

99. Patricia L. Hardyman et al., *Internal Prison Classification Systems: Case Studies in Their Development and Implementation* (Washington, DC: National Institutions of Corrections, 2002), from which some of the wording in this section is taken.

100. Ibid.

101. *Johnson* v. *California*, 543 U.S. 499 (2005).

102. U.S. Bureau of Prisons, *Facilities*, http://www.bop.gov/map.html (accessed February 2, 2005).

103. Some of the information in this section is derived from Bureau of Prisons, *About the Federal Bureau of Prisons* (Washington, DC: BOP, 2001).

104. Includes federal prisoners held in Bureau of Prisons facilities and privately operated institutions.

105. Bureau of Prisons, "The Bureau in Brief," http://www.bop.gov/ipapg/ipabib.html (accessed July 5, 2006).

106. Federal Bureau of Prisons, *State of the Bureau, 2005* (Washington, DC: U.S. Department of Justice, 2006), p. 19.

107. Most of the information in this section comes from telephone conversations with and faxed information from the federal Bureau of Prisons, August 25, 1995.

108. For additional information, see Dennis Cauchon, "The Alcatraz of the Rockies," *USA Today*, November 16, 1994, p. 6A.

109. "Congress OKs Inmate Fees to Offset Costs of Prison," *Criminal Justice Newsletter*, October 15, 1992, p. 6.

110. James J. Stephan, *State Prison Expenditures, 2001* (Washington, DC: Bureau of Justice Statistics, 2004), p. 3.

111. National Institute of Corrections website, http://www.nicic.org (accessed March 2, 2007).

112. Ibid.

113. Doris J. James, *Profile of Jail Inmates, 2002* (Washington, DC: Bureau of Justice Statistics, 2004), p. 2.

114. William J. Sabol, Todd D. Minton, and Paige M. Harrison, *Prison and Jail Inmates at Midyear 2006* (Washington, DC: Bureau of Justice Statistics, 2007).

115. Ibid, p. 5.

116. James, *Profile of Jail Inmates, 2002*, p. 1.

117. Sabol, Minton, and Harrison, *Prison and Jail Inmates at Midyear 2006.*

118. James J. Stephan, *Census of Jails, 1999* (Washington, DC: Bureau of Justice Statistics, 2001).

119. Ibid.

120. Ibid.

121. James, *Profile of Jail Inmates, 2002*, p. 2.

122. Ibid.

123. Stephan, *Census of Jails, 1999.*

124. See Gale Holland, "L.A. Jail Makes Delayed Debut," *USA Today*, January 27, 1997, p. 3A.

125. See Dale Stockton, "Cook County Illinois Sheriff's Office," *Police*, October 1996, pp. 40–43. The Cook County Department of Correction operates ten separate jails, which house approximately 9,000 inmates. The department employs more than 2,800 correctional officers.

126. Sabol, Minton, and Harrison, *Prison and Jail Inmates at Midyear 2006*, p. 7.

127. Ibid.

128. William Reginald Mills and Heather Barrett, "Meeting the Special Challenge of Providing Health Care to Women Inmates in the '90's," *American Jails*, Vol. 4, No. 3 (September/October 1990), p. 55.

129. Ibid., p. 21.

130. Ibid.

131. Ibid., p. 55.

132. American Correctional Association, *Vital Statistics in Corrections.*

133. Mills and Barrett, "Providing Health Care to Women Inmates," p. 55.

134. Ibid.

135. Linda L. Zupan, "Women Corrections Officers in the Nation's Largest Jails," *American Jails* (January/February 1991), pp. 59–62.

136. Linda L. Zupan, "Women Corrections Officers in Local Jails," paper presented at the annual meeting of the Academy of Criminal Justice Sciences, Nashville, TN, March 1991.

137. Ibid., p. 6.

138. "Jail Overcrowding in Houston Results in Release of Inmates," *Criminal Justice Newsletter*, October 15, 1990, p. 5.

139. Bureau of Justice Statistics, *Census of Local Jails, 1988* (Washington, DC: BJS, 1991), p. 31.

140. Kathleen Maguire and Ann L. Pastore, *Sourcebook of Criminal Justice Statistics, 1994* (Washington, DC: U.S. Government Printing Office, 1995).

141. Sabol, Minton, and Harrison, *Prison and Jail Inmates at Midyear 2006,* p. 19.

142. Ibid.

143. Harrison and Beck, *Prisoners in 2006.*

144. Christopher J. Mumola, *Suicide and Homicide in State Prisons and Local Jails* (Washington, DC: Bureau of Justice Statistics, 2005), p. 1.

145. George P. Wilson and Harvey L. McMurray, "System Assessment of Jail Overcrowding Assumptions," paper presented at the annual meeting of the Academy of Criminal Justice Sciences, Nashville, TN, March 1991.

146. Andy Hall, *Systemwide Strategies to Alleviate Jail Crowding* (Washington, DC: National Institute of Justice, 1987).

147. Ibid.

148. Linda L. Zupan and Ben A. Menke, "The New Generation Jail: An Overview," in Joel A. Thompson and G. Larry Mays, eds., *American Jails: Public Policy Issues* (Chicago: Nelson-Hall, 1991), p. 180.

149. Ibid.

150. Herbert R. Sigurdson, Billy Wayson, and Gail Funke, "Empowering Middle Managers of Direct Supervision Jails," *American Jails* (winter 1990), p. 52.

151. Byron Johnson, "Exploring Direct Supervision: A Research Note," *American Jails* (March/April 1994), pp. 63–64.

152. H. Sigurdson, *The Manhattan House of Detention: A Study of Podular Direct Supervision* (Washington, DC: National Institute of Corrections, 1985). For similar conclusions, see Robert Conroy, Wantland J. Smith, and Linda L. Zupan, "Officer Stress in the Direct Supervision Jail: A Preliminary Case Study," *American Jails* (November/December 1991), p. 36.

153. W. Raymond Nelson and Russell M. Davis, "Podular Direct Supervision: The First Twenty Years," *American Jails* (July/August 1995), p. 17.

154. Jerry W. Fuqua, "New Generation Jails: Old Generation Management," *American Jails* (March/April 1991), pp. 80–83.

155. Sigurdson, Wayson, and Funke, "Empowering Middle Managers of Direct Supervision Jails."

156. Duncan J. McCulloch and Tim Stiles, "Technology and the Direct Supervision Jail," *American Jails* (winter 1990), pp. 97–102.

157. Susan W. McCampbell, "Direct Supervision: Looking for the Right People," *American Jails* (November/December 1990), pp. 68–69.

158. For a good review of the future of American jails, see Ron Carroll, "Jails and the Criminal Justice System in the Twenty-First Century," *American Jails* (March/April 1997), pp. 26–31.

159. Robert L. May II, Roger H. Peters, and William D. Kearns, "The Extent of Drug Treatment Programs in Jails: A Summary Report," *American Jails* (September/October 1990), pp. 32–34.

160. See, for example, John W. Dietler, "Jail Industries: The Best Thing That Can Happen to a Sheriff," *American Jails* (July/August 1990), pp. 80–83.

161. Robert Osborne, "Los Angeles County Sheriff Opens New Inmate Answering Service," *American Jails* (July/August 1990), pp. 61–62.

162. Robert J. Hunter, "A Locally Operated Boot Camp," *American Jails* (July/August 1994), pp. 13–15.

163. James Austin, Michael Jones, and Melissa Bolyard, *The Growing Use of Jail Boot Camps: The Current State of the Art* (Washington, DC: National Institute of Justice, 1993).

164. See J. R. Dewan, "Regional Jail—The New Kid on the Block," *American Jails* (May/June 1995), pp. 70–72.

165. Tom Rosazza, "Jail Standards: Focus on Change," *American Jails* (November/December 1990), pp. 84–87.

166. American Correctional Association, *Manual of Standards for Adult Local Detention Facilities*, 3rd ed. (College Park, MD: ACA, 1991).

167. Ken Kerle, "National Sheriff's Association Jail Audit Review," *American Jails* (spring 1987), pp. 13–21.

168. Beck and Harrison, *Prisoners in 2000*, p. 7.

169. William J. Sabol, Heather Couture, and Paige M. Harrison, *Prisoners in 2006*, (Washington, DC: December 2007), from which much of the information in this section is taken.

170. Eric Bates, "Private Prisons: Over the Next Five Years Analysts Expect the Private Share of the Prison 'Market' to More Than Double," *The Nation*, Vol. 266, No. 1 (1998), pp. 11–18.

171. Gary Fields, "Privatized Prisons Pose Problems," *USA Today*, November 11, 1996, p. 3A.

172. Dale K. Sechrest and David Shichor, "Private Jails: Locking Down the Issues," *American Jails*, March/April 1997, pp. 9–18.

173. U.S. General Accounting Office, *Private and Public Prisons: Studies Comparing Operational Costs and/or Quality of Service* (Washington, DC: U.S. Government Printing Office, 1996).

174. Sechrest and Shichor, "Private Jails," p. 10.

175. James Austin and Garry Coventry, *Emerging Issues on Privatized Prisons* (Washington, DC: Bureau of Justice Statistics, 2001), p. ix.

176. For a more detailed discussion of this issue, see Austin and Coventry, *Emerging Issues on Privatized Prisons*.

177. *Richardson v. McKnight*, 117 S.Ct. 2100, 138 L.Ed.2d 540 (1997).

178. *Correctional Services Corporation* v. *Malesko*, 122 S.Ct. 515 (2001).

179. Ibid.

180. Quoted in Bates, "Private Prisons."

181. Judith C. Hackett et al., "Contracting for the Operation of Prisons and Jails," National Institute of Justice Research in Brief (Washington, DC: NIJ, June 1987), p. 6.

Chapter 14   Prison Life

i. Martha Stewart, *An Open Letter from Martha Stewart*, December 22, 2004, http://www. marthatalks.com (accessed July 15, 2007).

ii. Zebulon R. Brockway, *The Ideal of a True Prison System for a State* (1865).

iii. Jason DeParle, "The American Prison Nightmare," *New York Review of Books*, Vol. 54, No. 6 (April 12, 2007), http://www.nybooks.com/articles/20056 (accessed June 1, 2007).

1. Jason DeParle, "The American Prison Nightmare," *New York Review of Books*, Vol. 54, No. 6 (April 12, 2007), http://www.nybooks.com/articles/20056 (accessed June 1, 2007).

2. American Bar Association, Criminal Justice Section, *The State of Criminal Justice 2006* (Chicago, IL, ABA, 2007), p. 192.

3. Hans Reimer, "Socialization in the Prison Community," *Proceedings of the American Prison Association, 1937* (New York: American Prison Association, 1937), pp. 151–155.

4. Donald Clemmer, *The Prison Community* (Boston: Holt, Rinehart and Winston, 1940).

5. Gresham M. Sykes, *The Society of Captives: A Study of a Maximum Security Prison* (Princeton, NJ: Princeton University Press, 1958).

6. Richard A. Cloward et al., *Theoretical Studies in Social Organization of the Prison* (New York: Social Science Research Council, 1960).

7. Donald R. Cressey, ed., *The Prison: Studies in Institutional Organization and Change* (New York: Holt, Rinehart and Winston, 1961).

8. Lawrence Hazelrigg, ed., *Prison within Society: A Reader in Penology* (Garden City, NY: Anchor, 1969), preface.

9. Charles Stastny and Gabrielle Tyrnauer, *Who Rules the Joint? The Changing Political Culture of Maximum-Security Prisons in America* (Lexington, MA: Lexington Books, 1982), p. 131.

10. Erving Goffman, *Asylums: Essays on the Social Situation of Mental Patients and Other Inmates* (Garden City, NY: Anchor, 1961).

11. For a firsthand account of the prison experience, see Victor Hassine, *Life without Parole: Living in Prison Today* (Los Angeles: Roxbury, 1996); and W. Rideau and R. Wikberg, *Life Sentences: Rage and Survival behind Prison Bars* (New York: Times Books, 1992).

12. Gresham M. Sykes and Sheldon L. Messinger, "The Inmate Social System," in Richard A. Cloward et al., eds., *Theoretical Studies in Social Organization of the Prison* (New York: Social Science Research Council, 1960), pp. 5–19.

13. The concept of prisonization is generally attributed to Clemmer, *The Prison Community*, although Quaker penologists of the late eighteenth century were actively concerned with preventing "contamination" (the spread of criminal values) among prisoners.

14. Sykes and Messinger, "The Inmate Social System," p. 5.

15. Stanton Wheeler, "Socialization in Correctional Communities," *American Sociological Review*, Vol. 26 (October 1961), pp. 697–712.

16. Sykes, *The Society of Captives*, p. xiii.

17. John Irwin, *The Felon* (Englewood Cliffs, NJ: Prentice Hall, 1970).

18. Stastny and Tyrnauer, *Who Rules the Joint?* p. 135.

19. Ibid.

20. Sykes, *The Society of Captives*.

21. Clemmer, *The Prison Community*, pp. 294–296.

22. Irwin, *The Felon*.

23. Joseph L. Galloway, "Into the Heart of Darkness," *U.S. News* online, March 8, 1999, http://www.usnews.com/usnews/issue/990308/8pris.htm (accessed March 20, 2004).

24. Public Law 108-79.

25. Dee Halley, "The Prison Rape Elimination Act of 2003: Addressing Sexual Assault in Correctional Settings," *Corrections Today* (June 2005), pp. 30, 100.

26. Allen J. Beck and Timothy A. Hughes, *Sexual Violence Reported by Correctional Authorities, 2004* (Washington, DC: Bureau of Justice Statistics, 2005).

27. "Justice Department Issues Official Count of Prison Rapes," *Corrections Journal*, January 9, 2006, p. 7.

28. Halley, "The Prison Rape Elimination Act of 2003," p. 2.

29. Joanne Mariner, *No Escape: Male Rape in U.S. Prisons* (New York: Human Rights Watch, 2001), http://www.hrw.org/reports/2001/prison/report.html (accessed September 23, 2005).

30. Lee H. Bowker, *Prison Victimization* (New York: Elsevier, 1980).

31. Ibid., p. 42.

32. Ibid., p. 1.

33. Hans Toch, *Living in Prison: The Ecology of Survival* (New York: Free Press, 1977), p. 151.

34. Paige M. Harrison and Allen J. Beck, *Prisoners in 2006* (Washington, DC: Bureau of Justice Statistics, 2007).

35. Ibid.

36. Some of the information in this section comes from the American Correctional Association (ACA) Task Force on the Female Offender, *The Female Offender: What Does the Future Hold?* (Washington, DC: St. Mary's Press, 1990); and "The View from behind Bars," *Time* (fall 1990, special issue), pp. 20–22.

37. Much of the information and some of the wording in this section come from Barbara Bloom, Barbara Owen, and Stephanie Covington, *Gender-Responsive Strategies: Research, Practice, and Guiding Principles for Women Offenders* (Washington, DC: National Institute of Corrections, 2003).

38. Barbara Bloom, "Triple Jeopardy: Race, Class and Gender as Factors in Women's Imprisonment," paper presented at the American Society of Criminology annual meeting, San Diego, CA, 1997.

39. Joanne Belknap, *The Invisible Woman: Gender, Crime, and Justice* (Belmont, CA: Wadsworth, 2001).

40. C. W. Harlow, *Prior Abuse Reported by Inmates and Probationers* (Washington, DC: Bureau of Justice Statistics, 1999).

41. Ibid.

42. Ibid.

43. B. Owen and B. Bloom, "Profiling Women Prisoners: Findings from National Survey and California Sample," *Prison Journal*, Vol. 75, No. 2 (1995), pp. 165–185.

44. B. K. Jordan et al., "Prevalence of Psychiatric Disorders among Incarcerated Women," *Archives of General Psychiatry*, Vol. 53, No. 6 (1996), pp. 513–519.

45. A. Browne, B. Miller, and E. Maguin, "Prevalence and Severity of Lifetime Physical and Sexual Victimization among Incarcerated Women," *International Journal of Law and Psychiatry*, Vol. 22, Nos. 3–4 (1999), pp. 301–322.

46. A. Merlo and J. Pollock, *Women, Law, and Social Control* (Boston: Allyn and Bacon, 1995).

47. Center for Substance Abuse Treatment, *Substance Abuse Treatment for Incarcerated Offenders: Guide to Promising Practices* (Rockville, MD: U.S. Dept. of Health and Human Services, 1997).

48. Lawrence A. Greenfeld and Tracy L. Snell, *Women Offenders* (Washington, DC: Bureau of Justice Statistics, 1999).

49. Substance Abuse and Mental Health Services Administration, *National Household Survey on Drug Abuse: Population Estimates, 1992* (Rockville, MD: U.S. Department of Health and Human Services, 1993).

50. National Center on Addiction and Substance Abuse, *Behind Bars: Substance Abuse and America's Prison Population* (New York: Columbia University Press, 1998).

51. Quoted in "Report Cites Unfair Treatment of Female Drug Offenders," *Corrections Journal*, March 22, 2005, p. 4.

52. Lenora Lapidus et al., *Caught in the Net: The Impact of Drug Policies on Women and Families* (New York: American Civil Liberties Union, 2005).

53. L. Acoca, "Defusing the Time Bomb: Understanding and Meeting the Growing Health Care Needs of Incarcerated Women in America," *Crime and Delinquency*, Vol. 44, No. 1 (1998), pp. 49–70; and D. S. Young, "Contributing Factors to Poor Health among Incarcerated Women: A Conceptual Model," *Affilia*, Vol. 11, No. 4, (1996), pp. 440–461.

54. Acoca, "Defusing the Time Bomb."

55. A. L. Coker et al., "Childhood Forced Sex and Cervical Dysplasia among Women Prison Inmates," *Violence against Women*, Vol. 4, No. 5 (1998), pp. 595–608.

56. Allen J. Beck and Laura M. Maruschak, *Mental Health Treatment in State Prisons, 2000* (Washington, DC: Bureau of Justice Statistics, 2001).

57. L. A. Teplin et al., "Prevalence of Psychiatric Disorders among Incarcerated Women," *Archives of General Psychiatry*, Vol. 53, No. 6 (1996), pp. 505–512.

58. B. M. Veysey, *Specific Needs of Women Diagnosed with Mental Illnesses in U.S. Jails* (Delmar, NY: National GAINS Center, 1997); and M. Singer et al., "The Psychosocial Issues of Women Serving Time in Jail," *Social Work*, Vol. 40, No. 1 (1995), pp. 103–113.

59. Greenfeld and Snell, *Women Offenders;* and Mary K. Shilton, *Resources for Mother-Child Community Corrections* (Washington, DC: Bureau of Justice Assistance, 2001), p. 3.

60. Mary Jeanette Clement, "National Survey of Programs for Incarcerated Women," paper presented at the annual meeting of the Academy of Criminal Justice Sciences, Nashville, TN, March 1991, pp. 8–9.

61. B. Bloom and D. Steinhart, *Why Punish the Children? A Reappraisal of the Children of Incarcerated Mothers in America* (San Francisco: National Council on Crime and Delinquency, 1993).

62. Greenfeld and Snell, *Women Offenders.*

63. Ibid.

64. Ibid.

65. Barbara Bloom and Stephanie Covington, "Gendered Justice: Programming for Women in Correctional Settings," paper presented at the American Society of Criminology annual meeting, San Francisco, CA, November 2000, p. 11.

66. American Correctional Association, *The Female Offender.*

67. Marsha Clowers, "Dykes, Gangs, and Danger: Debunking Popular Myths about Maximum Security Life," *Journal of Criminal Justice and Popular Culture*, Vol. 9, No. 1 (2001), pp. 22–30.

68. D. Ward and G. Kassebaum, *Women's Prison: Sex and Social Structure* (London: Weidenfeld and Nicolson, 1966).

69. Esther Heffernan, *Making It in Prison: The Square, the Cool, and the Life* (London: Wiley-Interscience, 1972).

70. Rose Giallombardo, *Society of Women: A Study of Women's Prisons* (New York: John Wiley, 1966).

71. Ibid., p. 136.

72. For a summary of such studies (including some previously unpublished), see Lee H. Bowker, *Prisoner Subcultures* (Lexington, MA: Lexington Books, 1977), p. 86.

73. Giallombardo, *Society of Women*, p. 162.

74. Mary Koscheski and Christopher Hensley, "Inmate Homosexual Behavior in a Southern Female Correctional Facility," *American Journal of Criminal Justice*, Vol. 25, No. 2 (2001), pp. 269–277.

75. See, for example, Margie J. Phelps, "Sexual Misconduct between Staff and Inmates," *Corrections Technology and Management*, Vol. 12 (1999).

76. Heffernan, *Making It in Prison*.

77. Bowker, *Prison Victimization*, p. 53.

78. Giallombardo, *Society of Women*.

79. "Georgia Indictments Charge Abuse of Female Inmates," *USA Today*, November 16, 1992, p. 3A.

80. Ibid.

81. American Correctional Association, *The Female Offender*, p. 39.

82. American Correctional Association, "Correctional Officers in Adult Systems," in *Vital Statistics in Corrections* (Laurel, MD: ACA, 2000).

83. Kristen A. Hughes, *Justice Expenditure and Employment in the United States, 2003* (Washington, DC: Bureau of Justice Statistics, 2006); data table 5: Justice System Employment and Percent Distribution of Full-Time Equivalent Employment, by State and Types of Government.

84. Ibid. "Other" minorities round out the percentages to a total of 100%.

85. Ibid.

86. American Correctional Association, "Correctional Officers in Adult Systems."

87. Lucien X. Lombardo, *Guards Imprisoned: Correctional Officers at Work* (New York: Elsevier, 1981), pp. 22–36.

88. Leonard Morgenbesser, "NY State Law Prescribes Psychological Screening for CO Job Applicants," *Correctional Training* (winter 1983), p. 1.

89. "A Sophisticated Approach to Training Prison Guards," *Newsday*, August 12, 1982.

90. "Two Guards Taken Hostage by Inmates at Arizona Prison," *USA Today*, January 18, 2004, http://www.usatoday.com/news/nation/2004-01-18-prison-hostage_x.htm (accessed July 12, 2006).

91. Stastny and Tyrnauer, *Who Rules the Joint?* p. 1.

92. See Frederick Talbott, "Reporting from behind the Walls: Do It before the Siren Wails," *Quill* (February 1988), pp. 16–21.

93. "Ohio Prison Rebellion Is Ended," *USA Today*, April 22, 1993, p. 2A.

94. "Guards Hurt in Prison Riot," Associated Press, November 11, 2000.

95. "San Quentin Prison Riot Leaves 42 Injured," *USA Today*, August 9, 2005, p. 3A.

96. "Indiana Prison Riot Quelled," *USA Today*, April 24, 2007, http://www.usatoday.com/news/nation/2007-04-24-prison-riot_N.htm (accessed May 20, 2007).

97. See, for example, Reid H. Montgomery and Gordon A. Crews, *A History of Correctional Violence: An Examination of Reported Causes of Riots and Disturbances* (Lanham, MD: American Correctional Association, 1998); Bert Useem and Peter Kimball, *States of Siege: U.S. Prison Riots, 1971–1986* (New York: Oxford University Press, 1991); and Michael Braswell et al., *Prison Violence in America*, 2nd ed. (Cincinnati, OH: Anderson, 1994).

98. Robert S. Fong, Ronald E. Vogel, and S. Buentello, "Prison Gang Dynamics: A Look inside the Texas Department of Corrections," in A. V. Merlo and P. Menekos, eds., *Dilemmas and Directions in Corrections* (Cincinnati, OH: Anderson, 1992).

99. Ibid.

100. *Ruiz* v. *Estelle*, 503 F.Supp. 1265 (S.D. Tex., 1980).

101. Vernon Fox, "Prison Riots in a Democratic Society," *Police*, Vol. 26, No. 12 (December 1982), pp. 35–41.

102. Donald R. Cressey, "Adult Felons in Prison," in Lloyd E. Ohlin, ed., *Prisoners in America* (Englewood Cliffs, NJ: Prentice Hall, 1972), pp. 117–150.

103. The facts in this story are taken from *Hope* v. *Pelzer*, 122 S.Ct. 2508, 153 L.Ed.2d 666 (2002).

104. "Convictions Bar 3.9 Million from Voting," Associated Press wire service, September 22, 2000.

105. *Holt* v. *Sarver*, 309 F.Supp. 362 (E.D. Ark. 1970).

106. Vergil L. Williams, *Dictionary of American Penology: An Introduction* (Westport, CT: Greenwood Press, 1979), pp. 6–7.

107. Joint order issued in *McCray* v. *Sullivan*, Civ. Action 5620-69-H; *McCray* v. *Sullivan*, Civ. Action 6091-70-H; *White* v. *Commissioner of Alabama Board of Corrections*, Civ. Action 7094-72-H; *Pugh* v. *Sullivan, et al.*, Civ. Action 74-57N; and *James* v. *Wallace, et al.*, Civ. Action 74-203-N.

108. *Pell* v. *Procunier*, 417 U.S. 817, 822 (1974).

109. Ibid.

110. Title 42 U.S.C.A. 1997, Public Law 104-150.

111. Section 1997e.

112. American Correctional Association, *Legal Responsibility and Authority of Correctional Officers: A Handbook on Courts, Judicial Decisions and Constitutional Requirements* (College Park, MD: ACA, 1987), p. 8.

113. *Beard* v. *Banks*, U.S. Supreme Court, No. 04-1739 (decided June 28, 2006).

114. *Procunier* v. *Martinez*, 416 U.S. 396 (1974).

115. *McNamara* v. *Moody*, 606 F.2d 621 (5th Cir. 1979).

116. *Luparar* v. *Stoneman*, 382 F.Supp. 495 (D. Vt. 1974).

117. *Mallery* v. *Lewis*, 106 Idaho 227 (1983).

118. See, for example, *Pepperling* v. *Crist*, 678 F.2d 787 (9th Cir. 1981).

119. *Block* v. *Rutherford*, 486 U.S. 576 (1984).

120. *Overton* v. *Bazzetta*, 539 U.S. 126 (2003).

121. *Pell* v. *Procunier*, 417 U.S. 817, 822 (1974).

122. *Houchins* v. *KQED, Inc.*, 438 U.S. 11 (1978).

123. Ibid.

124. *Cruz* v. *Beto*, 405 U.S. 319 (1972).

125. *Aziz* v. *LeFevre*, 642 F.2d 1109 (2d Cir. 1981).

126. *Glasshofer* v. *Thornburg*, 514 F.Supp. 1242 (E.D. Pa. 1981).

127. See, for example, *Smith* v. *Coughlin*, 748 F.2d 783 (2d Cir. 1984).

128. *Campbell* v. *Cauthron*, 623 F.2d 503 (8th Cir. 1980).

129. *Smith* v. *Blackledge*, 451 F.2d 1201 (4th Cir. 1971).

130. *Dettmer* v. *Landon*, 617 F.Supp. 592, 594 (D.C. Va. 1985).

131. *Dettmer* v. *Landon*, 799 F.2d 929 (4th Cir. 1986).

132. *Lewellyn (L'Aquarius)* v. *State*, 592 P.2d 538 (Okla. Crim. App. 1979).

133. *Hill* v. *Blackwell*, 774 F.2d 338, 347 (8th Cir. 1985).

134. *Benning* v. *State*, No. 04-10979 (11th Cir. 2005).

135. *Cutter* v. *Wilkinson*, 544 U.S. 709 (2005).

136. For a Supreme Court review of the First Amendment right to petition the courts, see *McDonald* v. *Smith*, 105 S.Ct. 2787 (1985).

137. *Bounds* v. *Smith*, 430 U.S. 817, 821 (1977).

138. *Lewis* v. *Casey*, 516 U.S. 804 (1996).

139. *Johnson* v. *Avery*, 393 U.S. 483 (1968).

140. *Bounds* v. *Smith*, 430 U.S. 817, 821 (1977).

141. *Taylor* v. *Sterrett*, 532 F.2d 462 (5th Cir. 1976).

142. *In re Harrell*, 87 Cal. Rptr. 504, 470 P.2d 640 (1970).

143. *Guajardo* v. *Estelle*, 432 F.Supp. 1373 (S.D. Tex., 1977).

144. *O'Brien* v. *U.S.*, 386 U.S. 345 (1967); and *Weatherford* v. *Bursey*, 429 U.S. 545 (1977).

145. *U.S.* v. *Gouveia*, 104 S.Ct. 2292, 81 L.Ed.2d 146 (1984).

146. *Estelle* v. *Gamble*, 429 U.S. 97 (1976).

147. Ibid., pp. 105–106.

148. *Hudson* v. *McMillan*, 503 U.S. 1 (1992).

149. *Ruiz* v. *Estelle*, 503 F.Supp. 1265 (S.D. Tex. 1980); aff'd in part, rev'd in part, 679 F.2d 1115 (5th Cir. 1982); amended in part, vacated in part, 688 F.2d 266 (5th Cir. 1982); cert. denied, 460 U.S. 1042 (1983).

150. *Newman* v. *Alabama*, 349 F.Supp. 278 (M.D. Ala. 1972).

151. *In re Caulk*, 35 CrL. 2532 (New Hampshire S.Ct. 1984).

152. Ibid.

153. *Bee* v. *Greaves*, 744 F.2d 1387 (10th Cir. 1984).

154. *Washington* v. *Harper*, 494 U.S. 210 (1990).

155. *Pennsylvania Department of Corrections* v. *Yeskey*, 524 U.S. 206, 209 (1998).

156. U.S. Code, Title 42, Section 12132.

157. *U.S.* v. *Georgia*, U.S. Supreme Court, No. 04-1203 (decided January 10, 2006); and *Goodman* v. *Georgia*, U.S. Supreme Court, No. 04-1236 (decided January 10, 2006).

158. *Holt* v. *Sarver*, 309 F.Supp. 362 (E.D. Ark. 1970).

159. *Farmer* v. *Brennan*, 114 S.Ct. 1970, 128 L.Ed.2d 811 (1994).

160. Ibid.

161. *Helling* v. *McKinney*, 113 S.Ct. 2475, 125 L.Ed.2d 22 (1993).

162. *U.S.* v. *Ready*, 574 F.2d 1009 (10th Cir. 1978).

163. *Katz* v. *U.S.*, 389 U.S. 347, 88 S.Ct. 507, 19 L.Ed.2d 576 (1967).

164. *Hudson* v. *Palmer*, 468 U.S. 517 (1984).

165. *Block* v. *Rutherford*, 104 S.Ct. 3227, 3234-35 (1984).

166. *U.S.* v. *Lilly*, 576 F.2d 1240 (5th Cir. 1978).

167. *Palmer* v. *Hudson*, 697 F.2d 1220 (4th Cir. 1983).

168. *Jones* v. *North Carolina Prisoners' Labor Union*, 433 U.S. 119, 53 L.Ed.2d 629, 641 (1977).

169. *Wolff* v. *McDonnell*, 94 S.Ct. 2963 (1974).

170. Ibid.

171. Ibid.

172. *Ponte* v. *Real*, 471 U.S. 491, 105 S.Ct. 2192, 85 L.Ed.2d 553 (1985).

173. *Vitek* v. *Jones*, 445 U.S. 480 (1980).

174. American Correctional Association, Standard 2-4346. See ACA, *Legal Responsibility and Authority of Correctional Officers*, p. 49.

175. *Wilson* v. *Seiter et al.*, 501 U.S. 294 (1991).

176. *Estelle* v. *Gamble*, 429 U.S. 97, 106 (1976).

177. *Sandin* v. *Conner*, 63 U.S.L.W. 4601 (1995).

178. *Wolff* v. *McDonnell*, 94 S.Ct. 2963 (1974).

179. *Hewitt* v. *Helms*, 459 U.S. 460 (1983).

180. Laurie Asseo, "Inmate Lawsuits," Associated Press wire service, May 24, 1996; and Bureau of Justice Statistics, "State and Federal Prisoners Filed 68,235 Petitions in U.S. Courts in 1996," press release, October 29, 1997.

181. See, for example, "The Great Prison Pastime," *20/20*, ABC News, September 24, 1993, which is part of the video library available to instructors using this textbook.

182. Ibid.

183. Asseo, "Inmate Lawsuits."

184. Public Law 104-134. Although the PLRA was signed into law on April 26, 1996, and is frequently referred to as the Prison Litigation Reform Act of 1996, the official name of the act is the Prison Litigation Reform Act of 1995.

185. *Edwards* v. *Balisok*, 520 U.S. 641 (1997).

186. American Civil Liberties Union (ACLU), *Prisoners' Rights—An ACLU Position Paper*, fall 1999, http://www.aclu.org/library/PrisonerRights.pdf (accessed March 5, 2006).

187. *Booth* v. *Churner*, 532 U.S. 731 (2001).

188. *Porter* v. *Nussle*, 534 U.S. 516 (2002).

189. *Woodford* v. *Ngo*, U.S. Supreme Court, No. 05-416 (decided June 22, 2006).

190. John Scalia, *Prisoner Petitions Filed in U.S. District Courts, 2000, with Trends 1980–2000* (Washington, DC: Bureau of Justice Statistics, 2002).

191. F. Cheesman, R. Hanson, and B. Ostrom, *A Tale of Two Laws Revisited: Investigating the Impact of the Prison Litigation Reform Act and the Antiterrorism and Effective Death Penalty Act* (Williamsburg, VA: National Center for State Courts, 2004).

192. ACLU, *Prisoners' Rights*.

193. Laura M. Maruschak, *HIV in Prisons, 2005* (Washington, DC: Bureau of Justice Statistics, 2007).

194. Ibid., p. 1.

195. Dennis Cauchon, "AIDS in Prison: Locked Up and Locked Out," *USA Today*, March 31, 1995, p. 6A.

196. Maruschak, *HIV in Prisons, 2004*, p. 16.

197. Centers for Disease Control and Prevention, "HIV Transmission among Male Inmates in a State Prison System: Georgia, 1992–2005," *Morbidity and Mortality Weekly Report*, Vol. 55, No. 15 (April 21, 2006), pp. 421–426.

198. Theodore M. Hammett, *AIDS in Correctional Facilities: Issues and Options*, 3rd ed. (Washington, DC: National Institute of Justice, 1988), p. 37.

199. At the time of this writing, California, Massachusetts, New York, Wisconsin, and the District of Columbia were among those jurisdictions.

200. "Mississippi Eases Policy of Separating Inmates with HIV," *Corrections Journal*, Vol. 5, No. 6 (2001), p. 5.

201. Cauchon, "AIDS in Prison."

202. See "Court Allows Restriction on HIV-Positive Inmates," *Criminal Justice Newsletter*, Vol. 25, No. 23 (December 1, 1994), pp. 2–3.

203. Ibid.

204. Darrell Bryan, "Inmates, HIV, and the Constitutional Right to Privacy: AIDS in Prison Facilities," *Corrections Compendium*, Vol. 19, No. 9 (September 1994), pp. 1–3.

205. Alexandria Sage, "Doctor Shot at Los Angeles-Area Hospital," Associated Press, September 20, 2003.

206. Lincoln J. Fry, "The Older Prison Inmate: A Profile," *Justice Professional*, Vol. 2, No. 1 (spring 1987), pp. 1–12.

207. Harrison and Beck, *Prisoners in 2006*.

208. Bureau of Justice Statistics, "The Nation's Prison Population Grew by 60,000 Inmates Last Year," press release, August 15, 1999.

209. Jim Krane, "Demographic Revolution Rocks U.S. Prisons," APB online, April 12, 1999, http://www.apbonline.com/safestreets/oldprisoners/mainpris0412.html (accessed January 5, 2006).

210. Ronald Wikbert and Burk Foster, "The Longtermers: Louisiana's Longest Serving Inmates and Why They've Stayed So Long," paper presented at the annual meeting of the Academy of Criminal Justice Sciences, Washington, DC, 1989, p. 51.

211. *Disability Advocates, Inc.* v. *New York State Office of Mental Health*, Complaint No. 02 CV 4002 (SDNY, May 28, 2002).

212. Allen J. Beck and Laura M. Maruschak, *Mental Health Treatment in State Prisons, 2000*, Bureau of Justice Statistics Special Report (Washington, DC: BJS, 2001), p. 1, from which most of the information in this paragraph and the next is derived.

213. *Washington* v. *Harper*, 494 U.S. 210 (1990).

214. Paula M. Ditton, *Mental Health and Treatment of Inmates and Probationers* (Washington, DC: Bureau of Justice Statistics, 1999).

215. Robert O. Lampert, "The Mentally Retarded Offender in Prison," *Justice Professional*, Vol. 2, No. 1 (spring 1987), p. 61.

216. Ibid., p. 64.

217. George C. Denkowski and Kathryn M. Denkowski, "The Mentally Retarded Offender in the State Prison System: Identification, Prevalence, Adjustment, and Rehabilitation," *Criminal Justice and Behavior*, Vol. 12 (1985), pp. 55–75.

218. "Opening Session: Kerik Emphasizes the Importance of Corrections' Protective Role for the Country," http://www.aca.org/conferences/Winter05/updates05.asp (accessed July 22, 2007).

219. Jess Maghan, "Intelligence-Led Penology: Management of Crime Information Obtained from Incarcerated Persons," paper presented at the Investigation of Crime World Conference, 2001, p. 6.

220. Keith Martin, *Corrections Prepares for Terrorism*, Corrections Connection News Network, January 21, 2002, http://www.corrections.com (accessed June 15, 2005).

221. Quoted in Meghan Mandeville, "Information Sharing Becomes Crucial to Battling Terrorism behind Bars," Corrections.com, December 8, 2003, http://database.corrections.com/news/results2. asp?ID_8988 (accessed July 11, 2005).

222. "FBI: Al-Qaida Recruiting in U.S. Prisons," United Press International, January 7, 2004, http://database.corrections.com/news/results2.asp?ID_9148 (accessed July 1, 2005).

223. Institute for the Study of Violent Groups, "Land of Wahhabism," *Crime and Justice International*, March/April 2005, p. 43.

224. Office of the Inspector General, *A Review of the Federal Bureau of Prisons' Selection of Muslim Religious Services Providers* (Washington, DC: U.S. Dept. of Justice, 2004).

225. Ibid., p. 8.

226. Ibid.

227. Federal Bureau of Prisons, *State of the Bureau, 2004* (Washington, DC: BOP, 2005).

228. Associated Press, "Attorney, Three Others Indicted for Alleged 'Support of Terrorism,'" *Dallas Morning News*, April 9, 2002, http://www.dallasnews.com/latestnews/stories/040902dnnatterrorindictment.66910.html (accessed July 25, 2005).

229. The questions in this Web Quest were adapted from "Building Your Career in Corrections," *Keeper's Voice*, Vol. 18, No. 1, http://www.oict.org/public/toc.efm?series-KV (accessed February 20, 2002).

Chapter 15 Juvenile Justice

i. Tina Chiu and Sara Mogulescu, *Changing the Status Quo for Status Offenders: New York State's Efforts to Support Troubled Teens* (New York: Vera Institute of Justice, 2005).

ii. Jeffrey A. Butts and Ojmarrh Mitchell, "Brick by Brick: Dismantling the Border between Juvenile and Adult Justice," in Phyllis McDonald and Janice Munsterman, eds., *Criminal Justice 2000, Vol. 2: Boundary Changes in Criminal Justice Organizations* (Washington, DC: National Institute of Justice, 2000), pp. 167–213.

iii. Jeffrey A. Butts and Adele V. Harrell, *Delinquents or Criminals: Policy Options for Young Criminals* (Washington, DC: Urban Institute, 1998).

iv. Howard N. Snyder and Melissa Sickmund, *Juvenile Offenders and Victims: 2006 National Report* (Washington, DC: Office of Juvenile Justice and Delinquency Prevention, 2006).

v. John W. Whitehead, *The Stealing of America* (Wheaton, IL: Crossway Books, 1983).

1. Elliot Grossman, "Toughlove Parents Scared," *Allentown (PA) Morning Call*, March 7, 1995, p. B1.

2. Many of the details for this story come from David Karp, "Boy, 13, Found Guilty of Rape," *St. Petersburg (FL) Times*, September 8, 2001.

3. Ibid.

4. "Judge Sentences 13-Year-Old to 15 Years for Daytime Park Rape," Associated Press, November 9, 2001.

5. "9-Year-Old Pleads Guilty to Manslaughter," Associated Press, October 8, 2005, http://www.msnbc.com/id/9626361 (accessed May 20, 2006).

6. "Florida Girls Charged with Attempting to Drown Classmate," Associated Press, March 14, 2001.

7. Office of Juvenile Justice and Delinquency Prevention, *OJJDP Research, 2000* (Washington, DC: OJJDP, 2001).

8. Federal Bureau of Investigation, *Crime in the United States, 2006* (Washington, DC: U.S. Dept. of Justice, 2007).

9. Ibid.; and U.S. Census Bureau, *Age, 2000: A Census 2000 Brief* (Washington, DC: U.S. Census Bureau, 2001), http://www.census.gov/prod/2001pubs/c2kbr01-12.pdf (accessed January 2, 2005).

10. The term *juvenile* refers to people under 18 years of age.

11. H. Snyder, C. Puzzanchera, and W. Kang, *Easy Access to FBI Arrest Statistics, 1994–2002* (Washington, DC: Office of Juvenile Justice and Delinquency Prevention, 2005), http://ojjdp.ncjrs.org/ojstatbb/ezaucr (accessed November 11, 2007).

12. A reform movement, now under way, may soon lead to changes in the way juvenile records are handled.

13. For an excellent review of the handling of juveniles through history, see Wiley B. Sanders, ed., *Juvenile Offenders for a Thousand Years* (Chapel Hill: University of North Carolina Press, 1970).

14. Robert M. Mennel, *Thorns and Thistles: Juvenile Delinquents in the United States, 1925–1940* (Hanover, NH: University Press of New England, 1973).

15. Thomas A. Johnson, *Introduction to the Juvenile Justice System* (St. Paul, MN: West, 1975), p. 1.

16. Charles E. Springer, *Justice for Juveniles*, 2nd ed. (Washington, DC: Office of Juvenile Justice and Delinquency Prevention, 1987), p. 18.

17. Ibid., p. 50.

18. See Sanford Fox, "Juvenile Justice Reform: An Historical Perspective," in Sanford Fox, ed., *Modern Juvenile Justice: Cases and Materials* (St. Paul, MN: West, 1972), pp. 15–48.

19. *Ex parte Crouse*, 4 Whart. 9 (Pa., 1838).

20. Fox, "Juvenile Justice Reform," p. 27.

21. Anthony Platt, *The Child Savers: The Invention of Delinquency*, 2nd ed. (Chicago, IL: University of Chicago Press, 1977).

22. Ibid., p. 29.

23. *People ex rel. O'Connell* v. *Turner*, 55 Ill. 280, 8 Am. Rep. 645 (1870).

24. Johnson, *Introduction to the Juvenile Justice System*, p. 3.

25. Ibid.

26. Ibid.

27. Fox, "Juvenile Justice Reform," p. 47.

28. Ibid., p. 5.

29. Principles adapted from Robert G. Caldwell, "The Juvenile Court: Its Development and Some Major Problems," in Rose Giallombardo, ed., *Juvenile Delinquency: A Book of Readings* (New York: John Wiley, 1966), p. 358.

30. See, for example, *Haley* v. *Ohio*, 332 U.S. 596 (1948).

31. *Kent* v. *U.S.*, 383 U.S. 541 (1966).

32. *In re Gault*, 387 U.S. 1 (1967).

33. *In re Winship*, 397 U.S. 358 (1970).

34. *McKeiver* v. *Pennsylvania*, 403 U.S. 528 (1971).

35. *Breed* v. *Jones*, 421 U.S. 519 (1975).

36. *Schall* v. *Martin*, 467 U.S. 253 (1984).

37. *Thompson* v. *Oklahoma*, 487 U.S. 815, 818–838 (1988).

38. *Stanford* v. *Kentucky*, 492 U.S. 361 (1989).

39. Ibid., at 370–371.

40. *Roper* v. *Simmons*, 543 U.S. 551 (2005).

41. Death Penalty Information Center, "Juvenile Offenders Currently on Death Row, or Executed, by State," http://www.deathpenaltyinfo.org/article.php?scid527&did5882 (accessed September 10, 2007).

42. "Drug Bill Includes Extension of OJJDP, with Many Changes," *Criminal Justice Newsletter*, Vol. 19, No. 22 (November 15, 1988), p. 4.

43. The Formula Grants Program supports state and local delinquency prevention and intervention efforts and juvenile justice system improvements. Through this program, OJJDP provides funds directly to states, territories, and the District of Columbia to help them implement comprehensive state juvenile justice plans based on detailed studies of needs in their jurisdictions. The Formula Grants Program is authorized under the JJDP Act of 2002 (U.S. Code, Title 42, Section 5601 *et seq.*).

44. See "OJJDP Eases Rules on Juvenile Confinement," *Corrections Compendium* (November 1996), p. 25.

45. The Juvenile Justice and Delinquency Prevention Act of 2002 (Public Law 107-273).

46. Howard N. Snyder and Melissa Sickmund, *Juvenile Offenders and Victims: 2006 National Report* (Washington, DC: Office of Juvenile Justice and Delinquincy Prevention, 2006).

47. Ibid, p. 97.

48. *Fare* v. *Michael C.*, 442 U.S. 707 (1979).

49. *California* v. *Prysock*, 453 U.S. 355 (1981).

50. *New Jersey* v. *T.L.O.*, 105 S.Ct. 733 (1985).

51. Charles Puzzanchera et al., *Juvenile Court Statistics, 2000* (Washington, DC: Office of Juvenile Justice and Delinquency Prevention, 2005), p. 52.

52. National Center for Juvenile Justice, *State Juvenile Justice Profiles*, http://www.ncjj. org/stateprofiles (accessed August 10, 2006).

53. Charles M. Puzzanchera, *Delinquency Cases Waived to Criminal Court, 1990–1999* (Washington, DC: Office of Juvenile Justice and Delinquency Prevention, 2003).

54. "Young Killer Lionel Tate Held in Pizza Delivery Robbery," Associated Press, May 24, 2005.

55. Terry Aguayo, "Youth Who Killed at 12 Will Return to Prison, But Not for Life," *New York Times*, March 2, 2006, http://www.nytimes.com/2006/03/02/national/02tate.html (accessed May 20, 2006).

56. "Lionel Tate's FHP Mother Reprimanded for Gun Lapse," CBS4.com (Ft. Lauderdale, FL), March 28, 2006, http://lionel-tate-news.newslib.com/story/201-3137189 (accessed May 20, 2006).

57. Brian Skoloff, "Lionel Tate Sentenced to 30 Years," *Ledger Online*, May 18, 2006, http://www.theledger.com/apps/ pbcs.dll/article?AID=/20060518/BREAKING/60518010 (accessed May 22, 2006).

58. Adapted from Peter Greenwood, *Juvenile Offenders*, National Institute of Justice Crime File Series Study Guide (Washington, DC: NIJ, n.d.).

59. Bureau of Justice Statistics, *Report to the Nation on Crime and Justice*, 2nd ed. (Washington, DC: U.S. Government Printing Office, 1988), p. 78.

60. Ibid.

61. Ibid.

62. Puzzanchera et al., *Juvenile Court Statistics, 2000*, p. 52.

63. Ibid.

64. Ibid.

65. *McKeiver* v. *Pennsylvania*, 403 U.S. 528 (1971).

66. Some states, like West Virginia, do provide juveniles with a statutory right to trial.

67. Other early peer juries in juvenile courts began operating in Denver, Colorado; Duluth, Minnesota; Deerfield, Illinois; Thompkins County, New York; and Spanish Fork City, Utah, at about the same time. See Philip Reichel and Carole Seyfrit, "A Peer Jury in the Juvenile Court," *Crime and Delinquency*, Vol. 30, No. 3 (July 1984), pp. 423–438.

68. Ibid.

69. Tracy M. Godwin, *A Guide for Implementing Teen Court Programs* (Washington, DC: Office of Juvenile Justice and Delinquency Prevention, 1996).

70. Charles M. Puzzanchera, *Juvenile Delinquency Probation Caseload, 1990–1999* (Washington, DC: Office of Juvenile Justice and Delinquency Prevention, 1999).

71. Puzzanchera et al., *Juvenile Court Statistics, 2000*, p. 52.

72. Bethany Gardner, "Successful Pennsylvania School-Based Probation Expands," *Corrections Compendium*, Vol. 19, No. 8 (August 1994), pp. 1–3.

73. Puzzanchera, *Juvenile Delinquency Probation Caseload, 1990–1999*, p. 1.

74. Melissa Sickmund, T. J. Sladky, and Wei Kang, *Census of Juveniles in Residential Placement Databook*, 2004, http://www.ojjdp.ncjrs.org/ojstatbb/cjrp (accessed July 5, 2005).

75. Office of Juvenile Justice and Delinquency Prevention, *Census of Juveniles in Residential Placement, 2001* (Washington, DC: OJJDP, 2005).

76. See, for example, Blair B. Bourque et al., "Boot Camps for Juvenile Offenders: An Implementation Evaluation of Three Demonstration Programs," National Institute of Justice Research in Brief (Washington, DC: NIJ, 1996).

77. Melissa Sickmund, *Juvenile Offenders in Residential Placement, 1997* (Washington, DC: Office of Juvenile Justice and Delinquency Prevention, 2002), p. 110.

78. Ibid.

79. Ibid.

80. Ibid.

81. Sickmund, Sladky, and Kang, *Census of Juveniles in Residential Placement Databook.*

82. Ibid.

83. "Juvenile Offenders in Residential Placement, 1997," Office of Juvenile Justice and Delinquency Prevention Fact Sheet (Washington, DC: OJJDP, 1999).

84. Dale G. Parent et al., *Conditions of Confinement: Juvenile Detention and Corrections Facilities* (Washington, DC: Office of Juvenile Justice and Delinquency Prevention, 1994).

85. *Corrections Compendium* (December 1993), p. 14.

86. Ibid.

87. Ibid., p. 22.

88. Office of Juvenile Justice and Delinquency Prevention, *National Juvenile Custody Trends, 1978–1989* (Washington, DC: U.S. Dept. of Justice, 1992), p. 2.

89. Section 59 of the Uniform Juvenile Court Act recommends the granting of a right to appeal for juveniles (National Conference of Commissioners on Uniform State Laws, Uniform Juvenile Court Act, 1968).

90. Mark Memmott, "Release of Ark. School Killer Raises Questions of Justice," *USA Today*, August 12, 2005, p. 1A.

91. Patricia Torbet et al., *State Responses to Serious and Violent Juvenile Crime* (Washington, DC: Office of Juvenile Justice and Delinquency Prevention, 1996).

92. Snyder and Sickmund, *Juvenile Offenders and Victims: 2006 National Report*, pp. 96–97.

93. Jeffrey A. Butts and Ojmarrh Mitchell, "Brick by Brick: Dismantling the Border between Juvenile and Adult Justice," in Phyllis McDonald and Janice Munsterman, eds., *Criminal Justice 2000, Vol. 2: Boundary Changes in Criminal Justice Organizations* (Washington, DC: National Institute of Justice, 2000), p. 207.

94. Ibid., p. 167.

95. Ibid., pp. 167–213.

96. Barry C. Feld, "Abolish the Juvenile Court: Youthfulness, Criminal Responsibility, and Sentencing Policy," *Journal of Criminal Law and Criminology* (winter 1998).

97. Cindy S. Lederman, "The Juvenile Court: Putting Research to Work for Prevention," *Juvenile Justice Bulletin,* Vol. 6, No. 2 (Washington, DC: Office of Juvenile Justice and Delinquency Prevention, 1999), p. 23.

98. Public Law 107-273.

99. Activities funded under the legislation fall under Juvenile Accountability Block Grants (JABG) program.

100. See Cheryl Andrews and Lynn Marble, "Changes to OJJDP's Juvenile Accountability Program," *Juvenile Justice Bulletin* (Washington, DC: Office of Juvenile Justice and Delinquency Prevention, 2003).

Chapter 16   Drugs and Crime

i. Bureau of Justice Statistics, *Drugs, Crime, and the Justice System* (Washington, DC: BJS, 1992), p. 20.

ii. Jimmy Breslin, "Crack," *Playboy*, December 1988, pp. 108–110, 210–215.

iii. Bureau of Justice Statistics, *Drugs, Crime, and the Justice System*, p. 21.

iv. Ibid.

v. U.S. Department of Treasury, *2000–2005 Strategic Plan* (Washington, DC: U.S. Government Printing Office, 2000), p. 1.

1. Gary E. Johnson, "Bad Investment," MotherJones.com, July 10, 2001, http://www.motherjones. com/prisons/investment.html (accessed January 30, 2006).

2. "New Drug Czar Targets 'Unacceptably High' Rates of Drug Use among Students," Office of National Drug Control Policy press release, December 19, 2001, http://www.whitehousedrugpolicy. gov/news/press01/121901.html (accessed February 3, 2005).

3. Peter D. Hart Research Associates, *Drugs and Crime across America: Police Chiefs Speak Out—A National Survey among Chiefs of Police* (Washington, DC: Police Foundation, December 2004).

4. National Association of Drug Court Professionals, *The Facts: Facts on Drug Courts* (Alexandria, VA: NADCP, 2001).

5. Sentencing Project, *The Federal Prison Population: A Statistical Analysis* (Washington, DC: Sentencing Project, 2005).

6. Paige M. Harrison and Allen J. Beck, *Prisoners in 2003* (Washington, DC: Bureau of Justice Statistics, 2004). See also Barbara Owen, "Women in Prison," Drug Policy Alliance, 2005, http://www.drugpolicy.org/communities/ women/womeninprison/ (accessed May 14, 2005).

7. Peter D. Hart Research Associates, *Drugs and Crime across America*, pp. 1–2.

8. Ibid.

9. The term *recreational user* is well established in the literature of drug abuse. Unfortunately, it tends to minimize the seriousness of drug abuse by according the abuse of even hard drugs the status of a hobby.

10. Howard Becker, *Outsiders: Studies in the Sociology of Deviance* (New York: Free Press, 1963).

11. Jay Tokasz, "Eight of 11 People in Car Die in Crash," *USA Today*, June 20, 1995, p. 2A.

12. In most states, individuals may also be arrested for driving under the influence of other drugs and controlled substances, including prescription medicines.

13. Fiscal year 2001 Transportation Appropriations Bill (H.R. 4475), signed by the president on October 23, 2000.

14. "Drunk Driving Limit Lowered," *Lawyers Weekly USA*, October 16, 2000.

15. Federal Bureau of Investigation, *Crime in the United States, 2006* (Washington, DC: U.S. Dept. of Justice, 2007).

16. James B. Jacobs, *Drinking and Crime*, National Institute of Justice Crime File Series Study Guide (Washington, DC: NIJ, n.d.).

17. Rajesh Subramanian, *Alcohol Involvement in Fatal Motor Vehicle Traffic Crashes, 2003* (Washington, DC: National Highway Traffic Safety Administration, 2005).

18. Ibid.

19. FBI, *Crime in the United States, 2006.*

20. Bureau of Justice Statistics, *Report to the Nation on Crime and Justice*, 2nd ed. (Washington, DC: U.S. Government Printing Office, 1988), p. 50.

21. Jeffrey A. Roth, "Psychoactive Substances and Violence," National Institute of Justice Research in Brief (Washington, DC: NIJ, February 1994), p. 1.

22. Christopher J. Mumola, *Substance Abuse and Treatment, State and Federal Prisoners, 1997* (Washington, DC: Bureau of Justice Statistics, 1999).

23. Ibid.

24. Howard Abadinsky, *Drug Abuse: An Introduction* (Chicago, IL: Nelson-Hall, 1989), p. 32.

25. Charles E. Terry and Mildred Pellens, *The Opium Problem* (New York: Committee on Drug Addiction, 1928).

26. Ibid.

27. Office of National Drug Control Policy, *Heroin*, ONDCP Fact Sheet (Washington, DC: ONDCP, 2003), p. 1.

28. Terry and Pellens, *The Opium Problem*, p. 76.

29. David Musto, *The American Disease: Origins of Narcotic Control* (New Haven, CT: Yale University Press, 1973).

30. Becker, *Outsiders*.

31. Franklin E. Zimring and Gordon Hawkins, *The Search for Rational Drug Control* (New York: Cambridge University Press, 1992).

32. Ibid., p. 9.

33. President's Commission on Organized Crime, *Organized Crime Today* (Washington, DC: U.S. Government Printing Office, 1986).

34. *Webb* v. *U.S.*, 249 U.S. 96 (1919).

35. Michael D. Lyman and Gary W. Potter, *Drugs in Society: Causes, Concepts, and Control* (Cincinnati, OH: Anderson, 1991), p. 359.

36. Drug Enforcement Administration, *Drug Enforcement: The Early Years* (Washington, DC: DEA, 1980), p. 41.

37. White House Conference on Drug Abuse, *Commission Report* (Washington, DC: U.S. Government Printing Office, 1963).

38. For a good summary of the law, see Drug Enforcement Administration, *Drugs of Abuse* (Washington, DC: U.S. Government Printing Office, 1997).

39. Drug Enforcement Administration, *Drug Enforcement Briefing Book* (Washington, DC: DEA, n.d.), p. 3.

40. A number of states now recognize that marijuana may be useful in the treatment of nausea associated with cancer chemotherapy, glaucoma, and other medical conditions.

41. DEA, *Drug Enforcement Briefing Book*, p. 3.

42. Ibid.

43. Ibid., p. 4.

44. Ibid.

45. DEA, *Drugs of Abuse*.

46. Ibid.

47. Anti-Drug Abuse Act of 1988, P.L. 100-690, Section 5251.

48. This provision became effective on September 1, 1989.

49. "Congress Gives Final OK to Major Antidrug Bill," *Criminal Justice Newsletter*, Vol. 19, No. 21 (November 1, 1988), pp. 1–4.

50. The U.S. Supreme Court upheld that legislation in the 2002 case of *Department of Housing and Urban Development* v. *Rucker*, 122 S.Ct. 1230, 152 L.Ed.2d 258 (2002).

51. "Congress Gives Final OK to Major Antidrug Bill," p. 2.

52. "Drug Lord Sentenced to Death," *USA Today*, May 15, 1991, p. 3A.

53. Ibid.

54. Public Laws 101-647, 103-322, 105-20, and 109-177.

55. USA PATRIOT Improvement and Reauthorization Act of 2005 (Public Law 109-177). The act was signed into law by President George W. Bush on March 9, 2006.

56. *California* v. *Greenwood*, 486 U.S. 35, 108 S.Ct. 1625 (1988).

57. Ibid.

58. *Abel* v. *U.S.*, 363 U.S. 217 (1960).

59. *Oliver* v. *U.S.*, 466 U.S. 170 (1984).

60. *Hester* v. *U.S.*, 265 U.S. 57, 44 S.Ct. 445 (1924).

61. *U.S.* v. *Dunn*, 480 U.S. 294, 107 S.Ct. 1134 (1987).

62. *California* v. *Ciraolo*, 476 U.S. 207, 106 S.Ct. 1809 (1986).

63. *Florida* v. *Riley*, 488 U.S. 445, 109 S.Ct. 693, 102 L.Ed.2d 835 (1989).

64. Substance Abuse and Mental Health Services Administration, *2006 National Survey on Drug Use and Health: National Results* (Rockville, MD; Office of Applied Studies, NHSDA, 2007).

65. ONDCP, *Heroin*, p. 1.

66. Office of National Drug Control Policy, *General Counterdrug Intelligence Plan* (Washington, DC: ONDCP, 2000), http://www.fas.org/irp/ops/le/docs/gcip/index.html.

67. Information in this section comes from the National Drug Intelligence Center, http://www.usdoj.gov/ndic.

68. Office of National Drug Control Policy, *Pulse Check: National Trends in Drug Abuse—Marijuana* (Washington, DC: ONDCP, 2002), http://www.whitehousedrugpolicy.gov/publications/drugfact/pulsechk/nov02/marijuana.html (accessed August 4, 2003).

69. See Anita Manning and Andrea Stone, "How States Will Face Regulating Marijuana as Medicine," *USA Today*, November 7, 1996, p. 3D.

70. *U.S.* v. *Oakland Cannabis Buyers' Cooperative*, 532 U.S. 483 (2001).

71. Ibid., syllabus.

72. *Gonzales* v. *Raich*, 545 U.S. 1 (2005).

73. Department of Health and Human Services, "Trends in Annual Prevalence of Use of Various Drugs, for Eighth, Tenth, and Twelfth Graders," http://www.monitoringthefuture.org/data/04data/pr04t2.pdf (accessed May 30, 2005).

74. National Narcotics Intelligence Consumers Committee, *The NNICC Report, 1998* (Washington, DC: Drug Enforcement Administration, 2000), preface.

75. Ibid.

76. Ibid.

77. ONDCP, *Pulse Check*.

78. NNICC, *The NNICC Report, 1998*.

79. Ibid.

80. Ibid.

81. Drug Enforcement Administration, *Crack Cocaine Drug Intelligence Report, 1994* (Washington, DC: DEA, 1995).

82. National Institute of Justice, JUSTINFO Online (e-mail version), July 5, 1995.

83. NNICC, *The NNICC Report, 1998*.

84. Sam Vincent Meddis, "Arrests 'Last Rites' for Cali Cartel," *USA Today*, August 7, 1995, p. 1A.

85. DEA, *Drugs of Abuse*, p. 14.

86. Ibid., p. 12.

87. Ibid., p. 15.

88. Office of National Drug Control Policy, *The National Drug Control Strategy: Executive Summary* (Washington, DC: ONDCP, 1995), p. 13.

89. DEA, *Drugs of Abuse.*

90. NNICC, *The NNICC Report, 1998.*

91. National Institute of Justice, JUSTINFO Online, July 5, 1995.

92. ONDCP, *Pulse Check.*

93. Ibid.

94. Much of the information in this section comes from the National Institute on Drug Abuse's website at http://www.nida.nih.gov (accessed July 4, 2007).

95. National Institute on Drug Abuse, *NIDA InfoFacts: Methamphetamine,* http://www.nida.nih.gov/Infofacts/methamphetamine.html (accessed May 9, 2007).

96. Donna Leinwand, "DEA Sees Flavored Meth Use," *USA Today,* March 26, 2007, p. 3A.

97. Much of the information on club drugs in this section comes from Drug Enforcement Administration, "An Overview of Club Drugs," *Drug Intelligence Brief, February 2000,* http://www.usdoj.gov/dea/pubs/intel/20005intellbrief.pdf (accessed March 2, 2007).

98. "'Rophies' Reported Spreading Quickly throughout the South," *Drug Enforcement Report,* June 23, 1995, pp. 1–5.

99. Public Law 104-305.

100. Sentencing enhancement information in this section comes from the congressional testimony of Asa Hutchinson, administrator of the Drug Enforcement Administration, before the Senate Caucus on International Narcotics Control, December 4, 2001, http://www.usdoj.gov/dea/pubs/cngrtest/ct120401.html (accessed February 3, 2006).

101. Substance Abuse and Mental Health Services Administration, *The DAWN Report,* http://www.samhsa.gov/oas/dawn.htm (accessed March 10, 2007).

102. Substance Abuse and Mental Health Services Administration, *Drug Abuse Warning Network 2005: National Estimates of Drug-Related Emergency Department Visits* (Washington, DC: U.S. Dept. of Health and Human Services, December 2007), p. 19.

103. Public Law 106-310.

104. DEA, "An Overview of Club Drugs," from which some of the wording in this section is taken.

105. Carolyn Banta, "Trading for a High: An Inside Look at a 'Pharming Party,'" *Time,* August 1, 2005, p. 35.

106. Office of National Drug Control Policy, *The Economic Costs of Drug Abuse in the United States, 1992–2002* (Washington, DC: ONDCP, December 2004).

107. Office of National Drug Control Policy, *National Drug Control Strategy, Fiscal Year 2008 Budget Summary* (Washington, DC: ONDCP, February 2007), http://www.whitehousedrugpolicy.gov/ publications/policy/08budget (accessed May 10, 2007).

108. Office of National Drug Control Policy, *The National Drug Control Strategy 2003: Executive Summary* (Washington, DC: ONDCP, 2003), p. 12.

109. Material in this paragraph is taken from ONDCP, *The Economic Costs of Drug Abuse in the United States, 1992–2002,* pp. iii–18.

110. FBI, *Crime in the United States, 2006.*

111. Ibid.

112. Ibid. Unfortunately, UCR data combine arrests for heroin and cocaine possession into one category. They do the same for sale and manufacture arrests.

113. Bernard A. Gropper, "Probing the Links between Drugs and Crime," National Institute of Justice Research in Brief (Washington, DC: NIJ, February 1985), p. 4.

114. J. C. Ball, J. W. Shaffer, and D. N. Nurco, *Day to Day Criminality of Heroin Addicts in Baltimore: A Study in the Continuity of Offense Rates* (Washington, DC: National Institute of Justice, 1983).

115. "ONDCP Finds Americans Spent $57 Billion in One Year on Illegal Drugs," Office of National Drug Control Policy press release, 1997.

116. Office of National Drug Control Policy, *What America's Users Spend on Illegal Drugs* (Washington, DC: ONDCP, 1991), p. 4.

117. Mark Motivans, *Money Laundering Offenders, 1994–2001* (Washington, DC: Bureau of Justice Statistics, 2003).

118. Public Law 105-310.

119. Motivans, *Money Laundering Offenders,* p. 1.

120. U.S. Code, Title 18, Section 1957.

121. NNICC, *The NNICC Report, 1998.*

122. Ibid.

123. *Ratzlaf* v. *U.S.,* 114 S.Ct. 655, 126 L.Ed.2d 615 (1994).

124. Public Law 107-56.

125. Motivans, *Money Laundering Offenders,* p. 10.

126. ONDCP, *The National Drug Control Strategy, 2007.*

127. Ibid., p. 33.

128. Ibid., p. 3.

129. James Q. Wilson, "Drugs and Crime," in Michael Tonry and James Q. Wilson, eds., *Drugs and Crime* (Chicago, IL: University of Chicago Press, 1990), p. 522.

130. Drug Enforcement Administration, "DEA Announces Major Takedown of Online Drug Dealers," April 20, 2005, http://www.pushingback.com/archives/042005_2.html (accessed July 4, 2005).

131. "Twenty Arrested in Crackdown on Internet Pharmacies," CNN.com, April 20, 2005, http://www.cnn.com/2005/LAW/04/20/internet.drugs.ap (accessed July 4, 2005).

132. U.S. Code, Title 21, Section 881(a)(6).

133. Michael Goldsmith, *Civil Forfeiture: Tracing the Proceeds of Narcotics Trafficking* (Washington, DC: Police Executive Research Forum, 1988), p. 3.

134. *U.S.* v. *$4,255,625.39 in Currency,* 762 F.2d 895, 904 (1982).

135. Bureau of Justice Assistance, *Asset Forfeiture Bulletin* (October 1988), p. 2.

136. Ibid.

137. Goldsmith, *Civil Forfeiture.*

138. *U.S.* v. *92 Buena Vista Ave.,* 113 S.Ct. 1126, 122 L.Ed.2d 469 (1993).

139. *Austin* v. *U.S.,* 113 S.Ct. 2801, 15 L.Ed.2d 448 (1993).

140. *Alexander* v. *U.S.,* 113 S.Ct. 2766, 125 L.Ed.2d 441 (1993); and *U.S.* v. *James Daniel Good Real Property,* 114 S.Ct. 492, 126 L.Ed.2d 490 (1993).

141. *Bennis* v. *Michigan,* 116 S.Ct. 1560, 134 L.Ed.2d 661 (1996).

142. *U.S.* v. *Ursery,* 116 S.Ct. 2135, 135 L.Ed.2d 549 (1996).

143. Statement by the Honorable Henry J. Hyde, "Civil Asset Forfeiture Reform Act," http://www.house.gov/judiciary/161.htm (accessed March 10, 2007).

144. National Briefing: "Largest Drug Seizure at Sea," *New York Times,* April 24, 2007, http://query.nytimes.com/gst/fullpage.html?res=9801EEDD143EF937A15757C0A9619C8B63 (accessed May 10, 2007).

145. "Cocaine Found Packed in Toxic Chemical Drums," *Fayetteville (NC) Observer-Times*, November 5, 1989.

146. "Raid on Boat in Pacific Seizes 13 Tons of Cocaine," Associated Press, May 15, 2001.

147. Mark Moore, *Drug Trafficking*, National Institute of Justice Crime File Series Study Guide (Washington, DC: NIJ, 1988), p. 3.

148. Ibid.

149. Ibid.

150. Ibid.

151. In 2003, a California appellate court ruled that Proposition 36 does not apply to inmates in the state's correctional system. See *People* v. *Ponce*, Court of Appeals of California, First Appellate District, Division Five, No. A096707, March 7, 2003.

152. "Governor Signs Final Round of Bills," Kansas Governor's Office, April 21, 2003, http://www.ksgovernor.org/news/docs/news_rel042103.html (accessed August 3, 2006).

153. Michael S. Goodstadt, *Drug Education*, National Institute of Justice Crime File Series Study Guide (Washington, DC: NIJ, n.d.), p. 1.

154. See Federal Advisory Committee, *Methamphetamine Interagency Task Force: Final Report* (Washington, DC: Office of National Drug Control Policy, 2000), p. 5, from which some of the wording in this paragraph is adapted.

155. "DARE Not Effective in Reducing Drug Abuse, Study Finds," *Criminal Justice Newsletter*, October 3, 1994, pp. 6–7.

156. The government version of the study was first reported as *The DARE Program: A Review of Prevalence, User Satisfaction, and Effectiveness*, National Institute of Justice Update (Washington, DC: NIJ, October 1994). The full study, as published by NIJ, is Christopher L. Ringwalt et al., *Past and Future Directions of the DARE Program: An Evaluation Review* (Washington, DC: National Institute of Justice, 1995).

157. Fox Butterfield, no headline, *New York Times* wire service, April 16, 1997, citing Office of Justice Programs, *Preventing Crime: What Works, What Doesn't, What's Promising* (Washington, DC: U.S. Dept. of Justice, 1997).

158. Donald R. Lynam et al., "Project DARE: No Effects at 10-Year Follow-Up," *Journal of Consulting and Clinical Psychology*, Vol. 67, No. 4 (1999).

159. Goodstadt, *Drug Education*, p. 3.

160. *USA Today*, September 6, 1990, p. 8A, citing a report by the U.S. Senate Judiciary Committee.

161. Ibid.

162. RAND Corporation, *Drug Policy Research Center: Are Mandatory Minimum Drug Sentences Cost-Effective?* (Santa Monica, CA: RAND, 1997).

163. John S. Goldkamp and Doris Weiland, "Assessing the Impact of Dade County's Felony Drug Court," National Institute of Justice Research in Brief (Washington, DC: NIJ, December 1993).

164. National Association of Drug Court Professionals, *Facts on Drug Courts*, http://www.nadcp.org/whatis/facts.html (accessed July 15, 2007).

165. ONDCP, *The National Drug Control Strategy, 2005*, p. 37.

166. Ibid.

167. Ross Deck, "A New Way of Looking at the Drug War," in *Enhancing Capacities and Confronting Controversies in Criminal JusticeProceedings of the 1993 National Conference of the Bureau of Justice Statistics and the Justice Research and Statistics Association* (Washington, DC: Bureau of Justice Statistics, 1994), p. 12. Ross Deck, "A New Way of Looking at the Drug War," in *Enhancing Capacities and Confronting Controversies in Criminal JusticeProceedings of the 1993 National Conference of the Bureau of Justice Statistics and the Justice Research and Statistics Association* (Washington, DC: Bureau of Justice Statistics, 1994), p. 12.

168. Peter D. Hart Research Associates, *Drugs and Crime across America*, p. 5.

169. James C. McKinley, Jr., "Mexico Passes Law Making Possession of Some Drugs Legal," *New York Times*, April 29, 2006.

170. Paul H. Blachy, "Effects of Decriminalization of Marijuana in Oregon," *Annals of the New York Academy of Sciences*, Vol. 282 (1976), pp. 405–415. For more information on the decriminalization of marijuana, see James A. Inciardi, "Marijuana Decriminalization Research: A Perspective and Commentary," *Criminology*, Vol. 19, No. 1 (May 1981), pp. 145–159.

171. Arnold S. Trebach, "Thinking through Models of Drug Legalization," *Drug Policy Letter* (July/August 1994), p. 10.

172. For a more thorough discussion of some of these arguments, see Ronald Hamowy, ed., *Dealing with Drugs: Consequences of Government Control* (Lexington, MA: Lexington Books, 1987).

173. See Kurt Schmoke, "Decriminalizing Drugs: It Just Might Work," *Washington Post*, May 15, 1988.

174. "Should Drugs Be Legal?" *Newsweek*, May 30, 1988, p. 36.

175. Ibid., p. 37.

176. Ibid., pp. 37–38.

177. Trebach, "Thinking through Models of Drug Legalization," p. 10.

178. For a more detailed discussion of the two-market system, see John Kaplan, *Heroin*, National Institute of Justice Crime File Series Study Guide (Washington, DC: NIJ, n.d.).

179. Ibid., p. 3.

180. Ibid., p. 4.

181. Donna Leinwand, "Deadly Abuse of Methadone Tops Other Prescription Drugs," *USA Today*, February 13, 2007, p. 1A, citing a representative of the Food and Drug Administration.

Chapter 17   Terrorism and Multinational Criminal Justice

i. Testimony of Director of Central Intelligence Porter J. Goss before the Senate Select Committee on Intelligence, February 16, 2005.

ii. Andre Bossard, "Crime and Globalization," *Crime and Justice International*, Vol. 19, No. 71 (March 2003), p. 38.

iii. Ibid.

iv. Daniel Mabrey, "Human Smuggling from China," *Crime and Justice International*, Vol. 19, No. 71 (March 2003), p. 5.

v. Federal Bureau of Investigation, Counterterrorism Section, *Terrorism in the United States, 1987* (Washington, DC: FBI, 1987).

vi. Adapted from Federal Bureau of Investigation, *FBI Policy and Guidelines: Counterterrorism*, http://www.fbi.gov/contact/fo/jackson/cntrterr.htm (accessed March 4, 2007).

vii. Ibid.

viii. Adapted from Dictionary.com, http://dictionary.reference.com/search?q5infrastructure (accessed January 10, 2007).

ix. United Nations Department of Public Information, "The United Nations versus Transnational Crime," April 1995, http://www.un.org/ecosocdev/geninfo/crime/dpi1744e.htm (accessed January 15, 2004).

x.   As quoted in Joan Biskupic, "Attention Turns Back to Liberty," *USA Today,* November 1, 2002, p. 17A.

1.   Richard H. Ward, "The Internationalization of Criminal Justice," in Phyllis McDonald and Janice Munsterman, eds., *Boundary Changes in Criminal Justice Organizations,* Vol. 2 of *Criminal Justice 2000* (Washington, DC: National Institute of Justice, 2000), p. 267.

2.   Office for Victims of Crime, *Report to the Nation, 2003* (Washington, DC: OVC, 2003), p. 83.

3.   Donna Leinwand, "N.J. Store Clerk Foiled Attack on Fort Dix, FBI Says," *USA Today,* May 9, 2007, p. 2A.

4.   David Kocieniewski, "6 Men Arrested in a Terror Plot against Fort Dix," *New York Times,* May 9, 2007, http://www.nytimes.com/2007/05/09/us/09plot.html (accessed May 10, 2007).

5.   Robert Lilly, "Forks and Chopsticks: Understanding Criminal Justice in the PRC," *Criminal Justice International* (March/April 1986), p. 15.

6.   Adapted from Carol B. Kalish, *International Crime Rates,* Bureau of Justice Statistics Special Report (Washington, DC: BJS, 1988).

7.   Ibid.

8.   Ibid.

9.   For information about the latest survey, see *The Tenth United Nations Survey on Crime Trends and the Operations of Criminal Justice* (New York: United Nations, 2007), http://www.unodc.org/unodc/crime_survey_ tenth.html (accessed July 11, 2007).

10. As quoted in Lee Hockstader, "Russia's War on Crime: A Lopsided, Losing Battle," *Washington Post* wire service, February 27, 1995.

11. Roy Walmsley, *Developments in the Prison Systems of Central and Eastern Europe,* HEUNI papers No. 4 (Helsinki, 1995).

12. J. Schact, "Law and Justice," *The Cambridge Encyclopedia of Islam,* Vol. 2, p. 539, from which most of the information in this paragraph comes. Web available at http://www.fordham.edu/halsall/med/schacht.html (accessed July 1, 2007).

13. Sam S. Souryal, Dennis W. Potts, and Abdullah I. Alobied, "The Penalty of Hand Amputation for Theft in Islamic Justice," *Journal of Criminal Justice,* Vol. 22, No. 3 (1994), pp. 249–265.

14. Parviz Saney, "Iran," in Elmer H. Johnson, ed., *International Handbook of Contemporary Developments in Criminology* (Westport, CT: Greenwood Press, 1983), p. 359.

15. This section owes much to Matthew Lippman, "Iran: A Question of Justice?" *Criminal Justice International* (1987), pp. 6–7.

16. "Life Sentence for Burning Koran," BBC News, October 18, 2004, http://news.bbc.co.uk/1/hi/world/south_asia/3754276.stm (accessed May 21, 2007).

17. Souryal, Potts, and Alobied, "The Penalty of Hand Amputation."

18. Afshin Valinejad, "Iran Flogs, Hangs Serial Killer Known as 'The Vampire,'" *USA Today,* August 14, 1997, p. 11A.

19. For additional information on Islamic law, see Adel Mohammed el Fikey, "Crimes and Penalties in Islamic Criminal Legislation," *Criminal Justice International* (1986), pp. 13–14; and Sam S. Souryal, "Shariah Law in Saudi Arabia," *Journal for the Scientific Study of Religion,* Vol. 26, No. 4 (1987), pp. 429–449.

20. Max Weber, in Max Rheinstein, ed., *On Law in Economy and Society* (New York: Simon and Schuster, 1967), translated from the 1925 German edition.

21. Ibid.

22. Souryal, Potts, and Alobied, "The Penalty of Hand Amputation."

23. Paul Friday, "International Organization: An Introduction," in Elmer H. Johnson, ed., *International Handbook of Contemporary Developments in Criminology* (Westport, CT: Greenwood Press, 1983), p. 31.

24. Ibid., p. 32.

25. Gerhard O. W. Mueller, "The United Nations and Criminology," in Elmer H. Johnson, ed., *International Handbook of Contemporary Developments in Criminology* (Westport, CT: Greenwood Press, 1983), pp. 74–75.

26. Roger S. Clark, *The United Nations Crime Prevention and Criminal Justice Program: Formulation of Standards and Efforts at Their Implementation* (Philadelphia: University of Pennsylvania Press, 1994).

27. Ibid., pp. 71–72.

28. "International News," *Corrections Compendium* (June 1995), p. 25.

29. Khaled Dawoud, "U.N. Crime Meeting Wants Independent Jail Checks," Reuters, May 6, 1995.

30. "Protocol to Prevent, Suppress, and Punish Trafficking in Persons, Especially Women and Children, Supplementing the United Nations Convention against Transnational Organized Crime," *Report of the Ad Hoc Committee on the Elaboration of a Convention against Transnational Organized Crime on the Work of Its First to Eleventh Sessions,* U.N. GAOR, 55th Sess., Agenda Item 105, U.N. Document Number A/55/383 (2000), Annex II.

31. For additional information, see Mohamed Y. Mattar, "Trafficking in Persons, Especially Women and Children, in Countries of the Middle East: The Scope of the Problem and the Appropriate Legislative Response," *Fordham International Law Journal,* Vol. 26 (March 2003), p. 721, http://209.190.246.239/article.pdf (accessed August 2, 2006).

32. See "Interpol: Extending Law Enforcement's Reach around the World," *FBI Law Enforcement Bulletin* (December 1998), pp. 10–16.

33. "Interpol Member Countries," http://www.interpol.int/Public/Icpo/Members/default.asp (accessed June 9, 2007).

34. "Interpol at Forty," *Criminal Justice International* (November/December 1986), pp. 1, 22.

35. "Interpol Conference Agrees on Measures to Fight Bio-Terrorism," Interpol press release No. 11/2005, March 2, 2005.

36. Interpol General Secretariat, *Interpol at Work: 2003 Activity Report* (Lyons, France, 2004).

37. Marc Champion, Jeanne Whalen, and Jay Solomon, "Terror in London: Police Make One Arrest after Raids in North England," *Wall Street Journal,* July 12, 2005, http://online.wsj.com/article/0,,SB112116092902883194,00.html?mod5djemTAR (accessed August 15, 2007).

38. Ibid.

39. ICPO-Interpol General Assembly Resolution No. AG-2001-RES-07.

40. See the Coalition for an International Criminal Court, "Building the Court," http://www.iccnow.org/buildingthecourt.html (accessed July 30, 2007).

41. Much of the information and some of the wording in this section are adapted from "The ICC International Criminal Court Home Page," http://www.iccnow.org/index.html

(accessed July 4, 2007); and the ICC "Timeline," http://www.iccnow.org/html/timeline.htm (accessed April 12, 2007).

42. *Convention on the Prevention and Punishment of the Crime of Genocide,* adopted by Resolution 260 (III) A of the U.N. General Assembly on December 9, 1948, http://www.preventgenocide.org/law/convention/text.htm (accessed July 4, 2007).

43. *Plenipotentiary* is another word for "diplomat."

44. Rome Statute of the International Criminal Court, United Nations Diplomatic Conference of Plenipotentiaries on the Establishment of an International Criminal Court, Rome, Italy, June 15–July 16, 1998. U.N. Document Number A/CONF.183/9 (1998), art. 7, http://www.un.org/law/icc/statutw/romefra.htm (accessed July 4, 2007).

45. Jan M. Olsen, "EU Welcomes U.S. Compromise on War Crimes Tribunal," Associated Press, July 13, 2002.

46. United Nations Security Council Resolution No. 1422 (July 1, 2002).

47. "Decision of Pre-Trial Chamber I on the Prosecutor's Request under Article 56 of the Rome Statute," International Criminal Court press release, April 26, 2005, http://www.icc-cpi.int/press/pressreleases/105.html (accessed May 20, 2007).

48. "A Milestone for Justice," *Japan Times,* February 12, 2007, search.japantimes.co.jp/print/ed20070212a1.html (accessed May 10, 2007).

49. Much of the information in this paragraph and the next comes from David J. Lynch, "Belgium Plays Global Prosecutor," *USA Today,* July 16, 2001, p. 7A; and Katie Nguyen, "Cubans Use Belgian Law to File Case against Castro," Reuters, October 4, 2001.

50. Adapted from "Globalization," *Encyclopedia Britannica, 2003,* http://www.britannica.com/eb/article?eu5369857 (accessed July 28, 2006).

51. Federal Bureau of Investigation, "The Case of the Snakehead Queen: Chinese Human Smuggler Gets 35 Years," March 17, 2006, http://www.fbi.gov/page2/march06/sisterping031706.htm (accessed May 11, 2007).

52. Laurie Robinson, address given at the Twelfth International Congress on Criminology, Seoul, Korea, August 28, 1998.

53. National Institute of Justice, *Asian Transnational Organized Crime and Its Impact on the United States* (Washington, DC: NIJ, 2007), p. 1.

54. Robert S. Gelbard, "Foreign Policy after the Cold War: The New Threat—Transnational Crime," address at St. Mary's University, San Antonio, TX, April 2, 1996.

55. NIJ, *Asian Transnational Organized Crime,* p. 1.

56. Barbara Starr, "A Gangster's Paradise," ABC News Online, September 14, 1998, http://more.abcnews.go.com/sections/world/dailynews/russiacrime980914.html (accessed January 24, 2004).

57. As quoted in Starr, "A Gangster's Paradise."

58. Raymond Bonner and Timothy L. O'Brien, "Activity at Bank Raises Suspicions of Russia Mob Tie," *New York Times,* August 19, 1999, p. 1A.

59. Public Law 108-193.

60. Sex trafficking is defined separately under U.S. Code, Title 22, Section 7102 (8); (9); (14) as "the recruitment, harboring, transportation, provision, or obtaining of a person for the purpose of a commercial sex act."

61. Kevin F. Ryan, "Globalizing the Problem: The United States and International Drug Control," in Eric L. Jensen and Jurg Gerber, eds., *The New War on Drugs: Symbolic Politics and Criminal Justice Policy* (Cincinnati, OH: Anderson, 1997).

62. Foreign Relations Authorization Act, U.S. Code, Title 22, Section 2656 f(d)(2).

63. In the words of the act: "The term 'terrorism' means premeditated, politically motivated violence perpetrated against noncombatant targets by subnational groups or clandestine agents." U.S. Code, Title 22, Section 2656 f(d)(2).

64. Federal Bureau of Investigation, Counterterrorism Section, *Terrorism in the United States, 1987* (Washington, DC: FBI, 1987), in which the full definition offered here can be found. See also *FBI Policy and Guidelines: Counterterrorism,* http://www.fbi.gov/contact/fo/jackson/cntrterr.htm (accessed January 15, 2008), which offers a somewhat less formal definition of the term.

65. Gwynn Nettler, *Killing One Another* (Cincinnati, OH: Anderson, 1982).

66. Ibid., p. 253.

67. Adapted from *FBI Policy and Guidelines.*

68. Ibid.

69. The death penalty was imposed for the first-degree murders of eight federal law enforcement agents who were at work in the Murrah Building at the time of the bombing. While all of the killings violated Oklahoma law, only the killings of the federal agents fell under federal law, which makes such murders capital offenses.

70. "Terry Nichols Receives Life Sentences for Each of 161 Victims in 1995 Oklahoma City Bombing," Associated Press, August 9, 2004.

71. Michael E. Wiggins, "Rationale and Justification for Right-Wing Terrorism: A Politico-Social Analysis of the Turner Diaries," paper presented at the annual meeting of the American Society of Criminology, Atlanta, GA, October 1986.

72. "Rudolph Agrees to Plea Agreement," CNN Law Center, April 12, 2005, http://www.cnn.com/2005/LAW/04/08/rudolph.plea (accessed May 21, 2007).

73. Bruce Frankel, "Sheik Guilty in Terror Plot," *USA Today,* October 2, 1995, p. 1A. Sheik Abdel-Rahman and codefendant El Sayyid Nosair were both sentenced to life in prison. Other defendants received sentences of between 25 and 57 years in prison. See Sascha Brodsky, "Terror Verdicts Denounced," United Press International, January 17, 1996.

74. "Qaeda Suspect Dead, Suicide Eyed," CBSNews.com, July 3, 2003, http://www.cbsnews.com/stories/2003/06/26/world/main560618.shtml (accessed July 10, 2003).

75. Philip Stephens, "All Nostalgia Is Futile at the Beginning of History," *Financial Times,* May 27, 2005, p. 13.

76. See Barry Collin, "The Future of Cyberterrorism," *Crime and Justice International* (March 1997), pp. 15–18.

77. John Arquilla and David Ronfeldt, *The Advent of Netwar* (Santa Monica, CA: RAND Corporation, 1996).

78. Mark M. Pollitt, "Cyberterrorism: Fact or Fancy?" *Proceedings of the Twentieth National Information Systems Security Conference,* October 1997, pp. 285–289.

79. The White House Office of the Press Secretary, "Executive Order on Critical Infrastructure Protection," October 16, 2001, http://www.whitehouse.gov/news/releases/2001/10/20011016-12.html (accessed May 21, 2007).

80. President's Critical Infrastructure Protection Board, *The National Strategy to Secure Cyberspace* (Washington, DC: U.S. Government Printing Office, September 18, 2002).

81. Department of Homeland Security, "Ridge Creates New Division to Combat Cyber Threats," press release, June 6, 2003, http://www.dhs.gov/dhspublic/display?content5916 (accessed May 28, 2007).

82. Daniel Boyce, "Narco-terrorism," *FBI Law Enforcement Bulletin* (October 1987), p. 24; and James A. Inciardi, "Narcoterrorism: A Perspective and Commentary," in Robert O. Slater and Grant Wardlaw, eds., *International Narcotics* (London: Macmillan/St. Martins, 1989).

83. Details for this story come from "Alleged Afghan Drug Kingpin Arrested," *USA Today*, April 26, 2005, p. 3A.

84. The term *narcoterrorism* was reportedly invented by former Peruvian President Fernando Belaunde Terry; see James A. Inciardi, "Narcoterrorism," paper presented at the 1988 annual meeting of the Academy of Criminal Justice Sciences, San Francisco, CA, p. 8.

85. Boyce, "Narco-terrorism," p. 24.

86. Ibid., p. 25.

87. U.S. Department of State, *Terrorist Group Profiles* (Washington, DC: U.S. Government Printing Office, 1989).

88. Inciardi, "Narcoterrorism."

89. "U.S. Government Lacks Strategy to Neutralize International Crime," *Criminal Justice International,* Vol. 10, No. 5 (September/October 1994), p. 5.

90. *National Strategy for Combating Terrorism* (Washington, DC: White House, 2003).

91. Emilio C. Viano, Jose Magallanes, and Laurent Bridel, "Transnational Organized Crime: Myth, Power, and Profit," *Crime and Justice International,* May/June 2005, p. 23.

92. *National Strategy for Combating Terrorism,* p. 6.

93. Ibid.

94. The actual language of the act sets a standard for metal detectors through the use of a "security exemplar" made of 3.7 ounces of stainless steel in the shape of a handgun. Weapons made of other substances might still pass the test provided that they could be detected by metal detectors adjusted to that level of sensitivity. See "Bill Is Signed Barring Sale or Manufacture of Plastic Guns," *Criminal Justice Newsletter,* Vol. 19, No. 23 (December 1, 1988), pp. 4–5.

95. National Commission on Terrorism, *Countering the Changing Threat of International Terrorism* (Washington, DC: U.S. Dept. of State, 2000).

96. Mimi Hall, "Report: USA Left Open to Attack," *USA Today,* December 6, 2005, p. 1A.

97. U.S. Department of Homeland Security, "DHS Organization: Building a Secure Homeland," http://www.dhs.gov/dhspublic/theme_home1.jsp (accessed August 28, 2007).

98. On March 1, 2003, the Immigration and Naturalization Service became part of the U.S. Department of Homeland Security, and its functions were divided into various bureaus within that department.

99. The information in this section comes from U.S. Department of Homeland Security, "DHS Organization: Department Components," http://www.dhs.gov/dhspublic/display?theme59&content5858 (accessed August 22, 2007).

100. *National Strategy for Combating Terrorism.*

101. The NCTC was established by executive order in 2004, although Congress codified the NCTC in the Intelligence Reform and Terrorism Prevention Act of 2004 and placed the NCTC within the Office of the Director of National Intelligence.

102. National Counterterrorism Center, *NCTC and Information Sharing* (Washington, DC: NCTC, 2006), p. i, from which some of the wording in this paragraph is taken.

103. U.S. Code, Title 8, Section 1-1599.

104. Public Law 108-408.

105. U.S. Code, Title 8, Section 219.

106. Information in this paragraph comes from U.S. Department of State, *Patterns of Global Terrorism, 2002,* http://www.state.gov/s/ct/rls/pgtrpt/2002/ (accessed August 2, 2005); and U.S. Department of State, "State Sponsors of Terrorism," http://www.state.gov/s/ct/c14151.htm (accessed July 2, 2007).

107. Central Intelligence Agency, National Foreign Intelligence Council, *Global Trends, 2015: A Dialogue about the Future with Nongovernment Experts* (Washington, DC: U.S. Government Printing Office, 2000).

108. Ibid.

109. Central Intelligence Agency, National Foreign Intelligence Council, *Mapping the Global Future: Report of the National Intelligence Council's 2020 Project* (Washington, DC: U.S. Government Printing Office, 2005).

Chapter 18   The Future of Criminal Justice

i. Jonathan Littmann, "In the Mind of Most Wanted Hacker, Kevin Mitnick," *Computer World,* January 15, 1996, p. 87.

ii. "President Bush Calls on Senate to Back Human Cloning Ban," White House press release, April 10, 2002.

iii. Centers for Disease Control and Prevention, *Bioterrorism: An Overview,* http://www.bt.cdc.gov/documents/PPTResponse/laboverview.pdf (accessed August 5, 2007).

iv. Thomas J. Cowper and Michael E. Buerger, *Improving Our View of the World: Police and Augmented Reality Technology* (Quantico, VA: Police Futurists International/Federal Bureau of Investigation, 2003), p. 5.

v. *Imus in the Morning,* MSNBC, May 10, 2005.

vi. Thomas J. Cowper and Michael E. Buerger, *Improving Our View of the World: Police and Augmented Reality Technology* (Washington, DC: Federal Bureau of Investigation, 2003), http://www.fbi.gov/publications/realitytech/realitytech.pdf (accessed October 7, 2006).

vii. Ayn Rand, "The Lessons of Vietnam," *The Ayn Rand Letter,* August 26, 1974.

viii. Adapted from Entrust, Inc., "Secure Identity Management: Challenges, Needs, and Solutions," http://www.entrust.com (accessed August 5, 2007).

1. Quoted in Susan W. Brenner, "Is There Such a Thing as 'Virtual Crime'?" *California Criminal Law Review,* Vol. 4 (June 2001). Web posed at http://www.boalt.org/CCLR/v4/v4brenner.htm (accessed July 10, 2007).

2. Information for this story comes from "Hacker Hunters: An Elite Force Takes on the Dark Side of Computing," *Business Week,* May 30, 2005, pp. 74–82.

3. Deborah Gage, "Head of Shadowcrew Identity Theft Ring Gets Prison Time," *Baseline,* June 30, 2006, http://www.baselinemag.com/article2/0,1540,1984283,00.asp (accessed May 11, 2007).

4. Ibid.

5. Thomas J. Cowper, "Foresight Update 49," http://www.foresight.org/Updates/Update49/Update49.4.html (accessed August 5, 2007).

6. Ibid.

7. University of Minnesota Center for Infectious Disease Research and Policy, "All H2N2 Flu Virus Samples Destroyed, CDC Says," May 3, 2005, http://www.cidrap.umn.edu/cidrap/content/influenza/general/news/may0305h2n2.html (accessed July 10, 2005).

8. "Stem Cells Extracted from Human Clone," MSNBC News, February 12, 2004, http://www.msnbc.msn.com/id/4244988 (accessed July 8, 2006).

9. "President Bush Calls on Senate to Back Human Cloning Ban," White House press release, April 10, 2002.

10. "Bush Condemns Embryonic Cloning," Fox News, May 21, 2005, http://www.foxnews.com/story/0,2933,157163,00.html (accessed July 18, 2007).

11. H.R. 222, Human Cloning Research Prohibition Act.

12. Many other countries, such as England, permit therapeutic cloning, although they often criminalize or severely restrict human cloning efforts.

13. Dolly was euthanized in 2003 after falling ill with lung disease.

14. S. 658, the Human Cloning Prohibition Act of 2005.

15. House Committee on Energy and Commerce, Subcommittee on Health, "Prepared Witness Testimony," June 20, 2001, http://energycommerce.house.gov/107/hearins/06202001Hearing291/Allen449.htm (accessed August 15, 2006).

16. "Bush Backs Total Ban on Human Cloning: Declares Life Is a 'Creation, Not a Commodity,'" April 10, 2002, http://usgovinfo.about.com/library/weekly/aa041102a.htm (accessed August 10, 2006).

17. Linda Rosencrance, "Cyberscam Strikes Massachusetts State Lottery," *Computerworld,* July 24, 2003.

18. "Are You Vulnerable to Cybercrime?" *USA Today,* February 20, 1995, p. 3B.

19. "Most Wanted Hacker Released from Prison," *USA Today,* January 21, 2000, http://www.usatoday.com/news/ndsfri02.htm (accessed January 28, 2006).

20. Elinor Abreu, "Kevin Mitnick Bares All," *Industry Standard,* September 28, 2000, http://www.nwfusion.com/news/2000/0928mitnick.html (accessed January 26, 2002).

21. Pia Turunen, "Hack Attack: How You Might Be a Target," CNN.com, April 12, 2002, http://www.cnn.com/2002/TECH/ptech/04/12/hack.dangers (accessed August 3, 2006).

22. Nikola Krastev, "East: Many Nations Lack Effective Computer Crime Laws," *Radio Free Europe,* December 19, 2000, http://www.rferl.org/nca/features/2000/12/15122000153858.asp (accessed April 28, 2006).

23. Ibid.

24. "'Love Bug' Prompts New Philippine Law," *USA Today,* June 14, 2000.

25. "Cybercrime Treaty Gets Green Light," BBC News Online, November 12, 2001.

26. Details for this section come from the Council of Europe, Convention on Cybercrime signatories website, http://conventions.coe.int (accessed April 8, 2007).

27. Susan Schaibly, "Files for Ransom," *Network World,* September 26, 2005, http://www.networkworld.com/buzz/2005/092605-ransom.html (accessed May 12, 2007).

28. Ibid.

29. For suggested computer crime categories, see Peter Grabosky, "Computer Crime: A Criminological Overview," paper presented at the Workshop on Crimes Related to the Computer Network, Tenth United Nations Congress on the Prevention of Crime and the Treatment of Offenders, Vienna, Austria, April 15, 2000, http://www.aic.gov.au/conferences/other/compcrime/computercrime.pdf (accessed January 12, 2007). Also see David L. Carter, "Computer Crime Categories: How Techno-Criminals Operate," *FBI Law Enforcement Journal,* July 1995, pp. 21–26.

30. Grabosky, "Computer Crime."

31. Kevin Johnson, "Hijackers' E-Mails Sifted for Clues," *USA Today,* October 11, 2001.

32. Lawrence A. Gordon et al., *2006 CSI/FBI Computer Crime and Security Survey* (Southampton, PA: Computer Security Institute, 2007), p. 9, http://i.cmpnet.com/gocsi/db_area/pdfs/fbi/FBI2006.pdf (accessed August 1, 2007).

33. "Focus on Physical Security, Too," *eWeek,* January 27, 2003, p. 6a.

34. Ibid., p. 5.

35. Ibid., p. 6.

36. Ramona R. Rantala, *Cybercrime against Businesses: Pilot Test Results, 2001 Computer Security Survey* (Washington, DC: Bureau of Justice Statistics, 2004).

37. "Invasion of the Data Snatchers!" *Time,* September 26, 1988, pp. 62–67.

38. "Virus Infects NASA, Defense, University Computer Systems," *Fayetteville (NC) Observer-Times,* November 4, 1988, p. 19A.

39. Barbara E. McMullin and John F. McMullin, "Hacker Morris Sentenced," Newsbytes News Network, May 4, 1990, http://findarticles.com/p/articles/mi_m0NEW/is_1990_May_8/ai_9831055 (accessed June 23, 2007).

40. "First HTML Virus Detected," Andover News Network, http://www.andovernews.com/cgi-bin/news_story.pl?95529/topstories (accessed January 16, 2006).

41. Sophos Antivirus, "The First JAVA Virus," http://www.sophos.com/virusinfo/articles/java.html (accessed January 5, 2006).

42. Net IQ, "Virus Protection," http://marshal.netiq.com/0195/solutions_virusprotection.html (accessed August 1, 2005).

43. Gregg Keizer, "Microsoft Says Phishing Bad, Offers Little New for Defense," *TechWeb News,* March 15, 2005, http://www.techweb.com/wire/159900391 (accessed July 7, 2005).

44. Avivah Litan, "Phishing Victims Likely Will Suffer Identity Theft Fraud," Gartner, Inc., May 14, 2004, http://www.gartner.com/DisplayDocument?ref5g_search&id544811 (accessed July 6, 2007).

45. Software Information Industry Association, *Report on Global Software Piracy, 2000,* http://www.siia.net/piracy/pubs/piracy2000.pdf (accessed August 1, 2007).

46. See the music industry's reaction to the court's decision at http://www.nmpa.org/pr/NMPAPressRelease.doc (accessed August 1, 2003).

47. *Metro-Goldwyn-Mayer Studios, Inc.* v. *Grokster, Ltd.,* 259 F.Supp.2d 1029 (C.D. Cal. 2003).

48. Motion to dismiss denied, 243 F.Supp.2d 1073 (C.D. Cal. 2003).

49. *MGM* v. *Grokster,* 545 U.S. 913 (2005).

50. *Sony Corporation of America* v. *Universal City Studios, Inc.,* 464 U.S. 417 (1984).

51. Public Law 108-187.

52. Peter Firstbrook, "META Trend Update: The Changing Threat Landscape," Meta Group, March 24, 2005, http://www.metagroup.com/us/displayArticle.do?oid551768 (accessed July 5, 2007).

53. Virginia Statutes, Section 18.2-152.3:1.

54. Jack McCarthy, "Spammer Sentenced to Nine Years in Prison," *InfoWorld,* April 11, 2005.

55. Some of the technological devices described in this section are discussed in G. Gordon Liddy, "Rules of the Game," *Omni,* January 1989, pp. 43–47, 78–80.

56. Central Intelligence Agency Directorate of Intelligence, *Terrorist CBRN: Materials and Effects* (Washington, DC: CIA, 2003).

57. Radiological Weapons Working Group, Harvard Project on Managing the Atom.

58. The information in this paragraph comes from a June 30, 2003, General Accounting Office report. See "Continuing Radioactive Materials Seizures," Nuclear Threat Initiative website, http://www.nti.org/e_research/cnwm/overview/cnwm_home.asp (accessed August 1, 2003).

59. Matthew Bunn, Anthony Wier, and John P. Holden, *Controlling Nuclear Warheads and Materials: A Report Card and Action Plan* (Cambridge, MA: Nuclear Threat Initiative and Harvard University, 2003).

60. *Fact Sheet: The Biological Weapons Convention* (Washington, DC: Bureau of Arms Control, 2002), http://www.state.gov/t/ac/rls/fs/10401.htm (accessed August 8, 2007).

61. Ali S. Kahn et al., *Biological and Chemical Terrorism: Strategic Plan for Preparedness and Response* (Atlanta, GA: Centers for Disease Control and Prevention, April 21, 2000), http://www.cdc.gov/mmwr/preview/mmwrhtml/rr4904a1.htm (accessed August 2, 2007).

62. Council on Foreign Relations, "Terrorism: Questions and Answers—The Anthrax Letters," http://www.terrorismanswers.com/weapons/anthraxletters.html (accessed August 23, 2007).

63. See Rick Weiss, "DNA by Mail: A Terror Risk," *Washington Post,* July 18, 2002.

64. Peter Eisler, "High-Tech 'Bait Cars' Catch Unsuspecting Auto Thieves," *USA Today,* November 29, 2004, p. 1A.

65. Paul McClellan, "Automatic Plate Recognition Evaluation Ends with Positive Results," Ohio State Highway Patrol, December 22, 2004, http://www.statepatrol.ohio.gov/colcolumn/2004/AutoScanner-2.htm (accessed July 9, 2005).

66. Toni Locy, "Thieves Target Auto Identification," *USA Today,* May 20, 2005, p. 1A.

67. For an excellent overview of technology in criminal justice, see Laura J. Moriarty and David L. Carter, eds., *Criminal Justice Technology in the Twenty-First Century* (Springfield, IL: Charles C. Thomas, 1998).

68. National Law Enforcement and Corrections Technology Center, electronic press release, April 7, 1995.

69. Lester D. Shubin, *Research, Testing, Upgrading Criminal Justice Technology,* National Institute of Justice Reports (Washington, DC: U.S. Government Printing Office, 1984), pp. 2–5.

70. Simon Dinitz, "Coping with Deviant Behavior through Technology," *Criminal Justice Research Bulletin,* Vol. 3, No. 2 (1987).

71. See, for example, Laurence P. Karper et al., "Antipsychotics, Lithium, Benzodiazepines, Beta-Blockers," in Marc Hillbrand and Nathaniel J. Pallone, eds., *The Psychobiology of Aggression: Engines, Measurement, Control* (New York: Haworth Press, 1994), pp. 203–222.

72. Harry Soderman and John J. O'Connell, *Modern Criminal Investigation* (New York: Funk and Wagnalls, 1945), p. 41.

73. The system was invented by Lambert Adolphe Jacques Quetelet (1796–1874), a Belgian astronomer and statistician.

74. For more on Bertillon's system, see Alphonse Bertillon, *Signaletic Instructions* (New York: Werner, 1896).

75. Robert D. Foote, "Fingerprint Identification: A Survey of Present Technology, Automated Applications, and Potential for Future Development," *Criminal Justice Monograph Series,* Vol. 5, No. 2 (Huntsville, TX: Sam Houston State University Press, 1974), pp. 3–4.

76. Soderman and O'Connell, *Modern Criminal Investigation,* p. 57.

77. Ibid.

78. Francis Galton, *Finger Prints* (London: Macmillan, 1892).

79. Foote, "Fingerprint Identification," p. 1.

80. Office of Technology Assessment, *Criminal Justice: New Technologies and the Constitution: A Special Report* (Washington, DC: U.S. Government Printing Office, 1988), p. 18. Electro-optical systems for live fingerprint scanning were developed by Fingermatric, Inc., of White Plains, New York.

81. T. F. Wilson and P. L. Woodard, *Automated Fingerprint Identification Systems—Technology and Policy Issues* (Washington, DC: U.S. Dept. of Justice, 1987), p. 5.

82. Kristi Gulick, "Latent Prints from Human Skin," *Law and Order Magazine,* http://www.lawandordermag.com/magazine/current/latentprints.html.htm (accessed September 26, 2001).

83. Los Angeles Police Department, *Annual Report, 1985–1986,* p. 26.

84. Ibid., p. 27.

85. American National Standards Institute, *American National Standard for Information Systems—Fingerprint Identification—Data Format for Information Interchange* (New York: ANSI, 1986). Originally developed as the Proposed American National Standard Data Format for the Interchange of Fingerprint Information by the National Bureau of Standards (Washington, DC: NBS, 1986).

86. Dennis G. Kurre, "On-Line Exchange of Fingerprint Identification Data," *FBI Law Enforcement Bulletin,* December 1987, pp. 14–16.

87. Jon Swartz, "Ins and Outs of Biometrics," *USA Today,* January 27, 2003, p. 3B.

88. In 1998, ruling for the first time on polygraph examinations, the U.S. Supreme Court upheld the military's ban on the use of polygraph tests in criminal trials. In refusing to hear a case, Justice Clarence Thomas wrote, "[T]he aura of infallibility attending polygraph evidence can lead jurors to abandon their duty to assess credibility and guilt."

89. Details for this story come from *USA Today,* Nationline, March 16, 2000, p. 3A.

90. "NYC Seeks to Indict Rapists by DNA Alone," *USA Today,* August 5, 2003, p. 3A.

91. Francis X. Clines, "DNA Clears Virginia Man of 1982 Assault," *New York Times,* December 10, 2001.

92. U.S. Department of Justice, *Understanding DNA Evidence: A Guide for Victim Service Providers* (Washington, DC: DOJ, 2001).

93. Tim Schellberg and Lisa Hurst, *DNA Resource Report,* March 19, 2004, http://www.dnaresource.com/03-192004%20Summary.pdf (accessed July 4, 2007).

94. See Alec J. Jeffreys, Victoria Wilson, and Swee Lay Thein, "Hypervariable 'Minisatellite' Regions in Human Nature," *Nature,* No. 314 (1985), p. 67; and "Individual-Specific 'Fingerprints' of Human DNA," *Nature,* No. 316 (1985), p. 76.

95. Peter Gill, Alec J. Jeffreys, and David J. Werrett, "Forensic Application of DNA Fingerprints," *Nature,* No. 318 (1985), p. 577. See also Craig Seton, "Life for Sex Killer Who Sent Decoy to Take Genetic Test," *London Times,* January 23, 1988, p. 3. A popular account of this case, *The Blooding,* was written by crime novelist Joseph Wambaugh (New York: William Morrow, 1989).

96. Bureau of Justice Statistics, *Forensic DNA Analysis: Issues* (Washington, DC: BJS, 1991).

97. "Genetic Fingerprinting Convicts Rapist in U.K.," *Globe and Mail,* November 14, 1987, p. A3.

98. *Daubert* v. *Merrell Dow Pharmaceuticals, Inc.,* 509 U.S. 579, 113 S.Ct. 2786 (1993).

99. *Frye* v. *U.S.,* 54 App. D.C. 46, 47, 293 F. 1013, 1014 (1923).

100. For the application of *Daubert* to DNA technology, see Barry Sheck, "DNA and *Daubert,*" *Cardozo Law Review,* Vol. 15 (1994), p. 1959.

101. In 1999, in the case of *Kumho Tire Co.* v. *Carmichael,* 526 U.S. 137 (1999), the Court held that *Daubert* factors may also apply to the testimony of engineers and other experts who are not, strictly speaking, "scientists" and that a trial judge determining the admissibility of an engineering expert's testimony may consider one or more of the specific *Daubert* factors.

102. Violent Crime Control and Law Enforcement Act of 1994, Section 210301.

103. "National DNA Index System Reaches 1,000,000 Profiles," FBI press release, June 14, 2002.

104. Edward Connors et al., *Convicted by Juries, Exonerated by Science: Case Studies in the Use of DNA Evidence to Establish Innocence after Trial* (Washington, DC: National Institute of Justice, 1996).

105. The nonjury case involved a guilty plea from a defendant who had mental disabilities.

106. Stephen Strauss, "Fingerprints Leaving Fingerprints of Their Own," Simon and Schuster NewsLink, June 20, 1997.

107. Public Law No. 108-405.

108. U.S. Code, Title 18, Chapter 213, Section 3297.

109. "Time Line '98," *Yahoo! Internet Life,* January 1999, p. 90. To access the database, visit http://www.publicdata.com.

110. William S. Sessions, "Criminal Justice Information Services: Gearing Up for the Future," *FBI Law Enforcement Bulletin,* February 1993, pp. 181–188.

111. OTA, *Criminal Justice,* p. 29.

112. Ibid.

113. For more on the system, see Craig Stedman, "Feds to Track Sex Offenders with Database," *Computerworld,* September 2, 1996, p. 24.

114. "Saving Face," *PC Computing,* December 1988, p. 60.

115. See Dawn E. McQuiston and Roy S. Malpass, "Use of Facial Composite Systems in U.S. Law Enforcement Agencies," http://eyewitness.utep.edu/Documents/McQuiston%20APLS%202000.pdf (accessed March 25, 2007).

116. "Security or Privacy? DARPA's Total Information Awareness Program Tests the Boundaries," InformationWeek.com, http://www.informationweek.com/story/showArticle.jhtml?articleID510000184 (accessed August 2, 2007).

117. Information in this paragraph comes from "U.S. Sensors Could Track Any Car, All Passengers in Foreign Cities," WorldTribune.com, July 30, 2003, http://www.worldtribune.com/worldtribune/breaking_8.html (accessed August 5, 2007).

118. See, for example, Jeffrey S. Hormann, "Virtual Reality: The Future of Law Enforcement Training," *FBI Law Enforcement Bulletin,* July 1995, pp. 7–12.

119. See, for example, Thomas F. Rich, *The Use of Computerized Mapping Crime Control and Prevention Programs* (Washington, DC: National Institute of Justice, 1995).

120. Matt L. Rodriguez, "The Acquisition of High Technology Systems by Law Enforcement," *FBI Law Enforcement Bulletin,* December 1988, p. 10.

121. Office of the Inspector General, Department of Homeland Security, *Semiannual Report to the Congress* (Washington, DC: DHS, 2006).

122. Frank J. Murray, "NASA Plans to Read Terrorists' Minds at Airports," *Washington Times,* August 17, 2002.

123. Ibid.

124. The information in this section comes from Thomas J. Cowper and Michael E. Buerger, *Improving Our View of the World: Police and Augmented Reality Technology* (Washington, DC: Federal Bureau of Investigation, 2003), http://www.fbi.gov/publications/realitytech/realitytech.pdf (accessed October 27, 2006).

125. "Xybernaut and ZNQ3, Inc. Team to Deliver Secure Mobile Wearable Computing Solutions to State and Local Governments," *Business Wire,* July 29, 2003.

126. See the fictional discussion of such an advanced device in Dan Brown, *Deception Point* (New York: Simon and Schuster, 2002).

127. See "Nanotechnology in Crime Prevention and Detection," Institute of Nanotechnology, http://www.nano.org.uk/crime2.htm (accessed August 5, 2007).

128. Winston Chai, "Radio ID Chips May Track Banknotes," CNET News.com, May 23, 2003, http://news.com.com/2100-1019-1009155.html (accessed August 12, 2005).

129. The 2005 World Exposition website, http://www1.expo2005.or.jp/en/whatexpo/index.html (accessed August 3, 2005).

130. William L. Tafoya, "Law Enforcement beyond the Year 2000," *Futurist* (September/October 1986), pp. 33–36.

131. Ibid.

132. See Rodriguez, "The Acquisition of High Technology Systems," pp. 11–12.

133. *Hancock* v. *State,* 402 S.W.2d 906 (Tex. Crim. Appl. 1966).

134. Stanley S. Arkin et al., *Prevention and Prosecution of Computer and High Technology Crime* (New York: Matthew Bender, 1988), Section 3.05.

135. The Computer Fraud and Abuse Act (Public Law 98-473, Title II, Section 2102 [a], October 12, 1984). The act was substantially revised in 1986 and again in 1988.

136. William J. Hughes, "Congress versus Computer Crime," *Information Executive,* Vol. 1, No. 1 (fall 1988), pp. 30–32.

137. Because of significant modifications introduced into the legislation in 1986, the law is often referred to as the Computer Fraud and Abuse Act of 1986.

138. Section 225 of the Homeland Security Act, Public Law 107-296.

139. U.S. Code, Title 18, Section 2311.

140. U.S. Code, Title 18, Section 641.

141. U.S. Code, Title 18, Section 1905.

142. U.S. Code, Title 17, Sections 101, 117.

143. Public Law 106-160.

144. Public Law 105-304.

145. Public Law 105-147.

146. U.S. Code, Title 18, Section 2510.

147. U.S. Code, Title 18, Sections 1341, 1343, and 1344.

148. N.Y. Penal Law, Sections 156.30 and 156.35.

149. Christine Dugas, "Federal Survey: Identity Theft Hits 1 in 4 U.S. Households; Scope of Crime Much Worse Than Previously Thought," *USA Today,* September 4, 2003, p. B10.

150. Information in this paragraph comes from "Two Arraigned on False ID Charges Involving Hijackers," CNN.com, October 3, 2001, http://www.cnn.com/2001/US/10/03/inv.virginia.hearing (accessed August 6, 2003).

151. eEurope, "One World: Smart Cards," p. 2, http://eeurope-smartcards.org/Smart20Cards.pdf (accessed August 20, 2007).

152. Eric Duprat, "Smart Cards, Payment Terminals and the Point-of-Transaction," *Hyperline,* 1 (2003), p. 6.

153. OTA, *Criminal Justice,* p. 51.

154. U.S. Code, Title 47, Section 151 et seq.

155. *Reno* v. *ACLU,* 117 S.Ct. 2329 (1997).

156. *United States* v. *American Library Association,* 539 U.S. 194 (2003).

157. "Supreme Court Upholds Use of Porn Filters in Libraries," Associated Press, June 23, 2003.

158. *Helen Remsburg, Administratrix of the Estate of Amy Lynn Boyer* v. *Docusearch, Inc.,* No. 2002-255 (D.N.H., 1993).

159. *Bearden* v. *Georgia,* 461 U.S. 660 (1983).

160. The material in this section is adapted from Nancy M. Ritter, "Preparing for the Future: Criminal Justice in 2040," *NIJ Journal,* No. 255 (November 2006).

Glossary

1. Bureau of Justice Statistics, *Dictionary of Criminal Justice Data Terminology,* 2nd ed. (Washington, DC: U.S. Government Printing Office, 1982).

2. Federal Bureau of Investigation, *Uniform Crime Reporting Handbook, 2004* (Washington, DC: U.S. Dept. of Justice, 2005).

3. BJS, *Dictionary of Criminal Justice Data Terminology,* p. 5.

4. Adapted from U.S. Code, Title 28, Section 20.3 (2[d]). Title 28 of the U.S. Code defines the term *administration of criminal justice.*

5. Thomas J. Cowper and Michael E. Buerger, *Improving Our View of the World: Police and Augmented Reality Technology* (Washington, DC: Federal Bureau of Investigation, 2003), http://www.fbi.gov/publications/realitytech/realitytech.pdf (accessed October 7, 2007).

6. *People* v. *Romero,* 8 Cal. 4th 728, 735 (1994).

7. Technical Working Group on Crime Scene Investigation, *Crime Scene Investigation: A Guide for Law Enforcement* (Washington, DC: National Institute of Justice, 2000), p. 12.

8. Centers for Disease Control and Prevention, *Bioterrorism: An Overview,* http://www.bt.cdc.gov/bioterrorism/overview.asp (accessed August 15, 2007).

9. Howard N. Synder and Melissa Sickmund, *Juvenile Offenders and Victims: 2006 National Report* (Washington, DC: Office of Juvenile Justice and Delinquency Prevention, 2006).

10. *State* v. *Cross,* 200 S.E.2d 27, 29 (1973).

11. Adapted from Gerald Hill and Kathleen Hill, *The Real Life Dictionary of the Law,* http://www.law.com (accessed June 11, 2007).

12. Ibid (accessed February 27, 2007).

13. Community Policing Consortium, *What Is Community Policing?* (Washington, DC: Community Policing Consortium, 1995).

14. Michael L. Benson, Francis T. Cullen, and William J. Maakestad, *Local Prosecutors and Corporate Crime* (Washington, DC: National Institute of Justice, 1992), p. 1.

15. Office of Justice Programs, *The National Criminal Intelligence Sharing Plan* (Washington, DC: U.S. Dept. of Justice, 2005), p. 27.

16. Wayne W. Bennett and Karen M. Hess, *Criminal Investigation,* 6th ed. (Belmont, CA: Wadsworth, 2001), p. 3. Italics in original.

17. Violence against Women Office, *Stalking and Domestic Violence: Report to Congress* (Washington, DC: U.S. Dept. of Justice, 2001).

18. Sam W. Lathrop, "Reviewing Use of Force: A Systematic Approach," *FBI Law Enforcement Bulletin,* October 2000, p. 18.

19. Adapted from Larry R. Leibrock, "Overview and Impact on 21st Century Legal Practice: Digital Forensics and Electronic Discovery," http://www.courtroom21.net/FDIC.pps (accessed July 15, 2007).

20. Adapted from Federal Bureau of Investigation, *FBI Policy and Guidelines: Counterterrorism,* http://jackson.fbi.gov/cntrterr.htm (accessed March 24, 2007).

21. Bureau of Justice Statistics, *Drugs, Crime, and the Justice System* (Washington, DC: BJS, 1992), p. 20.

22. Adapted from Technical Working Group for Electronic Crime Scene Investigation, *Electronic Crime Scene Investigation: A Guide for First Responders* (Washington, DC: National Institute of Justice, 2001), p. 2.

23. Henry Campbell Black, Joseph R. Nolan, and Jacqueline M. Nolan-Haley, *Black's Law Dictionary,* 6th ed. (St. Paul, MN: West, 1990), p. 24.

24. Lawrence W. Sherman, *Evidence-Based Policing* (Washington, DC: Police Foundation, 1998), p. 3.

25. International Association of Chiefs of Police, *Police Use of Force in America, 2001* (Alexandria, VA: IACP, 2001), p. 1.

26. Adapted from "Globalization," *Encyclopedia Britannica, 2003,* http://www.britannica.com/eb/article?eu5369857 (accessed July 23, 2003).

27. Black, Nolan, and Nolan-Haley, *Black's Law Dictionary,* p. 1003.

28. *The American Heritage Dictionary and Electronic Thesaurus on CD-ROM* (Boston: Houghton Mifflin, 1987).

29. Adapted from Entrust, Inc., "Secure Identity Management: Challenges, Needs, and Solutions," p. 1, http://www.entrust.com (accessed August 5, 2007).

30. Identity Theft Resource Center website, http://www.idtheftcenter.org (accessed April 24, 2007).

31. Adapted from Dictionary.com, http://dictionary.reference. com/search?q5infrastructure (accessed January 10, 2007).

32. Angus Smith, ed., *Intelligence-Led Policing* (Richmond, VA: International Association of Law Enforcement Intelligence Analysts, 1997), p. 1.

33. Adapted from Federal Bureau of Investigation, *FBI Policy and Guidelines: Counterterrorism*, http://jackson.fbi.gov/ cntrterr.htm (accessed March 24, 2007).

34. Jeffrey A. Butts and Ojmarrh Mitchell, "Brick by Brick: Dismantling the Border between Juvenile and Adult Justice," in Phyllis McDonald and Janice Munsterman, eds., *Boundary Changes in Criminal Justice Organizations*, Vol. 2 of *Criminal Justice 2000* (Washington, DC: National Institute of Justice, 2000), p. 207.

35. David A. Garvin, "Building a Learning Organization," *Harvard Business Review* (1993), pp. 78–91.

36. U.S. Department of Treasury, *2000–2005 Strategic Plan* (Washington, DC: U.S. Government Printing Office, 2000), p. 1.

37. Adapted from Robert M. Shusta et al., *Multicultural Law Enforcement*, 2nd ed. (Upper Saddle River, NJ: Prentice Hall, 2002), p. 443.

38. The Organized Crime Control Act of 1970 (Public Law 91-451).

39. BJS, *Drugs, Crime, and the Justice System*, p. 20.

40. Carl B. Klockars et al., *The Measurement of Police Integrity*, National Institute of Justice Research in Brief (Washington, DC: NIJ, 2000), p. 1.

41. This definition draws on the classic work by O. W. Wilson, *Police Administration* (New York: McGraw-Hill, 1950), pp. 2–3.

42. National Institute of Justice, *Use of Force by Police: Overview of National and Local Data* (Washington, DC: NIJ, 1999).

43. National Council on Crime and Delinquency, *National Assessment of Structured Sentencing* (Washington, DC: Bureau of Justice Statistics, 1996), p. xii.

44. Bureau of Justice Statistics, *Prisoners in 1998* (Washington, DC: BJS, 1999), p. 7.

45. *Private Security: Report of the Task Force on Private Security* (Washington, DC: U.S. Government Printing Office, 1976), p. 4.

46. Samuel Walker, Geoffrey P. Albert, and Dennis J. Kenney, *Responding to the Problem Police Officer: A National Study of Early Warning Systems* (Washington, DC: National Institute of Justice, 2000).

47. BJS, *Drugs, Crime, and the Justice System*, p. 21.

48. Gerald Hill and Kathleen Hill, *The Real Life Dictionary of the Law* (Santa Monica, CA: General Publishing Group, 2000), http://dictionary.law.com/lookup2.asp (accessed February 28, 2007).

49. Deborah Ramierz, Jack McDevitt, and Amy Farrell, *A Resource Guide on Racial Profiling Data Collection Systems: Promising Practices and Lessons Learned* (Washington, DC: U.S. Dept. of Justice, 2000), p. 3.

50. *Victor v. Nebraska*, 114 S.Ct. 1239, 127 L.Ed.2d 583 (1994).

51. As found in the California jury instructions.

52. The term *superpredator* is generally attributed to John J. DiIulio, Jr. See John J. DiIulio, Jr., "The Question of Black Crime," *Public Interest* (fall 1994), pp. 3–12.

53. Adapted from Darl H. Champion and Michael K. Hooper, *Introduction to American Policing* (New York: McGraw-Hill, 2003), p. 166.

54. Sam S. Souryal, *Police Administration and Management* (St. Paul, MN: West, 1977), p. 261.

55. Federal Bureau of Intelligence, Counterterrorism Section, *Terrorism in the United States, 1987* (Washington, DC: FBI, 1987).

56. Daniel Oran, *Oran's Dictionary of the Law* (St. Paul, MN: West, 1983), p. 306.

57. Lawrence A. Greenfeld, "Prison Sentences and Time Served for Violence," *Bureau of Justice Statistics Selected Findings*, No. 4 (April 1995).

CASE INDEX

NAME INDEX

SUBJECT INDEX